최악의 폭염에도
마음껏 시원하게!

초절전 회오리 바람으로
유례 없는 폭염에도
진정한 시원함을 느낄 수 있도록
세 개의 바람문 조절로
전기료 걱정까지 시원하게-

삼성 스마트에어컨 Q9000
air 3.0 PROJECT

삼성 스마트에어컨 Q9000 air 3.0 PROJECT

❚ 세 개의 바람문 개별 제어로 초절전 냉방
❚ 온도, 습도, 청정도까지 보여주는 air 3.0 DISPLAY

성 스마트에어컨 Q9000
형명 : AF18J9975WW
소비 효율 : 에너지 프론티어

SAMSUNG

HERALD

헤럴드의
Re-imagine!
시작됩니다.

지식과 정보를 넘어 생활과 환경으로, 언론을 넘어
'Life beyond Media'로 헤럴드가 새로운 상상을 시작합니다.

국민이 행복한 변화가 시작됩니다

젊음에 희망을! 지역에 활기를! 행복주택

경제혁신
3개년계획

3년의 혁신
30년의 성장

매일 아침

자신과 가족을 위해

첫 걸음을 나서는 당신을

행복주택이

응원하겠습니다

집값 걱정에서 벗어나
편리한 교통과 문화생활을 누릴수 있는 곳,
미래를 향한 첫 걸음을 행복주택에서 시작하세요.

LH 한국토지주택공사

A COMPREHENSIVE
HANDBOOK ON KOREA

KOREA ANNUAL
2015

Korea's only and most authoritative
English-language yearbook

published by
YONHAP NEWS *AGENCY*

KOREA ANNUAL 2015

44th Annual Edition   Copyright 2015 by Yonhap News Agency   All Rights Reserved
Printed in Korea in June 2015   Publisher : Park No-hwang   Editor : Shim Soo-hwa

Korea Annual is the sole English-language almanac and book of facts published in Korea by Yonhap News Agency. Headquartered in Seoul, Yonhap is the nation's representative news agency providing news and information to all local newspapers, broadcasting firms and other subscribers as well as foreign news organizations and various readers. Yonhap also publishes Korean-language yearbook "Yonhap Yongam" and monthly journal "Imazine."

About Yonhap News Agency

Yonhap News Agency plays a central role in the Korean press by delivering news and information to its customers in various parts of the world, as well as to newspapers, broadcasting firms, government agencies, business organizations and Internet portals on a real-time basis.

Yonhap's News service provides some 3,000 multimedia news items each day covering politics, the economy, society, culture, entertainment, sports, science and other topics, helping readers access news from the global village.

Yonhap has over 600 journalists and photographers posted at the Seoul head office, regional offices and overseas bureaus, comprising the largest news-gathering network in Korea.

Under a 2003 law passed by the South Korean parliament, Yonhap has been charged with promoting the country's image and distributing information -- a task deemed critical to addressing the domination of information by major Western news media.

Yonhap dispatches news and information to international media organization in foreign languages to help the international community access clear and accurate information on the Korean Peninsula. Yonhap's foreign-language news service is distributed English, Chinese, Japanese, Arabic, Spanish and French. Launched in 1981 with the merger of several commercial news agencies, Yonhap keeps its customers abreast of the latest news and information by sending out fast, reliable reports. In 1988, Yonhap became the first of the Korean press to establish an electronic system for writing and releasing news articles to its clients.

With state-of-the-art equipment and a superior workforce, Yonhap successfully undertook its role as the key news agency for the 1988 Seoul Olympics, the 2000 Asia Europe Meeting (ASEM) in Seoul, the 2002 Korea-Japan FIFA World Cup and the 2005 summit of the Asia-Pacific Economic Cooperation (APEC) forum.

PROVIDING NEWS TO 82 FOREIGN NEWS AGENCIES

Yonhap currently has 60 correspondents in Washington, Paris, Moscow, Tokyo, Beijing and 31 other major countries around the world, and employs 17 local correspondents in 16 other cities to cover stories not only Korean affairs, but also other international issues from the Korean perspective.

Yonhap maintains contracts for the exchange of news services with over 82 global news agencies, including such major news companies as the Associated Press, Reuters, United Press International, Agence France-Presse, China's Xinhua News Agency, Japan's Kyodo News Agency, Deutsche Presse Agentur of Germany, Itar-Tass of Russia and Press Trust of India.

Yonhap also provides North Korean news under a contract to exchange news services with the Korean Central News Agency (KCNA) of North Korea, signed in December 2002.

WINDOW TO KOREA

Yonhap is a channel for foreign readers to get real-time information and news on Korea in English, Chinese, Japanese, Spanish, Arabic and French. The multi-language news service is very meaningful as the country is on the verge of becoming an advanced nation.

Yonhap's English-language news service reaches over 82 news agencies worldwide. In addition, international organizations, 160 government overseas missions and Internet users access the service via Yonhap's Web site.

LARGEST PROVINCIAL COVERAGE NETWORK

Over 130 reporters posted in 13 major provincial cities write articles that help narrow the information divide between Seoul and provincial cities, balancing regional development and promoting unity.

01

President Park Geun-hye meets reporters at Cheong Wa Dae to outline her administration's policy goal for the year on Jan. 6.

02

President Park Geun-hye chairs a joint meeting of government officials and private-sector experts at Cheong Wa Dae on March 20 to work out detailed reform measures.

03

President Park Geun-hye visits the site of the new Cheil Industries Inc. in Deagu and briefed by Samsung Electronics vice chairman Lee Jay-yong and head of the conglomerate's communication's team Rhee In-yong on Sept. 15.

2014 IN
PICTURES

01 02 03 04 05 06

Nuclear Security Summit 2014
The Hague, the Netherlands

01
President Park Geun-hye poses with other leaders at the Nuclear Security Summit in the Hague on March 25.

02
President Park Geun-hye holds a joint press conference with German Chancellor Angela Merkel during her state visit to the European country on March 26.

03
President Park Geun-hye delivers a keynote speech at the United Nations general assembly on Sept. 24.

04
President Park Geun-hye and U.S. President Barack Obama observe a moment of silence for those killed in the Sewol ferry tragedy during their summit meeting at the presidential office Cheong Wa Dae on April 25.

05
China's President Xi Jinping, on an official visit to South Korea, waves to elementary school children at a welcoming ceremony at the presidential Cheong Wa Dae on July 3.

06
President Park Geun-hye delivers a speech at the Korea-ASEAN special summit meeting at BEXCO in Busan on Dec. 12.

2014 IN
PICTURES

01 02 03 04 05 06

01
Reps. Kim Han-gil(R) and Ahn Cheol-soo shake hands during a press conference at the National Assembly after announcing the creation of a unified party ahead of the June 4 local elections on March 2.

02
Rep. Kim Moo-sung delivers a speech at the ruling Saenuri Party's national convention after being tapped as the party's new chairman on July 14.

03
Former Gyeonggi Province governor Sohn Hak-gyu holds a press conference during which he announced his retirement from politics after he lost parliamentary by-election on July 31.

04

Constitutional Court Chief Justice Park Han-chul reads the court's decision to dissolve the left-leaning Unified Progressive Party for being pro-North Korean on Dec. 19. The ruling stripped party five lawmakers of their parliamentary seats.

05

Long-separated sisters hug each other at a family reunion event held at Mount Kumgang Hotel in North Korea on Feb. 20. Hundreds of thousands of Koreans remain separated in the two Koreas since the division of the Korean Peninsula in 1945.

06

Korean-American peace activist Jonathan Lee holds a one-man protest outside the Japanese embassy in Seoul on March 24 demanding compensation for Korean and other Asian women used by Japan as sex slaves for its soldiers during World War II.

2014 IN
PICTURES

01
02 03
04 05 06

01
High-ranking North Korean officials
meet with South Korean officials,
including national security adviser
Kim Kwan-jin and Unification Minister
Ryoo Kihl-jae, after they arrived in
Incheon, a port city west of Seoul, to
attend the closing ceremony of the
Asian Games on Oct. 4.

02
Korean-American author Shin Eun-
mi (R) holds a press conference
in downtown Seoul on Dec. 2. She
arranged the gathering with a
progressive lawmaker after remarks
she had made during a talk concert
drew flak for being pro-North Korean.

03
Jeong Yun-hoe, a former adviser to
President Park Geun-hye, appears
before the state prosecutors' office on
Dec. 10 to give testimony in regards
to allegations that he had meddled in
state affairs.

04

Finance Minister Hyun Oh-seok outlines new government measures to ease South Korea's tight home rental market on Feb. 26.

05

KRX CEO Choi Kyoung-soo pushes the button to launch the gold trading market in Busan, South Korea's second largest city, on March 24.

06

People attentively watch TV news at the Samsung Medical Center in Seoul on May 12 where Samsung Group Chairman Lee Kun-hee is undergoing treatment after suffering a heart attack.

2014 IN
PICTURES

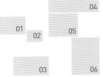

01 Daum Communication chief Choi Se-hun (L) and Kakao head Lee Sirgoo leave a press conference in Seoul where they announced the merger of the two companies on May 26.

02 Health and Welfare Minister Moon Hyung-pyo outlines the government's anti-smoking policy plan that calls for hiking up cigarette prices by 2,000 won at the Central Government Building in Seoul on Sept. 11.

03 Government officials, teachers rally in Seoul on Nov. 1 protesting government plans to reform the deficient-laden pension funds for public employees.

04
Coast Guard officers carry out rescue operations for passengers from the 6,825-ton Sewol ferry when it was listing rapidly off South Korea's southwestern coast on April 16.

05
Students from Danwon Highschool pay respects to colleagues killed in the Sewol ferry disaster during a memorial service in Ansan on April 23.

06
Police patrol the express bus terminal in Incheon after publically announcing they are looking for Sewol ferry owner Yoo Byung-eun on May 22.

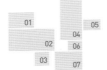

01 President Park Geun-hye receives Pope Francis at Seoul Airport on Aug. 14.

02 Pope Francis holds a mass at the Daejeon World Cup Stadium on Aug. 15.

03 Pope Francis gives blessing to a child by kissing its forehead as he heads for mass in downtown Seoul on Aug. 16.

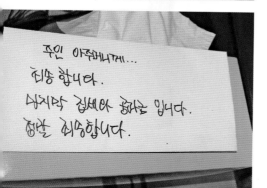

주인 아주머니께...
최송 합니다.
마지막 집세와 공과금 입니다.
정말 최송합니다.

04
Quarantine official herd ducks that must be culled at a farm in North Chungcheon Province after a nearby farm tested positive for bird flu on Feb. 2.

05
The collapse of the Mauna Ocean Resort in Gyeongju left 10 people dead and 100 others injured on Feb. 17. The disaster occurred when the resort structure collapsed under the weight of the snow.

06
A meteorolite that crashed into a farming greenhouse in Jinju on March 10.

07
Mother and daughters commit suicide in their home after suffering from deprivation for a long time. A memo found at the site of the suicide read 'our last rent and utility fees.'

01
The burning remains of a firefighting helicopter that crashed in a neighborhood in Gwangju on July 17.

02
Kim Hyung-sik, a Seoul city councilman accused of murdering a wealthy creditor leaves a police station in southern Seoul on July 3 without responding to reporters' questions.

03
Police escort a 50-year-old woman suspected of killing two person in Pocheon north of Seoul on Aug. 1.

04
An army sergeant, named. Lee who was implicated in the death of a private first class at the 28th infantry division is being escorted by military police after trial at a military court on Aug. 5.

05

A lead investigator explains the creation sinkholes near Seokchon lake in Seoul on Aug. 14.

06

Mourners lay flowers at the site that left 16 people dead when a ventilation duct collapsed during a rock concert in Bundang, a satellite city of Seoul, on Oct. 19.

07

Cho Hyun-ah, former Korean Air Lines Co. vice president and the daughter of the airline's CEO apologizes to the public on Dec. 12 for an uproar she caused by ordering a taxiing passenger plane to return to the gate at JFK Airport. The incident, dubbed the "nut rage" by the press, has raised questions about the management of family-run conglomerates.

2014 IN
PICTURES

01
A local curator explains the background behind the painting of a Buddha donated by a U.S. museum on Jan. 7.

02
Andrew Yeom Soo-jung waves to onlookers after he is formally appointed as South Korea's third cardinal at Myeongdong Cathedral in downtown Seoul on Jan. 13.

03
Dongdaemun Design Plaza opens to the general public on March 21 after 5 years of construction.

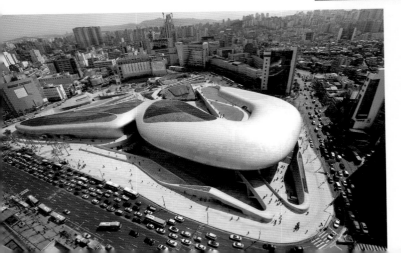

04

Leader actors from the hit drama "My Love from the Star" pose at SBS TV station in Seoul on Dec. 16, 2013. The Washington Post highlighted them in an article on March 8, saying that the popularity of the TV drama fueled another wave of Hallyu in China.

05

A pedestrian passes by an advertizing poster of "Roaring Currents" in Seoul on Aug. 19. The movie attracted more than 15 million viewers.

06

Stars of drama "Misaeng (An incomplete life)" pose for the cameras in southern Seoul on Dec. 11.

2014 IN
PICTURES

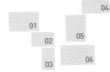

01
02
03
04
05
06

01
Speed skater Lee Sang-hwa
stands atop the podium at the
Sochi Olympics in Russia after
winning the women's 500-meter
event on Feb. 18.

02
South Korean female short
track skaters wave flowers after
winning the Olympic gold in the
3,000-meter event in Sochi on
Feb. 18.

03
Kim Yu-na waves to fans after
taking part in a farewell ice show
in southern Seoul on May 6.

04
South Korea's new national football team coach Uli Stielike holds a press conference in Goyang, a Seoul suburb, on Sept. 9.

05
Kim Ja-in becomes the first South Korean to win IFSC Climbing Worldcup in Spain on Sept. 15.

06
The first contingent of North Korean athletes and officials head to their quarters after registering their ID with the Welcome Center at the Asian Games athlete's village on Sept. 11.

2014 IN
PICTURES

01
02
03

01
Teammates rush towards Kim Ji-yeon after she defeated a Chinese rival to grab the gold in women's sabre team event at the Incheon Asian Games on Sept. 23.

02
South Korea's star rhythmic gymnast Son Yeon-jae sheds tears after receiving her gold medal at the Incheon Asian Games on Oct.2.

03
South Korea footballers celebrate after beating North Korea at the gold medal match of the Incheon Asian Games on Oct. 2.

Table of Contents

CULTURE

SPORTS

PROVINCIAL GOVERNMENT

Chronology 2014

JANUARY

Jan. 1 The National Assembly endorses 355.8 trillion won budget for 2014. It passes deadline for the second straight year. Budget for national defense grows 4% on-year to 35.7 trillion won.

Jan. 2 KOSPI closes down 44.15 points or 2.2% at 1,967.19 on the first trading day of the year.

Jan. 3 Ji So-yun signs 2-year contract with Chelsea Ladies in England.

Jan. 5 Independent lawmaker Ahn Cheol-soo announces that he launches a committee that will spearhead preparation for establishing a new party.

Jan. 6 The government makes an official proposal to the North Korea for the reunion of separated families and proposes holding working-level talks on the issue on Jan. 10.

Jan. 7 Prosecutors request warrants to arrest Hyun Jae-hyun, chairman of Tongyang Group, and its three former high-ranking officials on corruption charges.

Jan. 8 Foreign Minister Yun Byung-se holds a meeting with U.S. Secretary of State John Kerry, "sharing the view to strengthening cooperation in enhancing peace and stability.

Jan. 9 The Bank of Korea maintains its previous 2014 growth estimate at 3.8 % and raised the prospects for next year to 4.0%.

Jan. 10 South Korea and the United States hold the 10th high-level talks in Seoul to sign the Special Measures Agreement on jointly shouldering the cost of keeping the USFK on South Korean soil.

Jan. 12 The government protests Japan's alleged push to include its territorial claim over South Korea's easternmost islets of Dokdo in its guidelines on textbooks for middle and high schools.

Jan. 13 Pope Francis appoints Andrew Yeom Soo-jung. the archbishop of Seoul, as a new cardinal for South Korea. An official ceremony is scheduled for Feb. 22.

Jan. 15 The education ministry says that it will scrap the Korean style TOFEL for highschool students from this year, which was developed with an investment of 37.1 billion won from 2008-2013.

Jan. 16 President Park Geun-hye and

India's Prime Minister Manmohan Singh hold summit talks and promise to improve bilateral partnership and expand trade and investment between the two countries.

Jan. 18 A professor of Chungbuk National University who has participated in reviewing the quality of wood used in rebuilding the Sungyemun commits suicide by hanging himself.

Jan. 19 The Financial Supervisory Service launches on-spot investigation into KB Kookmin Card, Lotte Card and NH Nonghyup Card in connection with customer data leak.

Jan. 20 The government lambastes a Japanese official for referring to an independence fighter as a "terrorist," saying that it represents a lack of common sense and historical knowledge for a Cabinet member who represents the Japanese government's stance.

Jan. 21 The government endorses a law revision that would impose up to 3 years imprisonment or a fine of 30 million won for doing transactions with terror financiers.

Jan. 22 A Seoul court sentences Won Sei-hoon, a former spy chief, to 2 years in prison and a fine of 162.72 million won for receiving bribery.

Jan. 23 Comfort women send about 60,000 petition cards to the UN and Japan, reclaiming their tarnished reputation.

Jan. 24 The Senate of the State of Virginia passes a bill by a large margin that makes it mandatory to use both "East Sea" and "Sea of Japan" in public school textbooks.

Jan. 26 Hwang Keum-ja, a victim of Japan's sexual enslavement, dies at the age of 90.

Jan. 27 The government proposes holding a reunion of separated families at Mt. Geumgang.

Jan. 28 The government grants special pardons to 2.9 million people.

Jan. 29 The State of Georgia unanimously passes a resolution that supports the use of the East Sea along with the Sea of Japan to describe the waters between South Korea and Japan.

Jan. 31 A Singapore-registered tanker clashes with a pier, causing a oil spill into waters off Yeosu.

FEBRUARY

Feb. 2 South Korea and the U.S. sign the renewal of the Special Measure Agreement in which Seoul's defense cost sharing will grow 5.8% on-year to 920 billion won.

Feb. 3 North Korea proposes holding working-level talks on a reunion of separated families either on Feb. 6 or Feb. 6.

Feb. 4 KOSPI falls through the 1,900 mark on U.S. economic woes

Feb. 5 South and North Korea agree to hold a reunion of separated families on Feb. 20-25 at Mt. Geumgang.

Feb. 6 President Park Geun-hye dismisses Maritime Affairs Minister Yoon Jin-sook who has been under fire for making controversies over an oil leak accident.

Feb. 7 A Seoul high court overturns a lower court ruling on Ssangyong Motor's dismissal of 153 workers.

Feb. 9 Jeju City opens the country's first medical resort "Hotel We" where medical checkup, treatment and other services will be provided.

Feb. 10 South Korea and Australia initial a free trade agreement. (FTA)

Feb. 11 A team led by Hwang Woo-suk, a former Seoul National University professor, obtains a U.S. patent on the human embryonic stem sell.

Feb. 12 South and North Korea hold high-ranking talks for the first time in seven years but the meeting ends with little progress.

Feb. 13 A liquid nitrogen storage tank at a Bingrae factory in Namyangju City explodes, leaking hazardous ammonia gas. Three people were injured with one missing.

Feb. 14 South and North Korea agree to hold a reunion event for separated families at the truce village of Panmunjeom on Feb. 20-25.

Feb. 15 An oil tanker collides with a freighter ship off the coast of Busan, resulting in leaking 237kℓ of bunker C oil.

Feb. 16 Independent lawmaker Ahn Cheol-soo renames the new party preparatory committee as the "New Political Party."

Feb. 17 A resort in Gyeongju collapses under the heavy weight of snow on its roof, killing 10 students and injuring 128 others.

Feb. 18 Hanwha Group Chairman Kim Seung-youn resigns from all the posts of subsidiary companies.

Feb. 19 The National Assembly adopts a confirmation report on Cho Hee-dae, a nominee for Supreme Court justice.

Feb. 20 South and North Korea hold the first round of a reunion of separated families on Mt. Geumgang.

Feb. 21 North Korea fires four rounds of 300㎜ KN-09 launcher from Wonsan into the East Sea that fly around 150㎞

Feb. 22 Andrew Yeom Soo-jung becomes a cardinal at an official ceremony held in Vatican.

Feb. 23 South Korea and Australia sign a 5-trillion-won currency swap deal.

Feb. 24 South Korea and the U.S. start joint military drill Key Resolve and Foal Eagle to brace for any local provocations.

Feb. 25 President Park Geun-hye announces three-year economic innovation plans under which the government will inject 4 trillion won to stimulate business start-ups, raising the growth potential to 4%, employment rate to 70% and national income to exceed US$30,000 and beyond.

Feb. 27 North korea fires four rounds of missiles into the East Sea that can fly over 200㎞.

MARCH

March 1 Park Tae-hwan wins a gold in men's 200-meter freestyle at the 2014 NSW State Open Championship held in Sydney, Australia.

March 2 "Frozen" draws more than 10 million viewers for the first time as a foreign animation in South Korea.

March 3 President Park Geun-hye exchanges views with George W. Bush, a former U.S. president, on how to strengthen alliance and cooperation.

March 4 South Korea, China and Japan hold the fourth round of free trade agreement talks in Seoul.

March 5 The government proposes

holding working-level talks on March 12 with the North to discuss regular reunions of separated families, an offer later rejected by Pyongyang.

March 6 South Korea and Indonesia sign a 10.7 trillion won currency swap deal.

March 7 The government urges the North to respond to the proposal to hold working-level talks for Red Cross officials.

March 9 The National Intelligence Service(NIS) apologizes for allegations that it manipulated evidence in the espionage case.

March 10 The government announces a package of measurers aimed at preventing personal information leaks from happening again.

March 11 South Korea and Canada conclude free trade agreement talks in which they promise to lift tariffs on vehicles within two years.

March 12 Police raids KT headquarters to secure evidence in a lobby scandal involving Seoul City's transportation card business.

March 13 KT and LG Uplus start their 45-day business suspend. SK Telecom plans to suspend its operation from May.

March 14 Number of poultry slaughtered due to avian influenza infections tops 10 million.

March 15 Prosecution arrests a NIS official in connection with an espionage scandal involving a Seoul City public servant.

March 16 Kia Motors recalls 186,950 vehicles of four different models including Ray and Morning on defective emission parts.

March 17 241 military weapon makers are found to supply defective parts to the military by using fabricated certification documents.

March 18 The presidential office and the government officials in Sejong hold their first video conference for a Cabinet meeting.

March 19 The Korea Communications Commission (KCC) re-approves the channel operation rights for four broadcasting companies including News Y and JTBC.

March 20 SK Telecom's communications and data service suffer disruptions for five hours and 40 minutes.

March 21 The Dongdaemun Design Plaza designed by Iraqi-British architect Zaha Hadid opens.

March 22 North Korea fires 30 rounds of short-range rockets with an range of around 60㎞ into the East Sea.

March 23 North Korea fires an additional 16 rounds of short-range rockets from an area near Wonsan, Gangwon Province.

March 24 A unmanned plane equipped with a small-sized camera is found on a mountain side in Paju. It was turned out to be from North Korea.

March 26 North Korea fires 2 rounds of ballistic missiles from an area near the north part of Pyongyang into the East Sea.

March 27 South Korea and the U.S. start the Team Sprit joint military drill which will last until April 7.

March 28 The government sends back remains of 437 Chinese soldiers killed during the Korean War back to their homeland.

March 29 President Park Geun-hye returns home following a week-long visit to the Netherlands.

March 30 The U.S. movie Avengers is shot on the Mapo bridge, which is closed for cars on both directions from 6 a.m. to 5:30 p.m.

March 31 A unmanned plane crashes in the Yellow Sea near Baeknyeong Island. It is presumed to be a North Korean plane.

APRIL

April 1 A magnitude 5.1 earthquake, centered about 100㎞ northwest of West Gyeongnyeolbi Archipelago off Taean, strikes parts of South Korea.

April 2 South Korea tentatively concludes that two unidentified drones found near the border with North Korea are from the communist nation.

April 3 South Korea names career diplomat Hwang Joon-kook as its new chief negotiator for the six-party talks.

April 4 South Korea files a strong protest with Japan for laying a fresh territorial claim to its easternmost islets of Dokdo.

April 6 South Korea finds a third suspected North Korean drone on a mountain on the east coast.

April 7 An Army private first class, surnamed Yoon, dies after being beaten by his colleagues at a front-line barracks.

April 8 South Korea and Australia officially sign a free trade agreement.

April 9 The foreign ministry says a South Korean woman abducted earlier in the Philippines is found dead.

April 10 The top court rejects an appeal by an ailing smoker seeking compensation from the nation's leading tobacco maker.

April 11 The Daegu District Court sentences a 36-year-old woman to 10 years in prison for beating her 8-year-old stepdaughter to death.

April 13 South Korean rhythmic gymnast Son Yeon-jae wins the silver in clubs and the bronze in ball in the World Cup in Pesaro, Italy.

April 14 South Korean prosecutors bring charges against two state intelligence agents for their alleged role in forging Chinese government documents to frame a North Korean defector for espionage.

April 15 President Park Geun-hye apologizes for the spy agency's alleged forgery of evidence used in charging a North Korean defector with espionage.

April 16 The 6,325-ton Sewol sinks off South Korea's southern coast, killing 295 people and leaving nine others missing.

April 17 President Park Geun-hye pays a visit to the site where a ferry sank off South Korea's southern coast.

April 18 Rescuers attempt in vain to enter the sunken ferry Sewol 20 times.

April 19 The first body found in the fourth-floor of the sunken Sewol.

April 20 Funeral services are held for some victims of the sunken ferry Sewol. Most of the victims are students from Danwon High School in Ansan near Seoul.

April 22 The death toll of the Sewol ferry disaster reaches 121, with 181 still listed as missing.

April 23 Prosecutors raid 17 companies and houses related to Yoo Byung-eun, the owner of Cheonghaejin Marine Co. that owned the Sewol ferry.

April 24 Yoo Byung-eun, the owner of Cheonghaejin Marine Co. that operated the Sewol ferry, claims his asset only stands at 10 billion won, and that he is willing to give it up.

April 25 South Korean President Park Geun-hye meets U.S. President Barack Obama in Seoul and agrees that the two allies can reconsider the timing of the transfer of wartime control of South Korean troops to Seoul.

April 26 Yongin subway line opens amid controversies over its budget.

April 27 Prime Minister Chung Hong-won offers to step down from his post, holding himself responsible for the deadly sinking of the Sewol.

April 28 A joint investigation team raids the situation room of the local Coast Guard to seize documents and recordings from the day of the ferry Sewol's sinking.

April 29 President Park Geun-hye apologizes over the deadly sinking of the ferry Sewol, saying the government failed to prevent the disaster and bungled its initial response.

April 30 Around 70 students who survived the Sewol ferry disaster are discharged from hospital after treatment.

MAY

May 2 A ferry with around 400 passengers on board connecting the eastern island of Ulleung and the easternmost islets of Dokdo returns to its port of origin due to an engine malfunction.

May 4 South Korea's figure skating icon Kim Yu-na makes her last appearance on ice as a figure skater,

May 6 A civilian diver dies of fatigue and overwork while searching for the missing from the Sewol.

May 7 Prosecutors confirm former Prosecutor General Chae Dong-wook fathered an illegitimate son.

May 8 A joint team of prosecutors and police arrests Kim Han-sik, chief executive of Chonghaejin Marine Co. that owns the ill-fated ferry Sewol.

May 9 Five people are killed in a gas explosion at one of POSCO's facilities.

May 11 Lee Kun-hee, the de facto head of Samsung Group, is taken to hospital after suffering a heart attack.

May 12 Chung Mong-joon, a seven-term ruling party lawmaker, is elected as his party's candidate for Seoul mayor after winning 71.1 percent of the votes at a party meeting.

May 13 The death toll in the ferry Sewol disaster reaches 276.

May 14 Investigators seek murder charges against the captain and three crew members of the sunken ferry Sewol for prematurely abandoning the sinking vessel.

May 15 South Korea says Japan should dispel doubts and concerns shared by its neighboring countries as it moves closer to exercising the right to "collective self-defense."

May 16 The families of the victims of the Sewol disaster demand a special law authorizing the establishment of an independent fact-finding body.

May 17 An Ansan-based activist group commences a campaign to gather 10 million signatures to urge the government to implement a special law for the families of the victims of the Sewol disaster.

May 18 President Park Geun-hye attends a mass at Myeongdong Cathedral in downtown Seoul to pay tribute to the Sewol victims.

May 19 President Park Geun-hye vows to dismantle the Coast Guard, holding it responsible for responding poorly to the Sewol disaster.

May 20 South Korean President Park Geun-hye inspects the construction site of a nuclear power plant being built by South Korea in the United Arab Emirates.

May 21 South Korea's Cardinal Andrew Yeom Soo-jung pays a landmark visit to the North Korean border city of Kaesong to meet with South Korean Catholics working at a joint inter-Korean factory park there.

May 22 North Korea fires off two artillery shells near a South Korean warship on patrol in the tensely-guarded western sea border.

May 23 President Park Geun-hye

meets EU foreign policy chief Catherine Ashton, discussing ways to promote co-operation.

May 24 Protestors hold a rally in central Seoul, denouncing the government for its botched rescue operations in the Sewol ferry disaster.

May 25 Prosecutors raise its bounty on Yoo Byung-eun, the owner of Cheonghaejin Marine Co. on the run, to 500 million won.

May 26 Daum Communications announces its merger with Kakao Corp., the operator of South Korea's No. 1 messenger, Kakao Talk.

May 27 The eldest daughter of the de facto owner of the sunken ferry Sewol is arrested in France.

May 28 Ahn Dai-hee resigns as the nominee for prime minister following criticism that he had made too much money as a lawyer by allegedly taking advantage of his status as a former Supreme Court justice.

May 29 Lebanese ambassador to South Korea dies in a traffic accident.

May 30 A civilian diver dies inside the sunken ferry Sewol during a search operation.

May 31 Psy's global mega-hit "Gangnam Style" gathers 2 billion views on YouTube.

JUNE

June 1 Samsung General Chemicals Co. absorbs Samsung Petrochemical Co.

June 2 South Korea's national archives releases a list of 318 Korean victims killed by Japan after a powerful earthquake in Japan in 1923.

June 3 Daewoo Engineering & Construction wins 941.2 billion won deal from Qatar to build a highway.

June 4 Voter turnout in South Korea's local elections reaches 56.8%, with 23.4 million of the 41.2 million eligible voters casting ballots.

June 5 The ruling Saenuri Party claims eight seats in the local elections, while the main opposition New Politics Alliance for Democracy takes up nine seats.

June 6 North Korea arrests a U.S. tourist, named Jeffrey Edward Fowle, for violating visa regulations.

June 7 The Jury of the 14th International Architecture Exhibition of la Biennale di Venezi grants the golden lion prize to South Korea.

June 8 Bae Chun-hee, a South Korean woman who was forced into sexual slavery for the Japanese imperial army during World War II, dies at the age of 91.

June 9 South Korean rapper Psy uploads the video of his latest song "Hangover" on YouTube.

June 10 The captain and crew members of the sunken ferry Sewol go on trial.

June 11 A team of prosecutors and some 4,000 riot police, armed with court-issued warrants, raids a religious compound to arrest Yoo Byung-eun.

June 12 South Korea and Canada initial their bilateral free trade agreement (FTA). It, among other things, calls for the elimination of tariffs on automobiles in two years after the deal takes effect.

June 13 President Park Geun-hye replaces about half of her 17-member Cabinet, her first major shake-up since taking office last year.

June 14 A Cambodian vessel clashes with a South Korean ship off the coast of South Korea's southern city of Yeosu. No casualties resulted.

June 16 Hyundai Engineering & Construction Co. extends retirement age to 60 from the previous 58.

June 17 South Korean President Park Geun-hye and her Uzbek counterpart Islam Karimov hold a summit, agree to push for new joint projects in gas development and solar power.

June 18 South Korea plays Russia to a one-all draw in their opening Group H showdown at the 2014 FIFA World Cup in Brazil.

June 19 A local court rules that the Korean Teachers and Education Workers Union is not a legitimate labor group.

June 20 South Korea expresses deep regret over Japan's review of its 1993 statement acknowledging its wartime sexual enslavement of Korean and other Asian women, saying the move could undermine the credibility of the apology it had made at the time.

June 21 Five soldiers are killed and seven others are wounded after a soldier went on a shooting spree at a front-line Army unit.

June 22 An ancient mountain fortress in South Korea made the UNESCO world heritage list.

June 24 South Korea's prime minister nominee Moon Chang-keuk steps down amid mounting public and media criticism over his alleged pro-Japanese views.

June 25 The U.S. National Transportation Safety Board concludes pilots' mismanagement as the main cause of the 2013 Asiana Airlines passenger jet crash in San Francisco.

June 26 North Korea fires off three short-range projectiles into the East Sea from its east coast.

June 27 South Korea decides to raise the country's minium hourly wage to 5,580 won in 2015, up 7.1% from the previous 5,210 won.

June 28 Activists hold a rally in Seoul to protest the government's move to open its rice market.

June 29 North Korea fires off two short-range missiles into the East Sea ahead of Chinese President Xi Jinping's planned visit to Seoul on July 3-4.

June 30 North Korea proposes that the two Koreas stop all military hostilities against each other, and demands South Korea to scrap joint military drills with the United States.

JULY

July 1 The government launches a new pension program under which senior citizens in the lower 70% income bracket will receive 200,000 won in cash in monthly allowances.

• Local mobile carriers start the long-term evolution (LTE)-A service which is three times faster than the old LTE network.

July 2 Families of victims of the Sewol ferry disaster start a nationwide signature-collecting campaign to call for the enactment of a special law.

• The Korean won closes at 1,009.2

won against the U.S. dollar, sinking below the 1,010 won mark for the first time in six years.

July 3 South Korean President Park Geun-hye meets with her Chinese counterpart Xi Jinping.

• The education ministry files a lawsuit against a progressive teachers' union for participating in political rallies.

July 4 On his South Korea trip, Chinese President Xi Jinping visits the National Assembly and Seoul National University.

• North Korea declares that it will set up a special fact-finding panel to investigate cases of Japanese citizens it is alleged to have abducted decades ago. In response, Japan partly lifts its sanctions in effect against Pyongyang.

July 5 The 8th World Taekwondo Culture Expo kicks off in Jeonju, North Jeolla Province, with athletes from 26 countries competing.

July 7 Armed gangsters attack Samsung Electronics Co.'s Brazil plant to take away laptop computers and smartphones worth 6.5 billion won.

July 8 The Board of Audit and Inspection (BAI) says the government's negligence and corruption contributed to the tragic Sewol ferry disaster that left more than 300 passengers dead.

July 10 Hong Myung-bo, head coach of the national football team, steps down, holding himself responsible for his team's poor performance at the 2014 Brazil World Cup.

July 11 The National Assembly's foreign affairs committee adopts a resolution denouncing Japan's move to expand its military role.

• Hyundai Heavy Industries Co. wins a US$1.9 billion deal to build offshore oil development facilities in the United Arab Emirates.

July 14 Ruling Saenuri Party elects Kim Moo-sung, a fourth-term lawmaker, as its chairman.

• Pitcher Ryu Hyun-jin of the Los Angeles Dodgers becomes the first South Korean player to earn 10 wins before the All-Star break.

July 15 President Park Geun-hye appoints five cabinet members, including Finance Minister Choi Kyung-hwan after the parliament endorses their nomination after confirmation hearings.

July 16 South Korea's envoy to the six-party talks meets with his Japanese counterpart in Tokyo to discuss North Korean nuclear issues.

• South Korea and the United States kick off their five-day joint naval exercises in waters off South Korea's southwestern and east coasts.

July 17 A firefighting helicopter crashes into a residential area in South Korea's southern city of Gwangju, killing five firefighters on board. The chopper was on its way to the site of the ferry Sewol's sinking for rescue operations.

July 18 Archer Oh Jin-hyek scores a perfect 360 points at the men's 30-meter competition in a local archery competition.

July 19 Director Cho Keun-hyun's "Late Spring" wins two prizes including the Best Foreign Language Feature Film at the 2014 Madrid International Film Festival.

July 21 President Park Geun-hye has a summit meeting with her Portugese counterpart Aníbal António Cavaco Silva.

July 22 Two passenger trains collide on the east coast, killing one passenger and injuring 91 others.

July 24 South Korea confirms an outbreak of foot-and-mouth disease (FMD) for the first time in over three years.

July 25 Yoo Dae-kyun, the eldest son of the Sewol ferry owner, is arrested at his hideout in Yongin, south of Seoul, after months-long escape.

July 26 Cho Yang-ho, chief of Hanjin Group, is appointed as the chairman of the 2018 PyeongChang Winter Olympics Organizing Committee.

July 27 The Fair Trade Commission imposes 433.5 billion won in fine on 28 builders for price-fixing in a state-funded railroad project.

July 28 The government unveils online payment simplification programs to remove the troublesome authentification process at local internet shopping malls.

July 30 The ruling Saenuri Party wins 11 seats and the oppositions earn four at parliamentary by-elections.

July 31 Co-chairmen of the main opposition party New Politics Alliance for Democracy resign to take responsibility for the crushing defeat at the July 30 parliamentary by-elections.

AUGUST

Aug. 1 The government issues a travel warning for Ebola-hit Liberia and Sierra Leone.

Aug. 4 Hyundai Group Chairperson Hyun Jeong-eun visits North Korea to attend the memorial service of her late husband Chung Mong-hun who actively pushed cross-border tourism projects with North Korea.

Aug. 6 Samsung Electronics Co. and Apple Inc. agree to end all ongoing patent lawsuits outside of the United States.

Aug. 7 The ruling and opposition parties agree to pass the special law to set up an independent panel to examine the cause of the Sewol disaster.

Aug. 8 The government issues a travel warning on Ebola-hit Nigeria.

Aug. 10 The foreign minsters of the Unites States, South Korea and Japan meet on the sidelines of a regional security meeting in Myanmar.

Aug. 11 South Korea suggests holding high-level talks with North Korea on Aug. 18.

• The South Korean government unveils a plan to contribute US$133 billion to international organizations to help North Korea.

Aug. 12 Flames of the Incheon Asian Games are lit at Ganghwa Island on South Koreas's west coast.

Aug. 14 Pope Francis arrives in South Korea on a five-day visit.

Aug. 15 Samsung Electronics Co. acquires SmartThings Inc., a U.S. firm that specializes in the Internet of Things (IoT).

Aug. 16 Pope Francis beatifies 124 Korean martyrs at an open-air Mass in downtown Seoul.

Aug. 18 Pope Francis wraps up his five-day trip to South Korea.

• South Korean golfer Park In-bee wins the LPGA Championships.

Aug. 19 Police wrap up an investigation into the death of Yoo Byung-eun, the owner of the sunken Sewol. They said nothing suspicious was found in his death.

Aug. 21 The communications watchdog imposes 58.4 billion won in fine on three mobile carriers for squandering illegal subsidies.

Aug. 22 North Korea informs South Korea of its plan to send a 273-member sporting squad to the Incheon Asian Games.

Aug. 23 Lee June-hyoung finishes first at the 2014 Junior Grand Prix series in France, becoming the first South Korean male figure skater to win a competition sanctioned by the International Skating Union (ISU).

Aug. 25 South Korea's Little League baseball team wins the 2014 Little League World Series after beating Cuba 8-4 in the final.

Aug. 27 A merger between Daum Corp. and Kakao Corp. is endorsed by their shareholders meetings.

Aug. 28 North Korea says it will not send a cheering squad to the Incheon Asian Games.

SEPTEMBER

Sept. 1 The Ministry of Land, Infrastructure and Transportation announces a plan to stimulate the real estate market. The plan includes measures to encourage the redevelopments of old apartments.

• LG Display Co. completes an 8.5-generation liquid-crystal display factory in Guangzhou, China.

Sept. 2 China designates as a national monument the remains of a building in Hangzhou that was used by anti-Japanese Korean independence fighters as their government-in-exile in China in the early part of the 20th century.

Sept. 3 Girl group Ladies' Code is involved in a car accident on a slippery highway in the outskirts of Seoul. Two of its members were killed.

Sept. 4 South Korea and the United States agree to establish a combined division of their troops in 2015 as part of their programm to boost their combat strength.

Sept. 5 German Uli Stielike is named as the head coach of South Korea's national football team.

Sept. 6 North Korea fires off three short-range missiles into the East Sea.

Sept. 9 Seoul and Washington call on North Korea to hold inter-Korean family reunions and release foreigners detained in the reclusive country.

Sept. 11 Senior diplomats from South Korea, China and Japan hold a regular meeting in Seoul.

• The first group of North Korean athletes arrives in South Korea to compete at the Incheon Asian Games.

Sept. 12 An appellate court sentences CJ Group Chairman Lee Jay-hyun to three year in prison for tax evasion and embezzlement.

Sept. 15 North Korea sends a message to South Korea's presidential office, calling for an end to a leaflet campaign being waged by anti-Pyongyang activists in the South.

• Debris of a North Korean drone is discovered on the western border island of Baekryeong.

• South Korean female golfer Kim Hyo-ju wins the LPGA 2014 Evian Championship.

Sept. 17 A U.S. citizen is caught trying to swim across a border riverr into North Korea.

Sept. 18 President Park Geun-hye meets with International Olympic Committee (IOC) President Thomas Bach.

• Hyundai Motor Group wins a deal to buy a prime land in southern Seoul for 10.5 trillion won.

Sept. 19 The 2014 Incheon Asian Games kicks off to run through Oct. 4, with 9,700 athletes from 45 countries competing.

Sept. 20 President Park Geun-hye leaves Seoul to make a state visit to Canada and attend the United Nations General Assembly.

Sept. 22 South Korea and Canada sign a free trade agreement(FTA).

Sept. 24 President Park Geun-hye delivers a keynote speech at the United Nations Climate Summit.

• South Korea decides to buy 40 F-35A fighter jets from U.S. defense firm Lockheed Martin.

Sept. 26 Foreign ministers of South Korea and Japan meet in New York without making progress on pending is-

sues.
• Samsung Electronics Co.'s latest phablet Galaxy Note 4 hits showrooms of South Korea.

Sept. 30 Jessica leaves Girls Generation, citing that she wants to focus on fashion business.

OCTOBER

Oct. 1 South Korea and Japan hold a senior-level strategy meeting in Tokyo.
• The Terminal Distribution Structure Improvement Act takes effect, aiming to lower prices and correct pricing distortions in the market.

Oct. 2 South Korean men's football team wins the gold medal for the first time in 28 years at the Incheon Asian Games, beating North Korea 1-0 in the final.

Oct. 3 North Korea pays US$191,682 in accommodation costs for its athletes at the Incheon Asian Games.

Oct. 4 Three North Korean high-ranking officials surprisingly visit South Korea to attend the closing ceremony of the Incheon Asian Games. They are Hwang Pyong-so, vice chairman of the National Defense Commission; Choe Ryong-hae, secretary of the Workers' Party of Korea, and Kim Yang-ho, head of the United Front Department.

Oct. 6 The government announces the results of its probe into the ferry Sewol's sinking, saying that the disaster was caused by a combination of cargo overloading and an illegal redesigning of the ship.

Oct. 7 Rapper Psy's "Gangnam Style" music video tops a record 2.1 billion views on YouTube.

Oct. 8 Prosecution indicts a reporter of Japanese Sankei Shimbun newspaper on charges of defaming President Park Geun-hye by reporting rumors about her whereabouts at the time of the April 16 sinking of the Sewol ferry.

Oct. 9 The main opposition New Politics Alliance for Democracy elects three-term lawmaker Woo Yoon-keun as its new floor leader.

Oct. 10 New national football head coach Uli Stielike makes his triumphant debut at a friendly against Paraguay in Cheonan. South Korea beats the South Americans 2-0.

Oct. 13 The co-CEO of Daum Kakao Corp. vows not to respond to warrants from prosecutors seeking to access private messages on the company's flagship chat service KakaoTalk.
• South Korean golfer Bae Sang-moon earns his second PGA victory at the Fry. com Open.

Oct. 14 The floating Rubber Duck goes on display at a lake in southern Seoul.
• North Korean leader Kim Jong-un makes his first public appearance in 40 days amid rumors of a serious ankle disease.

Oct. 15 Two Koreas hold a military meeting in the neutral border town of Panmunjeon.
• The Bank of Korea cuts its key rate to 2% from 2.25%t and revises down the 2014 growth outlook to 3.5% from 3.8%.

Oct. 16 President Park Geun-hye meets with French President Francois Hollande and Danish Prime Minister Helle Thorning-Schmidt on the sidelines of the 10th Asia-Europe Meeting (ASEM) in Italy.

Oct. 17 A ventilation grate collapses during an outdoor concert at a multipurpose complex in Seongnam, just southeast of Seoul. Sixteen people were killed and 11 others injured.
• Nexen Heroes' second baseman Seo Geon-chang establishes a new KBO record of 200 hits in a single season.

Oct. 19 South Korean golfer Baek Kyu-jung wins the LPGA KEB–Hana Bank Championship.

Oct. 20 The International Telecommunications Union (ITU) conference kicks off in the southern port city of Busan, attended by thousands of officials and businessmen for discussions on ICT issues.

Oct. 21 North Korea releases Jeffrey Edward Fowle, one of three U.S. detainees.

Oct. 22 Unionized workers of leading shipbuilder Hyundai Heavy Industries Co. vote for a general strike for the first time in 18 years.

Oct. 23 An appellate court sentences

former president Chun Doo-hwan's second son to three years in prison for tax evasion.

Oct. 27 South Korea is elected to ITU Council for the seventh consecutive time.

• South Korean golfer Park In-bee regains her No. 1 title in the world rankings.

Oct. 29 One more body is recovered from the Sewol ferry that sank in the the sea off South Korea's southwestn coast. Nine people are still missing.

• Samsung Group heir Lee Jae-yong meets with Chinese President Xi Jinping in Bejing, their third meeting this yaer.

Oct. 30 South Korea's vehicle registrations top 20 million for the first time since 1945.

• New U.S. ambassador to South Korea Mark Lippert arrives in Seoul to take up his post. Lippert, 41, is the youngest U.S. envoy ever to Seoul.

NOVEMBER

Nov. 1 Labor unions of public and education workers hold a joint rally in Yeouido, west of Seoul, in protest against the government's move to reform the public servants' pension program.

Nov. 2 The bereaved families of the victims of the Sewol ferry sinking pledge to respect a bi-partisan agreement on a special law under which an independent panel will be set up to investigate the cause of the accident.

Nov. 3 President Park Geun-hye meets with Willem-Alexander, the king of the Netherlands.

• The Korean won soars to a 6-year high of 950 won against 100 Japanese yen in the aftermath of Tokyo's additional quantitative easing.

Nov. 4 Hyundai Motor Co. and Kia Motors Corp. agree with the U.S. environment authorities to pay a fine of US$100 million won for inflating mileage.

Nov. 5 President Park Geun-hye meets with Sheikh Hamad bin Khalifa Al Thani of Qatar.

• A local court sentences Yoo Dae-kyun, the eldest son of the Sewol ferry owner, to three years in prison on charges of embezzling 7 billion won in corporate funds.

• LG Electronics Inc. and Google Inc. agree to share each others' patent rights for the coming 10 years.

Nov. 6 The U.S. Army announces to replace the 1st Armored Brigade Combat Team, a permanent brigade in South Korea, from June 2015 with a rotational unit of the 2nd Brigade Combat Team of the 1st Cavalry Division, stationed at Fort Hood, Texas.

• The government announces to send an advance team of officials to Sierra Leone, charged with handling logistical affairs for South Korea's medical assistance to the Ebola-hit country.

Nov. 7 The ITU conference closes.

• The United States slaps 6.88% of anti-dumping duties on non-oriented electrical steel products from South Korea.

• South Korea seeks to buy PAC-3 interceptor missiles and related equipment for US$1.4 billion as part of its Korean Air and Missile Defense (KAMD) project.

Nov. 8 North Korea releases two U.S. detainees, Kenneth Bae and Matthew Todd Miller, after U.S. spy chief James Clapper made a secret trip to the reclusive country.

• Football club Jeonbuk Motors regains the K-League Cup in three years.

Nov. 9 President Park Geun-hye starts a nine-day trip to China, Myanmar and Australia before attending the summit meetings of the Asia-Pacific Economic Cooperation (APEC), the ASEAN+3 and the Group of 20.

Nov. 10 South Korean President Park Geun-hye and Chinese President Xi Jinping announce the conclusion of South Korea-China free trade negotiations.

Nov. 11 The government officially terminates the search for those still missing from the sunken ferry Sewol, 209 days it sank.

• A local court sentences the captain of the sunken ferry Sewol to 36 years in prison for abandoning passengers at the time of the deadly sinking.

• Baseball club Samsung Lions wins the Korean Series for four straight years.

Nov. 12 President Park Geun-hye meets with Indian Prime Minister Narendra Modi in Myanmar on the sidelines of the ASEAN+3 summit meeting.

Nov. 13 The advance team of government officials for handling logistics affairs in Ebola-hit Sierra Leone departs to Britain.

• No. 2 mobile carrier KT Corp. launches a 4th generation long-term evolution (LTE) service in Rwanda.

Nov. 14 Asiana Airlines Inc., South Korea's No. 2 flag carrier, gets a 45-day flight suspension on its Seoul-San Francisco route. The airline was penalized after one of jets crashed in the U.S. city last year, killing three people.

• The South Korean and U.S. air forces start their biannual joint military exercise, Max Thuner, for a nine-day run, with 1,200 military servicemembers taking part.

• Samsung SDS Co., Samsung Group's key IT unit, makes its debut on South Korea's main bourse, closing far above its initial public offering price.

Nov. 15 South Korea and New Zealand reach full agreement on their bilateral free trade deal, five years after they started negotiations.

• A fire in a holiday cottage in a southern resort area of Damyang kills five and wounds another five.

Nov. 17 South Korea's main bourse operator KRX resumes trading of stock options in the derivatives market after a 40-month hiatus.

Nov. 18 Nexen Heroes second baseman Seo Geon-chang wins the honor of the KBO's most valuable player of the year. His feat includes 200 hits.

Nov. 19 The government disbands the Coast Guard and the National Emergency Management Agency and place them under the control of the newly created Public Safety Agency.

Nov. 20 A local court sentences the head of the sunken ferry Sewol operator to 10 years in prison for involuntary manslaughter in the deaths of more than 300 people.

Nov. 21 Two Koreas agree on former first lady Lee Hee-ho's North Korean visit.

• South Korea's former national football coach Hong Myung-bo is inducted into the Asian Football Confederation (AFC) Hall of Fame.

Nov. 22 Prime Minister Chung Hong-won embarks on an eight-day trip to Egypt, Morocco and Azerbaijan.

Nov. 23 South Korea rescues a North Korean fishing boat drifting in the waters of East Sea.

Nov. 24 A parliamentary subcommittee introduces a bill on North Korean human rights issues.

Nov. 26 Samsung Group announces plans to sell its four chemicals affiliates, including Samsung Total Prochemicals Co. and Samsung Thales, to Hanwha Group for a combined 1.9 trillion won.

Nov. 27 Tatsuya Kato, a former Seoul bureau chief of Japan's Sankei Shimbun newspaper, pleads not guilty to defamation charges during a court hearing..

Nov. 28 South Korea's overall trade volume surpasses US$1 trillion for four straight years.

• UNESCO adds "nongak", traditional Korean music performed by farmers, to its intangible cultural heritage list.

Nov. 30 Representatives of Vietnam's Communist Party visit South Korea for the first time in 22 years since the two countries began diplomatic relationship.

DECEMBER

Dec. 1 The won-yuan swap market officially launches in Seoul, with the South Korean currency closing at 180.3 won against tits Chinese counterpart.

• The 40,500-ton South Korean fishing boat Oryong 501 sinks in the Bering Sea, leaving 27 crewmembers dead and 26 others missing. The ship was carrying 60 crew members.

• Veteran football striker Lee Dong-gook of Jeonbuk Hyundai Motors is awarded the K-League's most valuable player of the year, his third career top prize.

Dec. 2 The National Assembly passes bills on the South Korea-Canada and South Korea-Australia free trade agreements.

Dec. 4 The communications watchdog imposes 2.4 billion won in fine on three mobile carriers for violating the new handset subsidy law.

• Michael Sandel, the well-known author of the best-selling book "Justice," is awared Seoul's honorary citizenship.

Dec. 5 Cho Hyun-ah, vice president of Korean Air Lines Co., orders a taxiing Korean Air plane back to the gate to deplane a flight attendant in a fit of temper over what she though was an improper in-flight passenger service at New York's John F. Kennedy Airport.

Dec. 7 South Korea wins the Korea-Japan Women's National Golf Team Match Play Competition for three straight years. Kim Hyo-joo was chosen as the most valuable player.

Dec. 8 Kim Hyo-joo wins the KLPGA Player of the Year award and Baek Kyu-jung earns the Rookie of the Year prize.

Dec. 9 Prof. Chung Chang-ho is elected as a judge of the International Criminal Court (ICC).

Dec. 10 South Korea and Vietnam declare the conclusion of negotiations for their proposed bilateral free trade agreement.

• The Korea Development Institute (KDI), a state-run think tank, slahses its 2015 economic growth outlook of South Korea to 3.5% from 3.8%.

Dec. 11 A special summit of leaders from South Korea and the Association of Southeast Asian Nations (ASEAN) kicks off in the southern port city of Busan.

• Prosecution raids the headquarters of Korean Air Lines Co. and issues a travel ban on its executive, Cho Hyun-ah, who was engulfed in the so-called nut-rage scandal.

Dec. 12 The Seoul-Canberra free trade agreement takes effect, eliminating a 15% tariff on Australian wine, among other goods.

Dec. 13 President Park Geun-hye meets with Cambodian Prime Minister Hun Sen.

Dec. 14 A Navy captain and a Navy commander are arrested for receiving bribes from a local company in exchange for helping it win a contract to supply substandard parts to a Navy salvage vessel Tongyeong.

Dec. 15 The benchmark KOSPI plunges to below the 1,900 point level in intra-day trading.

Dec. 16 Rep. Park Ji-won visits North Korea to deliver a wreath in commemoration of the third anniversary of late leader Kim Jong-il on behalf of Lee Hee-ho, the wife of former President Kim Dae-jung.

• South Korea's defense industry firm Samsung Techwin Co. agrees to sell the K-9 self-propelled howitzers to Huta Stalowa Wola, the Polish public defense company, in a US$320 million deal.

Dec. 18 Swedish furniture firm IKEA opens the first South Korean showroom in Gwangmyeong on the southern outskirts of Seoul.

• Cheil Industries Co., Samsung Group's de facto holding company, debuts on the benchmark KOSPI, becoming the 15th biggest share by market capitalization.

• Confidential data about two nuclear reactors leak from the state-run Korea Hydro and Nuclear Power Co. (KHNP), South Korea's sole nuclear power plant operator.

Dec. 19 The Constitutional Court rules in favor of dissolution of the Unified Progressive Party (UPP), a minor leftist party accused of being pro-North Korea. The UPP became the first South Korean political party to be disbanded since the country's constitution was adopted first in 1948.

Dec. 23 Samsung Electronics Co. starts mass production of 8-gigabit mobile memory chips based on its 20-nanometer technology

Dec. 24 Prosecutors seek an arrest warrant for Cho Hyun-ah, a vice president of Korean Air Lines Co., for violating the aviation law in a so-called nut-rage incident.

Dec. 26 Three workers die apparently after inhaling toxic gas at the construction site of New Gori No. 3 nuclear reactor in the southern port city of Ulsan.

Dec. 30 South Korea sends a P-3 surveillance plane to join the Indonesia-led search for an AirAsia plane that went missing in the Indian Ocean.

Dec. 31 NH Investment & Securities Co. becomes South Korea's biggest brokerage house after merging with Woori Investment & Securities Co.

Highlights in Korea

Yonhap News Agency

THE SEWOL DISASTER

■ Never Forget the Sewol That All Koreans Want to Forget

The Sewol was a 6,825-ton passenger ferry operated by Chonghaejin Marine Co. that traveled from the western port city of Incheon to the southern resort island of Jeju two times a week. The trip took 13 hours and 30 minutes.

The boat was built in June 1994 at Hayashikane Shipbuilding & Engineering in Nagasaki, Japan. It arrived in South Korea in Oct. 2012, and was put into service in March 2013 after six months of repairs. Before being sold to South Korea, the ship had plied between Kagoshima and Okinawa between June 1994 and Sept. 2012, under the flag name of Ferry Naminoue, meaning top of the wave in English.

The Sewol, at 145m long by 22m wide, was one of the biggest passenger vessels in South Korea, with a maximum speed of 21 knots. It could carry 921 passengers, with a legal capacity of 180 vehicles and 152 regular cargo containers at the same time. There were royal rooms, family rooms and dormitories along with lounges, a cafeteria, restaurants, game rooms and bathrooms.

■ What Happened on the Morning of April 16?

At 9 p.m. on April 15, 2014, at the Incheon Seaport, 325 students and 14 teachers from Danwon High School went aboard the Sewol for their field trip to Jeju. Carrying 476 people, including other passengers and crew members, the Sewol left the Incheon port some two hours and 30 minutes behind schedule due to foggy weather.

At 8:25 a.m. on April 16, the Sewol entered the Maenggol Channel, which is notorious for its strong underwater currents, a condition that was exacerbated that day by the full moon from the night before. At 8:48 a.m., after leaving the channel, the ship made a sharp turn and started to sink. The late Choi Duk-ha, a senior at Danwon High School on board the Sewol, called 119, the national emergency service call, at 8:52 a.m., saying "The boat is capsizing."

Although the boat was sinking, Sewol crew members, including captain Lee Joon-seok, took no emergency actions to rescue their passengers but made announcements to order them not to leave their cabins. The crew members escaped the sunken ship faster than any other students and passengers on board.

All 304 students and passengers waiting in their cabins for other directions drowned. "The boat is sinking. Mom, Dad, I miss you." This was the last SNS message that came from the Sewol. It was made by a student at 10:17 a.m.

■ Helter-skelter Rescue Operation

The Jeollanam-do Fire Service was first informed of the Sewol ferry sinking from the national emergency service call after student Choi reported the accident. But it sent a firefighting helicopter 21 minutes after receiving the information, saying that it was the business of the Coast Guard.

▲ A family member of a missing passenger of the sunken ferry Sewol bursts into tears aboard a Coast Guard ship off South Korea's southwestern coast on April 17 as search and rescue work is delayed by unfavorable sea and weather conditions.

The Jindo vessel traffic service (VTS), highly responsible for detecting a maritime accident, was aware of the Sewol sinking at 9:06 a.m., after the Mokpo Coast Guard informed it of the case.

The Coast Guard could not avoid the responsibility. The Mokpo Coast Guard dispatched patrol vessel No. 123 in response to the first report of the incident but it did not call people to abandon ship and jump into the water. It focused on rescuing crew members, including captain Lee. The captains of the Sewol and the patrol vessel never tried to evacuate the passengers from the sinking ferry.

■ Prosecutors' Probe

The prosecution said the ferry sinking was caused by a combination of cargo overloading, illegal redesigning of the ship to increase its cargo load and the steerman's poor helmsmanship.

A total of 399 people were booked and 154 were arrested on charges of overloading, illegal redesigning, delayed rescue operations and embezzlement, including Yoo Byung-eun, the owner of the Sewol.

■ Investigation into Yoo Byung-eun Family

Prosecutors widened their investigation into irregularities and mismanagement by Yoo Byung-eun, the de facto owner of the sunken Sewol, and his relatives. They found that Yoo's mismanagement had caused the Sewol disaster as his relatives owned tens of billions of won in assets in South Korea but badly managed Chonghaejin Marine Co., the operator of the Sewol.

Investigators said Yoo and his family had illegally acquired 183.6 billion won through money laundering, using affiliate companies and paper companies. They registered copyrights and trademarks of company and boat names, and lent them to Chonghaejin Marine Co. and other affiliates in return for massive rental fees.

But the probe had been impeded by uncooperative suspects, who refused to respond to the prosecution's summonses. Investigators had requested help from Interpol to arrest Hyuk-kee, Yoo's second son and Som-na, the eldest daughter, who fled overseas. Dae-kyun, the eldest son, had also been at large.

The prosecution launched a project to search for the whereabouts of the oldest Yoo in cooperation with the police. It raided houses of Yoo's followers, offices of affiliate companies and a retreat of the Evangelical Baptist Church of Korea.

▪ Hide-and-seek

On the morning of June 12, police discovered a decayed body on a farm in South Jeolla Province. They did not take it seriously as they thought it was the death of a homeless person.

The National Forensic Service conducted an autopsy and found out that the remains were those of Yoo Byung-eun. But it said that it could not determine the exact cause of Yoo's death due to the heavy decomposition of the body. On July 25, Yoo's first son, Dae-kyun, was arrested in his hideout three months after fleeing.

The prosecutors pledged to search for the Yoo family's hidden properties, but it was difficult to seize them all as they concealed their fortune under borrowed-name accounts.

▪ Trials

The Gwangju District Court sentenced captain Lee Joon-seok to 36 years in prison for abandoning passengers at the time of the deadly sinking. It also convicted the ship's chief engineer, identified only by his surname Park, of murder, giving him a 30-year jail term.

Prison terms ranging from five years to 20 years were handed down to 13 other crew members, including the first engineer surnamed Sohn, who were charged with abandonment and violation of a ship safety act. The court dismissed prosecutors' earlier demand for the death penalty on the murder charges.

The Incheon District Court sentenced Yoo Dae-kyun, the eldest son of the late shipping tycoon blamed for the ferry disaster, to three years in prison for embezzlement. It also sentenced Yoo Byung-ill, the elder brother of Byung-eun, to one year in prison, with a two-year stay of execution, for embezzlement.

The court also handed down a prison term of two years to Yoo Byung-ho, the younger brother of the deceased tycoon, for borrowing 3 billion won from one of the affiliates run by his elder brother's family. In a separate ruling, the court handed down prison terms ranging from 18 months to four years to 10 of Yoo's close aides, including chiefs of the company's affiliates.

▪ The Government's Measures

A month after the Sewol incident, President Park Geun-hye issued a special statement on the reform of South Korea's disaster management system. The government took follow-up measures, including disbanding the Coast Guard and the establishment of the Ministry of Public Safety and Security.

After months of discussion and wrangling in the parliament, three follow-up bills passed the National Assembly to establish the Ministry of Public Safety and Security, which allows the government to seize a criminal's assets, even if those assets have already been bequeathed to their children, and to set up an independent fact-finding panel on the Sewol disaster. The bills were endorsed by the Cabinet on Nov. 18, 216 days after the ferry sank, killing more than 300 people.

POPE FRANCIS' VISIT TO SOUTH KOREA

■ Francis is First Pontiff to Visit South Korea in 25 Years

Pope Francis made his first visit to South Korea in Aug. 2014, for five days, or 100 hours. He made a great impression on the South Korean people, who were struggling in a deep sorrow in the aftermath of the Sewol ferry tragedy, which killed more than 300 people.

In the beginning of the year, some foreign news reports had hinted that Pope Francis would visit South Korea and in January, Federico Lombardi, a Holy See spokesman, mentioned the possibility of such a trip. Two months later, the South Korean presidential office and South Korea's Catholic diocese officially announced that the pope would visit from Aug. 14 to 18.

Pope Francis chose South Korea for his third overseas trip and his first Asian tour since his inauguration in March 2013. There have been two popes who visited South Korea, including Pope Francis. Pope John Paul II first came to South Korea in 1984 and he visited the Asian country again five years later.

Pope Francis came to South Korea to attend the 6th Asian Youth Day in the central city of Daejeon and to carry out a beatification ceremony for 124 Korean martyrs.

■ Pope's Five-day Stay Comforts South Korean People

On his first day Pope Francis arrived in South Korea at 10:16 a.m. on Aug. 14. He started his trip by meeting those "in need of consolation in Korean society," like the families of the Sewol victims, North Korean defectors, disabled people and immigrant workers. The Holy Father shook hands with each of the Sewol families who came to the airport and said, "I keep the pain of the victims deep in my mind. My heart aches."

In the afternoon, he had a brief talk with President Park Geun-hye and delivered a short speech to South Korean government officials. In the speech, the pope said the quest for peace represents a challenge, but said efforts for reconciliation and stability are the only sure path to lasting peace. "May all of us dedicate these days to peace, to praying for it and deepening our resolve to achieve it," the pontiff said.

▲ *South Korean President Park Geun-hye meets with Pope Francis at the presidential office Cheong Wa Dae in Seoul on Aug. 14.*

On his second day Pope Francis went to the central city of Daejeon via KTX, the South Korean bullet train. He presided over the first open-door Mass on the feast day of the Assumption of Mary held at a packed stadium in Daejeon. The Holy Father had a few minutes before the Mass to meet survivors and family members of the victims who lost their loved ones in the April 16 ferry sinking that left more than 300 people dead.

In the afternoon, the pope met and addressed participants of the 6th Asian Youth Day at the Solmoe Holy Ground, the birthplace of Korea's first priest, Kim Tae-gon, in the western port city of Dangjin.

On his third day Pope Francis started the day briefly visiting Seosomun Martyrs' Shrine, a historical site where the largest number of early Korean Catholics were executed. The pontiff held an open-air Mass at Gwanghwamun Square before 170,000 Korean Catholics and beatified 124 Korean martyrs.

During a parade down the boulevard in an open car from Seoul City Hall to the Gwanghwamun intersection, he occasionally stopped his parade to kiss children on the forehead, which brought claps and cheers from the crowd every time.

After the Mass, Francis met with some of the sick and disabled people living in Kkottongnae, a sanitarium center for the disabled in Eumseong, 131km south of Seoul, and thousands of Korean ascetics and representatives of lay people there.

On his fourth day Pope Francis started the day by baptizing the father of one of the children killed in April's ferry disaster at the Vatican Embassy in Seoul, where he is staying during his Korean visit. Lee Ho-jin, a 56-year-old who lost his youngest son in the ferry sinking, asked the pope on Friday to baptize him and received his baptismal name of Francisco.

Later in the afternoon, he headed to Seosan, south of Seoul, and celebrated a Mass that wrapped up the 6th Asian Youth Day at the nearby Haemieupseong Fortress, an old army post during the Joseon Dynasty (1392-1910), where some 1,000 Catholics were executed for their faith.

On his last day Pope Francis held a special Mass on peace and reconciliation on the Korean Peninsula at Seoul's Myeongdong Cathedral, which wrapped up his first official visit to Asia.

On hand at the special Mass were some 1,000 figures representing all walks of life in South Korea, including seven Korean women forced to serve as sex slaves by the Japanese military during World War II and five defectors from North Korea. Shortly before the Mass at the cathedral, the pontiff had time to briefly meet leaders of South Korea's 12 leading religious orders. Pope Francis departed Seoul aboard a Korean Air charter plane in the afternoon, wrapping up his five-day visit.

■ Pope Laments the Sewol Tragedy

The papal visit offered comfort to broken-hearted South Koreans and minors who needed love and condolences. Among the first people he greeted upon arriving on Aug. 14 were four South Koreans, out of hundreds, who lost their loved ones in the ferry tragedy.

The ferry Sewol capsized off South Korea's southwestern coast on April 16, leaving more than 300 people dead. Most of them were high school students on a field trip, making the tragedy one of the country's worst peacetime disasters. He kept donning a yellow ribbon on his chest in solidarity with the victims during his entire five-day visit.

In a press conference aboard his flight back to the Vatican, Pope Francis said he was unable to maintain neutrality before the victims of a South Korean ferry tragedy because their suffering was "human."

The Holy Father also gave special messages on peace and reconciliation on the Korean Peninsula. He continued to put a strong emphasis on peace, saying, "May all of us dedicate these days to peace, to praying for it and deepening our resolve to achieve it," upon his arrival.

■ Legacy of Pope Francis' Visit

His five-day itinerary was packed with meetings with the country's marginalized -- not surprising for a pontiff who espouses building a "poor Church for the poor."

Upon arrival, there was no special welcoming ceremony at the airport. Instead, underprivileged people, including the families of Sewol victims, immigrant workers and North Korean defectors and a few Catholic believers were there to greet Pope Francis.

He took a small, humble car produced by a South Korean carmaker

▲ Pope Francis blesses a Korean child during the "Mass of the Assumption of Mary" at Daejeon World Cup stadium in Daejeon, South Korea, on Aug. 15.

during his stay, instead of a luxurious bullet-proof vehicle. He stood in an open car to have face-to-face contact with ordinary people.

When the pope visited a center for the sick and disabled in Eumseong, 131km south of Seoul, he stood for nearly 50 minutes to watch a performance by disabled children.

His every message and movement touched the hearts of South Koreans who had experienced an unprecedented tragedy before his visit. The pope also comforted those who had been hurt and isolated in a materialized and polarized society.

■ Message for Religious Harmony

Pope Francis used the word 'love' most on public occasions during his five-day visit. He spoke 8,518 words in 12 speeches and Masses, with 'love' appearing 166 times. The pope's message was welcomed by other religious communities. In a meeting with Pope Francis, other religious leaders hailed the Holy Father's move to have interest in peace and underprivileged people.

DISSOLUTION OF UPP

■ Legal Developments

South Korea's Constitutional Court ordered the dissolution of the Unified Progressive Party (UPP), a pro-North Korean minor opposition party, on Dec. 19, 2014, 40 days after the Ministry of Justice filed a suit before the court. No political party had been banned by a court decision in the nation's modern history.

The government held a Cabinet meeting on Nov. 5, 2013, and passed a petition calling for the disbandment of the left-leaning minor opposition party. The petition was filed with the Constitutional Court upon approval from President Park Geun-hye.

The Constitutional Court had the first hearing on Dec. 24, 2013, and held two hearings each month. For the nearly one-year period, 12 people appeared in the court as witnesses and six as references.

The Justice Ministry submitted 2,907 pieces of written evidence and the UPP handed in 908 pieces. It totaled 175,000 pages, weighing 931kg. The Justice Ministry submitted a book previously owned by a former official of the leftist Democratic Labor Party (DLP) and seized by the ministry. The book is about North Korea's 'military first' ideology.

Justice Minister Hwang Kyo-ahn said in the final hearing that a small hole in a bank could destroy the entire riverbank. UPP Chairperson Lee Jung-hee argued that the government was oppressing the minor party just because of political differences.

■ Dissolution of UPP

The UPP was dissolved by the Constitutional Court three years after its establishment in 2011, when it was separated from the DLP. Upon the ruling, assets of the UPP were confiscated by the National Election Commission (NEC), the election watchdog. The party has been forced to forfeit all state subsidies and its assets have been frozen.

The court also ruled that five UPP legislators be stripped of their seats, regardless of whether they were elected through popular vote or the proportional representation system. Reps. Kim Mi-hyui, Kim Jae-yeon, Oh Byung-yun, Lee Sang-kyu and Lee Seok-ki were immediately stripped of their parliamentary seats.

The establishment of an alternative party with similar policies was also prohibited. A party is banned from using the name UPP for good.

■ Justices of Constitutional Court

According to the South Korean Constitution, six out of nine justices must rule on the dissolution of a party. Their political tendencies and inclinations were very important in meeting the quorum. Out of the nine justices, three are designated by the president and another three are recommended by the Chief Justice of the Supreme Court.

The ruling and opposition parties choose one each, with the last member is selected on the two parties' consent.

Eight out of the nine justices ruled in favor of the Justice Ministry, while the only one voted against it. The majority said that the party's dissolution was the only way to eliminate the threat it posed to South Korean democracy.

"The genuine goal and the activities of the UPP are to achieve progressive democracy and to finally adopt North Korea-style socialism," chief justice Park Han-cheol said, reading out the landmark ruling that was broadcast live on television.

He said the court came to the conclusion that the UPP's principles and activities were in violation of the "basic democratic order" stipulated by the Constitution of South Korea, which remains technically at war with North Korea.

The court also accepted the government's argument for the need to safeguard the country's democracy and national security by banning an unconstitutional political party. "The UPP, with a hidden agenda to adopt North Korea's socialism, organized meetings to discuss a rebellion. The act goes against the basic democratic order of the Constitution," Park said. "There is no other alternative to banning the UPP as the party causes real harm," Park added.

The only dissenting justice, Kim Yi-su, cautioned against making generalizations, saying that only some members of the UPP were engaged in activities supportive of Pyongyang. He maintained that a political party should only be outlawed when it is absolutely necessary to protect the country.

■ UPP Seeks to Overturn Disbandment Ruling

In February, the dissolved UPP asked the Constitutional Court to review its decision to dissolve their political party, which was embroiled in a pro-North Korean plot, arguing that the decision was "wrong."

It is the first time in the country's modern history that a disbanded party filed such a petition for a retrial of a ruling by the Constitutional Court. The South Korean Constitutional Court currently does not allow appellate trials.

"We will re-file a petition with the Constitutional Court since the Supreme Court upheld an acquittal of conspiracy charges," said Lee Jung-hee, a former UPP chief. She further argued that the Constitutional Court delivered the wrong decision, urging sitting justices to amend the court's "mistake." The UPP's filing is based on a separate ruling by the Supreme Court.

In January, the Supreme Court acquitted Rep. Lee Seok-ki of charges that he had conspired to plot a rebellion, and only found him guilty of instigating the members to stage a rebellion. It said there was no proof that a secret organization existed in which the 53-year-old and other UPP members convened to discuss insurgency plans.

▲ Lee Jung-hee, the head of the minor opposition Unified Progressive Party (UPP), speaks to reporters in front of the Constitutional Court in Seoul on Dec. 19 after the court ordered the disbandment of the party, which holds five seats in the 300-member parliament.

The UPP latched onto this discrepancy as a basis for their request for a retrial. Its legal representatives said they submitted the request earlier in the day. "How the majority treats a minority shows how mature a democratic nation is," read the request. "It's about time that South Korea returned to being the mature democracy that it once was."

EX-PRESIDENTIAL AIDE'S MEDDLING IN STATE AFFAIRS

■ Unveiling

On the front page of its Nov. 18 paper, the vernacular daily Segye Times ran an article under the headline "Jeong Yun-hoe's meddling in state affairs is true," claiming the former aide held regular meetings with a group of 10 other people, including three of President Park Geun-hye's closest secretaries, to exchange information on state affairs.

The report, citing an internal document of the presidential office dated Jan. 6, also claimed that Jeong instructed the group to inform the press and other news outlets of plans to replace Park's then chief of staff, Kim Ki-choon, so that the right mood could be created for his replacement.

The former aide holds no official title in the current administration but was reported to still wield enormous influence in the running of state affairs.

■ Presidential Office Denies Allegations

Park's spokesman, Min Kyung-wook, strongly denied the allegations, saying the presidential office plans to take legal action against those involved, which could include the newspaper and some of the officials cited in the article.

"The report regarding Cheong Wa Dae in today's Segye Times is not true," he said in a press briefing. "The reported (allegations) are nothing but a collection of groundless rumors." The internal document cited in the article was a report on rumors that were circulating in the financial community at the time, not a formal report for the alleged internal inspection, Min said.

The chief of staff received a verbal report on the rumors at the time but the presidential office found them to be untrue and took no action against those cited in the article, the spokesman added. Later in the day, Min said three of the 10 presidential officials decided to lodge a complaint with the prosecution against the daily on charges of libel.

The presidential office will also ask the prosecution to investigate a former official at the presidential office, who authored the internal document, about whether he violated the law on the management of public records, Min added.

The main opposition party New Politics Alliance for Democracy (NPAD) immediately attacked the administration, claiming that the allegations it has raised about the existence of a secret group of aides controlling Cheong Wa Dae were proven to be true.

"The (10 members of the reported group) and those involved in writing up the document must (testify) before the National Assembly's steering committee," NPAD spokesman Kim Sung-soo said in a press briefing. "Our party will focus our powers on this issue."

The presidential office had earlier launched an inspection in January into allegations that Jeong took hundreds of millions of won (hundreds of thousands of U.S. dollars) in bribes in exchange for favors in high-level government appointments.

The paper also claimed that the inspection was halted in February after the police official in charge was abruptly sent back to the police from his assignment at the presidential office. Cheong Wa Dae denied those allegations, saying it will take "strong measures" against articles that are not true.

■ Revelations

The scandal snowballed as the people in question had press interviews and disclosed their secrets behind the scenes. Jeong, who served as the president's chief of staff when she was a lawmaker, argued that the internal document of the presidential office dated Jan. 6 was fake and groundless. But Cho Eung-chun, another presidential official on the other side of Jeong, said the document carried quite highly reliable information.

The Jeong-Cho arguments spread to rumors about a power struggle between Jeong and Park Ji-man, President Park's younger brother. According to the rumors, the younger Park was supporting Cho, who tried to hold the trio of President Park's closest secretaries in check, and the trio was instructed by Jeong.

Cho, a former state prosecutor, had first encountered Ji-man when he was indicted for drug intake in 1994, and has continued a close relationship with the president's brother.

Jeong, however, refuted the rumors. He said that he has not been in contact with the three presidential secretaries, or with President Park. "The report that I had regular meetings with 10 officials and meddled in state affairs is totally untrue and false," Jeong said.

Meanwhile, Yoo Jin-ryong, former Minister of Culture, Sports and Tourism, had a media interview, hinting that President Park has exerted influence over the ministry's personnel affairs.

A local media report said that Jeong's daughter, a horseback rider, had received better-than-expected results in a local equestrian competition, suspecting her father's influence on the sport's jurors and the overseeing ministry. An official in charge of the equestrian affairs was dismissed from his position after the controversial contest.

■ President Park's Firm Response

President Park Geun-hye lamented the snowballing scandal over allegations that a group of her core aides meddled in state affairs behind the scenes and asked that people wait for the results of prosecution probe.

"I think it's a shame that the entire country is swayed by the type of stories that are typically mentioned in private papers," said Park during a luncheon with the ruling party leadership, referring to unofficial chit sheets, mostly carrying unconfirmed rumors, that are made for circulation in the stock market.

"Jeong had left me a long time ago and I lost contact with him. And I don't let my brother come to Cheong Wa Dae," said Park. "It's nonsense that these people have meddled in state affairs." Park, during the luncheon meeting, asked the participants to play a role in preventing the "consuming" controversy from impeding state management, especially at a time when the economy is on the brink of a crisis.

"After a daily reported the suspicions without properly confirming them, other news media are continuing to make absurd allegations. I want you to watch the result of the prosecution's probe (into the case) without being swayed by such unilateral allegations," she said.

■ Prosecution's Investigation

The prosecution widened its investigation into the case, focusing on the leak of the internal document. It arrested two police officers who had allegedly brought out an internal document from the presidential office when they had worked for Cheong Wa Dae, and gave it to the media.

On Dec. 10, prosecutors summoned Jeong, who said he would do his best to make clear who was behind the entire situation. Five days later, investigators summoned Park Ji-man.

In January of the next year, the prosecution wrapped up its months-long probe, concluding that the presidential document

▲ Jeong Yun-hoe, a former close aide to President Park Geun-hye, answers reporters' questions after arriving at the Seoul Central District Prosecutors' Office in Seoul on Dec. 10 to face questioning over suspicions that he had meddled in state affairs behind the scenes.

claiming a former aide to President Park Geun-hye tried to exert undue influence on state affairs was fabricated by Superintendent Park Kwan-cheon.

Investigators said that Supt. Park authored and leaked the document. The document was then handed over to the president's younger brother, Ji-man, under the orders of Cho, former presidential secretary.

Cho was indicted on charges of leaking confidential information, and violating the Presidential Records Management Act, prosecutors said.

Despite the prosecution's probe outcome, the scandal had rocked the nation for quite long time and pushed down President Park's approval ratings to a record low of 37% in mid-December.

MILITARY MIRED IN SCANDALS

■ Overview

The South Korean military faced severe public criticism over a series of deadly incidents that laid bare chronic problems with bullying in the barracks and a rigid order-and-obey culture.

In April, an Army private first class died after long suffering physical, mental and sexual abuse by six of his senior comrades at the barracks. Two months later, an Army sergeant who had been bullied by his comrades went on a shooting spree at a border outpost on the east coast, killing five soldiers and wounding seven others.

Pervasive corruption in the defense industry further tarnished the military's image. The country's first indigenous salvage ship, the Tongyeong, failed to be mobilized for a rescue mission during the tragic sinking of the ferry Sewol in April because its delivery was delayed due to the use of substandard parts.

■ Young Soldier Dies after Beating from Seniors

A 23-year-old Army private first class, surnamed Yoon, died on April 6 after being hit in the chest by his colleagues serving with front-line troops in Gangwon Province, while eating snacks at their barracks.

An initial investigation found that the deceased recruit had suffered severe physical abuse as well as sexual harassment for about a month after joining the 28th Infantry Division in March. Bruises from numerous beatings were found all over his body.

In addition, allegations have been raised that the military tried to cover up the incident. His death was found to be the result of damage to his skeletal muscles caused by repeated brutal assaults for about a month.

It was later revealed that Yoon's seniors often had him stay awake until 3 a.m. and forced him to swallow a tube of toothpaste. They poured water over his face while having him lie on the floor, and even ordered him to lick their spit off the ground, according to the authorities.

Following the incident, five soldiers, including two sergeants and a staff sergeant, were arrested on manslaughter charges. A total of 16 officers at the unit also faced punishment, with the regiment chief being dismissed from the position and the head of the squadron being suspended for three months.

Yoon's death, which was brought to light belatedly in a media report, is the latest in a series of incidents that have laid bare the chronic problem of bullying in barracks and rigid military culture.

■ Shooting Rampage by Military Deserter

On June 21, a 22-year-old sergeant, identified only by his surname Lim, detonated a grenade and shot at his comrades with his K-2 rifle at a front-line outpost, killing five and wounding seven others. He fled following the shooting spree and was captured two days later after an unsuccessful suicide attempt. He was to be discharged in September 2014.

Lim reportedly had difficulty in adapting to military life and had not associated much with his colleagues, suggesting that bullying may be one of the reasons for the shooting rampage.

Lim had been on a list of soldiers requiring extra care after undergoing personality tests. Although he had been classified as a Class-A soldier, under which he had been banned from front-line duties, he was later classified as Class-B, which meant he still required special at-

▲ On July, 8 army investigators bring a sergeant, identified only by his surname Lim, to the general outpost(GOP) in the inter-Korean border town of Goseong, some 250 kilometers east of Seoul, where the shooting took place, and have him reconstruct his alleged crime.

tention but was capable of carrying out normal duties. He was later found to have left a memo, which read: "Anyone would be in distress if they were in the situation I was in."

A week later, President Park Geun-hye expressed condolences Monday to the families of the victims, calling for the military to thoroughly determine the cause of the rampage and come up with measures to ensure that a similar incident does not recur.

The incident was not the first time that a South Korean soldier has attacked his comrades. In 2011, a Marine Corps corporal went on a shooting spree at a seaside unit on Ganghwa Island, west of Seoul, killing four soldiers and wounding one.

A series of deadly incidents at barracks forced the Army chief to step down from his post. Political watchers said that the decision by the Army chief to step down comes in the context of the incident generating negative publicity that has the potential to distract attention from President Park's drive to boost the economy.

The main opposition New Politics Alliance for Democracy called Kwon's resignation a ploy to deflect blame from incumbent national security adviser Kim Kwan-jin, who was the defense minister at the time of the recruit's death. The ruling Saenuri Party said the Army chief's resignation shows that the government is serious about dealing with the incident in a firm manner.

Following a series of incidents, the defense ministry introduced a system of compensating conscripts for reporting violence at barracks as part of efforts to eradicate deep-rooted ills and reform an outdated military culture.

The ministry said it plans to offer incentives for those who report any physical and verbal abuse in barracks, while coming up with ways to protect whistle-blowers. The military set up an online system to allow soldiers who are victims and their families to ask for help in an easier fashion.

■ Military Brass Embroiled in Bribery, Salvage Ship Project

In November, the government launched a joint investigation team amid growing allegations of bribery and other underhanded dealings between military officials and defense firms, as well as cozy relations between the arms procurement agency and retired service personnel at private defense companies.

Amid the widening investigation, two weapons acquisition officers were arrested in December on charges of taking bribes from a local company that supplied faulty parts to a Navy rescue and salvage ship.

Two Navy officers, a captain and a commander, were suspected of receiving kickbacks from a contractor in 2011 while serving at the Defense Acquisition Program Administration, the state arms procurement agency.

The local company won a 63 billion won contract in January 2011 to supply a sonar system to the nation's first indigenous salvage ship, the Tongyeong. The Tongyeong was completed in 2012 but was found to be fraught with problems at the peak of efforts to rescue those missing from the April 16, 2014, disaster in which a ferry capsized in southwestern waters and killed more than 300 people.

The military said the Tongyeong's sonar system was insufficient and that its remotely operated vehicle was unable to properly scale underwater structures, prompting an investigation in May to find out why the 3,500-ton vessel could not be used when it was needed most.

Earlier, the joint investigation team detained a retired Navy captain on charges of receiving some 400 million won from the company in return for business favors. Despite controversy over substandard equipment on the Tongyeong, the military said it will push to put the salvage vessel into service to replace aging ships.

The next-generation rescue and salvage ship was launched in September 2012, two years after the sinking of the warship Cheonan by North Korea, to enable the military to effectively carry out rescue operations and tow away damaged vessels.

The 160 billion won ($154 million) vessel, however, had not been delivered to the Navy as its remotely operated vehicle (ROV) and hull mounted sonar (HMS) failed to meet the standards set by the military.

Prosecutors found that retired and current military officers in private defense companies had been involved in fabricating documents for parts and committing other irregularities. In April, the military came under fire for failing to send the 3,500-ton ship to the scene of the sinking of the Sewol ferry in waters near the southern island of Jin. The disaster claimed more than 300 lives.

"We need to put the Tongyeong into service to prevent a possible vacuum caused by aging rescue vessels. Despite some hiccups, the Tongyeong is able to serve its basic duties of towing and recovering hulls as well as supporting divers' underwater operations," said an officer of the Joint Chiefs of Staff (JCS).

South Korea now operates two salvage ships, one built in 1968 and the other made in 1972, although such rescue vessels usually have a life cycle of 30 years. "After having the Tongyeong delivered, we will fix the ROV and the sonar systems over the next one or two years to make them perfect," he said.

Critics said it is improper to deliver a flawed ship to the Navy, claiming that no one can be sure whether the Tongyeong will be able to perform in another emergency like the ferry disaster. They also suspect that the authorities' hurried delivery of the ship is aimed at minimizing simmering criticism over alleged corruption in its construction.

BOTCHED PM NOMINATIONS WEAKEN PARK ADMINISTRATION

A chain of botched nominations of prime ministers called into question the personnel selection system of the presidential office Cheong Wa Dae as President Park Geun-hye marked her second year in office.

At the center of the personnel crisis were the successive withdrawals of two prime minister nominees -- Ahn Dai-hee, a prosecutor-turned-lawmaker, and former right-wing journalist Moon Chang-keuk.

Park's first choice for prime minister, Ahn Dai-hee, withdrew his name from consideration amid criticism that he had made too much money as a lawyer last year by allegedly benefiting from his status as a former Supreme Court justice.

Ahn is a veteran prosecutor who also served as a Supreme Court justice before joining the election camp of President Park. He became widely known for investigating a number of high-profile social corruption issues in the construction industry and private education institutions.

In 2012, he joined Park's election camp to help her come up with ideas on how to reform local politics. Ahn had suggested the curtailment of the president's powers and the removal of lawmakers' privileges. After Park's election victory, Ahn left the party, practicing law and working as a law school professor, when he made a massive amount of money.

Park's next choice was Moon Chang-keuk, a former journalist known for his hard-hitting, right-leaning political commentaries. The 65-year-old joined the JoongAng Ilbo, one of South Korea's major newspapers, in 1975 and spent most of his career writing for the political desk before retiring last year. He has since worked as a chair professor at Seoul's Korea University and a visiting professor at Seoul National University in media studies.

Moon's political commentaries and editorials have often offered a conservative view on key political controversies, a characteristic that could suit the conservative Park administration well but prompt fierce backlash from liberal opposition parties.

In a column written shortly after the suicide of former liberal President Roh Moo-hyun in May 2009, the prime minister nominee clearly expressed his opposition to holding a state funeral for the late president, saying Roh's final action was inappropriate for a public figure.

In March 2010, Moon expressed clear disapproval of the liberal camp's election pledge to provide free school meals, saying the promise was a socialist concept. Moon soon faced public opposition the following month over his remarks sympathizing with Japan's 1910-45 colonization of the Korean Peninsula.

Local media reported that Moon said in a 2011 speech at a local church that Japan's 1910-45 colonial rule of the Korean Peninsula and the subsequent division of the peninsula into capitalistic South Korea and communist North Korea were God's will.

Moon, an elder of a big church in Seoul, also described a bloody clash between the government and citizens in 1948 as a revolt, a sensitive comment in a country that has long been divided along ideological lines. Historians claim tens of thousands of people on the southern resort island of Jeju were killed or injured and three-quarters of the island's villages destroyed in the violence.

In 2003, then President Roh Moo-hyun apologized to the victims of the military crackdown and promised to restore their honor, though some conservative South Koreans still view the incident as a revolt as labeled by past authoritarian governments.

Moon's church speech clouded his prospects of winning parliamentary confirmation at a time when Park was struggling to restore public confidence in her administration, which has been battered by the fallout from a deadly ferry disaster.

The strong backlash underscored sensitivity among many South Koreans toward Japan and its previous colonial rule. Many South Koreans still harbor deep resentment against Japan, which critics say keeps trying to whitewash and glorify its past wrongdoing.

It is not the first time that religious comments by a high-profile official have stirred controversy in a religiously diverse country. In 2004, then Seoul Mayor Lee Myung-bak, a devout Christian, said he would "dedicate Seoul to God," during a prayer service, sparking harsh public criticism, especially from the Buddhist community. Lee is Park's immediate predecessor.

South Korea has a Buddhist community of more than 10.7 million, followed by Protestants numbering more than 8.6 million and Catholics numbering more than 5.1 million as of 2005, the latest year for which religious statistics are available, according to the country's statistics office.

Following the repeated botched attempts, President Park decided to retain Prime Minister Chung Hong-won, who had offered to resign in the aftermath of April's tragic ferry accident.

COLLEGE EXAM ERRORS
HIT EDUCATION SCENE

Overturning a lower court decision, the Seoul High Court on Oct. 16 ruled in favor of students who challenged the accuracy of one question in the world geology section of the college admission exam for the 2014 school year.

The education authority revised scores for world geography test-takers who marked the wrong answers in accordance with the ruling, affecting the grades of close to 10,000 students. Those who had failed to win a spot in college due to the flawed questions were admitted to their initial college of choice if they were qualified after the re-scoring.

The authority came under more public criticism, however, after the Korea Institute for Curriculum and Evaluation in charge of making the exam questions later acknowledged that two biology and English questions in this year's annual exam were flawed. In response to growing criticism, educational authorities decided to accept multiple answers for two disputed questions on the national college entrance exam for the 2015 school year.

The chief of the Korea Institute for Curriculum and Evaluation (KICE) in charge of administering the nationwide test offered to resign to take responsibility for the flawed questions. He became the third chief of the KICE to resign over problems with the CSAT.

The exam, which is similar to the American Scholastic Aptitude Test (SAT), is considered to be a crucial factor in determining a student's future career opportunities as Korean society places great importance on educational background. It is administered only once a year.

The KICE revealed the outcome of its discussion on the two questions from two sections -- one from biology II and another from English language -- of the College Scholastic Aptitude Test (CSAT). The KICE's website was flooded with complaints from students questioning the accuracy of the two questions days after the exam on Nov. 13.

After hearing advice from relevant academic societies and having meetings with experts in and out of the agency, the agency said on Monday that it will recognize two out of five choices each from the two faulty questions. The decision will affect the overall score as the exam is based on a relative grading system that divides all test-takers into nine groups.

Some 640,000 high school seniors and graduates took the nine-hour standardized CSAT that was administrated at 1,216 testing sites across the country.

According to local private institutions, the decision will likely raise the average score for biology by 1.3 points and the grades of between 3,600 and 4,000 exam takers. More than 60 percent of the biology test takers selected the disputed second answer while only 10 to 12% chose the correct answer initially presented by the KICE, they said.

The score change is expected to lead to more intense competition among those in the top-tier group as students are required to submit biology II scores to enter medical schools, a popular choice among the group. But a far smaller impact is expected in the English section as a preliminary rating by private institutions put the rate of students who got the right answer at 70%.

The recognition of multiple answers marks another setback for the education agency also responsible for a mistake in one question of the world geology section on the last college admission exam.

After a local appeals court ruled in favor of students who challenged the accuracy of the question, the KICE made a public apology and announced earlier this month that it would revise scores for test-takers who marked the wrong answers, affecting the grades of about 5,000 students.

JUNE 4 LOCAL ELECTIONS END IN DRAW

The June 4 local elections ended in a draw as the ruling Saenuri Party won eight of the 17 metropolitan mayoral and gubernatorial seats up for grabs, while the main opposition New Politics Alliance for Democracy won the remaining nine.

As the first nationwide elections under President Park Geun-hye, the polls were seen as a crucial test of public support for the conservative administration that drew fire for its botched handling of April's deadly ferry sinking, which left more than 300 people dead. The results were seen as a boost for the ruling party and a blow to the opposition party, which failed to properly take advantage of the disaster.

Despite a wave of anti-government sentiment in the wake of the deadly ferry disaster, South Korea's ruling party managed to avoid a crushing defeat in the June 2 nationwide local elections that were seen as a midterm vote on Park.

The ruling Saenuri Party won eight of the 17 key races for big-city mayors and provincial governors, while the main opposition New Politics Alliance for Democracy (NPAD) won the other nine races, including the Seoul mayorship, according to the National Election Commission.

As the first nationwide elections under Park, the polls were seen as a test of public support for the conservative administration that has drawn heavy fire for its botched handling of the sinking of the ferry Sewol.

Despite the widespread criticism of the government, however, the results were not as lopsided in favor of the opposition as had been expected. Regionalism demonstrated its power during the elections again, with the ruling and opposition parties sweeping races in their home turf regions.

The ruling party won mayoral races in Busan, Daegu, Incheon and Ulsan, and races for governor in Gyeonggi Province, North Gyeongsang and South Gyeongsang provinces and the island of Jeju.

The main opposition NPAD won mayoral races in Seoul, Gwangju, Daejeon and Sejong, and races for governor in Gangwon Province, North Chungcheong and South Chungcheong provinces and North and South Jeolla provinces.

Regional education chiefs were also elected. Though the candidates ran without party affiliations, liberal and opposition-leaning contestants clinched victories in 13 out of the 17 races, a result seen as reflecting parents' anger at the ferry disaster that claimed the lives of hundreds of high school students.

The Seoul mayorship carries extra weight in South Korean politics as it is often deemed a steppingstone to the presidency. Former Seoul Mayor Lee Myung-bak was elected president in 2007, running on his accomplishments as the top administrator of the city.

In the run-up to the votes, opposition parties called for judgment on the incumbent administration, saying the government failed to protect the lives of the public. The ruling party campaigned on a promise to fix the social abnormalities revealed through the ferry tragedy.

Voter turnout in the local elections reached a provisional 56.8 percent, according to a preliminary count by the election watchdog.

The turnout was the highest for nationwide local elections since the first such polls in 1995, when it reached 68.4 percent.

SAMSUNG CHAIRMAN HOSPITALIZED
AFTER HEART ATTACK

■ **Overview**

South Korea's top conglomerate, Samsung Group, fell into unexpected turmoil after its chief, Lee Kun-hee, was hospitalized in May following a near-fatal heart attack in May. The 72-year-old received cardiopulmonary resuscitation (CPR) at the time, and later underwent a procedure to widen his blood vessels and was put into hypothermia for the rest of the month.

Lee Kun-hee, the youngest son of Samsung founder Lee Byung-chull, has developed the group into a sprawling business empire that commands products ranging from phones and flat screen TVs to insurance and construction, accounting for about one-quarter of the nation's exports.

Samsung Electronics Co., Samsung Group's flagship unit, booked a net profit of 23.4 trillion won in 2014, down 23.2% from a year ago. The operating profit fell 32% to 25 trillion won last year, confirming its weakest performance since 2011, when it logged 15.6 trillion won in operating income.

The world's largest handset maker has been losing its edge to Chinese upstarts, including the world's No. 3 player, Xiaomi Inc., in the low-end market as these new firms have gained a greater share by cranking out cheaper handsets.

The Korean tech firm is also facing challenges from its U.S. rival, Apple Inc., in the premium market, as the U.S. firm has picked up sales with its latest iPhone 6 lineup that touts a bigger screen size.

■ Third-generation Transfer

Lee Jae-yong, the heir apparent of Samsung Group, has come under the spotlight after his 72-year-old father was hospitalized in May after a heart attack. The junior Lee, 46, has been serving as acting chairman since then, meeting foreign CEOs and political leaders over the past months.

Despite his increased public appearances and high-profile meetings, he faced the critical question of whether he can lift Samsung Electronics' struggling handset business, which is being sandwiched between Apple's premium iPhones and nimble Chinese rivals in the lower-end market. Its operating income and net profit both plunged to their lowest levels in three years in the July-September quarter.

■ Samsung Group Reshuffle

In November, Samsung Group clinched a deal to sell four chemical and defense units to Hanwha Group in a deal estimated at 1.9 trillion won as it continues its business reorganization for an eventual management transfer to the next generation of the owner family.

Samsung said it will sell its defense affiliate, Samsung Techwin Co., and chemical unit, Samsung General Chemicals Co., to Hanwha, another South Korean family-run conglomerate whose main businesses include defense and solar power.

Analysts saw the move as part of Samsung's reorganization, which ultimately aims for the smooth transfer of group chief Lee Kun-hee's US$13 billion fortune to his son and two daughters.

Samsung will sell a 32.4% stake in Samsung Techwin for 840 billion won, as well as a 57.6% stake in Samsung General Chemicals for 1.06 trillion won. Two other affiliates, Samsung Thales Co. and Samsung Total Petrochemicals Co., were automatically included in the sale-acquisition deal because they are half-owned by the companies being sold to Hanwha.

The bigger focus, however, is on what the deal brings to Samsung Group, troubled by a marked fall in profit in its IT business and preparing for a transition after its chief, Lee Kun-hee, was hospitalized in May after a heart attack. Market watchers said the business group, the country's largest, is anxious to sort out the businesses that aren't productive so that it can focus more on those that are profitable and promising.

With the chairman's only son, Jay-yong, effectively serving as the chief, corporate watchers are also closely following a large-scale personnel reshuffle and business restructuring expected to be announced next month. The sales of the affiliates, however, was considered to have little impact on the future of Samsung's ownership structure, analysts said, given the few stakes in the units owned by Lee's children.

■ Samsung's Struggling Handset Business

Samsung Electronics booked a net profit of 23.4 trillion won (US$21.6 billion) in 2014, down 23.2% from 30.5 trillion won the previous year, the company said in a regulatory filing.

The operating profit fell 32% on-year to 25 trillion won in the January-December period, confirming the weakest performance since it logged 15.6 trillion won of operating income in 2011. Overall sales slid 9.9% on-year to 206.2 trillion won last year.

Profit from the mobile business, the company's cash cow, plunged 64% to 1.96 trillion won in the fourth quarter, compared with 5.47 trillion won a year earlier. Samsung has been losing its share to Chinese upstarts, including the world's new No. 3 player, Xiaomi Inc., in the low-end market as these new firms have grown fast by cranking out cheaper handsets.

The Korean tech firm is also facing challenges from its rival Apple Inc. in the premium market, as the U.S. firm has picked up sales with its latest iPhone 6 lineup that touts a bigger screen size. Apple posted a record-high quarterly net income of US$18 billion in the quarter ending in December, selling 74.5 million units of handsets, up 46% from a year ago.

Analysts here predict Apple has likely caught up with Samsung in smartphone shipments, as Samsung is expected to have sold 76 million units in the fourth quarter. Market tracker Strategy Analytics said the two firms tied in their smartphone sales in the quarter.

Robert Yi, the IR head of Samsung Electronics, said in a conference call that followed the earnings disclosure that the company sold 95 million units of handsets in the fourth quarter, while declining to give an exact figure for smartphone sales.

The Suwon-based company said it plans to roll out an "innovative premium handset" this year that comes with a "special function," hinting that it will maintain a two-track strategy for the smartphone segment -- focusing on both premium and low-end lineups. The person at the IR panel didn't elaborate further.

The firm said it will extend the launch of the mid- to low-end A5 and A3 lineup, which debuted in India late last year, globally, while increasing shipments of metal-clad budget phones to target the younger generations in emerging markets.

Samsung's display and memory chip segments arrested a further decline in earnings, as firm demand for LCD, OLED panels and DRAM chips generated an operating profit of 9.43 trillion won in 2014.

Analysts projected a moderate recovery for the tech bellwether in 2015, as the mobile division is forecast to break out of its slump and the chip sector holds high prospects on the back of an increase in production of the advanced 20-nanometer technology.

PROLONGED ECONOMIC RECESSION AND WELFARE DEBATES

■ Economy Loses Steam

South Korea's consumer prices grew at the slowest pace in more than a year in December mainly due to a drop in oil and agricultural prices, as the country fights to overcome deflation worries. The country's consumer price index edged up just 0.8% last month from a year earlier, marking the lowest increase since October 2013.

For the whole of 2014, consumer prices rose 1.3% the same as the year before, with core inflation numbers gaining 2%.

The latest price data raised concerns that the country may be entering a long-drawn-out period of deflation that can adversely affect the country's growth, despite the government claiming that consumer prices will advance 2% on-year in 2015.

To cope with deflation concerns and boost growth, economic policy makers have stressed that an expansionary spending policy coupled with efforts to boost household income will be maintained until people can actually feel a positive change in their everyday lives. Facilitating the flow of money generates demand that can help raise consumer prices.

Another move that can help push up consumer prices in the new year is the decision to hike cigarette prices. Lawmakers agreed to raise the price of a pack of cigarettes by an average of 2,000 won (US$1.80) in January, in a move the government estimated could add 0.62%p to consumer prices in 2015.

■ **Bank of Korea Lowers Interest Rates**

South Korea's central bank cut its key interest rates in August and October by 50 basis points to a record-low 2% to shore up Asia's fourth-largest economy. The Bank of Korea's monetary easing was in line with the quantitative easing measures in other nations.

Following Japan's surprise move to further expand its monetary easing in late October, China also cut its benchmark one-year loan interest rate and one-year deposit rate in mid-November, the first cut in more than two years.

The rate cuts, however, fueled further concerns over the country's already-sizable household debt. A low lending rate is seen as further stoking household debt as more home buyers opt to borrow money to take advantage of the borrowing costs.

Recent central bank data showed that household credit in South Korea reached a record 1,060.3 trillion won (US$948.1 billion) as of end-September on the back of increased mortgage lending. Outstanding household loans came in at 1,002.9 trillion won in the same period, breaking the 1,000 trillion won mark for the first time.

In December, financial authorities vowed to rein in rising loans extended by non-bank institutions in their efforts to control household debts mounting from low borrowing costs and eased mortgage lending. Measures would include stricter guidelines on lending backed by commercial buildings and lands.

Non-bank institutions, and cooperative financial entities in particular, have accelerated their lending backed by property as customers were taking advantage of mortgage lending rules eased in August.

According to industry data, outstanding household loans extended by cooperative financial institutions reached 210.3 trillion won (US$191 billion) as of end-September, compared with 117.3 trillion won in 2008. In September, their household loans increased 11.3%, far exceeding the 6.2% gain in household loans extended by banks.

Household debt has been growing sharply as the government has tried to prop up domestic demand and property transactions to boost growth. Household loans extended by South Korean lenders increased 6.9 trillion won in November from the previous month, following a six-year-high gain of 6.9 trillion won in October, according to preliminary data by the BOK.

BOK Gov. Lee Ju-yeol also expressed concerns over rising levels of debt held by households. Lee said the central bank and financial regulators are looking into the problem in a "serious" manner and said efforts from both sides are needed to cope with the issue.

The BOK governor mentioned earlier that growing household debt may dampen consumption. Speaking to lawmakers in an Oct. 27 parliamentary audit, Lee said there are concerns that household debt may be nearing the critical level that could limit consumption.

■ **Rising Budget Shortfall**

South Korea's gross tax revenue fell 11 trillion won short of forecast in 2014, the largest shortfall on record, as slower-than-predicted growth affected the collection of dues. The finance ministry, which completed calculations on gross revenue and expenditures for the 2014 fiscal year, said tax earnings came to 298.7 trillion won. This represents a gain of 5.8 trillion won from the year before but still below the budget target of 309.7 trillion won.

Tax revenue amounted to 205.5 trillion won, 10.9 trillion won shy of the goal. In non-tax related areas, state revenue reached 93.2 trillion won, 100 billion won short of expectations. The 10.9 trillion won deficiency in 2014 marked the third year in a row that tax earnings fell short of the budget target. It marks the largest annual tax revenue shortfall to date, exceeding the 8.5 trillion won reported for 2013.

Lower interest rates and sluggish stock market transactions further affected taxes levied on financial interest earnings and those on the selling and buying of stocks.

- ## Controversy over 'Free Welfare' Program

A familiar dispute over who should bear the costs of providing welfare services for free re-emerged ahead of the National Assembly's approval of the 2015 government budget.

The trigger for the latest dispute came when Gov. Hong Joon-pyo of South Gyeong-sang Province, a southern province on the peninsula, announced he would stop funding free school lunch programs in the province after the local education office refused to undergo an inspection of its spending on the program, calling it "interference."

The idea of "free welfare," or universal welfare, has long been a trademark policy of the liberal opposition camp. The conservative ruling party called for "selective welfare" tailored to the needs of different income groups.

One of President Park's welfare pledges during the 2012 presidential campaign was to provide free child care services for all children between the ages of 3 and 5. Her office declared that the free child care program must be funded by local governments and education offices under relevant laws.

Opposition lawmakers accused Park of breaking her campaign pledge and demanded that the government fill the gaps in local budgets. The main opposition party also revealed plans to eliminate about 5 trillion won from 2015's budget earmarked for projects pushed by the Park administration in order to spend it on providing free child care services and school lunches.

Rep. Lee Wan-koo, the ruling Saenuri Party's floor leader, called for cooperation between central and regional governments as well as education offices to draw up measures to handle their diminishing budgets and growing welfare expenditures. Rep. Moon Hee-sang, the opposition party's chief, proposed an increase in taxes as a solution to the problem.

Considered too unrealistic by many economists from the outset, and even questioned by her own party, critics said Park's welfare goal may be derailed as her administration comes under growing pressure for a tax overhaul to meet the growing demand for a better social safety net.

- ## Listed Firms Post Sluggish Earnings in 2014

South Korean companies listed on the main stock market saw their combined net profit fall nearly 7% on-year in 2014 due mainly to a plunge in earnings by market bellwether Samsung Electronics Co.

The combined net profit of 496 companies traded on the main KOSPI market dipped 6.9% on-year to 61.1 trillion won (US$55.4 billion), while operating profit sank 12.7% to 91.4 trillion won, according to the data by the Korea Exchange (KRX). Their combined sales came at 1,821 trillion won last year, down 0.4% from 2013, showed the data based on an analysis of consolidated financial statements.

Samsung, the world's largest handset maker, led the overall decline as its bottom line tumbled 23.2% on-year to 23.4 trillion won last year in the face of increased competition with global rivals in both the high- and low-end smartphone markets.

The ratio of Samsung's net profit fell from 49.4% to 38.3% of the total over the cited period, while its operating profit and sales tumbled to 32 percent and 23.2 percent, respectively.

Excluding Samsung, the combined net profit of the KOSPI firms rose 7.1% on-year in 2014 and sales inched up 0.9%, while operating profit slid 2.3%. The data also showed earnings of small and mid-sized firms traded on the tech-laden KOSDAQ market increased last year, driven by strong performances by IT software firms and service providers.

The combined net profit of 671 KOSDAQ companies climbed 7.6% to 3.4 trillion won, with sales edging up 1.2% to 122.7 trillion won. Their operating profit declined 4.3% on-year to 6 trillion won.

- ## Bigger Dividend Payouts

Six out of 10 listed firms in South Korea paid dividends for their 2014 earnings, with the total amount rising under growing pressure for them to return more to shareholders.

Of 721 listed companies, 481 paid a combined 15.05 trillion won (US$13.76 billion) to investors for the 2014 fiscal year, up 27.3% from the previous year, according to the Korea Exchange.

The average dividend yield rate -- the ratio of dividends per share to the current share price -- was 1.69% last year, the bourse operator said. Local firms gave back more to investors in line with the government's policy aimed at spurring an increase in dividend payouts.

The government has revised the tax code to levy taxes on excessive corporate cash reserves in a broader effort to encourage companies to spend more on wages, dividends and investment.

Korean companies have been stingy in paying dividends, a key reason why South Korean stocks are undervalued. Their dividend payout ratio stands at 22.4%, far below the average of 47.7% of other countries. Despite higher dividend payouts, nudged by growing pressure from the government and investors, market watchers questioned whether it will have a lasting effect on the dull local stock market.

The government in December passed a law to tax corporate cash reserves held in excess of an understandable amount, hoping that more spending by companies will put more cash in people's pockets and drive up consumption. Analyst say investors do welcome bigger cash handouts, but the small rise from the miserable level of dividends isn't making any splashes.

Unlike start-up companies that invest their income for growth, market watchers say mature companies with strong balance sheets should return more to shareholders to compensate for their sluggish stock performance in the past years. KOSPI has been limited to between 1,900 and 2,100 points for the past three years, with no clear momentum to break out of the boxed range.

Market watchers say more cash returns in the form of dividends is good news for investors amid low interest rates, but dividends cannot be sustained without solid profit because they go hand in hand.

Some have expressed concern that if too much cash is returned instead of being invested in research and development, it may undermine the long-term competitiveness of companies, and they have recommended a balance that considers industry prospects and company balance sheets.

KOREAN AIR HEIRESS IN "NUT RAGE" INCIDENT

■ **Korean Air VP Enraged over Serving of Macadamia Nuts**
Cho Hyun-ah, a vice president of Korean Air Lines Co., faced a national uproar after ordering a flight attendant to deplane from a flight on Dec. 5 over the way she was served macadamia nuts -- in an unopened pack instead of on a plate. The eldest daughter of Korean Air Chairman Cho Yang-ho ordered the return of the Seoul-bound flight from New York, which had already been taxiing.

The flight was subsequently returned to the gate to deplane the purser, causing an 11-minute delay in its arrival at Seoul's main gateway, Incheon International Airport. More than 250 passengers were on board. She was angry because she believed the crew did not follow the proper procedure for serving nuts to first-class passengers.

The incident sparked national outrage and forced the vice president to resign and prompted prosecutors to look into whether she violated aviation safety regulations, including changing flight plans as well as coercion and interference of a pilot's official duties.

Following the widening investigation into Cho's charges and other company officials accused of covering up the case, Korean Airlines Chairman Cho made an open apology to the public to appease public anger. Regardless of the incident, the former vice president received 1.47 billion won in pay and severance allowances from the air carrier, while the firm posted 205.5 billion won in net losses in 2014.

■ "Nut Rage" Raises Worries over Untested Chaebol Scions

The Korean Air heiress' bratty behavior not only left Cho with aviation rule violation charges but also hurt the brand image of South Korea's No. 1 air carrier.

Brandstock, a South Korean market researcher that determines rankings of the top 100 local brands, said in its latest survey that Korean Air earned 860 points to stand at 45th place for the first quarter of this year, down from the No. 6 spot for all of 2014. In contrast, the country's No. 2 air carrier, Asiana Airlines Inc., jumped up three spots to stand at 19th place, outshining its local rival.

The strong sentiment against the chairman's daughter illustrated growing public uneasiness as the nation's major family-run conglomerates, known locally as chaebol, get ready to hand over management to the grandchildren of their founders -- the young and untested third-generation members of the owner families.

According to the Korea Employers Federation, 28 grandchildren of founders at 15 major conglomerates began working at group affiliates at an average age of 28 and were promoted to executive positions about three years later.

A study of 210 companies showed that it took rank-and-file workers about 22 years to become an executive-level official. Economists say the rapid promotion of chaebol scions without enough vetting and training poses risks to Korean business groups, which in turn bodes ill for the national economy.

Corporate founders get much credit for raising their businesses from nothing after the 1950-53 Korean War, helping South Korea leap to become the world's 10th-largest trading country. The companies have since branched out in size under their second-generation leaders, becoming the key drivers of the export-oriented economy. Their children, however, have faced skeptical investors, with not much of a track record to prove them wrong.

N. KOREAN OFFICIALS ATTEND ASIAN GAMES CLOSING CEREMONY

■ Kim Jong-un's Aides Attend Asian Games Closing Ceremony

Top-ranking North Korean officials made a surprise visit to South Korea on Oct. 4 to attend the closing ceremony of the Asian Games, which were held in the western port city of Incheon. It was the first time for high-ranking North Korean officials to visit since President Park took office in early 2013.

The visit by close confidantes of North Korean leader Kim Jong-un has raised speculation that the trip may be a wish to send a reconciliatory message to Seoul. Pyongyang made the request to send the delegation to the South just one day before the closing ceremony.

Hwang Pyong-so, Choe Ryong-hae and Kim Yang-gon held talks with South Korean Unification Minister Ryoo Kihl-jae and Seoul's national security adviser, Kim Kwan-jin.

Hwang, who holds the rank of vice marshal in the Korean People's Army, was promoted to the director of the military's General Political Bureau, the top military post. He is widely viewed as the No. 2 man in the communist country after leader Kim Jong-un.

Kim Yang-gon is the long-standing head of the United Front Department of the ruling Workers' Party of Korea (WPK), tasked with overseeing the activities of sleeper agents operating in South Korea.

Choe, a secretary of the WPK and head of the Physical Culture and Sports Guidance Committee, was believed to have significant power despite stepping down from his post of vice chairman of the powerful National Defense Commission.

The North's delegation was ostensibly in the country to meet North Korean athletes and attend the closing ceremony of the Incheon Asian Games, but Pyongyang watchers think they have been dispatched to send a message to the South and try to ease inter-Korean tensions. During the high-level talks, the two Koreas agreed to hold another round of high-level talks in late October or early November.

In February, the two sides had their first senior-level talks since the launch of their current leadership. In August, the South offered a second round, but the North had rejected it, taking issue with Seoul's "hostile policy" toward Pyongyang.

The North Koreans, as scheduled, flew back to Pyongyang on a special plane after the closing ceremony. As the last formal activity in their 12-hour stay here, the North's delegation had a farewell meeting with South Korean Prime Minister Chung Hong-won just before their departure. Pyongyang had sent a 273-member team to the Incheon games.

■ Koreas Exchange Fire Shortly after NK Delegation's Visit

Despite rising optimism following the delegation's visit, South and North Korean patrol boats briefly exchanged fire on Oct. 7 after a North Korean naval vessel violated the western maritime border.

The exchange of fire took place at around 9:50 a.m. in waters near Yeonpyeong Island in the Yellow Sea, after a North Korean patrol boat crossed the Northern Limit Line (NLL) into the South's waters, the Joint Chiefs of Staff said.

Though the South Korean military fired some 90 shots, including 10 shots with 76 mm guns, most of the artillery did not have a long enough range to reach the North Korean patrol boat. North Korea fired dozens of rounds in return and not a single one fell near the South Korean vessel.

The two sides did exchange fire, but the Seoul government did not view the incident as a battle as the two Koreas did not aim at each other.

Drawn by the U.S.-led United Nations Command at the end of the 1950-53 Korean War, the NLL acts as the de facto sea border between the two Koreas. Pyongyang does not recognize the border, and the two sides fought bloody battles there in 1999, 2002 and 2009. North Korean fishing vessels often wander into the area and are frequently chased away by South Korean patrol vessels.

People in Focus

Yonhap News Agency

OVERVIEW

In politics, Rep. Kim Moo-sung came into the spotlight by becoming the new chairman of the ruling Saenuri Party. In the main opposition New Politics Alliance for Democracy, Rep. Park Young-sun grabbed attention by becoming the first woman floor leader of a major political party in South Korea. But her debut was unsuccessful as she stepped down mid-term.

Later in the year, Jeong Yun-hoe, President Park Geun-hye's chief of staff during her term in parliament, emerged as the nucleus of the media, on allegations that he meddled in state affairs through regular meetings with a group of key presidential officials without holding an official title.

A total of 261 students and teachers at Danwon High School in Ansan, Gyeong-gi Province, were killed or went missing as the ferry Sewol sank in waters near the southwestern port of Jindo.

Kim Young-oh, whose daughter Yoo-min was a student victim in the ferry sinking, fasted for 46 days, demanding a probe into the accident. Yoo Byeung-eun, a religious figure and ex-convict whose family owns ferry operator Cheonghae-jin Marine Co., was found dead. Captain Lee Jun-seok enraged the public by abandoning the ship without saving the passengers.

Kim Soo-chang, the former chief of the local prosecutors' office, shocked the public with charges of masturbating in public while rock singer Shin Hae-chul's sudden death grieved many of his fans.

In the economics scene, Choi Kyung-hwan, who doubles as deputy prime minister for economic affairs and finance minister, launched the so-called 'Choinomics.' Lee Dong-chan, honorary chairman of Kolon Group, and ex-Daenong Corp. Chairman Park Yong-hak passed away. Hanwha Chairman Kim Seung-youn, who served a jail term for embezzlement, was released after an appeals court suspended his sentence.

Daum Kakao Corp. founder Kim Beom-su created an IT giant whose market capitalization is valued at 10 trillion won by leading the merger between Daum and Kakao. Min Won-ki, South Korea's ministry assistant minister, played a key role while chairing the International Telecommunications Union (ITU) conference in Busan, the country's largest port city.

Park Ji-sung, former captain of the South Korean men's football team who was the first Korean to play in the Premier League, retired after a 25-year career, while ice-skating legend Kim Yu-na also retired after competing at the Sochi Olympics.

Actress Jeon Ji-hyeon and actor Kim Soo-hyun, created a huge buzz throughout Korea and China as stars of the hit drama "My Love from the Stars." Actress Kim Ja-ok, 63, passed away after suffering from cancer.

In North Korea, Hwang Pyong-so, director of the general political department of the Korean People's Army, emerged as a key power in the Kim Jong-un regime. Kim's only sister Yo-jong, also began her activities as the regime's nucleus by taking post as the vice department director of the Central Committee.

POLITICS

▪ Jeong Yun-hoe

Jeong Yun-hoe shook the political scene following allegations that he meddled in state affairs through regular meetings with a group of key presidential officials.

The report claimed that Jeong, with no official title in the government, plotted to oust the president's current chief secretary, Kim Ki-choon. Reports also

▲ Jeong Yun-hoe, a former close aide to President Park Geun-hye, answers reporters' questions after arriving at the Seoul Central District Prosecutors' Office in Seoul on Dec. 10 to face questioning over suspicions that he had meddled in state affairs behind the scenes.

claimed that he exerted influence on the national horseback riding association for his daughter and tried to meddle in a reshuffle at the cultural ministry.

Jeong is the son-in-law of late pastor Choi Tae-min who was dubbed as President Park Geun-hye's mentor. He is known to have supported Park as a research officer and secretary between 1998-2007. Due to their history, Jeong was quoted as a 'hidden power' when Park took office.

▪ Saenuri Party Chaiman Kim Moo-sung

▲ Kim Moo-sung, the newly elected leader of the ruling Saenuri Party, speaks in an interview with Yonhap News Agency at his office at the National Assembly in Seoul on July 16.

Rep. Kim Moo-sung was elected as the ruling party's chief. beating Rep. Suh Chung-won, a seven-term lawmaker and key confidant of Park. Kim, who was once categorized as a pro-Park lawmaker, later on became a minority in the ruling party's power mechanics but still managed to grab the top post.

Kim, who calls himself 'the icon of the conservative innovation' is pushing for an open primary. He has also scouted former Gyeonggi Province Gov. Kim Moon-soo, a potential presidential candidate rival, to chair the party's innovation committee.

In a business trip to China in October 2014, his remark that "talks on constitutional amendment will start to pour out once the regular session of the National Assembly ends" caused a stir, clashing with President Park's position.

Kim also was in charge of the reform of civil service pension, which emerged as a key task for the incumbent administration.

■ **Rep. Park Young-sun of New Politics Alliance for Democracy (NPAD)**

Park broke the glass ceiling as she became the first woman floor leader of a major political party in South Korea in May 2014. She activated a regular conversation channel between the floor leaders of the main opposition and ruling parties and held talks with President Park Geun-hye in early July.

But taking post as the party's special committee set up after its crushing defeat in the July 30 parliamentary by-elections hurt her career. She faced the biggest crisis in her political career when talks on the Sewol bill were stalled.

▲ *Park Young-sun, interim chief of the No.1 opposition party New Politics Alliance for Democracy, proposes on Aug. 24 to create a trilateral dialogue channel with the ruling party and bereaved families of April's deadly ferry sinking to shed light on what caused the tragedy.*

She suffered another rough period when her plan to appoint Lee Sang-don, professor emeritus at Chung-Ang Univ., faced fierce internal opposition among hard-liners.

She resumed her position as floor leader but stepped down from the post on Oct. 2, roughly five months after she was elected. She is cited as one of the country's politicians who went through a extremely turbulent career in 2014.

ECONOMY

■ **Choi Kyoung-hwan, Deputy Prime Minister for Economic Affairs and Finance Minister**

▲ *Finance Minister Choi Kyoung-hwan speaks to a news conference at the Central Government Building in Seoul on July 16, immediately after his inauguration ceremony.*

Choi Kyoung-hwan is a pivotal figure in the Park Geun-hye administration's second cabinet reshuffle conducted in June 2014.

He was 'a big shot deputy prime minister' for his close ties with President Park Geun-hye. His expansionary fiscal policy, which has been aimed at boosting growth and innovating the economy, has coined the term "Choinomics."

In efforts to prop domestic demand, he focused on the property market by easing rules on lending such as loan-to-value and debt-to-income ratios.

The 2015 budget plan was processed within the legal deadline and other bills were also passed without undergoing alterations. But Choi has been facing a tough situation as the impact of his property measures were weaker than expected and a series of economic data deteriorated.

The success of "Choinomics" is likely to be decided this year. Recently, Choi has unveiled plans to boost the economy through structural reforms and service industry growth.

Bank of Korea Gov. Lee Ju-yeol

Lee Ju-yeol took office in April 2014 following a hearing requested under a revised rule for the Bank of Korea. His four-year term is expected to finish in March 2018, in line with the end of President Park Geun-hye's five-year single term.

Lee kicked off his career smoothly, with lawmakers from both the ruling and opposition main party giving the nod to his appointment on the day of the hearing. Lee had a 35-year career at the central bank as a monetary policy specialist between 1977-2012 ahead of making a come back as its chief in 2014.

But public assessment of Lee began to fray after he failed to stand by his remark that a forward signal is necessary ahead of a rate adjustment.

POSCO Chairman Kwon Oh-joon

Kwon took the top post at the steel giant, the country's sixth-largest conglomerate, on March 14. Kwon suggested "Innovation POSCO 1.0," a management reform campaign, as well as a new company vision "POSCO the great." His management vision was also reflected in a restructuring of business units aimed at bolstering competitiveness.

It may be too early to evaluate Kwon Oh-joon's management less than one year after he took the top post. But it is raising anticipation on a faster-than-expected improvement in earnings and financial structure.

A native of Yeong-ju, North Gyeongsang Province, Kwon majored in material science and engineering and earned his doctor degree in Pittsburgh University. He entered POSCO in 1986 and has since served top posts at its European Union office, technology institute as well as Chief Technology Officer.

Hanwha Chariman Kim Seung-youn

With the announcement of a major deal in end-November to acquire four Samsung units, Hanwha Chairman Kim Seung-youn resumed work after serving a jail term. Kim, who was taken up for a trial in January 2011 for embezzlement charges, faced a crisis after he was sentenced to three years in prison. But he was released in February 2014 after an appeals court suspended his sentence. Until November, he fulfilled a 300-hour volunteer service at a social facility ordered by the court and had preparing for his comeback.

The announcement of the deal, which includes the purchase of Samsung Techwin, Samsung Thales, Samsung General Chemicals and Samsung Total, signaled his return to the company. Kim, who had sold Kyung-In Energy to Hyundai Oilbank in 1999, in the face of the Asian financial crisis, had said the move "felt like undergoing surgery without anesthetics," drawing attention to how the Samsung Total acquisition would impact its business.

Dongbu Group Chairman Kim Jun-ki

Dongbu Group Chairman Kim Jun-ki stepped down from his post as chief executive officer on Oct. 23, 2014. Dongbu Steel, which entered an agreement with creditors for management normalization, has entered a restructuring phase. Kim has lost management over the firm. The group's Dongbu Special Steel was sold to a consortium led by Hyundai Motor Group in end-November. The company has also put up Dongbu HiTek for sale despite pouring billions of dollars into the semiconductor firm since the late 1990s.

In contrast to most top 30 conglomerates that are now managed by second or third-generation entrepreneurs, Dongbu is a rare case in which Kim is the founder. Kim became an entrepreneur in his late 20s when he established a construction firm while attending Korea University. Buoyed by the overseas construction boom, he expanded the group by adding affiliates such as Dongbu Fire Insurance.

He also tapped into business areas such as steel, electronics and semiconductor. But the massive investment prompted a liquidity crisis. Kim now only holds owner management in the group's manufacturing and financial affiliates.

Kolon Group Honorary Chairman Lee Dong-chan

Lee Dong-chan, honorary chairman of Kolon Group, who was dubbed as 'the star of the local textile industry' passed away on Nov. 8 at the age of 92.

such as Midopa Department Store and in 1973 established the group Daenong, which was among the country's top 30 conglomerates until the 1990s.

But Daenong's financial structure worsened as it excessively borrowed to expand and the group was dismantled in 1998 during the Asian financial crisis. Park served as the chairman of the Korea Federation of Textile Industries in 1980-1983 and the chairman of the Korea International Trade Association in 1991-1994.

▲ Lee Woong-yeul, chairman of Kolon Group, pays a tribute to Lee Dong-chan, his father and honorary chairman of Kolon Group, at a funeral parlor at Severance Hospital in Seoul on Nov. 9.

He entered the industry with an aim to provide apparel to South Koreans who were lacking appropriate clothing in the aftermath of the Korean War. In 1957, he established Kolon, supplying the country's first nylon.

He served as head of the Korea Employers Foundation in the 1980-1990s when labor disputes worsened, contributing in setting a cornerstone in bolstering ties between companies and laborers. He was also an enthusiastic marathon runner who helped Korea win its first Olympics medal in the 1992 Barcelona Olympics.

A famous anecdote of Lee involves leather slippers he wore for 50 years since 1947. He is said to have reproached employees who replaced it with new slippers and retrieved the old slippers from the trash can.

"I do not own the company. It is a living field for employees. A badly performing company is a betrayal to the society and a breach of duty," he said in a broadcasted lecture in the 1980s.

■ Former Daenong Corp. Chairman Park Yong-hak

Park who was dubbed 'a social butterfly in the South Korean conglomerate scene' died at the age of 99 on Aug. 2. He served as the head of the Korea International Trade Association. Born in Gangwon Province, he established a machineries firm and a fertilizer company after graduating high school. He expanded his business by purchasing companies

■ Former Korean Air Vice President Cho Hyun-ah

Cho Hyun-ah, the eldest daughter of Hanjin Group Chairman Cho Yang-ho, ignited public rage over changing the planned route of a flight due to discontent over the way nuts were served on the plane.

Cho, who was a first-class passenger on Korean Air's flight departing New York, ordered a senior crew member to deplane after being served her macadamia nuts in an unopened bag instead of on a plate. The Seoul-bound flight had already been taxiing when she had it return to the gate.

The event became a national topic as Cho did not apologize and instead blamed the senior crew member, stoking an unprecedented wave of public anger.

The public fury and ongoing prosecutors' investigation pushed Cho to step down from her posts in Hanjin Group. She was also extensively parodied over the macadamia nut brawl.

The event inflicted massive damage to Korean Air's corporate image as it unraveled inappropriate remarks by the group owner's family members to employees.

■ Former Lotte Shopping head Shin Heon

Shin Heon, the former head of Lotte Shopping, the country's largest department store chain, was sentenced to two years in prison on charges of receiving kickbacks from suppliers. The sentence shed light on another case of notorious ties between buyers and suppliers.

Shin, who began his career at Lotte Shopping in 1979 has worked at marketing and product divisions. He served as chief executive officer of Lotte Home Shopping between 2008 and 2012 and later on was promoted as the head of Lotte Shopping's department store business head.

The prosecutors' office began its probe on the case after finding evidence that former and incumbent executives at Lotte Shopping received kickbacks from suppliers between 2008 and 2012 for providing products for its TV shopping programs. Shin stepped down in April, immediately after being summoned by the prosecutors' office and was arrested for receiving such kickbacks as well as embezzling company funds.

On Nov. 21, he was sentenced to two years in prison and 88 million won in forfeit for receiving 106 million won from venture firms and catalogue producers between October 2007 and February 2014.

■ HomePlus Chief Executive Officer Do Sung-hwan

Do is under prosecutors' probe on charges of a fraud over a customer raffle event as well as leaking customer information. Since entering Samsung C&T in 1991, he has only worked in the retail business and has been the center of attention on charges over manipulating a customer raffle event. Ongoing issues over HomePlus' sale also stoked attention on Do.

The prosecutors' office began probing Do when the discount chain was alleged of manipulating its raffle event for customers. It started off with an employee at the company's insurance service team that schemed with a partner firm so that their acquaintants can win imported luxury sedans. It also led to allegations that winners of customer events in recent year did not actually receive their prizes.

A government team has launched an investigation into HomePlus on allegations that it has illegally sold hundreds of thousands of customer information to insurance companies for marketing purposes. Do has been summoned by the prosecution but has delayed his attendance, citing business schedule conflicts.

SCIENCE, TECHNOLOGY AND IT

■ Min Won-ki, chair of International Telecommunications Union (ITU)

Min Won-ki, South Korea's ministry assistant minister, played a key role in successfully hosting the three-week International Telecommunications Union (ITU) conference in the country's biggest port city of Busan. At the meeting, South Korea managed to become a board country for the seventh time in a row and successfully campaigned its agendas such as "Promotion of Internet-of-Things (IoT)" and "Connect 2020."

▲ Min Wonki, chairman of the International Telecommunications Union (ITU) Plenipotentiary Conference 2014, presides over a session of the conference in Busan on Nov. 5.

Meanwhile, South Korea's Lee Chae-sub, a specialist in IT convergence, was elected as the head of the ITU's Telecommunications Standardization Bureau, becoming the first Korean to take one of the top seats at the organization.

Min served key posts at the telecommunications ministry and also as the first spokesman for the Ministry of Science, ICT and Future Planning. He also chaired the telecommunications service policy committee at the Organization for Economic Cooperation and Development (OECD).

■ Kim Beom-su, head of Daum Kakao Corp.

Kim Beom-su, who played a key role

in merging Internet portal Daum Communications Corp. with mobile messaging giant Kakao Corp., is a first-generation entrepreneur in the South Korean venture scene. Kim, who became the head of the merged entity on Oct. 1, 2014, is striving to nurture Daum Kakao into an IT heavyweight that can compete with top Internet portal operator Naver. He is the biggest shareholder of Daum Kakao, ranking eighth among the country's biggest shareholders, with a holding valued at 1.7 trillion won, according to Chaebul.com, which tracks information of conglomerates.

Kim, who entered Seoul National University as an industrial engineering major in 1986, joined Samsung SDS before quitting to found game firm HanGame in 1998. He took post as the co-head of NHN when HanGame merged with NHN but stepped down in 2007. Kim hit the jackpot with the phenomenal success of mobile messaging app "Kakao Talk" in 2010 and helped build an IT giant with a market capitalization of 10 trillion with the latest merger.

■ KT Chairman Hwang Chang-gyu

KT Chairman Hwang Chang-gyu is an expert on semiconductors, who coined the term "Hwang's Law," referring to a hypothesis that the density of the top-of-the-line memory chips will double every 12 months. Hwang, who took the top post as one of the country's biggest telecommunications giants, is leading management reforms at KT.

As part of the plan to normalize KT, which has been suffering weakening profits, Hwang suggested a reform of human resources as well as restructuring. He combined business divisions into nine divisions and cut the number of executives to 100 from 130. He also led the first voluntary retirement program since 2009 and announced contingency plans to cut the salary of executives, including himself.

His efforts have slowly been paying off as KT's earnings are recovering after bottoming out. Hwang has set an ambitious goal of becoming a global top-tier firm based on its "gigatopia" strategy. He plans to herald the giga Internet era by offering service that is 10 times faster than the current level.

SOCIETY

■ Kim Young-oh, father of Sewol victim

Kim Young-oh lost his daughter, Yu-min, who was a student at Danwon High School in the April 16 Sewol disaster. He fasted for 46 days, demanding the government properly investigate the reasons behind the deadly disaster, which left more than 300 people missing or killed. He first started fasting on July 14, as he requested a meeting with President Park Geun-hye.

▲ Rep. Moon Jae-in (R) of the main opposition New Politics Alliance for Democracy meets with Kim Young-oh, the father of one of the Sewol ferry victims, at Gwanghwamun Square in downtown Seoul on Aug. 19.

He was rushed to a municipal hospital in Dongdaemun, a central Seoul district, on Aug. 22, 40 days after he started fasting. However, he refused to resume eating and continued to fast for six more days, only relying on medication. He then stalled fasting and started to take part in a move demanding the legislation of special bills related to the ferry sinking.

On Aug. 16, he was consoled by Pope Francis who was in Korea for a 100-hour-long stay. In November, Kim published a book "Bad Father," in which he shared family pictures and activities by families of Sewol victims.

■ Actress Kim Boo-seon

Actress Kim Boo-seon raised social awareness on making utilities costs at apartments transparent. On Sept. 12, she was indicted without detention on charges of mutually inflicting physical damages with a neighbor during their quarrel over heating costs.

Kim was initially criticized for hurting her neighbor. But the public started supporting the actress as it turned out that she had been fighting for irregularities in calculating utilities costs. Some 300 residents even signed a petition and submitted it to Seongdong Police Station requesting fair and just investigation into the case.

Testifying at parliament over utilities costs, she said she even considered leaving the country and her career as an actress due to the incident. Kim was recognized by Transparency International Korea for her efforts in raising awareness on utilities costs at apartments.

■ Kim Soo-chang, former chief of local prosecutors' office

Kim Soo-chang, the former top prosecutor on South Korea's southern island of Jeju, created a stir after committing lewd behavior in public. Kim was arrested on charges of masturbating in public near his residence on the resort island on Aug. 13. He concealed his identity in the police probe. The former prosecutor also visited the Seoul Supreme Prosecutors' Office and denied such charges.

Kim offered to resign and was immediately dismissed. When an analysis of closed circuit television(CCTV) footage by the national forensic agency showed that Kim was the man who committed the lewd behavior, he acknowledged his charges and issued an apology.

Police referred the case to prosecution. But the prosecution suspended the case on condition that Kim seek psychiatric treatment.

■ Yoo Byeung-eun, former chairman of Semo Group

Yoo, the former chairman of Semo Group, had been sought by prosecutors following the sinking of the ferry Sewol but was later found dead. Born in 1941 in Japan, Yoo began religious activities in 1961 with late pastor Kwon Shin-chan, his father-in-law. In 1981, he established the Evangelical Baptist Church, widely known as the Salvation Sect. In 1976, he acquired a firm called Sam-woo Trading and eventually established Semo Group, expanding his business into sectors such as health products and ferries.

He stepped aside from management after the Odaeyang mass suicide-murder in 1987 where he was a suspect. More than 30 people from the cult were found dead, bound and gagged in a factory outside of Seoul. Investigators found no direct evidence tying the event to Yoo. Later on, he started working as a photographer under the name "Ahae."

He became a wanted criminal following the Sewol disaster. The prosecution found him guilty of embezzlement, breach of duty and tax evasion, with the total amount worth 145 billion won.

He was registered as the chairman of Cheonghaejin Marine Corp. which operated the ferry Sewol. He was given a monthly stipend of 15 million won by working as an advisor for the company.

Yoo's body was found on June 12 in a plum field in the southern city of Suncheon, about 300 kilometers south of Seoul. Police identified him via DNA tests.

■ Sewol victims: 261 Danwon High School students and teachers

The 6,825-ton ferry Sewol sank in waters near the southwestern port of Jindo on April 16 en route to the southern resort island of Jeju. Of the 476 people on board, 295 were killed and nine went missing. Of the total, 246 were sophomore students from Danwon High School in Ansan, Gyeonggi Province who were on a school trip. The death toll at the school hit 255, as nine teachers were also killed.

▲ *A mourner pays tribute to the victims of the ferry Sewol's sinking at a joint incense-burning altar set up at Ansan Olympic Memorial Hall in Ansan, south of Seoul, on April 23.*

48

Four students and two teachers are still missing in addition to three other passengers. A total of 75 students and three teachers were rescued.

Survivor testimonies and video clips recorded on smartphones of student victims showed that the students consoled and helped each other as the ferry sank.

Jung Cha-woong took off his life vest for another friend and was killed as he went off to rescue his peers. Choi Duk-ha was the first to call the authorities to report the case, a move which saved 174 passengers. The Sewol disaster renewed the Korean society's sense of safety and prompted inspections of safety systems and facilities.

▲ This undated Yonhap file photo shows South Korea's archbishop Andrew Yeom Soo-jung of Seoul. On Jan. 12. The 71-year-old Yeom will be the country's third cardinal, following the late Kim Sou-hwan(1922-2009) and Cardinal Nicholas Cheong Jin-suk.

■ **Lee Joon-seok, captain of ferry Sewol**

Lee Joon-seok, the captain of the ferry Sewol, sparked pubic fury over the disaster that killed nearly 300 people and left nine people missing. A photo of Lee in his underwear waiting to be rescued at the steering wheel especially ignited nationwide fury in contrast with the massive death toll.

Lee, who was rescued without looking after his passengers first, testified in court that he was "half out of his mind and didn't know that he was only wearing his underwear." Lee, who started working as a sailor in 1972, had worked as a captain for Semo Group since 1985.

Prosecutors brought murder charges against Lee and demanded the death penalty. But a district court later acquitted him of murder charges and sentenced him to 36 years in prison for abandoning passengers at the time of the deadly sinking.

CULTURE

■ **Cardinal Andrew Yeom Soo-jung**

Cardinal Andrew Yeom Soo-jung became the country's third cardinal in South Korea with his appointment in February. The cardinal follows other cardinals, the late Stephen Kim Sou-hwan (1922-2009) and Nicholas Cheong Jin-suk. In May 2012, Cardinal Yeom was appointed as the archbishop of Seoul, the country's largest parish, as well as the apostolic administrator in Pyongyang.

Since the age of 71 in 2014, he is given the right to vote and to run for an election under a church law that mandates the rights for cardinals younger than the age of 80 in the case that the pope has deceased or is absent. Cardinal Yeom is known for his slightly conservative stance and strict interpretation of church law.

In 2013, he voiced a view that dissents the intervention of priests in current affairs following a mass organized by the left-wing Catholic Priests' Association for Justice that called for the resignation of President Park Geun-hye.

In May, he became the first cardinal to enter North Korea with his visit to the industrial complex in the North's western border city of Kaesong in May. Cardinal Yeom's two younger brothers are also serving as Catholic priests at the Seoul parish, which made them famous as the trio of priest brothers.

■ **Artist Kim Heung-sou**

Artist Kim Heung-sou, who coined the term "harmonism," passed away at the age of 95 on June 9. He was noted for his unique artistic sense that harmonized female nude figures with abstract figures.

After graduating from Tokyo Art School, he lectured at Seoul Arts High School and Seoul National University. In 1955, he departed for Paris to study art where he started using nudes as an important part of his art pieces. After returning home, he received the spotlight for harmonizing abstract figures with spherical figures.

"As yin and yang together create completion, the two artistic worlds of realism and abstractionism create a mystical artistic world that goes beyond the area of shape," he was quoted saying. He was a member of the National Academy of Arts of the Republic of Korea and was famous for continuing to draw despite being in a wheelchair.

▪ Rock singer Shin Hae-chul

Rock singer Shin Hae-chul created a stir when he unexpectedly died at the age of 46. He passed away on Oct. 27, five days after he had fallen into a coma as a result of medical malpractice.

Some 16,000 fans visited his mortuary, with those in their thirties and forties who spent their teenage years with his music mourning the most.

On Oct. 31, his family stalled the cremation of his body to implement an autopsy to identify the exact cause of his death. His death caused a rift between his family and the hospital that implemented his surgery, raising social awareness on medical malpractices.

Shin debuted in 1988 by winning the grand prix at a national song contest for university students. He was one of the country's most acclaimed musicians of the 90s, with dozens of his songs that he performed solo or with his band N.E.X.T.

He was nicknamed 'the devil' and was known for his lyrics that reflected social activism. Shin was a so-called "socialtainer," an entertainer who participates actively in social affairs and was noted for his wry sense of speech.

▪ Jun Ji-hyun and Kim Soo-hyun

"My Love from the Stars," televised by SBS, was a phenomenal TV drama hit in 2014. Its two protagonists Jun Ji-hyun (role of Cheon Song-i) and Kim Soo-hyun (role of Do Min-joon) saw their popularity soar and reignited a second round of Hallyu boom in China.

The number of views that replayed the TV hit on Chinese video streaming sites hit 4 billion and the two celebrities became instant stars in China. "Chi-maek" (a compound of chicken and beer) often enjoyed by Jun in the TV series became another hit product in China.

Clothes that Jun wore in the TV hit instantly became bestsellers in both China and Korea. The TV series was also mentioned at a Chinese political event and even prompted the country's first lady Peng Liyuan to remark that Chinese President Xi Jinping resembled Do Min-joon in his younger days.

▪ Actress Kim Ja-ok

Actress Kim Ja-ok who was loved for her girlish image died on Nov. 16 at the age of 63 due to cancer. Kim debuted in 1970 as an actress for TV broadcaster MBC and soon became a major celebrity, starring in major TV hits in the 70s and 80s.

Her cute and pretty image earned her the nickname "princess" and she even debuted as a singer in 1996 with the song "A princess is lonely." The song became a hit, giving her a comedic image in addition to her pretty presence.

SPORTS

▪ Korea's first Premier Leaguer Park Ji-sung

South Korean soccer icon Park Ji-sung retired from the sport on May 14 following an athlete career spanning 25 years. Park made his professional debut with Japan's Kyoto Purple Sanga in 2000 and has also played for Dutch side PSV Eindhoven, England's Manchester United, Queenspark Rangers and has been dubbed as the most successful Korean soccer player in Europe since star football player Cha Bum-keun.

Park became the first Korean to compete at the Premier League when he signed with Manchester United in 2005. He was loved by European soccer fans and earned the nicknames "the man with three lungs" and "two hearts" for his diligence and vitality.

He debuted for the Korean national team in 2000 and supported South Korea's historic run to the semifinals at the 2002 FIFA World Cup. Park retired from international play after winning his 100th cap (13 goals) in the semifinals of the 2011 AFC Asian Cup. He chose to retire after playing for the Queenspark Rangers and PSV Eindhoven.

He scored 27 goals while playing 205 matches as a Manchester United member and was the first non-European and the first Asian to be appointed as the team's honorary ambassador.

■ 'Figure Queen' Kim Yu-na

Figure skater Kim Yu-na retired from the sport after playing at the Sochi Winter Games in February. In her final Olympics, Kim earned 219.11 points on the ladies' singles event, settling for silver behind Adelina Sotnikova of Russia.

She emerged as a star in the Korean figure skating scene, which was considered a barren land, and reshaped the local sports landscape. In 2010, she earned the country's first Olympic gold at the Vancouver Winter Games with a record high 228.56 points. Kim also generated a breed of wannabes nicknamed "Kim Yu-na kids."

She played a decisive role in helping PyeongChang win the bid to host the 2017 Winter Olympics and has also built a solid image as a advertising model. Kim competed at the Sochi Winter Games despite her injuries but failed to reclaim the gold amid a major judging controversy in free skate.

In May, she performed at an ice show that doubled as her retirement ceremony. She now focuses on charity work and is pursuing a masters degree at Korea University to become a sports administrator.

NORTH KOREA

■ Hwang Pyong-so, Director of the General Political Dept. of the Korean People's Army

Hwang Pyong-so, director of the general political department of the Korean People's Army, emerged as a key power in the Kim Jong-un regime.

In March, Hwang was promoted as a vice director of the Organization and Guidance Department, one of the most powerful bodies in the communist country. In end-April, he was promoted to a vice marshal, putting him in the same rank as Choe Ryong-hae, the military's top political officer, along with four other senior officials. In September, Hwang was appointed vice chairman of the National Defense Commission.

▲ Hwang Pyong-so, the top political officer of the Korean People's Army and the vice chairman of the all-powerful National Defense Commission, arrives at Incheon International Airport along with two other officials, Choe Ryong-hae and Kim Yang-gon.

In October, the North Korean official visited the South to attend the closing ceremony of the Incheon Asian Games along with other high-ranking officials -- Choe Ryong-hae and Kim Yang-gon.

Hwang, 65, has been promoted to higher posts since Pyongyang officially launched its plan to convey leadership to Kim Jong-un. He has since emerged as Kim's key confidant, accompanying the North Korean leader in numerous visits and drills.

■ Kim Yo-jong, Deputy Director of Workers' Party of Korea

Kim Yo-jong, the only sister of North Korean leader Kim Jong-un, made her debut in the Pyongyang political scene in 2014. She quickly became a core figure in the Kim Jong-un regime, filling the vacuum created with their aunt Kim Kyong-hui's weakening presence following her husband Jang Song-thaek's execution.

Kim's name first appeared on North Korean media in the communist country's first election held after the Kim Jong-un regime was launched. She has since accompanied her brother to key events, solidifying her political role.

In November, North Korea unveiled her official title for the first time, calling her a deputy director of the North's ruling Workers' Party of Korea.

She is speculated to work in the party's propaganda department or hold a de facto top secretary role in the regime.

Land, Climate, Population

Yonhap News Agency

LAND

■ **Location and Area**
The country consists of a peninsula that stretches from the eastern end of the Eurasian Continent. It is 1,100㎞ long from north to south and about 300㎞ wide on average. It also consists of around 3,300 islands (South Korea alone).

Location of Land Area

	Extreme of longitude and latitude	
	Name of place	Extreme
Eastern extremity	East extreme of Dokdo islets in Ulleung-eup, Ulleung-gun, North Gyeongsang Prov.	East longitude 131° 52′ 22″
Western extremity	West extreme of Bidan island in Sindo-gun, North Pyeongan Prov.	East longitude 124° 10′ 51″
Southern extremity	South extreme of Marado island in Seogwipo City, Jeju Special Self-Governing Prov.	North latitude 33° 06′ 43″
Northern extremity	North extreme of Poongseo-ri in Yupo-myeon, Onseong-gun, North Hamgyeong Prov.	North latitude 43° 00′ 42″

In terms of longitude and latitude, the southern end of the country is the southern tip of Marado island in Seogwipo City, Jeju Special Self-Governing Province, that has a north latitude of 33°06′43″ and the country's northern end is the northern tip of Poongseo-ri in Yupo-myeon, Onseong-gun, North Hamgyeong Province, which has a north latitude of 43°00′42″.

Land Area by Region *Unit : ㎢*

Region	2011	2012	2013
Seoul Metropolitan City	605.2	605.2	605.2
Busan Metropolitan City	768.4	769.7	769.8
Daegu Metropolitan City	883.7	883.6	883.5
Incheon Metropolitan City	1,032.4	1,040.8	1,040.9
Gwangju Metropolitan City	501.2	501.2	501.2
Daejeon Metropolitan City	540.0	540.1	540.2
Ulsan Metropolitan City	1,060.0	1,060.2	1,060.5
Sejong Special Self-governing City	-	464.9	464.9
Gyeonggi Prov.	10,171.7	10,172.3	10,172.6
Gangwon Prov.	16,787.2	16,790.2	16,829.8
North Chungcheong Prov.	7,433.3	7,406.2	7,407.2
South Chungcheong Prov.	8,630.1	8,204.0	8,204.5
North Jeolla Prov.	8,067.1	8,066.6	8,066.4
South Jeolla Prov.	12,256.6	12,270.0	12,303.9
North Gyeongsang Prov.	19,029.6	19,028.8	19,029.0
South Gyeongsang Prov.	10,533.6	10,534.9	10,537.3
Jeju Special Self-governing Prov.	1,849.2	1,849.3	1,849.3
Nation's total land area	100,148.2	100,188.1	100,266.2

Source : Ministry of Land, Infrastructure and Transport
Note: 1) recording on end of December every year
2) excluding unrestored land area of nonregistered border region on cadastral record

The western end of the country is the westernmost part of Bidan island in Sindo-gun, North Pyeongan Province, which has a longitude of 124°10′51″ and the eastern end of the country is the easternmost Dokdo islets in Ulleung-eup, Ulleung-gun, North Gyeongsang Province, which has a longitude of 131°52′22″.

As of end-Dec. 2013, the combined area of South Korea came to 100,266 ㎢, up 78㎢ from the 100,188㎢ posted at end-2012. From 10 years earlier, the area expanded 649㎢.

The increase in the territory followed reclamation projects that added 30.8㎢, while the expansion of the Gwangyang steel plant also added 1.2㎢. As of end-2013, North Gyeongsang Province held the largest amount of land at 19,029㎢, or 18.9% of South Korea's land. Sejong Special Autonomous City, meanwhile, held the smallest land at 464.9㎢, or 0.5% of the combined territory.

■ Mountains

About three quarters of the country's total land are mountainous regions with the Taebaek mountain range in South Korea and the Nangrim mountain range in North Korea creating a backbone-like mountain range along the eastern coast.

Most of the mountainous regions with peaks over 1,000m in height sit on the eastern side of the Korean Peninsula, creating a steep slope to the east but a gentle, gradual slope to the Yellow Sea in the west.

Mountains

Rank	Name	Height(m)	Location
1	Halla	1,947.27	JeJu Special Self-Governing Prov.
2	Jiri	1,915.40	S. Gyeongsang, S. Jeolla, N. Jeolla
3	Seorak	1,707.86	Gangwon Prov.
4	Deokyu	1,614.20	S. Gyeongsang, N. Jeolla
5	Gyebang	1,579.06	Gangwon Prov.
6	Hambaek	1,572.10	Gangwon Prov.
7	Taebaek	1,566.70	Gangwon Prov.
8	Odae	1,565.11	Gangwon Prov.
9	Gariwang	1,561.80	Gangwon Prov.
10	Sobaek	1,439.50	N .Gyeongsang, N. Chungcheong

Source : National Geographic Information Institue

■ Rivers

Due to the country's geographical features, most of the rivers that flow to the west or south flow slowly while those that flow out to the East Sea tend to have strong currents.

Because of the high precipitation during the summer and low precipitation during the winter, seasonal changes to river currents are relatively more dramatic than those of rivers in other countries. Such seasonal changes are unfavorable for hydroelectric power generation and steady water supply, which is why many artificial lakes can be found along the rivers.

Rivers

Rank	Name	Length(km)
1	Nakdong	510
2	Han	494
3	Geum	398
4	Seomjin	224
5	Yeongsan	137
6	Mangyeong	81
7	Hyeongsan	63
8	Anseong	60
9	Sapgyo	59
10	Dongjin	51

■ Plains

Cities were developed around flat hill plains that were created by the erosion of granite. Farmlands were developed around flood plains and delta areas of major rivers, such as the Gimpo, Anseong, Nonsan, Honam, Naju and Gimhae plains.

■ Coastlines

The coastlines of the east, west and south each have unique features. On the east coast, the steep slope of the Hamgyeong mountain range and the Taebaek mountain range continue to the bottom of the sea, making a deep but simple coastline that consists of sand dunes, lagoons and semicircular beaches.

The south coast is a ria that has an extremely complex coastline with some 2,300 islands scattered around the area, making an archipelago. The west coast has a relatively gentle and flat seabed and a very large tide range, creating a vast area of tideland.

▪ Roads

Road networks consist of highways and national roads between major cities and regions, as well as local streets that connect different districts within a region.

As of the end of Dec. 2013, the total extension of roads reached 106,414km with 82.5% of total roads paved. The total road extension grew 1.2 times from the 88,775km in 2000 with the pavement rate also growing 6.5%p from 76%.

▪ Water Resources

By category, the country belongs to the Asian monsoon region and has an average annual rainfall of 1,270㎜ (1978-2007 average). When including Jeju Island, the figure rises to 1,277㎜.

The average annual rainfall is 1.6 times higher than the global average of 807 ㎜, but the country's per capita rainfall of 2,629㎥ is only about one-sixth of the global average of 16,427㎥. For Japan, the figure stands at 4,993㎥ per capita, with the combined amount of rainfalls reaching 1,690㎜.

By major areas adjacent to rivers, the region near the Han River has an average rainfall of 1,260㎜. Nakdong has 1,203 ㎜, Geum 1,271㎜, Seomjin 1,457㎜ and Yeongsan 1,340㎜. The eastern coast also has an average precipitation of 1,270㎜, while the western part has 1,272㎜. The southern coast held 1,496㎜, with that of Jeju standing at 1,683㎜.

▪ Land Use

Efficient use of land requires a systematic plan that allows for full utilization of land. To this end, the country has been operating a comprehensive law on the planning and use of the land since Jan. 1, 2003, when it was established.

The government set up comprehensive plans for the entire area of the country with provincial governments establishing and maintaining plans for the land in their respective regions. City and district offices also set up their own plans for the land within their administrative regions with plans for cities renewed every five years.

The government has also reorganized the five categories in the land-planning rules into four categories in order to improve efficiency in the use of land and to also encourage strategic development of different areas.

At end-December 2013, South Korea held 49,403㎢ of agricultural area, while 27,093㎢ were under supervision. Cities accounted for 17,593㎢, while the environment preservation zones stood at 12,017㎢.

Of urban areas, 14.6%, or 2,580㎢, were residential, and 1.8%, or 325㎢, were commercial. The industrial zones came to 1,122㎢, or 6.4%, and the green zones came to 72%, or 12,682㎢.

At end-December 2013, the combined size of cities came to 17,593㎢, up 6㎢ from a year earlier. The number of population living in such areas came to 47.23 million, up 405,654 from a year earlier.

The figures imply the country's urbanization rate, which shows the proportion of people who live in urban areas to total population, stands at 91.5%, maintaining its growth trend. However, the growth started to slow, as it only edged up 0.7%p from 90.8% posted in 2009. From 1960 to 2000, the rate jumped from 39.1% to 88.3%.

The government also rolled out a new development strategy to tackle climate changes and seek green growth with less carbon emissions. In order to deal with the escalating global competitions, the government also sought after open-development strategies.

Also to deal with various changes in terms of society and economy, including the low birthrate along with the aging population, the government has rolled out the fourth comprehensive land development plan since 2011, which will continue through 2020.

CLIMATE

▪ Summary

The country's average temperature in 2014 came to 13.1℃, 0.6℃ higher than average while its annual precipitation reached 1,173.5㎜, 10.2% lower than average.

▪ Temperature

The national average temperature in 2014 came to 13.1℃, which was 0.6℃ higher than average. The highest average

2014 Whole Country's Mean Climate by Month

Period	Mean Air Tem. [℃]	Average Highest Tem. [℃]	Average Lowest Tem. [℃]	Precipitation(mm)	Number of Days with Precipitation (day)	Duration of Sunshine(hr)
Jan.	0.5	6.3	-4.8	10.1	4.4	202.1
Feb.	2.5	7.9	-2.1	28.7	6.5	145.0
Mar.	7.7	13.5	2.2	74.1	9.1	212.3
Apr.	13.4	19.8	7.6	85.6	7.7	212.3
May	18.4	25.0	12.1	56.2	7.6	291.4
Jun.	21.9	26.8	17.9	78.2	10.4	172.8
Jul.	25.1	29.7	21.4	152.6	15.3	181.5
Aug.	23.8	27.7	20.8	369.0	18.2	128.0
Sep.	20.9	26.5	16.4	119.6	7.1	201.1
Oct.	14.8	21.2	9.5	116.6	6.5	227.1
Nov.	8.8	14.5	4.1	56.8	8.3	177.7
Dec.	-0.5	4.3	-5.0	26.1	10.7	190.3
Annual Average	13.1	18.6	8.4	1,173.5	111.9	2,341.6

Source : Korea Meteorological Administration

temperature was 18.6℃, which is 0.5℃ higher than average, but its lowest average was 8.4℃, which is 0.7℃ higher than that of the average year.

Seoul's annual average temperature was 13.4℃, up 0.9℃ from the normal figure. The highest average temperature came to 18.3℃, which is 1.3℃ higher than usual with the lowest average coming to 9.3℃, which is 0.7℃ higher than average.

Long-term changes show South Korea's annual temperatures are steadily rising with the lowest average temperature rising at a faster rate than the highest average temperature. In the 2000s, Seoul's lowest average temperature was 9.1℃, which is 1.2℃ higher than the lowest average of the 1970s and 3.1℃ higher than that of the 1920s.

Areas with new daily highest average temperatures were Euisung (July 25, 30.0℃), Ganghwa (Aug. 2, 30.5℃), Baengnyeongdo (Aug. 2, 28.5℃). Gangwha set a new daily highest temperature of 35.8℃ on Aug. 2.

■ Precipitation

The country's annual precipitation came to 1,173.5mm, which is 10.2% lower than that of the average year (1,307.7mm). There were 111.9 rainy days last year, which is 8.4 days more than the average for the year (103.5 days).

The number of days with more than 30mm of precipitation per hour came to 1.2 days, 0.5 day less than the average year (1.7 days). The number of days with more than 80mm of precipitation came to 1.5 days, which is 0.8 day less than that of the average year. The number of days with more than 150mm of precipitation came to 0.3 day, which is 0.1 day less than the average year.

Seoul's annual precipitation total came to 808.8mm, compared with 1,450.5mm on average. The number of days with rain or snow came to 101 days, which is 7.9 days less than that of the average year (108.9 days).

The number of days with precipitation of more than 30mm per hour was one day, two less than that of the average. There was not a day with daily precipitation over 80mm, down from the average 3.2 days. Precipitation of more than 150mm per hour did not take place last year, compared with 0.6 day in the average year.

■ Typhoons

In 2014, a total of 23 typhoons were formed, which is lower than the annual average of 25.6 formed between 1981 and 2010. The average number of typhoons in the past 10 years dropped from the average of 1971-2000, but the intensify of each typhoon has been showing an upward trend.

Last year, there was no severe damage caused by typhoons. Typhoon Vongfang knocked out power in some parts of Jeju, and Typhoon Nakri swept through the southern and western coasts but didn't cause major damage.

■ **Earthquakes**

The number of earthquakes with a magnitude of 2.0 or greater that occurred in the country came to 49 in 2014, which is higher than the annual average of 47.7 for the 1999-2012 period. Earthquakes with a magnitude of 3.0 or greater occurred eight times. The number of earthquakes that could be felt by people came to 11, slightly up from the average of 8.7.

Earthquakes took place inland and offshore 23 times and 26 times, respectively. By region, earthquakes were most frequent in the western sea, occurring 12 times, followed by North Gyeongsang Province at 10 times. The strongest earthquake of 3.5 magnitude occurred in Gyeongju, North Gyeongsang Province, on Sept. 23, which shook buildings and windows. It didn't cause major damage.

POPULATION

■ **General Summary**

In the past, South Korea was a typical country with a high birthrate based on its male-dominated agricultural communities. However, the combined population

remained almost unchanged due to war, famine and diseases.

After industrialization, however, due to improvements in public hygiene and health care, the death rate decreased and the average lifespan went up, leading to an increase in population. Baby boomers, who were born between 1955 and 1963, especially led to the population increase after the Korean War.

As the population started to explode in the 1960s, the government rolled out various restrictive measures to curb the growth. Such efforts were fruitful when coupled with urbanization, even sparking concerns as the population rapidly fell. The average birthrate, which came to 6.0 in 1960, fell to 2.1 in 1983. While the figure was maintained through the mid-1990s, it again plunged in 1997, when South Korea experienced a financial crisis.

In 2001, the birthrate came to an extremely low level of 1.3. The figure slid to an all-time low of 1.08 in 2005. Due to the government's move to promote more children, the figure recovered to 1.19 in 2008 and 1.3 in 2012. The number again lost ground, falling to 1.19 in 2013, but then advanced to reach 1.21 in 2014.

■ **Changes in Demographics**

According to the data compiled by Statistics Korea, the South Korean population stood at 50,423,955 as of 2014. After breaking the 30-million level in 1967, it took 16 years to reach the 40-million level. It took another 29 years to reach

Total Population & Population Increase Rate

Unit : person, Percent

| Year | Total Population | | | Population increase rate | Structuring Factor of Population Growth | | |
	Total	Male	Female		Births	Deaths	The rate of a natural increase[1]
1990	42,869,283	21,568,181	21,301,102	1.0	649,738	241,616	9.5
1995	45,092,991	22,705,329	22,387,662	1.0	715,020	242,838	10.3
2000	47,008,111	23,666,769	23,341,342	0.8	634,501	246,163	8.2
2005	48,138,077	24,190,906	23,947,171	0.2	435,031	243,883	3.9
2010	49,410,366	24,757,776	24,652,590	0.5	470,171	255,405	4.3
2013	50,219,669	25,132,612	25,087,057	0.4	436,455	266,257	3.4
2014	50,423,955	25,219,810	25,204,145	0.4	435,300	268,100	3.3
2030	52,160,065	25,901,365	26,258,700	0.0	-	-	-
2060	43,959,375	21,766,652	22,192,723	-1.0	-	-	-

Source : Statistics Korea
Note : 1) The rate of a natural increase per 1000

the 50-million level in 2012. South Korea became the world's 26th country to post such a number.

The country will reach its peak in terms of population at 52,160,065 in 2030 and gradually lose ground to reach 43,959,375 in 2060. With the number of females hovering above that of males starting in 2015, South Korea is expected to experience changes in its structure coupled with the aging population.

According to Statistics Korea, the number of females is set to reach 25.31 million, compared with the 25.30 million estimated for males. It will mark the first time since the government started to gather such data that females will outnumber males, especially in a country where boys used to be preferred over girls due to the Confucius culture.

While the number of females is expected to reach a peak at 26.26 million in 2031 and gradually decrease starting in 2032, the number of males is set to reach a peak of 25.91 million in 2029 and start to decline in 2030.

The number of South Koreans aged 65 or older will sharply increase. While there were 6.39 million seniors in 2014, the number will hover above the 7-million mark in 2017 to reach 7.12 million, outnumbering the number of youths (aged below 14) for the first time.

This number will then grow to 8 million in 2020, 9 million in 2023 and 10 million in 2025. South Korea is estimated to set new million-level records faster in the future.

Of the total population, the portion of seniors will reach 12.7% in 2014 and rise to 14% in 2017. The figure will make South Korea an "aged" society, just 17 years after it entered the "aging" level in 2000.

The proportion of seniors in the population will continue to rise, reaching 20.8% in 2026, with South Korea becoming a "super-aged" society. Accordingly, the number of economically active population, which stood at 36.84 million in 2014, will reach its peak at 37.04 million in 2016, and gradually decline starting in 2017.

Those aged between 25 and 49, who are considered the most active age group, are already declining. In 2010, there were 20.43 million of such population, but the figure fell below the 20-million mark to 19.78 million in 2010. It continued to lose ground, declining to 19.58 million in 2014, with 19.4 million estimated for 2015. It is expected to reach 18.84 million in 2019.

■ **Birth**

There were 435,300 newborns in South Korea in 2014, down 0.3%, or 1,200, from the 436,500 posted a year earlier. The 2014 figure marked the second-lowest number since the South Korean government started to compile such data in the 1970s. The lowest record was posted in 2005 when only 435,000 babies were born. The number of births rose between 2010 and 2012, but it resumed a downward trend starting in 2013.

The 2014 rate translates into 8.6 babies per 1,000 people, staying unchanged from the 2013 rate to tie the record low. A South Korean woman was estimated to give birth to 1.21 babies during her lifetime in 2014, up 0.02 from a year earlier.

South Korea's combined birthrate came to 1.08 in 2005 but rose to 1.24 in 2011, and managed to recover to 1.3 in 2012. But the figure again dropped to 1.19 in 2013, which is recognized as a "superlow" birthrate. The figure marks the lowest level among the members of the Organization for Economic Cooperation and Development.

By age group, women in their 20s had fewer births while those in their 30s had more children. The average birthrate per 1,000 women between the ages of 35 and 39 came to 43.2 in 2014, up 3.7 on-year.

Due mainly to people delaying weddings, South Korean women gave birth at the average age of 32.04 in 2014, up 0.2 on-year. Such figures are setting new records every year. Mothers aged 25 and above accounted for 21.6% of all births in 2014.

For every 100 girls born, there were 105.3 males born, remaining almost unchanged from a year earlier. Figures between 103 and 107 are considered to be appropriate.

■ **Death**

In 2014, the number of deaths reached 268,100, up 0.7% from a year earlier. The figure translates to 735 deaths per day. There were 5.3 deaths per 1,000 South

Birth · Death 1984~2014

Unit : person, per 1000 population

Year	Births	Deaths	The number of a natural increase	Crude birth rate(per 1000)	Crude death rate(per 1000)	Crude death rate(per 1000)
1984	674,793	236,445	438,348	16.7	5.9	10.8
1985	655,489	240,418	415,071	16.1	5.9	10.2
1986	636,019	239,256	396,763	15.4	5.8	9.6
1987	623,831	243,504	380,327	15.0	5.9	9.1
1988	633,092	235,779	397,313	15.1	5.6	9.5
1989	639,431	236,818	402,613	15.1	5.6	9.5
1990	649,738	241,616	408,122	15.2	5.6	9.5
1991	709,275	242,270	467,005	16.4	5.6	10.8
1992	730,678	236,162	494,516	16.7	5.4	11.3
1993	715,826	234,257	481,569	16.0	5.2	10.8
1994	721,185	242,439	478,746	16.0	5.4	10.6
1995	715,020	242,838	472,182	15.7	5.3	10.3
1996	691,226	241,149	450,077	15.0	5.2	9.8
1997	668,344	241,943	426,401	14.4	5.2	9.2
1998	634,790	243,193	391,597	13.6	5.2	8.4
1999	614,233	245,364	368,869	13.0	5.2	7.8
2000	634,501	246,163	388,338	13.3	5.2	8.2
2001	554,895	241,521	313,374	11.6	5.0	6.5
2002	492,111	245,317	246,794	10.2	5.1	5.1
2003	490,543	244,506	246,037	10.2	5.1	5.1
2004	472,761	244,217	228,544	9.8	5.0	4.7
2005	435,031	243,883	191,148	8.9	5.0	3.9
2006	448,153	242,266	205,887	9.2	5.0	4.2
2007	493,189	244,874	248,315	10.0	5.0	5.1
2008	465,892	246,113	219,779	9.4	5.0	4.4
2009	444,849	246,942	197,907	9.0	5.0	4.0
2010	470,171	255,405	214,766	9.4	5.1	4.3
2011	471,265	257,396	213,869	9.4	5.1	4.3
2012	484,550	267,221	217,329	9.6	5.3	4.3
2013	436,455	266,257	170,198	8.6	5.3	3.4
2014[p]	435,300	268,100	167,200	8.6	5.3	3.3

Source : Statistics Korea

Koreans, maintaining similar levels for the past three years. Such rates stayed around 5 between 2004 and 2009 but gradually increased starting in 2010 to 5.1. In 2014, the death rate remained almost unchanged throughout all age groups. For those aged 90 and above, there were 188.1 deaths per 1,000 people, down 6.6 from a year earlier.

Males outnumbered females by 1.2 times in terms of death. When it comes to those in their 50s, the death ratio between males and females came to 2.8 times. In 2014, 73.1% of deaths occurred in medical institutions. Of the remaining amount, 16.6% died at home and 10.3% died at social welfare centers or other places.

In 2014, the number of newborns outnumbered deaths by 167,200, down 3,000 from 17,200 a year earlier. The natural increase of population per 1,000 people remained at 3.3, posting an all-time low for the second consecutive year.

■ Marriage and Divorce

In 2014, the number of marriages came to 305,600, down 5.3% from a year earlier. By month, January held 26,900, February 25,100, March 25,000, April 238,000, May 28,300, June 24,800, July 25,000, August 22,300, September 19,300, October 27,100, November 23,600 and December 34,300.

In 2009, there were 309,000 weddings, and it gradually increased to 329,000 in 2011. The figure, however, commenced its downward trend in 2012 by posting 327,000 cases, leading to 322,000 cases in 2013.

The number of divorces came to 115,600 in 2014, up 0.3% from a year earlier. By month, there were 9,100 divorces in January, 9,300 in February, 9,500 in March, 9,600 in April, 9,900 in May, 9,600 in June, 10,400 in July, 9,200 in August, 9,900 in September, 10,000 in October, 9,300 in November and 9,900 in December. In 2009, there were 124,000 divorces, followed by 116,000 in 2010 114,000 in 2011, 114,000 in 2012 and 115,300 in 2013.

■ **Life Expectancy**

According to Statistics Korea, the average life expectancy for babies born in 2013 stood at 78.5 years for males and 85 years for females. The combined average stood at 81.9 years.

From a year earlier, the number edged up 0.6 years for males and 0.4 years for females. From 10 years earlier, it increased 4.7 years and 4.2 years, respectively. The combined life expectancy also increased 4.5 years for all genders.

The gap between males and females in terms of life expectancy stood at 6.5 years in 2013, the lowest since the government started to compile such data in 1970. It reached a peak in 1985 at 8.4 years.

Babies born in 2013 are most likely to die of cancer. For males, 28.1% of deaths were caused by cancer, up 0.5% from a year earlier, while that for females came to 16.6%, up 0.3% on-year. The next highest threat for babies was cerebrovascular diseases, which caused 9.1% and 11.9% of the deaths of male and female babies, respectively.

For most age groups, cancer was the biggest killer. For females aged 80 and above, however, heart-related diseases were the No. 1 cause of death. If a cure for cancer is discovered, the average life expectancy of babies born in 2013 will be extended by 4.7 years for males and 2.8 years for females. For those aged 65 and above, their lives will be extended 3.9 years and 2 years, respectively.

■ **Population and Households Structures**

While the number of households with three or more members came to 7.73 million units in 1985 to account for 80.8% of the total, the 2010 census showed 48.2%, or 8.34 million households, held one or two members. Of the households with two members, 860,000 were one-parent families in 2015, a twofold growth from the 390,000 posted in 2010.

Between 1995 and 2010, the South Korean population grew by 8.9%. But the number of households jumped 33.8%, indicating households split apart. An average household held 3.4 members in 1995, but it decreased to 2.69 in 2010.

As more people have decided to live alone, while the number of divorces and seniors living alone has increased, only 66.6% had spouses, down from 77.6% posted in 1995.

Households with females as the head came to 25.9% in 2010, up from 16.6% posted in 1995. There were 2.22 million single female households, hovering above males, of which there were 1.92 million. Such one-member households have increased rapidly in provincial areas.

Government

Yonhap News Agency

OVERVIEW

The year 2014 was hit hardest by the Sewol ferry disaster that claimed 304 lives - most of them high-school students - off the southwest coast on April 16.

The government and the main ruling Saenuri party were determined to push forward their pledges and policies in the second year of the Park Geun-hye administration. But the ferry sinking nearly paralyzed the political circles.

In particular, the June 4 provincial election was regarded as a mid-term review on the Park government, but the general public didn't pay much attention to the election due to a huge ripple effect of the Sewol tragedy on the economy.

Initially, the ruling party seemed to be better positioned to win the election helped by President Park's high approval rating compared to the main opposition New Politics Alliance for Democracy (NPAD) and other opposition parties. But neither the ruling nor opposition parties were winners in the election.

The government and the ruling party were criticized for failing to handle the Sewol incident properly, while the opposition parties came under criticism for their attempts to use the disaster for their political gains.

At any rate, the disaster threw cold water on consumer sentiment, which weighed on the country's economic growth. The government's stimulus packages worth 40 trillion won announced in August to boost the lackluster economy didn't have any tangible results.

In the June election, some non-mainstream politicians were elected to fill seats of the Saenuri Party and in July Kim Moo-sung, who was not a close aide to President Park, was elected to lead the ruling party. The results were widely translated into signs of power transfer from close aides to Park to "non-Park" politicians.

Worse still, the ruling party leader Kim voiced for constitutional amendment in a press conference held in Shanghai in October and in November, there were widespread speculations that Chung Yoon-hoe, a close aide to Park, was influencing

Park when she makes policies. They hit another blow to Park and politicians.

■ Politics Paralyzed after Sewol, No Winner in Provincial Election

In fact, the June election was regarded as prelude to the general election in 2016 and the presidential election in 2017. So the Saenuri Party was determined to win as many seats possible in the election to maintain the momentum of the Park government in its second year in office.

A victory in the election could have paved the way for the ruling party's return to power in 2017. The main opposition NPAD Party sought to recapture the power in the election, but neither the ruling nor opposition party could claim victory in the election.

As the election was held 50 days after the Sewol sinking, the ruling party was expected to lose the election. But the Saenuri and NPAD Party won eight and nine districts, respectively.

In the Metropolitan areas, the barometer of public sentiment, the NPAD Party beat the ruling Saenuri Party. In Incheon and Gyeonggi Provinces, ruling party candidates won over opposition party rivals. There was no clear winner in the June 4 provincial election.

The results were a shock to the Saenuri Party as President Park's approval rating remained between 50% to 60% and the ruling party was traditionally better positioned than opposition parties in provincial elections.

No doubt, the Sewol disaster gravely affected the results. The general public turned against the government and the ruling party as the maritime police didn't do its job to rescue passengers when the ship was going down with 250 high-school students trapped inside.

Moreover, the government's lack of control and mismanagement of the incident disappointed the whole nation. It's safe to say the ruling party deserved all the criticisms and no victory in the election.

To soothe public disappointment, President Park was in tears making an apology to the nation and drummed up support from the conservatives. The NPAD party called on voters to judge the current government by voting against it. It was like a tight see-saw game for

two months before the June election. Some voters were still supporting the Park government, but others were not.

Unlike expectations that "angry moms" who were enraged with the government's mishandling of the incident would vote against the ruling party, there was no clear winner.

Young voters in their 20s and 30s voted for the NPAD party, but those in 60s and older gave their unchanged support to the Saenuri party. Given the results, Park managed to avoid becoming a lame duck president.

In the July 30 by-election held two months after the June election, the ruling Saenuri scored a landslide victory over the NPAD party by winning 11 seats out of 15. But the outcome was not seen as support for the incumbent government but seen the results of internal conflicts in the NPAD party.

Back then, the NPAD party pushed ahead with "Gwangju's daughter" Kwon Eun-hee, the then-chief investigator at Seoul's Suseo Police Station, as the candidate for a district in Gwangju, 329km southwest of Seoul. The recommendation faced criticism because Kwon had been a part of the investigation team of the National Intelligence Service's allegedly illegal intervention to make Park Geun-hye the president in the 2012 presidential election.

Some politicians in the ruling and opposition parties emerged as potential presidential candidates for the upcoming 19th presidential election through the June election.

They include Gyeonggi Province Governor Nam Kyung-pil, Incheon Mayor Yoo Jeong-bok, South Gyeongsang Province Governor Hong Joon-pyo and Jeju Island Governor Won Hee-ryong all from the Saenuri Party and Seoul Mayor Park Won-soon and South Chungcheong Governor Ahn Hee-jung.

In the June 4 provincial election that also selected the superintendent of education for the Seoul government, hawkish candidates outperformed dovish ones. Progressive candidates won in 13 out of 17 districts in 2014, in a sharp reversal from four years earlier when conservative candidates won 10 out of 16 districts.

Ruling, Opposition Vying for Political Overhaul

Faced with the nation's deepening distrust toward politicians, the ruling and opposition parties entered the race to overhaul their organizations. If not drastic changes, they took out the "innovation card" because they would never win the upcoming general and presidential elections.

The Saenuri Party was quick to take a step to innovate itself. In September, two months after Kim Moo-sung took the helm at the ruling party in July, the innovation committee led by the former Gyeonggi Province Governor Kim Moon-soo came into existence. The committee largely composed of non-mainstream and young politicians announced a series of innovation measures which included giving up some privileges given to lawmakers.

In other suggested measures, arrest warrants should be automatically issued within 72 hours for politicians involved in crimes; politicians should be fully barred from holding a publishing ceremony for their books; there should be the "no labor, no wage" rule for all lawmakers; the lawmakers' budget needs to be frozen for the year of 2015; lawmakers should not be allowed to have a side job on top of their four-year policymaker role; and stricter rules should be adopted for the National Congress ethics committee.

But all the suggestions were rejected by lawmakers as widely expected in a lawmakers' meeting on Nov. 11, putting a brake on the ruling party's innovation drive. Some lawmakers criticized the measures were no other than populism.

Through a month of discussions, lawmakers agreed to accept six innovative measures in their December meeting. The approved measures didn't include the shortened process to arrest lawmakers and two other suggestions opposed by most of lawmakers.

The NPAD sought survival through innovation after they failed to win the June election. NPAD representative Moon Hee-sang has set up a politics innovation committee in September to compete with the ruling party. But the committee made a slow start as it took a month for them to invite outside experts. Moreover, there were no fresh innovation-related pledges that drew the attention of the general public.

Major innovative measures banned lawmakers from intervening in internal votes within the ruling or opposition party and recommended to invite an outsider to the chairman post of each party's ethics committee. Other measures that drew attention were unveiling the financial status of each party and cutting all the attention fees for lawmakers who miss more than one fourth of lawmakers' general meetings.

Call for Constitutional Amendment and Aides' Influence on Park's Decisions

Saenuri Party leader Kim Moo-sung sought to be in line with the Blue House by taking a low-profile attitude. But during his visit to Shanghai in October, he called for constitutional amendment, which made the presidential house uncomfortable.

President Park pledged to amend the constitution during the 18th presidential campaign but she put getting the economy back on track before anything else. Kim and many ruling party members took issue with Park's position change towards the constitutional amendment.

When he came back to Seoul, Kim immediately made an apology about his "wrong comments" in China. But their position toward constitutional amendment remained unchanged, being a potential apple of discord.

Meanwhile, allegations that former chief presidential adviser Chung Yoon-hoe pulled strings behind the scenes on key state affairs drove up the demand to reshuffle the Blue House.

Chung allegedly regularly met Park associates to try to exert influence on Park's personnel management. Those reports are based on leaked documents and came from an office headed by another presidential aide, reportedly close to Park's brother.

Not only the ruling but also the opposition party increasingly expressed their complaints about personnel matters. In the second year of Park's administration, the "non-Park" Saenuri politicians voiced for a cabinet reshuffle amid lack of communication between the Blue House and the ruling party.

▪ Presidential Candidates in the Making

Summary In the second year of the Park government, presidential candidates from the Saenuri and NPAD parties began to emerge. It was a bit early to say who will make the most competitive presidential candidate but there was not any unrivaled candidate.

No strong candidates in Saenuri Party For the 19th presidential election, there seemed to be no such strong ruling-party candidates as Lee Hoe-chang in the 2002 presidential election, the neck-and-neck race between Park Geun-hye and Lee Myung-bak in 2007 and Park Geun-hye's overwhelming lead in 2012.

Experts viewed a politician who has an interest in issues of the general public and offer solutions will ultimately make it to the presidential election.

Currently, Kim Moo-sung, a non-Park politician, emerged a potential presidential candidate in the Saenuri Party, but he still has to wisely handle a "power struggle" with politicians who support Park in the Saenuri Party.

Former Gyeonggi Province Governor Kim Moon-soo, in charge of the Saenuri innovation committee, focused on strengthening his presence in the party.

The former lawmaker Chung Mong-joon, a son of the late Hyundai Group founder Chung Ju-young, focused on putting the beleaguered Hyundai Heavy Industries back on track after the Ulsan-based shipbuilder was hit hardest by the 2008 financial crisis. He failed to beat the current Seoul Mayor Park Won-soon in the June provincial election.

Kim Moon-soo and Chung Mong-joon are expected to run for the 2016 general election in Daegu and Seoul's Jongro-gu, respectively, a prelude to the 2018 presidential election.

South Gyeongsang Province Governor Hong Joon-pyo, the "issue maker," often made the headlines due to major issues. South Gyeongsang became the first province in the country to withdraw the free meal program in April due to funding problems.

Former Seoul Mayor Oh Se-hoon is looking for opportunities to return to the political circles from 2015 after serving a member of advisors to the Korea International Cooperation Agency (KOICA)'s mid and long-term development plan in Rwanda in 2014. As he did when he served as Seoul mayor from July 2006 to Aug. 2011, Oh helped the African country improve environment, designs and city administration processes.

Gyeonggi Province Governor Nam Kyung-pil and Jeju Governor Won Hee-ryong are also regarded as potential presidential candidates, but they are expected to focus on their governor roles while seeking opportunities to run for the upcoming presidential election.

Three potential candidates in NPAD Party In the main opposition NPAD party, lawmaker Moon Jae-in announced he will re-run for the presidential election in 2018. He was defeated by President Park Geun-hye in the 19th presidential election by narrow margins. Political maneuvering by the National Intelligence Service reportedly affected to the result of the presidential election.

Moon was once besieged due to criticisms that he should take the responsibility for the loss of a conversation record between heads of North and South Korea in 2007. But he is expected to seek a "frontal breakthrough" to run again for the presidential election.

But the major stumbling block for the NPAD party is how to raise its low popularity ratings and internal disputes over major issues. If Moon succeeds in raising the approval ratings and stitching up the split party, he will be better positioned to run for the presidential election, according to experts.

Lawmaker Ahn Cheol-soo, the founder of the AhnLab which is an antivirus software company, failed to earn a seat in the July 30 by-election and stepped down as co-representative of the NPAD party.

He was once emerged as "dark horse"politician before the 18th presidential election but he soon lost his shine as a "rising star" in the political scenes. In 2015, he has to find a breakthrough to regain his foothold in the National Assembly.

In June 2014, Seoul Mayor Park Won-soon beat his archrival Chung Mong-joon to serve another four years as Seoul mayor. The result showed he could manage to win a major election without joining hands with an influential politician. In 2011, Park Won-soon won the election to select the Seoul mayor with the help of Ahn Cheol-soo who dropped out of the race for the mayoral position to support Park.

Distancing himself from mud-slinging politicians in Yeoido, Park Won-soon has built up his approval ratings by focusing on meeting Seoul citizens' demands in the past year.

But the Seoul City government's failure to pass the "Seoul Citizen's Human Rights Charter," which bans discrimination against homosexuality, may remain an obstacle to Park's possible bid for the presidential election in 2018, experts say.

South Chungcheong Province Governor Ahn Hee-jung was re-elected in the July 30 by-election. Ahn's re-election was translated into a sign that he was no longer a novice in the political scenes but a potential next-generation politician.

Sohn Hak-kyu, a former NPAD lawmaker, decided to discontinue his political career in the July 30 by-election after he lost to a young entry-level Saenuri Party candidate Kim Yong-nam in the Suwon district. After he retired from political circles, Sohn barred himself from the outside world and is not likely to return to the political scene.

UN secretary-general Ban Ki-moon leads in poll for president Un Secretary-General Ban Ki-moon also emerged as one of the potential presidential candidates. Ban led other candidates in a series of polls for some time. The "National Competitiveness Strengthening Committee" under the umbrella of the Saenuri Party first mentioned the possibility of Ban's bid for the 2018 presidential election due to his popularity among Koreans.

Although he does not belong to the Saenuri Party nor the NPAD Party, he is still regarded as one of the most competitive presidential candidates. But he denied all the allegations. He made it clear that he didn't have any interest in running for the presidential election in response to rumors and reports in Korea.

His term as UN secretary-general ends in 2016. Most of the presidential candidates are expected to make a bid for the presidential election. It remains to be seen whether the public will continue to support Ban enough for him to join other candidates for the presidential race.

PRESIDENT

■ **Overview**

In her second year in office, President Park Geun-hye focused on "reviving the economy" throughout the year but went nowhere hit by the April Sewol ferry disaster and the allegations that former chief aide Chung Yoon-hoe meddled behind the scenes in key state affairs.

In the new-year press conference held in Cheong Wa Dae on Jan. 6, Park proposed the three-year economic innovation plan and put the top priority on activating the lackluster economy and stimulating the sluggish domestic spending.

Moreover, she underlined the importance of unification between North and South Korea, calling the unification between the two Koreas a "bonanza." Park also vowed to improve the estranged inter-Korean relations while trying to put the economy back on track.

In a speech to celebrate her one-year anniversary as chief of state on Feb. 25, Park outlined the details of the three-year economic innovation program. During her visit to Germany in March, she unveiled detailed strategies to back up the "unification jackpot" theory.

▲ *President Park Geun-hye reads a statement on a three-year economic innovation plan at the presidential office Cheong Wa Dae in Seoul on Feb. 25.*

In April, however, the Sewol ferry sinking brought all those efforts and commitments to a nearly full-scale halt. In particular, the government's mishandling of the incident in its initial response and some loopholes in the country's disaster control and management system provoked criticisms from the general public. Public trust in the Park Geun-hye government nearly fell to rock bottom following the Sewol sinking.

Worse still, Park's subsequent two prime minister nominees -- Moon Chang-geuk and Ahn Dae-hee -- stepped down shortly after they were nominated due to ethical issues. Moon resigned due to his questionable historical perception of the Japanese colonial rule of Korea.

On April 20, Prime Minister Lee Wan-koo offered to resign amid mounting criticisms against him for allegedly receiving bribes from the late businessman Sung Woan-jong, who killed himself during prosecutors' probe into his bribery scandal.

When Lee Wan-koo counted, Park made five nominations for the second highest-ranking position in her administration as of April 22, 2015. Two of them resigned while in office and three quit even before their National Assembly confirmation hearing began. Such personnel failures made it difficult for the government to wrap up the Sewol incident and public sentiment towards the Park government grew worse.

But the ruling Saenuri Party managed to finish the June 4 provincial election in a draw, avoiding a major defeat to the main opposition NPAD Party. In the July 30 by-election attended by influential politicians from the ruling and opposition party, the Saenuri Party won over the NPAD Party allowing the Park government to push forward its drive again to revive the economy.

Making putting the nearly frozen spending back on track the top priority, Park met major businessmen, ministers, government officials and economic advisors from the private sector to discuss measures to jumpstart spending. She launched the "creative economy innovation center" in the cities of Daegu and Daejeon as well as in the North Jeolla Province to help generate new growth engines.

Moreover, she held unification-focused meetings three times with related parties and met Pope Francis when he paid a visit to Korea in August to express her strong commitment to improve the inter-Korean relations. She reiterated her commitment in an Aug. 15 Liberation Day speech.

On the diplomatic fronts, Park took part in the UN General Assembly in September, the Asia-Europe Meeting (ASEM) in October, the Asia Pacific Economic Cooperation (APEC) meeting and the G-20 Summit composed of 20 traditional economic powers in November not only to drum up support for her government's efforts to seek stability on the Korean peninsula but also to quickly react to the rapidly changing diplomatic scenes in Northeast Asia.

Park made a major achievement in the Korea-China summit on the sidelines of the APEC summit talks in November. Park and China's President Xi Jinping signed the free-trade agreement between the two countries after 30 months-long negotiations. China is Korea's biggest exporter and has emerged as one of the world's two biggest markets together with the United States.

On Nov. 7, the Sewol Special Law designed to help the victim's families and to punish those who are responsible for the tragedy passed the National Assembly. But the allegations that former presidential aide Chung Yoon-hoe was behind Park's major decisions made headlines only 20 days after the Sewol Special Law was passed. It was a major hit to President Park's leadership and her people.

Calling the allegations "totally groundless," Park ordered prosecutors to make a thorough investigation into the rumors but it was hard to make all the rumors clear. Park was criticized for lack of communication and lack of transparency in personnel management throughout the year of 2014.

■ New-Year Press Conference in 2nd Year in Office

In the new-year press conference held at Cheong Wa Dae on Jan. 6, Park stressed the importance of preparations for the age of unification between two Koreas. She told Korean and foreign journalists that unification was nothing less than a "bonanza." To make an overhaul and another leap, she vowed to push ahead with the three-year plan for economic innovation.

As for inter-Korean issues, she offered a reunion of separated families from North and South Korea around the Lunar New Year holidays early in 2014. She reiterated her existing stance towards the summit between North and South Korean leaders. "I can meet North Korean leader Kim Jong-un, but the summit meeting should not be a meeting for a meeting," she said.

Under the three-year economic innovation, Park announced three major principles: fundamentally-strong economy, innovative economy filled with power and potential and balanced economy between domestic demand and exports.

When it comes to the government's push to "normalize things that have gone abnormal," she ordered public organizations to cut their heavy debts and shed some advantages public officials have enjoyed compared to workers at private-sector companies. She also suggested innovation in the fiscal and tax systems to increase tax revenue.

But she stood against the need for constitutional amendment and for a special investigation into the allegations that the National Intelligence Service's (NIS) involvement in the 18th presidential election to help Park to be elected as president.

Back then, Park beat Moon Jae-in, her rival from the NPAD Party, but rumors had it that the NIS intervened to make Park president. When it comes to raising taxes, she put reviving economy before easing regulations to help support the economy.

As for criticisms that Park lacks in communication with opposition parties and opposing voices, she dismissed such controversies. "Reacting to any illegal pushes with principles should not be translated into lack of communication," she said.

The New Year address was hailed by the Saenuri Party as a message seeking support from the NPAD Party, while the opposition party undervalued the speech as unilateral.

■ State Visit to India, Switzerland… "Trade Diplomacy" Kicks off

President Park made her first overseas trip to India and Switzerland for eight days from Jan. 15. She attended the 44th World Economic Forum annual meeting held in Davos, Switzerland to attract investment in Korea and its companies.

In the first overseas tour in her second year in office, she focused on "trade diplomacy" to draw foreign investment in Korea and help resolve complaints Korean companies were suffering in countries they have advanced to.

In India, Park agreed to improve the Comprehensive Economic Partnership (CEPA) between India and Korea. The two countries signed a strategic partnership agreement in 2010 when the former President Lee Myung-bak visited India. But their bilateral trades were slowing down in recent years.

▲ President Park Geun-hye (L) poses with Indian Prime Minister Manmohan Singh prior to their summit talks at a state guest house in New Delhi on Jan. 16. Park arrived in India the previous day for a four-day state visit.

In Switzerland, she signed an initial agreement on 12 business and technology partnership projects between Korea and Switzerland. She also made efforts to appeal Korea as a good investment site when she met chief executives from major multinational companies during the Davos forum.

■ National Security Council Comes into Existence

President Park named Kim Kyu-hyun, the former vice minister at the Ministry of Foreign Affairs, and former unification ministry official Cheon Hae-sung in charge of unification policies to lead the National Security Council (NSC) and Cheong Wa Dae's national security team, respectively.

The NSC was established on Feb. 3. In Dec. 2013, the government announced its plan to set up the NSC to tackle increased security concerns following the execution of North Korea's No. 2 man Jang Song-thaek.

Kim Kyu-hyun reportedly was appointed to head the NSC helped by the former defense minister Kim Jang-soo. Kim Kyu-hyun came to know the then minister in 2006 when he worked in the ministry's international affairs team. Kim's appointment to the key position at NSC drew a sharp attention because Kim Jang-soo, NTS Director Nam Jae-joon, Defense Minister Kim Kwan-jin were all soldier-turned-politicians.

As Kim Kyu-hyun was regarded as expert in diplomacy and unification, he was expected to offer some flexibility to the government's diplomatic and security policies largely determined by the hawkish politicians who carry a military background.

But Cheon Hae-sung was replaced only a week after his appointment with Korea Institute for National Unification President Jeon Seong-hoon for unknown reasons. It was another setback for the Park government already criticized for personnel issues.

Ex-KBS Newscaster Named Presidential Spokesman

President Park named Min Kyung-wook, a former prime time news anchor at the Korean Broadcasting System, as presidential spokesman on Feb. 5. Min replaced former spokeswoman Kim Haing, who left the post citing personal reasons in Dec. 2013.

Kim was one of two presidential spokespeople appointed by Park early in 2013. But she held the post on her own after the other presidential spokesperson Yoon Chang-joong was sacked for his alleged sexual harassment of a Korean-American intern during the president's state visit to the U.S. in May 2013.

Min was expected to help Park better

communicate within the ruling party and with opposition party members. But the allegations came up that he delivered some information about the 2007 presidential election to a U.S. intelligence agency when he worked as a reporter for the state-run broadcasting company.

Oceans and Fisheries Minister Sacked

On Feb. 6, President Park sacked Minister of Oceans and Fisheries Yoon Jin-sook over her inappropriate conduct and comment in dealing with an oil spill in Yeosu, South Jeolla Province.

Following the accident that leaked large quantities of crude oil in the sea along the southern city's coastline, Yoon drew fire from all sides for her controversial comments and actions. While inspecting the accident site, Yoon was seen holding her nose to avoid smelling the spill and made questionable comments including one in which she called GS Caltex, the facility from which the oil leaked, a "victim."

Prime Minister Chung Hong-won asked Cheong Wa Dae to dismiss her and Park immediately gave an approval to the request when she received a call from Chung. It was the second time for the country's prime minister to make an offer to dismiss the minister of oceans and fisheries.

In Oct. 2003, then Prime Minister Koh Gun demanded then President Roh Moo-hyun sack then oceans and fisheries minister Choi Nak-jung for his "inappropriate" comments about President Roh and his families' attending a musical performance near Cheong Wa Dae on the day when the typhoon Maemi hit the nation in Sept. 2003. Choi said the president's watching the musical didn't affect the country's efforts to minimize the impact of the typhoon.

Yoon Jin-sook became the second minister to take responsibility for their inappropriate conduct and comments by stepping down, following the former Health and Welfare Minister Chin Young, who also quit his job in 2013 under the Park government. Park named the Saenuri Party's four-term lawmaker Lee Ju-young as new health and welfare minister 12 days after Yoon's dismissal.

■ **Three-Year Economic Plan, Unification Committee Launched**

On Feb. 25, when her government celebrated its first year in office, Park outlined the details of the three-year economic innovation plan. Under the "474 plan," the government aimed to achieve a potential growth rate of 4%, employment ratio of 70% and the per-capita income of US$40,000. In the ambitious program, the government planned to inject 4 trillion won over the next three years to generate an "ecosystem" to support venture startups.

It also planned to encourage companies to increase their investment in research and development to 5% of the country's gross domestic product by 2017, a move to strengthen science technology which is the cornerstone of the "creative economy," a concept promoted by President Park to generate new business opportunities through the integration of different industries.

When it comes to the innovation of the public sector, the government said it will seek a spinoff or an establishment of an affiliate to improve competitiveness of the public services such as railways. Among others, the government said it will focus on reducing debt-to-equity ratio of public companies to 200% by 2017. As for the public officials pension, it offered measures to have public officials pay more and receive less due to lack of funds.

To help boost domestic spending, the government will make efforts to cut the ratio of household debts to overall debts by 5%p by 2017. To promote home transactions, it will ease regulations on the transfer sales of homes built by private construction companies and allow landlords to pay less tax on their rental income.

Park said the government will launch the unification preparation committee under the wing of Cheong Wa Dae to study "systematic and constructive" ways to unify the two Koreas. She explained private-sector experts in diplomacy, security, economics and society and culture and civilian organizations will participate in the committee to discuss the ways and future inter-Korean exchanges.

■ **Ministers' Meeting to Tackle Complaints Involving Regulations**

On March 20, President Park held a meeting with ministers and business leaders to discuss ways to tackle complaints involving regulations in the private sector. The "marathon" meeting lasted for seven hours from 2 p.m.

Some 60 businessmen asked for deregulations in the fields where they suffer and Park ordered chiefs of respective ministries tackle the complaints as soon as possible.

Park viewed easing or lifting regulations as helping the Korean economy take a step forward and helping companies create jobs. She said the government will offer some incentives to public officials who try to innovate the economy and punish those who oppose the government's move and only take care of their own interests.

The government is aiming to reduce the number of regulations by 20% from the current level of regulations by 2016. On Sept. 3, Park reiterated the importance of easing regulations to generate jobs and promote convenience in the private sector.

■ **Nuclear Security Summit in Netherlands, State Visit to Germany**

In her second overseas visit in 2014, Park chose Germany and the Netherlands. She attended the 3rd Nuclear Security Summit held in the Hague, the Netherlands, from March 24-25. She also held trilateral summit talks with leaders from the U.S. and Japan.

During the summits, Park and world leaders reaffirmed the principles of jointly dealing with North Korean nuclear arms issues and that the rogue state must give up its nuclear weapons program in a verifiable, irreversible and complete way.

In her keynote speech on March 24, Park stressed the international community should take joint responsibility to keep peace and stability on the planet from any nuclear attacks. She proposed joint efforts to make the world free from nuclear weapons.

She also said it was not acceptable that North Korea pushes to develop nuclear weapons and at the same time to promote its economy. The South Korean government will make efforts to make the Korean Peninsula free of nuclear

68

weapons, she added.

In the Hague, Park had a summit with China's President Xi Jinping on March 23 to discuss pending issues such as North Korea's nuclear arms and the free trade agreement between China and Korea. They shared views that North Korean nuclear weapons were not acceptable and the Korean Peninsula should be nuclear weapon-free territory. They agreed to strengthen communication and cooperation in effort to seek peace and stability on the peninsula.

She had a trilateral meeting with U.S. President Barack Obama and Japanese Prime Minister Shinzo Abe in the Hague. It was Park's first meeting with Abe since she took office in Feb. 2013.

In her state visit to Germany, she stressed the need to learn from the unification of two Germanys and asked for full-scale support and guidelines from the German government in Korea's preparations for unification.

In her summit with German Chancellor Angela Merkel, Park asked for cooperative measures between the two governments for the future inter-Korean unification and agreed on joint efforts to make the North give up its nuclear arms and become a responsible member of the international community.

In her speech in the former East German city of Dresden, Park made three proposals to North Korean authorities.

박근혜 대통령 명예박사 학위수여식

TECHNISCHE UNIVERSITÄT DRESDEN

▲ President Park Geun-hye delivers a speech after receiving the honorary doctorate in legal sciences in Dresden, Germany, on March 28. Park unveiled a package of proposals calling for bolstering exchanges with North Korea as first steps toward building trust between the two sides to lay the groundwork for unification.

Park initially took up the agenda for humanity, the concerns of everyday people, saying "we must help ease the agony of separated families" for decades after the 1950-53 Korean War.

In her second proposal, she said an agenda for co-prosperity through the building of infrastructure that supports the livelihood of North Korean people. "South and North Korea should collaborate to set up multi-farming complexes that support agriculture, livestock and forestry in areas in the north suffering from backward production and deforestation," she said.

Lastly, she mentioned an agenda for integration between the people of South and North Korea, saying efforts should be made to narrow the distance between the two Koreas in terms of language, culture and living habits.

"To achieve this, those from South and North Korea must be afforded the chance to interact routinely. We will encourage exchanges in historical research and preservation, culture and the arts and sports -- all of which could promote genuine people-to-people contact -- rather than seek politically-motivated projects or promotional events," she said.

In Frankfurt, the last leg of the trip, Park met 18 miners and nurses who left their home country for Germany to make money 50 years ago and have since lived there.

■ Cabinet Reshuffle amid Criticisms

On April 2, Park named Kang Byung-kyu to replace Security Minister Yoo Jeong-bok, who quit to run for the Incheon mayoral election.

Although Kang and his wife were found to have registered their addresses falsely twice to have their children to go to a prestigious school and the opposition parties rejected approving his appointment in a hearing, Park pushed ahead with her appointment. But Kang was soon replaced with the "reform-minded" Chong Jong-sup due to mounting criticisms against Kang.

■ Major Government Projects Nearly Paralyzed after Sewol Disaster

The April 16 Sewol ferry disaster threw a major blow to the Park government, which was stepping up its drive to put the lackluster economy back on track under the three-year economic innovation plan in its second year in office.

In the afternoon of April 16, she visited the central disaster control tower in Government Complex to be briefed on the incident. She ordered the rescue team to save as many passengers as possible from the sinking ship, using all available workforce and equipment.

On the same day, she went to Paengmok Harbor in Jindo County, South Jeolla Province, to look around the incident site and meet families and relatives of missing passengers. She promised to make all-out effort to rescue the missing people and to punish those responsible for the incident through a thorough investigation.

As the probe into the Sewol sinking went by, however, the government's initial responses to rescue Sewol passengers turned out to fall far short of meeting the basic manual. Public officials in charge of supervising the safety of car ferries turned a blind-eye to the Sewol's overloading and illegal structural change. As the government focused on handling the Sewol disaster for months after April, its major projects were brought to a halt.

The opposition NPAD Party took issue with Park's whereabouts on the morning of the Sewol disaster. Rumors had it that Park was under going a skin treatment in Cheong Wa Dae during the morning or she was with her boyfriend, who is reportedly her former close aide Chung Yoon-hoe.

Park's approval ratings sharply plunged after the rumors. According to market research company Realmeter, Park's ratings fell to 56.5% on April 23, a week after the Sewol incident, from 71% on April 18. Her government's crisis management capability was harshly criticized.

On April 27, Prime Minister Chung Hong-won, the No. 2 man after President Park, offered to resign to take responsibility for the mismanagement and lack of control. Park said she will accept his resignation after the handling of the Sewol ferry sinking was completed. She picked two candidates to replace Chung -- Moon Chang-geuk and Ahn Dae-hee. Ahn withdrew from consideration after it was revealed that the used connections made as

a Supreme Court justice to earn millions of dollars in his private legal practice.

After Ahn, former journalist Moon also withdrew just before his confirmation after controversial comments he made during his media career were revealed. So Park ordered Chung to continue his job as prime minister.

In a cabinet meeting held on April 29, Park said the Ministry of Public Safety and Security will be built as the country's disaster control tower. She expressed her deep regret about all the confusion and lack of management in handling the Sewol sinking.

▲ President Park Geun-hye speaks to a news conference at the presidential office Cheong Wa Dae in Seoul on May 19. Park apologized to the nation for the poor handling of the April 16 sinking of the ferry Sewol that left more than 300 passengers dead or missing.

In her address to the nation on May 19, she made an apology to the nation about the government's mishandling of the incident, which took lives of more than 300.

She announced the Korea Coast Guard will be dissolved due to its failure to rescue more than 200 passengers from the sinking ship. She also proposed to make a special law to form a committee composed of ruling and opposition party and private-sector experts for a thorough investigation into the Sewol incident.

■ Obama Visits Seoul, Renews Partnership

Park had a summit with U.S. President Barack Obama, who paid a visit to Seoul from April 25-26. They discussed North Korea's nuclear issues, bilateral ties between Seoul and Washington, follow-up measures to the free-trade agreement between the two countries, and Korea's joining the U.S.-led Trans-Pacific Partnership (TPP).

The TPP agreement is aimed at reducing trade barriers and promoting greater economic cooperation, currently among 12 nations bordering the Pacific. The idea has been under negotiations since 2006, and it got started with relatively small economies like New Zealand and Brunei. It now includes very big economies such as the U.S., Japan and Australia. The 12 nations make up about 40% of the world's GDP.

In particular, Park and Obama agreed to reconsider the transition period of the military controlling rights during a war on the Korean Peninsula. Currently, the U.S. is expected to return the controlling rights to Korea in Dec. 2015. They warned there will be punishment against North Korea if it makes any provocations such as a nuclear test.

They paid a 30-second silent tribute to the victims of the Sewol sinking before their summit.

Obama delivered the U.S. flag, which was hoisted at the White House on the day of the Sewol incident and the magnolia seedling, which was planted on the same day, to Park. Nine national treasures such as a great seal of the Korean Empire from 1897-1910 were returned from the U.S. to Korea on the sidelines of the summit. They visited the Republic of Korea-US Combined Forces Command to show the two countries' strong ties to the North.

▪ President's Appointments Fail to Pass

Park's government continued to suffer as two prime minister candidates failed to replace Chung Hong-won who offered to resign taking the responsibility of the mishandling of the Sewol incident.

To replace Chung, Park named the former Supreme Court justice Ahn Dae-hee on May 22. In an unexpected personnel appointment, she dismissed the national security chief Kim Jang-soo and National Intelligence Service (NIS) Director Nam Jae-joon.

But Ahn voluntarily gave up the position six days before the National Assem-

bly hearing following speculations that Ahn used his connections for his own interests after his retirement as justice. It was a hit for the president and her government.

On June 10, Park named former journalist Moon Chang-geuk as prime minister candidate and Korean Ambassador to Japan Lee Byung-kee as new chief of the NIS. Personnel changes in Cheong Wa Dae and the cabinet reshuffle followed.

On June 1, Park named former National Defense Minister Kim Kwan-jin as new national security chief and R.O.K. Joint Chiefs of Staff Chairman Han Min-koo as defense minister. On June 8, she named YTN Plus President Yoon Doo-hyun as her chief spokesman instead of the outgoing Lee Jung-hyun.

On June 12, Minister of Gender Equality & Family Cho Yoon-sun was named as presidential senior secretary for political affairs and Saenuri Party Rep. Ahn Jong-beom was named chief economic advisor to the president. On June 13, Park appointed her close aide and three-term Saenuri Party Rep. Choi Kyung-hwan as deputy prime minister and strategy and finance minister.

Among the appointments, Moon's withdrawal on June 24, 14 days after his appointment, was a major hit to the Park government. Moon came under fire for his comments in 2011 about the Japanese colonial rule from 1910-1945. He said it was "God's will that Korea became a colony of Japan and Korea has become the only divided country in the world."

So Park decided to keep Chung Hong-won as prime minister, the first of such a decision in Korea's history, on June 26. To avoid further appointment failures, Park ordered the generation of a position in charge of personnel matters at Cheong Wa Dae.

▪ Tour of 3 Central Asian Countries in "Eurasia Initiative"

From June 16-21, Park made a tour of three central Asian countries - Uzbekistan, Kazakhstan and Turkmenistan in the "Eurasia Initiative" aimed at promoting diplomatic and economic ties with the less developed countries.

In the summit with Uzbekistan, Park paved the way for 13 trillion won worth of existing and future economic partnerships with the central Asian country whose economy grew by more than 8% in recent years despite global economic uncertainties.

In Kazakhstan, she signed a 20-year contract to buy 19 trillion won worth of electricity produced at a local coal-fired power plant, which is 75% owned by Samsung C&T, a conglomerate of Samsung Group. She also signed an initial agreement with the gas-rich Turkmenistan to seek economic ties worth 12.7 trillion won.

Park drummed up support from Kazakhstan President Nursultan Nazarbayev for South Korea's call on North Korea to give up its nuclear weapons and heads of Uzbekistan and Turkmenistan. Nazarbayev led Kazakhstan's economic growth by attracting a great deal of financial aid from the international community instead of giving up its nuclear weapons.

▪ Xi Jinping Visits Seoul, Voices against Pyongyang's Nuclear Programs

Park announced a joint statement with China's President Xi Jinping to stand against North Korea's nuclear programs after she had a summit meeting with him at Cheong Wa Dae on July 3. In her fifth meeting with the Chinese leader, Park and Xi agreed to sign the free-trade pact between China and Korea at an earliest date.

Xi made a return visit to Seoul following Park's visit to Beijing in June 2013. It was meaningful for the Chinese president to choose Seoul over Tokyo or Pyongyang for his state visit when the North continued to threaten the stability of Northeast Asia and Japan continued to make provocations by denying its war crimes during the World War II.

In the summit talks, the two leaders agreed to build a mature and strategic partnership based on mutual trust and strengthen ties to promote peace and stability on the Korean Peninsula and Northeast Asia.

On July 4, Park and Xi had an informal lunch meeting at a furniture museum in Seoul and shared their worries about Japan's push to strengthen its collective self-defense right and its denial of forcing Korean and other Asian women to serve as sex slaves for Japanese soldiers during the 2nd world war.

They didn't include their concerns about Japan's right-wing moves in the joint statement released a day earlier and the press conference held the same day. But in the informal meeting, they expressed grave concerns about Japan's rightward shift.

▪ Meeting with Political Leadership amid Miscommunication Worries

On July 10, Park called in the leadership of the ruling Saenuri and main opposition NPAD Parties for the first time since she took office in early 2013. The meeting was aimed at regaining her declining approval ratings after the Sewol disaster and push forward major political projects with support from the opposition party.

The president and the two parties' leadership agreed to pass the Sewol Special Law not only to punish those responsible for the Sewol incident but also to support the families of 304 Sewol victims. They also agreed to establish the Ministry of Public Safety and Security to avoid another Sewol disaster.

▲ President Park Geun-hye (C) meets with floor leaders of the ruling and main opposition parties at the presidential office Cheong Wa Dae in Seoul on July 10 to discuss pending political issues. At left is Rep. Lee One-koo, the floor leader of the ruling Saenuri Party. Rep. Park Young-sun of the main opposition New Politics Alliance for Democracy is at right.

▪ Unification Preparation Committee Launched

On July 15, Park officially launched the Unification Preparation Committee in order to make systematic preparations for the unification of North and South Korea. Some 50 professors, government officials and chiefs of state-run research institutes also formed the committee chaired by the president. The committee came into existence to support Park's unification push between the two Koreas.

The committee is composed of four divisions - diplomacy and security, economics, society and culture, and politics, law and system. And the committee focuses on making tangible results from North Korea-related projects in the four sectors. The committee plans to run an advisor group composed of 30 civilians, journalists and unification experts. Park chaired three meetings on Aug. 7, Oct. 13 and Dec. 2 to discuss ways to promote inter-Korean cooperation and exchanges.

■ Saenuri Rep. Hwang Woo-yea Named Education Minister

On July 15, Park named Saenuri Party Rep. Hwang Woo-yea as education minister after she scrapped her nomination of Kim Myung-soo, professor at Korea National University of Education, who allegedly plagiarized his student's paper.

On the following day, Jeong Seong-geun, the minister candidate for culture, sports and tourism, voluntarily withdrew amid escalating criticisms about his false testimony at a National Assembly hearing and drinking bomb shots over lunch during the hearing period.

On July 25, Park appointed Strategy and Finance 1st Deputy Minister Choo Kyung-ho as government policy coordination minister and Seoul Regional Tax Office chief Lim Hwan-soo as National Tax Service commissioner. She also filled 10 other vice minister-level positions.

Joo Hyung-hwan, the economy and finance secretary at Cheong Wa Dae was named as 1st vice finance minister and Bang Moon-kyu in charge of the finance ministry's budget team was named as 2nd vice minister. Jang Ok-joo, health and welfare secretary at Cheong Wa Dae, was named health and welfare minister and Kim Nak-hoe in charge of the tax system at the finance ministry was named as Korea Customs Service commissioner.

■ Park Welcomes Pope Francis at Airport

Park paid special attention to receiving Pope Francis who visited from Aug. 14-18. She went to the Seoul Airport in Seongnam, Gyeonggi Province, to greet him in person. In the welcoming ceremony and summit talks held at Cheong Wa Dae in the afternoon of Aug. 14, Park welcomed the head of the Catholics with special treatment.

In the welcoming address she delivered after the summit talks, Park said "Pope Francis is the top leader of the world's 1.2 billion Catholics and his visit to Korea is a big blessing to the Korean Catholics as well as the Korean people. We believe the Pope's visit will serve as momentum which heals the decades-long wounds resulting from the division of the Korean Peninsula and open the era of unification."

Pope Francis said as North and South Korea use one language, it will be the seed of peace and they need to plant it and grow it well. As he believes the two Koreas are becoming one, he will pray for the unification.

Park dropped by the mass for peace and reconciliation held at the Myeong-dong Cathedral, central Seoul, carried out by the Pope before he left the country to say goodbye to him.

■ State Visit to Canada, U.S., Keynote Speech at UN General Assembly

Park paid a state visit to Canada from Sept. 20-22 to have a summit with Canadian Prime Minister Steven Harper. In the meeting, they signed the free trade agreement between Korea and Canada and agreed to cooperate in energy technology and research and development of the North Pole.

▲ *President Park Geun-hye speaks to a session of the United Nations General Assembly in New York on Sept. 24. She urged North Korea to improve its human rights record and end its nuclear weapons programs.*

And then she moved to New York to consecutively attend the UN Climate Change Summit held at the United Nations' New York headquarters, the 69th UN General Assembly, the UN Security Council summit talks, the Global Education First Initiative high-ranking official meeting. She made a successful debut at those UN meetings in the U.S.

In her keynote speech at the UN General Assembly, Park explained the South Korean government's strenuous efforts to seek unification on the Korean Peninsula and peace and stability in Northeast Asia to the world. Her speech was well accepted by the participants, according to Cheong Wa Dae's self analysis.

She wrapped up her schedules in New York by meeting representatives from think tank organizations such as the Korea Society, the Council on Foreign Relations, the National Committee for American Foreign Policy, and the Foreign Policy Association.

▪ Makes Debut at ASEM Summit in Italy, Meets Pope Francis

Park paid a visit to Italy and the Vatican from Oct. 14-18 to attend the Asia-Europe Meeting (ASEM) and meet Pope Francis. During the ASEM period, Park proposed the "Eurasia Initiative"again in which the unified Korea will play the role of connecting Asia and Europe in her keynote speech and free speech session. She also expressed South Korea's strong willingness to have dialogue with North Korea.

In his meeting with Park, China's premier Li Keqiang said "inter-Korean dialogue and exchanges are helpful in Northeast Asia so we support improved relations between the two Koreas." His comments showed China's support to promote any progress in inter-Korean talks.

But what awaited her when she returned to Korea from the trip were the 2nd inter-Korean talks of high-ranking officials, an accident and the ruling Saenuri Party leader's demand for constitutional amendment.

Saenuri leader Kim Moo-sung asked for the constitutional amendment and an accident during a concert at Pangyo Techno Valley in Seongnam, Gyeonggi Province, claimed 16 lives. Around 27 on-lookers fell 20m when a ventilation grate that they were standing on near the outdoor concert venue collapsed in September. Park had no choice but to wrestle with the issues right after she returned home, instead of resting to overcome the jet leg from her trip.

▪ Park Pushes Reform of Public Officials' Pension

At a speech in the National Assembly on Oct. 29, Park said as the country's economy is in a crisis, the government was determined to revive the lackluster economy by increasing the national budget. She explained the government increased the budget for 2015 by 20 trillion won as it focuses on activating the economy.

She asked the ruling and opposition party members to pass laws involving deregulation, reform of public officials' pension, and reorganization plans of government agencies by the end of Dec. 2014.

Park made her second speech regarding the budget at the National Assembly. It was the first time for the president to deliver a speech on budget for two consecutive years at Yeoido. Following the speech, Park met with representatives of the ruling and opposition parties at the VIP restaurant in the National Assembly. They agreed to pass the 2015 budget by Dec. 2, the deadline stipulated by the law.

▪ Multilateral Diplomacy

From Nov. 9-16, Park attended global summit meetings such as the Asia Pacific Economic Cooperation, the East Asia Summit, the Association of Southeast Asian Nations and the Group of 20 Summit held in countries such as China, Myanmar and Australia.

Through the multilateral talks, she reconfirmed their support for South Korea's efforts to bring peace and stability on the Korean Peninsula and in Northeast Asia.

During the tour, Park signed two separate free trade agreements with China and New Zealand. The free trade deal with China, with the world's biggest population of 1.3 billion, opened the gate of its huge domestic market to Korean companies.

Park shared views with leaders from China, the U.S. and Japan over pending diplomatic and economic issues. Her move was aimed at helping Korea make its voice in the rapidly-changing diplomatic world in Northeast Asia. During the EAS and ASEAN plus 3 meetings in Myanmar, there was even a proposal for a trilateral meeting between China, Japan and Korea.

■ Public Safety Minister, Personnel Chief Named

On Nov. 18, Park named the former ROK. Joint Chief of Staff vice chairman Park In-yong as minister of public safety and security. A new emergency control tower was built to better deal with disasters such as the Sewol sinking and innovate extravagant spending on public officials' benefits and lax management in public organizations.

Lee Geun-myeon, formerly in charge of Samsung Electronics' human resources team, was named to head the Ministry of Personnel Management.

Fair Trade Commission Vice Chairman Cheong Jae-chan was appointed as chairman of the antitrust regulator and Kim Sang-ryul, who taught English literature at Sookmyung Women's University, was appointed as chief advisor of education and culture in the presidential office. Lee Sung-ho, the 2nd vice minister of the Ministry of Government Administration and Home Affairs, was named as vice minister of the Ministry of Public Safety and Security.

All the safety-related appointments were made a day after the revised laws aimed at strengthening safety systems and preventing former government officials from getting a job after retirement at companies he once supervised or worked with passed the cabinet council meeting.

■ Close Aide behind Park Pulling Strings behind Scenes

Segye Ilbo, a local daily, reported on Nov. 28 that the former chief presidential advisor Chung Yoon-hoe influenced key national affairs based on leaked internal documents from the presidential Blue House. The Chung Yoon-hoe scandal drove up the demand to reshuffle the Blue House.

Chung was also alleged to have feuded with Park's younger brother, Park Ji-man, who denied allegations that he tried to influence state affairs. The scandal pulled down Park's approval ratings and led to a political gridlock.

Cheong Wa Dae was quick to call the allegations "totally groundless." In the Dec. 1 chief advisors' meeting, the president said the allegations intended to put the whole nation into disorder. The rumors didn't die down for some time.

The opposition party called it "Chung Yoon-hoe gate" and asked Park to tell the truth. But prosecutors found all the rumors were not true, but Park's approval ratings fell sharply due to the suspicions.

■ Park Meets Leaders from ASEAN Member Countries in Busan

Park presided over meetings with 10 heads of states from the Association of Southeast Asian Nations (ASEAN) in Busan, a southern port city of Korea, from Dec. 11-12. The Korea-ASEAN summit was the second reunion after the first in 2009.

▲ South Korean President Park Geun-hye and ASEAN leaders pose before attending the first session of the ASEAN-South Korea Commemorative Summit at Bexco in Busan on Dec. 12.

The participants made an analysis of the 25-year-long partnership between Korea and the ASEAN countries. Park had discussions with 10 participating leaders to further cooperate and exchange with the ASEAN nations in the future.

The Korea-ASEM summit was the first multilateral meeting hosted by the incumbent government. It successfully wrapped up multilateral meetings in 2014 following the UN General Assembly in September, ASEM summit in October, APEC and ASEAN plus 3, EAS, and G-20 summit.

On Dec. 12, Park and 10 ASEAN leaders announced a "joint statement for strategic partnership and future vision." In the statement, they agreed to maximize the fre -trade agreement signed among them and increase their mutual trade volumes to US$200 billion in terms of value by 2020.

As for the joint statement, the Blue House said the leaders' analysis on the past 25 years of partnership will help them make a "blue print" for future cooperation and a "road map" to carry out their goals. It said Korea and ASEAN countries, as new growth engines, are expected to play a key role in putting the world economy back on track.

THE BOARD OF AUDIT AND INSPECTION OF KOREA

■ **Composition**

The Board of Audit and Inspection of Korea (BAI) is a constitutional institution established under the Article 97 of the Constitution. BAI is in charge of auditing the government's tax income and tax spending and is also responsible for supervising accounting reports of organizations designated by the government and law. The BAI is comprised of seven members, including the BAI chairman. BAI Chairman Hwang Chan-hyeon took office on Dec. 2, 2013, replacing his predecessor Yang Kun.

■ **Key Activities**

BAI asks 50 Korea Coast Guard officials to be punished after Sewol On Oct. 10, the BAI called on the Ministry of Oceans and Fisheries to take disciplinary measures against Kim Seok-kyun, then head of the Korea Coast Guard (KCG) for his inadequate role in supervising rescue operations following the Sewol ferry disaster that took place on April 16.

It also demanded disciplinary actions against 46 officials at the KCG and made a request for an immediate dismissal of four supervising officials in the Vessel Traffic Service (VTS) center in Jindo.

In its audit from May 14 to June 20, 50 inspectors from BAI looked into whether the Sewol ferry captain and crewmen took proper action to rescue its passengers when it began to sink on April 16. The audit agency also inspected how the authorities were supervising the safety control of car ferries such as the Sewol ship.

On top of the 50 KCG officials at KCG and the VTS center, the BAI also gave a warning against 59 officials involved in the tragic incident. But the BAI came under fire as it concluded that the Blue House's response to the incident was appropriate. The opposition parties and the bereaved families of the Sewol victims criticized the conclusion.

The sinking of Sewol occurred on the morning of 16 April 2014 en route from Incheon to Jeju Island. The ferry capsized while carrying a total of 476 people, mostly schoolchildren from Danwon High School in Ansan, Gyeonggi Province. The 6,825t vessel sent a distress signal from about 2.7km north off the Byeongpungdo islands at 08:58 a.m.

Even though there was enough time to rescue a lot more passengers from the sinking ship, 304 passengers died in the disaster. Of the approximately 172 survivors, many were rescued by fishing boats and other commercial vessels that arrived at the scene approximately 30 minutes earlier than the national coast guard or the Republic of Korea Navy ships.

The BAI reported its findings on the Sewol ferry disaster and related disciplinary recommendations to the National Assembly. The BAI said in the report to lawmakers, "We demand disciplinary actions for all involved officials for their poor safety management and supervision on passenger ships, and poor initial responses to the Sewol incident".

Lax management at state firms, reckless spending on overseas resources pointed out The BAI also found that state-owned financial companies' lax management was at a serious level, revealing that despite falling profitability, the public companies had paid extraordinary salaries and welfare benefits to its employees compared to financial firms in the private sector.

The BAI's findings were announced on Oct. 7, when it compared 13 state-owned financial firms to eight private financial firms. The BAI said that employees at public financial firms were paid higher than their counterparts at private financial firms despite lack of competition and continued financial support from the government.

Job security at public financial firms was mostly at top levels and working hours were shorter than those of private firms. The income gap between the two sectors was widening further, the BAI report showed.

According to the findings, the average number of years of service at a public financial company reached 25.9, 4.2 years more than in a private financial firm. But labor costs at the former were 1.2 times higher that the latter and welfare benefits were 31% higher.

For example, average wages at the state-owned Korea Development Bank reached 89 million won, 13% higher than the average salary of four major banks. Average salaries at the Korea Exchange (KRX), the country's main bourse, were 113 million won, 67% higher than the average wage of 68 million won at private-sector brokerages.

Labor costs at private financial firms were on the decline since 2011. In contrast, those in public financial firms were on the rise. The wage gap between the two sectors expanded to 16 million won in 2013 from 7 million won in 2011.

Separately, the BAI on Jan. 2, 2015 reported former Korea National Oil Corporation (KNOC) President Kang Young-won to the police with regard to the KNOC's acquisition of Harvest Energy, a Canadian oil firm, and filed a lawsuit against Kang for damages that arose from the acquisition.

In 2009, the KNOC took over Harvest and its subsidiary North Atlantic Refining Limited (NARL), but the acquisition incurred losses of over 100 billion won each year. So KNOC sold NARL at 1 trillion won.

On Oct. 23, National Assembly's Trade, Industry and Energy Committee chair Kim Dong-chul said "the acquisition of Harvest was nothing more than a power-related corruption case committed by the Lee Myung-bak government."

BAI's demand for both civil and criminal actions against a chief of a state-run institution for his mismanagement was the first of its kind in its history. The BAI sounded an alarm bell to the government's reckless pursuit of raw materials overseas with taxpayers' money without conducting a proper survey.

Disciplinary actions asked against marine chief In May, the BAI conducted an audit to find out why the "Tongyoungham," an offshore rescue ship was not hired for the Sewol ferry rescue and search operations. And it expanded its audit to other related institutions such as each military headquarters, the Defense Acquisition Program Administration (DAPA) and the Agency for Defense Development.

On Dec. 17, the BAI found that Navy Chief Hwang Ki-chul, then department head of the DAPA, which was in charge of buying sonar for the Tongyoungham, or Tongyoung warship, was negligent in his duty of carefully examining a sonar supply proposal. The DAPA budgeted about 70 billion won in national budget since Sept. 2008 to buy the sonar used for the Tongyoungham.

However, the Defense Acquisition Program Administration spent only 4.1 billion won of the planned budget to purchase the sonar equipment, which was similar to the sonar used for the Pyeongtaek warship built in the 1970s. So the Navy refused to accept the Tongyoungham for its use.

The BAI also found that documents were forged in the process of DAPA's sonar purchases. "The Marine Commander Hwang neglected his duties because he signed off on the documents without recognizing they were amended in the process of purchase," a BAI official said.

The BAI set up a team dedicated to auditing any misdeeds related to defense deals. The special audit team was comprised of 33 experts from related organiza-

01234567

89012345678

tions such as the National Tax Service and Financial Supervisory Service. The BAI announced follow-up audit results for defense-related corruptions on Jan. 6, 2015.

According to the findings made over the May-July period in 2014, at least 600 billion won in national budget was wasted due to the authorities' poor supervision and special favors they delivered to companies in defense industry and poor supervision.

Tong Yang Securities crisis attributable to financial authorities' negligence of duties On July 14, the BAI said the financial authorities' negligence of duties made 40,000 investors suffer from 1.7 trillion won in losses from their investments in products sold by Tong Yang Securities in the several years through 2013.

The BAI pointed out the authorities were aware of incomplete sales at the securities company well ahead of the breakout of the "Tong Yang Securities Crisis" at the end of 2013 but failed to prevent the crisis from taking place.

The BAI asked chief of Financial Supervisory Service (FSS) to punish related officials in the financial regulator for their negligence of duties. According to the findings, the FSS confirmed such incomplete sales several times since 2008 but did not check them thoroughly in a comprehensive examination conducted in Nov. 2011.

The FSS also looked the other way regarding Tong Yang Securities' incomplete sales of 1 trillion won in commercial papers with speculative ratings issued by the brokerage's affiliates.

The Financial Services Commission (FSC) was also to blame, as even after it being reported to such incomplete CP sales, the commission erased a provision such as banning support to affiliates in Aug. 2008 when it incorporated related regulations and made regulations regarding financial investment operations.

NATIONAL INTELLIGENCE SERVICE

▪ Composition

The National Intelligence Service (NIS) is an organization under the direct control of President Park. It is in charge of information gathering, security, and crime investigation. Before turning into the NIS in Jan. 1999, it was National Security Planning since Dec. 1980. The NIS head is appointed by the president.

The NIS is the chief intelligence agency of South Korea. The agency was officially established in 1961 as the Korean Central Intelligence Agency (KCIA), during the rule of President Park Chung-hee's military Supreme Council for National Reconstruction, which displaced the Second Republic of South Korea.

The original duties of the KCIA were to supervise and coordinate both international and domestic intelligence activities and criminal investigation by all government intelligence agencies, including that of the military. The agency's broad powers allowed it to actively intervene in politics.

The agency took on the name Agency for National Security Planning (ANSP) in 1981, as part of a series of reforms by then President Chun Doo-hwan. Besides trying to acquire intelligence on North Korea and suppress South Korean activists, the ANSP, like its predecessor, was heavily involved in activities outside of its sphere, including domestic politics and even promoting the 1988 Summer Olympics in Seoul.

▪ Aftermaths of Interfering in 2012 Presidential Election

The National Intelligence Service (NIS), which was at the center of political turmoil in 2013 on charges of interfering in the 2012 presidential election, remained a controversial issue in 2014.

In the wake of interfering in the Dec. 2012 presidential elections, the National Assembly sharply cut budget for the NIS at its national budget for 2014. The Assembly also passed seven bills related to reforming the NIS-the first of its kind since the election interference scandal at end-2012.

The centerpiece of the legislations was to tighten the National Assembly's control of the NIS and prevent the NIS from engaging in politics. The revised laws prohibited NIS officials from being involved in any political activities in cyberspace through social network service channels.

The National Assembly gave its Intelligence Committee the authority to tighten the budget for the NIS. It also voted for a bill that strengthens protection of whistle blowers inside the NIS.

Both the ruling and opposition parties decided to come up with the second NIS reform bill by the end of February in areas of counterterrorism and overseas information gathering on North Korea.

To that end, the National Assembly's special NIS reform committee visited key nations' intelligence organizations such as Israel's Mossad, U.S.' CIA, and Germany's BND, and National Assemblies in the countries as well, to look at the former's management systems and the latter's intelligence organization control systems, but to no avail.

The committee failed to narrow differences on key issues, such as ways to prevent the NIS from revealing confidential information and the president's winning National Assembly's approval when the president appoints the head of NIS. In all, the special committee failed to reach an agreement on second NIS reform measures by the February deadline, walking out empty handed.

Embroiled in building a spying case against a former Seoul City official who escaped to South Korea from the North in 2004, the spy agency chief stepped down to take responsibility for the allegations.

In mid-February, which was when both the ruling and opposition parties were engaged in fierce battle over introducing an independent counsel team to investigate NIS' interference in the 2012 presidential elections, the NIS was again accused of forging a spying case against a former Seoul City official who escaped to South Korea from the North in 2004.

The case was brought back in January 2013. The NIS then arrested the Seoul City official on charges of infiltrating South Korea, saying that he turned over the information of about 200 North Korean defectors living in Korea to North Korea.

The prosecution brought charges on him in Feb. 2013 based on the confession made by the Seoul City official's younger sister. Lawyers for Democratic Society, however, in April raised doubt that the spying case was forged as the younger sister made a false confession.

The Seoul City official was found not guilty in the first trial held in Aug. 2013, which triggered the prosecution to appeal. In the appeals court, the prosecution presented Chinese data on the official's moving between North Korea and China.

Lawyers for Democratic Society in Jan. 2014 again raised doubt that the Chinese data was also forged, which prompted the court to ask China to verify the data.

China on Feb. 14 replied that the data was forged, which hit another blow to the NIS. The embattled prosecution set up a special investigation team and found that an NIS official working in Shenyang, China provided the forged document. The NIS' spying forgery case created huge public outcry.

The special prosecution team found that all evidence was forged and forged documents were presented to the court as if they were issued by Chinese authorities. The prosecution team also seized and searched the NIS, the third raid of its kind since 2005.

Faced with public uproar, a high-ranking NIS official on April 14 resigned over the case, and President Park accepted the resignation due to the seriousness of the case. NIS director Nam Jae-joon on April 15 made a public apology to the public and the president on the same day also did so.

Though the public's demand for Nam's resignation was high, his and the President's public apology seemed to appease the public anger for some time. However, the Sewol ferry disaster, which took place a day after the apologies, changed everything.

The government's poor rescue operations again caused public outcry, resulting in massive government reshuffling and several high-profile resignations, including Nam Jae-joon.

■ Lee Byung-kee Named as New NIS Director

The President on June 10 appointed former Korean ambassador to Japan Lee Byung-kee, known as a dovish and professional diplomat, as new director of the NIS, which was wrecked by the forgery case.

In National Assembly confirmation hearing, he several times promised no NIS engagement in politics, recognizing that the NIS was at the center of controversy since the launch of the Park Geun-hye government due to the interference in the 2012 presidential elections and 2013 spying forgery.

▲ *President Park Geun-hye (L) gives a letter of appointment to Lee Byung-kee, the new director of the National Intelligence Service, at the presidential office Cheong Wa Dae in Seoul on July 18.*

At the July 18 inauguration ceremony, he asked all NIS employees to commit-tee themselves to their original duties by erasing the words 'political engagement.' He also said that he will be committed to political neutrality. The NIS in August carried out organizational reshuffling, with key focus given to minimizing domestic political engagement and strengthening counterterrorism.

As signs of preventing any engagement in political activities, the NIS banned its information officials' unlimited access to the National Assembly, political parties, and mass media outlets, and the agency reshuffled its organization.

NATIONAL UNIFICATION ADVISORY COUNCIL

▪ Composition and Goal

The National Unification Advisory Council is a constitutional organization (under direct control of the President), which gives advice or recommendations to the President regarding establishment and implementation of unification policies.

It is composed of local representatives elected by locals, and key members of political parties and social organizations appointed by the President. The President takes the chairmanship, and the Council has one senior vice chairman and 20 vice chairmen. It has a lot of regional and overseas subdivisions.

The National Unification Advisory Council is the constitutional organization, established in accordance with the Article 92 of the Constitution of the Republic of Korea and the National Unification Advisory Council Act (Korea) to advise the President of South Korea on the formulation of peaceful unification policy.

This was organized in October 1980. The Chairperson of the Council is President of South Korea and the Executive Vice-Chairperson is a minister-level officer. In 2013, the 16th National Unification Advisory Council was launched.

▪ 2014 Goals

To establish the basis for peaceful unification on the Korean Peninsula, the Council had the 2014 goals of making more political proposals, building public consensus for unification, unifying the public, supporting North Korean defectors, and strengthening collaboration with international communities.

To make more political suggestions, the Council strived to diversify unification-related public opinion gathering channels, and boost Council members' capability of raising political suggestions. Moreover, to consolidate public interest in unification, it decided to take unification-related businesses with the public.

To help North Korean defectors' settlement in Korea, it decided to expand legal, medical and academic assistance and boost youth's interest in unification. Finally, to bolster the international community's cooperation, it decided to hold unification forums in key overseas nations.

The Korean Peninsula was divided into South Korea and North Korea due to the result of the 1945 Allied victory in World War II. The United States and the Soviet Union agreed to temporarily occupy the country as a trusteeship with the zone of control along the 38th parallel.

The purpose of this trusteeship was to establish a Korean provisional government which would become "free and independent in due course", as set forth in the Cairo Conference.

■ Directions of Policy Proposals for 2014

The Council held meetings on Jan. 16 to discuss the direction of making policy proposals for 2014. Attendees of the meetings pointed out the needs to discuss more the institutionalization of the unification of the Korean Peninsula and put the Council into an organization aimed at consulting unification laws.

At the meetings, the Council - under the grand topic of establishing the basis for unification era - selected subtopics by committee and decided to carry out policy studies with consistency.

The Council also agreed to select as agendas promotion of strong security environment, bolstering of international cooperation for denuclearization, nurturing of agricultural cooperation, boosting of unification education at schools, enhancement of human rights in North Korea and promotion of welfare for North Korean defectors as well as raise policy ideas centered on them.

■ Domestic Regional Meetings Held in 17 Cities

To celebrate the one year anniversary of the 16th Council, the Council held domestic regional meetings in 17 cities and provinces. About 16,423 advisory members attended the meetings, which started with Daejeon gatherings on June 16 and lasted until July 7, with total gatherings hitting 17 in areas such as Incheon, Daegu, Seoul, Jeju, and Busan.

Regional meeting topic was direction and challenges for Korean Peninsula unification era, and focus was given to setting direction for making unification preparations. In the Seoul meeting held on June 24, 2,200 members gathered, with attendees reporting unification policy measures and announcing resolutions for helping unification preparations.

■ Overseas Regional Meetings also Held

The Council also held overseas regional meetings on Sept. 2. About 570 unification advisors from 61 countries attended the meetings. Opinion gathering on inter-Korean unification and building consensus for unification among Koreans residing outside of Korea were discussed.

In small group meetings, attendees discussed ways to support overseas North Korean defectors, boost humanitarian support and exchange with the North through international non-government organizations (NGOs). About 560 advisers out of the 570 attendants had a meeting with President Park in the Blue House on Sept. 2 and shared their views on the government's peaceful unification policies.

■ Policies Recommended for Unification and North Korean Policy

The Council on Dec. 4 adopted a policy recommendation on the government's unification and North Korean policies. "To boost denuclearization, the recommendation said that South Korea, the U.S. and China should have strategic discussions, and that considering U.S. and China's passive attitude, the discussion should be focused on the Korean Peninsula," the recommendation said.

The recommendation also said that to minimize China's intervention in the course of inter-Korean unification, there should be strategic discussions between three parties - the U.S., China and South Korea.

In the Korean Peninsula-type denuclearization model, the recommendation proposed a complex model such as, adopting a Ukrainian model for security and economic exchange, a Libyan model for mediation and political big deals and a South African model for security environment change and political power change.

The Council made an official request for the two Koreas to meet to improve the human rights conditions in Pyongyang. The Council also adopted the human rights resolution for North Korea, urging the North to be more responsible for North Korean people's human rights and adopt the UN General Assembly's resolution involving human rights.

■ Conferring Medal and Commendation on Advisory Committee Members

In an event held at Kim Koo Museum

and Library on Dec. 9 in central Seoul, the Council delivered medals and commendation to 45 advisory committee members who were aggressive in pushing forward a peaceful unification on the Korean Peninsula and unifying the general public. Medals were given to 42 members. Commendation was also given to 34 regional organizations which were actively engaged in efforts to seek unification.

THE CABINET

THE EXECUTIVE BRANCH

▪ Government Organization

As of the end of 2014, the government is made up of two bureaus, 17 ministries, five administrations, 16 agencies, five offices and six commissions. The president is assisted by the office of presidential staff (headed by a minister-level chief of staff), the Presidential Security Service and the office of national security. Under the direct control of the president are the Board of Audit and Inspection, the National Intelligence Service and the Korea Communications Commission. There are 16 presidential committees that are responsible for carrying out the government's policy tasks.

They are the presidential committees for unification preparation, national cohesion, youth affairs, regional development, cultural prosperity, development of regional autonomy, creation of a hub city of Asian culture, library information and policy, national construction policy, national life and ethics deliberation, space issues, intellectual property, low birthrate and aging society, protection of personal information, regulatory reform and the tripartite commission for economic and social development.

The constitutional advisory bodies -- the National Security Council, the National Unification Advisory Council, National Economic Advisory Council, and the Presidential Advisory Council on Science and Technology -- are placed under the president. Under the prime minister are the Office for Government Policy Coordination and the Prime Minister's Secretariat.

The Ministry of Government Legislation, the Ministry of Patriots and Veterans Affairs, the Ministry of Food and Drug Safety, the Ministry of Public Safety and Security, the Ministry of Personnel Management, the Fair Trade Commission, the Financial Services Commission, the Anti-Corruption and Civil Rights Commission, and the Nuclear Safety and Security Commission are placed under the prime minister.

The government offices headed by a minister are: the Ministry of Strategy and Finance; the Ministry of Science, ICT and Future Planning; the Ministry of Education; the Ministry of Foreign Affairs; the Ministry of Unification; the Ministry of Justice; the Ministry of National Defense; the Ministry of Government Administration and Home Affairs; the Ministry of Culture, Sports and Tourism; the Ministry of Agriculture, Food and Rural Affairs; the Ministry of Trade, Industry and Energy; the Ministry of Health and Welfare; the Ministry of Environment; the Ministry of Employment and Labor; the Ministry of Gender Equality and Family; the Ministry of Land, Infrastructure and Transport; and the Ministry of Oceans and Fisheries.

The government offices headed by an official of vice-minister rank are: the National Tax Service, the Korea Customs Service, the Public Procurement Service, Statistics Korea, the Supreme Prosecutors' Office, the Military Manpower Administration, the Defense Acquisition Program Administration, the National Police Agency, the Cultural Heritage Administration, the Rural Development Administration, the Korea Forest Service, the Small and Medium Business Administration, the Korean Intellectual Property Office, the Korea Meteorological Administration, the Multifunctional Administrative City Construction Agency and the Saemangeum Development Agency.

At the bureau level are the Board of Audit and Inspection and the National Intelligence Service. At the office level are the office of presidential staff, the Presidential Security Service, the Presidential Office of National Security, the Office for Government Policy Coordina-

Organization Layout of Government
(17 ministries, 5 administrations, 16 agencies)

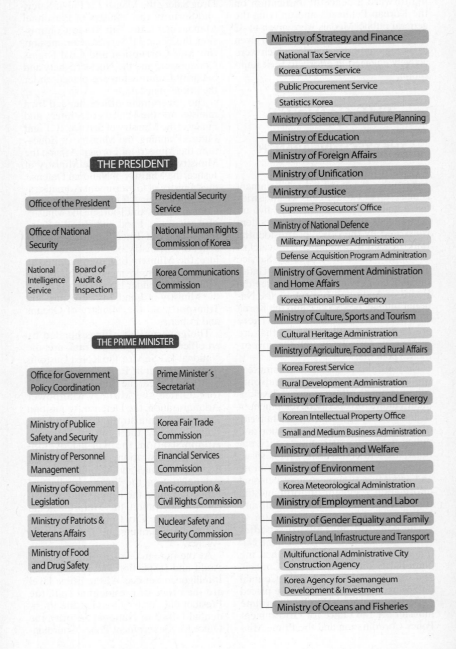

THE PRESIDENT

Office of the President

Presidential Security Service

Office of National Security

National Human Rights Commission of Korea

National Intelligence Service | Board of Audit & Inspection

Korea Communications Commission

THE PRIME MINISTER

Office for Government Policy Coordination

Prime Minister´s Secretariat

Ministry of Publice Safety and Security

Korea Fair Trade Commission

Ministry of Personnel Management

Financial Services Commission

Ministry of Government Legislation

Anti-corruption & Civil Rights Commission

Ministry of Patriots & Veterans Affairs

Nuclear Safety and Security Commission

Ministry of Food and Drug Safety

Ministry of Strategy and Finance
- National Tax Service
- Korea Customs Service
- Public Procurement Service
- Statistics Korea

Ministry of Science, ICT and Future Planning

Ministry of Education

Ministry of Foreign Affairs

Ministry of Unification

Ministry of Justice
- Supreme Prosecutors' Office

Ministry of National Defence
- Military Manpower Administration
- Defense Acquisition Program Admintration

Ministry of Government Administration and Home Affairs
- Korea National Police Agency

Ministry of Culture, Sports and Tourism
- Cultural Heritage Administration

Ministry of Agriculture, Food and Rural Affairs
- Korea Forest Service
- Rural Development Administration

Ministry of Trade, Industry and Energy
- Korean Intellectual Property Office
- Small and Medium Business Administration

Ministry of Health and Welfare

Ministry of Environment
- Korea Meteorological Administration

Ministry of Employment and Labor

Ministry of Gender Equality and Family

Ministry of Land, Infrastructure and Transport
- Multifunctional Administrative City Construction Agency
- Korea Agency for Saemangeum Development & Investment

Ministry of Oceans and Fisheries

tion and the Prime Minister's Secretariat. At the commission level are the Korea Communications Commission, the Fair Trade Commission, the Financial Services Commission, the Anti-Corruption and Civil Rights Commission and the Nuclear Safety and Security Commission.

The National Human Rights Commission of Korea is an independent commission and excluded from the list of government offices.

■ Government Reorganization

Summary The Park Geun-hye administration was launched with two bureaus, 17 ministries, three administrations, 17 agencies, five offices and six commissions. Following the launch of the Saemangeum Development Agency in Sept. 2013, the government was reorganized into two bureaus, 17 ministries, three administrations, 18 agencies, five offices and six commissions.

However, following the Sewol ferry sinking in the second year of the administration's term, the government was reorganized just a year after its launch. On May 19, President Park Geun-hye announced plans to reorganize the government while stating her will to achieve a grand reform of the country and determine the truth behind the Sewol ferry tragedy.

The reorganization plan centered on newly establishing the Ministry of Public Safety and Security under the Prime Minister's Office to oversee disaster and safety issues, placing the coast guard and firefighting agency under it, and newly establishing the Ministry of Personnel Management to carry out government reforms.

The plan also included the appointment of a deputy prime minister for social affairs to oversee non-economic areas, such as education, society and culture. Although Cheong Wa Dae claimed the reorganization aimed to accomplish "responsible administration," critics argued that the government's reorganization at the start of its term had been short-sighted.

Rival parties discussed the government's reorganization bill along with a package of bills related to the Sewol ferry disaster. However, as the parties wrangled over the ferry bills, the reorganization bill was passed through the National Assembly along with the ferry bills on Nov. 7, 2014, 205 days after the tragedy occurred.

On Nov. 18, the Cabinet passed the revised government organization act, and on Nov. 19, President Park proclaimed the law, leading to the government's current structure of two bureaus, 17 ministries, five administrations, 16 agencies, five offices and six commissions.

Cheong Wa Dae At the start of the Park Geun-hye administration, the presidential office Cheong Wa Dae was comprised of one chief of staff, one chief of national security, one chief of the presidential security service and nine senior secretaries (for state affairs planning, political affairs, civil affairs, foreign affairs and national security, public relations, economic affairs, future strategy, employment and welfare, and education and culture). Following the establishment of an office for personnel affairs in June 2014, the number of senior secretaries increased to 10.

The reorganization was announced as Park decided to retain Prime Minister Chung Hong-won, who had offered to resign over the Sewol ferry disaster, following the successive nominations and withdrawals of prime minister nominees Ahn Dai-hee and Moon Chang-keuk.

At the start of its third year in office, the Park administration carried out another reorganization of Cheong Wa Dae on Jan. 23, 2015. The move was interpreted as a means to regain public confidence and restore momentum in the running of state affairs following an alleged power struggle among some of Park's key aides and backlash over the government's new tax settlement scheme.

Cheong Wa Dae kept the number of senior secretaries at 10, but expanded the office for state affairs planning to the office for policy coordination. It also established a new team of special advisers for political affairs, civil affairs, society and culture, security and public relations.

A total of 16 presidential committees have been in operation, including the unification preparation committee launched in Feb. 2014.

Deputy Prime Minister After President Park Geun-hye's public statement over the Sewol ferry tragedy, the government created the new post of deputy prime minister for social affairs to oversee issues related to education, society and culture.

This provided the framework for "responsible administration" in which the economy would be handled by the deputy prime minister for economic affairs and non-economic areas excluding foreign affairs, unification and national defense would be handled by the education minister who would double as the deputy prime minister for social affairs.

This marked the revival of what was six years earlier the deputy prime minister for education, which had been introduced under then President Kim Dae-jung in 2001 and later scrapped under then President Lee Myung-bak.

■ Current State of Civil Servants

As of the end of June 2013, the quota for civil servants in the country's executive, legislative and judicial branches was 991,481 people. This was 1,058 more than the quota of 990,423 people at the end of the Lee Myung-bak government's term. By the end of 2014, the number of civil servants was believed to have exceeded 1 million.

In the central government, 96,307 people (9.7%) worked in the general administration, while 346,446 people (34.9%) worked in the education sector. More than 138,000 (13.9%) people worked in the judicial and public safety sectors, such as in the police and fire departments, while 31,300 people (3.2%) worked at the Korea Post. There were 354,863 civil servants (35.8%) working in the provinces.

The legislative branch employed 3,974 civil servants, while the judicial branch employed 17,431 people and the Constitutional Court employed 277. The National Election Commission employed 2,721 people.

Including the 22,605 civil servants working at constitutional institutions such as the presidential office, the Prime Minister's Office and the Board of Audit and Inspection, the total number of civil servants in the country reached 1,044,086.

As of 2013, the average age of civil servants in the country was 43.2, which was 2.1 years greater than the average age of 41.1 in 2008. Those aged 40 or above accounted for 64.1%, up 8.8%p from the 55.3% tallied in 2008, indicating a rapidly aging labor force.

Women accounted for 41.4%, up 0.8%p from the 40.6% recorded in 2008. More than 56% of the women worked in the education sector, while 29.7% worked in local governments and 11.7% worked in the central government.

For those joining the civil service as a low-ranking public servant at the age of 29, the average monthly salary was 1.56 million won pre-tax. Those who had worked for 10 years earned 2.74 million won, while those who had worked for 20 years earned 3.56 million won. Those who had worked for 30 years earned 4.42 million won.

The average salary received by college graduates at their first job was 2.66 million won. Of the civil servants, 48.4% were college graduates, while 21.9% went to graduate school. About 14% graduated from two-year colleges or high school, while 2.1% received middle school education or less. More than 70% of civil servants received college education or more, while the percentage among people aged 25 or above was 24.4%.

About 80% of civil servants were married, while 66.8% of them were working couples. Of the married civil servants, 27.4% had a spouse who was a civil servant. The percentage of civil servants owning a house was 67.9%.

About 4% of civil servants, or 20,235 people, were able to freely give a speech or hold a debate in English. That number was fewer than the 39,888 civil servants who have experience living abroad. It was also one of the lowest rates among member nations of the Organization for Economic Cooperation and Development (OECD).

According to OECD statistics, 6.5% of South Korea's economically active population worked in the general government, including the central government, regional governments, social security funds and non-profit organizations. This was the lowest rate among OECD member nations, whose average was 15.5%. Norway recorded the highest rate with 30.5%.

PRIME MINISTER'S OFFICE

▪ Successive Resignations of Prime Minister Nominees

Prime minister nominee Moon Chang-keuk stepped down on June 24, leaving the Park Geun-hye administration with a record of three prime minister nominees stepping down before undergoing the parliamentary confirmation process.

Moon's resignation marked the first time that two successive nominees stepped down as the nominee before him, Ahn Dai-hee, had also stepped down. In 2002, two prime minister nominees were forced to step down as the National Assembly vetoed their appointment. But that took place toward the end of the then administration's term.

The successive withdrawals of Ahn and Moon dealt a large blow to President Park Geun-hye's running of state affairs as it came only in the second year of her term. Her efforts to start anew with a new lineup following the Sewol tragedy were hampered by the successive resignations of two prime minister nominees.

Moon, who had been chosen to tackle the negative public opinion of the government following the ferry disaster as the first journalist-turned-prime minister nominee, chose to step down 14 days after his nomination due to public disapproval of him.

The day after his nomination on June 11, reports emerged of his controversial views of history, ultimately leading to his resignation. Although it was technically a voluntary resignation, it was widely seen as Park's withdrawal of her nomination as she did not request parliamentary endorsement of him.

Ahn, the nominee before Moon, had a reputation as a "people's prosecutor" and formerly served as a Supreme Court justice. Despite expectations he would push through reforms, such as the eradication of corrupt practices within bureaucratic circles, revelations that he received a salary of 1.6 billion won during his five months as a lawyer prompted accusations he received special favors in consideration of his past career.

Ahn promised to donate his earnings to society, but the opposition party called it a new form of buying public office with money, leading him to eventually step down on May 28, six days after he was named and two days after Park requested parliamentary endorsement of the nomination.

This marked the third time in 17 months that a prime minister nominee stepped down. The first nominee, former Constitutional Court chief Kim Yong-jun, stepped down in Jan. 2013 when Park was the president-elect over allegations he received special favors in consideration of his past career and speculated in real estate.

With Moon's resignation, the number of prime minister nominees who have stepped down since the parliamentary confirmation process was introduced in 2000 increased to six. Of the six, Moon was the third, after Kim Yong-jun and Ahn Dai-hee, to step down even before undergoing the parliamentary confirmation process.

▪ PM Chung Retained after 60 Days

On June 26, Park turned down Prime Minister Chung Hong-won's resignation offer 60 days after he submitted it and decided to retain him. It was the first time in South Korean history that a prime minister who had offered to resign was retained.

Park's decision reflected the difficulty she experienced in choosing personnel following the successive resignations of Ahn Dai-hee and Moon Chang-keuk. It was also seen as a reflection of her apparent concern that state affairs would remain in limbo if she remained tied down with choosing a prime minister.

However, by retaining Chung, Park failed to keep her promise to normalize state affairs following the ferry disaster by appointing a prime minister with high moral standards and the ability to eradicate deep-rooted social ills revealed through the tragedy.

▪ Handling Aftermath of Ferry Sinking

Prime Minister Chung Hong-won heard of the ferry Sewol's sinking en route to South Korea from a visit to China and Pakistan. He made a phone call from Bangkok to the then home affairs minister, Kang Byung-kyu, to order the rescue of passengers.

He then convened an emergency meeting of relevant ministers to check progress in search and rescue operations and assign the role of each ministry.

He also proposed the designation of Ansan and Jindo, the areas most affected by the tragedy, as special disaster zones and established institutional support measures. Through 13 visits to the site of the accident, he comforted the victims' families and took steps to meet their demands.

▲ Prime Minister Chung Hong-won hugs a family member of a missing passenger of the sunken ferry Sewol during his visit to Jindo Indoor Auditorium in Jindo Island off southwestern South Korea on June 27.

He promised to turn the tragedy into an opportunity to change the world and ensure it is remembered forever. He also ordered relevant ministries to swiftly take steps to designate some of the victims who sacrificed their lives to save others as martyrs.

On Jindo, he visited the fishermen who put aside their work to help search for the missing and expressed his thanks while asking for their continued cooperation.

On Sept. 23, Chung presided over a Cabinet meeting and passed a plan calling for the prime minister to head the central disaster control headquarters in the event of major disasters such as the Sewol tragedy.

On July 25, Chung also launched an anti-corruption team under the Prime Minister's Office tasked with leading national reform efforts. Five months later, the government uncovered 1,643 cases of corruption, including 583 cases posing a threat to safety, 456 cases of financial loss

and 211 cases of partiality. A total of 6,046 public and business officials were caught in connection with those cases, of whom 412 were put under arrest.

UNIFICATION

■ **Overview**

The Unification Ministry endeavored to put the Korean Peninsula Trust-Building Process in full-fledged operation in 2014, the second year of the Park Geun-hye administration.

President Park Geun-hye presented a new policy agenda in her New Year speech saying the reunification of the two Koreas is a "bonanza." Expectations for improved inter-Korean relations ran high as South and North Korea held high-level contact and opened a family reunion event on the occasion of Lunar New Year's Day.

But there was no further progress as North Korea fiercely protested the South Korea-U.S. joint military drills and the international community's pressure on Pyongyang for its human rights record.

On Oct. 4, Hwang Pyong-so, director of the general political department of the Korean People's Army (KPA), Choe Ryong-hae, the Workers' Party of Korea secretary, and Kim Yang-gon, director of the North's United Front Department in charge of South Korea affairs, made a surprise visit to South Korea to attend the closing ceremony for the Incheon Asian Games.

During their trip, the two Koreas agreed to hold the second round of high-level talks, again raising hopes for a breakthrough in the deadlocked inter-Korean ties. However, North Korea did not return to the talks on the pretext of the scattering of propaganda leaflets by the South's activists across the border.

Nonetheless, the Unification Ministry expanded humanitarian assistance for North Korea, as shown its decision to provide North Korea with aid worth 3 billion won through civilian groups. It marked South Korea's first government-led aid for North Korea since it imposed sanctions, known as the May 24th Measure, on North Korea.

▪ South-North High-Level Contact

South and North Korea had high-level contact at the truce village of Panmunjom on Feb. 12 and Feb. 14, in which they produced a three-point agreement: efforts for improving bilateral ties, suspension of slandering each other and opening of family reunion event as planned.

The talks were arranged as the South's Cheong Wa Dae accepted an offer by the North's National Defense Commission delivered via the Yellow Sea military hotline on Feb. 8. It was the first contact between senior officials from South and North Korea since the launch of the Park Geun-hye administration.

In the high-level talks, South Korea was represented by Kim Kyou-hyun, deputy chief of the presidential office of national security, and his counterpart was Won Dong-yon, the deputy head of the United Front Department. The South and the North failed to produce a deal despite nearly 14 hours of talks from 10 a.m. to midnight on Feb. 12.

The South Korean delegation explained the purpose of the Korean Peninsula Trust-Building Process, a key policy of its government. It also said holding the family reunion event would be the first step to improved relations. It also reportedly underlined the need to resolve the North Korea nuclear problem in order to achieve substantive progress in inter-Korean ties.

But North Korea linked the issue of family reunion with the South Korea-U.S. joint military training and demanded the South postpone the Key Resolve and the Foal Eagle exercises, scheduled to begin on Feb. 24. North Korea also called on South Korea to accept its call for halting criticism and slandering each other and what it calls "militarily hostile acts."

Finally, South and North Korea reached a three-point deal at the high-level meeting which resumed on Feb. 14 at Panmunjom. ① The South and the North would hold the reunion of separated families as planned. ② The South and the North would stop slandering each other in order to promote mutual understanding and trust. ③ The South and the North would continue consultations on issues of mutual concerns and make active efforts to develop bilateral ties. The two sides would hold another round of high-level contact at their convenience.

▪ Family Reunion

Hundreds of separated families from South and North Korea were reunited with each other at Mount Kumgang between Feb. 20-25, the first face-to-face reunion since November 2010.

In the first round of reunion from Feb. 20 to Feb. 22, 82 South Koreans met with their families in North Korea and 88 other North Koreans met with their families from South Korea in the second round held from Feb. 23-25. The families had individual and group reunions as well as joint lunch over six times, lasting a total of 11 hours.

On Jan. 24, North Korea's Red Cross proposed a family reunion and the two sides had working-level talks on the matter on Feb. 5. On Jan. 6, the South Korean government proposed a family reunion, but North Korea rejected it three days later.

▪ Humanitarian Aid for North Korea

The Unification Ministry announced on July 15 that it would provide North Korea with aid worth 3 billion won through civilian organizations in the fields of agriculture, livestock industry and medical services.

It marked the first time for South Korea to use government funds for North Korea assistance since the May 24th Measure was implemented. The sanctions on North Korea was imposed after the North's torpedo attack on a South Korean warship on March 26, 2010, which killed 46 sailors.

A Unification Ministry official said, "The government has decided to use South-North Cooperation Fund for North Korea aid on the basis of its position to provide it with effective humanitarian assistance."

In August, the government received applications from civilian groups for plans to fund aid in three fields, 1 billion won each. A total of 28 groups applied for 37 projects. After a review, the government selected 13 of them for 17 projects.

The related groups had consultations with North Korea over their aid plans, but only one of them was granted consent by the North as of the end of 2014.

North Korea is viewed as taking a dim view of such aid programs funded by the South Korean government as it is apparently against the Dresden Declaration by President Park Geun-hye.

▪ Test-Run of Rajin-Khasan Project

In November, the two Koreas and Russia conducted a test operation of the trilateral Rajin-Khasan logistics project in line with South Korea's 'Eurasia Initiative.'

The projects is designed to bring in Russian coal through the North Korean port city of Rajin. A 54km railway that reconnected in 2013 between the Russian town of Khasan and Rajin. In the first-ever trial operation, 40,500t of Russian coal was transported to Rajin by rail and then shipped to Pohang, a South Korean port city.

South Korea's top steelmaker POSCO has formed a consortium with two other South Korean firms -- Hyundai Merchant Marine Co. and Korail Corp. It is pushing to purchase about half of Russian stake in the RasonConTrans, a joint venture between Russia and North Korea launched in 2008. Russia holds 70% stake in it.

The Rajin-Khasan program, if implemented, is expected to save 10-15% in time and cost, which would be reduced more under a stable, long-term contract, South Korean officials said.

▪ School Education on Reunification

The Unification Ministry, together with the Education Ministry, carried out a survey of 116,000 students and 3,130 teachers at 200 schools nationwide on unification-related education.

According to the results of the poll, announced by the Unification Ministry in August 53.5% of the students said the reunification of Korea is "necessary." Also, 19.7% said reunification is unnecessary, with 26.1% was neutral.

The survey results came as a surprise to government officials, as most adults in South Korea believe reunification is not an option but a must. In a 2013 poll of adults by the Center for International Studies at Seoul National University, 71.6% said reunification is necessary.

On the reason why reunification is necessary, 25.8% of the students cited security risks, including the possibility of war, and 24.7% cited the need for strengthening national power. Among those who answered that reunification is unnecessary, 45.4% expressed worries over economic burden and social unrest.

As to perceptions on North Korea, 48.8% said cooperation is needed, while 26.3% said it is an enemy and 14.5% supported assistance for the impoverished communist neighbor. In addition, 58.7% of the students said there is a high possibility that North Korea will cause another war. As to obstacles to reunification, 38.4% picked North Korea's military threats. Meanwhile, 81.6% of teachers said students are learning about reunification at schools, mostly less than five hours a week. The survey was conducted from June 23 to July 11 and it was the first-ever government-led poll on unification-related education. The margin of error is plus and minus 0.28%p for students and 1.17%p for teachers.

▪ DMZ Peace Park Project

The Unification Ministry launched an ambitious project to create a world peace park inside the Demilitarized Zone (DMZ), which President Park Geun-hye proposed in May 2013.

In its New Year report to the president, the Unification Ministry said it aims to strike a deal with North Korea on the matter within the year. The ministry earmarked 30.2 billion won in budgets.

The Unification Ministry formed a task force and carried out a basic site survey of candidate areas including Paju, Gyeonggi Province, Chorwon, Gangwon Province, and Goseong in the same province. In August, an inter-agency team of more than 20 officials from unification, land and environmental ministries as well as experts conducted an on-site survey.

But there has been progress in efforts to consult with North Korea, the most important part of the project. North Korea is strongly protesting against President Park's initiative.

▪ Action Plan for Developing South-North Relations

The Unification Ministry gave a report on Aug. 18 to the National Assembly on the government's action plan for the development of inter-Korean relations. The government said it would consider resuming economic cooperation projects and allowing investment in North Korea if appropriate conditions are met.

In particular, the government said it would push for support for the renovation of the Pyongyang-Kaesong highway and the Kaesong-Sinuiju railway and efforts to prevent floods in Imjin River as well as measures to help the fisheries industry via the Food and Agriculture Organization (FAO) and promote inter-Korean maritime cooperation.

It was the first time that the South Korean government formally specified its plan to participate in large-scale infrastructure projects in North Korea, although it attached some preconditions.

The government also said it is open to assistance for economy-related education for North Koreans in cooperation with international agencies and NGOs abroad. The government added it has the intention of pushing for joint development of natural resources if conditions are met.

With regard to the Rajin-Khasan project, the government said it would step up efforts to reconnect railways with North Korea as part of President Park's campaign for "Silk Road Express (SRX)," which is aimed at connecting Busan, South Korea, North Korea, Russia, China, Central Asia and Europe.

In the report, the government said it will try to establish standing dialogue channel with North Korea in order to discuss and resolve pending issues in a comprehensive manner.

In an effort to recover homogeneity of South and North Koreans, the government said it would promote social, cultural and sports exchanges and seek joint works to preserve ancient cultural assets. It also unveiled plans to boost environmental cooperation with North Korea such as the establishment of channel for experts' cooperation.

The report to the National Assembly included the government's commitment to holding the reunion of separated families, resolving the issues of prisoners of war and the abducted, creating a peace park in the DMZ, handling the North

Korean Human Rights Act, providing North Koreans with humanitarian aid, developing the Kaesong Industrial Complex, building up political and military trust and making substantive progress in efforts to resolve the North Korean nuclear program.

A Unification Ministry official said it's of great significance that a pan-governmental action plan on inter-Korean relations has been presented.

■ **Website on South-North Cooperation**

On Dec. 28, the Unification Ministry revised its website on inter-Korean exchanges including cross-border travel and the authorization of cooperation projects.

The website, http://www.tongtong.go.kr, opened in 2002, but there had been public opinions that it's rather hard for ordinary citizens to use.

The Unification Ministry said it focused efforts on making the use of the website easier. Also, it enabled foreigners, not just locals, to log onto the website, in line with efforts to globalize the Kaesong Industrial Complex.

DIPLOMACY

■ **Overview**

South Korea and four powers were actively engaged in diplomacy last year. China tried to set a new oder in Asia based on its economic growth while the U.S. pursued "Pivot to Asia" policy. Japan made efforts to move from the post-war system and Russia turned its eye to the Far East.

Security landscape in Northeast Asia was characterized by competition between Washington and Beijing last year. China actively sought to change a U.S.-led security scheme while the U.S. tried to keep its influence in Asia based on its strong alliance with Seoul and Tokyo.

North Korea, which conducted a third nuclear test in 2013, moved closer to Russia as its relations with China turned sour.

South Korea maintained its alliance with Washington while it also made efforts to strengthen cooperation with China, which has leverage in pressing North

Korea into giving up nuclear weapons.

Seoul and others sought to revive the stalled multilateral denuclearization talks, but there has been no substantive progress as the North has not shown sincerity toward denuclearization.

South Korea ramped up efforts to preach for the Northeast Asia Peace and Cooperation Initiative to promote cooperation in the region. It also actively joined global efforts to tackle Ebola by sending medical staff to Sierra Leone last year.

▪ North Korea's Nuclear Weapons Program

South Korea and other member countries to the six-party talks sought to revive the denuclearization talks in 2014, but no major progress has been made. The six-party talks involving the two Koreas, the United States, China, Japan and Russia have been dormant since late 2008.

South Korea and the U.S. said that North Korea should first demonstrate its willingness for denuclearization, but North Korea called for the resumption of the six-party talks without any preconditions.

In May, North Korea agreed to reinvestigate the fate of Japanese people it abducted in the 1970s and 1980s. In return, Japan lifted some of its unilateral sanctions on North Korea. Japan's move raised concerns that it could hamper trilateral coordination between Seoul, Washington and Tokyo over North Korea's nuclear arsenal.

On July 3, South Korean President Park Geun-hye and her Chinese counterpart Xi Jinping held a summit in Seoul where they reaffirmed zero-tolerance stance toward the North's nuclear ambitions. Seoul has created the so-called Korean Formula, an initiative to resume the six-party talks in a "multifaceted and creative" manner. Details about the Korean Formula have not been disclosed.

Except for North Korea, Seoul and the other four members have reached consensus over conditions for the resumption of the six-party talks and the need to do so at an early date. But there has been some limitation for China to use its leverage to push North Korea into returning to the negotiation table in a sincere manner as the Beijing-Pyongyang relations have been strained since the death of Jang Song-thaek

In October, North Korea released one of the three detained American citizen, Jeffrey Edward Fowle, in what was seen as a gesture of goodwill toward Washington amid stalled nuclear negotiations.

In November, U.S. Director of National Intelligence James Clapper made an unannounced trip to the North to win the release of two other detainees: Kenneth Bae and Matthew Todd Miller. But the visit little affected the strained relations between Washington and Pyongyang.

But as the deadlock has prolonged without any breakthrough, Seoul and Washington shared the view about the need to have so-called exploratory talks with the North to test whether Pyongyang is willing to denuclearize.

In 2014, North Korea's dismal human rights conditions garnered great attention from the global community. The U.N. Commission of Inquiry (COI) released a report in February that accused Pyongyang of "systematic, widespread and grave violations of human rights."

The U.N. Human Rights Council adopted a resolution that calls for the Security Council to refer to the North Korean leadership to the International Criminal Court (ICC) for taking responsibility for the human rights violation.

In December, the U.N. General Assembly passed a landmark resolution on North Korea's human rights that calls for the Security Council to refer the North's rights situation to the ICC. The Security Council also decided to put the North's human rights issue on its official agenda for the first time.

North Korea has been engaged in brisk diplomacy to counter the global community's move to slam its rights situation. North Korean Foreign Minister Ri Su-yong delivered a speech at the U.N. session and Kang Sok-ju, secretary of the Central Committee of the Workers' Party of Korea, made a rare trip to Europe in early September. The North has increasingly been moving to Russia as its ties with China have been frayed.

▪ Strained Relations between Seoul and Tokyo

The relations between South Korea

and Japan reached one of the lowest points in 2014 following Japanese Prime Minister Shinzo Abe's visit to a controversial war shrine in Dec. 2013.

Abe visited Yasukuni war shrine that honors 14 Class-A war criminals, which is considered by many as a symbol of Japan's past militarism. The move, the first visit of its kind by a Japanese prime minister since 2006, sparked fierce criticism from Seoul and Beijing, victims of Japan's wartime aggression.

Throughout 2014, Seoul and Tokyo had not seen improvement in their ties as Abe has been walking on the path of historical revisionism. The main diplomatic tension between the two came from Japan's refusal to sincerely resolve Tokyo's sexual enslavement of Korean women for its troops during World War II.

Amid Seoul's continued criticism for Japan to whitewash its history, the two nations agreed to hold senior official-level talks on the sex slaves in April. Since then, the two countries have held such talks on a regular basis, but no major progress has not been made.

The Seoul government demands that Japan show sincerity by resolving the sex slave issue. But Japan has long dismissed Seoul's demands, saying that all grievances related to its colonial rule were settled through a 1965 treaty that normalized their bilateral ties.

In June, Japan announced the result of a review for its 1993 key apology over Tokyo's wartime sex slaves, indicating that the Kono Statement was the outcome of a political compromise between Seoul and Tokyo. The Seoul government strongly denounced Japan for glossing over its wartime wrongdoing.

Japan's rightest politicians gained traction as Japanese newspaper Asahi Shimbun retracted an article on the sex slave issue in August. Asahi acknowledged some errors of its past reports containing late Seiji Yoshida's accounts that Korean women were forcibly dragged into brothels in Korea's southernmost islands of Jeju. Since then, right-wing Japanese politicians have claimed that the 1993 Kono statement should be revised or nullified.

South Korean President Park Geun-hye has not held a summit with Abe since taking office in early 2013, citing Japan's refusal to apologize for the sex slave issue.

At the global stage, Seoul has been also ramping up efforts to highlight the issue of Japan's wartime sex slave as a matter of women's human rights violation under conflict. But also, the Seoul government maintained high-level contacts with Japan on the grounds that other cooperative mechanism needs to be kept separately from the history issue.

▲ *South Korean Foreign Minister Yun Byung-se makes a keynote speech at a U.N. Human Rights Council session in Geneva on March 5. Yun denounced Japan for denying its wartime atrocities of sexually enslaving Korean women, calling on it to strive for a swift resolution on the issue.*

Meanwhile, Abe is seeking to expand its military role by exercising the right to "collective self-defense," which would allow Tokyo to fight alongside its allies and beyond its borders, a departure from its pacifist constitution.

In July, the Japanese cabinet approved a proposal to reinterpret its war-renouncing Constitution that has banned Japan from exerting the right to collective self-defense, a major shift in Japan's postwar security policy. Seoul and Beijing have been raising concerns that Tokyo tries to revive its militarism without a proper apology for its wartime atrocities. The U.S., is supporting Japan's move, apparently to keep a rising China in check.

China has expressed its hope to coordinate with Seoul when it comes to the shared history issue at a time when China's relations with Japan have been frayed due to history and territorial disputes. Their relations have deteriorated in recent years over the disputed islands, known as Senkaku in Japan and Diaoyu in China, in the East China Sea.

Xi proposed to his S.korea counterpart President Park at a July summit that the two countries would jointly commemorate the 70th anniversary of China's victory against Japan's aggression as well as of Seoul's liberation from the Japanese 1910-45 colonial rule.

Seoul has focused on reviving trilateral cooperation between Seoul, Beijing and Tokyo. The foreign ministers from the three nations held a meeting in Seoul on March 21, 2015 for the first time in almost three years.

In November, Park expressed her hope to meet with the Chinese and Japanese leaders someday. Some analysts said that a possible three-way summit is seen as using it as a leverage to create the atmosphere for the improvement in the strained Seoul-Tokyo ties.

But many experts said that it is not clear if bilateral relations could improve by the year of the 50th anniversary of the normalization of their diplomatic ties.

■ Seoul-Washington Alliance

South Korea's strategic interest was tested last year as it is sandwiched by competitions for bigger clouts between the U.S., Seoul's key ally, and China, its largest trading partner.

The case in point was the controversy surrounding Washington's possible deployment of an advanced missile defense system in South Korea and Seoul's joining of a China-led regional infrastructure bank.

China has explicitly voiced concerns about Washington's possible move to deploy a Terminal High-Altitude Area Defense (THAAD) battery on Korean soil, home to about 28,500 American troops. Seoul and Washington said that there have been neither consultations nor decisions over the issue, but China has expressed its opposition to the possible deployment. Xi is known to have requested Park to carefully review the move during the summit in July.

Touching on the Asian Infrastructure Investment Bank (AIIB), the U.S. raised the issue of the bank's opaque decision-making process and governing structure. Washington sees China's bid to set up the bank as its intent to increase economic clouts in Asia and further in global financial markets that are currently dominated by the U.S. and other advanced countries.

Seoul decided to join the AIIB in late March, 2015, becoming the founding member of the new regional bank. The row reflects challenges facing Seoul between the world's two powers. Some experts said that Washington has some concerns that South Korea is tilting toward China.

South Korea and the U.S. also agreed in late October to delay the planned transfer of wartime operational control (OPCON) of South Korean forces from Washington to Seoul until it improves capabilities to counter nuclear and missile threats from North Korea.

The two allies have also been negotiating for more than four years to revise the 1974 accord over Seoul's civilian nuclear energy use, also known as the "123 agreement." The two nations have "effectively" concluded their nuclear cooperation accord that would allow Seoul to reprocess spent nuclear fuel for the purpose of research and development (R&D), albeit in a limited way.

In addition, Mark Lippert, a key aide to U.S. President Barack Obama, became the U.S. ambassador to Seoul in late October with the pledge to deepen and broaden the alliance.

■ Summit Diplomacy

When Obama visited Seoul in April, Park and he reaffirmed the zero-tolerance toward North Korea's nuclear weapons program and appreciated the value of the alliance.

Obama called Japan's sexual enslavement of Korean women during World War II a "terrible and egregious violation of human rights." He also expressed deep condolence to the victims of the deadly ferry sinking.

Meanwhile, Xi's visit to Seoul in July marked the first time that a Chinese leader travels to South Korea before visiting North Korea, China's long-time ally.

▲ *President Park Geun-hye (R) shakes hands with Chinese President Xi Jinping at the presidential office Cheong Wa Dae in Seoul on July 3, prior to a summit meeting.*

Park and Xi reaffirmed the zero-tolerance toward North Korea's nuclear weapons program and warned against Japan's move to whitewash its wartime history. The two sides agreed to open a won-yuan market and to embark on a meeting on demarcating their maritime border.

In the second half, Park was busy in attending a series of multilateral summits to appeal to the global community to pay more attention to the inter-Korean relation and unification issues.

In September, she delivered a speech at the U.N. General Assembly. In October, President Park joined a biennial summit of the Asia-Europe Meeting, known as ASEM, in Milan and in November, she participated in the Asia-Pacific Economic Cooperation (APEC) summit in Beijing, the ASEAN+3 Summit as well as the East Asia Summit that were held in Myanmar. She also attended the G20 summit held in Australia in November.

But Seoul and Tokyo failed to hold a summit last year due to the long-running history row. Amid American efforts to mend ties between Seoul and Tokyo, the leaders from South Korea, the U.S. and Japan held a three-way summit in The Hague, Netherlands in March 2014 on the sidelines of the Nuclear Security Summit. But the atmosphere was icy due to Japan's intransigence toward the history issue.

Park and Abe had a brief encounter at a gala dinner when they attended the APEC summit in Beijing. They agreed to

encourage the ongoing bilateral talks on the sex slaves to gain traction down the road, but it is still unclear whether the historical grievance will be resolved.

In December, South Korea held a commemorative summit with ASEAN countries in the country's southernmost port city of Busan. The commemorative summit marked the first multilateral conference that South Korea held since Park took office in February 2013. The summit came as ASEAN plans to launch the ASEAN Community by the end of 2015 in a bid to deepen integration in the region.

JUDICIAL AFFAIRS AND PROSECUTION

■ Scandals in Prosecution

Within four months of the prosecution-general's resignation over having an illegitimate child, the justice ministry was once again embroiled in a scandal from the beginning of 2014.

On Jan. 22, the Supreme Prosecutors' Office charged a prosecutor with intimidation after allegations emerged that he helped an actress settle disputes with a plastic surgeon in 2012. A court sentenced him to eight months in prison with a two-year stay of execution.

In August 2014, the top prosecutor on South Korea's southern island of Jeju was arrested for masturbating in public at night. Kim Soo-chang, the 52-year-old former chief of Jeju District Prosecutors' Office, was accused of masturbating in public near his residence on the resort island on Aug. 12. Prosecutors decided not to indict Kim on condition that he seek psychiatric treatment.

■ Investigations into Ferry Disaster

On April 20, four days after a ferry capsized off the southwest coast with more than 300 passengers on board, a special task force was formed to investigate the family who owned the ferry operator.

More than 40 members of the late Yoo Byeong-eun's family were banned from leaving the country. Yoo was the owner of Cheonghaejin Marine Co., the operator of the ferry Sewol.

On July 25, prosecutors learned through DNA analysis that a badly decayed body found in a plum field in Suncheon, South Jeolla Province, in June belonged to Yoo. The state forensic lab, however, failed to determine the cause of Yoo's death, as his body was badly decayed.

On that same day, police concluded a three-month manhunt for Yoo's eldest son, Yoo Dae-kyun, who was at an apartment hideout in Yongin, Gyeonggi Province. He was arrested on charges of colluding with his father to embezzle.

The prosecution later announced April's deadly ferry sinking was caused by a combination of cargo overloading, an illegal redesigning of the ship to increase its cargo load and the steersman's poor helmsmanship.

▪ Evidence Tampering in Espionage Case

Prosecutors came under media scrutiny after the evidence they submitted to prove a North Korean defector a spy was found to have been fabricated. Yoo Woo-seong, a former Seoul city government official, had been charged for espionage in 2013.

On March 27, prosecutors admitted three of the documents submitted as evidence were fake and withdrew them. A lower court found Yoo not guilty, a ruling confirmed by the appellate court on April 25.

▪ Probe into Defense Industry Corruption

South Korea launched an inquiry into corruption in the defense industry after an indigenous rescue and salvage ship failed to function during the rescue operations for the Sewol ferry victims.

On April 18, the military announced it would be unable to deploy the salvage ship, Tongyeong, due to substandard sonar and underwater detection systems.

Investigators found that South Korea's military procurement agency fabricated the quality evaluation of Tongyeong's parts supplier in return for billions of won from these officials. President Park Geun-hye subsequently announced an all-out war on deep-seated corruption in the defense industry.

▪ Controversy over Cyber-censorship

Following the Supreme Prosecutors' Office announcement on Sept. 18 to bolster response to online libel cases, suspicions grew that the government may start keeping tabs on private messages exchanged on the popular mobile messaging app Kakao Talk.

The prosecution created a special investigation team and expanded its manpower on online libel cases. The news sparked controversy, as they followed President Park Geun-hye's complaint over insults hurled at her.

Prosecutors offered an explanation on Sept. 25, saying that they were only focusing on slandering on public domains. On Oct. 13, Justice Minister Hwang Kyo-ahn told lawmakers it was "technically impossible" to monitor private messages on a real-time basis, adding he himself is a frequent user of Kakao Talk.

▪ Justice Minister's Controversial Remarks

On Sept. 24, Justice Minister Hwang Kyo-ahn told local newspapers that the government should seriously consider freeing convicted businessmen if it can help turn the economy around. A day later, Finance Minister Choi Kyung-hwan expressed his full support for Hwang's controversial remark.

A civic group immediately filed a complaint with the prosecution against the justice and finance ministers for "abusing their power." Pardoning CEOs, especially heads of the nation's family-controlled conglomerates, is a contentious issue in South Korea, where the president typically grants special pardons to them at the end of the year or national holidays.

The presidential office Cheong Wa Dae refused to comment, saying pardoning was the responsibility of the justice ministry. No businessmen were pardoned in 2014.

▪ Probe into Presidential Document Leak

In late November, the local daily Segye Times reported allegations that a former aide to President Park Geun-hye with no official title in the government meddled in state affairs through regular meetings with a group of key presidential officials.

The report, citing a presidential document dated Jan. 6, claimed that Jeong Yun-hoe, Park's chief of staff during her term in parliament, plotted to oust the president's current chief secretary, Kim Ki-choon.

The newspaper said Jeong had regularly met with a coterie of 10 key presidential aides since October 2013 to receive briefings on state affairs. The presidential document also read Jeong hired a man to follow the president's younger brother Ji-man.

The allegations raised a political storm as opposition parties accused the Park administration of monopolizing power, while Park dismissed the leaked document as a mere collection of groundless rumors circulating in the financial community.

Eight of the presidential aides mentioned in the report filed a libel suit against the Segye Times. In Jan. 2015, prosecutors concluded the presidential document was fabricated by police superintendent Park.

NATIONAL DEFENSE

NORTH KOREA'S SUCCESSIVE PROVOCATIONS

■ N. Korea Fires 111 Projectiles in Saber-Rattling

North Korea fired off a total of 111 short- and mid-range projectiles between Feb. 21 and Sept. 6 in an apparent saber-rattling against annual joint military drills between South Korea and the United States.

With the projectiles including 300㎜ multiple-rocket launchers and the medium-range Nodong missiles, Pyongyang also fired novel tactical missiles with a range of some 200㎞, longer than its existing KN-02.

The communist country has continued military provocations by firing off missiles mainly by claiming that annual joint exercises between South Korea and the United States is a rehearsal for their invasion of the North. The allies, however, rejected the call from Pyongyang to stop the drills, stressing the regular joint exercises are defensive in nature.

■ Over 100 N.K. Shells Cross into South, Two Koreas Exchange Fire

On March 31, North Korea fired around 500 rounds of artillery shells into waters north of the Northern Limit Line (NLL) in the Yellow Sea as part of its large-scale maritime live-fire drill, and some 100 rounds fell south of the NLL.

Upon their landing, South Korea evacuated residents of border islands, and shot around 300 artillery shells into North Korean waters with K-9 self-propelled howitzers. No casualties or injuries were reported.

The incident caused the United Nations Command's Military Armistice Command to urge Pyongyang to stop the live-fire drill and propose a general-level meeting to ease tension, which failed to get any response from the North.

■ 3 N. Korean Drones Fall on S. Korea's Border Regions

Between March and April, three small drones were found near the inter-Korean border regions of Paju, the Yeonpyeong Island in the Yellow Sea, and the eastern city of Samcheok, and they were found to have been sent from North Korea.

The unmanned aerial vehicles, equipped with a cam-

▲ The number 35 is written on a suspected third North Korean drone found on a remote mountain in Samcheok, Gangwon Province, on April 6. (Photo courtesy of defense ministry)

era and a parachute, departed from North Korea and flew southward to prearranged coordinates to take photos of key facilities and military installations along their routes, according to the investigations by South Korea and the U.S.

Paju drone, in fact, took photos of key installations in the Seoul metropolitan area, including the presidential office in the capital city, while Baengnyeong Island drone took photos of troops on two western border islands. North Korea is believed to have made the drones based on Chinese UAVs it had acquired via Hong Kong.

Despite being programmed to return to their departure point, they failed to complete their mission, as one crashed due to an engine problem and the other two due to fuel shortage.

The drones could carry about 3-4kg of ammunition, a payload that some say is too little to cause substantial damage compared with other conventional weapons.

The North is estimated to have about 300 spy drones, less than 10 attack UAVs and about 10 Russian-made Shmel UAVs, while currently developing a multipurpose UAV, according to the ministry.

■ N. Korea Fires Artillery near S. Korean Warship in Yellow Sea

On May 22, North Korea fired two artillery shells near a South Korean warship on patrol in the Yellow Sea.

The shells fired from north of the Northern Limit Line, the de facto sea border between the two Koreas, fell in waters 14km south of Yeonpyeong Island, prompting a South Korean Navy corvette patrolling near the area fired back five shells into North Korean waters, targeting a patrol ship located nearest to the border.

The South Korean gun boat was sailing some 9.9km south of the NLL at the time of the North's attack, and the North's patrol ship targeted by the South was some 2km north of the sea border.

No casualties or property damage from the South Korean side were reported, though some 20 South Korean fishing boats and 20 vessels from China had been operating in the area at the time.

North Korea is presumed to have fired the shells with coastal artillery, according to Seoul's Joint Chiefs of Staff. It is the first time that Pyongyang has carried out this kind of maritime attack against the South.

■ N. Korea Fires Artillery Shells into East Sea

On July 14, North Korea fired about 100 artillery shells into the East Sea from a place near the demilitarized zone (DMZ) in Goseong, Gangwon Province. They landed in the sea, some 1 to 8km north of the Northern Limit Line, the de facto inter-Korean maritime border, with no shells flying into South Korean territory.

The South Korean military said most of them were likely fired from the North's 122mm or 240mm launchers, and around 10 of them flew at the maximum of 50km. Though it is not unusual for Pyongyang to carry out such a shelling on its east coast, it is rare that the North has done that near the military demarcation line.

■ N. Korean Boat Violates Border, Causing Exchange of Fire

On Oct. 7, South and North Korean patrol boats briefly exchanged fire in waters near Yeonpyeong Island in the Yellow Sea, after a North Korean naval vessel violated the western maritime border of the Northern Limit Line.

To force the North Korean vessel to retreat, the South Korean military issued warning messages and fired five warning shots. But the patrol boat fired back rather than backing down, which caused the South to fire again. Then the ship made a retreat. The exchange of gunfire lasted for about 10 minutes.

Though the South Korean military fired some 90 shots, including 10 shots with 76mm guns, most of the artillery did not have a long enough range to reach the North Korean patrol boat. North Korea shot dozens of rounds in return and not a single one fell near the South Korean vessel, with Seoul's patrol boat not sustaining any damage.

■ Two Koreas Exchange Gun Fire after S. Korea's Leaflet Campaigns

On Oct. 10, North Korea fired some 10 rounds of 14.5mm anti-aircraft machine guns aiming at balloons South Korea's civic groups flew to the North that carried anti-Pyongyang propaganda leaflets.

As some of the North Korean rounds landed south of the inter-Korean border, the military here broadcast warning messages and fired back around 40 rounds from the K-6 machine gun toward the North's guard posts along the border.

Minutes later, a handful of bullets flew from the North, which caused the South Korean service personnel to fire back nine shots again.

The North apparently fired shots first with the aim of shooting down the 10 balloons carrying 200,000 anti-Pyongyang leaflets which were floated from South Korea's border village of Paju, but Seoul officials said they could not confirm whether the attempt was successful.

North Korea has long bristled at the leaflet campaign by civic groups in South Korea and demanded that the Seoul government ban their activities.

■ **Koreas Exchange Fire Near Heavily Fortified Border**

On Oct. 19, South and North Korea exchanged fire across the heavily fortified border in the city of Paju. Some 10 North Korean soldiers approached the military demarcation, which led South to broadcast warning messages. Undeterred by the broadcast, they continued to march toward the border, promping the South to fire warning shots against them.

After South Korea's warning shots, the North fired back, which caused the South to launch additional firing. The exchange of fire lasted for about 10 minutes. There were no reports of casualties or property damage in South Korea, though no details were immediately known about the situation in the North. It was not known what prompted the North Korean soldiers to try to advance toward the military demarcation line.

LAUNCH OF BIG-TICKET MILITARY PROJECTS

■ **S. Korea to Buy 40 F-35As, 4 Global Hawk Block 30s**

On March 24, South Korea decided to buy 40 F-35As manufactured by Lockheed Martin, a deal expected to be worth about 7.4 trillion won (US$6.8 million). Negotiations over price and other conditions have been under way with the U.S. government, as the deal is supposed to be done through the U.S. foreign military sales (FMS) process.

▲ *Shown is a file photo of the F-35A fighter jet. South Korea said on Sept. 24, it has decided to purchase 40 F-35A fighter jets from the U.S. defense firm Lockheed Martin in a deal worth 7.3 trillion won (US$7.04 billion).*

South Korea also approved a plan to buy RQ-4 Global Hawk Block 30s from Northrop Grumman through the FMS to improve surveillance of North Korea. The high-altitude, long-endurance unmanned aerial vehicle (UAV) operates at considerable stand-off distances and in any weather or light conditions and can carry up to 1,360kg of internal payload.

■ **S. Korea to Deploy 5 Spy Satellites in Early 2020s**

On June 11, South Korea decided to develop a military reconnaissance satellite with its indigenous technology to boost its capacity to reconnoiter North Korea. In accordance with the so-called 425 project, five spy satellites will be then deployed in the early 2020s, with the government to earmark some 1 trillion won (US$983 billion) for their development and production.

The satellite is capable of securing imagery intelligence on the Korean Peninsula and the surrounding regions, which is expected to serve as a useful tool not only for military purposes but for civilian uses such as disaster prevention.

■ **S. Korea Opts for Double-Engine Platform for Indigenous Fighters**

On July 18, South Korea's Joint Chiefs of Staff decided to adopt the C-130 double-engine platform for its indigenous warplane project, which is expected to boost combat capabilities and ensure long-term economic feasibility.

Codenamed KF-X, the 8.67 trillion won (US$7.84 billion) project calls for South Korea to develop fighter jets of the F-16 class to replace its aging fleet of F-4s and F-5s. Some 120 jets are to be put into service starting around 2025, with the production to cost another 9.3 trillion won.

Though the dual-engine platform costs more, the Air Force has been in support of the two-engine concept, which is expected to boost the aircraft's combat capabilities with its large weapons and fuel capacity, long-term economic feasibility and pilot safety features. Indonesia joined South Korea for the project, vowing to meet 20% of the costs.

MILITARY UNDER FIRE FOR GRUESOME INCIDENTS

■ Soldier Dies after Severe Abuses by Comrades

On April 7, a 23-year-old Army private first class died after being severely abused by their comrades at their frontline unit on the east coast. According to investigations, six of his colleagues hit his chest while eating snacks at their barracks and the assault caused a piece of food to obstruct his airway, leading the victim to die of asphyxiation.

His death was also found to be the result of damage to his skeletal muscle caused by repeated brutal assaults for about a month. After being dispatched to the 28th Infantry Division in the northern border town of Yeoncheon, the soldier, surnamed Yoon, allegedly had been beaten almost 100 times per day. The suspects also often forced him to stay awake overnight, hold a horse-riding stance for hours during the night, swallow a tube of toothpaste and even lick their spit from the ground.

The suspects were charged with murder, and the prosecution sought a death penalty for some of them.

■ Soldier Goes on Deadly Shooting Spree

On June 21, a 22-year-old enlisted soldier detonated a grenade and went on a shooting rampage, killing five and wounding seven others, at his frontline

outpost. He, surnamed Lim, fled following the shooting, but was captured two days later after a botched suicide attempt.

▲ An Army soldier, identified only as Sgt. Lim, who was arrested on charges of killing five fellow soldiers in a shooting rampage in June, leaves a military court in Wonju, Gangwon Province, on Oct. 23 after trial. Lim claimed he committed the rampage after being ostracized for years.

Lim told investigators that he had been bullied by his comrades, and military officers said the suspect had difficulty in adapting himself to military life and had not socialized much with his colleagues.

He had been on the list of soldiers requiring extra care after undergoing personality tests, which caused public criticism for the military authorities' failure to properly manage the service personnel.

■ Female Service Personnel Victimized by Sexual Abuses by Male Colleagues

The year 2014 saw a series of sex crimes where senior service personnel victimized their female subordinates, drawing strong criticism for the public.

In April, a Navy officer was arrested on charges of harassing a female officer working at a same patrol boat by inappropriately touching her. Another naval officer in charge of convoy was dismissed from his post in July after allegedly groping the buttocks of two of his female subordinates after heavily drinking. In September, an Army lieutenant colonel was caught for allegedly raping a female officer at a motel after drinking together.

Shocking the nation, a one-star general was under detainment without a court warrant on October for allegedly sexually abusing a female subordinate multiple times in his office. Two months later, he was sentenced to a six-month jail term on sexual molestation charges.

In the wake of successive shameful incidents, the military came up with comprehensive countermeasures, vowing a "zero-tolerance" policy.

■ **Military Reform Committee Recommends Incentives for Military Service**

In December, a joint committee of the civil society, the government and the military for military culture reform recommended that the government give extra points to job applicants who complete military service.

It is part of efforts to reform the military culture in the wake of a series of gruesome incidents at the barracks including the deadly shooting spree by an enlisted soldier and the death of a draftee after suffering from severe abuses.

According to the recommendations, such applicants shall be given a bonus 2% on company examinations to help encourage draftees to successfully carry out their military duty, though only 10% of successful applicants at a single company can receive the benefit.

The move, however, could draw opposition from women, who are not obligated to serve in the military, at a time when the job market remains tight. In 1999, the Constitutional Court ruled as unconstitutional the law giving males who served in the military an advantage in applying for public service positions, saying it was unfair to women and the disabled.

The committee also recommended the defense ministry reduce the current four ranks of conscripts to two or three to try to root out pervasive abuse and to revamp the hierarchy-based culture in barracks.

■ **Corruption Involving Navy's Salvage Ship, Tongyeong**

South Korea's first indigenous salvage ship Tongyeong was launched in Sept. 2012, but it failed to be deployed for the all-out rescue efforts following the country's worst ferry tragedy on April 16 that killed more than 300 passengers.

The subsequent prosecution probe found that its sonar system and a remotely operated vehicle for underwater maneuvers were riddled with problems due to a collisive link between their suppliers and former and current naval officers involved in the project.

The revelation prompted the country to launch an extensive investigation into the overall defense industry by setting up a pan-governmental task force in November. With the probe under way, a handful of officers were arrested, including former Naval chief, Adm. Hwang Ki-chul.

In November, the military lowered the requirements to pave the way for the vessel to be deployed to replace aging fleets based upon the judgement that the faulty parts are not critical, affecting the Tongyeong's serving of its key roles.

REORGANIZATION OF U.S. FORCES KOREA WITH INCREASING ROTATIONAL PRESENCE

■ **S. Korea, U.S. to Form Wartime Combined Unit**

On Sept. 4, South Korea said it agreed with the United States to establish a combined division of their troops in 2015 that will be tasked with carrying out wartime operations.

While the unit will be comprised of the U.S. 2nd Infantry Division and a South Korean brigade-level unit, the 2nd Division commander plans to head the newly-made joint staff of the combined unit, with South Korea's brigadier general-level officer to be its vice chief.

In time of war, the two entities will get together to carry out diverse "strategic operations" such as eliminating weapons of mass destruction as well as civil missions against North Korea, while being operated in a separate fashion in peacetime, the 2nd Division and the Korean brigade will carry out joint exercises when necessary, according to the ministry.

The agreement, however, does not mean any revision to their ongoing plan of relocating the U.S. Forces Korea bases south of Seoul.

The 2nd Division and the headquarters of the envisioned joint unit will be based in Uijeongbu, north of Seoul, and after the relocation project is completed, they will then be moved to Pyeongtaek altogether, in accordance with the 2004 agreement of relocating the U.S. military bases in central and northern Seoul to Pyeongtaek by the end of 2016.

■ U.S. Cavalry Regiment Rotates into S. Korea

On Nov. 1, the U.S. deployed its 3rd Battalion, 8th Cavalry Regiment from Texas to South Korea on a rotational basis, which is the fourth U.S. Army rotational unit to deploy to the Asian nation for a nine-month tour. The regiment brings some 800 soldiers to replace its sister unit of the 1st Battalion, 12th Cavalry Regiment who had been deployed to South Korea since 2013.

A trained and combat ready force, the regiment deployed with mechanized Infantry and armor assets, will utilize vehicles and equipment already in place from the previous rotational unit. Upon completion of its nine-month rotation, the squadron will return back to its homestation.

U.S. Army Pacific routinely schedules and deploys forces on a rotational basis to South Korea. These routine deployments support the U.S. security commitment to South Korea as specified by our mutual defense treaty and presidential agreements.

They are also designed to meet the U.S. National Security Strategy in support of a strong and capable partnership in the Asia-Pacific region, according to the U.S. army.

■ U.S. to Disband Armored Unit in South Korea

On Nov. 7, the U.S. Forces Korea said that the country has decided to disband the 1st Armored Brigade Combat Team under its 2nd Infantry Division in South Korea and instead bring in a new 4,600-strong rotational combat unit.

The armored brigade combat team, currently based in Camp Casey in Dongducheon, north of Seoul, is to be deactivated in June 2015 when the rotational team arrives here.

The new team is to operate on a nine-month rotational basis, which does not mean any cut in the number of the troops dispatched on the Korean Peninsula, according to the USFK, adding the new unit will keep its equipment here and only its personnel will be rotated.

The decision comes as the U.S. seeks to curtail the number of its combat brigades to 32 from 45 as part of the military realignment scheme promoting the rotational troop operation to more flexibly manage its forces.

DELAY IN WARTIME OPERATIONAL CONTROL

■ S. Korea, U.S. Delay Transfer of Wartime Troop Control

On Oct. 23, South Korea and the United States agreed to delay again a plan to give Seoul wartime operational control (OPCON) of its troops until it improves capabilities to counter nuclear and missile threats from North Korea. The allies did not specify a target year for the transfer of wartime operational control (OPCON), but officials from both sides anticipate that it could be around the mid-2020s.

The transfer was scheduled for late 2015 after being postponed four years earlier. Citing growing threats from North Korea, South Korea asked for another delay in 2013, with Seoul and Washington agreeing in April to reconsider the transfer date.

South Korea currently has peacetime control of its approximately 639,000 servicemembers, but control in case of war transfers to a U.S. four-star general under the Combined Forces Command.

The agreement, reached at the annual Security Consultative Meeting (SCM) between South Korean Defense Minister Han Min-koo and his U.S. counterpart, Chuck Hagel, was seen as an expression of Washington's security commitment to the Korean Peninsula and a stern message to Pyongyang, which has threatened to carry out "a new form of nuclear test" and test-launch long-range rockets.

The allies set three conditions for the transfer: First, the handover will come when the overall security situation can guarantee the stable transition; when

South Korea is equipped with core military capabilities to lead the combined defense posture; and when it is able to effectively guard against North Korea's nuclear and missiles attacks in the early stages of local provocations and full-scale wars.

Based upon the regular assessment of the conditions and the recommendations by the two defense chiefs, the South Korean and the U.S. presidents will set the appropriate date, according to officials.

As part of efforts for stronger deterrence against the North, South Korea has been developing the preemptive strike apparatus of the Korea Air and Missile Defense (KAMD) and the "kill chain" systems, according to the allies.

The two sides also agreed to establish a comprehensive operational concept to counter North Korea's missile threats, which will be the basis for their joint operational plan.

▪ S. Korea, U.S. Agree to Exclude Joint Command from Relocation Plan

On Oct. 23, South Korea and the United States agreed to keep the Combined Forces Command (CFC) located in Seoul and the 2nd Infantry Division near the tense inter-Korean border in a move that could spark controversy over an earlier plan to move U.S. troops south of the South Korean capital.

In 2004, the allies agreed to move the joint command, U.S. Forces Korea and the United Nations Command -- located in a sprawling military base in central Seoul -- to Pyeongtaek, some 70km south of Seoul, by the end of 2016, and to relocate the American artillery brigade north of Seoul to a new location south of the Han River that runs through the South Korean capital.

The agreement was made during the annual Security Consultative Meeting between South Korean Defense Minister Han Min-koo and his U.S. counterpart Chuck Hagel, resulting in the postponement of a bilateral plan to give South Korea wartime operational control (OPCON) of its troops.

The joint command, set up in 1978, was supposed to be dissolved upon transfer of the OPCON, which was scheduled for late 2015 after a delay, but Seoul and Washington agreed to keep it at the current location until the OPCON transition takes place "for effective joint operations between the two to bolster deterrence against North Korea," according to the Seoul ministry. The two countries estimated the transfer could take place around the mid-2020s.

The allies also agreed to retain the 210th Fires Brigade under the 2nd Infantry Division at its current location of Dongducheon, north of Seoul, near the Demilitarized Zone (DMZ) that separates the two Koreas until "around the year 2020" when South Korean forces' counter-fires reinforcement plan is completed.

The decision was based upon the judgement that counter-fire fights are one of the most crucial functions during the early phases of war that decide the very existence of a nation.

According to officials, if the brigade is based in Pyeongtaek, it would take several days for its manpower and weapons to be deployed near the DMZ, which would cost a lot. The brigade's artillery, including the Multiple Launch Rocket System (MSLR) and the ATACMS surface-to-surface missile system, is seen as a strong deterrent to North Korea's long-range artillery threats.

▪ S. Korea to Shrink Armed Forces to 522,000 by 2022

On March 6, South Korea announced its defense reform plan with a gist of cutting its standing forces from the current 640,000 to 522,000 by 2022, while increasing the ratio of non-commissioned officers with specific technical expertise and skills.

The defense reform plan for 2014-2030 takes into account the shrinking birth rate in a country where all able-bodied men must complete at least two years of military service to counter North Korea's 1.2 million strong army.

The key is to recruit more non-commissioned officers, who are professional soldiers, to keep pace with the current trend. Most of the reduction will come from the Army, which heavily relies on conscripts.

The number will be cut from 498,000 to 387,000 in the next eight years, while the manpower of the other branches will remain unchanged at 41,000 for the Navy, 65,000 for the Air Force and 29,000 for the Marine Corps.

By rank, the number of soldiers will shrink to 300,000 from 446,000, while the number of non-commissioned officers will increase to 152,000 from the current 116,000.

Under the plan, the Navy will establish a submarine headquarters as South Korea is expected to have over 20 submarines, including nine 3,000t submarines after 2020. The Air Force also plans to set up a satellite surveillance unit under another plan to acquire five multi-purpose satellites capable of monitoring all parts of North Korea by 2022.

■ S. Korea, U.S., Japan Sign Info-sharing Pact on N.K. Nukes

On Dec. 29, South Korea, the United States and Japan signed a pact on sharing their military intelligence about North Korea's nuclear and missile programs in the face of Pyongyang's evolving security threats.

The three countries have been working on the signing of an agreement on sharing military secrets since May, when they agreed to launch working-level discussions during their defense ministers' talks in Singapore. The conclusion comes two years after a bilateral information-sharing pact between Seoul and Tokyo was ruptured due to fierce public criticism in South Korea.

The scope of military information to be shared among the three will be confined to intelligence on threats from North Korea in such various forms as documents, photos and digital electronic data, according to the Seoul ministry, noting that it will exchange secrets with Japan not directly but via the U.S.

It is in an apparent move to circumvent expected opposition from the public, which has opposed any military cooperation with Japan, its former colonial ruler.

Seoul and Washington have a bilateral military intelligence-sharing agreement, as do the U.S. and Japan. Seoul and Tokyo had worked to sign such a deal in 2012, but the deal fell apart at the last minute due in part to negative public sentiment in South Korea.

The three-nation arrangement will be legally binding as it is based on the Seoul-Washington and Washington-Tokyo treaties on sharing confidential information. So far, South Korea has signed similar information-sharing arrangements with 29 countries, including Russia.

PUBLIC ADMINISTRATION AND NATIONAL POLICE

PERSONNEL MANAGEMENT

■ Tighter Public Servants' Ethics Law

A tighter ethics law on public servants was passed in the National Assembly in Dec. 2014 and went into office on March 31, 2015. The law is aimed at rooting out cozy public-private ties following a deadly ferry disaster that claimed more than 300 lives, mostly students, on April 16.

The law calls for tighter rules on former government workers' entrance into private firms. It further limits public workers from working for non-profit organizations related with safety inspection, regulation management and procurement as well as social welfare foundations, universities and general hospitals that deal with such issues. The law has thus far mainly limited public workers' employment in the private for-profit sector.

The new law tightens the standard under which the government allows or bans public servants' non-government sector employment, while also extending the number of years by which former government workers are prohibited from private sector jobs from two to three. Violators are subject to receiving a jail term of less than two years and below 10 million won (US$18,290) in fine.

■ Heated Competition to Become Public Servants

The number of applicants for the class-seven public servants reached 61,252 last year for the 730 vacancy, which means one applicant should beat 84 rivals to become public servants. The number of applicants for the class-nine civil servants, the lowest ranking, reached 193,840 last year, making the competition ratio of 64.6 to one. The competition ratio of the class-five public servants hit the lowest of 32 to one since 2000.

■ **The Largest Recruitment of New Public Servants**

The number of newly recruited public servants reached 4,160 last year, up 412 from a year earlier and the largest since 2008. Increases in application for maternity leave and retirement raised the need to recruit more employees. Starting from 2011, parents whose children are aged under eight are eligible to apply for maternity leave, compared with parents with children aged under six previously.

The number of applicants has been on the rise with it hitting 6,671 in 2012.Last year, the number of newly recruited class-nine public servants, the lowest ranking, reached 3,000 and that of class-seven public servants hit 730. The number of class-five public servants reached 430.

■ **Flexible Work-Hour System for Public Servants**

The Ministry of Government Administration and Home Affairs recruited 200 public servants who will work in a flexible work-hour system for the first time in 2014. The government introduced the system last year in the first half of last year to employ civil servants who cannot work full-time. The flexible work-hour system calls for working for about 20 hours per week, half of working hours for full-time public servants.

An average age of applicants who passed an exam reached 35.2 and women accounted for 74.5%. Those aged in the 30s made up for 69% of the total, followed by those in the 40s with 18.5% and those in the 20s with 11%. Three people aged in the 50s also passed the examination. The results showed that more women who left the workforce due to marriages and childcare could return to work due to the system, experts say.

■ **Public Servants in Provincial Governments**

Provincial governments recruited a total of 17,561 new public servants last year, up 3,474 from a year earlier as demand for more civil servants in social and welfare services rose. The government also increased the recruitment of physically challenged people, those in the low-income bracket and high school graduates.

The newly employed number of the disabled reached 786 last year, up 107 from the previous year. Those from low-income families rose by 70 to 537 last year among the total civil servants working for provincial governments. Three North Korean defectors were selected and the number of high school graduates reached 284 last year, up 17 from 2013.

Those who will work under a flexible work-hour system reached 1,317 last year. The system calls for selected public servants to work for four hours per day or 20 hours per week.

■ **Improvement in Public Servants' Working System**

The government enhanced the system of hiring public servants by opening more spots to civilians as the ferry sinking revealed that a bungled response by the government increased casualties.

The government designated 2,739 posts requiring expertise as long-term work positions which allow civil servants on those posts to work at least for four years. It also designated 17,516 posts calling for flexibly managing personnel as rotation duty.

■ **Recruitment of Public Servants Handling Disaster Management**

The Daejeon City Hall and the South Chungcheong Province hired class-nine public servants on disaster management in June 2014. In 2012, the government announced its plan to hire such public servants to raise its capacity for disaster response, but it managed to implement the plan two years after its announcement. The move came as the government came under fire for its poor response to the April ferry sinking.

■ **Establishment of the Ministry of Personnel Management**

South Korea set up the Ministry of Personnel Management in Nov. 2014 with the task of reforming the government's personnel affairs following the deadly ferry sinking in April last year.

Around 300 people died in the ferry Sewol that sank off the country's southwest coast en route to the southern resort island of Jeju. Poor initial rescue operations were largely blamed for the heavy death toll.

The ferry accident called into question the effectiveness of the country's safety control system as well as the government's personnel management. Critics say that corruptive government personnel decisions have contributed to the botched rescue operations by national rescue agencies.

Lee Geun-myun, a former Samsung Electronics official who handled human resources, took office as the head of the new agency responsible for human resources.

PUBLIC SAFETY

■ Large-sized Incidents Including Sewol Ferry Sinking

Oil spill in waters off the coast of Yeosu On Jan. 31, a speeding Singapore-registered tanker collided into pipelines operated by GS Caltex Co., the country's second-largest refiner, causing up to 754 kℓ of oil to spill into waters off the coast of Yeosu, 455㎞ south of Seoul. While the oil tanker was to blame for the accident, the refiner has also been under fire for belatedly responding to the case and underplaying the size of the spill.

Gym collapse in the city of Gyeongju On Feb. 17, ten people were killed and 128 others were injured after the roof of a hotel gymnasium packed with students collapsed in the southern city of Gyeongju, according to the police.

The roof of the gymnasium at the Mauna Ocean Resort in Gyeongju, a historical tourist city 370㎞ southeast of Seoul, caved in on some 560 incoming freshmen of the Busan University of Foreign Studies on Feb. 17 during a welcoming party.

Officers at the Gyeongju Police Station said that the collapse was the result of overall poor construction and lax management of the building.

▲ Rescue workers search for survivors at the scene of resort roof collapse in Gyeongju, southeastern South Korea on Feb. 18. Ten people were killed and more than 100 injured in the disaster.

Sewol ferry sinking On April 16, the 6,825t ferry Sewol capsized and sank in waters near the southwestern port of Jindo en route to the southern resort island of Jeju. The deadly ferry sinking killed 295 people, mostly students on a field trip from one high school with nine still remaining missing. The ferry sinking, one of the nation's worst maritime disasters, sparked nationwide soul-searching.

The captain, Lee Joon-seok, and 14 other crew members of the ferry were accused of abandoning the ferry.

Prosecutors alleged that ferry operator Chonghaejin, motivated by profit, routinely overloaded the ship with passengers and cargo even though its balance was substantially compromised after a remodeling.

The ferry disaster has been a major political issue in South Korea as critics argue that the government's poor initial response to the tragedy contributed to the high death toll.

A joint altar was set up at a gym in Ansan, just south of Seoul, to voice deep condolence to the dead high school students. Most of the victims were students from a high school in Ansan who were on a field trip to the southern resort island of Jeju. In Incheon, a memorial altar for other victims was also erected. The bereaved families of the ferry sinking victims have been rallying to muster signatures to identify what caused the ferry sinking.

In November, ruling and opposition lawmakers passed a package of bills aimed at preventing a disaster similar to the Sewol ferry sinking. The victims' families demanded that the fact-finding committee should have the right to independently probe into the case and indict those who are responsible, but the demand was rejected.

Prosecutors had sought a death penalty for the captain and life imprisonment for three crew members in charge of steering the ship and jail terms ranging from 15 to 30 years for 11 other crew members.

But a district court sentenced the captain Lee to 36 years in jail, clearing him of manslaughter and other major charges in November. The 14 others were given jail terms ranging from five to 30 years, while the ferry's operator Chonghaejin Corp. was fined 10 million won (US$9,161).

Ferry owner Yoo Byung-eun -- the co-founder of the sect and an ex-convict -- was found dead on a remote mountain in southern South Korea in June, two months after he was put on the wanted list in connection with the ferry sinking. His family members were put in jail on various corruption charges related to the tragedy.

Yoo's daughter, Som-na, is fighting an extradition bid from Paris, and his second son, Hyuk-ki, is also wanted on corruption charges but is hiding abroad.

Subway train collision and fire at bus terminal On May 2, two trains collided on one of Seoul's major subway lines, injuring 238 passengers, police and firefighters said. No fatalities were immediately reported.

The collision happened at Sang-wangsimni Station on Subway Line 2 at around 3:30 p.m. when a train ran into the back of another train that had stopped at the station due to a mechanical problem.

According to Seoul Metro, the operator of the subway line, it was the first time that subway trains had collided in South Korea. Service on the subway line was partially restricted following the accident. Seoul city officials said a failure in the following train's automatic distance control system (ATS) could have been the cause of the collision. The ATS should have activated when the two trains approached within 200m of each other.

On May 26, eight people were killed and more than 60 others were injured in a fire at a local bus terminal near Seoul, fire and hospital officials said.

The blaze occurred at an underground construction site of the Goyang bus Terminal in Goyang, just northwest of Seoul, firefighters said. Firefighting authorities said they suspect the fire was started by sparks from welding work.

Widespread safety insensitivity Despite the deadly ferry sinking in April last year, there were a lot of incidents caused by people's insensitivity toward public safety and lax supervision by authorities.

On May 28, a fire ripped through a nursing home in southern South Korea, killing at least 21 people, mostly elderly patients, and injuring eight others, police and fire officials said. An 82-year-old man, who suffered from dementia, was accused of setting an arson attack on the hospital. The suspect, surnamed Kim, was also a patient at the hospital.

A firefighting helicopter also crashed into a residential area of South Korea's southern city of Gwangju on July 17, killing five firefighters on board, fire officials said. The chopper crashed into a road near the city's housing area of Gwangsan-gu. The firefighters were returning from an operation to search for those still missing from the ferry Sewol that sank on April 16.

On July 22, two passenger trains collided on the east coast, killing one passenger and injuring 93 others. KORAIL, the state-run railroad operator, said the accident happened between its O-Train, a sightseeing train that travels to parts of Gangwon, and a normal-speed Mugunghwa train. The operator of the sightseeing train was blamed for chatting on a mobile messenger while driving.

On Oct. 17, sixteen people were killed and eleven others were injured as a ventilation grill gave way due to their weight on it during a pop concert at Pangyo Techno Valley, a multipurpose complex, just southeast of Seoul.

On Nov. 15, a fire occurred at a camping ground in Damyang, 193km south of Seoul, killing five people and injuring another five. They had a barbecue on an unauthorized campground.

Fifty workers were injured after a lethal chemical was leaked at a plating factory on Dec. 10 in the southeastern city of Daegu on Wednesday. Hypochlorite was leaked at the Yeongnam Metal Co. plating factory when some workers mistakenly poured the chemical from a truck into a tank filled with sulfuric acid, which produced toxic gas.

■ Establishment of the Ministry of Public Safety and Security

South Korea launched a new government entity dealing with public safety in the aftermath of the deadly ferry sinking on Nov. 19, 2014. The Ministry of Public Safety and Security was established to ensure citizens' safety and operate an effective integrated disaster response system at the earliest time possible. The new ministry consisted of more than 10,000 public servants, the fifth-largest among South Korea's government agencies.

CENTRAL GOVERNMENT'S ADMINISTRATION

■ Personnel Reorganization

President Park Geun-hye conducted a reshuffle of government organizations following the Sewol disasters. The main plans include the establishment of a control tower on disaster management and the overhauling of a disaster response system.

The government set up the Ministry of Public Safety and Security and the Ministry of Personnel Management. South Korea also appointed a deputy prime minister on social affairs and education who will also double as the education minister.

■ 'Substitution Holiday' System

South Korean allows one more holiday to be given to its citizens when its national holidays such as the Chuseok fall harvest day or the Lunar holiday overlap a weekend. The system made the 2014 Chuseok holiday into five-day long holiday.

■ Sejong Administrative Capital

The era of "Sejong City" has opened in a full-fledged manner as 10-year long construction of government complex buildings and the movement of government agencies wrapped up in December 2014. The three-phased movement plans were completed since South Korea's blueprint

to re-locate its government agencies was first announced in October 2005.

South Korea spent 1.77 trillion won (US$1.63 billion) in building the government's U-shaped complex buildings in Sejong, 150km south of Seoul between 2006 and 2014. The construction of 17 buildings was first started in December 2008. A total of 18 ministries and 18 government agencies were moved into the complex with about 13,000 public servants working.

The government set up a video conference system and smart working scheme to improve the work efficiency. In the first half of 2015, the Presidential Archives will be opened and a cultural art center will also be established in 2018.

■ Making Public Gov't Documents

The government began to make public its original documents in March 2014 if deemed appropriate in being revealed to the public. Except documents dealing with in the presidential office, government documents approved by director general or above began to be open to the public. But if documents contain private individual's information or contents about national security or diplomacy, they will not be made public for security concerns.

■ Banning Random Collection of Resident Registration Number

A new law on protection of individuals' information went into effect on Aug. 7, 2014 in a bid to curb random collection of resident registration numbers and crack down on violators. If found to violate the law, one is subject to receive a fine worth up to 30 million won.

PROVINCIAL GOVERNMENTS

■ No. of Registered Citizens in Seoul Dips below 10 mln

The number of registered citizens in Seoul declined to the 10 million mark for the first time in 2014. As of January 2014, the number of Seoul citizens stood at 11.4 million, down 481 compared with a year earlier. If excluded with those whose residencies were not recorded, the number of Seoul citizens reached 9.99

million.

The number of Seoul citizens has been on the decline since peaking at 19.4 million in 1992. But those living outside of Seoul, in particular, the Gyeonggi Province rose by reaching 12.2 million last year. The number of Gyeonggi residents has been on the rise since it surpassed the 10 million mark for the first time in 2003.

■ **Provincial Governments' Financial Soundness**

As of 2013, combined income by provincial governments amounted to 70.3 trillion won and their budget reached 140.4 trillion won, making their financial independence rate hit 50.06%. A combined debt reached 32.9 trillion won with their debt ratio reaching 13.15%.

The average ratio of debt to asset by 17 provincial governments reached 6.98%. Incheon reported the highest debt ratio with 10.16% while Seoul's debt ratio was the lowest with 3.01%.

Seoul reported the financial independence ratio of 86.7% and the city of Ulsan with 69.97% and Gyeonggi Provincial government with 69.33%. But the South Jeolla Province government recorded the corresponding ratio of 25.48% and the North Jeolla Province government with 27.01% and the North Gyeongsang government with 29.9%.

■ **Rise in Local Public Firms' Debt**

As of end-2013, a combined debt held by 26 public firms in provincial areas under high supervision amounted to 51.3 trillion won with their debt ratio hitting an average of 157.9%. Their total debt accounted for 69.6% of the combined debt of 73.9 trillion won held by a total of 394 public firms in provincial areas as of the end of 2013.

Among the 26 public firms, SH Corp. held the largest debt worth 18.4 trillion won, followed by Gyeonggi Urban Innovation Corp. with 8.3 trillion won and Incheon Development & Tourism Corp. with 7.8 trillion won.

The Ministry of Government Administration and Home Affairs notified the troubled public firms of unveiling their plans to clean debt in February 2014. The 26 public firms should cut a combined 11.8 trillion won in debt by the end of 2017. If the debt reduction is made as planned, their debt ratio will fall below 200%.

■ **Local Tax Reform**

In Dec. 2014, the National Assembly finalized a law aimed at reforming the payment of local taxes. So tourist hotels, funds on real estates, project financing ventures and other agencies should pay local taxes starting from 2015.

POLICE

■ **Overview**

The Sewol sinking tragedy also heavily affected South Korean police. The disaster led the chief of the state policy agency to step down as police were criticized for a bungled manhunt for the fugitive shipping tycoon wanted for the ferry disaster. The Korea Coast Guard was also disorganized.

■ **New Police Chief Named following Ferry Sinking**

In August, Kang Sin-myeong became the National Police Agency (NPA) commissioner, replacing his predecessor Lee Sung-han as police came under fire over a bungled manhunt for the fugitive shipping tycoon wanted for April's ferry disaster.

▲ *Kang Shin-myung, new commissioner of the National Police Agency, gives a salute during his inauguration ceremony at the agency's headquarters in western Seoul on Aug. 25.*

Lee had offered to step down over a delay in identifying the body of Yoo Byung-eun, a 73-year-old billionaire whose family owns Sewol operator Chonghaejin Marine Co. Yoo is partly blamed for the disaster as the de facto owner.

Kang, who previously headed the Seoul Metropolitan Police Agency (SMPA), took office on Aug. 25 as the new chief of the police agency. He vowed to restore public trust in the police. Kang, a graduate of the Korean National Police University, took the helm of the SMPA in 2013.

▪ Police Undertake Several Roles by the Coast Guard

The Korea Coast Guard underwent dissolution due to its poor handling of the ferry sinking. Police undertook the coast guard's several roles including investigation, security and intelligence. For this goal, the National Police Agency set up two teams tailored to probing into intellectual crime and five provincial policy agencies. Sixteen police stations set up additional investigative teams. For smooth transition, police decided to employ 300 new police officers in 2015.

▪ Nationwide Crackdown on Village Gangs

New police chief Kang Sin-myeong vowed to strengthen crackdown on gangsters. On Sept. 3, police kicked off a 100-day special crackdown on gangsters who frequently rob and beat people nearby their residences. They arrested 3,136 gangsters, among which 960 were taken into custody.

Police found that half of the arrested so-called village gangsters had criminal records of being punished on more than 11 accounts. The most frequent crime committed by village gangsters was obstruction of business with 35.2%. Extortion ranked second with 32.5%, followed by violence with 16.3%.

▪ Response to So-called "Four Social Evils"

Police have been seeking to eradicate so-called "four social evils" -- sexual violence, domestic violence, school violence and unsanitary food. Police set a five-year plan to root out such ills until 2017.

In 2014, police set four specific goals to achieve that target: strengthening driving forces to eradicate the four social evils, focusing on preemptive and preventive policing, supporting victims' protection and expanding candidates subject to social protection, such as children and senior citizens.

Police expanded the number of investigative teams on sexual violence to 126 police stations from 52. The number of police officers on school violence were also increased to 1,078 from 606. They also began to designate special police officers who will help support victims of sexual violence. Efforts to curb child violence were increased.

As a result, the recurrence rate of sexual violence reached a target ratio of 6.3%. The recurrence rate of domestic violence reached 11.1%, below the target of 11.4% and the rate of reporting school violence reached 1.3%, lower than the target of 2%.

▪ Strengthened '112' Emergency Call System

Starting in September, police began to operate the 112 emergency all-out response system that calls for traffic police officers to respond to 112 emergency call.

If serious crime cases take place, police officers who are in charge of traffic control or drunk driving control should be dispatched to the scene of such crime for quick responses.

The code zero indicates criminal cases that call for dispatch of police officers from multiple police stations on concerns that violators will flee. Traffic police officers should be armed with guns, laser rifle or tear gas guns for a possible dispatch.

The National Police Agency also enhanced the 112 emergency call system so that traffic police officers are able to find out reported crime cases via their mobile checkers on a real-time basis.

NATIONAL ASSEMBLY

▪ 322nd Extra Session of National Assembly

The 322nd extra session of the National Assembly ran for 26 days from

Feb. 3 to Feb. 28. During this period, plenary sessions were held 10 times, while a total of 198 items were passed, including 158 bills and 30 resolutions. Plenary meetings of standing committees were held 80 times for a total of 266 hours and 34 minutes.

During a plenary session on Feb. 28, the National Assembly passed 139 items, including 132 bills. Among them was a bill calling for the establishment of a special inspector system, one of President Park Geun-hye's campaign pledges. The bill passed 83-35, with 42 abstentions. The plenary session had been unscheduled and the quorum of 150 lawmakers was barely met.

A bill calling for the payment of basic pensions to senior citizens aged 65 or above starting in July failed to pass through the parliament as it got stuck at the level of the relevant standing committee, the parliamentary committee for health and welfare.

▪ 323rd Extra Session of National Assembly

The 323rd extra session of the National Assembly ran for 30 days from March 20 to April 18. During this period, plenary sessions were held seven times, while a total of 28 items were passed, including 18 bills and 6 resolutions. Plenary meetings of standing committees were held 50 times for a total of 208 hours and 1 minute.

During a plenary session on April 16, the National Assembly ratified the 9th Special Measure Agreement calling for South Korea to share the cost of stationing 28,500 American troops in South Korea. The agreement, valid from 2014 to 2018, passed 131-26, with 35 abstentions. This resolved the absence of an agreement that had begun at the start of 2014.

During the same plenary session, the National Assembly also passed an amendment bill calling for the joint chiefs of staff to oversee decisions related to the cost and modification of weapons systems. Previously, the defense minister made such decisions upon the recommendations of the Joint Chiefs of Staff.

Meanwhile, passage of a bill calling for basic pension payments to all senior citizens aged 65 or above starting in July fell through. The bill had been one of President Park's campaign pledges.

The Saenuri Party proposed as a final compromise the monthly payment of basic pensions between 100,000 and 200,000 won depending on the period of subscription to the national pension plan. For the 120,000 people in the low-income bracket and with a long subscription period to the national pension plan, the party proposed an increased monthly payment of 200,000 won.

Some lawmakers of the New Politics Alliance for Democracy, however, raised objections and the party deferred a decision on the issue in order to concentrate on the Sewol ferry disaster that took place that day.

▪ 324th Extra Session of National Assembly

The 324th extra session of the National Assembly ran for 30 days from April 19 to May 18. During this period, two plenary sessions were held, while a total of 202 items were passed, including 188 bills and eight resolutions. Plenary meetings of standing committees were held 27 times for a total of 72 hours and 19 minutes.

During a plenary session on April 29, the National Assembly passed a resolution calling for compensation measures following the Sewol ferry disaster and the determination of the truth behind the accident. Of the 253 lawmakers present, 250 voted in favor of the resolution, while three abstained.

The resolution called on the government to make utmost efforts to rescue those who remained missing in the ferry disaster and offer a sincere apology for failing to properly respond to the accident.

It also called for emergency rescue measures and psychological treatment for the victims, their families and residents of the areas affected by the tragedy. It urged the government to draw up measures to financially support those affected, and resolved to build a memorial park and memorial monument in Ansan, Gyeonggi Province, which lost the most lives in the ferry sinking.

The resolution especially called for strict punishment against those public officials who neglected their duties and those involved in illegal acts related to the sinking.

The National Assembly also passed an amendment bill requiring school chiefs to check safety measures and carry out other necessary measures when organizing school trips or other hands-on activities. During a plenary session on May 2, the National Assembly passed the basic pension plan 140-49, with six abstentions.

The bill's passage marked the realization of the basic pension plan pledged by both the ruling and opposition parties during the 2012 presidential campaign. It came more than five months after the government submitted its proposal to the National Assembly in November 2013. Still, critics argued that the bill was a retreat from President Park Geun-hye's pledge to pay a basic pension to all citizens aged 65 or above.

On the same day, the Assembly also passed an amendment bill on ensuring the safety of nuclear power plants and radioactive material, which had caused a controversy ahead of President Park's participation in the Nuclear Security Summit held in The Hague in March.

The amendment bill was aimed at establishing the necessary legal basis for two international treaties -- one against nuclear terrorism and the other for the physical protection of nuclear material and facilities -- which the Assembly had ratified in 2011.

■ **325th Extra Session of National Assembly**

The 325th extra session of the National Assembly ran for 30 days from May 19 to June 17. During this period, plenary sessions were held five times, while a total of six items were passed, including three resolutions. Plenary meetings of standing committees were held nine times for a total of 17 hours and 43 minutes.

During a plenary session on May 29, the National Assembly passed a plan to carry out a parliamentary investigation to determine the truth behind the sinking of the ferry Sewol. The plan passed with 224 votes in favor, and two abstentions.

On the issue of whether to include presidential chief of staff Kim Ki-choon as a witness in the investigation, the rival parties agreed to include the office of presidential secretaries as a subject of the investigation and require the head of each organization to appear before the National Assembly. A list of witnesses, which the New Politics Alliance for Democracy had insisted on, was not included in the plan.

However, the rival parties agreed to select witnesses through bipartisan consultations and also to include the National Intelligence Service as a subject of the investigation.

During the same plenary session, five-term lawmaker Chung Ui-hwa of the ruling Saenuri Party was chosen as the new parliamentary speaker to lead the second half of the 19th National Assembly's four-year term. As deputy speakers, Rep. Jeong Kab-yoon of the Saenuri Party and Rep. Lee Seok-hyun of NPAD were jointly selected.

▲ *Rep. Chung Eui-hwa of the ruling Saenuri Party speaks at the podium of the National Assembly in Seoul on May 29, after being elected to be speaker of the National Assembly for the next couple of years.*

It was the first time that the speaker for the second half was chosen during the term of the speaker of the first half since the parliamentary speaker's term was decided under a revision to the National Assembly Act in 1994.

■ **326th Extra Session of National Assembly**

The 326th extra session of the National Assembly ran for 30 days from June 18 to July 17. During this period, plenary sessions were held four times, while a total of 11 items were passed, including three resolutions. Plenary meetings of standing committees were held 105 times for a total of 483 hours and 30 minutes. Under a plan for a parliamentary investigation into the ferry disaster, the investigation committee met a total of eight times.

During a plenary session on June 24, the National Assembly selected the chairs of each standing committee, thereby completing its formation for the second half of the 19th Assembly's term.

The Saenuri Party was assigned the chairmanships of the parliamentary steering committee, and the committees for political affairs; strategy and finance; science and communication; foreign affairs and unification; national defense; security and public administration; intelligence; budget and accounts; and ethics.

The New Politics Alliance for Democracy was assigned the chairmanships of the parliamentary committees for judicial affairs; education, culture, sports and tourism; agricultural and maritime affairs; industry and trade; health and welfare; environment and labor; land and transport; and gender equality and family.

- ### 327th Extra Session of National Assembly

The 327th extra session of the National Assembly ran for 30 days from July 21 to Aug. 19. During this period, no plenary sessions were held. Plenary meetings of standing committees were held 31 times for a total of 90 hours and 5 minutes. The rival parties wrangled over who should have the right to recommend an independent special counsel to look into the ferry tragedy but failed to reach an agreement.

- ### 328th Extra Session of National Assembly

The 328th extra session of the National Assembly ran for 10 days from Aug. 22 to Aug. 31. During this period, no plenary sessions were held. Plenary meetings of standing committees were held three times for a total of 8 hours and 37 minutes. No progress was made during the session due to an escalating row between the parties over legislation of a special bill on the ferry disaster.

- ### 329th Regular Session of National Assembly

The 329th regular session of the National Assembly ran for 100 days from Sept. 1 to Dec. 9. During this period, plenary sessions were held 14 times, while a total of 289 items were passed, including 237 bills and 16 resolutions. Plenary meetings of standing committees were held 168 times for a total of 483 hours and 31 minutes.

Veto of arrest motion for Rep. Song Kwang-ho On Sept. 3, the National Assembly vetoed the arrest of Rep. Song Kwang-ho of the Saenuri Party, who had been accused of taking 55 million won in bribes from local railway parts supplier AVT in exchange for business favors.

His arrest was subject to parliamentary consent as lawmakers in South Korea are immune from detention while the National Assembly is in session. Song's arrest motion, which was put to a secret vote during a plenary session, was rejected 118-73, with eight abstentions and 24 votes deemed invalid. In a separate vote, the Assembly approved the appointment of Kwon Soon-il as a justice of the Supreme Court.

On Sept. 26, a plenary session was convened in the absence of all opposition parties, including NPAD. The session was adjourned without handling the 90 items that had been scheduled for handling. Speaker Chung Ui-hwa declared the session's adjournment nine minutes after its opening, saying the items would be handled during a plenary session on Sept. 30.

First passage of bills in 151 days During a plenary session on Sept. 30, the National Assembly passed a total of 90 items, including 85 bills. It marked the first time in 151 days that the Assembly passed a bill as the rival parties sparred over a special bill on the Sewol tragedy.

Despite concerns that the plenary session would be attended only by the ruling party due to a boycott by NPAD, the opposition party joined the session after reaching a breakthrough deal with the rival party on the special Sewol bill.

Largest ever number of agencies subject to parliamentary audit On Oct. 2, the National Assembly convened a plenary session and decided to carry out a parliamentary audit of 672 government agencies during the audit period that would last 20 days starting on Oct. 7.

The number was 42 greater than the 630 agencies that were subject to the audit in 2013, and the largest ever since the audits were reintroduced in 1988.

During the same session, the Assembly passed the government's accounts for 2013 and a request for an inspection by the state audit agency of safety regulations for vessels, management of disaster relief funds, management of various permit systems, and projects supporting the contents industry.

Sewol bills passed 205 days after tragedy On Nov. 7, the National Assembly passed a package of bills aimed at preventing a disaster similar to April's ferry sinking that left more than 300 people dead or missing. One bill called for an independent investigation into the cause of the disaster through the appointment of an independent counsel and a fact-finding team.

Also passed was a bill calling for the dismantlement of the Coast Guard and the National Emergency Management Agency. Both organizations would be placed under a new government ministry to be charged with overseeing disaster management.

The final bill of the package called for measures to swiftly retrieve the wealth of those found to have caused people's deaths through illegal activities, including any wealth hidden by a third party. The retrieved wealth would be used to compensate victims' families.

The special Sewol law passed 212-12, with 27 abstentions, while the government reorganization bill passed 146-71, with 32 abstentions and the wealth retrieval bill passed 224-4, with 17 abstentions.

Budget bill passed before deadline On Dec. 2, the National Assembly passed the government's 2015 budget bill, meeting the legal deadline for the first time in 12 years.

The bill called for increasing the government budget by 5.51% to 375.4 trillion won in 2015 from 355.8 trillion won in 2014. It fell slightly short of the 376 trillion won requested by the government.

▲ Lawmakers applaud after passing the government's 2015 budget bill during the National Assembly's plenary session in Seoul on Dec. 2.

■ **330th Extra Session of National Assembly**

The 330th extra session of the National Assembly ran for 30 days from Dec. 15 to Jan. 13, 2015. During this period, plenary sessions were held four times, while a total of 259 items were passed, including 212 bills and 24 resolutions. Plenary meetings of standing committees were held 22 times for a total of 55 hours and 45 minutes.

During the year's last plenary session on Dec. 29, the Assembly passed a total of 148 items, including a package of bills related to the housing market. It also passed plans to form a special committee tasked with reforming civil service pensions and a committee to investigate overseas resource development projects carried out under past administrations.

POLITICAL PARTIES

SAENURI PARTY

■ **Outline**

For the Saenuri Party, 2014 was a year that made the stable running of state affairs top priority in the second year of the Park Geun-hye administration.

However, with the paralysis of state affairs in the aftermath of the Sewol ferry sinking in the first half of the year, and the leak of classified presidential documents alleging the existence of behind-the-scenes powers in the second half of the year, crisis management became a pressing issue for the ruling party.

A rapid reorganization of the power structure within the party took place after the non-mainstream Kim Moo-sung won the chairmanship in a landslide victory over Suh Chung-won, who represented the pro-Park faction.

The local elections and the July 30 by-elections, which were seen as mid-term referenda, went smoothly. The June 4 local elections were seen as a tie between the ruling and opposition parties after each won about the same number of seats for local government chiefs. The by-elections, which were seen as a mini general election, ended in a victory for the Saenuri Party.

Those classified as presidential aspirants began to raise their profiles. With Chairman Kim Moo-sung holding power within the party, former Gyeonggi Governor Kim Moon-soo returned to the political scene as chief of the party's conservative reform committee.

Former Rep. Chung Mong-joon ran for Seoul mayor but lost to incumbent Mayor Park Won-soon.

Those classified as presidential aspirants in future elections, such as Nam Kyung-pil, Hong Joon-pyo and Won Hee-ryong, all ran in the local elections.

■ Launch of Kim Moo-sung Regime

In the July 14 national convention, five-term lawmaker Kim Moo-sung, who had served as the pivot of the non-mainstream faction, won the chairmanship for a two-year term. Kim, at the national convention held inside an indoor gymnasium in Jamsil, won a total of 52,702 votes, beating his rival Suh Chung-won, who won 38,293 votes.

Rep. Kim Tae-ho came in third, while six-term lawmaker Rhee In-je came in fourth, becoming members of the Supreme Council. Two-term lawmaker Kim Eul-dong also joined the Supreme Council under a regulation that requires a woman to be elected as a member, beating Hong Moon-jong, who came in fifth in the number of votes.

Kim Moo-sung and Suh Chung-won carried out fierce campaigns rivaling the presidential campaigns in the run-up to the national convention.

▲ Rep. Kim Moo-sung of Saenuri Party waves a party flag at the party national convention held at Jamsil Stadium in southeastern Seoul on July 14, after winning an election to be the new leader of the ruling party.

Following Kim's inauguration, the Saenuri Party's power structure, which had been dominated by the pro-Park mainstream faction, rapidly changed along the lines of the non-mainstream and branch factions.

Kim named Rep. Lee Gun-hyeon of the faction affiliated with former President Lee Myung-bak as secretary-general, Rep. Kim Young-woo of the non-mainstream faction as spokesman, and Rep. Kim Hak-yong as his chief of staff.

Kim, who won the chairmanship after vowing to say what needs to be said to President Park and the presidential office Cheong Wa Dae, invited former Gyeonggi Governor Kim Moon-soo as chief of the conservative reform committee and launched his reform drive.

He also formed a special committee to strengthen the party and conducted an inspection of party members' associations to clean up any shoddy associations ahead of the 20th general elections.

In the process, he faced backlash from those who claimed he was out to wipe out the pro-Park faction, which led him to cancel inspections of party associations affiliated with the electorates of incumbent lawmakers.

■ Non-Mainstream Chung Mong-joon Wins Seoul Mayor Candidacy

In the primaries for the Seoul mayorship in the June 4 local elections, the non-mainstream seven-term lawmaker Chung Mong-joon beat former Prime Minister

Kim Hwang-sik, who was reportedly endorsed by the president, by a landslide.

Rep. Chung won the primary on May 12 after garnering a total of 3,198 votes against the 958 votes of former Prime Minister Kim and 342 votes of Supreme Council member Lee Hye-hoon.

Kim received repeated requests from the party leadership to run for mayor even before the primary campaign began in earnest, leading to controversy over his alleged favor with President Park.

However, as he visited the United States starting on Feb. 11 to help found a Korean law center at UC Berkeley's law school, there were views that he had missed the right time. Upon returning home on March 14, he announced his bid for Seoul mayor, vowing to reclaim the mayorship from the opposition party, but as a latecomer, he lacked the ability to beat Rep. Chung.

The "non-mainstream wind" was strong among candidates for local government chiefs, including Seoul mayor. In the party's stronghold of Daegu, Mayor Kwon Young-jin of the pro-Lee faction beat his rivals, Suh Sang-kee and Cho Won-jin of the pro-Park faction. Of the 15 local government chief candidates, eight were classified as belonging to non-pro-Park factions.

Draw in Local Elections

The local elections, which were held 50 days after the Sewol ferry disaster, were expected to end in a crushing defeat for the ruling party. However, the party won 8 of the 17 local administration chief seats up for grabs, putting on a better-than-expected performance.

Especially in the capital area seen as a barometer of public sentiment, the opposition party won Seoul, but the ruling party won Incheon and Gyeonggi Province, making it difficult for either side to claim a clear victory.

Before the Sewol tragedy, the Saenuri Party was expected to do well in the local elections despite the common notion that they are the "ruling party's grave." That was because no one knew that President Park Geun-hye's approval rating would fall from the 50-60% range.

But after the Sewol tragedy, circumstances changed. Public opinion turned cold as the government revealed its incompetence in failing to rescue the young students who drowned with the sinking ferry.

However, the election mood changed completely once again as conservative voters joined forces after President Park's tearful apology. The main opposition New Politics Alliance for Democracy, which struggled to find an appropriate tool to win the election, mounted calls for judgment of the administration, while the Saenuri Party appealed to voters using Park's popularity.

When the ballot boxes were opened, contrary to expectations that "angry moms" who watched students die would come out to cast their votes, it appeared that the generational trend determined the result.

Exit polls showed that in Seoul, the New Politics Alliance for Democracy won 15%p more among voters in their 20s and 30s, compared to 2010, while the Saenuri Party gained nearly 8%p among those aged 60 or above.

Landslide Victory in July 30 By-elections

In the July 30 by-elections that were held two months after the local elections, the Saenuri Party won a landslide victory with 11 out of the 15 parliamentary seats up for grabs.

The by-elections were seen as a mini general election and a midterm referendum following the local elections that ended in a tie.

▲ Kim Moo-sung (front), chairman of the Saenuri Party, tries to carry Rep. Lee Jung-hyun on his back during the ruling party's supreme council meeting at the National Assembly in Seoul on Aug. 11. Lee won a parliamentary by-election in Suncheon and Gokseong in South Jeolla Province, a traditional stronghold of the liberal camp, on July 30.

The Saenuri Party got Lee Jung-hyun, a close aide to President Park Geun-hye who served as her senior secretary for political affairs and then senior secretary for public relations, elected in its traditional wasteland of South Jeolla Province. It was the first time the party won a seat in the Honam region since the current election system came into being in 1988.

In Seoul's Dongjak district, which was seen as the biggest battleground in the elections, the Saenuri Party nominated former lawmaker Na Kyung-won, who had been taking a break from politics after losing to Park Won-soon in the Seoul mayoral election, after much contemplation and succeeded in getting her elected.

Former lawmaker Yim Tae-hee, who served as chief of staff to former President Lee Myung-bak, was defeated in Suwon district D, but former lawmaker Jeong Mi-kyung, who lost in the 19th general elections in Suwon district B, ran again and this time succeeded.

The general view inside and outside political circles was that this was the result of the opposition party's "own goal," rather than full public support for the Park administration.

The NPAD created a controversy by nominating Kwon Eun-hee, a former senior investigator who conducted an investigation into the state spy agency's alleged smear campaign during the 2012 presidential election, in Gwangju, while in Seoul's Dongjak district, the party's merger of candidacies with the Justice Party drew criticism that it was a failure in terms of reasoning and timing.

■ Pro-Park Figures Enter Cabinet

As President Park Geun-hye struggled with personnel nominations amid the repeated resignations of prime minister candidates following the Sewol tragedy, she began to build her second Cabinet around pro-Park lawmakers within the Saenuri Party.

Rep. Choi Kyung-hwan, a former party floor leader and a confidant of the president, was named deputy prime minister for economic affairs and minister of strategy and finance, spearheading efforts to revive the economy in the second year of the Park administration under the so-called "Choinomics" policy.

Hwang Woo-yea, former chairman of the Saenuri Party, was named deputy prime minister for social affairs and minister of education, after being unexpectedly defeated by Chung Ui-hwa of the former pro-Lee Myung-back faction in the race for parliamentary speaker.

With Hwang's inauguration, the new Cabinet was characterized as a pro-Park two-top system under Hwang and Choi. Also, Rep. Kim Hee-jung, who served as former President Lee's spokesperson, was named minister of gender equality and family in a surprise nomination.

An Chong-bum, who played a large role in drawing up President Park's campaign pledges on the economy, gave up his seat in the National Assembly to join the presidential office as Park's senior secretary for economic affairs, while Cho Yoon-sun also gave up her post as minister of gender equality and family to serve as senior presidential secretary for political affairs.

■ Chungcheong Representative Lee Wan-koo Chosen as Floor Leader

In the second half of the 19th National Assembly, three-term lawmaker Lee Wan-koo was chosen floor leader of the Saenuri Party. Lee, whose electoral district is Buyeo and Cheongyang of South Chungcheong Province, was the sole candidate for floor leader and unanimously approved without a vote on May 18.

Three-term lawmaker Joo Ho-young, whose electoral district is Suseong district B in Daegu, was chosen as the chief policymaker.

In terms of region, it was a combination of Chungcheong and Saenuri's stronghold of Daegu. In factional terms, it was a combination of the pro-Park faction and the non-pro-Park faction. It was the first time that a lawmaker from the Chungcheong region became the Saenuri Party's floor leader.

Lee, who previously served as governor of South Chungcheong, is a leading politician of the region. Although he began his career as a public official for economic affairs, Lee later worked as commissioner of North Chungcheong and South Chungcheong and joined the National Assembly as a lawmaker during the 15th and 16th Assemblies.

In 2006, he was elected South Chungcheong Governor but stepped down in 2009 in protest of the government's revision of a plan to relocate the administrative capital to Sejong.

Joo, a former judge, served as a minister during the previous Lee Myung-bak administration and is considered to have a large network of personal connections beyond factional divides thanks to his rationality.

Lee and Joo led negotiations with the opposition party on a set of bills related to the Sewol ferry disaster, and smoothly led negotiations to pass the government's budget bill before the legal deadline.

■ Non-Mainstream Faction Grows in Stature

Following Kim Moo-sung's election as chairman, the pro-Park mainstream faction within the Saenuri Party experienced a rapid deterioration of their power and stronger consolidation around the core.

In a situation where the ruling party needed to secure stable momentum in the early phase of the Park Geun-hye administration, Park's leadership style of keeping a distance from the National Assembly prompted complaints within her party that she was being uncommunicative and making the mainstream pro-Park faction feel left out.

The mainstream pro-Park faction that appeared to be getting intimidated released their frustrations during an end-of-year gathering and nearly triggered an all-out factional war.

A forum aimed at strengthening national competitiveness, comprised of pro-Park lawmakers, had an end-of-year luncheon on Dec. 30 and poured out criticism on the Kim Moo-sung leadership.

Three-term lawmaker Yoo Ki-june directed his criticism at Kim Moo-sung, saying the chairman was imposing his own standards for reform on the people, rather than carrying out reforms demanded by the people.

Signs of a factional conflict increased when it became known that President Park invited seven pro-Park lawmakers to dinner at the presidential office Cheong Wa Dae on the second anniversary of her election on Dec. 19.

■ Rep. Chung Ui-hwa Elected National Assembly Speaker

The election of five-term lawmaker Chung Ui-hwa as speaker of the National Assembly in the second half of its term was another unexpected event for the party.

Rep. Chung became the party's candidate for parliamentary speaker after beating pro-Park former Chairman Hwang Woo-yea with 101 votes against Hwang's 46 votes in a party contest.

Chung, of the non-mainstream faction, won a landslide victory on the back of full support from the non-mainstream faction and first-term lawmakers, against Rep. Hwang who had the support of the mainstream pro-Park faction.

A former neurosurgeon, Chung entered the National Assembly toward the end of former President Kim Young-sam's term in 1996 and was re-elected for four more consecutive terms.

Shortly after his election as parliamentary chief, he resisted the Saenuri Party's demands to convene a plenary session amid a row with the opposition party over the Sewol ferry disaster, and urged both sides to reach a compromise over the government's budget bill despite the ruling party's repeated requests for unilateral passage of the bill.

NEW POLITICS ALLIANCE FOR DEMOCRACY

■ Launch of NPAD

In 2014, NPAD struggled through rough waters. The first signal was the merger of the then Democratic Party with the new party under creation by independent lawmaker Ahn Cheol-soo. On March 2, then Democratic Party leader Kim Han-gil and Ahn Cheol-soo, chief of what would become the "New Political Vision Party," announced the creation of a new party through their merger.

Kim proposed the merger to Ahn at the end of February, and the two held two meetings on March 1 before agreeing to merge their parties.

The biggest factor behind the decision was the realistic concern that the opposition would lose in the June local elections if they were conducted as a three-way race among the Saenuri Party, Democratic

Party, and the New Political Vision Party.

The merger was also in the interests of the Democratic Party, which was struggling to raise its approval rating, and the new party, which was struggling to launch the party.

The two sides agreed to participate in the new party's formation with a 50:50 share, create a preparatory committee for the party's launch, create a basis for the new party with a party platform, and each join the new party in succession.

The Democratic Party was the No. 1 opposition party with 126 lawmakers, while Ahn's emerging party only had two seats in the parliament, leading to views that the agreement was the result of the DP's respect for the principle behind the merger and consideration for Ahn, a leading contender in the next presidential election.

Kim and Ahn became co-heads of the new party and created four subcommittees under the party's preparatory committee to each handle the party platform, party regulations, administration and political planning.

On March 16, the preparatory committee held a meeting to formally launch the organization and named the party "New Politics Alliance for Democracy."

After holding launching meetings in six areas -- Gyeonggi, Daejeon, Gwangju, Incheon, Busan and Seoul -- the party was officially launched on March 26. Kim and Ahn were elected co-chairs, while the leadership was comprised of nine Supreme Council members from each side, including the two co-chairs.

▲ A ceremony is underway in Seoul on March 26, to launch the New Politics Alliance for Democracy, a coalition of the main opposition Democratic Party and the minor opposition group led by independent lawmaker Ahn Cheol-soo.

In its launching declaration, the party laid out the goals of a just society, united society, prospering nation, peaceful Republic of Korea and the restoration of democracy. Independents Park Joo-sun and Kang Dong-won joined the new party to give it a total of 130 seats in the National Assembly.

▪ Park Young-sun Elected Floor Leader

On May 8, three-term lawmaker Park Young-sun was elected floor leader, becoming the first female floor leader of a major political party in South Korea.

In the first floor leader election since the party's merger, four-term lawmaker Lee Jong-gul and three-term lawmakers Roh Young-min, Park Young-sun and Choi Jae-seong entered the race. Park won 69 votes in a run-off against Roh Young-min, who won 59 votes.

Park, with no clear affiliation to any faction, won the race on the back of support from first- and second-term lawmakers demanding a hardline stance against the ruling party, and the new mainstream faction headed by party co-chairs Kim Han-gil and Ahn Cheol-soo.

As the counterpart of Saenuri Party floor leader Lee Wan-koo, who was selected the same day, Park was assigned the task of leading negotiations for the determination of the truth behind the Sewol ferry disaster and measures to prevent its recurrence. She also became responsible for leading the party to victory in the June 4 local elections and July 30 parliamentary by-elections.

▪ June 4 Local Elections

The June 4 local elections determined the political fates of co-chairs Kim Han-gil and Ahn Cheol-soo. The party leadership, which had already faced backlash over its decision to reverse an earlier pledge not to field candidates for lower-level administration chiefs and councilors, vowed to win the local elections through a reformed nomination system.

It also launched a so-called "rainbow election campaign committee" made up of the two co-chairs and former presidential contenders, Moon Jae-in, Sohn Hak-kyu, Chung Sye-gyun, Chung Dong-yeong and Kim Doo-kwan.

However, controversy over the nomination system persisted during the primaries.

As a result, out of the 17 mayoral and gubernatorial seats up for grabs, NPAD won nine seats, including those for Seoul, Gwangju and the Chungcheong provinces.

By winning all four seats in the Chungcheong region -- Daejeon, Sejong, North Chungcheong Province and South Chungcheong Province -- the party secured a firm hold on the politically neutral region and gained one more seat than in the 2010 elections.

However, there were voices within the party that viewed the results as an "incomplete victory" as the party lost two of the three seats in the capital area, seen as the barometer of public sentiment, and failed to make the most of the public disillusionment with the ruling party following the ferry disaster.

■ Crushing Defeat in July 30 By-Elections

The July 30 by-elections, conducted in 15 districts nationwide, were viewed by both the ruling and opposition parties as a mini general election.

In the initial stages of the elections, there was confidence within and outside the party that it would win. A series of unsuccessful personnel nominations following the ferry disaster and the failure to arrest Yoo Byung-eun, a key suspect implicated in the ferry disaster, all seemed to work in favor of the opposition party.

However, the result was a shocking loss. Out of the 15 seats being contested, NPAD won only four seats in Gwangju, Suwon, and two electoral districts in South Jeolla Province.

In particular, it lost a seat in its stronghold South Jeolla to Lee Jung-hyun of the Saenuri Party, while former party leader and presidential aspirant Sohn Hak-kyu lost to the Saenuri Party's political novice Kim Yong-nam in Suwon.

The crushing defeat in the July 30 by-elections was attributed to the controversy over candidate nominations in the election process. After the elections, NPAD conceded defeat, saying it accepts the people's will with a heavy and humble heart.

The day after the elections, on July 31, co-leaders Kim Han-gil and Ahn Cheol-soo stepped down to take responsibility for the crushing defeat. Their resignations came only four months after they took office. On the same day, former chairman Sohn Hak-kyu, who had run for a seat in Suwon, announced his retirement from politics.

UNIFIED PROGRESSIVE PARTY

■ Dissolved 3 Years after Launch

The Unified Progressive Party disappeared into history three years after its launch following a Constitutional Court ruling on Dec. 19, 2014 that ordered its dissolution.

The UPP was launched in December 2011 through the merger of three parties but it faced continuous trouble, including a split over allegations of irregularities in the selection of proportional representatives in the 2012 general elections.

In August 2013, the party faced dissolution amid allegations that one of its lawmakers, Lee Seok-ki, plotted to overthrow the government in the event of war with North Korea.

The party was labeled as pro-North Korean following reports in the media that Lee led a clandestine group called the Revolutionary Organization, whose members spoke of guns.

NPAD and other opposition parties claimed they had no affiliation with a party that denied the Constitution, leaving the UPP surrounded by enemies on all sides.

The UPP fought to save the party amid an ongoing trial over Lee's case and the Constitutional Court's review of a petition for the UPP's dissolution, but no rally or legal struggle could block the party's disbandment.

■ UPP's Dissolution

On Nov. 5, 2013, the government passed during a Cabinet meeting a petition for a trial on the UPP's disbandment, citing the party's alleged violation of the Constitution.

In January 2014, UPP leader Lee Jung-hee had a fierce debate with Justice

Minister Hwang Kyo-ahn during the first public debate of the trial. In February, however, the Suwon District Court sentenced Lee Seok-ki to 12 years in prison on charges of plotting a rebellion and violating the National Security Act.

Faced with a looming a crisis, the UPP put in its best efforts to turn the situation around. In March, Lee Jung-hee proposed that North Korea express its condolences over the loss of lives in the sinking of the warship Cheonan in March 2010. North Korea has been accused of bringing down the ship with a torpedo attack. Other members of the party also tried to rid the party of its image as being pro-North.

In August, party members fasted for 10 days to urge legislation on the Sewol ferry disaster. Despite such efforts, public sentiment toward the party did not change, and the party made no remarkable achievement either in the June local elections or the July by-elections.

On Dec. 19, the Constitutional Court ordered the UPP's dissolution in a 8-1 vote, stripping all five UPP lawmakers of their seats in parliament. The UPP has been working to reunite its supporters ahead of the April 29 by-elections. Political circles expect the now-dissolved party to have an influence in the elections by splitting the opposition vote, if not by winning seats.

COURT

■ **"Emperor's Labor" Controversy Sets New Guidelines**

The nation's top court set up general guidelines in the current prison labor system on March 28 in response to criticism that a convicted property developer had exploited legal loopholes to dodge levied fines.

The Supreme Court established guidelines for determining the value of labor costs and sentences so that the daily cost of prison labor would not be fixed too high.

The controversy began when a district court in 2010 allowed Huh Jae-ho, the former chairman of the now-bankrupt Daeju Group convicted of embezzle-

ment and tax evasion, to pay off a 25.4 billion won fine with just 50 days of prison labor.

The decision valued the disgraced tycoon's daily labor, mainly manual work such as making tofu, at 500 million won, about 10,000 times higher than the usual pay of 50,000 won a day for other convicts.

Huh was released from a prison labor facility after the prosecution, in an unprecedented move, scrapped a 2010 court decision to give Huh the option of working off the 25.4 billion won (US$23.66 million) fine with just 50 days of prison labor.

Amid controversies, prosecutors overturned the court's decision and released him from the facility, vowing to levy the remaining 22.4 billion won in fines after deducting six days of prison labor.

Prosecutors and tax authorities also said they have begun tracking down Huh's assets, believed to be hidden in New Zealand where he had maintained an extravagant lifestyle as a fugitive.

Daeju, a business group based in Gwangju with 15 subsidiaries, collapsed in 2010 when its main construction arm went bankrupt due to a slump in the property market.

■ **Leftist Lawmaker Didn't Plot Rebellion but Encouraged It**

An appeals court on Aug. 11 commuted a leftist lawmaker's prison term to nine years for plotting an armed rebellion against the Seoul government in the event of an inter-Korean war.

Rep. Lee Seok-ki, affiliated with the minor opposition Unified Progressive Party (UPP), was indicted in September 2013 on charges of conspiring with members of a clandestine organization to topple the government if a war with North Korea broke out.

Overturning a lower court's verdict of a 12-year jail sentence, the Seoul High Court acquitted the 53-year-old UPP legislator of charges that he had plotted the rebellion and only found him guilty of instigating the members to stage the rebellion. The court also stripped the 53-year-old UPP legislator of his civic rights, such as suffrage, for seven years following his eventual release from prison.

Prosecutors allege that Lee discussed plans to blow up key infrastructure in South Korea, including communication lines and railways, with about 130 other members of the secret underground organization, Revolutionary Organization (RO), during late-night secret meetings in central Seoul in May 2013.

In the same ruling, the court also commuted the prison terms of all six other UPP members, including Hong Sun-seok, vice chairman of the UPP's Gyeonggi branch.

Past military-backed governments used insurgency charges to suppress political dissidents. However, there have been no indictments under similar charges in recent years since democratically elected leaders replaced the country's past military dictators.

In 1980, former South Korean President Kim Dae-jung, the winner of the 2000 Nobel Peace Prize, was put behind bars on the same charge but later was acquitted in a retrial.

In an unprecedented move, the government had filed a petition with the Constitutional Court calling for the disbandment of the UPP. The ruling was expected to be delivered by the end of the year.

On Aug. 22, the Seoul High Court, upholding a lower court ruling, also found Lee guilty of a separate charge of sympathizing with North Korea, in violation of the South's anti-communist National Security Law.

Enacted in 1948 to fight communism, the draconian security law bans any "anti-state" activities that attempt to praise, encourage or propagandize North Korean political ideals.

The lawmaker made remarks sympathetic to North Korea and sang North Korea's "revolutionary" propaganda songs before hundreds of members who attended the organization's meetings held between March and August of last year, court documents showed. Lee also possessed publications praising the communist regime.

Lee Seok-ki, a former student activist, was elected to the National Assembly as a proportional representative in the 2012 general elections.

■ Spy Agency Accused of Framing Defector as Spy

A Seoul court sentenced a mid-ranking state intelligence agent to two and a half years in prison on Oct. 28 for instructing other agents to forge documents to frame a North Korean defector as a spy.

The 48-year-old National Intelligence Service (NIS) agent, surnamed Kim, was convicted of instructing other agents to fabricate the Chinese immigration records of Yoo Woo-seong, a 34-year-old defector who was then an employee of the Seoul municipal government, to charge him with espionage.

The court also sentenced a 54-year-old ranking NIS official, surnamed Lee, to one and a half years in prison for colluding with Kim, while two other agents -- a mid-ranking official surnamed Kwon and Lee In-cheol, an official working as a South Korean consul in China -- were sentenced to one and one and a half years in jail with a two-year stay of execution, respectively.

Two Korean-Chinese collaborators received jail sentences of one year and two months, and eight months, respectively. The high-profile case began when Yoo was indicted on charges of espionage in early 2013. A local district court acquitted Yoo of the charges in August 2013, at which point allegations emerged that the NIS may have forged evidence to frame him.

■ Top Court Rejects Appeals for Tobacco Damages

The top court rejected the last legal appeals for ailing smokers seeking compensation from the nation's leading tobacco maker on April 10, saying there is no causal connection between smoking and lung cancer.

Upholding a lower court's ruling and ending a 15-year-long legal battle, the Supreme Court threw out two damages suits brought on by 30 lung cancer patients and their families against the government and KT&G Corp.

"Lung caner is not a disease solely caused by smoking, but a disease that is caused by a host of exterior reasons such as physical, biological and chemical factors," the court said in its ruling.

Seeking 474.7 million won (US$454,700)

in compensation, a total of 36 people initially launched the separate two suits in 1999, arguing that long-time smoking caused the fatal disease and that the company did not fulfill its duty of informing them of the dangers of smoking by concealing most of its manufacturing records.

Four patients have died and others have dropped out of the suits since the filing of the suit as the legal battle continued for more than a decade.

The manufacturer, meanwhile, refuted the causal relationship between smoking and the plaintiffs' disease, citing a lack of scientific evidence.

■ Top Court Says Night Rally not Crime

The nation's top court on July 10 overturned a lower court's conviction of a local civic activist for launching a rally at night and ordered a retrial.

The Supreme Court said the Daegu District Court should reconsider its guilty verdict against human rights activist Seo Chang-ho. It said the decision goes against the Constitutional Court's earlier ruling that a current law banning nighttime rallies is unconstitutional.

The Constitutional Court ruled in March that two clauses of the assembly law that ban holding rallies before sunrise or after sunset greatly infringe upon the right to freedom of assembly guaranteed by the Constitution. Sitting judges viewed the clause of "before sunrise or after sunset" as too vague and subject to interpretation.

Seo was found guilty of launching street rallies in the downtown area of the southern city of Daegu between 7:15 p.m and 9 p.m in September 2009 and ordered to pay a fine of 700,000 won (US$690).

■ Teachers' Union Maintains Legal Status but Awaits Constitutional Decision

Upholding a lower court ruling, a Seoul high court said on Sept. 19 that a progressive teachers' union, outlawed by the government, should be recognized as a legal trade union until it makes its decision on the matter.

In Oct. 2013, the government outlawed the Korean Teachers and Education Workers Union (KTU) due to its repeated refusal to deny membership to fired teachers. In a landmark ruling in June, the Seoul Administrative Court approved the decision, depriving the KTU of its 14-year-old status as a legal trade union.

Despite the government's decision, the union had maintained its legal status until the June ruling was made as it won an injunction against the government's move from the same court in November.

In September, the Seoul High Court upheld the injunction, ruling that the union's legal status should remain intact until its judge decides on the matter. The court also accepted a request from the union that the Constitutional Court review whether the law governing the status of teachers' unions based on which the labor ministry outlawed the KTU goes against the Constitution.

Article No. 2 of the law prevents dismissed teachers from being members of their trade union. The 60,000-strong KTU has as members dozens of teachers who were sacked for signing statements against the former Lee Myung-bak government in 2009.

■ Agency Accepts Multiple Answers for College Exam Questions

Educational authorities announced on Nov. 24 that they have decided to accept multiple answers for two disputed questions on the national college entrance exam for the 2015 school year, a decision that could change scores for thousands of students.

The chief of the Korea Institute for Curriculum and Evaluation (KICE) in charge of administering the nationwide test offered to resign to take responsibility for the flawed questions.

The exam, which is similar to the American Scholastic Aptitude Test (SAT), is considered to be a crucial factor in determining a student's future career opportunities as Korean society places great importance on educational background. It is only administered once a year.

The KICE unveiled the outcome of its discussion on the two questions from two different sections -- one from biology II and another from English language -- of the College Scholastic Aptitude Test (CAST). The KICE's Website was flooded with complaints from students questioning the accuracy of the two questions days after the exam on Nov. 13.

After hearing advice from relevant academic societies and having meetings with experts in and out of the agency, the agency said that it will recognize two out of five choices each from the two faulty questions.

According to local private institutions, the decision will likely raise the average score for biology by 1.3 points and the grades of 3,600-4,000 exam takers. More than 60% of the biology test takers selected the disputed second answer while only 10 to 12% chose the correct answer initially presented by the KICE, they said.

Some 640,000 high school seniors and graduates took the nine-hour standardized CSAT that was administrated at 1,216 testing sites across the country.

■ Lawmakers Mired in Graft Cases

A Seoul court sentenced an incumbent opposition lawmaker on Jan. 15, 2015 to three years in prison for taking bribes in exchange for favors.

Rep. Kim Jae-yun of the main opposition New Politics Alliance for Democracy was found guilty of taking 48 million won (US$44,000) in cash and gift certificates from a local vocational training school in return for helping pass a bill in favor of the school.

The passage of the bill to revise the vocational education law in April helped change the name and upgrade the status of what is now known as Seoul Art College. Kim will lose his legislative seat if the sentence is upheld through the Supreme Court.

A former aide to an opposition lawmaker, meanwhile, was arrested to face questioning over allegations that he had been involved in the legislator's creation of illegal political funds.

Rep. Shin Hak-yong of the main opposition New Politics Alliance for Democracy (NPAD) is under suspicion of taking illegal funds worth tens of millions of won (tens of thousands of U.S. dollars) from his political aides in exchange for spots on the party's proportional representation ticket, prosecutors said.

A ruling party lawmaker received a jail sentence for taking bribes from a railway parts supplier in exchange for business favors.

The Seoul Central District Court handed down a four-year jail term and a fine of 70 million won (US$64,060) to Rep. Song Kwang-ho of the Saenuri Party and ordered him to pay 65 million won in restitution for the crime. He would be stripped of his parliamentary seat if the sentence is confirmed through the top court.

Another ruling Saenuri Party lawmaker was sentenced to five years in jail for taking bribes from a railway parts supplier in exchange for business favors.

Rep. Cho Hyun-ryong was indicted on charges of taking 160 million won (US$146,000) from the head of Sampyo E&C from December 2011 to July 2014.

Prosecutors said the 70-year-old helped one of Sampyo's products pass a qualification test and landed the company a deal with the state railway authority, which Cho headed until December 2011. The Seoul Central District Court found Cho guilty of the charges, citing convincing testimony from Sampyo officials.

■ Japanese Reporter Accused of Defaming Park

South Korea's prosecutors indicted a Japanese reporter from a conservative Tokyo newspaper without detention on Oct. 3 on charges of damaging President Park Geun-hye's reputation for raising questions about her whereabouts on the day of April's deadly ferry sinking.

Tatsuya Kato, head of the Seoul bureau of Japan's Sankei Shimbun newspaper, was indicted on defamation charges for reporting that Park and an unidentified man had an alleged secret meeting on the day of the ferry disaster, citing rumors circulated in Korea's financial community.

In August, the Sankei Shimbun cited a column carried by the Chosun Ilbo in mid-July, in which South Korea's largest-circulation newspaper said Park's whereabouts were unknown for seven hours, a development it said caused rumors that she met a man at an undisclosed location.

A local civic group filed a complaint against Kato and prosecutors have summoned him three times for questioning, concluding that the newspaper's move to raise questions about Park's whereabouts are groundless.

The presidential office refuted the newspaper's claim, saying that Park "was inside the presidential compound."

■ Lower Courts Hand down Sentences for Ferry Tragedy Contributors

A district court on Nov. 11 sentenced the captain of the sunken ferry Sewol to 36 years in prison in November for abandoning passengers at the time of the deadly sinking.

▲ *Lee Joon-seok, the captain of the sunken ferry Sewol, stands during a trial at Gwangju District Court in Gwangju, South Jeolla Province, on Nov. 11. The court sentenced him to 36 years in prison for abandoning passengers. Lee, however, was acquitted of murder charges, although he left the passengers behind while he was the first to be rescued when the ship was sinking off South Korea's southern coast on April 16, leaving 295 people dead and nine others missing. The court also delivered prison terms ranging from 5 to 30 years for 14 other crew members.*

Lee Joon-seok, however, was acquitted of charges that he murdered 304 passengers as he left them behind while he was the first to be rescued when the ill-fated ship was sinking off South Korea's southern coast on April 16.

The Gwangju District Court in this southern city convicted the 68-year-old skipper of gross negligence and dereliction of duty, including abandoning his ship while the passengers, most of them high school students on a school trip, remained trapped inside the ship.

Prosecutors, who had earlier sought the death penalty against Lee, said they would immediately appeal the verdict. In the same ruling, the Gwangju District Court sentenced the ship's chief engineer, only identified by his surname Park, to 30 years in prison, convicting him of murder.

Prison terms ranging from five years to 20 years were delivered to 13 other crew members, including the first engineer surnamed Sohn, who have been charged with abandonment and violation of a ship safety act.

The ruling came just hours after the government terminated the nearly seven-month search for the sunken vessel, with nine passengers still unaccounted for, citing the collapsing interior and worsening sea conditions.

A district court also sentenced the wife of the late shipping tycoon blamed for April's ferry disaster to one and a half years in prison with a two-year stay of execution.

Kwon Yun-ja -- the wife of Yoo Byung-eun, the late 73-year-old religious figure and ex-convict whose family owns ferry operator Chonghaejin Marine Co. -- was indicted on charges of embezzling funds from the religious sect in which the owner family remains as an influential member.

Prosecutors allege that Kwon helped her younger brother, Kwon Oh-kyun, funnel funds worth nearly 30 billion won into his business after taking out loans using collateral assets belonging to the Evangelical Baptist Church in 2010.

The Incheon District Court also handed a five-year prison term for the younger Kwon. The eldest son of the late shipping tycoon blamed for April's ferry disaster was sentenced to three years in prison for embezzlement.

Yoo Dae-kyun, 44, the son of Yoo Byung-eun, was convicted of misappropriating 7.39 billion won (US$7.28 million) from the ferry Sewol operator Cheonghaejin Marine Co. and six other affiliates between May 2002 and December 2013.

Law enforcement authorities had sought Yoo Byung-eun and Dae-kyun, believing that their alleged corruption may have contributed to the April 16 disaster that left more than 300 people, mostly high school students, dead or missing.

The younger Yoo was arrested at a hideout in a town just outside Seoul together with Park Soo-kyung, a 34-year-old female bodyguard, on Jul. 25, three days after the discovery of his father's badly decomposed body.

The 6,825-ton ferry Sewol sank in waters near the southwestern port of Jindo en route to the southern resort island of Jeju. A total of 295 people, mostly teenage students on a field trip, have been confirmed dead, with nine remaining unaccounted for.

■ **Ex-Spymaster Guilty of Violating Election Laws**

Upholding a lower court ruling, a Seoul appeals court on June 5 acquitted a former Seoul police chief of charges that he impeded a police probe into a high-profile election-meddling scandal.

The scandal centers around allegations that the nation's intelligence agency meddled in the 2012 presidential election by swaying public opinion in favor of President Park Geun-hye, the then ruling party candidate.

The Seoul High Court delivered a not-guilty verdict to Kim Yong-pan, the former chief of the Seoul Metropolitan Police Agency (SMPA), citing a lack of evidence and the credibility of the testimony from a key witness.

Kim was indicted on charges of abusing his authority to cover up the case by deliberately hiding key evidence alleging that the National Intelligence Service (NIS) systematically intervened in the presidential election.

Meanwhile, a Seoul district court sentenced a former government intelligence chief to two years and six months in prison for spearheading an online smear campaign in favor of President Park Geun-hye, then ruling party candidate, ahead of the 2012 presidential election, but stayed the sentence for four years.

Won Sei-hoon, former director of the National Intelligence Service (NIS), was found guilty of ordering agents to post politically sensitive comments not only on major Internet bulletin boards but also on Twitter, with NIS agents posting and retweeting a total of 780,000 messages, in violation of the law governing the status of NIS officials. The law strictly prohibits NIS officials from intervening in domestic politics.

The court, however, acquitted Won of violating the Public Official Election Act, which bans public officials from intervening in local elections by abusing their status. The court ruled that Won did not give orders that directly aimed to have specific candidates elected or not. Won, a close aide to then-President Lee Myung-bak, had headed the NIS for about four years until early 2013.

CONSTITUTIONAL COURT

■ **Jurisdiction and Organization**

The Constitutional Court of Korea is an independent and specialized court in South Korea, whose primary role is the reviewing of constitutionality under the Constitution of the Republic of Korea. It has jurisdiction over impeachment, dissolution of a political party, competence dispute between state agencies, between a state agency and a local government, between local governments and constitutional complaints.

The Constitutional Court consists of nine Justices. The Justices are appointed by the President of the Republic. Among the Justices, three are elected by the National Assembly, and three are designated by the Chief Justice of the Supreme Court.

The President of the Republic, with the consent of the National Assembly, appoint the President of the Constitutional Court among the Justices. The term of Justices is six years and may be renewed.

The presiding Justice of the Full Bench is the President of the Constitutional Court. The Full Bench reviews a case by and with the attendance of seven or more Justices. The Full Bench makes a decision on a case by the majority vote of Justices participating in the final discussion.

It requires a vote of six or more Justices when it makes a decision of upholding on the constitutionality of statutes, impeachment, dissolution of a political party or constitutional complaint; and when it overrules the precedent on interpretation and application of the Constitution or laws made by the Constitutional Court.

- **Major Decisions in 2014**

Parties with no seat may stay The Constitutional Court said on Jan. 28 that an article in the Political Party Law that prohibits parties without parliamentary seats is unconstitutional.

Article 44 Section 1 Clause 8 of the Political Party Law had banned parties that garnered less than 2% of the vote in the general election. Article 41 Section 4 had also prohibited parties from using their previous names in the upcoming general election.

The Constitutional Court, however, said Article 44 violated the principle of minimal intervention. It is unfair if the parties that reaped promising results at regional or presidential elections are dissolved because of the outcome of a general election, the court ruled.

The Green Party Korea and other minor parties had filed a constitutional appeal during their dissolution trials at the Seoul Administration Court. These parties were able to keep their names for the June 4 regional election.

Voting rights may be maintained during probation The Constitutional Court ruled unanimously on Jan. 28 that an article in the Public Official Election Act, which bans people from voting during probation, is unconstitutional. A man, surnamed Ku, had filed a constitutional appeal, saying Article 18 Section 1 Clause 2 of the law violates rights to happiness and equality.

The court said restricting voting rights for all convicted criminals regardless of the gravity of their crimes violated the principle of minimal intervention. The ruling allowed more than 110,000 on probation to vote for the June 4 regional election.

Mandatory military service for men 'constitutional' The Constitutional Court unanimously ruled on March 10 that an article in the military service law that mandates only men to service in the military is constitutional.

Article 3 Section 1 of the law says all able-bodied men in South Korea must serve military duty. In 2011, a 22-year-old man, surnamed Lee, filed a constitutional appeal against the article, saying he was losing a crucial time in his life that he can use to get a job.

The court, however, said men are more physically suitable for combat, and even women who have stellar stamina may not be able to fully commit themselves to military duty due to pregnancy, birth or other physiological traits unique to women.

The court had previously ruled similarly twice before -- in November 2010 and June 2011. In both instances, at least one justice delivered an opinion of unconstitutionality. None did in 2014, however.

Overnight rally partially allowed The Constitutional Court on March 27 ruled by a 6-3 majority that an article that bans protests between sunset and midnight is partially unconstitutional. Six said Article 10 and 23 of the protest law were partially unconstitutional, while three said it were wholly unconstitutional.

The court said Article 23, which penalizes those who hold protests between dusk and midnight, is unconstitutional. The reason was the article practically excluded workers and students' participation.

Still, the court said whether the law should ban rallies after midnight is a question that should be left to the citizens' sentiment and the decision of lawmakers, justifying the "partially constitutional" opinion.

Gov't workers, teachers banned from political activities The Constitutional Court ruled on March 27 that articles in the Political Party Law and the National Public Service Law that ban civil servants and teachers from political activities is constitutional.

Article 22 of the Political Party Law and Article 65 of the National Public Service Law state that civil servants and elementary and middle school teachers shall not be part of a political party.

Violators of the Political Party Law article are punishable by up to one year in prison or a maximum fine of 1 million won. Those who offend the National Public Service Law article may face up to a year in prison or a maximum fine of 3 million won.

In a 5-4 majority, the court said the articles did not violate the principle of minimal violation because they maintain the political neutrality of civil servants and teachers.

Late-night gaming banned for teenagers The Constitutional Court said on April 24 that an article that bans adolescents below 16 from playing online games late at night is constitutional.

Article 26 Section 1 of the Juvenile Protection Act prohibits online game providers from allowing teenagers to play between midnight and 6 a.m. Article 59 Section 1 of the same act subjects violators to up to two years in prison or a maximum fine of 10 million won.

In a 7-2 opinion, the court said the articles served their legislative purposes of promoting healthy development of teenagers and preventing them from game addictions, Two justices, however, said the articles were unconstitutional because they harmed autonomy and diversity of people.

Full-time union members should not be paid for regular work The Constitutional Court said on May 29 that an article that only allows full-time union members to be paid for union activities and not their regular jobs is constitutional.

Article 24 Section 2 of the Labor Union Law states that full-time union members should not be paid for work. Article 11 Section 2 of the same law, however, allows a limited number of union members payment based on the scale of the union and the nature of their role within it.

In a 9-0 decision, the court said the articles served their legislative purposes because they allowed each union autonomy and independence.

South Korea adopted the so-called "Time-Off" system, which allows labor unions to pay full-time members in 2010. The purpose was to prevent union activities from contracting because the management is not obligated to pay full-time union members.

Prisoners on trial may participate in religions congregations The Constitutional Court ruled unanimously on June 26 that prohibiting prisoners on trial from joining religious congregations is unconstitutional.

A man, surnamed Kim, who was detained in a Busan detention center on violence charges had filed a constitutional appeal after the center banned him from holding a religious service inside.

The court said religious activities "contribute to order within detention centers" and called on authorities to provide not only the convicted but also prisoners on trial a chance to hold religious services.

DNA collection of sex offenders constitutional The Constitutional Court ruled on Aug. 28 that an article that allows authorities to collect DNA samples of suspected sex offenders for the purpose of preventing the crime is constitutional.

The article was enacted in January 2010 and was put into effect in July that year. Article 5 of the DNA Identification Law says authorities may collect DNA samples of suspects of 11 violent crimes including murder, robbery, rape and violence. Article 2 of the law allows authorities to collect samples of convicted prisoners.

In a 5-4 decision, the court said it was appropriate to collect samples of suspects who commit crimes that have a high risk of recidivism. Regarding Article 2, the court said the common good outweighed the costs the article would inflict on the suspect.

Smoking ban in internet cafes constitutional The Constitutional Court said on Sept. 25 that an article that bans smoking at Internet cafes is constitutional. Article 9 Section 4 Clause 23 of the National Health Promotion Act says Internet cafes should be no-smoking.

A man, surnamed Jin, had filed a constitutional appeal, saying the article violated the rights to pursuit of happiness, privacy and equality. The court said the article was legislated to promote the health of citizens by preventing secondhand smoking and reducing the number of smokers.

■ First Court-Ordered Dissolution of Party

The Constitutional Court on Dec. 19 ordered the dissolution of a pro-North

Korean minor opposition party, outlawing a political party here for the first time since the country adopted its first constitution in 1948. The 8-1 ruling effectively spelled the immediate demise of the Unified Progressive Party (UPP) created in 2011.

All five sitting lawmakers of the party also lost their seats, with by-elections slated for April 2015. The establishment of an alternative party with similar policies is also prohibited. The party has been forced to forfeit all state subsidies and its assets have been frozen, according to the National Election Commission.

"The genuine goal and the activities of the UPP are to achieve progressive democracy and to finally adopt North Korea-style socialism," chief justice Park Han-cheol said, reading out the landmark ruling that was broadcast live on television.

He said the court came to the conclusion that the UPP's principles and activities were in violation of the "basic democratic order" stipulated by the Constitution of South Korea, which remains technically at war with North Korea. No political party has been banned by a court decision in the nation's modern history.

Constitutional Court Hosts 3rd World Congress

The Constitutional Court hosted the 3rd Congress of the World Conference on Constitutional Justice from Sept. 28 to Oct. 1.

The event, being the first gathering since the World Conference became a permanent body with the entry into force of its statute, was attended by the heads of constitutional courts, supreme courts, constitutional councils and representatives of international organizations from almost 100 countries.

The main topic, "Constitutional Justice and Social Integration", was divided into five sub-topics and was discussed in five plenary sessions.

The participants of the Congress adopted the Seoul Communique as an outcome document summarizing the results of the two-day sessions, which also contains the proposal of Chief Justice Park Han-chul to promote discussions on international cooperation in human rights, including the possibility of establishing a human rights court in Asia.

Decisions Expected in 2015

The Constitutional Court is expected to rule on the constitutionality of a decades-old anti-adultery law in 2015. South Korea has been one of the few remaining countries in Asia that prohibits infidelity, next to North Korea and Taiwan. Extramarital affairs here had been banned under the criminal law since 1953, and before that, only women were held accountable for extramarital affairs.

Sentences have been relatively heavy, with jail time ranging up to two years being the only fate a cheater and the affair partner could face. In Taiwan, the sentences range up to just one year in prison.

Previously, the court had turned down petitions to repeal the law four times from 1990 to 2008. In 2008, however, the judges supporting personal freedom became a majority, but were only one vote shy of realizing a change.

Some 100,000 South Koreans have been convicted of adultery since 1953. But the conviction rate dwindled from two-thirds between 1985 and now, to below 1% between late 2008 and early this year. The Constitutional Court, meanwhile, is also expected to deliberate on the constitutionality of a law banning sex trafficking in 2015.

In South Korea, both buying and selling sex are offenses punishable by up to a year in prison or a maximum fine of 3 million won. In Germany and the Netherlands, however, prostitution is legal as long as it is for one's livelihood.

A 44-year-old woman accused of sex trafficking in 2012 for what she claims was for a living had filed a petition with the court, questioning the constitutionality of the current law.

The sex trafficking law in South Korea was first legislated in 2004, after fires in the red light district in Gunsan, 274 km south of Seoul, in 2000 and 2002, revealed the poor conditions in which prostitutes worked.

NATIONAL ELEC-
TION COMMISSION

▪ Overview

The National Election Commission (NEC) was established based on the self-examination of the illegal election held on March 15, 1960 and became a constitutional agency following the enactment of the Fifth Constitutional Amendment during the Third Republic of Korea.

The term and status of each Election Commissioner is strictly guaranteed as prescribed by the Constitution and Act to ensure fair execution of duties without any external interference or being affected.

The Election Commission has a four-stage organizational structure, consisting of the National Election Commission, 17 Si/Do election commissions, 250 Gu/Si/Gun election commissions and 3,481 Eup/Myeon/Dong election commissions.

Overseas Voting Committee is temporarily established at overseas embassies for the presidential election and the National Assembly elections to be conducted following the termination of office.

▪ Organization

The National Election Commission is an independent constitutional agency composed of nine members. Three members are appointed by the president, three elected by the National Assembly and three nominated by the Chief Justice of the Supreme Court.

The Chairperson and the Standing Commissioner are elected from among the Commissioners and as is its custom, the Justice of the Supreme Court is elected to be the Chairperson.

The Standing Commissioner of State Minister level is a full-time position unlike the Chairperson, supports the Chairperson and oversees the Secretariat as directed by the Chairperson. Six-year term of office is guaranteed by the constitution.

The Secretariat, the Internet Election News Deliberation Commission and the Election Debate Broadcasting Commission are the NEC's affiliated institutions.

The term of office of the members of the Commission shall be six years.

No member of the Commission shall be expelled from office except by impeachment or a sentence of imprisonment without prison labor or heavier punishment.

The members of the Commission shall not join political parties, nor shall they participate in political activities. The Commissioners endorsed by the National Assembly shall have a social position of that of general Commissioners.

▪ Key Responsibilities

In accordance with Article 114 of the Constitution, the Election Commission was established as an independent constitutional agency compatible with the National Assembly, the government, courts and the Constitutional Court of Korea for the purpose of managing elections and national referendums fairly and dealing with administrative affairs concerning political parties and political funds.

In 2014, it managed the sixth regional elections and the July 30 by-elections. The ruling Saenuri Party won eight of the 17 key races for big-city mayors and provincial governors, while the main opposition New Politics Alliance for Democracy (NPAD) won the other nine races, including Seoul mayorship, according to the National Election Commission.

As the first nationwide elections under Park, the polls were seen as a test of public support for the conservative administration that has drawn heavy fire for its botched handling of the sinking of the ferry Sewol in April that claimed the lives of more than 300 people.

Despite the widespread criticism of the government, however, the results were not as lopsided in favor of the opposition as had been expected. Regionalism demonstrated its power in this week's elections again, with the ruling and opposition parties sweeping races in their home turf regions.

According to the election watchdog, the ruling party won races for mayors of Busan, Daegu, Incheon and Ulsan, and governors of Gyeonggi Province, North Gyeongsang and South Gyeongsang provinces and the island of Jeju. The main opposition NPAD won contests for mayors of Seoul, Gwangju, Daejeon and Sejong, and governors of Gangwon Province, North Chungcheong and South Chungcheong provinces and North and South Jeolla provinces, according to the results.

Also elected in the June votes were regional education chiefs. Though the candidates ran without party affiliations, liberal and opposition-leaning contestants clinched victories in 13 out of the 17 races, a result seen as reflecting parents' anger at the ferry disaster that claimed the lives of hundreds of high school students.

One of the most-watched contests was the race for Seoul mayor. Current Mayor Park Won-soon of NPAD won re-election after beating Chung Mong-joon of the ruling party. Park thanked Seoul's citizens for their support, vowing to work together with all citizens including those who didn't vote for him.

The Seoul mayorship carries extra weight in South Korean politics as it is often deemed a stepping stone to the presidency. Former Seoul Mayor Lee Myung-bak was elected president in 2007, running on his accomplishments as the top administrator of the city.

In the run-up to the votes, opposition parties called for judgment on the incumbent administration, saying the government failed to protect the lives of the public, while the ruling party campaigned on a promise to fix the social abnormalities revealed through the ferry tragedy.

Analysts had offered the view that the older and more conservative generations, who traditionally support the ruling party, would come out of their "covers" after having kept a low profile during the mourning period that followed the tragedy. The effect of the elections on the political landscape remains to be seen.

Some offered the view that the Park administration would regain confidence to push forward major policies. The president could also limit the scope of a planned government reshuffle to just the prime minister and several other Cabinet members, and retain her chief of staff, Kim Ki-choon, and other key presidential staff despite earlier calls for their dismissal.

South Korean presidents have often used government shakeups as a key political tool to overcome trouble and start anew as such reorganizations are taken as an acknowledgment of fault and an expression of commitment to work harder with a new lineup.

Voter turnout in June's local elections reached a provisional 56.8%, according to a preliminary count by the election watchdog. The turnout was the highest for nationwide local elections since the first such polls in 1995 when it reached 68.4%.

Economy

Yonhap News Agency

ECONOMIC TREND

■ **Overview**

In 2014, South Korea was hit hard by the shock of the Sewol ferry sinking and a slower-than-expected pace of global economic recovery.

The government's action to front-load spending in the first half and implement expansionary fiscal policies helped keep alive modest growth momentum and permitted Asia's fourth-largest economy to pull off 3.3% growth. This growth was helped to some extent by the lowering of interest by the Bank of Korea.

On the external front, the United States started showing clear signs of recovery that helped exports, but such developments were tempered by sluggish economic conditions in the European Union (EU), China and Japan.

Last year, South Korea's economy clearly showed that it was different from developing countries by attracting a steady inflow of foreign funds after the U.S. Federal Reserve's decision to scale back its bond-buying monetary easing program. The Korean won also appreciated against the U.S. dollar, which was not the case with other currencies.

In addition, despite adverse conditions, South Korean export volume broke new records, with outbound shipments totaling US$560 billion, and the country's current account surplus hitting an unprecedented US$89 billion.

The country's consumer prices moved up 1.3% with weak international crude oil prices helping stabilize inflation.

In regards to the job market front, the government's goal of attaining a 70% employment rate as well as providing more opportunities to young people and women resulted in 533,000 new positions being created for the whole of the year. This is the highest increase since 2002, with employment rates hitting a high of 65.3%.

In the realm of finance, the weak Japanese yen and concerns triggered by the rolling back of the quantitative easing program raised uncertainty and coupled with a relatively poor showing by local companies there was a general offloading of local stocks by foreign investors that caused the bourse to backtrack.

The fall in stock prices toward the end of the year came after the benchmark KOSPI started the year weak, then rebounded after the new economic team led by Finance Minister Choi Kyung-hwan announced a string of economic revitalization measures in July, which caused the index to peak at 2,082 points on July 30. The KOSPI ended the year at 1,915.

The drop came after the Bank of Korea (BOK) lowered key rates twice, in August and October, after measures taken by the government failed to properly revive growth.

▪ Economic Growth

In 2013, South Korea managed to pull off 3% growth. After hitting bottom in the first quarter, numbers started accelerating throughout the year, hitting 3.7% in the October-December period. Such growth was on par with numbers reached before the global financial crisis and raised hopes that the country was on track to a full recovery.

Another sign that fueled confidence was the fact that the "flow of growth" was very stable from quarter to quarter, with numbers closing the gap with global figures. In 2013, South Korea's national growth was on par with the rest of the world, which not the case in 2012, when the country's economy grew just 2.3%, vis-a-vis 3.1% for the global community as a whole.

By industry, construction slowed down, amid sluggish domestic housing demand, with the slack being taken up by manufacturing, which grew steadily throughout the year. Domestic consumption overtook exports as the largest contributing factor to growth during the year, the first since 2011. The service sector also managed to expand at a good pace.

Such trends remained unchanged coming into 2014, but the advent of the Sewol ferry disaster poured cold water on progress with consumption nose-diving in the second quarter of last year. The country experienced a slight rebound over the summer months, but this was short-lived as weak sales of mobile phones in the fourth quarter again caused a tapering of growth.

On the plus side, compared to 2013, demand for new homes triggered a spike in the number of people buying real estate, which boosted investment in the construction sector. The gains, however, were weakened as less money invested in social overhead capital projects restricted growth, with investment growth hitting just 1.1%.

Facility investment, another measure of economic health, expanded 5.9% on-year from -1.5% in 2013. A rise in exports and money poured into the automobile industry and transportation equipment helped spur growth.

▪ Exports

The steady pace of global economic recovery played a part in stimulating demand that bolstered South Korea's exports. The country, which posted two-way trade in excess of US$1 trillion for the first time in 2011, was able to maintain this volume for the fourth consecutive year in 2014, while also managing to post the largest current account surplus in its history.

Last year's data then showed more and more small and medium enterprises (SMEs) exporting more and diverse goods abroad. In addition, the country was shipping products to a wider range of countries, which can better insulate South Korea in the event that one or more of its major trading partners suffered a setback.

Semiconductors, mobiles phones and other information technology (IT) products led growth, along with certain steel goods. Toward the end of the year, ships contributed to export growth. By region, outbound shipments to the United States grew 13.3% on-year, while exports to China, its No. 1 trading partner, contracted 0.4%.

Numbers for the European Union advanced 5.7% for the whole year, although in the fourth quarter alone, it contracted 4.1%. Exports to Japan contracted for the third year in a row as the weak yen hurt that country's purchasing power and made South Korean products more expensive. In 2014, exports to Japan dropped 7.2% on-year.

Imports, notwithstanding weak global crude oil prices, grew for the first time in three years. Inbound shipments expanded 1.9% on-year in 2014.

■ **Employment**

South Korea's job market rebounded gradually throughout the year with more people becoming economically active. The number of new positions added to the workforce reached the highest level since 2002. Demographically, people in their 50s and women contributed to more people getting

hired. In addition, the number of youths entering the workforce grew for the first time since 2000.

In terms of quality of work, there was a steady increase in full-time workers, while the percentage of non-regular workers declined. On the downside, growth in the wholesale and retail sectors as well as the hospitality sector and service industries caused a rise in the number of temporary positions.

The employment rate hit 60.2% last year, up 0.7%p from 2013, with the numbers for people between 15 and

Summary Table of Economically Active Population

yoy, Unit : 1,000 persons, %, %p

	2012	2013	Changes	Percentage change	2014	Changes	Percentage change
Population 15 years and over	41,582	42,096	514	1.2	42,513	417	1.0
Economically active population	25,501	25,873	373	1.5	26,536	663	2.6
(Participation rate)	(61.3)	(61.5)	(0.2p)		(62.4)	(0.9p)	
Male	14,891	15,071	180	1.2	15,387	315	2.1
(Participation rate)	(73.3)	(73.2)	(-0.1p)		(74.0)	(0.8p)	
Female	10,609	10,802	193	1.8	11,149	347	3.2
(Participation rate)	(49.9)	(50.2)	(0.3p)		(51.3)	(1.1p)	
Employed persons	24,681	25,066	386	1.6	25,599	533	2.1
Employment/ population ratio	59.4	59.5	0.1p		60.2	0.7p	
Employment/ population ratio in 15 ~ 64 Years old	64.2	64.4	0.2p		65.3	0.9p	
Agriculture, forestry & fishing	1,528	1,520	-8	-0.5	1,452	-68	-4.5
Mining & manufacturing	4,120	4,200	80	1.9	4,343	143	3.4
Manufacturing	4,105	4,184	79	1.9	4,330	146	3.5
Construction	1,773	1,754	-19	-1.1	1,796	42	2.4
Wholesale & retail trade	5,595	5,630	35	0.6	5,889	259	4.6
Electricity, transport, telecom & finance	2,997	3,059	62	2.1	3,041	-18	-0.6
Business, personal, public service & others	8,668	8,903	235	2.7	9,079	176	2.0
Regular employees	11,097	11,713	615	5.5	12,156	443	3.8
Temporary employees	4,988	4,892	-96	-1.9	5,032	140	2.9
Daily workers	1,627	1,590	-37	-2.3	1,555	-35	-2.2
Independent businessman	5,718	5,651	-67	-1.2	5,652	1	0.0
Unpaid family workers	1,251	1,221	-30	-2.4	1,205	-16	-1.3
Unemployed persons	820	807	-13	-1.6	937	130	16.1
Unemployment rate	3.2	3.1	-0.1p		3.5	0.4p	
Male	504	498	-6	-1.2	548	50	9.9
(Unemployment rate)	(3.4)	(3.3)	(-0.1p)		(3.6)	(0.3p)	
Female	316	309	-7	-2.2	389	80	26.0
(Unemployment rate)	(3.0)	(2.9)	(-0.1p)		(3.5)	(0.6p)	
Not a high school graduate	126	105	-21	-16.7	118	13	12.7
(Unemployment rate)	(2.5)	(2.2)	(-0.3p)		(2.6)	(0.4p)	
High school graduate	359	347	-12	-3.3	416	69	19.9
(Unemployment rate)	(3.6)	(3.4)	(-0.2p)		(4.0)	(0.6p)	
Bachelor's degree or more	335	355	-20	5.9	402	47	13.3
(Unemployment rate)	(3.2)	(3.3)	(0.1p)		(3.5)	(0.2p)	
Economically inactive population	16,081	16,223	141	0.9	15,977	-246	-1.5

64 hitting 65.3%, for a gain of 0.9%p. There were a total of 2.56 million people employed last year with manufacturing, healthcare, social services, retail and hospitality sectors contributed the most to the increase.

Unemployment stood at 3.5%, a 0.4%p gain from the year before with the number of people out of work hitting 937,000, an increase of 130,000. The government said the rise in jobless figures came as more people taking advantage of growth sought jobs.

Going into details, the number of full-time workers grew by 443,000 last year, with the number of temporary posts rising by 140,000. The number of daily or hourly workers decreased by 35,000, with the number of non-wage workers and those working for free at family-run stores growing.

Official data said the number of people who were classified as economically inactive in 2014 dropped by 246,000. This is the sharpest drop since the government started compiling data. The largest number of people who dropped out of the workforce who were inactive economically were homemakers, followed by those that simply did not want a job and those that have been trying to find work in the past but were unable to do so for various reasons.

In addition, the number of people who gave up trying to find work reached 394,000. This is a sharp increase compared to 172,000 tallied for 2013, but the change is partly due to the way the government calculated data last year.

■ **Consumer Prices**

Consumer prices grew just 1.3% throughout the year, helped by stable farm and crude oil prices. Not calculating volatile food and energy prices, the country's core inflation reached 2%, with the cost of basic necessities index edging up 0.8%.

■ **The Balance of Payment and Trade**

In 2014, South Korea's current account surplus improved markedly over the year before, despite a spike in the service sector deficit. The country's balance of goods account also improved, thanks to a rise in exports and a decline in imports.

The service sector account remained firmly in the red, with transportation and construction-related deficits compounding the imbalance.

Current account(Yearly)   *Unit : 100 million US$*

	2009	2010	2011	2012	2013	2014
Current account	335.9	288.5	186.6	508.4	811.5	892.2
Goods	478.1	479.2	290.9	494.1	827.8	926.9
Services	-95.9	-142.4	-122.8	-52.1	-65.0	-81.6
Primary income	-24.4	4.9	65.6	121.2	90.6	102.0
Secondary income	-21.9	-53.2	-47.2	-54.7	-41.9	-55.0

On the financial front, outbound assets eclipsed inbound funds by US$90.39 billion, an increase of US$10.26 billion compared to the year before. The increase was mainly due to money going abroad in the form of foreign direct investment and to purchase shares.

Product exports, helped by solid demand for goods from the United States and the EU, grew 2.3% on-year to reach more than US$572.6 billion last year. Imports grew 1.9% to US$525.5 billion to allow the country to enjoy a surplus of US$47.2 billion.

Summary of Exports and Imports

Unit : 100 million US$, %

	Amount(rate of increase)			
	2011	2012	2013	2014
Exports	5,552	5,479	5,596	5,727 (2.3)
Imports	5,244	5,196	5,156	5,255 (1.9)
Balance of trade	308	283	441	472

Yearly Average CPI by Specialized Classification

Unit : % (2010=100)

	Items	Weight	growth rate						
			2008	2009	2010	2011	2012	2013	2014
Living necessaries	142	555.7	5.3	2.1	3.4	4.4	1.7	0.7	0.8
Foods	78	167.3	4.7	5.8	4.8	6.3	2.4	0.8	0.5
Excluding foods	64	388.4	5.6	0.4	2.7	3.5	1.5	0.7	1.0
Excluding agricultural products & oils	429	891.6	4.3	3.6	1.8	3.2	1.6	1.6	2.0
Fresh foods	51	40.7	-5.8	7.6	21.3	6.3	5.8	-1.3	-9.3

Outbound shipments were led by semiconductors, steel and ships, while further growth was tempered by the poor showing for refined petroleum goods and petrochemicals.

Exports to the United States and the EU grew, with the number of ships for China, Japan and Latin American countries declining.

Data showed that exports to the United States grew 13.3%, with numbers for the EU gaining 5.7%. On the other hand, a slowdown in growth for China caused exports to dip 0.4% on-year, with shipments to Japan contracting 7.2%.

In regards to imports, the purchase of capital and consumer goods increased last year, but commodities contracted sharply as international crude oil prices fell throughout the year. As a result, the country reported record high trade volume, export and surplus numbers last year.

▪ Financial Market

In the first half of 2014, South Korea's financial market fluctuated after fallout from the U.S.'s decision to scale back its quantitative easing programs and heightened geopolitical risks abroad. Coming into the second half, the market took a further beating from the net selling of shares by foreign investors and poor earnings reports filed by local companies.

The country's bourse hit bottom in February, then rebounded in July, as the government released a host of economic revitalization measures. The KOSPI lost steam again toward the end of the year on disappointing corporate turnouts, with the main index ending the year at 1,915 points, down from a year earlier.

The country's interest rates had been falling steadily throughout the year, with rates falling in the second half as the impact of the Sewol ferry sinking delayed a recovery. The BOK's decision to lower rates in August and then again in October further accelerated the drop in rates.

The country's foreign exchange rates were affected by policy measures taken by large economies with the won appreciating against the U.S. dollar in the first half. It traded at 1,008.9 won to the dollar on July 7. In the second half, the Fed's move to scale back its bond-purchasing program caused the dollar to appreciate,

with the Korean currency trading at 1,183 won to the greenback.

▪ Foreign Exchange Market

The foreign exchange market in 2014 was rocked by the scaling back of quantitative easing by the United States, developments in Ukraine and South Korea's current account surplus.

At the start of the year the won lost ground as the Chinese economy showed signs of slowing down, but with concerns about growth in the world's second-largest economy dissipating later on in the year, the Korean currency rose to 1,008.5 won to the U.S. dollar.

In the second half, with the U.S. reining in its stimulus program that pumped large sums of money into the market and Tokyo moving to stimulate its economy, the won ended the year at 1,099.3 to the dollar.

Such developments were not restricted to the South Korean currency alone, since legal tenders of all the G-20 countries lost ground vis-a-vis the U.S. dollar. Last year, the move by the U.S. to reduce the amount of money poured into the market also raised volatility in daily foreign exchange rates.

South Korea's foreign reserve, meanwhile, stood at US$363.6 billion in late 2014, up US$17.1 billion from the year before. The increase was brought about by foreign investors buying up more local shares and the country's solid current account surplus.

Last year, the country's total overseas debt rose US$1.9 billion to US$425.4 billion, with short-term debt rising 0.7%p on-year to account for 27.1% of all debt. The increase is much smaller than in the past.

The country's ability to repay debt, which is measured by dividing the amount of short-term debt by total foreign currency reserves, stood at 31.7%, the lowest reading since 2008.

Data showed that while short-term debt rose, medium- and long-term debt decreased last year, as the value prices of foreign invested bonds declined and local banks issued less bonds abroad. Economic actors also took active steps to pay back short-term loans during the year, which helped reduce their exposure.

Overall, while short-term debt did increase last year, South Korea's ability to service its debt remains solid.

Average Monthly Income and Expenditure(2 persons and over)

Unit : %, %p

year	Income	(real)	Consumption expenditure	(real)	Non-consumption expenditures	Disposable Income	Surplus	Propensity to income
2009	1.2	-1.5	1.7	-1.1	3.7	0.7	-2.4	0.7p
2010	5.8	2.8	6.4	3.4	7.6	5.4	2.2	0.7p
2011	5.8	1.7	4.6	0.6	7.2	5.5	8.3	-0.6p
2012	6.1	3.8	2.7	0.5	5.1	6.4	18.4	-2.6p
2013	2.1	0.8	0.9	-0.4	2.8	1.9	4.7	-0.7p
2014	3.4	2.1	2.8	1.5	3.0	3.5	5.2	-0.4p

Note : Percent change over the same quarter of previous year

▪ Households

The average monthly income of a South Korean household stood at 4.3 million won in 2014, up 3.4% from the year before. Excluding a rise in inflation, actual earnings rose 2.1%. The rise comes as more people found work, and a steady increase in salaries, which pushed up wage earnings by 3.9%. Pension and transfer incomes also increased 4.2%, while earnings generated by assets fell 3.1% on falling deposit interest rates.

In 2014, average outlays per household reached 2.55 million won each month, an increase of 2.8% and a gain of 1.5% if inflation is calculated. Of the increase, the amount of money spent on transportation, services, recreation and cultural activities all rose, along with purchases of household goods and services, and outlays on food and lodging. Data showed that South Korea spent less on communications, utilities and alcoholic beverages last year compared to the year before.

On average, each household spent 805,000 won a month on non-living expenditures such as taxes and money poured into pensions. The total represents a 3% increase on-year. Earned income tax stood at 136,000 won, while various social security payments hit 124,000 won, with other miscellaneous expenses standing at 212,000 won. Money paid to cover interest on debt stood at 89,000 won, down 5.2% thanks to a drop in bank interest rates.

Average disposable income for each household per month reached 3.49 million won, an increase of 3.5% on-year. Disposable income is measured by deducting non-living expenditures from the overall income of a household.

The increase in earnings also helped improve the balance sheet for households last year, with each on average having 947,000 won left over every month after covering outlays. The number represents a 5.2% increase vis-a-vis 2013. This translated into a surplus rate of 27.1%, a gain of 0.4%p from the year before.

The country's average consumption propensity, or the ratio of total consumption spending to disposable income, stood at 72.9%, a dip of 0.4%p from the year before.

ECONOMIC GROWTH

OVERVIEW

In 2014, South Korea's economy grew 3.3%, up from 3% growth tallied in the previous year. The rise in gross domestic product (GDP) is noteworthy because it came amid unfavorable times at home and abroad. Last year's growth was mainly led by a rebound in facility investments.

Data showed that construction sector backtracked during the year, with the slack being taken up by the manufacturing and service sectors. In the expenditure sector, the sinking of the Sewol ferry hurt consumer demand, with construction-related investment also taking a beating.

In the face of such challenges business investment rose compared to the year before, along with exports, which posted weak yet positive gains.

In the first quarter of 2014, the national economy moved up 1.1% on-quarter and 3.9% from the year before. By sector, output in farming and fisheries declined, but the manufacturing, construction and service areas reported improved numbers.

In output, facility investments dipped, while the amount of money poured into the construction sector spiked. Exports and consumption rose with gross national income (GNI) advancing 1% from the previous three-month period. This translated into a GNI hike of 4.8% on-year.

In the second quarter, the country's real GDP edged up 0.5% from the previous quarter and moved up 3.4% from the year before. From a production perspective, manufacturing, construction and services moved up, but the pace of acceleration dipped. On the issue of outlays, the ferry disaster that left more than 300 people dead caused people to withhold spending, with investment in construction dropping sharply in the April-June period.

On the plus side, government spending on various projects, along with facility investments and exports, propped up growth that would otherwise have been stunted. Real GNI growth reached 1% compared to the year before, and was up 3.5% from the year before.

Coming into the third quarter, GDP moved up 0.8% from the previous three-month period and 3.3% on-year, with manufacturing suffering a setback, while construction and services did relatively well. Exports declined, with consumer spending rebounding from a low in the second quarter, with South Korea's GNI edging up 0.2% on-quarter and 3.2% from the third quarter of 2013.

In the October-December period, the national economy only managed to pull off 0.3% growth from the previous quarter, and moved up 2.7% on-year. Construction backpedaled in terms of output, but agriculture and fisheries did well, along with manufacturing. The service sector also saw growth.

Exports again rebounded, along with business investment figures, although private consumption and government spending dropped. The latter is due to the government front-loading budget spending in 2014, to arrest the slowdown caused by the ferry sinking disaster.

Growth/Decline for Each Economic and Spending Activity

Unit : At Chained 2010 Year Prices, %

	Annual		2014^p (Seasonally-adjusted Data)				2014^p (Original Data)			
	2013	2014^p	1/4	2/4	3/4	4/4	1/4	2/4	3/4	4/4
Gross Domestic Product(GDP)	2.9	3.3	1.1	0.5	0.8	0.3	3.9	3.4	3.3	2.7
Agricultural, forestry and fishing sector	3.1	2.6	-2.2	-2.0	2.0	2.8	5.6	3.3	1.4	1.3
Manufacturing	3.6	4.0	2.2	1.1	-0.9	0.0	5.1	5.1	3.3	2.4
Construction	3.0	0.6	1.4	0.1	0.9	-3.0	2.1	0.4	1.5	-1.0
Service	2.9	3.1	0.9	0.3	1.2	0.6	3.5	2.7	3.2	3.1
Private consumption	1.9	1.8	0.4	-0.4	0.8	0.5	2.6	1.7	1.5	1.4
Government consumption	3.3	2.8	0.1	0.6	2.1	0.2	3.0	1.6	3.6	3.1
Construction investment	5.5	1.0	5.3	0.5	0.9	-7.8	4.1	0.2	2.3	-1.5
Facility investment	-0.8	5.8	-1.4	1.3	0.2	4.0	7.2	7.7	4.2	4.2
Export	4.3	2.8	1.4	1.3	-1.7	0.4	4.2	3.4	2.2	1.4
Import	1.7	2.1	-1.1	1.2	-0.7	0.7	3.2	2.9	2.3	0.1
Gross National Income(GNI)	3.7	3.8	1.0	1.0	0.2	1.6	4.8	3.5	3.2	3.7

Source : The Bank of Korea(Ecos)
Note : Quarterly comparison for seasonally adjusted data, yearly comparison for original data

SEASONALLY ADJUSTED DATA

- ### GDP as Measured by Economic Activity

In the first three months of 2014, agro-fisheries posted 2.2% losses, mainly due to a drop in the number of pigs and cattle. On the other hand, manufacturing, propped up by electricity and electronic equipment, petrochemicals and metal products, grew 2.2%. Construction grew 1.4% thanks to demand for large buildings, while the service sector edged up 0.9% on health care, social welfare, transportation and storage-related operations. On the other hand, restaurants and hospitality businesses suffered losses.

In the second quarter, a drop in the number of livestock again hurt agro-fisheries by some 2%, with utilities dropping 2.3%, mainly due to a warmer climate that reduced demand for heating. Manufacturing advanced 1.1%, bolstered by a rise in production for chemicals, autos and LCDs, while construction posted 0.1% growth. The service sector as a whole struggled with weak demand in hospitality, transportation and storage businesses, yet managed to grow 0.3% on social welfare and health care.

For the third quarter, manufacturing backtracked 0.9% on poor showings by LCDs and smartphones, but power production centered on nuclear power and certain utilities advanced 4.7%. Construction gained 0.9% on large infrastructure projects. The service sector, buoyed by financial operations including insurance, advanced 1.2% in the three-month period.

In the last three months of the year, output in manufacturing stood pat, while construction was down 3%. Utilities, again helped by nuclear power generation, expanded 5%, while the service sector managed to pull off 0.6% growth.

- ### Expenditure Compared to GDP

In the first quarter of 2014, private consumption in autos, durable goods and services edged up 0.4%, with construction-related investment expanding 5.3%, buoyed by demand for homes. Facility investment contracted 1.4% on weak demand for machinery, while the amount of money poured into intellectual property rights rose 2%, thanks to a solid increase in private sector research and development (R&D). Exports moved up 1.4% on shipments of electricity, electronics and refined petroleum products, but imports were off 1.1% due to less demand for machinery products. South Korea is a major importer of precision machinery that is used to make finished goods for export and local consumption.

In the second quarter, private consumption of products and demand for services all fell 0.4%, while construction pulled off 0.5% growth, on orders for more buildings. Facility investment numbers moved up 1.3%, helped by funds allocated to transportation equipment and machinery, while the licensing of foreign patents caused intellectual property-related investments to dip 0.1%. Exports of LCDs allowed outbound shipments to advance 1.3%.

In regards to the third quarter, private consumption, demand for quasi-durable goods and services all increased to push up overall numbers by 0.8%. Facility investment was up 0.2%, while construction rose 0.9% with the help of more building orders and civil engineering projects. Investment in intellectual property was down 0.3%, while exports backtracked 1.7% on weak overseas demand for LCDs. Imports were also down 0.7% on poor demand for machinery and a sharp drop in natural gas prices.

In the last three months of 2014, consumer demand for both durable and non-durable goods went up to push up numbers by 0.5%. Facility investment, helped by transportation equipment and machinery demand, rose 4%, while construction sector numbers nosedived 7.8%. Investment into intellectual property rights products were off 0.5%, while exports and imports increased 0.4% and 0.7% each.

ORIGINAL NON-ADJUSTED DATA

In the first quarter of 2014, South Korea's GDP rose 3.9% on-year. By industry, manufacturing rose 5.6% on the strength of electricity and electronics and with metal products. Construction, a key source of jobs, rose 2.1% on-year, helped by solid demand for homes, while the service sector, buoyed by growth in health care, social welfare and hospitality, advanced 3.5%.

By spending, private consumption rose 2.6% vis-a-vis January-March of 2013 on demand for cars, communication equipment and services. Facility investment soared 7.2% on businesses pouring money into semiconductors, manufacturing equipment and automobiles. Construction-related investment also advanced 4.1% on strong building orders, while funds injected into intellectual property production areas jumped 7.2%.

In exports, a rise in outbound shipments of smartphones and metal goods pushed up numbers by 4.2%, while local demand for cars and machinery helped imports move up 3.2%. There has been a steady rise in demand for foreign-made cars in recent years.

Non-adjusted original data figures for the second quarter showed South Korea's GDP rising 3.4% on-year, with manufacturing advancing 5.1% on output of chemical products and LCDs. In construction, civil engineering suffered losses, but the slack was taken up by housing demand, with overall numbers edging up 0.4%. The country's service industry moved up 2.7% on stronger demand for social welfare and health care.

In the area of spending, private consumption rose 1.7% on-year, helped by the purchase of cars, durable goods and medical and service-related outlays. Investment in facilities jumped 7.7%, thanks to money spent to make cars, airplanes, telecommunication and broadcasting equipment. Despite weak demand for civil engineering projects, the construction sector posted 0.2% growth, while newfound interest in software caused intellectual property-linked investment to rise 5.6%. Exports rose 3.4%, with imports increasing 2.9%.

As for the third quarter, the country's GDP was up 3.3%, with the manufacturing sector also rising 3.3%. Construction suffered from weak civil engineering growth, but nevertheless grew 1.5%, while the service sector expanded a respectable 3.2%.

In spending, demand for cars and durable goods helped private sector spending rise 1.5%, with investment in business facilities going up 4.2%. Investment in construction was up 2.3%, with numbers for intellectual property-centered investment jumping 4.9%. Exports buoyed by machinery and metal products rose 2.2%, while imports gained 2.3% on more crude oil brought into the country along with cars.

For the last quarter, the country's GDP grew 2.7% on-year, with manufacturing expanding 2.4% on the output of metal products. The construction industry backtracked 1%, while services and agro-fisheries rose 3.1% and 1.3%, respectively.

In terms of spending, consumption helped by both durable and non-durable goods purchases rose 1.4%, with government purchases expanding 3.1%, which propped up the economy. Critical business investment that is linked to job creation rose a solid 4.2%, although the construction sector posted a 1.5% loss. Exports of goods were up 1.4%, with imports advancing 1%, in the three-month period vis-a-vis the year before.

CONSUMER PRICES

■ **Movement of Consumer Prices**
Consumer Prices Consumer prices rose 1.3% on-year in 2014, showing overall signs of stability. By product, good weather conditions and better harvests helped agriculture and fisheries prices to fall 2.7% compared to 2013. In the manufactured goods sector, prices of processed foods jumped 3.7%, but a sharp drop in international crude oil prices limited overall gains. Crude oil prices contracted 4.3% vis-a-vis the year before, with all manufactured goods edging up just 1.3%.

Prices for city gas advanced 6.4% on-year, with electricity costs gaining 2.2%. Public utility costs that encompass heating, sewerage and tap water use rose 3.9%, while prices associated with housing rent moved up 2.3%. The rise in rent was brought on by the sharp rise in "jeonse" a local property lease system in which a tenant pays a large deposit in place of monthly rent.

CPI(Customer Price Indexes) by Items

Unit : %

	No. of Items	No. of Summation	Flucturation Rate Compared with Last Year						
			2008	2009	2010	2011	2012	2013	2014
Total Items	481	1000.0	4.7	2.8	3.0	4.0	2.2	1.3	1.3
Commodities	327	453.2	6.3	3.3	4.6	5.7	3.1	1.0	0.9
Agricultural, Marine & Livestock Products	71	77.6	0.5	6.4	10.0	9.2	3.1	-0.6	-2.7
Industrial Products	252	326.6	7.8	2.5	3.2	4.9	2.8	0.9	1.3
Electricity, Water Supply, Gas	4	49.0	-	-	-	4.8	5.0	4.5	3.9
Service	154	546.8	3.7	2.4	1.9	2.7	1.4	1.5	1.6
Renting for Housing	2	92.8	2.3	1.6	1.9	4.0	4.2	2.7	2.3
Public Service	29	142.6	2.5	2.0	1.2	-0.4	0.5	0.7	0.8
Personal Service	123	311.4	4.7	2.8	2.2	3.7	1.1	1.6	1.7

Cost of living index and core consumer price index In 2014, the cost of living index that measures price changes in 142 products frequently bought by consumers rose 0.8%, while fresh produce prices dropped 9.3% on-year, mainly due to a 17.2% plunge in the price of fresh vegetables. This drop is more than the 1.3% contraction reported for 2013.

In regards to core inflation, which is used as a measure to gauge longer-term movement in consumer prices, numbers gained 2%, which is a faster pace of growth than the 1.6% increase tallied for the year before. Core inflation does not take into account the movement of highly volatile fuel and agricultural prices, with the government checking the prices of 429 products.

Consumer price shifts by region Consumer prices rose differently in 16 major cities and provinces last year, with Seoul, Gwangju, Daegu, Incheon and South Gyeongsang Province rising 1.4% to 1.6%. Other regions such as Busan, Ulsan, as well as Gyeonggi, North

Chungcheong, North Jeolla, Jeju, South Jeolla and North Gyeongsang moved up 1.0% to 1.3%, while inflation numbers for Daejeon, Gangwon and South Chungcheong edged up 0.5% to 0.9%.

■ Movement of Producer Prices

In 2014, producer prices fell 0.5% compared to 2013, marking the second year in a row that numbers fell compared to the year before. The dip is attributed to the weaker international commodity prices that stabilized prices of manufactured goods. By quarter, producer prices gained 0.4% in the January-March period, but contracted 0.1% in the second quarter and 0.1% in the following three months. For the October-December period, inflation backtracked 1.5%.

By product, farm and fisheries-based goods rebounded from -6% growth in 2013 to a gain of 0.7% in 2014. Inflation numbers for manufactured goods were also in negative territory due to weak raw material prices. Manufactured goods prices were down 2.1% last year from

Growth rate of Producer Price

Unit : %

	Weight	2013 Annual	2014				
			Annual	1/4	2/4	3/4	4/4
Producer Price	⟨1,000.0⟩	-1.6	-0.5	0.4	-0.1	-0.1	-1.5
Goods	⟨665.1⟩	-2.5	-1.4	0.4	-0.4	-0.3	-2.1
Agricultural, forestry & marine products	⟨32.3⟩	-6.0	0.7	6.2	-1.5	0.1	-1.9
Manufacturing products	⟨566.5⟩	-3.0	-2.1	-0.3	-0.4	-0.3	-2.4
Electric power, gas & water supply	⟨64.0⟩	5.7	5.3	3.9	0.1	-0.4	0.0
Services	⟨334.9⟩	0.4	1.5	0.6	0.5	0.4	0.0

Note : Percent change over the same quarter of previous year

-3% in 2013. Prices for public utilities such as electricity, gas, water and sewerage advanced 5.3% in 2014, from 5.7% reached the year before. Utility prices were directly affected by weak global energy prices.

■ **Export, Import Prices**

In 2014, inflation numbers for both exports and imports fell compared to the year before. Export prices contracted 6%, accelerating from a loss of 4.3% tallied for 2013, while import prices dipped 7.5% from -7.3% the year before.

Export prices were bolstered by semiconductors, but any gains were offset by sharp drops in petroleum and chemical prices. Import numbers contracted because raw materials and intermediate goods prices backtracked last year from the year before.

■ **Key Developments in 2014 that Contributed to Fluctuating Consumer Prices**

In 2014, consumer prices remained stable at 1.3%, on par from gains reached the year before. In the first quarter, consumer prices rose 1.1% on-year, while numbers rose to 1.6% in the second quarter and 1.4% in the July-September period, with numbers coming down to 1.1% in the last three months.

Farm produce prices as well as energy costs brought down consumer prices while public and private services played a part in pushing up numbers. Agricultural

prices plunged 10%, with the drop only being arrested by a rise in meat prices.

Manufactured goods remained weak, mainly due to cheap crude oil prices, which brought down production costs, although overall inflation numbers gained 1.3% last year on the strength of processed food and textiles. The prices of refined petroleum products such as gasoline fell 4.8%, as a result of sharp drop in crude oil prices. Diesel prices also fell 5.1%, despite a rise in consumer demand. Prices of processed foods, including bread and other wheat-based goods, gained 3.7%, while textiles, fueled in part by demand for sportswear, advanced 4%.

An increase in city gas and electricity prices caused public utilities to rise 3.9% on-year, with public services, including transportation costs, edging up 0.8% last year. The cost of rent moved up 2.3% to bolster consumer prices. Private services, which includes the amount of money spent on people eating out and private education, rose last year.

While stable consumer prices do mean that people are not paying more for products they need, a sluggish gain is at the same time triggering new concerns about deflation, which can sap demand and adversely affect investment.

The government has said that while consumer inflation numbers have generally grown at a slower pace than before, core inflation numbers clearly indicate that there is consumer demand.

Officials added that deflation concerns

Growth rate of Consumer Price by Items

Unit : %

	Weight	2011	2012	2013	2014				
					Annual	1/4	2/4	3/4	4/4
Consumer Price	⟨1,000.0⟩	4.0	2.2	1.3	1.3	1.1	1.6	1.4	1.1
Agricultural, Marine & Livestock products	⟨77.6⟩	9.2	3.1	-0.6	-2.7	-4.7	-2.2	-3.3	-0.3
(Agricultural products)	⟨44.1⟩	8.8	8.8	-1.0	-10.0	-12.6	-10.6	-10.5	-6.0
(Livestock products)	⟨22.1⟩	10.3	-7.4	-0.9	9.5	9.7	13.2	7.8	7.5
(Marine products)	⟨11.3⟩	8.5	2.6	1.3	2.0	1.3	1.2	1.5	4.2
Industry products	⟨326.6⟩	4.9	2.8	0.9	1.3	1.6	2.0	1.6	-0.1
(Petroleum products)	⟨56.7⟩	13.6	3.7	-3.3	-4.3	-2.7	-1.6	-4.5	-8.4
Electricity, Water Supply, Gas	⟨49.0⟩	4.8	5.0	4.5	3.9	5.4	4.2	3.4	2.5
Rentals for housing	⟨92.8⟩	4.0	4.2	2.7	2.3	2.5	2.4	2.3	2.2
Public Service	⟨142.6⟩	-0.4	0.5	0.7	0.8	0.7	0.7	0.9	0.7
Personal Service	⟨311.4⟩	3.7	1.1	1.6	1.7	1.2	1.8	1.9	1.8

Note : Percent change over the same quarter of previous year

are exaggerated because in order for a country to be classified as being in deflation, it must post minus growth for two consecutive years, which is not the case in South Korea.

MONEY SUPPLY AND FINANCE

▪ Money Supply

South Korea's monetary policy in 2014 was accommodative, with two rate cuts and an expansion of the central bank's loan facility. The Bank of Korea's monetary policy committee lowered the rate twice, in August and October, on concerns that a slump in consumer sentiment following the deadly sinking of the ferry Sewol may hamper economic recovery. With the two quarter percentage point rate cuts, the seven-day repo rate, used as the base rate, fell to 2% from 2.5%.

In efforts to prop up capital investment by small and medium enterprises, the central bank raised the ceiling of its loan instrument for companies to 15 trillion won from 12 trillion won in July.

In April, the central bank lowered the interest rate for a loan program aimed at the self-employed to 0.5% from 1%. As part of efforts to normalize the corporate bond market, it supplied loans to Korea Investment Corp. so that the state-run firm can finance up to 100 billion won (US$94 million) to Korea Credit Guarantee Fund.

South Korea's M2 money supply

gradually rose in 2014, up 6.6% from the previous year. The on-year rise came on a continued surplus streak in the current account as well as credit growth in the private sector amid a low rate trend. The M1 money supply increased 10.9%.

Reserve money climbed 13.1% in 2014, picking up from 11.3% growth in 2013. The liquidity aggregate of financial institutions rose 7%, staying mostly unchanged from a 6.9% gain in the previous year.

Key Figures on Money Supply

Average, yoy, %

	2013	2014				
		Year	1/4	2/4	3/4	4/4
Lf	6.9	7.0	6.5	6.5	7.1	7.9
M2	4.8	6.6	5.3	5.9	7.1	8.0
M1	9.5	10.9	8.8	8.4	11.0	14.3
Base money	11.3	13.1	13.4	12.5	12.4	14.0

Source : The Bank of Korea(Ecos)

▪ Interest Rates

The long-term interest rate, which soared on jitters over the global financial market in early 2014, quickly fell as external risks stabilized and anticipation over the central bank's rate cut built up. It moved in the 2.00 to 2.20% range.

The rate soared to an annual high of 2.92% on Jan. 3, but trended lower on views that the U.S. Federal Reserve would sustain its accommodative policy as well as concerns over geopolitical risks in Ukraine. But the fall was limited as

Trends of Key Bond Yields, Market Rates

Unit : %

	2013	2014				
		Year	1/4	2/4	3/4	4/4
Treasury Bond(3yrs)	2.79	2.59	2.87	2.82	2.50	2.17
Corporate Bond(3yrs, AA-)	3.19	2.98	3.30	3.25	2.89	2.51
CD(91days)	2.72	2.49	2.65	2.65	2.51	2.16
CP(91days)	2.81	2.60	2.79	2.75	2.58	2.29
Call Rate(1day)	2.56	2.32	2.47	2.47	2.34	1.99
Bank Deposit Rate	2.73	2.43	2.63	2.59	2.38	2.15
Bank Lending Rate	4.64	4.26	4.48	4.41	4.24	3.93
Yield Spread	0.23	0.27	0.40	0.35	0.16	0.18

Source : The Bank of Korea(Ecos)
Yield Spread=Treasury Bond(3yrs)-Call Rate(1day)

142

pressure weighed on its narrowing gap with the base rate.

In the second half, the rate quickly declined as a delay in economic recovery, stemming from the sinking of the ferry Sewol, stoked hopes for a rate cut. After the base rate fell to 2%, the lowest since the global financial crisis, following rate cuts in August and October, the rate moved in a narrow range amid eased hopes for an additional rate cut. The short-term rate moved in a narrow range in the first half but trended lower on two rate cuts in the second half.

The CD rate, which averaged 2.72% in 2013, fell to 2.49% in 2014. The savings deposit rate on new loans also tumbled to 2.43% in 2014 from 2.73% in 2013. The call rate moved in a stable manner despite tightened regulation on securities firms' borrowing of call money in April. But it trended lower after the two rate cuts. Bond rates also trended lower in 2014 from a year earlier. The yield on three-year treasury bonds slipped to 2.59% in 2014 from 2.79% in 2013.

In the first half, rates fell gradually on hopes that the Fed's tapering will be orderly. The pace of the decline picked up in the second half as hopes for the Bank of Korea's rate cut picked up. In July, the rate on three-year Treasury bonds even fell lower than the base rate.

Bank deposit and lending rates also extended their falls. Lending rates fell on an expansion of fixed-rate mortgage loans and the central bank's rate cut. Deposit rates fell in tandem with falling market rates.

■ **Stock Market**

The stock index fell from the previous year on concerns over a number of factors -- the Fed's tapering, geopolitical risks in Ukraine and an outflow of foreign funds. It moved up and down throughout the year and ended lower than the previous year on concerns over corporate earnings and increased net selling by foreigners.

The stock market started off on a weak note amid worries over slowing growth in China and weak corporate earnings. On Feb. 4, the benchmark KOSPI index hit an annual low of 1,887 points. It then remained range-bound amid jitters over an earlier-than-expected rate normalization by the Fed as well as geopolitical risks in Ukraine and the Middle East.

The KOSPI, however, gained ground in the second half on the government's stimulus measures as well as hopes for the European Central Bank's quantitative easing. On July 30, it hit an annual high of 2,082 points. But starting in October, the KOSPI trended lower as foreign funds exited on sluggish corporate earnings and a strengthening U.S. dollar. The benchmark index ended 4.8% lower from a year earlier at 1,915 points.

In the first half of 2014, daily trading volume averaged between 3 billion won and 4 trillion won amid risks at home and abroad, including the Fed's tapering and sluggish earnings by local companies. But it increased to 6 trillion won, slightly increasing from a year earlier, as investor sentiment recovered in the second half. The KOSPI's daily trading volume stayed mostly unchanged from a year earlier at 4 trillion won, while that of the KOSDAQ rose to the 2 trillion won level from around 1.8 trillion won.

In 2014, foreigners moved in and out of the market amid the Fed's tapering move

Stock Price Index(KOSPI and KOSDAQ)

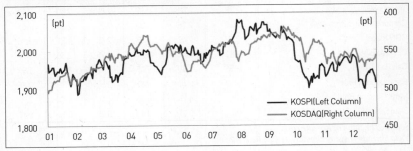

and a downbeat outlook for corporate earnings in South Korea. But overall, their net investment totaled 11.5 trillion won, gaining from 8.2 trillion won in the previous year.

In the January-March period, foreigners' net selling reached 3.2 trillion won amid possibilities of an earlier-than-expected rate hike by the U.S. Federal Reserve as well as external geopolitical risks in areas like Ukraine.

But they shifted to net buying in the second quarter on U.S. recovery hopes as well as eased external risks. They sustained their net buying mode into July, when the government, which newly appointed Choi Kyung-hwan as finance minister and deputy prime minister for economic affairs, announced a number of stimulus measures. They briefly turned to net selling in September on earnings jitters as well as a strengthening won, but overall net purchased 6.3 trillion won throughout the year.

By country, Britain's net selling totaled 7.4 trillion won, while net buying by the U.S. and Japan reached 3.8 trillion won and 3.2 trillion won, respectively.

Foreigners continued to buy in the local bond market, with their net investment totaling 5.2 trillion won in 2014. Mid- to long-term fund inflow increased on a relatively high interest rate, stable economic fundamentals compared with emerging economies and a continued streak of current account surplus.

By country, net outflow by investors in the U.S. and Luxembourg each totaled 1.4 trillion won and 2.5 trillion won, while net investment by investors in China and France reached 2.2 trillion won and 1.7 trillion won.

Stock Market Daily Average Turnover

Unit : Trillion Won

	2009	2010	2011	2012	2013	2014
Kospi	5.8	5.6	6.9	4.8	4.0	4.0
Kosdaq	2.1	1.9	2.3	2.2	1.8	2.0
Total	7.9	7.5	9.1	7.0	5.8	6.0

Source : Korea Exchange

■ Foreign Exchange Market

The won-dollar exchange rate was affected by a number of factors, such as monetary policy changes in major economies, geopolitical risks in Ukraine and a continued streak of current account surplus.

Early in the year, the won weakened amid financial and political instability in some emerging markets, concerns over an earlier-than-expected rate hike by the Fed as well as slowing growth in China. But as worries over a slowdown in China's growth eased and foreigners increased their stock investments on a continued current account surplus trend and improved investor sentiment, the won strengthened to 1,008.5 against the U.S. dollar on July 3.

In the second half, the Fed's tapering stoked the greenback's value. Japan's additional easing, meanwhile, led to a further depreciation of the yen. On Dec. 8, the won weakened to 1,117.7 against the U.S. dollar and slightly strengthened to end at 1,099.3 at the end of the year. The currencies of all G-20 member countries weakened against the U.S. dollar with the Fed's tapering.

External risk factors affected the volatility of the won-dollar exchange rate. But volatility slightly slipped from a year earlier, with average intraday volatility falling to 4.9 won in 2014 from 5.2 won in 2013. Average volatility from the previous day also slipped to 3.5 won from 3.7 won in the cited period.

Uncertainties over the U.S. Federal Reserve's tapering as well as geopolitical risks in some emerging economies increased daily volatility by affecting foreign investment. Rising foreign exchange volatility is a global trend following the Fed's tapering. South Korea's volatility was slightly lower than the G20 average of 0.38%.

Foreign exchange reserves reached US$363.6 billion as of the end of 2014, growing US$17.1 billion from the previous year. Supply was more dominant as foreigners increased their stock investment on a number of factors, such as a continued streak of current account surplus, which eased worries that the Fed will start hiking rates earlier than expected.

South Korea's foreign debt totaled US$425.4 billion as of the end of 2014, growing US$1.9 billion from a year

Exchange Rates to US Dollars and Yen

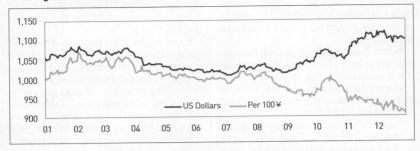

earlier. The on-year gain is mostly due to a rise in short-term debt. The portion of short-term debt against overall debt gained 0.7%p to 27.1%, but it is still at a lower level compared with the past.

The portion of short-term foreign debt against foreign exchange reserves, which is seen as a country's external payment capacity, reached 31.7%, the lowest level since the 2008 global financial crisis as foreign exchange reserves expanded.

Long-term foreign debt declined as banks and companies scaled back their overseas bond issuances. The fall in value of bond investments held by foreigners also affected the amount. In contrast, short-term foreign debt increased in the first half as local branches of overseas banks increased their borrowing. But it trended lower in the second half as they repaid their loans.

Despite an overall rise in foreign debt, the low portion of short-term foreign debt against overall foreign debt and short-term foreign debt against foreign exchange reserves, are seen as indicators that point to a relatively stable level of payment capacity and financial health for the South Korean economy.

■ Money Movement

Cash inflows into local financial institutions in 2014 gained from the previous year. Banks posted a 115 trillion won rise in cash inflows, sharply up from a 41-trillion won gain in the pervious year.

Local asset managers saw their cash inflows surge 47 trillion won in 2014, sharply accelerating from a 17.7 trillion won increase in 2014. Money market funds saw a net inflow of 16 trillion won, also picking up from a 3.3 trillion won

increase in the previous year.

Cash inflows into bond-type funds and other new types of fund products increased 14.8 trillion won and 17.4 trillion won on-year, respectively, as uncertainties in the financial market and a continued low-rate trend stoked demand by investors searching for financial products with medium risk and medium return. Stock funds declined for the second straight year as resale volume increased amid uncertainties in the stock market.

Cash inflows into securities firms rose 2.2 trillion won on-year. Money trusts at banks and asset managers gained 40.7 trillion won, with their growth accelerating from a year earlier. A rise in customer deposits at brokerages came as investors offloaded their holdings amid a lack of strong momentum in the stock market.

■ Corporate Financing

Bank lending to companies increased in 2014 compared with the previous year, while direct financing shrank in the cited period. Overall corporate financing was sound, with the dishonored bill rate remaining at a low level and corporate default rate slipping.

Banks' corporate lending to both large corporations and small and medium enterprises increased in 2014, bringing the total to 52 trillion won from 34.8 trillion won a year earlier.

Lending to large firms increased to 18.5 trillion won from 8.2 trillion a year earlier as the direct financing market was sluggish. Most of the lending growth was concentrated in the first half and growth slowed in the second half as the corporate bond market recovered and companies stepped up efforts to secure financial health.

Lending to small and medium enterprises sharply gained to 33.5 trillion won from 26.6 trillion won, backed by government policies aimed at supporting smaller firms as well as eased lending attitude by banks.

Corporate bond issuance in the direct financing market was sluggish in the first half but started to increase in the second half as a fall in the corporate bond rate in July stoked demand for issuance. Net issuance of corporate bonds slipped to 1.8 trillion won from 3.1 trillion won in 2013. High-rated companies continued to flourish in the corporate bond market, accounting for 80% of overall issuance.

Commercial paper shifted to a net redemption of 2.1 trillion won, turning around from a net issuance of 1 trillion won on increased efforts to rein in debt by state-run firms. Stock issuance, however, increased to 9.6 trillion won in 2014 from 6.5 trillion won a year earlier on eased regulations on corporate listings. The dishonored bill rate slightly increased to 0.16%, while the corporate default rate slipped to 1.11%.

▪ Household Credit

South Korea's household debt is still high at 1,089 trillion won as of the end of 2014. During the year, it increased by 67.6 trillion won. This marks the biggest on-year growth since 73 trillion won in 2011. It also marked a faster growth, 6.6%, compared with 6% in 2013.

The spike in household debt is seen to have been affected by eased mortgage lending rules in August as well as two rounds of rate cuts in August and October. Property transaction growth also hit the highest level since 2006. These factors mostly became apparent in the second half, prompting a whopping 49 trillion won rise in household debt compared with a 18.6 trillion won growth in the first half.

Household loans increased in both the banking and non-banking sectors. But growth in the banking sector was sharper compared with the non-banking sector following policy changes.

The portion of fixed interest rate loans, which accounted for only 0.5% of all loans in 2010, following a policy program aimed at supporting the soft landing of

household debt, rose to 15.9% as of the end of 2013. It further increased to 23.6% as of the end of 2014.

The default rate on banks' household loans fell to 0.49% in 2014 from 0.63% a year earlier, supported by an economic recovery. The default rate on mortgage loans also stabilized to 0.41% in end-2014 from 0.58% in the previous year.

Household Credit   *Unit : Trillion won*

	2012	2013	2014			
			1/4	2/4	3/4	4/4
Credit to Households	963.8	1,021.4	1,024.9	1,038.3	1,059.2	1,089.0
Loans to Household	905.9	962.9	976.8	980.8	1,001.7	1,029.3
Merchandise Credit	57.9	58.5	57.1	57.5	57.4	59.6

Source : The Bank of Korea(Ecos)

TRADE AND BALANCE OF PAYMENTS

▪ Overview

Korea's current account surplus reached a record high of US$89.22 billion in 2014. While the deficit in the service account widened, an increase in trade pushed the figure to a record high and up US$8.07 billion from the previous year.

The weight of the current account surplus against the country's gross domestic product reached a provisional 6.4% last year, hitting the highest level since 10.7% in 1998. Despite improved domestic demand, sliding oil prices led to a 1.3% decline in imports, while exports gained 0.5%.

The goods balance increased by US$9.91 billion to US$92.69 billion. Exports of goods gained 0.5% on-year to US$621.5 billion while imports of goods fell 1.3% to US$528.6 billion.

On a customs-cleared basis, Korea posted a trade surplus of US$47.15 billion in 2014, but the goods balance, calculated under the balance of payments, logged a surplus of US$92.69 billion.

The main difference mainly comes as the current account data was compiled based on the day of changes in ownership. But the customs-cleared trade data

Exports and Imports(Customs Clearance Basis)

Unit : 100 million US$, %

	2013				2014				
	Yearly	2/4	3/4	4/4	Yearly	1/4	2/4	3/4	4/4
Exports	5,596.3	1,411.6	1,367.9	1,463.6	5,726.6	1,375.3	1,456.7	1,417.6	1,477.0
(Growth rate, %)	2.1	0.7	2.8	4.7	2.3	1.6	3.2	3.6	0.9
Imports	5,155.8	1,267.6	1,260.3	1,330.6	5,255.1	1,323.7	1,309.6	1,328.4	1,293.5
(Growth rate, %)	-0.8	-2.8	0.3	2.5	1.9	2.0	3.3	5.4	-2.8
Excess of exports and imports(-)	440.5	144.0	107.6	133.0	471.5	51.6	147.1	89.2	183.5

was compiled based on when documents on verifying exports and imports were accepted. In terms of ship delivery, the timing of customs clearance differs from that of changes in ownership.

Customs-cleared trade data also includes freight charges and insurance fees while imports of goods subtract such costs. The difference in calculating the methods of exports and imports results in a larger surplus in goods balance under the current account rule.

■ Exports and Imports

Korea's exports gained 2.3% on-year to US$572.6 billion. Export growth expanded from the previous year in tandem with economic recoveries in major economies. On-quarter growth gradually gained throughout the first three quarters, reaching 1.6% in the first quarter, 3.2% in the second quarter and 3.6% in the third quarter. But it sharply fell to 0.9% in the fourth quarter as sliding oil prices affected shipment prices.

By product, exports of semiconductors, steel products and ships improved, while that of oil and chemical products slipped on low oil prices. By region, exports to the United States jumped 13.3%, while those to the Middle East and the European Union each gained 7.7% and 5.7%. In contrast, exports to China and Japan fell 0.4% and 7.2%, respectively.

A recovery in the U.S. economy drove exports. Exports to the European Union also surged in the first half but slowed in the second half on the region's deflation and sluggish growth. Exports to Japan continued to fall on a weakening yen following the Bank of Japan's quantitative easing. Imports gained 1.9% on-year to US$525.5 billion. While imports of consumer goods increased, those of raw materials fell on weakening oil prices.

■ Trade Balance

Korea posted a trade surplus of US$47.15 billion, up US$3.1 billion from the previous year, as exports rose more steeply than imports. The country posted a trade surplus in the United States, China and ASEAN, and saw its surplus of imports to the Middle East and Japan

Balance of Payments

Unit : 100 million US$

	2013		2014				
	Annual	4/4	1/4	2/4	3/4	4/4	Annual
Current account	811.5	239.4	151.9	242.4	225.7	272.3	892.2
Goods	827.8	245.9	177.5	264.3	216.8	268.4	926.9
Services	-65.0	-24.0	-35.0	-18.4	-9.0	-19.2	-81.6
Primary income	90.6	32.4	19.1	13.3	31.4	38.2	102.0
Secondary income	-41.9	-14.9	-9.6	-16.8	-13.5	-15.2	-55.0
Financial account	-801.3	-263.4	-171.8	-242.1	-224.8	-265.3	-903.9
Direct investment	-155.9	-48.9	-36.6	-75.5	-39.1	-55.4	-206.6
Portfolio investment	-93.4	-16.6	-136.6	-58.7	-47.6	-93.8	-336.1
Other investment liabilities Financial derivatives	44.1	18.7	8.9	20.8	15.3	-8.0	37.0
Other investment assets & liabilities	-432.8	-124.9	62.1	-17.0	-95.1	-169.3	-219.4
Reserve assets	-163.0	-91.7	-70.2	-111.7	-58.3	61.4	-178.9

Source : Statistics Korea

shrink. The country posted record trade, exports and imports for the second consecutive year.

By company, smaller firms saw a 5.9% growth in their exports compared with a 0.3% rise for large corporations. The category of products that are exported are also diversifying from technology products to medical and food products.

■ Service Account

Korea posted a deficit of US$8.2 billion, widening by US$1.6 billion from the previous year. While the deficit in its travel account sharply fell, its surplus in the construction and logistics sectors also shrank.

The deficit in the travel account narrowed by US$1.7 billion to US$5.3 billion in tandem with a sharp influx of Chinese tourists into the country. Its surplus in the construction sector shrank US$1.7 billion to US$13.8 billion as overseas construction deals declined.

■ Primary Income Account

Korea posted a surplus in the primary income account of US$10.2 billion, up US$1.1 billion from the previous year, due mainly to an increased surplus in its investment income account. The primary income account tracks wages of foreign workers and dividend payments overseas.

■ Capital and Financial Account

Korea's capital and financial account posted a net outflow of US$90.4 billion in 2014, up US$10.3 billion from the previous year. Direct investment logged a net outflow of US$20.7 billion, up US$5.1 billion from the previous year. Last year, the country's foreign exchange reserves grew by US$17.1 billion on-year to US$363.6 billion.

PUBLIC FINANCE

■ Fiscal Management Conditions

In the first quarter of 2014, the economy grew 0.9%, raising hopes that it was regaining some of its lost momentum but in the aftermath of the Sewol ferry sinking in mid-April that left more than 300 people dead, growth plunged to 0.5% in the second quarter, effectively halting any hope of serious gains for the whole year.

In July, with the arrival of the new economic team led by deputy prime minister Choi Kyung-hwan, the economy received a much-needed boost in the form of aggressively expansionary policies, but the overall pace of recovery has not met expectations, with gains remaining weak and inconsistent.

The reversal in economic conditions raised fears that state revenues will drop, which could result in a mismatch between earnings and outlays. Last year, the government increased outlays to pick up the slack caused by a sharp drop in consumer spending that accounts for about 60% of the gross domestic product.

South Korea's growth, which was originally forecast to expand 3.9%, actually grew just 3.3% for the whole of last year, according to estimates released by the Bank of Korea in January 2015.

■ Tax Revenue

The government in 2014 forecast that state earnings, including profits generated by various funds, would reach 369.3 trillion won, up 2.4% from the year before. Of the total, it predicted that tax revenues would hit 216.5 trillion won, with non-tax earnings topping 27.3 trillion won. These figures, however, were found to have been overly optimistic, with tax earnings falling short by 10.9 trillion won to 205.6 trillion won. The shortfall has been attributed to sluggish growth that hurt the collection of value-added and corporate taxes.

■ State Spending

In 2014, total state expenditures set by the National Assembly stood at 355.8 trillion won, up 2% vis-a-vis the 349 trillion won tallied for the previous year. The sum spent was used to bolster economic growth throughout the year.

In the parliamentary review process, some expenditures were adjusted to ensure fiscal health, with cuts being made to childcare, medical support and livelihood subsidies for some underprivileged households. On the other hand, more assistance was provided to the elderly and women along with key social overhead capital (SOC) projects.

Overall, the 2014 budget was tailored to revitalize the economy, help create jobs, strengthen the country's growth potential and stabilize the living conditions for ordinary people. In the wake of the Sewol ferry tragedy, more attention was paid to public safety, along with efforts made to boost the country's fiscal health.

■ Fiscal Balance and State Debt

The consolidated public sector finance balance for 2014 stood at 13.5 trillion won in the black, or 0.9% of the gross domestic product (GDP). The operational budget balance on the other hand was in the red by 25.5 trillion won. The deficit in the operational balance comes as this account deducts earnings from social security-related funds that will be used in the future to pay for pensions.

This method can give a better picture of the state of fiscal health. In 2014, state debt hovered at 527 trillion won. This is equal to 35.1% of the annual GDP, or a rise of 0.8%p from the year before.

■ Future Fiscal Management Plans for 2014-2018

The government is in the process of enhancing the efficiency of its fiscal management to ensure sustainability and is forging a detailed five-year plan to meet these goals.

The 2014-2018 national fiscal management plan aims to breathe new life into the economy in the short run, while at the same tackling more systemic problems such as job creation, and supporting efforts to transform South Korea into a "creative economy" through aggressive investments. In the longer term, the aim is to strengthen the country's basic economic health by implementing tough fiscal reforms and boosting outlay-related transparency.

For the five-year period, the government aims to increase revenues by 5.1% annually, while expenditures will rise by an average of 4.5% in the 2013-2017 period. The numbers represent a slight increase from the 3.5% target set for the four-year period, and reflects the expansionary policy stance of policymakers. The general goal is to keep outlays below earning levels to ensure a positive fiscal balance sheet.

The government said it wants to keep any expenditure growth at least 1.5%p lower than a rise in earnings in the coming years, which should prevent a rise in state debt. State debt is a source of concern for all countries because it can become a serious burden to future generations and limit a government's options in the event of an unforeseen and severe economic downturn.

Despite such efforts, the government estimated that the operational budget balance will suffer as a result of the expansionary policy stance. The government claimed that while it will spend more than originally forecasted, state debt will be maintained at the mid 30-percent level in the coming years, which is viewed as being manageable for the country.

On the matter of allocating resources and funds, priority has been given to vitalizing the economy, giving hope to people and creating a safer country. The government said it will concentrate on creating more jobs, fuel regional economic growth, build up the service sector that can all stimulate domestic spending. In addition, more attention will be paid to improving the work condition of non-regular workers and helping small-time entrepreneurs who have been hurt by stunted growth.

Policymakers have argued that the "dual labor market" in South Korea is adversely affecting the labor market and hindering the hiring of young people. The dual market refers to the gap between full-time regular employees who enjoy "excessive" job security and good pay vis-a-vis non-regular workers whose employment is tenuous and are usually paid less than their regular employee counterparts.

The country will also move to expand the social security net, and implement measures that can reduce outlays of people with low income that can stabilize their livelihoods.

In light of the Sewol ferry sinking, the government will spend money to carry out inspections of all major public facilities and transportation infrastructure so that members of the general public can go about their everyday lives without worrying about their safety.

Meanwhile, the government said that it will greatly improve fiscal health by carefully checking outlays to prevent unnecessary money from being spent. Under the plan, South Korea aims to slash a tenth of all state-funded projects in 2016, which will allow more resources to be diverted to welfare outlays.

The budget guidelines call for a stringent "zero-base" review of all 2,000 state-subsidized projects receiving taxpayer money. Each government ministry and agency will be required to examine their projects and halt support for 10% of them starting in 2016. The government will aim to eliminate projects that have failed to generate results or are redundant, and programs that customarily got assistance in the past.

Another way the government aims to enhance the country's fiscal balance is to check the current rules on government non-taxable earnings and favorable tax relief programs and get rid of those that are no longer needed. This move can expand the country's tax base, allowing more revenues to be collected without raising the burden on taxpayers. The government has said on numerous occasions that the goal is not to raise taxes if it can be avoided.

To further strengthen the country's fiscal balance sheet, the government will strive to manage public sector debt and pro-actively deal with other dangers that can imperil fiscal health down the road. It said that to better control debt, more effort will be paid to carrying out in-depth feasibility studies on all future projects that public corporations want to engage in to make certain that the stated goals can be met and to check whether an excessive amount of money is being poured into such efforts, which can burden taxpayers and worsen fiscal health.

TAXATION

■ **State Tax Revenue in 2014**

In 2014, South Korea's tax office collected 205.5 trillion won in dues from taxpayers, up 360 billion won from the previous year. The total includes both general and special accounts. Despite the increase, the amount collected fell shy of the national budget of 216.4 trillion won by 5.1% or 10.9 trillion won.

The main reason for the shortfall in earnings is the result of mediocre corporate earnings in 2014 compared to 2013, along with unfavorable exchange rates and a drop in imports that adversely affected import duties. Lackluster consumption also hurt value-added taxes collected from the sale of goods.

Looking at the general account, the country collected 199.3 trillion won in taxes, a gain of 3.9 trillion won from the 195.4 trillion won tallied for 2013. The special account, on the other hand, showed numbers falling by 300 billion won to 6.2 trillion won, vis-a-vis 6.5 trillion won a year earlier.

By tax item, the total amount of income tax collected topped 53.3 trillion won, up 5.5 trillion won from 47.8 trillion brought in the year before. Going into more detail, the country's tax office said that earned income tax reached 25.4 trillion won, a gain of 3.4 trillion won from 21.9 trillion won the year before. The increase is due to a rise in the number of hired workers, a rise in nominal salaries and an upward adjustment of tax rates for those earning the most money.

Besides such developments, a spike in real estate transactions resulted in capital gains tax earnings increasing by 1.4 trillion won on-year, while more diligent reporting by people who are self-employed and run their own businesses caused aggregate income tax numbers to go up 600 billion won. On the minus side, a drop in interest rates on deposits hurt taxes levied on interest earnings by 400 billion won compared to the year before.

Corporate taxes shrank as companies reported less overall earnings. Compared to 2013 when the state collected 43.9 trillion won in taxes, numbers for 2014 dipped 1.2 trillion won to 42.7 trillion won. In regards to value-added taxes collected, state earnings moved up 1.1 trillion won to 57.1 trillion won in 2014 from 56 trillion won the year before. The rise is a sign that people spent more last year than the year before.

Import duties, meanwhile, reached 8.7 trillion won last year, a decrease of 1.9 trillion won from 10.6 trillion won reported for 2013.

2014 Tax Collection

Unit : Trillion won

Tax item	2013 Collection	2014	
		Plan	Collection
Total national tax	201.9	216.4	205.5
General account	195.4	209.2	199.3
Income tax	47.8	54.4	53.3
Corporate tax	43.9	46.0	42.7
Inheritance tax	4.3	4.6	4.6
Value-added tax	56.0	58.5	57.1
Selective excise tax	5.5	6.0	5.6
Security transaction tax	3.1	4.0	3.1
Stamp tax	0.6	0.7	0.7
Revenue from past fiscal year	4.8	5.5	4.1
Transportation tax	13.2	13.5	13.5
Customs duty	10.6	10.6	8.7
Education tax	4.5	4.5	4.6
Comprehensive real estate holding tax	1.2	1.1	1.3
Special account	6.5	7.2	6.2
Liquor tax	2.9	3.0	2.9
Special tax for rural development	3.6	4.2	3.3

Source : Ministry of Strategy and Finance

■ **Key Changes to South Korea's Tax Code in 2014**

The government made changes to the country's tax codes to support economic vitalization and fair and reasonable taxation. It also focused on stabilizing the livelihoods of ordinary citizens and assisting ongoing efforts to promote business investment, create jobs and assist small and medium enterprises (SMEs).

Besides such guidelines, measures were taken to allow ordinary citizens to amass wealth, ensure that people have the means to support themselves in old age and increase safety and welfare-related expenditures.

■ **Economic Vitalization**

In 2014, the government announced a three-tiered tax program designed to push up earnings for households that could lead to more consumer spending. The plan calls for tax benefits for earned income, dividend-related earnings and corporate income recirculation taxation that can prod companies to invest more on facilities.

SMEs that increase wages for workers could get tax deductions for up to 10% of the hike, while large conglomerates

can get 5% deductions. The tax burden for small-time shareholders and their transactions were lowered from 14% to 9%, which can permit such investors to take home more money. On the recirculation taxation, companies that fail to spend a set percentage of their operating profits on investment will be levied taxes on such holdings.

The new programs will be maintained for three years, which could allow more money to reach households and the market. The rise in liquidity and disposable income can help jump-start the economy, which has grown at a slower-than-expected pace.

In addition, the government moved to revise the employment-related investment deduction scheme that can create a market environment more conducive to creating more jobs. Job creation is critical for a country's sustainable growth and forms the foundation for economic expansion.

On the business front, tax reforms gave more deductions to SMEs and small service-oriented companies. Other measures that aim to fuel growth through consumer spending include extending the earnings deduction benefits given to credit card purchases by two years and temporarily raising the tax deduction rate for check or debit card users from 30% to 40%.

In addition, SMEs that have grown in size and would normally have been excluded from various tax breaks will continue to benefit. Previous rules on "tax support graduation" based on the number of employees have been eased, with only the total sales limit being maintained at 500 billion won per year.

So-called angel investments involving promising SMEs and tech venture firms will get more tax deductions, while rules dealing with government stock options have been adjusted to make it possible for companies to attract more talented workers.

■ Stabilizing Livelihoods of Ordinary People

South Korea in 2014 pushed forward a host of measures designed to make it easier for ordinary people to amass wealth by reforming special tax-exemption bank accounts and raising the amount that can be deposited in such accounts from 30 million won to 50 million won.

The country also postponed value-added taxes from being slapped on diapers and baby formula until late 2017, as part of an ongoing effort to reduce the cost of raising children.

Asia's fourth-largest economy has one of the lowest birthrates in the Organization for Economic Cooperation and Development. Such a development can pose serious social and economic problems down the line.

On other issues aimed at helping ordinary people, the tax office overhauled tax codes for retirees and will take steps to not penalize pensioners if they opt to receive their severance pay in a lump sum.

The country, moreover, made it possible for people to take out more money through mortgage loans and offered tax deductions on such borrowing. It then moved to provide more tax breaks for real estate and home rental companies so as to get them to build new homes. The building of more homes can stabilize prices and make it easier for people to secure living quarters.

In the wake of the Sewol ferry disaster, the government has decided to give a special deduction on investments made to strengthen safety-related infrastructure, which includes fire prevention.

Besides such measures, tax authorities said funds to help SMEs by large conglomerates will be eligible for tax deductions. On the other hand, an excise tax has been slapped on the sale of cigarettes as part of an ongoing effort to keep people from smoking.

■ Fair Taxation

In the past several years, South Korea has persistently taken steps to reduce various non-taxable systems that have been cited for being unfair, with particular emphasis given to rectifying complaints that foreign-invested companies were getting hefty breaks when local companies could not. In regards to SMEs, whose annual operating profits exceeded 2 billion won, the tax rate has been marked up from the previous 9% to 12%.

The country, moreover, extended the waiving of value-added taxes on clearing, maintenance and security services for apartments for three more years, but exempted homes that are larger than 135㎡ from such benefits.

The tax office said that it plans to check various rules so it can ferret out those that no longer need benefits. Such a move can increase the country's tax base, which is directly linked to state revenues. A wider tax base can make it possible for the country to bring in earnings needed to finance growing social security demands without raising tax rates.

To ferret out businesses that try to dodge paying their proper dues, the government is moving to make it mandatory for all operations that generate a certain amount of sales to issue electronic receipts for payments made with cash. It added that more businesses, such as those related to automobiles, will be required to issue receipts that can make it easier for tax authorities to keep tabs on earnings.

As an extension of such efforts to catch tax delinquents, the government said it will beef up its inspections of people who habitually try not to pay taxes and raise the reward money for people who report false name bank accounts that have been set up to avoid paying taxes.

The maximum limit for reward money has been marked up to 3 billion won from 2 billion won for major cases, while the reward for smaller cases has been doubled to 1 million won.

In addition, the South Korean government took steps to deal with efforts by people and businesses to hide their wealth in overseas tax havens. Authorities took steps to tighten requirements on what constitutes Korean nationals living abroad. In the past, the minimum requirement was six months but this was raised to one year.

People living abroad can receive more money sent from South Korea. In another move to track people attempting to hide wealth in foreign lands, the government changed tax breaks given to people who pay transfer or gift taxes abroad.

Under the old system, those that paid taxes to a foreign government and can provide documentation were exempted from paying similar taxes in South Korea. Under the new arrangement, the government will not give an exemption but only offer tax deductions, with such transactions still subject to local taxes.

In regards to overseas bank accounts that are not reported to authorities, Seoul will strengthen penalties such as fines and other administrative actions. At the same time, people who eventually report such accounts after the reporting deadline will be given deductions on fines they have to pay the government as part of an effort to get people to come clean about such asset holdings. Getting a clearer picture of such accounts can make it easier for tax authorities to track the movement of wealth that can be taxed.

On the issue of tax dodging that involves the movement of money that crosses international borders, the government has opted to extend the period in which the government can levy fines from the current 10 years to 15 years and to take tougher measures against people who habitually try to hide their taxable assets and income in foreign countries.

■ **Rationalization of Taxes**

The government has taken steps to rationalize the way taxes are levied so as to offer the maximum benefits to ordinary people.

For land that is bought to meet public demand, the transfer tax exemption rate has been marked up from 15% to 20%. In addition, the maximum limit imposed on the amount of taxes that can be paid by businesses through credit cards has been lifted, which could help those suffering from temporary liquidity problems. In the past the maximum limit was set at 10 million won.

In order to facilitate growth of the country's real estate market, which is closely linked to the construction sector, the government will defer a policy that would slap a transfer tax and other dues on land that is not used by individuals or companies for one year to late 2015. This move can give more breathing room for property owners and those wanting to invest in land but who, for the time being, do not have the resources to do so.

To boost private consumption that took a beating last year, but which is essential for the country's long-term growth, authorities opted to raise the amount of duty-free goods that can be brought into the country from US$400 per person to US$600 in 2014. The move reflects changing times and a rise in goods prices since the old limit was set.

The move was taken at the same time as efforts taken by customs officials to check travelers' baggage to see whether or not they have undeclared goods. On the matter of levying additional taxes for small businesses, the government said it will put off taking such a step until late 2016, a delay of two years, which should give people more time to adjust.

FAIR TRADE

■ **Summary**

The Fair Trade Commission (FTC) spent 2014 upholding market economy principles as South Korea's rapid growth fostered unfair trading by companies in search of ever more profit.

Large companies, using their advantageous status, have been compelling smaller companies to accept losses or forcing them to agree to unfair business arrangements. To counter such developments, the FTC took stern remedial actions to enforce the country's subcontract law during the year. It also took action against public corporations that had engaged in similar unfair actions against private-sector companies.

In addition, the anti-trust watchdog ferreted out price-rigging practices and collusion between companies that distorted the fair market, and checked practices by owners of large conglomerates, who swindled money from the companies they ran for personal profit.

On the downside, efforts by the incumbent Park Geun-hye administration to revitalize the economy at all costs have raised questions about the government's willingness to push forward "economic democracy," which was a key focal point in the 2012 presidential race.

■ Correcting Irregular Transactions

The FTC allocated its resources to correcting irregular transactions between large and small and medium enterprises (SMEs) in 2014. It conducted sweeping probes to find problems and detected unfair practices being perpetrated by 128 companies throughout the one-year period.

It even signed a memorandum of understanding (MOU) in December with the police, patent office and Small and Medium Business Administration to prevent big companies from unilaterally using technologies developed by SMEs.

As part of this effort, the FTC slapped a fine of 1.38 billion won on Lotte Mart for transferring various advertisement costs to its suppliers. The corporate regulator then took action against local franchise operators who were found to have engaged in unfair trading with the owners of their franchise outlets.

In the realm of the Internet, the FTC took pro-active steps to root out unfair practices in the search engine and software market areas. When the watchdog found illegal activities being committed by portals Naver and Daum, the former agreed to set aside a 100 billion won fund to help smaller operators make headway in the highly competitive market.

In regards to clamping down on unfair practices by public companies, the FTC slapped hefty fines on Korea Land & Housing Corp., KEPCO, Korea Express-way Corp., Korea Railroad Corp. and Korea Gas Corp.

The country's land and housing corporation was fined 14.6 billion won, while electricity power monopoly KEPCO was ordered to pay 10.6 billion won. The highway and railroad operators were fined 1.9 billion won and 1.7 billion won, respectively.

Amid such actions, the FTC welcomed a new chairman who vowed to push forward measures to strengthen an open and free market.

■ Enforcement of Fair Trade Laws Directly Linked to the Livelihoods of People and Public Work Projects

The number of fair trade violations that impacted the livelihoods of ordinary people or involved large-scale public work projects hit 56 last year.

The FTC said of these, high-profile cases involving price-rigging by large builders resulted in huge fines exceeding 666 billion won being slapped on perpetrators. These companies were engaged in the building of metro lines in Incheon, a canal linking Seoul to the Yellow Sea and a high-speed bullet train line connecting the capital city to the country's Jeolla region.

Investigations showed that builders such as Hyundai E&C, Daewoo E&C, Samsung C&T Corporation and SK E&C effectively rigged the open bidding process to safeguard profit margins at the expense of both the central and regional governments. Because of their illegal actions, taxpayers had to pay more for the infrastructure work they undertook.

Related to such actions, local builders complained that the intensity of the probes was seriously affecting normal business operations and stirred up controversy. Construction companies conceded that they engaged in "limited" price fixing during the bidding process but claimed that such practices had been common practice in the past and to some extent they had no choice in order to ensure minimum profit margins.

Besides construction companies, the FTC detected unlawful collusion in the rent-a-car, unmanned security service provider and household boiler industries last year and ordered remedial actions.

Such measures directly impacted the everyday lives of citizens.

The corporate regulator, moreover, discovered unfair trading in the country's film distribution network, where large movie theaters such as CJ CGV and Lotte Cinema allocated screen time to favor films made by one of their affiliates. This practice put independent filmmakers at a disadvantage and infringed on fair trade.

The FTC levied 5.5 billion won in fines on the companies involved and reported the matter to the state prosecutors' office for criminal investigation. The FTC, moreover, took steps to better protect the privacy of people making on-line transactions by changing standard commerce rules.

In a move to better protect the intellectual property rights of artists, the agency even took action against various app stores and Web operators. Despite such efforts, a court ruling that favored companies canceled out efforts made by the FTC to deal with unfair trade violations while the loss of some cases triggered criticism that the regulator was "overzealous" about tackling cases in the absence of strong incriminating evidence.

Economic Democratization

The FTC said that despite receiving some flak it has been steadfast in pursuing economic democratization and has sent officials to conduct on-site inspections to determine whether large companies or powerful actors were using their strength to force smaller partners to suffer losses.

It said that such activities conducted by special task force members have been instrumental in reducing complaints filed by SMEs and small store owners by an average of 30% to 40% during the year compared to 2013.

Supporting this view, a poll conducted by the Korea Federation of Small and Medium Business in November showed that 84.3% of companies checked said that the number of unfair subcontract cases has been reduced.

On combating criminal actions by large corporate owners, the FTC said it completed revising related laws that would impose stiffer penalties on violators.

Related to big business groups, or chaebol, the anti-trust agency said it screened the regulatory filing records of 100 listed companies belonging to six top conglomerates and found 57 violations of disclosure rules. These companies were fined a total of 1.12 billion won for their actions.

Notwithstanding such measures, there has been persistent complaints that companies were still breaking rules and thereby hurting the rights of partner companies and ordinary consumers.

The main reason for this problem lies in the fact that most of the FTC's work is centered on finding unfair trading practices between large companies and their smaller subcontractors. It said that because subcontractors are fearful of losing future orders, many are reluctant to report unilateral and unfair actions taken by large companies with whom they have business relations.

On the issue of the FTC losing interest in pushing forward economic democracy agendas amid mounting concerns of an economic slowdown, the commission's chief argued that every single action to rectify unfair trading can be seen as a move to enforce the principles of economic democracy in the country.

As the FTC tried to alleviate concerns about economic democracy, it also had to contend with attacks that its actions were "suffocating" the business community at large. Proponents of this view said that the commission's actions hurt the operating profits of many companies at a time of slow growth that on the whole exerted a negative influence on economic recovery efforts.

Dealing Effectively with Globalization of Competition-Related Laws

In light of market globalization and the competition laws that need to take into account development taking place in foreign countries to be effective in South Korea, the FTC took active steps to engage in closer dialogue with foreign regulatory authorities in 2014. This move had a two-fold purpose of protecting local companies operating abroad from unfair discrimination while at the same time clamping down on multinationals that disrupt the local market.

The commission last year inked bilateral agreements with the United States, the European Union (EU) and Japan and reached a memorandum of understanding on fair trade rules with Brazil. It also represented Seoul's views on free trade in free trade agreement negotiations with China and Vietnam, emphasizing the importance placed on fair trade by Asia's fourth-largest economy.

Reflecting such efforts, the 8th Seoul International Competition Forum hosted by the FTC in September brought together corporate regulators from the United States, the EU, China and Japan, along with officials from the Organization for Economic Cooperation and Development (OECD). From the corporate side, executives from global information technology giants such as Samsung Electronics and Google were present at the event.

At the forum, participants debated policy direction that will be taken in regards to companies sometimes abusing intellectual property protection guidelines to restrict competition, how to ensure that public companies remain neutral players in the marketplace and the future of competition law in Asia.

The FTC, meanwhile, took tough steps to penalize multinationals that break fair trade rules, which hurts local companies and South Korean consumers. In November, the commission levied 77.8 billion won in fines on Japanese and German bearing companies that have been fixing prices and controlling supply for 14 years. The two companies that were found to have engaged in illegal practices between 1998 and 2012 were reported to the state prosecutors' office for criminal investigation.

In addition, fines totaling 11.4 billion won were slapped on U.S., French and Dutch chemical additive suppliers who have been found to have worked together to set prices in advance.

The FTC said that in 2014, it has received calls to play a larger role in protecting local consumers who purchase products online for foreign shopping malls and businesses. The increase in orders has resulted in an upsurge of consumer complaints.

Complaints lodged with the FTC center around long shipment delays, wrong products being sent, difficulty in returning items, as well as unfair rules regarding refund policies by foreign shopping malls.

The agency said that because it does not have legal jurisdiction abroad, there is little it can do for consumers at present, although it has started to take part in talks with the United Nations Commission on International Trade Law. This can allow it to play a part in the setting of international standards for handling liabilities related to products bought online from foreign countries.

As part of this role, the FTC said it has beefed up monitoring over foreign shopping malls and companies that buy products on behalf of customers. In the case of the latter, which has gained popularity because some local consumers are adverse to handing over credit card information or suffer from a language barrier, the state watchdog said that because such companies are local firms, any breaches of fair trade rules can result in action being taken to correct the problem.

On foreign shopping malls that have been cited for shoddy service, the FTC, through the Korea Consumer Agency, will issue advisories to local consumers to not buy products from such sites.

The FTC, however, said that there is a lack of concerted effort between all related government agencies, local governments and consumer groups to better protect local consumers from overseas shopping malls. It said that because of such shortcomings the country as a whole cannot effectively deal with complaints regarding online transactions at present.

ECONOMIC COOPERATION

▪ Expansion of Free Trade Agreements

Overview In 2014, South Korea and Turkey initialed a free trade agreement (FTA) for their investment and service sectors. It also initialed bilateral trade agreements with New Zealand, China and Vietnam. The country's FTAs with Australia and Canada went into effect.

S. Korea and Turkey initial free trade agreement South Korea and Turkey reached a de facto agreement on free trade in the investment and service sectors in their seventh round of talks held between June 30 and July 4. The move follows a free trade pact for products that went into effect on May 1, 2013. The agreement marks Turkey's first-ever free trade pact in the service and investment sector. It has so far signed 17 FTAs that only deal with products.

The two countries decided to opt for a positive-list approach while surpassing the boundary of the World Trade Organization (WTO)'s Doha Development Agenda (DDA). Under the deal, Turkey agreed to open 18 additional sectors -- such as construction, culture and environmental services -- to South Korea.

Meanwhile, in addition to the DDA, Seoul agreed to permit the transfer of financial information and the entrance of university graduates. The deal was partly aimed at the potential establishment of Turkish financial firms in the country.

In the investment sector, the two countries agreed to adopt the investor state dispute settlement in which investors can file for an international arbitrage should they suffer a financial loss due to the country of investment's infringement of the free trade deal. They also agreed not to give benefits to paper companies owned by a third-country party that are operating in either South Korea or Turkey.

South Korea opened its investment market to the non-service sector, while Turkey secured the right to delay the opening of several markets such as property, energy, coal and agricultural products.

South Korea's exports to Turkey jumped 24.3% to US$5.66 billion in 2013. Its imports gained 2.9% to US$4.97 billion, leading to a current account surplus. Service trade between the two countries reached US$740 million in 2012, with South Korea reaping a US$170 million surplus.

S. Korea, New Zealand initial bilateral FTA South Korea and New Zealand initialed their FTA in December, a month after South Korea and New Zealand struck the deal on Nov. 15 on the sidelines of a summit between President Park Geun-hye and New Zealand Prime Minister John Key.

In 2013, bilateral trade between the two countries reached US$2.8 billion, making New Zealand the 44th-largest trading partner of South Korea while South Korea became New Zealand's 41st-largest trading partner.

Under the move, New Zealand will be scrapping 92% of its tariffs in terms of import volume and will expand it to 100% of its tariffs within seven years. By product category, New Zealand will be immediately scrapping its 5% to 12.5% tariffs on tires and 5% tariffs on washing machines.

South Korea, meanwhile, plans to immediately abolish 48.3% of its tariffs in terms of import volume, and expand it to total exports within 20 years. Some 199 product categories, including fruits and vegetables, are excluded from the agreement.

S. Korea and Canada's FTA goes into effect A free trade pact between Seoul and Canada went into effect on Jan. 1, 2015, after it was struck and initialed in March 2014. It marked Canada's first FTA agreement in Asia, with South Korea becoming Canada's 12th FTA partner.

Under the deal, the two countries agreed to gradually lower the tariff rate on most products over the next decade. By product, it will affect 97.5% of the two countries' tariffs. In terms of import volume, it will affect 98.7% of Seoul's tariffs and 98.4% of Ottawa's tariffs.

Canada will remove the current 6.1% tariff rate on auto exports and completely scrap it within two years after the FTA has gone into effect. Automotive vehicles account for a significant 42.8%, or US$2.23 billion, worth of Seoul's exports to the country.

Ottawa will also be scrapping the 6% tariff on auto parts and a 6 to 8% tariff on refrigerators and washing machines within three years.

South Korea excluded some 211 products, such as rice and cheese, from the category of products whose tariffs will be removed. It still will be removing the 40-percent rate on beef imports within 15 years and the 22.5 to 25-percent rate on pork imports within five to 13 years.

Excluding chicken, all meat imports' origin of destination will be based on the place of their butchery process. They will also discuss whether products made in the Kaesong Industrial Complex in North Korea's border city of the same name will be considered as products of South Korea.

The two sides agreed on a mutual safeguard which enables the countries to introduce measures to protect certain industries that have gravely suffered losses from increased imports. They also agreed to introduce an investor state dispute settlement in which investors can file for an international arbitrage should they suffer a financial loss due to the country of investment's infringement of the free trade deal.

Canada is South Korea's 25th-largest partner. The two sides started their FTA negotiations in July 2005. The Seoul-Ottawa FTA deal took the longest time among FTAs involving South Korea as Canada filed a suit against the country with the World Trade Organization in April 2009 to force it to open its beef market.

S. Korea and Australia's FTA goes into effect The FTA between Seoul and Sydney was signed on April 8, 2014, and went into effect on Dec. 12. Under the deal, the 40% tariff on Australian frozen beef imports will be lowered gradually over 15 years. The tariff was reduced by 2.7%p immediately after the bilateral trade pact went into effect and another 2.7%p on Jan. 1, lowering the rate by 5.4%p within a three-week period.

The 15% tariff on Australian wine was also immediately abolished after the trade pact went into effect. Iron ore and bituminous coal, which accounted for the biggest portion of imports from Australia, had already been mostly tariff-free. The impact on local steelmakers, such as POSCO, was minimal.

The FTA is expected to benefit exports of Korean products to Australia. The tariff on small and mid-sized cars that run on gasoline and cargo trucks that run on diesel, as well as televisions and refrigerators, are expected to boost exports as the tariff on these products will be immediately scrapped once the trade pact goes into effect. The trade deal, especially, is expected to bolster local exporters' footing as it went into effect ahead of the FTA between Australia and Japan.

Australia scrapped tariffs on compact cars and sedans that run on gasoline, both made in South Korea and Japan,

once the trade pact goes into effect. Its approach is to eliminate tariffs on auto parts immediately or within three years after the trade pact goes into effect.

Australia is the world's 12th-largest economy with a gross domestic product (GDP) of US$1.5 trillion and a per-capita GDP of US$65,000. Trade between the two countries totaled US$30.3 billion in 2013. Negotiations for the Korea-Canada FTA were first held in May 2007. The agreement was signed in September after 14 rounds of negotiations.

Seoul, Beijing sign FTA Seoul and Beijing announced their free trade agreement at the APEC summit held on Nov. 10 in Beijing.

▲ South Korean Trade Minister Yoon Sang-jick (L, front) shakes hands with his Chinese counterpart, Gao Hucheng, at the Great Hall of the People in Beijing on Nov. 10, after signing a free trade agreement. South Korean President Park Geun-hye (L, rear) and Chinese President Xi Jinping witness the signing ceremony.

The agreement was struck across 22 chapters that include products, service, investment, finance and telecommunications. China included finance, telecommunications and online commerce in the FTA for the first time.

The two countries agreed to open the market for more than 90% of their products. Beijing plans to scrap the tariffs for 91% of all products and 85% in terms of import amount. Korea, meanwhile, plans to scrap the tariffs for 92% of all products and 91% in terms of import amount.

Product categories whose tariff was immediately removed accounted for 44% of China's imports and 52% of Korea's imports. Both countries excluded vehicles from their agreement and also agreed to abolish the tariff on liquid crystal displays within 10 years.

A major remaining issue for South Korea was the level of its market liberalization for agricultural and fishery products. Trade ministry officials said market opening for agricultural goods under the Korea-China FTA will be minimal when compared to the other major FTAs that South Korea has signed.

Under the China deal, South Korea will eliminate its import tariffs on 40% of agricultural and fishery products, in terms of value, shipped from China. The figure compares with 92.5% and 98.4% under the country's bilateral FTAs with the United States and Australia, respectively, according to the trade ministry.

In addition, 30% of all agricultural and fishery products, in terms of value, have been permanently excluded from market liberalization in any future negotiations, it added.

Seoul and Beijing agreed to apply tariff benefits to products manufactured in the Kaesong Industrial Complex in the North Korean border city of the same name.

They also agreed to expand the initial residential permit for South Korean employees in China and give benefits to films and television programs co-produced by the two countries.

In the service sector, they agreed to take a negative list approach to liberalize all sectors, excluding those that have been agreed not to be open for the next two years.

S. Korea, Vietnam sign FTA South Korea and Vietnam struck an FTA on Dec. 10, 2014, two years and four months after they announced the start of talks.

With the move, Seoul inked FTA deals with two of the regional economic group ASEAN's biggest trading partners, Singapore and Vietnam. Vietnam is an emerging economy that is posting an average growth of 5% to 6% each year, raising hopes the trade pact will increase demand for consumer goods.

The trade agreement is also seen as a boon for South Korean companies that lagged behind Japanese firms in terms of price competitiveness due to a pact between Japan and Vietnam that was signed in 2009. The two countries reached an agreement on 17 chapters, including product, service, investment and intellectual property.

With the Korea-Vietnam FTA, Vietnam's liberalization rate, in terms of the number of products, rose to 89.2% from 87% compared with the Korea-ASEAN FTA. The rise came as the two countries agreed to open markets for trucks, auto parts, cosmetics products and electronic goods such as washing machines and rice cookers.

Korea's liberalization rate rose to 94.7% from 91.7%. In terms of import amount, Seoul also agreed to scrap tariffs for up to 15,000 tons of shrimp. In terms of the number of products, Korea's liberalization rate rose to 95.4% from 91.3%. Newly added products include dried or refrigerated goods such as garlic and ginger. Rice was excluded.

■ South Korea Logs Record Exports, Trade Surplus, Trade Amount

South Korea successfully set record exports, trade surplus and trade amount in 2014 despite a global economic slowdown. Exports rose 2.4% on-year to US$573.1 billion, while imports gained 2% to US$525.7 billion, leading to a trade surplus of US$47.5 billion. Both exports and trade surplus hit a record high.

The amount of trade reached US$1.1 trillion, surpassing the US$1 trillion threshold for the fourth straight year and setting a fresh high.

By area, exports to the United States jumped the most by 13.4%. Exports to the European Union gained 5.9%, while that to the ASEAN rose 3.5%. But an economic recession and a weakening yen lowered exports to Japan by 6.9%. Exports to China slipped 0.4%, falling for the first time since 2009.

By product, semiconductor exports increased 9.7% to US$62.7 billion. Steel product exports rose 9.3% while telecommunications product exports gained 7.1%. In contrast, exports of oil and chemical products each fell 3% and 0.1% amid sliding global oil prices.

The volume of oil imports, meanwhile, gained 1.2%, but fell 4.2% in terms of amount as prices slipped. Imports from the European Union and China each rose 9.9% and 7.9%, while those from Japan and the Middle East slumped 10.7% and 5.7%.

By area, South Korea's trade surplus was the biggest in China at US$53.5 billion, followed by the ASEAN at US$30.6 billion and Hong Kong at US$24.5 billion. The country, however, posted a trade deficit of US$82.6 billion in the Middle East and US$20.7 billion in Japan.

The trade ministry forecasts exports to grow 3.7% and imports to rise 3.2% in 2015. It projected a favorable trade environment for the country, backed by a U.S. economic recovery and stabilizing oil prices.

▪ Foreign Direct Investment Hits Record High

Foreign direct investment (FDI) soared 30.6% on-year to a record US$19 billion in 2014. The figure is 16.6% higher than the previous record set in 2012.

By country, FDI by Singapore spiked 288%, followed by 147.2% by China, 35.4% by the European Union and 2.4% by the United States. Japan's FDI, however, fell 7.5%.

By sector, FDI in the manufacturing sector jumped 64.6% to US$7.7 billion, while that in the service sector gained 13.6% to US$11.2 billion.

The government aims to increase FDI to US$20 billion this year on the back of a U.S. economic recovery and recently signed FTAs.

▪ Inter-Korean Trade Grows

Inter-Korean trade volume hit a record high of US$2.3 billion in 2014, growing 106.2% from a year earlier.

The gain was mostly fueled by a rise in exchanges at the Kaesong Industrial Complex even as Seoul has imposed punitive sanctions that bans economic exchanges with North Korea since 2010 following the North's deadly sinking of a South Korean warship.

The joint factory park, which opened in 2004, is the last remaining symbol of inter-Korean reconciliation. It has served as a major revenue source for the cash-strapped communist North, while South Korea has utilized cheap but skilled North Korean laborers.

A total of 124 South Korean small- and medium-sized enterprises have hired about 53,000 North Korean workers at the industrial complex in the border city of the same name.

AGRICULTURE, LIVESTOCK AND FORESTRY

AGRICULTURE AND LIVESTOCK

▪ Overview

In 1975, there were 13.24 million people in the agriculture or farming industry, accounting for 37.5% of the country's total population. In 2013, however, the number plunged to reach 2.85 million in 2013, accounting for only 21.5%.

In 2013, the average income of agricultural households came to 34.5 million won per year, with returns generated from farms taking up 10 million won, or 29.1%. The average debt held by such households, on the other hand, soared to reach 27.3 million won in 2013, compared to 140,000 won posted in 1975.

While farm households were richer than urban households, with the ratio standing at 111.1%, it plunged to 97.4% in 1990, and reached 76.7% in 2010. In 2013, it managed to inch up to 82.1%. The decrease was attributable to the rising cost of farm machinery and the workforce.

The combined area of farms is also decreasing. In 1990, the area covered 2.1 million hectares, but it shrank to 1.7 million hectares in 2013. The size hovers far below the 170 million hectares in the United States or the 142.6 million hectares in China.

An average farm household had 1.5 hectares of land, compared to 82.5 hectares in the United States and 1.6 hectares in Japan. About 55% of farm households in South Korea owned a farm with less than 1 hectare of land. Local farms are also aging, as 56% of the population is 65 or older.

While South Korean farms have been making efforts to cut costs and beef up competitiveness to tackle the free trade agreements which opened the local rice market, there are limits due to poor environments.

The country's food substantiality also was low. South Korea's self-sufficiency rate in terms of rice came to 89.2% in 2013, but the rate in terms of other grains came to 23.1%, an all-time low figure. Japan held a comparable figure of 30.7%, while the United States and Canada were at 129.4% and 143.5%.

■ Liberalization of Rice Market with 513% Tariff

The biggest issue in the South Korean agricultural realm in 2014 was the liberalization of rice. On July 19, Agriculture Minister Lee Dong-phil said the country will open the rice market starting in January 2015, adding that it is "inevitable" to do so considering the future of the rice industry.

▲ Agriculture Minister Lee Dong-phil speaks to a news conference after a meeting of economy-related ministers at the government building in Seoul on July 18. He said the government decided to open the country's rice market with tariffication from Jan. 1, 2015.

Two months later, the government decided to levy a tariff of 513% on rice imports, and reported the plan to the World Trade Organization. In a bid to protect the local market from soaring import volumes, the government also built legal grounds to roll out a special agricultural safeguards (SSGs), which allow temporary import restrictions if imports exceed 5% of the three-year average import volume.

While local agricultural activists protested against the liberalization, the higher-than-expected tariff of 513% limited woes.

The 513% tariff is high enough to limit the influx of U.S. and Chinese rice. As the price of 80kg of U.S. rice stands at 63,303 won and the price of Chinese rice stands at 85,177 won, the tariff will increase the price to 388,049 won and 522,134 won, respectively, allowing South Koran rice to maintain its competitiveness. The price of 80kg of South Korean rice stands at 160,000 to 170,000 won.

The government will also make efforts to protect rice from other free-trade agreements to come in the future. The government also moved up the fixed subsidy of rice farms to 1 million won from the previous 900,000 won per hectare, while rolling out incentives to farms seeking double-cropping. It will also ban sales of South Korean rice mixed with imports, and implement other financial instruments for the local rice industry.

However, the United States, China, Australia, Thailand, and Vietnam have protested against South Korea's move, making complaints to the World Trade Organization that a tariff of 513% is too high. Japan and Taiwan also expressed interest in such a joint move. Seoul needs to reach an agreement with each and every one of the countries that have objected to the tariff rate before obtaining an official WTO approval.

Chronology of Rice Tariffs

▲ 1994 April = The Uruguay Round agreement reached, the rice tariff delayed for 10 years (1995-2004).

▲ 2004 Jan. = Talks begin with the World Trade Organization on opening the rice market.

▲ 2004 Dec. = The rice tariff delayed for the second time from 2005 through 2014.

▲ 2005 May = The National Assembly commences an investigation on the opening of the rice market.

▲ 2010 Sept. = The rice-tariff plan is scrapped due to delayed reports to the World Trade Organization.

▲ 2014 June 20 = The South Korean government opens a public hearing on the rice-tariff plan.

▲ 2014 July 11 = The National Assembly opens a public hearing on the rice-tariff plan.

▲ 2014 July 18 = The agricultural ministry announces tariffs on rice.

▲ 2014 Aug. 14 = A commission on the development of the rice industry kicks off with government and agricultural experts.

▲ 2014 Sept. 10 = The South Korean government insists on a rice tariff of 513%.

▲ 2014 Sept. 30 = South Korea hands in the 513% tariff plan to the World Trade Organization.

▲ 2014 Dec. 31 = The United States, China, Australia, Thailand and Vietnam file complaints with the World Trade Organization, arguing that the 513% rate is too high.

▲ 2015 Jan. 1 = South Korea kicks off the tariff.

Background of 513% Tariff

South Korea decided to adopt a 513% tariff to protect the local rice industry. The calculation was based on the Uruguay Round agreement, which suggested "(domestic price-import price)/import price x 100." The government applied data compiled by Korea Agro-Fisheries & Food Trade Corp. and the price of imported Chinese rice.

Subsidy of 885 Billion Won to 1.23 Million Agricultural Households

In 2014, combined agricultural subsidies worth 885 billion won were distributed to 1.23 million agricultural households which cultivate 1.13 million hectares of land. The figure translates into 718,000 won per household, up 47,000 won from a year earlier. The amount moved up 15.9%, or 1.21 billion won from 2013. The increase came as subsidies per hectare moved up 100,000 won.

Implementation of Flexible-Rate Rice Subsidy for First Time in Four Years

Due to the falling price of rice, the government is estimated to have rolled out a flexible subsidy worth 140 billion won for the first time in four years to local agricultural households growing rice. The subsidy came as the average price of an 80kg bag of rice came to 167,600 won in the October-December period.

The flexible subsidy is rolled out when an 80kg bag of rice falls below 188,000 won. The government insures 85% of the gap between the median price fixed by the agricultural ministry.

The amount of the flexible-rate subsidy rolled out in 2005 came to 900.7 billion won, 437.1 billion won in 2006, 279.1 billion won in 2007, 594.5 billion won in 2009, 750.1 billion won in 2010. In 2008, 2011, 2012, and 2013, there were no subsidies due to an increase in rice prices.

Rice Production Reaches 4.24 Million Tons

The combined area of rice farms reached an all-time low level in 2014, but production reached 4.24 million tons, up 0.3% from a year earlier. Favorable weather conditions also lent support to the increase. Productions per 10a (unit area) reached 508kg in 2014, hovering above the average of 496kg.

Due to the rise in rice production, South Korea's self-sufficiency rate in terms of rice is expected to reach 95% in 2014, hovering above 90% for the first time in four years. When adding the mandatory import volume, South Korea is expected to experience an oversupply of rice for the second consecutive year in 2015. In order to stabilize prices, the government decided to purchase 24t.

The size of the country's rice fields, however, moved down 2.1% on-year in 2014 to reach an all-time low of 815,506 hectares. South Chungcheong Province produced the most rice at 836,000t last year, trailed by South Jeolla Province and North Jeolla Province with 809,000t and 679,000t.

Rice Consumption Per Capita Falls Below 50 Pct of 1970

In 2013, a South Korean consumed 184g of rice. Considering a bowl of rice (300kcal) holds 100g, the figure implies South Koreans consume less than two bowls everyday. It continued to hover below 200g after posting 202.9g in 2009. The yearly rice consumption also reached an all-time low in 2013 at 67.2kg, accounting for 49.3% of the 136.4kg posted in 1970. It first fell below the 100kg mark in 1998 at 99.2kg, continuing its downward trend to break the 80kg mark in 2006 at 78.8kg.

The consumption of non-glutinous rice stood at 62.4kg, down 4.2% or 2.8kg from a year earlier, but the consumption of glutinous rice came to 4.8kg, up 0.2kg, or 4% on-year.

The consumption of other grains, such as potatoes, sweet potatoes, millet and kaoliang, came to 8.1kg per capita, up 11% from a year earlier. Potatoes and sweet potatoes accounted for 2.7kg, followed by beans with 2.1kg, barley with 1.3kg, wheat with 1.3kg, and mixed grains with 0.8kg.

FTA Feared to Weigh on Agricultural Industry

In 2014, South Korea sought free-trade deals with Canada, China and Vietnam. Such moves sparked concerns over the country's agriculture industry. On Dec. 12, the FTA with Australia came into effect. Another agreement with Canada also became effective as of January 2015.

In 2012, the combined trade volume in the agricultural and livestock sector with Australia came to US$2.99 billion, with the trade deficit standing at US$2.7 billion, reflecting a severe trade imbalance.

In 2013, the amount of imported Australian beef came to 147,173t, accounting for 55% of combined beef imports. The United States had 92,145t, or 34.5%, and New Zealand beef accounted for 9.5%, or 25,000t.

The 40% tariff imposed on Australian and Canadian beef will be completely abolished by 2030. Those on Australian pork will be abolished in 10 years (excluding frozen products), and those from Canada will be free of tariffs in next 10 years.

Following the FTAs with Canada and Australia, the combined production of South Korea's agricultural and livestock sector will suffer a 2.1 trillion won decline in production, with the livestock sector taking up 1.75 trillion won, the Korea Rural Economic Institute estimated.

The FTA with New Zealand is set to kick off by the first half of 2015 after earning approval from the parliament. In 2013, South Korea imported US$114 million worth of beef from New Zealand, along with US$102.2 million worth of cheese. If the FTA takes effect, South Korea must import 1,500t of evaporated milk and powdered milk every year tariff-free, and increase the amount by 3% every year over the next decade to reach 1,957t.

The tariff on mixed milk powder will be abolished over the next 10 to 15 years, and that on cheese will be lifted. While that on cheese will be eliminated over the next seven to 15 years, South Korea must instead increase its tariff-free volume by 3% every year from 7,000t.

The agricultural ministry estimates the combined damage on local agricultural households over the next 15 years after the implementation of the FTA with New Zealand will reach 40 million won to 50 million won, an amount similar to losses from the FTA with Canada.

Concerning the FTA deal with China, South Korea has been making efforts to limit the scope of market liberalization in fear of Chinese goods dominating the local agricultural sector. Despite such struggles, however, damages on spices and garden goods are inevitable, as China is geographically adjacent to South Korea and grows similar crops. The influx of alternative-import agricultural goods is also set to spark a secondhand impact on the local industry.

South Korea will be obligated to import 10,000t of beans, 24,000t of sesames, 5,000t of sweet-potato starch, and 3,000t of red beans from China annually. The tariff on kimchi, however, will be 19.8%, down 0.2%p from the previous 20%. The tariff on mixed sauces is estimated to be fixed at 44.5%, industry watchers forecast.

The FTA with Vietnam will also allow several sensitive products to go tariff-free, including tropical fruits such as guava and mango, along with dried or frozen garlic and ginger, over the next 10 years. Vietnamese honey will benefit from the agreement, with its tariff being abolished over the next 15 years, sounding an alarm for the local beekeeping industry.

South Korea also seeks to expand the scope of tariff cuts related to the existing FTAs with the European Union and the United States, which will spark a further increase of imported goods, casting a gloomy outlook over local agricultural households.

■ **South Korea Loses Status as Foot-and-Mouth-Disease-Free Nation**

South Korea confirmed an outbreak of foot-and-mouth disease (FMD) in Uiseong, North Gyeongsang Province, in July 2014. The last FMD outbreak was in April 2011. South Korea had regained the status of an FMD-free country just two months before the latest case.

The government had planned to roll out a long-term strategy to expand exports of local livestock goods after it had regained the status, which ended in vain. It will take two years for South Korea to recover its FMD-free status, during which time 80% of its livestock must be injected with FMD vaccines regularly, and it must prove that there has not been a virus outbreak for a one-year period.

However, South Korea confirmed an additional case of FMD at a pig farm in the southeastern city of Hapcheon in August. A cow at a farm in Anseong, 77km south of Seoul, tested positive for the animal disease, the first such case among cattle since early 2011.

Chronology of Local Foot-and-Mouth Disease (FMD)

▲ 2000 = 15 cases of outbreak

▲ 2002 = 16 cases of outbreak

▲ 2010 = 17 cases of outbreak

▲ 2010 Nov. 29 = Two pigs found with FMD in Andong, North Gyeongsang Province.

▲ 2011 April 21 = FMD breaks out in Yeongcheon, North Gyeongsang Province.

▲ 2011 May 16 = South Korea finishes burial procedures, declares elimination of FMD.

▲ 2014 May 24 = South Korea regains its FMD-free status from the 82nd World Organization for Animal Health gathering.

▲ 2014 July 23 = A pig farm in Uiseong, North Gyeongsang Province, reports the possibility of an outbreak of FMD.

▲ 2014 July 24 = After pigs are diagnosed with FMD in Uiseong, North Gyeongsang Province, South Korea loses its FMD-free status.

■ Fear Continues to Rise over Avian Flu; 14 Mln Birds Slaughtered

South Korea suffered from bird flu throughout 2014 regardless of the season, sparking woes over the disease being naturalized to the country. There was also the possibility that the disease may have come from China or other nearby Asian countries.

Taking such a phenomenon into consideration, South Korea decided to keep a closer watch on bird flu not only during winter, but all year long. The country designated 1,700 households raising birds, or 35% of the total. The number of birds being monitored came to 35 million, or 20% of the total.

Following such moves, the agricultural ministry declared that the bird flu was eliminated in the country as of September. But only 20 days later, there was another outbreak in South Jeolla Province.

From January to November in 2014, the number of birds slaughtered due to the disease came to 14.46 million, reaching an all-time high level. The previous record was posted in 2008 at 100.2 million units. In 2014, the disease also occurred in the following countries: Japan, China, Russia, Britain, India, the Netherlands, Canada and Germany.

■ Implementation of Pork-Tracking System

Starting on Dec. 28, 2014, South Korea implemented a new tracking system for pork being sold in markets. Following the move, the government can keep track of all local pork meat, including the slaughter date of the animals or packaging details, which will be provided to consumers.

The move aims to promptly deal with an outbreak of animal diseases by collecting and disposing concerned products. A company which fails to provide such information will be subject to a fine of 5 million won. The data can be found at www.mtrace.go.kr. South Korea already has been implementing similar rules on beef since June 2009.

FORESTRY

■ Overview

As of the end of 2010, forest areas in the country amounted to 6.37 million hectares, making up 63.7% of the country's total land. Of the total, national forests totaled 1.54 million hectares, or 24.2% of the entire forest land, with public forests totaling 488,000 hectares, or 7.7% of the total. Privately-held forest areas amounted to 4.33 million hectares, or 68.1% of the total.

The proportion of forest land in the country's total area is the fourth-highest among the members of the Organization for Economic Cooperation and Development after Finland (72.9%), Sweden (68.7%) and Japan (68.5%).

The total area of woodlands shrank by 1,461 hectares from 2009. The decrease was attributable to construction of roads, which took up 1,357 hectares. Factories were responsible for the decrease of 620 hectares.

By type, coniferous forests amounted to 2.58 million hectares, or 40.5% of the total woodlands with broadleaf forests accounting for 27% of the total, or 1.71 million hectares.

Forests with a mixed population of coniferous and broadleaf trees amounted to 1.86 million hectares, accounting for 29.3% of total forest lands, with bamboo forests and others making up 204,000 hectares, or 3.2% of the total.

The amount of trees aged 30 years or below took up 2.02 million hectares, or 31.8% of the total, while 65% was held by trees older than 31 years. Bamboo forests took up the remaining 3.2%, or 204,000 hectares.

■ **Forestry Industry**

Overview In 2013, the combined output from the forestry industry came to 6.9 trillion won, up 2.4% from 6.7 trillion won posted in 2012. Compared to 2012, the production of herbs and wildflowers increased, while that of mushrooms and vegetables decreased.

Economic value of forests The economic value of forests represents the physical growth of trees within a given year converted into its monetary value. In 2010, the economic value of forests neared 2.51 trillion won at 37 million cubic meters. Such growth shows a rise in the country's forest resources, which may also positively affect the country's efforts to secure permits for greenhouse gas emissions.

Materials for landscape architecture Materials for landscape architecture, which includes wildflowers, took up 11.1% of the combined forestry production. In 2013, the sector generated 763.6 billion won, up 12.6% from a year earlier. Landscape trees held the largest amount at 715.7 billion won, followed by wildflowers with 25 billion won and potted plants with 22.9 billion won.

Forest crops The total output of forest crops, such as chestnuts, walnuts, acorns, mountain berries and wild grapes, dropped 5.8% to 718.1 billion won on-year in 2013. Output of chestnuts reached 64,184t, followed by persimmons with 148,100t, jujube with 10,583t, pine nuts with 2,435t, and walnuts with 1,282t.

Mushrooms and wild greens The total output of mushrooms grown, including pine mushrooms, fell 24.9% on-year to reach 19,742t in 2013, with the production valued at 196.1 billion won, down 31.7% from 2012. By sector, shiitake mushrooms took up 19,239t, pine

mushrooms 86t, and other mushrooms accounted for 417t. They each generated profits of 176.8 billion won, 16.5 billion won, and 2.8 billion won, respectively.

The production of wild greens moved down 15.8% on-year to reach 38,676t, while its value moved down 4.6% over the cited period to reach 370.7 billion won.

Timber The combined production of timber reached 3.8 million cubic meters in 2013, down 18.3% from a year earlier. Its monetary value, however, moved up 8.8% to 389.6 billion won.

Soil The combined production of soil-related goods came to 3.17 million cubic meters, with its monetary value standing at 1.15 trillion won. The figures mark a 43.9% and 10.8% increase from 2012.

■ **Forestry Policies**

Overview From end-February to April 2013, the government promoted the planting of more trees to foster the country's forestry. In that year, the country added 47.2 million trees on 20,000ha of land.

South Korea has successfully completed two development plans for the forest industry. The first generation (2004-2008) of the plan aims at absorbing more carbon and generating more jobs. The second phase (2009-2013) put priorities on tackling climate change. Starting in 2014, the government rolled out the third-stage plan that will run through 2018 to develop forests by functions.

Bolstering carbon absorption to tackle climate change South Korean forests absorbed 53.2 million tons of carbon dioxide in 2012. The government also implemented a new rule that plans to promote the absorption of gases starting in February 2013. Based on the law, it kicked off the first-stage comprehensive plan on the promotion of gas absorption in 2015 that will run through 2019.

Expanding revenue for forestry workers South Korea aimed to foster the chestnut industry to help give more profits to workers in the forestry industry by using such measures as replacing old trees and upgrading the quality of soil.

As for shiitake mushrooms, the government made efforts to adopt more modern methods of production, also opening 33 support centers through 2014 to develop more popular cultivation models. South Korea has also been expanding facilities to support high-profit forestry goods such as wood-cultivated ginseng, pine mushrooms and walnuts.

Promoting sustainable timber use
South Korea enacted a new law in May 2013 to add sustainability to the local forestry industry. It included providing subsidies to firms using home-grown timber products and opening academies for students.

Based on the legal grounds, the government ① established a comprehensive plan on sustainable timber use ② will open a commission and promotion agency regarding forestry use ③ will adopt a timer production registration system ④ will manage the quality of timber goods and implement a private-police system for quality control. As such, South Korea has boasted various achievements in the forestry sector, and built grounds to foster the industry.

South Korea also promoted the use of domestic timber products, rolling out incentives to facilities which aimed at meeting the goals. To expand the ground for timber-related cultural assets, the government rolled out a promotion campaign and promoted various classes for kindergarten, elementary and middle school students as well as for adults. By joining forces with regional government, South Korea also held various exhibitions and events to promote the industry.

Diversifying forestry leisure services
In 2014, the government established 14 leisure facilities (six recreational forests, five forest-therapy facilities, and three ecosystem and cultural experience zones).

In order to take advantage of the forests' self-healing function, the government also rolled out a forest-therapy program and educated 171 experts in 2014 to operate related programs. The program is available throughout the country.

The government also made efforts to prevent the damage of forests by cemeteries by promoting cremation. It also operates a state forestry cemetery to foster a sound funeral culture. In 2014, the government also drew up plans to expand related facilities and improve rules.

Starting in 2007, the government has been making efforts to build tracking roads on major mountains, including Mount Halla, Mount Jiri, and the Demilitarized Zone to establish a forest-road network among major tourist sites, allowing people to enjoy forestry culture.

Also, breaking out from traditional hiking tracks, which only focused on reaching the peak, the government seeks to open more safe tracks aimed at enjoying regional history, culture, and natural heritages for everyone. It aimed at paving 7,614km of such roads by 2021. They have been under construction since 2012.

The government also continuously renovated existing hiking tracks to provide a better environment. In 2014, 8,166 km of hiking roads were renovated, with 747 staff members from 27 rescue squads on hand in case of possible accidents.

In order to make use of forestry resources and profits of residents, the government had pushed forward a village development program since 1995, which continued through 2010, to build 240 centers.

Establishing strategical preservation plan for mountains Following the first mountain management plan rolled out in April 2013, the government has established a strategical plan to preserve and utilize mountains in relation to the country's land and environment policies on a long-term basis.

The government has also been collecting the public's opinion since 2013 to apply changes in the society to mountain-related policies. It also sought standardization of study methods, and boosted credibility of its research by promptly reflecting improvements.

It also made efforts to ease regulations to foster more investment, in line with the outcomes of the trade-promotion meeting presided over by President Park Geun-hye. Officials at the meeting urged the deregulation of seven sectors, including the construction of cable cars.

As the new government promoted forestry policies that came in line with its efforts to promote investment, it came out with an improvement proposal. Such moves led to an investment of 1 trillion won through 2017, with an additional 1.4 trillion won after 2018.

South Korea also established a so-called "mountain forum" composed of members from academia, organizations, and institutions, which stands as a human resources network of experts in forestry.

Prevention of disasters Forest fires, pests and landslides are often called the three major disasters in forests. Despite having a smaller workforce due to the spring vacation season, the provincial election, and an outbreak of pine wilt disease, the country's forestry authority still focused its efforts on preventing forest fires by making use of helicopters and other systems related to forest fires.

During spring and fall, which are considered as vulnerable seasons for forest fires, related South Korean authorities maintained a close cooperation system, with 23,000 fire monitoring staff members expanding inspections on weak spots. Helped by such efforts, the combined damage of forest fires came to 137㏊ in 2014, which only accounts for 18% of the decade-average of 776㏊. The number of cases, however, moved up 26% to 492 in 2014, compared to the decade-average of 389 cases.

In 2014, the government also built evacuation and inspection systems in areas vulnerable to landslides. Following such efforts, the amount of landslide-damaged areas moved down 22% in 2014 from 312 ㏊ posted a year earlier. The 2014 figure was also 15% lower than the decade-average of 456㏊. The government will continue its efforts to protect the lives of citizens as well as their assets from landslides by rolling out pre-emptive projects in vulnerable places, and build an emergency evacuation system.

Expansion of national forests The government purchased 7,055㏊ of privately-owned woodlands in 2014 and plans to purchase an additional 8,620 ㏊ in 2015. Purchasing privately-owned woodlands is part of efforts to promote the public use of forests, secure an additional and stable source of carbon absorption and also help preserve forest wildlife.

The government has been making efforts to purchase unmanaged private lands and secure direct control of forests to implement a planned and sustainable forestry management. Also, to protect various species living around the United Nations Educational, Scientific and Cultural Organization (UNESCO)-designated Mount Halla of Jeju Island, the government has secured 378㏊ of land since 2009, and plans to acquire an additional 60㏊ in 2015.

MARITIME AFFAIRS AND FISHERIES

MARITIME AFFAIRS

■ Maritime Minister Lee Ju-young Resigns over Sewol Sinking

South Korean Maritime Minister Lee Ju-young resigned less than a year after his inauguration, due mainly to the sinking of the Sewol ferry on April 16, 2014. Lee was nominated to take the post after his predecessor, Yoon Jin-sook, was fired after she failed to cope properly with an oil spill that occurred in Yeosu, 455㎞ southwest of Seoul.

Lee was known as a close aide to President Park Geun-hye, and was expected to solidify the maritime organization. But as Lee failed to cope with the sinking of ferry Sewol, he came under fire from the public regarding his rescue and search missions. He even had to spend nights surrounded by families of the missing.

As Lee stayed on the southern island of Jindo and took the lead in dealing with the disaster, he gradually bought trust from the families. Some considered him as a "politician with communication" by the time he stepped down from the disaster commission on Nov. 18.

Lee's resignation was accepted on Dec. 23. He later returned to the ruling Saenuri Party and ran for a representative election but lost. Lee's vacancy was taken by the vice-minister as the acting minister.

■ Efforts to Be Excluded from Illegal-Fisher Status by EU, U.S.

As South Korea was designated as an illegal, unreported and unregulated (IUU) nation by the European Union and the United States, the government has been making efforts to not be named as an official IUU state, which could have an adverse impact on the local fisheries industry.

If designated as an IUU nation, South Korea would be banned from exporting fishery goods processed in the country, and entering ports of the EU and the U.S.

As such a move would also damage South Korea's reputation around the globe as it will give the impression of a "piracy country," the country has been making a full-fledged effort to stop the designation.

The EU has been claiming that South Korean fishing boats have been involving in illegal fishery activities in the waters near Western Africa, adding that Seoul does not have disciplinary systems to punish such boats. Thus, the EU designated South Korea as a potential IUU state.

The ministry explained to the EU delegate who visited South Korea in June 2014 that a monitoring center in Busan operates to prevent such activities. It also said that the country has improved related policies to track fishing boats and their records when issuing certificates.

South Korea also stopped issuing certificates to five fishery firms that were involved in illegal activities near Western Africa, and punished 22 boats.

Penalties for illegal fishing were also increased due to criticism that they were too weak. Under the revision implemented in July 2013, an illegal fishing activity can lead to imprisonment of up to three years, or a fine of up to three times the amount of the profits gained from violations.

Although the final announcement by the EU was scheduled for September 2014, the procedure has been delayed. The government expects the announcement to be made in April 2015.

South Korea was excluded from preliminary IUU status in February 2015, about two years after being designated as such in January 2013 after a local boat was involved in illegal fishing activities near the Antarctic Ocean.

The U.S. National Oceanic and Atmospheric Administration released the final report that took South Korea's efforts for improvements into consideration.

■ Jang Bo-Go Antarctic Research Station Kicks Off

South Korea opened its second research center in Antarctica in February.

Following the move, South Korea now has the King Sejong Station and the Jang Bo-go Station in the South Pole region. It became the 10th country to own two or more residential bases in the area. The stations will conduct various studies on asteroids, volcanoes and sub-glacial lakes.

▲ *South Korean government and parliamentary officials pose for the camera after attending a dedication ceremony for the nation's second antarctic research station in Terra Nova Bay, East Antarctica, on Feb. 12. (local time).*

Jang Bo-go Station has collected some 81 asteroid samples, including one weighing 36kg, which are used to conduct studies on the evolution of materials in various solar systems.

South Korea also detected an emission of gas from Mount Melbourne in January 2015 for the first time in 25 years, allowing the country to conduct studies that could have not been done at home.

The country made efforts to stabilize the operation of the base over the past year, and built a cooperation center with New Zealand. It also established an emergency management system on a real-time basis.

South Korea seeks to establish a 2,000 km-long "Korean Route" to reach the geographic South Pole from King Sejong Station. King Sejong Station, which has been in operation since 1998, currently has 17 members, including Asia's first female chief researcher.

■ Deep-Ocean Water Available for Soju, Beer, and Other Food Stuffs

While deep-ocean water has only been allowed for use in the making of a few products, such as tofu and kimchi, the government lifted regulations and allowed its use on all foodstuffs.

Deep-ocean water refers to clean water whose temperature is maintained below 2 degrees Celsius at 200m deep. It is known to be free from germs.

The ministry said it plans to expand the use of such resources and make a next-generation blue ocean, as South Korea currently uses only 3.4 million tons every year, despite having 4 trillion tons.

Because Japan and Taiwan have 1,000 and 250 varieties of deep-ocean water-related products, the ministry believes that South Korea can also expand the number it has from the current 69. Along with coffee, green tea, and beverages, the resource is believed to be also applicable for snacks, instant noodles, instant rice, rice cakes, spices, fermented or marinated goods, and other processed goods.

The ministry plans to open a deep-ocean water industry support center between 2016 and 2018, which will be capable of conducting studies on the resource, while establishing an industrial cluster in Gangwon Province.

In the long run, South Korea also plans to build venture-support centers, where companies can produce samples of new products. The government will also establish a water amusement park that uses deep-ocean water.

■ Maritime Ministry Hosts Investment Conference

The maritime ministry held an investment conference in September for small- and medium-size companies. At the gathering, the ministry said that although South Korea has the world's 12th-strongest maritime industry, and has kept its crown in the marine plant and shipbuilding sector, the country needs to diversify its scope of business to cover the telecommunications or biological sectors.

The government also urged local companies to develop seafood products that meet the demand of Chinese consumers following a free trade agreement with China that lifted tariff barriers.

The conference was held in three sessions with 15 topics and covered maritime research, maritime security, leisure, and marine resources sectors. The ministry suggested about 200 business opportunities for the maritime sector.

■ Consulting Center Opens for Those Seeking to Return to Rural Areas

The government opened a support center in Busan to provide consulting services to those wishing to return to farms and fishing towns from urban regions. The five experts deployed at the center will provide visitors with details on maritime polices and technologies, providing one-stop services from preparations to settlement.

Similar support will also be provided by the existing National Fisheries Research & Development Institute and other maritime organizations.

■ Expanding Income of Fishery Villages

The ocean ministry rolled out a development plan to improve the income of residents of fishery villages by making use of the tourism resources of their area.

Under the plan, the ministry will expand the number of fishery-experience villages and improve the scenery of such towns, pushing up the current average income of 37 million won to 50 million won by 2018. It also plans to generate 8,278 more jobs over the next five years.

The number of fishery-experience villages is expected to increase to 134 from the current 100. The government will also spend 90 billion won over the next five years on the project.

The ocean ministry also decided to lift related regulations to vitalize the tourism of fishery villages at a regulation improvement meeting held in September that was presided over by President Park Geun-hye.

It also decided to reveal the grades of such villages and tourists facilities to prevent visitors' inconveniences in accomodations and attractions.

FISHERIES

■ Overview

The number of South Koreans involving in the fishery industry came to 1.16 million in 1970, or 3.6% of the population. The number, however, plunged to 147,000 in 2013, accounting for 0.29% of the combined population in South Korea.

Amid the expansion of free trade agreements with fishery big-players such as China and Vietnam, the combined import of marine goods came to US$3.8 billion in 2013.

Of such imports, Chinese goods took up US$1.02 billion, followed by Russian products with US$590 million. The country also imported US$480 billion worth of goods from Vietnam.

While South Korea's fishery industry was facing challenges due to its small size, the number of registered fishing boats came to 71,287 units in 2013, down from the 75,031 units posted in 2012.

The number of deep-sea fishing boats came to 315 units, while that of coastal fishing boats came to 2,780 units. Others included: inshore fishing boats with 44,713 units, aquaculture boats with 16,772 units and inland fishing boats with 2,908 units.

■ Chinese Illegal Fishing and Joint Surveillance

The South Korean and Chinese government started joint surveillance on waters as illegal fishing activities by Chinese boats emerged as a serious problem.

The surveillance was originally planned to be started in October 2014 following the South Korea-China summit held in 2013. But after the death of a Chinese fisherman who fought against the South Korean coastal authority's crackdown, it was postponed to December.

The inspection was conducted by vessels from two countries. Each country conducted its own inspections in the respective waters, and exchanged outcomes of the surveillance.

Following the surveillance, South Korea detected 19 Chinese boats which failed to follow regulations, such as exposing their vessel name, but no Chinese boats were found to be involved in illegal fishing.

The ocean ministry plans to expand the number of such surveillance to two to three times in 2015 before October, which is considered as the peak season for the fishery industry. The government will also operate an inspection team armed with helicopters and troops to seize unregistered fishing boats.

The ministry estimates that 2,000 to 3,000 Chinese boats are involving in illegal fishing between October and December in the Yellow Sea, while 1,800 others operate in the East Sea in North Korean waters.

■ Oryong 501 Sinking

A 1,753-ton ship, the Oryong 501, sank in the western Bering Sea. Seven crewmen -- one Russian inspector, three Filipinos and three Indonesians -- were rescued. There were 11 South Koreans aboard. It was owned by a local fisheries firm, Sajo Industries. Investigators said the ship likely sank because it failed to drain an influx of water properly.

▲ Executives of Sajo Industries bow to families of the missing sailors of the South Korean fishing boat Oryong 501, which sank in the western Bering Sea on Dec. 1, during a briefing session at the company's branch office in Busan on Dec. 2.

MARINE TRANSPORT AND PORTS

■ Port Cargo Volume Reaches All-Time High of 1.41 Billion Tons

In 2014, the country's combined volume of cargo handled at ports reached 1.4 billion tons, marking an all-time high. The figure was a 3.9% increase from a year earlier. By sector, timber and automobiles moved up 32.9% and 12.4%, respectively, while that of scrap metals shed 13%.

■ Number of Marine Passengers Falls after Sewol Tragedy

In 2014, the number of marine passengers fell 11% on-year to reach 14.27

million in 2014, compared to the 16 million posted a year earlier. The decline apparently came as less visitors traveled to islands after the sinking of the Sewol ferry. The number of tourists fell 15% to reach 10.6 million.

MANUFACTURING

■ Overview
The South Korean economy remained mired in a slump because of lackluster demand and exports in 2014. In 2014, the Korean economy expanded 3.3%, accelerating from 3% the previous year. In 2011 and 2010, the economy grew 3.7% and 6.5%, respectively.

Industrial output increased 1.1% last year, the slowest pace since 2000, when related data began to be compiled. The trade surplus reached a record US$47.5 billion last year with exports rising 2.4% to US$573 billion and imports gaining 2.4% to US$526 billion.

The country's employment rate rose 0.7%p to 60.2% last year, the highest since 1997, when the comparable figure was 60.9%. The number of the employed increased 533,000 to 25.59 million, the largest gain since 2002, when the figure rose by 597,000.

■ Real Economy
The country's GDP expanded 3.3% in 2013. In 2010, the economy increased 6.5%, after rising 3.7% and 2.3% each in 2011 and 2012.

Private spending increased 1.7% in 2014, slowing from the 2% expansion a year earlier, and construction investment increased 1.1% last year, sharply slowing from the 6.7% gain a year earlier, and export growth slowed to 2.8% from 4.3% over the cited period.

In contrast, facility investment surged 5.9% last year, a turnaround from a 1.5% drop. The manufacturing sector grew 4% in 2014, while the service segment expanded 3.2%.

The country's gross domestic income increased 3.8% in 2014, slowing from the 4.1% gain a year earlier, but its growth rate hovered above the GDP growth thanks to improved terms of trade.

■ Export-Import
Exports increased 2.4% on-year to reach US$573.1 billion in 2014, while imports gained 1.9% to US$525.6 billion over the cited period.

By item, steel products, telecommunications equipment and ships posted sharp growths, while petrochemicals and electronic goods suffered drops in their outbound shipments.

By region, exports to the U.S., the Middle East and Australia led the overall gains, while shipments to China, Japan and Canada declined.

The country logged US$47.5 billion in trade surplus in 2014. Imports of alcohol, garments and automobiles surged, while imports of crude oil and resources declined.

■ Key Industrial Sectors
Machinery sector The country's machinery sector, excluding the shipbuilding-related one, increased slightly in 2014 as a slump in emerging countries and a decline in facility investment offset a sharp growth. The sector logged a growth rate of 1.4% last year to reach 101.6 trillion won in 2014 despite a global economic slump.

Exports gained 4.7% on-year to reach US$452.7 billion last year, while imports declined 2.4% to US$110.6 billion over the cited period.

The country's machinery sector is expected to post a mild recovery in 2015 on the back of moderate growth in the U.S. and rising demand from emerging countries. But China's economic slowdown and increased competition could pose threats to the sector's much-awaited recovery.

In particular, the sector's exports could drop to US$422 billion from US$475 billion if the yen-dollar rate rises 20% on an annual basis. Also, if crude oil prices fall by 20% annually, the segment's exports could fall to US$463 billion from US$475 billion.

Steelmaking sector South Korea emerged as the world's fifth-largest steel producer in 2014, with its crude steel production capacity topping the 70-million-ton mark. Data compiled by the World Steel Association show that global crude steel output gained 1.2% in 2014 to reach 1.6 billion tons.

South Korea's crude steel production surged 7.5% last year to reach 71 million tons, ranking fifth among major countries. In 2013, South Korea's crude steel production slipped 4.4% to reach 66 million tons.

China maintained its top spot with 822.7 million tons, followed by Japan with 110 million tons, the U.S. with 88.3 million tons, and India with 83.2 million tons.

South Korea's crude steel output topped 40 million tons, 50 million tons and 60 million tons, respectively, in 1997, 2007 and 2011.

China accounted for 49.5% of the global crude steel output in 2014, followed by Japan with 6.7% and the U.S. with 5.3% and India with 5% and South Korea with 4.3%.

Due to a global economic slump, global steel demand reached 1.5 billion tons in 2014, up 2% from a year earlier, but fell short of crude steel production of 1.6 billion tons, showing that the global steel industry is suffering a supply glut.

In 2015, global steel demand is expected to rise 2% to reach 1.6 billion tons, but a constraint in demand from China would not work to help resolve a global supply glut.

The local steel industry is expected to continue to face unfavorable business conditions such as strict regulations and weak demand.

Automobile sector South Korea's automobile sector enjoyed sharp growth in domestic sales, but suffered a slump in its exports. According to the Korea Automobile Manufacturers Association, or KAMA, South Korea's automakers produced 4.52 million units in 2014, up 0.1% from a year earlier.

Of the manufactured, 3.06 million units were exported, down 0.8% from a year earlier, largely due to increased competition. But in terms of value, automobile exports gained 0.6% on-year to reach US$48.9 billion last year on the back of a surge in outbound shipments of large cars and SUVs.

By region, exports to the U.S. surged 17.7% to 893,580 units last year, with shipments to the Middle East gaining 4.3% to 619,435 units. In contrast, shipments to Europe, Africa and other regions suffered sharp downturns.

In the U.S., sales of South Korean-made cars surged 4% on-year to reach 1.3 million units last year, driven by strong demand for SUVs and large cars.

Hyundai Motor Co., and its smaller affiliate, Kia Motors Corp., produced 4.41 million units at their overseas plants, up 7.4% from a year earlier, which marks the highest-ever figure on an annual basis.

Domestic sales gained 5.8% on-year to reach 1.46 million, on the back of aggressive marketing and reduced tax rates. The sales of large cars jumped 16.6% on-year to reach 180,633 units, while SUVs and minivans logged growth rates of 15.1% and 12.9% in their sales last year. Small-sized cars witnessed a 2.6% growth in sales, and commercial vehicles logged a 4.7% rise in sales as well.

Sales of imported cars surged 25.5% last year to reach 196,359 units, a record high, on the back of aggressive marketing and diversified customer needs. Volkswagen's Tiguan 2.0 TDI Bluemotion was the best-selling model with 8,106 units sold.

Shipbuilding sector South Korea's shipbuilding industry had its worst-ever year in 2014 as low oil prices and the global economic slump reduced demand for new ships.

According to the data compiled by Clarkson, a total of 39.69 million CGTs were placed around the world in 2014, down 34.7% from a year earlier. In 2012, the comparable figure was 26.15 million CGTs.

South Korea clinched a total of 11.78 million CGTs last year, a sharp fall of 36.4% from a year earlier, trailing China, which bagged 15.31 million CGTs.

South Korea's market share stood at 29.7% last year, down from 30.5% in 2013 and 32.1% in 2012. China held a 38.6% market share in 2014, with the comparable figure for Japan being 19.7%.

Hyundai Heavy Industries Co., the world's largest shipyard, saw its new vessel-building contracts fall 28% to reach US$19.83 billion last year. The figure fell sharply short of its annual target of US$29.56 billion.

Hyundai Heavy also logged more than 3 trillion won in losses last year due to reserves against offshore plants projects, which led the shipbuilder to undertake massive restructuring moves such as staff cuts.

Samsung Heavy Industries Co. targeted deals worth US$15 billion last year, but its actual deals received totaled US$7.3 billion. In contrast, Daewoo Shipbuilding & Marine Engineering Co. surpassed its annual target last year to clinch US$14.9 billion worth of deals.

Petrochemical sector South Korea's petrochemicals industry faced a variety of headwinds such as the global economic downturn and shale gas developments in 2014.

In particular, falling crude oil prices were the biggest reason for an industry-wide slump as players had to produce goods with high-priced raw materials.

According to the Korea Petrochemical Industry Association, production of synthetic resine and synthetic rubbers and others fell 2.6% last year to reach 21.27 million tons, while demand for those goods fell 2.7% to reach 10.51 million tons.

Exports of petrochemicals fell 2.1% to reach 11.78 million tons last year, largely affected by a slowdown in China and its expanded capacity.

South Korea's production of synthetic resine fell 0.2% to reach 12.70 million tons last year, while demand shed 0.9% to reach 5.49 million tons.

The country's output of synthetic materials dropped 6.6% to reach 7.54 million tons, with demand for those goods falling 7.4% to 4.57 million tons.

Synthetic rubber output also shed 1% to reach 1.03 million tons, while demand for the good jumped 4.2% to 440,000t.

Synthetic rubber output fell despite an expanded capacity and steady domestic demand. Exports of the goods also remained weak because of China's expanded output and a slowdown in its economy. Exports of styrene-butadiene rubber to China shed 8.2% in the first 11 months of last year to 106,000t.

For 2015, the petrochemical industry is expected to continue to face a down cycle in line with strict environmental regulations and a global economic downturn.

Semiconductor sector The semiconductor industry enjoyed its heyday in 2014. Exports surged 9.6% on-year to reach US$62.65 billion.

Outbound shipments of DRAM spiked 45.7% to reach US$20.06 billion, with that for NAND flash memory soaring 10.9% to US$3.97 billion. Exports of memory chips gained 33.2% to US$33.99 billion.

The boom was driven by strong demand for memory chips and Samsung Electronics Co. and SK hynix Inc. upgraded their chip-making technologies, thus reducing costs.

But exports of system semiconductors shed 9.8% to reach US$22.52 billion last year mainly because of a slump in weak demand for mobile application processors.

The semiconductor maintained its top spot as the best export item for a second consecutive year in 2014. Its exports topped US$10 billion in 1994, and surpassed the US$20 billion mark in 2000. Its outbound shipments again broke the US$30 billion mark and the US$50 billion mark, respectively, in 2006 and 2010.

The stellar growth was led by Samsung Electronics and SK hynix. Samsung's chipmaking-sector logged a 6.1% rise in its 2014 sales at 39.73 trillion won, and operating income surged 27.4% to 8.78 trillion won. SK hynix also enjoyed a 21% spike in its 2014 sales at 17.12 trillion won with its operating income soaring 51% to 5.1 trillion won.

The global chipmaking sector is expected to grow 6.4% this year, according to market researcher IHS.

IT/Display sector The telecommunication sector saw continued growth in the smartphone business, while suffering a slump in the tablet market. According to Strategic Analytics, the global sales of smartphones reached 1.18 billion units last year, up 30% from a year earlier, led by growth in emerging markets such as China and India.

Samsung Electronics held on to its rank as the top smartphone seller last year with shipments of 312 million units, which marks a decline of 2.6 million units from a year earlier. Samsung had a 24.7% share of the global smartphone market last year.

Apple Inc., Samsung's archrival, sold 192.7 million smartphones last year, up 40 million from a year earlier to grab a 15% market share. Lenovo-Motorola came next with 92.7 million units.

Hit by a slump in smartphone sales, Samsung's mobile unit saw its operating income fall to 1.75 trillion won during the third quarter of last year, from 4.42 trillion won and 6.4 trillion won, respectively, in the first and the second quarters. Outbound shipments of mobile handsets, in contrast, surged 6.3% to US$26.44 billion last year.

Sales of tablet PCs showed signs of a fatigue last year with their shipments gaining 4.4% to reach 229.6 million units, according to market researcher IDC. The deceleration in growth was mainly due to consumers switching to so-called phablets.

The global panel market posted steady growth last year, driven by firm demand for large and high-definition flat screens. According to market researcher Display-Search, South Korean makers accounted for a combined 47.3% of the large-sized LCD market last year, followed by Taiwanese rivals with 34.7% and Chinese counterparts with 11.4%.

South Korean flatscreen makers also led the mid-to-small sized LCD panel market last year with a 33% market share, followed by Japanese firms with 29% and Taiwnese rivals with 20.5%.

LG Display Co., the country's biggest flatscreen maker, logged sales of 26.46 trillion won last year, down 2.1% from a year earlier, while its operating income surged 16.7% to 1.36 trillion won.

Samsung Electronics also saw its display panel business's sales drop 13.7% on-year to 25.73 trillion won last year. Its operating income also sank 77.9% to 660 billion won.

The global TV market was also led by South Korean firms such as Samsung and LG. According to Wits View, a market researcher, LCD TV shipments increased 5.5% last year to reach 215 million units.

Samsung Electronics posted a 22.8% market share last year, up 1.8%p from a year earlier. LG Electronics saw its market share expand 1.2%p to 14.9% last year. Their combined market share reached 37.7% last year, trailed by Japan's Sony Corp. with 6.8% and TCL of China with 6.1%, according to the data.

Textile sector The textile industry posted decent growth with its exports gaining 0.1% to US$15.9 billion. Imports surged 8.4% on-year to reach US$14.65 billion, resulting in a trade surplus of US$1.28 billion.

Overseas sales of garments surged 6.2% last year, and shipments to Vietnam gained 9.2% to US$2.73 billion, the largest among other countries. Shipments to China came in at US$2.52 billion last year, up 7.9% from a year earlier, followed by the U.S. with US$1.43 billion, Indonesia with US$1.34 billion and Japan with US$870 million.

Imports of textiles from China came in at US$6.59 billion, followed by Vietnam with US$2.76 billion, Indonesia with US$760 million and Italy with US$630 million.

For 2015, exports of textiles are expected to rise 2.9% to reach US$16.4 billion, while imports advanced 9.3% to US$16 billion, resulting in a surplus of US$400 million.

A steady recovery in the U.S. economy and steady demand from Vietnam and other Southeast Asian countries will help boost exports. Also, a series of free trade deals with other countries will help solidify firm outbound shipments.

Foodmaking sector Government data show that the country's milk inventory almost tripled to 232,000t last year from 92,000t a year earlier, as milk production increased in line with a rise in the number of milk cows.

Also, higher prices of domestically-produced milk was cited as one of main reasons for the increased inventory of milk and South Korean consumers' reduced demand for milk as well.

The price gap between imported milk and domestically-produced milk runs high, with the price of powdered milk standing at between 4,000 won and 5,000 won. Also, the hike in prices of milk by processing companies was cited as another factor behind a drop in milk consumption.

The data show that the price of a 200-milliliter milk pack cost 727 won in 2014, compared with 650 won in 2012 and 672 won in 2013. The drop in milk consumption led to a cull of milk cows in 2014, the first since 2003.

Ramen The sales of ramen dipped to below the 2-trillion won level last year, affected by weak domestic demand and a rising appetite for fast food. South Korea's ramen market is estimated at 1.97 trillion won last year, down 2% from 2.01 trillion won a year earlier.

Weak consumer sentiment and an increased amount of fast food being substituted for ramen were cited as key factors for a slump in the local ramen market. Nongshim Co. maintained its top status as the No. 1 player with a 62.4% market share, followed by Ottogi with 16.2% and Samyang with 13.3%.

Exports of ramen also declined, with shipments reaching 48,803t last year, down 0.6% from a year earlier. In terms of value, its exports also declined 1.9% to US$208 million last year, ending its upward trend.

Exports of ramen declined as Japanese consumers reduced purchases of Korean-made ramen over territorial and historical disputes. In terms of value, shipments to Japan dropped 23.5% to US$24.47 million last year, with the volume also down 26% to 5,534 tons.

Consequently, Japan was relegated to being the second-largest importer of South Korean ramen. The U.S. became the No.1 buyer of South Korean ramen with 7,135t or US$26.1 million.

Liquor The local alcohol beverage market suffered a decline last year amid the economic slump, but imported beers drew a strong reaction from local consumers.

Shipment of whisky reached 1.78 million boxes (500milliliters/18 bottles) last year, down 3.4% from 1.85 million boxes. The consumption of whisky logged a minus 12.8% growth in 2013, after suffering an 11.6% decline and a 4.8% contraction, respectively, in 2012 and 2011.

Diagio Korea, the No. 1 player, shipped 705,000 boxes last year, down 2.1% from a year earlier. Pernorika Korea also suffered a 13.5% drop in its sales last year, with local firms such as Lotte Liquor and Hite Jinro also suffering negative growth last year. In contrast, imported beers swept the country last year as consumers' choices diversified.

Imports of beers reached US$112 million last year, up 24.5% from a year earlier, but in terms of volume, slipped to 111,000t last year for the first time in four years.

Import of Japanese beers reached 31,914t last year, the largest amount, followed by Dutch beers with 17,812t, German beers with 16,688t and Chinese beers with 11,490t.

Wine imports remained strong last year. A total of 33,100t of wine were imported last year, up 1.6% from a year earlier. In terms of value, wine imports increased 6% to US$182 million last year.

Outdoor gear South Korea's outdoor product market suffered a sharp downturn last year as the sector is saturated.

The sector's sales were estimated at 6.9 trillion won last year, little changed from a year earlier. In 2000, the market was valued at 200 billion won, but posted sharp growth to reach 4 trillion won in 2011 and 6.9 trillion won in 2013.

Northface, the No. 1 player, logged sales of 240 billion won last year, maintaining its top spot for the 12th consecutive year, according to an industry source. Kolon Sports ranked second with sales totaling 150 billion won, followed by K2 with 120 billion won and Nepa with 75 billion won.

Cosmetics South Korea's cosmetics firms logged record sales last year on the back of strong demands from foreign visitors, especially from Chinese travelers.

Amore Pacific Co., the country's top cosmetics firm, racked up sales of 3.87 trillion won last year, a 25% jump from a year earlier, with its operating income surging 52.4% to 564 billion won.

Its domestic sales spiked 23.5% on-year to reach 2.58 trillion won. Its sales at duty-free shops more than doubled to 703 billion won from 348 billion won over the cited period.

Overseas sales surged 52.8% to reach 833 billion won, with operating income reaching 61.8 billion won, a shift from a loss of 5.7 billion won a year earlier.

LG Life and Household, the No. 2 player, also enjoyed its largest-ever sales last year. Its sales gained 8.1% last year to reach 4.68 trillion won with its operating income rising 2.9% to 511 billion won. Its sales at duty-free shops tripled to 300 billion won last year from 98.7 billion won a year earlier. Its overseas sales also jumped 16% to 399 billion won.

Affected by hallyu, exports of cosmetic products reached US$740 million during the first half of last year, up 34.5% from a year earlier.

CONSTRUCTION AND TRANSPORTATION

CONSTRUCTION

▪ Construction Industry Trends

South Korea's construction industry has shown a mild recovery since 2009, but the sector's recovery was short-lived, with a protracted slump running through 2012.

The sector's spending has increased for the seventh consecutive quarter in the third quarter of 2014.

Builders' orders have been on a rise since the fourth quarter of 2013 for four straight quarters. The number of construction firms that went belly-up dropped to 100 last year from 137 posted a year earlier.

▪ Registration of Construction Firms

South Korea saw the number of construction firms gain 0.6% to 56,132 last year, which breaks down to 10,949 general builders and 45,183 companies specialized in small-sized projects.

The number of builders sanctioned reached 3,666 last year, sharply down from 10,005 in 2013, 6,291 in 2012 and 5,578 in 2011.

▪ Domestic Construction Orders

Domestic construction orders gained 2.6% last year to reach 71.3 trillion won. Orders from the private sector surged 34% on-year to reach 32.1 trillion won, while those from the public sector gained 23.4% to 17.9 trillion won.

▪ Overseas Construction Orders

South Korean builders secured US$66 billion worth of overseas construction orders in 2014, the second highest annual tally after the country won a United Arab Emirates nuclear plant deal four years earlier.

In 2010, overseas construction orders soared to a record US$71.6 billion but fell to US$59.1 billion the following year before rising to US$65.2 billion in 2013.

By region, the Middle East accounted for 47.5% of all orders secured last year, followed by 24.1% for Asia and 13.6% for Africa and Europe. Latin America made up 10.2% with North America and the Pacific Rim accounting for the rest.

Last year's strong numbers were attributable in part to state financial institutions such as the Export-Import Bank of Korea and Korea Trade Insurance Corporation increasing the amount of funds opened to builders to 32.3 trillion won, up 5.2% from the year before.

For 2015, business conditions are expected to get tougher as political instability in the Middle East and volatile oil prices may sap demand for new projects.

▪ Backbone Cities

In November 2014, the government unveiled a set of plans to spearhead the so-called backbone cities across the country, a shift from its previous plan to foster the so-called large-scale cities, in order to boost quality of life and customized urban life. The focus is placed on interconnecting a key city and areas nearby and developing them with more organized plans.

▲ *President Park Geun-hye speaks at a meeting of government officials and businessmen at the presidential office Cheong Wa Dae on March 12 to promote investment and regional development. Park called on provincial governments to take the initiative in the development of provincial regions.*

▪ Public Houses

The Park Geun-hye administration sought to expand the number of public houses for university students, newly-married couples and wage earners with low incomes. The public houses are built in areas which are close to subway stations and commuting zones, and their prices are much lower than those houses offered by private construction companies.

In 2014, the government issued permits for 26,000 public houses, and plans to issue permits for 140,000 more houses by 2017. In 2014, the government designated 55 construction areas for 36,000 public homes, approved projects for 26,000 homes and broke ground on 6,000 houses.

▪ Builders' Declining Profit

Data show that 124 listed construction firms logged a combined 86 trillion won in sales last year, up 3.2% from a year earlier, led by overseas orders clinched by the top three builders, including Hyundai Engineering & Construction.

Their debt-to-equity ratio increased 5.8%p to 175.8% last year, with the ratio of operating income to sales standing at 1%. In particular, the interest coverage ratio shed 33.6%p to 37.5%, indicating that most of the builders are suffering from cash shortages.

▪ Heavy Fines on Builders over Collusion

South Korea's antitrust watchdog levied fines of 849 billion won on 42 construction companies for colluding to fix bidding prices on 18 projects. But the hefty penalty dealt a blow to the builders reeling from a protracted recovery of the local property and housing markets.

TRANSPORTATION

▪ Railroads

South Korea boasted 3,587.8km of railroads at the end of 2013 with 90 lines. Of them, about 69.1% were subway railroads. In 2013, 1.23 billion passengers used railroads, little changed from the previous year's level. But the number of passengers who used the Saemauel, Mugunghwa and commuting lines increased 5.2% to 77.28 million.

The government is seeking to connect the Kyongbu Express Railroad Line with the Pohang Line in the first half of 2015, and planned to open the Ohsong-Gwangju-Songjeong section on the Honam Express Railroad Line in April 2015.

Also, the government is planning to complete the Suseo-Pyongtaek Express Railroad Line by the end of 2015, whose services will cover Seoul and its adjacent areas. South Korea plans to spend 7.4 trillion won for construction of more express railroads, interconnection lines, and maintenance.

By 2020, the government plans to extend the railroad lines to 4,934km with the portion of subway lines reaching 85%. In 2015, the government plans to build 227 km of railroad.

▪ City Railroads

South Korea had 615km of city railroads at the end of 2013 in the country's six major cities and some urban areas. Currently, 100.5km of city railroads are being built, and the lines will be extended to 715.5km when railroads currently under construction are completed by 2018.

A total of 2.47 billion passengers, which could translate into 6.78 million a day, used the railroads in the nine cities with 591 stations in total. There were 5,535 compartments in total.

On Aug. 15, 1974, Seoul Subway Line 1, which connects Seoul Station and Cheongryangni Station, was opened. Line 2 started its service on Oct. 31, 1980, and Line 4 went into full-fledged service on April 20, 1985. Busan's Subway Line 1 opened on July 19, 1985.

There are nine subway lines in the Seoul Metropolitan City network, covering 327.1km. There are 302 stations, and an average of 1.87 billion passengers use the lines every year. By 2016, 100.5km of subway lines will be added.

▪ Expressways

In 2014, South Korea had 4,139km of express highway roads, achieving some 64.5% of its target. In 2015, some 230 km of express roads will be expanded or newly built.

Also, the government plans to start the construction of some 200km of express roads in 2015. According to the government data, some 24km of express roads will be newly opened, with 4,162km of roads under construction in 2015.

▪ National Highways

South Korea had 23,843㎞ of roads in 2013, and added 238㎞ in 2014, including the Masan-Shineum Expressway. In 2015, 3.63 trillion won was earmarked for the construction of roads, with 480㎞ scheduled to be newly opened in 2015. Also, 155㎞ of roads will be newly built in 2015 alone.

▪ Automobiles

The number of registered vehicles in South Korea exceeded 20 million for the first time in 2014, doubling in 17 years. A list of records showed that South Korea is the world's 15th and Asia's fourth nation to surpass the 20 million mark. In Asia, Japan, China and India have reached that number.

As of the end of last year, the number of registered cars in the country came to 20,117,955, up 3.7% from a year earlier. The government began collecting related data in 1945. Since then, it took 52 years to reach 10 million. The growth in the number of registered vehicles reflects the size and importance of the country's automobile market.

South Korea is one of the world's largest automobile producers with its local industry leader, Hyundai Motor Co., posting annual sales of US$75 billion, the world's eighth-largest, in 2013. Together with its smaller affiliate, Kia Motors Corp., the company makes up the world's fifth-largest automotive group, Hyundai Motor Group.

South Korea has three other automakers -- GM Korea, Renault Samsung Motors and Ssangyong Motor, the local units of U.S., French and Indian automakers, respectively. Of the total registered, 78%, or some 15.74 million cars, are passenger vehicles.

Sales of imported vehicles surged 34.3% on-year to reach 57,000 units last year, with the number of foreign vehicles registered totaling 1.11 million. Foreign-made vehicles accounted for some 5.5% of the total in the country.

▪ Airlines

South Korea's air passenger traffic surpassed the 80 million mark for the first time in 2014 on an increase in both inbound and outbound travelers as ticket prices became more affordable due to the lower cost of jet fuel.

A report by the Ministry of Land, Infrastructure and Transport showed the number of people entering and leaving the country by plane surpassed 81.46 million, up 11% from 73.34 million the year before. International passenger traffic jumped 11% on-year to 56.78 million, while domestic numbers advanced 10.3% to 24.64 million.

Last year's good showing was helped by more routes being offered by both full-service and budget carriers, an increase in the number of planes used to ferry passengers and the popularity of South Korean pop culture, which is attracting more visitors from abroad.

With the exception of visitors from Japan, there was a general increase in the number of people visiting the country from all over the world, led by travelers from China and Southeast Asia.

The number of people on South Korea-China routes rose by 26.7% on-year in 2014. In contrast, the number of people traveling to and from Japan decreased by 1.6%.

The number of passengers serviced by South Korean airlines rose 6.9%, while corresponding numbers for foreign carriers jumped 19.8%. Of all passengers on international flights, 62.6% flew on South Korean planes, of which 11.5% used no-frills airlines such as Jeju Air.

On domestic routes, more vacation time and more flights offered by low-cost carriers (LCC) contributed to the higher number of travelers. The number of travelers using regional airports in Daegu, Jeju and Gwangju all rose by double digits.

Air cargo, both international and domestic, rose from 350t in 2013 to 369t last year, boosted by local and overseas demand for semiconductors and mobile telecommunication services. International cargo traffic alone reached 341t, up from 325t a year earlier.

There are downside risks, including fluctuations in foreign exchange rates and stiffer competition from foreign carriers, but the industry is expected to grow in 2015, with a steady rise in the number of tourists as well as local travelers going abroad.

As of end-2014, there are 15 airports across the country. Of them, Incheon, Kimpo and six others are international airports.

HOUSING AND REAL ESTATE

▪ Real Estate Policy

From 2008 to 2013, South Korea's real estate market continued to plunge due to economic uncertainties and an imbalance in the supply of additional housing. The lackluster trade of housing sales led to the increase in demand for "jeonse," which led to unstable jeonse market conditions in the second half of 2013. Jeonse is a local property lease system in which tenants pay a large deposit in place of monthly rent.

The government made efforts to normalize the housing market and recoup housing stability of the low-income bracket, as the prolonged slump in the real estate market may lead to burdens and give an adverse impact on the macro-economy.

Thus, South Korea puts its priority on normalizing the housing market by recouping self-adjustment capability of the market by controlling supply, while easing excessive regulations imposed earlier.

The country promoted a real-estate promotion law in 2013, exempting first-time buyers of houses from paying an acquisition tax and helping to spur demand for properties. It also induced those with purchasing power to buy new houses.

Helped by such efforts, the country's housing trading has moved to the recovery phase from the doldrums, but the market's sentiment remained weak and it has not yet jumped into the full-fledged recovery phase.

The government in August 2014 also had eased the loan-to-value (LTV) ratio and the debt-to-income (DTI) ratio, both aimed at widening access to home mortgages. It has pushed forward what it calls "the plan to stabilize housing of the low-income bracket and revitalize the property market through lifting regulations."

Such efforts to normalize the housing market were also partially fruitful, as it limited the downward phase of the property prices, while the trade volume also increased.

▲ Seo Seoung-hwan, the minister of land, infrastructure and transport, speaks at a news conference in Sejong, South Chungcheong Province, on Sept. 1. He announced a set of measures aimed at stimulating the country's real estate market that include cutting the minimum age of housing units subject to reconstruction by up to 10 years.

The government also made efforts to establish a universal housing welfare system, and stabilize low-income brackets' living environments by expanding the supply of state-run rental houses.

It has joined forces with private construction firms to build houses where the middle-income class can live for more than eight years at a reasonable amount of rent.

In order to expand the number of public rental houses in urban areas, the government has been pushing its "happiness housing" project, while handing out "housing vouchers" to the low-income bracket to ease their burden related to rental costs.

The government also provided customized welfare to different groups, supplying jeonse-dormitories to university students, one-room public apartments to low-income singles, and permanent public houses for seniors and people with disabilities.

▪ Overview of Real Estate Market

The housing market continued to gain ground after the government established grounds for revitalization in 2013, coupled with the rising anticipation in the market for the recovery, leading to an increase in the amount and price of housing transactions.

According to the state-run Korea Appraisal Board, the average price of local housing moved up 1.7% on-year in 2014. The figure hovers above the five-year average of 2.1% posted between 2009 and 2013.

By region, Seoul and its surrounding area saw an increase of 1.5%, while provincial cities rose 2.5%. Housing prices in other provincial areas increased 1.6%. By size, the demand for small-and-medium sized houses continued to remain high as observed over recent periods.

As for apartments, the sales of houses between 85 and 102㎡, the sales price increased 2.3% on-year. For those between 102 and 135㎡, the increase came to 1.3%. However, the sales price of houses larger than 135㎡ edged down 0.2%, implying that demand for large-sized houses remained weak, while the demand for small- and medium-sized houses remained strong to maintain growth.

The demand for smaller houses rose following an increase in the number of households with one or two members. The trend followed rising divorce rates and low birth rates, while the size of families became smaller. The sluggish housing market also reduced the number of investors seeking property assets, thus the actual demand for small- and medium-sized homes increased. Such a trend is anticipated to continue for the time being.

The price of "jeonse," a local property lease system in which tenants pay a large deposit in place of monthly rent, also increased due to shortages, while the demand for new houses moved up following the government's district redevelopment plans. It advanced 3.4% from end-2013, rising at a steeper pace than actual sales prices. The increase, however, still remained lower than 4.7% on-year rise tallied in 2013. The increase rate also stood at 6.2% annually on average between 2009 and 2013.

The lack of jenose-based houses led to "jeonse shortages," which induced more people to buy properties instead. The decline of jeonse properties in the market apparently came as leaseholders sought monthly rents for higher profit, coupled with the rising seasonal demand and higher preferences for prestigious school districts.

■ Sales of Apartments

In 2014, the combined sales of apartments came to 344,887 units, up 15.4% from 298,851 posted in 2013. It also marked a 17.3% rise from the three-year average of trade volumes.

In provincial areas, sales declined in Ulsan, Sejong, and South Chungcheong. But as sales leaped in Busan, Gwangju, and South Gyeongsang by 131.7%, 124.7%, and 128.3%, respectively, the combined performance moved up 30.6%.

The rising demand in the provincial areas reflects the rising preference for newly-built houses. South Korea's top five metropolitan cities saw their combined sales jump 50.4% on-year.

As for Seoul and surrounding areas, their sales declined 4.4%. Sales moved down 17.5% in Seoul, and 26.4% in Incheon. Gyeonggi Province, however, posted a 5.2% rise to reach 82,943 units.

As apartment sales remained robust through 2014, the number of unsold houses drastically decreased. While there were 61,091 units of unsold new apartments at end-2013, the number decreased by 20,712 units to reach 40,379 units at end-2014.

The number of unsold new apartments in Seoul came to 1,356 units at end-2014, down 1,801 units from the 3,157 posted in 2013. Busan had 2,060 units of unsold new apartments in 2014, down 2,199 units from the 4,259 posted a year earlier. Gyeonggi Province had a comparable figure of 14,732 units, down 10,037 units from the 24,760 posted at end-2013.

Sejong City, where the supply of new houses was high, the number of unsold new apartments came to 433 units, up 179 from 54 units posted at end-2013. North Gyeongsang Province had 2,023 units of unsold homes, up 618 units from a year earlier.

■ Land Prices

The price of land, which had lost

ground immediately after the 2008 economic crisis, resumed its growth since April 2009. Its growth trend stabilized through 2014, advancing about 1% annually.

In 2014, the government rolled out real-estate plans to normalize housing prices, while lifting regulations related to properties in order to revitalize investment. It also announced reform plans related to urban and construction regulations, which led to the combined trading of 2.64 million pieces of land.

It marked the highest number since 2006. The fluctuation rate of land prices came to 1.96%, with that of Seoul and the surrounding area reaching 1.91% while other rural regions came to 2.06%. Moving up from the 1.14% posted in 2013, it hovered above the inflation rate of 1.3%.

Sejong led the increases in land prices by jumping 4.53%, posting the highest level for the third consecutive year. Jeju Island, Daegu and Seoul had comparable figures of 3.73%, 3.15% and 2.26% respectively, also leading the growth of land prices.

By specific districts, Dalseong County of Daegu Metropolitan City had the highest growth, at 4.71%, trailed by Sejong Metropolitan Autonomous City with 4.53%, Seogwipo City of Jeju Island with 4.48%, Naju City of South Jeolla Province with 4.46%, and Gangnam of Seoul Metropolitan City with 0.11%. Ganghwa County of Incheon Metropolitan City, on the other hand, saw its land prices edge down 0.11% over the cited period. Taebaek City and Sokcho City of Gangwon Province saw their real-estate values inch up 0.19% and 0.26%, posting sluggish growth compared to other areas.

The combined trade volume of land reached an all-time high for the first time since 2006, helped by the increasing trade of housing-purpose buildings. It reached 2.64 million pieces of land to cover 1.9 billion square meters, up 17.9% in units and 7.8% in area from a year earlier.

■ **Construction of Homes**

In 2014, 515,251 units of houses were approved for construction throughout the country. Seoul and its surrounding area had 241,889 units while provincial areas accounted for 273,362 units. The figure marks a 17.1% increase from 440,106 units in 2013. The rise apparently followed the government's various efforts to lift regulations that aimed to create a positive effect in the market.

The figure hovers far above the 374,000 units originally planned, but it is still 2% lower than the three-year average of 525,531 units. Thus, it is believed that the market does not have to be worried about a possible oversupply of houses.

The number of new constructions fell 15.9% in Seoul and that of Incheon slid 28.2%. However, that of Gyeonggi Province surged 69.7% following the government's large-sized housing zone development plans.

Concerning provincial areas, the number of new constructions fell in Busan, Sejong and North Chungcheong Province, but the performance in other areas, including Ulsan, North Gyeongsang Province and Jeju gained ground, leading to a combined growth of 10% since 2003.

By sector, the construction of new public houses reached 63,320 units, maintaining its downward trend to fall 20.5% from 2013. It also marks a 37.6% decline from the three-year average. The private sector raised 451,931 units, up 25.4% from a year earlier, and up 6.6% from the three-year average.

ENERGY AND RESOURCES

■ **Energy Consumption**

South Korea is estimated to have consumed 281.92 million TOEs (tons of oil equivalents) in 2014, up 0.6% from a year earlier. Last year, the country's economy expanded 3.3%.

Petroleum consumption edged down 0.4% on-year to reach 822 million barrels last year, while demand for liquefied natural gas(LNG) dropped 9% to 36.64 million tons.

Coal consumption is estimated to have risen 2.9% to 133.36 million tons last year, and nuclear power generation gained 12.7% to 156TWh.

In terms of energy sources, oil accounted for 37.3% of the total last year, down 0.5%p from a year earlier, with the comparable figure for coal being 30.1%, up 0.85%p.

LNG consumption accounted for 16.9% of the total energy use, down 1.79%p from a year earlier, while nuclear power use rose 1.26%p to 11.7%.

Meanwhile, South Korea said in December it would seek to reduce its use of energy by 4.1% from its business-as-usual (BAU) level in 2017, which will also help cut its greenhouse gas emissions.

The government said it will seek to keep the annual growth of the country's total energy use under 1%, which will help reduce the country's overall use of energy to 218.2 billion tons of TOEs from the anticipated BAU level of 227.5 billion TOEs.

The move comes as the country imports nearly all of its energy. Imports of raw materials, including energy, currently account for nearly 60% of the country's overall imports.

The government seeks to require all new large, energy-dependent facilities to be equipped with a power management system, such as an energy storage system. It also seeks to increase the minimum requirements for vehicle fuel efficiency to those of advanced nations, such as the European Union, which are expected to reach 26.5km per liter in 2020. In addition, the government will seek to promote the use of clean energy vehicles, such as electric cars, in the public transportation sector.

The government has already implemented a new regulation that requires all public offices, including state-run universities, to choose at least 25% of all their new vehicles from electric cars.

The ministry said such efforts will also help reduce the country's overall greenhouse gas emissions by 88 million carbon dioxide equivalent tons over the 2013-2017 period.

■ Energy Demand

The final amount of energy provided to consumers is estimated to have increased 1.8% on-year to 213.97 million TOEs last year. The amount excludes consumption by energy-related companies.

By sector, the industrial sector is expected to have consumed 136.54 million TOEs last year, up 4.3% from a year earlier.

The logistics sector, however, saw its energy consumption slip 0.12% to 139.1 TOEs, while households, commercial and the public sector consumed an estimated 40.14 million TOEs last year, also down 4.5% from a year earlier.

By source of energy, coal consumption increased 10.8% last year in line with a rise in demand from power generation companies. Electricity consumption edged up 0.6% to 477,592 GW last year over the cited period. Gas consumption, however, dropped 7.4% on-year to reach 22.13 billion cubic meters last year, while oil use increased 1.3% to 80.9 million barrels.

■ Oil Price Movement

▲ Gasoline price is marked below 1,600 won per liter at a gas station in Goyang, north of Seoul, on Nov. 28, amid the falling international oil prices.

In 2014, global crude oil prices shed some 8% to average US$96.56 per barrel because of a supply glut. The stronger U.S. dollar, a fall in demand for oil amid the global economic slump, and geopolitical risks worked to drive oil prices lower.

The price of Dubai crude, South Korea's benchmark, stayed at US$107.79 per barrel in the first week of January, but surged to US$111.23 per barrel in the fourth week of June. In the last week of December, the price stood at US$53.60 per barrel.

In line with falling crude oil prices, the average gasoline price in South Korea fell to 1,594.92 won per liter in the fourth week of December, from 1,889.07 won per liter seen in early January.

■ **Petrochemical Goods**

Consumption of petroleum products in South Korea hit a three-year low in 2014, despite a sharp fall in oil prices as the domestic economy remained tepid.

A total of 823 million barrels of refined petroleum products were sold domestically last year, down 0.38% from 2013, according to data by the Korea National Oil Corporation (KNOC).

Domestic consumption had been on a steady rise from 2009 to 2012 after a steep slide in the wake of the 2008 financial crisis, but it slumped from 2013 to 2014 as the domestic economy moved sideways.

By product, gasoline consumption inched up 0.08% on-year to 73.4 million barrels in 2014, and diesel increased 1% to 144.7 million barrels, data showed.

In contrast, sales of liquefied petroleum gas(LPG) shed 3.6% to 89.67 million barrels, and kerosene plunged 18% to 15.41 million barrels in the period.

The state-funded Korea Energy Economics Institute (KEEI) forecast that domestic petroleum consumption will increase 1.8% in 2015, assuming the Korean economy grows 3.4% and the average price of Dubai crude stays at US$63.30 per barrel.

■ **Electricity Market**

The average system marginal price (SMP) for electricity sold last year stood at 141.78 won per kwh, compared with 151.56 won per kwh in 2013 and 160.12 won per kwh in 2012.

There were 913 members of the Electricity Exchange, and the country's power generation capacity increased 8.2% on-year to reach 94.10 million kilowatts last year.

The country's electricity consumption peaked at 80.15 million kilowatts on Dec. 17, while its summer peak was 76.05 million kilowatts on July 25. For all of last year, electricity sales reached 477.6 billion kwh, or a gain of 0.6% from 2013.

The ministry said that while there were two fewer working days last year, a rise in exports and facility investment pushed up demand and sales.

INFORMATION AND TELECOMMUNICA-TIONS

INFORMATION-RELATED POLICY

■ **Creative Economy Innovation Center Opens**

The government decided to build 17 Creative Economy Innovation Centers across the nation, with an aim to encourage larger firms to lend support to venture startups, from helping them initiate business ideas, get their footing and expand abroad.

It is the government's plan to have each city and province partner up with a key conglomerate and set up a one-on-one support system with the venture firm. Starting with Daegu in March, the Creative Economy Innnovation Center was established in Daejeon the following month, in North Jeolla Province in November and North Gyeongsang Province in December.

Forty-five companies moved into the innovation complex. The government set up an investment fund worth 160 billion won (US$146.2 million) as part of its efforts in assisting the nascent companies to grow.

On its online site, dubbed Creative Economy Town, more than 18,000 business ideas were submitted by the public, reflecting eagerness to revitalize the economy through the Creative Economy's initiative, pushed by President Park Geun-hye.

The government had previously pledged to create a business model with the best fit for each designated region and complete the construction of the innovation centers by the first half of 2015.

Some of the business models being discussed include hydrogen-fueled vehicles in Gwangju, building a bio hub in North Chungcheong Province and a global lifestyle and retail culture in Busan.

■ **ICT Exports Hit Record US$173.9 Billion**

Exports of Information and Communications Technology (ICT) hit a record high last year to surpass the US$170 billion mark for the first time.

The Ministry of Science, ICT and Future Planning said the outbound shipments in the ICT sector rose 2.6% on-year to US$173.8 billion in 2014. Imports increased 8.3% to US$87.5 billion over the cited period, putting the industry in the red with a US$86.3 billion surplus.

The ICT exports accounted for 30.3% of the country's total exports (US$573.1 billion) in 2014, contributing to the overall trade surplus.

Sales of memory chips and handsets increased, while shipments of display panels and digital TVs saw a slide. Smartphone sales fell 3.3% last year from a year earlier, weighed down by intense competition. In the two previous years, Korea's smartphone sales had surpassed the US$12 billion mark consecutively.

The sales of smartphone components such as chips came to US$13.9 billion, outpacing those of handsets for the first time.

■ State-Run TV Shopping Channels Open

The ICT ministry came to a decision by which a publicly-run TV shopping channel will be allowed to operate with a focus on distribution and sales of agricultural and livestock products produced by small- and medium-sized companies.

The consortium, picked by the ministry, consists of related bodies representing smaller firms and the National Federation of Fisheries Cooperatives. It will invest 800 billion won (US$73.1 million).

The home-shopping channels will be banned from paying out dividends to investors, nor will they be permitted to earmark a lot of spending for network transmission fees in order to get more channels, since the purpose of the establishment is grounded upon serving the public interest.

■ Seoul Hosts International Congress of Mathematicians (ICM)

The International Congress of Mathematicians (ICM) was held in COEX, Seoul, in August. The tournament, one of the most renowned academic events in basic science, has taken place for 117 years, since 1897.

Some 5,000 participants from more than 120 countries attended, despite concerns over the deadly Ebola virus that swept through West Africa.

The organizing committee in Seoul and the International Mathematical Union were quick to take necessary steps so that all expected attendees could make the trip to the Seoul event.

The 77th Seoul ICM was meaningful as the Fields Medal was awarded to a female scientist and a Latin American for the first time. Maryam Mirzakhani, a Stanford University professor, and Artur Avila, a Brazilian mathematician, were among the winners.

Hwang Jun-mook, a math professor at the Korea Institute for Advanced Study, made the keynote speech, with five other Korean experts invited to each speak on a topic.

It was also the first time that the keynote speech was done by a Korean. Upon the hosting of the ICM, South Korea has stepped up efforts to enter the fifth string of the IMU, which is considered the world's top mathematical league.

■ ITU Conference

The International Telecommunication Union (ITU) conference was held in Seoul for three weeks in October 2014.

▲ Delegates from 170 countries listen to South Korean President Park Geun-hye during the opening ceremony of the 2014 International Telecommunication Union Plenipotentiary Conference at Bexco in Busan on Oct. 20.

The conference, which is held every four years, is the top decision-making meeting attended by ministers from key member countries. It was the first time for Seoul to have hosted the event.

More than 3,000 government representatives, including 140 ministerial officials from 170 countries, attended the conference. There were more than 800 conferences held over the 19-day period to discuss various agendas in the global ICT field.

As the host country, Korea was successful to have Lee Jae-seop, a senior research fellow at the KAIST Institute for IT Convergence, elected as the ITU chief director in charge of global standardization.

Korea also retained its post as an ITU member country for the seventh consecutive year. Korea joined the ITU in 1952, when the country was in the middle of the Korean War. It first became a member country in 1989.

The ITU council unanimously passed a resolution put forward by Korea, in which it proposed nurturing the Internet-of-Things (IoT) and ICT convergence. Min Won-ki, the director of the ITU conference, has been elected as the council director to lead the board in 2015.

■ Gov't Vows to Build a "SW-Oriented Society"

The government announced a plan in July to build a software-focused society, in which national infrastructure and industrial systems are upgraded with a stronger software capability.

Among the measures were creating a new software market, an upgrade of the national system with better software and a revamp of the software industry.

The government said it plans to add software as a mandatory subject required as part of the courses in primary and secondary school.

Seventy-two schools were designated by the government as test schools for software education, with four universities to build an institute for the gifted in software-related fields. Some high schools will be transformed into software-focused schools.

The government plans to designate wearables, robots, sensors and 3-dimensional printing as four key new growth engines to nurture the software industry.

It also said it plans to bolster efforts to protect software copyrights, build a business-friendly environment for software distribution and spread the importance of software copyright issues.

■ Gov't-Funded Research Institutes Join Forces with Biz Groups

The ICT ministry and the National Research Council of Science & Technology founded two research groups in partnership with local businesses in December. Each research group will focus its study on sinkholes, which have become a problem in Korea recently as a few cases happened in a row, and the energy sector.

The monitoring group for underground facilities in IoT-based cities will be formed by the Electronics and Telecommunications Research Institute, the Korea Institute of Civil Engineering and Building Technology, the Korea Railroad Research Institute, the Korea Institute of Geoscience and Mineral Resources, and 11 companies, including SK Telecom Co.

It will work to come up with preventive measures against sinkholes based on collected data, analysis and prediction using the IoT. The other group, in charge of research and development in energy and chemical materials for large-scale plant projects, will focus on the commercialization of economical and eco-friendly processing of core chemical materials.

■ Korea-China TV Channels Co-produce First Documentary

South Korea and China have agreed to co-produce their first historical documentary in July. The two sides signed a preliminary deal to produce two documentary films.

The Korean Broadcasting System (KBS) and CCTV will together make five episodes that depict the Japanese invasion of Korea in 1592, and the Munhwa Broadcasting Corporation (MBC) will produce a four-episode documentary tentatively named "Climate's Revolt".

The ICT ministry has sought to extend the mutual exchanges on digital content between the two countries since 2013, under the name of "Pengyou (朋友-meaning a companion) Content Project" and clinched deals with related government agencies in China on hopes of taking the relationship further.

The ICT ministry said the preliminary

deal is significant as it has paved the way for the two countries to actually move onto the documentary production based on the mutual trust they have built through the Pengyou Project. The funding for the production will be shared 50-50 by each country.

TELECOMMUNICATIONS POLICY

▪ Handset Subsidy Law Enacted for Industry Overhaul

A new law was enacted in October to curb illegal cellphone subsidies and better serve the public interest. The reform on handset distribution is aimed at providing the benefit of a subsidy to all cellphone users regardless of their monthly rate plan.

Retail stores had offered a higher subsidy to those who buy a premium phone with a higher rate plan, as opposed to others who get a budget phone and sign a cheaper contract.

The new law seeks to bring transparency in the execution of subsidy payments by mobile carriers, which will lead to the reduction of handset prices, which are being criticized for excessiveness in a market dominated by Samsung and LG.

The new law stipulates that mobile carriers must disclose the factory price, the subsidy amount and the market price for each handset via their websites. Retail stores are required to do the same at their shops.

It bans mobile carriers from discriminating against customers with the subsidy based on certain criteria such as age, place of residence or rate plan. The government has set the subsidy at 345,000 won (US$316).

The Korea Communications Commission (KCC), the country's telecom watchdog, has decided the threshold should be 300,000 won, with an additional 15% discretionary offer by a retail store.

For those who bought their cellphones before July 2013, there is no limit on the subsidy. But the rule of disclosure on mobile carriers' subsidies and the amount of sales incentives at manufacturers has been removed from the provisions, stoking worries that the new handset law may no longer be effective.

▪ Mobile Carriers Accused of Illegal iPhone 6 Subsidies

The KCC referred three South Korean mobile carriers -- SK Telecom Co., KT Corp and LG Uplus Inc. -- and their executives to the prosecution on allegations that they violated the new handset law and gave customers a subsidy through retail stores.

The move by the KCC comes on the sidelines of the 2.4 billion won penalty it imposed on the three firms and their 22 affiliated retail stores. The watchdog said the telecom firms violated the law by offering excessive subsidies to the merchants, prompting hundreds of people to line up in a queue because they were told they could buy a 16GB iPhone 6 for between 100,000 and 200,000 won.

The KCC took the matter seriously as it happened less than a month after the new handset rule was put into effect. The watchdog said it will set up a special nine-member probe team in collaboration with the police to catch the illegal distribution of subsidies.

▪ Broadcasting Channels Set Up Automated Seismic Alarm System

The KCC and 10 local broadcasting companies completed setting up an automated seismic alarm system in December. The alarm system will automatically transmit a text message via TV should there be any seismic activity detected by the national weather agency.

The tele-text will be sent over to TVs within 10 seconds, the KCC said. Yonhap News TV, the television arm of Yonhap News Agency, adopted the transmission system in August 2014. EBS, another public broadcasting channel, and cable news channel MBN also provide such a system.

▪ Gov't Moves to Boost Budget Phone Biz

The ICT ministry said in June it will boost the budget phone business in the country to provide a wider range of mobile phones to the public at a reasonable price.

The government advised that the rate plan offered by budget phone-selling businesses should be about half of what big mobile carriers have set for their rate plans.

Those major mobile carriers must keep their stake in the budget-phone business under 50%, while the budget phone sellers, whose network services are borrowed from those owned by major players, can seek a further cut in their fees paid for the network coverage.

The ministry said it will bring additional measures to curb big mobile carriers from encroaching on the budget phone market, with a possible suspension of business for up to 13 months and a penalty.

FIXED-LINE SERVICE AND INTERNET

▪ Market Competition in High-Speed Internet Market Gets Intense

KT Corp., the country's largest fixed-line carrier, is the top player in the high-speed Internet market with a 42.3% share, or 8.13 million subscribers, out of 19 million nationwide.

SK Telecom Co. and its affiliate, SK Broadband Co., hold a 25.1% share with 4.93 million subscribers, followed by LG Uplus Inc. with 15.7%, or 3.01 million users.

Cable channels have 3.16 million subscribers with a 16.4% share, standing alone in a battle against the mobile carriers.

Such a cutthroat market, however, has been challenged in recent years by the rise of SK Telecom. The largest mobile carrier acquired SK Broadband in 2008 and took over the affiliate in March 2015.

Since 2010, SK Telecom has been selling a combined mobile and high-speed Internet package, with its market share only standing at 2.3% at the start.

It took less than a year for SK Telecom to catch up fast, on the back of its share in the mobile market that tops 50%. In 2011, its share in the high-speed Internet business rose to 5%, and 7.3% in 2012, 9.2% in 2013, before it hit 10.7% last year.

In 2014, 334,000 new subscribers, representing 72.4% of the total, signed up with SK Broadband's high-speed Internet service, giving a boost to SK Telecom's market presence.

Sales from high-speed Internet service reached 259.3 billion won in 2013, soaring 690% from the 32.8 billion won tallied in 2010. The fast growth of SK Telecom's high-speed Internet business has stoked worries about market dominance led by one company.

LG Uplus, the smallest mobile carrier in the country, has been saying that SK Telecom is again monopolizing the high-speed Internet market, as it has done in the mobile sector.

The KCC, wary of such changes in the market, set up a task force in pursuit of fair trading in the sector. The watchdog pledged to keep close tabs on the issue as one of its main agenda items for 2015 in its report to the presidential office early this year.

▪ The Advent of Giga-Internet Age

The commercialization of the giga-Internet is one of the hottest topics in the wire communication business. Giga-Internet has the highest speed of 1Gbps, 10 times faster than the high-speed Internet introduced to the market in 2006. This means a user can download a full HD movie (about 4GB in size) in 33 seconds.

KT has been a pioneer in the expansion of the giga-Internet business in South Korea. The telecom company announced its plan in late October 2014 that it will start the giga network service nationwide, the first to carry out such a plan.

It is considered the first achievement by KT since the new chief executive, Hwang Chang-gyu, took over the top post. KT said the commercialization of the giga-Internet will be the stepping-stone to the opening a new age of IoT, or what the company has named "Gigatopia."

SK Broadband and LG Uplus joined the race in late October and a month later, respectively, to commercialize the high-speed Internet service.

Market watchers expect that nationwide coverage of the giga-Internet will be possible by the end of 2015. KT plans to provide the network coverage to more than 3 million households in the next five years.

▪ The Merger of IT Portal Giants Daum, Kakao

Daum Communications Corp., a major search engine operator, and Kakao Corp., the creator of South Korea's top mobile messenger, KakaoTalk, announced in May a merger plan of the two companies, taking the industry by surprise for what was going to be the biggest consolidation in the country's IT sector.

▲ Daum CEO Choi Sae-hoon (L) poses at a news conference at the Plaza Hotel in downtown Seoul on May 26, to announce Daum's merger with Kakao Corp. Kakao CEO Lee Seok-woo is at right.

The merger process took four months. The merged entity, Daum Kakao Corp. was born Oct. 1, 2014, to be co-run by former Daum Communications chief Choi Sae-hoon and ex-Kakao CEO Lee Sirgoo.

The merger, however, practically gave Lee the leadership control, as it was a reverse takeover by the then unlisted Kakao, which had sought ways to go public at a lesser cost. Kakao made a backdoor listing via its merger with Daum, one of the top-listed companies on the secondary KOSDAQ.

The merger made Kim Beom-su, the chairman and founder of Kakao, one of the top 10 stock-rich people in Korea, with his holdings increased to 2 trillion won following the backdoor listing.

The establishment of Daum Kakao casts a shadow on Naver Corp., the No. 1 Internet portal provider in the country. Daum, although its business has dwindled in recent years, is one of the first-generation IT ventures that has built the know-how and technology in Internet portals. Kakao's messenger platform has more than 35 million users, in a country with a population of 50 million.

Six months into the merger, Daum

Kakao has rolled out a string of new mobile platforms as part of efforts to make further inroads into offline businesses as well as online.

Its release of BankWalletKakao, a mobile wallet that provides money transfers, and KakaoPay, a mobile payment tool, have raised the possibility that Daum Kakao may get into the banking business.

It also unveiled its first cab-hailing app, KakaoTaxi, in cooperation with local taxi drivers as a way of expanding the platform business to an existing industry.

Shares of Daum Kakao rose to the extent that the company became the top-cap KOSDAQ firm, but they lost ground in recent weeks as investors began to worry the company has not shown a visible performance.

Co-CEO Choi said in the fourth-quarter earnings conference call in February that the company will keep its payout ratio low for the time being to spend it on investments.

■ Naver's Mobile Messenger, Line, Becomes Global Hit

Mobile messenger Line, run by Japan-based Line Corp., a wholly-owned subsidiary of Naver Corp., has seen robust growth across the globe, with its monthly active users (MAU) increasing by 49 million to 181 million at the end of 2014 from a year earlier.

Thirteen countries saw the number of Line downloads reach more than 10 million, with Turkey as the latest.

Line has established a solid footing in Japan with a string of popular life-focused platforms such as Line Pay and Line Taxi. Its shopping service Line Deal and Line Pay made a local debut in Seoul.

As the market share of Line messenger remains low in South Korea, Line intends to focus on overseas expansion through aggressive marketing for Line characters and games that use LINE as an operating platform.

Naver posted 10% annual growth in its 2014 earnings, attributing the expansion to Line's global sales, which increased 62% on-year to 221.7 billion won in the cited period.

■ **Security Issues in ICT Age**

In April, the personal data of more than 100,000 customers at Shinhan Card Co., Kookmin Card Co. and Nonghyup Card Co. were leaked by a hacker.

The network systems at foreign banks and financing companies, including Standard Chartered Bank Korea, were also hacked, resulting in a leakage of personal data of thousands of accounts.

Confidential information from the state-run Korea Hydro & Nuclear Power Co. was spilled over the Internet, prompting the government to vow to take all-out action against the hacking group responsible for the leakage. But they still have not found who carried out the illegal operation.

Since then, there have been calls for stiffer management requirements for personal data at financial and public companies. But businesses have been reluctant to increase spending on security since it is still considered a cost rather than an investment.

The Korea Internet & Security Agency published a report in 2014 in which it said that 97% of firms earmark less than 5% of their budget on IT-related facility investment.

Those that answered that they earmark more than 5% dropped 0.5%p to 2.7% compared with 2013, while others that had invested on a new security system stood at 7.7% of the total.

The report also showed that Korea's IT security business will likely post a pullback in growth of 7.1% in 2014, sharply down from 18.1% two years earlier. Exports of IT security systems grew 22.5% on-year in 2011, before slowing to 1.7% in 2014.

The government pledged to rev up efforts to set up a control tower that manages security issues so that swift communications can be made between ministries in the event of another security breach.

MOBILE COMMUNICATIONS

■ **Handset Law Takes Effect to Revamp Market**

The legislation on the distribution of mobile communication devices was put into effect Oct. 1, 2014, in a bid to improve transparency in the mobile market and help households reduce the burden of increasing phone bills.

The new law stipulates a mandatory disclosure of subsidies on retail stores by mobile carriers, a raise on the subsidy to 300,000 won from 270,000 won per handset, a ban on discrimination against customers with subsidies and stiffer rules on the distribution of illegal subsidies.

In the past, telecom companies had given customers a big subsidy that exceeded the limit for a certain period of time in a specific region to lure more consumers away from rival firms.

Such an outlawed practice has caused a discrepancy among cellphone buyers. Those with access to such information had the advantage of getting a brand new phone with a big discount, while others who did not know about the benefit had to buy a cellphone for the full price.

The handset law aims to root out such a practice by disclosing the amount of the subsidy for each type of cellphone so that all customers can enjoy the benefit. This will eventually help households save on their phone bills, the government said earlier.

The policy, at first, made the market stagnant as mobile carriers had set the subsidy at a minimum level, while consumers took a wait-and-see approach.

But the market began to gain ground about three months after the adoption of the handset law. Data showed that the daily number of new subscribers came to 60,570 in December, eclipsing the 58,363 that was tallied for the January-September period.

■ **Mobile Carriers in Race for LTE-A Network**

Mobile carriers joined the race to gain an upper hand in the broadband long-term evolution (LTE)-advanced network in 2014, following a heated battle with LTE-A in 2013 and in 2012 when the competition for the superfast network began for the telecom companies with the introduction of LTE in the country.

The broadband LTE-A, known for its speed that is three times faster than LTE, uses what is called Carrier Aggregation (CA) technology, which refers to a way of expanding the bandwidth by combining 20MHz frequency with 10Mhz, to provide a speed of up to 225Mbps.

SK Telecom commercialized the broadband LTE-A as the first in the world. KT and LG Uplus quickly joined the race by kicking off their own services the following month.

In December last year, the local telecommunication market was in a flareup with the 3-band LTE-A service, an advanced version of broadband LTE-A and is four times faster than the LTE.

It has applied a CA using 3 bandwidths to realize 300Mbps. That is, equivalent to downloading a 1GB movie in 28 seconds.

SK Telecom published a press release on Dec. 28 in which it claimed itself to be the first to provide the 3-band LTE-A service to the public. KT released a similar statement later in the day to inform of its test run of the service.

KT accused SK Telecom of providing false information about its first-ever commercialization of the network in the globe, saying that offering the service to a certain group of consumers who volunteered for a test use cannot be regarded as the world's first commercialization.

When SK Telecom advertised it on TV, KT took the issue to court and asked to put a ban on the advertisement since it contains erroneous information. The court ruled in favor of KT and decided that SK Telecom's ad should be suspended.

■ Mobile Carriers Face Suspension after Subsidy War

The old habit of stealing away customers from rivals with a sweet inducement of a handset subsidy recurred in 2014. It happened only three months after the three major mobile carriers were slapped with a combined fine of 106.4 billion won at the end of 2013.

The ICT ministry also put SK Telecom and KT on a 45-day suspension. The mobile communication market jolted. KT's March market share fell below the 30% mark for the first time in decades. During the month of April, when the two players were not in business, No. 3 LG Uplus saw its share jump to more than 20%.

Nonetheless, the habit of giving customers subsidies continued even after the handset distribution law took effect Oct. 1. Between Oct. 31 and Nov. 2, SKT, KT and LG Uplus handed out massive incentives to retail stores, who promised customers that came to buy a new iPhone 6 to pay back a certain portion if he or she paid for the smartphone in full.

This led the KCC to impose a penalty of 2.4 billion won on the three mobile carriers. The KCC, in a rare move, took the matter further and referred it to the prosecution to investigate the executives at the three firms on criminal charges. The watchdog also imposed a fine of between 1 million and 1.5 million won on 22 retail stores involved in the illegal subsidy offers.

The outcome of the suspension had negative repercussions on the mobile carriers. SK Telecom saw its 2014 operating profit drop 9.2% to 1.83 trillion won from a year earlier, while marketing costs increased 4.2% on-year to 3.57 trillion won.

KT logged 291.8 billion won in net losses, turning to the red for the first time. Its marketing costs surged 17.6% to 3.15 trillion won. LG Uplus fared well with a 6.3% increase in operating profit to 576.3 billion won.

■ Ex-Samsung Chip Head Hired to Take Helm of KT

Hwang Chang-gyu, the former chief executive of Samsung Electronics' memory chip division, took the helm of KT, the country's second-largest mobile carrier, in December 2013.

▲ Hwang Chang-gyu, chairman of KT Corp, South Korea's second biggest mobile carrier and top fixed-line operator, speaks at a news conference in Seoul on May 20. Hwang said KT will invest 4.5 trillion won (US$4.38 billion) in the development of the Giga-speed Internet connections in broadband, 10 times faster than the current 100 Mbps connection, for the coming three years to ensure faster delivery of high quality video broadcasts.

Hiring him raised the question among industry watchers as to whether he will be able to reconstruct KT, a company Hwang diagnosed as being "slow and too large," which is losing its competitive edge.

As soon as he came to the top post, Hwang came up with the catch phrase "Global No. 1 KT" and undertook an aggressive restructuring that led to voluntary retirements and a 30% reduction of executive staff members.

Some industry watchers described Hwang's drive for the big reshuffle as a Samsung way of reform. Hwang vowed to take a selective approach for the company overhaul, focusing on mobile communications as KT's mainstay business instead of branching out into other sectors. The Giga-Internet stemmed from his plan.

He set out to slim down KT's businesses, starting off with the sale of the entertainment arm Sidus FNH in 2014 and a takeover plan on KT Media Hub under way. In 2015, it sold car rental unit KT Rental to an affiliate of Lotte Group.

Hwang has pushed for smart energy, security, next-generation media, health care and intellectual traffic management as new drivers for growth, using the telecommunication infrastructure that KT has built over the years.

Nonetheless, the remaining two years of his tenure still may come as a challenge for Hwang. KT's mobile sector has plummeted on a falling number of subscribers, while its smaller rival, LG Uplus, has caught up a lot. It stands at the top of the fixed-line business but it's been trailed behind by rivals also.

■ Budget Phone Market Sees Rapid Growth, Becomes Game-Changer

In 2014, the budget phone market has proved itself to be a game-changer in the mobile communication industry as it saw robust growth, with the number of subscribers soaring 85% to 4.6 million as of end-December from a year earlier. Its share of the entire telecom market here doubled to about 8% at the end of 2014, up from 4.5% a year ago.

Market analysts said that the strategy of offering phones at a nearly 50% discount, while keeping the level of mobile service similar to that provided by existing mobile carriers, has paid off to attract customers.

The ICT ministry said it expects a big shift in the telecom market if the budget phone share grows to more than 10%. Analysts say that in order for the budget phone carriers to expand that much, they need to gain enough presence in the long-term evolution (LTE) network market, which makes up 63% of the entire telecom industry.

The saturated 2G and 3G markets will no longer do them any good because the bulk of mobile phone users have moved to the LTE network.

Some of the budget phone providers that are affiliated with conglomerates -- CJ HelloVision and KT IS -- have been swift to introduce market LTE-based monthly plans to woo customers.

Yet, concerns remain about whether they can achieve further growth in the LTE market when it's been a stronghold for the three major mobile carriers. There are about 30 budget phone carriers in South Korea, which means the players are likely to get into an intense marketing battle.

MOBILE PHONES

■ Samsung Electronics Co.'s Profit Crashes in 2014

2014 was a bad year for Samsung Electronics Co., the world's top smartphone maker, as the new Galaxy S5 that debuted in March ended up as a disappointment with lackluster sales. In terms of both design and function, the Galaxy S5 failed to impress consumers.

Samsung also failed to read the market trend, finding itself squeezed by U.S.-based Apple Inc. in the premium market and Chinese upstarts in the mid- to low-end market.

This led to a plunge in Samsung's share of the global smartphone market for the first time in three years. Samsung had taken away the top spot from Apple in the third quarter of 2011, but it tied for first place with its archrival in the fourth quarter of 2014, ending its reign.

Samsung also saw a setback in China, where up-and-coming smartphone makers quickly expanded their footing by cranking out cheaper phones. Samsung fell behind to place third in the ranking.

As Samsung's cash-cow mobile sector faltered, the company was faced with its worst earnings in three years. Its operating profit fell below 5 trillion won in the third quarter, which more than halved compared with the record-high of 10 trillion won logged for the third quarter of 2013.

The South Korean tech giant admitted that the profit slide came largely from sluggish smartphone sales. It fared better in the following quarter, but failed to meet market estimates of 2 trillion won in operating profit.

■ Apple Fights Back with Larger-Size iPhone 6

Apple returned with a bigger-screen iPhone 6 and iPhone 6 Plus. Its new line-up swept across the globe with upbeat responses, earning the Cupertino, California-based firm a record-high profit.

Some said that it was a work of magic done by CEO Tim Cook, who ditched Steve Job's long-held principle of sticking to a 3.5-inch screen for Apple smartphones. For the iPhone 5 series, Cook increased the screen size to 4 inches, and further extended it to 4.7 inches for the new iPhone 6. In November 2014, Apple's market share in South Korea rose to 44%, pushing LG Electronics Inc. to third place.

Apple's return made Samsung's domestic share fall from 60% to 50%. Analysts say its bold choice to go bigger in size worked for Korean consumers, or even Asians. Apple also pushed Samsung to No. 3 in China with a 10.9% share in the fourth quarter.

Apple shipped out 74.5 million units of handsets in the fourth quarter, up 46% from a year earlier. The figure beat the earlier market estimate by 10 million units.

■ Xiaomi's Rise Threatens Samsung, Apple

Neither Samsung nor Apple was at the center stage of 2014; instead, there were three Chinese players that rose to challenge the big two in the global smartphone market: Xiaomi, Lenovo, and Huawei -- all of which make smartphones and electronic devices.

The three Chinese players cranked out cheaper phones and grew rapidly last year, trailing closely behind Samsung and Apple. Notably, Xiaomi beat out LG Electronics and Huawei in the third quarter and ranked third in the industry, grabbing the market's attention. On its home turf, Xiaomi trumped Samsung and was in first place for the second straight quarter in the fourth quarter.

Xiaomi had hardly been known until a couple of years ago, and was often referred to as "Fake Apple" by its rivals in derision of its low recognition. But it began to steal away market share from Lenovo, ZTE, Coolpad and Samsung and Apple. The word "xiaomi" in Chinese means "millet", a grain. A U.S.-based market tracker described the firm as "a millet turned into a star performer."

■ Samsung, Apple End Patent Suits in All Countries Except U.S.

Samsung Electronics Co. and Apple Inc. decided to end all lawsuits over patent rights in countries besides the United States. Both companies announced the agreement on Aug. 6.

Their long legal dispute, which stretches to regions around the world, first began in April 2011, when the U.S. smartphone maker sued its Korean rival in a U.S. court. The suits then spread to nine countries, including Korea, Germany and Japan.

In June, the battle seemed to be shifting toward a settlement when both companies withdrew their appeals to a ruling by the U.S. International Trade Commission.

Apple dropped an appeals suit against Samsung for one of the early rulings in the U.S. and the market began to project that the two rivals may be headed for a settlement.

For the last two years, neither of the two firms has filed for a fresh suit against each other in any of the courts around the world. Yet, the suits filed in the U.S. court are still under way and it seems it will take some more time until they reach a final settlement.

Some market watchers said that the withdrawals in non-U.S. courts are simply to reduce unnecessary costs and focus on the U.S. suits because they will matter the most to their businesses in future. Samsung and Apple may have concluded that an ITC ruling would have little impact on their patent protection.

■ Cash-Strapped Pantech Put Up for Sale

Pantech Co., a mid-sized South Korean smartphone maker, has been put up for sale after struggling with financial difficulties. Pantech, founded by an ordinary salesman, Park Byung-yeop, once grew into the second-largest handset maker in the country, where phone manufacturing is dominated by conglomerates.

However, cutthroat competition and a spate of business suspensions on local mobile carriers caused Pantech to experience a cash shortage, and it later filed for court receivership after undergoing a series of workout programs.

Even under a state of court protection, Pantech strived for a turnaround, including efforts from its own employees, who voluntarily returned a portion of their income to the management in a bid to save costs.

They included some staff members who returned 10 to 35% of their monthly wages. At the end of the year, all Pantech employees gave back 20% of their monthly income. About half of the 1,500 workers, or 700 of them, took a paid leave.

Pantech stepped up to salvage itself by offering some handsets at a bargain price ahead of its preliminary bidding. In November, it was put up for a final bidding, which ended up a botched attempt after foreign buyers that were widely expected to take part in the bid -- India's Micromax Informatics Ltd. and some Chinese players -- backed away from it.

Lee Jun-woo, the Pantech CEO, went on to attempt another takeover bid, despite a report on the ailing company by its sale managers in which it said it's worth more to sell off than to revive it, based on its valuations.

The court and its creditor banks have been of one mind with Lee, given that the significance of the tech firm as the country's first mid-sized smartphone producer that had once stood on its own feet makes the sale process worthwhile.

■ Battle of Smartwatches...Platforms or Designs?

As the market for smart wristwatches grew, tech firms joined the race to make the best wearable device to woo consumers. Samsung Electronics and LG Electronics released the Gear S and G Watch R in Germany in early September. Apple unveiled its first smartwatch, the Apple Watch, in Cupertino, California.

The smart wristwatch market first opened with Sony Corp. and Pebble Technology Corp., but they were soon overrun by bigger players as the competition got fiercer.

There are already at least eight different smartwatches made by key players: Samsung's Gear and Gear S; the G Watch series by LG; Motorola's Moto 360; Pebble's namesake smartwatch; ZenWatch by Asus; and Apple's Apple Watch.

The operating platforms (OS) include five types, mainly led by Samsung's own Tizen and the Android platform by Google Inc. Pebble, Sony and Apple have adopted their own OS into their wearable devices. China's Xiaomi Inc., Acer Inc. of Tawian and Japan's Toshiba Corp. have been tapping into the smartwatch market.

Analysts say the expansion of the smartwatch market is similar to how smartphones first began to bulge. It was introduced in a market where various PDAs and Window-based mobile products were making good headway, when the BlackBerry smartphone emerged as the first case that started to hit the road, until iPhones and Android handsets came to commercialize the market.

Over the course of such a shift in market trends, a spate of other operating platforms came along, including BlackBerry OS, Tizen, Bada and FireFox OS. But Android and iOS were survivors while others either went into extinction or are still struggling to gain a presence.

Analysts say smartwatches could follow suit or go a different way. Some say that it will hinge on which operating system will gain an upper hand in the market, while others say that a wearable device like a wristwatch may be more dependent on its design because it's more of an accessory than a product itself.

FINANCIAL INDUSTRY

▪ Overview

South Korea ushered in an unprecedented era of ultra-low interest rates as the Bank of Korea cut its base rate twice in 2014 to help pump up the country's slowing growth momentum, which also had an impact on money market rates.

The country's low borrowing costs led to a surge in household debt, which got a further boost from eased lending regulations aimed at boosting the country's sagging property market. The nation's household debts surpassed the 1,000-trillion won level, which many observers claim could pose a threat to Asia's fourth-largest economy.

The country's financial sector was also roiled by a series of events such as a massive data leak and an internal feud at KB Financial Group. Also, the so-called fintech and a direct won-yuan trading system heralded a new chapter for the country's financial sector.

The U.S. Fed's much-awaited rate hike drew keen attention through 2014, and the government's drive to privatize Woori Financial Group was again pushed back due to a lack of possible investors.

▪ Ultra-Low Interest Rate

The South Korean economy's growth remained weak as the global economy was dragged down by the aftermath of the global financial crisis.

The Bank of Korea's growth estimate for the year was cut to 3.8% in July from the 4% estimate in April, and again to 3.5% in October. Asia's fourth-largest economy grew 3.3% in 2014.

The Bank of Korea came under growing pressure to cut the rate to help the economy get back on a recovery track. In particular, market speculation over a rate cut ran high after Choi Kyong-hwan took office in July.

The Bank of Korea cut its rate by a quarter percentage point in August and October to reach a record low of 2% for the first time since February 2009. Deposit rates at banks and government bond yields fell to record lows with the average deposit rate standing at 1.97% in October.

▪ Soaring Household Debt

Record low borrowing costs and a series of measures to boost the sagging property market helped boost household debt. The amount of household debt hit 1,060 trillion at the end of September, up 6.7% from a year earlier.

Also, households' capability to repay debt fell to record lows, with the ratio of household debt to disposable income reaching an all-time high of 137% at the end of September. That figure compares with 135% in 2013, 133% in 2012 and 131% in 2011.

Household debt growth was led by a surge in mortgage lending as the country's financial regulator eased lending criteria for home-backed loans. The authorities took steps to rein in the ballooning household debt, vowing that they would pay close attention to the soaring problem.

▪ Real-Name Financial Transaction

All types of ill-intended money transactions under borrowed names were banned in South Korea starting in November as the government closed loopholes in the law to tighten the real-name financial system.

The revisions to the Act on Real Name Financial Transaction and Confidentiality enable the punishment of all parties involved in transactions using the names of others. Previously, only financial institutions were held accountable in confirming the identities of the real clients behind the transactions.

The real-name transaction system was first introduced in 1993 to root out shady and hidden financial activities and help enhance transparency. But a series of slush fund scandals using borrowed names by politicians and business tycoons sparked public demand to revise the mechanism and stiffen penalties.

Borrowed names were also being used by the rich to evade taxes by dividing the wealth into pieces and depositing them into accounts held by another individual. Even when tax authorities discovered such activities, they were only able to levy additional taxes.

Under the revised law, those who engage in such ill-intended transactions can be imprisoned for up to five years or fined 50 million won. Those who lent their names can be also punished if they knew if it was for illegal financial activities.

The revisions include an assumption that the assets belong to the individual whose name is on the account, rather than the actual owner. Banks reported a flurry of withdrawals and deposits ahead of the law revisions taking effect.

Their data showed that lump-sum deposits decreased while money put into savings accounts increased as customers switched over to financial products with lower tax rates. The amount of money put into savings accounts rose to 562 trillion won in October from 555 trillion won six months earlier, according to the data.

■ Data Leak from Credit Card Firms

In January, some 20 million bank clients' personal data, including bank account numbers, addresses and credit ratings, was leaked from three credit card firms -- KB Kookmin, Nonghyup and Lotte. A leak also occurred at Kookmin Bank, which shared its customer data with its affiliated credit card firm.

The largest-ever data theft came to light when an employee from a personal credit ratings agency, the Korea Credit Bureau, and two others were indicted for illegally obtaining and distributing confidential data from the three card firms while working as temporary consultants for the financial institutions.

In March, the financial regulator unveiled a set of measures to better protect clients from data breaches, including a regulatory framework under which top executives at financial firms could face suspension or dismissal.

The measures also include strengthened monitoring of staff at financial firms and their contractors in areas related to data protection, and strictly regulating the sharing of customer information between affiliates. In cases of data breaches, financial firms will face hefty penalties and business suspensions.

A financial institution will be levied a fine of up to 1% of its revenue if its customer data are stolen or when it uses illegally obtained personal information to sell financial products. Under the proposed measures, clients will be given the choice to opt out of information-sharing among affiliates and third parties.

Financial service providers will be required to end their decade-long practice of asking for "too much" personal information, including citizen registration numbers. Also, credit card firms will be forced to delete all data during a given grace period if their customers cancel their plastic cards.

The financial regulator also handed down a three-month business suspension to the three card firms, and took punitive measures against their top executives.

Following the scandal, top executives at KB Financial Group Inc. and its mainstay banking unit, Kookmin Bank, and three other credit card firms tendered their resignations and promised to fully cover any financial losses if their clients are scammed because of the stolen data.

■ Internal Feud at KB Financial

In September, the board of KB Financial Group Inc. dismissed the group's chairman, Lim Young-rok, who was accused of a series of management lapses but refused to step down.

Lim, who took the helm of the country's No. 2 banking group by market value in July 2013, came under mounting pressure to resign over a series of scandals such as massive data leaks and illegal loans.

The banking group has been also embroiled in an ugly internal feud over a computer system change at its mainstay banking unit, Kookmin Bank.

In April, the bank's board approved the expensive transition to a new computer system, based on reports compiled by the bank that were full of fabricated information.

The reports underestimated the risks of the system change and scaled down the related expenses, according to the Financial Supervisory Service (FSS), the country's financial watchdog.

The FSS had censured Lim and Kookmin Bank president Lee Kun-ho, but the Financial Services Commission (FSC), the regulator, upped the level of punishment, citing the gravity of their misconduct. By law, only the regulator, the FSC, can finalize the punishment of CEOs of financial groups.

Kookmin Bank chief Lee resigned after being sanctioned, but Lim insisted he did nothing wrong in handling the computer system change and vowed to take all possible measures to clear his name, including legal action.

The FSC has been going all-out to oust Lim from his post by lodging a complaint with the prosecution against Lim and other executives over irregularities in the computer system transition. Critics say the regulator is meddling excessively in a private firm's management with its arm-twisting to replace CEOs who clash with regulators.

The case came to light in May this year when Kookmin Bank CEO Lee asked for a probe into the system change at the bank, claiming that the decision process needed to be thoroughly inspected because of rule violations and other irregularities.

▪ Insurers' Refusal to Pay Suicide Insurance

Local life insurers came under fire last year for their repeated denial of insurance payments related to suicides, although they were ordered to pay contracted money to the families of policyholders who kill themselves.

More than 10 life insurers had sold policies for accidents that cover disaster-caused deaths as well as suicides between 2003 and 2010 before it changed the terms of the policies to exclude suicide.

Under the previous contract terms, the families of policyholders who commit suicide received far higher payments than those for general death.

But insurers denied the payouts, arguing that the suicide provision was incorrectly inserted into the contract and that payments for suicide would encourage people to kill themselves.

The insurers took the case to court in November, defying instructions from the Financial Supervisory Service (FSS) to pay the insurance money in arrears. Market watchers estimated that the combined amount of unpaid policies for suicide cases is more than 200 billion won.

According to 2011 data compiled by the Organization for Economic Cooperation and Development (OECD), South Korea's suicide rate was 28.4 per 100,000 people, the highest among OECD countries, followed by Hungary with 19.8 and Japan with 19.7.

▪ Won-Yuan Direct Trading

On Dec. 1, South Korea launched a market for direct trading of its currency with China's yuan, a move that could facilitate trade based on their currencies and reduce their dependence on the U.S. dollar.

The new currency market was expected to help develop the local financial market as a hub for offshore yuan transactions and cushion South Korea against a global currency shock by diversifying currencies used in trade settlements.

The currency market could be helpful for South Korea in reducing its dependence on the dollar in its deals with China. In 2013, South Korea's trade with China reached US$229 billion, up from US$215.8 billion tallied the year before.

The launch was a follow-up on an agreement reached during a summit between South Korean President Park Geun-hye and her Chinese counterpart, Xi Jinping, in July.

The government has selected 12 banks, including five foreign bank branches, as market makers in the run-up to the launch of the won-yuan direct market.

The banks are tasked mostly with proposing selling and buying prices for transactions and inducing money flows, a move intended to lay the groundwork for the currency market, which could face a lack of supply and demand in its early stage.

The government launched a similar won-yen transaction market in 1996, but it failed to take off due in large part to a lack of demand.

▪ Burgeoning Fintech

South Korea braced for the fast-growing financial technology, or fintech, in 2014. The South Korean financial regulator vowed to remove hurdles and fully support the sector to refresh the country's long-sluggish financial industry.

Fintech is a new type of information technology linked with financial services, ranging from mobile payments and remittances to asset management, and the industry is sharply growing across the world by absorbing money from wealthy tech-savvy individuals.

Leading mobile messenger and portal service provider Daum Kakao Corp. launched mobile payment systems called "Bank Wallet Kakao" and "Kakao Pay," through which users can send money or shop online.

The Financial Services Commission, the country's financial regulator, has been focusing on boosting the mobile-based e-commerce market and pushing to remove regulations in related areas to promote IT-finance consolidation.

It promised to remove the compulsory authentication requirements for online purchases and introduce alternative online payment systems to offer foreign shoppers easier access to local shopping malls.

■ **Repeated Bids to Sell Woori Bank**

An auction to sell state-run Woori Bank failed in November due to a lack of bidders, the fourth such failed attempt by the government to privatize South Korea's No. 3 bank. "Only China's An-bang Property & Casualty Insurance Co. applied for it," said the Financial Services Commission (FSC).

At least two bidders were needed to make the auction valid, but only China's Anbang Property & Casualty Insurance Co. applied for it. Anbang Insurance is a leading Chinese insurer, with assets of 121 trillion won.

Kyobo Life Insurance Co., South Korea's third-biggest life insurer by assets, had expressed its interest in buying the bank, but did not submit a bid.

The South Korean government has tried to privatize Woori Bank and its affiliates since 2010 to recoup some 13 trillion won in bailout money invested in the aftermath of the 1997 Asian financial crisis.

After the three previous attempts to sell the bank during the Lee Myung-bak administration failed, the FSC came up with a new sales plan.

Under the plan, of the nearly 57% stake held by the state-run Korea Deposit Insurance Corp. (KDIC), a controlling 30% would go to a single buyer, with the remaining 27% to be sold to multiple investors.

STOCK MARKET

■ **Overview**

The benchmark KOSPI index ended down 4.8% in 2014 from a year earlier, the first fall in three years. The secondary KOSDAQ, in contrast, soared more than 8% in the same period, posting the biggest gain since 2008 in the aftermath of the financial crisis spurred by the collapse of Lehman Brothers.

Last year, the South Korean stock market saw a bullish run in small and mid-caps, a departure from its strong dependence on large-cap firms.

The government policy, dubbed "Choinomics", led by finance minister Choi Kyung-hwan, influenced the local market, along with the sharp fall of global crude oil prices.

A spate of key rate cuts led the market to keep the low-rate policy, which raised interest for dividend payouts and had investors scurrying to increase bets on mid-risk, mid-return products. China-based stocks caught investors' attention, with some of them going public backed by Beijing's support for corporate IPOs.

■ **KOSPI Down 4.8 Pct, KOSDAQ Up 8.6 Pct**

The Korea Exchange (KRX), the country's bourse operator, said the KOSPI and the KRX100 index fell 4.8% and 9.5% each last year, decoupling from other key global benchmarks. On the last trading day of 2014, the KOSPI finished at 1,915.59, sliding 4.76% from a year earlier.

The KOSPI's gain was the second slowest among the Group of 20 nations. Argentina marked the biggest gain of 56.6%, coming first in the group, followed by China with 49.7% and India's 29.4%.

Turkey came behind with 24% and Indonesia rose 21.1%. Japan logged an 8.8% gain, with the United States rising 8.8%. Russia was the biggest decliner with a 44.9% on-year fall.

The bearish run mainly stemmed from the developed economies, whose recovery pace had been slower than expected, while the global currency market fluctuated and companies posted weak earnings.

The KOSPI rose to its yearly high of 2,082.61 on July 30, 2014, while dropping to its lowest point of 1,886.85 on Feb. 4. The index lost ground sharply at the beginning of the year on growing uncertainties from emerging markets, but it gained momentum and hit the 2,000-point mark at the end of the first half. In July-August, expectations over Choinomics -- a set of measures announced by finance minister Choi Kyung-hwan that aims to boost the economy -- lifted market sentiment to nearly touch the 2,100-point level.

But renewed concerns about a U.S. exit strategy to end its easy-money policy, poor corporate earnings, a sudden fall of crude oil prices and a weaker yen sent the KOSPI tumbling to below 2,000 points.

Still, the market capitalization of the KOSPI hit a record high of 1,192 trillion won, on the back of a slew of big-scale initial public offerings (IPOs) by a few key companies here, including Samsung SDS Co. and Cheil Industries Inc.

The tech-laden KOSDAQ continued a rally throughout the year. It ended the last day at 542.97, up 8.6% from the previous year. Its market cap also grew to the highest level in history to 141.35 trillion won as of end-December, from 119.3 trillion won in end-2013.

The combined market cap of the two key benchmarks came to 1,335 trillion won, equivalent to 94% of the country's gross domestic product (GDP). The number of listed firms on the main KOSPI slid by 18, or 1.97% to 898 in 2014.

■ Three Keywords: Dividends, Management Structure, China

Keywords that described the South Korean stock market in 2014 were dividends, management structure and China. Choinomics, a measure spearheaded by finance minister Choi Kyung-hwan, raised hopes for an increase in dividend payouts last year.

The ministry brought a stick-and-carrot policy, in which it proposed "a flowback tax" levied on company profits, while offering a tax break for those who pay out more dividends.

Such a policy caught investors' attention since they have been looking for investments amid a low-rate and low-growth trend. In October, the KRX released four new indices that have been improved from the earlier version of dividend-focused stocks.

The ownership structure of major conglomerates, known as chaebol here, became a fresh agenda. Lee Kun-hee, South Korea's richest man and the chairman of Samsung Group, suffered a heart attack in May and has since been bedridden. His illness stoked jitters over the next generation of leadership that controls the biggest conglomerate in the country, with more than 70 affiliates under its wing.

Analysts were busy publishing reports with predictions on stocks that will benefit from the leadership transfer at Samsung. Such a move pushed the shares of Samsung affiliates up, with their combined market cap surpassing 300 trillion won in June, from 280 trillion won at the beginning of the year.

Shares lost ground as concerns about their earnings grew. But the initial public offering (IPO) of Samsung SDS Co., a key unit of the group, again spurred momentum.

China was another hot issue. A surge in the number of Chinese tourists in Korea drove up shares of cosmetics, home appliance and baby product makers. Amore Pacific Corp., the top cosmetics producer, jumped to 2,220,000 won per share on the main bourse by the end of 2014, up from 1,007,000 won at the beginning of the year.

Investor appetite for Chinese assets increased as Beijing began to allow a cross-trading of shares between the Shanghai and Hong Kong markets starting this year.

■ Foreigners on Buying Binge, while Institutions, Individuals Selling

The stock turnover at the benchmark KOSPI came in at 4 trillion won on a daily basis in 2014, slowing the drop for the first time in three years. Trading volume stood at an average of 280 million shares daily last year, down 15.3% from 330 million shares in 2013, marking the second consecutive fall.

The yearly turnover and trading volume reached 975.92 trillion won and 68.1 billion shares, falling 1.06% and 15.99%

from the previous year, respectively.

On the KOSPI market, foreigners bought more shares than they sold at 4.8 trillion won. Institutions and individuals, however, unloaded a net 700 billion won and 2.8 trillion won each. Offshore investors remained net buyers of local equities for the third straight year last year, extending their market clout as a key driver of stocks.

Institutions turned to a net seller for the first time in four years. Pension funds scooped up 5 trillion won worth of shares last year, extending their buying spree for a fifth consecutive year, whereas asset managers dumped shares worth 1.1 trillion won as a net seller for the seventh straight year and financial investors also offloaded a net 1.1 trillion won. Retail investors have remained as net sellers for the last six years.

■ Small- and Mid-Caps Bullish; Large-Caps Lose Ground

Large-cap firms fell 7.2% last year, while small- and mid-caps each rose 2.5% and 21.2%. The portion of large-caps in the KOSPI's entire market cap slid to 74.7% in 2014, from 81.2% a year earlier. That of mid-caps, in contrast, rose to 12.6% from 11.4%, with the figure for small-caps also rising to 4.1% from 3.3% over the cited period.

The market cap of key conglomerates showed that Samsung Group affiliates saw theirs increase by 8.4 trillion won, with those of SK Group and Hanjin Group also growing by 9.5 trillion won and 3.1 trillion won.

But Hyundai Motor Group saw its combined market cap sink by 24.1 trillion won. The market cap of major seven conglomerates all decreased: Hyundai Heavy Industries Group shrank by 13.1 trillion won, with Lotte Group losing 7.5 trillion won.

Posco Group's market cap shed 5.6 trillion won, LG Group lost 3.8 trillion won, and GS Group dropped 2.1 trillion won, with that of Hanhwa Group falling by 800 billion won.

■ Revitalizing IPOs

The volume of initial public offerings (IPOs) on the KOSPI reached 3.5 trillion won in 2014, up by 2.8 trillion won from the previous year. This is the second-largest amount since 2010, when the figure came to a record 10.9 trillion won after blue-chip Samsung Life Insurance Co. went public in that year.

IPOs in South Korea remained sluggish in 2012 and 2013, with only 1.09 trillion won and 1.4 trillion won worth, respectively. But in 2014, the IPOs of Samsung SDS Co. and Cheil Industries Inc. helped boost the volume.

Due to the fact that the two Samsung affiliates are closely related to the group's leadership transfer to Lee Jay-yong, Chairman Lee's son, investors showed huge interest in its stock subscription.

The application for Cheil stocks had a 195:1 chance of winning. The amount of deposits made for the Cheil Industries subscription reached 30.6 trillion won, outpacing the corresponding figure of 19.8 trillion won for Samsung Life Insurance back in 2010.

Shares of Samsung SDS rose as high as 428,000 won at one point, before falling back to 293,500 won at the year-end. Cheil Industries tripled to 158,000 won from its initial subscription value of 53,000 won.

■ KONEX Market

The KONEX, South Korea's third bourse for ventures and startups, has seen its market cap grow steadily this year since its launch in 2013, reaching 1.4 trillion won as of end-2014, up 50% from 916.4 billion won a year ago.

Opened in July 2013, 45 firms joined the KONEX market and another 34 were added to the list. Now there are 79 companies listed on the KONEX, whose main businesses are bio, software or semiconductors.

Individual investors were the biggest net buyers of KONEX stocks in 2014, accounting for 70.4% of the total, up from 19% in 2013. Institutions took up 16.3% as of end-2014.

Since the market opened, 22 KONEX-listed companies have raised a combined 81.4 billion won, of which 67.8 billion won was raised in 2014. The daily turnover came to 390 million won, with the trading volume reaching an average of 49,000 shares on a daily basis.

Bond Issuances Up, Their Turnover Drops

South Korea's bond issuance increased 0.77% to 602.1 trillion won in 2014 from a year ago. The country sold Treasuries worth 146.6 trillion won, up 8.19% on-year, as part of a measure to boost the economy. But sales of special debts and those floated by public firms decreased, leading to the overall drop in debt issuance.

Corporate bonds reached 78.9 trillion won, down 10.03%, with nearly 80% of them accounting for those rated above A, while only 3% took up BBB-rated or under.

The yields dropped to a record-low level with three-year government bonds at 2.073% on Dec. 1, largely due to two-time rate cut by the Bank of Korea.

Investors Seek Mid-Risk, Mid-Return; Brokerages Face Belt-Tightening

Equity-oriented mutual funds saw an outflow worth 2.6 trillion won of assets, marking a net sell-off for the third straight year as of end-2014, according to a local market tracker. In contrast, investors scooped up debt-related funds worth 2.9 trillion won as they sought profits from the central bank's rate cuts.

Equity-focused funds posted a minus 5.35% return rate as the local stock market sagged, while debt-linked funds logged a 4.69% annual return rate last year, on the back of a strong bond market.

An overall downturn in stock markets had local brokerage houses taking stiff restructuring steps. Major players, including Samsung Securities Co., reduced their staffs in the beginning of the year.

Data showed that the number of executives in the industry fell by 4,000 to 37,000 at the end of September, which compared with an increase in staff numbers at banks and insurers, by 2,500 and 300, respectively, in the same period.

RETAIL INDUSTRY

Overview

The country's retail business sector logged 267.54 trillion won in sales last year, a 1.37% rise or 3.63 trillion won, from the previous year's 263.91 trillion

won. The 2014 expansion marks a slow-down from a 1.55% gain in 2013 and a 4.16% rise in 2012 and an 8.36% increase in 2011.

Department stores strived to attract Chinese visitors while venturing into the outlet and shopping mall businesses to beef up their falling profitability.

The local convenience stores, meanwhile, logged a decent growth last year on the back of a demographic change in the country -- a growing number of single households -- and the variety of items sold.

Online shopping continued to grow last year as mobile devices such as smartphones helped more consumers tap Internet shopping sites.

Department Stores

Department stores saw their sales decline 1.9% on-year to reach 29.23 trillion won last year, marking the first contraction in four years. In 2013, the sector grew 2.6%, slowing from a 5.4% expansion in 2012. The comparable figure for 2011 was 11.4%.

Lotte Department Store, the country's top player, logged sales of 14.2 trillion won last year, up 3.6% from a year earlier. The department store suffered a 0.9% decline in its sales in 2013 because of an economic slump.

Shinsegae Department Store Co., the country's No. 2 player, suffered a 2.6% fall in its 2014 sales at 4.044 trillion won, marking a decline for the second consecutive year. Its operating income also slipped 6.5% on-year to reach 190 billion won.

Consumers remained reluctant to buy luxury goods amid a protracted economic slump, while flocking to foods, as local department stores rolled out a series of imported food brands.

The local department stores also ventured into shopping mall business and outlets, in a bid to beef up falling profits in their traditional businesses.

Larger Retailers

Large-sized retailers such as Homeplus and E-Mart faced difficulty in expanding their outlets because of an economic slump and enhanced restrictions, but logged a 3.37% rise in their sales at 46.64 trillion won last year.

When the online shopping segment was excluded, the large-sized marts were the only retailers that grew. But their sales growth slowed from a 5% expansion in 2012 and a 10.9% gain in 2011. E-Mart, the No. 1 player, saw its sales increase 1.8% on-year last year.

By product, sales of fresh foods and home-meal replacement (HMR) foods and electronic goods led the overall growth, while daily goods and fashion sports suffered a sharp decline in their sales amid an economic slump.

Processed foods also suffered a mild decrease in their sales, and sales of dairy products such as milk and coffee and soda declined because of a growing number of health-conscious consumers.

■ Supermarkets

The sales of supermarkets in the country is estimated at 36.07 trillion won last year, slightly growing from 35.8 trillion won a year earlier. The 2014 expansion marks a slowdown from the 5% growth seen in 2011 and 2012.

Large-sized supermarkets also faced a deadlock in expanding their presence because of laws banning them from excessively setting up stores. Mid-sized supermarkets, meanwhile, enjoyed a mild growth in their sales because of enhanced restrictions on large-sized retailers.

■ Convenience Stores

South Korean convenience stores continued their modest growth last year on the back of a demographic change in the country -- a growing number of single households -- and the variety of items sold.

They dwarfed their bigger and traditional retail channels in expansion. The market size was estimated at 12.6 trillion won last year, compared with 11.73 trillion won a year earlier. The 7.4% expansion compares with a 7.8% rise in 2013, and an 18.3% gain in 2012.

CU, run by BGF Retail Co., posted 3.37 trillion won in sales last year, up 7.6% from a year earlier, with its operating income also spiking 18% on-year to 124 billion won and the number of its outlets rising by 469 to 8,408.

GS25, managed by retail giant GS Retail, logged 8.8% growth in its 2014 sales at 3.5 trillion won, while suffering a 7.7% fall in its operating income at 111 billion won. The number of its outlets rose 516 last year to reach 8,290, according to the data.

Lotte affiliate Korea Seven, which runs 7-Eleven and Buytheway, saw a 5.1% rise in its sales last year at 2.68 trillion won, accelerating from a 4.3% expansion a year earlier. But it suffered a 33% drop in its operating income to 38 billion won due to increased marketing costs.

The number of convenience stores newly opened across the nation is estimated at 16,000 last year, compared with 500 in 2013 and 3,300 in 2012.

Their decent growth came as local convenience stores have introduced their own store brands, known in the country as "private brands," which have an edge over traditional and multinational labels in terms of price and costs.

They have also been shifting away from their conventional product mix of instant food and drinks to non-food items to foster loyal customers.

■ Online Shopping

In 2014, online shopping increased 17.5% to 45.24 trillion won, with mobile shopping accounting for 14.81 trillion won, a 125.8% increase. Corresponding figures for 2013 were 38.49 trillion won and 6.56 trillion won.

Transactions in travel and reservation services moved up 31.1%, on-year, with cosmetics gaining 26.8% in 2014. Everyday goods and car-related products advanced 20.9% with 19.9% gains for electronics and communications equipment.

During the fourth quarter, online shopping sales surged 20.1% on-year with total transactions reaching 12.74 trillion won, which also marks a gain from 11.45 trillion won in the previous quarter.

The stellar growth was driven by a surge in use of mobile devices such as smartphones. Also, the economic slowdown led consumers to flock to cheap products offered by online retailers, in particular, by social networking services such as Coupang.

The Korea Chamber of Commerce and Industry forecast that Internet shopping market is expected to surge 14.3% in 2015, as mobile shopping continued to rise.

SMALL AND MEDIUM ENTERPRISES

▪ Number of Fresh SMEs Hits Record High

The number of newly-established small and medium enterprises (SMEs) in South Korea surpassed 80,000 for the first time in 2014, according to government data. A bad job market stemming from the slowing economy and an increase in the number of retirees from the baby boomers (born between 1955-1963) are cited as main reasons.

The number of new SMEs reached 84,697 as of end-2014, up 12.1% from a year earlier, marking the biggest yearly gain since the government began to compile data in 2000.

Service companies increased the most by 53,087, followed by manufacturers with 19,509, builders with 8.145 and agricultural/fisheries/mining with 2,593.

More than 50,000 smaller firms were created by baby boomers in their 40s and 50s, suggesting that they have opened companies that fall into the service category, such as transportation, accommodation or restaurants.

The growth in SMEs came as the baby boomer generation turned to self-employment after retiring early amid a slump in the job market. Also, the government's policy drive to bolster the creation of venture firms lent support to the increase.

▪ Kaesong Complex into Its 10th Year

Last year marked the 10th year for the Kaesong Industrial Complex, an economic zone co-run by the two Koreas near the border of the namesake city in the North. The Kaesong complex kicked off with initially 15 smaller firms from the South that signed up to set up their business in the designated area in June 2004.

Since then, the complex has been regarded as a symbol of inter-Korean economic cooperation that could lay the groundwork for the unification process. In December 2004, the complex unveiled its first set of products.

According to the unification ministry, the cumulative value of production at the Kaesong complex has mounted to US$2.3 billion over the last decade, with the value of trade reaching US$9.45 billion. There are now 125 firms running their businesses there. Textile companies accounted for more than half, followed by 24 machinery companies, 13 electronics businesses and nine chemical firms.

The annual production grew by 30-fold over the years to US$369 million at the end of 2012, with 52,000 North Korean employees working at the site, which is also a big increase from the initial 6,000 workers at the start.

The production value, however, had once halved in 2013 when the complex was shut down after Pyongyang cut off the inter-Korean military communication hotline. The site resumed operation in August.

There are currently a high percentage of North Korean female workers at the complex, representing about 71%. Their average age came to 37.9 years old, with 0.4% being teenagers.

The monthly minimum wage, which was US$50 at the start, rose 5% every year and is now US$130 a month. With a set of other costs like insurance coverage included, a North Korean worker is paid about US$144 a month.

As part of a bid to boost the industrial zone, the Seoul government has pushed for improving communication, customs and transportation procedures with the North, while seeking ways to open the complex to foreign investors.

A few groups of foreign entrepreneurs and related public officials visited the Kaesong complex. A German firm agreed to open a retail arm as the first foreign company, while Seoul set up a support center for foreign investment in the area.

As for improvement of the three sectors mentioned above, the infrastructure is all ready for a final agreement between the South and North, but little headway has been made since Pyongyang stayed reluctant over the move.

In November last year, North Korea unilaterally removed a provision regarding labor at the Kaesong complex that limits the upper ceiling of the workers' minimum wage.

■ IKEA Lands in S. Korea, Faces Backlash from Neighboring Shops

Swedish furniture retail giant IKEA opened its first branch on the outskirts of Seoul in December 2014. The IKEA branch in a city southeast of the capital comprises three buildings and a three-story parking lot which can accommodate 2,000 vehicles. Its size altogether adds up to 131,500㎡.

The warehouse store sells more than 8,600 items, including furniture, bedding, daily and kitchen supplies, and has 65 exhibition halls inside.

▲ People line up in front of the Swedish furniture brand IKEA store in Gwangmyeong City, south of Seoul, on Dec. 18. IKEA plans to open four more stores in South Korea in the near future.

There was a negative perception about the furniture retailer making inroads to the local market, since the company caused controversies on "the Sea-of-Japan" written on its map of the Korean Peninsula. Also, the difference between the prices of items sold here and abroad sparked anger among Korean consumers. There were also concerns that the business will eat into the profits of smaller stores.

A business association here representing small and medium-sized firms said in a survey that 55% of smaller stores have seen their profit drop 31.1% on average since December last year.

The majority of them said they don't think IKEA will be of help to the neighboring stores in terms of boosting their businesses. They worried that the foreign company could be the source of a capital outflow, and as smaller stores lose ground, it can lead to staff layoffs.

Most of them agreed with the idea that the government should classify IKEA as one of those that are required to close their stores every two weeks. If a store is categorized as a supermarket by the metropolitan government, it must close the store on a biweekly basis, a measure to protect smaller businesses.

Currently, IKEA is classified as a special store instead of a supermarket, which frees it from any kind of administrative limits on running its business.

■ Change in Definition of SME

The government passed a revised ordinance for an Act that defines an SME in South Korea. According to the ordinance, a company will be classified as an SME based on its average revenue for the last three years, instead of including all production elements such as workers and capital.

A startup that is less than 3 years old will be determined based on its annual revenue. Depending on the type of industry, the company must fit into the 40 billion, 60 billion, 80 billion, 100 billion or 150 billion-won group.

The government abolished the upper ceiling of 1,000 workers/100 billion won in capital that were needed for the firm to be an SME. But the threshold of 500 billion won in assets will continue to be applied.

A company can only once "delay" its status as an SME when it grows to a size too big to stay as a smaller firm. In that case, its SME status is retained for another three years. Such a rule came as many companies prefer to stay as SMEs due to many government benefits and less stiff regulations, even if they grow bigger.

■ Pro-SME Policy Stokes Adverse Effect on Large Firms

The government had designated certain types of businesses as "fit for SMEs." In other words, smaller companies had priority if they wanted to enter one of several types of businesses and large firms would be banned from tapping into the industry.

It was a policy that aimed at helping smaller companies keep their footing solid. But soon there were voices complaining that such a policy resulted in reverse discrimination for big companies. Large firms claimed that the policy overlooks foreign firms that stand in the grey area and are fully exempt from any restrictions.

For instance, makgeolli, a traditional Korean alcohol made of rice, was designated for an "SME-fit" sector, when it was selling well in other countries like Japan. But since it was categorized as a limited business for SMEs, the industry began to falter and led to a slowdown, industry sources say.

CHAEBOL

▪ Overview

In 2014, South Korean businesses were locked in a prolonged earnings slump stemming from an overall economic slowdown, with the absence of many of the conglomerate owners as a result of an illness or arrests by law enforcement authorities.

It came with the utmost importance that businesses focus on how to brace against the slowing economy amid the government's policy drive to revitalize the economy and to ease rules.

Later in the year, a so-called "nut rage" incident, in which a daughter of the chairman of top flight carrier Korean Air Lines Co. forced a flight crew chief off a plane at New York's JFK airport bound for Seoul, because she was served macadamia nuts in a package instead of on a plate, which she claimed was against regulations.

The case, which ended with Cho Hyunah, Korean Air's ex-vice president of cabin service, behind bars on charges of violating flight rules, stirred hostile public sentiment toward conglomerates, also known here as chaebol, and raised calls among the inner circle of the chaebol to reflect upon themselves and show regret over their distorted way of wielding power that results in wealth.

Hyundai Motor Group took the market by surprise when it won the bid to buy a site owned by the state-run Korea Electric Power Corp. for an astronomical 10 trillion won. Hyundai Heavy Industries Co. faced the worst time in its history with more than 1 trillion won in net losses.

In 2014, Tong Yang Group collapsed after suffering a cash shortage, while Dongbu Group also struggled with liquidity problems. Samsung and Hanwha clinched a "big deal" in which the latter agreed to buy four units of Samsung.

▪ Lee Kun-hee's Illness, Samsung's Reshuffle

Lee Kun-hee, the patriarch of South Korea's top conglomerate, Samsung Group, suffered a heart attack at his home on May 10, 2014. The chairman was resuscitated, and sent to the Samsung Medical Center, where the 73-year-old tycoon has been ever since.

He's been on hypothermia treatment, which prevents the generation of toxic material in blood vessels by slowing the cell metabolism. According to his medical officials and Samsung Group, Lee is in a stable condition.

His illness sparked worries about the future of the top South Korean chaebol, whose flagship unit, Samsung Electronics, began to show a slowdown in profit. But at the same time, Chairman Lee's absence gave his 47-year-old son, Jay-yong, a chance to embark on his own way of reorganization as well as to put himself to the test on leadership.

The younger Lee, the vice president of Samsung Electronics, didn't wait. He pushed forward a management reshuffle and M&As, through which he sought to slim down the conglomerate.

In later 2013, the materials unit of Cheil Industries Inc., formerly known as Samsung Everland Inc., was absorbed into Samsung's battery-making arm, Samsung SDI Co. The building-management and security division of Samsung Everland was transferred to S-1 Corp., the group's security unit. Samsung Everland's food distribution business was spun off to Samsung Welstory Inc.

In November last year, Samsung announced a plan to sell Samsung Techwin Co., Samsung General Chemicals Co., Samsung Thales Co. and Samsung Total Petrochemicals Co. -- its petrochemical and defense industry units -- to Hanwha Group, the 10th-largest family-run conglomerate in the country, in what market watchers said is the biggest deal in a decade.

▪ The "Owner Risk" and Leadership Change

A spate of legal arrests on some chiefs of conglomerates continued in 2014, casting a shadow on their business outlooks. Chey Tae-won, the charman of No. 3 chaebol SK Group, has been in jail since January 2013. Chey and his younger brother, Jae-won, the chief vice president, were sentenced to four years in prison.

It was the first time in Korea that an incumbent chief of a top conglomerate got a prison term. Many business moguls have been indicted for embezzlement charges in the past, but most of them got off with no jail time as the court gave them an extended probation period.

Lee Jae-hyun, the chief executive of food and entertainment conglomerate CJ Group, was sentenced to three years in prison at an appellate court in September, for embezzling 200 billion won worth of company assets and tax-dodging charges.

In the following month, Kang Duk-soo, the head of STX Group, the shipping and shipbuilding firm, was given a six-year prison term on charges of cooking the books and misappropriation of funds.

Hyun Jae-hyun, the chief of Tong Yang Group, was sentenced to 12 years in prison at his first trial in October, on charges of fraud. He was alleged to have ignored his financial affiliate, Tongyang Securities Inc., selling junk-level bonds worth 1.3 trillion won to individual investors who claimed they were given wrong information about the debts they bought. This is the heaviest punishment handed down on a chaebol in the last decade.

▪ 'Nut Rage' Incident Puts Chaebol and Their Heirs Under Fire

It took the public by surprise when Chey Min-jung, the younger daughter of SK Group Chairman Chey Tae-won, enlisted in the Navy as an officer in August, a very rare case for a child from a chaebol family in Korea.

She passed all her tests and training, and was commissioned as a second lieutenant in November. Her choice of career came as a contrasting example to the nut rage case involving Cho Hyun-ah, the daughter of Cho Yang-ho, the CEO of Korean Air Lines Co.

She went on trial on charges of violating aviation rules when she forced a chief purser off a plane because she was served macadamia nuts in a pack instead of on a plate.

The plane, with 250 passengers on board, had already headed out on the runway at New York's JFK airport, but made its way back to drop the staff member off on Cho's order.

Since the incident was reported by media, the public has shown deep resentment toward the way that a chaebol family treated staff members of the company like their servants.

Cho's case fueled anti-chaebol sentiment in Korea, with growing calls for appropriate legal actions to be taken against her. She resigned all her positions at Korean Air as the vice president and the head of on-board service and hotel business, asking for a pardon, but she was arrested in December and has been imprisoned since.

▪ Hyundai Motor Wins KEPCO's Land for 10.5 Trillion Won

Hyundai Motor Group won the bid to buy the lucrative land asset of the state-run Korea Electric Power Corp. (KEPCO) by offering 10.5 trillion won in September.

The carmaker beat Samsung Electronics to buy the 79,345-square-meter site, seen as the last sizable piece of land available for development in Seoul, to build its new global business center in the affluent Gangnam district.

It was estimated to be worth more than 3.3 trillion won. Hyundai bid for the land through a consortium with two of its affiliates -- Kia Motors and Hyundai Mobis -- who had expressed strong interest in buying the KEPCO site to build a business center to put auto affiliates together, and pursue hotel- and convention-related businesses.

The property was put up for sale as KEPCO is scheduled to move its headquarters to Naju, 350km south of Seoul, in November as part of the government's plan to relocate state-run companies for balanced national development.

But such a high bid offer by Hyundai Motor was a blow to its corporate valuations, sending its shares tumbling and shrinking its market cap. Samsung Group, the top conglomerate, also tendered a bid, but at a much lower price.

The carmarker said the new Seoul headquarters will bring its 18,000 employees from 30 affiliates together in one building. It also revealed a plan to set up an auto theme park, for which it said is envisioning a Korean version of "Autostadt".

Retail giant Lotte Group finally realized its long-held wish of opening the second Lotte World in Seoul in October. But a series of accidents at its construction site and its aquarium raised serious questions about the safety of the new shopping mall.

A few workers at the construction site were either injured or killed from a fall. The building's walls, including those at the aquarium, were found to have had cracks and apparently people saw water leak from inside the silicon. Media reports on such issues followed, and shoppers stopped going to the new mall.

Merchants that run a shop at the second Lotte World filed a complaint with police against Lotte, claiming that they've been losing money since the firm failed to prevent the accidents.

▪ Dismal Earnings Lead to Corporate Defaults

Dongbu Group, ranked 28th in the corporate list in South Korea, went under a painful restructuring due to liquidity problems from its steel and construction units. It is expected to see a big scaledown in size as Dongbu Steel handed over management to its creditors and two of its other affiliates were sold off.

Pantech Co., a mid-sized smartphone maker, is on the verge of a liquidation. It applied for a workout program in March, seeking to salvage itself from financial difficulties but took only six months for the ailing tech firm to go under court receivership in September.

The three mobile carriers -- SKT, KT and LG Uplus --, on whom Pantech had depended for the bulk of its sales, declined to help Pantech, which was the final blow to the smartphone maker's balance sheet.

South Korean companies suffered from the prolonged slump in domestic demand, while the rapid growth of Chinese rivals and resurgence of Japanese firms on the back of a cheaper currency weighed on their profits. The fluctuation of the won-dollar exchange rate added pressure on Korean companies.

Such unfavorable conditions led key conglomerates to overhaul their business strategies and revise their blueprint for future growth. Samsung Electronics, whose mobile division was hit hard by Chinese upstarts, took belt-tightening measures in which it reduced the number of its mobile executives by half and relocated staff to other sectors to slim down the cash-cow division that once had accounted for more than 60% of Samsung Electronics' revenue.

Hyundai Motor Group reorganized its affiliates, reducing its seven units to three within only a month in August. The company said it was a decision to cut costs and improve effectiveness by combining businesses that overlapped between some units.

Hyundai Heavy Industries Co., the world's largest shipyard, which booked a cumulative 3 trillion won in net losses at the end of 2014, laid off 31% of its 262 executives in its massive staff reshuffle.

Social Affairs

Yonhap News Agency

NATIONAL LIFE

■ **Household Income**

South Korean household income grew 3.4% on-year in 2014, with net income going up 2.1%, according to a report by Statistics Korea. Inflation-adjusted household income also moved up 2.1% over the same period.

While their earned income rose 3.9% thanks to an increase in the employment rate and wage hikes, property income fell 3.1% due to lower interest rates. Household spending also moved up compared to the previous year. Monthly consumption expenditures -- household spending on services and products that include daily necessities -- rose 2.8% to 2.55 mil-

lion won in 2014.

The findings showed people spending more on transportation and recreation and other services, while cutting back on telecommunication, housing and utilities. Transportation outlays were buoyed by more people buying cars, while utilities were affected by lower energy prices. Non-consumption expenditures, which include payments on taxes, pensions and insurance, expanded 3% on-year to 800,500 won.

Households' monthly disposable income -- total income minus non-consumption spending -- stood at 3.35 million won, up 3.5% from a year earlier. In 2013, disposable income grew 1.9%. The average monthly surplus for a household stood at 947,000 won, a solid gain of 5.2% on-year.

But the numbers for households' "average consumption propensity" -- the ratio of total consumption spending to disposable income -- dropped to 72.9%, a 0.4%p difference from the previous year. It marks the fourth year in a row that it contracted compared to the year before, which indicates that people are withholding spending, despite a rise in earnings.

■ **Income Distribution**

In 2014, the average monthly income per household rose in all classes of the population, and the expenditure also moved up in all classes except among those the lowest 20% of the population.

Households' average consumption propensity -- the ratio of total consumption spending to disposable income --

dropped to the lowest level, indicating that people tended to tighten their purse strings amid lingering worries over the economic slump.

The consumption propensity stood at 74.1%, down 0.7%p from the previous year, marking the third straight year that the figure has dropped on a year-on-year basis and also represented the lowest level since related data started to be released in 2003.

▪ Consumer Prices

South Korea's consumer price index (CPI) stood at 1.3% in 2014. The core price, which excludes volatile oil and food prices, rose 2% on-year; excluding food and energy prices, it went up 1.7%. CPI for living edged up by 0.8%, and the index for fresh food plunged 9.3% on-year.

By expenditure, consumers spent more on housing and utilities (2.9%), clothing and shoes (4%), food and accommodation (1.4%) and education (1.5%), among others, while cutting spending on such items as transportation (-1.6%) and telecommunication (-0.1%).

By item, the amount of products grew 0.9% on-year, and service items rose by 1.6%. Of the products, agricultural, livestock and fishery products saw a 2.7% decrease, while utilities rose 3.9% and industrial goods increased 1.3%. Of service items, prices for housing climbed 2.3%, public services edged up 0.8% and private services went up by 1.7%.

▪ Real Estate

Land prices across the country rose 1.96% in 2014, the sharpest increase since the financial crisis in 2008. It was the first time since 2007 that the land price growth rate exceeded the inflation rate. The Ministry of Land, Infrastructure and Transport determined that land prices are on a steady upward trend, given that the small but steady rise has continued for 50 straight months.

The capital area saw its land prices rise by 1.91% while the prices for regional areas increased by 2.06%. Land prices in Seoul have inched up for 16 months in a row, but the growth rates in Gyeonggi Province and Incheon stood at 1.24% and 1.35% respectively, underperforming the average recorded for the country. The city

of Sejong recorded the steepest growth rate of 4.53% while Jeju Island jumped by 3.7% with Daegu rising 3.15%.

The annaul volume of land transactions came to 2.64 million plots of land in 2014, rising 17.9% from a year earlier. It was the highest reading recorded since 2006. The city of Sejong posted the sharpest on-year growth in the volume of land transactions, with a growth rate of 57.6%, followed by Jeju Island, Seoul and Incheon.

▪ Performance of House Construction

Construction permits for 515,000 new houses were approved during 2014, 17.1% more than the 440,000 houses permitted a year earlier. (The number came to 550,000 in 2011, 587,000 in 2012 and 440,000 in 2013). After the approval, outcome swung to a downward trend in the second half of 2014, bringing the annual number down 2% from the three-year average of 526,000 houses recorded from 2011 to 2013.

The downward turn indicated that the local house market is free of oversupply concerns. Seoul and Incheon saw their numbers of new house permits decrease by 15.9% and 28.2% respectively, but Gyeonggi Province saw its number rise by 25.6%.

The number of construction permits for apartments grew by 24.7% year-on-year to a total of 347,687 houses, while the number of non-apartment house construction permits came to 167,564, up 3.8% from a year earlier. But it marked a drop of 11% in comparison with the three-year average of 188,000 houses recorded from 2011 to 2103.

▪ Quality of Life

Statistics Korea's (KOSTAT) Statistical Research Institute (SRI) began its on-line services on June 30 to provide data which show the real 'quality of life' of the general public. SRI selected 81 indicators in 12 fields to measure the nation's quality of life and data on 70 indicators began to be available on June 30 on KOSTAT's website.

The existing economic indicators based on gross domestic product (GDP) didn't show the entire picture of the nation's quality of life. So, the new measurement program was adopted. Considering social issues such as declining birth rates, never-ending social conflicts and an increasing number of suicides, the government began to transfer its focus to improving the quality of life of the public via economic development. In the 21st century, countries increasingly measure the quality of their peoples' lives and social development.

As part of efforts to offset the limitations of GDP-based measurement with social and environmental indicators, more governments joined to measure their people's quality of life following reports from the Stiglitz Commission in 2009 and the Organization for Economic Cooperation and Development in 2011.

Out of the 70 measurement indicators, 34 showed improvement in terms of the nation's quality of life. When it comes to income, consumption, assets, employment, culture and leisure activities, education and environment, respondents replied that there was improvement. But they said their health worsened due largely to tougher competition.

KOSTAT expects the quality of life measurement services will make related government agencies and the society have a bigger interest in the quality of life. It also hopes policymakers and researchers will continue to have an interest in improving the measurement system to help the nation live a happy life.

■ **Health Insurance**

As of the third quarter of 2014, 50.23 million people are under health service coverage. Salaried workers accounted for 35.65 million, or 71%, of the total beneficiaries. Non-salaried workers accounted for the remaining 29%. There were 5.94 million people aged 65 and older, an increase of 4.8% compared to 2012.

Medical insurance premiums paid by the 50.23 million subscribers reached 31.815 trillion won last year, up 6.5% from a year earlier. By sector, salaried workers paid 26.26 trillion won, or 83%, in insurance premiums and non-salaried workers paid 5.555 trillion won. The former paid an average of 98,328 won per month and the latter paid 80,749 won. Overall households paid an average of 92,351 won per family each month. Per-capita insurance premiums were 41,430

won per month.

Out of medical insurance subscribers, the ratio of salaried workers increased to 66.4% in the third quarter of 2014 from 60% at the end of 2009. The insurance premiums paid by salary workers also climbed 5.2% to 82.5% from 77.3% during the same period. In contrast, the ratio of non-salaried workers and the insurance premiums paid by them all declined.

A total of 40.36 trillion won was spent for the subscribers' medical treatment in 2014, up 7.2% from a year before. Medical spending on those aged 65 or older accounted for 36.7% of the total spending, up 9.5% from a year earlier. Per-capita medical spending was up 6.5% to 89,497 won during the same period. Interestingly, spending on those aged 65 or older was more than four times higher than spending on those aged 64 or younger.

The National Health Insurance Service spent 31.57 trillion won in 2014 in insurance payments to its subscribers. The figure was up 7% from a year ago. Reflecting the fact that Korea is rapidly becoming an aging society, medical care benefits for the aged subscribers reached 30.254 trillion won, a 7.3% rise from a year earlier. In 2014, there were 86,308 medical care facilities, and the number jumped 9.9% compared to a year earlier.

The Ministry of Health and Welfare decided to increase the insurance premiums by 1.35% in 2015, the lowest level of increase except for its decision to hold the premiums steady in 2009. Under the downward revision, salaried workers saw their insurance premiums rise to 95,550 won from 94,290 won per household. Non-salaried workers saw their premiums increase to 83,400 won from 82,290 won in 2015.

The ministry also started to provide long-term medical treatment services for the aged people who suffer mild symptoms of Alzheimer's disease on July 1, 2014. As a result, the long-term medical care program was well accepted by the aging society, given that eight out of 10 families who have dementia patients were happy with it.

■ **National Pension**

As of the end of 2014, a total of 21.13 million people were covered by the national pension system. Compared to the end of

2013, the total number of subscribers grew by 380,000, or 1.8%.

The number of pensioners came to 3.75 million in 2014, increasing 3.1% from a year earlier. The number of people receiving a pension (elderly, people with disabilities) came to 3.59 million in 2014, jumping 4.2% from a year earlier.

Of them, the number of elderly increased by 3.8% to 2.95 million. The number of people receiving a lump sum payment dropped by 16.4% to 160,000. The average payment to elderly pensioners came to 334,000 won, while the highest payment was 1.73 million won.

The National Pension Service has been conducting a program that pays half the pension premium of low-income employees and employers of small businesses. Starting in 2015, the program will be expanded to cover employees of businesses with fewer than 10 employees who earn a monthly salary of less than 1.4 million won.

The government plans to continue efforts to help those unable to benefit from the national pension plan by expanding support for low-income workers of small business in the form of subsidizing their pension premium.

■ **Basic Pension**

In 2014, the basic pension program was introduced. The program was discussed amid claims that payments should be raised and more closely linked to the national pension in order to relieve poverty among senior citizens. The poorest 70% of pensioners aged 65 and older had been receiving a monthly basic pension of 100,000 won.

In 2013, the government proposed a bill centered on linking Category A payments of the national pension with the basic pension. After discussing the proposal for a long time, the National Assembly passed the bill in May 2014. In July, the basic pension program was fully implemented.

The basic pension is paid to the poorest 70% of senior citizens. As of July 2014, it was paid to citizens with an income of 870,000 won or less, or couples with a joint income of 1.39 million won or less.

The amount is determined based on the pensioner's national pension plan.

Those with no pension receive 200,000 won, while the rest receive between 100,000 and 200,000 won, depending on their national pension.

Starting in 2015, the basic pension will be paid to citizens with an income of 930,000 won or less, or couples with a joint income of 1.49 million won or less.

■ **Basic Living Guarantee**

In 2014, there were large changes to the basic living guarantee system. An amendment to the relevant law was submitted to the National Assembly in May 2013 and passed on Dec. 9, 2014.

The revised law reflects the concept of relative poverty, making it possible for low-income citizens to continue to receive benefits even after their incomes exceed the minimum level.

It also encourages people to support their low-income relatives by helping them maintain a middle-income standard of living even after they support a beneficiary of the system.

The revised system is scheduled to be enacted on July 1, 2015. It is expected to lead to an increase in the number of recipients from 1.34 million to 2.1 million, and an increase in cash payments from an average of 423,000 won to 472,000 won.

■ **Job Creation for The Youth**

The government unveiled measures to boost the country's youth employment rate on April 15, 2014, amid a prolonged economic slowdown. South Korea's overall employment rate has risen steadily and job creation has also improved. But the youth employment rate is on the decline as more young people are delaying finding jobs.

The government said it drew up the measures to help promote the youths' early employment and encourage young people to work at one workplace longer.

As part of such efforts, it unveiled a plan to introduce an apprenticeship system similar to that of Switzerland, where students can receive education or training while also working.

The government also sought to create synergy in the labor market. Companies with less than five workers will be allowed to use young people as interns if those companies are in the sectors favored by the youths. The on-the-job training will be started from the fall semester of the second year at colleges from the spring semester of the third year. The moves were aimed at increasing connectivity between what they learn at universities and what they learn from workplaces.

South Korea also made efforts to eliminate blind spots for the job market. Job training for regular high school graduates will be reinforced and a set of basic security benefits will be expanded to those who are aged between 18 and 24 and work without going to schools.

It also drew up measures to ease a phenomenon in which youths undergo a cut in their career due to compulsory military service.

▪ Reform of Retirement Pension

The government said in August last year that it will make it mandatory for companies to subscribe to private retirement pension programs in phases by 2022 in an effort to provide a stronger safety net for retirees.

Companies with 300 or more employees will have to subscribe to retirement pension programs for their workers starting in 2016. Other firms with smaller workforces are required to subscribe by 2022, according to the finance ministry.

Under the plan, 672 companies will be subject to mandatory subscription in 2016. About 1.3 million firms will have to introduce private retirement pension programs by 2022, according to the ministry.

The move is part of a series of measures meant to help solve growing concerns that the state-run public pension might not be enough to support the senior population after retirement. Fiscal pressure is mounting that welfare spending on senior citizens could become too heavy for future generations due to the fast-aging population and chronically low birth rates.

The retirement pension was first introduced in 2005 but only 16% of companies have it. The ratio is particularly low among small- and medium-sized companies that have less financial resources.

Along with the mandatory subscription, the government also plans to ease regulations related to retirement pension fund operation to allow companies to "strike a balance between safety and profitability" by investing in stocks and other riskier assets.

In a related move, the government will introduce a fund-type pension in July 2016, allowing a company committee comprised of management, labor and outside experts to determine how it will operate the company pension money.

This is intended to encourage more employees to participate in the operation of the fund, unlike the current system in which companies usually hire financial agencies to manage the money.

The fund-type pension is expected to give more leeway to large companies such as Samsung and Hyundai to maximize profitability in running their trillions of won worth of accumulated retirement pension deposits.

The government also plans to ease the ceiling of risky asset ownership for defined contribution-typed retirement pension programs to 70% from the current 40%, allowing for more investment in stock markets. These measures, while designed to help pension operators maximize their profitability, come with worries that the leeway also increases the overall risk of losses.

▪ Job Creation Efforts

On Oct. 15, 2014, the government unveiled follow-up measures to boost the creation of flexible part-time jobs. In November 2013, South Korea said it plans to create 16,500 flexible part-time jobs in the public sector by 2017 as part of efforts to raise the country's overall employment rate to 70%.

Flexible part-time jobs refer to those that offer workers the same treatment in terms of hourly wages and promotions as those afforded to full-time workers, ministry officials said. Workers can choose to work four to six hours a day and flexibly decide their work schedules.

The government raised its target of hiring civil servants at provincial governments by 1%p. By ministry, the government will make efforts to select exemplary cases for flexible part-time jobs.

To support the private sector, the government plans to help small and medium-sized enterprises ease labor costs. It also overhauled standards for hiring nurses to expand the employment of nurses on a flexible part-time basis.

The government plans to ramp up efforts to expand the flexible part-time job system in both the public and private sectors. Starting in March 2015, teachers will be able to work on a flexible part-time basis.

The government plans to facilitate the implementation of the system for the public sector. If the private sector follows suit, companies will receive financial benefits such as support for personnel costs.

Temporary workers who work flexible part-time jobs at multiple work places will be able to receive social safety benefits based on a combined number of working hours.

The government will also prevent workers from being disadvantaged when they receive retirement severances even if they decide to become flexible part-time workers. Korea will provide financial support worth 50% of the burdens of increased income to small and medium-sized companies if they allow existing flexible part-time workers to become unlimited contract-based workers.

LABOR

▪ Overview

In 2014, the labor circle was embroiled in a heated debate over such major issues as labor market reform, measures for non-regular workers and a Supreme Court ruling on ordinary wages.

The government began to push for the reform of the overall structure of the labor market in earnest, focusing on making it easier for companies to adjust salaries and working hours for regular workers, which has drawn strong opposition from unions.

Last year's ruling on ordinary wages caused a series of conflicts at workplaces, with labor and management failing to resolve differences on how to apply the new guidelines. Despite the need to reform the overall wage system ahead of the extension of the retirement age starting in 2016, the two sides also differed widely on the implementation of the wage-peak system.

Active consultations among labor, management and the government did not take place in the first half of 2014, as the Federation of Korean Trade Unions (FKTU), one of the country's two major umbrella unions, walked out of the trilateral committee in opposition to the government's use of force to arrest union leaders of Korea Railroad Corp. in December 2013.

Dialogue began in mid-August upon its return to the committee, and the representatives agreed on basic principles of their future discussions on reforming the labor market. They also decided to conclude negotiations on pending topics, including easing discrimination against irregular workers, by March.

The Korean Confederation of Trade Unions (KCTU) launched a general strike against the government to protest its alleged oppression of workers and moves to privatize public firms.

▪ Labor Circle Opposes Gov't Push for Reform Plan

Labor and management were in a tug of war over such key pending issues as labor market reform measures and ways to boost flexibility in employment.

The controversy was sparked by Finance Minister Choi Kyung-hwan, who called in November for structural reform in the labor market, where regular workers are being "overprotected." He said that it causes companies to shun recruitment and instead rely on irregular workers that they can fire more easily.

According to a survey by the labor ministry in 2013, irregular workers at conglomerates earned some 66% of what their regular counterparts received, and regular workers at small- to medium-sized firms earned 54%, and non-regular workers there took 37%.

As of March, the salary for regular workers at large-sized companies which have their own labor union earned 3.92 million won (US$3,649) per month on average, while their counterparts earn some one-third of that.

The number of irregular workers in South Korea came to 6.08 million as of August, accounting for 32.4% of the country's total number of salaried workers. It is the first time that irregular workers have exceeded 6 million since related data started to be compiled in 2002.

The government and management have stressed the need to devise specific standards and procedures to prevent labor disputes regarding the termination of employment contracts and to better manage employees. The aim is to give flexibility to companies ahead of the mandatory extension of the retirement age to 60 starting in 2016.

The move, however, instantly drew strong backlash from the labor side, which claimed that the government is demanding sacrifices from regular workers, not trying to deal with root causes. Critics also pointed out that the government is aiming to lower the overall level of protection for workers in the name of helping irregular workers.

According to the report by the Korea Labor Institute, a South Korean worker serves at one company for 5.1 years on average, far short of the average 10-year period seen among the OECD member countries. The ratio of employees who work for one company for more than 10 years was 18.1%, while the OECD average was 36.4%.

▪ Gov't Pushes to Extend Maximum Employment Period for Irregular Workers

On Dec. 29, the labor ministry announced a plan to allow irregular and subcontract workers aged 35 or older to work for up to four years at the same workplace as part of efforts to improve their working conditions and eliminate discrimination against them. Currently, the maximum employment period for irregular workers is two years.

Irregular and subcontract workers will also be able to receive retirement allowance if they work for at least three months for one firm, though the minimum requirement now is one year, according to the government plan. The government also vowed to push for the permission of particular types of irregular workers, such as insurance agents, tutors and golf caddies, to enable them to subscribe to the employment insurance program.

While the government said the goal of the measures is to provide job security for irregular workers as companies tend to replace them with other non-regular workers after the two-year contract term ends with existing employees, the unions said they are far from fundamental and would rather increase the number of non-regular workers.

As fundamental solutions, the FKTU called on the government to enforce companies to hire workers to be in charge of major and consistent duties on a permanent basis, and to strengthen monitoring and oversight of management to root out illegal subcontracting practices.

▪ Confusion Lingers over Ordinary Wages

In December 2013, the Supreme Court ruled that regular bonuses paid to workers constitute "ordinary wages," siding with labor in the prolonged dispute. Setting a final guideline on the controversial issue, the top court recognized that regular bonuses paid at intervals exceeding one month should also be included in calculating ordinary wages.

An ordinary wage refers to a fixed amount of wage paid to an employee on a regular basis and is used as the basis for calculating certain employee benefits, such as overtime pay, holiday shifts, paid annual leave, severance pay and other allowances.

So far, the government has customarily recognized regular bonuses as part of ordinary wages only when they are paid on a monthly basis. With no clear provisions on the scope of regular wages, labor and management had been at odds over whether bonuses and other severance payments paid out every other month should be included in calculating ordinary wages.

Despite the ruling, however, confusion continues as local courts have applied different criteria when making relevant rulings. According to a survey by the Federation of Korean Industries, 44 out of 100 companies ranked among the country's top 300 firms in sales were successful in adjusting the wage via discussions with their labor union. Of them, 77.3% raised the amount of the ordinary wage by an average of 17.9%.

▪ Labor, Management at Odds over Shorter Working Hours

Labor, management and the government failed to reach a meaningful agree-

ion Social Affairs **213**

ment on the reduction of the maximum number of weekly working hours. The three, as well as the country's rival political parties, agreed in principle to shorten the number of working hours from the current 68 to 52 hours in a bid to create more jobs. But they have differed on when to implement the new policy and how long the grace period will be before the full implementation.

After three-month consultations on the issue at the parliament went nowhere, relevant bills are still pending. The labor side calls for a reduction in the working hours without a wage cut, while the management demands that the policy be introduced in phases.

In December, the government said it is considering a gradual reduction in the legally permitted work time of employees to 60 hours a week from the current 68 hours by including holiday work in statutory overtime.

■ Labor Density Remains Unchanged

In 2013, South Korea's union density remained unchanged at 10.3% from the previous year, according to government data. Union density is defined as the percentage of workers in the nation who belong to a union.

The union density fell to a single-digit rate of 9.8% for the first time in 2010 after peaking at 19.8% in 1989. It recovered to a two-digit rate in 2011 at 10.1%, thanks mainly to the introduction of a government policy that allowed for more than two unions at a single company.

The number of workers enrolled as members of trade unions increased by 3.7% to 1.84 million, and the total number of trade unions grew to 5,305 in 2013, up from the previous year's 2.5%.

Among umbrella unions, the Federation of Korean Trade Unions (FKTU) remained the largest organization, representing 43.6% of all trade union members, followed by the Korean Confederation of Trade Unions (KCTU) with 6.7%, while the third umbrella union, the Korea Labor Union Confederation (KLUC) took up 1.9% of the total. The remaining 47.8% had no affiliation with an umbrella union in 2013, according to the data.

The KLUC was launched in 2011, calling

for a different type of labor movement. But the entity was merged with the FKTU in December after losing momentum.

■ Labor Dispute Rises 54 Pct, No Progress in Peak Wage System

In 2014, there were no major labor disputes that could affect the overall economy. But small-scale ones staged mainly by workers in service sectors and subcontractors took place more often than before. According to government data, 111 disputes occurred throughout the year, up 54.2% from the previous year.

Some 82.5% of companies reached an agreement between labor and management on wages, slightly higher than the 80.6% in 2013, with the average rate of increase coming to 4.1%. Only 45.2% out of the 9,905 companies that hired more than 100 employees reached wage agreements with their workers, edging down from the previous year's 46%. Wages rose by 4.4%, or 0.9%p more than 2013.

With the government's plan to extend the mandatory retirement age to 60 to be implemented in 2016, less than 10% of business entities across the nation adopted the wage peak system as of the end of 2014. The wage peak system is a job-sharing measure that aims to provide job security for older employees through a gradual wage cut after a certain age. The money saved can be used to hire more young people.

■ Deaths by Industrial Accidents on Decrease

The number of deaths caused by industrial disasters came to 756 in 2014, down 16.6% from a year earlier.

By sector, deaths in the construction field decreased 22.5%, marking the largest margin of all fields, followed by a 20.7% fall in deaths in the manufacturing industry.

The decrease in the death toll appears to be attributable to the government's stronger measures to guarantee safety, such as the strengthening of regulations and heavier punishments for violators.

■ Trilateral Panel agrees on Labor Reform Principles

In December, the trilateral committee

of labor, management and government representatives agreed on the basic principles of their future discussions on reforming the labor market and to wrap up discussions on three key topics, including easing discrimination against irregular workers, by March. The Economic and Social Development Commission adopted a basic agreement on labor market reform at the end of a main session held in Seoul.

The three parties shared the need to reform laws and systems introduced to support the country's fast economic growth in the past in "a future-oriented way" to overcome the crisis of the present and the future. They also agreed to share their social responsibilities and burdens based on the accountability of the reality of the labor market.

In addition to the two basic principles of discussions, the agreement included five agenda items and 14 detailed topics. The committee also decided to finish discussing three of the five items as priorities by March.

The three entities also eased the so-called "dual structure" of the labor market, settling pending labor issues over wages, working hours and retirement age, and mending the nation's weak social safety net.

The agreement came after the finance ministry called for structural reforms to make the labor market more flexible as part of key economic policy plans for next year to improve national competitiveness and fuel growth. The government has been striving to ease inflexibility in employment at large businesses and public companies as part of its structural reform of the economy.

■ KCTU Holds 1st Direct Election to Choose Chief

In December, the Korean Confederation of Trade Unions (KCTU) held its first direct election to choose the leadership, and Han Sang-gyu, the former chief of Ssangyong Motor's labor union, was chosen to lead the entity until 2017.

The 52-year-old had vowed to launch an instant general strike against what he called the government's anti-labor policy. It was the first time in the country's labor movement history that union members chose the leader of the umbrella union. South Korea also became the world's third nation to do so.

Han is known for his hard-line steps while leading strikes by Ssangyong's union workers since 2009. After spending three years in prison since 2009 for leading a massive walkout, he stayed atop a transmission tower for 171 days, demanding the reinstatement of his colleagues to their previous jobs.

■ S. Korea's Number of New Hires Reaches 12-yr High in 2014

According to Statistics Korea, the number of new hires in South Korea is estimated to have reached a 12-year high in 2014. The number of new hires came to a monthly average of 543,000 in the first 11 months of 2014.

Once December figures are factored in, the average may fall but still remain above 530,000. The estimated number marks a 21% rise from 438,000 in 2013. It would also be the highest increase since 2002, when 597,000 new jobs were added on a monthly average.

The country's overall employment rate for people between the ages of 15 and 64 is expected to have reached 65.3%, up from 64.4% in 2013. Such a rise, however, is attributable to a large increase in the number of people, especially those aged 60 and older, finding part-time jobs.

In the January-November period, the number of people in their 30s who found new jobs dropped by about 20,000 from a year earlier while those in their 20s increased by 58,000. Those in their 50s and 60s who found new employment rose by 241,000 and 200,000, respectively, accounting for more than 80% of all new hires last year.

Among those 60 or older, less than one-third, or about 541,000, held full-time jobs, up 5.3% from 2013, while more than 1.18 million had temporary or part-time jobs. The number of part-time workers of the age class marked an 11.1% increase on-year.

For the entire workforce, the number of part-time jobs gained 2.2% on-year to some 6.07 million in 2014, breaching the 6 million mark for the first time.

PUBLIC HEALTH AND DRUGS

■ **S. Korea Has 60,899 Medical Institutions, 109,563 Doctors**

According to the data by the health ministry, South Korea had 60,899 medical institutions as of the end of 2013, up by an average of 4.6% on-year since the 1990s. Of them, clinics took up the largest share with 29,054, followed by 15,779 dental clinics, and 13,019 hospitals for oriental medicine, with the country having 3,047 general hospitals. The total number of sickbeds came to 633,087, a 5.7% increase compared to the previous year.

There are 109,568 licensed doctors, which is a 2.1% increase from the previous year. In sum, the country has 403,341 medical staff members, up 29.5% over the past five years.

Some 49,999 people in the country enjoyed the benefit of the national health insurance. They received 39.32 trillion won (US$36.61 billion), a per person average of 783,306 won for the insurance program for the year.

The health expenditure, meaning the total health and treatment-related expenses of the people, reached 97.1 trillion won as of the end of 2012, accounting for 7.6% of the gross domestic product.

■ **Doctors Go on First Massive Walkout in 15 Yrs**

One of the most eye-catching issues in the medical field was a one-day strike by doctors, the first of its kind in 15 years. On March 10, thousands of doctors, involving medical clinics, interns and resident physicians working in hospitals around the country, staged the strike in protest of the government's plan to introduce a new medical system.

The Korean Medical Association (KMA), which represents more than 100,000 doctors here, made clear its opposition to the state plan to allow remote medical examinations and treatment, as well as for-profit hospitals.

While doctors argue that the government's plan will accelerate their management woes and undermine public health,

the government says the new telemedicine system aims to offer benefits to the elderly, the disabled and patients in remote areas, along with people with chronic diseases.

Some 20.9%, or 5,991 clinics, out of the 28,660 around the country closed down for the day to take part in the collective action, according to the Ministry of Health and Welfare, while the KMA estimated that some 49.1% of the clinics participated in the strike.

Though doctors vowed to hold another round of walkout for six days from March 24-29, they canceled it after the association reached an agreement with the government on whether and how to implement the new medical system.

■ **Renewed Controversy over Medical Privatization**

South Korea saw a heated debate over whether to privatize medical services. In December 2013, the government announced a comprehensive plan to promote investment in the sector in which medical institutions will be allowed to set up subsidiaries for profits and to make inroads into relevant industries.

The move drew instant protests from civic groups, which said it will facilitate the privatization of medical services and push up the costs for necessary medical services for the public. More than 100,000 petitions were received against the policy, though the government went ahead with the law revision in June.

■ **S. Korea Nixes Plan for Chinese-Invested Hospital Plan**

On Sept. 15, South Korea's health ministry said it has rejected a Chinese medical group's plan to build the nation's first for-profit foreign hospital, named Shaner Hospital, on the southern resort island of Jeju, as doubts grew over the firm's financial status and emergency medical system.

China Stem Cell Health Group has been seeking Seoul's approval since early 2013 to build the hospital on Jeju with a 50 billion won investment pledge, but the health ministry turned down the proposal because the Chinese firm was not qualified as an investor and the proposed hospital does not have an appropriate emergency medical system.

The decision also comes as the CEO of CSC's parent company, Tianjin Huaye Group, was arrested the previous year in China on fraud allegations, and the hospital's largest shareholder, Xidanmu Shaner Bio, has also been shut down. What concerned the Seoul government is whether the Chinese hospital will keep its promise not to use stem cell therapy, which is a concern because local authorities lack a monitoring system to keep it in check.

Despite the problems surrounding the Chinese health care company, South Korea in August announced its plan to ease regulations on foreign hospitals to attract investment in the health industry, raising hopes for the approval of Shaner Hospital. Faced with criticism over its hasty verification process, the government said it will continue to make efforts to attract foreign hospitals to the free economic zones like Jeju Island to develop the nation's health care industry.

■ 'Two-Strike-Out' Regulations Against Die-Hard Rebate Practices

The government has continued efforts to root out pervasive bribery practices in the pharmaceutical industry, where doctors allegedly accept money or other undue favors, known as "rebates" from drug makers in exchange for prescribing their products.

One of the countermeasures is the introduction in July of a "two-strike-out system" that calls for the banning of a drug found to have been involved in such illegal practices from being covered by the national health insurance. The measure is deemed powerful as the elimination would lead to a stiff reduction in the number of prescriptions by doctors, which could cause huge losses to the firms.

Following the move, the pan-government task force indicted Dongwha Pharm Co. Ltd. and its officials on charges of providing illegal kickbacks worth 5.07 billion won to doctors in the country's 923 clinics, the largest such case since 2008.

■ Yuhan Corp. Becomes 1st Domestic Drugmaker to Break 1 Tln. Won in Sales

Yuhan Corp. surpassed 1 trillion won in sales for the first time in South Korea's pharmaceutical history. According to the company, its sales volume came to 1.01 trillion won as of 2014. South Korea's first drugmaker opened in 1897.

The company attributed the achievement to its efforts for business diversification and exports of raw material medicines, which also helped it to avert impacts of the government's strong regulations against pervasive rebate practices and the fall in the overall medicine prices.

The milestone carries significance, as it means that the company has achieved the baseline for the "economy of scale" that could enable a domestic pharmaceutical company to grow into a global business.

Meanwhile, another of the country's pharmaceutical firms, Green Cross Corp., said its exports topped US$200 million in 2014, becoming the first South Korean drugmaker to reach the mark.

Green Cross said its outbound shipments were led by a surge in demand for vaccine products, which totaled US$60 million in 2014, up 60% from a year earlier. In 2010, the drug firm started delivering a seasonal flu vaccine to the Pan American Health Organization in the wake of an influenza outbreak, and its exports of the vaccine amounted to US$38 million last year.

■ Controversy Surrounding Tobacco

In April, South Korea's National Health Insurance Service filed a 54 billion won (US$52 million) lawsuit against three tobacco companies -- Philip Morris International Inc., British American Tobacco Plc., and KT&G Corp. -- to seek compensation for health care costs for diseases related to smoking.

The state-run health insurer said the sought damages are based on data of its payments to patients diagnosed with three types of lung cancer between 2003 and 2012 who smoked at least a pack of cigarettes a day for more than 20 years, adding that the amount of the compensation claims can be increased during the legal process.

Meanwhile, the government announced a plan in September to nearly double cigarette prices starting in 2015 in a move to cut the country's high smoking rate. The prices will be raised by 2,000 won per pack from the current average of 2,500 won, with the government vowing to introduce a pricing system in which cigarette prices will be pegged to other consumer prices. The last price hike for cigarettes was in 2004, when it was raised by 500 won.

The proposed price hike, coming mostly from a tax increase, was expected to lead to a 34% drop in the overall sales of tobacco products, and will likely generate an additional 2.8 trillion won in tax revenues, according to the government.

In further efforts to reduce the smoking population, the government will require all cigarette manufacturers to print picture-based warnings on tobacco products and prohibit promotions and advertisements of tobacco by manufacturers and retailers, including convenience stores.

ENVIRONMENT

- ## Overview
In the environmental sector in 2014, a big issue was the government-set carbon-emission quota for companies ahead of the implementation of a carbon-emission trading system in 2015.

Controversy also erupted over the results of the government's audit of the four-rivers project, which found that water quality deteriorated in some rivers and large-scale dredging works were inappropriate.

A basic air quality control plan was finalized to sharply reduce the amount of ultrafine particles in metropolitan areas. A bill was introduced to require environmental safety checks for the building and remodeling of daycare facilities.

The habitat of an endangered species of leopard cat on Mount Bukhan was confirmed, and cymbidium, a species of orchid called hanran, was regenerated for the first time after a freeze. But an Asiatic black bear and foxes released for species restoration were killed by traps.

- ## Carbon-Emission Quota for Companies Draws Backlash
In connection with the carbon-emission trading system to go into effect in 2015, the government set related quotas for companies and informed them of the decision on Dec. 2. A total of 525 firms were affected and many strongly protested the government's decision.

Under the system, the government allocates emission permits to firms and allows them to trade surpluses or buy them if needed. In cases of excessive emissions, firms will be fined.

A total of 15.98 billion KAU (Korean Allowance Units) were allocated by the Ministry of Environment. It distributed emission quotas to petrochemical, steel, and power generation and energy companies, with POSCO, KOSEP, and Hyundai Steel on the list of 10 firms with the biggest quotas.

The firms filed a complaint that the quotas are insufficient. The Federation of Korean Industries and other business lobby groups issued a joint statement arguing that the current plan will raise the financial burden on companies.

They urged the government to craft additional supply measures, saying they will face an additional financial burden of more than 12.7 trillion won from 2015 to 2017 even if the price is maintained at 10,000 won per KAU as the government promises.

The Ministry of Environment responded to the claim, saying it is premature to judge the appropriate level of reserves. It added that it is inappropriate to assume fines will be imposed as firms will face no fines if they make proper reductions in carbon emission.

- ## Audit of Four-Rivers Project
The Four Rivers Project Evaluation Commission announced on Dec. 23 that there was some deterioration in the water quality of four rivers due to a related project by the Lee Myung-bak administration and a change in water quality is also expected due to the changing groundwater environment.

The commission said water quality in the Han River, Nakdong River and Geum River has improved generally. Biochemical oxygen demand (BOD) and algae concentration (Chl-a) have decreased, it said.

But the water quality in the upstream portion of the Nakdong River (Andong-Gumi) and Yongsan River has deteriorated somewhat.

With regard to predictions of water quality from the four-rivers project, there was an allegation that the Ministry of Environment made wrong and distorted predictions in crafting a master plan. But the commission concluded the ministry's sample selection and study on water quality predictions was appropriate.

But the ministry took some unrealistic scenarios into consideration, said the commission. The commission also said large-scale dredging work was not appropriate.

■ Air Quality Control in Metropolitan Area

On Jan. 1, 2014, the Ministry of Environment announced the second basic plan aimed at improving air quality in the metropolitan area. It said it would reduce the amount of fine dust (PM-10) by 34% from an expected amount and that of ultrafine particles (PM-2.5) by 45%.

It plans to reduce the concentration of fine dust levels in Seoul to that of London ($30\mu g/m^3$) and keep ultrafine particle concentration to $20\mu g/m^3$ lower than environmental standards ($25\mu g/m^3$).

Ozone was added to the list of pollutants subject to close monitoring on top of fine dust, nitrogen oxides, sulfur oxides, and volatile organic compounds.

To attain this goal, the Ministry of Environment will spend 4.5 trillion won over the next 10 years, starting in 2015, to expand the supply of environmentally-friendly electric cars and emissions reduction equipment.

First, 2 million eco-friendly cars will be provided by 2024, 20% of the total number of registered vehicles in the metropolitan area.

■ Environmental Safety Checks on Daycare Facilities

Environmental safety checks are required for childcare centers, kindergartens, and schools if they remodel or enlarge their facilities. The Ministry of Environment issued such a notice on some amendments to the Legislative Decree and Enforcement Regulations of the Environment Act on May 20.

Expanding children's activity space to more than $33m^2$ and remodeling more than $70m^2$ of space using wall paint, finishing materials, synthetic rubber flooring, etc., is subject to environmental safety checks.

Childcare centers, kindergartens and elementary schools should go through environmental safety checks before being authorized in accordance with relevant laws.

■ Gov't Seeks to Increase Use of EVs

In a meeting of the Government Committee on Green Growth, the government crafted a comprehensive plan for commercializing electric vehicles.

First, single charge mileage will increase significantly. Currently, electric vehicles can run about 150km with a single charge, equivalent to the distance between Seoul and Daejeon. If a heater is used, it drops to 120km.

The government plans to double the mileage in 2020 by investing 22.2 billion won in high-efficiency motor technology and battery temperature control technology. State subsidies will be expanded as well to help reduce the burden on customers and promote the initial market.

The government will provide subsidies of 15 million won for two years starting in 2015, 12 million won starting in 2018, and 10 million won in the next two years. In addition to subsidies, tax incentives will be offered for individual consumption.

In 2015, 100 electric taxies will be supplied for Jeju Island, along with 40 for Seoul and 28 electric buses. Starting in 2015, at least 25% of the cars purchased by public agencies should be electric ones. The number of fast recharge facilities, currently 177, will increase to 1,400 by 2020 and those will be installed in service areas on highways nationwide.

■ 'Gangwon Declaration' Adopted in Biological Diversity Forum

The 12th Conference of the Parties to the Convention on Biological Diversity was held in Pyeongchang, Gangwon Province, from Oct. 15-16. It ended with the adoption of the Gangwon Declaration on Biodiversity for Sustainable Development.

The 16-point declaration called on the United Nations to set the post-2015 development agenda on the issue of biodiversity. It also contains a message welcoming the "Peace and Biodiversity

Dialogue Initiative" proposed by South Korea for the conservation of biodiversity in border areas.

Advanced nations maintained a lukewarm attitude toward developing countries' demand that they expand financial support for the conservation of biodiversity, but participating nations shared the view that lack of funding is an obstacle to attaining the goal of the Convention on Biological Diversity

The Ministry of Environment expected the Gangwon Declaration to serve as a basic direction in South Korea's role as chair nation of the convention over the next two years.

■ Cymbidium Resurrected after Freeze

The National Institute of Biological Resources announced on May 28 that cymbidium, a species of orchid called hanran, was resurrected for the first time in South Korea after a freeze in an experiment intended to explore ways to save the endangered species.

■ Leopard Cat Confirmed to Be Living on Mount Bukhan

It was confirmed that an endangered species of leopard cat, one of the top predators in South Korea's ecosystem, is living on Mount Bukhan in Seoul. Korea National Park said on May 13 that it filmed a leopard cat in the Wooyiryeong district of the mountain. The park authorities installed seven cameras in the area.

In its 2001 research report, park authorities believed that there was a low possibility that the habitat of the leopard cat existed on the mountain. However, in 2010, after some maintenance work was performed, a leopard cat's feces was found for the first time in the area. Leopard cats eat rats or birds. The leopard cat is categorized into Class II of protected endangered wildlife.

■ Asiatic Black Bear, Foxes in Trouble

An Asiatic black bear and several foxes, released for the protection of the endangered species, were killed by traps or pesticides. Among 18 foxes released on Mount Sobaek over three instances starting in 2012, 12 were killed and only six are left as of the end of 2014.

The Ministry of Environment released two foxes in October 2012, six in September 2013 and 10 others in October 2014. Five were found killed by traps and pesticides were detected in the bodies of three others. The reason for the deaths of four of the foxes remains unknown.

An Asiatic black bear was also found snared and dead on Mount Jiri. It marked the fifth time that an Asiatic black bear died after being snared on the mountain.

■ Gov't Says Pectinatella Magnifica "Not Toxic"

A government study found that pectinatella magnifica is not toxic and does no harm to the ecosystem. On Dec. 17, the Ministry of Environment announced the results of research on the impact to aquatic organisms from pectinatella magnifica that appeared in four rivers in the summer of 2014.

On-site research and a laboratory experiment showed the same results that there is no harm from pectinatella magnifica, according to the ministry.

■ 168 Victims of Humidifier Fungicides Receive Gov't Compensation

The Environmental Ministry's Center for Disease Control and Prevention has decided to pay compensation to victims of humidifier fungicides. The lung diseases of 168 people were regarded as related to humidifier fungicides "almost certainly" or "highly possibly."

PUBLIC WELFARE

■ "One Step Forward, but a Long Way to Go"

This summarizes the level and geography of South Korea's public welfare in 2014. There were some improvements, including the guarantee of a minimum living wage for low-income senior citizens under the basic pension program. However, South Korea is still seen as being very far from a welfare state.

Many problems arose due to the gap between reality and the ideal world as politicians continued to promise welfare without an increase in taxes. The central and regional governments argued over who should shoulder the burden of growing welfare costs. As the two sides argued, the groans of the poor grew louder, with some taking their own lives.

▪ Ping-pong Game over Shouldering Welfare Costs

The dispute over universal welfare and selective welfare continues, especially among politicians. However, one thing is clear. South Korea is a low burden-low welfare state. It can be proven through statistics.

According to the Korea Institute for Health and Social Affairs, 9.1% of the country's GDP in 2011 was spent on public welfare. This amounts to less than half (42.1%) of the average of 21.7% among member states of the Organization for Economic Cooperation and Development (OECD). South Korea is a low-welfare state. Of the OECD nations, Mexico is the only country that has a lower rate than South Korea.

The total tax rate is also 25.9%, much lower than the OECD average of 34.1%. This is the reason South Korea is called a low-burden state. To summarize, as people pay a small amount in taxes and get back a small amount in social welfare, South Korea is classified as a low-burden, low-welfare state. However, compared to the OECD average, South Koreans pay more in taxes relative to the amount they receive back in social welfare spending.

What could be the reason South Korea is in this low-burden, low-welfare state? It is because of the lack of fairness in the taxation system and the unbalance in spending. In particular, employers' contributions to social security and the low income tax rate are key factors behind the low welfare funds.

In a situation in which welfare funds were far short due to the low burden, the Park Geun-hye administration stuck to its principle of expanding welfare without tax hikes and made little effort to fill up the welfare funds through an increase in tax rates, and in particular, an increase in the corporate tax rate. In this way, it tried to maintain the status quo in welfare in line with its campaign pledge. This led to conflicts with regional governments over sharing welfare costs.

In July 2014, the Park administration implemented an expanded basic pension plan. Of course, it failed to keep its initial promise to pay a monthly basic pension of 200,000 won to all citizens aged 65 or above. As a result, the legislation process was not smooth. The pension plan was introduced only after a tug-of-war with the opposition party that almost led to its cancellation.

Still, the government began to pay between 100,000 and 200,000 won each month to the poorest 70% of senior citizens. The size of the payment depended on the period of time a citizen has been subscribed to the national pension plan, leading to lower public confidence in the national plan, but it provided a basis to improve the poverty rate among the elderly, which stood at 49%, the highest among OECD nations.

Although it is early to rush to conclusions, the basic pension plan had a visible effect by raising the income of low-income citizens, at least in terms of statistics. According to household data for the third quarter of 2014, released by Statistics Korea on Nov. 21, 2014, the average household's monthly income rose 3% from the same period a year earlier to 4.39 million won.

However, even a basic pension that fell far short of the administration's campaign pledge raised doubts about its sustainability. The central and regional governments engaged in a bitter dispute over how to shoulder the enormous financial burden caused by maintaining the basic pension program.

Local administrations protested that they would not be able to finance the basic pension plan with the current level of tax collection and the state subsidy.

The central government claimed the local administrations had earmarked an excessively small amount of their budgets for welfare-related projects and claimed the administrations would be able to resolve the issue by drawing up a supplementary budget.

According to the National Assembly's budget policy bureau, if the government maintains its subsidy level at 74.5% and continues to run the basic pension plan, the state's financial burden would expand from 9 trillion won in 2018 to 74 trillion won in 2040 and 170 trillion won in 2060.

The amount that would need to be shouldered by local administrations would also increase from 3 trillion won in 2018 to 25 trillion won in 2040 and 58 trillion won in 2060.

Adding to the rapidly aging population and inflation, the government could face a much larger financial burden than what it had planned for its basic pension program. It is only a matter of time before such concerns become reality.

■ Social Safety Network Reveals Hole

In early 2014, the suicides of a mother and her two daughters sent shockwaves across the nation and revealed a hole in South Korea's social safety network.

The mother and her two daughters could not receive any help within the social security system established by the state or local administration. The mother, who had been the family's breadwinner, quit her job after being injured a month earlier, while the two daughters in their 30s were credit delinquents but unable to receive help from anywhere.

They did not qualify for any of the social security plans, while the emergency support system failed to identify the family. They were not classified as being within the vulnerable group, which is comprised of the disabled, elderly people and families with one parent, and had very little contact with their neighbors.

The fact that even the emergency welfare system did not operate properly spoke to the large area of blind spots in South Korea's welfare system.

■ Revisions to Welfare System Still Insufficient

The emergency welfare system came into operation in 2006. It aimed to help low-income households overcome crisis situations by swiftly providing the necessary welfare services, such as living expenses, medical costs, electricity costs and education costs. By providing such services, it aimed to prevent family breakups and chronic poverty.

As part of such efforts, the system was designed to first provide support and then review the recipient's circumstances. This was different from other welfare programs. The problem is that contrary to the aim of providing emergency support within three days after it has been requested, in many cases, the support is delayed.

The Ministry of Health and Welfare recognized the problem and set out to fix the system. It lowered the criteria for "crisis situations" and expanded the scope of support to enable more people to benefit from the emergency welfare system.

Despite such revisions to this and other welfare programs, critics argued that they were insufficient to help the poor. For example, those with family members are still not qualified to receive basic subsidies even if the families cannot be reached and are unable to help.

PATRIOTS AND VETERAN AFFAIRS

■ Veterans

As of the end of 2014, the total number of veterans and their family members was 857,107, down from 858,834 in 2013. The figure included 7,378 patriots, 186,570 former and incumbent war veterans, 154,683 veterans killed during the 1950-53 Korean War, and 207,230 veterans who participated in the Vietnam War.

■ Compensation to Veterans

A total of 3.44 trillion won was paid to war veterans, independence fighters and their bereaved family members in 2014, up from the previous year's 3.29 trillion won. Some 2.29 million veterans also received 2.36 trillion won as a separate monthly payment.

■ Employment Support

In 2014, the government helped 8,264 family members of war veterans find work. Of the total 106,624 people looking for jobs, 32,862 landed jobs in government-related agencies and the remaining people got positions in local businesses. The government also carried out job-training programs for 347 high school graduates and job seekers.

Some 2,880 family members of the veterans also enjoyed benefits in taking various exams such as TOEIC, TEPS,

JPT, JLPT, HSK and other related certificate tests in 2014, in accordance with the state system to help those job seekers with free training, which was adopted in 2007. The government also revised a bill to support war veterans in which they can be employed as civilian workers in 35 fields.

Education Support

A total of 35,291 people enrolled in middle school, high school or college are categorized as family members of war veterans. In 2014, 96.2 billion won was paid to help with the tuition fees of university students who are family members of war veterans. Also, the government provided scholarships to 700 people worth 572 million won who are studying for their postgraduate and doctoral degrees.

Medical Support

In consideration of the trend in which a growing number of veterans are getting old and suffering from chronic diseases, the government set up a medical system at Seoul Veterans Hospital to provide services as a general hospital. After remodeling its building, the number of sickbeds there nearly doubled, from 800 to 1400. Five hospitals for veterans in the country got state qualification for their services.

The government also designated 300 hospitals across the country as places where war veterans and their families can receive medical service if the Veterans Affairs Medical Center is too far away from where they live.

Supporting Veterans' Associations

South Korea has 14 official veterans' associations, with 2,052 branch offices across the country. They've launched diverse projects to help more people bear patriotism and to contribute to the development of the country and local communities.

Housing Support

The government provided 145.01 billion won to 4,384 families of war veterans to help them to purchase houses. The money was used in either the purchase of houses, renting or other related matters.

Livelihood Support

The government also gave 116.4 billion won to be used to help 28,278 households involving war veterans secure their livelihoods. The money was used to purchase land, lend money for their businesses and other related matters.

Welfare Programs for Elderly Veterans

The Ministry of Patriots and Veterans Affairs has provided diverse welfare programs for veterans, especially for elderly veterans. The average age of veterans is now 69. While expanding support in using welfare facilities, the ministry has also been pushing to build new nursing and recreation centers.

Since 2010, the government has employed a new system for the welfare of the elderly to effectively manage the service, and more than 710,000 rounds of relevant services were offered to 12,858 veterans in 2012 alone.

Supporting War Veterans

The Ministry of Patriots and Veterans Affairs holds an annual event honoring war veterans. Diverse commemoration ceremonies also take place to honor their sacrifice, with some 750 million won being earmarked on average for such projects per year. The ministry has gradually increased veterans' monthly allowances, which are set at 180,000 won (US$135) in 2014.

Supporting discharged service personnel

In 2014, the Ministry of Patriots and Veterans Affairs supported 6,089 service personnel discharged from the military after serving the military for more than five years in their job seeking and opening businesses. To help 7,903 servicemembers to be released, the government spent 4.35 billion won. Some 2,701 soldiers to be discharged after serving longer than 10 years received 15.84 billion won for housing and living costs.

The government has been trying to provide servicemembers with customized training programs to help them better adjust to the social life, while trying to find more vacancies in which former soldiers can play a key role by maximizing their military experience.

■ **Launch of Hotline Service for Veterans**

In October 2004, the Ministry of Patriots and Veterans Affairs opened a hot line to provide better services for veterans and deal with their complaints and other petitions in a faster and easier fashion. Since then, more than 2.78 million petitions have been received, with a growing number of users expressing satisfaction with the service.

■ **Expansion of Capacity of National Cemeteries**

Amid a growing demand on the back of the increased population of elderly veterans, the government has been trying to boost the capacity of national cemeteries. The Yeongcheon National Cemetery in North Gyeongsang Province established a charnel house that can house 25,000 remains. Three other major cemeteries in the country -- in Daejeon, Icheon, and Imsil -- also expanded their capacity by an additional 6,000 remains.

To allow those living in the southern part of the country to be buried in the cemetery, the government has been building a new one in Sancheong, South Gyeongsang Province, set to open in 2015. It is also pushing to make two more national cemeteries -- one in the central part of the country and the other on the southern resort island of Jeju.

As of the end of December, 71,507 remains have been placed in the Daejeon National Cemetery, 39,530 in Yeongcheon, and 35,544 in Icheon.

THE ELDERLY, WOMEN AND YOUTH

THE ELDERLY

■ **Poverty Rate of The Elderly Close to 50%**

The elderly in South Korea tend to work even after retirement but their poverty rate is close to 50%. According to an analysis of data from the Korea Institute for Health and Social Affairs and Statistics Korea, the poverty rate of the elderly stood at 48% in 2013. This is 3.5 times higher than the total poverty rate of 13.7%.

The general poverty rate decreased by 0.3% from 14% in 2012, but that of the elderly remained the same. The poverty rate is the ratio of the number of people who fall between the poverty line based on disposable household income.

According to London-based HelpAge International's 2014 Global AgeWatch Index, South Korea ranked 80th among 91 countries surveyed in the income security field, which takes the elderly poverty rate into account.

South Korea ranked 50th behind China and Kazakhstan in general welfare for the elderly. It's a dominant view that it's attributable to the immaturity of the public pension system and the lackluster private pension market.

Only 31.8% of the 'baby boomer' generation, or those born between 1955 and 1963, has a public pension and just 15.8% has a private pension.

Most of the elderly in South Korea have no assets other than real estate and they are forced to search for jobs after retirement.

■ **Longer Life Expectancy, Medical Costs for Elderly Soar**

The 'qualify of lifespan' is getting more important than the 'quantity of life." But South Korea has no adequate social infrastructure to meet the trend.

According to a report by the Korea Institute for Health and Social Affairs, the life expectancy of South Korean people is 81.2 years but their 'health lifespan' is 70.74. It means South Koreans suffer illness about 10 years on average.

The difference between the life expectancy and the health lifespan is mainly attributable to periodic chronic illness, which is a big financial burden on the public health care insurance system.

According to the Health Insurance Statistics Yearbook 2013, 3.7 trillion won was spent to cover the five major illness suffered by South Koreans, including essential hypertension and chronic kidney disease.

In addition, medical costs for the elderly increased 9.9% to 18.1 trillion won in 2013. It is a 2.5-fold increase in seven years from 2007. The elderly accounted for 11.5% of the total population, but their medical costs covered by public health care funds stood at 35.5% of the total.

The annual average medical expense for the elderly rapidly grew from 1.8 million won per person in 2006, to 2.33 million won in 2008, and 3.22 million won in 2013. It was three times more than per capita medical fee of the total population, which was 1.02 million won.

Health spending for the elderly who live longer but who are unhealthy will inevitably become a big burden to individuals as well as society.

According to a study in 2014 by the Health Industry Development Institute, medical spending by people aged 65 and older reached 908,670 won on average. Some elderly people with no proper health care service often make extreme choices, including suicide.

WOMEN-YOUTH

■ Overview

Kim Hee-jung was sworn in as the minister of gender equality and family, replacing Cho Yoon-sun. Kim reaffirmed that her ministry's aim is to promote work-family balance, gender equality, youth ability and endeavored to expand the role of the ministry.

For work-family balance, a full child day-care policy was implemented and legislation on a subsidy for childcare service was passed. In connection with gender equality, the ministry implemented a measure to undertake a public gender effect analysis and assessment. The ministry continued efforts to address sexual violence and harassment.

As to problems associated with youths, a 'healing school" for addicts to the Internet and cell phone use was founded and legal measures were taken to raise the safety of youth camping after the Taean Marine Corps camp tragedy.

In addition, the Ministry of Gender Equality and Family took continued steps to counter Japan's provocative words and actions on the issue of its sexual enslavement of Korean and other Asian women during World War II.

The ministry, in charge of supporting victims, sought the listing of archives related to 'comfort women' with UNESCO

and the publication of a white paper on Japan's atrocity.

■ Inauguration of Kim Hee-jung as Gender Equality Minister

In a reshuffle of the Cabinet and presidential staff carried out amid the aftermath of the Sewol ferry incident, Minister Cho Yoon-sun moved to the post of senior presidential secretary for political affairs. And Kim Hee-Jung took the baton from Cho as the minister of gender equality and family.

▲ New Gender Equality Minister Kim Hee-jung attends an inauguration ceremony at the ministry's headquarters in Seoul on July 16.

Cho, a close aide to President Park Geun-hye, was widely expected to take a high-profile position in the Park administration. But Kim, who served as Cheong Wa Dae spokeswoman during the Lee Myung-bak administration, is not viewed as a politician close to President Park.

Minister Kim Hee-jung, who was re-elected in the 2012 parliamentary elections, is known for her legislative work to prevent sex crimes against children and youths. In her inauguration speech on July 16, Kim said her ministry should provide support for the happiness of the people.

■ Expansion of Daycare Service for Babies

The Ministry of Gender Equality and Family expanded government-funded daycare services for babies. In 2014 alone, 4,244 households benefited from the system. The Ministry of Gender Equality and Family increased pay for nannies from 5,000 won to 5,500 won per hour.

Legislation on Child-Rearing Expenses

In February, the National Assembly passed legislation calling for the government to help parents who are raising their children after a divorce receive support from their ex-spouses. It will take effect in March 2015.

In accordance with the law, the government set up a related office to provide counseling, support for locating ex-spouses and finding their financial data as well as assist child support payment-related litigation and debt collection.

Also, a committee was established in the Ministry of Gender Equality and Family to deal with relevant affairs, including punishments for those who default on their child support debt and cooperation with other authorities.

Gender Impact Analysis and Evaluation

A revision law passed in the National Assembly in February that requires government agencies to make public the records of their implementation of rules to craft policies and carry out them in consideration of gender equality.

Gender impact assessment and evaluation is designed to encourage central and local governments to analyze and evaluate the characteristics of gender and social and economic gaps in pushing for policies and projects, thus contributing to the realization of gender equality.

Until the legislation was introduced, government agencies just reported their implementation of general impact assessment and evaluation to Cabinet meetings and submitted related documents to the National Assembly.

Protecting Foreign Women with Arts and Entertainer Visas

The government held its 35th anti-prostitution meeting in March and decided to review on a regular basis the human rights situation of foreign women who work in South Korea on E-6 visas.

On-site surveys of 10-20 bars, night clubs and other facilities were conducted at least once every quarter. The government took administrative measures against those who violate the human rights of foreign women.

Safety of Youth Campaign Activities

The Ministry of Gender Equality and Family enforced an ordinance on promoting youth activities after a 2013 accident at a private Marine Corps camp in Taean. It was designed to tighten regulations on organizing and operating youth camps in order to enhance the safety standards of related activities and facilities.

It has restricted individuals or groups without reports, records, or authorization from hosting youth camps. In addition, it has mandated that camp operators have staff with professional training in first aid or safety measures in camping sites. Camping facilities have become subject to comprehensive safety inspection and assessment at least once every two years and are required to make public the results.

Measures Against Internet, Smartphone Addiction

The Ministry of Gender Equality and Family remodeled a closed school in Muju and established the National Youth Internet Dream Village there in August for healing youths who suffer troubles from excessive use of the Internet and smartphones.

Set up on a 9,134m² site, it is equipped with counseling, education and accommodation facilities. It offers tailored services to participants so that they can increase their communication ability and recover self-confidence, while staying there with no access to the Internet and smartphones. In 2014, 200 students took part in the eight-day healing program.

'Comfort Women' Issue

The government made efforts in earnest to counter a move by Japan's Shinzo Abe administration to review the so-called Kono Statement.

The Foreign Ministry was in charge of the direct response to Japan's move to modify the Kono Statement, which acknowledged the suffering endured by sex slaves for Japanese troops during World War II, dubbed 'comfort women.'

The Ministry of Gender Equality and Family Ministry also supported the Foreign Ministry. As Japan continued to claim that there is no evidence on the sexual enslavement, the ministry said it would help find more historical materials.

Above all, the Ministry of Gender Equality and Family announced plans to put records related to comfort women into UNESCO's Memory of the World Register. It is continuing work to find the relevant materials to submit an application to the Cultural Heritage Administration in 2015.

The Ministry of Gender Equality and Family is reviewing documents and other materials related to comfort women in China, Southeast Asia and Japan. If records related to comfort women are listed on UNESCO's Memory of the World Register, the government expects it to help enhance international attention on the matter.

The government also announced in June that it published a white paper on Japan's sexual enslavement of women during World War II in a way to counter Japan's attempt to water down the Kono Statement.

To be jointly published by the Ministry of Gender Equality and Family, Kookmin University's Institute of Japanese Studies and Gender Equality, and Sungkyunkwan University's East Asia Institute, the white paper will contain newly discovered materials after a similar report in 1992 and other findings by international organizations, civic groups and foreign parliaments.

The white paper, scheduled to be published at the end of 2015, will clarify that Japan's atrocity in connection with the comfort women issue was in clear violation of international law.

The Ministry of Gender Equality and Family has formed a publication team composed of 10 experts and researchers on South Korea-Japan relations, history, diplomacy and international law. In addition, a 19-member advisory group has been created to include officials from the Foreign Ministry and Northeast Asian History Foundation. It is headed by a vice minister of gender equality and family.

In addition, the Ministry of Gender Equality and Family sponsored a special exhibition, titled "Korean Cartoons on Comfort Women Victims" during the International Comics Festival held in Angouleme, France, in January 2014.

The Ministry of Gender Equality and Family, which is in charge of supporting the victims of Japan's wartime sexual enslavement, is also providing a tailored program to help them.

■ Anti-Prostitution Campaign

The 'Prostitution Prevention and Victim Protection Act' (Prostitution Act) amendment took effect on Sept. 28. It calls for the Ministry of Gender Equality and Family to evaluate the results of prostitution prevention education at state agencies, local governments, schools and other public organizations. Evaluation results are revealed through the media.

The legislation also includes the designation of a week of the year as a special campaign week to root out prostitution and produce a video on Prostitution Prevention and Victim Assistance. It also calls for the chatting windows of websites for adults and mobile applications to carry a warning message that prostitution is illegal. Violators face fines of up to 5 million won.

CONSUMER PROTECTION

■ Mobile Device Sales Law

As confusion continued in the mobile phone market, symbolized by illegal subsidies and high service fees, the government enacted new legislation aimed at addressing the situation.

The law, which went into effect on Oct. 1, calls for a cap on subsidies of mobile devices, including smartphones, and the disclosure of related details such as service type, region, and age in a transparent manner for the purpose of ending discrimination and bursting the bubble in regards to the prices of mobile devices.

But consumers continue to complain about costs. Especially in the early weeks, criticism was raised as customers received less subsidies and were forced to pay more to buy handsets. However, the markets gradually stabilized as additional measures were taken, such as a reduction in service fees and hikes in legal subsidies.

▪ Hikes in Meat Prices and Utility Bills

Although annual inflation rates stood at the 1% level, meat prices and some utility bills, which are closely associated with the livelihoods of the people, continued to soar.

According to Statistics Korea, consumer prices jumped 1.3% in 2014 from a year earlier, the lowest level since 1999. But the prices of some items increased more than 10%.

Pork prices rose 15.9% year-on-year, the highest increase since 2011 (28.1%). And the prices of imported beef (10.7%) and domestic beef (6.2%) sharply rose as well, seen as attributable to a reduction in supply.

Egg and milk prices also rose by 7.4% and 8.2%, respectively. Powdered milk prices increased 7.1%, raising the burden on families with infants. Chocolate (16.7%), choco pies (15.3%), biscuits (13%) and other snack prices also jumped a lot.

Some utility bills also jumped significantly. Sewer bills recorded an 11.6% rise, a big jump from 7% in 2013. Local governments steadily raised sewer bills, citing high production costs. City gas rates rose 6.4%. Among industrial products, the prices of toothpaste (11.7%), handbags (11.6%), notebooks (10.3%) and women's coats (7.5%) recorded big hikes.

▪ Popularity of Budget Carriers

The market share of low-cost airliners on domestic routes grew to 35% in 2010, 48% in 2013, and 54.7% in December 2014, outdoing Korean Air Lines and Asiana Airlines. The market share of budget carriers on international routes reached 12.2% in December 2014.

The fierce competition among airliners led to a decline in international airline ticket prices. According to data compiled by Interpark, the average fares for America, Europe, Oceania, Southeast Asia, Japan and China fell 9% from 749,075 won in 2011 to 684,981 won in 2014.

But with the demand for international travel growing, there were increased reports of complaints of airline services. According to the Korea Consumer Agency, 510 cases were reported between January and September 2014, up 24.7% from the same period in 2013.

▪ Overseas Direct Purchases

Overseas direct purchases grew popular, especially during the 'Black Friday' period in the United States. Cheaper prices, various products, simplified purchase procedures and tariff reductions from the South Korea-U.S. free trade agreement were cited as main factors.

According to the Korea Customs Service, the number of overseas direct purchases in 2014 amounted to 15.5 million, totaling US$1.54 billion, up 39% and 48%, respectively, from a year earlier. 73% of the purchases came from the United States, 11% from China and 5% from Germany.

By item number, clothing (19%) topped the list, followed by health products (14%), footwear (13%), food (11%), cosmetics (11%), handbags and other bags (8%), toys and dolls (4%), household appliances (2%), clocks (2%) and books (1%). By purchase price, 37% of people spent between US$50 and US$100.

Amid a surge in overseas direct purchases, there are a growing number of reports of damages. In a survey by the Korea Internet & Security Agency (KISA), 56.6% of the respondents who bought foreign goods on the Internet said they suffered damages or inconveniences. The most common damage types were delays in delivery and loss of goods with 50.5%.

▲ Customs officials handle a heap of South Korean televisions bought by domestic consumers through foreign shopping malls during the so-called Black Friday Deals Week at Incheon International Airport on Dec. 1.

▪ Mobile Buying Surge

Mobile shopping markets have grown significantly as consumers buy goods via smartphones without space and time constraints.

According to the Korea Online Shopping Association, the Internet and mobile shopping sales more than doubled to 13.1 trillion won in 2014, up from 5.9 trillion won in 2013. In particular, purchases of fresh foods such as fruit and vegetables, in addition to the traditional commodities, increased.

Meanwhile, with the key channel of online shopping shifting to mobile devices, sales using desktop PCs declined 5.4% to 31.9 trillion won in 2014 from 33.7 trillion won in 2013. TV home shopping sales through IPTV, cable TV and satellite TV increased only 2.3% to 9.3 trillion won.

In line with the change in buying patterns, retailers tried to develop mobile-shopping apps and strengthen warranty and delivery services. The overall online shopping market, including TV home shopping and online shopping, amounted to 55 trillion won in 2014, up 11% from a year earlier.

■ Growing Phishing, other Financial Scams

Voice phishing and other financial scams using smartphones were prevalent.

According to the National Police Agency, the number of voice phishing cases soared from 5,455 in 2010 to 8,244 in 2011 and it fell to 5,709 in 2012 and 4,765 in 2013 due to police crackdowns and an improved financial system. But it rose to 7,635 in 2014.

The methods of financial scams have become diverse. The number of fraudulent bank accounts being detected by police and financial authorities has also grown. According to the Financial Supervisory Service (FSS), the number of such accounts used for phishing jumped 16.3% from 38,437 in 2013 to 44,705 in 2014.

OVERSEAS KOREANS AND MULTICULTURAL SOCIETY

OVERSEAS KOREANS

■ Overseas Koreans Foundation's Budget Exceeds US$50 Billion

The Budget of the Overseas Koreans Foundation, which supports Korean nationals abroad, topped US$50 billion for the first time.

Its 2015 budget was the largest-ever at 51.8 billion won, an increase of 5.1 billion won, or 11%, from 2014. Of the total, 50.3 billion won was funded by the government and 1.5 billion won came from its own revenue.

The foundation earmarked 2 billion won to support ethnic Koreans in China and help Koreans in the U.S. increase their political influence there. Five billion won was allocated for events to celebrate the 50th anniversary of Koreans' immigration to Argentina and Paraguay.

■ Overseas Koreans' Economic Value Estimated at 144 Trillion Won

There are more than 7 million Koreans residing abroad, about 10% of the total population of South and North Korea. How much would be their economic value? Baek Myoung-ok, professor of Myongji University, said it is estimated to reach US$130 billion.

In a forum held at the Korea National Diplomatic Academy on Nov. 28, 2014, Baek said the economic value of overseas Koreans accounts for 56.8% of foreign direct investment. They can play a pivotal role in drumming up international support in the event of reunification and drawing economic investment, Baek said.

In order to transform North Korea's economy into a market economy for the integration of the South and North Korean economies, overseas Koreans' investment in North Korea will be the key, said the professor. In fact, enterprises run by ethnic Koreans in China accounted for more than 80% of investment in the Rajin-Sonbong Special Economic Zone.

"As the Korean Peninsula is a place where the national interest of four nearby regional powers is intertwined, overseas Koreans can exert influence in winning the hearts of policymakers and people there," Baek said.

As of December 2013, the number of Korean nationals living abroad was estimated at 7 million, 86% of whom live in the U.S., China, Japan and Russia.

■ 'East Sea' Name Bill Passes in Virginia Legislature

An East Sea name bill gained ground

as local politicians and Korean residents' groups teamed up in 2012. Peter Kim, the head of the Voice of Korean Americans (VOKA), played a key role.

He was shocked that his son in elementary school called the East Sea the "Sea of Japan." Kim began a petition campaign on the "We the People" site of the White House home page.

He launched the VoKA in December 2012 and created a bipartisan mood to submit the East Sea name bill with the help of two Virginia state senators, David Marsden from the Democratic Party and Richard Black from the Republican Party.

But the Japanese government attempted to foil the bill with lobbyists and a series of meetings between Ambassador Kenichiro Sasae and local politicians.

Japan even pressured Virginia Gov. Terry McAuliffe with a threat to withdraw Japanese firms doing business in Virginia. But Japan's lobbying was outdone by ceaseless efforts by Koreans living in Virginia. On Jan. 24, 2014, the bill passed the state senate, followed by passage in the House of Delegates on March 5.

Gov. McAuliffe signed the bill in the same month, ending related legal procedures. It went into effect on July 1, mandating public school textbooks in Virginia to use the name East Sea as well as the Sea of Japan to describe the waters between South Korea and Japan.

■ Impact on Other States, Monuments for 'Comfort Women' Gain Momentum

With passage of the bill in Virginia, the East Sea name campaign spread to New Jersey and New York. Local politicians, supported by South Koreans there, submitted similar bills.

Koreans in the U.S. also became more active in raising the issue of Japan's sexual enslavement of Korean and other Asian women during World War II.

A monument for "comfort women" was erected in the Peace Memorial Garden in Fairfax County, Virginia, on May 30 2014. The monument carries a message that women were mobilized as sex slaves by Japan.

In July, a similar monument was established in New York City, which is more

meaningful because local authorities took the lead for that, not the Korean community there.

Koreans are continuing grass-roots campaigns despite the Japanese government's call for the dismantlement of monuments for comfort women in Palisades Park and Bergen County in New Jersey, Long Island in New York, Glendale in California, and Fairfax in Virginia.

■ Korean Bizmen Abroad Visit Kaesong Industrial Complex

A group of Korean businessmen and women abroad visited the Kaesong Industrial Complex in 2014. Thirty-five members of the World Federation of Overseas Korean Traders Associations (OKTA) made a one-day group tour of the complex in May. They were on a trip to Korea to attend the 13th World Korean Business Convention organized by the Overseas Koreans Foundation. Some of them expressed their intention to set up factories in the Kaesong zone.

The OKTA also held a road show in Dalian, China, for ethnic Korean businessmen and women in China in the middle of September. Also on hand were several North Korean officials, including Kim Kyung-soo, vice chairman of the Korea Investment & Foreign Economic Cooperation Committee, and Oh Kyung-chol, vice chairman in charge of international organizations for the Korea Trade Promotion Committee.

■ 150th Anniversary of Ethnic Koreans' Emigration to Soviet Union

This year marks the 150th anniversary of ethnic Koreans' emigration to the former Soviet Union. To commemorate, Korean descendants living in Central Asia visited South Korea.

A variety of events were held in 2014 to mark their emigration. Those events took place not only in Moscow, Vladivostok and Central Asian nations, but also in South Korea.

In South Korea, a related committee was formed by some ruling and opposition party lawmakers and civic groups. It organized various ceremonies and events, including festivals, concerts, academic forums, and cultural events.

In particular, 130 ethnic Koreans living in the Russian Far East, dubbed "Goryeoin," visited South Korea in June. Another highlight event was a trans-Eurasian auto-trek rally. The team made a road trip by car from Russia through Central Asia and North Korea to South Korea.

The team set off from Moscow on July 7. Forty days later, they arrived at the Dorasan Inter-Korean Transit Office in Paju, Gyeonggi Province, at the inter-Korean border on Aug. 16. The 32 members and the eight vehicles of the rally team also passed through Khabarovsk, Sakhalin and Vladivostok in the Russian Federation, before passing into North Korea.

They entered North Korea by train and crossed the Military Demarcation Line (MDL) by car on Aug. 16.

▲ Ethnic Koreans residing in Russia pose with Busan citizens in the South Korean port city on Aug. 19, after completing their international auto rally, which began in Moscow on July 7, went through Russia and North Korea, and ended in Busan in anticipation of unification on the Korean Peninsula.

■ U.N. Panel Urges Japan to Curb Anti-Korea Protest

Throughout 2014, hate speech was rampant in Japan. Ethnic Koreans in Japan suffered big damages from hate speech by some Japanese people.

Representatives from the Korean Residents Union in Japan, or Mindan, visited the UN Committee on the Elimination of Racial Discrimination in Geneva and asked it to take measures against the spread of hate speech and racist demonstrations in Japan.

Thanks to such efforts by ethnic Kore-

ans in Japan, the United Nations called on Japan to take legal steps against hate speech and racist protests. It is watching the situation closely with the hope that the Japanese government will make efforts to get rid of prejudice and discrimination against Koreans there.

■ New I.D. Registration Rule on Koreans Abroad

Starting on Jan. 22 2015, South Koreans living in foreign countries became eligible for personal identification cards. Under a new regulation, overseas Koreans can apply for the cards if they enter South Korea for stays of 30 days or longer.

However, they will also face tougher income tax rules. If they stay in South Korea for more than six months, they will be subject to income taxes.

■ Mindan Pushes for Incorporation

Members of the Korean Residents Union in Japan, or Mindan, are pushing for the incorporation of the organization. Founded in 1946, a year after Korea's liberation from Japan's colonial rule, Mindan has branches across Japan.

It is working to strengthen the legal status of ethnic Koreans in Japan and protect their rights. It has been immune from the supervision of the Japanese government for the past 68 years. But it is considering incorporating in a bid to enhance transparency in its operation.

Mindan receives 8 billion won in financial support annually from the South Korean government. Because it is based in Japan, however, there is a restriction on the South Korean government's audit of the group.

During a parliamentary audit of the South Korean Embassy in Japan in October 2014, Rep. Lee Hae-chan of the New Politics Alliance for Democracy voiced worries that Mindan's assets will be owned by individuals.

The South Korean government asked Mindan to consider incorporation. In this regard, some Mindan officials are concerned that their activities will be restricted if the organization is incorporated in Japan and comes under the supervision of the Japanese government.

MULTICULTURAL SOCIETY

▪ Number of Foreigners in S. Korea Close to 1.8 Million

The number of foreigners staying in South Korea increased more than 2.5 times over the past 10 years and neared 1.8 million. According to the Justice Ministry, the number of foreigners in South Korea as of the end of 2014 jumped 14.1% to 1.79 million. It accounts for 3.5% of South Korea's population. In 2004, the number was 718,000.

Until the late 1990s, the number of foreigners in South Korea stood at around 380,000. It constantly rose in the 2000s, topping 1 million in 2008 and 1.5 million in 2013.

By nationality, China topped the list with 898,654 in 2014, followed by the United States with 136,663, Vietnam with 129,973 and Thailand with 94,314. By the purpose of stay, visiting workers such as migrant workers were the most common with 617,145, overseas Koreans (286,414 people) and immigration by marriage (15,099).

▪ Number of Illegal Immigrants Reaches 208,000

The number of illegal immigrants rose to 208,778 as of Dec. 31, 2014, up 14% from 183,106 in 2013. It marked the largest number since 2007, when there were 223,464 illegal immigrants.

The increase is connected with a rapid increase in the number of overall immigrants. The ratio of illegal immigrants to total immigrants is on the decline. It reached 27.9% in 2004 and decreased to 11.6% in 2014.

By nationality, China, including ethnic Koreans there, represented the largest number with 70,311, followed by Thailand (44,283), Vietnam (26,932) and the Philippines (12,814).

▪ S. Korea Accepts 94 Refugees

In 2014, South Korea accepted its largest-ever number of refugees. The government granted refugee status to 94 people among 2,896 applicants. The government recognized 47 foreigners as refugees in 2010, 42 in 2011, 60 in 2012 and 57 in 2013. In addition, the number of those who were allowed to stay legally

in South Korea on a humanitarian basis, if not as refugees, jumped to 539 in 2014 from six a year earlier.

It is because the government gave residence permits to people who escaped the civil war in Syria. Of the 539 people who were given humanitarian residence permits in 2014, 502 were Syrians.

Meanwhile, a growing number of foreigners are seeking asylum in South Korea after the introduction of a refugee law in 2013. The number of applicants increased from 423 in 2010 to 1,011 in 2011, 1,143 in 2012 and 1,574 in 2013.

▪ Multicultural Families Taking Root

Multicultural family life seems to be on course to become relatively stable. According to data released by Statistics Korea in November 2014, the number of multicultural marriages involving South Koreans dropped 7.8% to 26,948 in 2013 from a year earlier. The number stood at 35,098 in 2010, 30,695 in 2011 and 29,224 in 2012.

The average marriage age was 35.5 years for men in their first marriage and 27.2 for women with gap of 8.3 years. It was 6.8 years in 2011 and 9.1 years in 2012. But the age gap for remarried couples rose to 7.3 years from 6.7 in 2012.

The number of divorces involving multicultural couples fell by 1.6%, to 13,482 cases from 13,701 in 2012. The average duration of those marriages was 4.9 years in 2011, 5.4 years in 2012, and 5.8 years in 2013.

The number of births from multicultural families declined to 21,290, down 7.1% from 2012, accounting for 4.9% of the total number of new births in South Korea.

▪ Protection of Immigrants' Children

The political circles produced a series of bills on protecting the basic rights of children of immigrants regardless of their legal status.

Rep. Jasmine Lee of the ruling Saenuri Party submitted a bill on protecting the basic rights of children of undocumented immigrants. The bill would allow them to register new births with South Korea and be granted special residence status. It also enables children to receive mandatory education and medical support in South Korea.

Rep. Jung Chung-rae of the main opposition New Politics Alliance for Democracy and Rep. Lim Su-kyung of the same party submitted similar bills. An estimated 20,000 undocumented children of illegal immigrants live in South Korea.

▪ Healthcare for Overseas Koreans

Starting in November 2014, the government imposed a health care premium on overseas Koreans staying in South Korea for a long time in accordance with their income and asset level, just like South Korean citizens.

The measure was introduced in a revised rule on "extended stay overseas Koreans and their health insurance coverage criteria."

▪ Call Center for Female Immigrants

In April 2014, the Danuri Call Center (☎1577-1366) to help multicultural families and immigrants by marriage and the Emergency Support Center for Migrant Women were incorporated.

The Danuri Call Center, which opened in June 2011, provides immigrants with marriage counseling, emergency assistance and other information. Since the merger with the Emergency Support Center for Migrant Women, it operates around the clock and has expanded the number of service languages from 10 to 13.

CRIMES

▪ Ex-Korean Air VP in 'Nut Rage'

In the incident referred to as "nut rage" in South Korea, a former vice president of Korean Air Lines ordered the chief purser of a Korean Air Airbus A380 jet, with some 250 passengers aboard, to leave the plane on Dec. 5 after a spat over how nuts were served.

Cho Hyun-ah was reportedly angered when a first-class flight attendant served her an unopened package of macadamia nuts instead of on a plate. She then took issue with the purser over his lack of knowledge of the service manual.

Cho and Korean Air took a lot of flak over the incident, with some predicting the negative publicity will invariably hurt the carefully built-up image of the full-service airline.

Officials at South Korea's transportation ministry said the return to the gate delayed departure from New York's John F. Kennedy International Airport by some 20 minutes, with the plane arriving 11 minutes behind schedule at Incheon International Airport. The plane had pushed back from the gate and was on the taxiway heading for the runway when it turned around.

State prosecutors raided Korean Air's headquarters to "safeguard" possible evidence related to the incident. They have said that Cho will be barred from leaving the country until the case is resolved.

In an interview with state-run broadcaster KBS, the purser, named Park Chang-jin, claimed that Cho showered abuse on him at the time and even jabbed the back of his hand multiple times with the sharp edge of a file that contains in-flight service guidelines.

▲ Cho Hyun-ah, the eldest daughter of Korean Air Chairman Cho Yang-ho and former vice president of the airline company, appears at Aviation and Railway Accident Investigation Board in western Seoul on Dec. 12, to be questioned for ordering a crew member to leave a plane over an alleged breach of snack-serving protocol.

▪ Slavery at Salt Farm

Two disabled people were rescued on Jan. 28 from a salt farm after years of slavery-like labor. The two in their 40s, one of them mentally handicapped and the other visually impaired, were coaxed with job promises to the salt farm on an island off the southwest coast in 2008 and 2012, respectively, and were forced to work like slaves with little sleep and no pay. Their attempts to escape were met by beatings.

Their ordeal came to light after one of them, the 40-year-old visually impaired man who was identified only by his surname Kim, secretly mailed a letter to his mother calling for help. The mother alerted police and both of them were rescued.

■ City Councilor Detained in Slaying of Millionaire

A member of the Seoul municipal council was arrested on June 24 on charges of abetting the murder of a wealthy man to whom he owed hundreds of thousands of dollars.

The 44-year-old Seoul city councilor, identified only by his surname Kim, is charged with instigating a friend to kill the 67-year-old man, surnamed Song, in early March.

After borrowing 500 million won (US$493,000) from Song between 2010 and 2011, Kim had been pressured to repay the money since late 2012, police said, adding that Song, worth hundreds of millions of dollars, threatened Kim not to run for the June local elections, according to police.

In the June 4 local polls, Kim ran as a candidate of the main opposition New Politics Alliance for Democracy and won a seat on the Seoul city council. He left the party after being arrested by police.

Kim's friend has also been arrested on charges of killing Song at his office in western Seoul by hitting him on the head with a blunt object dozens of times, police said.

The friend said he had committed the murder on Kim's promise to write off 70 million won he owed to the councilor, police added. The suspected killer, who fled to China three days after the murder, was arrested by Chinese police in Shenyang a week ago and repatriated.

■ Top Jeju Prosecutor Caught in Lewd Act

A former top prosecutor on the southern island of Jeju stepped down after being accused of indecent exposure. Kim Soo-chang, the former chief of the local prosecutors' office, was suspected of masturbating in public near his residence on Jeju Island on Aug. 12.

The Jeju District Prosecutors' Office, however, said it has accepted a jury's decision to suspend the case on the condition that Kim, 52, seek psychiatric treatment.

"Kim didn't target anyone in particular and committed the acts at night where he could not be easily seen," prosecutors said. "Witnesses and closed-circuit TV footage have confirmed that, at the time of his arrest, Kim didn't know someone had been watching him."

In South Korea, public indecency typically calls for a prison sentence of up to a year or a fine of up to 5 million won (US$4,491).

■ Korean-Chinese Man Held in Dismemberment of Woman

Police arrested a 55-year-old Chinese man of Korean ethnicity on Dec. 13 on charges of murdering a woman whose chopped upper body was found in Suwon, just south of Seoul.

The suspected, identified as Park Chun-bong, is accused of killing the woman believed to be his ex-girlfriend, also of Korean-Chinese origin, and brutally butchering her body before abandoning it, police said.

The upper body of the woman without its head, arms, and internal organs, except for both kidneys, was found in a black plastic bag on a hiking trail in Suwon, 46 km south of Seoul.

ACCIDENTS AND DISASTERS

■ Deadly Ferry Disaster Kills Hundreds

Sending shock waves throughout the nation, the 6,825-ton ferry Sewol sank

▲ A rescue helicopter flies over the passenger ship Sewol, which is sinking in waters off South Korea's southwestern coast on April 16, with 477 people aboard. A lifeboat is seen near the ship, which was en route from Incheon, west of Seoul, to Jeju Island. (Photo courtesy of contributor)

in waters off the southwestern island of Jindo on April 16, leaving more than 300 people dead or missing.

A total of 295 people, mostly high school students on a field trip to the resort island of Jeju, were found dead, with nine others still missing and presumed dead.

Prosecutors concluded in October that the sinking was caused by a combination of cargo overloading, an illegal redesigning of the ship to increase its cargo load and the steersman's poor helmsmanship.

Announcing the outcome of a five-month-long probe into one of the nation's worst maritime disasters, the Supreme Prosecutors' Office (SPO) also said the Coast Guard's botched initial response had led to the high death toll.

"The disaster resulted from overloaded cargo, an illegal change in the ship's structure, the steersman's lack of ability to handle the ship and the botched initial response of Coast Guard officials," said Cho Eun-suk, a senior prosecutor who was in charge of the investigation.

According to the results, the redesigning of the ship to increase its cargo load impaired its stability, and the poorly trained crew members made a sharper-than-recommended turn when the ship was passing through strong currents.

The ill-fated ferry was found to have been carrying 3,606 tons of freight and cars, more than three times its recommended maximum cargo, at the time of the accident. The ship's operator, Chonghaejin Marine Co., reportedly depended on cargo to compensate for declining passenger revenue.

A patrol boat of the Mokpo Coast Guard, named the 123, had failed to move swiftly to save more lives, even though it was the first ship to arrive at the scene, prosecutors said.

Twelve Coast Guard officials at the vessel traffic service (VTS) on Jindo Island were also found to have neglected their duty to properly monitor the ferry as it sailed nearby and failed to follow proper procedures in registering the Sewol's distress call.

Kim Kyoung-il, the captain of the Coast Guard, has been indicted on charges of negligence of duty, and removing some of the work records written on the day of the ferry sinking and filing new content, possibly out of fear that his rescue team's poor initial response would be disclosed, prosecutors said.

■ Gym Packed with Students Collapses

A poorly built resort facility in southeastern South Korea collapsed on Feb. 17, killing 10 university students. The snow-covered roof of the gymnasium facility at the Mauna Ocean Resort in the historical tourist city of Gyeongju, about 370km southeast of Seoul, caved in during a freshmen welcoming party. The incident also injured 204 others.

Announcing the final result of an investigation into the case, a special police investigation team said arrest warrants have been sought for two executives of the gymnasium operator and four other men involved in the building of the gymnasium on manslaughter charges.

An additional 16 people will be booked without physical detention on charges of negligence and forgery of official documents. "Heavy snow weighing on the roof as well as the shoddy construction of the main pillars supporting the roof were the causes of the collapse," the team said.

The wrong bolts and shoddy materials were illegally used for the construction of the gymnasium due to the lax supervision of the builders and some false official documents.

Those who were in charge of maintenance did not remove snow piled up on the roof after days of heavy snowfalls, resulting in the fatal collapse of the one-story building, the team added.

■ Ventilation Grate Collapses at Pop Concert

Sixteen people were killed and eleven others were injured on Oct. 17 as a ventilation grill gave way due to their weight on it during a pop concert.

The victims, who plunged four stories to the basement of a parking lot, were on top of the grate to get a better view of the concert that took place at 5:53 p.m. at Pangyo Techno Valley, a multi-purpose complex for technology firms in Seongnam, Gyeonggi Province, just southeast of Seoul.

"Twelve people were killed at the scene, two others were killed while they were being rushed to the hospital. The other two are assumed to have passed away while receiving medical treatment," said a fire official.

Kim Nam-joon, a spokesman for a temporary headquarters set up to deal with the accident, said some 700 people were attending the concert where various South Korean musicians, including girl group 4Minute, were performing.

Kim, who identified the main cause of the accident as excessive weight on the ventilation grill, said that the list of victims does not include any teenagers.

In 2005, 11 people were killed and 70 others were injured in the southern city of Sangju, 270km south of the capital, as some 10,000 people gathered to see a televised concert. Investigation results showed that no police officer or safety official was at the site of the accident.

■ South Korean Ship Sinks in Russian Waters

The 1,753-ton Oryong 501 carrying 60 crew members sank in the western Bering Sea on Dec. 1. One Russian inspector and six crew members -- three Filipinos and three Indonesians -- survived the sinking, with 27 crew members confirmed dead and 26 others still missing.

South Korea, the United States and Russia conducted a search for the missing crewmen, but no major progress was made due mainly to inclement weather.

A ranking official at Seoul's foreign ministry said that the government will end the search operation in January 2015, given freezing water temperatures and security concerns for rescuers aboard a 5,000-ton patrol ship dispatched to the area.

Two South Korean surveillance aircraft and the patrol ship were involved in the search operation. The patrol vessel ended its mission at the end of the year.

South Korean fishing vessels, which have been engaged in the operation, were withdrawn from the accident scene as they are permitted to do fishing only until the end of the year.

A Russian ship carrying six survivors and 21 bodies of Southeast Asian victims arrived at South Korea's southeastern port of Busan after sailing for more than two weeks.

The bodies of six other South Koreans have not been brought home yet at the request of their bereaved families, who asked for the search to be finished first.

■ Seoul Subway Trains Collide

Two trains collided on one of Seoul's major subway lines on May 2, injuring 238 passengers, police and firefighters said. No fatalities were immediately reported.

Most of the injured were not reported to be in a serious condition. Some of the wounded passengers were taken to one of 13 nearby hospitals, mostly with minor scratches, with one of the two train drivers receiving surgery for a fractured shoulder, officials said. About 43 passengers were hospitalized. Some 1,000 other passengers escaped safely about 10 minutes after the accident, they added.

The collision happened at Sangwangsimni Station on Subway Line 2 at around 3:30 p.m. when a train ran into the back of another train that had stopped at the station due to a mechanical problem, they said.

According to Seoul Metro, the operator of the subway line, it was the first time that subway trains had collided in South Korea. Service on the subway line was partially restricted following the accident.

Seoul city officials said a failure in the following train's automatic distance control system (ATS) could have been the cause of the collision. The ATS should have activated when the two trains approached within 200m of each other.

Some of the rings connecting cars of the struck train were damaged and three wheels of the other train were knocked off the track by the collision, according to Seoul Metro. Passengers said there was no announcement telling passengers to leave the trains following the crash so they pulled emergency levers to open the subway doors and exit.

The accident comes as the country is still reeling from a ferry tragedy on April 16 that has left 304 people dead or missing. The 6,825-ton Sewol carrying 476 people sank off South Korea's southwestern island of Jindo, sending the nation into grief and shock. A total of 174 people were rescued in the accident.

Education

Yonhap News Agency

OVERVIEW

■ **New Deputy Prime Minister & Education Minister**
Hwang Woo-yea, a former head of the

▲ *Hwang Woo-yea, former head of the ruling Saenuri Party, speaks to reporters at his office in Seoul on July 15, after President Park Geun-hye tapped the judge-turned-lawmaker to be the new education minister on the day.*

ruling Saenuri Party, became South Korea's education minister in August 2014. Hwang also doubled as the country's deputy prime minister on social affairs and education.

The 68-year-old Hwang, a former five-term lawmaker, also worked on the parliamentary education committee. Hwang entered local politics in 1996 after serving as a judge for more than 20 years.

Hwang became the country's deputy prime minister, along with Choi Kyung-hwan, deputy prime minister on economic affairs. Hwang smoothly passed the parliament's hearing.

■ **Efforts to Improve the Education System**
The Ministry of Education has decided to lower the number of elementary school students per class to 21 and that of middle and high school students per class to 23 by 2020.

The government launched a review on the trends of students at elementary, middle and high schools; available space to increase the number of classrooms; and plans to boost the number of schools. The education ministry is consulting with the Ministry of Government Administration and Home Affairs and the Ministry of Strategy and Finance on how to hire more teachers in the long term.

South Korea has been pushing to enhance the education system since July 2001. The education ministry injected 11.5 trillion won between 2001 and 2004 and raised the number of teachers by

Education **237**

23,600 between 2002 and 2003.

The government's efforts to cut the number of students per class and the low birthrate caused the number of students per class to fall to 23.2 at elementary schools, to 31.7 at middle schools and to 31.9 at high schools. In particular, the number of elementary school students per class has been on the decline since 2008 when it fell below 30 for the first time.

The government established free compulsory education for middle school students in 2004 with investments of 266.4 billion won in 2002, 532.8 billion won in 2003 and 799.3 billion won in 2004.

In December 2009, the education ministry laid out a blueprint for the curricula, which called for reducing the required number of subjects per semester and for allowing students to learn several subjects intensively for one semester or for one year. The new education plan was introduced in 2011.

A law on lifelong learning was revised in 2004 to allow adults who did not receive elementary education to acquire it at lifelong education facilities. The education ministry also opened a portal site on lifelong education and related contents (www.everyday.go.kr) with the National Institute for Lifelong Education in December 2014.

■ Education Policy under President Park's Administration

The administration of President Park Geun-hye expanded the "free semester" system, a key pillar of her government's education policy in 2014. Education Minister Hwang Woo-yea also vowed to successfully implement the free semester system when he took office in August last year.

The free semester system allows students to join discussions, field classes or other on-the-job training without taking midterm or final exams. The system is one of Park's key education pledges that allows middle school students to explore what they want to be in the future, at least for one semester.

The education ministry is aiming to introduce the free semester system in a full-fledged manner in 2016 after operating it on a pilot run and accepting applications from hopeful schools in 2014 and 2015.

Minister Hwang visited a school that is operating the free semester system on the country's southern resort island of Jeju in December 2014. He said that the government will make legal grounds to implement the system in a bid to institutionalize it so that the operation of the system will not be swayed by changes in the government.

Vocational education has also gained traction. The education ministry unveiled nine special schools that will operate vocational education, similar to that of Switzerland and Germany on a pilot run. The government also unveiled its plan that calls for college students to receive on-the-job training for one semester.

The education ministry also finalized its plan to conduct a complete evaluation of English during the nationwide college entrance exam. It announced the basic guidelines to reform colleges and universities to brace for a decline in the number of students. The government also created a blueprint to reduce school violence.

EDUCATION POLICY

■ Expansion of the 'Free Semester System'

The education ministry designated 811 middle schools nationwide as model schools for the "free semester system" in 2014. The 811 schools accounted for 25% of all middle schools nationwide. The government sharply expanded the number of model schools for pilot operations from 42 middle schools.

The free semester system is one of President Park Geun-hye's key education pledges that allows middle school students to have a chance to explore what they want to be in the future, at least for one semester.

The model schools and schools hoping to get into the program abolished midterm and final exams. Instead, students are allowed to receive self-reflection evaluations and assessments from their teachers. Teachers will also document how their students have explored potential career paths in their middle school transcripts.

Teachers will be given flexibility in operating their classes. Basic subjects, which include Korean, English, mathematics and science, will be taught to help students improve their foundation. But when it comes to more complicated areas, such as conducting experiments, receiving practical training and working on projects, teachers will focus on enhancing students' creative thinking and learning.

Students will undertake all-day field activities more than twice per semester. Teachers will be allowed to conduct various classes. For example, several teachers can hold a joint class together or they can teach a combination of basic subjects, as well as art, music and physical education, during one class.

The government plans to provide financial support worth up to 40 million won to model and aspirant schools. The government positively assessed the system, citing student satisfaction.

Education Minister Hwang visited Seogwi Jungang Girls' Middle School on Jeju Island on Dec. 8, 2014. The school test ran the free semester system for the past two years. A total of 44 middle schools on the island have operated the free semester system. On Jeju, Hwang vowed to make a law on the free semester system, saying that the government will earmark more budget for it in 2015. "As demand for the free semester system has shot up, the government plans to raise the percentage of participating schools to 70% of all middle schools in 2015," Hwang said.

But experts say there is a long way to go before the system is fully implemented. It is not easy for students to get experience toward selecting a career and there are concerns that if the system is implemented in 2016, students in rural and fishing areas will have difficulty in exploring career options due to a lack of infrastructure.

▪ Gov't Efforts to Curb School Violence

The government approved the 2015-2019 blueprint on eradicating school violence in December 2014. To accomplish its goal, the government decided to strengthen measures to enhance family education. The government is considering requiring parents to receive education on school violence in accordance with their children's development.

It is also considering creating mandatory online or offline courses on school violence for parents that they would take every three years after the birth of their children is registered. To this end, the government plans to push for the revision of related laws and regulations. The government is also considering giving incentives to parents who take the courses or fining those who do not.

It also plans to strengthen anti-violence education for school parents. The government will set up a pan-government consultative body on the prevention of social violence that includes officials from the education ministry, the defense ministry and the justice ministry. The government will also offer a class on the prevention of violence at workplaces at least once per year.

"There is a prevailing view that school violence results from a lack of education on humanism at home," an education ministry official said. When new schools are built or existing schools are expanded, they will be required to create an atmosphere that can prevent violence. The move is aimed at reducing blind spots where school violence can occur by changing the design of the buildings.

The government said it plans to adopt a four-week-long program to help bullies and victims restore their friendship via counselling. It also plans to include more content on the prevention of school violence in curricula.

South Korea will also push to create a theme park, where materials on the prevention of school violence will be displayed. It also unveiled plans to install more CCTVs in schools, dispatch police officers on school violence and push for the "Wee Project" that offers counseling to bullies.

▪ Absolute Evaluation for English during College Entrance Exam

The education ministry unveiled its plan to introduce an absolute evaluation for English on the nationwide college entrance exam starting in late 2017. If adopted, students will only receive one letter grade. The move is aimed at reducing households' growing burden on private tutoring.

But there are mixed responses to the government's plan. Supporters say that the move could ease households' high costs for private tutoring and relieve students' stress. But opponents claim that demand for private tutoring for English could be shifted to other key subjects, such as mathematics and Korean.

▪ Reforming Colleges and Universities

The education ministry finalized a blueprint for reforming local colleges and universities in December 2014. The government is seeking to cut the entrance quota by 160,000 by 2023. In the first phase of the plan, the government plans to reduce the number of new college students by 40,000 by 2017.

It will evaluate the performances of 18 universities and 16 colleges and classify them into grades, which will also affect the government's financial support to those universities. The government plans to unveil a list of universities eligible for state financial support in August 2016.

It will also push for taking a graded approach to decide on the entrance quota for each university based on the results of the evaluation. Education experts expressed opposition against the government's plan, saying that the practice of ranking universities will be intensified and provincial private colleges are more likely to bear the brunt of the university reform drive.

▪ Nurturing Universities in Local Provinces

A law on the balanced nurturing of universities in provincial areas was passed at the National Assembly at the end of 2013. The Cabinet also approved an enforcement ordinance on fostering provincial universities in July 2014.

The moves paved the way for universities in regional areas to pick some high school graduates from specific areas. The enforcement ordinance on the so-called regional allocation of admitting high-qualified students allows local universities to select students in six provinces, including Chungcheong, Honam and Jeju.

If public institutions and companies that have more than 300 permanent workers fill more than 35% of their new positions with talented people with regional backgrounds, they will be eligible to receive financial and other benefits from provincial governments.

According to the education ministry, the employment rate for graduates from regional universities stood at 55.8% in 2013, compared with 56.7% in universities located in and around Seoul. But in 2014, the corresponding rate for regional universities came in at 55.1%, compared with 54.3% for their rivals in Seoul's metropolitan area.

▪ Strengthening Vocational Education

The education ministry made efforts to increase vocational training for high school students. In November 2014, the government announced its decision to select nine model high schools that will specialize in vocational training similar to those in Switzerland and Germany.

A total of 50 students at the designated schools will be able to receive intensive apprentice-type training in companies during their second and third year.

The government plans to operate such vocational education in 2015 and to expand the specialized high schools to 41 in 2016. The education and labor ministries announced the master plan to create a merit-based society by strengthening education via on-the-job training.

The government will introduce the in-the-field semester on a pilot operation that calls for college students to receive on-the-job training at companies for one semester. In addition, junior colleges are expected to adopt the high-skill master program, under which students will be apprenticed to experts.

The government also plans to help university students take a long-term break for at least six weeks to undergo on-the-job training. The move will help college students connect what they learn at colleges to what they learn at workplaces. In particular, several smaller firms will be able to establish in-house colleges together. The move is aimed at giving more workers a chance to learn.

PRE-SCHOOL EDUCATION AND PRIMARY, SECONDARY SCHOOLS

■ **Pre-school Education**

The number of kindergartens shot up to 8,453 in 1990 from 901 in 1980 but has been on the decline since 2000 due to the low birthrate. The establishment of new kindergarten has followed such a trend.

Since the number of kindergarteners reached 19,566 in 1965, it had been on the overall rise until 2013 when the number hit 659,265. But in 2014, the number of kindergarteners reached 652,546, down 6,719 from the previous year, affected by South Korea's low birthrate.

The number of kindergarten students increased between 2011 and 2013, which analysts said results from an expansion of the government's education for pre-schoolers.

South Korea adopted the "Nuri Process," which calls for the government to provide preschool fees and child care benefits regardless of parents' income level. In 2012, the government gave such benefits to those aged five and in 2013, the benefits were expanded to those aged between three and four. The move helped more parents send their kids to kindergartens.

■ **Primary Schools**

The number of primary schools reached 6,519 in 1985 after hitting 2,834 in 1945 and 5,125 in 1965. The number of primary schools declined after 1985, reaching 5,267 in 2000. Since then, the number has been on a slight rise, reaching 5,913 in 2013 and 5,934 in 2014.

The number of primary school students came in at 2.78 million in 2013, compared with 4.94 million in 1965. The number of primary school students peaked at 5.75 million in 1970 and since then, the number has dropped. In 2011, the number reached 3.13 million and 2.95 million in 2012. Last year, the number of primary school students came to 2.72 million, compared with 2.78 million a year earlier.

The number of primary school teachers reached 182,672 last year, up from 181,585 in 2013. The number of teachers at elementary schools reached 79,164 in 1965 and 180,625 in 2011.

By gender, the number of male teachers came to 58,957 in 1965 while that of female teachers reached 20,207. But in 1990, the number of female teachers reached 68,604, outweighing that of male teachers at 68,196. In 2014, the number of female teachers accounted for 76.7% of the total elementary school teachers.

The number of students per class reached 29.2 in 2008, marking the first time it fell below 30. The number of students per class declined to 23.2 in 2013 and 22.8 in 2014. The number of students per teacher also has been declining. The corresponding data reached 28.7 in 2001, 19.8 in 2009 and 14.9 in 2014.

■ **Middle Schools**

In 1965, only one in five people had entered middle schools, but that drastically increased to 95.8% in 1980. Since 1995, the entrance rate has been 99.9%.

The number of middle schools amounted to 1,208 in 1965 and 3,166 in 2012. It then reached 3,173 in 2013 and 3,186 in 2014. The number of middle school students peaked at 2.78 million in 1985 after being at 761,341 in 1965. The number of such students declined after 1985, hitting 1.71 million in 2014.

The number of middle school teachers reached 99,931 in 1995, 112,690 in 2013 and 113,340 in 2014. By gender, the portion of male teachers accounted for 83.9% of the total in 1965, but since 1995, the number of female teachers has outnumbered that of male teachers. In 2014, female teachers accounted for 67.9% of all middle school teachers.

The number of students per class has been falling since 1965 when it hit 60.7. The corresponding data reached 38 in 2000, 33 in 2011 and 30.5 in 2014. The number of students per teacher also has been on the decline. In 2014, it reached 15.2, down from 16 in 2013.

■ **High Schools**

The number of high schools, which reached 389 in 1965, has been on the rise and surpassed the 1,000 mark by hitting

1,096 in 1990. In 2010, the number of high schools in South Korea rose to 1,561. The number of specialized high schools reached 692 in 2010, up from 312 in 1965.

Since 2011, different types of high schools have been created. The number of regular high schools reached 1,520 in 2014, while 164 newly designated autonomous private schools were established. The number of high schools with a special purpose reached 143, and that of specialized schools amounted to 499.

The number of high school students reached 254,095 in 1965 and 1.47 million in 1990. That of specialized high school students came in at 172,436 in 1965 and 466,129 in 2010.

In 2014, the total number of high school students reached 1.84 million. The number of regular high school students reached 1.31 million and that of high schools with special purposes reached 66,928. The number of specialized high school students reached 313,449 and that of autonomous private schools came in at 10,442 in 2014.

The number of teachers at regular high schools reached 90,735 in 2010, up from 7,894 in 1965. That of teachers at specialized high schools came to 35,688 in 2010, up from 6,214 in 1965.

In 2014, the number of teachers at regular high schools reached 90,174 and that of teachers at high schools with special purposes came in at 6,934. The number of teachers at specialized high school reached 26,939 and that of autonomous private schools reached 10,442 in 2014.

TERTIARY EDUCATION

■ College

The number of colleges rose to 128 in 1980 from 48 in 1965. The number has since fluctuated, falling for 12 years before rising and reaching 161 in 1999 and then falling again, reaching 139 in 2014. The number of college students reached 23,159 in 1965. The number then increased to 925,963 in 2003. It declined to 76,929 in 2009 due to a fall in the overall number of students. In 2014, it reached 74,801.

The employment rate for college graduates rose to 72.6% after hitting 57.5% in 1965. But it declined to around 50-60% between 1975 and 1985. The employment rate began to rise in the 1990s and hit 86.5% in 2009. In 2014, the rate stood at 61.4%.

■ Universities and Graduate Schools

The number of universities reached 70 in 1965 and 100 in 1980. It has been on the sustained rise and reached 189 in 2014. The number of state and public universities reached 14 in 1965 and rose to 35 in 2014. That of private universities reached 56 in 1965 and rose to 154 in 2014.

The number of university students hit 105,643 in 1965 and surpassed the 1-million mark in 1990 with 1.04 million. In 2012, there were 2.1 million students and 2.12 million in 2013. Last year, the number stood at 2.13 million. The portion of male to female students came in at 3.4 to 1 in 1965 and 1.5 to 1 in 2014.

The employment rate for university graduates reached 65% in 2005, 67.3% in 2006 and 68.9% in 2008. But the rate hit 68.2% in 2009 and declined to 55.6% in 2013. In 2014, the employment rate for university graduates fell to 54.8%.

KEY DEVELOPMENTS IN EDUCATION CIRCLES

■ Suspension of Field Trips Following Ferry Sinking

Negative sentiment toward field trips has increased since the deadly ferry sinking in April last year claimed the lives of high school students on a field trip. The incident raised concerns about student safety.

Many parents expressed opposition against field trips, calling on education authorities to abolish them. Due to growing concerns about safety, local schools canceled plans to go on field trips or suspended them.

The education ministry and related agencies launched the plan to check student safety. The government ordered schools to cancel field trips in the spring semester last year.

The government again permitted schools to resume field trips starting in July last year and drew up measures aimed at securing the safety of students on field trips.

Schools resumed their field trips in the fall semester gradually, but the landscape has been totally changed since the ferry sinking as schools put a priority on safety and planned field trips with small groups.

Seoul operated a new program that assigned rescue workers for safety education for field trips arranged by 30 designated schools between September and November.

Rescue workers conducted safety education for teachers and students before going on the field trips, such as cardiopulmonary resuscitation. They also dealt with emergency relief and first aid when accidents occur and checked safety of lodgings and buses that students used.

But parents' concerns about safety persisted, causing schools to delay or cancel trips. The number of schools that canceled field trips increased due to stringent safety standards.

■ Anti-Gov't Protest by Progressive Teachers' Union

The Korean Teachers and Education Workers Union (KTU), a progressive teachers' union, lodged a protest with the government as it was outlawed by the labor ministry in 2013.

On Oct. 24, 2013, the labor ministry notified the union it needed to revise its rules that allowed fired teachers to enter the union. But as the teachers' union defied the order, the government decided to outlaw the KTU due to its repeated refusal to deny membership to fired teachers.

The 60,000-strong KTU currently has 22 teachers who were sacked for signing statements against the former Lee Myung-bak government in 2009 as members.

The union filed a lawsuit with the Seoul Administrative Court against the labor minister last year, but the court ruled on June 19 last year that the union is not a legitimate labor group because it allows membership of fired teachers.

In a ruling statement, the court said the decision by the Ministry of Employment and Labor is not unconstitutional. The education ministry quickly ordered the union's 78 full-time staff members to return to their teaching jobs.

Should the ruling be upheld by the top court, the KTU would be prohibited from using the title "labor union" and from engaging in negotiations with school authorities.

Even as the ruling came out, 13 newly elected superintendents vowed to recognize the union as a legitimate labor group, raising tension with the government. A large number of the superintendents expressed opposition against the government's follow-up measures that came after the ruling.

The KTU appealed the ruling and filed an injunction. In June last year, it declared the launch of an "all-out struggle" against the government, starting with a partial walkout of teachers. The constitutional court will now decide whether the union can be recognized as a legitimate labor group.

■ Era of Progressive Superintendents

After a law revision in 2006, progressive education superintendents were elected in 13 areas out of 17 in a local election in June 2014. The number was a rise from 2010 when progressive superintendents were elected in six areas out of 16. Eight out of the elected progressive superintendents were members of the KTU.

During an election campaign, they laid out key campaign pledges to eliminate irregularities in education circles and normalize public education. After the elections, progressive education policies gained traction, including environment-friendly free school lunches and an ordinance on students' human rights.

Since Jang Huy Kook, Gwangju's education superintendent, was elected as the head of a nationwide group of superintendents, education superintendents' opinions about education policies and related issues were actively delivered to the central government.

Progressive superintendents rejected the government's punitive actions against the KTU, lending support to the progressive union's protest against the government.

Movement to Going to School at 9:00 a.m.

On Sept. 1, 2014, an education policy to allow students to go to school at 9:00 a.m. was first implemented in Gyeonggi Province, outside of Seoul. The policy was aimed at guaranteeing students' right to sleep and live a healthy life. On the first day, 90.1% of schools in the province implemented it.

As progressive education superintendents are supportive of such a policy, the number of schools adopting the policy is expected to increase, experts say. The policy led to more students having breakfast at home in Gyeonggi Province.

The number of students who dozed off at school also fell as they got enough sleep at home. But there are many schools that voiced complaints about the policy as the provincial office of education adopted the policy by force without garnering enough consensus from schools.

Anti-Discrimination Protest by Irregular Workers at School

A group of some 600,000 irregular workers at schools staged an all-out walkout on Nov. 20-21, 2014, to call for the elimination of discrimination at schools.

In response, workers who did not join the strike provided lunch to students at school cafeterias. Students were also advised to bring their own lunch to school or were given bread and milk by schools.

The number of schools that could not offer lunch reached 900 nationwide on the first day of the walkout. but the number declined to about 620 on the second day as provincial offices of education reached a deal with regional sections of the group.

The strike ended without big mayhem, but the group vowed to wage another all-out strike if the government does not offer measures to improve their working conditions.

Sharp Rise in Voluntary Retirement

The number of teachers applying for voluntary retirement shot up in opposition of the government's reform of the public servant pension system. But a lack of budget allocated to central and provincial offices of education made it difficult for them to accept the applications.

Experts said that a rise in applications for voluntary retirement resulted from the government's move to reform public servants' pension scheme and growing frustration faced by teachers at school.

As of end-February, 5,164 teachers applied for early retirement to 17 city and provincial offices of education, but only 2,818 applications, or 54.6%, were accepted. The number was dwarfed by the 90.3% recorded in 2013.

The Seoul Metropolitan Office of Education received 3,644 of such applications in 2014, but the acceptance ratio reached 15% due to a lack of budget. The office secured 256 billion won in budget via a bond sale to prepare for teachers' early retirement in 2015.

Wrangle over Budgets for Kindergartens

Last year, the government and provincial offices of education locked horns over budget allocation for kindergartens related to support for pre-schoolers.

South Korea adopted the "Nuri Process," which calls for the government to provide pre-school fees and child care benefits regardless of parents' income level. In 2012 the government gave such benefits to those aged five, and in 2013 the benefits were expanded to those aged three and four.

The provincial offices of education called for the government to offer state funds for the operation of the Nuri Process. But the government repeated its stance that it is impossible to give state financial support. In October, an association of education decided not to allocate part of budget to support kindergartens in protest of the government.

Amid growing concerns about a "debacle" over child care, the government issued bonds worth 1.1 trillion won in November to provide money for paying retirement allowance to provincial offices of education.

The provincial offices of education had decided to partially allocate the budget to support kindergartens. The Seoul Metropolitan Office of Education set aside such budget for three months while other provincial offices of education allocated money at their disposal.

Support for the Nuri Process is given to kindergartens in loans by mayors and governors. But education offices in Seoul, Gwangju and some other cities could not allocate the budget for two or three months, raising concerns about their financial soundness.

■ Tension Surrounding Autonomous Private School

Cho Hee-yeon, superintendent at the Seoul Metropolitan Office of Education, pushed ahead with the move to abolish autonomous private schools, his key election campaign, pitting himself against the education ministry.

A total of 25 autonomous private schools across the country should be reviewed for eligibility by relevant offices of education every five years. The Seoul office assessed 14 autonomous private schools in Seoul last year based on their performances over the past four years to decide whether to re-designate them as such schools.

The schools in question gained a passing mark in June when Cho's predecessor led the office. But Cho conducted the second review on those schools after his inauguration, with more than half of them not passing.

Raising the issue of fairness over assessment standards, a group of parents whose children went to autonomous private schools and an association of principals at such schools threatened to take legal actions. In response, Cho announced the plan to unveil the final results at end-October based on another assessment by revising the scoring criteria.

But the 14 schools vowed not to take

▲ *Seoul's top educator Cho Hee-yeon speaks during a press conference at the Seoul Metropolitan Office of Education on Oct. 31. Cho said that six schools will lose their licenses to be "autonomous" private high schools and become ordinary schools.*

the test, claiming that they passed the first assessment. In October, the Seoul Metropolitan Office of Education revoked its designation of six autonomous private schools and suspended the cancelation for two years.

The education ministry ordered the Seoul office to cancel its decision to revoke the designation. As the office disobeyed, the education ministry cancelled the education office's decision. The education ministry said that Cho overused its authority and discretionary power, violating related laws.

The move helped the six autonomous private schools keep their status even after 2016. But the Seoul Metropolitan Office of Education filed a lawsuit with the Supreme Court in December last year, calling for the lower court to cancel the education ministry's decision.

Culture

CULTURE POLICY

■ **Overview**

The core policy direction of the Ministry of Culture, Sports and Tourism for the year 2014 called for cultural prosperity that can cater to common citizens.

The ministry's main achievement connected with the 2014 policy direction included the event "Culture Day", which was hailed for its drawing of public attention to culture, as well as welfare measures to help artists and the introduction of a fixed price system for book sales.

But the abrupt dismissal of former Culture Minister Yoo Jin-ryong, the first minister selected from inside the ministry, and the following one-month vacancy of the top position drew criticism.

■ **Laying Groundwork for Everyday Cultural Enjoyment**

Designed by the Presidential Committee for Cultural Enrichment and the culture ministry, the Culture Day event provided free or discounted admission to various cultural programs every Wednesday from January for 12 weeks with the aim to help citizens gain access to more cultural activities.

With increased participation by cultural institutions and a favorable reaction from citizens, the event expanded in size every month. A largely increased budget of 9 billion won was earmarked for the program for 2015 amid the success.

The National Hangeul Museum opened in October with an aim to publicize the cultural value of the local language.

The King Sejong Institute, which provides overseas education programs for hangeul and Korean culture, saw the number of its overseas offices expand by 10 in three more countries in 2014 from 120 in 51 foreign countries as of 2013. The accumulated number of students at the King Sejong Institute also grew to 40,000.

Following the launch of more welfare assistance intended for artists, a total of 820 artists benefitted from occupational health and safety insurance programs in 2014. Another 1,600 low-income artists also received emergency welfare assistance intended to help their creative activities.

The introduction of a new law aimed at boosting the so-called Mecenat, or corporate assistance to the art sector, in July, also helped sharply increase corporate sponsorship to the art industry. Corporate-artist collaborations expanded by 65% on-year to a total of 192 cases in 2014, while the annual size of corporate donation exceeded 5 billion won.

■ Forming a Fair Environment for the Contents Industry

The Ministry of Culture, Sports and Tourism increased efforts to pave a level playing field for the file, broadcasting and contents industry by setting up guidelines for forging business contracts.

Especially, an agreement was made with the movie industry to rationalize the process to allocate movie screens in order to guarantee diversity in film screenings.

The groundwork was laid for efforts to formulate a sound publishing culture by putting a fixed book price system into force on Nov. 11. The system prohibits price discounts of more than 15% on all books. Although the regulation is basically designed to control excessive price competition in book sales and to help boost business for small book sellers, it also drew criticism for higher book prices.

In a bid to better support business ventures in the cultural contents sector, the culture ministry established the so-called Contents Korea Lab in five regions including Seoul, Busan and Incheon under a three-year plan. Other investment encouragement programs were also active including the launch of a 20 billion won fund to boost contents development.

■ Personnel Problems Including Replacement of Minister

Chung Sung-keun, who was nominated to replace former Culture Minister Yoo Jin-ryong, resigned during a parliamentary confirmation hearing in July and the minister seat was then left empty for a month. Kim Jong-deok, an art professor from Hongik University, later filled the vacancy in late August.

A flurry of personnel measures was taken in the following 100 days after Kim took office in order to stabilize the troubled ministry. But it was again thrust into the spotlight as former Minister Yoo was involved in a political meddling scandal surrounding presidential aides in late 2014.

MASS COMMUNICATION

NEWSPAPER

■ Journalists Decried as Trash Following a Ferry Accident

Public outcry over the press reached its peak after the tragic sinking of the ferry Sewol on April 16. The press churned out heady stories in heated competition in the aftermath of the tragic accident.

The press only repeated the government's unilateral announcement on the disaster, leading to false reports that incorrectly said all the passengers aboard the ferry were safely rescued. This led to heightened public outcry and criticism. The public denounced the entire press industry as trash and the unfavorable notion still remained in many citizens.

The Korean Association of Newspapers and four other media associations jointly established media guidelines on national disaster stories, which included ways to respect victims' human rights and to bolster the safety of journalists, all in efforts to raise media standards in a disaster situation. The guidelines endorsed by 15 media associations put accuracy ahead of speed in covering disaster situations.

■ Scandal Involving Seoul Branch of Sankei Daily and Segye Ilbo

Japan's Sankei Shimbun daily claimed in its Aug. 3 issue that President Park Geun-hye had disappeared for seven hours the day the ferry Sewol sank on April 16, citing a local newspaper column.

In the story, the Sankei indicated that Park's chief of staff Kim Ki-choon said in a parliamentary session in July that he did not know the whereabouts of the president on the day of the accident and that President Park is in a relationship with Jeong Yun-hoe, her former aide who was often reported to hold unofficial power in the government.

In return, the presidential office Cheong Wa Dae filed a lawsuit against Tatsuya Kato, the former chief of Sankei's Seoul unit, and the prosecution indicted him on online defamation charges, leading to wild criticism for violation of free expression from media at home and abroad, as well as civil rights groups.

▲ Tatsuya Kato, former head of the Seoul bureau of Japan's conservative Sankei Shimbun newspaper, enters a courtroom in Seoul on Nov. 27. He has been accused of libel after he reported that President Park Geun-hye held a secret meeting with an unidentified man during the early hours of April's deadly ferry sinking.

Segye Ilbo carried in its Nov. 28 issue a document tilted "The rumor on the replacement of the presidential chief of staff and latest information on VIP's closest aide (Jeong Yun-hoe)," created by Cheong Wa Dae's government official discipline office as well as the photo of the document.

The report said that Jeong met with Park's three key aides to share information on personnel and state affairs, and that Jeong tried to exert influence on personnel decisions for presidential officials, including chief of staff Kim Ki-choon.

In response, the presidential office dismissed the report, saying the reported document is only a minor compilation of stock market rumors. It also expressed a plan to take legal action against the newspaper.

On the same day, Cheong Wa Dae filed a defamation suit against Segye Ilbo, but the prosecution failed to raid the newspaper's headquarters in the face of the opposition bloc's strong criticism.

■ The Electronics Times Co.'s Defeat in Fight Against Samsung

The Internet-based Electronics Times Co. reported on March 17 that Samsung was short in its camera lens production for the Galaxy S5 and the problem may undermine the electronics firm's production schedule for the Galaxy S5 line.

Samsung Electronics rejected the report as groundless and demanded a revision, but the Internet media published a similar report, leading to a long series of news reports followed by rebuttals.

With The Electronics Times showing no sign of surrender, Samsung filed a compensation suit on April 3 against the Internet news site and its journalists. Samsung also discontinued its advertisement relations with the media outlet, further adding pressure.

Ending six months of fighting, The Electronics Times admitted on its homepage for two days from Sept. 25 that Samsung's camera lens production was stable at the time of the initial report and Samsung had no difficulties in churning out the Galaxy S5 model.

Following the admission, Samsung dropped its legal suits against The Electronics Times and its reporters, but people in the media said the result was not only a surrender to Samsung, but also a death sentence for Internet media.

■ Decrease in Newspaper Market and Increase in Number of Journalists

The newspaper market has shrank in size for two years in a row, but the overall number of journalists gained ground on the back of growth in online media.

The Korean Press Foundation said in its 2014 research of the newspaper market that the total sales of the press sector -- newspapers and Internet outlets -- stood at 3.54 trillion won in 2013, down 5.2% from a year earlier.

Newspapers accounted for 88.8% of all press sales with revenue of 3.15 trillion won, while combined sales of Internet news media reached 396 billion won. The newspaper market recorded a 3.5% drop on-year while their online rivals posted a decline of 16.9%.

For the newspaper sector, sales from advertisement stood at 1.98 trillion won while subscription sales came to 584.4 billion won, a on-year drop of 5.2 and 11.7%, respectively.

As of 2013, a total 33,495 people were working for the newspaper sector, down 10.6% from a year earlier. Among the total, the number of journalists grew 2.7% from the previous year, a result attributable to more journalists being employed by Internet news outlets.

Chosun Ilbo was the No. 1 seller in terms of the number of copies published as of 2013, according to the Korea Audit Bureau of Circulation or KABC. Chosun published a total of 1.76 million copies in 2013.

Combined copies published by the top 10 of the total 153 local newspapers reached 6.42 million, down 5.75% from a year earlier.

BROADCASTING

▪ Overview

The year 2014 started with a wild fever over popular TV series "My Love from the Star," produced by Seoul Broadcasting System, and ended with an influx of so-called "China money" into the local popular culture market.

The TV series, aired from Dec. 18, 2013 to Feb. 27, 2014, turned out to be a viral sensation in China and this led to a revival of the Korean Wave, or Hallyu, there. Against this backdrop, investment from China or China money, which has been

▲ *An exhibition featuring the sets and props of SBS drama "My love from the star" opens in the Dongdaemun Design Plaza from Oct. 10 to Oct. 15, 2014.*

expanding worldwide, also infiltrated Korean popular culture.

South Korea and China also saw their pop cultures come closer with the marriages of Korean director Kim Tae-yong to Chinese actress Tang Wei, and Korean actress Chae Lim to Chinese actor Gao Zi Qi.

The forging of a free trade agreement between the two countries also prompted Korea to move its Hallyu sales pitch completely to China from Japan.

Fluent Korean-speaking foreigners adorned local TV entertainment programs while the formats of popular local TV programs were exported overseas.

▪ Growth of Korean Drama Series Exports, Korean Stars Tapping Chinese Market

Thanks to the success of "My Love from the Star," the export of Hallyu drama series to China posted sharp growth in 2014. While one episode of a Korean series was sold to China for about US$10,000 in early 2013, the corresponding price tag for another popular series, "The Heirs" starring Lee Min-ho and Park Shin-hye, was US$30,000, while the price of "My Love from the Star" further rose to US$40,000.

With the steep export growth of Korean soap opera series, another series called "Pinocchio" again broke the record by exporting its 20-episode program for a total of 6.2 billion won. This translated into US$280,000 per episode.

More Korean stars tapped into the Chinese market. Lee Min-ho, Kim Soo-hyun and Jun Ji-hyun emerged as popular commercial market models, while Song Hye-kyo, Kim Tae-hee, Rain and other actors were cast in Chinese productions.

▪ Growth in Export of TV Program Format, Entrance into U.S. Market

A number of local TV variety shows, including "Gag Concert," "Dad! Where Are We Going?," "Running Man," and "Grandpas Over Flowers" saw their program formats exported to China and produced into Chinese versions in 2014.

The Chinese show "Running Man China: Hurry Up Brother," jointly produced by SBS and Zhejiang Television, posted over 1% viewing rating for its inaugural airing and jumped to the mostly viewed program when aired the second time.

The story lines of local drama series "Good Doctor" and "My Love from the Star" were also exported to U.S. broadcasters CBS and ABC while local variety show "Grandpas Over Flowers" was sold to NBC in the United States.

TV Market Swept with Foreigners and Hit Drama Series

The local TV variety show market was also inundated with Korean-speaking foreigners in 2014. JTBC's "Non Summit" and MBC's "Hello, Stranger" focused solely on foreigners' stories and other reality shows like "Real Man" also included foreigners in the main cast.

Following the mega hit "My Love from the Star," the local drama industry had been dormant with just moderate success of MBC drama "Jang Bo-ri is Here!" and KBS' "Jeong Do-jeon."

Cable Channels registered a better performance with tvN making a sensational hit with its drama series "Misaeng," which depicts a young office worker's life at a trading company.

NEW MEDIA

Rise of New Media in the Era of Mobile First Environment

Eric Schmidt, Google's chairman, declared that the future of the media sector is the mastery of mobile gadgets, by saying in November 2014 that it is "about not just mobile first, but mobile only." The declaration is based on the widespread adoption of smartphones and tablets as well as the fast development of mobile networks.

The "mobile first" phenomenon was mostly pronounced in the broadcasting sector with the development of streaming technology. Increased video footage service led to more heated competition in telecommunications, Internet connection, cable TV and other media markets. Mobile users dominated content markets like music and online games. The change also led to the sharp growth of the mobile advertisement market.

Mobile Video Service OTT (Over the Top)

OTT (over the top) means additional gadgets attached to electronic devices. An OTT dongle connected to an Internet-connected PC or digital TV provides access to VOD and TV programs in real-time through streaming services.

Google's Chromecast, launched in 2013, is one example that enables users to watch TV broadcasting for only 49,000 won. Chromecast was launched in May 2014 in South Korea, with the device launching in 27 foreign nations overall. For 2014, a total of 10 million units were sold worldwide, and users used the device an accumulated 1 billion times.

About 6,000 developers from around the world came up with over 10,000 applications for Chromecast, including domestically developed Tving and Hopping.

Local cable broadcasting operator CJ Hellow Vision was the most active player for the OTT business locally. Just three months after the launch of Chromecast, the local firm launched Tving Stick in August 2014, in competition against the device.

Like Chromecast, Tving Stick, when connected to a TV or computer monitor, provides access to about 150 broadcasting channels and 50,000 VODs. The local firm plans to launch a remote-controlled OTT device in 2015 to gain a edge in the market.

Another cable channel operator, HCN, which operates Everyon TV, also launched OTT dongle 'Everyon TV Cast' in February 2014, and plans to launch a second version in 2015.

The domestic OTT market, which totaled 149 billion won as of 2013, will expand four-fold to 634.5 billion won by 2019, market research firm Strabase forecast in its research into the OTT industry.

The number of smartphones in use exceeded 40 million units as of 2014 locally. As the local communications network advanced to long term evolution (LTE), the quality and stability of OTT service also improved. Strengthening video services on major portal sites also helped the speedy spread of OTT service.

Naver's TVcast began offering broadcasting content from January 2015 and

Daum Kakao is also expected to launch a similar service within the year. At the instruction of chairman Kim Bum-soo, Daum Kakao embarked on a plan to bolster video service. So far the video service market had been dominated by YouTube.

More changes are expected for the year 2016 as the most successful N-screen video streaming platform Netflix is set to enter the local market.

Netflix reportedly has dispatched a team to South Korea to prepare for the local launch. Upon the monthly payment of US$8.99, users gain access to an unlimited number of films and TV series. The firm has secured about 57 million subscribers in 50 foreign countries while its 2014 sales reached 4.8 trillion won.

■ Downtrend of Paid Broadcasting Service, Spread of Zero TV

As smartphones made it possible to watch real-time broadcasting or VOD at anytime anywhere, people began to leave the sofa in front of TV sets at home. Instead, they now can enjoy videos at their desired time.

According to a survey by DMC Media in 2014, 89% of the 500 people polled said they watch VOD on their smartphones. One out of every three people said they have used N-screen service.

As Netflix gained popularity in the U.S., the so-called "cord cutting" phenomenon began to spread. According to market research firm Experian, a total of 7.6 million U.S. people ended their subscriptions to television service during 2013.

About 12.4% of TV viewers aged 35 or younger cut the cord, a reading which is double the average recorded for the entire group. The trend is also visible at home with the growth of N-screen-based video services like Tving, Everyon TV and Africa TV.

Tving, serviced by CJ Hello Vision, saw the number of subscribers reach 6.8 million as of February 2015. It was a growth of 20 times since the number stood at 300,000 in 2010. It is expected to grow further to 7 million in the first half of 2015.

SK Planet's Hopping and Pooq, the joint platform for ground wave broadcasters, gathered subscribers of 4.5 million and 3 million, respectively. The combined subscribers of mobile IPTV services by three mobile carriers -- KT, SK Broadband and LG UPlus -- reached over 5 million as of early 2015.

As the growth of N-screen-based video streaming service combined with the spread of OTT service, the notion of so-called "zero TV" emerged. U.S.-based Nielsen Media Research highlighted the emergence of the zero TV era in which more people view broadcasting without any payment.

Zero TV refers to the phenomenon in which TV programs are streamed on smartphones, tablet PCs or desktop PCs on the back of the growth of smart media. It is called zero TV because viewer ratings are not recorded since most TV contents are consumed without subscriptions.

About 4% of local households belong to the zero TV group, according to a recent survey. The ratio of the zero TV group may not shrink down the road given that 55% of the households that do not currently subscribe to paid broadcasting services have not paid for subscription broadcasting services for the past four years, according to the Korea Information Society Development Institute.

■ IPTV Subscribers Exceed 10 Million, Growth of T-Commerce Market

The number of subscribers to IPTV services offered by the three local telecommunications firms exceeded the 10 million mark as of August 2014.

First put into public service in January 2009, IPTV service quickly amassed subscribers and surpassed the 1 million mark in September the same year. The number of subscribers again rose to 3 million in December 2010 and 5 million in April 2012.

Further growth pushed the number to 10 million, five years and seven months after the first launch. Continuing launches of new services combined with discount offers contributed to such fast growth, industry watchers said.

Despite the quantitative growth, growth in quality is being held back because of the growing cost of supplying content with scarce income in broadcasting, critics said.

Amid decreasing advertisement revenue in 2014, ground wave broadcasters demanded a 50% hike in the price of one VOD program to 1,500 won a piece, stirring tension with IPTV service providers and cable TV broadcasters.

The IPTV sector is racing to the T commerce market, or TV-based electronic commerce, in order to break out of the loss-making structure and to create added value. A meager subscription base had previously made it hard to vitalize the T commerce market, but the speedy growth of subscribers to the 10 million mark boosted the developed of the sector.

SK Broadband, which operates B tv, launched in November 2014 the shopping channel 'B Shopping' through Olleh TV as well as its mobile web.

■ Sensational Popularity of Streamed Music and Radio

Listening to music or radio through streaming services was as popular as watching streamed video. The merit of a random collection of free music pushed Samsung Electronics and KT, as well as other electronics makers and wireless carriers to race to join the market.

After launching its first radio streaming service "Milk" in the U.S. in March 2014, Samsung Electronics launched the service locally in September. Four months after the local launch, a total of 3 million downloads were recorded. About 1.5 million people were estimated to use Milk on mobile devices every month.

KT's "Music Hug" also saw the number of users double in the past 10 months. One Music Hug user listened to an average of 47 songs over a duration of 188 minutes every day.

Free radio streaming application "Beat," listed among the top 30 applications chosen by Google in 2014, exceeded 2 million in membership 11 months after it first launched.

■ Advertisement Sales by Ground Wave Broadcaster Down, Those by Mobile Media in Steep Growth

According to a 2014 survey by the Korea Broadcast Advertising Corp. (KOBACO), South Korea's total advertisement revenue came to 10.97 trillion won in 2014, up 1.6% from 10.8 trillion won recorded a year earlier.

Advertisement revenue by KBS stood at 522.9 billion won in 2014, 10.9% less than 580 billion won posted a year earlier. That by MBC also fell 8.2% on-year to 664.8 billion won.

The advertisement revenue by newspapers and magazines dropped by 4.1% and 7%, respectively, from a year earlier, recording a combined decrease of 4.8%.

On the other hand, advertisement revenue by smart media like smartphones, smart TVs, Internet or IPTV jumped 11.3% from 2013 to post 3.3 trillion won in 2014. Advertisement in mobile media especially skyrocketed 52.4% to post 725 billion won in 2014.

PUBLISHING

■ Overview

The publication industry in 2014 was dominated by the implementation of the long-pursued fixed-price book sale system. One-source-multi-use production, which uses one story line for publication and video production, became a major trend.

The comic book series that was the base story for web cartoon "Misaeng" and the subsequent TV series with the same name, posted sales of 2 million units. Chronic financial problems festering in the publication and circulation industries remain tasks to be addressed as well as hoarding and royalty issues.

■ Introduction of Fixed Book Price System

The fixed book price system was put into force on Nov. 21, 2014, prohibiting book discounts of more than 15%. It had been feverishly pushed by the publication industry for the past seven years. The new system is also designed to regulate the prices of old books that have been on sale for more than one and a half years, paving the way for competition based on value rather than price.

The implementation of the new system also helped bring together the government, the publication and distribution industries, as well as writers and private book buyers to jointly pledge efforts to work toward the creation of sound reading culture. But criticism remains that the fixed price system passes the burden of higher book prices on to consumers.

■ Popularity of Publication Based on History, Rise of Stories of Historic Heroes

The key word dominating best-selling books was history, with stories based on historial figures likes Jeong Do-jeon and Yi Sun-sin gaining popularity.

The success of the film "The Admiral: Roaring Currents" in the second half of 2014 led to brisk sales of writer Kim Joon's best-selling book "The Song of the Sword." The film based on the historic admiral also led to the publication of a flurry of books on Yi Sun-sin.

Along with outstanding history-themed books like "The Annals of the Joseon Dynasty" by Park Si-baek and "My Korean Contemporary History" by Rhyu Si-min, "The Hundred-Year-Old Man Who Climbed Out of the Window and Disappeared" and "The Girl Who Saved the King of Sweden," both by Jonas Jonasson, were all based on primary moments of contemporary history.

The comic book fever brewing around Yoon Tae-ho's "Misaeng" series continued into 2014 from 2013, and was even boosted further following the TV series adaptation. The nine-volume comic book series exceeded sales of 2 million books, opening a new chapter for the local comic book industry.

Thomas Piketty's book "Capital in the Twenty-First Century" became one of best-selling translated academic pieces. Publisher SallimBooks' Sallim Knowledge series issued its 500th book despite the largely unfavorable market environment.

■ Scandal Hits Star Publishing Firm

After a successful year with best-selling self-help books, rising star publishing firm SamNParkers faced a major sexual harrassment scandal involving its executive in charge of marketing.

It was a tepid year for the electronic book industry. But online bookseller Yes24's ambitious acquisition of reference book publisher Doosan Donga boosted expectations by heralding the online firm's entry into the electronic book market.

ADVERTISING

■ Local Advertisement Remains Languid Despite Big Sports Event

Domestic advertisement grew little in 2014 when many high-profile sports events were held, including the Winter Olympics, World Cup and Asian Games. The total local advertisement sales in 2014 reached 9.65 trillion won, according to a tally by ad agency Cheil Worldwide. It was growth of only 0.6% from a year earlier.

The gloomy mood from the national tragedy of the sinking of the ferry Sewol in April led to the contraction of companies marketing operations and South Korea's unsuccessful bid in the World Cup round of 16 also discouraged consumers' appetite. Growing household debt and other economic uncertainties at home and abroad also hampered private spending.

Ground wave broadcasters registered 1.7 trillion won in advertisement revenue in 2014, down 8% from a year earlier. The decline came in the aftermath of the rise of Internet protocol television and the so-called Nscreen service. Advertisement revenue by cable TV operators rose 3.8% on-year to 1.4 trillion won.

Popular drama series and variety shows also led the growth of general cable TV channels run by four newspapers. All of the four -- TV Chosun, JTBC, Channel A and MBN -- posted sales revenue 10% higher than the previous year.

On the back of increased subscription and expanded popularity of VOD (video on demand), advertisement revenue by IPTV also jumped 67% on year.

The mobile advertisement market also posted steep growth, with its advertisement revenue rocketing 82.4% from 2013 to reach 839.1 billion won in 2014. It was the biggest rate of growth compared to other sectors.

Continuing popularity of the professional baseball league and an increase in advertisement in big shopping malls also led to a gain of 4.6% in out of home advertisement revenue. The size of the public transportation advertisement segment, however, dropped 11.5% on year.

Cheil Worldwide, meanwhile, forecast that the ground-wave broadcasting advertisement market will overcome the blow from the ferry tragedy and IPTV and the mobile markets will continue their upward trend, pushing total advertisement sales up 3.2% to nearly 10 trillion won in 2015. The mobile advertisement industry may increase 20% to a 1 trillion won market.

▪ SK Telecom Commercial Listed as Most Unforgettable Ad in 2014

In a consumer survey by Korea Broadcast advertising Corp., SK Telecom's TV commercials ranked as the most impressive advertisement, by getting 15.5% of the votes.

Three popular commercial models -- Jeon Ji-hyun, Kim Yu-na, and Lee Jung-jae -- appearing in the commercials as well as the easy-to-remember CM song primarily impressed consumers, the KOBACO said.

KT's commercial was listed as second while third place went to the Vita500 commercial that cast Suzy, one of the hottest idols today. LG Uplus' advertisement was ranked fourth with its casting of G-Dragon and soccer star Park Ji-sung.

Jeon Ji-hyun ranked as the most impressive commercial model with 15.9% of the vote. It was her first time to make top three status in the survey.

Suzy came in second place with strong support from male fans, with Kim Soo-hyun listed as the third most popular model. Kim Yu-na stepped down to fourth place after having taken the top position three times previously.

▪ Downtrend in the Volume of Daily Publication

According to a report by the Korea Audit Bureau of Circulation, the total number of circulation by 148 local newspapers came to 10,271,000 in 2014, down 13.7% from a year earlier.

Chosun Ilbo published a total of 1,757,000 copies, the largest number among the 46 national newspaper companies, followed by Joongang Ilbo (1,264,00) and Donga Ilbo (907,000).

Among provincial newspaper publishers, Busan Ilbo ranked as the biggest player with 151,000 copies, followed by Maeil Shinmun based in Daegu (147,000) and Busan-based Kookje Shinmun (10,000).

▪ Legislature on Flexible Advertising System for Ground Wave Broadcasters, Shock Wave Korea Communications Commission Lifted Regulations

The Korea Communications Commission in December announced the introduction of a revised ordinance which gives ground wave broadcasters more leeway in deciding the time and types of advertisement.

The commission had previously put the advertisement of programs at 6 minutes, short advertisements at 3 minutes and caption advertisements at 40 seconds in strict regulations for each type. But the change allowed each broadcaster to determine for itself what type of advertisement will be aired how many times and for how long under the total advertisement time allowed by the new revision.

But the associations for newspapers, magazines and cable TV broadcasters demanded the withdrawal of the new revision which they say will further strengthen the status of ground wave broadcasters. They claimed more advertisements on ground wave channels will lead to a drop in their advertisement sales.

The Korean Broadcasters Association countered that the revision would not have any real effect amid the stagnant economic condition which they fill only 50% of the total advertisement time allowed. The communications watchdog plans to put the new broadcasting ordinance into effect sometime between March and May 2015.

▪ Compulsory Commercial Marking in Text Message and Email Ads

New ordinance and law required advertisers to head their mobile text message or email advertisements with the marking (AD) from November.

Advertisers were also required to make it easy for consumers find how to block advertisements, with the violation of the rule subject to a fine of 30 million won or less.

■ Animation Characters Approved for Broadcasting Advertisement

The Korea Communications Commission relaxed its advertisement regulations to allow the use of animated characters in broadcasting advertisement. Before the revision, animated characters were prohibited for use in advertisements that come after animation programs because of the possible negative impact on children.

The decision came amid criticism that the restriction discourages the animation industry which is struggling to make ends meet.

■ Relaxed Rules on Outdoor Advertisement

A revised ordinance passed through a Cabinet meeting in December to allow street advertisement boards as well as wrapping advertisement on the back of vehicles.

Street advertisement boards were widely used before the revision although it was illegal in principle. The revision requires that the street boards should be used in a way they don't spoil the street landscape or public safety and be placed within the advertisers' building site.

■ VOD Watching to be Included to TV Viewer Rating Counting from 2016

The Korea Communications Commission ruled that from 2016, television programs watched on PCs, smartphones or through VOD services will be counted in when calculating viewer ratings, according to a new viewer rating count system announced by the communications watchdog in December.

ACADEMIA

■ Overview

Following the controversy over the right-leaning high-school history textbook by Kyohak Publishing Co. in 2013, another controversy over claims for state-published history books hit the academic world in 2014.

The shocking tragedy of the Sewol ferry sinking also called for sour searching in the local academic sphere. Academic papers delved into different perspectives on how the Sewol accident affected South Korean society.

■ Controversy over State-designated History Textbooks after Controversy over Kyohak Publishing Co.

Kyohak Publishing Co. came under fire for its controversial high-school textbook that was accused of embellishing pro-Japan figures and the dictatorship. Only one school decided to use the controversial textbook.

Amid rising public criticism, several other high schools withdrew their decisions to adopt the textbook with only Buseong High School in the southern port city of Busan sticking to its adoption of the book. After spearheading the decision to adopt the controversial Kyohak textbook, the Busan high school's headmaster ran for a regional election held on June 4 under the banner of eradicating pro-North Korea leftists and reform of the right wing.

The controversy over the Kyohak textbook was followed by a new push to publish state-approved history textbooks, which roiled the academic and education sectors throughout the year.

The idea of state-approved history textbooks, proposed by the ruling party and conservative bloc, was based on claims that the current history book adoption process is subject to frequent ideology disputes and the front-line education segment is forced to sustain damage from the dispute.

The current approval system allows each school to freely choose from among history course books approved by education authorities. And the ruling party and the conservative bloc claimed the current system should be changed to allow only one kind of history textbook to be published by the government and to be used nationwide.

The idea of a state history textbook was first mentioned by former Prime Minster Chung Hong-won and ruling

Saenuri Party leader Kim Moo-sung amid the controversy over the right-leaning textbook in 2013, and the issue gained further traction the following year.

The opposition parties, however, denounced the proposal as a return to the Yushin era. Major historical academic groups also bitterly criticized the proposal, saying that will limit students' learning of a wide spectrum of historical perspectives.

■ Sewol Ferry Tragedy Left South Korea Society Soul Searching

The tragedy of the Sewol ferry sinking left big homework for the local academic world. Scholars have agreed that the maritime accident shed light on South Korea's problems in individual ethics, incriminate profit-seeking by companies, the non-permanent employee sector and media reporting as well as the corruption front.

Under the environment, academic quarterlies attempted to address the academic meaning of the incident. Both conservative and progressive papers shared the assessment that the Sewol tragedy laid bare South Korean society's deep-rooted problems.

■ S. Korea-Japan Ties Further Worsen, Scholars from Two Countries Concerned

Local scholars continued to express concerns over worsening South Korea-Japan relations since the beginning of 2014 when some Japanese politicians' rash historical remarks strained bilateral ties.

In January, the Northeast Asian History Foundation hosted an academic conference in which scholars from both countries voiced concerns over souring bilateral ties as well as calls for repairing them.

In August, former Japanese Prime Minister Tomiichi Murayama visited South Korea. Revisiting his apology issued in 1995, the former prime minister suggested the two neighbors would need a summit meeting to resolve the bilateral issues including the imperial Japanese army's war-time sexual enslavement of Korean women.

▲ *Japan's former Prime Minister Tomiichi Murayama gives a keynote speech during a seminar on historical and other disputes between South Korea and Japan at the Northeast Asian History Foundation in Seoul on Aug. 22.*

■ Controversy over Colonialist Historical View

A group of historians denounced the mainstream historical perspective on ancient Korean history as a colony of China and banded together to fight back against the Northeast Asian History Foundation, a sub-organization of the culture ministry.

The historians took issue with the foundation's academic paper titled "The Han Commanderies in Early Korean History," published by Harvard University's Korea Institute.

The stated location of the Han Commanderies makes the northern part of the Korean Peninsula a colony of China, a point which the historians say corresponds to China's Northeast Project. The group of historians launched a campaign in March and requested an audit of the foundation.

The Han Commanderies generally refers to four administrative districts Han' Wu-ti established after overthrowing Wiman Joseon. Where the Han Commanderies were located is a long-running debate in the ancient history sector.

Mainstream historians claim the commanderies were located in the northern part of the Korean Peninsula while minor groups say they were in China's Liaodong.

Recognition of the commanderies' station in the northern part of the peninsula supports China's provocative claims that they controled the peninsula in the past, the minor historian groups said.

The Northeast Asian History Foundation countered that the paper does not try to limit the history of Ancient Joseon because it said the origin of ancient Korean history remained intact despite the overthrowing.

SCIENCE AND TECHNOLOGY

- ■ **The Successful Hosting of the International Congress of Mathematicians: Quoted as the Most Successful Hosting**

The quadrennial International Congress of Mathematicians(ICM), billed as the mathematics olympics, was held in Seoul from Aug. 13-21, bringing together 5,200 mathematicians from 122 foreign countries as well as 20,000 participants under the banner of "Dreams and Hopes for Late Starters."

In terms of headcount, the Seoul event exceeded the previous event hosted by India, which gathered about 4,000 participants. The event venue of COEX and other management programs were highly lauded.

Since the first launch in Zurich, Switzerland in 1897, the world's biggest academic gathering in the sector of natural science marked its fourth event following Japan in 1990, China in 2002 and the 2010 event in India.

In an opening speech, President Park Geun-hye said, "Mathematics is the study with the longest history, a great expectation which the entirety of mankind can share. This event, I hope, could expand the horizon for mathematics and contribute to human civilization."

The Fields Medal, known as the "Novel Prize for mathematics," awarded by the president of the hosting country, went to Maryam Mirzakhani, a 37-year-old professor at Stanford University in the U.S.

Honors went to: Artur Avila, a 35-year-old mathematician and a senior researcher at the National Center for Scientific Research, Manjul Bhargava, a 40-year-old chair professor at Princeton University in the U.S. and Martin Hairer, a 38-year-old professor at the University of Warwick in Britain.

▲ South Korean President Park Geun-hye (4th from L) poses with award winners during the opening ceremony of the 2014 International Congress of Mathematicians at COEX in southern Seoul on Aug. 13.

The next ICM is scheduled for 2018 in Rio de Janeiro, Brazil. The latest ICM in Seoul was acclaimed for laying the groundwork for the popularization of mathematics and confirming the possibility of Korea's mathematics sector entering the world stage.

Following the hosting of the world event, the local mathematic sector stepped up efforts to become a level five International Mathematical Union (IMU) group, known as one of the world's most advanced clubs in mathematics.

The Korean Mathematical Society, a member of the International Mathematical Union, set the goal of entering the level five group at the next 2018 event in Brazil and was to set up a task force to work toward the goal.

Only 10 countries -- the U.S., Britain, Canada, France, Germany, Italy, Russia, Japan, China and Israel -- belong to the level five group. After its membership started in 1981, South Korea became a level two group in 1998 and rose to level four in 2007.

- ■ **Development of Technology to Cultivate Brain Cells of Alzheimer's Disease Patients**

A joint South Korea-U.S. research team succeeded in cultivating brain cell characteristics in Alzheimer's disease patients.

Kim Doo-yeon and Rudolph Tanzi

of Harvard Medical School and Kim Young-hye from the Korea Basic Science Institute said in their article, published by Nature on Nov. 13, that they developed the technology to grow brain cells of Alzheimer's patients.

The result provides the first clear evidence supporting the hypothesis that the deposition of beta-amyloid plaques in the brain is the first step in a cascade leading to the devastating neurodegenerative disease.

New Technology in Expediting The Commercialization of New Material Graphene

A local research team succeeded in developing cutting edge technology to speed up the much-hoped commercialization of the dream material Graphene for sectors like semi-conductors or displays.

Hwang Sung-woo from Samsung Advanced Institute of Technology and Sungkyunkwan University professor Hwang Dong-mok announced in Science magazine issued on April 4 that they have developed large, single-crystal Graphene.

Graphene is an allotrope of carbon in the form of a two-dimensional, hexagonal lattice in which one atom forms each vertex. Two-dimensional Grapene is as thin as 0.2 nanometer and is capable of moving electrons more than 100 times faster than silicon does, making it a very promising future material to be used as flexible products.

Large Graphene was produced previously, but only in a polycrystalline form. Monocrystal Graphne is far easier to commercialize. In the case of silicone, one of the major materials for semiconductors, monocrystal silicone carries electrons 10 times faster than polycrystalline silicone does and excels in terms of uniformity.

The researchers developed a way to produce wafer-size monocrystal Graphene by using germanium. Previously metal was added as a catalyst when compounding monocrystal Graphene, but the researchers used silicone wafers coated with germanium. Germanium wafers are eco-friendly and economic because they can be re-used.

Researcher Hwang Jung-woo said

"The latest monocrystal Graphene technology may become an important skill in speeding up the application of Graphene in an electronic device. Through follow-up research, the size of monocrystal Graphene will be further enlarged for commercialization."

Development of New Nanomaterial Capable of Improving Safety of Photothermal Therapy for Cancer

A local research team developed a new nanomaterial that can enhance the effectiveness and safety of photothermal therapy which is used to kill cancer cells.

Korea University's professor Lee Ji-won and a research team led by Dr. Kim Kwang-myong at the Korea Institute of Science and Technology announced in the June 8 issue of the Advanced Materials journal the development of the nanomaterial that combines only with cancer cells, not with normal cells, and decompose by itself before being emitted from human body.

Photothermal therapy is a way of necrosing cancer cells with the use of gold nanoparticles which absorb near-infrared ray to make heat. But the use of gold nanoparticles has been deemed unsafe because they are not easily emitted from the human body.

The newly developed nanomaterial was extracted from a rat's body in experiments easily after killing cancer cells that had grown in its organs. The researchers expect their new technology will help solve the issue of nano toxicity caused by nanoparticles staying inside the body without being emitted.

Professor Lee said "The latest development of new nanomaterial will help maximize the effectiveness of photothermal therapy while providing the key to solving the issues cause by the accumulation of gold nanoparticles inside the body."

Establishment of South Korea's Second Antarctic Research Station, Jang Bogo

South Korea's second Antarctic research station Jang Bogo opened on Terra Nova Bay on the southeastern tip of Antarctica, 26 years after the first research station Sejong was established in 1988. The opening of the second station made South Korea the world's 10th country to maintain two antarctic research stations.

▲ *An international milepost set up at South Korea's second antarctic research station in Terra Nova Bay, East Antarctica. The station, named Jang Bo Go, was dedicated on Feb. 12 (local time).*

In a completion ceremony on Feb. 12, President Park Geun-hye said in a video message that the new research station could hopefully open the new chapter in South Korea's exploration of the Antarctic.

A total of 104.7 billion won has been invested since 2006 to build the research station spanning some 4,458㎡ with the capacity of accommodating 60 people.

Hydromechanics were applied to the design to enable the station to endure temperatures as low as minus 40 degrees Celsius as well as strong winds blowing at the speed of 65 meters per second. The station was also designed to use solar energy and wind power as second sources of energy in consideration of the environment.

With the addition of the new research station, the Sejong station now can focus its research on the maritime environment and other coastal subjets while Jang Bogo is dedicated to land-based research like glacier, meteorite and ozone layer.

MEDICINE

▪ Overview

Following the stir created by former Jeju district attorney Kim Soo-chang's obscene act in a public space, exhibition-

ism and sexual contact disorder became a major focus of interest in the medical sector.

The death of singer Shin Hae-chul and the following legal dispute over his death drew heavy public attention. The hospital who treated Shin and his bereaved family were involved in a fierce fight that led to an examination of the association of doctors and the Korea Medical Dispute Mediation and Arbitration Agency. But the result of the investigation failed to attain public acceptance and the case is expected to become a long legal fight.

▪ About 16 Percent of People Aged 10-40 Encountered an Exhibitionist

A local report said about 16% of South Koreans aged from 10 to 40 have experienced trauma from exhibitionists. The report by Dankook University psychology professor Lim Myung-ho said that most victims were women. In a survey of 441 people, 15.6% -- 69 people -- said they had been victims of exhibitionists. Of those, 54 were women. School and workplace were most frequently cited places where respondents said they experienced trauma.

▪ Death of Singer Shin Hae-chul and Following Legal Fight

Singer Shin Hae-chul died five days after undergoing surgery for intestinal stricture at a local hospital on Oct. 17, 2014. After suffering cardiac arrest, Shin was rushed to Asan Medical Center for emergency surgery, but died on Oct. 27.

The Korea Medical Association later said in its analysis that perforations on his pericardium and small intestine did not directly constitute medial malpractice, but more attention should have been paid to noticing the perforations and dealing with them.

The police investigating the case sought medical advice from the medical association and the association formed a nine-member committee to conduce an examination of the evidence.

On the question of whether a gastroplication surgery had been conducted, the association said surgery was indeed carried out to reduce the volume of the stomach and it is something that requires approval from the patient.

The troubled hospital had only insisted that the surgery was not conducted, although another surgery was carried out in order to strengthen the stomach walls.

Touching on the cause of death, the medical association also noted that manmade damage inflicted during the surgery led to the perforations, which then caused perforative peritonitis.

The perforations are usual complications that can develop from surgery therefore they do not automatically constitute medical malpractice. But still, efforts to prevent and treat the complications were not enough because a previous examination showed symptoms of pneumopericardim, they said.

▪ Controversy on Ebola Virus Infection upon Contact with Syringe

Controversy erupted locally after one South Korean medical worker was reported to have come in contact with a syringe used to draw blood from an Ebola patient in Sierra Leone, Africa. The controversy was over how likely the medical worker could have been infected with the virus.

Many experts said infection was unlikely because the needle just brushed the palm without piercing the skin. But others were still worried of a possible infection. Fortunately, the concerned medical worker tested negative for the Ebola virus.

▪ Controversy over Excess Tests for Breast Cancer

Controversy arose among medical experts over the effectiveness of the so-called mammogram, widely recommended to women age 40 and up for the early detection of breast cancer.

For certain age groups the test is effective to a certain point, but for other age groups the test could be excessive and likely lead to a misdiagnosis, experts claimed.

The issue was discussed by a committee tasked with revising guidelines on breast cancer diagnosis during a cancer forum hosted by the National Cancer Center in the winter of 2014.

According to the state program of five cancer tests, women aged 40 and over are advised to undergo a mammogram and other breast cancer tests every two years for the purpose of early diagnosis.

The mammogram had moderate effectiveness in preventing death among women aged 40-69, but its effectiveness has not been proven in preventing breast cancer deaths of all age groups, Shin Myung-hee, a medical professor at Sungkyunkwan University, said. The professor said the test is likely to be effective in detecting breast cancer in early stages, but that also has not been proved scientifically.

Mammograms, meanwhile, have the risks of radiation exposure. Accepting such claims, the revision committee modified the guidelines, requiring that only women aged 40-69 undergo the test every two years. With the change, the test is no longer recommended for women aged 70 or higher.

▪ Three out of Every 100 Soldiers Treated for Mental, Behavior Disorders

In the aftermath of a private first class beaten to death by his seniors, the medical sector released data showing that a total of 2,158 conscripted soldiers received medical treatment for anxiety disorders for three years since 2011.

According to a report by the Armed Force Medical Command, from January 2011 to December 2013, a total of 66,481 cases of mental or behavior disorders in 19,066 new soldiers were treated in the 19 local military hospitals across the country. This accounts for about 3% of the country's total 650,000 military population. It was the first report on the mental health of South Korean soldiers.

LITERATURE

▪ Overview

The Sewol ferry sinking left deep wounds in the local literary world. Authors were reluctant to release new works for a while, gazing at the wounds left by the disaster.

While the entire domestic literary circle was in sorrow, foreign novels, including Japanese mystery novels, quickly dominated the market in 2014.

Amid the slump in the publication of Korean novels, lots of realist novels shedding light on Korean society in the 1970s and 80s hit bookstores. Books by young writers such as Kim Ae-ran and Lee Ki-ho were introduced to overseas markets in a series, bringing the wind of Korean literature.

■ **Korean Literary Circle in Sorrow**

Writers lost words after the ferry tragedy. They lost the desire to write, feeling guilty about the many children who were killed or unaccounted for in the ship sinking.

Some popular novelists such as Kim Ae-ran and Park Min-gyu halted plans to release new books. Some others took to the street to share the pain of the families of those killed in the sinking and to find the truth. They had a cultural festival and a relay hunger strike and published books of poems, all in memory of the victims. Kim Hoon, Kim Ae-ran and other writers visited the bereaved families camping out at a port near the scene of accident to share their pain.

On the contrary, foreign novels, including Japanese, swept the local list of best-selling books. "The 100-Year-Old Man Who Climbed Out the Window" by Swedish author Jonas Jonasson and Murakami Haruki's new book "The Men Without Women" captured local fans, taking the top two spots on the best-seller list in turn.

Japanese novels, especially, performed strong. Latest works by popular Japanese novelists such as Keigo Higashino, Kaori Ekuni and Banana Yoshimoto as well as Haruki poured into the market to take high rankings on the list.

Some novels took advantage of the recent popularity of film adaptations in the local box-office. According to the Kyobo Book Center, the original novel of the 2013 Swedish film, "The 100-Year-Old Man Who Climbed Out the Window," topped the best-seller list shortly after the movie opened in the local market. "The Chronicle of a Blood Merchant" by Chinese writer Yu Hua saw its monthly average sales almost tripled upon the release of news that popular Korean actor Ha Jung-woo will direct a local film adaptation of the novel.

Sales of "Fingersmith," a 2002 historical crime novel by Sarah Waters, soared from 4.75 copies a month to 150.2 books a month after news reports that Korean director Park Chan-wook will make the book into a movie.

■ **Globalization of Korean Literary Works**

Translations of young Korean writers armed with sensible and witty writing styles were made briskly as their works received a lot of attention in overseas markets.

"My Palpitating Life" by Kim Ae-ran, whose short story collection "Run, Daddy, Run" entered the spotlight in the local market, is currently being translated into English following the release in February 2014 of the book's French edition. In particular, "I Go to the Convenient Store," one of the short stories in "Run, Daddy, Run" drew attention for receiving the 2014 "Prix de l'inapercu" award from French critics and journalists in June. The award recognizes excellent literary works which have not yet reached a wide audience. Shin Kyung-sook won the prize in 2009 for "A Lone Room," the first Korean writer to do so.

Han Kang's novels "The Vegetarian" and "Here Comes the Boy" were released in the U.S. and British markets, respectively. Park Min-gyu debuted in the French market with his novel "Pavane for a Dead Princess."

Works by veteran novelists such as Shin and Lee Seung-u were also translated and released in overseas markets in a series. Shin, who drew attention among American readers for "Please Look After Mom" in 2011, is expected to hit the American market again with her autobiographical novel "A Lone Room." Lee's novel "The Gaze of Meridian" was published in France.

■ **Writers Association Marks 40th Anniversary**

The Writers Association of Korea announced "a declaration of young literature" marking its 40th founding anniversary. The association vowed to "more intensely raise problems with the world," saying that "literature has lost human problems."

Launched on Nov. 18, 1974 as the Council of Writers for Freedom and Practice when the nation was under the rule of authoritarian leader Park Chung-hee, the association has taken a big role in enhancing the freedom of expression and pro-democracy movement in the country's modern history.

Novels shedding new light on Korea in the 70s' and 80s' also hit the market in a series. Han's "Here Comes the Boy" drew attention with its message of advocating for human dignity through the story of a young boy who was killed in the May 18, 1980 Gwangju pro-democracy uprising.

"World History of Second-born Sons," a satirical novel by Lee Gi-ho, a professor at Gwangju University, and writer-poet Choi Young-mi's latest novel, "Bronze Garden," were also among the books that painted a grim picture of the 1980s.

Veteran novelist Yi Mun-yol, who published a revised edition of his epic novel "The Border" about South Korean society in the 60s in July, is now working on a new epic novel set in 1980s Korea.

Poet Lee Seong-bok published a book of poems titled "Poems in Darkness," a collection of unpublished poems from the 70s and 80s. Song Sok-ze sophisticatedly depicted the dark side of the era of industrialization through his latest novel "Invisible Man."

Jeong Gwa-ri, a literary critic and a professor at Seoul's Yonsei University, published a collection of his book reviews on works by leading Korean poets of the 80s' like Lee Seong-bok and Hwang Ji-woo.

FINE ART

■ Overview

After a years-long slump, the year 2014 enlivened the dullness of the Korean art world. South Korea won the top award in the Venice Architecture Biennale for the first time in history. More Korean artists advanced to overseas markets with Lee U-fan having an exhibition at France's Versailles Palace, a rare chance for a Korean artist.

But there also were dark sides in the local art scene. Chung Hyung-min, the director of the National Museum of Modern and Contemporary Art (MMCA), was accused of being involved in the

illegal hiring of one of her students and a former subordinate as curators.

Lee Yong-woo, president of the Gwangju Biennale Foundation, resigned after the biennale's decision to postpone the display of a painting critical of President Park Geun-hye for a special exhibit marking the 20th anniversary of the biennale, stirring protests from participating artists.

■ S. Korea Tops Venice Architecture Biennale

The Korean pavilion received the Golden Lion for Best National Participation at the 14th Venice Architecture Biennale. Commissioned and curated by Cho Min-suk, the pavilion was highly acclaimed by the world architectural circle with the exhibit, "Crow's Eye View: The Korean Peninsula" shedding light on architectural differences between the two Koreas. This marked the first time for Korea to win the prestigious award.

Lee U-fan, a master of Korean contemporary art, held a private exhibition at France's Versailles Palace from June, the first time for an Asian artist since Japanese pop artist Takashi Murakami in 2010.

Lee was the only Korean on the international art resource Artnet's list of the world's top 100 living artists. Lee ranked 47th on the list in terms of the value of all works sold, having brought in around $37.6 million at art auctions between January 2011 and August 2014.

One of his works was sold for about 2.3 billion won at Sotheby's "Contemporary art evening sale" in New York in November, the highest price for his works that have been sold in New York.

▲ South Korean artist Lee Ufan gives an explanation on his works of art displayed at the Versailles Palace in France on June 12. His private exhibition will take place at the palace from June 17 to Nov. 2.

"Dansaekhwa," or Korean monochrome painting, was re-illuminated internationally and fetched millions of dollars at auctions. Dansaekwha refers to the art movement born in Korea in the 1970s characterized by the use of one color or similar colors.

In 2014, works by Korea's first-generation Danseakhwa artists such as Park Seo-ho, Yoon Hyong-keun, Chung Sang-hwa and Ha Chong-hyun were introduced at many overseas art fairs and auctions.

Galerie Perrotin in Paris had a retrospective of Park while Ha held a solo exhibit at Blum & Poe gallery in New York.

Kim Chang-il, internationally noted art collector and gallery owner, opened four art museums in 2014. He opened one in Shanghai in August and Arario Museum in Space, which transformed the iconic Space Building in central Seoul, the following month. In October, he unveiled three more museums on Jeju Island which were built through the remodeling of abandoned buildings.

■ Biennales

Two biennales enlivened the Korean art scene in the year 2014. The 10th edition of the Gwangju Biennale brought in some of the most abstract creations from all over the world under the theme "Burning Down the House." The event was directed by Jessica Morgan, curator at Tate Modern.

But the biennale was marred by a controversy over a political painting rejected for a special exhibition to mark the anniversary. After the Gwangju Biennale decided to postpone the display of the painting by artist Hong Seong-dam, which portrays President Park Geun-hye as a scarecrow controlled by her late father President Park Chung-hee and presidential chief of staff Kim Ki-choon, many artists pulled out of the event in protest, citing the decision as a "violation of the freedom of artistic expression and creation." The controversy led to the resignation of Lee Yong-woo as president of the Gwangju Biennale Foundation.

This year's Busan Biennale, considered one of the two largest biennales in Korea, was hit by a dispute over whom to select as the director. Olivier Kaeppelin, French art critic and director of Fondation Maeght in Saint-Paul de Vence, was finally chosen. He, however, came under harsh media criticism for presenting an uninspiring exhibition under the theme "Inhabiting the World."

■ MMCA Director Resigns over Corruption

Chung Hyung-min, the director of the National Museum of Modern and Contemporary Art (MMCA), was sacked from her post in October after state auditors found that she unjustly hired her student and a former subordinate as curators of the museum's new Seoul branch. According to the Board of Audit and Inspection, Chung illicitly ordered officials to rig the result of a document screening process and intervened in the interview of applicants to hire the two.

It was the first time an MMCA director has been removed from the post and investigated by the prosecution in its 45-year history.

Hong Song-won, the head of Gallery Seomi, was jailed in September for selling hidden artwork from Tongyang Group on behalf of the conglomerate and failing to hand over part of the sales money. Hong previously was imprisoned in 2011 for helping Orion Group hide illegal funds.

MUSIC

POP MUSIC

■ Overview

The Korean music world had a year mixed with joy and sorrow. Singers' release of new albums and concerts were halted in the aftermath of the Sewol ferry sinking. The gloomy mood continued in the second half with the death of seasoned rock star Shin Hae-chul and two members of K-pop girl group Ladies' Code.

But many legendary singers from the 90s made a comeback after years of hiatus, vitalizing an otherwise dull local market. "Sum" sung by Girl group Sistar's Soyou and male singer JunggiGo made a big hit, bringing a boom of collaboration between singers.

The base of the Asianwide boom of Korean pop music known as "hallyu" has shifted from Japan to China as the relations between South Korea and Japan fell to one of their lowest levels. South Korea's largest entertainment agencies such as S.M., YG and JYP, accelerated their efforts to advance into the Chinese online music market in partnership with China's leading information-technology firms.

But a red light was turned on in the local system to cultivate hallyu stars as members of such idol groups as EXO and B.A.P. filed lawsuits to nullify exclusive contract with their management agencies.

■ Return of Veteran Singers

The return of seasoned singers continued all year long. The boom began when popular boy band from the 90s "g.o.d." made a comeback in 2014 marking the 15th anniversary of its debut. Following the group's successful reformation, the male duo "Fly to the Sky" and boy group "Buzz" followed suit, releasing new albums.

▲ Members of the South Korean pop group g.o.d. pose for a picture during a press conference before their "reunion concert" in Seoul on July 12.

Seo Tai-ji, a legendary singer nicknamed the "cultural president" of the 90s, returned to the music scene after five years of hiatus with his 9th full-length album.

Hip-hop artist MC Mong, who was once mired in controversy over draft evasion, topped major local music charts for over a week after his return to the local music scene. The 35-year-old rapper kept low for nearly four years after being charged with deliberately delaying his military duty in 2010. His unexpectedly strong performance on the music charts also sparked anger from netizens who opposed his comeback.

Besides them, female divas who were household names in the 70s such as Kim Chu-ja, Gye Eun-sook and Yang Hee-eun released new albums for their now middle-aged or older fans. Kim, in particular, resumed activity nearly 33 years after she stopped domestic activities. Gye, nicknamed "queen of Enka," began working again in her home country for the first time since 1982 when she debuted in the Japanese market.

In addition, big-name singers of the 80s and 90s such as Lee Seon-hi, Lee Seung-hwan, Lee So-ra, Kim Dong-ryul, Yoo Hee-yol, Yoon Sang and Lim Chang-jeong showed a strong presence in the K-pop scene by releasing new albums.

Peaking the retro boom in the K-pop scene was a special program "Saturday, Saturday is for Singers (Totoga)" aired Dec. 27 as a segment of MBC TV's long-running reality show "Infinite Challenge." Totoga reenacted a TV music show from the 90s, bringing together the pop icons of the time. It provided a chance for popular singers of the 90s such as Turbo, S.E.S. and Jinusean to perform, evoking a nostalgic response from their fans.

On the other side of the scene, there was a boom of collaboration between singers. After "Sum" by Sistar's Soyou and singer JunggiGo made a big hit, staying for 40 days at the top of major domestic charts, many other singers, including pop diva IU and boy band "High4," joined the collaboration trend.

■ Music World in Gloomy Mood

As the entire nation was in grief over the sinking of the Sewol ferry, the pop music world virtually came to a standstill. Singers postponed planned releases of new albums and concerts all together and stopped working to join the nationwide mourning.

The gloomy mood continued in the second half of the year. Girl group Ladies' Code was involved in a car accident in September that left members EunB and RiSe dead.

In October, legendary rocker Shin Hae-chul, who was widely called "the Devil" for his charismatic stage presence, died following a bowel operation. The autopsy led to accusations of medical malpractice. After his death, over 16,000 mourners, including top K-pop artists, actors and fans, visited Shin's memorial that was set up at Asan Medical Center in Seoul.

▲ Mourners pay tribute at the altar of the late South Korean singer Shin Hae-chul at the Asan Medical Center in southern Seoul on Oct. 28.

▪ Idol Group Members in Disputes with Management Agencies

The local system to cultivate "hallyu" stars came to a slight halt as members of idol groups such as EXO and B.A.P. began filing lawsuits to nullify exclusive contracts with their management agencies. K-pop boy band EXO's popular Chinese members Kris and Luhan filed lawsuits in May and October, respectively, demanding their exclusive contracts with S.M. Entertainment be nullified. Boy group B.A.P. also filed a suit to end their management contract with T.S. Entertainment.

In September, Jessica, a member of Girls' Generation, left the girl group after allegedly being in a feud with the group's management agency, S.M., due to her privately-run fashion business.

Moon Joon-young, leader of the boy band ZE:A, evoked controversy after he fiercely criticized his agency's alleged exploitation of its singers in posts on Twitter.

Girl group 2NE1's Park Bom came under fire after a local news outlet reported that she had attempted to bring illegal drugs into Korea four years ago and did not face charges. Her agency, YG Enter-

tainment, later refuted the report saying that the drugs in question were not illegally obtained, but officially prescribed by doctors in the U.S.

Singer Lee Seung-chul sparked controversy in November by claiming that Japan denied him entry in apparent retaliation for his recent performance of a song on South Korea's easternmost islets of Dokdo, which are also claimed by Tokyo. Lee performed the song "The Day," which talks of Koreans' long-cherished aspiration for inter-Korean reunification, with a choir composed of young North Korean defectors in South Korea on Aug. 14, one day before the anniversary of Korean liberation from 1910-1945 Japanese colonial rule.

Despite troubles with some of their artists, large music agencies stepped up moves to advance into the Chinese market. They began providing K-pop content to Chinese online music services under partnership deals with IT companies there. S.M. Entertainment formed a strategic alliance with Baidu Inc., operator of China's biggest search engine, to jointly promote "legal" music downloads and K-pop in China.

YG Entertainment signed an exclusive deal with the Chinese online giant Tencent to jointly distribute and produce K-pop and other content in the booming Chinese market. JYP Entertainment also signed a contract with Baidu to provide K-pop songs in China while producing a reality show jointly with Youku, one of China's largest streaming video sites.

CLASSICAL MUSIC

▪ Overview

For the Korean classical music scene, the year 2014 was characterized by local orchestras' advance onto the world stage. Although many rising Korean artists have so far performed on foreign stages and won big in international competitions, little has been known about Korean orchestras among the world's classical music fans.

The Seoul Philharmonic Orchestra was invited to perform in four major European music festivals, including BBC Proms, while the Bucheon Philharmonic

Orchestra and Suwon Philharmonic Orchestra made concert tours of European countries, the home of classical music.

■ Seoul Phil Invited to Overseas Music Festivals

The Seoul Philharmonic Orchestra led by maestro Chung Myung-whun made its debut at BBC Proms as the first Korean orchestra to take part in the event's 120-year history. It also was the second Asian orchestra to perform there next to Japan's NHK Symphony in 2001.

The BBC Proms is one of the world's greatest classical music festivals, founded in 1895, and all Proms concerts are broadcast live on BBC Radio 3. Since then, the annual event showcases the most prestigious orchestras and musicians. With the London performance, the Seoul Phil wrapped up its 2014 European Tour, spanning four music festivals, including the Grafenegg in Austria and the Merano in Italy.

The Bucheon Phil, which celebrated its 25th founding anniversary in 2013, made a concert tour of European countries in August as part of efforts to become a world-class orchestra. Conducted by Lim Hun-joung, the orchestra performed at Smetana Hall, a celebrated concert hall in Prague, the Czech Republic; the Hercules Hall in Munich, Germany; and the Musikverein Golden Hall in Vienna, Austria.

The Suwon Philharmonic Orchestra also went on a European tour in February, visiting Vienna, Budapest, Prague and Munich. In September, it was formally invited to the 2014 Italy Merano Festival.

■ Visits of Famous Foreign Orchestras

World-class orchestras conducted by maestros continued to visit South Korea for concerts in 2014. The list of foreign orchestras performed here is as follows: New York Philharmonic led by Alan Gilbert, Germany's Kölner Philharmonie, London Symphony Orchestra led by Daniel Harding, the Bavarian Radio Symphony Orchestra conducted by maestro Mariss Jansons and the Deutsche Kammerphilharmonie Bremen (or the Bremen German Chamber Philharmonic) led by Paavo Jarvi.

▲ New York Philharmonic conductor Alan Gilbert (L) speaks about his orchestra's Seoul concert in a news conference at the Seoul Arts Center in southern Seoul on Feb. 6.

Lesser known orchestras to local music fans but still with long-lasting reputation overseas such as the Tonhalle Orchestra Zurich, Swiss Romande Orchestra and the Czech Philharmonic also held concerts in South Korea and received a hot response from audiences.

Visits by world renowned performers continued. They included the Canadian pianist Angela Hewitt, Hungarian-born pianist András Schiff, the Russian pianist and conductor Mikhail Pletnev.

■ Seoul Phil in Trouble over Chief's Abusive Words, Sexual Harassment

The Seoul Philharmonic Orchestra (SPO) was mired in trouble after the orchestra's administrative staff demanded the resignation of the chief Park Hyunjung, accusing her of sexually harassing and verbally abusing some of the staff members. Park, in the process of defending herself, raised issues with the poor management of the SPO and with the director Chung Myung-whun.

The internal strife ended as Park offered to resign on Dec. 29 which the SPO board accepted nearly a month after the dispute began. But the incident tarnished the SPO's reputation, disappointed the orchestra's fans and sponsors, and left questions about whether the orchestra run with taxes paid by Seoul citizens is being managed properly.

The Seoul city government temporarily extended a contract with the conductor Chung by one more year to readjust the terms of contract although his three-year contract with the SPO expired in December, 2014.

The conductor has been in the hot seat over his salary level and alleged misuse of air tickets and other perks. A local group even filed a complaint with the police, asking the authorities to investigate him over embezzlement. After the investigation, Seoul city auditors said some of the allegations raised against Chung were found to be true and that the city government needs to readjust his salary level.

THEATER PLAYS AND MUSICALS

■ Overview

It was a tough year for the local theater and musical circles. They were hit by the nationwide mood of mourning after the Sewol ferry disaster.

As the year marked the 450th anniversary of William Shakespeare's birth, a number of plays shedding new light on his literary world were staged. Despite overall dullness in the scene, some creative works performed well. The strength of established musical theater stars, not rising stars, remained strong in the year.

■ Performing Arts Hit by Ferry Disaster

The Sewol ferry sinking that engulfed the entire nation in shock and sorrow directly hit the local performing arts world. After the sinking, various promotional events for new plays and musicals were canceled in a series.

Schools also canceled programs intended to provide students chances to collectively attend cultural performances after educational authorities ordered them to refrain from all kinds of school trips for fear of similar incidents. The case was same with programs prepared by individual companies.

Industry officials say the ferry disaster created an unprecedentedly hard situation for the local performing arts world. According to the online ticket reservation service, Interpark, ticket sales for concerts, musicals, plays and dance performances actually dipped in the first half of the year in the aftermath of the ferry sinking but quickly recovered in the second half.

■ S. Korea Celebrates 450th Birth Anniversary of Shakespeare

In celebration of the 450th anniversary of William Shakespeare's birth, a series of performances, from plays and operas to films and musicals, were shown throughout the year. The National Theater Company of Korea staged "Macbeth," "Singing Shylock," "The Tempest," while the Myeongdong Theater presented another Shakespeare tragedy, "Julius Caesar," and "Ophelia," a musical adaptation of the play "Hamlet."

■ Established Singers Enjoy Popularity in Musicals

In the year 2014, it was hard to find a rookie actor or actress who rose to stardom. Continuing popularity were well-known box-office powerhouses such as Kim Jun-soo, a member of K-pop boy band JYJ, and Ryu Jeong-han of the musical "Dracula," Ock Ju-hyun, who was the main vocalist of K-pop girl group Fin. K.L, Jeong Seon-ah and Park Hye-nah of the musical "Wicked," and Jo Seung-woo of "Hedwig and the Angry Inch."

Despite the unfavorable environment, some creative musicals received favorable responses from critics and audiences alike. The musical "Frankenstein," British playwright Nick Dear's stage adaptation of Mary Shelley's novel of the same name, attracted more than 80,000 viewers, an unusually big success for creative musicals. Also drawing popularity was the musical "Sherlock Holmes Bloody Game," based on a detective novel by Arthur Conan Doyle.

The musical adaptation of "Woyzeck" written by German playwright Georg Buchner, drew attention as the first attempt to make it into a large-scale stage musical and as a rare local project launched with the global stage in mind.

More K-pop artists advanced to theater musicals in 2014. They include Girls' Generation's Seohyun, Super Junior's Kyuhyun, Kahi from After School, BEAST's Jang Hyun-seung, Mblaq's Jio and EXO's Baekhyun.

DANCE

▪ Overview

In the year 2014, the Korean dance circle made new attempts in many aspects to better adapt to changes of the times and to reach broader audiences.

The Korean National Ballet led by renowned ballerina Kang Sue-jin from February kick-started efforts to further develop. It presented modern ballet pieces, a departure from its earlier focus on classical ballet.

The National Dance Company of Korea, which has drawn attention for its various experiments in combining traditional and modern pieces, continued its challenge toward new areas and stepped up preparations to go abroad, announcing a plan to do a performance tour of France in 2015.

▪ 'Experiment' of Korean National Ballet

The Korean National Ballet received a warm welcome from its fans as it presented a variety of works, including neoclassical and modern ballet pieces. The ballet company originally planned to stage "Madam Butterfly" as its first performance of 2014 starring its music director Kang, but cancelled due to controversy over the quality of the performance.

▪ National Dance Company Continues Changes, Reaps

The National Dance Company of Korea, which performed before sold-out audiences for the first time in its 52 years of history with "Chum, Chunhyang" in 2013, kept drawing public attention with fresh quality works. They include "Twister," produced through the company's first-ever collaboration with a foreign choreographer, and the modern dance extravaganza "Tournament."

"Twister," in particular, was invited to be the opener to the 2015 International Dance Festival in Cannes, one of France's largest dance festivals, opening the way for Korean dance to reach out to the world.

The company is set to go on a tour of four French cities in 2015 to stage "The Scent of Ink," a 2013 work which drew media attention in South Korea for the stage design by fashion designer Jung Ku-ho. It also plans to co-produce a new dance piece with the Chaillot National Theater in Paris in 2015.

▪ Korean Dancers Working on World Stage

South Korean ballerina Park Se-eun, who works for world prestigious Paris Opera Ballet, became the first Korean soloist at the company. She played the lead role of Naila in the company's piece "La Source," which was performed at a Paris theater from Nov. 29 to Dec. 31.

Lee Soo-bin, a 16-year-old ballerina from South Korea, won the grand prize in the girls' and boys' category of the 26th International Ballet Competition Varna 2014, one of the world's three largest ballet competitions. She also received a special "Emil Dimitrov" award for young talent and another special award in the competition.

▪ Return of Korean Ballet Stars Abroad

Kang Sue-jin, who was named chief of the Korean National Ballet in February, made a comeback to the local stage as a dancer in July. Kang played the lead character of Cio-cio San in the Austrian ballet company of Innsbruck's performance of "Madam Butterfly" in Seoul in 2013.

The Korean National Ballet's performance of "Madam Butterfly" drew much anticipation from local ballet fans as the work was choreographed by the company director Enrique Gasa Valga reportedly with only Kang in mind for the role.

It also was widely seen as a rare chance to see a performance by the nation's oldest ballerina before her retirement in 2016. But despite Kang's beautiful dancing, the performance failed to receive good marks from critics and audiences alike.

The annual homecoming performance of Korean ballet stars abroad was held in July. Hosted by International Performing Arts Project, the Korea World Dance Stars Festival invited Korean dancers -- either soloists or principal dancers at acclaimed ballet companies or dance groups across the globe -- to show off the skills they have accumulated overseas.

The 2014 event invited six Korean dancers -- Han Seo-hye of the Boston Ballet, Choi Young-kyu of the Dutch National Ballet, Rhee Hyon-jun and Son You-hee of the U.S. Tulsa Ballet, Kwon Sae-hyun of the Norwegian National Ballet and Lee Hye-rin from the modern U.S. dance troupe Leesaar the Company. They showcased a variety of works ranging from classical ballet to contemporary dance.

MOVIES

■ Overview

"Roaring Currents," a homegrown film about a 16th century Korean naval hero's crushing victory against the Japanese navy, saved the Korean film industry against a strong performance by foreign films. Thanks to "Roaring Currents," which drew a record high number of viewers, a Korean film topped 10 million in annual viewers for the third year in a row.

The animated Disney film "Frozen" led box-office sales in the first half of the year amid the lack of popular Korean films. The sci-fi film "Interstellar," which topped 10 million in attendance, and action flick "Transformers: Age of Extinction" were also among the films that led Hollywood films.

South Korea also experienced a boom of indie and art-house films with the popularity of "Han Gong-ju," "My Love, Don't Cross That River," "Begin Again" and "The Grand Budapest Hotel."

■ Local Film Industry Passes 2 tln in Annual Sales

The Korean film industry raked in over 2 trillion won ($1.84 billion) in annual box-office sales for the first time in 2014. The sales increased by 7.6% from the previous year thanks to box office revenues and overseas and digital sales, according to the Korean Film Council.

Also in 2014, over 200 million movie tickets were sold in the local box-office for the second consecutive year. This means each Korean watched an average of 4.19 films.

Box office sales were driven by foreign movies, while audiences for domestic movies shrank. The attendance for Korean films dropped 15.4% on-year to 107.7 million people. The number of tickets sold for foreign films increased 24.8%, generating an all-time high of 107.36 million ticket sales.

The local film industry's overseas sales increased 6.1% to $63.08 million. In addition, the digital online market -- which includes mobile, Web-based platforms and TV channels via IPTV and digital cable networks -- grew 11% from a year earlier to 297.1 billion won.

■ "Roaring Currents" Reignite Boom of Adm. Yi

The historical film "Roaring Currents" rewrote the history of the Korean film industry. Starring veteran actor Choi Min-shik, the historical drama tells the story of Joseon Dynasty (1392-1910) Admiral Yi Sun-shin's victory in the battle of Myeongnyang against Japan in 1597. In the decisive naval battle, Yi, who had 12 ships under his command, defeated more than 300 Japanese warships.

The film attracted the largest number of movie-goers on its first day of release in South Korea at 680,000. It then broke all previous audience records before surpassing the 10 million mark only 12 days after release. In August, it became the most-viewed film in the country, breaking the previous record of 13.62 million viewers held by Hollywood blockbuster "Avatar."

That was not the end of the story. "Roaring Currents" ended up drawing 17.61 million viewers in local theaters, collecting a record of 135.7 billion won in sales.

Thanks to the box-office smasher, the monthly number of visitors to local theaters reached the all-time high number of 25 million in August while theaters earned 539.9 billion won in the third quarter. The film also helped the total number of tickets sold for Korean films top 100 million for the third consecutive year in 2014.

The boom of Adm. Yi was spread to other fields of culture. The movie's popularity pushed up sales of steady-selling novels about the hero, including "Song of the Sword" by Kim Hoon, books of history about the naval war as well as toys replaying the hero's crushing victories against Japanese invaders.

Strength of Hollywood Films

After a slump in the first half, sales of Korean films picked up in the second half thanks to the success of "Roaring Currents" and "The Pirates." In the first half, "Miss Granny" was the only Korean film that exceeded the 4 million audience mark, considered a box-office success for average budget films.

Benefiting from the dull sales of domestic films were Hollywood films led by "Frozen," an animated Disney film that sold more than 10 million tickets in local theaters. It surpassed the 1 million mark only four days after release on Jan. 16 and became the most successful animated film in South Korea, beating "Kungfu Panda 2," and drawing slightly more than 6 million viewers 17 days after release. "Kungfu Panda 2" recorded 5.44 million audiences in 2011.

"Frozen" later surpassed the 10 million mark, becoming the second-most viewed foreign film of all time in South Korea next to "Avatar" (2009). As the movie hit the box office, "Let It Go," the title track of the movie's soundtrack album, swept the nation's online music services.

In the second half, Christopher Nolan's sci-fi epic "Interstellar" succeeded "Frozen" as a box-office hit. "Interstellar" features a team of space travelers who travel through a wormhole in search of a new habitable planet. Although it opened in November, a traditionally slow season for the film industry, the film attracted as many as 220,000 moviegoers on its opening day.

It then surpassed the 1 million mark on its third day and 3 million on its eighth day and eventually topped the 10 million later. Besides those two films, "Transformer: Age of Extinction" also performed well, attracting about 5.3 mililon movie-goers in South Korea.

Boom of Diversity Films

A homegrown documentary film about an elderly couple became the talk of the town for its unexpected box-office success. Released on Nov. 27, "My Love, Don't Cross That River" by director Ji Mo-young became the first local indie film to draw 100,000 viewers in seven days after release. The film then exceeded 1 million on the 18th day, 2 million six days later. On the 29th day, it surpassed 3 million, becoming the most-viewed docu film of all time in the country.

The previous record was 2.92 million set by "Old Partner" (2009). For indie films, an attendance of 100,000 is considered comparable to 10 million for commercial films and a huge box-office success. Critics say the film has appealed to all generations with its true story of love between a 98-year-old man and 89-year-old woman who have lived as a couple for 76 years.

▲ South Korean director Jin Mo-young (R) responds to reporters' questions during a publicity event for the new movie "My Love, Don't Cross That River" in Seoul on Dec. 18. The movie was released in South Korea on Nov. 27.

"Han Gong-ju," a domestic indie film by director Lee Su-jin, also was a box-office hit, drawing 220,000 viewers. The film tells the story of a high school girl named Han Gong-ju who moved and changed schools after being involved in a nasty situation.

Among non-Korean films that led the boom of small films were "Begin Again," an American musical comedy-drama film written and directed by John Carney and starring Keira Knightley and Mark Ruffalo, and "The Grand Budapest Hotel," a comedy film directed by Wes Anderson. The two films drew 3.4 million and 773,887 viewers, respectively.

Influx of Chinese Investment

The South Korean and Chinese film industries accelerated their moves to co-produce films and advance to each other's market. CJ E&M, a leading Korean content and media company, said it is co-producing with China "20, Once Again," the Chinese version of the South Korean box-office hitter "Miss Granny" and "The Peaceful Island," a Chinese-language thriller by director Chang Yoon-hyun.

China's Huace Film & TV Co. purchased 15% of new stocks worth 53.5 billion won (US$49 million) in NEW, a leading South Korean film company known for making such box-office hits as "The Attorney" and "Miracle in Cell No. 7." The investment made the Chinese company the distributor's second-largest shareholder. This marks the largest investment from any foreign firm to a local film company.

■ **Korean Films Win Prizes in Overseas Film Festivals**

Master director Im Kwon-taek received a lifetime achievement award during the 25th Singapore International Film Festival. "Han Gong-ju" by director Lee Su-jin won major prizes at the 28th Fribourg International Film Festival in Switzerland, the 43rd International Film Festival Rotterdam, and the 47th Sitges International Film Festival in Spain.

Director July Jung won the Best First Film award at the Stockholm International Film Festival for her feature directorial debut "A Girl at My Door."

"Late Spring" by director Cho Geun-hyun won the best actress and best cinematography awards at the 14th Milan International Film Festival.

RELIGION

■ **Overview**

The dominating issue in Korean religious circles in the year 2014 was Pope Francis' visit to South Korea. The first papal visit to South Korea since 1989 when Pope John Paul II visited the country, brought a big impact to the society transcending all religious sects, delivering a message of peace and healing.

In February, Andrew Yeom Soo-jung, the archbishop of Seoul, was named South Korea's third-ever cardinal after the late Stephen Kim Sou-hwan (1922-2009) and Nicholas Cheong Jin-suk.

In October, the Catholic Bishops' Conference of Korea, the top decision-making body of the local church, appointed Hyginus Kim Hee-joong, archbishop of Gwangju, as its chairman succeeding Bishop Peter Kang U-il.

■ **Appointment of Third-ever Korean Cardinal**

▲ *South Korea's archbishop Andrew Yeom Soo-jung of Seoul holds up a bouquet during a ceremony to celebrate his appointment as cardinal at the Myeongdong Cathedral in Seoul on Jan. 12.*

In February, Andrew Yeom Soo-jung, the archbishop of Seoul, was named South Korea's new cardinal. He is the third-ever Korean cardinal after the late Stephen Kim Sou-hwan (1922-2009) and Nicholas Cheong Jin-suk.

The 71-year-old Yeom was one of 19 new cardinals worldwide named by Pope Francis on Jan. 21. Yeom was installed as a new cardinal in a Vatican ceremony on Feb. 22.

South Korea has a Catholic community of more than 5 million, a sizable portion of its population of nearly 49 million people whose religious heritage is largely based on Buddhism. The appointment of another Korean cardinal is seen as a reflection of the Catholic Church's expectations for South Korea's bigger role in the Asian and world church.

Since Cardinal Nicolas Cheong is over 80, which is the canonical retirement age, Yeom will be the only Korean representative to the conclave to elect the next pope, which is a cardinal's most important task.

▪ Pope Francis Visits S. Korea

Pope Francis made a five-day trip to attend a gathering of Asian Catholic youth and beatify Korean martyrs in August. It was his third international trip and first to Asia since he took over the papacy in March last year.

▲ *Pope Francis waves to the crowd on Aug. 16 as he heads to the altar in Seoul's city center where the beatification of 124 Korean martyrs will take place.*

His 100-hour-long stay in South Korea left an impression on the Korean people as it was packed with meetings with the country's marginalized -- grieving families who lost loved ones in April's ferry disaster, disabled people living in a rehabilitation center, North Korea defectors settled in the country and migrant workers mostly from Southeast Asian countries.

During a Mass he led at the Myeongdong Cathedral in central Seoul, Francis delivered a message of peace and reconciliation for the divided Korean Peninsula, calling on the two Koreas to unite in the spirit of mutual forgiveness.

▪ Protestant, Catholic Churches Appoint New Leaders

The Christian Council of Korea (CCK), an association of conservative Protestant churches, fell into crisis as a number of its members bolted from the organization amid accusations of financial mismanagement, bribery and corruption.

In May, Cho Kwang-jak, a co-vice chairman of the CCK, came under fire for remarks about the victims of the April 16 ferry sinking that claimed more than 300 lives.

The pastor drew strong public indignation for saying during a meeting of the council in Seoul that he does not understand why the children from poor families chose to travel to the southern resort island of Jeju instead of going to a popular inland destination such as Mount Seorak on the east coast or Bulguk Temple in Gyeongju, an ancient city in the southeastern part of the country. The controversy led to Cho's resignation.

On Sept. 2, the CCK elected Lee Young-hoon, senior pastor of the Yoido Full Gospel Church, as its new chairman amid the controversies.

The Communion of Churches in Korea, another association of conservative Protestant churches, appointed pastor Yang Byeong-hee as its fourth chairman in December. The communion was formed in 2012 by churches that left the CCK.

The National Council of Churches in Korea, an association of progressive Protestant churches, decided to name pastor Kim Young-joo for another four-year term as its leader.

In Catholicism, the Catholic Bishops' Conference of Korea, the top decision-making body of the local church, appointed Hyginus Kim Hee-joong, archbishop of Gwangju, as its chairman succeeding Bishop Peter Kang U-il.

▪ Gov't Delays Taxation on Clergy Earnings for One More Year

The long-pending controversy over taxing clergy earnings continued in 2014, too. The government originally scheduled to start levying taxes on the earnings of clergy members from the start of 2015 amid mounting calls that they should not be an exception from the principle that all income earners should pay taxes.

But the government decided to delay the taxation on clergy earnings for one more year as some conservative Protestant ministers strongly opposed the plan. The Catholic Church in Korea has already been paying income tax voluntarily since 1994, and Buddhist sectors in the nation support the taxation.

However, some are concerned that the January 2016 start date could be pushed back as politicians are probably unwilling to brave protests from clergy members to start the measure ahead of the local elections in 2016 and the presidential election in 2017.

▪ Cheondo-gyo Marks 120th Year of Donghak Revolution

The indigenous Korean religion called Cheondo-gyo marked the 120th anniversary of the Donghak Peasant Revolution in 1894 with a ceremony attended by followers and descendents of the Donghak peasants on Oct. 11.

Prior to the meeting, church officials reached an agreement in the North Korean border town of Kaesong with their North Korean counterparts to jointly hold a ceremony and various other events to commemorate the anniversary. But the plan was eventually not carried out as inter-Korean relations worsened afterwards.

CULTURAL ASSETS

▪ Overview

The corruption-ridden ancient gate restoration project continued to dog the local cultural heritage circle in the year 2014. An expert who took part in the project killed himself while state auditors and police released the outcome of their intensive audit and probe results.

Also in the year 2014, there were remarkable results in government-led efforts to discover ancient ruins. They included a gilt bronze crown and shoe from the Baekje Kingdom (18 B.C. - 660 A.D.) and a complete fossilized skeleton of a small carnivorous dinosaur.

Controversy erupted in Chuncheon where a Legoland theme park is under construction as ruins dating back to the prehistoric age were massively discovered in an archeological survey into the site.

▪ Corruption-ridden Project to Restore Ancient Gate

The gloomy mood that has shaped the local cultural heritage circle appeared to peak with the suicide of a professor who took part in the national project to restore the fire-damaged ancient gate.

One of the four gates that surrounded the capital city during the Joseon Dynasty (1392-1910), Sungnyemun reopened in 2013 after undergoing five years of repairs following an arson attack in 2008.

Suspicion, however, has mounted over its shoddy reconstruction, with cracks in some of its pillars, mismatched parts and damaged paintwork, prompting the parliament to demand the audit by the Board of Audit and Inspection (BAI).

As the police looked into the suspicions, the professor of Chungbuk National University who analyzed the wood used for the gate restoration as a member of the project's advisory team, was found dead on Jan. 18. He was found to have killed himself, according to police. The professor's aides say he was under much mental stress as he was grilled intensively from the authorities over the corruption-ridden project.

After months of an extensive audit into nine relevant government agencies, state auditors found in May that the project to rebuild the gate in downtown Seoul was riddled with flaws and corruption, calling for rebuilding part of the structure in accordance with its original form.

The BAI also said the Cultural Heritage Administration failed to carry out thorough research and get enough advice on its original form as it rushed the project to meet the deadline.

The heritage agency also hired inexperienced, private pseudo-craftmen, who employed untested methods and applied poor-quality materials in painting the national symbol. The head in charge of the painting job even turned out to have pocketed some 300 million won in illicit profits by using cheap glue, according to the BAI.

The heritage administration was also found to lay the foundation of the gate without enough research, causing the southern gate to be built up to 145cm above the original foundation. The contractors also didn't use Sungnyemun's original, unique tiles on the roof, as the agency arbitrarily adopted modern-style, uniformed ones.

Based upon its audit results, the BAI called for the gate to be returned to its original form, particularly in terms of its foundation, coloring and tiles. The auditor also called for punitive measures against five officials who led the project and asked for a police investigation into the painting chief for embezzlement.

The audit results once again disappointed and enraged people here, as police earlier this year arrested 17 people, including a veteran carpenter in charge of the carpentry work for the project, on diverse corruption charges related to the shoddy reconstruction.

▪ Historical Ruins Discovered in Theme Park Construction Site

A large set of ruins dating back to the prehistoric age have been discovered at a site for the construction of a Legoland theme park on Jungdo Island of Chuncheon, Gangwon Province. In the preliminary excavation of the 122,025㎡ site, which began in October 2013, experts found 101 dolmens and 917 ruins of homes dating from the Bronze Age, among other items.

The discovery erupted into controversy over whether to go ahead with the development plan or preserve the site. After a heated debate, the cultural heritage authority decided to approve the construction plan on the condition that the dolmens be moved to the south of the current site and be well preserved. Despite the decision, however, controversy over the site continued as civic groups opposed the development plan.

▪ Baekje-era Gilt-bronze Shoes Unearthed in Naju

A pair of gilt-bronze shoes dating back to the Baekje Kingdom were recovered in the best preserved condition to date from a tomb in Naju, South Jeolla Province, in October. The Naju National Research Institute of Cultural Heritage

▲ *A pair of gilt bronze shoes presumably from the ancient Baekje Kingdom (18 B.C.-A.D. 660), which was unearthed from an ancient tomb in Naju, South Jeolla Province, are unveiled to the media on Oct. 23.*

also unearthed gold earrings, plates, ornaments, tools, pottery and other precious relics in its latest survey of three of the nine tombs it discovered in 2013.

The shoes -- 32㎝ in length, 9.5㎝ in width and 9㎝ in height -- bear a dragon image paired with the image of a lotus blossom, in delicate gilt-bronze work.

▪ Ruins of Goryeo Pond Unearthed

Large-scale ruins of a pond and garden from the Goryeo Dynasty (918-1392) was discovered at Silsang Temple in Namwon, North Jeolla Province, in almost perfect condition. A cultural heritage research institute under the Jogye Order, the largest Buddhist sect in South Korea, made the discovery in a survey of areas outside the fence of the temple.

The institute found ruins of a uniquely oval-shaped pond, intact outbound and inbound waterways and two buildings believed to be related to the pond. The pond and waterways attracted much attention for its scale, near-perfect preservation condition and beautiful style.

The oval-shaped pond is about 16m long and 8m wide with the bottom covered with river stones laid flat. The same type of stones were used to build a bank around the pond.

▪ Joseon-era Shipwreck Found in Western Waters

A shipwreck presumed to date back to the Joseon Dynasty has been found in western waters in what archaeologists say could be the first discovery of a Joseon-era ship. The National Research Institute of Maritime Cultural Heritage said that its underwater research team discovered the shipwreck on the seabed off Mado Island, Taean County, South Chungcheong Province.

A total of 111 pieces of white ceramic, all thought to date back to the Joseon era, were also found on the sea floor near the shipwreck site. Inside the vessel, two Buncheong Sagi ceramics were discovered. Buncheong Sagi refers to ceramics with a gray or bluish-green body, decorated with white. The style emerged in the early Joseon Dynasty, largely replacing celadon in common use. It all but disappeared from Korea after the 16th century due to the popularity of white porcelains.

Three shipwrecks have previously been discovered on the seabed off Mado Island alone but all are thought to be from the Goryeo era which preceded Joseon. The recently found ship, nicknamed "Mado No. 4," is thought to measure 11.5m long and 6m wide and has a shape that is typical to ancient Korean ships.

▪ Dinosaur Fossil Discovered

A complete skeleton of a small carnivorous dinosaur was found in southern South Korea, the first such discovery in the country. The National Research Institute of Cultural Heritage said the fossil was discovered in a Mesozoic geologic formation in Hadong, South Gyeongsang Province, with the skull and the lower jaw intact. Theropods, or "beast-footed" dinosaurs, are of the same family as the Tyrannosaurus, one of the largest land carnivores to have lived on Earth.

The fossil has a 5.7㎝-long and a 2.6㎝ -wide skull and is about 28㎝ tall, making it one of the smallest dinosaurs to have ever been discovered in South Korea. Previously, paleontologists in South Korea had only managed to find fragments of bones belonging to theropod dinosaurs.

▪ Mountain Fortress Wins UNESCO Heritage Status

An ancient mountain fortress in South Korea made the UNESCO world heritage list. The 38th meeting of the World Heritage Committee decided during a meeting in Doha, Qatar, to give World Heritage status to the Namhansanseong mountain fortress in Gwangju, Gyeonggi Province. The inscription brought the number of South Korean items on the UNESCO list to 11 as of the end of 2014. If North Korea is included, the number would rise to 14.

Located at an elevation of 480m above sea level, Namhansanseong is one of two mountain fortresses built during the Joseon Dynasty (1392-1910) to defend the capital Seoul, along with Bukhansanseong.

The committee said the fortress provides a good understanding of ancient Koreans' different styles and techniques of fortress construction as it was used as military facilities for a long period of time spanning from the 7th to 19th century. The fortress has about 200 historic sites and buildings, including Haenggung, a temporary palace where Joseon kings stayed during their trips out of Seoul and during wars.

▪ Nongak Listed as UNESCO's Intangible Cultural Heritage

UNESCO added "nongak", traditional Korean music performed by farmers, to its intangible cultural heritage list on Nov. 27 for its creativity and cultural identity. The music was inscribed as Intangible Cultural Heritage of Humanity during the 9th session of UNESCO's Intergovernmental Committee for the Safeguarding of the Intangible Cultural Heritage in Paris.

▲ An event is underway in Gangneung City, Gangwon Province, on Dec. 14, to demonstrate "nongak," the traditional Korean music of farmers. The event was held to commemorate UNESCO added "nongak" to its intangible cultural heritage list in November for its creativity and cultural identity.

Nongak -- comprising drums, gongs, dancing and acrobatic feats -- was originally performed by farmers, but nowadays it is a popular performing art seen nationwide, especially during the holidays. The committee said the music, characterized by independence, openness and creativity, has served to provide a cultural identity to both performers and audiences.

Nongak became South Korea's 17th item on the UNESCO list that includes ancestral royal rites, a percussion instrument performance known as "pansori" and a 5,000-year-old dance called "ganggangsullae," and "Arirang," a traditional folk song. "Arirang" is not just one song but a variety of local versions handed down generation after generation on the Korean Peninsula.

A group of six North Korean provincial versions of Arirang was separately added to the intangible heritage list during the same meeting, making it the North's first-ever inscription on the list.

- ### Recovery of Stolen Korean Cultural Assets

There was a remarkable outcome in the national efforts to recover Korean cultural assets illegally taken out of the country. The U.S. government returned a set of nine Korean royal seals timed for President Barack Obama's visit to South Korea in April.

▲ Displayed at the National Palace Museum of Korea in Seoul on May 12, are national seals of the Korean Empire (1897-1910) and signets of the Joseon Royal Court of the Joseon Dynasty (1392-1910). They were retrieved recently from the U.S. after customs authorities there seized the seals illegally taken by U.S. soldiers during the 1950-53 Korean War.

In November 2013, U.S. customs authorities seized the seals from the family of a deceased U.S. Marine lieutenant who served in the 1950-53 Korean War. South Korea's Cultural Heritage Administration was later handed over information on the seized items and found that they were royal seals from the Joseon Dynasty and the ensuing Korean Empire.

Among the returned items were Hwangjebibo (Seal of the Emperor), the national seal made upon the establishment of the Korean Empire in 1897. It is deemed highly significant both academically and historically as it symbolizes King Gojong's will for independence.

In July, Najeon Gyeongham, a lacquered box inlaid with mother-of-pearl, was donated to the National Museum of Korea. Presumed to be made in latter

years of the Goryeo Dynasty, the item is considered to represent the pinnacle of Goryeo arts and crafts.

The Friends of the National Museum of Korea, a private support group, bought the box from a Japanese citizen months earlier and donated to the museum. "Gyeongham" means a box to contain Buddhist texts, while "najeon" is a Korean word indicating mother-of-pearl inlays. The wooden box is 41.9cm long and 20cm wide and 22.6cm high and weighs 2.53kg.

TOURISM

- ### Overview

In 2014, the number of foreign tourists who visited South Korea topped 14.2 million people, the highest of all time. Chinese tourists tallied at 6.12 million, up 41.6% from 2.83 million in 2013. They accounted for 43.1% of the foreign groups that visited South Korea, an increase of 35.5% from 2013.

Despite the increase in foreign tourists coming to visit South Korea, the nation's tourism profits recorded a deficit for the 14th consecutive year.

Yeongjong Island, the nation's main gateway, gained attention regarding whether it would become a Korean version of Macau as the government and private firms unveiled a series of plans to build foreign-exclusive casino resorts in a free economic zone on the island.

As more and more people opt to travel freely rather than using package tour programs, so-called "smartphone tourism," in which people reserve air tickets and hotel rooms on their mobile sets, became a trend.

- ### Chinese Emerges as Largest Group of Foreign Tourists to S. Korea

The number of foreign tourists coming to visit South Korea hit the all-time high of 14.2 million in 2014. Among them, the Chinese made up the largest group with 6.12 million for the second consecutive year.

Chinese tourists were found to have spent US$2,204.5 per person, the highest amount of money spent by foreign tourists, according to a survey released by the Korea Tourism Organization.

The number of Japanese tourists fell 17% on-year to 2.28 million, mainly because of the worsened diplomatic relations between South Korea and Japan and the weaker yen.

■ S. Korea Posts Tourism Deficit for 14th Straight Year

South Korea logged a deficit in its tourism balance for the 14th consecutive year in 2014 as outbound travelers outnumbered inbound visitors. According to industry data, the tourism deficit reached US$1.7 billion but the amount of deficit was smaller than US$2.8 billion marked a year earlier.

The deficit came as South Korea's outbound travelers spent some US$19.7 billion in total, exceeding the US$18 billion spent by foreigners visiting the country.

Researchers of the Korea Culture and Tourism Institute attributed the fall in yearly tourism deficit to the sharp rise in Chinese tourists, thanks to the strength of the Korean currency and thriving businesses of budget airlines.

■ S. Korea in Casino Battle

The government decided to permit the creation of two large-scale casino resorts worth about 1 trillion won each to improve the global competitiveness of local casinos. It planned to select the operators in the second half of 2014 with a goal of beginning construction as early as 2016.

The gambling business is thriving in South Korea with 16 foreigner-exclusive casinos currently in operation with only one open to locals. After topping 1 trillion won in 2010, annual sales of foreigner-only casinos have risen sharply from 1.12 trillion won in 2011 to 1.25 trillion won in 2012 and to 1.37 trillion won in 2013. The number of visitors to these casinos reached 2.7 million a year, according to industry tallies.

Kangwon Land, located in Jeongseon, Gangwon Province, saw its annual sales shoot up to 1.36 trillion won in 2013 with the number of guests reaching 3.07 million. The sales figure for 2014 is estimated at 1.59 trillion won.

The envisioned creation of two integrated casino resorts is expected to bring a synergy effect to the already booming casino business. Construction of two integrated resorts are already underway on Incheon's Yeongjong Island, a location considered to be the strongest candidate for the government-run casino resorts.

Paradise Group, in cooperation with Japanese Sega Sammy Holdings, began building an integrated casino resort called "Paradise City" on the island in November 2014. An integrated resort caters for both business people and tourists with casinos, hotels, shopping malls, convention halls, performance halls, gaming venues and theme parks.

The first-stage construction project of Paradise City is set to be completed in the first half of 2017 with a total budget of 1.3 trillion won. When the first-stage project is over, preparations for the second-stage construction are expected to begin.

Lippo and Caesars Consortium (LOCZ Korea), a joint venture between U.S. firm Caesars Entertainment and Indonesian company Lippo, plans to set up a casino resort, which is estimated to cost around $794 million, on the island by 2018. For this, the consortium received a license from the government in March 2014 and bought land to build the resort recently.

Industry experts say should the new casino resorts be created on Yeongjong Island, this can create a synergy effect arising from their integration, causing an influx of Chinese tourists due to the island's geographical proximity to China.

Of the 14.2 million foreign tourists who visited South Korea in 2014, 6.2 million were Chinese. The number of Chinese tourists who visit casinos in South Korea has risen 15% annually.

Grand Korea Leisure (GKL), the local operator of a foreigner-only casino, and several Chinese capitals are known to have interest in the government-led resort project on the island. But some showed skepticism over the project. They say the casino resorts to be built on the island are for foreigners only, so there will be limits in making profits and they can suffer from oversupply.

Japan's push to create casinos for all ahead of the 2020 Tokyo Olympics and the Chinese government's recent declaration of a war on corruption and a crackdown on gambling are also feared to pose a risk to the local casino business.

■ 'Smartphone Tour' Becomes a Trend

As more and more people prefer individual travel to group travel, the so-called "smartphone tour" became a trend in the tourism industry. Individual travelers use smartphones to book air tickets and hotels and search for popular tourist destinations and restaurants.

Boosted by this trend, the sales of air tickets and accomodations on mobile phones have greatly increased. For instance, of the 399,000 flight tickets put on sale by Hana Tour, one of the leading tourism agencies in the country, in the summer peak season of 2014, 43% or 171,000 tickets were sold on the agency's mobile app service for ticket reservation. The figure 171,000 was up 25.8% from the same period in 2013.

According to Interpark Tour, another local tour agency, reservations for accommodations made on its mobile booking app accounted for only 13.5% of the total online reservations in February 2013. But the rate jumped to 39.3% in February 2014 and to 60% in June.

■ International Flight Ticket Prices Decline

Prices of international flight tickets fell an average of 9% for the past three years mainly due to overheated competition among airlines fueled by the emergence of a number of low-cost carriers at home and abroad.

According to an analysis of ticket prices on major overseas routes, average air fare fell 9% from 749,075 won in 2011 to 684,981 won in 2014.

By region, air fare to Japan experienced the largest decline with 24% during the period, followed by Oceania (17 percent), Southeast Asia (15%), China (15%) and the Americas (11%).

FASHION

■ Overview

The economic recession continued to affect the local fashion market in 2014. Outdoor fashion brands were hit the hardest after years of fast growth while SPA brands got more popular than before among consumers with reasonable consumption behaviors.

On TV homeshopping channels, the wind of fashion items was stronger than before but consumers showed a consumption pattern that is typical for a recession. Direct shopping on overseas online shopping malls has been on a steady rise.

■ Direct Overseas Purchasing Booms

As online overseas purchasing steadily drew public attention, such purchases reached 1 trillion won in the first eight months of 2014, easily surpassing 1.1 trillion won recorded in 2013. The purchases, if this trend continues, are expected to hit 8 trillion won in 2018.

A padded jacket from Polo drew the most popularity among direct shoppers in 2014. The number of foreigners who buy items on domestic shopping sites also increased thanks to the runaway hit of the smash-hit local TV series, "My Love from the Stars," in China.

■ Growth of Outdoor Brands Slows Down

After years of fast growth, the local market for outdoor clothing slowed down in 2014 due to the lingering economic recession. The market for outdoor fashion products soared from 2 trillion won in 2000 to 4 trillion won in 2011.

But in 2014, the market was estimated at 6.9 trillion won, gaining almost no growth from the previous year. The North Face ranked No. 1 as the best-selling outdoor brand for the 12th straight year since it first took the post in 2003.

■ Growth of SPA Brands Continued

Global SPA brands such as G.U. of Uniqlo, COS of H&M and Joe Fresh, a Canadian SPA brand, pushed to expand their reach to the domestic market. The SPA brands from various foreign countries sought to increase their grip on the Korean fashion market, taking advantage of their management knowhow and marketing strategy gained from the global market.

Industry experts say SPA brands have totally changed the local fashion market as consumers who had purchased high-priced and quality products are no longer affordable for such products amid the protracted recession. South Korean conglomerates that had led the local fashion market have launched their own SPA brands from a few years ago. They are now expanding their products to women's casual wear, underwear, children's wear, outdoor and men's wear, against global SPA operators' introduction of family brands. The industry is now watching with interest the second round of war between the global and domestic SPA brands.

■ Fashion, Still Hottest Items on TV Homeshopping

Fashion continued to be an important part of major TV homeshopping channels, accounting for almost half of the most-selling products on them. For instance, the number of fashion items on the top 10 best-selling list for 2014 was five for CJ O Shopping and six for GS Shop.

■ Mobile Becomes Key Part of Fashion Market

A recent study found that women may be purchasing more on mobile shopping malls rather than online as far as clothes and fashion-related products are concerned.

As shoppers who used to drop department stores, street shopping malls to purchase clothing moved to the mobile market that provides a great accessibility, operators of mobile shopping malls devised a variety of marketing strategies to make the shoppers visit the malls more frequently and stay longer.

Some brands even developed an app-based mobile payment system to differentiate them from other brands. Also noteworthy is a study that found that the growth of mobile shopping more than doubled on-year in 2014.

According to the Korean Online Shopping Association, Korea's mobile shopping market is expected to be worth about 10 trillion won, up more than 100% from the previous year. The association attributed the fast growth to the popularity of smart devices and social networking services and the wider use of e-money.

Sports

Yonhap News Agency

OVERVIEW

It was an action-packed 2014 for South Korean sports. Figure skating Olympic champion Kim Yu-na retired. The country had a disastrous campaign at the FIFA World Cup in Brazil. The western city of Incheon hosted the Asian Games, with North Korea also taking part.

In Major League Baseball, Ryu Hyun-jin of the Los Angeles Dodgers and Choo Shin-soo of the Texas Rangers had decidedly mixed fortunes. Park Ji-sung retired from football, ending his European club career.

At the end of 2014, Yonhap News Agency polled 48 newspapers and broadcasters (19 national and 29 regional outlets) on the top 10 sports-related news of the year. Kim Yu-na's retirement and the judging controversy surrounding her final Olympics came out on top.

Kim had long set out to retire after the Sochi Winter Games. She led the field after the short program and seemed well on her way to her second consecutive Olympic gold.

Kim also put together a flawless free skate, but the gold medal went to Adelina Sotnikova (224.59 points) of the host Russia, who'd trailed Kim by 0.28 point after the short program. Kim ended with 219.11 points. Foreign media and figure skating experts cried foul over judging. The Korea Skating Union appealed to the International Skating Union to no avail.

▲ *South Korean figure skater Kim Yu-na performs her free skate program in ladies' singles competition during the 2014 Winter Olympics in Sochi, Russia, on Feb. 20.*

Whereas Kim settled for silver, speed skater Lee Sang-hwa dominated the women's 500-meter race and claimed her second straight Olympic gold. The Vancouver Olympic champion posted a combined time of 74.70 seconds after two races, becoming the first Asian skater, male or female, to defend an Olympic speed skating gold.

Also in Sochi, South Korean-born short track star Viktor Ahn competed for Russia after getting naturalized. He received his Russian passport in 2011, after enjoying a memorable career in South Korea.

Ahn won the bronze in the 1,500m for Russia's first-ever Olympic short track medal, and then won the 1,000m gold medal for his first Olympic title in eight years. Ahn swept up two more golds in the 500m and the 5,000m relay to raise his career Olympic medal total to a record-tying eight. While Ahn proved he was far from finished, the South Korean men left without a medal for the first time in a dozen years.

At the FIFA World Cup in Brazil, South Korea was a major disappointment. Coached by Hong Myung-bo, South Korea set its sight on making the quarterfinals for the first time at an away World Cup.

Yet it failed to win a match in the group stage with one draw and two losses. After such a lethargic showing, Hong's selection of players and his lack of tactical acumen came under the microscope. It was also reported that Hong might have compromised some training hours just before the World Cup when he purchased real estate, and that his squad had a team dinner with alcohol being served immediately following the elimination.

The Korea Football Association at first gave Hong its vote of confidence, but Hong, under mounting pressure from the still-angered public, decided to step down. German-native Uli Stielike took over the national team, becoming the first foreign head coach for South Korea since the Dutchman Pim Verbeek in July 2007.

At the Asian Games that kicked off at home in September, South Korea grabbed 79 gold, 71 silver and 84 bronze to finish second for the fifth consecutive event. Archery, shooting, taekwondo, judo, wrestling and fencing, among some other traditional gold mines, once again delivered the goods.

South Korea also excelled in ball sports. Baseball defended its gold, while the men's and the women's teams both won the gold medal for the first time. The men's football team defeated North Korea in the final with a dramatic last-gasp goal in extra time, bringing home the first Asiad title in 28 years. More gold medals came from women's volleyball, women's handball and women's field hockey.

Rhythmic gymnast Son Yeon-jae, the nation's sweetheart, was one of the competition's biggest stars, becoming the first South Korean in the event to win an Asian Games gold.

North Korea competed in its second straight Asiad south of the border, after the 2002 Busan Asian Games. North Korea picked up four gold medals in weightlifting and also won the women's football tournament. It ended with 11 gold, 11 silver and 14 bronze, good for seventh place overall.

In domestic professional sports, the Samsung Lions won both the KBO pennant and the Korean Series for the fourth straight year. Their accomplishments ranked third on Yonhap's survey.

After clinching their fourth pennant in a row, the Lions fended off the Nexen Heroes to win the Korean Series in six games. They're the first club to claim the pennant and the Korean Series for four years in a row. Seo Geon-chang of the Heroes, a former practice squad player, became the first player to get more than 200 hits in a season and was voted the MVP.

In Major League Baseball, Ryu Hyunjin shook off the sophomore jinx and established himself as a viable big league starter. In 2013, Ryu went 14-8 as a rookie with a 3.00 ERA. In 2014, he was 14-7 with a 3.38 ERA as a key member of the Dodgers' rotation.

He was shut down early in the regular season with an injury, but he came back for the National League Division Series against the St. Louis Cardinals. In Game 3, Ryu held the Cards to one earned run in six innings.

Choo Shin-soo signed a seven-year, $130 million contract with the Rangers, but injuries held him back. He was nagged by left elbow and left ankle pains all year. He could never get used to the ever-changing strike zone. He finished the season with a .242 average, a .340 on-base percentage and 13 home runs.

▲ *Park Ji-sung is tossed into the air by players of PSV Eindhoven after a friendly between the Dutch team and South Korea's Suwon Bluewings at the World Cup Stadium in Suwon, Gyeonggi Province, on May 22. Park played with the Dutch team in the match to mark his retirement.*

Park Ji-sung, an Asian football icon plying his trade in Europe, announced his retirement, citing debilitating knee injuries. Park rose to international fame during the 2002 World Cup, co-hosted by South Korea and Japan. And Guus Hiddink, who'd coached South Korea at that tournament, brought Park back to his Dutch club, PSV Eindhoven.

In 2005, Park became the first South Korean in the English Premier League when he signed with Manchester United. In seven seasons with Man United, Park scored 27 goals in 205 matches. He is the first South Korean to score a goal in the tournament stage at the UEFA Champions League, the first Asian to win a Premiership title and the first to win the UEFA Champions League.

In women's golf, Kim Hyo-joo had a sensational season. On the KLPGA Tour, Kim won the money title, the scoring title (average of 70.26 per round) and the Player of the Year honors, while also leading the tour in victories. At the ripe age of 19, Kim became a force to be reckoned with.

Top 10 Sports News Stories of 2014

❶ Kim Yu-na retires from figure skating amid a judging controversy at the Sochi Winter Olympics (330 points)

❷ South Korea eliminated in group stage at the World Cup ... Hong Myung-bo resigns as Uli Stielike comes on board (326 points)

❸ Samsung Lions win the pennant and the Korean Series for fourth straight year (208 points)

❹ Lee Sang-hwa defends her Olympic gold in the women's 500m speed skating (202 points)

❺ Seo Geon-chang writes history as ex-practice squad player, surpasses 200 hits for the season and wins the MVP (198 points)

❻ Incheon hosts the Asian Games ... North Korea competes (191 points)

❼ Viktor Ahn's success at the Sochi Winter Olympics and its aftermath (138 points)

❽ Ryu Hyun-jin wins 14 games for second straight season ... Choo Shin-soo struggles after signing mega free agent deal (133 points)

❾ Park Ji-sung retires from football (119 points)

❿ Sensational season by golfer Kim Hyo-joo ... Youth served well (100 points)

2014 INCHEON ASIAN GAMES

(Sept. 19~Oct. 4, 2014, Incheon)

The Asian Games, the largest multi-sport competition on the continent of 4.5 billion people, kicked off on Sept. 19 and finished on Oct. 4 in Incheon. South Korea sent its largest Asia delegation ever with 1,068, including 831 athletes in all 36 sports.

South Korea won 79 gold, 71 silver and 81 bronze to rank second. China swept up 151 gold, 108 silver and 83 bronze medals, once again reaffirming its status as the dominant powerhouse.

▪ Partial Success in Medal Race

South Korea finished second in the medal standings for the fifth consecutive Asian Games, though many felt the result represented only a partial success.

South Korea did excel in its traditional gold mines, which include archery, shooting, taekwondo, judo, wrestling and fencing, along with some other combat events. South Korea took home eight gold medals in shooting, while its archers won five of the eight gold medals up for grabs. South Korea also dominated fencing with eight gold medals.

In combat events, the host did better than in the past. Popular professional sports, such as baseball and football, delighted fans with gold medals. In the baseball final, South Korea came from behind against Taiwan in the eighth to clinch the gold.

In men's football, South Korea edged out North Korea with a dramatic last-gasp goal in extra time. More gold medals came from women's handball, basketball and volleyball. The women simply rocked.

Rhythmic gymnast Son Yeon-jae, one of the country's most beloved athletes, became the first South Korean to win an Asian Games gold in her sport. She emerged as the darling of the entire competition.

▲ South Korean rhythmic gymnast Son Yeon-jae performs with the ribbon during the 2014 Asian Games at Namdong Gymnasium in Incheon on Oct. 1.

During the Asiad, South Korea conceded the No. 2 spot in the medal race to Japan. Yet gold medals from bowling and soft tennis, among other lesser-known sports, lifted South Korea past its rival.

However, with some of the established stars coming up short of expectations, South Korea couldn't accomplish its goal of winning 90 gold medals.

Pistol shooter Jin Jong-oh, gymnast Yang Hak-seon and swimmer Park Tae-hwan were all hugely disappointing. Jin managed a gold medal in a team event, while Yang and Park failed to win a gold.

South Korea was shut out of gold in athletics and swimming, two of the fundamental sports in multisport competitions. Critics also noted that sports that rely too heavily on one or two stars, such as swimming, artistic gymnastics and rhythmic gymnastics, should strive for more balanced development.

▪ South Korea Lags Behind in Fundamentals

The South Korean national anthem was not played once at Park Tae-hwan Aquatics Center, the venue for swimming competitions, and the Incheon Asiad Main Stadium, which hosted track and field events. It was a solemn reminder of South Korea's standings in two of the most fundamental sports.

Swimming offered the most gold medals with 53, followed by athletics with 47. And for the first time since the 1978 Bangkok Asiad, South Korea failed to win a gold in both swimming and athletics. In artistic gymnastics, South Korea failed to get gold for the first time since 1982 in New Delhi.

In track and field, South Korea is falling further from relevance in Asia. The likes of Qatar and Bahrain have become more competitive by naturalizing African-born athletes. China, still the Asian athletics powerhouse, led the way with 15 gold medals. Japan earned three. South Korean, meanwhile, settled for four silver and six bronze medals. The country had set out to capture three gold medals, but it seemed a tad unrealistic.

There were some bright spots, however. In the men's 110m hurdles, Kim Byoung-jun set a national record of 13.43 seconds to win the silver. The men's

4x400m relay team of Seong Hyeok-je, Park Bong-go, Park Se-jung and Yeo Hosua set their own national record of 3:04.03 to win the silver. Yeo also won the bronze in the men's 200m, becoming the first South Korean man to win an Asiad sprint medal in 28 years.

Lim Eun-jin was the first South Korean Asian Games medalist in the women's pole vault. In the men's 50km race walk, Park Chil-sung got the silver, while in the men's and the women's 20km race walk, Kim Hyun-sub and Jeon Yeong-eun each got the bronze.

Despite these small victories, things were disappointing for South Korea for the most part. The host couldn't place anyone in the finals of the men's and women's 100m. Its athletes ranked well out of contention in throwing events too.

Yeo, the only South Korean to win more than one athletics medal, called for stronger support to develop athletics at the grassroots level.

In swimming, South Korea earned two silver and six bronze medals. Of those eight, six (one silver and five bronze) came in Park Tae-hwan's races. Park was going for his third consecutive Asiad gold in the 200m free and the 400m free but only got bronze in both. He was the reigning Asiad champ in the 100m free but settled for silver this time.

Kosuke Hagino of Japan was a quadruple gold medalist, while Ning Zetao and Shen Duo each won four gold medals for China. South Korea simply couldn't compete.

In artistic gymnastics, another fundamental event, South Korea drew blanks. Yang Hak-seon, the man they call "God of Vault," failed to defend his vault gold medal. South Korea won silver in the men's team event, while Lee Sang-wook got the bronze in the men's individual all-around and Park Min-soo earned the bronze in the men's pommel horse.

Yoon Na-rae emerged as the future of women's gymnastics in South Korea. However, getting shut out of gold for the first time in 32 years was a big letdown. Despite China and Japan not sending their best gymnasts, with the top names choosing instead to prepare for the world championships, South Korea still played second fiddle.

The conclusions of each Olympics and Asian Games are often followed by calls for nurturing athletes for these fundamental sports. So far, though, the country has relied on a few gifted athletes to carry the load. Overall South Korea regressed at the Incheon Asian Games.

■ Changing Landscapes of Gold Mines

In Incheon, South Korea struggled in sports it had thrived in the past, while the athletes in some lesser-known sports took major steps forward.

South Korea finished second in fencing medal tallies at the 2012 London Olympics, and the sport was expected to once again deliver the goods in Incheon.

It was a sign of things to come. From Sept. 20 to 25, South Korea swept up eight of 12 gold medals at stake, getting the host off to a blazing start early in the Asian Games. No other country has ever won eight fencing gold medals at an Asiad. It was also a balanced performance: four gold medals each came from individual and team events, with six silver and three bronze medals also being won.

There were three all-South Korean finals in individual events. South Korea won seven fencing titles at the 2010 Guangzhou Asian Games, and thanks to another strong performance at home, it further established itself as a major strength for South Korea.

In equestrian, South Korea won four out of six gold medals available, along with a silver and a bronze. It was the country's best-ever Asiad performance. Song Sang-wuk, the first South Korean champ in eventing, led the way with two gold medals. Hwang Young-sik got his two gold in dressage, one apiece in the individual and team competitions.

In sailing, South Korea picked up multiple gold medals toward the end of September. Park Sung-bin became the Asiad's youngest gold medalist in the men's optimist. The host also won titles in the men's laser, the men's 470 and the Hobie-16. South Korea added silver in open match racing and bronze in the women's 420. In total, South Korea led all countries with four gold, one silver and one bronze.

Some of the usual suspects delivered the goods again. Bowlers got off to a slow start but walked away with seven out of 12 gold medals available, along with one silver and six bronze medals. South Korea has been the top bowling nation at every Asiad since 2002. Female bowler Lee Na-young was the only South Korean to win four gold medals in Incheon.

South Korea has been a perennial powerhouse in archery, and the host overcame rule changes among other obstacles to earn five out of eight gold medals at stake. South Korea was able to fend off some emerging nations to stay on top.

Wrestling, golf, shooting and taekwondo, which could always be counted on for a slew of gold medals, were disappointments in Incheon. There were three golds and 12 medals overall from wrestling, and it was a measure of redemption for a country that was shut out of gold in Guangzhou in 2010.

Kim Hyeon-woo completed his grand slam of international titles. Yet, South Korea can no longer be expected to win five or more gold medals consistently, and those concerned about the future of the sport say South Korea should have bolstered its lineup of freestyle wrestlers.

In golf, South Korea swept up all four gold medals in 2006 and in 2010. In Incheon, Chinese Taipei snatched a pair of gold medals while Thailand had one, limiting South Korea to just one gold medal.

In shooting, the host earned eight gold, 11 silver and eight bronze. The gold medal total actually exceeded the original target of five to seven, but South Korea had to watch as China gobbled up 27 golds. Perhaps it was only a flash in the pan that South Korea claimed 13 golds in Guangzhou. Taekwondo produced six champions from the host, up from four in Guangzhou.

■ Victories in Ball Sports Delight Home Crowds

Strong performances in football, baseball, basketball and volleyball ramped up the excitement in the stands. Professional stars in football and baseball thriving on the international stage delighted the crowds. Both baseball and football had dramatic finishes for the gold medal.

In the baseball final, South Korea was trailing Chinese Taipei 3-2 in the eighth but scored four runs in that inning to charge out in front 6-3. It stood as the final score, as South Korea defended its Asiad gold and claimed its fourth baseball title overall.

The men's football team faced North Korea in the final, and Rim Chang-woo netted the thrilling winner in the dying seconds of the extra period for an improbable 1-0 victory. It was South Korea's first Asiad gold in men's football since the 1986 competition in Seoul.

Both the women's basketball and women's volleyball teams defeated China to end the country's 20-year Asiad drought. In women's basketball, South Korea lost to China in the final in 2002 and again in 2010. The third time proved to be the charm, as South Korea prevailed 70-64. The women's volleyball team lost to China 3-2 in Guangzhou but exacted its revenge with a convincing 3-0 victory for the gold, behind Kim Yeon-koung's 26 points.

The men's basketball team pulled off a major upset over the Asian champ Iran, erasing a five-point deficit with two minutes to play to win 79-77. It was the country's first Asiad men's hoops gold since 2002.

The men's volleyball team earned the bronze with a win over China. Though the host came up short of sweeping gold medals in its four major professional sports, it was still the best performance in ball sports since 2002, when South Korea won golds in baseball, men's basketball and men's volleyball.

On the flip side, these professional athletes faced their share of criticism. In baseball, Japan, South Korea's usual rival, only sent amateurs. Chinese Taipei built a team of young prospects. Because of the obvious gap in talent, South Korea's gold medal was rendered that much less impressive. There were also people who wondered aloud if some of the little-used players deserved to receive exemptions to the mandatory military service with the rest of the team.

In the men's football quarters, South Korea struggled against the Japanese team made up entirely of under-21 players before eventually winning. In women's basketball and women's volleyball, China and Japan, both strong title contenders, sent their best athletes to the world championships, which overlapped with the Asian Games. Both nations boast such depth that their "B" teams are just as strong as their top squads. Still, beating the reserves for gold medals couldn't exactly be considered monumental feats.

Women's handball and hockey, while overshadowed by more glamorous sports, delivered fine performances. South Korea was upset by Japan in the women's handball semifinals in Guangzhou but defeated Japan 29-19 this time for the country's sixth Asiad gold.

In the women's hockey final, Kim Darae scored the winner against China, as South Korea avenged a painful loss to the Chinese in the final four years earlier. It was South Korea's first Asian Games gold in women's hockey in 16 years.

■ Bright Youngsters Show Promise for Bright Future

The Asian Games saw the emergence of some promising athletes who are expected to dominate the continental and also global competitions for years to come.

Lee Ha-sung, the host country's first gold medalist at the Asiad, is one of them. On Sept. 20, Lee upset gold medal contenders in the men's changquan event to bring South Korea its first wushu Asiad gold in 12 years. Lee once appeared on a television program as a child wushu prodigy, and he put his nerves of steel on full display to capture the surprise gold.

New stars also rose in shooting. Kim Cheong-yong, the teenage sensation, became the first multiple gold medalist, taking home the individual and team titles in the men's 10m air pistol. He was also the youngest Asiad shooting gold medalist for South Korea. His boyish good looks and the fact that he'd lost his father at an early age further endeared him to fans.

Kim Jun-hong was just blossoming into a star after finishing his mandatory military service and picked up a gold in the men's 25m rapid fire pistol, while adding the individual and team silvers in the 25m standard pistol.

In fencing, where South Korea snatched eight out of a dozen golds, star-struck underdogs finally had their moments. In the women's sabre, Lee Rajin stunned the reigning Olympic champ Kim Ji-yeon, her first win over the former middle school and high school teammate in an international event.

In the women's foil, Jeon Hee-sook, who'd been long overshadowed by the Olympic medalist Nam Hyun-hee, defeated Nam in the semifinals and then went on to win the gold. Jeon later admitted she concentrated extra hard in that semifinal showdown because she didn't want to play second fiddle again. Jung Jin-sun, a seasoned veteran in the men's epee, defeated his teammate Park Kyoung-doo for the first individual gold medal of his career.

In archery, Jung Dasomi captured both the individual and the team titles in the women's recurve. In bowling, Lee Na-young, a late bloomer who only made the national team in 2013, became South Korea's only quadruple gold medalist.

Rhythmic gymnast Son Yeon-jae stole the show in the late stages of the event. She guided her teammates to South Korea's first Asiad silver in the team competition. In the individual all-around, Son edged out China's Deng Senyue for her first gold. Son admitted to feeling stressed out by malicious online messages, and she let her history-making performance do the talking.

Among foreign athletes, young champions emerged in swimming and gymnastics. In the men's 200m freestyle swimming, Kosuke Hagino of Japan stunned the two established stars, Park Tae-hwan of South Korea and Sun Yang of China, for the gold. Hagino then added golds in the 200m individual relay and 4x200m freestyle relay to become Incheon's first triple medalist. He added the 400m individual medley title to his tally.

Japan had long dominated the breaststroke, but it was Dmitriy Balandin of Kazakhstan who swept up golds in the 50m, the 100m and the 200m breaststroke. Ning Zetao of China also won four gold medals in swimming (the men's 50m and the 100m freestyle, the 4x100m medley relay and the 4x100m freestyle relay). Yao Jinnan, also of China, claimed four golds in artistic gymnastics: the women's floor exercise, uneven bars, individual all-around and team.

■ **North Korea, Determined to Become Sports Power, Returns to Top 10**

North Korea performed admirably at the Asian Games. Ever since its leader Kim Jong-un began the push to build North Korea into a sports power, this was the second-largest international multisport competition, behind the 2012 London Olympics.

At London, North Korea came away with four gold and two bronze, its best Olympic performance in 20 years. North Korea picked up right where it left off in Incheon, capturing 11 gold, 11 silver and 14 bronze for seventh place.

North Korea ranked ninth with nine gold medals at the 2002 Busan Asian Games, but in Doha in 2006 and in Guangzhou in 2010, it only could manage six gold medals each, finishing 16th and 12th, respectively.

Weightlifting played the biggest role in North Korea's ascent. Om Yun-chol, Kim Un-guk, Ri Jong-hwa and Kim Un-ju were gold medalists, and they combined for five world records. In light weight classes, North Korea held its ground against China, long considered the best in the world. North Korea also did well in football, the one sport in which Kim Jong-un had taken the most interest.

In women's football, North Korea came from behind to beat South Korea and then got past Japan for the gold medal, the country's third Asiad title. Korean Central TV carried the item in a news flash, and it was a major cause for celebration in the North.

▲ *North Korean female footballers celebrate after defeating Japan 3-1 in the final of the 2014 Asian Games at Munhak Stadium in Incheon on Oct. 1.*

The men's team lost to South Korea in the gold medal match but still left a strong impression with some spirited play. North Korea won two golds in artistic gymnastics and picked up one each in shooting, wrestling and boxing.

Thanks to a strong Asian Games, Kim Jong-un's sports-centric policy should get a much-needed push. In the North, sports are often used to inspire patriotism in people and rally the public.

During the competition, North Korea also showed its more flexible and open side. Its traveling journalists stayed inside the media village with other members of the press. The female football players received flower bouquets along with their gold medals and were generous enough to share the flowers with the volunteers.

The North Korean female athletes were all fashionably dressed, decked out in skirts and heels. Kim Yong-hun, Pyongyang's minister of physical culture and sports and the head of its Olympic committee, stayed in Incheon for the duration of the Asian Games, a sign of the country's overall interest in the event. He visited venues for weightlifting and football to cheer on his athletes.

There weren't any formal talks between officials of the two countries. Kim Yong-hun was the North's highest-ranking official to travel to the South since President Park Geun-hye took office in Seoul, but no surprise meeting materialized.

■ **Organizing Committee under Fire for Shoddy Operations**

The organizing committee for the Asian Games did such a shoddy job running the event it was at times embarrassing. The organizers poured in 2.2 trillion won to build 16 venues. Yet it turned out they didn't quite have the know-how to run the show, and they hadn't paid attention to detail.

The identity of the final torch bearer, often kept secret until the very last minute in most competitions, was leaked. It was a prime example of the organizers' lack of understanding of the operations and of the communication breakdown within. A mishap such as that was actually foreseen before the opening ceremony.

With about 10 days left before the start of the competition, journalists from across the continent began to check in at the Main Press Center (MPC).

However, the organizers simply weren't ready to welcome them. One foreign journalist said, "We discussed some of the things with the organizers that needed to be taken care of months before the competition. But the Internet connection was set up three days after we opened our office."

Members of the operating staff and vol-unteers who didn't receive proper training ended up causing major headaches during the event. After the end of the opening ceremony, the participating athletes found themselves stuck among the crowds outside the main stadium, waitingly hopelessly for the shuttles to the athletes' village that didn't come on time.

The organizing committee also did an inadequate job running mixed zones, and for some press conferences, it didn't have appropriate interpreters in place.

The volunteers and interpreters often bore the brunt of criticism, while at the same time they had to endure subpar working conditions.

Transportation was a major source of problems. Venues were placed all over Incheon, but the organizers just weren't ready to accommodate the athletes and the media. On more than a few occasions, athletes who'd completed their training or competitions were forced to wait outside for more than half an hour, as their bodies cooled, for buses to the athletes' village.

As the event wore on, the organizers showed a steady improvement in their operations. There's little doubt, however, that they should have done a better job preparing for the big event down to the final detail.

Such poor operations by the Incheon Asian Games organizers provided an example of what not to do for the organizers of upcoming athletic events in South Korea: the 2015 Summer Universiade in Gwangju and the 2018 Winter Olympics in PyeongChang. The lesson is this: You may be hosting a competition for amateur athletes, but you can't be amateurish about it.

The 17th Asian Games Incheon 2014

Rank	Country	Gold	Silver	Bronze
1	China	151	109	83
2	South Korea	79	71	84
3	Japan	47	76	76
4	Kazakhstan	28	23	33
5	Iran	21	18	18
6	Thailand	12	7	28
7	North Korea	11	11	14
8	India	11	9	37
9	Chinese Taipei	10	18	23
10	Qatar	10	0	4
11	Uzbekistan	9	14	21
12	Bahrain	9	6	4
13	Hong Kong	6	12	24
14	Malaysia	5	14	14
15	Singapore	5	6	13
16	Mongolia	5	4	12
17	Indonesia	4	5	11
18	Kuwait	3	5	4
19	Saudi Arabia	3	3	1
20	Myanmar	2	1	1
21	Vietnam	1	10	25
22	Philippines	1	3	11
23	Pakistan	1	1	3
	Tajikistan	1	1	3
25	Iraq	1	0	3
	United Arab Emirates	1	0	3
27	Sri Lanka	1	0	1
28	Cambodia	1	0	0
29	Macao	0	3	4
30	Kyrgyzstan	0	2	4
31	Jordan	0	2	2
32	Turkmenistan	0	1	5
33	Bangladesh	0	1	2
	Laos	0	1	2
35	Afghanistan	0	1	1
	Lebanon	0	1	1
37	Nepal	0	0	1

PROFESSIONAL LEAGUES·OTHER SPORTS

PROFESSIONAL FOOTBALL

■ **Summary**

In professional football in 2014, we saw runaway champions in both the first and the second divisions. In the top-flight K League Classic, Jeonbuk Hyundai Motors climbed to first place in August and never came down. On Nov. 8 in Jeju, Jeonbuk defeated the home club Jeju United 3-0 to clinch the league title with three matches to spare. Jeonuk opened a 13-point lead over the second-place Suwon Samsung Bluewings.

Sangju Sangmu finished dead last in 12th place and got relegated to the second-tier K League Challenge for 2015. Daejeon Citizen dominated the second division. Ansan Police FC made a push, but on Nov. 5, following a 1-1 draw with FC Anyang, Daejeon opened an eight-point lead with two matches remaining to secure the league title.

Daejeon earned an automatic promotion to the top division. Gwangju FC also punched a ticket to the K League Classic. Gwangju finished fourth in the regular season, and knocked out Gangwon FC and then Ansan in the playoffs. Gwangju then took on Gyeongnam FC, the 11th-ranked team from the K League Classic, in the promotional playoff, and came away victorious.

■ Jeonbuk without Peer···Seoul·Pohang with Mixed Fortunes Late

Even as other teams cut down on their spending, Jeonbuk kept its wallet open, building a spanking new club house and acquiring players with abandon to strengthen its roster. Well before the start of the season, Jeonbuk was considered the prohibitive title favorite.

Head coach Choi Kang-hee, who briefly left the team to lead the national team in late 2011, returned during the 2013 season. By 2014, Jeonbuk once again became Choi's team.

The star striker Lee Dong-gook continued to perform at a high level. New faces, such as Kim Nam-il, Han Kyo-won and Caio, blended seamlessly with the rest of the squad. Lee Jae-sung was one of the promising youngsters on the rise.

Jeonbuk reached first place on Aug. 3 and never let up. Jeonbuk closed out the season on a 15-match undefeated streak, starting with the match against Sangju Sangmu on Sept. 6. Jeonbuk at one point reeled off eight consecutive clean sheet victories, a streak that started with a win over Jeju on Oct. 1 and went all the way to a win over Pohang on Nov. 15.

Jeonbuk led all 12 K League Classic clubs with 61 goals and also gave up the fewest goals with 22. The team was a complete package.

Suwon ended in fifth in 2013, but in the second season with Seo Jung-won as head coach, the team improved in every facet despite a shrinking budget. Suwon finished second to Jeonbuk.

FC Seoul overcame some early season woes to finish third. On the final day of the season, FC Seoul came from behind to defeat Jeju 2-1. Pohang Steelers fell to Suwon 2-1 on the same day, allowing FC Seoul to overtake them for third place and secure a ticket to the Asian Football Confederation (AFC) Champions League playoff.

Pohang, the 2013 champ, played its second straight season without a foreign player but had a disappointing finish to the season. Suwon's Santos led the competition with 14 goals, and Jeonbuk's Lee Seung-gi topped the league with 10 assists.

■ Sangju·Gyeongnam Relegated···Daejeon·Gwangju Promoted

Sangju Sangmu, a military club where conscripted players can only stay on for two years, finished dead last in the K League Classic. Lee Keun-ho and other key players were discharged, and the club slipped to last place in September, unable to bounce back the rest of the season.

Gyeongnam FC brought in the veteran Lee Cha-man as head coach and acquired goalkeeper Kim Young-kwang among other players to try to join the upper tier. The club, though, finished in 11th place and lost to Gwangju FC in the promotion playoff to be relegated for the first time.

In the K League Challenge, Daejeon Citizen started out with 12 wins, two draws and one loss. The team had a dry spell in September and October with a six-match winless skid (four draws and two losses) but managed to win the league.

Adriano, the Brazilian attacker, scored a whopping 27 goals in only 31 contests to lift the team to the championship.

Gwangju FC secured the fourth spot on the final day of the season to squeeze into the playoff. Then Gwangju rolled over the competition in three playoff matches, the final being the promotion playoff against Gyeongnam and returned to the top league for the first time in three years.

Both teams are led by relatively young coaches still in their 40s: Jo Jin-ho for Daejeon and Nam Ki-il for Gwangju. Their ability to communicate effectively with the players was considered a major force behind the clubs' emergence.

■ 10-Game Point Streak·Oldest Player Takes Field

Lee Myung-joo of Pohang Steelers recorded at least a goal or an assist in 10 consecutive matches, with five goals and nine assists starting with a match on March 15.

His streak ended in a match on May 10. Four players had shared the previous record of a nine-game point streak: Radivoje Manic (six goals and five assists for Busan in 1997), Everaldo De Jesus Pereira (seven goals and five assists for Gyeongnam in 2007), Eninho (eight goals and four assists for Daegu in 2008) and Lee Keun-ho (nine goals and four assists for Sangju in 2013).

Despite his record, Lee wasn't picked for the national team for the 2014 FIFA World Cup in Brazil. During the K League's World Cup break in June, Lee joined Al-Ain in the United Arab Emirates and couldn't extend his streak.

Jeonbuk forward Lee Dong-book scored a goal and set up two against Sangju on July 20, becoming the third player in the league ever, after Shin Tae-yong and Eninho, with at least 60 goals and 60 assists for their career. Lee is also the all-time leader in goals and netted 13 goals in 2014 to increase his tally to 167.

Park Soo-chang of Jeju United poured in four goals in the first half of the Sept. 6 match against Jeonnam Dragons FC, becoming the first K League player to score four goals in the first half.

Kim Byung-ji, the veteran Jeonnam goalkeeper, took the field against Sangju on Nov. 22 at the age of 44 years, seven months and 14 days, becoming the oldest

player ever to play in a K League match. Shin Eui-son held the previous record by five days. Kim then appeared in the next match a week later to rewrite his own record. Kim also holds the league record for most career games with 679.

2014 K League Classic Final Table

Pos.	Team	Pts	W	D	L	GF	GA	GD
1	Jeonbuk	81	24	9	5	61	22	39
2	Suwon	67	19	10	9	52	37	15
3	Seoul	58	15	13	10	42	28	14
4	Pohang	58	16	10	12	50	39	11
5	Jeju	54	14	12	12	39	37	2
6	Ulsan	50	13	11	14	44	43	1
7	Jeonnam	51	14	9	15	48	53	-5
8	Busan	43	10	13	15	37	49	-12
9	Seongnam	40	9	13	16	32	39	-7
10	Incheon	40	8	16	14	33	46	-13
11	Gyeongnam	36	7	15	16	30	52	-22
12	Sangju	34	7	13	18	39	62	-23

2014 K League Challenge Final Table

Pos.	Team	Pts	W	D	L	GF	GA	GD
1	Daejeon	70	20	10	6	64	36	28
2	Ansan	59	16	11	9	57	47	10
3	Gangwon	54	16	6	14	48	50	-2
4	Gwangju	51	13	12	11	40	35	5
5	Anyang	51	15	6	15	49	52	-3
6	Suwon	48	12	12	12	52	49	3
7	Daegu	47	13	8	15	49	46	3
8	Goyang	47	11	14	11	36	41	-5
9	Chungju	34	6	16	14	37	57	-20
10	Bucheon	27	6	9	21	33	52	-19

※ *Teams ranked based on points-goal difference-goals scored-wins-superior head-to-head record*

PROFESSIONAL BASEBALL

■ Samsung Builds Dynasty, Wins Fourth Straight Championship

For the fourth year in a row, the South Korean baseball season ended with the same picture. The Samsung Lions' players sprinted out on to the ground to celebrate their championship, and their manager Ryu Joong-il shook hands with his coaches. Ryu had the wide smile of a champion. On Nov. 11, 2014, when the season ended, Ryu once again found himself in the spotlight.

The Lions were the champions of South Korean baseball in 2014 again. Their impressive streak of winning both the pennant and the Korean Series started back in 2011. In 2014 the Lions fended off the Nexen Heroes in the championship series.

▲ Players of the Samsung Lions rejoice after pounding the Nexen Heroes 11-1 at Jamsil Stadium in Seoul on Nov. 11, to capture the Korean Series in six games. The Lions became only the second team to win four consecutive Korea Baseball Organization (KBO) titles in the league's 32-year history.

"People say it's the same every year, but to me, this championship is new and special," Ryu said. "I woke up on the morning of Nov. 11, the day of Game 6 of the Korean Series. A friend texted me and said, 'There are four 1's today,' as in the 11th day of the 11th month. I guess I was destined to clinch my fourth title. I will never forget Nov. 11."

Samsung reached first place on May 16 and never came down the rest of the regular season. They kept it up in the postseason to capture the Korean Series. Ryu led the national team to the gold medal at the Asian Games in September, shaking off the disappointment of an early elimination at the 2013 World Baseball Classic. He has joined the ranks of the country's greatest managers.

■ New Faces on Rise, Traditional Powers in Decline

The Heroes, though they came up short, made a valiant run at the title. The NC Dinos, which only joined the league in 2013, became the fastest expansion franchise to make the postseason. On the other hand, the Doosan Bears, the Lotte Giants and the Kia Tigers, the original franchises of the league that started in 1982, struggled among the upstarts.

The Heroes, which were founded in 2008, dominated the regular season along with the Lions. They finished in second place, one better than a year ago, and reached the second round of the playoffs and then the Korean Series for the first time.

The Dinos were even more impressive. The Dinos finished seventh in their inaugural season in 2013 and then became the first KBO expansion franchise to make the postseason in the second year.

The original members had seasons that they'd rather forget. The Bears, the league's inaugural champion in 1982, missed the postseason for the first time since 2011. The Tigers, who have won a league-leading 10 titles, missed the postseason for the third straight year.

The Giants once made the playoffs in five consecutive years starting in 2008 but missed out on the postseason for the second straight year in 2014, much to the chagrin of the enthusiastic fans in Busan. The Hanwha Eagles spent most of the season near the bottom of the standings and ended up in dead last for the third straight year.

■ Revolving Door for Managers···Kim Sung-keun Takes Over Hanwha as Fans' Wishes Come True

The five non-playoff clubs all changed their managers after the end of the regular season.

Kim Sung-keun, the veteran dubbed "Baseball God," who took over the Hanwha Eagles, came under the brightest spotlight. He had been managing the Goyang Wonders, South Korea's first independent baseball club, but when the Wonders folded, Kim's future became a hot potato in baseball.

Fans of the Eagles began an online petition calling on the club to hire Kim, and they even picketed in front of Hanwha's headquarters in Seoul. The club went on to ink Kim to a three-year deal.

Kim had last managed in the KBO with the SK Wyverns in August 2011. He ran the Eagles into the ground during their season-ending camp, and in a highly unusual turn of events, the last-place club began making headlines in the offseason. Kim Sung-keun mania was in full swing almost from Day 1.

The Kia Tigers at first re-signed manager Sun Dong-yol after his contract expired, but Sun himself stepped down under mounting pressure from angry fans. Kim Ki-tai was hired as Sun's successor. The Lotte Giants saw Kim Si-jin resign after the season, and several executives also left the club amid allegations that the team illegally reviewed CCTV footage at road hotels to monitor its players. When the dust settled, Lee Jong-woon emerged as the new manager.

The Doosan Bears dismissed Song Il-soo after only one season and replaced him with Kim Tae-hyung. The Wyverns decided not to retain Lee Man-soo after his contract expired, and Kim Yong-hee was hired as the new manager.

■ Seo Geon-chang Reaches over 200 Hits, Writes History as Undrafted Free Agent

Seo Geon-chang had been released and had to do his mandatory military service. Then he entered an open tryout to resume his baseball career. But there truly was light at the end of the tunnel.

Seo, the Nexen Heroes' second baseman who once was an undrafted free agent, was voted the most valuable player of the 2014 KBO season after setting the league's single-season hits record with 201.

Seo beat out some impressive candidates, who all happened to be his teammates. Park Byung-ho became the first since 2003 to hit 50 homers in a season; Kang Jung-ho set a league record with 40 home runs by a shortstop; and Andy Van Hekken was the KBO's only 20-game winner. Yet all three of them lost out to Seo.

Seo broke records previously held by two KBO legends: Lee Jong-beom and Lee Seung-yuop. Lee Jong-beom once owned the record for most hits in a season with 196, and Seo ended the year with 201. Lee Seung-yuop was the owner of the record for most runs scored in a season with 128, and Seo scored 135 runs in 2014. In addition to these two categories, Seo won his first batting title with .370.

That Seo had overcome so much adversity added poignancy to his improbable success story. After graduating from high school in 2008, Seo joined the LG Twins through a tryout. Yet after striking out in one pinch-hit at-bat, he was released.

Seo failed in his tryout for the National Police Agency baseball squad, which would have given him a chance to keep playing baseball while completing his mandatory duty. Instead, he ended up taking up active combat duties. Seo joined Nexen also as an undrafted free agent and went on to win the Rookie of the Year in 2012. Two years later, Seo wrote even more history.

■ Free Agents' Contracts off the Charts ⋯Kang Jung-ho joins big leagues

In 2014, a record 19 players declared free agency. In total, they signed for 63.6 billion won, easily surpassing the previous mark of 52.4 billion won for an all-time record. Big-ticket free agents signed for 8 billion won.

Kang Min-ho of the Giants had possessed the record free agent deal with 7.5 billion won over four years, yet three players signed for more than 8 billion. SK's infielder Choi Jeong, a consistent performer still in his prime, re-signed for 8.6 billion won over four years.

With a dearth of starting arms, left-hander Jang Won-jun and right-hander Yun Sung-hwan hit the jackpot. Jang signed for 8.4 billion won over four years to leave his Giants for the Bears. It was the largest free agent contract handed out to a pitcher. Yun remained with his Lions after signing for 8 billion won in a four-year deal.

The players who were posted for big league clubs all had conflicting situations. A pair of lefties, SK's Kim Kwang-hyun and Kia's Yang Hyeon-jong, had to put their major league dreams on hold. Nexen shortstop Kang Jung-ho signed a four-year deal worth $11 million, becoming the first position player to go from the domestic competition to the majors.

Regular Season Standings

1. Samsung Lions	78W	47L	3D
2. Nexen Heroes	78W	48L	2D
3. NC Dinos	70W	57L	1D
4. LG Twins	62W	64L	2D
5. SK Wyverns	61W	65L	2D
6. Doosan Bears	59W	68L	1D
7. Lotte Giants	58W	69L	1D
8. KIA Tigers	54W	74L	0D
9. Hanwha Eagles	49W	77L	2D

Playoffs and Korean Series Results

▲ **First Round**
LG Twins 3-1 NC Dinos

▲ **Second Round**
Nexen Heroes 3-1 LG Twins

▲ **Korean Series**
Samsung Lions 4-2 Nexen Heroes

PROFESSIONAL BASKETBALL

■ Men's Basketball

There was some positive momentum heading into the 2013-2014 men's pro basketball season. The national team finished third at the Asian championships in Manila, the Philippines, and earned a berth for the 2014 FIBA Basketball World Cup.

This would be South Korea's first international appearance in men's hoops since the 1996 Summer Olympics in Atlanta. Hot shot rookies Kim Jong-gyu, Kim Min-goo and Doo Gyeong-min joined the pro ranks together, giving the league a breath of fresh air.

In the Professional-Amateur Championship, a preseason summer event, Korea University, led by Lee Seung-hyeon and Lee Jong-hyeon, got past professionals to take the title. The emergence of Kim Jong-gyu, Kim Min-goo and Doo Gyeong-min added excitement to the annual rookie draft in September. It was a golden opportunity for pro basketball to strike big at the gates.

Kim Jong-gyu went first overall to Changwon LG. Kim Min-goo was picked by Jeonju KCC. Doo was drafted by Wonju Dongbu.

LG in particular turned heads with a series of offseason moves. The team signed high-scoring forward Moon Tae-jong as a free agent, as well as drafting Kim Jong-gyu with the No. 1 pick. Then LG traded for guard Kim Si-rae. In the foreign player draft, LG selected former Russian league scoring champ Davon Jefferson.

The non-playoff team in 2013 quickly became a title contender on paper in 2014. LG tied Ulsan Mobis with a 40-14 regular season record but finished in first place thanks to a superior head-to-head record. This was LG's first-ever regular season title.

Mobis and Seoul SK enjoyed strong seasons, but Wonju Dongbu, considered among the title favorites, instead finished dead last at 13-41. Lee Choong-hee, formerly a sharp-shooting scoring machine who took over the team before the season, stepped down before the end of the season.

LG clinched first place on the final day of the regular season. In the first round of the playoffs, the third-seed SK and the sixth-seeded Goyang Orions clashed, while Incheon ET Land and Busan KT, seeded fourth and fifth, respectively, met on the other side of the bracket.

In the end, Mobis emerged as the champion. They got past SK in the semifinals and then knocked off LG in six games in the championship series for their second consecutive title. LG's Moon Tae-jong was named the MVP of the regular season. His younger brother, Moon Tae-young of Mobis, was voted the playoffs MVP.

Kim Jong-gyu beat out Kim Min-goo for the Rookie of the Year honors. Thanks to some positive vibes for hoops before the season, the league drew just over 1.18 million fans, the second-largest single-season attendance in its history.

Regular Season Standings

1. Changwon LG	40W	14L
2. Ulsan Mobis	40W	14L
3. Seoul SK	37W	17L
4. Incheon ET Land	28W	26L
5. Busan KT	27W	27L
6. Goyang Orions	27W	27L
7. Jeonju KCC	20W	34L
8. Seoul Samsung	19W	35L
9. Anyang KGC	19W	35L
10. Wonju Dongbu	13W	41L

Playoffs and Finals Results

▲ **First Round**

Seoul SK 3-1 Goyang Orions

Busan KT 3-2 Incheon ET Land

▲ **Semifinals**

Changwon LG 3-0 Busan KT

Ulsan Mobis 3-1 Seoul SK

▲ **Finals**

Ulsan Mobis 4-2 Changwon LG

■ **Women's Basketball**

In the 2013-2014 season, Chuncheon Woori Bank established itself as the new force to be reckoned with in women's basketball. Ansan Shinhan Bank won its sixth straight championship in the 2011-2012 season, but Woori Bank went "last to first" in 2012-2013 to end the streak.

Woori Bank chose ex-Shinhan Bank coach Wi Sung-woo as its new head coach and another former Shinhan assistant joined Wi as an assistant. Woori Bank was the chased in 2013-2014.

The table had turned and Shinhan Bank became the chaser. Woori Bank was without Tina Thompson, an integral part of the team's championship run the previous season, and it was expected to deal a huge blow to the team's title aspirations.

Yet, Woori Bank boasted a tight-knit group of domestic stars, including Park Hye-jin, Lim Young-hee, Lee Seung-ah and Yang Ji-hee, while the two new foreign players, Sasha Goodlett and Noelle Quinn, did admirable work. Shinhan Bank, though, didn't go away easily.

Choi Yoon-ah, Kim Dan-bi, Ha Eun-joo and Kwak Joo-young were the established stars, joined by the skilled Shekinna Stricklen. In the regular season, Woori Bank finished first at 25-10, followed by Shinhan Bank at 21-14.

Starting in the 2013-2014 season, only the top three regular season teams reached the postseason, down from four. Yongin Samsung Life would have competed in the playoffs in the past, but not this time. Shinhan Bank and Kookmin Bank, the second and third seeds, met in the opening round, and Shinhan Bank captured two quick victories to dispatch its opponent. In Game 2, Stricklen poured in 37 points to set a single-game playoff scoring record.

Woori Bank proved too much for Shinhan Bank in the finals. Shinhan Bank players were exhausted after playing a tough playoff series, and Woori Bank easily handled them 80-61 in Game 1. Woori prevailed again 58-54 in Game 2.

On the brink, Shinhan came home for Game 3 and won 76-71 in overtime. Yet Woori came out on top 67-66 in the decisive Game 4 to clinch its second straight title.

Regular Season Standings

1. Chuncheon Woori Bank	25W	10L
2. Ansan Shinhan Bank	21W	14L
3. Cheongju Kookmin Bank	20W	15L
4. Yongin Samsung Life	17W	18L
5. Guri KDB Life	14W	21L
6. Bucheon KEB-HanaBank	8W	27L

Playoffs and Finals Results

▲ **First Round**

Ansan Shinhan Bank 2-0 Cheongju Kookmin Bank

▲ **Finals**

Chuncheon Woori Bank 3-1 Ansan Shinhan Bank

PROFESSIONAL VOLLEYBALL

■ Samsung Fire Becomes 1st Korean Sports Franchise to Win 7 Consecutive Titles

Samsung Fire was once again the champion of the men's V-League in 2013-2014. Despite losing key players and the rise of rivals, Samsung still finished first in the regular season and then dispatched Hyundai Capital in four games in the finals. It was the third straight season in which Samsung captured both the regular season crown and the championship finals.

And Samsung has won every championship series since the 2007-2008 season, a string of seven in a row. Samsung is the first franchise in four major sports (baseball·football·basketball·volleyball) to win those many titles consecutively. Samsung previously shared the record with Ansan Shinhan Bank in women's basketball, which had won six consecutive championships starting in the 2007 Winter League.

Samsung Fire has always had a great eye for foreign talent, and its "systematic" brand of volleyball, built on a rigid delegation of responsibilities, helped keep the team on top. Yet it was Samsung's most trying season in a while. Libero Yeo Oh-hyun joined the archrival Hyundai Capital, and left wing Seok Jin-wook retired. The system was shaken at its core. Samsung still finished first in the regular season but ranked last in team reception and fifth in team digs. The team's total of receptions plus digs was also the worst in the league, with an average of 18.296 per set.

The dynasty, however, stayed strong. Leo Martinez, the "Cuban Express," came back even better than the season before. After playing in 29 regular season games, Martinez finished first in points (1,084), total attacks (58.57%), open attacks (57.36%), quick open attacks (70.73%) and delayed spiking (74.16%). He also became the first player ever to win back-to-back regular season MVP honors.

Lee Seon-gyu, who joined as a compensation player for Yeo, and the rest of the offense blended in perfectly with the setter Yoo Gwang-woo, and head coach Shin Chi-yong never wavered in his belief that hard work would surely pay dividends.

Hyundai Capital put up a good fight but came up short of a championship. Kim Ho-chul was back as the head coach. By snatching Yeo Oh-hyun from Samsung and signing Liberman Agamez of Colombia, one of the world's most lethal attackers, Hyundai Capital showed it meant business. Yet it had to settle for its first finals appearance since the 2009-2010 season.

Korean Air, which lost regulars to the mandatory military service, ended in third place. Woori Card started out hot but faded away to fourth place.

The new club, Rush & Cash, acquitted itself in its inaugural season. It managed to reach double figures in victories to avoid being in the league cellar but played the role of a spoiler later in the season.

Jeon Gwang-in, the first overall pick by KEPCO, was named the Rookie of the Year on the men's side, while Ko Ye-rim of Korea Expressway Corp. had the honor for the women. Jeon led all South Korean players with 616 points, a promising start to a burgeoning career.

■ GS Caltex Back on Top after Six Years Away

In the women's V-League, GS Caltex, which had been struggling since winning the championship in the 2007-2008 season, returned to the top after six years. IBK finished atop the regular season standings and seemed on the verge of its second straight championship.

GS Caltex, despite finishing 13 points behind IBK in second place in the regular season, got the last laugh in the championship series. The two clubs went the distance before GS Caltex prevailed in five matches.

GS Caltex won its inaugural title in 2008 and finished first in the following regular season. Yet, Heungkuk Life Insurance upset GS Caltex in the championship final in 2009, and things quickly went downhill for GS Caltex. It finished third in 2009-2010, and then ranked last among five teams in 2010-2011. The following season, when the league expanded to six teams, GS Caltex finished at the bottom again.

On the positive side, Han Song-yi, who'd developed into a complete player after the 2012 London Olympics, took the leadership role. Bethania de la Cruz, a Dominican Republic star, rejoined GS Caltex for the first time since 2008-2009 and powered the team to second place in 2013. It was a sign of things to come. In 2013-2014, the veterans and the youngsters came together at just the right time to snatch another championship.

Prior to the season, starting setter Lee Sook-ja suffered an injury and Lee Na-youn was released. GS Caltex acquired new setter Jeong Ji-yoon from a semi-pro club. De la Cruz, a blue chip attacker, led the offense, backed capably by Han Song-yi and the reigning Rookie of the Year Lee So-young. Along with Lee Sook-ja and Jeong Ji-yoon, veteran setter Jeong Dae-young provided stability and savvy to the club.

Hyundai E&C dropped from third in 2013 to fifth in 2014. KGC jumped from sixth to third. For Hyundai E&C, Yang Hyo-jin led a solid offense, but the defense ranked last in receptions and digs. The team missed the postseason for the first time since 2009.

In the offseason, Lee Hyo-hee, the veteran setter who won the regular season MVP after guiding IBK to first place in the regular season, signed with Korea Expressway Corp. as a free agent. Kim Sa-ni returned from a stint in Azerbaijan and signed with IBK. Jeong Dae-young moved from GS Caltex to Korea Expressway Corp., while Kim Soo-jin left Hyundai E&C to join Heungkuk Life Insurance.

Hyundai E&C promoted senior assistant Yang Cheol-ho to the head coaching job. Park Mi-hee, a former TV commentator, took over Heungkuk Life Insurance. Yang led his team to the 2014 Ansan·Woori Card Pro Volleyball Cup title, Hyundai's first championship in eight years. Park's team was the runner-up for the cup, after ending the 2013 season second to last.

PROFESSIONAL GOLF

■ **<KPGA> Kim Seung-hyuk Enjoys Banner Year, Wins Money, Top Player Honors**
Kim Seung-hyuk dominated the 2014

Korean PGA (KPGA) Tour season.

Kim won the tour's money title with 589 million won and also earned the points race for the Ballantine's Player of the Year honors. Kim became the first player to sweep both awards since Bae Sang-moon in 2009.

Kim, a former national team member, turned pro in 2005 but remained a largely unknown golfer who didn't get his first victory through 2013. He finally got into the winner's circle at the SK Telecom Open in May 2014. In October, Kim also captured the Japan Golf Tour Organization's Tokai Classic. He kept his torrid pace and captured the Korea Open, the national tournament of South Korea. Kim all but secured the money title with the victory.

At the season-ending Shinhan Donghae Open, Park Sang-hyun, who was battling Kim for the money title, struggled. Yet the two were still fighting for the Player of the Year award.

On the par-5 18th, Kim putted from just off the green and made a long birdie putt to finish tied for fourth. After clinching the KPGA money title, Kim said his goal was to also lead the Japanese tour in money in 2015.

Park, who won twice in 2014, settled for leading the tour in scoring average (69.86). Park Il-hwan was the Rookie of the Year.

Along with Kim Seung-hyuk, Kim Woo-hyun emerged as a promising youngster. He earned two victories and gave the tour a much-needed breath of fresh air.

There were only 14 tournaments in 2014 -- none in the entire month of September -- and the KPGA Tour has a long way to go to return to respectability.

■ **<KLPGA> Kim Hyo-joo Rules 2014 Season, Captures Four Season-End Awards**
The 2014 Korea LPGA (KLPGA) Tour season was all about Kim Hyo-joo. With former main attractions Shin Ji-yai and Seo Hee-kyung now playing overseas, the KLPGA Tour went through a stretch with no one dominant super star.

Kim single-handedly took care of that. In 2014, the teenager topped the money list with 1.2 billion won, led the tour with

2014 KPGA Tour Champions

Dates	Title	Location	Champion
4.17~20	Dongbu Insurance Promi Open	Wellihilli CC	Dongmin LEE
5.8~11	The 33rd GS Caltax Maekyung Open	NamSeoul CC	Junwon PARK
5.15~18	SK telecom OPEN 2014	Sky 72 GC	Seunghyuk KIM
5.22~25	Descente Korea Munsingwear Matchplay Championship	88 CC	Kisang LEE
5.29~6.1	The 2nd Happiness Songhak Construction Open	Happiness CC	KIM Woo Hyun
6.12~15	2014 Bosung CC Classic	Bosung CC	KIM Woo Hyun
6.26~29	Gunsan CC Open	Gunsan CC	Heungchol JOO
7.10~13	YAMAHA HANKYUNG The 57th KPGA Championship	Sky 72 GC	Matthew GRIFFIN
8.7~10	The 1st Maeil Dairies Open	Yuseong CC	Junggon HWANG
8.21~24	Vainer-Pineridge Open	Pineridge CC	Sanghyun PARK
10.9~12	KJ CHOI INVITATIONAL presented by CJ	Lake Hills Suncheon CC	Sanghyun PARK
10.23~26	Kolon The 57th Korea Open	Woojeong Hills CC	Seunghyuk KIM
10.30~11.2	Hearld KYJ Tour Championship	Lotte Sky Hill Jeju CC	Hyungjoon LEE
11.6~9	The 30th Shinhan Donghae Open	Jack Nicklaus Golf Club Korea	Sangmoon BAE

Source : KPGA

five victories, had the best scoring average with 70.26 strokes and then earned the Player of the Year honors.

Kim first rose to fame as a promising star in 2012 but went winless in 2013, much to the disappointment of her fans. But in 2014, Kim won five times, starting with a major championship: the Kia Motors Korea Women's Open. Kim earned two more major titles: the Hite Jinro Championship and the KB Financial Star Championship.

▲ *Kim Hyo-joo poses after winning the Evian Championship in France on Sept. 14, edging out veteran player Karrie Webb of Australia by one shot for her first career LPGA major championship.*

Kim broke the 1 billion-won mark in earnings to set the tour's single-season record. On the LPGA Tour, Kim won the fifth major, the Evian Championship, as a non-member, setting the stage for a full season on the U.S. circuit in 2015. Rock steady from start to finish, Kim is seen as a viable threat to the top South Korean on the LPGA Tour, Park In-bee.

Baek Kyu-jung, another teenager, also enjoyed a strong season. Baek, who made her pro debut a year later than Kim, won three times on the KLPGA Tour and then captured her maiden LPGA title at the KEB-HanaBank Championship held in South Korea. Like Kim, Baek earned her LPGA playing privileges for 2015. It marked the first time two KLPGA players claimed LPGA Tour wins in the same year. Baek also came out on top in the tight battle for the Rookie of the Year honors, getting past Kim Min-sun and Ko Jin-young. Baek, a long hitter who averaged nearly 260 yards off the tee in 2014, is also a fearless competitor who is fit for a bigger stage in the United States. Kim and Baek will be gone from the Korean tour in 2015, but it won't be short of homegrown stars.

Chun In-gee won three tournaments in 2014, including the season-ending Cho-

2014 KLPGA Tour Champions

Dates	Title	Location	Champion
4.10~13	7th Lotte Mart Women's Open	Lotte Sky Hill Jeju CC	Lee MinYoung2
4.25~27	Nexen-Saintnine Masters 2014	Gaya CC	Baek Kyu Jung
5.2~4	4th KG-Edaily Ladies Open	Muju Anseong CC	Lee Seung Hyun
5.16~18	2014 Woori investment&securities Ladies Championship	Ildong Lake CC	Kim Sei Young
5.22~25	2014 Doosan Matchplay Championship	Ladena CC	Yoon Seul A
5.30~6.1	E1 Charity Open	Phoenix Springs CC	Heo Yoon Kyung
6.6~8	4th Lotte Cantata Women's Open	Lotte Sky Hill Jeju CC	Baek Kyu Jung
6.13~15	8th S-OIL Champions Invitational	Elysian Jeju CC	Chun In Gee
6.19~22	Kia Morors the 28th Korea Women's Open	Bearsbest Cheongna CC	Kim Hyo Joo
7.4~6	Kumho Tire Ladies Open	Weihai Point CC	Kim Hyo Joo
7.18~20	Jeju Samdasoo Masters	Ora CC	Yoon Chae Young
7.31~8.3	Hanhwa Finance Classic 2014	Goldenbay CC	Kim Hyo Joo
8.8~10	Kyochon Honey Ladies Open	Interburgo CC	Lee Jung Min
8.14~17	Nefs Masterpiece 2014	Hilldeloci CC	Ko Jin Young
8.21~24	MBN Women's Open with ONOFF	The star hue CC	Kim Sei Young
8.29~31	2014 Charity High1 Resort Open	High1 CC	Jang Ha Na
9.12~14	YTN-Volvik Women's Open	Kosca CC	Lee Jung Min
9.18~21	Metlife-Hankyung 36th KLPGA Championship	Island CC	Baek Kyu Jung
9.26~28	KDB Daewoo Classic 2014	Phoenix Park CC	Chun In Gee
10.3~5	OKSavingsBank SE RI PaK Invitational	Solmoro CC	Lee MinYoung2
10.9~12	The 15th HiteJinro Championship	Blueheron CC	Kim Hyo Joo
10.16~19	LPGA KEB · HanaBank Championship	Sky 72 GC	Baek Kyu Jung
10.23~26	KB Star Championship	Namchon CC	Kim Hyo Joo
10.31~11.2	Seoul Economic daily Ladies Classic	Lake hills Yongin CC	Heo Yoon Kyung
11.7~9	ADT CAPS Championship 2014	Lotte Sky Hill Kimhae CC	Kim Min Sun5
11.14~16	Chosun-Posco Championship 2014	Jack Nicklaus Golf Club Korea	Chun In Gee
12.6~7	Korea-Japan Women's National Golf Team Matchplay Competition 2014	Moyoshi CC	
12.12~14	Hyundai China Ladies Open 2014	Shenzhen Mission Hills CC	Kim Hyo Joo

Source : KLPGA

sun Ilbo-POSCO Championship. Heo Yoon-kyung, Lee Jung-min and Kim Sei-young are other young guns who will be vying for the throne in 2015.

■ <LPGA Tour> Lydia Ko·Stacy Lewis Lead Way in 2014

The 2014 LPGA Tour came to an end Nov. 23, with the CME Group Tour Championship in Naples, Florida. Lydia Ko, a South Korea-born Kiwi, and American veteran Stacy Lewis led the way.

Ko took the Tour Championship on the fourth playoff hole to cap off an impressive season.

She cashed in $500,000 for that victory and also earned a $1 million bonus for taking the Race to the CME Globe points race.

Ko won back-to-back CN Canadian Women's Opens as an amateur. She began playing on the LPGA Tour as a pro in 2014 and picked up three victories en route to becoming the youngest Rookie of the Year ever.

Ko made $2.08 million to finish behind Lewis ($2.53 million) and Park In-bee ($2.22 million). Ko is the first rookie to surpass $2 million in earnings.

Lewis lost out on that $1 million bonus to Ko, but she led the tour in money, scoring average and the Player of the Year points race. Lewis was also the Player of the Year in 2012, but she'd conceded the money and the scoring titles to Park. In 2014, Lewis completed the trifecta. She is the first U.S.-born player to pull off that feat since Betsy King in 1993.

There were other Americans who thrived on the tour in 2014, including Jessica Korda and Lexi Thompson, as the tour grew more popular among the U.S. audience. Of the 32 tournaments in 2014, the Americans combined to win 13, their highest total since 1999.

The South Koreans held their ground too. The Americans claimed three of the five majors in 2014, and the South Koreans won the other two. Among the three American winners was Michelle Wie, the U.S. Women's Open champ whose parents are Korean natives.

The players of Korean descent -- Ko, Wie and Christina Kim -- combined for six victories. The South Korean nationals claimed a total of 10 victories. In 2013, the South Koreans also won 10 times, after combining for eight wins in 2012.

Park In-bee had a relatively quiet season in 2014, a year after winning three consecutive majors. Still, she counted a major, the Wegmans LPGA Championship, among her three wins. Park ended the 2014 season ranked No. 1 in the world.

Kim Hyo-joo and Baek Kyu-jung were the two KLPGA Tour members who got their first LPGA victories in 2014. Kim took the Evian Championship, the fifth major of the season, while Baek won on home soil at the LPGA KEB-HanaBank Championship. The two could go toe-to-toe for the LPGA Tour's Rookie of the Year honors in 2015.

The 2015 season kicked off with the Coates Golf Championship in Florida in January.

■ **<PGA Tour> McIlroy's Comeback Fuels 2014 PGA Tour**

The 2013-2014 PGA Tour season wrapped up on Sept. 14, 2014, as the champion of the playoffs emerged. Billy Horschel, a relative unknown, captured the $10 million bonus as the playoff winner. Yet it was Rory McIlroy who dominated the season.

Anointed the next big thing, McIlroy struggled for most of 2013. Then in July 2014, McIlroy captured the Open Championship, and the game was on. McIlroy then won the WGC-Bridgestone Invitational and captured the PGA Championship, the season's final major, to cap off a remarkable stretch. He was firmly entrenched as the world No. 1 at the season's end.

McIlroy led the tour in money and in scoring average too. He entered the FedEx Cup playoffs at No. 1 in the points race but failed to win any of the four events as Horschel came out on top. Horschel won twice during the playoffs for the $10 million jackpot. He'd made $4.5 million in his career through the previous season.

For Tiger Woods, this was a season to forget. He injured his back and failed to win a tournament. He also failed to qualify for the playoffs.

Woods missed the first two majors -- the Masters and the U.S. Open -- while recovering from back surgery, and only finished 69th at the Open Championship. He then missed the cut at the PGA Championship to end the season on a sour note.

Among South Koreans, Noh Seung-yul earned his first PGA Tour win at the Zurich Classic of New Orleans in April. A bomber, who routinely drives the ball over 300 yards, Noh became the youngest-ever South Korean winner on the tour.

Yang Yong-eun, the shocking winner of the 2009 PGA Championship, lost his tour card. Another veteran, Choi Kyoung-ju, went winless in 2014.

BADUK

■ **Kim Ji-seok Wins Samsung Fire & Marine Insurance World Masters··· Named MVP**

Kim Ji-seok, the nation's second-ranked player, was the biggest star of the 2014 season. The 9-dan captured the

Samsung Fire & Marine Insurance World Masters for the country's first major title in nearly two years.

In 2013, South Koreans were shut out of individual titles at seven international competitions, the first such calamity in 18 years. The country had produced at least one champion every year from 1996 to 2012. Then in 2014, Kim restored some of the pride. This was Kim's first world title in his 11-year career.

In the final, Kim defeated Tang Weixing of China 2-0. Kim parlayed that victory into the MVP honors at the 2014 Baduk Awards.

In 2014, Kim went 17-2 internationally. At domestic competitions, Kim defended his crown at the 19th GS Caltex Cup. He also made the final at the LG Cup World Baduk Championship but fell to the No. 1-ranked Park Jung-hwan 2-1.

Kim served as captain on the successful national team. Coached by Yoo Chang-hyuk, the four South Koreans made up the semifinals at the LG Cup, and Kim was the Samsung champ.

▪ Lee Se-dol Defeats Gu Li in 10-Game Match... Wins Money Title

In the "Jubango (10-game match) of the Century," South Korean 9-dan Lee Se-dol defeated Chinese 9-dan Gu Li. The showdown opened in Beijing in January, and Lee prevailed 6-2. He took home 5 million yuan, or some 890 million won. Gu settled for 200,000 yuan. This clash saw the top baduk players from South Korea and China go toe-to-toe.

Lee clinched his win in Gu's hometown of Chongqing by taking the eighth game. Lee only lost the third and fourth games and closed out the 10-game match with relative ease. Thanks to the victory, Lee earned a record 1.41 billion won. Kim Ji-seok finished a distant second with 560 million won.

▪ 'Misaeng' Fever···Baduk Enters Pop Culture Realm

In 2014 the TV series "Misaeng" and other shows and films dealing with baduk enjoyed huge success. Misaeng, based on a webtoon series by Yoon Tae-ho, follows a former baduk player named Jang Geu-rae, as he throws himself into the corporate world.

The 20-part series nearly reached double figures in ratings, and the webtoon books sold more than 2 million copies. The Korea Baduk Association presented Yoon with its Special Achievement Award. "The Stone" and "The Divine Move" were two films centered on baduk.

▪ Choi Jung Reigns Supreme as Queen of Baduk

Choi Jung, a 5-dan, upset Chinese 9-dan Lui Naiwei to capture her first international title. Choi won the fifth Konglyung Mountain Cup to become only the third South Korean female player, after 9-dan Park Ji-eun and 5-dan Yoon Young-seon, to win an international competition. Choi also became the first South Korean woman to surpass 100 million won in earnings in one season.

▪ T-Broad Wins Baduk League

T-Broad became the national baduk championship team in its seventh season. T-Broad finished first in the regular season of the 2014 Kookmin Bank Baduk League, and in the championship final, it prevailed over Jeonggwanjang 2-1 for the title.

T-Broad was the first team to win the regular season crown in two straight years. T-Broad also captured the second-tier "Futures Baduk League" to complete its sweep of national baduk trophies.

▪ Baduk Contested as Demonstration Sport at National Sports Festival

Baduk was contested at a national multisport competition for the first time. On Nov. 1 and 2, baduk was a demonstration sport at the 95th National Sports Festival. The tournament featured 223 players and officials from 17 cities and provinces, and South Jeolla Province won.

▪ Korea Baduk Association Chair Hong Seok-hyun Named Int'l Head

Hong Seok-hyeon, chairman of JoongAng Ilbo·JTBC, became the 18th president of the Korea Baduk Association in December 2013. Two months later, Hong was elected the fourth head of the Korea Baduk Federation.

As the integrated leader of the two

organizations, Hong was elected the new president of the International Go Federation (IGF) during the board of directors meeting held in Gyeongju in July. The general congress promptly approved the decision, making Hong the first South Korean head of the IGF. His term is two years.

CLIMBING

▪ Overview

The year 2014 in climbing belonged to Kim Ja-in. In a memorable season, Kim swept three consecutive World Cup events, won the world championship, captured her 10th Asian title and finished the year ranked No. 1 in the world. Some tragic news came from the Himalayas, where an avalanche on Annapurna left 43 dead and 50 missing.

▪ Kim Ja-in, "Queen of Climbing," Remains No. 1 for 3rd Straight Year, Takes First World Championships

This was truly Kim Ja-in's year. For the third straight year, Kim finished as the No. 1 lead climber in the International Federation of Sport Climbing (IFSC) rankings.

In lead climbing, the climbers must ascend within a time limit. Kim started the season with a bang, taking the opening leg of the IFSC Climbing World Cup in Haiyang, China, in June.

The following month, Kim also won the second World Cup in Chamonix, France, and then extended her winning streak to three at Briancon, France. Kim failed to keep it going at the fourth World Cup in Imst, Austria, as her archrival Magdalena Rock of Austria finished first.

Yet it turned out Kim only took a step back before taking two steps forward. At the IFSC World Championships in Gijon, Spain, Kim became the first South Korean to win the lead event.

For this "Queen of Climbing," it was the maiden world title in lead. Kim was the overall champ in 2012, but in the lead, Kim was the runner-up in 2009 and 2011.

The competition took place at Palacio Deportes, which means "Palace of Sports," and Kim lived up to her moniker as the climbing queen. She had her share of difficulties -- she had to get her uniform delivered -- but she still enjoyed her coronation.

Kim wasn't done. At the IFSC Asian Championship in Lombok, Indonesia, in October, Kim captured the 10th lead title of her illustrious career. Kim only missed out on the 2013 event with injuries, and she's been the event's only champ since 2004.

At the fifth World Cup in Mokpo, South Korea, and then the sixth World Cup in Wujiang, China, Kim ranked sixth and 10th, respectively. In Mokpo, Kim had a chance to showcase her talent before home fans but struggled on a route that put shortish climbers like her at a disadvantage.

At the seventh World Cup in Inzai, Japan, Kim was the only woman to complete her lead climb in a dominant performance. At the eighth and last World Cup in Kranj, Slovenia, in November, Kim finished in second place. That was still good enough to clinch the overall World Cup title and the No. 1 ranking.

The 2014 season will go down as the greatest season of Kim's career. In a sport that demands explosiveness and endurance at the same time, Kim just might have peaked in 2014.

Among the top 10 lead climbers at the world championships, only two were older than Kim. Kim started making a name for herself by finishing seventh at the World Cup in 2004, and she's been in the sport for a decade.

Bumps and bruises are a badge of honor and a hindrance. After hurting her knee in bouldering at the World Cup in 2013, Kim didn't compete in bouldering in 2014.

Lead and bouldering are two different animals and require the use of different muscles, making it difficult for one climber to excel in both.

Kim became the first female climber to win both events at the 2011 World Cup in Milan, and the knee injury was certainly frustrating.

Kim insists, after each victory, that her ultimate goal is not to win but to finish her climb. It'll be fascinating to watch where the sport of climbing will take her next.

■ **Himalayan Avalanche Leaves 43 Dead, 50 Missing**

A snowstorm and avalanche in the Nepalese Himalayas caused what was believed to be the worst trekking disaster ever in the area on Oct. 14, 2014. Trekkers in the Mustang and Manang regions on the way to Thorong La in the Annapurna range (5,416 meters above sea level), and the base camp at Mt. Dhaulagiri were most affected.

Though the relatively warm October climate in the Himalayas is said to be perfect for trekking, a huge cyclone that tore through eastern India led to unseasonable amounts of rain and snow, according to the Nepalese authorities.

A 1995 avalanche on Mt. Everest claimed 42 lives, including 13 members of a Japanese crew. In this 2014 disaster, 43 people were confirmed dead and 50 missing. No South Korean is said to have been killed or injured. The tragic incident was a solemn reminder of the dangers of mountaineering.

THE 95TH NATIONAL SPORTS FESTIVAL

(Oct. 28~Nov. 3, 2014. Jeju)

The 95th National Sports Festival went on for a week on Jeju Island starting on Oct. 28, 2014. Some of the athletes that represented the country at the 2014 Asian Games returned to the heat of the battle barely a month after the Asiad.

A world record was set at a National Sports Festival for the first time in four years.

Kim Woo-jin in men's archery was among the outstanding athletes. In the 30-meter event, Kim scored a perfect 360 to tie the world record. In the 70m, he set a new world record with 352 points.

He earned a combined 1,391 points in four distances, also a world record. In the individual and team competitions, with the set system in effect, Kim couldn't grab a gold. With his three gold medals and world records, Kim was named the MVP of the entire competition.

Jin Jong-oh, one of South Korea's leading shooters, lived up to his name,

winning three gold medals. Jin swept the individual and team titles in the 10m air pistol and got another in the 50m pistol. Since the 50m pistol didn't have a team portion, Jin won gold in every event he entered. There were no national records set in shooting in 2013, but four national marks were broken at the 2014 event.

Yang Hak-seon, the "God of Vault," claimed his fourth consecutive gold in the men's vault, shaking off a disappointing Asiad campaign.

Sa Jae-hyouk, a weightlifter who's undergone seven operations in his career, led the field in snatch, clean and jerk, and total weight in the men's 85kg division. Though Sa was drained after the Asian Games, he competed for his club and the home province of Jeju, much to the delight of the partisan crowds.

Kim Jae-bum, the double judo gold medalist at the Asian Games, captured his third straight national gold. Lee Yong-dae, the Olympic badminton champ, won two silver medals. Oh Jin-hyek, who won two archery gold medals at the 2012 London Olympics, settled for two bronze medals.

Inclement weather affected the competition. Rainstorms brought down the temperature, and many athletes had up-and-down days. In archery, there were unusually low scores of 5s and 6s, and one particular archer, Chang Hye-jin, had the dubious distinction of shooting a zero. Chang somehow overcame that donut and ended up winning a gold medal. Preliminary baseball games in the senior and high school divisions were rained out, and draws determined the winners.

Athletics was dealt the hardest blow. Rainy and windy conditions resulted in poor times in marathon. Those in throwing events struggled to stay dry. Kim Min-ji, an up-and-coming sprinter, had been expected to set a new national record in the 200m but came up short. There were no Korean records established in track and field, and only seven competition records were set.

New faces stepped up their game. Promising swimmer Lim Da-sol set a national record with 2:11.69 in the 200m backstroke in the high school division.

In archery, Kim Jong-ho matched his own world record in the men's 70m. He beat out such veterans as Oh Jin-hyek,

Kim Woo-jin and Im Dong-hyun for the gold medal in the senior division.

Park Ji-soo, the youngest member of the women's national basketball team, chipped in 7 points and 18 rebounds in the high school final, helping her Bundang Management High School beat Insung Girls' High School.

In the men's high school football final, POSCO High School's goalkeeper Kim Ro-man made some spectacular saves, including two stops in the penalty shoot-out, against Hyundai High School to lift his team to the gold.

Seasoned veterans also stood their ground. Cho Ho-sung, the elder statesman in Korean cycling, retired from the sport after the competition. He won a gold at the 1994 Hiroshima Asian Games and then captured a silver 20 years later at the Incheon Asian Games. At the national event, Cho grabbed two gold medals, in the men's 4km mass start ranking event and the final, and added a bronze in scratch.

Lee Hyung-taik, a tennis star who retired in 2009 but returned four years later, made his first appearance in three years. He was eliminated in the first round in the men's singles, however, after not being able to train extensively due to an injury.

With the e-sports competition added for the first time, the competition's website crashed with heavy traffic. League of Legends, StarCraft, Crazy Racing Kart Rider and FIFA Online 3, four of the most popular e-sports games, were part of the program.

Though they weren't medal events and thus the results weren't available on the event's website, e-sports fans still flocked to the site, causing it to crash.

THE 95TH NATIONAL WINTER SPORTS FESTIVAL

(Feb. 26 ~ March 1, 2014. Gangwon Province)

The 95th edition of the National Winter Sports Festival, the largest winter sports competition in the country, closed with Gyeonggi Province claiming its 13th consecutive overall title. Gyeonggi captured 99 gold, 73 silver and 71 bronze medals for 1372.5 points, and has topped the points race every year since 2002.

Gangwon Province, which will host the 2018 Winter Olympics in PyeongChang, earned 975 points to beat Seoul (960.5 points) for second place. It had finished behind the capital city the past two years. North Jeolloa (605), Busan (490.5), Daegu (429), North Gyeongsang (304), North Chungcheong (298), South Jeolla (291.5), Gwangju (257), Incheon (253), Daejeon (172), South Chungcheong (143), South Gyeongsang (86), Ulsan (64), Jeju (10) and Sejong (4) followed.

Sejong entered the competition for the second straight year but is still looking for its first medal. Jeju competed for the third time, and speed skater Lee Seung-hoon set two competition records en route to capturing two gold medals himself.

Cho Yong-jin, who won four titles in cross-country skiing, was named the top athlete of the competition. There were

The 95th National Sports Festival

Rank	City/Province	Score	Gold	Silver	Bronze
1	Gyeonggi Prov.	60,801	130	108	139
2	Seoul City	48,704	93	82	102
3	S. Gyeongsang Prov.	47,603	69	89	99
4	N. Gyeongsang Prov.	44,557	82	68	90
5	Incheon City	40,641	77	59	79
6	Busan City	40,420	64	74	90
7	S. Chungcheong Prov.	39,492	50	60	84
8	N. Chungcheong Prov.	35,102	56	48	79
9	Gangwon Prov.	32,670	60	46	85
10	Daejeon City	32,449	38	57	64
11	Jeju Prov.	31,860	52	54	61
12	S. Jeolla Prov.	31,546	38	52	95
13	Daegu City	27,916	37	37	68
14	N. Jeolla Prov.	27,386	37	46	58
15	Gwangju City	27,022	35	44	56
16	Ulsan City	21,643	45	35	47
17	Sejong City	5,415	6	5	10

six quadruple gold medalists, 16 triple champions and 46 double gold medalists.

Stars from the 2014 Sochi Winter Games shined, while those hoping to represent the country at the 2018 PyeongChang Winter Olympics also offered a glimpse into their bright future.

In figure skating, Park So-youn, hoping to follow in the footsteps of Olympic champion Kim Yu-na, won the ladies' singles in the high school category. Two Olympic short trackers, Park Sei-young and his older sister Park Seung-hi, both grabbed gold medals.

In cross-country skiing, veteran Lee Chae-won won two gold medals in the women's senior competition, raising her career total to 53. In the men's alpine skiing, Jung Dong-hyun swept up four gold medals.

Other quadruple gold medalists were Kim Hyun-soo in men's high school alpine skiing, Cho Yong-jin in men's high school cross-country skiing, Lee Eui-jin in women's middle school cross-country skiing and Bae Min-joo in women's high school cross-country skiing.

Magnus Kim bagged five medals: three gold medals in men's middle school cross-country skiing, and one gold and one silver in biathlon.

Kim was born to a Norwegian father and a Korean mother. Maria Abe, who has a Japanese father, was another athlete from a multicultural family, and she won three gold medals in the women's middle school biathlon.

No national records were set. There were 26 new competition records set in short track and 21 competition records in speed skating.

The 95th National Winter Sports Festival

Rank	City/Province	Score	Gold	Silver	Bronze
1	Gyeonggi Prov.	1,372.5	99	73	71
2	Gangwon Prov.	975.0	56	60	59
3	Seoul City	960.5	45	60	42
4	N. Jeolla Prov.	605.0	14	18	17
5	Busan City	490.5	4	6	10
6	Daegu City	429.0	7	2	11
7	N. Gyeongsang	304.0	5	2	9
8	N. Chungcheong Prov.	298.0	4	5	7
9	S. Jeolla Prov.	291.5	5	4	4
10	Gwangju City	257.0	1	0	3
11	Incheon City	253.0	1	3	3
12	Daejeon City	172.0	2	3	2
13	S. Chungcheong Prov.	143.0	8	4	7
14	S. Gyeongsang	86.0	1	1	0
15	Ulsan City	64.0	0	2	1
16	Jeju Prov.	10.0	2	0	0
17	Sejong City	4.0	0	0	0

MAP OF KOREA

Hamgyeongbuk-do

Ryanggang-do

Jagang-do

Hamgyeongnam-do

Pyeonganbuk-do

Pyeongannam-do

Pyeongyang

Nampo

East Sea

Hwanghaebuk-do

Gangwon-do

Hwanghaenam-do

Gaeseong

Demilitarized Zone

Incheon

Seoul

Gangwon-do

Gyeonggi-do

Chungcheongbuk-do

Chungcheongnam-do

Ulleungdo

Dokdo

Sejong

Daejeon

Gyeongsangbuk-do

Yellow Sea

Daegu

Jeollabuk-do

Ulsan

Gyeongsangnam-do

Gwangju

Busan

Jeollanam-do

Jeju-do

Note : *For the name of province in Korea Annual, two different names are used as belows;*

- Gyeonggi-do = Gyeonggi Province
- Gangwon-do = Gangwon Province
- Chungcheongbuk-do = North Chungcheong Province
- Chungcheongnam-do = South Chungcheong Province
- Jeollabuk-do = North Jeolla Province
- Jeollanam-do = South Jeolla Province
- Gyeongsangbuk-do = North Gyeongsang Province
- Gyeongsangnam-do = South Gyeongsang Province
- Jeju-do = Jeju Special Self-Governing Province

Provincial Government

Yonhap News Agency

Area(㎢) : 605.21
Population(persons) : 10,386,339
Number of Households : 4,195,210
Flower : Forsythia
Bird : Magpie
Tree : Ginkgo
Character : Haechi
Address : 110, Sejong-daero, Jung-gu, Seoul, Korea
Mayor : Park Won-soon

SEOUL METROPOLITAN CITY

■ **Overview**
History Seoul was referred to as Wiryeseong during Kingdom of Baekje (18 BC-660 AD). It changed its name to Hansanju during Unified Silla (668-918). By the time of the Goryeo Dynasty (918-1392), it got the name Yangju, Nam-kyeong(1067) and Hanyangbu (1308). When the Joseon Dynasty moved its capital from Kaesong to Hanyangbu in 1394, it again got a new name, Hansungbu.

Seoul was called Hansungbu for 500 years during the Joseon Dynasty, and changed its name to Gyunsangbu in 1910 following the Japanese invasion. Following independence in 1945, the city got its current name, Seoul.

It was raised to the status of a metropolitan city in 1946, and was put under the supervision of the Prime Minister's Office in 1962. By 1995, Seoul became a gigantic city with 25 "gu" and a population of 10.38 million.

Area & administrative districts The combined size of Seoul stands at 605.20 ㎢, accounting for 0.61% of the South Korean territory. As of Dec. 12, it has consisted of 25 "gu" and 423 "dong."

Population & households As of end-December 2014, there are 10,386,339 people living in Seoul, with South Ko-

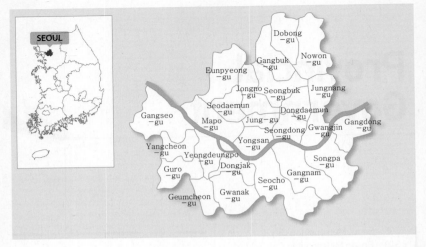

reans accounting for 10,122,661 and foreigners taking up 263,678. Compared to 2013, the figure moved down 0.02% by 1,716. The number of South Korean households came to 4,195,210, up 0.3%, or 12,859 on-year. An average household had 2.41 people. By gender, there are 5,119,324 males and 5,267,015 females. The figures translate into 97.2 males per 100 females.

By district, 11 "gu" south of the Han River had 5,365,168 residents, or 51.7% of the total, while 14 "gu" north of the river had 5,021,171, or 48.3% of the combined population, with the southern region outpacing the north by 343,997.

■ Finances

Overview The combined budget for 2015 came to 25.5 trillion won, up 4.5%, or 1.1 trillion won from 2014. Of the combined amount, the general budget took up 18.2 trillion won, up 7.9% on-year. The special budget went down 3% over the cited period to 7.2 trillion won. Each citizen held a tax burden of 1.22 million won. The value of per-capita liabilities came to 295,000 won.

By sector, social welfare took up 34.3%, or 7.8 trillion won. Subsidies to each "gu" accounted for 15.3%, or 3.5 trillion won. Others are as follows: education with 2.45 trillion won (10.7%), roads and transportation with 1.85 trillion won (8.1%), parks and environment with 1.72 trillion won (7.6%), security

with 1.06 trillion won (8.1%), culture and tourism with 502.1 billion won (2.2%), industry and economy with 472.3 billion won (2.1%), city planning and residential organization with 221.6 billion won (1%), general administration with 388.2 billion won (1.7%), administration costs with 1.48 trillion won (6.5%), financial costs with 1.1 trillion won (5.1%), and reserve fund with 172.2 billion won (0.8%).

Financial and expenditure plans

Firstly, the city plans to support projects which aim to establish a safe environment, generate jobs and vitalize the regional economy, which can benefit the citizens.

Second, the city will plan to expand tax revenue by building strong sources of profit. Fees and commissions will gradually be adjusted to be imposed on beneficiaries, and find omitted tax sources. It will also make efforts to abolish and reduce unnecessary tax incentives.

Third, it will ask the central government to improve its financial support plans on regional areas, and expand its support to Seoul. The city will find new projects that can win support from the government, and have Seoul's key projects be reflected in the parliament's decisions.

Fourth, Seoul will maximize the efficiency of the budget expenditure through strict management. It will try to raise as much budget as possible for security, welfare, creative economy and urban revitalization.

Seoul will focus on finishing large-sized social overhead capital (SOC) projects, but will aggressively invest in SOC projects that aim to improve safety, environment and the quality of citizens' livlihood.

- ### Key Projects
Seoul-style basic pension The policy aims at guaranteeing a quality of life for those living with below the minimum cost of living, but can not receive support from the government due to qualifications. The Seoul-style pension program will provide beneficiaries with a livlihood, education and birth-death subsidies. In 2014, 31,959 were provided with such supports.

Expanding public-run daycare centers Seoul added 87 public daycare centers, but mostly focused on districts without such facilities. Only 15 dongs do not have a daycare center as of end-2014, narrowing gaps among districts. The Seoul-style daycare centers are built by making use of private territories or unused public facilities, which makes cost 1/12 cheaper compared to previous models.

Bolstering public healthcare In order to expand accessibility to the public health, Seoul built 22 more healthcare centers, while rolling out a handful of precautionary projects such as promoting vaccinations and quitting smoking. The city also operated a healthcare call center and received 16,738 reports, and opened 56 night-and-holiday medical centers.

Protecting traditional markets and small retailers Seoul injected 16.7 billion won in modernizing 30 traditional markets, while providing loans worth 15 billion won to small retailers in 75 markets. The city also operated an academy for retailers to help bolster their competitiveness. In order to add vitality to traditional markets and have them stand in the center of the regional economy, Seoul selected five traditional markets and rolled out retailer-oriented projects that aimed to develop market-based business models. Seoul also regulated operating hours and days of large supermarkets and their branches to lend support to traditional markets. It also built logistics centers for mid-and-small retailers.

Eradicating challenges on livlihood
Seoul plans to root out challenges against citizens' livlihood by taking pre-emptive, crackdown and damage relief measures, rolling out all-out war against top 10 areas including loan sharks. The city aims to provide education and advertising of potential threats.

It also visited 1,001 loan sharks, 40 mutual-aid firms, 2,094 job offices and 5,424 real-estate offices to investigate potential threats. The city also helped debtors reduce 890 million won worth of debt through 359 cases of mediation efforts. It also operated free legal consulting and other help lines to support those suffering in these 10 areas.

Revitalizing urban agriculture Seoul operates $55,617 m^2$ of farms in 3,783 areas, along with 28,652 box gardens, 8,397 m^2 roof-top gardens, and 27 themed-farms throughout the city. Generating 645 jobs related to the urban agriculture, the city also rolled out related expositions, markets and other centers to promote the system among citizens, and made efforts to foster specialists regarding to the field.

Seoul-style new deal jobs The New Deal project, which aims to find jobs that are necessary to the public center and bring practical help to the livelihoods of the people, has provided 2,123 jobs to young, females, as well as the elderly through 27 businesses. Each participant also received an average of 98 hours of vocational education.

Promoting tourism and conventions
In order to make attractive tourists' destinations with themes, Seoul has developed five key points of interest, and developed projects to make the places popular. It also made efforts to eradicate scams on foreign tourists, while expanding the number of accomodations and improving foreign-language signs. The city also plans to foster its convention business, aiming to host 350 international events by 2018, and become the world's No. 3 host of global conventions.

Pedestrian-friendly city In order to make clean, safe, convenient and themed streets, the city has made 30 all-day pedestrian-exclusive streets. It also designated 24 and 13 streets that become pedestrian-exclusive on a daily and hourly basis, respectively. Seoul also banned automobiles in children-exclusive streets during school hours, allowing children to freely walk around. It also imposed a slower speed limits in central areas.

10 commandments for streets An upgraded version of the rules rolled out in 2012 to make people-first convenient roads, the city aimed to reorganize 1.1 million facilities on streets to recover the rights of Seoul citizens. The 10 commandments for streets were released on December 2014.

Open administration 2.0 Seoul made efforts to open more information through "open data square," and established the so-called m-Voting system which is aimed at using smartphones for voting. It also made a long-term strategy to make use of bid data. In 2014, around 19,000 participated in voting, and the results were reflected in around 50 policies.

It also aimed to open more administrative information, and continued to expand the scope of such data. Websites were also reorganized to meet the needs of citizens, and the city's open-document system allowed users to read authorized papers.

Revitalizing village community Seoul built legal grounds to revitalize the community and implemented 12 projects suggested by citizens. In 2014, 1,529 businesses were suggested by residents, to which Seoul supported 704 cases. Citizens also conducted various village projects in 18 "gu," including parents, community and childcare.

Improving housing conditions and providing public houses Seoul operates jeonse-support centers (Jeonse refers to a local property lease system in which tenants pay a large deposit in place of monthly rent. Tenants receive the money back after the contract ends.) to support tenants in the low-income bracket.

It also provided citizens with various financial loans to help them secure housing. It has provided citizens with a combined 81,624 public homes since 2010 through 2014. By 2018, it plans to provide 80,000 additional homes.

New town development plan Seoul has been making efforts to mediate discord among residents regarding development plans, and allowed them to choose whether to continue or end such projects. The city aimed to break out from traditional all-out destruction development and focus on protecting residents and maintaining existing communities, while inducing citizens to improve such regions themselves and maintain their regional identities. Seoul also provides consulting and financial aid regarding to such districts.

Seoul safety headquarter Seoul operates a control office that oversees all disasters, traffic and other issues, located in the basement of its head office. It takes the lead in all safety-related situations, including flood and mountainside accidents, and cope with disasters through real-time monitering. Up to 112 staffs are deployed to the situation room sized 472㎡, the headquarters will remain intact from earthquake and chemical attacks, maintaining its full capacity even during war.

Saving energy In order to make a sustainable and safe city, Seoul has rolled out its flagship energy campaign dubbed "Reduce a nuclear plant." It aims to reduce 2 million TOE of energy, which is equal to the capacity of a nuclear power plant. It started in August 2014, and aims to post an energy-independency rate of 20 percent by 2020. The city aims to bolster three values through the campaign, namely "Energy Independence, Sharing, and Participance."

■ **Industry**

Commerce At end-2014, there were 426 large shops, including 63 supermarkets, 32 department stores, 24 speciality stores, 41 shopping malls, and 266 other large shops. There were also 331 traditional markets, with 31 being located in Jung-gu, followed by 27 in Youngdeungpo-gu and 24 in Jongno-gu.

Manufacturing At end-2012, there were 4,540 businesses with 10-or-more employees, reaching up to the combined number of 115,385 workers. The annual revenue stands at 32.6 trillion won, generating added-value of 14.7 trillion won. The number of businesses moved down 285 compared to a year earlier, with the number of employees also decreasing 16,790. The revenue also fell 248.3 billion won from the 32.8 trillion won posted in 2011.

■ **Society**

Housing At end-2013, the number of houses stood at 3.54 million, up 49,774 from the 3.49 million posted in 2012. The housing penetration rate also moved up 0.2 percentage point to 97.5%, compared to the 97.3% posted in 2012.

By category, the number of detached houses came to 1.27 million, or 35.9% of the total. The number of apartments reached 1.57 million to account for 44.5%. There were also 143,370 town-house and 526,172 multiplex housings. Others took up 24,435, or 0.7%.

Traffic As of 2012, buses took up 27.4% of the city's transportation methods, while rail and subway accounted for 38.2%. Taxis, automobiles and others held 6.9%, 23.1%, and 4.4%, respectively. At end-2013, the number of automobiles came to 2.97 million units, up 4,000 from 2012.

Privately owned cars came to 2.33 million units, up 21,000 from 2.31 million units posted in 2012. In 2014, the length of bus-reserved roads came to 117.5㎞. The number of passengers using public transportation came to 10.9 million in 2013, up 8.5% from 2007.

Environment Concerning air condition, the pollution rate posted by sulfurous acid gas came to 0.006ppm in 2014, helped by the city's efforts to adopt more environment-friendly sources of energy. The figure stood at 0.051ppm in 1990s. As for carbon monoxide(CO), the figure came to 0.5-0.7ppm after 2003, compared to 2.6ppm posted in the 1990s, boasting conditions equal to those of advanced countries.

The density of fine particulate matter with 10 microns or less in diameter, commonly referred to as PM10, reached 46 $\mu g/m^3$ in 2014, up from $41\mu g/m^3$ and $45\mu g/m^3$ posted in 2012 and 2013, due mainly to dust from Northern Asia regions. The amount of nitrogen dioxide in the air stood at 0.033ppm in 2014, standing unchanged from 2013.

Waste disposal At end-2013, the city produced daily trash of 8,559t, with 64%, or 5,481t, being recycled, while 27%, or 2,304 tons, was incinerated. Around 774t, or 9% is buried underground. An average citizen produces 0.88 kg of trash everyday. There are 3,049 staff involved in collecting and transporting trash in the private sector with 1,540 automobiles, 570 wagons and 22 heavy machineries. In the public sector, there are 2,711 staff, 1,079 cars, 1,151 wagons and 54 heavy machineries.

There are four disposal facilities that generate energy. In 2006, they only operated at 33% of capacity, but the figure increased to reach 85% in 2013, generating 49 million kilowatts of power by burning 78,000t of trash. The amount is enough to provide power to 180,000 households for a year and worth 1.4 million barrels of crude.

Park and forest There are 2,782 designated forests in Seoul, including Namsan Park, with a combined size reaching 170.8㎢, or 28.1% of the combined area of the city. The figure translates into a 16.37㎡ park per capita. The size of green belts stand at 149.61㎢. There are 151 streets specially designated for forestry, with the combined length standing at 854 ㎞. There are 6,323 greenzones in Seoul which are estimated at 14,148㎢.

Natural environment Seoul designates environmental areas as restrictive zones controlled by law. Those include the Han River Bamsum, Dunchon-dong, Bangi-dong, Tancheon, Jingwan-dong, Amsa-dong, Cheonggye Mountain, Huninreung, Namsan, Bulamsan, Changdeokgung, Bongsan, Inwangsan, Sungnae stream, Gwanaksan, and Baeksashil Valley, with the 17 areas of such zones adding up to 4.82㎢. Wild fauna and flora sanctuary habitats include Umyunsan, Suraksan, Jingwan, and Nanji Han River Park, with the seven zones sized at 1.46㎢. The city plans to add more regions in the future.

Health and welfare At end-2014, there were 16,381 medical institutions with 83,344 beds. There are 57 general hospitals, 206 smaller hospitals, 7,689 private clinics, 98 long-term care facilities, nine elderly clinics, six mental institutions, one tuberculosis clinic, 4,696 dental clinics, 3,562 Chinese alternative herbal clinics, and five maternity hospitals.

There were 24,256 distributers of medical supplies, with pharmacies taking up 5,079, trailed by drug retailers with 726, Chinese herb retailers with 182, Chinese herb dealers 61, and one medicine dealer.

Around 5,101 sold emergency medicines, while 12,526 sold and rented medical instruments. There were also 580 medical equipment repair centers.

■ **Education and Culture**
Education As of April 2014, there are 884 kindergartens in Seoul, with 185 of them being public-owned and 699 being private. There are also 599 elementary schools, 559 public and 40 private. The number of middle schools came to 383, with 274 being public and 109 being private. High schools reached 318, with 118 being public and 200 being private.

There are also 29 speciality schools, 10 public and 19 private. The number of colleges reached 9, while that of universities came to 39. Five of the universities were public-owned. There are also 399 graduate schools and 21 others, reaching the combined number of 2,681 educational institutions.

Cultural heritage At the end of December 2014, there were 1,558 assets designated and registered as cultural properties. Of these, 1,055 are nationally designated, with 503 registered with the city. Compared to 2013, national cultural heritage moved up by 10 and the city's cultural properties grew by 30, raising the combined figure to 40.

Nationally designated assets include 157 national treasures such as Sungnyemun, Wongaksa Pagoda and 591 treasures such as Heunginjimun. There are also 69 historical sites and three scenic places, as well as 40 folk heritages, 13 natural monuments, 42 intangible assets and 141 registered heritages. The city also designated 334 tangible assets, 37 monuments, 45 intangible assets, 30 folk heritages, and 57 cultural data.

Cultural facilities As of end-December 2014, there are 118 museums, 338 auditoriums, 39 art galleries and 215 public libraries, leading to the combined number of 710 cultural facilities. The most famous ones include the Seoul Museum of History in Gyeonghui Palace, Seoul Museum of Art, Sejong Center for the Performing Arts, Namsan Hanok Village, Bukchon Hanok Village and Unhyeon Palace.

Cultural event Seoul has a variety of cultural events, including Jongmyo Daeje in May and Sajik Daeje in September. There is also Seoul Dream Festival in August, as well as a traditional music festival in October. Seoul rolls out various citizen-oriented festivals in all areas to provide people with various opportunities to enjoy culture.

The HiSeoul Festival, which held its 12th anniversary in 2014, held various programs in major squares in central Seoul, allowing citizens to participate in various activities involving sharing, natural preservation, and art. In November, Seoul hosts a lantern festival for 23 days on Cheonggye Stream, attracting some 3.1 million visitors. Seoul also hosts various programs to promote the city's beauty to the globe all year long, including fireworks and photo festivals.

Accommodations There are 237 hotels and 6,343 tourism agencies, leading to the combined number of 7,783. The number of "special" grade luxury hotels came to 56, while 97 also received grades one through three, with one being the highest. There are also nine family hotels and 16 hostels, with the number of rooms standing at 34,576. There were also 570 urban lodges and 27 amusement facilities.

BUSAN METROPOLITAN CITY

Area(㎢) : 769.82
Population(persons) : 3,519,401
Number of Households : 1,421,648
Flower : Camellia
Bird : Seagull
Tree : Camellia
Character : BUVI
Address : 1001, Jungang-daero, Yeonje-gu, Busan, Korea
Mayor : Suh Byung-soo

■ **Overview**
History It is believed that people started to live in the port region of Haeundae in Busan as early as the Late Paleolithic, since ruins from that era have been

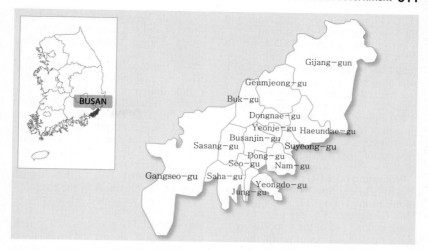

found. Neolithic culture and Bronze Age culture had a profound impact on the foundation of Japanese culture. Busan is also presumed to have been a port for iron exports in ancient days.

In February 1876, Busan debuted a modern international trading port. In early 1900, harbor and urban construction began to take place, and the Gyeongbu Line railway first opened in 1905. In April 1925, the provincial capital was moved to Busan, expanding its administrative region in 1936-1942.

During the 1950-1953 Korean War, Busan functioned as the temporary capital city. In March 1995, more parts of various regions were incorporated into Busan. As of December 2014, Busan consists of 15 districts, one county and 214 towns and boroughs.

Area & administrative districts The combined administrative district stands at 769.82㎢, taking up 0.8% of the combined South Korean territory. The urban planning zone is 993.54㎢, with 141.01 ㎢ being residential, 24.10㎢ commercial, 60.07㎢ industrial, and 554.77㎢ green area. Around 160.88㎢ are undesignated and 52.71㎢ are considered natural preservation zone.

■ **Finance**

In 2015, the combined budget stands at 13.4 trillion won, with 9.1 trillion won allocated for the city and 4.2 trillion won reserved for autonomous towns and boroughs. The general budget takes up 74.9% at 6.8 trillion won, while the special budget stands at 2.3 trillion won, or 25.1%.

Of tax revenue, 3.2 trillion won came from the city. By expenditure, 1.08 trillion won was spent on public safety, 587.9 billion won on education, 239.4 billion won on tourism, 84.6 billion won on environment protection, 2.6 trillion won on welfare, 153.2 billion won on the marine industry, 278 billion won on industry and small companies, 974.5 billion won on transportation, and 326.5 billion won on regional development. The reserves fund stood at 549.6 billion won.

■ **Key Projects**

Generating 200,000 good jobs In 2014, Busan has created a combined 155,000 jobs. It has rolled out a direct-job creation project to hire 27,000, and educated 30,000 in vocational skills. The city also provided education to 1,000 youths seeking to open start-ups. It also created 47,000 temporary jobs. In 2015, Busan is set to implement a master plan that aims to create 200,000 quality jobs.

Hosting competitive firms from home and abroad Busan has been making efforts to attract competitive companies from home and abroad through various programs, such as creating a 500 billion won fund with Busan Bank, while hosting various international events such as the International Telecommunications Union

(ITU) Plenipotentiary Conference and the South Korea-ASEAN summit.

Establishing Busan R&D zone In 2014, Busan received a 10 billion won fund from the central government, which was used to support 63 projects, build five research institutes and designate two high-tech firms. In 2015, Busan will create a 400 million won fund to speed up the growth of competitive firms. It also plans to establish a so-called "global tech business center" that will support researchers of marine plant machineries.

Promoting post-ITU projects In 2014, Busan held the International Telecommunications Union (ITU) Plenipotentiary Conference. The city plans to continue making use of the opportunity to generate new sources of profit, through establishing the ITU University and operating the Internet-of-Things center and ITU Youth Center.

New airport project In order to solve safety and noise issues with Gimhae International Airport, South Korea is seeking to build a new airport. The city will make efforts to narrow the gaps among other cities through having its opinions be reflected in the government's plan.

Establishing international industry-logistics city Busan is going through a development project that is divided into two phases. It is being conducted on 33 km², with the budget standing at 16 trillion won. Kicked off in 2008, it is scheduled to be completed in 2020.

Busan innovative city In 2015, the 10-year project to relocate state firms to the provinces will be completed. Ten institutions relocated through 2014, with three more to come. By end-March, 2,526 staff from 12 institutions, including Korea Housing Guarantee Co., Korea Securities Depository, and Korea Hydrographic and Oceanographic Administration.

■ **Economy**
Economy index Due to the Sewol ferry disaster in 2014, the Busan economy went through setbacks amid lackluster domestic demand. By index, the export of autoparts, automobiles and steel products gained ground despite the weak Japanese yen. China remained the biggest trading partner, but shipments to the United States also rose helped by the

Free Trade Agreement. Trade with Japan, however, did not have a full-fledge recovery, although it increased for the first time in three years.

With the increase of imports, mainly driven by raw materials, Busan posted a trade deficit of US$190 million. The shortfall reduced from US$280 million posted in 2013. The production of cars gained ground despite the falling domestic demand due to robust exports. Production of ships and machinery also gradually recovered.

Employment Due to the sluggish economy, employment in the manufacturing sector decreased, while employment in the food and tourism industries also suffered. The public, as well as tech, transportation, telecom and financial sectors, however, gathered ground, improving from 2013.

Manufacturing At end-2013, the number of manufacturers with 10 or more employees came to 4,643, which employed a total 139,332 staff. Their revenue stands at 40.2 trillion won, with the added value reaching 13.9 trillion won.

By sector, metal and machinery companies took up 41%, followed by shoes and fabrics with 18.4%. Automobile firms reached 9.5%. Companies with less than 300 employees took up 99.5% of the combined Busan-based firms.

Finance At end-2013, there were 630 banks, with 266 private, 240 regional-based and four foreign-owned. There are also 120 special banks and 1,929 non-banking financial institutes. At end-2014, the combined deposits came to 115.7 trillion won, with loans standing at 108 trillion won.

Agriculture The combined agricultural territory stands at 6,145ha, including 7,178 households with 20,486 members.

Livestock industry The number of households involved in the livestock industry came to 361 in January 2015, raising 2,942 cows, 6,782 pigs and 153,732 chickens and ducks.

Port and fishery The combined logistics handled at Busan ports came to 4.59 million twenty-foot-equivalent units (TEU) for imports, while that of exports came to 4.65 million TEU. Transshipment took up 9.41 TEU, leading to 18.65 million TEU, up 5.5% from 2013, or 75% of the combined amount posted by South

Korea. There are 48 fishing ports, with three owned by the state government, 13 owned by the provincial government and 32 other smaller ones.

■ **Society**
Housing At end-2014, the number of detached houses came to 483,765 units, while apartments reached 706,428. Townhouses came to 139,812 units, and there were also 39,513 multiplex housings, which all adds up to 1.36 million living accomodations. The housing penetration rate stands at 105.9%.

Water supply Busan is capable of producing 2.14 million cubic meters of water every day. At end-2014, the city was producing 1.07 million cubic meters of water on a daily basis, which translates into 303 liters per capita. The water supply penetration rate stands at 100%.

Sewerage At end-2014, the sewerage system covered 99.2% of Busan, and the sewer penetration rate is 79.6%. The coverage of the sewerage system is set to reach 99.9% by 2030. Total sewage pipe facilities extend 7,886km, while that of wastewater pipeline stretches 1,506km. It is an urgent task for Busan to separate the sewage pipe system from the current combined one.

Health and hygiene There are 27 general hospitals, 2,472 clinics, 1,201 dental clinics, 1,097 Chinese alternative herbal clinics, 10 attached hospitals, and four maternity centers. This adds to 4,811 medical facilities with 24,311 doctors and 24,015 nurses and other medical-related workers. There are 6,467 facilities dealing with medicine.

International exchange In 2014, Busan joined forces with Japan's Nagasaki prefecture and China' Shanxi and Hubei provinces. The Busan delegation also visited Myanmar, Thailand, and Cambodia to roll out official development assistance (ODA) projects.

■ **Education and Culture**
Education There are 403 kindergartens, 306 elementary schools, 172 middle schools, 167 high schools, 22 universities and colleges and 11 lifetime education institutions, which adds up to 701,000 students in 1,081 schools.

Religion There are 2,000 Buddhists'

facilities, 1,800 christian locations, 106 Catholic sites, 53 for won Buddhism, 9 Cheondoism and 2 Confucianism places.

Clergy are estimated to number approximately 7,000.

Cultural heritages Busan has a total of 388 cultural heritage assets: six national treasures including the gilt bronze Bodhisattva figurine placed at the Municipal Museum of Cultural Property, the three-story Beomeosa stone pagoda, four historical landmarks including Dongrae shell mounds, seven natural monuments and two scenic spots such as Taejongdae.

DAEGU METROPOLITAN CITY

Area(㎢) : 883.48
Population(persons) : 2,518,467
Number of Households : 970,739
Flower : Peony
Bird : Eagle
Tree : Fir
Character : Fashiony
Address : 88, Gongpyeong-ro Jung-gu, Daegu, Korea
Mayor : Kwong Young-jin

■ **Overview**
History It is estimated that people started to live in Daegu some 10,000-20,000 years ago, as remains of stone tools and arrowheads from the Paleolithic era were found. Daegu dwellers had possibly resided in villages between two small streams which are now called Seobyeondong and Daebongdong. At the time of the Bronze Age, the dwellers in the villages formed communities and tribes, and began to call their region "Dalgubul" or "Dalgubeol."

Daegu first earned its current name in A.D. 757, but the name did not show up until A.D. 1778 in the Joseon Dynasty, during which it developed as the central region in the southern area of the country. In July 1, 1981, Daegu was put under direct municipality of the central

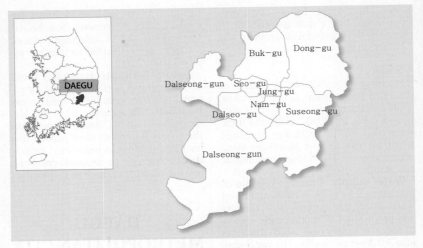

government, incorporating seven nearby regions. In 1995, it was renamed Daegu Metropolitan City, integrating Dalseong-gun which includes the Nakdong River.

Area, population and administrative districts The combined area of Daegu stands at 883.48㎢, accounting for 0.9% of the South Korean territory. Development restricted zones, however, take up 401.35㎢, accounting for 45.4%. The total population stands at 2.51 million, with seven administrative districts.

■ **Finance**

In 2015, the combined budget stood at 9.1 trillion won, with the general budget taking up 7.6 trillion won and special budget accounting for 1.5 trillion won.

The combined budget for the city headquarters stands at 6.1 trillion won, with the general budget standing at 4.6 trillion won. Of the general budget, social welfare takes up 35.5%, followed by general administration with 13.81%, transportation with 11.27%, education with 8.98%, and industrial sector 4.06%.

■ **Key projects**

Establishing grounds to revitalize Daegu Daegu operates 64 centers to communicate with citizens that aim to build ground for the happiness of people. It also lifted a handful of barriers to host investment.

Building ecosystem for creative economy After opening a creative

economy center in April, Daegu also joined forces with Samsung to beef up the city's efforts to join the creative economy drive promoted by the central government. Daegu has strengthened its corporate supportive systems to foster new ICT-based growth engines.

Bolstering competitiveness of regional firms Daegu has opened a one-stop corporate support center, and provides local companies with customized support, aiming to build a business-friendly environment. Following such efforts, regional exports are growing. In 2014, exports came to US$7.8 billion, up 11.4% from US$7 billion posted in 2013. The growth hovered above the country's average of 2.4%. The city's 42 firms attracted 843.1 billion won, and generated 65,237 jobs.

■ **Industry**

In 2015, Daegu received a 3.2 trillion won budget from the central government. Of that amount, 10 billion won was used for water industry cluster projects, while 7.6 billion won was allocated for the World Water Forum. Attracting a combined investment of 853.3 billion won, Daegu joined hands with Samsung Electronics and opened an exclusive office to consult business-related problems.

Manufacturers The manufacturing sector made up 23.3% of the regional economy in 2013, down from the 23.7% posted in 2012. The output, however, advanced 2.4% on-year over the January-

November period of 2014, hovering above the average minus 0.1% decline observed throughout the country.

Combined exports also stood at US$7.07 billion as of November, which already hovers above the all-time high annual record of 2013. As such, the manufacturing sector maintained its stable growth despite challenges.

Retail In Daegu, there are eight department stores, five shopping centers, 18 large supermarkets and 136 traditional markets, reaching a combined 236 retail facilities. The city has been making efforts to revitalize the competitiveness of traditional markets by modernizing their facilities and promoting gift certificates. It also regulated operating hours of conglomerate-owned supermarkets in order to protect smaller retailers.

Finance There are 726 financial institutions in Daegu, with combined deposits of 84.6 trillion won. Combined loans stands at 70.1 trillion won. Daegu is making efforts to foster human resources and adequate information for financial firms. It also supports small-and-medium firms to modernize their facilities.

Trade In 2014, Daegu saw its exports reach US$7.8 billion and imports US$3.6 billion, reaching a trade surplus of US$4.1 billion. While the stronger Korean won, prolonged economic slump and cheaper Japanese yen had adverse impacts on exporters, last year's export volume set a new record. Major export products included machinery, which took up 42.6%. Electronic goods, fabrics and chemicals took up 19.9%, 16.4% and 7.9%, respectively.

The city's biggest trading partner is China at 22.2%. The United States accounted for 13.9%, followed by Japan, Vietnam and Mexico with 6.6%, 5.5% and 4.5% respectively. Daegu said its record-high exports came as the city has continuously supported local exporters, as well as rolled out prompt measures against free trade agreements. It also supported overseas market research while providing interpretation services to exporters.

■ **Society**

Park and greenery Daegu plans to expand the size of parks to reach 80.1km² in the future. As of end-2013, the total size of 449 parks reached 51.8km². It plans to add 19.2km² at 59 locations in the future. The city plans to make use of such parks to improve the quality of life of citizens.

Waterworks The city is capable of producing 1.64 million tons of water through six facilities per day. The waterwork penetration rate stands at 99.9%, with production per capita standing at 304 liters per day.

Sewerage The city's sewage facility has a disposal capacity of 1.87 tons per day.

Health and hygiene Daegu has 3,439 medical institutions, 4,979 drug and medical instrument dealers, 11,270 health and hygiene establishments, 51,003 food hygiene facilities and 3,291 music and games businesses. The city is making efforts to expand its surveillance on retail of food-related products.

Environment Daegu has been making efforts to improve the environment by tackling global warming and reducing waste, while building nature-friendly facilities.

Social welfare The number of those receiving basic pension came to 93,539 from 54,306 households. The number of shelter facilities came to 318, along with 26 social welfare centers, 1,426 senior centers, 88 places for the disabled, and one shelter for the homeless.

■ **Education and Culture**

Education Daegu has 857 educational institutions, which includes 373 kindergartens, 219 elementary schools, 124 middle schools, 92 high schools, nine colleges, four universities and 26 graduate schools. The combined number of students stand at 298,250. There are 30 public libraries in the city.

Tourism As the city aims to have 10 million tourists by 2020, Daegu will roll out various measures in 2015 to make the city more attractive. The plans include improving the quality of accomodations and developing measures to attract Chinese tourists.

Science technology Hosting the 7th World Water Forum, the city will continue to foster new growth engines for the future.

INCHEON METROPOLITAN CITY

Area(㎢) : 1,046.27
Population(persons) : 2,957,931
Number of Households : 1,136,280
Flower : Rose
Bird : Crane
Tree : Tulip tree
Address : 29, Jeonggak-ro, Namdong-gu, Incheon, Korea
Mayor : Yoo Jeong-bok

▪ Overview
History It is presumed that people started to live in Incheon in the Neolithic age because of various discoveries made around Munhak Mountain and Gyeyang Mountain. In the Bronze Age, given the findings of graveyards in what is now the central city areas, it is believed that tribes resided there.

According to ancient literature, Incheon used to belong to Baekje in the Three Kingdoms era, before it became a territory of Silla in King Jinhung's time. During the Goryeo Dynasty, Incheon was promoted a few times to an upper grade in terms of city classification because it was the city the king's mother was born in.

After Korea was liberated from the Japanese colonial rule of 1910-1945, Incheon earned its status as a city as Korea began its regional autonomous governments on Aug. 15, 1949. It later incorporated nearby regions -- Gimpo, Gyeyang, Ongjin, Yeongjong -- before it became a metropolitan city on Jan. 1, 1995.

Area & administrative districts As of January 2015, the combined size of Incheon stands at 1,046.27㎢, accounting for 1% of South Korean territory. It is divided into eight districts.

▪ Finance
In 2015, the combined budget stands at 11.4 trillion won, up 1.14% from 11.3 trillion won posted in 2014. Around 7.7 trillion won is allocated for the city headquarters, while 3.7 trillion won is reserved for autonomous regions.

In terms of the general budget, the administrative sector took up 672.3 billion won, down 21.37% on-year. The social welfare sector added 21.62% to 1.5 trillion won, while the agricultural and fishery sector was allocated 102.8 billion won. The transportation and science sectors were given 650 billion won and 42.9 billion won, respectively.

▪ Key Projects
Establishing sound financial health Incheon seeks to build healthier financial ground starting in 2015, and eradicate inefficient businesses while taking a stra-

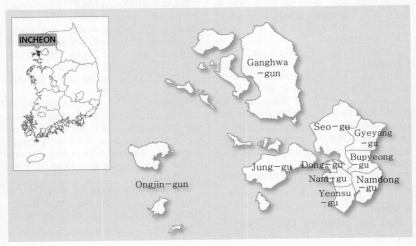

tegic approach in making expenditures. It will implement a self-evaluation on the performance of financial management, and roll out new policies that can bring more responsibility on spending.

Also, the city will make efforts to host more funds from the central government to avoid any delay in administrative management. It will refrain from issuing additional bonds and make efforts to reduce interest expenditures by reducing debt. Incheon will also make efforts to find new sources of tax income.

Revitalizing economy through investment The city will operate a special commission on hosting investment, and bolster cash inflow into the Incheon Free Economic Zone. It will also lift various regulations, and bolster the city's role in hosting investment.

Incheon will persuade companies, which have already left the city, to return, and seek to host a real estate investment convention in 2015. It will promote investment especially in shopping malls and resort sectors, as well as make efforts to bring in high-tech companies.

Generating performances from existing projects Incheon aims to bring visible performance to on-going projects. It aims to find various solutions toward delayed projects, such as the new bridge that will connect Yeongjongdo with central Incheon. The construction of the bridge has been delayed due to financial restraints.

Bolstering competitiveness by building new rail The city aims to open a KTX bullet train line that will kick off in Incheon. It has also opened a validity study into the Seoul-Songdo railway line, along with extending Subway Line 7 to bolster the competitiveness of Cheongna International City. Incheon also seeks to relocate the Gyeongin Subway Line to underground for efficiency.

Revitalizing the value of Incheon In 2015, the city was designated as the World Book Capital by the United Nations Educational, Scientific and Cultural Organization. Incheon will also host the World Education Forum this year, and continue its efforts to take the lead in hosting international events, which will lend support to the city's convention industry.

Developing city centers with history and tradition Incheon will develop new tourism programs and make efforts to revitalize the city's cultural heritage. It will eventually become a role model for revitalizing urban economy through creative recovery of modern-day assets.

■ **Industry**

Industry Incheon has the best environment for business on the back of its seaports and airports, and aims to become a key city of South Korea that leads overall growth. The first export industry complex was established in Bupyeong, Incheon, in October 1969.

Since 1971, Incheon has been operating 10 industrial zones, with two more to come. In such zones, there are 9,512 companies hiring 14,192 workers. At 10,453 factories, 190,434 workers are involving in metal, machinery, electronics, electric, chemical and timber industries.

Commerce As of end-2014, there are five department stores, nine shopping centers, 27 large supermarkets, five specialized stores and 76 super-supermarkets. There are also 83 traditional markets and two agricultural wholesalers and distributors.

■ **Society**

Housing As of 2014, the city has built a total of 18,020 houses, with 8,663 privately owned and 9,357 publicly owned. The number of detached houses came to 223,727 at end-2014, along with 558,329 apartments, 26,629 town houses, 214,446 multiplex houses, which adds up to 1.03 million units.

Transportation At end-2014, the number of registered automobiles came to 1,247,485 units, up 105,134, or 9.2%, from 1,142,351 units posted in 2013. By sector, the number of sedans came to 1,010,828 units, followed by vans at 58,644, trucks at 172,696 and special purpose vehicles at 5,317.

Health and hygiene The number of healthcare facilities came to 2,949. There are 19 general hospitals, 53 hospitals, 1,404 clinics, 769 dental clinics, 608 Chinese medicine clinic and 59 rehabilitation centers. There are also 1,001 pharmacies, 28 herbal medicine stores, 76 medicine wholesalers and 1,675 medical instrument sellers.

There are also 26 senior facilities and

300 nursing homes for the elderly, which accommodate a total of 8,682 seniors. The number of state-run child care facilities came to 132, along with 815 privately run centers. When combining other forms of day care centers, including those at workplaces, the number of child care-related facilities reach 2,308 units.

■ **Education and Culture**
Education Incheon is home to four graduate schools, four universities, four colleges, 122 high schools, seven special schools, 133 middle schools, 242 elementary schools, 403 kindergarten and 10 other type of institutions.

Cultural heritages There are 75 national heritage properties: one national asset, 28 national treasures, 18 national heritage sites, 14 natural monuments, six important intangible assets, one scenic site and seven registered cultural heritages. There are also 177 pieces of heritage designated by the city, which are: 58 tangible assets, 65 monuments, 27 intangible assets, two folklore records and 25 heritage records.

Tourism There are 541 tourism agencies based in Incheon, along with 81 accomodations, 32 tourism facilities, 11 international convention centers, one casino, 21 amusement facilities and 172 tourists' convenience facilities.

Cultural event Cultural events include: New Year's Concert (January), the Incheon Calligraphy Exhibition (July), 2015 Incheon Pentaport Rock Festival (August), Incheon Photo Festival (September), Incheon K-POP Concert (September), Incheon-China Cultural Tourism Festival (October), Incheon Soraepogu Festival (October) and other various cultural and art festivals year around.

GWANGJU METROPOLITAN CITY

■ **Overview**
History Gwangju used to be called Mujinju in the Mahan era before the Three Kingdoms, when Baekje had the

Area(㎢) : 501.18
Population(persons) : 1,475,884
Number of Households : 573,043
Flower : Royal azaleas
Bird : Dove
Tree : Ginkgo
Character : BitDoli
Address : 111, Naebang-ro, Seo-gu, Gwangju, Korea
Mayor : Yoon Jang-hyun

region under its control. It was the 33rd year of Goryeo that Mujinju changed its name to Gwangju. In 1893, when the country was reorganized into 13 provinces, Gwangju became the capital of South Jeolla Province.

Four years after the establishment of the Republic of Korea, Gwangju expanded its area to 214.92㎢ comprising 45 boroughs. In 1986, Gwangju was promoted to the fourth city under the direct control of the central government with 72 boroughs. As of Dec. 12, Gwanju consists of five autonomous "gu," and 95 boroughs in total.

Area and population The combined area of Gwangju stands at 501.18㎢, taking up 0.5% of the South Korean territory. Its population stands at 1.47 million, accounting for 2.9% of the country's total population. Women outnumber men in Gwangju at 50.4% to 49.6%.

■ **Finance**
In 2015, the combined budget came to 3.84 trillion won, with the general budget standing at 3.1 trillion won and special budget posting 745.2 billion won. Its financial independency reached 39%, relatively lower than the average of 47.6% posted by metropolitan cities. The city's revenue includes 1.4 trillion won along with 184.6 billion won from municipal bond issuances.

■ **Key Projects**
Establishing direct-participation system for citizens The city has kicked off the so-called "Gwangju Community Citizen Commission" to exchange ideas on key policies of the city among experts and citizens. Through this, the

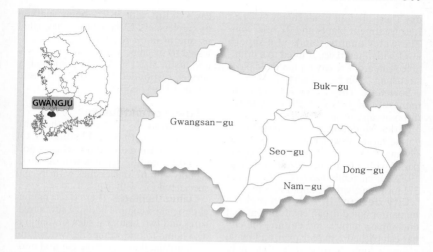

citizens shared and exchanged issues regarding Gwangju. The city also conducted on-site investigations into 1,785 reports to solve civil complaints. It also analyzed such complaints through big-data systems to be used as grounds for new policies.

Building grounds to become international sports city Gwangju will host the 2015 Summer Universiade and the 2019 World Aquatics Championships, emerging as a global sports city.

Communicating the world with culture Gwangju will open Asian Culture Complex in 2015, and is preparing for the official opening.

■ **Industry**

Economic index The combined regional gross domestic product stands at 29.6 trillion won, accounting for 2.1% of South Korea's economy. The figure translates into 19.5 million won per capita. Of the output, the service sector takes up 71.2%, followed by manufacturing with 28.3 percent and agriculture with 0.5%. There are 7,816 manufacturing firms in the city, with 14 being conglomerates and 189 mid-sized. There are also 7,613 small firms. Each hires 21,310, 19,526 and 37,743, respectively. The population aged 15 and above came to 1.26 million in 2014, up 0.9% on-year.

The economically active population came to 744,000 in 2014, up 0.1% from 2013. Of them, 726,000 had jobs, down 0.3% on-year. The unemployment rate stands at 2.4%, up 0.3 percentage point on-year.

Finance There is one central bank, seven commercial banks, one regional bank and 34 special banks operating in Gwangju. There are also nine non-banking financial organizations.

Retail There are three department stores, 14 large supermarkets, 15 super-supermarkets operated by large retailers, three special stores, and eight shopping centers, which add up to 41 retail outlets.

■ **Society**

Housing The housing penetration rate stands at 103.2%, with apartments taking up 63%. In order to revitalize reconstruction, the city provides incentives to designated areas.

Roads and traffic Gwangju is currently seeking to build a second subway line. The combined length of roads stands at 2,337km, with highways, state roads and city roads taking up 28, 87 and 560km, respectively. Its roads cover 71.4% of the territory.

At end-2014, the number of registered vehicles stood at 589,334 units, up 3.75%, or 21,000 units from 2013. Subways and buses provide free transfer systems.

Waterwork The combined length of water pipes stands at 3,798km, with the coverage reaching 99.56% of the area. The production is enough to provide each citizen with 322 liters of water every day. There are four water supply facilities, four treatment plants and 21 reservoirs. The water quality stands at a superb level, with filtered water fitted to a drinkable standard. The city replaced old pipes stretching 289㎞ from 2005 to 2014.

Sewerage The city has a sewer treatment rate of 91% with the daily sewer disposal capacity at 736,000 tons.

Parks Mudeungsan National Park is 75.4㎢ large, of which 47.6㎢ belong to Gwangju. The city plans to establish 606 parks, with a combined size standing at 19.7㎢. It currently has 8.6㎢ of parks at 371 locations, with 235 more to come.

City design In order to make a human-oriented urban environment that encompass nature and culture, the city has established a master plan, and made efforts to improve roads to become more pedestrian-friendly. It also tried to revitalize the cultural aspect of old industrial zones, and improve public design. Based on public-design related rules, the city has made efforts to improve the quality of life, and become a happy, creative city with quality culture.

Social welfare The number of beneficiaries of basic pension stands at 59,598, taking up 4.1% of its population. Those aged 65 and above reached 59,598, making up 10.7% of the total population. The number of registered citizens with disabilities reached 68,288, or 4.6% of the city population. There are 168 social welfare living facilities, 102 social welfare benefit facilities, 1,269 child care centers and 27 public health and medical facilities.

Health and hygiene There are 22 general hospitals, 951 general practitioners and private clinics, 560 dental clinics, 382 Chinese and herbal medicine clinics and one maternity clinic, which adds up to 1,970 medical institutions.

Food-related stores include 20,466 hospitality establishments, 2,745 manufacturers, 2,681 health food imports and manufacturers, 2,971 food sale and transportation businesses, and 1,397 food suppliers. Health and hygiene entities include 835 accommodations, 239 public baths, 605 barbers, 3,929 hairdressers, 1,164 dry cleaners and 396 hygiene-management firms.

Fire control In 2014, there were 1,010 cases of fire, with 58.7% being sparked by carelessness. Electricity was also cited as one of main reasons at 22.6%, followed by machinery malfunction at 5.8% and arson at 3.1%. The 119 emergency service responded to 10,095 cases and rescued 3,194 people.

■ **Education and Culture**

Education As of end-2014, there are 328 schools with 327,772 students. Of them, 150 are elementary schools, followed by middle schools with 88, high schools with 67, universities with 18, and special schools with five.

Cultural heritages There is one national-designated cultural heritage, seven treasures and two historical sites. Gwangju is also home to one scenic site, two natural monuments, one intangible cultural heritage and three folklore heritages.

Culture and art Gwangju has 20 libraries, 10 museums, 11 art centers, 51 galleries, 39 performance centers and 16 theaters.

International exchange Gwangju has forged ties as sister cities with San Antonio in the U.S., Taiwan's Tainan, China's Guangzhou and Changzhi, Indonesia's Medan and Japan's Sendai.

DAEJEON METROPOLITAN CITY

Area(㎢) : 540.24
Population(persons) : 1,531,809
Number of Households : 592,508
Flower : White Magnolia
Bird : Magpie
Tree : Pine Tree
Character : Hankkumi
Address : 100, Dunsan-ro, Seo-gu, Daejeon, Korea
Mayor : Kwon Sun-taik

■ **Overview**

History Daejeon had belonged to the periphery of Mahan, and was called Usul in the Baekje period during the Three

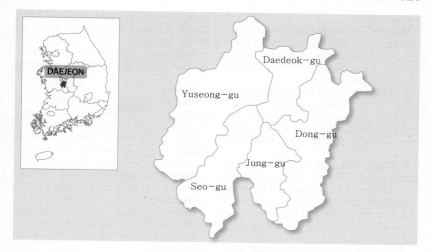

Kingdoms era. In 1905, as Daejeon Station was launched as part of the development of the Gyeongbu railway, the city saw an inflow of Japanese residents settling in the area at the start of Japan's colonial rule of Korea. In 1932, the regional city council of South Chungcheong Province moved to Daejeon from Gongju.

In 1949, it was promoted to the city of Daejeon, before it was promoted to metropolitan city status in 1995. Four years later, as some of the government agencies moved to Daejeon, the city began its new era as an administrative capital. In 2005, Daeduk Research & Development Cluster helped the city develop further into a symbol of a growth engine in science in Korea. In 2013, the city became the base for the government's creative economy drive. Daejeon continued to build grounds for the future growth.

Area and population At end-2014, the combined size of Daejeon stands at 540.24㎢, with the population reaching 1.53 million with 592,508 households.

■ **Finance**

In 2014, the combined general budget of the city came to 3.41 trillion won, with the general budget taking up 2.55 trillion won and special budget took up 860 billion won. The city's revenue included 1.1 trillion won worth of regional tax and 73.6 billion won worth of non-tax income. It depended on 1.17 trillion won from other sources of income, including a 724.7 bil-

lion won subsidy from the central government.

It has also issued 35.5 billion won worth of municipal bonds, having its financial independency reach 51.5%. Of its expenditures, the general public administration costs took up 292.3 billion won, while the public safety sector accounted for 27.5 billion won. The education area called for 253.4 billion won, and the culture sector was allocated 164.2 billion won.

Others are as follows: natural protection 71.9 billion won, social welfare 981.2 billion won, public health 45.6 billion won, agricultural and fisheries 29.5 billion won, industry and small-medium firms 49.1 billion won, transportation 231.7 billion won, regional development 98.7 billion won, science technology 31.2 billion won, and reserve fund 270.4 billion won.

As for the 860.8 billion won worth of special funds, the waterworks called for 109 billion won and sewerage works took up 137.2 billion won. Others are as follows: regional development 293.2 billion won, residential development 400 million won, traffic business 33.6 billion won, metropolitan transportation system 1.7 billion won, medical pension 179.5 billion won, urban development 241.2 billion won, industrial zone 50.3 billion won, urban rail development 2.2 billion won, school territory payment 11 billion won, compensation for delays in development plans 1.2 billion won, and 300 million won for infrastructure.

- **Key Projects**
Disaster-crime free Daejeon Daejeon operates 3,482 units of close-circuit cameras in vulnerable places, 24 hours a day, 365 days a year, making efforts to build a convenient and safe city.

Building grounds to create quality jobs The city continues efforts to attract corporate investment to sustain growth and create 100,000 quality jobs, as well as lend support to livelihood of low-income bracket.

Building safe and easy transportation system The city has designated nine key areas to improve the environment for pedestrians. It also added more public transportation to meet the rising need, while expanding call taxi services for the handicapped.

Human-oriented sustainable city Daejeon has been making efforts to revitalize outdated facilities and create new value by adding cultural touch. It also struggles to improve underdeveloped areas and seek a balanced growth among each parts of the city.

- **Industry**
Industry There are 2,200 manufacturers in the city, with 115 of them being food and tobacco producers, followed by textile and leather firms at 139. The figure also includes 20 timber firms, 78 paper producers, 241 chemical businesses and 37 nonmetal firms. Such firms have 46,328 employees. As of end-November 2014, the combined export came to US$4.3 billion, with imports standing at US$3.1 billion.

Agriculture At end-2014, there were 9,518 households involved in the agricultural sector with 28,816 people. They cultivated 4,616ha -- 1,837ha of rice farms and 2,779ha in gardens -- producing 8,925t of rough grain, 86t of non-rice grains, 321t of beans, 3,104t of root crops, 21,370t of vegetables, 262t of special crops and 6,446t of fruits.

Commerce There are 14 large supermarkets, four department stores, 39 traditional markets, two wholesalers and 39 super-supermarkets, which are operated by large retailers.

Finance At end-2013, the financial institutions in the city were as follows: one Bank of Korea office, 153 commercial banks, 44 special banks, 253 trust companies, 264 asset management firms, six saving banks, 45 credit cooperative, 15 mutual finance firms and 43 offices of the Korea Federation of Credit Cooperatives.

- **Society**
Housing At end-2014, detached houses numbered 222,452 units, while apartments reached 315,278 units. Town houses came to 43,104 units, which leads to combined 580,834 units of houses. The housing penetration rate stands at 101.4%.

Waterworks and sewerages The daily production of water reached 514,000 m³, reaching 99.7% of the city. The 1.51 million population covered by the network receives 340ℓ of water per day. The sewerage system reached 97.5% of the population.

Traffic The number of registered cars came to 621,035 units. Sedans took up 508,266 units, while the number of vans came to 25,942 units. Others included 85,083 units of cargo trucks, 1,744 units of special cars, and 35,726 units of motor bikes. There are 38,049 parking lots capable of handling 626,282 cars. Daejeon has 2,267km of streets, which include 76km of highway and 84km of state roads. The traffic coverage rate stands at 100 percent.

Social welfare The city provides subsidies to 2,562 citizens from 2,396 households. It has also provided 6,320 jobs to women through employment conventions, while allowing citizens to enjoy various welfare services to enjoy their lives.

Environment The city undertook an administrative inspection of 1,748 buildings and offices for pollution, discovering about 61 entities had committed wrongful acts that harmed the environment. The levels of various toxic elements in the air were as follows: sulfur dioxide at 0.04ppm/year, monoxide at 0.5ppm/year, nitrogen dioxide at 0.02 ppm/year, and ozone at 0.026ppm/year.

Health and hygiene There are 2,085 medical institutions, including nine general hospitals with 5,465 beds, and 34 hospitals with 3,464 beds. There are also 993 clinics, five special hospitals, 48 nursing hospitals, six dental hospitals, 488 dental clinics and five Chinese and herbal practices. Recipients of basic living benefits stand at 40,133 from 24,618 households, and 3,336 from 134 facilities also receive subsidies.

■ **Education and Culture**
Education At end-2014, the number of schools stand at 319. There are 145 elementary schools, 88 middle schools, 62 high schools, five special schools and 19 colleges and universities, with 343,166 students.

Cultural heritages National cultural assets numbered 208 in total, which include 10 national treasures, one national heritage site, 18 registered cultural properties, 52 tangible cultural assets, 21 intangible assets, 46 monuments, three folklore cultural assets and 56 cultural asset materials.

Cultural facilities The city has built Daejeon Culture and Arts Hall and the Museum of Modern Art. These institutes have become a central area serving the citizens' needs for culture. There are 23 public libraries with 214 smaller libraries. There are 10 movie theaters, 53 performance theaters and 62 exhibition facilities.

Gym facilities Daejeon has 28 sports stadiums, three golf driving ranges, seven sports complexes, 23 swimming pools, 53 martial arts academies and 603 billiards halls, among others.

Sister cities Daejeon has forged friendship with 13 cities from 11 countries, including Seattle in the U.S., Hungary's Budapest, and South Africa's Durban.

ULSAN METROPOLITAN CITY

Area(㎢) : 1,060
Population(persons) : 1,192,262
Number of Households : 442,250
Flower : Rose
Bird : White Heron
Tree : Bamboo
Character : Haewuri
Address : 201, Jungang-ro, Nam-gu, Ulsan, Korea
Mayor : Kim Gi-hyeon

■ **Overview**
History Ulsan has been presumed to be the land of affluence since prehistoric times. It had belonged to Jinhan during the Three Hans era. In the Goryeo Dynasty and through the Joseon Dynasty, the region was called Uljoo, until it changed its name to Ulsan in 1413. In 1962, Ulsan was promoted to a city after the government embarked on a project to develop Ulsan into an industrial complex.

Area and administration zone The area of Ulsan stands at 1,060㎢ with a population of 1.19 million. It consists of four "gu," one "gun," and 56 boroughs.

■ **Finance**
In 2015, the combined assets of the city stands at 2.91 trillion won, up 4.74%, or 132 billion won from a year earlier. The general fund stood at 2.1 trillion won, taking up 73%, while the special fund stood at 787.9 billion won. Of its general fund, tax revenue took up 1.1 trillion won, or 52.88%, while non-tax revenue accounted for 74.2 billion won, and 531.8 billion won came from the central government.

■ **Key Projects**
Building new Ulsan port Since 1997, Ulsan has been making efforts to build a new port sized at 679,000㎡ with a budget of 6.4 trillion won. Currently, 31% of the project is finished at the size of 242,000㎡. It will be completed by 2020.

Establishing innovative Ulsan The city plans to welcome 10 public organizations with around 20,000 staff into the 2.98 million-square-meters innovative zone in Ulsan. Seven have already moved in as of end-2014.

Ulsan free-trade zone Ulsan has been making efforts to build an 837,000㎡ free trade zone since 2009, and it has began construction of buildings that aim to be completed in 2015. The area will host export-oriented local firms, as well as foreign investment, logistics and trade firms. They will be given various tax incentives.

Rising Northeast Asian oil hub Ulsan plans to rise as the world's No. 4 oil trader along with the United States, Europe and Singapore. It will invest 1.9 trillion won through 2020 and establish facilities capable of reserving 28.4 million barrels of oil.

Connecting academies and corpo-

324

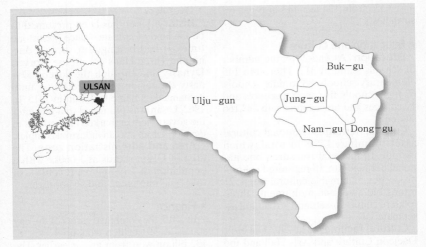

rations Ulsan will establish a South Korean version of the U.S.' Silicon Valley. Under the plan, the city will foster 200 small-and-medium ventures over the next five years, educating 4,000 experts.

Establishing Ulsan-technology industrial zone On 1.278 million square meters of land, the city will build what it calls Ulsan Techno General Industrial Zone. It will join forces with various research and development organizations, including Ulsan National Institute of Science and Technology. It will be home to 32 research institutes or firms and 30 industrial organizations.

Establishing city library Ulsan will build a city library that will be three stories high on 31,125㎡ of land. It has commenced planning in August 2014, and the ground-breaking ceremony will be held in October 2015. It will be completed by end-2017.

Lifting regulations In 2014, Ulsan selected 218 regulations and is under way in lifting the unnecessary ones through exchanging ideas with other state organizations in order to lend support to the city economy.

■ **Economy**
Tax In 2014, Ulsan collected 1.6 trillion won in regional tax. Of that amount, acquisition tax took up 405.7 billion won, followed by registration fees with 35.5 billion won, residence tax with 47.1 billion won, automobile tax with 181.8 billion won, property tax with 174 billion won, tobacco tax with 73.8 billion won, regional consumption tax with 253.9 billion won, regional income tax with 283.1 billion won, resources tax with 28 billion won, and regional education tax with 120.2 billion won.

Industry The city's industrial area covers 88,435㎡. There are 1,624 firms generating 217.2 trillion won and employing 157,724 workers. Ulsan has been working to create 14 more industrial zones, with 10 currently completed and four under construction.

Retail As of end-2014, there are three department stores, 12 large supermarkets, five shopping centers, one agricultural and fisheries wholesaler, one agricultural and fisheries retail center, and 53 traditional markets. Ulsan has been making efforts to boost the competitiveness of traditional markets by installing parking lots along with other measures.

Housing As of end-2013, the number of houses came to 428,454 units, with detached houses taking up 165,385. Others include apartments at 235,541 units, town houses at 7,635 units, and multiplex houses at 19,893 units, with the housing penetration rate standing at 107.5%.

Construction The number of registered construction firms came to 222. There were also 110 companies that lease construction equipment, 44 repair firms, 22 dealers and eight machine scrappers.

Transportation There are 504,604 registered automobiles in Ulsan, with 416,326 sedans, 17,255 vans, 68,682 trucks and 2,305 special cars. As for commercial vehicles, there are 855 buses, 2,159 corporate taxis, 3,623 private taxis and 8,540 cargo trucks.

Export-import In 2014, the city's exports reached US$92.4 billion, up 1% from 2013. Ulsan's top five products -- petroleum goods, automobiles, ships, petrochemicals and auto parts -- take up 82.5% of the export volume. Ulsan's import volume reached 79.7 billion won, down 5% from 2013.

Agriculture At end-2013, the combined agricultural area reached 11,441 ha, with rice farm taking up 6,887ha and others types of gardens reaching 4,554ha. There are 11,997 households with 32,114 members involved in the agricultural sector, which takes up 2.8% of Ulsan's population. The figures translate into 1ha per each household.

Livestock There are currently 33,140 Hanwoo cattle, a Korean specialty breed, 1,299 regular cattle, 36,547 pigs and 534,199 chickens in the city. In 2014, 20,248 cattle and 127,904 pigs were slaughtered for meat consumption.

■ **Society**

Social welfare At end-2014, the city provided 44.7 billion won in subsidies to 15,363 beneficiaries from 10,193 households. It has also provided 1.4 billion won to 466 elementary school students, 560 middle school students and 824 high school students.

Corporate-labor union relationships In 2014, the tension between companies and their workers escalated due to changes in the global environment and management conditions. Therefore, Ulsan has been making various efforts to mediate such discord and joined forces with both parties to find solutions that can bring stability.

Fire At end-2014, the number of fire outbreaks came to 890 cases, taking six lives and injuring 38. The incidents led to losses of 7.4 billion won in assets. The 119 emergency service worked 14,813 cases and rescued 2,515 people.

Waterworks The waterworks penetration rate stood at 98% as of end-2014. The daily production of water reached 286ℓ per capita. Its sewerage penetra-

tion rate reached 98.06%.

Roads At the end of 2014, the combined length of roads reached 3,555km with 6,483 different roadways.

Health There are six general hospitals, 91 hospitals, 546 clinics, 283 Chinese herbal medicine practices, and 354 dental clinics and other health-related institutions, which combined come to 1,312 health facilities. There were also 1,135 medicine-related institutions, including 383 pharmacies.

■ **Culture**

Cultural facilities There are nine museums, four literature institutes, 14 libraries, five cultural centers, seven performance centers and 520 parks. Ulsan Culture Art Center has a large auditorium with 1,484 seats, and a smaller concert hall with 472 seats. It also has an outdoor stage with 650 seats. Ulsan is also currently building a long-anticipated art gallery, which is scheduled to be completed in 2016.

Cultural heritages Ulsan is home to two state-designated treasures, six treasures, six historical sites, four natural monuments, two folklore heritages, six registered assets, four city-designated intangible assets, 34 city-designated tangible assets and other types of cultural heritage.

SEJONG METROPOLITAN AUTONOMOUS CITY

Area(km²) : 464.8
Population(persons) : 158,844
Number of Households : 62,807
Flower : Peach Blossom
Bird : Blue Bird
Tree : Pine Tree
Character : Saebichi, Saenari
Address : 93, Guncheong-ro, Jochiwon-eup, Sejong Metropolitan Autonomous City, Korea
Mayor : Lee Chun-hee

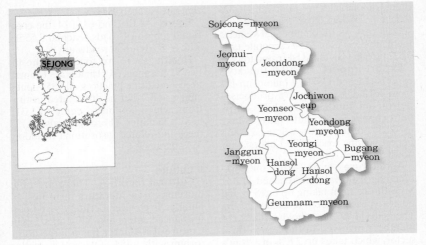

- **Overview**

  History Sejong Metropolitan Autonomous City was created as a new location for state organizations and Seoul's population to seek balanced growth throughout the country. The city was a part of the ancient Baekje Kingdom (18 B.C.-668 A.D.) and received its initial name Yeongi in 1895 during the Joseon Dynasty (1392-1910).

  South Korea's plan to relocate administrative bodies first came up during the Park Chung-hee government (1961-1979), but it was scrapped after Park's death. In 2002, former President Roh Moo-hyun made a pledge that he would relocate the country's administrative center to Chungcheong Province.

  During the Roh Moo-hyun government (2003-2008), a special law was passed at the National Assembly to move the country's capital. However, South Korea's Constitutional Court announced in 2004 that the law was unconstitutional, which downsized the extent of the relocation.

  In 2006, the region received its name Sejong and people started to move into Sejong Metropolitan Autonomous City starting 2011. In April 2012, mayors and council members were elected, and Sejong Metropolitan Autonomous City officially launched in July 2012.

  In June 2014, the city went through its second election, where Lee Chun-hee was elected its second mayor. At end-2014, the city government had a staff of 1,214, including 985 general workers, 182 firemen and other researchers.

  Area and population The city is composed of one town, nine townships and 14 villages. It is located near North Chungcheong Province to the east, South Chungcheong Province to the west and north and Daejeon Metropolitan City to the south. Its combined size stands at 464.8km². In 2014 its population came to 158,844 people from 62,807 households, with foreigners accounting for 2,719 residents.

- **Finance**

  In 2015, the city's combined budget stood at 917 billion won. The general budget took up 695 billion won and the special budget came to 220 billion won. Of its tax revenue, regional tax accounted for 303.2 billion won. It depends on 305.4 billion won from other sources, making its financial independency 43.9 percent.

  Of its general expenditures, public administration costs took up 45.7 billion won, and spending on the security sector reached 24.8 billion won, while that of education reached 45.1 billion won. Sejong will spend 20.3 billion won on culture and tourism, 43.8 billion won on environment protection, 153.2 billion won on social welfare, 14 billion won on public health, 71.6 billion won on agriculture and fisheries, 35.7 billion won on small-and-medium firms, 38 billion won on transportation, 93.9 billion won on regional development, and 200 million won on science technology, while 108.8 billion won was allocated as a reserves fund.

Of the special budget, 34.3 billion won was used for waterworks, 44.6 billion won on sewerage systems, and 52.7 billion won was used for public developments.

■ Key Projects

Solidifying reputation as administrative city Sejong has emerged to become a proud administrative city of South Korea. It has established grounds to become a functioning administrative city, acquiring 102.2 billion won from the central government for special budgets.

Building grounds for balanced growth The city has rolled out various programs to seek balanced growth throughout the region, also joining hands with SK Group to build a creative city that co-exists with farms.

Establishing grounds for self-function The city held numerous events to host investment. It has attracted 31 companies, including Hanhwa. It also expanded incentives to foster strategic industries, such as auto parts. It also continued to expand the number of medical institutions and supermarkets to increase citizens' convenience.

Expanding welfare and security The city has paid out basic pension to secure post-retirement lives for its citizens. It has also opened various support centers to create a safer environment.

Adding transparency and efficiency The city bolstered transparency of its policies through expanding communication with residents. It also secured 110 experts to build grounds for more efficient management.

■ Industry

Industry As of end-2013, the number of manufacturers came to 761, which employ 17,811 workers. Of them 365 had four or less employees, while 21 had between 100 and 299 workers. Nine companies hired more than 300 employees.

Agriculture At end-2014, the number of households involving in the agricultural business came to 6,673 with 17,939 workers. The combined area came to 11,790ha.

■ Society

Housing At end-2014, the number of detached houses came to 31,685 units. There are also 42,401 apartments, 708 town houses, and 1,224 multiplex houses. The housing penetration rate stood at 120%.

Waterworks and sewerage As of end-2014, the daily water production capacity reached 47,731㎥, reaching 82.2% of the population. The production per capita reached 365ℓ on a daily basis. In 2014, the sewerage system covered 88,667 residents, or 71.1% of the total population.

Transportation The number of registered automobiles came to 67,881. The combined length of roads stands at 45,142km, with highways taking up 18.53 km, state roads 57.64km and city roads 241.57km, covering 84.6% of the territory. There are 40 parking lots that can hold 102,721 automobiles. The city's public buses operate 270 times a day, with four lines in Jochiwon and 38 lines in Daepyeongdong. From Jochiwon, buses depart 15 times a day to Seoul. Buses connecting Osong Station, located near the city, and Banseok Station of Daejeon operate 110 times a day.

Social welfare There is a welfare center that accommodates 3,661 people, along with one homeless shelter that holds 113 people. There is also a regional self-support center that accommodates 209 people. The number of volunteers working at such facilities came to 22,744.

Environment Sejong covers trash disposal for over 465km² An average citizen in Sejong creates 402g of trash every day, with the combined amount reaching 63.8t. Of this refuse, 18% is buried, 13.2% is recycled and 68.8% is incinerated.

Health The city has 153 medical institutions, although it does not yet have a general hospital. It has eight private hospitals, 76 clinics, 37 dental clinics, 32 Chinese herbal medicine practices, and 69 pharmacies.

■ Education and Culture

Education At end-December 2014, Sejong had 80 schools, which break down as follows: 27 kindergartens, 28 elementary schools, 13 middle schools, eight high schools and four colleges and universities. There are 35,798 students, excluding graduate school students.

Cultural heritages Sejong is home to four state-designated cultural assets, which include a treasure, natural monument and an important folklore heritage. The city has also designated its own 43 assets, which are 19 tangible heritages, one intangible heritage, 10 monuments and 13 cultural records.

Cultural facilities The city has three performance facilities, which are two movie theaters and one performing arts center. It also has a cultural center. The Sejong Cultural Art Center, which is three stories with a basement, has a 765 m^2 stage with 870 seats, along with a 295.8 m^2 exhibition hall.

Gym facilities Sejong has two registered golf centers, along with 49 gymnasiums, 17 golf-practice centers, 14 fitness center, 72 billiard halls and 6 dancing institution.

Cultural events Yongam Gangdarigi, a tug-of-war festival, and Jochiwon Peach Festival are just some of the main annual events of the city. Yeongpyeongsa Siberian Chrysanthemum Festival is held around end of September. "The Sejong Festival" is also held every October at Sejong Lake Park.

Tourism The combined park area of the city stands at 1 million square meters. There are a handful of tourist attractions where visitors can enjoy cultural heritage and natural environments, which are part of the long history of the Baekje Kingdom. Gobok Natural Park has a statue park and cherry blossom street. The 460m high Unju mountain has an ancient fortress. The Milmaru Observatory also provides a view of the administrative city. Sejong Lake Park, the largest artificial lake in South Korea, also offers five different themed islands.

GYEONGGI PROVINCE

■ **Overview**

History In 1967, the Gyeonggi provincial government building located in Seoul moved to the city of Suwon. In 1973,

Area(㎢) : 10,172
Population(persons) : 12,709,201
Number of Households : 4,786,718
Flower : Forsythia
Bird : Dove
Tree: Gingko
Character : Blue Ring
Address : 1, Hyowon-ro, Paldal-gu, Suwon-si, Gyeonggi Province, Korea
Governor : Nam Kyung-pil

Blue Ring

the administrative districts of Gyeonggi Province expanded to six cities and 18 counties. In 1981, as the population increased, Incheon was promoted to under the direct control of the central government, separated from Dongducheon, Songtan and Gwangmyeong, all three of which were promoted to city status in the same year.

In 1991, the Bundang Newtown development project kicked off, and later in 1992, Goyang was promoted to a city, bringing the total number of administrative districts for Gyeonggi Province to 19 cities and 17 countries. By 2001, the province expanded to include 25 cities and six counties. In 2013, Yeoju was promoted to city status. As of 2014, the area covers 10,171㎢, with 28 administrative cities, three counties, 33 towns and 413 boroughs.

Financial and expenditure plans The 2015 budget for Gyeonggi Province stands at 15.99 trillion won, of which 14.81 trillion won is under the general budget and 1.17 trillion won is under the special budget. The total budget for the 28 cities and three counties comes to 25.78 trillion won.

■ **Key Projects**

Recovering financial health The province declared a financial crisis in August 2013, so delayed payments of 831.8 billion won were transferred to the 2014 supplementary budget as well as the budget for 2015. The amount includes 400.7 billion won for cities and districts' fiscal compensation, 304.7 billion won for education-related budget, and 126.4 billion won for development purposes.

Development of northern sector

As a practical means to balance out development of the province's northern sector and match it with other parts of the region, the provincial government relocated its economic department to an office in the region. More than 40 billion won was set aside each year for the development of the province's northeastern regions and their economies, industries and social overhead capital.

■ Economy
Economically-active population

The number of economically active people over the age of 15 totals 6.44 million, of which 6.23 million are currently employed. About 142,000 work in the agricultural and fishery sectors, 1.22 million are in mining and manufacturing, and 4.87 million work in social overhead capital businesses and other industries.

Industrial complex There are three national industrial complexes, 74 general industrial complexes and one agro-industrial complex, with a combined 24,343 entities, or 455,000 employees, based there.

Agriculture The number of farmers stands at 133,000 households with a population of 390,378. Their working area of land stands at 177,000ha. Livestock include 279,662 beef cattle, 165,298 dairy cattle, 182,257 pigs and 32.9 million chickens.

Fishery The number of households in the fishery sector stands at 853, totaling a population of 2,433. They have a combined 1,444 ships, and their production comes in at 17,956t.

Forestry Forests cover 526,985ha of Gyeonggi Province, with 96,738ha owned by the state, 30,622ha by the province, 10,721ha run by counties and towns, and the remaining 388,904ha under private ownership.

■ Society

Houses The number of households stands at 4.22 million, and the number of houses is 4.16 million with its distribution ratio coming in at 98.7%.

Traffic There are 4.53 million registered vehicles in Gyeonggi Province, of which 3.57 million are sedans, 246,912 are vans, 698,313 are trucks and 110,399 are special automobiles. There are 302,000 parking areas to accommodate a combined 4.72 million vehicles, with a 104.3% ratio of parking spots to the number of cars.

There are a total of 27,600 routes stretching 12,823km with a road coverage ratio of 88.4%. There are 15 highways at 669km, 18 national highways at 1,553 km, 55 regional roads of 2,712km, and 22,918 routes of 7,889km. There are 4,517 bridges, 116 tunnels and 516 streams that stretch for 3,489km.

Water supply The distribution ratio for water supply stands at 97.5%, with the daily per capita supply at 319ℓ and the amount of total daily supply reaching 3.9 million tons. Sewage facilities reach 24,034km, with its supply penetration ratio standing at 93.4%.

Environment There are 37 public recycling centers that produce 1,767t of waste per day, and 24 food waste facilities with a daily output of 1,785t. There are 24 garbage incineration facilities with a daily capacity of 5,014t, and nine landfills that cover 8.38 million square meters, with 132 landfills currently filled to capacity at 24.1 million ㎡.

Medical care There are 55 general hospitals, 261 hospitals, 5,893 general practitioners, 35 special hospitals, 3,523 dental clinics, 2,438 Chinese medicine clinics, 2,609 nursing homes and 42 other facilities. There are 45 state-run health centers, 122 branch offices, and 161 health care centers. There are also 4,394 pharmacies and 126 traditional Chinese medicine stores.

Welfare The number of those receiving basic living support reached 188,103. The number of elderly people came to 677,618, while that of those registered as disabled came to 506,464. There are 1,831 living facilities, including 30 foster care services, 1,831 welfare centers for the elderly, 198 for the disabled and 14 centers for the homeless.

■ **Education and Culture**

Education There are a total of 4,667 education institutions -- 2,137 kindergartens, 1,195 elementary schools, 604 middle schools, 418 high schools, 33 specialized schools, 36 community colleges, one educational college, 36 universities and 188 graduate schools.

Cultural assets There are 902 cultural assets, of which 283 are nationally designated, 462 are regionally designated, and 53 are registered cultural properties.

Cultural facilities There are 124 museums, 46 art galleries, 31 arts and literature centers and 31 cultural institutions. There are 71 public theaters, 23 private theaters and 73 movie theaters.

Tourism The number of tourism businesses reached 2,569, including 1,861 travel agencies, 116 accommodations, 49 service facilities for tourists, 90 amusement facilities, 765 convenience facilities for tourists and 16 international convention centers.

Sports facilities There are a total of 3,577 sports facilities, including 41 track and field stadiums, 177 indoor gymnasiums, 129 tennis courts, 65 swimming pools and one shooting range. Among registered facilities, there are 159 golf courses, six ski resorts and one motor racing track. Among licensed facilities, there are six ice rinks, 52 horse-riding facilities, 64 comprehensive sports centers, 160 swimming pools, 3,619 physical education centers, 2,478 golf practice centers, 5,618 billiard halls and 36 sled parks.

GANGWON PROVINCE

Area(㎢) : 16,873.50
Population(persons) : 1,558,885
Number of Households : 673,978
Flower : Royal Azalea
Bird : Crane
Tree : Nut Pine
Character : Ban-B
Address : 1, Jungang-ro, Chuncheon-si, Gangwon Province, Korea
Governor: Choi Moon-soon

■ **Overview**

History Gangwon Province was one of the ten provinces of the Goryeo Dynasty (918-1392), then named Sakbang Province. It received its current name in 1395, during the Joseon Dynasty (1392-1910). In October 1986, Samcheok, a border town about 90km northeast of Seoul, was promoted to a city. In January 1989, Wonseong changed its name to Wonju, and Chunseong, located 85km east of Seoul, was altered to Chuncheon.

Population In October 2007, the population of Wonju surpassed the 300,000 mark for the first time, making it Chuncheon and Gangneung the three major cities and growth engines of Gangwon Province. The population of Gangwon

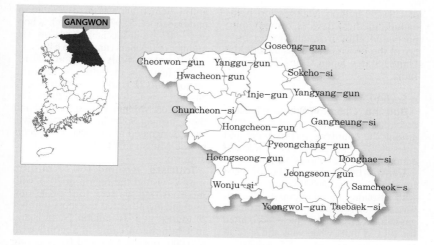

Province reached 673,978 households in December 2014, with 785,023 men and 773,862 women.

Land The total area of the province is estimated at 20,569㎢. Around 82% of the area, 16,873.50㎢ is located below the inter-Korean border, and accounts for 16.8% of South Korean territory. Woods and fields take up 82%, while farmlands account for 7.4%. Rice paddies account for 39.3% of the farmland, while fields take up the rest.

Gangwon Province is located in the eastern part of the Korean Peninsula, and is divided into east and west by Mount Taebaek. The land stretches 150㎞ from east to west, and 243㎞ north to south. Its administrative districts are composed of seven cities and 11 counties as of January 1995.

■ **Finance**

Gangwon Province's 2015 budget came to 11.64 trillion won, with 4.56 trillion won allocated for the provincial government.

■ **Major Projects**

The year 2014 was designated as the year for developing the province into one of the core regions, with strategies including globalization, modernization of technology, regionalization, continentalization, and creating a community-centered society.

■ **Industry**

Agriculture Gangwon Province has 71,203 households working in the agricultural sector, equivalent to 6.2% of the country's farming families. Gangneung has the most number of such households, followed by Hongcheon. Cheorwon has the largest farming area per household, while Sokcho has the smallest.

Forestry Woods and fields account for 82% of the province with 1.37 million hectares as of 2014. There are 20,141 workers in the forestry industry within the region, or about 7.8% of the country's workers. Major forestry goods include lumber, wild greens, seeds, medical herbs and mushrooms.

Fishery Around 0.5% of the population, or about 8,365 people, are involved in the fishing industry. Sokcho has the most number of fishing boats with a combined 4,049t, followed by Gangneung and Goseong. There are 64 fishing ports in the region, with the majority located in the northern part of the province.

Mining Gangwon Province is also home to the mining industry, producing goods such as steel, agalmatolite, Kaolin mineral, limestone, quartzite, coal and dolomite. The region also resumed production of tungsten in 2013, which is anticipated to become a flagship export item along with limestone.

Exports As of 2014, exports amounted to US$2.07 billion, while imports totaled US$2.86 billion, resulting in a net of US$790 million. Main export items include medical devices, cement, auto parts and alloy iron, and major buyers of the province's goods include the United States, Japan, China, Russia and India.

■ **Society**

Housing Gangwon Province has the seventh-highest house distribution ratio among the country's 16 provinces and cities at 107.5% in 2013. Houses accounted for 67% of the region's buildings.

Transportation The number of registered cars totaled 667,144 units in 2014, with gasoline cars taking up 42.8%, followed by diesel and liquified petroleum gas models. Passenger vehicles accounted for 491,038 units, while vans and specialized vehicles stood at 33,273 and 20,038, respectively, with the addition of 140,795 trucks. The length of roads in the regions reached 10,147km, or 9% of the country's combined length.

Medical care Gangwon Province has 764 hospitals and 633 pharmacies as of 2014, along with public health centers, dental clinics, oriental medicine clinics, and hospitals for the elderly which accounted for 48% of the total at 711.

Welfare The number of welfare facilities came to 200, with 37 in Chuncheon, 36 in Wonju, and 25 in Gangneung. The number of child-headed households came to 15, and the number of people with disabilities stood at 98,970, equivalent to about 6% of the province's total. There are 68 facilities for the disabled with a capacity of 1,641 people. Wonju is home to the highest number of facilities for the elderly at 412, followed by Chuncheon and Gangneung at 350 and 312, respectively.

Waste disposal Chuncheon has the highest amount of wastewater flow in the region at 141,616t, while Wonju and Gangneung trailed at 138,482t and 62,835t. Gangneung has the highest amount of waste emission at 10,016t, followed by Wonju and Chuncheon at 699t and 511t, respectively.

■ **Education and Culture**

Education The number of students in Gangwon Province is 205,356. Of the total, 15,947 are in kindergarten, 80,458 are in elementary school, 51,976 are in middle school, 55,973 are in high school and 1,002 are in specialized schools. The number of teachers came to 15,649.

Cultural festivals There are 92 regional festivals, including 48 focusing on tourism, 22 traditional festivals, 15 cultural arts festivals and 7 others. The Hwacheon Mountain Trout Festival and the Yangyang Songi Mushroom Festival were designated as the best such events by the Ministry of Culture, Sports and Tourism.

Tourists Around 100.57 million tourists visited the region in 2013, with most visiting via free tour programs. Gangneung attracted the most number of tourists at 15.01 million. Nami Island in Chuncheon came in second with 670,000 tourists, followed by Goseong Daemyung Resort and PyeongChang Phoenix Park with 140,000 and 80,000, respectively.

Cultural properties Gangwon Province has 10 national treasures, 73 treasures, 17 historical sites, 42 national monuments, 11 folklore data, and four intangible cultural properties. The region also designated 614 cultural properties of its own.

Cultural facilities As of 2014, the province has 49 public museums, 19 performing arts facilities, four public art galleries and 52 public libraries.

NORTH CHUNG-CHEONG PROVINCE

Area(km²) : 7,407.21
Population(persons) : 1,609,588
Number of Households : 656,321
Flower : Yulan
Bird : Magpie
Tree : Zelkova

Character : Godeumi, Bareumi
Address : 82, Sangdang-ro, Sangdang-gu, Cheongju-si, North Chungcheong Province, Korea
Governor : Lee Si-jong

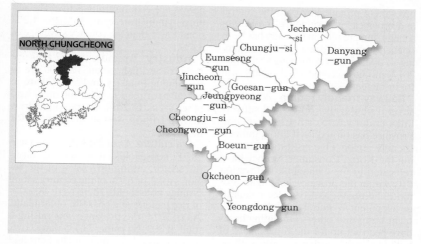

Overview

History North Chungcheong Province lies in the center of Mount Sobaek. The land was divided into three parts during the Three Kingdoms era (57 B.C.-688 A.D.). The region first received its name during the Goryeo Dynasty (918-1392) in 1106, and while its name was changed to Yanggwang Province in 1171, it took back its original name in 1356. In 1896, Chungju became the capital of the province, but later it was relocated to Cheongju in 1908. Cheongju was promoted to city status in 1949, followed by Chungju in 1956 and Jecheon in 1980.

Land North Chungcheong Province is the only province in the country that is not adjacent to the ocean. The total area of the province is 7,407.21㎢, with 11 cities and counties, and 153 towns. As of December 2014, the region's population reached 1,609,588 including registered foreigners, up 9,428 from a year earlier.

Major Projects

Creating a happy life The province has set out to realize its goal of creating a happy life for its residents. Despite the Sewol ferry disaster and the grief that was brought with it, the province successfully kicked off the Cheongju self-governing body, and also demonstrated the unity of its residents via large-scale events such as Pope Francis' visit to the region. In 2014, North Chungcheong Province posted an an-

nual economic growth rate of 7.4%, the highest among all cities and provinces within the country.

New growth engine industry The province has taken over six major new growth engine industries - bio, solar power, cosmetics, organic food, information and communications technology as well as airports and aviation maintenance businesses - and has come up with a goal to achieve exports worth US$20 billion, attract 30 trillion won of investment, create 40,000 jobs and accomplish an employment rate of 72% during the tenure of the current provincial government administration.

Establishing Economic take-off project Also, the province will secure a bridge to entering the Chinese market by pushing ahead with the establishment of a North Chungcheong branch office in Shanghai. North Chungcheong Province is working to give more vigor to the people's economy. Some 350 billion won will be used to support small businesses, five local markets will be fostered for tourism, and the province has newly designated 22 social enterprises and 12 town businesses.

Inland expressway The Chungcheong inland expressway was in its working design stage in 2014 after its basic designs were finished. The Chojeong-Miwon, Miwon-Unam, Boeun-Yeongdong sections of the Chungcheong expressway are currently under construction with investment provided by both the central and provincial governments. The Euomseong-Chungju section highway has been opened for use, and the province is aiming to open a Oksan-Ochang section by 2017, and has secured 137.1 billion won for its budget.

Railway-friendly region Also, with several new train routes and subway lines underway, North Chungcheong Province has turned itself into a railway-friendly region. Five institutions including the Korea Consumer Agency have relocated to the Chungbuk Innovation City within the province, helping to promote the region as a base for balanced development in central South Korea. All-night buses and other commuting buses have been set up for the convenience of both provincial residents as well as those outside.

Organic farming complex The province is pushing to nurture a high-value organic food business. The province has begun preparations for the 2015 International Organic Expo and Industry Fair to be held in Goesan, secured business expenses to be used for setting up a service providing complex regarding organic farming, and also began construction for a organic farming research center. Thanks to such efforts on its part, the province was able to register US$520 million in agricultural exports despite the free trade agreements pushed ahead by the South Korean government.

Realizing wish of artists The province established an arts center and realized a long-cherished wish of the region's artists, and also secured the budget necessary for expanding its culture and tourism infrastructure. Also, the province built seven additional cultural facilities including museums and art galleries, expanded its culture and arts platform business, conducted some 80 concerts for areas that otherwise lacked the means to enjoy cultural events, distributed 24,000 culture cards that provide benefits to residents such as going to concerts and other culture-related activities.

■ **Industry**
Population In North Chungcheong Province, about 59.7%, or 788,000 people of the region's population aged 15 and above, are economically active. The unemployment rate came to 2.2%, 1.2% point lower than the country's average of 3.4%.

Industry By industry, 52,000 are farmers and fishermen, 167,000 are in the mining industry, and 551,000 are in social overhead capital business and other areas. In 2014, the province drew in 5.46 trillion won in investment for businesses.

Agriculture As of 2013, the region had 78,717 households involved in the farming sector, taking up 12.2% of the region's total, or 6.9% of the country's total farming households. There were 48,000ha of rice paddies and 66,000ha of farmland. As of 2014, the province was raising a total of 203,954 cattle, 23,435 dairy cows, 61,4581 pigs, 11.27 million chickens and 1.37 million ducks.

Mining There are two metal mines and 41 non-metal mines as of October 2014, with 672 miners.

■ **Society**
Housing North Chungcheong Province had 632,347 houses as of end-2013. Individual houses took up 192,559 units, while apartments accounted for 280,485 units.

Transportation As of the end of 2014, a total of 699,797 cars were registered in the province, with passenger cars accounting for 519,581 units, followed by vans and special-purpose cars with 34,105 units and 143,169 units.

Infrastructure The province has 8,000 public places with WiFi access, with plans to set up 348 more by 2017.

Medical care There are 11 general hospitals, 37 hospitals, four oriental medicine clinics, one dental clinic and 43 rehab and psychiatric hospitals as of 2014.

■ **Culture**
Cultural Properties In end-2014, North Chungcheong Province had 12 national treasures, 82 treasures, 19 historical sites, 23 natural monuments, 21 folklore data and three intangible cultural properties. It also has 301 cultural properties and 27 intangible ones designated by the province.

SOUTH CHUNG-CHEONG PROVINCE

Area(㎢) : 8,213.36
Population(persons) : 2,063,050
Number of Households : 872,450
Flower : Chrysanthemum
Bird : Mandarin Duck
Tree : Weeping Willow
Character : Chungcheonggi, Chungnami
Address : 21, Chungnam-daero, Hong buk-myeon, Hongseng-gun, South Chungcheong Province, Korea
Governor : An Hee-jung

▪ Overview
History and administrative district

South Chungcheong Province, which was the center of the Baekje Dynasty (12 B.C.-660 A.D.), received its current name during the Goryeo Dynasty (918-1392). The Chungcheong area was divided into North and South in 1896. In July 2012, a part of Gongju City and Yeongi-gun was incorporated into Sejong City, reducing the total area of South Chungcheong Province by 8,213.36㎢. In January 2013, the provincial government building moved from Daejeon to Hongseong-gun.

▪ Finance
Budget Budget and expenditure

South Chungcheong Province's yearly budget for 2015 came to 12.72 trillion won. The region allocated 773.5 billion won for general administration, 369 billion won for public safety, 341 billion won for education, 624.3 billion won for culture and tourism businesses, 976.3 billion won for preserving the environment, and 2.97 trillion won for social welfare.

▪ Major Projects
Customized welfare and education

for life The type of welfare that South Chungcheong Province promotes is doing its best to realize ethical communal living for social minority groups. The province has pushed ahead with projects such as creating communities for senior citizens who live alone, setting up centers for the elderly, and operating hospital services so that patients can stay at clinics without the help of their own guardians. The province also provides endless opportunities for learning as a means to improve quality of life for residents, whose lives have been extended to 100 years or more thanks to technological advances made today.

Dignified culture and tourism to wow the world The province is currently taking care of and keeping up management for its cultural assets, including its famous mud flat in the west coast, setting up a culture center on Confucianism in Chun-

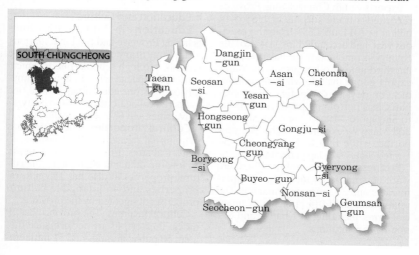

gcheong, as well as registering the Baekje Historical Site as a UNESCO world heritage site.

■ Industry

Agriculture In end-2013, there were 153,418 households, or 377,533 people, working in the agricultural and fishing sectors. Farmland came to 232,000ha, of which 166,000ha are rice paddies and 66,000ha are farmland. As of end-2013, 823,000t of rice was produced, while 52,000t of wheat was produced. As of end-2012, the region's production of vegetables and fruits came to 987,000 metric tons and 85,207 metric tons, respectively.

Forestry The combined area of South Chungcheong Province's woods and fields reached 414,000ha in end-2014, with national forests accounting for 31,000ha, public and private forests accounting for 20,000ha and 361,000ha. Major forestry goods include chestnuts, walnuts, pine nuts, jujube, acorns, persimmons and gingko nuts.

Fishery The number of people in the fishing industry came to 21,375 people, or 9,385 households, as of end-2013. Their annual production stood at a combined 146,000 metric tons worth 521.4 billion won, including 51,000 metric tons of fish, 15,000 metric tons of crustaceans, and 5,000 metric tons of mollusks.

Manufacturing In end-2013, the province had 13,452 manufacturing firms with a combined 257,231 employees.

Exports South Chungcheong Province recorded a trade surplus of US$65.14 billion in 2014, up 1.3% from the previous year, and accounted for 11.4% of the country's combined trade balance, ranking third among other provinces. Major export goods include wireless communication devices, computers, electronics parts, and petroleum products. Exports to Singapore, Mexico, Vietnam, Slovakia and Malaysia expanded in the one-year period, while that to Hong Kong, the United States and Japan declined.

Businesses At the end of 2014, there were 66 traditional markets, 22 supermarkets and 36 super-supermarkets. The region also has 1,014 branches of financial firms, including 197 banks and 817 non-bank institutions.

■ Society

Housing In end-2012, South Chungcheong Province had 857,673 houses, with individual houses accounting for 52.5% and apartments accounting for 47.5%.

Water supply Around 91.1%, or 191,000 people, have access to the province's water supply in end-2013. Its sewer system supply rate came to 71.6% over the cited period, and some 46.1 billion won was charged for its use.

Transportation The province's roads came to a combined distance of 7,510.6 km at the end of 2013. As of 2014, a total of 924,651 cars were registered, including 675,335 passenger cars, 46,110 vans, 199,842 trucks and 3,364 vehicles for special purposes. In end-2013, there were 2,066.8t of residential waste disposed of per day.

Medical care As of end-2013, there were 12 general hospitals, 39 hospitals, 981 clinics, 16 psychiatric hospitals, 450 dental clinics, 465 oriental medicine clinics, 48 rehab facilities and six facilities for the elderly. There are a total of 18,204 medical staff in the region, including 2,570 doctors, 757 dentists, 596 oriental medicine doctors, 15 maternity nurses, 13,083 nurses and medical technicians, and 1,183 pharmacists.

Fire and rescue services South Chungcheong Fire Service Headquarters has 2,142 firefighters and 10,060 volunteer firemen, with one fire school, 15 fire stations, 15 emergency rescue centers and 66 safety centers.

■ Education and Culture

Education In 2014, South Chungcheong Province had 502 kindergartens, 421 elementary schools, 188 middle schools, 116 high schools, one technical school, six special schools, nine community colleges, one educational college, one industrial college, one cyber university, 17 universities and 62 graduate schools.

Cultural properties The region has 27 national treasures, 105 treasures, 48 historical sites, 14 natural monuments, 24 folklore data and eight intangible cultural properties. It also has 183 cultural properties and 46 intangible cultural properties designated by the province.

Cultural facilities The province has 19 movie theaters, 17 art performance theaters, 56 public libraries and 51 museums and art galleries. Regarding sports facilities, the region has 25 indoor gymnasiums, 12 sports complexes, 13 smaller gyms, four sport facilities for the disabled, 21 golf courses and one horse-riding course.

Accomodation South Chungcheong Province also has 17 hotels for tourists, 15 condos, two family-friendly hotels and other facilities.

Cultural festivals The region is home to key festivals including the Cheonan PAN Festival, Buyeo Seodong Lotus Flower Festival and the Hansan Ramie Fabric Culture Festival.

NORTH JEOLLA PROVINCE

Area(km²) : 8,067.25
Population(persons) : 1,871,560
Number of Households : 687,803
Flower : Crape Myrtle
Bird : Magpie
Tree : Gingko Tree
Character : Shinmyeonggi
Address : 225, Hyoja-ro, Wansan-gu, Jeonju-si, North Jeolla Province, Korea
Governor : Song Ha-jin

■ Overview

History The Jeolla region received its current name during the Goryeo Dynasty (918-1392), and it was divided into north and south in 1896. In 1995, Okgu, Jeongeup, Namwon, Gimje and Iksan counties, and Gunsan, Jeongju, Namwon, Iri cities were incorporated in the respective order of Gunsan, Jeongeup, Namwon and Gimje cities. Currently, North Jeolla Province is composed of administrative districts for six cities and eight counties.

Area and population The total area of the region stands at 8,067.25km², accounting for 8.1% of the country. Farmland accounts for 26.9%, and woods and fields take up 55.7%. As of 2014, the population in the region stood at 1.87 million, down 1,405 from a year earlier.

■ Finance

Budget The annual budget for 2015 came to 12.82 trillion won, up 4.83% from the previous year. After collecting opinions from various experts and different social groups, the budget was planned for policies regarding agriculture, tourism, carbon businesses, welfare and development of the Saemangeum seawall project. For the economic sector, the government will work to expand R&D investment and create more jobs via attracting more businesses to the province.

Of the annual budget, 356.9 billion won will be allocated to general administration, with 128.6 billion won set aside for public safety, 179 billion won for education, 199.6 billion won for culture and tourism, 347.5 billion won for preserving the environment, and 1.53 trillion won to be used for social welfare.

■ Major Projects

Global companies North Jeolla Province has succeeded in attracting several global firms to set up or conduct business in the region, including Japan's chemical materials company Toray as well as French pet food giant Royal Canin. Also, despite the not-so-rosy investment sentiment, the province has drawn in investment from 13 local mid-size companies.

■ Industry

Economically active population Among the 1.51 million people aged 15 and over living in North Jeolla Province, about 893,000 people, or 59.3%, are currently economically active, with 876,000 people employed. The unemployment rate stands at 2%. By sector, 139,000 people were working in the agriculture and fishery industry, while 126,000 worked in the mining and manufacturing sectors. The remaining 612,000 people, or about 69.9% of the total number of those employed, worked in social overhead capital businesses or service industries.

Agriculture Farmland take up about 25.4%, or 204,593ha, of the province's entire land area, of which rice paddies account for 141,875ha. A total of 258,880 people, or about 105,880 households, are involved in the farming sector.

Fishery The number of people working in the fishing industry stood at 5,673

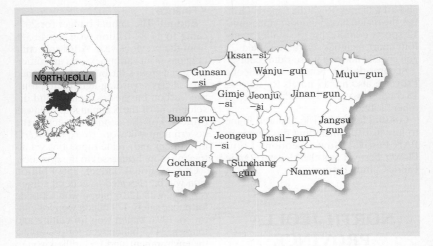

people, or 2,376 households, as of 2014, down by 7,239 people from a year earlier.

Agriculture and fisheries export Exports of agriculture and fisheries goods to Japan was the highest at US$38.65 million, followed by China at US$36.87 million. The United States, Vietnam, Hong Kong and Thailand trailed behind in that respective order. Processed goods such as confectionery goods were the top export item for the region, reaching US$67.81 million.

■ **Society**

Housing North Jeolla Province has a total of 687,803 households living in 767,146 housing units. Of the houses, individual houses stood at 275,929 units, while there were 342,564 apartments. In the year 2013, apartments totaling 5,974 homes with a living space of 135㎡ per unit were built.

Transportation A total of 807,368 vehicles were registered in the province, of which 592,166 units were passenger cars. Vans came to 36,752 units, while trucks and special-purpose vehicles stood at 175,753 units and 2,697 units, respectively.

Health and welfare In North Jeolla Province, there are a total of 2,220 hospitals with a combined 35,852 beds. Of the hospitals, there were 11 general hospitals and 69 private hospitals. There were a total of 1,068 clinics, 491 dental clinics, 473 oriental medicine clinics and seven specialized hospitals.

Of the 9,554 welfare facilities within the province, 417 were living facilities in which a combined 11,707 people were currently residing. Facilities for the elderly were the most common with a total of 236, followed by those for the disabled and children at 73 and 62, respectively. A total of 7,098 elderly people were living in such facilities, followed by disabled people with 1,938 people, children with 998 and the mentally ill with 751 people.

Fire, rescue and emergency medical service In the year of 2014, there were 1,652 cases of fire, from which there were 13 casualties and 57 injuries. There were a total of 22,896 dispatches with 5,802 rescues made. In terms of emergency medical services, there were 69,389 dispatches with rescue efforts made for 71,684 people.

■ **Education and Culture**

Education There are a total of 1,293 schools with 267,058 registered students within North Jeolla Province. There are 20,743 teaching staff. Of the education facilities, 526 are kindergartens, 414 elementary schools, 209 middle schools, 132 high schools and 12 are specialized schools. There are also 10 community colleges with 18,494 students, one education college with 1,258, and nine universities with 74,956 students. The province has 51 public libraries with 382,256 books and data, and an average of 9.39 million residents use the library per year.

Cultural assets North Jeolla Province has eight national treasures, 88 treasures, 31 natural monuments, 13 folklore data and nine intangible cultural properties. It also has 435 other cultural assets designated by the province.

National parks North Jeolla Province has four national parks, including Jirisan National Park, the top national park in South Korea. There are also four other provincial parks, including the Daedunsan Provincial Park.

Tourism North Jeolla Province is known as the home for taste, style and sound. There are a total of 21 sites designated as tourist attractions related to mountain resorts, historical and cultural sites, traditional arts, and marine culture.

Local specialties North Jeolla Province is home to one of the representative traditional Korean foods, bibimbap, a dish of rice mixed with vegetables, meat and hot pepper paste. Sunchang, one of the famous brands of pepper paste used in the bibimbap is also from the province. Other items including rice, dried seaweed, apple, ginseng, watermelon, walnut, dried persimmon, jujube and others.

Cultural events North Jeolla Province is known for key festivals such as the Jeonju Sori Festival, Jeonju International Film Festival and the World Calligraphy Biennale of North Jeolla Province.

SOUTH JEOLLA PROVINCE

Area(㎢) : 12,309
Population(persons) : 1,905,780
Number of Households : 823,667
Flower : Camellia
Bird : Turtledove
Tree : Gingko Tree
Character : Namdo and Nami
Address : 1, Oryong-gil, Samhyang-myeon, Muan-gun, South Jeolla Province, Korea
Governor : Lee Nak-yon

■ **Overview**
 History South Jeolla Province received its current name in 1896, when the Jeolla region was divided into north and south. In 1947, Jeju Province was separated from the region. In 1981, Geumseong City was established after merging Naju and Yeongsanpo. In 1986, Gwangju City was separated as Gwangju Metropolitan City, and Songjeong achieved city status. In 2005, the provincial government building was relocated to the current address in Muan.

 Area The total area of the region stands at 12,309 ㎢, the third-largest in South Korea, occupying 12.3% of the whole country. Farmland accounts for 26.4% at 3,233㎢ while woods and fields occupy 57% of the region at 7,004㎢. South Jeolla consists of five cities, 17 counties, and 296 smaller towns and villages.

■ **Finance**
 Budget The budget for 2015 came to 6.28 trillion won, with 394.1 billion won allocated for public administrative affairs, 162 billion won for education, 292.4 billion won for culture and tourism, 467.3 billion won for preserving the environment, and 1.59 trillion won for social welfare.

■ **Major Projects**
 The goal starting in July 2014 is to create a province where life is created and where the young will like to return. In order to realize this goal, the provincial government has come up with creating a lively regional economy, agriculture and fisheries industry with a higher income, attractive culture and tourism, welfare that provides warmth, and policies with creativity and communication.

 The detailed goals include creating a strong foothold for regional economy, managing and preserving a clean environment, coming up with government policies with the opinion of the people, realizing an effective welfare system, balancing out development throughout the region, and setting up a base for tourism in northeastern Asia.

■ **Industry**
 Agriculture As of 2013, South Jeolla Province had 371,000 people in the agriculture industry. The area of farmland came

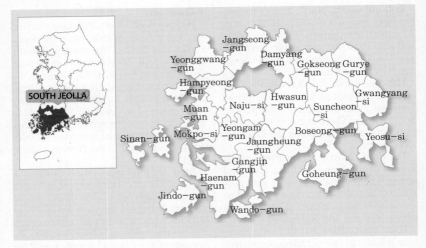

to 309,000ha, with rice paddies taking up 191,000ha. Annual rice production in 2014 stood at 809,000t, accounting for 19.1% of the country's total production. Production of barley accounted for 34% of the nation's entire production at 45,000t.

Forestry Forests take up 10.9% of South Korea's land at 695,000ha as of end-2014, with national forests standing at 83,000ha, public forests 31,000ha and private forests accounting for 581 ha. Mushroom production in the forests came to 26.2 billion won, while that of landscape materials and grass came to 39.8 billion won and 26.9 billion won.

Fishery As of 2014, there were 22,000 households, or 53,000 people, involved in the fishery business. Production in this sector in end-2013 came to a combined 1.22 million tons, accounting for 47% of the country's entire production.

Manufacturing As of September 2014, there were a total of 97 industrial complexes in the province, with 1,836 companies currently doing business within the complexes. In 2013, there were 100,995 manufacturing firms with employees totaling 104,818 people.

Industry structure As of the end of 2014, agriculture and fisheries accounted for 25.8% of all businesses in the province, while mining and social overhead capital businesses took up 8.5% and 65.7%, respectively. A total of 921,000 people were employed, with an economically active population of 936,000.

Exports The size of the province's exports in 2014 reached US$39.16 billion, down 5.4% from a year earlier, dragged down by plunging oil prices, weakening of the Japanese yen and slowed growth in China. The exports include US$38.86 billion worth of manufactured goods, US$148 million of agricultural products and US$158 million of fisheries goods. Major export items are petrochemicals, accounting for 37.7%, followed by petroleum products with 36.2%, steel goods with 12.6% and ships with 6.5%.

■ **Society**
Housing As of end-2013, there were a total of 801,628 housing units, including 467,728 individual houses and 295,522 apartments.

Welfare As of end-2014, those receiving basic living support in the province came to 75,501 people, equivalent to about 4% of the region's population. Those receiving medical support stood at 84,140 people, while the number of registered disabled people and elderly people came to 144,324 and 383,808 people, respectively. The province had 11,731 social welfare facilities, including living facilities for the elderly at 319, those for the disabled at 47, and also those for children and women at 57 and 14, respectively.

Health care As of 2014, the number of public medical facilities came to a combined 564. The number of private medical facilities stood at 1,857, including 192 hospitals, 888 clinics, 348 oriental medicine clinics, 424 dental clinics and five maternity clinics.

■ **Education and Culture**

Education In 2014, there were 552 kindergartens with 19,081 children attending, 424 elementary schools with 95,722 students, 249 middle schools with 64,300 students, and 148 high schools with 70,238 students. There also were 10 community colleges with 22,625 students, 10 universities with 32,599 students, and eight special-education schools with 984 students.

Cultural properties As of end-2014, South Jeolla Province had 20 national treasures, 172 treasures, 44 folklore data, 62 natural monuments, 18 historical sites and 18 intangible cultural properties. It also had 224 cultural properties, 47 intangible cultural properties, 193 monuments and 232 data on cultural assets designated by the province.

Cultural and sports facilities As of 2014, the province was home to 10 broadcasting stations, 1,112 publishers and printing houses, 19 performing arts theaters, 64 public libraries, 52 museums, nine movie theaters, 22 art galleries, 31 public sports centers, 24 gymnasiums and 32 gold courses.

Tourism South Jeolla Province is home to six of the country's 21 national parks. Top tourists' destinations include 2,219 islands, a coastline expanding 6,475km, as well as a vast mud flat spanning 1,037km².

NORTH GYEONG-SANG PROVINCE

Area(km²) : 19,029
Population(persons) : 2,700,794
Number of Households : 1,153,559
Flower : Garden Zinnia
Bird : Heron
Tree : Zelkova Tree
Character : Sinnari
Address : 40, Yeonam-ro, Buk-gu, Daegu, Korea
Governor : Kim Kwan-yong

■ **Overview**

History The region first received its name in 1314 during the Goryeo Dynasty (918-1392). In 1896, Gyeongsang Province was divided into North and South. In 1949, Daegu, Pohang, and Gimcheon were promoted to the status of cities. In 1963, Uljin-gun separated from Gangwon Province and merged with North Gyeongsang Province.

Area and administrative zone The combined area of the region stands at 19,029km², with the forest taking up 13,628 km², or 71.6%. The combined area of rice farms came to 1,787 km² to take up 9.3% of the province, trailed by gardens with 1,266km². North Gyeongsang Province consists of 10 cities, 13 counties and other smaller districts.

■ **Finance**

In 2015, the combined budget of North Gyeongsang Province came to 19.2 trillion won, with 38.1%, or 7.3 trillion won, allocated for the provincial government, while the remaining 11.9 trillion won is allocated for other regions within the province.

■ **Key Projects**

Building grounds for manufacturing sector North Gyeongsang Province kicked off the so-called "1+1 Creative Economy Innovation Centers" that aims to provide small-and-medium firms as well as ventures with financial, legal and technology consulting services. President Park Geun-hye also attended the opening ceremony of the centers. The centers, opened under cooperation with Samsung Group and POSCO, will take the lead in fostering the local economy by providing one-stop services.

The Samsung-led center will roll out various projects that aim to develop seven new growth engines for the local economy. The POSCO-led center will also lend support to the province's goal to establish a high-tech material cluster, and provide technology and capital needed by small firms with strong competitiveness.

Building grounds for the balanced growth among regions By injecting 4 trillion won, North Gyeongsang Province has paved the way for balanced growth

NORTH GYEONGSANG

among regions. In 2015, two new high-ways and two additional train lines will be added to connect North Gyeongsang Province with other regions. It also plans to establish a new airport on Ulleung Island by 2020, and has conducted studies to roll out the project.

Establishing research and development hub for nuclear studies North Gyeongsang Province is a step closer in establishing a nuclear-power cluster and is making efforts to foster experts.

Hosting investments and generating quality jobs Despite the slowing global economy and falling investors' sentiment, North Gyeongsang Province managed to host a combined 4.4 trillion won investment in 2014.

The foreign direct investment also jumped nine-fold on-year from 2013 to reach US$2.14 billion, with capital flowing in from the United States, Japan, the European Union and China. The province also created quality jobs for all brackets, including the elderly, handicapped and women, which added up to 69,000 jobs.

Establishing grounds to expand exchanges with Europe and Asia North Gyeongsang Province has been making efforts to develop the East Sea as a hub for exchanges with Europe and Asia, as the area holds three key infrastructure, namely transportation, logistics and resources. It has joined forces with Russia and North Korea along with top

steelmaker POSCO in a pilot project to expand such ties.

Expanding competitiveness to cope with FTAs In order to boost competitiveness of local agricultural households amid the free trade agreements with China, Canada, and Vietnam, the provincial government asked the central government to come up with measures to protect the local industry. It also made efforts to foster experts and improve the quality of produce.

■ **Industry**
Agricultural and livestock industry The combined area of rice farm within the province came to 141,000ha, with that of other gardens standing at 139,000ha. The areas produce 570,000t of rice, 2,000t of barley and 26,000t of beans.

Within the province, there are 138,000 units of cultivators and 45,000 units of tractors, along with 48,000 units of rice-planting machines and 214,000 units of other machinery, which adds up to 445,000 units. Around 10,000 households are fully devoted to the cultivation of rice. The province is raising 594,000 units of beef cattle, 37,000 units of dairy cattle, 1.25 million units of pigs and 20.3 million units of chickens.

Forestry The combined area of state-owned forest stand at 252,000ha, with 116,000ha also owned by the public and 975,000ha owned privately, which adds up to the combined forest area of 1.34

million hectares. Of the area, needle leaf trees take up 564,000ha, while broadleaf trees take up another 236,000ha. Another 519,000ha of land is covered with mixed vegetation.

Fishery There are 130 fishing ports within the province, with 14 of them designated by the central government. There are 3,613 ships stationed in the province, including 3,461 units of powerboats. The combined production of fishery goods of the province came to 113,000t through November 2014, which is estimated at 423.9 billion won.

Mining industry As of end-2014, there were 176 mining-related facilities, with 21 of them handling metal-related goods. The annual production of limestone came to 1.94 million tons, followed by kaolin minerals with 280,000t and silicon dioxides with 190,000t. Other mining products include zeolite, zinc and tungsten.

Industry Major industries in the region cover electronics parts, metal processing, auto parts and textiles. As of end-2012, the number of manufacturers in the province came to 11,989 units, which employ 271,591 workers.

Commerce There are 10 chambers of commerce within the province at major locations with 3,907 members. There are 98 public-run markets and 102 private markets within the province, along with two department stores, four shopping centers, 25 supermarkets and 64 super supermarkets (SSMs), which are commonly run by large retailers.

Finance There are 1,102 branches of financial organizations within the province as of end-2014, with banks accounting for 270.

■ **Society**

Housing As of end-December 2013, the number of houses in North Gyeongsang Province came to 1.18 units, with the housing penetration rate standing at 111.23%. Of those, detached houses take up 704,987 units, followed by town houses with 26,355 units and multiplex houses with 35,295 units.

Transportation As of end-December 2014, the number of automobiles in the province came to 1.25 million units, with sedans taking up 903,327 units, buses

55,209 units, trucks 291,550 units and special cars accounting for 5,817 units.

Health The number of general hospitals came to 19. There are also 2,602 other kinds of medical facilities in the province, which include 1,378 clinics, 607 dental clinics and 617 Chinese herb practices. There are 5,216 doctors in North Gyeongsang Province, with 818 of them being dentists and 923 of them involved in Chinese herb practices. There are a combined 39,178 beds to accommodate patients in such facilities. Some 1,392 pharmacists are also working at 1,031 pharmacies.

In terms of social welfare facilities, there are 88 institutions for the handicapped that can accommodate 2,536 people, and five mental-health facilities that can handle 1,069 people. North Gyeongsang Province also has five homeless shelters that can accommodate 411 people, along with 344 senior centers that can host 9,586 people.

■ **Education and Culture**

Education There are 716 kindergartens with 37,274 students, 478 elementary schools with 131,307 students, 287 middle schools with 85,118 students, 191 high schools with 92,328 students, eight special schools with 1,503 students, 16 colleges with 46,905 students, and 20 universities with 176,833 students, which adds up to 571,268 students in 1,716 education institutions

Religion There are 2,870 Protestant churches, 119 Catholic churches, 2,139 Buddhists' temples, and 93 other religious institutions, which add up to 5,211 facilities.

Cultural heritage North Gyeongsang Province is home to 56 national treasures, 319 treasures, 97 historical sites, 68 natural monuments, 15 scenic sites, 80 major folklore heritages and 12 major intangible assets, which add up to 682 articles of state-designated heritages. The province has also designated some 756 heritages, which are: 420 tangible assets, 148 monuments, 30 intangible assets and 158 folklore heritages. The province also takes care of 540 pieces of cultural property.

Cultural facilities There are 62 public libraries, 57 museums, and nine art galleries in the province.

344

SOUTH GYEONG-
SANG PROVINCE

Area(㎢) : 10,537
Population(persons) : 3,447,405
Number of Households : 1,343,984
Flower : Rose
Bird : White Heron
Tree: Zelkova Tree

Character : Geyongnami and Gyeongi
Address : 300, Jungang-daero, Uichang-
gu, Changwon-si, South
Gyeongsang Province, Korea
Governor: Hong Joon-pyo

▪ Overview
History The region first received its
name in 1314 during the Goryeo Dynasty (918-1392). In 1896, Gyeongsang Province was divided into North and South.
In 1963, the province moved its capital to
Changwon as Busan was separated from
the province. In 1997, Ulsan was elevated
to Ulsan Metropolitan City, also separating from the provincial government.
Area and administration zone The
combined area of South Gyeongsang
Province stands at 10,537㎢, occupying 10.5% of South Korea's territory.
It includes around 400 islands that are
responsible for 8.5% of the region's
territory. As of end-2014, the combined
population of South Gyeongsang Province came to 3.44 million, which includes
97,148 foreigners. The province is composed of eight cities, 10 counties and 315
smaller districts.

▪ Finance
In 2015, the combined budget of the
city stands at 6.99 trillion won, with the
general budget accounting for 5.9 trillion
won and special budget taking up 999.9
billion won. Its tax revenue came to 2.1
trillion won, while non-tax income came
to 129.5 billion won. It also received 3.4
trillion won from the central government, while earning 100 billion won from
municipal bonds.

By expenditures, general public administration came to 1.37 trillion won,
followed by public safety with 147.1
billion won, education with 474.7 trillion won, culture and tourism with 172.2
billion won, environment preservation
with 365.8 billion won, social welfare and
health with 2.3 trillion won, agricultural
and marine industries with 776 billion
won, supporting small-and-medium
firms with 146.2 billion won, transportation with 273.1 billion won, and regional
development with 316.5 billion won. The
tax burden on each resident came to
646,255 won, and its financial independency came to 34.2% in 2015, up from
the 32.3% posted in 2014.

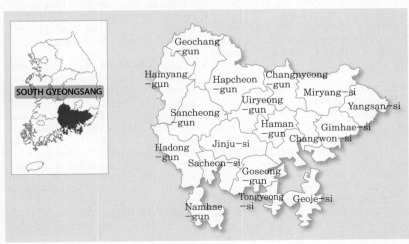

■ **Key Projects**
Public relations South Gyeongsang Province made efforts to promote key projects to residents by making use of various methods. It has established a comprehensive public-relations system that produces videos related to key policies, lending support in promoting the public's awareness. It has also utilized online media, blogs and Twitter to communicate better with the people.

Business and employment policies After opening the business support center in 2013, South Gyeongsang Province handled 538 civil complaints. It has also found 148 business-related problems, making headway in solving issues by thinking in entrepreneurs' shoes. It also focused efforts on generating new jobs under the slogan "creation of jobs is the best welfare." It has joined forces with 57 firms to hire more local college graduates and kick off a special committee aimed at helping students find stable jobs.

Economy and commerce policies Concerning the machinery sector, the mainstay industry of South Gyeongsang Province, the on-year growth continued to hover around 2.3% since the 2009 global economic crisis, hovering below the country's average of 8.9%. The region plans to invest 8.05 trillion in 21 businesses through 2023 to find a new growth engine that can re-create Changwon and the ICT-convergence smart industrial zone.

Agricultural policies As South Korea's agricultural industry is facing new challenges from free-trade agreements with China, New Zealand and Vietnam, South Gyeongsang Province is focusing its efforts to find solutions amid the rising competition in the industry.

Marine policies The region shipped US$10 million worth of fishery goods overseas, after tapping the U.S. market with its popular green-tea yellow mullet, building ground to diversify its exports. Amid the rising outlook over sea cucumbers, the province injected 5 billion won to foster the sector to add to local households' profits.

Welfare and health policies Under the slogan "making customized welfare for resident's happiness and hope," the province has allocated 23% of its annual budget to welfare, aiming to lend a hand to those in the low-income bracket, seniors and the handicapped.

■ **Economy**
Economy Index In 2014, South Gyeongsang saw its exports decrease 1.4 percent on-year to reach US$51.1 billion, while its imports also shed 5.9% to US$26.8 billion over the cited period, which led to a trade surplus of US$24.3 billion. The region's unemployment rate came to 2.5% in 2014, hovering below the country's average of 3.5%. The inflation rate came to 1.4%, which is 0.1 percentage point higher than South Korea's average of 1.3%.

Manufacturing sector In 2013, the number of manufacturers with 10 or more workers came to 7,101, encompassing various industries such as metal, fabric, leather, petrochemical, timber, electronics, automobile, food and paper-related segments. The companies hired 342,672 workers with their combined sales standing at 144.5 trillion won, generating added-value of 47.1 trillion won. Those with less than 300 workers came to 7,020, accounting for 98.8% of the total.

Agriculture In South Gyeongsang Province, there are 136,700 households involved in the agricultural industry with 320,000 members. Its area of cultivation came to 98,000ha for rice, with other goods taking up 58,900ha, leading to the combined area of 156,900ha.

Fishery South Gyeongsang Province holds 567 fishing ports, including 19 state-owned and 61 provincially-owned facilities. There are 14,845 fishing boats based in the region, accounting for 21% of the country's total fishing boats. The combined area of fish nurseries came to 11,646ha. In 2013, the region produced 525,000t of fishery goods, which takes up 16.6% of the country's combined production. There are 479 firms registered in the region for processing fishery goods.

Forestry The combined area of forest stands at 706,990ha, with state-owned area taking up 70,662ha, while private-owned areas stand at 588,088ha. Needle leaf trees take up 320,500ha, trailed by broadleaf trees with 136,838ha, mixed area with 233,144ha and bamboo taking up 1,996ha.

Livestock As of end-2014, the number of beef cattle in the region came to 262,549 units from 13,266 households. There were also 29,480 dairy cows from

340 households, 1.08 million pigs from 581 households, and 9.76 million chickens from 176 households.

■ **Society**

Housing The combined number of houses stands at 1,301,065 units in South Geyongsang Province. Of them, detached houses take up 363,213 units, followed by multiplex-houses with 283,594 units and apartments with 600,124 units. There are also 27,249 town houses, which adds up to a housing penetration rate of 106.6%.

Roads There are nine lines of highways that stretch 488km and 17 lines of state roads that are 1,554 kilometers long, with 71.4% of the region's 13,053km-long roads being paved.

There are 1.16 million sedans registered in the region, followed by 63,864 vans and 274,019 trucks. Of the combined 1.51 million automobiles, 77,110 are registered for commercial purposes while 1.43 million units are privately-owned.

Health There are 24 general hospitals in South Gyeongsang Province with 8,845 beds. There are also 149 private hospitals with 24,272 beds, 16 dental hospitals with 30 beds, four Chinese herbal medicine hospitals with 253 beds, and 98 nursing homes with 18,284 beds.

Welfare There are 52 child care centers that accommodate 1,142 children, and 32 facilities for the handicapped that can hold 1,581 people. Four homeless shelters accommodate 376 people as well. There are also 20 welfare centers for seniors with 12,819 visitors everyday. Around 90,500 people from 56,993 households receive basic-living pension.

■ **Education and Culture**

Cultural facilities There are 63 public libraries, 21 movie theaters with 151 screens, 20 cultural centers, 55 museums, eight art galleries and 19 art centers in South Gyeongsang Province.

Cultural heritages Gyeongsang Province has 10 national treasures, 159 treasures, 51 historical sites, 45 natural monuments, 19 intangible cultural properties, 12 folklore data and 41 registered cultural assets. It also has 21 folklore assets, 496 tangible cultural properties and 31 intangible cultural properties designated by the provincial government.

JEJU SPECIAL SELF-GOVERNING PROVINCE

Area(km²) : 1,849
Population(persons) : 621,550
Number of Households : 246,516
Flower : Korean rosebay
Bird : White-backed woodpecker
Tree : Camphor tree
Character : Dorhee & Sorhee (Dolharu bang & woman diver)
Address : 6, Munnyeon-ro, Jeju-si, Jeju Special Self-Governing Province, Korea
Governor : Won Hee-ryong

■ **Overview**

History Jeju Special Self-Governing Province first received its title during the Goryeo Dynasty (918-1392). The island was previously known as Tamna. In 1946, the country's southern resort island of Jeju was separated from South Jeolla Province, while Seogwipo and Jeju counties were made cities. In 2006, the region became a special self-governing province which holds two cities, seven towns, five townships and 31 neighborhoods.

Area As of end-2014, the combined area of the region came to 1,849km², taking up 1.85% of the combined South Korean territory. By purpose, 29.2% is being used as agricultural land, while 47.5% is forest. There are eight islands with inhabitants around Jeju, while 71 islands do not have inhabitants. The combined length of shorelines came to 530.09km, with the main island taking up 419.99km.

Natural environment Jeju Special Self-Governing Province is composed of sedimentary rocks, andesite, trachyte and pyroclastic rocks covered with volcanic ash soil. There are 77 kinds of mammals, 198 birds, eight reptiles, 873 insects and 74 spiders living on the island. There are also 2,000 kinds of plants, with Mount Halla being designated a national park.

The region has also won many titles

from its rich natural resources from the United Nations Educational, Scientific and Cultural Organization. There are also more than 50 kinds of natural resources that could be used commercially.

Population As of end-2014, there are 621,550 people living in the region from 246,516 households, including 14,204 foreigners. It marks a 2.7% increase from the 604,670 posted in 2013. Jeju City has 458,325 people from 179,090 households, while Seogwipo City holds 163,225 people from 67,426 households.

▪ Finance

In 2015, Jeju Special Self-Governing Province held a combined budget of 3.8 trillion won, with the general budget taking up 3.1 trillion won and special budget accounting for 689.4 billion won. It marked a 6.6% increase from the 3.58 trillion won allocated for 2014. Its fiscal independency rate came to 29.9%.

▪ Key projects

Overview Jeju Special Self-Governing Province attracted 122.7 million visitors in 2014 from home and abroad. The figure marked a significant increase from 2013, when the region attracted 100 million visitors for the first time. The region also made headway in promoting electric cars by rolling out subsidies, with the number of such automobiles reaching 451. The region also made efforts to produce water products by making use of lava seawater.

Attracting 10-million visitors The region has attracted 8.94 million South Korean tourists and 3.32 million foreign-

ers in 2014, marking the second consecutive year to attract more than 10 million visitors. The 2014 figure marks a 13.1-percent rise from a year earlier.

Establishing natural-friendly island Gapa Island, located in Seogwipo City, was turned into a "Carbon Free Island," taking a step closer to making Jeju a pollution-free environmental island. It also handed out incentives to those purchasing electronic cars, with 15 million won in subsidies from the central government and 8 million won from the regional government. The incentives were given for 451 units of electronics cars in 2014.

Development of lava-seawater Jeju established a lava-seawater facility in a 197,000 square-meter land to build industrial facilities to produce related commercial goods, including food and cosmetics.

▪ Key Achievements and Future Goals

Expanding airport infrastructure Jeju has been acknowledging the need to expand the existing airport or build a new one amid rising demand. Domestic travelers account for 80% of the combined flight demand for the island. The Gimpo-Jeju route has been cited as one of the busiest lines in the world.

Expanding the airport in the region is now the key task for the country's goal in improving accessibility for foreign travelers and developing the island as one of the world's top tourists' destinations.

Establishing rules for large-scale development Jeju welcomes any investment that can add value to the future of the province. The premise of such developments, however, is protecting the environment. Only after nature has been protected can a new value be created.

Establishing transparent casino watchdog Eight out of South Korea's 17 casinos are based in the province. Thus, Jeju has been making efforts to establish a quality watchdog which meets global standards to add transparency to the operation of such facilities.

▪ Industry

Economic index The region's annual economic growth came to 4.9% in 2013, with the Gross Regional Domestic Product (GRDP) per capita reaching 23.4 million won. In 2013, 20.6% of the population was involving in the agricultural sector, while 4.6% was in manufacturing and 74.8% in service segment. There are 51,727 firms based in the region, employing 226,734 workers.

Agriculture As of end-2013, the combined area of farms came to 62,855ha, with rice farms taking up 32ha. Around 80% of the households involved in the agricultural business, or 31,041 units, grew tangerines. In 2013, the combined production of tangerines came to 672,000t at 20,577ha.

Livestock There are 29,447 hanwoo, Korean native cattle, 1,567 beef cattle, 4,427 dairy cows, 541,465 pigs and 1.36 million chickens being raised in the region by 5,308 households. The combined area of grassland came to 65,695 hectares. In 2014, the combined export of livestock-related goods came to 1,352 tons, or US$1.38 million.

Forestry The combined area of forest came to 88,874ha, with 5,973ha public-owned, 29,990ha state-owned and 52,911ha privately owned.

Fishery At end-2013, the number of population involving in the fishery business came to 11,497 people from 4,752 households in the region. The number of fishing boats came to 1,982 units. The combined production came to 10,605 t, which is estimated at 855.5 billion won. The export came to US$56.1 million in the sector. There are 99 fishing ports, with six of them being state-owned.

Tourism In 2014, the number of tourists visiting the region came to 122.7 million, with foreigners accounting for 3.32 million. There are 1,570 tourism-related businesses in the area, including 947 tourism agencies, 222 accomodations, 101 tourists' facilities, 23 amusements facilities, 30 international convention facilities, eight casinos and 29 golf facilities.

▪ Society

Housing As of end-2013, the number of houses came to 192,693 households with 208,512 houses, leading to the housing penetration rate of 108.2%. By category, detached houses came to 112,600 units, apartments came to 59,222 units, while town houses came to 14,051 units. There were also 22,639 units of multiplex houses.

Transportation In 2014, the annual passengers of airplanes came to 20.9 million for domestic flights and 2.25 million for international flights. The combined amount of cargo handled by air came to 275,428t. There are two landing strips at the Jeju International Airport, which is capable of handling 172,000 flights every year. There are also 1,752 public cars, 31,997 personal cars and 71,368 units of commercial automobiles as of end-2014, which adds up to 384,117 vehicles. By category, there were 293,527 sedans, 20,634 vans, 69,117 trucks and 779 special cars. The combined length of roads stand at 3,215km in 4,393 lines, with 84%, or 2,719.7km of them being paved.

▪ Education and Culture

Education The province has 114 kindergartens, 111 elementary schools, 44 middle schools, 30 high schools, three special schools and three international schools. There are also two universities, two colleges and 22 public libraries.

Cultural heritage The province has six treasures, seven historical sites, nine scenic spots, 47 natural monuments, nine folklore data, five intangible cultural properties, and 22 registered cultural assets. It also has 33 tangible properties, 20 intangible properties, 127 monuments, 82 folklore data, and 10 heritage material designated by the provincial government.

Cultural facilities The province has three cultural centers, 57 museums, 19 art galleries, six movie theaters and 32 performance halls. There are also five newspapers, five broadcasting stations and 49 online media based in the province.

North Korea

Yonhap News Agency

TOP 10 NEWS STORIES OF NORTH KOREA IN 2014

■ **Surprise Visit to South Korea by Three North Korean Power Elites**

In the morning of the final day of the 2014 Incheon Asian Games on Oct. 4, big news from North Korea surprised South Koreans: A high-powered North Korean delegation would arrive in South Korea to attend the Asiad's closing ceremony.

In less than three hours after the announcement released by the unification ministry in Seoul, Pyongyang's three power elites arrived in Incheon International Airport. The top Pyongyang officials were Hwang Pyong-so, the newly

elected vice chairman of the mighty National Defense Commission and the director of the general political bureau of the (North) Korean People's Army; Choe Ryong-hae, the secretary of the Workers' Party Central Committee; and Kim Yang-gon, who heads the ruling party's United Front Department in charge of South Korean affairs.

Their sudden visit was interpreted by Seoul officials to seek a breakthrough in improving inter-Korean relations that had been soured for months. The North initially planned to send a large scale cheering squad together with athletes and sports officials. But their hopes for sending the cheerleaders vanished due to conflicting stance between the two Koreas.

The North Korean officials held a series of closed-door talks with Seoul's Unification Minister Ryoo Kihl-jae and Kim Kwan-jin, the chief of the national security office and former defense minister. But their meeting with President Park Geun-hye was not realized. At the closing ceremony, however, the North Korean officials met with South Korean Prime Minister Chung Hong-won.

North Korea's Hwang said "We have paved a small path this time. Let's make it lead to a bigger one." But the wide road was not open, with the rival Koreas only repeating their confrontational stance over the North's dire human rights situation and the South's scattering of anti-Pyongyang leaflets across the border.

▪ Kim Jong-un's Return after 40-day Hiatus

North Koran leader Kim Jong-un appeared again in mid-October after a 40-day absence from public eye. A few months before, Kim drew the attention of South Korean news media on July 8 when he appeared to be limping in his right leg slightly during a memorial ceremony for his grandfather and North Korean founder Kim Il-sung.

Kim last appeared to the public on Sept. 3 when he attended a Moranbong Band concert. Speculation that there was something wrong with Kim soared when he missed important political engagements such as the 2nd Session of the 13th Supreme People's Assembly (SPA) on Sept. 25. On that day, the North's Central TV admitted that Kim was "not well" when he missed the SPA meeting.

After a 40-day hiatus, Kim reappeared and gave "field guidance" at the Wisong Scientists Residential District, a newly built apartment complex in Pyongyang for satellite and nuclear scientists, according to North Korean media on Oct. 1. It was his first public appearance since Sept. 3, which suggests he has no critical health problems and he maintains a firm grip on power.

South Korean officials and U.S. authorities have dismissed speculation over political instability, citing their own intelligence. They say Kim either might have broken, or sprained, his ankle or he might have acute inflammation in his feet.

▪ Official Debut of Kim Jong-un's Younger Sister

Kim Yo-jong, the younger sister of North Korean leader Kim Jong-un emerged as a key figure in the socialist regime after being appointed vice director of the North's ruling Workers' Party. This was confirmed when the North's news agency unveiled on Nov. 27 the official title of Kim Yo-jong amid growing speculation over her political role and stature in the North.

As the only younger sister of the current leader, she was often seen accompanying him on public activities, but this was the first time that Pyongyang's state-controlled media had revealed her official title. Both Kim Jong-un and his sister Yo-jong were born to Ko Yong-hui, known as the fourth wife of late leader Kim Jong-il. They lived in Pyongyang together and went to the same boarding school in Switzerland.

Kim Yo-jong made her first official debut when he accompanied her brother Kim Jong-un in April to cast votes in the election of deputies to the Supreme People's Assembly, the North's rubber stamp parliament.

▲ North Korean leader Kim Jong-un's sister, Kim Yo-jong casts a ballot at a polling station at the Kim Il-sung University of Politics in Pyongyang on March 9 to elect the Supreme People's Assembly.

It was not confirmed which department Kim Yo-jong is responsible for, while media reports and North Korean experts speculate that she probably belongs to a department in charge of propagating the North Korea system, or a department for managing the leadership of the isolated state.

The confirmation showed that Yo-jong is apparently being groomed to play a key supporting role for her brother in the absence of their once-powerful aunt, Kim Kyong-hui. She disappeared from the public eye after her husband and former No. 2 man in the Kim Jong-un regime, Jang Song-thaek, was executed in December 2013.

Propaganda in the regime regularly describes the ruling Kim family as belonging to the bloodline of Paektu, the highest mountain in the North. The so-called Paektu bloodline refers to the royal bloodline descending from Kim Il-sung to his son, Kim Jong-il, and Kim Jong-un.

■ Frosty Relations between North Korea and China

The relationship between North Korea and China remained strained in 2014, despite their 65 years' history of formal diplomatic relationship. Their relations appeared to have plunged to the lowest level since the brutal purge of Jang Song-thaek, once powerful uncle of leader Kim Jong-un, in December 2013. Jang was known to have been a pro-Beijing figure, although he was executed on charges of treason and corruption, among others.

In 2014, not a single North Korean ministerial-level official visited Beijing. Instead, Chinese Vice Foreign Minister Liu Zhenmin and Special Representative for Korean Peninsular Affairs Wu Dawei visited Pyongyang.

The North's powerful National Defense Commission (NDC) showed its displeasure with China on July 21 when Beijing joined the U.N. Security Council in adopting a press statement denouncing the North's test launches of ballistic missiles.

The North's commission said "Some spineless countries are also blindly following the foul-smelling rear end of the U.S. and vainly attempting to embrace Park Geun-hye." The expression "some spineless countries" appears to have been aimed at China and Russia, which have permanent seats on the UNSC.

North Korea also criticized Chinese President Xi Jinping as a man obsessed with "big brother" as he visited Seoul in early July and held summit talks with President Park Geun-hye. Xi became the first Chinese leader to visit South Korea before visiting North Korea.

Kim Jong-un delivered a congratulatory message to Xi Jinping on the occasion of the 65th founding anniversary of the People's Republic of China on Oct. 1. In the three-paragraph message, Kim only wished China prosperity and its people's happiness. Kim, however, skipped routine words such as "friendship" often used for the importance of their communist alliance.

China remained silent on Oct. 6 about the 65th anniversary of establishing diplomatic relations with North Korea, apparently reflecting continued strain in the bilateral relationship. North Korea and China established diplomatic ties on Oct. 6, 1949 and their alliance was often described as being "forged in blood" as China fought alongside the North in the 1950-53 Korean War.

■ May 30th Economic Measures

North Korea announced May 30th economic reform policy seeking to reinforce market element from its strict state-control economy. The measures are aimed at imbuing vigors and competition among individuals in production sites by mitigating the element of state-controlled economy and giving greater autonomy to state corporations in terms of their production items, prices and amounts.

Under the measures, individuals and small-scale business owners were allowed to sell surplus agricultural grains and manufacturing output at the market after taking out their portion alloted for the state. In addition, the incentive system for workers were expanded in accordance with their achievements.

In 2012, the North announced the so-called "June 28 measures" that centered on allowing farmers to keep 30% of their production quota plus any excess over the quota. In 2014, a new set of reforms, known as "5.30 measures," were announced that call for increasing the farmers' portion to 60%.

Kim Jong-un regime sought changes in its economic policies so that its socialist economic system would have some sort of market elements. Outwardly, North Korea denies capitalistic market economy, but internally, it has been accepting the capitalistic elements in economic policies and corporate management system to effectively adapt to the changing realities.

The package, which analysts argue has moved further away from an inefficient socialist system, was aimed at improving economic conditions to keep the loyalty of a people growing disgruntled over an ever-worsening food crisis.

A pro-North Korean newspaper published in Japan reported in January 2015 that the sub-work team and individual ownership in agriculture and industrial work sites resulted in a significant increase in production. Some workers are paid far more wages than before through the reinforcement of autonomy at some of the factory sites, the Choson Sinbo newspaper said.

▪ Choe Ryong-hae's Trip to Moscow as Kim Jong-un's Special Envoy

In 2014, North Korea and Russia formed a new honeymoon relationship while Pyongyang's relations with Beijing remained strained. Kim Jong-un's special envoy, Choe Ryong-hae, visited Moscow in November, bolstering the friendship between the two nations and possibly arranging a summit between their two leaders.

Choe, a senior North Korean Workers' Party official, met with Russian President Vladimir Putin in Moscow on Nov. 18 and delivered a hand-written letter from Kim Jong-un. The envoy's Russia trip came as Pyongyang and Moscow appear to be joining forces to ease their international isolation as the former strives to strengthen the bilateral relationship in a frantic search for outside economic assistance and diplomatic support.

A Russian news agency quoted Putin as having said that deeper relations between Russia and North Korea are conducive to boosting regional security and stability, a day after he met with Choe, one of the closest aides to the North Korean leader. "The further deepening of political ties and trade-economic cooperation undoubtedly serves the interests of the peoples in both countries and ensuring regional security and stability," Putin was quoted by the Itar-Tass news agency as saying.

In Pyongyang, the North's official Korean Central News Agency (KCNA) quoted Putin as telling Choe that it is important to actively study ways to improve mutually beneficial cooperation, a sentiment Choe echoed.

President Putin and Choe also agreed to improve political, economic and military exchanges between the two countries in 2015, according to the KCNA. In 2015, Korea will commemorate the 70th anniversary of its liberation from Japan's colonial rule and Russia will mark the 70th anniversary of the allied victory in World War II.

Meanwhile, top North Korean and Russian military officials held talks in Moscow on ways to improve defense ties between the former communist allies, Pyongyang's state media reported on Nov. 21. No Kwang-chol, vice chief of the General Staff of the North's Army, met with his Russian counterpart, as No was accompanying Choe.

"Both sides had a wide-ranging exchange of views on putting the friendship and cooperation between the armies of the two countries on a new higher stage," it said in a dispatch from Moscow. The two nations also held a separate meeting between senior economic officials, added the KCNA.

North Korean Vice Economy Minister Ri Kwang-gun had talks with Alexander Galushka, minister for the development of the Russian Far East. They "discussed measures for further boosting cooperation between the two countries in economy and trade for more substantial results," the KCNA said.

Russian news media said the economic relations between the two countries have reached a new level, as they are carrying out transactions in Russian rubles following the write-off of the bulk of North Korean debt.

Russia's State Duma lower house on April 18 ratified a 2012 agreement to write off the bulk of North Korea's debt. Russia hopes to promote mutual projects in North Korea, including a proposed gas pipeline and a railway to South Korea and to develop North Korea's mineral resources after canceling the isolated state's debts.

▪ Election of Kim Jong-un as Deputy to the SPA

North Koreans went to the polls on March 9 to elect a new rubber-stamp parliament. As expected, North Korean leader Kim Jong-un was elected to the Supreme People's Assembly (SPA) together with key military and party officials, all of whom won unanimous approval.

In the tightly choreographed election, the first under the young leader, the 687 candidates for the SPA pulled in 100% of the vote with a 99.97% turnout, state media said.

All the voters of Kim's constituency voted for Kim, the North's official

KCNA said in a dispatch, citing election results from the Central Election Committee.

The dispatch said Kim's election demonstrated soldiers' and citizens' "absolute support and profound trust" in their young leader, who took over the country in December 2011 following the death of his father, long-time leader Kim Jong-il.

Kim ran for a seat in Constituency No. 111 Mount Paektu, the highest peak on the Korean Peninsula, which Pyongyang claims is the sacred birthplace of Kim's late father. North Korea's propaganda machine uses Mount Paektu as it refers to the country's royal bloodline.

The socialist state holds the election every five years, with the last one held in March 2009. Except for the physical voting, it is largely considered a formality because North Korean voters can cast their ballot for only one candidate standing for each of the 687 constituencies.

"This represents the absolute support and trust of all electors for the regime," the official KCNA said, adding that the absentees were mostly those who work overseas or at sea. The first Session of the 13th SPA held on April 9 elected Kim Jong-un as first chairman of the National Defense Commission.

■ Desperate Efforts to Fend off U.N.'s Human Rights Resolution

On Nov. 18, the U.N. General Assembly's Third Committee passed a resolution denouncing North Korea's human rights violations. It seeks to refer Pyongyang's rights violation record to the International Criminal Court (ICC) and to hold the country's top leaders responsible for alleged crimes against humanity.

North Korea made desperate diplomatic efforts to stop the U.N. move. North Korea's mission to the United Nations attended a human rights debate session held at the U.N. headquarters on Oct. 22 and made a furious debate with Michael Kirby, who served as chairman of the U.N. Commission of Inquiry, asking him to show any evidence of North Korean leaders' involvement in the human rights abuses.

The North struggled to tone down the resolution, offering to invite the special human rights investigator from the European Union to visit the socialist country in exchange for dropping any mention of referring the country to the ICC. North Korean diplomats in New York also stepped up public relations activities, including providing a rare briefing on the country's human rights situation for U.N. diplomats, attending private seminar to make the country's case.

In its brisk diplomatic activities, North Korea sent Foreign Minister Ri Su-yong to the U.N. and Kang Sok-ju, another secretary of the Workers' Party and veteran diplomat, to the European Union in September but no avail to stop the U.N. action. Ri was the first North Korean foreign minister to attend the U.N. meeting in 15 years.

After the U.N. resolution's passage, the North's state organizations such as the National Defense Commission and the foreign ministry rejected the resolutions, with North media ratcheting up threats. The Rodong Sinmun said that the North will use all of its political and military deterrence including the nuclear capability.

■ North Korea's Participation in Incheon Asian Games

North Korea achieved fairly good results at the 17th Asian Games held in the South Korean city of Incheon from Sept. 19-Oct. 4. North Korea recorded its best performance ever at the Asian Games, finishing seventh with 36 medals including 11 gold, 11 silver and 14 bronze medals.

It was the first time that the North had placed in the top 10 since 2002, when it finished in ninth place with nine gold, 11 silver and 13 bronze medals at the games held in Busan, South Korea.

North Korea was most successful in weightlifting, in which its athletes -- Om Yun-chol, Kim Un-guk, Ri Jong-hwa and Kim Un-ju -- won four gold medals and set five world records.

North Korean athletes were also brilliant in soccer, a sport that was particularly emphasized by Kim Jong-un. North Korea's women soccer team won the gold medal, beating Japan in the final, while its male counterpart finished in second place behind South Korea.

North Korea won two gold medals in gymnastics and one each from shooting, wrestling, boxing and table tennis. North

Korea offered a lavish welcome to its athletes and coaches who returned to the country from Incheon and the North's state media provided wide coverage of the games and athletes.

■ **Release of U.S. Detainees**

North Korea released its two last remaining American detainees in November upon a visit by Director of U.S. National Intelligence (DNI) James Clapper to Pyongyang in what appears to have been a decision aimed at improving its image tarnished by human rights violations and offering an olive branch to Washington. Clapper's office said on Nov. 8 that Kenneth Bae and Matthew Todd Miller had been allowed to depart North Korea to rejoin their families.

Bae, a Korean-American missionary, had been serving a sentence of 15 years of hard labor after being detained in late 2012 for unspecified anti-state crimes. Miller was detained in April and had been sentenced to six years of hard labor for committing hostile acts. Their release came after the North freed in a third American detainee, Jeffrey Fowle, in late October.

In Pyongyang, Clapper delivered President Barack Obama's personal letter to North Korean leader Kim Jong-un. Upon their release, Obama hailed the release, saying it was a "wonderful day" for them and their families. He also said that the U.S. was "very grateful for their safe release."

Clapper's trip to the North raised hopes for a breakthrough in U.S.-North Korea ties. But Obama said the visit was focused on the detainee issue and "did not touch on some of the broader issues that have been the source of primary concern when it comes to North Korea, in particular, its development of nuclear capacity."

INTRODUCTION

■ **History**

The Democratic People's Republic of Korea, the official name of North Korea, was established on Sept. 9, 1948 on the northern half of the Korean Peninsula under the patronage of the Soviet Union, whose troops occupied the area at the end of World War II on Aug. 15, 1945. Japan's defeat in the war naturally liberated Koreans from the 36-year Japanese colonial rule on the peninsula.

The inauguration of the Communist regime there was preceded by the birth of South Korea, on Aug. 15, 1948, known as the Republic of Korea, the official name of South Korea, in the southern half of the peninsula through free elections sponsored by the United Nations.

In June 1950, North Korean communists invaded South Korea, triggering the fratricidal three-year Korean War. But their attempt to bring the South under their control and unify the two Koreas was thwarted when the U.S.-led U.N. allied forces rushed to the peninsula a few weeks later to help the South repulse the invaders.

The collapse of the socialist camp led by the Soviet Union at the beginning of the 1990s dealt a heavy blow to the North Korean economy, resulting in continued minus growth for nearly a decade. The abrupt death of North Korea's founder, Kim Il-sung, in July 1994, combined with natural disasters such as floods, deteriorated the situation, touching off social unrest and famine. Upon the leader's death, his son Kim Jong-il took power and instituted military rule in 1998, under the name of "military-first politics."

Despite the economic hardships, North Korea poured its energy in developing weapons of mass destruction such as the inter-continental ballistic missiles. In October 2006, North Korea conducted its first atomic test, followed by the second detonation in April 2009, naming itself as the nuclear possession country.

Current North Korea's leader Kim Jong-un, who inherited power from his late father Kim Jong-il who died in December 2011, has reinforced the country's military-oriented policy to heighten tension on the Korean Peninsula. The belligerent country under Kim Jong-un succeeded in launching a long-range ballistic rocket in December 2012, and conducted the third nuclear test in February 2013.

The country has been continuously developing nuclear and missile capabilities despite international call for desisting them. North Korea appears to have achieved "a significant level" of technology to miniaturize nuclear warheads to fit on its ballistic missiles that could potentially reach the United States mainland, South Korea's defense ministry said. It has now threatened to conduct a "new form" of nuclear test, repeatedly vowing to develop its economy and nuclear arsenal in tandem.

■ **Geography and Climate**

North Korea occupies an area of 123,138km², a size similar to countries such as Cuba, Greece and Nicaragua, compared to 100,232km² for South Korea. It borders China and Russia to the north and South Korea to the south. The border with the South was fixed by the military demarcation line under the truce agreement halting the 1950-53 Korean War.

With mountains and hills accounting for about 80% of its land territory, North Korea has 2 million hectares of cultivated land, most in the four southern provinces. It has 2,495km of coastline.

North Korea is abundant with water resources. According to 2013 Year Book of North Korea published by the (North) Korean Central News Agency, the water resources of the country is estimated to be 10 million kilowatts. Together with some 2,000 lakes and reservoirs across the country, North Korea has long rivers such as Amnok and Taedong rivers that flow into Yellow Sea.

Its border with China runs 1,360km, while the one with Russia is 17.2km and the one with the South is 248km. The inter-Korean border has a 4km-wide buffer zone called the Demilitarized Zone established under the truce agreement.

North Korea has four seasons of almost equal length, but the temperature in most of its northern areas is improper for growing its staple grains, notably rice. The annual average temperature is 3.9℃ for Hyesan in the northern area, compared with 11.5℃ for Haeju, an area close to the border with the South. The North has an annual average rainfall of 1,100 to 1,300mm, with Pyongyang 1,289mm and Chongjin 635mm.

■ **Population**

According to the data from Statistics Korea in Seoul published in December 2014, North Korea had a total population of 24.54 million as of the end of 2013, compared to the South's 50.22 million.

But the Yearbook 2013, published by the (North) Korean Central News Agency in October that year, put the North's population in 2008 at 24.05 million, 3 million more than 1993 showing an annual increase rate of 0.85%. The U.N. Fund for Population Activities (UNFPA) also tallied the North's population as of October 2008 after conducting a population census of North Korea.

In a program aired on April 8, 2001, Radio Pyongyang put life expectancy in the North at 74.5 years. This compares with the U.S. CIA's 71.08 years for the total population, 68.38 years for men and 73.92 years for women. Rumor had it that a maximum of 3 million North Koreans starved to death in the mid-1990s under the period called "arduous march under trial."

According to Seoul's Statistics Korea, North Korea's life expectancy in 2015 for men is 66.0 while that of South Korea is 78.2 years. In the case of North Korean women's life expectancy is 72.7 while that of South Korea is 85.0.

North Korea has moved into an aging society with the portion of its elderly taking up more than 8% of the population and women in their 70s outnumbering their male counterparts, data showed on Jan. 1 in 2013

The number of North Koreans aged over 65 reached 2.09 million as of Oct. 1, 2008, or 8.7% of the 24.05 million in total population, according to the country's Population Census, published by the North's Central Statistic Bureau in 2008 with assistance from the UNFPA.

According to the UNFPA's date in 2013, North Korea's total population ranked 49th among the 202 countries in the world.

■ **Administrative Units**

North Korea's administrative units are comprised of 9 provinces, 3 province-level cities, 25 other cities, 146 counties, 31 county-level districts, a special administrative region and 2 special zones, plus towns and laborers' districts number about 4,700. The provinces are South and North Hwanghae, South and North Pyongan, South and North Hamgyong, Kangwon, Jagang and Ryanggang.

The three cities with special status are Pyongyang, which is the North's capital, Nampho and Rason. In particular, the size of Pyongyang was contracted in 2010 by 57% to be 1,747km². Still, the North Korean capital is almost three times larger in size than Seoul which has a total area of 605km².

Besides, the special administrative region in Sinuiju bordering China was established in 2002 in an effort to attract foreign investments. One of the two other special zones in the Mount Kumgang area is to attract South Korean investments and the other one in Kaesong is to house South Korean manufacturers.

■ Citizen's Basic Rights

The human rights situation in North Korea is said to be the worst in the world. Any North Korean who speaks ill of the country's ruler should expect to be sent to one of the country's political camps. Article 67 of the North Korean Constitution stipulates: "Citizens are guaranteed freedom of speech, of the press, of assembly, demonstration and association. The State shall guarantee conditions for the free activity of democratic political parties and social organizations."

But the actual situation facing North Korean citizens is much different, as testified by defectors from the North ruled by the socialist regime. Unconditional loyalty to their ruler Kim Jong-un is a fundamental requirement.

The case is the same for freedom of religious belief. Officially, North Korea says it guarantees the freedom of religion. Article 68 of the Constitution stipulates "Citizens have freedom of religious beliefs. No one may use religion as a pretext for drawing in foreign forces or for harming the State and social order." The North Korean rulers have considered religion to be an opiate of the masses.

It is estimated that there are 200,000-400,000 Christians in North Korea who risk harsh punishments and as many as 70,000 Christians suffering in prison camps. The North Korean authorities operate a showcase church and a Catholic cathedral in the capital city of Pyongyang. In reality, those engaged in North Korea missions say believers suffer the harshest treatment because religion goes against the worship of its deceased leaders, Kim Il-sung and his son Kim Jong-il.

There are two Christian churches in the North's capital, one of them built in memory of former leader Kim's mother, Kang Ban-sok, who was a devoted Christian. There also is a Catholic church. The North has a few religious associations, but all of them were organized by the state for propaganda directed against South Korea and the global community.

On Dec. 18 in 2014, the U.N. General Assembly formally adopted a landmark resolution calling for referring North Korea to the International Criminal Court for human rights violations. The resolution followed an action of the U.N. General Assembly's Third Committee the previous month. The resolution has drawn keen attention because it would be the first-ever U.N. resolution calling for the North's referral to the ICC.

However, chances of an actual referral are slim because General Assembly resolutions, unlike U.N. Security Council resolutions, are not legally binding. Still, the North has protested strongly against the resolution, threatening a nuclear test in response.

Pyongyang has long been labeled as one of the worst human rights violators in the world. The communist regime does not tolerate dissent, holds hundreds of thousands of people in political prison camps and keeps tight control over outside information. But the North has bristled at such criticism, calling it a U.S.-led attempt to topple its regime.

The North's human rights problem has drawn greater international attention after the U.N. Commission of Inquiry issued a report in February 2014 saying North Korean leaders are responsible for "widespread, systematic and gross" violations of human rights.

■ National Emblem, Flag and National Anthem

The North Korea's national emblem bears the design of a grand hydroelectric power station under Mount Paektu, called in the North the "sacred mountain of the revolution," and the beaming light of a five-pointed red star, with ears of rice forming an oval frame, bound with a red ribbon bearing the inscription "The Democratic People's Republic of Korea."

Its national flag consists of a central red panel, bordered both above and below by a narrow white stripe and a broad blue stripe. The central red panel bears a five-pointed red star within a white-circle. Its national anthem is called the "Patriotic Song."

▪ Industries

North Korea is suffering from extreme poverty mainly due to its closed economic system, while South Korea, rising from the debris of the Korean War, has become one of the most successful economic models in the world. This huge gap has resulted from the different economic development systems between the two sides, one by the capitalism and the other by the Communism.

According to Seoul's Statistics Korea in January 2013, North Korea's overall economic power in the 1950s doubled that of South Korea. But in 2009, South Korea's economy grew 40 times larger than the North. The North Korean economy has been in the doldrums as it suffers from chronic food and energy shortages, mismanagement and natural disasters.

Despite the abundance in power sources such as hydroelectricity and coal and underground resources such as iron, magnesite and tungstine, North Korea's industries have almost stopped growing due to its closed and outdated economic system.

The North Korean economy, however, grew a little in four years in 2012 on the back of increased production from the manufacturing sector and favorable performances in the agriculture and fisheries industry, South Korea's central bank said on July 12, 2013.

The South's Bank of Korea estimated the socialist country's economy grew 1.3% in 2012 in terms of the gross domestic product (GDP), quickening from a 0.8% on-year gain in the previous year.

The 2012 growth was the steepest advance since 2008 when the North's GDP was estimated to expand 3.1% thanks to favorable agricultural production and international assistance of heavy oil.

But the economic gap between South and North Korea widened in 2013 with the difference in their trade volumes remaining far apart. According to the data from Statistics Korea in December 2014, North Korea's nominal gross national income (GNI) came to 33.84 trillion won (US$30.87 billion) in 2013 with that of the South coming to 1.44 quadrillion won, or 42.6 times larger.

In 2012, South Korea's GNI was 38.2 times larger than the North's. On a per-capita basis, South Korea's GNI came to 28.7 million won, 20.8 times that of North Korea. South Korea also continued to greatly outperform the communist North in trade. In 2013, South Korea's overall trade volume came to about US$1.07 trillion, 146 times larger than North Korea's US$7.3 billion.

South Korea's overall rice production came to 4.23 million tons, while the North produced about 2.1 million tons. The two Koreas also showed significant gaps in social infrastructure. South Korea's road network totaled 106,414km, compared with the North's 26,114km.

According to a report in March 16 2014, North Korea's per-capita gross domestic product (GDP) rose 4.8% on-year in 2013 from an improved grain harvest and expanded investment in the mining, utility and other segments.

The North's per-capita GDP for 2013 is estimated at US$854, up US$39 from a year earlier, according to the report released by the Hyundai Research Institute, a South Korean private think tank. The North's 2013 per-capita GDP amounts to a mere 3.6% of South Korea's per-capita GDP of US$23,838 for the same year, it said.

Trade between North Korea and its strongest ally China jumped 10.4% on-year to reach US$6.5 billion in 2013, while inter-Korean trade sank 42% to US$1.1 billion due to a five-month halt of a jointly run industrial park. The 2013 inter-Korean trade figure is the lowest since 2005 when the comparable figure was US$1.06 billion.

POLITICS

■ **Overview**

North Korea's political formula is based on a "party-state system." In theory, North Korea is ruled by a socialist party, namely, the Workers' Party of Korea, as stated in Article 11 of its Constitution: "The DPRK (Democratic People's Republic of Korea) shall conduct all activities under the leadership of the Workers' Party of Korea."

The Party's charter, which was amended during its sixth congress in October 1980, says: "The Workers' Party of Korea is guided by the Juche Idea, a revolutionary ideology meaning self-reliance created by Great Leader, Comrade Kim Il-sung."

In reality, however, the country is governed by the monolithic ruling system of the Kim family, who have exercised absolute authority for over half a century. Still, the country is also called a military-oriented state in the name of "songun" or military-first politics.

After the death of Kim Il-sung in July 1994, his son, Kim Jong-il, inherited this dictatorship. Kim Il-sung became the "eternal state president" when the regime of Kim Jong-il was officially inaugurated during the first session of the sixth Supreme People's Assembly (SPA), the North's rubber-stamp parliament, in September 1998, more than five years after the senior Kim's death.

Kim Il-sung's death touched off extreme social unrest and deteriorated the situation facing the North Korean economy, a politics stressing the importance of the military role in developing the North emerged as Kim Jong-il's ruling idea. The North alleges that Kim Jong-il initiated military-first politics in January 1995. Despite growing military influence in the North, it has been actually under the Workers' Party of Korea's rule since 1994.

During the September 1998 SPA meeting, Kim Jong-il became the North's leader in his capacity as chairman of the National Defense Commission (NDC), while Kim Yong-nam, a veteran diplomat, was named president of the SPA Presidium, a ceremonial position mainly concerned with representing the North in dealings with foreign countries.

In that SPA meeting, Kim, the titular head of state, announced, "The NDC chairmanship is the highest post of the state with which to organize and lead the work of defending the state system of the socialist country and the destinies of the people, and strengthening and increasing the defense capabilities of the country and the state power as a whole through command over all the political, military and economic forces of the country."

North Korea revised the Constitution at its SPA meeting in April 2009 in which it reinforced the role and function of the National Defense Commission, defining the NDC chairman the supreme leader of the country.

In September 2010, the country held a meeting of the Party representatives and revised the party charter, wherein it formalized the three generation hereditary power succession from Kim Il-sung and Kim Jong-il to Kim Jong-un.

Since Kim Jong-il's death in December 2011, his son Kim Jong-un inherited the absolute leadership by taking top official posts of the country. Kim Jong-un was named the first chairman of the NDC during the Supreme People's Assembly session in April 2012. In that SPA session, the country rewrote its Constitution defining the socialist country of Juche (self-reliance) as materialized by the ideology and guidance of Kim Il-sung and Kim Jong-il.

In April 2012, the Workers' Party's representatives meeting named the late leader Kim Jong-il as the eternal secretary of the Party while Kim Jong-un was named the first secretary of the Party.

Since taking the reins, Kim Jong-un has challenged the military's iron grip on the country and begun restructuring the socialist state's economic strategy. The ruling Workers' Party and the Cabinet are now considered more important than the once-invincible military, which had formerly been the backbone of North Korea's power base.

Yet, Kim Jong-un still preserves the "songun" or the military-first politics, as a legacy of his late father Kim Jong-il. In line with it, the North Korean regime and state media have been increasingly placing emphasis on the idea of "military for the people."

■ Workers' Party of Korea

The Workers' Party of Korea (WPK) is the most powerful organization in North Korea, setting its main policies and political line. The party has a membership of about 3 million. The party charter, which was revised in October 1980, says: "The Workers' Party of Korea represents the interest of all Koreans." It also says the party's mission is to achieve the complete victory of socialism in the North and fulfill the revolutionary tasks of national liberation and forming a people's democracy.

The party's leading institution is its Congress and its highest body is its Central Committee, which heads the Party between congress sessions. The party charter calls for the Congress to convene once every six years and the Central Committee, once every six months.

The Political Bureau, or the Politburo, is Central Committee's top policymaking body, while the Bureau of Secretaries, or the Secretariat, is the office responsible for implementing policies established by the Politburo.

The ruling party revised its charter in April 2012, whereas it put forward the ruling theory of Kim Il-sung and Kim Jong-il as the principal ideology of the party, which is a little different from the previous Juche or self-reliance idea. It also made it clear through the party charter's revision that the current leader Kim Jong-un, the first secretary of the party, is the supreme leader of the country. It also defined that Kim Il-sung and Kim Jong-il are "eternal leaders" of the country.

In its revision in September 2010, the party charter says the ultimate goal of the party is to realize the juche ideology and the complete autonomy of the masses of the people. The party also revised its objective in a way to construct the powerful and prosperous socialist country, defining the party as "the Kim Il-sung's Party."

The Organization of Workers' Party

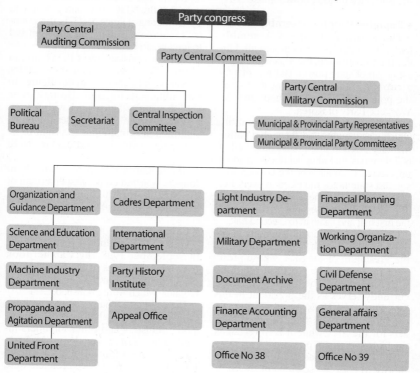

As of the end of 2012, there are a total of 20 departments under the Workers' Party such as the organizational guidance, information and instruction, and united front departments.

Provincial network of the party is tightly organized. All levels of party representative meetings and committees are placed at the provinces, counties, cities as well as special cities such as Pyongyang. These party organizations are also placed at major factories and business enterprises across the country. Under the party committees of the cities and counties, there are party cells, the party's smallest organizational blocks composed of five to 30 party members.

In January 2013, the North held a meeting of party cell leaders, the first convening of party cell leaders since October 2007. During the meeting, Kim Jong-un stressed the increased role of the ruling party's "grass-roots organizations" in building an economically powerful country, a main policy goal Kim has stressed since he took power in late 2011.

▪ Supreme People's Assembly

The Supreme People's Assembly (SPA) is North Korea's parliament. Under the Constitution, the SPA is the highest organ of state power. But it is merely a rubber stamp body that endorses the policies of the government and the Workers' Party of Korea.

The incumbent 13th-term Assembly, which was inaugurated through a parliamentary election in 2014, is composed of 687 deputies, including leader Kim Jong-un, elected from all over the country. The socialist state holds the election every five years, with the last one held in March 2014. The SPA holds two sessions a year, once in the first half and again in the second half.

Under a constitutional amendment on Sept. 5, 1998, North Korea established the Presidium of the SPA, whose president represents the North in relations with foreign countries. Kim Yong-nam, currently serves as the president of the SPA Presidium. He is also North Korea's ceremonial head of state. The Presidium acts for the SPA while it is in recess as the highest organ of power.

The Presidium has the duty and authority to convene sessions of the SPA, and examine and adopt new departmental bills and regulations raised when the SPA is in recess.

▪ National Defense Commission

North Korea's Constitution, revised in 1998, says in Article 100: "The National Defense Commission is the highest military leading organ of State power and an organ for general control over national defense." The NDC became an independent governmental body when the North revised its 1972 Constitution in 1992. The NDC, defined as it is in the Constitution, has sovereign control over national defense and significant administrative power.

North Korea revised its Constitution in April 2009 at the 12th-term of the Supreme People's Assembly and redefined the roles and duties of the NDC and NDC chairman. The new constitution empowered NDC chairman Kim Jong-il as the state's supreme leader, highlighting his songun, or military-first, politics and reemphasizing the importance of communism.

Article 100 in the amended statutes state that the NDC chairman, a post held by Kim Jong-il since 1993, is the country's "supreme leader," an apparent bid to lend greater authority to Kim.

Another revision states the chairman of the NDC "oversees all state affairs, appoints and dismisses major figures in the military sector, and also ratifies or abolishes important treaties with foreign nations." Article 103 stipulates the NDC chairman also maintains the right to issue special pardons and declare state emergencies.

North Korea's current leader Kim Jong-un was named the first chairman of the NDC in April 2012 after the death of his father Kim Jong-il in December 2011.

▪ Cabinet

Under a constitutional revision made in September 1998, the Cabinet took over most functions of the Central People's Committee and Executive Policy Council, which were abolished.

The Cabinet is composed of a premier, two vice premiers, chairmen of commissions, ministers and other members including heads of the Academy of Science and the Central Bank. But it was known later that a few more vice premiers were newly added.

The Cabinet is entitled to control not only commissions and the ministries but also local people's committee. It also institutes, amends and supplements regulations concerning state management.

Article 123 of the revised Constitution in 2009 stipulates that the Cabinet is the administrative executive body of the highest sovereignty and an overall state management organization.

Under the revised Constitution of 2009, the local people's committees are guided by the Cabinet as well as the higher central people's committee and also the Presidium of the Supreme People's Assembly.

Provincial (or municipalities directly under the control of the central authority), municipal (district), and county local people's committees are sovereign power organs when similar local people's assemblies are in recess. The term of each LPC is four years. An LPC has the duty and authority to convene people's assembly sessions and prepare for local assembly elections, among other things.

As of the end of 2014, the Cabinet is composed of 42 organizations including seven commissions and 31 ministries. Present Cabinet premier Pak Pong-ju succeeded Choe Yong-rim in April 2013.

(Members of DPRK Cabinet) As of April 2015

- Premier of the DPRK Cabinet = Pak Pong-ju
- Vice-Premier and Chairman of the State Planning Commission = Ro Tu-chol
- Vice-Premiers = Kim Yong-jin, Choe Yong-gon, Rim Chol-ung, Kim Dok-hun
- Vice-Premier and Minister of Chemical Industry = Ri Mu-yong
- Vice-Premier and Minister of Agriculture = Ri Chol-man
- Foreign Minister = Ri Su-yong
- Minister of Electric Power Industry = Kim Man-su
- Minister of Coal Industry = Mun Myong-hak
- Minister of Metallurgical Industry = Kim Yong-gwang
- Minister of Railways = Jon Kil-su
- Minister of Land and Maritime Transport = Kang Jong-gwan
- Minister of Mining Industry = Ri Hak-chol
- Minister of Light Industry = Choe Il-ryong
- Minister of State Natural Resources Development = Ri Chun-sam
- Minister of Oil Industry = Pae Hak
- Minister of Forestry = Han Ryong-guk
- Minister of Machine-building Industry = Ri Jong-guk
- Minister of Atomic Energy Industry = Ri Je-son
- Minister of Electronics Industry = Kim Jae-song
- Minister of Posts and Telecommunications = Sim Chol-ho
- Minister of Construction and Building-Materials Industry = Tong Jong-ho
- Minister of State Construction Control = Kwon Song-ho
- Minister of Food and Consumer Goods Industries = Jo Yong-chol
- Minister of Fisheries = Ri Hyok
- Minister of Finance = Ki Kwang-ho
- Minister of Labor = Jong Yong-su
- Minister of Foreign Trade = Ri Ryong-nam
- Chairman of the State Science and Technology Commission = Choe Sang-gon
- President of the State Academy of Sciences = Jang Chol
- Minister of Land and Environment Protection = Kim Kyong-jun
- Minister of Urban Management = Kang Yong-su
- Minister of Food Procurement and Administration = Mun Ung-jo
- Minister of Commerce = Kim Kyong-nam
- Chairman of the Education Commission and Minister of General Education = Kim Sung-du
- President of Kim Il Sung University and Minister of Higher Education under the Education Commission = Thae Hyong-chol
- Minister of Public Health = Kang Ha-guk
- Minister of Culture = Pak Chun-nam
- Minister of Physical Culture and Sports = Kim Yong-hun
- President of the Central Bank = Kim Chon-gyun
- Director of the Central Bureau of Statistics = Choe Sung-ho
- Secretary General of the Cabinet = Kim Yong-ho

362

(Members of Presidium of Supreme People's Assembly) As of April 2014

- President of the Presidium of the SPA of the DPRK = Kim Yong-nam
- Vice-Presidents = Yang Hyong-sop and Kim Yong-dae
- Honorary Vice-Presidents = Kim Yong-ju and Choe Yong-rim
- Secretary General = Hong Son-ok
- Members = Kim Yang-gon, Thae Jong-su, Jon Yong-nam, Hyon Sang-ju, Ri Myong-gil, Kim Jong-sun, Kim Wan-su, Ryu Mi-yong, Kang Myong-chol, Kang Su-rin and Jon Kyong-nam.

■ **Workers' Party Meeting**

North Korea convened a meeting of the political bureau of the Workers' Party Central Committee on April 8 to decide major agenda items including the party's organization and the party's leadership role.

▲ North Korean leader Kim Jong-un (at the podium) presiding over a meeting of Political Bureau of the Workers' Party of Korea's Central Committee in Pyongyang on April 8.

Chaired by leader Kim Jong-un, the meeting discussed the issue of reinforcing the organization for increasing the leadership role and function of the Party, according to the North's official KCNA. It discussed a proposal for forming the state leadership body to be submitted to the First Session of the 13th-term Supreme People's Assembly.

Kim Jong-un set forth important tasks to be fulfilled to further strengthen the WPK to be an invincible revolutionary party, firmly protect the dignity and sovereignty of the country and dynamically accelerate the work to improve the standard of the people's living and the building of a rich and powerful country.

The Workers' Party earlier held a key meeting to discuss ways to improve combat readiness and military capabilities, the country's state media said on March 17, in its latest show of force.

Participants of an enlarged meeting of the Party's Central Military Commission also discussed issues related to establishing the party's monolithic leadership system in the army and improving livelihoods of its soldiers, the Korean Central News Agency said.

The report came a day after North Korea fired 25 short-range rockets into waters off its east coast in what could be a routine military exercise. On March 14, the North vowed to keep up its efforts to bolster its nuclear deterrence and take additional measures to demonstrate its might continually as long as nuclear threats and blackmailing from the U.S. persist.

Leader Kim Jong-un chaired the enlarged meeting of the Party's Central Military Commission and "discussed issues arising in further developing the Korean People's Army (KPA) into the powerful Paektusan revolutionary army faithful to the party, the leader, the country and its people," according to the KCNA report on April 27.

"He stressed the need to enhance the function and role of the political organs of the KPA if it is to preserve the proud history and tradition of being the army of the party, win one victory after another in the confrontation with the U.S. and creditably perform the mission as a shock force and standard-bearer in building a thriving nation," the KCNA said.

In 2013, North Korea adopted a new strategic policy line that calls for building a stronger economy and an nuclear arsenal so that the country will emerge as "a great political, military and socialist economic power."

The KCNA said that the North's nuclear weapons are not a "political bargaining chip" nor a "thing for economic dealings," saying that the nuclear armed forces are its "life, which can never be abandoned as long as imperialists and nuclear threats exist on earth."

■ Reshuffle of Government Offices

North Korean leader Kim Jong-un maintained most of his inner circle of confidants without a massive power shake-up at the first session of North Korea's 13th-term Supreme People's Assembly held in Pyongyang on April 9. The rubber-stamp SPA re-elected leader Kim Jong-un as chairman of the NDC as widely expected.

Choe Ryong-hae, a top military official, became an influential figure second to only leader Kim Jong-un when the newly launched parliament elected him as new vice chairman of the socialist country's most powerful body, National Defense Commission (NDC).

The other two NDC vice chairmen remained the same. Choe, who served as the special envoy for Kim Jong-un and met with Chinese President Xi Jinping in May 2013, replaced Jang, the leader's late uncle who was previously a vice chairman. The North's state media called Choe's name first before the other two vice chairmen were announced, apparently in recognition of his position as the second most powerful figure in the regime.

With his NDC appointment, Choe has grabbed all of the No. 2 positions of the North's three core power bodies, the Political Bureau of the Workers' Party's Central Committee and the party's Central Military Commission.

Meanwhile, the North apparently opted for stability by making no dramatic changes in a Cabinet shakeup. "Kim Jong-un chose stability rather than change," a South Korean government official said. "He appears intent to minimize any internal instability that could be caused by the purge of Jang Song-thaek and manage state affairs stably, while the regime continues to be isolated by the international community."

The North's octogenarian titular head of state, Kim Yong-nam, retained his position as president of the Presidium of the Supreme People's Assembly, with Premier Pak Pong-ju also keeping his job.

What was notable is that the North replaced its foreign minister. Ri Su-yong, a former ambassador to Switzerland, was named to replace Pak Ui-chun as the top diplomat of the communist country.

Ri is known to have served as a guardian of leader Kim and his younger sister Kim Yo-jong when they studied at an international school in Switzerland in the 1990s. The appointment, however, is unlikely to lead to any dramatic change in the North's foreign policy toward the U.S. or its nuclear programs.

The parliamentary meeting came a month after Kim was elected to the new legislature in uncontested nationwide elections along with 686 deputies, including many who were considered close to Jang.

Most of those who were considered close to Jang were elected to the legislature in March, an indication that Kim is confident enough not to worry about any backlash from the execution of his uncle.

But Kim Jong-un's powerful aunt, Kim Kyong-hui, was not elected to any important position in the Assembly, according to KCNA's list of Assembly members. Since the death of her husband, Jang, she has been rumored to have stepped down from political life in North Korea.

Among those who died in 2014 was Chae Hui-jong, a former department director of the Workers' Party. Leader Kim Jong-un on Feb. 14 sent a wreath to the bier of Chae, a recipient of Order of Kim Il-sung and former department director of the Central Committee of the Workers' Party of Korea, expressing deep condolences on his demise, according to a report of the KCNA.

Meanwhile, Gen. Jon Pyong-ho, who played a key role in developing North Korea's nuclear weapons, died of a sudden heart attack at age 88, the country's state news agency said on July 9.

Jon had been a leading figure in North Korea's much-denounced nuclear weapons development, having served as the ruling Workers' Party secretary in charge of arms development.

Jon made a special contribution to converting North Korea "into a satellite producer and launcher and a nuclear weapons state," the obituary said. Jon was included in the United Nations' sanctions lists in 2013 following the country's third nuclear test in February.

■ Parliamentary Election

North Koreans went to the polls on March 9 to elect a new rubber-stamp parliament. As expected, leader Kim Jong-un was elected to the Supreme People's Assembly (SPA) together with key military and party officials, all of whom won unanimous approval.

North Korea unveiled a new roster of deputies for parliament on March 11. In the tightly choreographed election, the first under the young leader, the 687 candidates for the SPA pulled in 100% of the vote with a 99.97% turnout, state media said.

All the voters of Kim's constituency voted for Kim, the North's official Korean Central News Agency (KCNA) said in a dispatch, citing election results from the Central Election Committee.

The dispatch said Kim's election demonstrated soldiers' and citizens' "absolute support and profound trust" in their young leader, who took over the country in December 2011 following the death of his father, long-time leader Kim Jong-il.

Kim ran for a seat in Constituency No. 111 Mount Paektu, the highest peak on the Korean Peninsula, which Pyongyang claims is the sacred birthplace of Kim's late father. North Korea's propaganda machine uses Mount Paektu when it refers to the country's royal bloodline.

▲ A massive gathering at an unidentified location in North Korea on Feb. 3, to nominate North Korean leader Kim Jong-un as candidate in the "No. 111 Mount Paekdu constituency" for March's Supreme People's Assembly elections.

The socialist state holds the election every five years, with the last one held in March 2009. Except for the physical voting, it is largely considered a formality because North Korean voters can cast their ballot for only one candidate standing for each of the 687 constituencies.

According to the new roster of the SPA, there seemed no big surprise in the North's power shift. Rather, most of the officials close to North Korean leader Kim's executed uncle Jang Song-thaek were elected to the SPA, an outcome that suggests that Kim may be confident of having consolidated his power.

The elections had been widely seen as an opportunity to either eliminate or sideline Jang's supporters from the SPA. The results of the election showed that most officials believed to be close to Jang, including Kim Yang-gon, Pyongyang's point man on inter-Korean relations, were elected deputies to the legislature. Also included in the list is People's Security Minister Choe Pu-il, one of Jang's old associates and friends.

North Korea's ambassador to China, Ji Jae-ryong, was also elected as a new deputy to the legislature. Ji's political fate had been the focus of intense media attention because he was considered one of the closest aides to Jang.

However, two other officials close to Jang -- Mun Kyong-dok, a senior Workers' Party official in Pyongyang, and Ro Song-sil, former chairwoman of the Central Committee of the Democratic Women's Union of North Korea -- were removed from the legislature.

Mun, who was last seen in public in a massive rally on Jan. 6, appears to have been dismissed from his post or purged, said Cheong Seong-chang, a senior research fellow at the Sejong Institute, a private security think tank near Seoul. Cheong said the election results "indirectly confirmed that there aren't as many of Jang's proteges in the North's leadership as believed by the outside world."

Other high-profile officials who were elected to the parliament include Choe Ryong-hae, the chief political officer of the Korean People's Army, and Won Tong-yon, the vice head of the United Front Department of the Workers' Party, who represented North Korea during last month's high-level talks with South Korea.

The newly elected deputies also include Jang Jong-nam, minister of the People's Armed Forces; Kim Su-kil, vice director of the General Political Bureau of the Korean People's Army; Jo Yon-jun, senior vice director of the ruling Workers' Party's organization guidance department; and Ma Won-chun, vice director of the party's finance and accounting department.

Almost all of Kim Jong-un's confidants retained their seats, including Ri Yong-gil, chief of the military general staff; Kim Won-hong, minister of state security; Pak Pong-ju, Cabinet premier; and Kim Yong-nam, president of the SPA presidium.

Some old military officials, including Hyon Chol-hae, a former first-vice minister of the People's Armed Forces, were removed from the legislature in a sign of a shift in power.

Also missing were retired senior army personnel, apparently reflecting Kim Jong-un's drive to dilute the influence of the potent, rigid military within his regime.

■ Ideological Campaign to Consolidate Socialist System

North Korea has been intensifying its campaign to promote the country's "superior" socialist system, revolutionary ideology and monolithic ruling structure. Pyongyang's campaign is aimed at consolidating the people's loyalty -- an essential step for the dynastic country to maintain its unitary political system.

North Korean leader Kim Jong-un stressed the need to solidify his monolithic leadership during a meeting of the party's ideological officials held from Feb. 24-25, in which Kim also called for the construction of a thriving country through a self-reliance economy and the removal of toxic elements of capitalism from North Korean society.

The new tasks presented by the leader are follow-ups to the leader's policy goals and tasks made in his New Year's day address, in which Kim called on the two Koreas to work toward better relations and emphasized economic growth and ideological consolidation in the North to build a "thriving socialist country."

In his latest speech to the party, the North Korean leader warned against factionalism in the nation's ruling Workers' Party as part of ongoing efforts to reinforce the state ideology after the stunning execution of his uncle for treason.

"(We) failed to learn and root out the emergence of a modern-time faction within the party in advance" despite efforts to strengthen the monolithic ruling system, Kim was quoted as saying by the North's Korea Central News Agency. He made the remarks in his speech during the closing ceremony of the 8th Conference of the Ideological Officials of the Workers' Party on Feb. 25.

Kim stressed the need to concentrate all efforts on firmly establishing the Party's monolithic leadership. "All efforts of the party's ideological projects should be poured into the firm establishment of the monolithic control system... and to eradicate factionalism," he said.

Stressing that such sectarianism is caused by changes in ideology, the young leader called for "proactive operations to prevent the toxin of capitalism from encroaching on us and to nullify their imperialistic ideological movements."

The two-day conference in Pyongyang was the first in 10 years. The latest conference is its eighth, but North Korea attached significance to the meeting as Kim said the conference convened on a scale unprecedented in the history of the Workers' Party.

Kim said that the most powerful weapon for a party that wages a revolution shouldering people's destiny is ideology. "Without ideology, a party cannot be founded nor can it exist, and its work and revolutionary struggle are inconceivable separated from ideological work."

He said the revolutionaries of Korea rallied comrades and obtained weapons on the strength of ideology and on its strength they defeated imperialist powers and built a prospering form of socialism. Then he called for the party's ideological officials to conduct their work in an aggressive manner.

Kim also emphasized that the ideological work should ensure that "all shades of evil ideas and spirits never make inroads into our ranks by giving uninterrupted publicity to the Party's intentions and leading the continuous advance of the ideological struggle."

He then encouraged propaganda and agitation activities. "We must launch an information offensive to ideologically and morally overpower the imperialist reactionary forces who are trying to stamp out socialism by all means."

"The sector of ideological work and related units should work out elaborate plans for putting mass media and external publicity means on a modern and IT basis and make persevering efforts to carry them out," he said. "We should ideologically support the efforts to make a breach in imperialist maneuvers to monopolize high technology, and make advanced science and technology our own."

■ **Kim Jong-un's New Year's Message**

In his New Year's address on Jan. 1, North Korean leader Kim Jong-un called on the two Koreas to work toward better relations and emphasized economic growth and ideological consolidation in the North to build a "thriving socialist country."

▲ North Korean leader Kim Jong-un delivers a New Year's message through the North's Central Television Station in Pyongyang on Jan. 1.

Kim defined 2014 as a year of "grandiose struggle to make a fresh leap forward ushering in a golden age of songun (military-first) Korea."

In the message delivered live on the North's television and radio, the leader also pledged to rebuild the North's moribund economy in 2014 with emphasis on agriculture, food production, construction and science-technology.

North Korea, Kim said, will continue to build up its military. "We should continue to channel great efforts into building up the country's defense capabilities," he said.

"Strengthening defense capabilities is the most important of all state affairs,

and the country's dignity, people's happiness and peace rest on powerful arms."

Referring to the worsened inter-Korean relations, Kim said, "We will make aggressive efforts to improve relations between the North and South," Kim said in the speech that lasted 25 minutes. "The South side should also come forward to improve relations between the North and the South."

Kim's remarks appear to contain relatively clearer reconciliatory signals than the previous year's, which underscored the need for defused tension on the Korean Peninsula and efforts for national unification.

The young leader emphasized a robust economy buttressed by agriculture, construction and science as key to a "new leap into a strong, prosperous socialist nation" this year.

While 2013's speech focused on agriculture and light industries for economic development, the latest one singled out construction, fisheries and protection of underground resources and forests as core areas.

Notably, he placed emphasis on agriculture in the impoverished state, and even the development of "green energy." All of those economic policies would be under the control of the ruling party, he said, signaling a growth in the role of the Workers' Party.

Kim called for efforts to boost agricultural output. North Korea's food production is estimated to have been at about 5.03 million metric tons in 2013, up 5% from the previous year, the U.N. World Food Program said in a report posted on its website.

Still, the food security situation is serious, with 84% of all households having borderline or poor food consumption, the report said.

During the speech, however, Kim did not explicitly refer to the nuclear program, though he vowed to maintain a "strong deterrent" against "external threats of a nuclear war."

Kim lambasted frequent joint military exercises by South Korea and the U.S., calling them a rehearsal for a nuclear war against the North. He warned that any accidental military skirmish on the Korean Peninsula could lead to "a deadly nuclear catastrophe" and that "the United States will never be safe."

The United States, which fought against North Korea in the 1950-53 Korean War, still keeps about 28,500 troops in South Korea to deter threats from Pyongyang.

Reflecting on last year's achievements, Kim noted, "The entire party, the whole army and all the people waged an all-out offensive in support of the party's new line of developing the two fronts simultaneously and thus achieved brilliant successes in building a thriving socialist country and defending socialism."

He said that through last year's struggle "we clearly demonstrated that our ideology, our strength and our way are the best, and no force can check our sacred cause advancing to accomplish a far-reaching ideal and goal."

Also looking back on his achievements from 2013, Kim complimented North Korean scientists for developing state-of-the-art military technology for national defense and urged them to develop more modernized weapons that are "lightweight, unmanned, intelligent and precisely functioning."

Greeting the new year, Kim said, "Let us raise a fierce wind of making a fresh leap forward on all fronts of building a thriving country filled with confidence in victory! This is the militant slogan our party and people should uphold this year."

Referring to the country's economic plan for 2014, he said, "This year we should ensure that the sectors of agriculture, construction and science and technology hold the torch of innovations in the van and the flames of the torch flare up as flames of a leap forward on all the fronts of socialist construction."

Specifically, he underscored the need to build up the country's defense capabilities. He also stressed the political and ideological consolidation, saying that "the political and ideological position is a fortress that decides the victory and failure in the battle of defending socialism, and consolidating the revolutionary ranks politically and ideologically is the most important task facing us."

Then he said, "We should make fresh headway in the national reunification movement for this year," and noted that

"We can never just sit back with folded arms and see the dark clouds of a nuclear war against us hovering over the Korean Peninsula. We will defend our country's sovereignty, peace and dignity by relying on our powerful self-defensive strength."

"Holding fast on to the ideals of our foreign policy -- independence, peace and friendship -- our party and the government of the DPRK will strive to expand and develop relations of friendship and cooperation with all the countries that respect our sovereignty and are friendly to us, and safeguard global peace and security and promote common prosperity of mankind," Kim said.

Kim said the ruling Workers' Party had "eliminated the factional filth remaining in the party," apparently referring to the brutal executions of Jang Song-thaek and his confidants.

Still, he made no direct mention of Jang's purge in the speech, saying only that "the purge of anti-party and counter-revolutionary factionalists has strengthened the party." Without naming Jang, the leader alluded to him as "factional filth."

But Kim's call for improved inter-Korean relations during the speech is possibly part of the young leader's efforts to consolidate his grip on power in the aftermath of the execution of Jang in December.

In his speech, he said "It's time to stop all this useless slandering and swearing that hinders reconciliation and unity of the two Koreas." "The South Korean government should stop the reckless fratricidal confrontation and the fuss of cracking down the pro-North Korean people," he said. "We should achieve a new progress in the movement for national unification this year."

Despite Kim's verbal gesture, the young leader still warned that a trivial military clash could trigger an all-out war on the Korean Peninsula. "Those war-like people in the United States and the South are bringing all their nuclear weapons in full scale and crazily committing a North Korea-bound nuclear war exercise," he said.

"That creates a dangerous situation in which a trivial and accidental military clash could prompt an all-out war. ... If a war happens again on this land, it would bring about a huge nuclear disaster, and the United States would not survive from it either," he threatened.

Kim's New Year's message, widely seen as the North's equivalent of the U.S.' State of the Union address, is scrutinized by South Korea and other regional powers for clues to the North's policy goals in the new year.

■ Kim Jong-un's Public Appearances

North Korean leader Kim Jong-un made fewer public appearances in 2014 than the previous year due to his alleged ankle surgery, which had kept him out of the public eye for more than a month, according to the South Korean government data.

Kim made a total of 172 public appearances in 2014, 17.7% less than the total 209 outings registered in 2013, the data by the unification ministry showed. Economy-related activities stood at 62, followed by visits to military units with 56 and social and cultural outings with 29.

In 2013, Kim made 71 economy-related public appearances out of a total of 209 public outings. In 2012, Kim made 37 economy-related public appearances out of a total of 151 public appearances.

The young leader suddenly disappeared from the public eye in early September in 2014, triggering wild speculation over a possible coup in the dictatorship and health problems. He reappeared to the public about 40 days later, leaning on a walking stick.

South Korea's spy agency later said that Kim underwent surgery during his time in seclusion to remove a cyst in his left ankle. Hwang Pyong-so, the military's top political officer, accompanied Kim to 126 of the total 172 public outings in 2014, the largest number out of any North Korean official.

MILITARY

■ Overview

Ever since his grip of power after his father Kim Jong-il's death in late 2011, North Korean leader Kim Jong-un has consolidated his power through frequent reshuffles of the higher echelon of the Workers' Party, the Korean People's Army and the Cabinet.

In April, 2014, Kim reinforced his power base by replacing the director of the general political bureau of the KPA, Choe Ryong-hae, with Hwang Pyong-so. In March 2013, the North convened a full session of the Party's Central Commitee and adopted the so-called "byongjin line" for its simultaneous pursuit of nuclear weapons and economic growth.

North Korea continued to ratchet up tensions on the Korean Peninsula with wild rhetoric and military moves. Since its third underground nuclear test in Feb. 12, 2013, North Korea heightened military tensions in protest against the U.N. Security Council's move to impose strict sanctions on the belligerent regime.

Outwardly, the North's escalation of tension was a response to the annual South Korea-U.S. joint exercises, Key Resolve and Foal Eagle, but was interpreted as an aim to establish a strong leadership of Kim Jong-un by calming down the internal instability in his third year of autocratic rule.

North Korea fired seven short-range projectiles from its east coast on March 4 using multiple rocket launchers in a series of provocations as the U.S. and South Korea entered the second week of joint military drills.

The North's provocations came after its charm offensive toward Seoul proved to be ineffective. On Jan. 16, the North's powerful National Defense Commission formally proposed halting all cross-border slander starting Jan. 30 and called for mutual action to prevent a nuclear calamity on the Korean Peninsula.

The North's top decision-making organization, headed by leader Kim Jong-un, claimed that its "important proposal" clearly showed how Pyongyang wished to improve the frayed inter-Korean relations. The message came a day after the socialist country warned of an "unimaginable holocaust" if Seoul carried out the annual Key Resolve and Foal Eagle exercises from late February through April as scheduled.

North Korea's provocations continued even during the period of the reunion meeting of the separated families in February at Mount Kumgang resort on the North's east coast. It fired rocket and ballistic missiles in March and in April

Chronology of North Korean rocket, missile launches

China

North Korea

Musudan-ri

Dongchang-ri   Hamhung

Sukchon

Wonsan

The East Sea

650 km

Pyongyang   Gitdaeryeong

1 ~ **6**

South Korea

The Yellow Sea

Seoul

700 kg warhead
(nuclear payload)

1 Launches four Scud ballistic missiles from Gitdaeryeong on Feb. 27

2 Fires off two short-range ballistic missiles from Wonsan and Gitdaeryeong on March 3

3 Launches seven projectiles from a multiple rocket launcher from Wonsan on March 4

4 Launches 25 short-range missiles from Wonsan on March 16

5 Launches 30 short-range missiles from Wonsan on March 22

6 Fires off 16 short-range missiles from Wonsan on March 23

7 Launches two Rodong ballistic missiles into the East Sea from Sukchon, north of Pyongyang, on March 26

15 – 20 meters

Rodong missile (range of 1,200 km)

YONHAP NEWS AGENCY

drones were found in Paju and Baengnyeong Island near the border area with the North.

On March 31, North Korea fired some 500 artillery shells near the Northern Limit Line (NLL) with about 100 of them falling south of the de facto inter-Korean sea border. In its response, the South fired back some 300 rounds from its K-9 self-propelled howitzers.

The skirmish came after North Korea sent a rare fax message to the South Korean 2nd Navy Fleet Command, notifying it of a plan to hold live-fire drills in seven areas near five front-line islands close to the NLL.

In the following months, North Korea gave contradictory signals to its southern neighbor and the international com-munity with both missile launches and a peace gesture.

North Korea test-fired two ballistic mis-siles, assumed by Seoul to be Scud missiles, on June 29 toward international waters in the East Sea. The launch came just three days after the regime fired three 300-mm artillery shells in a similar direction.

On June 30, North Korea proposed that the two Koreas stop all military hostilities starting July 4 and urged Seoul to scrap planned joint military exercises with the United States scheduled for August.

The rare conciliatory gesture coincided with Chinese President Xi Jinping's planned visit to Seoul on July 3 and the 42nd anniversary of the July 4 Joint Com-munique between South and North Ko-rea calling for efforts for better relations and the future reunification of Korea.

Then Pyongyang regime asked Seoul to cancel the Ulchi Freedom Guardian (UFG) exercise ahead of the Asian Games in September. The UFG is an annual joint military exercise between South Korea and the United States held every summer.

South and North Korean patrol boats briefly exchanged fire on Oct. 7 after a North Korean naval vessel violated the western maritime border. The clash came three days after a high-powered North Korean delegation made a rare visit to South Korea and agreed to hold another round of high-level dialogue in the near future.

Dampening hopes for the inter-Korean talks, South and North Korea exchanged fire on Oct. 10 after the North began shooting heavy machine guns, apparently aiming at balloons launched by South Korean civic activists.

After some North Korean machine gun rounds were discovered south of the border, South Korea's military fired back about 40 K-6 machine gun rounds, which was followed by another round of the North's machine gun attack.

The two Koreas held a furtive five-hour military meeting at the truce village of Panmunjom on Oct. 15. Pyongyang's delegation was led by North Korean Gen. Kim Yong-chol, director of the Reconnaissance General Bureau.

This was the first time in three years and eight months that the two countries' military officials sat down at the negotiating table, but the Seoul government remained tight-lipped on what was discussed afterwards.

According to a lengthy report carried by the North's Korea Central News Agency (KCNA) about the inter-Korean talks, the communist country made several proposals to the South during the meeting on ways to prevent the recurrence of "the recent shameful incidents," including seeking ways not to cross the sensitive sea border, stopping the leaflet propaganda campaigns and resolving issues via dialogue.

▪ Korean People's Army

According to the North's Workers' Party charter, the Korean People's Army (KPA) is the revolutionary armed forces of the ruling party which succeeded the revolutionary tradition of the anti-Japanese armed struggle. This revolutionary character of the military is an illustration that the KPA contributes to the establishment of the North's dynastic rule through the hereditary power succession from the founding president Kim Il-sung to his son Kim Jong-il and to the current leader Kim Jong-un.

Overwhelmed by the U.N. allied forces during the three-year Korean War it started in June 1950, in a bid to unify the divided halves of Korea, North Korea formulated a military-oriented policy in December 1962.

The four-point military policy, which was endorsed during the fifth session of the fourth-term Central Committee of the Workers' Party held in December 1962, calls for the training of all army servicemen as cadres, the modernization of all army units, the armament of the entire populace and the fortification of the entire national territory.

This policy was written into the Constitution in April 1992, when it revised it, and was retained in the current Constitution amended in September 1998, when the North revised it while formally inaugurating the Kim Jong-il's regime in the first session of the 10th-term Supreme People's Assembly.

Article 60 of the Constitution reads: "The State shall implement the line of self-reliant defense, the import of which is to arm the entire people, fortify the country, train the army into a cadre army and modernize the army on the basis of equipping of the army and the people politically and ideologically."

Under this policy, the North has maintained a one million-strong army, while digging tunnels for military use, developing such strategic weapons as nuclear bombs and missiles, and maintaining an eight million-man reserve forces. The Kim Jong-il regime reinforced this policy by giving top priority to all military-related projects, including the munitions industry, under the so-called Songun or military-first politics.

The military-first policy was heralded by Kim Jong-il as a guideline for ruling the impoverished, socialist country. But the vision has been upheld by his son,

Jong-un, who is pursuing missile and nuclear weapons programs despite international warnings and strict sanctions.

Basically, Pyongyang's military policy intends to protect its political and social system from external challenges, but it is ultimately to unify and communize the divided Korean Peninsula by means of armed forces.

■ Key Military Offices

The National Defense Commission (NDC) is the top organization for military command control. The North's Constitution revised in 2009 stipulates that the commission makes final decision on defense projects of the country and make guidance on defense policies. Kim Jong-un, the first chairman of the commission, is the top military leader and also undertakes the position of the supreme commander of the KPA.

Under the NDC are Escort Command and Security Command. KPA's General Political Bureau and the General Staff of the KPA are on equal standing with the North's People's Armed Forces Ministry. The chief of the three military organizations are competing with each other to pay loyal through mutual restraints.

Under a constitutional amendment in April 1992, North Korea elevated the NDC status in a way to be on a par with the Central People's Committee (CPC) chaired by the state president. But in September 1998, the North abolished the CPC, while declaring the NDC the top office in the reclusive regime. It also moved the Ministry of the People's Armed Forces, namely the defense ministry, under the control of the National Defense Commission from the Cabinet.

The two key offices of the KPA are the General Staff and the General Political Bureau. The former controls the army militarily and the latter politically and ideologically. Though hard to understand by Western standards, the chief of the General Political Bureau is more influential than the chief of the General Staff, who is more influential than the people's armed forces minister.

Under orthodox Communist theory and system, the Central Military Commission of the Workers' Party should be top office as far as military affairs are concerned. But it is uncertain whether the Party is playing its role properly in this era of military-first politics.

Before the death of Kim Il-sung in July 1994, the General Political Bureau of the KPA was under the command channel of the Party. But it is also uncertain whether the channel is still being maintained.

The general political bureau has its own offices in every army organization, corps, division, regiment, battalion and company to supervise ideological behavior of officers and soldiers.

Of the key military organizations, there is the office of the supreme army commander, which was held by the state president before Kim Jong-il took over the office in December 1991. It is uncertain, however, whether the office of supreme commander belongs to the government or the Workers' Party, but presently leader Kim Jong-un serves as KPA's Supreme Commander.

■ Kim Jong-un's Frequent Visits to Military Units

North Korean leader Kim Jong-un made a series of visits to military units, giving field guidance to soldiers for improving the quality of the training and achieving results in combat readiness.

In December, Kim visited a naval unit and called for efforts to boost its combat capabilities for the year 2015. Calling for making 2015 "a year of bringing about a fresh turn in the strengthening of the navy," Kim stressed the need to employ "advanced training methods ... and set forth the tasks and ways for rounding off sub unit's war preparations."

There have been signs that Pyongyang has beefed up its naval power with a focus on boosting submarines' capabilities. Pyongyang has launched a new submarine capable of firing ballistic missiles, raising further concerns over the North's evolving missile and nuclear threats.

Earlier in December, Kim Jong-un visited a military unit to instruct winter training, calling for thorough preparations "to fight." During his visit to Unit 1313 of the Korean People's Army, the young leader was briefed on "the situation of the new year combat and political drill" and then guided a firing exercise.

With a goal to achieve national reunification in 2015, North Korea has geared up for all-out war by conducting tactical training and boosting its attack capabilities, according to the Seoul government.

The North Korean military has kicked off a winter exercise at the instruction of leader Kim Jong-un. Kim chose an artillery unit for his first "field guidance" during the defense exercise season.

Kim guided a joint military drill to highlight improved combat readiness, the country's official news agency said on Nov. 23, amid the North's repeated threats of retaliation against the United Nations resolution on its human rights situation.

Kim guided the combined drill of two Korean People's Army (KPA) units that included simulations of a coastal landing and attacks on enemy troops. He instructed his country's military to conduct frequent war rehearsals to be better prepared for modern warfare.

The North Korean leader inspected a flight drill by fighter pilots, the North's state media said on Oct. 30, his third drill guidance since he resumed public appearances after a 40-day hiatus. Saying that the North's pilots are very good at flying, Kim personally boarded a fighter plane to talk with its pilot.

In summer, Kim Jong-un inspected a military landing drill, warning against any provocations in the southwestern sea border with South Korea, the North's state news wire said on July 5.

Kim guided the landing drill by the Korean People's Army's ground, naval, air and anti-air forces on an island, which involved combatants, combat ships,

bombers and transport planes, the state-run KCNA said without disclosing the date of the inspection.

In a rare conciliatory gesture on June 30, the North proposed that the two Koreas halt military hostilities, including the joint Seoul-Washington military drill Ulchi Freedom Guardian planned for later in 2014. The North has since repeated the suggestion, although it was rejected by Seoul on the following day, which cited lack of Pyongyang's sincerity.

Marking the Armistice Day, which ended the Korean War six decades ago, North Korea continued its military threats against the United States and South Korea. The North also fired a short-range missile into the East Sea on July 26, the eve of the Armistice Day.

Kim Jong-un observed the test-firing of a short-range ballistic missile from a site close to the inter-Korean border. The rocket flew across North Korea and fell into the East Sea.

Pyongyang's state media said on July 27 that the North Korean leader guided the rocket firing drill pointed at U.S. forces based in South Korea, a day before the 61st anniversary of the signing of the Armistice Agreement that ended the 1950-53 Korean War.

Kim Jong-un guided a live-shell firing exercise by a front-line military unit, the North's media reported on July 15, one day after it fired about 100 artillery shells into waters near its eastern sea border with the South.

He also ordered heightened combat readiness of the military servicemen during the guidance visit, saying that "the hostile forces are now getting more undisguised in their moves to isolate and stifle the socialist country, but the Korean people can dynamically push forward the building of a thriving nation," according to the North's state news media.

■ Military Power

As of October 2014, North Korea had 1.2 million regular service personnel, some 10,000 more than two years ago, while South Korea has around 630,000 service members, according to the 2014 defense white paper published by South Korea's Ministry of National Defense.

North Korea's regular troops comprise

▲ *North Korean leader Kim Jong-un inspects a military landing drill participated by the People's Army's ground, naval, air and anti-air forces on July 5.*

1.02 million ground forces, 60,000 naval and 120,000 air force troops, according to the defense white paper. North Korea increased the number of its air force troops by 10,000 from previous number of 110,000.

Under the KPA's General Staff, the North's ground forces have 10 regular corps and five other corps-level units -- two mechanization corps, Pyongyang Defense Command, 11th Special Forces Corps and Strategic Rocket Command. About 70% of the ground forces are deployed south of Pyongyang-Wonsan line that is bordering with South Korea.

In an apparent move to strengthen defenses along the border and to better protect its military facilities, North Korea has set up a new military unit in its North Hamgyong Province upon the instruction of its leader Kim Jong-un, according to the defense paper.

The new unit, the Border Garrison General Bureau, is not under the control of the KPA but under the supervision of the State Security Ministry, the North's top spy agency. It is presumably tasked with cracking down on defectors, guarding munitions facilities and reinforcing troop strength near the border with China and Russia.

The communist country has also continued its military build-up by securing more armored vehicles, rocket launchers and battleships, and it is presumed to be building new types of submarines such as one capable of firing ballistic missiles. The white paper says the North is improving its capability to infiltrate South Korea with small submersibles and special-purpose vessels.

Intelligence authorities are citing something called a "Very Slender Vessel," a 30 meter-long stealth ship with defenses against radar detection. The North is also continuing to build small submersibles such as a 120t salmon-class submarine and a 300t shark-class submarine.

The North also dug shelters for special troops along the frontline near the demilitarized zone. South Korean military authorities were on the alert in November when there was a sudden increase in parachute jump exercises for special troops using AN-2 planes, the aircraft for low-altitude infiltration.

The North's military also increased the number of its aircraft by 230 to 1,580 and the navy has 810 ships, mostly small and aged ones, the ministry said in the report.

Under the Navy Command, North Korea operates two fleet commands of West Sea and East Sea, 13 squadrons, 40 naval bases and also two maritime sniper brigades capable of conducting special warfare.

Under the North's Air Force Command, there are four air divisions, two tactical transport brigades, two air force sniper brigades, and some air defense forces. North Korea's air forces are deployed in the four large spheres of southwest, northwest, east and northeast.

There has been no change in the number of North Korean submarines (about 70). But it seems that the regime has built several new ones, including those capable of carrying new torpedoes and even ballistic missiles, the white paper adds.

According to various reports, the North is estimated to have 70 submarines and midget subs, 260 landing ships, 30 mine sweepers, 30 support vessels, 820 fighter jets, 30 surveillance aircrafts, 330 parachute drop aircrafts and 170 training jets.

The North has increased the operations of its submarine fleets and the training of coastal artillery units, conducting amphibious landing operations targeting the South in the past years.

The communist state has already deployed about 70 air-cushion vehicles on its west coast and 60 of the amphibious vehicles in the east at its four hovercraft bases. Pyongyang has also put in place 200-ton new combatant ships with guns of longer ranges, while adding one or two submarine midgets every year to the fleet of 70 submarines.

Although North Korea's air force planes are mostly obsolete and outdated, some 820 fighters including MiG-21 are deployed at bases south of the Pyongyang-Wonsan line that is closer to inter-Korean border.

The North has stockpiled about 4,200 tanks. Although its number of artillery pieces changed little over the past years, its 170mm self-propelled artillery and 240mm multiple rocket launchers deployed on the front line are capable of carrying out a "massive surprise bombardment" on the South Korean capital of Seoul and its neighboring areas.

South Korea's military sources said the North Korean Army has deployed about 900 new tanks equipped with improved armament in the last nine years to modernize its aging vehicles. The new tanks, known as the "Chonma-ho 5" (sky horse) and the "Songun-ho" (military-first), are equipped with an advanced fire control system and turret guns, an upgrade compared to the Pokpung-ho (storm) tank, which was first revealed in October 2010 during a military parade.

The Chonma-ho 5 is the latest variant of North Korea's main battle tank, the Chonma, which was built based on the Soviet T-62 tank. "The North Korean military has deployed 900 new tanks from 2005 until 2013," according to a military source.

Beginning in the late 1970s, Pyongyang started to produce a modified version of the 115mm-gunned T-62 tank, and since then it is believed to have made considerable modifications to the basic Soviet and Chinese designs.

Military officials in Seoul said the North is increasingly focused on unconventional or "asymmetric" weapons, such as improvised explosives or low-cost missiles because the regime knows its aging conventional weapons are no match for the technologically superior South Korean and U.S. forces.

■ Strategic Weapons Development

North Korea appears to have achieved "a significant level" of technology to miniaturize nuclear warheads to fit on its ballistic missiles that could potentially reach the United States mainland.

The assessment was included in the 2014 edition of the South Korea's defense ministry's biennial white paper released on Jan. 6, 2015.

North Korea started to develop missiles in 1976 with a Scud-B missile it obtained from Egypt and succeeded in the development of an ICBM-level rocket in 36 years. The North first produced a Scud-B type missile in 1984 and test-fired a Scud-C type missile with a range of 500 km in 1986. It has deployed the missiles and sold some to foreign countries since 1988.

In the 1990s, North Korea made a strategic deployment of Rodong missile with a range of 1,300km. Then at the end of 1990s, it began to develop new ballistic missile named "Musudan" with a range over 3,000km that could reach the U.S. bases in Guam in the Pacific.

Based on the experiences of developing Scud missiles, North Korea developed the Rodong-1 missile with a range of 1,000km, which could strike Japan, in 1990. North Korea surprised the world in August 1998 by test-firing the Taepodong-1 missile, the Unha-1 rocket, which went more than 1,600 km, flying past Japan.

On July 4, 2006, North Korea fired the more advanced Taepodong-2 missile but it crashed within a minute after liftoff from the North's eastern coastal village of Musudan-ri.

North Korea launched the Unha-2 rocket at the launch site of Musudan-ri on April 5, 2009. North Korea claimed the rocket successfully put a satellite into orbit. South Korea, however, described the launch as a failure, although experts said the North appeared to have upgraded its missile technology and capabilities considerably. On April 13, 2012, the country fired off a long-range rocket, the Unha-3 rocket, from the Tongchang-ri launch site. The three-stage craft exploded in mid-air and crashed into the sea shortly after takeoff.

On Dec. 12, 2012, North Korea succeeded in launching a long-range rocket from the Tonchang-ri launch site in North Pyongan Province. Experts warned the Unha-3 rocket is believed to have a range of some 10,000km, which means it could fly as far as Los Angeles. Now, North Korea is presumed to have the technological prowess to develop a 10,000km-range intercontinental ballistic missile.

North Korea independently built most of the key parts of its long-range rocket launched in December 2012, with the exception of some commercially available materials imported from overseas, experts said. The fact that North Korea is close to developing long-range missiles capable of carrying nuclear weapons deepens security concerns on the Korean Peninsula and in other regions of the world.

Pyongyang claims the launch was aimed at placing an earth observation satellite in space, but many in the international community believe it was a disguised test of ballistic missile technology. The U.N. Security Council adopted a binding resolution against North Korea on Jan. 22, 2013, condemning its December rocket launch and expanding sanctions, which invited strong repercussion from North Korea.

The 15-member council voted unanimously to approve the 20-point resolution which calls for freezing the assets of six more North Korean entities, including the Korean Committee for Space Technology and the Bank of East Land, and a travel ban on four additional officials.

It also warned of "significant action" in the event of a future launch or nuclear test by North Korea. North Korea pledged on Jan. 23, 2013 to end any efforts at denuclearizing the Korean Peninsula, just hours after the U.N. Security Council adopted the resolution.

Despite repeated international warnings, North Korea carried out a long-threatened nuclear test on Feb. 12, 2013, exactly two months after its long-range rocket launch that sparked international condemnation and tightened sanctions.

Seoul's Korea Meteorological Administration detected a magnitude 4.9 tremor with its epicenter located in Kilju County. The area, located in North Hamgyong Province in the northeast of the socialist country, is home to the North's Punggye-ri nuclear test complex that was used in the 2006 and 2009 nuclear tests.

After the detonation, North Korea claimed that its third nuclear test forced the international community to recognize it as a "strategic rocket and nuclear weapons state."

Seoul's claim in the 2014 defense paper that North Korea has refined technology to miniaturize nuclear weapons is the first time the ministry has made the claim in such an emphatic form, although it admitted there are a lot of provisons.

The previous 2012 Defense White Paper merely mentioned the North's two nuclear tests in 2006 and 2009 but did not offer any evaluation of the technology to produce viable warheads for missiles. The 2014 white paper used the term "North Korea's nuclear weapons" for the first time, since there has long been a polite fiction that the North is not officially a nuclear-armed state.

The white paper also says that the maximum range of the North's Taepodong-2 missiles has increased from 6,700km to 10,000km. With a range of 6,700km, a North Korean missile could reach Alaska; and with a range of 10,000km, it could hit the west coast of the U.S. mainland.

Some nuclear experts even said that North Korea's nuclear stockpile could expand to as many as 100 weapons by 2020. Joel Wit, the chief analyst running the website 38 North at Johns Hopkins University, announced the projections during a seminar in February 2015, saying Pyongyang is currently believed to have 10-16 nuclear weapons, six to eight of them based on plutonium and four to eight based on weapons-grade uranium.

Wit also said the North is believed to have miniaturized the plutonium-based weapons enough to be mounted on medium-range Rodong missiles, which can strike South Korea and Japan, and on Taepodong-2 missiles that can achieve intercontinental ranges.

DIPLOMACY

■ Overview

North Korea has diplomatic relations with other countries based on the principle of self-reliance, peace and friendship. During the Cold War era, North Korea made efforts to have closer ties with socialist and nonaligned countries such as ones in Africa. However, the collapse of the Soviet socialist block at the turn of the 1990s, the North changed its diplomatic policy. It pushed for the improvement of relations with the United States and other Western countries.

North Korea's effort to establish diplomatic relations with the U.S. have made no progress due to its ambitious nuclear program. In October 2002, relations between the two countries turned sour because of the revelation by the U.S. of the North's covet nuclear program. This also put a crimp on the development of relations between the North and the European Union, with which it had contacts since 1998.

Pyongyang and Washington sought to improve their relations following the North's first nuclear test in 2006. But the North's second atomic denotation in 2009 and the third one in 2013 worsened their relations. The two countries remained chilly in 2014.

Pyongyang's relations with Beijing also underwent ups and downs due to the North's long-range rocket launches and nuclear tests. China joined the U.N. sanctions on the North's provocative actions, but the two allies maintained amicable ties in various fields.

From 2000, North Korea established diplomatic ties with the European Union and its member countries, but it has yet to set up diplomatic ties with Japan. According to Seoul's Statistics Office, North Korea was maintaining, as of December 2012, normal diplomatic relations with 162 countries and 323 international organizations.

■ **Relations with the U.S.**

Human right issues had a significance influence on the relations between Pyongyang and Washington for all of 2014. The North's human right issues came to the surface after the Commission of Inquiry on Human Rights in North Korea released its report on the North's human rights abuse on Feb 17 after a yearlong probe.

The report accused Pyongyang of making "systematic, widespread and grave violations of human rights." It added that North Korean leaders' crimes against humanity should be dealt with by the International Criminal Court (ICC).

The pressure from the U.N. agency to improve the human rights conditions of North Korea became the key issue of the relations with the North and the U.S. as the isolated country had maintained that the U.S. masterminded the international move to put pressure on the North to make its human right conditions better.

On Feb. 21, four days after the release of the report, an unidentified spokesman for the North's Foreign Ministry said the report was fabricated based on fallacious testimony North Korean defectors and criminals fleeing from the North. The

spokesman said in a statement released by the (North) Korean Central News Agency (KCNA) that the U.S. should back down from raising issue with the North's human right conditions.

Despite the North's strong reaction, the international community tightened its grip on the country's human right circumstances. On Nov. 18, the U.N. Third Committee passed a European Union-authored resolution, which for the first time called for the referral of North Korea's human rights violations to the International Criminal Court.

▲ A mass rally is underway at the Kim Il-sung Square in Pyongyang on Nov. 25, to denounce the United States for initiating the U.N. resolution adopted recently to sanction North Korea for its human rights violations.

In response to the move, North Korea on Nov. 23 refuted the resolution on its human rights conditions, threatening merciless retaliation against the U.S. and its allies that Pyongyang says were behind the vote at the international body. The North's reaction came from the North's powerful National Defense Commission (NDC). The resolution called on the U.N. Security Council to refer the country to the ICC over its dire human rights situation.

The U.N. General Assembly on Dec. 18 passed the resolution calling for the referral of Pyongyang's alleged human rights violations to the International Criminal Court (ICC) on Thursday by a vote of 116 to 20. Fifty-three countries abstained.

Another thorny issue between the two countries in 2014 was a U.S. comedy movie featuring an assassination attempt on the North's leader Kim Jong-un. North Korea had issued strong warnings against the release of the movie since the film's U.S. distributor Columbia Pictures released a trailer of the movie "The Interview" in June.

On June 25 the North's foreign ministry condemned the release of the trailer as "the most undisguised terrorism" and threatened to take "a strong and merciless countermeasure" if the movie is released in theaters.

North Korea also filed a protest with the United Nations against the U.S. movie, calling on the U.S. government to ban the release of the movie, a U.S. report said. In a letter sent to U.N. Secretary General Ban Ki-moon on June 27, North Korean Ambassador to the U.N., Ja Song-nam, called the movie "The Interview" an insult to the North Korean leader, the Washington-based Voice of America (VOA) said.

Pyongyang's hysterical reaction delayed the release of the movie to December from October. In November, the computer systems of Sony Pictures Entertainment, which produced the film, were hacked by the "Guardians of Peace," a group the FBI believed had connected with North Korea. U.S. President Barack Obama said on Dec. 19 the United States "will respond proportionally" against North Korea for its destructive cyberattacks on Sony Pictures.

Despite the group's threat of terrorist attack against cinemas that play The Interview, the movie was released at about 300 cinemas across the U.S. on Dec. 24.

The detention of two Americans by the North in 2014 raised tension between the two countries. North Korea detained two U.S. tourists-- Miller Matthew Todd and Jeffrey Fowle. Thanks to the U.S. government's effort to release its nationals via the Swedish embassy to Pyongyang, Jeffrey Fowle was freed on Oct. 21. However, Miller Matthew Todd and Kenneth Bae, who had been detained since November 2012, were not released until Director of U.S. National Intelligence James R. Clapper visited the country on Nov. 9.

After its third nuclear test in February 2013, the North hinted at an additional

nuclear test, tightening tensions with the U.S. in 2014. But no additional nuclear test occurred.

In 2014, Pyongyang and Washington failed to hold government-level talks. North Korea's Foreign Minister Ri Su-yong, however, visited New York on Sept. 21 for the first time in 15 years, when then Foreign Minister Paek Nam-sun made a visit there in 1999. While in New York, Ri attended the 69th U.N. General Assembly and denounced the pressure from the international community on the improvement of its human right conditions as little more than a political campaign.

Despite the stalled relations, two-way trade rose sharply in 2014. U.S. shipments to North Korea reached US$24 million, up three fold from US$6.6 million in 2013, but U.S. imports from the North had no record. U.S. exports to the North were mainly relief goods such as medicine and medical supplies.

■ Relations with China

China has remained North Korea's only ally in the post-Cold War era, although their relations turned sour after South Korea established diplomatic relations with Beijing in 1992. For decades, the Pyongyang-Beijing ties became close, lips-to-teeth relations when China dispatched 1 million troops to save the North, whose troops were overwhelmed by the 16-nation United Nations allied forces a few months after the North started the Korean War in June 1950.

China sent forces across the Yalu River that forms its border with North Korea on Oct. 19, 1950, about four months after the Korean War broke out, having earlier warned U.S.-led forces that it would intervene if they crossed the 38th parallel and pressed north toward the Sino-North Korean border.

In 2013, relations between the two countries turned chilly again after the North's third underground nuclear test in February. In protest, China joined the international community in imposing harsher sanctions on the North, including the suspension of Chinese banks' remittance to North Korea.

In this critical situation, North Korea sent key military official Choe Ryong-hae to Beijing as a special envoy of Kim

Jong-un from May 22-24. Choe delivered a letter from Kim to Chinese President Xi Jinping, in which Kim underlined the need to foster and consolidate the traditional friendship between the two countries. But the execution of pro-China Jang Song-taek, uncle of Kim Jong-un, in December left the two countries' relations in the doldrums.

In 2014, North Korea has made no improvement in relations with China. In July, Chinese President Xi Jinping visited South Korea, marking the first time that a Chinese leader visited the South ahead of the North. On July 3, the Chinese president arrived in Seoul and held a summit with his South Korean counterpart Park Geun-hye. During the summit, the leaders agreed to disapprove the North's nuclear weapons program.

In response to the agreement, the North showed a sensitive reaction via the statement by its highest power body National Defense Commission on July 21. In the statement, the North criticized China saying "Some backbone-lacking countries are blindly following the stinky bottom of the U.S., also struggling to embrace (South Korean President) Park Geun-hye who came to a pathetic state of being."

The chilly relations between the two countries were revealed in their trade in 2014. According to official statistics by the Chinese government, China's exports of crude to North Korea remained at zero. It was believed that China might have stopped providing crude to the North after it made a third nuclear test in February.

Two-way trade between the two countries fell unusually in 2014. Their trade dropped 2.4% to US$6.39 billion. The North's shipment of hard coal to China, which had been the North's top export goods to the neighbouring country, fell in 8 years in 2014. According to data by the Korea International Trade Association (KITA), the North's exports of hard coal to China reached 1.13 billion, down 17.6% from 1.37 billion in 2013.

Despite the chilled relations, the exchange of the two countries' high-level governmental officials took place in 2014. As part of efforts to seek ways to resolve the North's nuclear standoff with the United States, Chinese Vice Foreign Minister Liu Zhenmin began a four-day visit to North Korea on Feb. 17 according to the Norths' request.

One month later on March 17, China's top nuclear envoy, Wu Dawei visited Pyongyang, while Choi Son-hui, director general of the North Korean Foreign Ministry traveled to Beijing on March 25. China showed opposition against the anti-Pyongyang human rights campaign, which had prevailed in 2014 in the international community.

■ **Relations with Japan**

During the three-day talks starting on May 28, 2014 in Stockholm, Sweden, North Korea and Japan reached an agreement that Japan will lift its own sanction against the North, while the North will resume the investigation of the Japanese abductees by its agents.

North Korea had previously said the abduction issue was settled. In 2002, North Korea admitted to abducting 13 Japanese nationals in the 1970s and '80s. The North then let five of them return home but said eight others had died, though Japanese officials believe that some of them are still alive. One of those Japanese who North Korea claimed to have died is Megumi Yokota, who was abducted in 1977 at the age of 13.

After years of enmity since Korea's liberation from Japanese colonial rule, Pyongyang-Tokyo relations marked a new momentum in 2002 when North Korean leader Kim Jong-il and Japanese Prime Minister Junichiro Koizumi held their first summit on Sept. 17 in Pyongyang, where they made their "Pyongyang Declaration."

During the summit meeting, Kim Jong-il admitted North Korea's abduction of Japanese citizens in the past. North Korea admitted to abducting 13 Japanese nationals in the 1970s and '80s. The North then let five of them return home but said eight others died, though Japanese officials believe that some of them are still alive.

The summit also produced a four-point joint declaration, which called for, among other things, the resumption of their talks for diplomatic normalization. North Korea and Japan have never had diplomatic ties, and the abduction issue has long been a key stumbling block in normalizing their bilateral relations.

On July 1, 2014, North Korea started its full-scale investigation on its abduction of Japanese citizens by forming a special investigation committee. On the same day, Japan decided to lift part of its restrictions against the North.

The conciliatory gestures by the two countries were followed by the meeting of North Korean Foreign Minister Ri Su-yong and his counterpart Fumio Kishida at the ASEAN Regional Forum (ARF), Asia's biggest annual security conference that brought together top diplomats from 26 Asia-Pacific countries and the European Union held on Aug. 10, 2014 in Myanmar.

On October 27, a Japanese government delegation led by Junichi Ihara, chief of the Asia and Oceania Bureau of the Ministry of Foreign Affairs, arrived in Pyongyang to receive a briefing on the progress of the investigation on the Japanese abductees from the North.

Along with the government-level contacts, nongovernmental exchanges between the two countries were busy in 2014. On July 10, a Japanese Diet delegation headed by Kanji Inoki, member of the House of Councilors, visited Pyongyang and went around the Kaesong Industrial Complex.

The delegation visit followed a international pro wrestling contest on Aug. 30 in Pyongyang. Kanji Inoki played a pivotal role in arranging the rare event to take place. The rare event in Pyongyang was held for a two-day run with pro wrestlers and mixed martial artists including Bob Sapp of the U.S. and Jerome Le Banner of France in participation.

On Sept. 8, Masaki Fukuyama, president of Japan's Kyodo news agency also arrived in Pyongyang. The visit comes two days after Ho Jong-man, the head of a pro-North Korean organization in Japan, arrived in Pyongyang in his first trip to the North in eight years. In 2014, Japan allowed officials of the General Association of Korean Residents in Tokyo to visit the North as part of a deal between North Korea and Japan on the abduction issue.

Despite thawing conditions, the North maintained its criticism over Japan's

military and economic pressure on it. North Korea urged Japan on May 16 to stop seeking a greater security role abroad by exercising the right to collective self-defense, calling the move "a first step to overseas invasions." In a press conference a day earlier, Japanese Prime Minister Shinzo Abe called for a review of the interpretation of its pacifist constitution to permit the use of collective self-defense.

The move "is needed to realize its ambition of overseas expansion and re-invasion," the Rodong Sinmun, the main newspaper of the ruling Workers' Party of (North) Korea, said in a commentary. "It is needless to say that it will be the first step of Japan's overseas invasion to achieve its long-sought ambition to rule the world," the newspaper added.

▪ Relations with Russia

Pyongyang kept close ties with Moscow in 2014. Due to the sour relations with Beijing, North Korea approached Russia which sought to expand its influence on the Korean Peninsula. They made significant progress in various sectors such as politics, economy and culture. Their high-ranking officials visited Pyongyang and Moscow in turn. In early February, the North's titular head Kim Yong-nam attended the opening ceremony of the Sochi Winter Olympics.

In Sochi, Kim met with Russian President Vladimir Putin.

Kim's visit to Sochi was followed by the North's Trade Minister Ri Yong-nam's trip to Russia in May. Pak Myong-chol, president of the Supreme Court of North Korea, travelled to Moscow to discuss human rights and terror issues with Russia in June.

North Korean Foreign Minister Ri Su-yong stopped by Moscow on Sept. 30 after attending the U.N. General Assembly held in New York. While staying in Moscow for 10 days, Ri held meetings with Russia's high-ranking officials, including Foreign Minister Sergey Lavrov.

In November, Choe Ryong-hae, a governing party secretary, visited Russia as a special envoy of North Korean leader Kim Jong-un as part of efforts to improve relations. Choe's weeklong trip to Moscow, Khabarovsk and Vladivostok was highlighted by his meetings with President Vladimir Putin and Foreign Minister Sergey Lavrov in the Russian capital.

▲ Choe Ryong-hae (R), the Workers' Party of (North) Korea secretary, meets with Russian President Vladimir Putin at the Kremlin in Moscow on Nov. 18. North Korea's official Korean Central News Agency reported on Nov. 19 that Choe delivered North Korean leader Kim Jong-un's personal letter to Putin without elaborating on the content of the letter.

During his stay in Russia from Nov. 17-24, the North's special envoy to Russia met with Russian President Vladimir Putin in Moscow on Nov. 18 and delivered a hand-written letter from the North's leader Kim Jong-un.

The contents of the letter were unknown. But a Russian news agency quoted Putin as having said that deeper relations between Russia and North Korea are conducive to boosting regional security and stability, a day after he met with Choe.

"The further deepening of political ties and trade-economic co-operation undoubtedly serves the interests of the peoples in both countries and ensuring regional security and stability," Putin was quoted by the Itar-Tass news agency as saying.

President Putin and Choe agreed to improve political, economic and military exchanges between the two countries in 2015, according to a report released by the KCNA on Nov. 25.

Choe and Russian Foreign Minister Sergey Lavrov also decided to step up efforts to restart the six-way talks without any preconditions and discussed ways to set the stage for them, the KCNA said.

Choe was accompanied by Vice Foreign Minister Kim Kye-gwan, Vice Economy Minister Ri Kwang-gun and No Kwang-chol, vice chief of the General Staff of the North's military.

North Korea replaced its ambassador to Russia to Kim Hyong-jun from Kim Yong-jae in August in eight years since September 2006.

■ **Relations with Europe**

In 2014, the relations between North Korea and the European Union (EU) were deteriorated due to EU-led human right campaign to put pressure on the improvement of the North's human rights issue. Japan and the EU presented a resolution on the North's human rights situation to the United Nations Human Rights Council (UNHRC) on March 20. On March 31, the North's Foreign Ministry showed strong disapproval of it.

When the U.N. Third Committee passed a European Union-authored resolution, which for the first time called for the referral of North Korea's human rights violations to the International Criminal Court on Nov. 18, the North accused the EU of being a pawn of the U.S.

In 2000, North Korea began to establish diplomatic ties with European countries, starting with Italy, a key member of the EU and a member of the Group of Seven, known as the G-7. Normal relations with Britain came in December, with the Netherlands and Belgium in January the next year, with Spain in February, with Germany, Luxemburg and Greece in March, and with the EU in May. However, both sides' relations have remained meager due to the North's nuclear tests and dismal human rights conditions.

As part of efforts to improve the sour relations with the EU, Kang Sok-ju, the secretary handling international relations within North Korea's ruling Workers' Party, visited Germany, Belgium, Switzerland and Italy in September.

However, the EU retained its limitations on the operation of the North's national airline Air Koryo within Europe in 2014 following 2013. In 2011, the North's airline was banned from operating in Europe as it did not meet international safety standards.

▪ Relations with Other Countries

In 2014, North Korea stepped up the relations with its traditional ally Mongolia. Kang Sok-ju, the secretary handling international relations within North Korea's ruling Workers' Party met with Mongolian President Tsakhia Elbegdorj in Ulan Bator. They agreed to enhance their bilateral relations.

The Mongolian president visited the North in October 2013, marking the first time a foreign head of state visited the isolationist country since Kim Jong-un took power. But there was no report of a summit between the two leaders in Pyongyang.

North Korea also sought to improve relations with Southeast Asian countries in 2014. The North's Foreign Minister Ri Su-yong embarked on his tour to five Southeast Asian countries--Laos, Vietnam, Myanmar, Indonesia and Singapore--on Aug. 2. Ri said at a ministerial meeting of the ASEAN Regional Forum on Aug. 10 held in Myanmar that the country will make every possible effort to preserve peace and security in Asia.

The North sent a high-ranking delegation to the Middle East and Africa in 2014. On April 28, an economic delegation led by Vice Minister of Foreign Trade Ri Myong-san left Pyongyang to participate in the fourth meeting of the Inter-governmental Joint Committee of North Korea and Nigeria and to visit various countries of Africa including Angola.

On June 5, Foreign Minister Ri Su-yong and Gambian Foreign Minister Aboubacar Abudoullah Senghore held talks in the capital of Banjul. In October, the North's titular head Kim Yong-nam made his visit to African countries such as Ethiopia, Sudan and Congo.

Along with the enhancement of the relations with African countries, the North made efforts to beef up ties with the Middle Eastern countries. Foreign Minister Ri Su-yong visited Syria on June 18. He met with Syrian President Bashar al-Assad during his visit to the country.

An economic delegation of North Korea led by Trade Minister Ri Yong-nam visited Syria for an economic cooperation in mid May. A delegation of the Supreme People's Assembly (SPA), led by Deputy Kim Wan-su, presidium member of the Central Committee of the Democratic Front for the Reunification of Korea, travelled to the country in June.

Foreign Minister Ri Su-yong left Pyongyang on Sept. 11 to take part in the 53rd meeting of the Asian-African Legal Consultative Organization to be held in Iran and pay an official goodwill visit to Iran.

Meanwhile, North Korea named Jang Myong-ho its new ambassador to Syria, replacing Choe Su-hon in April, who started his diplomatic career in 1988 and had served in the post since 2008.

ECONOMY

▪ Overview

North Korea, in the third year of Kim Jong-un's reign, tried to expand the introduction of market economy and sought expansion of cooperation with foreign economies in 2014. In a letter to participants in the national meeting of sub-workteam heads in the field of agriculture in February, Kim stressed the achievements of a farming management system involving handing out a plot of land, called "Pojon," to small sub-workteams, usually comprising a family unit. which expanded individual's rights to dispose of farm products,

"Egalitarianism in the realm of distribution has no connection to socialist principles and has a detrimental impact that would reduce farmers' productivity." North Korea reportedly took an economic measure to expand autonomy of economic entities on May 30 and continued policies to expand international economic cooperation.

North Korea launched the Ministry of External Economic Affairs on June 16 in order to take care of external trade affairs by combining the Joint Venture and Investment Commission and the State Economic Development Committee with the Ministry of Foreign Trade. The North also designated six additional economic development districts to bring the number of such zones to 19.

While maintaining distance with China which has been alienated since the execution of Jang Song-thaek, the pro-Chinese uncle of Kim Jong-un, in December 2013, Pyongyang increased economic cooperation with Moscow substantially.

North Korea agreed with Russia to install or renovate railways in the North worth about US$25 billion and construction of railway linking Pyongyang and Moscow was under way.

North Korea utilized the tourism industry as a means of inducing foreign capital and activating the economy. North Korea offered new tourism products featuring golf and mountaineering, and opened a college to train tourism experts in Pyongyang. To allure overseas Koreans to visit North Korea, it launched domestic flights from Pyongyang to Hamgyong and Ryanggang provinces.

North Korea engaged in various construction works to build homes and other facilities for its people and launched large-scale propaganda that the constructions were thanks to the leader's policy of taking care of people.

Homes for scientists, apartments for educators of the Kim Chaek College of Technology and a rest facility for Yonpung scientists have been built one by one and the works were attributed to the Party's policy of regarding science and technology as important.

Kim Jong-un also made frequent visits to construction sites of an orphanage in Pyongyang and Songdowon international camping ground in order to spread his image as a leader who cares most about the people.

North Korea caused friction with South Korea in the operation of the inter-Korean factory park in Kaesong by unilaterally removing a 5% cap in the raise of wages for North Korean workers at the complex. About 120 South Korean small and medium-sized companies employ more than 50,000 North Korean workers at the joint industrial park.

■ Economic Growth

North Korean economy grows 1.1% in 2013. The Bank of Korea said North Korean economy recorded positive growth for the third straight year in 2013. North Korea's real gross national income (GNI) was estimated at 33.8 trillion won, one 42.6th of South Korea's GNI totaling 1,044.1 trillion won. Per capita GNI of North Korea was 1,379,000 won, one 20.8th of South Korea's 28,695,000 won,

recording a wider gap from 2002, according to the South's central bank.

The size of North Korea's external trade, excluding the trade with South Korea, rose 7.8% in 2013 to US$7.34 billion. Exports totaled US$4.13 billion, recording a 5% growth thanks to the growth of plastic goods (27.5%) and textiles (204%).

The growth rate of gross domestic product (GDP) in North Korea was estimated at 1.1%. The country saw its GDP grow 0.8% in 2011 and 1.3% in 2012. It recorded a minus growth of 0.9% in 2009 and 0.5% in 2010.

By industry, production of agriculture and fisheries, which accounted for 22.4% of the North's nominal GDP, rose by 1.9%. The livestock industry's production dropped but that of agriculture rose thanks to favorable weather. The mining industry also saw a growth of 2.1% thanks to the favorable production of coal and iron ore. Production in the manufacturing sector, which accounted for 22.1% of GDP, rose 1.1% while the production of the service industry (30% of the GDP) grew 0.3% from the previous year.

The volume of inter-Korean trade in 2013 dwindled by 42.4% from the previous year to US$1.14 billion, due to suspension of the Kaesong industrial park from April to September. Shipment to the North reduced by 42% while shipment to the South dropped 42.7%.

■ External Trade

Sharp growth of grain imports from China North Korea imported 58,387t of grains from China in the first half of 2014 or 8,730t a month on average, according to the (South) Korea International Trade Association and private think tank GS&J on Oct. 1. North Korea's grain imports from China rose sharply in the last half to 19,559t in July, and 25,217t in August. The high growth of grain imports in the second half was due to the unfavorable harvest at the end of June and the expectation for poor crops in August.

Imports of wheat flour accounted for 46.6% of all grain imports as of August, followed by rice at 42.3% and corn at 8.9%. The portion of corn dropped from 2013 while that of rice rose. North Korea's grain imports in the first eight months of 2014 totaled 115,337t, compared with 174,020t for the same period a year ago, showing the North's food grain situation improved from the previous year.

North Korea's imports of chemical fertilizer from China in the first eight months of 2014 also decreased 37% to 115,337t from 183,639t for the same period in 2013.

Sharp rise in digital TVs from China
According to statistics from KITA on May 25, China exported LCD TV sets worth US$4.82 million in April 2014. The figure is the fifth largest of North Korea's import items from China, after gasoline worth 12.58 million and diesel oil at US$7.73 million. North Korea's digital TV imports from China in the first four months of the year amounted to US$17.67 million, representing a growth of 338% from US$4.03 million in the same period in 2013.

Rare earth exports to China North Korea exported rare earth ores worth US$550,000 to China in May 2014 and US$1.33 million in June, according to KITA on July 27. North Korea first exported rare earth ores to China in January 2013 but had suspended the export until May 2014. North Korea boasts its ample reserve of rare earth.

Imports of Chinese rice grows sharply
According to statistics from KITA on Aug. 25, China exported 11,780 tons of rice worth US$7,019,738 to North Korea in July, 2014, up 115% from a year ago worth US$3,271,067. The figure is the biggest in terms of monthly rice imports since Kim Jong-un took power in 2012. China's grain exports to North Korea in the first half of 2014 totaled 58,387 tons or only 47% from the same period of a year ago. The growth of North Korea's rice imports from China may be intended to stabilize domestic rice prices.

Exports of anthracite coal to China
Statistics from KITA on Jan. 24 showed North Korea's exports of anthracite coal to China in 2013 totaled US$1,37 million in 2013, up 15.5% from US$1,19 million in 2012. North Korea's anthracite coal exports to China has risen for the seventh consecutive year since 2007. The total volume of the North's anthracite coal exports to China was 16,494,000 tons in 2013, up 39% in 2012.

■ **Construction**
Residential quarters for scientists and educators The Korean Central News Agency (KCNA) reported on Oct. 17 that the modern Wisong (satellite) Scientists Residential Quarter was dedicated in the Unjong science area in Pyongyang on the occasion of the 69th founding anniversary of the Workers' Party of Korea (WPK).

The residential quarter has multi-story town houses on 24 blocks, schools, hospital, nursery, kindergarten, various welfare service facilities and other public buildings and parks, it said. The Wisong Scientists Residential Quarter, the KCNA said, is the great creation of the WPK's idea and policy of attaching importance to science and technology.

North Korean media also reported a dedication ceremony for apartment complex for educators of Kim Chaek University of Technology. Construction of the apartment complex started in August 2013 at the instruction of Kim Jong-un.

The KCNA said a dedication ceremony was held for the Scientists' Rest Home in Yonphung, built on the picturesque shore of Lake Yonphung, on Oct. 24. Kim Jong-un visited the place two days before the ceremony to show his special concern for the welfare of scientists and technicians.

Construction of welfare facilities for children North Korea completed remodelling of a children's camping grounds at Songdowon on May 2. The remodelling work was completed after six months by a large number of soldiers at the instruction of Kim Jong-un. Dedication ceremonies were held for Pyongyang Baby Home and Orphanage were held on Oct. 27.

Construction of social infrastructure
An expressway linking the North's eastern coastal city of Wonsan and Hamhung was newly confirmed in 2014. Ahn Byung-min, a researcher for the Korea Transport Institute, said on Nov. 23 that North Korea mentioned the existence of the Wonsan-Hamhung highway for the first time in a document released to foreign investors.

North Korea announced a plan to renovate the Pyongyang railway station in January. The Pyongyang Station is a four-story building on a 3,500㎡ lot. The building was completed in 1958 and was designated as one of the 10 biggest buildings in Pyongyang by Kim Il-sung. North Korea also dedicated two hydro power plants on the Orangchon Stream in North Hamgyong Province and on the Yesung River in North Hwanghae Province.

Sports and Shopping Facilities North Korea started construction of a large-scale shopping mall in Pyongyang with Chinese capital, Russia's Itar-Tass news agency reported on Jan. 17. A ground-breaking ceremony for the shopping mall was attended by Kim Ki-sok, head of North Korea's State Economic Development Committee, senior officials of the Great China International Group and officials of Chinese embassy in Pyongyang, according to the Russian news agency.

North Korea is also constructing new buildings for the head offices of the Central Bank of Korea and Northeast Asian Bank.

An athletes' village was completed at the Chongchun Street in Pyongyang on March 19 after renovation work at the order of Kim Jong-un.

▪ Revision of Organizations, Systems

The Ministry of External Economic Affairs was launched on June 16 by combining the Joint Venture and Investment Commission and the State Economic Development Committee with the Ministry of Foreign Trade. The purpose of the new ministry was to take care of external trade affairs so as to support development of the economy.

Issuance of new 5,000-won bill A Chinese source, quoting a North Korean trade official, said on July 30 that North Korea distributed new 5,000-won bill from that day. The source said the existing 5,000-won bill has the portrait of only Kim Il-sung, but the new bill has portraits of Kim Il-sung and Kim Jong-il. The issuance of the new bill was intended to strengthen the idolization of the Kim family after the death of Kim Jong-il.

▪ Reshuffle of Ministers

North Korea conducted a series of reshuffles of key Cabinet officials following the execution of Jang Song-thaek on Dec. 12, 2013. North Korea's state media

on Jan. 5 introduced Mun Myong-hak as the head of the Ministry of Coal Industry.

Although little was known about the details of the reshuffle, North Korea watchers in Seoul speculated it may be related to the execution of Jang. North Korea condemned Jang for selling the country's precious mineral resources, including coal, at dirt-cheap prices.

The news of the new coal industry minister comes after the North confirmed change of the metal industry minister to Kim Yong-gwang from Han Hyo-yon, which was reported by the North's Korean Central TV Broadcasting Station on Jan. 2.

North Korea replaced its commerce minister in March, according to state-run media on April 5. Pyongyang Broadcasting Station reported that new Commerce Minister Kim Kyong-nam was in attendance at a food festival marking the birth anniversary of the country's founder. Kim replaced Ri Song-ho.

Pak Pong-ju cabinet retained The first session of the 13th Supreme People's Assembly retained Premier Pak Pong-ju and most of economy ministers on April 9. North Korea appointed Kim Dok-hun, Lim Chul-ung and Choi Young-gon as vice premiers under a decree of the SPA, the North state media reported on May 1.

Minister of external economic affairs North Korea had not revealed the head of the Ministry of External Trade Affairs when the ministry was launched in June. The KCNA confirmed Ri Ryong-nam as the minister of the new ministry in a report on July 15.

▪ Tourism Promotion

North Korea offered new tourism products as a means of earning more dollars in 2014. The KCNA said a ceremony took place on Oct. 30 to open the Chongsu Tourist Zone in North Pyongan Province.

A golf tour was introduced in January by Uri Tours based in the United States which allows tourists to enjoy 2.5 rounds of golf and tour Pyongyang, Kaesong and the demilitarized zone for three days.

Young Pioneer Tours, based in Beijing, said on March 12 that foreign tourists can stay a night in Sinuiju for sightseeing of northern North Korea. Previously only a one-day tour of Sinuiju has been allowed for foreigners.

North Korea in May also launched a one-day bus tour program for Chinese tourists to visit Hoeryong City of North Hamgyong Province. Tours of cities using trains and a city tour of Pyongyang aboard street cars were also launched.

North Korea restarted some of its regular domestic flight routes for the first time in years, according to Young Pioneer Tours on July 15, in another indication that the impoverished country was making efforts to boost tourism. Previously, foreign tourists had to charter flights to fly between cities, a journey which could take up to two days by rail or road, it said.

■ **Economic Development Zones**

North Korea designated six more economic development zones in 2014, including ones in the capital city of Pyongyang and a county near the border with South Korea, bringing to 19 the total number of economic zones in the country. The North also renamed a special economic zone in Sinuiju City, North Phyongan Province, an international economic zone.

"It was decided in the DPRK to establish economic development zones in some areas of Pyongyang, South Hwanghae Province, Nampho City, South and North Pyongan provinces," the KCNA said in an English-language dispatch on July 23, referring to the country by its official name, Democratic People's Republic of Korea.

The capital Pyongyang will host the Unjong technology development zone while an eco-friendly zone, export processing zone, tourism development zone, industrial development zone and agricultural development zone will be set up in other areas, according to the KCNA report.

"The sovereignty of the DPRK will be exercised in the zones," it said, adding that relevant decree of the Presidium of the Supreme People's Assembly (SPA) was promulgated on July 23.

The KCNA said Unjong cutting-edge technological development zone will be set up in some areas of Wisong-dong, Kwahak 1-dong and Kwahak 2-dong, Paesan-dong and Ulmil-dong in Unjong District, Pyongyang.

Kangryong international green model zone will be set up in some areas of Kangryong township in Kangryong County, South Hwanghae Province while Jindo export processing zone will appear in some areas of Jindo-dong and Hwadori, Waudo District, Nampho City, the KCNA said.

Chongnam industrial development zone will be set up in some areas of Ryongbuk-ri, Chongnam District, South Pyongan Province. Sukchon agricultural development zone will appear in some areas of Unjong-ri, Sukchon County and Chongsu tourist development zone in some areas of Chongsong Workers' District and Pangsan-ri, Sakju County, North Pyongan Province.

The KCNA said in another dispatch that the socialist country decided to rename the Special Economic Zone in some parts of Sinuiju City Sinuiju International Economic Zone, and the sovereignty of the DPRK will be exercised in the Sinuiju International Economic Zone. The relevant decree of the Presidium of the Supreme People's Assembly was promulgated on July 23.

Joint development of Sinuiju North Korea joined hands with a Hong Kong-based company to develop the country's northwestern border city of Sinuiju into a special economic zone, a North Korean official said in March.

Sinuiju, which borders China's Dandong city, has drawn much attention from foreign investors for its geographical advantage as North Korea's western gateway to China, Ri Chol-sok, the vice chairman of North Korea's economic development committee, said in an interview in the March issue of Kumsugangsan magazine, a North Korean government mouthpiece.

"Now a joint development company has been established for the development of (Sinuiju) and is striving to win back lost opportunities," said the North Korean official.

Hong Kong-based conglomerate Great China International Investment Groups Ltd. reportedly signed the deal with North Korea. North Korea is also making efforts to lure foreign investment to other special economic zones, including one in the Rason area in the northern tip of the country, according to Ri.

The foreign company already has deep ties with the North, having joined the country's project launched in January to renovate the eastern part of the capital Pyongyang.

■ Cooperation with Russia

North Korea began a joint venture with Russia to renovate its key railway network, according to Pyongyang's media, amid growing signs of closer ties between the former communist allies.

The North held a ground-breaking ceremony on Oct. 21 for re-building a railroad linking the logistical hub of Nampho and several areas rich in coal, cement and other natural resources, the KCNA reported.

The project is designed to modernize the aged Jaedong-Kangdong-Nampho railway, a key industrial transportation route running through the capital, Pyongyang. Nampo is the North's largest port city along the west and Jaedong is home to a number of coal mines.

Participants in the event, held at the East Pyongyang Railway Station, included the North's external economy minister Ri Ryong-nam and Russia's minister of Far East development Alexander Galushka. They chair the Inter-Governmental Committee for Cooperation in Trade, Economy, Science and Technology between the sides.

Both North Korean and Russian officials agreed to the significance of the joint work to refurbish the North's aged railway, said the KCNA. It quoted the Russian officials as describing it as "the first stage of realizing the large-scale cooperation project" and expanding economic partnership between the two nations.

A Russian broadcaster earlier reported that Pyongyang and Moscow signed a US$25 billion deal to modernize a combined 3,500km stretch of railways in North Korea. If confirmed, it would cover 60-70% of the North's railways.

The two nations have already teamed up to renovate the 54km double-track rail link between the town of Khasan in southeastern Russia and Rason in North Korea's northeastern tip. Many observers take note of growing economic coopera-tion between North Korea and Russia.

Pyongyang is viewed as reaching out to Moscow as its ties with Beijing are not as good as before. Seoul has also suspended most of its economic cooperation with Pyongyang.

Economic cooperation agreement North Korea and Russia signed an economic cooperation agreement on April 26, Pyongyang's state news agency reported, as part of the two countries' recent moves to strengthen bilateral relations.

"An agreement on trade and economic cooperation was signed between the DPRK Ministry of Foreign Trade and the Amur Regional Government of the Russian Federation," said the KCNA. The KCNA did not give any further details on the pact.

The bilateral agreement came after Russian Deputy Prime Minister Yuri Trutnev visited Pyongyang in a series of exchange visits of high-level officials between the two countries. Trutnev, who is also President Vladimir Putin's envoy to Russia's Far East, met with Ro Tu-chol, vice-premier of the DPRK cabinet, according to the KCNA in a separate report.

"At the talks both sides exchanged views on the issue of boosting the economic and cooperative relations between the two countries and other issues of mutual concern," said the KCNA.

In September, a 54km, double-track rail link reopened between Rason, in North Korea's northern tip, and the nearby Russian town of Khasan after several years of renovation.

Settlement in rouble North Korea and Russia agreed on June 5 to settle trade bills with Russian rouble in a meeting of trade, economy and science-technology cooperation between the two countries..

Alexander Galushka, Russia's minister of Development of Far East, said the two countries discussed in the meeting Russia's participation in underground natural resources development in North Korea and ways for North Korea to pay the trade bills in kind with natural resources.

■ Kaesong Industrial Park

Demand for pay raise North Korea in February demanded a US$30 pay raise for its workers at the inter-Korean industrial complex in exchange for sending more workers, officials at South Korean companies operating in the complex said on Feb. 12.

The base pay of North Korean workers at the Kaesong complex was set at a minimum of US$67 per month based on an inter-Korean agreement. South Korean companies give a 5% raise annually, and each company pays overtime.

Scrap of pay hike cap North Korea has removed the legal limit for wages paid to its workers at the Kaesong Industrial Complex, the North's propaganda Website said on Dec. 6, a move that could cause tension with South Korea, which co-runs the industrial park with the reclusive regime.

The North revised the Act on Kaesong Complex laborers late last month, scrapping the upper ceiling for workers' wages, according to Uriminzokkiri, one of the country's major propaganda sites. The site also said that raises will be set every year by the supervisory committee overseeing laborers at the complex.

The law, enacted in 2003, had stipulated that a North Korean employee working at the complex be paid at least US$50 per month, and any raise shouldn't exceed 5% of the monthly figure. The North and the South have together set the minimum wage for Kaesong complex workers through negotiations, with the figure standing at US$70.35. It has been raised by 5% every year since 2007.

SOCIETY

OVERVIEW

North Korea in 2014 made an all-out effort to step up propoganda work to strengthen idolization of its leader Kim Jong-un as a means of consolidating Kim's monolithic leadership.

It continued to strengthen indoctrination education of the people. Education of young generation was stressed among others and social organizations continued to hold rallies to pledge allegiance to Kim.

North Korea made a major reshuffle of

the heads of news media and publishing organizations to expedite the indoctrination of its people.

There were series of big incidents and accidents in 2014. Senior members of the WPK made rare apologies to the people after an apartment building under construction in Pyongyang's posh residential district collapsed, causing an unknown number of casualties. Internet sites operated by the Pyongyang authorities were disabled and restored for more than a week at the end of the year.

There were also moves to develop the North Korean society to meet the trend of the times. The Korean Central News Agency (KCNA) developed mobile applications to allow the readers news access on their phones while Kim Il Sung University introduced cyberlectures.

ACCIDENTS AND INCIDENTS

■ Collapse of Apartment Building

An apartment building under construction in the posh Pyongchon District in Pyongyang collapsed on May 13, causing an unspecified number of casualties. The KCNA said on May 18 the accident occurred as "the construction was not done properly, and officials supervised and controlled it in an irresponsible manner."

North Korea's top officials in charge of the construction, including Choe Pu-il, minister of People's Security, made a public apology, a very unusual act in the authoritarian country.

▲ *A North Korean official apologizes to citizens over an apartment building collapse at a construction site in Pyongyang on May 17.*

The KCNA reported that a "state emergency mechanism" was formed to rescue survivors and treat the wounded, and senior officials met with bereaved families and citizens in the district to express "deep consolation and (issue an) apology."

It is unusual for North Korean media to report such news of a massive accident. It is also rare for ranking officials to publicly apologize for a construction accident to the people, and the North's media reported it quickly, indicating that the North Korean leadership is very much concerned with the accident's consequences.

North Korea watchers in Seoul say the North Korean leadership may have been greatly concerned as the accident took place in the heart of the North's capital. The Pyongchon District is at the center of Pyongyang along with Chung and Potong River regions, and there are many prestigious schools in the region.

Families of senior military officers and middle- and upper-class citizens are living in the Pyongchon region. Most of the residents in the collapsed apartment are known to be families of key officials of the People's Security Ministry, one of the three top power organs of the socialist country.

■ Life imprisonment on S. Korean Missionary

On May 31, North Korea's Supreme Court held a trial for Kim Jeong-uk, a South Korean missionary who was arrested while entering the North in November 2013, and sentenced him to a lifetime of hard labor.

North Korea accused him of being an agent of South Korea's National Intelligence Service and that he was arrested while infiltrating into Pyongyang to commit hostile acts against the DPRK (North Korea) after crossing the border illegally.

During the trial, the accused admitted to all his crimes, the KCNA said. The South Korean government, political circle and social organizations urged the North to release Kim, but the North did not respond to the calls.

■ Ping-pong Legend Injured in Car Accident

Ri Pun-hui, a former North Korean table tennis star, has been seriously injured in a car accident in Pyongyang, an informed source in Seoul said on Oct. 2. The news surprised many South Koreans and dimmed hopes of Li's visit to the South for the Incheon Asian Para Games slated to take place from Oct. 18-24.

Ri, chief of North Korea's disabled athletes association, is popular not only in North Korea but also in the South. Li played on a unified Korea team in the 1991 world table tennis championships in Japan. She played with Hyun Jeong-hwa, a South Korean ping-pong legend, to win the women's doubles title.

Ri, 47, was driving a sedan, also carrying two disabled kids, when it hit a truck in the North's capital in late September, said the source with close ties with her.

The Voice of America (VOA) also reported the accident on the same day, quoting Lee Seok-hee, a pastor leading a London-based North Korea relief agency. Lee told the VOA that the British Embassy in Pyongyang has confirmed Li's injury.

■ N.K. Workers Arrested in Middle East

Five North Korean workers in the Middle East were arrested on charges of selling illegally brewed liquor and possessing drugs and some of them were expatriated, the Voice of America reported on Oct. 17 quoting local sources.

North Korean workers are mainly engaged in construction work in the Middle East and many of them are making various illegal operations like moonshining to make money to pay "loyalty funds" to the North Korean authorities.

■ N. Korea's Internet Downed

North Korea's Internet connections repeated outages and restorations for eight days in late December after U.S. President Barack Obama blamed the socialist nation for the massive hack on Sony Pictures and promised a "proportional response."

North Korea's main news organizations and propaganda websites, including the KCNA, the Rodong Sinmun, Uriminzokkiri, Ryugyong and Ryomyong, had been unstable until Dec. 30 since the servers were completely down at 1 a.m. on Dec. 23.

Speculation of a cyberattack by the U.S. has been spread because the outage came just days after U.S. President Barack Obama vowed a "proportional" response to the North's alleged hacking of Sony.

Pyongyang has threatened to retaliate against Sony's release of a movie, which portrays an assassination story targeting North Korean leader Kim Jong-un, but it has denied responsibility in the Sony hacking.

INDOCTRINATION EDUCATION

■ **Stepping up Education**

Since the execution of Jang Song-thaek in late 2013, North Korea pushed a drive to strengthen the ideology education of its people by Workers' Party officials in charge of propaganda.

The Rodong Sinmun, organ of the party, stressed in an editorial on Feb. 3 that the party's intention today is to renew the ideology and spirit of all the party members and workers and put spurs to the grand march toward the final victory for the construction of a strong thriving country.

■ **Education of Young Generation**

North Korea made special effort on education of young people in order to block the spread of captalistic ideology and culture among the young generation by holding seminars.

Officials of the youth league held a seminar on July 30 on the education of Kim Jong-il's patriotism, faith, the working class and morality at the hall of the youth league.

O Hye-son, director of the Kumsong Youth Publishing House, said that it is an important requirement of the struggle for defending socialism to intensify the working class education among the school youth and children, the KCNA said.

Although North Kroean authorities were all out to block the influx of capitalistic idea and culture, foreign cultural content like South Korean TV dramas, which were secretly introduced to the reclusive country via USB flash drives and DVDs, enjoy popularity among the North Korean youths.

SOCIAL ORGANIZATIONS

■ **Auxiliary Organs**

Social organizations in North Korea are auxiliary organs of the Workers Party and plays a role in bridging the party and the people. and educating the public. Major groups include the General Federation of Trade Unions of Korea (GFTUK), the Union of Agricultural Workers of Korea (UAWK), the Korea Democratic Women's Union (KDWU) and the Kim Il sung Socialist Youth League.

■ **Loyalty Rallies**

Various social organizations competed to hold general meetings to support the tasks set forth by Kim Jong-un in his New Year's address and pledge allegiance to Kim, the Rodong Sinmun reported on Feb. 4.

The GFTUK held an expanded meeting of its leaders in Pyongyang on Feb. 3 and evaluated Kim's address as a guideline to show a shortcut to the prosperity of the nation and discussed ways to put the tasks into practice.

The KDWU and the Kim Il-sung Socialist Youth League held general meetings in Pyongyang on the same day. Similar meetings followed across the country throughout the year.

The Kim Il-sung Socialist Youth League held the 4th meeting of primary organization cadres in Pyongyang on Sept. 18-19 to strengthen the youth league into the young vanguard organization of the Workers' Party. North Korea's top leaders like Kim Yong-nam, Choe Thae-bok, Choe Ryong-hae, exemplary officials of primary organizations of the youth league and its officials in Pyongyang and local areas attended the meeting.

Kim Jong-un sent a letter titled "Let Youth Become Vanguard Fighters Intensely Loyal to the Songun Revolutionary Cause of the Party" to the participants in the meeting.

Speakers at the meeting said that the officials of the youth league should deeply realize the great expectation of the party and the importance of the work of the youth league, decisively enhance the militant function and role of the primary organizations and make the youth league the young vanguard organization, upholding the Songun leadership of Kim Jong-un with loyalty.

TRANSPORTATION

An agreement on air service between the DPRK and Jordan was signed in Beijing on Sept. 15, the KCNA reported on Sept. 16 without revealing details of the agreement. North Korea established diplomatic relations with Jordan in 1974 and has maintained basic diplomatic ties such as exchanging congratulatory messages of their top leaders on each other's national holidays.

North Korea signed aviation agreements with the Czech Republic in 2004, with Syria in 2006 and with Kuwait in 2008.

An agreement on the joint building, management and protection of a new bridge between North Korea's Wonjong-ri, Rason City and Quanhe, Hunchun of China was concluded between the governments of the DPRK and China on June 27.

The agreement was inked by Pak Myong-guk, vice-minister of Foreign Affairs from the DPRK side and Liu Hongcai, Chinese ambassador to the DPRK, from the Chinese side upon the authorization of their respective governments, the KCNA reported.

LAND ADMINISTRATION AND ENVIRONMENTAL PROTECTION

▪ Adoption of Land Law

North Korea began to show interest in land administration in the 1960s. In April 1977. the Supreme People's Assembly adopted the Land Law, and in the 1980s the government launched the "Hometown Creation Project" and began the "Make Our Villages and Streets Beautiful" campaign as part of efforts to motivate the public to improve and beautify their living environment.

In April 1986, North Korea adopted the Environment Protection Law. After suffering severe droughts and floods in the mid-1990s, North Korea began to take serious interest in land administration and incorporated it into its policy agenda.

The first meeting of workers in sectors related to land and environmental protection was held in September 1996, when a resolution to turn forestation and river embankment construction into a nationwide effort with popular participation was adopted.

Despite the rhetoric about land administration and environmental protection, a U.N. report showed the area of North Korea's forests had fallen almost 31% in 20 years.

The U.N. Development Program announced in a report on March 15, 2013 that the area decreased 30.9% between 1990 and 2010, and the proportion of animal and plant species at risk of extinction came to 8.6%. North Korea also recorded substantial warming.

▪ Meeting of Environment Protection Officials

A meeting of officials in the field of land and environment protection was held at the People's Palace of Culture on Feb. 27, attended by Premier Pak Pong-ju, vice premiers, Kwak Pom-gi, Ro Tu-chol, Thae Jong-su, chief secretaries of provincial committees of the Workers' Party, and other related people.

The participants watched a video showing the successes made by the service personnel and people of North Korea in the work to facelift the land and environment in 2013, the KCNA said.

The meeting reviewed the successes and experience gained in the 2013 drive for the general mobilization for land management and for increasing strength of rails. It also discussed the issue to bring about bigger successes tin 2014.

Speakers at the meeting said the energetic leadership of Kim Jong-un served as a motivational force for encouraging all the people throughout the country to dynamically turn out in the drive for the general mobilization for land management in 2013 and called for conducting the more brisk drive for the general mobilization for land management across the country in 2014.

▪ Destruction of Forest in North Korea

A total of 160,000ha of forest have been destroyed in North Korea since 2001, the Voice of America reported on

March 18, quoting the World Resources Institute in Washington.

MEDIA

■ Responsibilities and Roles

The major responsibilities of the North Korean media are to convey the instructions of North Korea's founder Kim Il-sung, late leader Kim Jong-il and current leader Kim Jong-un; promote and defend the policies and "revolutionary works" of the Workers' Party of Korea; and communicate to the outside world the superiority of the North Korean system.

Therefore, it is inevitable that the media measures the news value of an event based on how effective it is at enhancing the status of the three Kims, promoting the party line and policies, mobilizing the public for various drives and indoctrinating the masses. The entire process of collecting, editing and reporting is controlled by the party, which censors newspaper articles and broadcasts before they are published or aired.

■ News Agency & Newspapers

The Korean Central News Agency is the only wire service and the socialist country's key mouthpiece. The KCNA is headed by Kim Chang-gwang, director general. There are five vice directors general and a chief editor. It has about 1,000 workers, including 700 in charge of reporting. It transmits 40 domestic news articles and about 50 foreign news articles a day. It has branches in six foreign countries, including China, India, Iran and Egypt.

The KCNA has news exchange agreements with Xinhua, Kyodo, Reuters and Yonhap News Agency of South Korea. It joined the Organization of the Asia and Pacific News Agencies (OANA) in 1981.

There are several newspapers published by the party, government and social organizations. Rodong Sinmun is the main newspaper published by the WPK. Minju Joson is the newspaper of the Cabinet.

■ Braodcasting

Broadcasting is the major method of arming North Koreans with the WPK's doctrine. It is estimated that there are about 1.3 million televisions in the country and about 5 million radio receivers.

North Korea's main broadcaster is the DPRK Radio and Television Broadcasting Station. There are also Pyongyang Municipal Cable Broadcasting Station and regional broadcasting stations.

North Korea started using Internet podcasts to propagandize about its socialist system. A list of podcasts was released on March 20 via propaganda website Uriminzokkiri.

■ Visit by Kyodo Head

Masaki Fukuyama, president of Japan's Kyodo News Service, visited North Korea from Sept. 8-11 and had meetings with top North Korean leaders, including Kim Yong-nam, president of the Presidium of the Supreme People's Assembly, in Mansudae Assembly Hall.

■ Media Cooperation with Mongolia

The KCNA agreed with Mongolia's Montsame News Agency to strengthen cooperation, the agency reported on Sept. 16. A KCNA delegation, led by Director General Kim Chang-gwang reached an agreement on the cooperation in Mongolia, the KCNA said but did not elaborate on the agreement.

EDUCATION

■ Summary

North Korea introduced a new schooling system that extends compulsory education to 12 years from the previous 11 years in 2013.

The Supreme People's Assembly (SPA), North Korea's parliament, approved legislation to extend the compulsory education period by one year at a meeting on Sept. 25, 2012.

"The ordinance of the DPRK (North Korea) Supreme People's Assembly on enforcing universal 12-year compulsory education was promulgated at the session," the KCNA said.

The education reform will create a system similar to that of the South. Previously, students in North Korea were given 11 years of compulsory education -- one year of kindergarten, four years of elementary school and six years of middle school.

North Koreans will now be required to complete one year of kindergarten, five years of elementary school, three years of middle school (junior middle school) and three years of high school (senior middle school), the KCNA said.

The new educational system is aimed at helping the younger generation round off secondary general education by teaching them general basic knowledge and basic knowledge of modern technologies, the report noted.

■ Education Reforms in Kim Il-Sung University

North Korea made reforms in the top-brand Kim Il-Sung University by strengthening education of foreign languages and young students. The Rodong Sinmun reported on Oct. 1, the 68th anniversary of the university's founding, that the university organized competitions for foreign language listening and conversation in September.

The paper also said the university is attaching big importance on the education of young geniuses especially in mathematics and physical science departments.

The university is also achieving progresses in computerizing the entire process of teaching and experimenting and opened cyberlecture courses. The paper said the university launched eight "electronic classrooms" in the economics college.

■ Economy-related Departments Installed

Major North Korean universities, including the Kim Il-Sung University, opened departments related to economy and business administration in 2014.

RELIGION

■ Summary

Christianity, including Catholicism and Protestantism, was introduced to North Korea even before it was introduced to South Korea. While the country was still under Japanese colonial rule, Christianity had a deep impact on various aspects of people's lives, along with traditional religions like Buddhism and Cheondoism. After Korea was liberated from Japan and divided into two countries, North

Korea suppressed all religion in the country as it was thought to be a hurdle to maintaining a monolithic system.

The hard-line policy against religion took a turn after 1972 when inter-Korean dialogue began and religious organizations such as the Korean Christian Association, Korean Buddhist Association and Central Guidance Committee of the Korean Cheondoist Association were revived in the reclusive country. Beginning in the 1990s, North Korea attempted repeated contact with Western religious organizations. Its dealings with South Korean religious organizations also increased in the process of getting food aid.

Outwardly, North Korea says it guarantees freedom of religion and there are a number of protestant churches and a Catholic church in Pyongyang, but only for propaganda purposes.

■ Remodelling of Chilgol Church

North Korea's propaganda Website Uriminzokkiri reported on July 25 the Pyongyang Chilgol Church has been reopened after remodelling. Chilgol Church is North Korea's third church built after Jangchung Catholic Church and Bongsu Church.

MEDICAL SERVICES

■ Summary

North Korea's socialist Constitution advocates the provision of free medical services for all. The concept of providing free medical services first appeared in 1946 but free medical treatment only became available to North Koreans in February 1960.

Hospitals in North Korea are divided into general hospitals, specialized hospitals and hygiene and prevention centers specializing in public health and quarantine. Most healthcare and quarantine workers are trained at medical or pharmacy universities.

North Korea made efforts to develop remote medical treatment systems. It hosted a Southeast Asia regional meeting of the World Health Organization from July 30-Aug. 1, 2013 in Pyongyang to discuss the remote treatment system.

There is a pharmacy open 24 hours and

year round in Pyongyang. The Pyongsu Pharma J-V Co., a joint venture between Switzerland's Parazelsus and the Pyongyang Pharmaceutical Factory, opened the Taedongmun outlet in the Mansudae area in August 2012. According to the company's homepage, the Taedongmun outlet is the only pharmacy open 24 hours a day, 7 days a week, in Pyongyang.

■ **High Smoking Rate**
The VOA reported on Jan. 11 that one of every four North Koreans smoke, much higher than international average smoking rate. A joint study by the Washington University of the United States and Australia's Melbourne University showed the North's smoking rate was 23.4% as of 2012, higher than the world's average of 18.7%. The rate was 45.8% for North Korean men, 14.7%p higher than 31.1% for the world average. North Korean women's smoking rate was tallied at just 2.6%.

■ **New TB Facilities**
Two recuperation centers for tuberclosis patients were built in North Korea with aid from Caritas Germany, the Radio Free Asia of the United States reported on July 30.

HOLIDAYS

In North Korea, there are 11 national holidays, a number of significant anniversaries and four traditional holidays. National holidays such as the Day of the Sun (April 15), or the birthday of North Korean founder Kim Il-sung, Day of Shining Star, or birthday of Kim Jong-il (Feb. 16), the anniversary of the founding of the Workers' Party of Korea (Oct. 10), anniversary of the government's establishment (Sept. 9) and the anniversary of the establishment of the Korean People's Army (April 25) are the most important holidays.
The birthday of current leader Kim Jong-un has not been made a national holiday but the North Korean army celebrated the day as an important anniversary. North Korea newly designated Aug. 25 as a national holiday to commemorate Kim Jong-il's first inspection of a field army unit in 1960.

The four traditional holidays are Seol, or Lunar New Year's Day, Hansik, Dano and Chuseok. Traditional holidays had been denounced as incompatible with the socialist way of life. However, since inter-Korean dialogue began in 1972, the North Korean government has allowed people to pay visits to their ancestors' graves on Chuseok. It officially designated Chuseok, or the Autumn Full Moon, a public holiday in 1989, along with Seol and Dano.

CULTURE AND SPORTS

CULTURE

■ **Performances, Dancing & Music**
Performances Various performances were held throughout 2014, but virtually all the performances were for North Korean leadership, including supreme leader Kim Jong-un and military and state leaders.
Kim attended performances by the North's civilian and military performers, some times along with his wife Ri Sol-ju and his sister Kim Yo-jong.
The KCNA said Kim watched a military art troupe's performance at the 534 Unit of the Korean People's Army (KPA) on Jan. 12 after reviewing the command post of the unit. Choe Ryong-hae, the secretary of the Workers' Party of Korea, and Hwang Pyong-so , director of the General Political Bureau of the KPA, accompanied Kim. Kim also attended a concert of the KPA military band on Jan. 17, the KCNA said.
Kim Jong-un and Kim Yo-jong enjoyed performance of the Moranbong Band, the KCNA reported on March 17 and Kim, accompanied by his wife and sister, was the guest of honor at another performance of the all-female music group on March 22.
Among the performances attended by Kim were congratulatory performances celebrating the second anniversary of recommending Kim as the first chairman of the National Defense Commission on April 11, the ninth national arts competition on May 19 and the 61st anniversary of

the "Victory of the Korean people in the Fatherland Liberation War" on July 27.

▪ Movies

Film festivals were held throughout 2014 to celebrate various occasions like the "Day of the Shining Star" (Kim Jong-il's birth anniversary) on Feb. 16 and the "Day of the Sun" (the birthday of Kim Il-sung) on April 15.

▪ Pyongyang Int'l Film Festival

About 100 films submitted from 40 world countries were screened during the 14th Pyongyang International Film Festival from Sept. 17-24, the KCNA said.

▲ The opening ceremony of the 14th Pyongyang International Film Festival is being held in Pyongyang, capital of the Democratic People's Republic of Korea (DPRK), on Sept. 17.

▪ Exhibitions

Exhibitions of historic relics were held from Feb. 6-28 across North Korea to celebrate the Day of the Shining Star at history museums in Pyongsong, Sinuiju, Sariwon, Chongjin and Hamhung.

There was an arts exhibition on April 10 to celebrate the Day of the Sun (April 15) at the Korea Arts Museum in Pyongyang. A national arts exhibition was held to celebrate the "victory of the Korean people in the Fatherland Liberation War" on July 17, showing 150 art works.

▪ Relics and Cultural Heritage

Goguryo relics found The North's propaganda Website Uriminzokkiri said on Jan. 24 an ancient Goguryo tomb with murals was discovered at Daesongdong in Pyongyang. Another Goguryo tomb

was found at Samsok District of Pyongyang, the Korean central TV reported on April 24. Uriminzokkiri said the tomb was in representative Goguryo style.

Researchers of Kim Il Sung University discovered the relics of salt manufacturing relics for the first time in Onchon County, the KCNA said on July 2. Various earthenware, bricks and debris of iron kiln were also found.

Arirang inscribed on UNESCO's intangible heritage list A group of North Korean versions of the traditional Korean folk song "Arirang" was inscribed on UNESCO's intangible cultural heritage list, on Nov. 26 during the 9th session of the Intergovernmental Committee for the Safeguarding of the Intangible Cultural Heritage that opened in Paris on Nov. 24 for a five-day run, Seoul's Cultural Heritage Administration said.

"Arirang folk song in the Democratic People's Republic of Korea (DPRK)" became the first North Korean item on the Representative List of the UNESCO Intangible Cultural Heritage of Humanity. DPRK refers to the official name of North Korea.

"Arirang" is not just one song but a variety of local versions handed down generation after generation on the Korean Peninsula. It is often dubbed an "unofficial national anthem" of Korea because, due to its easy melody and tune, virtually all Koreans, even those living in North Korea and abroad, can sing at least part of it. Experts say there are thousands of variations of "Arirang" carrying the refrain, "Arirang, arirang, arariyo."

The new entry on the list includes six versions of "Arirang" originated from Pyongyang, South Pyongan Province, South Hwanghae Province, Kangwon Province, South Hamgyong Province and Jagang Province in North Korea.

South Korea's "Arirang" was added to the list under the title "Arirang, lyrical folk song in the Republic of Korea" in 2012.

Meanwhile, North korea's official media did not made an immediate report of the news. The KCNA reported it belatedly on Dec. 3.

National meeting of artistes The ninth national meeting of artistes took place in Pyongyang on Sept. 17-18. Speakers said that the wise leadership of Kim

Jong-un is what keeps the Juche-oriented literature and art alive and the Songun revolutionary exploits of the Workers' Party of Korea are the eternal theme and seed in the creation of masterpieces.

They said they can create as many masterpieces as possible if everybody makes redoubled efforts to reach the high level of creation desired by Kim Jong-un.

The dynamic music presentation by the Moranbong Band playing the role of an engine for a revolution in literature and art in the new era and the choruses of military songs staged by the State Merited Chorus are putting strong spurs to the steady advance of the Juche revolutionary cause started in Mt. Paektu, making the hearts of all the service personnel and people burn with enthusiasm, the speakers said, calling for thoroughly implementing the important tasks set forth by Kim Jong-un in his letter to the participants in the meeting.

They deeply reflected on the fact that inactivity and stagnation manifested in the field of literature and art at present are attributable to the wrong ideological viewpoint and aesthetic outlook of creators and artistes and this is directly related to the faith in the victory of socialism in the final analysis.

Speakers called for ushering in a fresh heyday of literature and art by grasping again and reconfirming the issue of roles of literature and art at present and the importance of the mission and duty of the creators and artistes in the present era and making even a single movie or an article a powerful weapon in the party's ideological work, which can be a substitute for thousands of tons of food and tens of thousands of shells.

Choe Thae-bok made a closing address. The 9th national meeting of artistes will go down as a grand meeting which powerfully demonstrated the strong faith and will of the creators and artistes to fully display the might of the Juche-oriented literature and art and dynamically speed up the grand advance for modeling the whole society on Kimilsungism-Kimjongilism under the wise leadership of Kim Jong-un and marked a milestone for an epochal turning point in the development of the Songun revolutionary literature and art in the 21st century.

SPORTS

Summary
In a country like North Korea where the people are urged to offer "limitless" loyalty to the monolithic leader, sports has been used as a tool to divert people's discontent over the regime and induce their loyalty to the state and its leader.

Kim Jong-un and his regime have poured lavish efforts into promoting sports events and encouraging its athletes to achieve good results not only in domestic events but international competitions as well. At the end of 2013, North Korea highlighted its performance in sports in 2013 in an apparent bid to rouse loyalty among citizens for leader Kim Jong-un.

North Korean athletes competed in more than 70 global sports events and gathered over 160 gold medals in 2013, a 3.7-fold increase from the year before, the paper said. The country earned a total of 380 medals, up 3.2-fold from 2012, it added. The paper also praised successful athletes, including Kim Kum-ok, who finished first at the 14th Asian Marathon Championship, as the "archetypal athletes of the new generation."

Domestic Competitions
2014 DPRK Championships The April 25 Sports Team topped the team standings in the 2014 DPRK Championships by taking 111 gold medals, the KCNA said. In the championships, nearly 5,000 players from more than 80 teams had competed for over 500 gold medals.

Male and female players of the April 25 Sports Team finished first in basketball and volleyball, namely its players who won 23 gold medals out of 45 in weightlifting while setting six new records in women's weightlifting and swimming events.

Ro Un-ok, female marathoner of the team, retained a four-time championship and other players won the titles in table-tennis, track-and-field, wrestling, boxing and other events. Meanwhile, the Sports Team of the Ministry of Land and Marine Transport bagged 59 gold medals and Kigwancha Sports Team 47 golds in the championships.

- **International Competitions**

17th Asian Games North Korea won 36 medals, including 11 golds, in the 17th Asian Games held in Incheon, South Korea, from Sept. 19 to Oct. 4. North Korean women soccer team won the gold medal, beating South Korea. North Korea established new world and Asian games records in Weightlifting.

World Weightlifting Championships North Korea finished first in the 2014 World Weightlifting Championships held in Kazakhstan, winning 12 gold medals, the KCNA reported on Nov. 17. Competitions were made in 15 categories of weights (men's eight and women's seven) for a total of 45 gold medals at the championship.

Kim Un-guk of the April 25 Sports Team, who renewed world records at the 17th Asian Games, won three gold medals in men's 62kg while Ryo Un-hui took first place in women's 69kg snatch, jerk and total. Besides, Ri Jong-hwa and Kim Kwang-song finished first in women's 58kg and men's 77kg jerk and Kim Un-ju in women's 75kg jerk and total.

World record in weightlifting Female weightlifter Ri Song-gum set a new world record in 44kg category by lifting 93 kg in the jerk on the first day of the World Junior and Juvenile Weightlifting Championships in Thailand from March 4-12. She snatched 66kg, coming first in total points to bag three gold medals.

Ri Hyon-hwa placed second and third in the jerk and snatch coming second in total points in the girls' 44kg category while Kim Yong-gun placed second in the jerk and third in total points in the boys' 50kg category. Pak Jong-ju finished third in jerk and snatch respectively and came third in total points in the boys' 56kg category.

- **Sports Figures and Events**

North Korea-U.S. basketball game North Korean leader Kim Jong-un, along with his wife Ri Sol-ju, watched a friendly game between the North Korean team and a U.S. team led by former NBA star Dennis Rodman in Pyongyang on Jan. 8.

Kigwancha sports team Sportspersons of the Kigwancha Sports Team bagged more than 190 gold medals at domestic and international tournaments in 2013, the KCNA reported on Feb. 25.

Male and female weightlifters, including Jon Myong-song, Rim Jong-sim, Ryo Un-hui, Kim Un-ju and Jo Pok-hyang, won 37 gold medals at the Asian Weightlifting Championships, the Asian Cup and Interclub Junior and Senior Weightlifting Championships and other tournaments. It is equivalent to 22.6% of total gold medals won by the DPRK sportspersons at different international games in 2013, the KCNA said.

Rim Jong-sim and Kim Un-ju set new records in snatch and jerk events of women's 69kg and 75kg weightlifting categories of the 6th East Asian Games. Pak Kwang-ryong and Ju Kwang-min played a key role in taking the DPRK team to first place at the men's football game in the 6th East Asian Games.

The athletes of the Kigwancha Sports Team proved successful in more than 150 events of the Mangyongdae Prize Sports Games, the DPRK Championships and the Sports Contest for Pochonbo Torch Prize, setting five new records in weightlifting and field and track games.

Ro Chol-ok, vice director of the sports team, told KCNA that the team has prioritized training reserve athletes and improving the training conditions after putting sporting skills, training methods and tactics on a more scientific basis. The team, founded in January 1956, was awarded the Order of Kim Il-sung and produced lots of winners of the titles of the People's Athlete and Merited Athlete.

Medalists and coaches honored North Korea commended seven gold medalists and coaches who were successful in the Incheon Asian Games and world championships.

Kim Jong-il Prize was awarded to Kim Un-guk, wrestler of the April 25 Sports Team, Om Yun-chol, wrestler of the Amnokgang Sports Team, the title of Labor Hero to Kim Kwang-min, football coach of the April 25 Sports Team, Pak Ki-song, wrestling coach of the April 25 Sports Team, and Ra Un-sim, footballer of the Amnokgang Sports Team, the title of People's Sportsperson to Ho Un-byol, footballer of the April 25 Sports Team, and Order of National Flag First Class to Ri Se-gwang, gymnast of the April 25 Sports Team.

A decree of the Presidium of the Supreme People's Assembly to honor athletes was promulgated on Oct. 22, the KCNA said on Oct. 25.

INTER-KOREAN RELATIONS

▪ Overview

South and North Korea made little progress in their relations in 2014, which were at their worst in 2013. At the beginning of the year, they held the first reunions of families separated since the 1950-53 Korean War in three years and four months. In March, South Korean President Park Geun-hye announced the Dresden Declaration, which calls for laying the groundwork for the future reunification of the two Koreas.

In October, a group of high-ranking North Korean officials including Hwang Pyong-so, director of the general political bureau of the Korean People's Army (KPA), visited South Korea. The visit was followed by secret military talks between the two Koreas.

However, the widened gap between the two countries on thorny issues such as economic sanctions on the North by the South has made it difficult to take big strides in improving relations.

▪ Reunions of Separated Families

From the beginning of 2014, South Korea has proposed to North Korea that they resume the reunions of families separated by the 1950-53 Korean War.

On Jan. 10, the South suggested holding a working-level meeting on the North's side of the border village of Panmunjom to arrange the reunion. On the same day, President Park also called on the North to accept the South's proposal. However, the North kept mum.

On Jan. 16, the North's most powerful body, the National Defense Commission (NDC), proposed halting all cross-border slander starting Jan. 30 and called on Seoul not to go through with its planned military exercises with the United States. The "important proposal" made by the NDC came a day after Pyongyang threatened an "unimaginable holocaust" if

Seoul carried out the annual drills Key Resolve and Foal Eagle from late February through April as scheduled. One day after the North's proposal, the South dismissed the North's suggestion, saying the communist country tried to distort the facts.

In response to the South's chilly reaction, the North urged the South to accept its proposal, saying its Jan. 16 proposal is disguised peace propaganda. The North's call was dismissed by the South's refutation.

In a separate telephone message on Jan. 16, the North suggested holding the reunions of the separated families after the Lunar New Year. In response, the South proposed holding the reunions from Feb. 17-22 on Mount Kumgang. Following several working-level talks, the two Koreas agreed to hold the reunions from Feb. 20-25 at the North's scenic resort of Mount. Kumgang.

Under the agreement, hundreds of South and North Korean families separated by the 1950-53 Korean War met with each other. Millions of Koreans remain separated across the border as a legacy of the 1950-53 Korean War, which ended in a truce, leaving the peninsula still technically in a state of war.

▲ Park Un-hyung (L), a 92-year-old South Korean, raises a toast with his daughter and brother living in North Korea during the inter-Korean family reunions at the North's Mount Kumgang resort on Feb. 21.

▪ Inter-Korean High-Level Talks

South Korea's unification ministry announced on Feb. 11 that South and North Korea would hold their first high-level talks in seven years since 2007. Senior officials from the two Koreas exchanged views on issues of mutual interest in the rare talks held at the border village of Panmunjom from Feb.12-15.

According to the ministry, the sides listened to each other's positions on issues in a "sincere" manner at their meeting held on Feb. 12. They met for more than three hours before their chief delegates held separate talks for about 30 minutes. However, they failed to produce tangible results due to the wide gap of opinions over a military exercise between Seoul and Washington.

The North had urged the South to stop the military exercises with the U.S., saying they are a rehearsal for war. However, the South and the U.S. vowed to go ahead with the exercises, calling them defensive in nature.

The high-level talks resumed on Feb. 14 when they agreed to hold the reunions of families separated by the 1950-53 Korean War from Feb 20-25. On the third day of the talks on Feb. 15, they reached an agreement to stop mutual slander and hold high-level talks again in due course. However, the troubled relations between the two Koreas hamper efforts to hold more high-level talks in 2014.

▪ Visit of High-Ranking North Korean Officials to S. Korea

A North Korean delegation comprised of high-ranking officials made a roughly 12-hour trip to South Korea on Oct. 4 in order to attend the closing ceremony of the 17th Asian Games held in Incheon,

▲ Hwang Pyong-so, the top political officer of the Korean People's Army and the vice chairman of the all-powerful National Defense Commission, arrives at Incheon International Airport along with two other officials, Choe Ryong-hae and Kim Yang-gon, to attend the closing ceremony of the Incheon Asian Games and to hold talks with South Korean counterparts on Oct. 4.

South Korea's second-largest port city.

Among the officials were Hwang Pyong-so, director of the general political bureau of the (North) Korean People's Army (KPA); Choe Ryong-hae, secretary of the Workers' Party of (North) Korea; and Kim Yang-gon, director of the North's United Front Department in charge of South Korean affairs.

The delegation met with South Korea's Unification Minister Ryoo Kihl-jae and national security adviser Kim Kwan-jin. During the meeting, the delegation said the North intends to have high-level contact with the South in late October or early November, whichever the latter wants.

Earlier, the South proposed holding a second round of inter-Korean high-level talks, but the North dismissed the proposal, citing balloon messages sent by anti-North Korea civic groups and the North's human right issue raised by the South.

The delegation, however, failed to meet with South Korean President Park Geun-hye due to a lack of time. The North's delegation returned home at 10:25 p.m. that day after wrapping up its visit to South Korea.

▪ Inter-Korean Military Talks End Without Breakthrough

South and North Korea held their first high-level military talks in seven years on Oct. 15, but failed to reach an agreement on pending issues such as inter-Korean clashes near the tense western maritime border.

"The two Koreas held a closed-door meeting involving military officials from 10 a.m. at the truce village of Panmunjom after North Korea proposed it to discuss the recent exchange of fire between patrol boats in the Yellow Sea," defense ministry spokesman Kim Min-seok said.

The meeting, which ended at 3:10 p.m., failed to produce any meaningful agreements "due to the differences between the two sides," he added. South and North Korean patrol boats briefly exchanged fire on Oct. 7 after a North Korean naval vessel violated the NLL, the de facto maritime border in the Yellow Sea.

Heightening tensions further, the North on Oct. 10 fired anti-aircraft machine guns at balloons containing leaflets criticizing the authoritarian regime. After some of the shots landed south of border, the two sides traded machine gun fire.

During the Oct. 15 meeting, Pyongyang demanded the South "ban its ships from entering areas it claims as the inter-Korean sea border, stop civic groups from sending propaganda leaflets, and refrain from slander including in the press," Kim said.

Drawn by the U.S.-led United Nations Command at the end of the 1950-53 Korean War, the NLL acts as the de facto sea border between the two Koreas. It is not recognized by Pyongyang.

In response, South Korea called on the North to abide by the NLL, stressing that it is "not possible for the democratic government to control civic groups or the media," according to the ministry.

South Korea was represented by Ryu Je-seung, Deputy Minister for National Defense Policy, and the North by Kim Yong-chol, who leads the Reconnaissance General Bureau, he added.

Asked whether the two touched upon the North's sinking of the South Korean warship Cheonan near the Yellow Sea border in March 2010, the ministry said Seoul "reminded the North of the fact that Pyongyang should be held accountable" for the deadly incident. The two Koreas last held working-level military talks in February 2011 and general-level talks in December 2007.

The latest talks came some 10 days after high-ranking figures from the communist country made a surprise visit to South Korea and met with senior government officials here. The rare trip resulted in an agreement to hold another round of high-level talks in early November at the latest.

Visits of S. Korean Key Figures to N. Korea

Rep. Park Jie-won of the main opposition New Politics Alliance for Democracy visited Kaesong Industrial Complex on Dec. 16 on the third anniversary of former North Korean leader Kim Jong-il's death.

During his visit to the complex, Park delivered a wreath on behalf of Lee Hee-ho, the widow of late South Korean President Kim Dae-jung, in North Korea's border city of Kaesong to North Korean authorities. The city is home to the large inter-Korean factory park. Park's visit

reciprocates a similar gesture by North Korea in August to commemorate the fifth anniversary of the death of the late South Korean president.

The lawmaker applied for approval from the South Korean government to visit the North again on Dec. 19 at the invitation of Kim Yang-gon, secretary of the Workers' Party of (North) Korea. But the government dismissed his application.

On Dec. 24, Kim Sung-jae, who served as the culture minister under the Kim Dae-jung government from 1998-2003, visited the North's border city of Kaesong, leading a six-member delegation from the non-profit Kim Dae Jung Peace Center.

Kim met with Kim Yang-gon during his visit and received a personal letter from North Korean leader Kim Jong-un. The North Korean leader vowed to make active efforts to achieve the reunification of the Korean Peninsula in his personal letter sent to Kim Dae-jung's widow Lee Hee-ho in return of the flowers she sent earlier.

"Following their lofty willingness for unification and their life-time feat, we will continue to strive actively to achieve the long-cherished dream of unification down the road," said the young leader who inherited power from his father in 2009.

S. Korea's Humanitarian Aid to N. Korea

South Korea sought to expand its humanitarian aid to North Korea after the Dresden Declaration by South Korean President Park Geun-hye at Dresden University of Technology in Dresden, Germany on March 28, 2014. The Dresden Declaration includes new initiatives for the reunification of the two Koreas.

South Korea's aid to North Korea rose slightly to 5.4 billion won compared to 5.1 billion won in 2013 when inter-Korean relations were rocky due to a nuclear test by the North. In 2012, the South's aid to the North was 11.8 billion won.

10th Anniversary of First Shipment of Products in Kaesong

The Kaesong Industrial Complex located in Kaesong, a North Korean city near the inter-Korean border, marked the 10th anniversary of the first shipment of products on Dec. 15, 2014.

Despite a jump in its output, the industrial park remained susceptible to political and military factors, leaving the sole inter-Korean economic project incomplete.

According to South Korean government data, the output of the joint industrial complex reached US$230 million in the first half of 2014, compared with US$14.91 million for all of 2005. Some 53,000 North Koreans were employed by South Korean companies in 2014, up from roughly 6,000 in 2005.

The number of South Korean companies with factories in Kaesong has also surged to 124 from 15. South Korean companies were estimated to pay North Korean workers a combined US$87 million in wages and social insurance per year.

▪ Rajin-Khasan Project

The Xin Hong Bao, a 32,911t Chinese-flagged freighter, arrived in waters off Pohang, a South Korean port city, carrying 40,500t of Russian coal on Nov. 29.

▲ A Chinese cargo ship is anchored in the harbor of the southern port city of Pohang, 374 kilometers from Seoul, on Nov. 29. The vessel loaded with 45,000 tons of Siberian soft coal left North Korea's northeastern port city of Rajin two days ago.

The coal was transported from the Russian town of Khasan, a far eastern city near North Korea's northernmost port of Rajin. The two are connected by a 54km railway that was re-opened in 2013.

In July, a South Korean consortium comprised of the state-run railroad operator KORAIL, No. 1 steelmaker POSCO and the second-largest shipping company Hyundai Merchant Marine Co. carried out its second inspection of the North Korea-Russia economic project.

The consortium joined the project by purchasing stakes in RasonKonTrans, a North Korea-Russia joint venture, due to sanctions banning inter-Korean trade introduced in May 2010, after the deadly sinking of a South Korean navy ship that was blamed on the North.

North Korea owns a 30% stake in the joint venture, with Russia holding the rest. The South Korean firms are considering buying 50% of Russia's stake.

The project is closely linked to the "Eurasian Initiative," which is aimed at expanding South Korea's economic cooperation with Eurasian countries, proposed by South Korean President Park Geun-hye in 2013.

An 18-member team from the consortium conducted the first inspection of Rajin and the railway between Rajin and Khasan from Feb. 11-13.

▪ N. Korea Scraps Wage Ceiling for Kaesong Workers

North Korea revised the Act on Kaesong Complex Laborers on Nov. 20, which consists of 13 provisions including those on wages, scrapping the 5% upper ceiling for workers' wages. It escalated tension between the two Koreas.

The revised law stipulated that the pay increase will be set every year by the North, not by the South's committee overseeing the operation of the industrial complex. The law, enacted in 2003, had stipulated that a North Korean employee working at the complex be paid at least US$50 per month.

In protest against the North's unilateral decision, South Korea on Dec. 16 tried to deliver a fax that included the South's stance that the decision was unacceptable, as the working conditions for the Kaesong workers should be decided through inter-Korean agreement. But the North refused to accept the letter from South Korea.

▪ Inter-Korean Trade in 2014

The volume of inter-Korean trade hit a record high in 2014 on growth in exchanges at the Kaesong Industrial Complex in the North despite Seoul's punitive sanctions on Pyongyang.

The value of inter-Korean trade reached US$2.343 billion in 2014, up 106.2% from a year earlier, according to data by the South's unification ministry. The volume accounted for 99.8% of the total inter-Korean trade.

An increase in inter-Korean trade mainly resulted from a rise in exchanges at the inter-Korean industrial park, even as Seoul has imposed punitive sanctions that ban economic exchanges with North Korea since 2010 following the North's deadly sinking of a South Korean warship.

The joint factory park, which opened in 2004, was the last remaining symbol of inter-Korean reconciliation. It serves as a major revenue source for the cash-strapped communist North, while South Korea has utilized cheap but skilled North Korean laborers.

A total of 124 South Korean small- and medium-sized enterprises hired about 53,000 North Korean workers at the industrial complex.

■ Number of North Korean Defectors Tumble over the Past 3 Years

The number of North Koreans who defected to South Korea has fallen sharply over the past three years since the North's new leader took power. The number of the North Korean defectors came to 1,396, down nearly 50% from 2,076 in 2011. The number of North Korean defectors has been decreasing since reaching its peak of 2,914 in 2009.

In particular, the number of the North Korean defectors reached the 1,500 range between 2012-2013 as it had sharply dropped since late 2011 when Kim Jong-un took power. Analysts said that less North Koreans defected to South Korea as the North's economic situation improved thanks to its adoption of market economic factors.

■ N. Korea Continues to Detain South Korean Missionary

South Korea urged North Korea on Oct. 22 to set free a South Korean Baptist missionary, in a demand that followed Pyongyang's release of an American man. Kim Jung-wook, 50, was arrested by the North's authorities in October 2013, while traveling there. He was sentenced by North Korea to hard labor for life on charges of spying and setting up underground churches.

"Our government once again calls on (North Korea) to free the missionary and repatriate him," unification ministry spokesman Lim Byeong-cheol said at a press briefing. He was asked about Seoul's position on the issue of Kim as the North unexpectedly released Jeffrey Fowle, one of three Americans held there.

"Our government will make constant efforts, in cooperation with the international community, so that he will return to the arms of his family," added Lim.

Meanwhile, the White House and the State Department announced the release of the 56-year-old Fowle, but the North's state-controlled media have kept mum on it.

■ Inter-Korean Joint Dictionary Project

South and North Korea in October resumed a project to publish a joint Korean dictionary about five years after it last met in October 2009.

A group consisting of 28 South Korean lexicographers visited North Korea from Oct. 30-Nov. 8 to meet their North Korean colleagues. During their stay in the country, they discussed ways of publishing the dictionary.

Earlier, lexicographers from South and North Koreas held a meeting in the Chinese city of Shenyang from July 29-Aug. 6. It was the 21st session of its kind, since a related inter-Korean committee was launched in 2006.

The project started in 2005 with the aim "to integrate and compile words used by both Koreas and to expand the width and depth of cultural community for the reunification era and onwards," according to the committee's website.

The publication work, however, was officially suspended in 2010 after Seoul accused Pyongyang of torpedoing one of its warships killing 46 South Korean sailors onboard.

Officially, both sides speak the same Korean language, but the gap between daily used words has grown over the past decades not only because of differences in local dialects, but also due to an influx of foreign languages into the South. The North, on the other hand, has remained largely isolated and maintained the use of so-called pure Korean words.

The two Koreas plan to make a dictionary of the Korean language with over 300,000 entries by April 2019.

Chronology
of Korea (1900~2013)

Yonhap News Agency

1900

April 10 Hanseong Electric, the country's first electric energy producer, which was established two years earlier, installs street lights for the first time in Jongno, the central district of Seoul, where the royal palaces of the Joseon Dynasty are located.

1901

Feb. 12 The Currency Act is promulgated, adopting gold standard for the first time in Korea.

April Resident ministers are appointed for a number of foreign countries for the first time in Korea.

Aug. 17 Hansung Electric Co. holds a ceremony to mark the first time that electric lights are turned on in Seoul.

Aug. 20 Construction begins on a railroad connecting Seoul and Busan.

1902

March 14 A ground-breaking ceremony is held in Mapo, central Seoul, to mark the beginning of construction on the Gyeongui railway linking Sinuiju, a city on the Korean Peninsula's border with China, and Busan, a southeastern port city.

March 19 The first long-distance telephone line of the nation is inaugurated between Seoul and Incheon.

Dec. 21 A group of 121 Koreans leaves the port of Incheon to emigrate to Hawaii. They were the first Korean immigrants on the U.S. island and part of some 7,400 Koreans who permanently settled there, mostly as workers on sugar cane plantations, from 1902 to 1905.

1903

Jan. 13 A group of 102 Koreans lands in Honolulu, Hawaii, after traveling across the Pacific Ocean on the S.S. Gaelic, marking the first wave of Korean emigration to the United States.

Aug. 11 The Joseon Dynasty (1392-1910) signs a trade agreement with Denmark.

1904

Feb. 22 The Korea-Japan Protocol is signed, providing Japan a foot-hold in Korea.

May 18 The Korea-Russia Treaty is repealed under pressure of Japan.

Dec. 27 Korea's royal court under the Joseon Dynasty (1392-1910) appoints U.S. diplomat D.W. Stevens as its foreign affairs advisor.

1905

Jan. 1 The Seoul-Busan rail line is inaugurated.

Jan. 18 The royal authorities announce currency regulations that officially acknowledge the Japanese currency on the peninsula.

July 1 The Seoul branch of the First City Bank of Japan is made the central bank of the Kingdom of Joseon.

Aug. 1 The daily Daehan Maeil Sinbo issues its inaugural edition.

Oct. 27 The Korean National Red Cross is established.

Nov. 9 Japan forces the Korean court to sign the Korea-Japan Treaty. Emperor Gojong on Nov. 17 sends his emissaries to the United States, Russia, Germany and France with secret letters declaring the invalidity of the treaty.

Nov. 17 Japan signs a "Protectorate Treaty" with Korea's Joseon Dynasty (1392-1910), which led to Japan's 1910-45 colonization of the Korean Peninsula. The treaty was enforced despite opposition from the Korean emperor Gojong and ended the era of ruling dynasties in Korea. The treaty stripped Korea of its rights to sign international agreements, and a Japanese resident-general was dispatched to the peninsula to take charge of all diplomatic relations.

Dec. 20 The Japanese government recalls all Korean overseas resident ministers.

1906

Jan. 1 The Foreign Ministry of the Kingdom of Korea is abolished with its functions taken over by the Japanese.

Feb. 1 The Japanese Resident General's Office is established in Seoul.

April 3 A railway opens, linking Seoul, now in South Korea, and Sinuiju, now in North Korea.

April 16 An express train from the southeastern port city of Busan travels 450 kilometers to Seoul in 11 hours, a record speed for that era. In 2004, the nation's new high-speed Korea Train Express, or KTX, covered that distance in about two hours and 40 minutes.

April 22 The country's first bicycle race is held in Seoul.

May 19 An anti-Japan rebel army led by former Minister Min Jeong-sik occupies the Hongju Castle. In June Choe Ik-hyeon and Im Byeong-chan also revolt at Sunchang, southern Korea.

Nov. 11 Korea's first recognized modern drama, "Eunsegye" (Snow World), is staged at the Wongaksa Theatre.

1907

June 16 A group of Korean emissaries denounces the Japanese aggression at the second International Peace Conference held at The Hague, the Netherlands.

July 14 Lee Jun, a Korean patriot, commits suicide by slashing his belly with a knife in The Hague after he was blocked from attending an international peace meeting in the Dutch city where he wanted to protest Japan's colonial subjugation of the Korean Peninsula.

July 20 Emperor Gojong abdicates under Japanese pressure amid uproarious objections among the Korean people.

July 24 The third Korea-Japan Treaty is signed, vesting in the Japanese the right to supervise the internal affairs of Korea.

Aug. 1 The royal government is forced to announce the dissolution of the Korean armed forces.

Aug. 6 The Wonju Garrison troops clash with Japanese touching off widespread rebellion in the country in protest against the dissolution of Korean forces.

1908

Dec. 28 After colonizing the Korean Peninsula in 1905, the Japanese colonial government establishes the Oriental Development Company in Seoul as an economic base to control Korea's land and business.

1909

July 31 The Korean Defense Ministry is abolished by Japan.

Oct. 26 Patriot An Jung-geun shoots Hirobumi Ito, the first Japanese resident Gov. Gen., to death at the Harbin, Manchuria railway station.

1910

Feb. 14 Korean independence fighter An Jung-geun is sentenced to death for the assassination of Japanese Governor-General Hirobumi Ito in October of the preceding year.

Feb. 18 The first commercial movie theater opens in Seoul.

March 26 Ahn Jung-geun, a Korean independence fighter who resisted Japanese colonial rule, is executed at a prison in China by Japanese authorities. Ahn was arrested in 1909 for assassinating Ito Hirobumi, the Japanese resident-general in Korea, at a railway station in Harbin, a city in China's Heilongjiang Province.

April 15 Korean linguist Ju Si-gyeong publishes a grammar book that consolidates the modern-day usage of the Korean language.

June 24 The Japanese government takes over the police force in Korea.

Aug. 29 The Korea-Japan Annexation Treaty comes into force, marking a tragic end to the Joseon Dynasty.

1911

Aug. 23 The Japanese colonial government, which ruled the Korean Peninsula from 1910 until 1945, announces a new public education system in Korea to prohibit the use of Korean language at schools.

1912

March 18 The Japanese government establishes a judiciary system in Korea, a Japanese colony from 1910 to 1945. Under the system, defendants can make appeals three times as in Japan and European countries.

Aug. 13 The overall land survey of the country is set about. It was completed on June 18, 1918.

1913

May 13 The Heungsadan (Young Korean Academy) is organized in Los Angeles under the leadership of Dr. An Chang-ho to carry out an independence movement.

1914

Jan. 7 Ewha Hakdang (Ewha School), the first educational institute for women, establishes Korea's first modern kindergarten.

Aug. 16 A railway linking Seoul to Wonsan is opened.

1915

April 24 A group of South Korean journalists form an association of newspapers.

1917

Sept. Park Yong-man represents Korea at the International Conference of Small Nations held in New York.

1918

June 18 The Japanese colonial regime completes a research project on land ownership in Korea after eight years of collecting data. The large-scale project was aimed at documenting land ownership on the Korean Peninsula and modernizing data management, but ended up leading to the consolidation of land acquisitions by the Japanese, who had not been legally allowed to own land in Korea. Many Korean farmers lost their property during the registration process, and their land was sold to Japanese companies or individuals.

1919

Jan. 22 Abdicated Emperor Gojong dies amid widespread rumor that he was poisoned to death by the Japanese.

Feb. 8 Some 800 Korean students in Tokyo, Japan gather in secrecy to plot an independence movement.

Feb. 10 A group of Korean students in Japan denounces the Japanese colonial rule of the Korean Peninsula and holds a ceremony at the YMCA building in Tokyo to declare Korea's independence. Korea was occupied as a colony by Japan from 1910 to 1945.

March 1 The Samil (March 1) Independence Movement breaks out as 33 national leaders read the Declaration of Independence at Pagoda Park of Seoul.

• Independence movement leaders found the Korean Provisional Government in exile in Shanghai. Its cabinet was formed April 17, with Syngman Rhee as Prime Minister.

April 10 The provisional government of Korea, established in Shanghai, promulgates a provisional constitution and adopts a modern name for their country, "Daehanminguk", with Syngman Rhee etected provisional president.

April 15 The Daehan Dongnip Dan (Korea Independence Corps) is inaugurated at Liuho Hisen of Manchuria, and the National Society of Korean Residents in North Chientao of Manchuria.

• Japanese police kill a group of Korean villagers in Jeam-ri, Gyeonggi province, following their participation in street demonstrations for independence from the Japanese colonial regime. The Japanese police drove the villagers into a church, closed all the doors and opened fire before torching the building.

April 23 A group of 24 leaders from Korea's independence movement declare the establishment of a provisional government in Shanghai aimed at gaining freedom from Japanese colonial rule.

May Kim Gyu-sik, representing the Korean government in exile, appeals to the Peace Conference in Paris for independence of Korea.

May 3 Independence movement organizations found Sinheung School at Tunghua Hsien of Manchuria for training of army officers. This school became Sinheung Military Academy in May 1920.

Aug. 21 The Korean government in exile in Shanghai begins publishing its organ, the Dongnip Sinmun.

Sept. 2 Patriot Kang U-gyu hurls a bomb at Gov.-Gen. Minoru Saito at the Seoul railway station in an unsuccessful assassination attempt.

Sept. 10 Makoto Saito, the Japanese governor-general of Korea during his country's 1910-1945 colonization of the peninsula, announces "cultural governance," a scheme to deprive Koreans of their language and customs and replace them with those of Japan.

1920

Feb. The Gwangbok (Recovery of

Homeland) Army is activated at Kuanten Hsien of Manchuria.

March 5 The Chosun Ilbo begins publication. The newspaper later became one of the most popular dailies in South Korea.

April The International Socialist Conference held in Brussels, Belgium asks the League of Nations and world powers to recognize the Korean Provisional Government in exile in Shanghai.

April 1 The Dong-A Ilbo, now one of the oldest and largest dailies in the country, is founded with the aim of expressing Korean opinions, restoring Korean culture and promoting democracy in the face of Japanese colonial rule over Korea.

June An independence army belonging to the National Association of North Chientao defeats a large unit of the Japanese army in the battle of Fungwe Dong.

June An independence army called Guwolsan Budae (unit) is organized by Lee Myong-so and other independence fighters.

Oct. 20 An independence army led by Kim Jwa-jin and Lee Beom-seok annihilate a Japanese regiment in a battle at Chongshanri.

1921

Feb. 4 Korean independence movement leaders operating in Manchuria attack Japanese forces at Chongjin Port on the northeastern coast and kill about 40 Japanese soldiers. Korea was under Japanese colonial rule from 1910 to 1945.

March 19 Na Hye-seok becomes the first female Korean painter to hold an exhibition in Korea. The exhibition was held at the headquarters of the Gyeongseong Ilbo newspaper in Seoul.

June 1 The first fine arts exhibition in Korea opens.

1922

Aug. 22 Many independence movement groups including the Korean Independence Corps and the Gwangbok Army Command merge into Daehan Tonguibu.

Nov. 6 Korea's first recognized pilot, Ahn Chang-nam, succeeds in his maiden flight from Tokyo to Osaka.

1923

July 14 The Korean Revolutionary Committee is organized by followers of Chondogyo (a Korean native religion).

Sept. 1 Over 5,000 Koreans are murdered by Japanese mobs in Tokyo and neighboring areas in the chaos of the Great Earthquake of Kanto District.

Sept. 2 Anarchist Pak Yol is arrested after an unsuccessful attempt to assassinate the Japanese emperor.

1924

May Volunteers belonging to the Daehan Tonguibu headquartered in Manchuria attack Gov.-Gen. Saito in an unsuccessful assassination attempt.

1926

April 25 Dethroned King Sunjong dies amid rumors that he had been poisoned to death by the Japanese. On the occasion of the royal funerals on June 10 some 30,000 students of Seoul demonstrated against the Japanese.

April 27 King Yeongchin, the second son of King Gojong of the Joseon Dynasty (1392-1910), succeeds King Sunjong during Japan's colonial rule of the Korean Peninsula. He had lived and studied in Japan since the age of 11, and his marriage to a Japanese aristocrat was arranged.

April 28 Song Hak-seon, a Korean fighter for independence from Japanese colonial rule, makes an unsuccessful attempt to assassinate Makoto Saito, the Japanese governor general in Korea.

Dec. 14 Independence fighter Kim Gu is inaugurated as chief marshal of the Korean Provisional Government, which was set up in Shanghai, China.

Dec. 28 Independence fighter Na Seok-ju shoots himself to death after throwing bombs into a Japanese-owned bank and the Oriental Development Company in Seoul.

1927

Feb. 15 Nationalist Communist groups form a consolidated common front named Singanhoe.

1929

March The Joseon Revolutionary Party is organized in Chilin Province, Manchuria, and the Hankuk Revolutionary Party in Nanking, China.

March 24 Gyeongseong Imperial University, the predecessor of Seoul National University, holds its first graduation ceremony.

Nov. Independence leader Kim Jwa-jin organizes the Korean Autonomy Federation in Manchuria.

Nov. 3 An independence movement against Japanese breaks out among Korean students in Gwangju.

1930

Jan. 25 The Korean Independence Party is organized in Shanghai by Lee Dong-nyong, Lee Shi-yong, and Kim Gu.

April 16 The Dong-A Ilbo, one of the first dailies in Korea, is suspended from publishing by the Japanese colonial regime.

1931

Sept. 18 The Manchurian Incident (War) breaks out inflicting damage and casualties on Korean residents, heralding full-scale Japanese invasion of mainland China.

1932

Jan. 8 Patriot Lee Bong-chang throws a bomb at Japanese Emperor Hirohito in front of the Sakurada Gate in an unsuccessful assassination attempt.

March An independence army belonging to the Joseon Revolutionary Party defeats the Japanese Army at Yunglin Zeh, Shinpin Hsien.

April 29 Patriot Yun Bong-gil bombs Japanese dignitaries celebrating the birthday of the Japanese emperor at a park in Shanghai, killing Gen. Yoshinori Shirakawa.

July The Korean Independence Movement Youth Corps is organized in Shanghai.

1933

Feb. Syngman Rhee condemns the Japanese aggression on Korea and Manchuria as representative of the Korean Provisional Government at the League of Nations.

April 15 Korean independence army in Manchuria, in collaboration with a Chinese volunteer army, defeats a combined Japanese-Manchurian force at Shutaohotzu, and occupies the Tongkin Cheng in June.

July 5 Korean political parties including the Korea Independence Party merge into the Nationalist Revolutionary Party at Nanking, China.

Aug. 28 A combined force of Korea and China destroys the Japanese 72nd Regiment at Tatentsu Lin in east Manchuria.

Nov. 4 The Korean Language Society announces the first orthography for the Korean language.

1934

May 7 A group of writers and historians establishes "Jindan," a research institute dedicated to the study of Korean language and history. Use of the Korean language was partially banned under the Japanese colonial occupation of Korea, which lasted from 1910-1945.

1935

March 18 The first telephone switchboard in Korea begins operation at a post office in North Hamgyong Province, the northernmost region of the peninsula. The area later became part of North Korea.

1936

Aug. 9 Sohn Ki-jung wins the marathon race at the 11th Olympics in Berlin. A Korean, Sohn ran for Japan, which occupied the Korean Peninsula from 1910-1945.

Dec. The Anti-Japan People's Front is organized in Gapsan, South Hamgyeong Province.

1937

Feb. The Nationalist Revolutionary Party convenes an extraordinary convention in Shanghai, expels the leftist elements, and is reorganized as the Joseon Revolutionary Party.

March 10 Around 20,000 Koreans are forced to relocate to northeastern China by Japan, which colonized the Korean Peninsula from 1910 to 1945.

March 18 The Japanese governor-general orders government agencies in Korea to use Japanese as their official language. The announcement was part of the Japanese policy to eradicate Korean culture and language.

May 11 The Japanese colonial regime orders 100,000 Koreans to move to Manchuria in northeastern China in an attempt to make it easier for Japan to invade China and to weaken Korea's independence movement. The descendants of those Koreans, living in villages named after their hometowns, are now Chinese nationals.

1938

March 31 Sungshil High School in Pyongyang is closed after refusing to force students to worship at Japanese shrines. Japanese authorities introduced the requirement as part of cultural colonization efforts.

April 3 Sookmyung Women's College, the predecessor of Sookmyung Women's University, opens.

1940

Feb. 11 The Japanese colonial regime orders all Koreans to adopt Japanese names.

Aug. 10 The dailies of the Chosun Ilbo and the Dong-A Ilbo are closed. They are restored after the Japanese rule ended in Korea in 1945.

1941

March 31 The Japanese colonial government bans the teaching and use of the Korean language in schools.

Dec. 9 The Korean Provisional Government declares a war of independence on Japan.

1943

March 1 Japanese colonizers proclaim a system forcing young Koreans to fight for the Japanese Imperial Army during

World War II. Over a million Koreans are believed to have been forced into conscription or labor as a result.

Aug. The Korean Gwangbok Army dispatches guerrillas to the Indian and Burmese fronts to fight the Japanese army.

1944

June France and Poland recognize the Korean Provisional Government.

June 17 Imperial Japan enforces a rice collection order on Korean farmers across the country, forcing them to send their produce to Japan, which was spending extensively on its military during World War II. Brass household objects, such as spoons, chopsticks and kitchen knives, were also collected to make weapons. The excessive exploitation caused many Korean farmers to leave their homes for northeastern China or any place they could feed their families.

Feb. 8 Japanese colonial authorities in Korea begin conscripting Korean laborers for work in mines and factories overseas.

1945

Feb. 9 The Korean Provisional Government declares war against Japan and Germany.

Feb. 16 Poet Yoon Dong-ju dies in a prison in Japan at the age of 29. Japanese police arrested him as a "thought criminal" pursuing an anti-government drive. Serving his two-year jail term in a Fukuoka prison, Yoon died from harsh treatment.

July 26 The Potsdam Declaration demands unconditional surrender of Japan and real-firmed independence to be granted to Korea.

Aug. 14 Japan accepts the Potsdam Declaration and announces its unconditional surrender Aug. 15.

Aug. 15 Korea is liberated from Japan's colonial rule, which began in 1910. On the same day, Yeo Un-hyung (1886-1947), a left-leaning nationalist, sets up a national foundation preparation committee.

Aug. 24 A Japanese ship on its way to Korea's southern port of Busan from Japan, carrying 3,725 Koreans, explodes.

The Ukishima-Maru was returning Koreans who had been forced to leave home and work in Japan during the 1910-45 colonial era. The incident happened a little more than a week after Japan announced it would give up any rights to Korea following its defeat in World War II. More than 500 people died in the explosion, which survivors said was caused by a bomb. A statement from the Japanese government claimed the ship sank when it accidentally hit a mine. South and North Korean civic groups demand that the Japanese government take responsibility for the incident, saying it was premeditated.

Sept. 1 The Joseon Kukmin Party is inaugurated with An Jae-hong as chairman. It was reorganized into Kukmin Party Sept. 24.

Sept. 2 The Supreme Command of Allied Powers announces Korea would be divided into two halves under joint occupation by the United States and Soviet forces.

Sept. 3 U.S. forces land at Incheon to occupy the southern half of Korea below the 38th Parallel.

Sept. 11 The operation of a railway line linking Seoul and Sinuiju, a border city in what is now North Korea, is stopped amid deepening enmity between the rival political forces which controlled the southern and northern parts of the Korean Peninsula.

Oct. 24 All Japanese nationals are ordered to clear out of Korea.

Nov. 3 The right-wing Chosun Democratic Party is organized in Pyongyang with Cho Man-sik as chairman.

Nov. 13 The U.S. Military Government establishes the National Constabulary Command.

Nov. 23 A group of leaders of the Korean Provisional Government including Kim Gu returns home from their exile in Shanghai.

Dec. 20 The Hapdong News Agency is inaugurated as the first news agency in Korea.

Dec. 27 Top diplomats from the United States, Britain and the Soviet Union hold a meeting in Moscow and announce a five-year United Nations trusteeship over Korea.

Dec. 29 The Central Committee for

Anti-Trusteeship National Mobilization is organized mostly by former leaders of the Korean Provisional Government.

Dec. 31 Anti-trusteeship demonstrations and strikes sweep the country.

1946

Jan. 2 The Communist Party in Korea, in a sudden about-face, declares its support for the trusteeship plan under an instruction from the North Korean Communist Party.

Jan. 19 Rightist and leftist Korean students clash over whether the Korean Peninsula should be placed under a U.N. trusteeship.

Feb. 8 The North Korean Provisional People's Committee is organized in Pyongyang with Kim Il-sung as chairman.

March 5 The North Korean Provisional People's Committee announces a sweeping land reform effecting land confiscation and redistribution without any compensation.

March 7 An express train starts running on the Seoul-Busan line.

March 13 A group of students stages protests against communism, spreading in the northern part of the Korean Peninsula, in Hamheung, a city located in what is now North Korea. After Korea regained its sovereignty from Japan in 1945, fierce clashes between capitalists and communists continued until the country was divided by the 1950-53 Korean War.

March 20 The first U.S.-Russia Joint Committee is held in Seoul under the earlier big-four agreement on Korean trusteeship to decide the future of Korea.

July 17 The U.S. military government, which occupied the southern half of the Korean Peninsular at the end of World War II, places a ban on civilian passage across the inter-Korean border set at the 38th parallel. Following the surrender of Japan, which controlled Korea as a colony from 1910 to 1945, the southern half of the Peninsular was occupied by U.S. troops and the other half by the Soviet Union's military.

Aug. 22 The Seoul National University is founded.

Dec. 2 Korean independence fighter Syngman Rhee, who later became South Korea's first president, visits the United States with a proposal that his country set up its own government.

Dec. 12 The Korean Provisional Parliament is inaugurated with Kim Gyu-sik as speaker.

1947

June 3 A transitional government is established in southern Korea, separate from communist leadership in northern Korea.

June 21 The International Olympic Committee accepts South Korea's proposal for membership.

Sept. 17 The United States formally brings the Korean problem to the U.N. General Assembly, which resolves on Nov. 24 to establish a unified government through general elections under the supervision of the U.N. Temporary Commission on Korea (UNTCOK).

Dec. 16 North Korea implements its first currency reforms in an effort to strengthen its communist economic system, separate from that of the Soviet Union, and to prevent the inflow of the South Korean currency.

1948

Jan. 8 The United Nations Temporary Commission on Korea arrives in Korea.

Jan. 16 The first Korean opera, Chunhyang, is staged.

Jan. 31 A total of 2,068,073 Koreans return to Korea from overseas.

Feb. 26 The United Nations decides to conduct general elections in what is now South Korea, giving up on plans to establish a single Korean government after a Soviet-backed regime took control in the northern part of the peninsula.

Feb. 28 Kim Gu, an independence fighter and politician, publicly opposes the U.N.'s proposal to hold a separate general election in southern Korea. Kim said the election would lead to the division of the Korean Peninsula, and that communist-controlled northern Korea and U.N.-supervised southern Korea should set up a common government.

March 1 Lt. Gen. John R. Hodge, head of the United States Army Military Government in Korea, announces general elections are to be held in South Korea.

April 3 An uprising breaks out on Jeju, the largest island off the Korean Peninsula, when the U.S.-backed South Korean government attempts to hold elections separately from the communist North. Jeju residents attacked police stations on the island, prompting U.S. commanders in Seoul to dispatch 1,700 Korean police and thousands of soldiers. Historians estimate there were nearly 14,000 civilian deaths in the ensuing violence.

May 5 North Korea disconnects electric power lines to the South.

May 10 General elections are held in South Korea under the supervision of UNTCOK for establishing an independent government. The elections were boycotted by leftists and their fellow travelers.

May 31 The Constituent Assembly opens, resolves July 1 to christen the new nation the Republic of Korea, adopts the new constitution July 17, elects Dr. Syngman Rhee president of the new Republic July 20.

June 2 The United States House of Representatives decides to extend aid totaling US$ 170 million to South Korea.

June 22 South Korea sends its athletes to participate in the Olympic Games, held that year in London, marking the first time for the country to compete in the quadrennial event.

July 17 South Korea promulgates its first Constitution and designates July 17 as Constitution Day, a week ahead of the inauguration of Syngman Rhee as the country's first president.

July 20 The National Assembly elects Syngman Rhee president and Yi Shi-yong vice president.

Aug. 15 The government of the Republic of Korea, or South Korea, is established.

Aug. 25 North Korea holds a general election to establish a separate government. South Korea held its own election in May that year.

Sept. 3 The U.S. military in South Korea hands over police authority to the South Korean government.

Sept. 5 South Korean Army and Navy are inaugurated.

Sept. 9 North Korean communists found the Democratic People's Republic of Korea in Pyongyang with Kim Il-sung as premier.

Sept. 30 The National Assembly passes legislation on the use of Hangul (the Korean Alphabet).

Oct. 20 A group of soldiers in Yeosu, a port city 455 kilometers south of Seoul, rebels against the South Korean government, which had just been established. The soldiers, who supported reunification of the two Koreas, refused the government's order to put down civil protests on Jeju Island by residents who also opposed the government. The demonstrations spread to a nearby city, Suncheon, and the soldiers held the city, along with Yeosu, under their control for a number of days. The government proclaimed martial law to put down the rebellion and occupied the cities with support from the U.S. army stationed in South Korea. The exact number of civilian deaths during the rebellion has never been determined.

Nov. 20 The anti-communist National Security Law is put into effect. The law bans any activity that might assist North Korea and prohibits unapproved contact or sympathizing with North Korea.

Dec. 12 The U.N. General Assembly recognizes the Republic of Korea Government as the sole lawfully-elected one Korea.

1949

Jan. 1 The United States formally recognizes the Republic of Korea Government and appoints John J. Muccio as the first U.S. Ambassador to Korea.

Jan. 7 South Korea and Japan sign a secret pact calling on the latter to return cultural properties looted during Japan's 35-year colonial rule of Korea.

Jan. 18 South Korea establishes diplomatic relations with Britain.

March 3 South Korea establishes diplomatic relations with the Philippines.

March 18 North Korea and China sign a mutual defense treaty.

March 24 Chang Myon, the first South Korean ambassador to the United States, takes office in Washington.

March 31 South Korea outlaws trade with North Korea as an ideological rift deepens on the peninsula. The two sides established separate governments in 1948, and the deterioration of relations eventually led to the 1950-53 Korean War.

April 15 South Korean Marine Corps is inaugurated in Jinhae, South Gyeongsang Province.

April 23 Republic of Korea and Japan sign trade agreement.

April 27 The South Korean National Assembly passes a bill on farmland reform for the redistribution of land previously owned by Japanese colonizers and the registration of all landowners.

May 1 The first census shows there are 20,166,758 people in South Korea.

Aug. 7 South Korean President Syngman Rhee holds a summit meeting with Nationalist Chinese President Chang Kai-shek at Jinhae to work out joint strategy against communism.

Aug. 16 South Korea joins the World Health Organization.

Oct. 12 South Korea establishes its Air Force.

Oct. 29 The Communist Party and its affiliated organizations are outlawed in South Korea.

1950

Jan. 26 South Korea-U.S. Financial and Economic Cooperation Agreement is signed.

March 1 South Korean government designates Wednesday every week as 'No Liquor, No Meat Day.'

March 17 South Korea establishes diplomatic ties with Sweden.

April 12 Koreans sweep first, second and third places in the Boston Marathon.

May 25 South Korea joins the United Nations Educational, Scientific and Cultural Organization (UNESCO).

May 30 The second National Assembly is elected and opened June 19 with Sin Ik-hui as speaker.

June 2 South Korea and Japan sign a trade treaty, five years after Korea's recovery of its sovereignty from Japan.

June 12 The Bank of Korea is established.

June 25 The Korean War is provoked by North Korean communists who launched an all-out invasion across the 38th Parallel. The U.N. Security Council

ordered immediate cease-fire, but North Korea ignored it. The Security Council on June 27 resolved to sanction North Korea. The United States the same day ordered its army and navy elements to help defend Korea.

June 28 The North Korean Army occupies Seoul just three days after it crosses the 38th parallel, the pre-Korean War boundary between North and South Korea.

• The South Korean Army blows up the Han River Bridge in an effort to slow the advancing communist forces. Hundreds of people, including civilians, were killed in the explosion.

July 1 U.S. ground troops land in the port of Busan, 450 kilometers southeast of Seoul, and Canadian combat vessels leave for South Korea as part of U.N. coalition forces to join the Korean War, which broke out on June 25 when North Korea attacked South Korea. The U.N. Security Council, before that date, held an emergency meeting to pass a resolution to dispatch coalition troops to the South to help deter the North Korean communist forces. The war ended with an armistice agreement on July 27, 1953, leaving the two Koreas technically at war.

July 4 U.S. troops engage North Korean forces in Osan. The encounter marks the first clash between U.S. and North Korean soldiers in the Korean War.

July 16 As North Korean invaders advance on the nation in the early days of the Korean War, President Syngman Rhee moves his government from Daejeon in central South Korea to the southeastern city of Daegu. Rhee was later forced to move it further south to Busan, a port city.

July 26 About 300 South Korean civilian refugees are killed by retreating U.S. troops at Nogun-ri, a village in central South Korea, during the early weeks of the Korean War. In 1999, after repeated denials, the U.S. government under then President Bill Clinton acknowledged that the massacre took place and expressed deep regret.

Sept. 15 U.N. coalition troops led by U.S. General Douglas MacArthur carry out an amphibious landing at Incheon, a port city west of Seoul.

Sept. 28 South Korean and U.N. forces

hold a ceremony to officially declare the recapture of Seoul, two days after they retook the capital from North Korean forces.

Oct. 19 South Korean and U.N. Forces capture Pyongyang and hold it until Dec. 4.

Oct. 22 American-led U.N. forces advance to Korea's border with China a little more than a month after the Incheon landing.

Nov. 2 Communist China throws 600,000 troops into the Korean War in support of North Korea, launching 'human-sea warfare.'

Nov. 25 The Seoul Central Broadcasting Station starts regular broadcasting.

Dec. 10 500,000 North Korean refugees arrive in South Korea.

Dec. 14 The United Nations approves a resolution for the establishment of a U.N. committee to work toward signing an armistice to bring a ceasefire to the Korean War.

1951

Jan. 3 South Korea's government begins pre-censorship on publications.

Jan. 4 South Korean troops and U.N.-led coalition forces retreat from Seoul amid an offensive by North Korean and Chinese forces.

Jan. 16 China rejects a United Nations proposal for a cease-fire in the Korean War. The government signed the armistice that later concluded the 1950-53 conflict and therefore the North and South technically remain at war.

Feb. 11 Over 500 villagers are shot and killed in Geochang, a county in the southeast of the country, by South Korean soldiers who wrongfully identified them as collaborators with North Korean communists. The indiscriminate killings continued for several days.

March 1 The government announces allocation of farm land to 1.2 million sharecroppers.

March 5 The government counts 3,817,000 refugees in 939 camps in the South.

March 14 The South Korean army and United Nations forces retake Seoul after it was occupied by the North Korean People's Army during the Korean War.

March 24 South Korean forces advance north of the 38th Parallel, which roughly bisects the Korean Peninsula, during the three-year Korean War (1950-1953).

March 27 The Ministry of Education introduces a new school system -- six years for elementary school, three each for middle and high school, and four for university.

June 23 The Soviet delegate at the United Nations proposes a truce in Korea. The 16 Korean allies accepted it June 27.

July 10 Truce negotiations begin at Kaesong.

Aug. 16 Telephone line between Seoul and Busan opens.

Sept. 6 South Korea establishes the Women's Army Corps.

Oct. 8 Panmunjom, a small village near the 38th parallel that forms the border between South and North Korea, is selected as the site of armistice talks on ending the fratricidal conflict. Negotiations dragged on, and a formal cease-fire agreement was not signed until almost two years later.

1952

Jan. 18 President Syngman Rhee promulgates the 'Peace Line' in the East Sea.

Feb. 1 The Korea Veterans Association is launched.

Feb. 16 The first round of the Korea-Japan talks for normalization of their relations begins in Tokyo, but is disrupted Feb. 20 due to sharp differences between the two sides.

Feb. 18 North Korean prisoners of war being held at a jail on Geoje Island off South Korea's southern coast start a revolt. About 100 were killed during the conflict with anti-communist inmates and the rest were set free in 1953 when the Korean War ended with an armistice.

April 26 Six persons receive the nation's first Ph.D. degrees.

May 26 A large number of opposition lawmakers are arrested in a political turmoil over a constitutional amendment tabled by the governing party to have the president elected at the polls instead of at the National Assembly.

July 7 The National Assembly adopts the first revision of the Constitution.

Aug. 5 Elections for the presidency are held under the revised constitution which the ruling party had railroaded. Syngman Rhee was elected president, and Ham Tae-yong vice-president.

Sept. 1 South Korea introduces compulsory military service.

Dec. 2 U.S. President-elect Dwight D. Eisenhower visits the Korean front. He promises Korea military and economic assistance in return for an unwanted cease-fire.

1953

Jan. 5 South Korean President Syngman Rhee expresses his intention to resume diplomatic relations with Japan after meeting with the country's Prime Minister Shigeru Yoshida.

Feb. 15 The 'won' currency is replaced with the 'hwan' at the rate of 100-1 in the first money reform of the nation.

March 11 The U.N. General Assembly resolves to extend economic aid to South Korea.

March 28 North Korea agrees to exchange prisoners of war wounded during the ongoing conflict with South Korea. The war ended in a ceasefire signed in July later that year.

April 16 The government asks all artists and cultural personalities to register.

June 1 President Syngman Rhee orders the release of 27,000 North Korean and Chinese prisoners of war who wanted to remain in freedom in a bombshell gesture of his protest to a cease-fire which was about to be concluded.

June 8 The U.N. Command signs a treaty with the North Korean and Chinese forces to exchange prisoners captured during the 1950-53 Korean War.

June 18 The government releases 25,000 anti-Communist North Korean prisoners of war.

July 27 The Korean Armistice Agreement is signed.

Aug. 5 South and North Korea begin repatriating prisoners of war through the truce village of Panmunjom.

Aug. 8 The Korea-U.S. Mutual Defense Treaty is initialed in Seoul.

Oct. 27 The Korea-U.S. Mutual Defense Treaty is signed in Washington.

Nov. 27 President Syngman Rhee visits Taiwan, and releases a joint communique with Chinese President Chiang Kai-shek announcing their agreement on formation of a joint front against communists.

Dec. 14 The Korea-U.S. Agreement on Korea's economic reconstruction and financial stabilization is signed.

1954

Jan. 18 The South Korean government establishes a territorial marker on Dokdo, a group of uninhabited islets located in the East Sea.

Jan. 30 The United Nations Educational, Scientific and Cultural Organization (UNESCO) launches its Korean committee.

Feb. 3 South Korea designates a civilian-restricted area between 5 and 20 kilometers south of the Southern Limit Line (SLL). The SLL is just 2 kilometers south of the heavily fortified border between the two Koreas.

March 21 Korean Standard Time is set.

April 3 The Korea Development Bank, the nation's representative borrower of overseas funds, begins operations.

April 26 The Geneva Political Conference opens with 14 nations participating in to solve the Korean problem, but closed on June 20 without any result.

May 20 The third National Assembly is elected, and convened on June 8.

June 15 The first general meeting of the Asian People's Anti-Communist League is held at Jinhae, South Gyeongsang Province.

July 25 President Syngman Rhee visits the United States.

Nov. 29 The second revision of the Constitution is adopted after the result of votes rejecting the proposal was overturned.

Dec. 15 The first private broadcasting station, the Christian Broadcasting System (HLKY), begins broadcasting.

1955

Jan. 18 Lee Jung-seop, whose oil paintings were still new in his war-torn homeland, holds his first exhibition in a hall of the Midopa Department Store in Seoul. Born in Pyongyang in 1916 and educated in Tokyo, Lee's work depicts the indefatigable spirit of the Korean people through such images as a cow laboring tirelessly for farmers.

March 30 The Ministry of Education announces measures to check imports of foreign movies and provide for censorship.

May 25 The pro-Pyongyang General Association of Korean residents in Japan, commonly referred to as Chongnyeon, is established in Tokyo.

May 31 The United States signs an aid agreement to supply surplus farm products to Korea.

June 23 Rationing of grain in major cities begins.

Aug. 26 Korea joins the International Monetary Fund (IMF) and the International Bank for Reconstruction and Development (IBRD).

Sept. 19 The Democratic Party is inaugurated with Sin Ik-hui as its top leader.

Oct. 14 South Korea and Japan resume bilateral trade for the first time since Korea's liberation from Japanese colonial rule in 1945. The two countries normalized their diplomatic ties in 1965.

Oct. 19 North Korea and China sign a trade agreement.

1956

March 3 South Korea launches the Korea Stock Exchange, the country's first stock market operator for the main bourse.

May 15 Syngman Rhee is elected president, and Chang Myon of the opposition party vice-president in the presidential election.

May 18 Marshal Law is declared across the country.

June 16 South Korea's first television network, HLKZ-TV, starts broadcasting.

1957

Feb. 3 The government announces six-year economic plan.

April 7 The Korean Newspaper Editors Association is inaugurated.

1958

Jan. 1 The National Assembly passes Election Law that includes restrictions on the press.

Feb. 16 A Korean National Airlines (KNA) plane is hijacked by communists to North Korea while flying from Busan to Seoul with 26 persons aboard.

March 6 Twenty-six South Koreans return home after being held in North Korea for almost three weeks. They were taken to the North on Feb. 16 when a group of communist spies hijacked their plane en route to Seoul from Busan. The North did not return the plane.

March 20 A commercial airline starts flights between Seoul and Jeju.

May 21 The fourth National Assembly is elected and convened on June 7.

Dec. 24 Opposition lawmakers occupy the National Assembly hall to prevent the passage of a revision to the National Security Law allegedly designed to suppress the press. The ruling Liberal Party had them thrown out, and railroaded the bill.

1959

Jan. 27 Lee Dong-jun, a correspondent of the Soviet Union's Pravda newspaper in Pyongyang, defects to South Korea through the truce village of Panmunjom.

Feb. 13 The Japanese government decides to repatriate Korean residents in Japan to North Korea. The repatriation began on Dec. 24.

March 10 South Korean labor unions celebrate Labor Day for the first time in the country. It was later moved to May 1.

March 11 South Korea establishes diplomatic relations with Sweden.

March 31 South Korea establishes diplomatic relations with Denmark.

July 27 South Korea test-fires its first rocket.

1960

March 15 Syngman Rhee is elected president and Lee Gi-bung vice president.

April 4 South Korea and Japan resume trade although diplomatic relations were not normalized until 1965.

April 11 Kim Ju-yeol, a student at Masan Commercial High School who was arrested by police after participating in a pro-democracy demonstration the previous month, is found dead. His body is discovered in waters off Masan, a southeastern coastal city, adding fuel to mounting public protests against Syngman Rhee's dictatorial regime. A nationwide protest took place on April 19, pushing the president to step down.

April 19 Student uprising breaks out in Seoul, rapidly spreading throughout the country.

April 24 Vice President Lee Ki-boong resigns following the April 19 Revolution. The student-led popular uprising, which took place after the country's first president, Rhee Syng-man, revised the Constitution and rigged the election that year to extend his term of office, led to the end of Rhee's regime after 12 years in power.

April 25 A group of college professors issues a statement accusing the autocratic government of President Rhee Syng-man of using police force to crack down on pro-democracy student protesters.

Arpil 26 President Syngman Rhee announces his retirement. A caretaker cabinet was formed on April 28, with Ho Chong as acting president. He left Seoul on May 29 in secret for a self-imposed exile in Hawaii.

April 28 Lee Ki-boong, who stepped down as vice president after the April 19 student revolution for democracy, commits suicide with his family at the presidential residence in Seoul.

June 1 The government sets a grace period during which those who had illegally amassed personal wealth could surrender. Owners of nine conglomerates report tax evasions totaling 3.68 million 'hwan.'

June 15 The National Assembly amends the constitution to replace the presidential system with cabinet system of government.

June 19 U.S. President Dwight D. Eisenhower visits South Korea in his second trip to the nation after his visit to the Korean combat zone in December 1952.

July 29 The Houses of Representatives and Councilors are elected under the new constitution.

Aug. 8 The House of Representatives and the House of Councilors open.

Aug. 12 The National Assembly elects Yun Po-son president.

Aug. 23 Chang Myon of the Democratic Party is named prime minister under the new cabinet system.

Sept. 6 A goodwill mission led by Foreign Minister Kosaka arrives in Seoul as the first Japanese official to set foot in Korea since 1945.

1961

Feb. 8 South Korea and the United States sign an economic cooperation pact.

Feb. 24 South Korea and the Philippines sign a trade accord.

April 4 South Korea and the Netherlands establish diplomatic ties.

April 8 The government announces measures banning sales of foreign goods.

April 15 The government changes the school term, beginning the school year from March 1, instead of April 1.

April 22 South Korea and Japan sign a treaty on trade and commerce.

May 16 A military coup led by Maj. Gen. Park Chung-hee overthrows the government of Chang Myon.

May 18 Chang Myon cabinet resigns.

June 10 The Law on the Supreme Council for National Reconstruction (SCNR) and the Law on the Central Intelligence Agency (CIA) are promulgated.

July 2 The SCNR names Maj. Gen. Park Chung-hee its chairman.

Nov. 11 SCNR Chairman Park Chung-hee leaves Seoul, and confers with U.S. President John F. Kennedy Nov. 14-15 in Washington, D.C.

Dec. 30 KBS-TV, the first full-scale television service, is established in Seoul by the Government.

1962

Jan. 13 The First Five-Year Economic Plan (1962-1966) is announced.

Feb. 17 The government finalizes its five-year economic development plan for the nation's economy, still reeling from the effects of Japanese colonization and the Korean War. Economic revitalization was carried out through four five-year plans over 20 years until 1982, eventually achieving South Korea's globally touted economic miracle. In 1982, the project was renamed the "economic and social development plan" with a vision to improve the quality of individual lives as well as the nation's economy. The state project ended in 1996.

March 10 South Korea establishes diplomatic relations with Spain.

March 22 President Yun Po-son resigns in protest against the military government of Park Chung-hee.

March 26 South Korea establishes diplomatic relations with New Zealand.

April 9 South Korea establishes diplomatic relations with Israel.

April 15 The SCNR announces the names of 4,374 persons to be purged under the Political Purification Law.

June 10 The South Korean government implements its second currency reform, converting the basic monetary unit to the "won" from the "hwan" and devaluating it 10 to 1.

Aug. 17 Prime Minister Chang Myon is arrested without physical detention on anti-revolutionary conspiracy charges.

Dec. 17 A national referendum is conducted over a proposed constitutional amendment designed to restore a presidential system.

Dec. 27 Chairman Park Chung-hee of the SCNR announces process to revert to civilian rule.

1963

Jan. 1 KBS-TV begins broadcasting commercials, collecting fees for viewing.

Jan. 24 South and North Korea begin negotiations to form a unified Korean team for the Olympic Games.

Feb. 26 The Democratic Republican Party (DRP) is inaugurated.

April 1 South Korea establishes diplomatic relations with Peru.

May 14 The Minjong Party is inaugurated.

July 18 The Democratic Party is inaugurated.

Oct. 15 Park Chung-hee is elected president.

Nov. 26 The sixth National Assembly is elected with the Democratic Republican Party (DRP) capturing more than two thirds of its seats.

Dec. 17 The Third Republic is born as President Park Chung-hee is inaugurated under the new constitution.

Dec. 21 The nation exports manpower for the first time. The first group of 123 miners goes to West Germany to work.

1964

Feb. 6 South Korea establishes diplomatic relations with Kenya.

Feb. 7 South Korea and Kenya forge diplomatic ties.

Feb. 8 The government imports 250 Japanese cars for educational purposes.

March 10 Korean and Japanese agricultural ministers meeting is held.

March 17 Korean Air Lines Co. begins service between Seoul and Osaka, Japan.

March 24 Students of Seoul National, Korea and Yonsei universities launch demonstrations in protest against the low postured diplomacy in the Korea-Japan negotiations. Martial law is proclaimed in Seoul June 3-July 29.

June 3 10,000 university students in Seoul demonstrate, attack and destroy police substations, marshal law imposed on parts of Seoul.

Aug. 4 The National Assembly approves a government plan to dispatch combat troops to Vietnam. It opened the way for 300,000 South Korean soldiers to fight alongside the United States during the Vietnam War.

Oct. 9 North Korean athlete Sin Kum-dan who was participating in the Tokyo Olympic Games has reunion with her father for the first time in 14 years.

Dec. 6-15 President Park Chung-hee visits West Germany.

1965

Jan. 4 Korea's export in 1964 records US$ 120.7 million for the first time.

March 22 A unitary fluctuation foreign exchange system is introduced.

April 9 South Korea signs a trade agreement with West Germany.

April 16 University students in Seoul stage class boycotts to denounce the South Korean and Japanese governments' signing of a treaty on fishing, cultural, property and economic cooperation. The treaty, which was finally signed in June that year after 14 years of controversy, was criticized for yielding too much to Japan.

April 21 South Korea and Gambia establish diplomatic relations.

April 25 South Korea establishes diplomatic relations with Bolivia.

May 16-17 President Park Chung-hee visits the United States.

June 14 The Minjung Party is inaugurated with Mme. Pak Sun-chon as its head.

June 22 The Korea-Japan Basic Treaty is signed in Tokyo, and is ratified on Aug. 14 by the National Assembly.

July 17 Former President Syngman Rhee dies in Hawaii and is buried in the National Cemetery in Seoul.

July 24 The nation faces a foreign currency crisis.

Aug. 1 The government announces plans to dispatch 2,000 non-combatants to Vietnam.

Aug. 13 The National Assembly approves the government bill to deploy Korean troops in South Vietnam.

Sept. 30 Interest rates are adjusted to realistic levels.

Dec. 18 Korea and Japan normalize relations.

1966

Feb. 4 The Korea Institute of Science and Technology opens.

Feb. 22 U.S. Vice President Hubert Humphrey visits Korea, confers with Korean leaders on the dispatch of Korean troops to Vietnam.

Feb. 28 The cabinet decides to send Korean troops to Vietnam.

March 30 The Sinhan Party is inaugurated with Yun Po-son as leader.

June 14 The first ministerial meeting of the Asian and Pacific Council opens in Seoul.

July 9 The Korea-U.S. Status-of-Forces Agreement (SOFA) is signed in Seoul.

July 21 High-speed train service between Seoul and Busan opens.

July 29 The government announces the Second Five-Year Economic Development Plan (1967-1971).

Sept. 5 The first contingent of the "White Horse" division lands in South Vietnam, becoming the first South Korean military unit to take part in the Vietnam War.

Oct. 2 At the request of West Germany, the South Korean government dispatches 251 female nurses to the European nation, which experienced a shortage of workers amid the country's rapid economic growth.

Oct. 31 U.S. President Lyndon Johnson visits Korea.

1967

Jan. 30 The Korea Exchange Bank is founded.

Feb. 2 The Democratic Republican Party (DRP) nominates Park Chung-hee as its presidential candidate.

March 1 Direct telex service between Seoul and Hamburg, West Germany, opens.

March 26 West German President Heinrich Luebke visits Korea.

April 14 The General Agreement on Tariffs and Trade, a set of multilateral trade agreements aimed at the abolition of tariffs, quotas and subsidies, goes into effect in South Korea.

May 3 President Park Chung-hee is reelected, and is sworn in on July 1 for his second term.

May 17 Violinist Chung Kyung-hwa wins the 25th International Music Competition.

June 3 The seventh National Assembly is elected.

June 8 General elections are held to elect representatives to the seventh National Assembly.

July 21 Chase Manhattan Bank of the United States becomes the first foreign bank to open a branch in Korea.

Aug. 9-11 The first Korea-Japan Annual Ministerial Conference is held in Tokyo.

Dec. 13 All the 34 foreign-educated intellectuals, accused of involvement in an East Berlin-based North Korean spy ring, are convicted by the Seoul District Court.

Dec. 29 Mount Jiri is designated as South Korea's first national park.

1968

Jan. 21 A 31-man North Korean commando sneak into Seoul in an attempt on the life of President Park Chung-hee.

Jan. 23 U.S. intelligence ship Pueblo is seized by North Korean naval ships off Wonsan, North Korea.

Feb. 1 Ground is broken for the construction of the nation's second expressway to link Seoul and Busan. It opens for traffic on July 7, 1970.

April 1 Korea Reserve Forces are established.

April 18 President Park Chung-hee holds two rounds of talks with U.S. President Lyndon B. Johnson in Honolulu, Hawaii.

May 18-21 Emperor Haile Selassie of Ethiopia visits Korea.

May 27 The first Korea-U.S. Security Consultative Meeting is held in Washington.

May 30 Kim Jong-pil resigns his chairmanship of the Democratic Republican Party and National Assembly membership, declaring his retirement from politics.

June 20 The government rounds up gangsters to work on national development projects.

July 15 The Ministry of Education announces the termination of entrance examinations to middle schools.

Sept. 1 Foreign investment in Korea amounts to US$ 76 million in 98 cases.

Nov. 4 A group of some 30 North Korean guerrillas infiltrate into the country through the shore of Samcheok and Uljin counties on the east coast.

Dec. 21 The Seoul-Incheon Highway is opened.

1969

Jan. 24 The government announces an order to control the price of rice.

Feb. 12 The Korea-Japan Cooperation Committee opens its inaugural conference in Seoul.

Feb. 13 The Korean Central Intelligence Agency announces its arrest of Lee Su-geun, a North Korean spy who entered South Korea posing as a defector in 1967. Lee was executed on July 3, 1969.

March 19 The government decides to reinstate limits on foreign currency borrowing.

March 24 A research team led by Lee Yong-kak, a professor at the College of Medicine of Catholic University in Seoul, successfully completes the country's first kidney transplant.

March 28 Archbishop Stephen Kim Sou-hwan is ordained as South Korea's first cardinal.

April 15 North Korea shoots down a U.S. reconnaissance plane over the East Sea.

May 6 The Economic Planning Board announces the Third Five-Year Economic Development Plan (1972-1976).

May 15 The nation's first communication satellite station is built in Geumsan, South Chungcheong Province.

May 26 South Vietnamese President Nugyen Van Thieu visits Seoul.

June 19 Students demonstrate against a bid to revise the Constitution to allow Park Chung-hee to serve a third term.

July 21 The Seoul-Incheon Superhighway opens.

July 25 President Park Chung-hee issues statement on plans to hold national referendum on a constitutional revision allowing him a third term.

Aug. 20 President Park Chung-hee leaves for the United States to hold talks with U.S. President Richard Nixon in San Francisco, the United States.

Oct. 17 The proposed constitutional amendment is approved in the national referendum.

Dec. 6 More than 500 priceless cultural relics, including Goryeo celadon, being smuggled to Japan aboard a freighter, are seized by authorities.

Dec. 11 A Korean Air passenger flight from the eastern city of Gangneung to Seoul with 51 people aboard is hijacked by North Koreans and forced to land in Pyongyang. North Korea repatriated 39 of the hijacked people two months later.

Dec. 14 The International Monetary Fund (IMF) allows Korea to issue Special Drawing Rights (SDRs).

1970

Feb. 14 Thirty-nine passengers from a Korean Air aircraft hijacked by North Korea some two months earlier return to South Korea via the truce village of Panmunjom. North Korea still holds 12 crew members, including the pilot.

March 31 Japanese commercial airliner Yodo skyjacked by a group of Japanese leftist students with 99 passengers aboard makes an emergency landing at Gimpo airport. They heads for Pyongyang after releasing all passengers on April 3.

April 1 The government establishes Pohang Iron and Steel Company (POSCO), which later becomes South Korea's largest steelmaker.

April 22 President Park Chung-hee launches the "Saemaeul" (new community) movement aimed at restructuring the nation's economy.

May 26 The United States signs agreement on the last US$ 10 million grant-in-aid to Korea.

July 1 The postal zone number system is introduced.

July 7 The Seoul-Busan Superhighway opens.

Aug. 15 President Park Chung-hee declares his willingness to open gradual contacts with North Korea if the North renounce the use of force.

Sept. 29 The New Democratic Party holds national convention and names Kim Dae-jung as its presidential candidate.

Nov. 13 Jeon Tae-il, 22, a garment worker at Seoul's Pyeonghwa Market, commits suicide by self-immolation in protest for better pay and working conditions. His death sparked protests by labor activists in South Korea, which was then ruled by authoritarian President Park Chung-hee.

Dec. 24 The National Assembly passes an amendment of the Trade Law to legalize trade relations with non-hostile communist countries.

1971

Jan. 27 South Korea puts the Vienna Convention on consular relations into force.

Feb. West Germany asks Korea to send 17,000 nurses to work in German hospitals.

Feb. 9 The government announces the Third Five-Year Economic Development Plan (1972-1976).

March 12 The Korean ground troops assumes the defense responsibility for the entire 155-mile truce line in the wake of a partial U.S. military withdrawal.

March 19 The government begins construction on the nation's first nuclear power plant, Gori No. 1.

March 27 The U.S. Army 7th Division withdraws after being stationed for two years in South Korea.

March 31 Direct telephone lines between Seoul and Busan open.

April 27 President Park Chung-hee is reelected to his third consecutive four-year term.

May 25 General elections are held to choose representatives to the eighth National Assembly.

July 30 The government designates a greenbelt, an area of land protected from development, outside Seoul for the first time.

Aug. 6 North Korean Premier Kim Il-sung suggests for summit talks with President Park Chung-hee and inter-Korean meetings of political parties and social organizations.

Aug. 12 The Korean National Red Cross proposes to North Korea direct talks on ways of arranging reunion of family members living in separation in both sectors of Korea. The North accepted the proposal on Aug. 14.

Aug. 23 A group of 24 South Korean commandos trained on Silmido, an island off the west coast, to assassinate North Korean leader Kim Il-sung blow themselves up while trying to enter Seoul on a stolen bus.

Sept. 20 The first session of the inter-Korean preliminary Red Cross talks is held in Panmunjom to work out the agenda for the plenary conference.

Sept. 22 A telephone hotline between South and North Korea opens at the border village of Panmunjom, located in the Demilitarized Zone between the two countries.

Dec. 6 President Park Chung-hee declares a state of emergency in South Korea, citing a threatened invasion by North Korea. The move drastically curtailed the freedom of speech, thus helping him tighten his grip on power.

Dec. 10 The first civil defense excercise is held.

Dec. 25 The 22-story Daeyeongak Hotel in Seoul is gutted down in fire which claimed the lives of 167 persons.

1972

Jan. 24 South Korea publishes its first Trade White Paper.

Feb. 6 The Cheongryong unit, one of the main South Korean contingents that participated in the Vietnam War at the United States' request, returns home.

Feb. 25 The government signs an agreement to join the General Agreement on Tariffs and Trade (GATT) special tariff union.

March 7 South Korea and the United States begin a large-scale joint military exercise called "Team Spirit."

March 30 President Park Chung-hee presents a five-point peace principle to North Korea.

April 3 Pulcho chikchi shimche yojeol (The Select Sermons of Buddhist Sages and Zen Masters) dated 1377, the earliest extant book printed in movable type, is found in France.

April 11 The government adopts the Saemaeul (New Community) Movement program for 1972.

April 10 Fifteen members of a Korean mountaineering expedition are killed in an avalanche which swept them off the 7,156-meter Himalayan peak of Manaslu.

May 10 The country's first nuclear power plant in Gori, North Gyeongsang Province, is completed.

July 4 South and North Korea announce a historic agreement to end a quarter of a century of hostility and work together toward peaceful unification of the nation.

July 5 President Park Chung-hee orders universities to offer Japanese as second foreign language.

July 13 Rep. Kim Dae-jung urges South and North Korea to join the United Nations simultaneously.

Aug. 8 In an emergency presidential action, private assets of all corporations are frozen, interest rates reduced drastically.

Aug. 30 The first historic full-dress talks between South and North Korean Red Cross societies open in Pyongyang.

Oct. 12 Lee Hu-rak, director of the Korean Central Intelligence Agency and Pak Song-chol, vice premier of North Korea, hold their first official meeting in their capacity of co-chairmen of the South-North Coordinating Committee (SNCC) at Panmunjom.

Oct. 17 President Park Chung-hee imposes martial law throughout the nation and suspends some provisions of the constitution, dissolves the National Assembly and bans all political activities.

Oct. 27 A draft for a constitutional revision is announced. The draft amendment to the Constitution is approved in a national referendum on Nov. 21.

Nov. 22 The fourth full-dress talks between South and North Korean Red Cross societies are held in Seoul.

Nov. 30 The co-chairmen of the South-North Coordinating Committee, at their third official meeting in Seoul, formally inaugurate the South-North Coordinating Committee.

Dec. 23 President Park Chung-hee is elected the first six-year term president at the inaugural meeting of the National Conference for Unification.

Dec. 27 The Yushin (Revitalizing Reform) Constitution officially takes effect.

1973

Jan. 27 The Democratic Unification Party (DUP) is formally inaugurated.

March 3 The Korea Broadcasting Corporation (KBC) is established.

March 14 The second meeting of the inter-Korean Coordinating Committee is held in Pyongyang. The committee was organized to implement the inter-Korean joint communique of July 4, 1972 in which the two sides agreed to achieve the peaceful reunification of the peninsula.

April 10 Korea's women's table tennis team wins the championship in Yugoslavia.

March 10 Yujonghoe, a pro-government floor group, is inaugurated.

March 12 South and North Korea open their two-day political talks in Pyongyang.

April 16 An exhibition of 5,000 years of Korean arts opens.

June 12 The South-North Coordinating Committee opens its third full-dress conference in Seoul.

June 23 President Park Chung-hee declares in a seven-point foreign policy statement that the government would not object to simultaneous entry of South and North Korea into the United Nations.

July 3 Pohang Iron and Steel Company opens.

Aug. 8 Kim Dae-jung is kidnapped by a band of five Korean speaking men from Grand Palace Hotel in Tokyo. He turned up at his home in Seoul Aug. 13.

Sept. 14 The government takes nation-wide disciplinary action against men with long hair.

1974

Jan. 8 President Park Chung-hee issues the Emergency Measures No. 1 and No. 2 banning criticism of the Constitution.

Jan. 14 President Park Chung-hee issues Emergency Decree No. 3 in reaction to first oil crisis. It drastically cut taxes on low-income people.

Jan. 18 President Park Chung-hee proposes a pact of mutual non-aggression with North Korea.

Jan. 21 South Korea and West Germany sign a visa waiver accord.

Jan. 30 South Korea and Japan sign an agreement on the zoning of their continental shelves.

Feb. 22 A total of 157 seamen are drowned when a Navy YTL boat capsized off the southern naval port of Chungmu.

March 28 South Korea establishes diplomatic ties with Oman.

April 3 President Park Chung-hee issues Emergency Decree No. 4 outlawing the Mincheonghaknyeon (National Federation of Democratic Youth and Students), a student activist organization.

April 18 South Korea and Uganda establish diplomatic ties.

May 29 President Park Chung-hee issues special order to implement measures to foster healthier corporate environment.

July Chung Myung-whun wins second place in the piano section at the Tchaikovsky Music Competition in Moscow.

Aug. 15 President Park Chung-hee narrowly escapes an attempt by a Korean gunman, Mun Se-gwang, from Osaka, Japan, on his life during a ceremony marking the 29th anniversary of National Liberation at the National Theater in Seoul. The gunman's shots missed the president, but killed his wife, Yuk Young-soo.

Aug. 15 The first subway line in Seoul (Seoul Station-Cheongnyangni 9.5-km long) opens.

Nov. 15 The United Nations Command announces it has found an infiltration tunnel illegally built by North Koreans in the southern portion of the demilitarized zone (DMZ).

Nov. 22 U.S. President Gerald Ford arrives in Seoul en route to the Soviet Far Eastern port of Vladivostok.

1975

Feb. 12 President Park Chung-hee wins the popular confidence in his Yushin structure in a national referendum.

April 9 Eight South Korean university students convicted of trying to overthrow the government are executed just 20 hours after a court sentenced them to death. They were among 23 college students arrested on rebellion charges as part of a government crackdown on dissident movements.

April 11 A Seoul National University student, Kim Sang-jin commits suicide by disembowelment as a protest against President Park Chung-hee. The general-turned-president issued a set of emergency decrees aimed at banning public criticism of his regime and empowering a military court to deal with violations.

April 18 North Korean President Kim Il-sung visits China for the first time in 14 years and holds talks with his Chinese counterpart, Mao Zedong.

April 23 The National Assembly ratifies the Nuclear Non-Proliferation Treaty.

May 13 President Park lifts the Emergency Decree No. 7 and issues Emergency Decree No. 9 for bidding criticism of the Constitution.

Sept. 15 Some 700 pro-Pyongyang Korean residents in Japan arrive in Seoul to visit their ancestral tombs in Korea on the occasion of Chuseok (Korean version of Thanksgiving Day).

1976

Jan. 21 The Seoul District Prosecutor's Office charges Kim Young-sam with violation of Emergency Decree No. 9.

Feb. 29 Hyundai Motor Co. releases the country's first car, the Pony.

March 13 Choi Kyu-hah is sworn in as the 12th prime minister of the country.

March 26 South Korea signs a trade agreement with Guatemala.

April 17 South Korea establishes diplomatic relations with Bahrain.

June 14 The seventh general assembly of the World Trade Centers Association opens in Seoul.

July 22 U.S. Secretary of State Henry Kissinger proposes a conference of South and North Korea, the United States and China to discuss the Korean question.

Aug. 18 Two U.S. army officers are brutally hacked to death in an unprovoked attack by some 30 axe-wielding North Korean communist guards in the Joint Security Area of Panmunjom.

Aug. 28 The Seoul District Court sentences Kim Dae-jung and former President Yun Po-sun to five years in prison each for violating Emergency Decree No. 9.

1977

March 9 U.S. President Jimmy Carter announces that the U.S. ground combat forces would be pulled out of Korea over the next four to five years.

June 19 The nation's first ever nuclear generator with a capacity of 595,000kw is ignited in Gori, South Gyeongsang Province.

Nov. 11 The biggest ever explosion in history of Korea takes place in Iri, North Jeolla Province, when a freight car carrying dynamites blew up.

Dec. 22 The nation achieves US$ 10 billion export target (Export Day celebrated).

Dec. 31 The Korean and U.S. governments jointly announce a five-point agreement on the testimony in the U.S. of Park Tong-son, central figure in the alleged Korean in fluence-buying on Capitol Hill, on his role in the bribery scandal.

1978

Jan. 14 South Korean actress Choi Eun-hee is abducted by North Korean agents in Hong Kong, two weeks before her husband, movie director Shin Sang-ok, is also taken to the North. Choi and Shin later made movies that extolled the rule of former North Korean leader Kim Il-sung and his son Kim Jong-il while in North Korea before successfully seeking refuge at the U.S. Embassy in Vienna in March 1986.

Feb. 23 The Justice Ministry decides to issue entry visas to visitors from nonhostile communist countries and left-leaning nonaligned nations with which Seoul has no diplomatic relations.

April 14 The Sejong Center for the Performing Arts opens in Seoul.

April 11 The Ministry of Trade and Industry announces 321 products to be liberalized as part of efforts to open domestic markets to foreign products.

April 21 A Korean Air Lines Boeing 707 jetliner with 110 persons aboard is intercepted by the Soviet Union and forced to land about 354km south of Murmansk.

April 30 South Korea proclaims a 12-mile limit territorial waters.

July 6 President Park Chung-hee is re-elected to lead the nation for another six years as the ninth president.

• The National Conference for Unification (NCU) reelects Park Chung-hee to fill the six-year ninth presidential term.

Sept. 3 Minister of Health and Social Affairs Shin Hyon-hwak arrives in the Soviet Union to attend the WHO International Conference on Primary Health Care, becoming the first Korean cabinet member to set foot on the Soviet soil.

Sept. 8 The number of foreign tourists visiting Korea tops the one million mark for the first time.

Sept. 26 Korea successfully test-fires long-range ground-to-ground missiles of its own.

Sept. 27 The 42nd World Shooting Championships are opened in Seoul.

Nov. 7 The Korea-U.S. Combined Forces Command is formally activated.

Dec. 12 General elections are held to elect representatives to the 10th National Assembly.

Dec. 13 A group of 219 American soldiers leave for the United States to become the first U.S. ground combat troops to pull out of Korea.

Dec. 27 President Park Chung-hee is inaugurated; Kim Dae-jung is released from prison as part of a grand national amnesty.

1979

Jan. 19 President Park Chung-hee calls on North Korea to resume the stalemated inter-Korean dialogue 'at any place, at any time and at any level.'

Feb. 17 A Korean delegation of the South-North Coordinating Committee has a direct contact with a North Korean delegation of the Workers' (Communist) Party's Central Committee at Panmunjom.

Feb. 27 Pingpong representatives from South and North Korea have talks in Panmunjom to discuss the formation of a single Korean team to participate in the World Table Tennis Championships.

March 6 South Korea and Mexico sign a visa exemption agreement.

April 2 Local radio station KBS FM begins broadcasting in stereo.

April 25 Korea opens its international telephone services with the Soviet Union via London.

May 4 U.N. Sec.-Gen. Kurt Waldheim arrives in Seoul to exchange views on the stalemated inter-Korean dialogue and other global problems.

May 30 The New Democratic Party national convention elects Kim Dae-jung party president.

June 29 U.S. President Jimmy Carter arrives in Seoul. On July 1, Presidents Park and Carter agree to jointly propose a meeting of official representatives of South and North Korea and the United States as part of efforts to promote the inter-Korean dialogue and reduce tensions on the Korean Peninsula.

July 2 The fourth World Congress of Poets on the theme of 'East and West in Poetry' begins its five-day schedule in Seoul.

July 12 South Korean football player Cha Bum-kun starts his career in Germany's Bundesliga. In South Korea, Cha is greatly respected for his accomplishments in the Bundesliga in the 1980s and on the South Korean national team. Cha is also considered the best Asian striker that ever played in Europe.

Aug. 11 The metropolitan police storm the headquarters building of the New Democratic Party to disperse by force more than 190 girl workers of the Y.H. Trading Co. who had been demonstrating in protest against the company's lockout.

Aug. 21 The first World Air Gun Shooting Championships open at the Taeneung International Shooting Range in Seoul.

Oct. 4 Kim Young-sam, president of the New Democratic Party, is dismissed from the National Assembly led by the ruling Democratic Republican Party, because of the articles, "Kim asked Carter administration end to support President Park Chung-hee's governmen" that the New York Times was carrying.

Oct. 16 Students of Pusan National and Dong-A universities stage mass campus and street demonstrations for two days in Busan, denouncing the so-called Yushin (Revitalizing Reform) system to prolong the regime of President Park Chung-hee. Following the demonstrations, the government proclaimed a Martial Law in the city.

Oct. 18 The anti-Yushin demonstrations in Busan spread to the neighboring city of Masan, causing violent demonstrations joined by students, citizens and workers on Oct. 18 for two days.

Oct. 26 President Park is assassinated by Kim Chae-kyu, director of the Central Intelligence Agency.

Oct. 27 Martial Law is imposed on the entire nation. Prime Minister Choi Kyu-hah becomes acting president.

Dec. 6 Acting President Choi Kyu-hah is elected the 10th president.

1980

Jan. 14 North Korean Prime Minister Lee Jong-ok sends a letter to Prime Minister Shin Hyun-hwak proposing a meeting in Seoul, Pyongyang, Panmunjom or any third country. Shin on Jan. 24 called for a preliminary meeting to arrange necessary procedures for the proposed Prime Ministers' meeting.

Jan. 25 A High Military Court Martial upholds death sentences handed down to Kim Jae-kyu, who assassinated President Park Chung-hee, and five others.

Feb. 6 The first preliminary meeting for the projected Prime Ministers' meeting between South and North Korea is held in Panmunjom.

Feb. 27 Korea implements a full-fledged floating foreign exchange system.

Feb. 29 President Choi Kyu-hah restores the civil rights of former President Yun Po-son,

April 14 President Choi Kyu-hah appoints Chun Doo-hwan, defense security

424

commander, as the acting head of the Korean Central Intelligence Agency, predecessor of the National Intelligence Service.

April 16 The nation's first hydro-electric power plants are completed in Cheongpyeong, Gyeonggi Province.

April 21 Some 700 miners of the Dong-won Coal Mine in Sabuk-eup, Gangwon Prov. stage a four-day demonstration.

May 17 The government proclaims nationwide Martial Law based on a resolution at an extraordinary cabinet session. The Martial Law Command issues Martial Law Decree No. 10 banning all kinds of political activities and other politics-oriented assemblies and rallies.

May 18-27 Tens of thousands of students and citizens stage massive demonstrations in Gwangju calling for the lifting of Martial Law and the release of dissident leader Kim Dae-jung, clashing with police and Martial Law troops.

May 31 The government formally inaugurates the Special Committee for National Security Measures (SCNSM). Lt. Gen. Chun Doo-hwan, commander of the Defense Security Command, was named to head the Standing Committee of the SCNSM.

July 30 The SCNSM announces a set of drastic educational reforms which include the abolition of written tests at each school for college entrance.

Aug. 16 President Choi Kyu-hah steps down from his post about nine months after he assumed the presidency on Dec. 6, 1979.

Aug. 27 Gen. Chun Doo-hwan, ret., is elected the 11th-term president in a by-election by the delegates to the National Conference for Unification, and is inaugurated on Sept. 1.

Sept. 17 Kim Dae-jung, standing Advisor to the president of the New Democratic Party, indicted for anti-state activities and plotting rebellion by the Army court-martial, is sentenced to death, and released in 1982.

Sept. 29 The government makes public the draft constitution to steer the upcoming Fifth Republic. It is adopted in a referendum on Oct. 22

Oct. 3 President Chun Doo-hwan urges North Korea to accede to a proposal the Seoul government forwarded Sept.

26 for the early opening of the inter-Korean prime ministers' talks.

Oct. 27 All four Korean political parties are disbanded under the addendum to the new Constitution.

Nov. 14 The press, including news agencies, news papers and broadcasting companies, are compulsorily merged by the military authorities across the country.

Nov. 25 A total of 286 persons of the 835 who had been ordered to stay out of politics regain their political eligibility.

Dec. 1 KBS-TV begins Korea's first color TV broadcasting.

Dec. 31 The government promulgates the basic law on the press.

1981

Jan. 4 The Yonhap News Agency begins operations.

Jan. 12 President Chun Doo-hwan proposes the exchange of visits by top leaders of South and North Korea. North Korea turned down the proposal Jan. 19.

Jan. 15 The Democratic Justice Party (DJP) is inaugurated, the Democratic Korea Party (DKP) Jan. 17, and the Korea National Party (KNP) Jan. 23.

Jan. 23 South Korea's military government reduces opposition leader Kim Dae-jung's death sentence to life in prison. Kim was sentenced to death the previous year for allegedly instigating an insurgency in the southwestern city of Gwangju that year.

Jan. 24 The government fully removes the Martial Law which had been in effect since Oct. 27, 1979.

Jan. 28 President Chun Doo-hwan embarks on a 10-day trip to the United States at the invitation of President Ronald Reagan.

Feb. 11 An election committee to elect South Korea's 12th president is set up with 5,278 members. The committee, representing 40 million South Koreans, elected as head of state Chun Doo-hwan, a former army general, who was later convicted of amassing hundreds of billions of won in slush funds.

Feb. 12 South Korea opens diplomatic ties with Lebanon.

Feb. 25 President Chun Doo-hwan is elected the 12th-term president in electoral college voting.

March 3 Chun Doo-hwan, a former army general, takes office as South Korea's 12th president after being elected by a hand-picked electoral college. Chun seized power in a coup in 1980 after his predecessor, Park Chung-hee, was assassinated. Chun ruled from 1981-88.

April 11 The 11th National Assembly is inaugurated.

June 19 Korean Olympic Committee president Cho Sang-ho proposes that South and North Korea form a single athletic team to send to the 1984 Los Angeles Olympics.

June 25 President Chun Doo-hwan embarks on a tour of the five ASEAN member countries.

Sept. 27 Canadian Prime Minister Pierre Trudeau visits Korea.

Sept. 30 Seoul is chosen as the venue for the 1988 Summer Olympic Games.

Oct. 17 Okpo Shipyard of Daewoo Shipbuilding and Heavy Machinery Ltd. is inaugurated with annual capacity of 1.2 million gross tons. Korea becomes the 5th largest shipbuilding country in the world.

1982

Jan. 5 The government lifts the 37-year-old midnight-to-4 a.m. curfew.

Feb. 1 National Unification Minister Son Jae-shik proposes to North Korea a set of 20 'pilot projects' to help improve the relations between South and North Korea. North Korea turned down the proposal Feb. 10.

Feb. 26 The U.S. Air Force announces the deployment of 10 units of the A-10 close support aircraft to South Korea.

March 18 A group of civic activists carries out an arson attack against the American Cultural Center in Busan, some 450 kilometers southeast of Seoul, to protest the alleged involvement of the United States in the Gwangju massacre. Hundreds were killed in the 1980 massacre when forces of the then military government cracked down on citizens of Gwangju, 330 kilometers southwest of the capital, who were protesting against the military regime.

March 27 The South Korean professional baseball league launches with the opening game taking place in Seoul.

May 23 Australian Prime Minister Malcom Fraser visits Korea.

Aug. 3 The Foreign Ministry conveys a memorandum to the Japanese government calling for the correction of erroneous historical accounts of past Korea-Japan relations in Japanese high school textbooks.

Aug. 16 President Chun Doo-hwan embarks on a two-week tour of Africa (Kenya, Nigeria, Gabon, Senegal) and Canada.

Sept. 4 The 27th World Amateur Baseball Championship opens in Seoul. Korea won the 10-nation tournament.

Sept. 9 Korea puts into service its first domestically assembled fighter aircraft in a public test flight.

Sept. 21 The 23rd International Council of Women (ICW) opens at Seoul Sejong Cultural Center.

Oct. 16 Indonesian President Suharto visits Seoul.

Nov. 3 The 37th Jaycees International (JCI) world congress opens for two weeks in Seoul.

Nov. 4 No. 2 shipyard of the Hyundai Mipo Dockyard Co. is dedicated, bringing Hyundai Mipo Dockyard to the rank of the world's largest ship repairing shop.

1983

Jan. 11 Japanese Prime Minister Yasuhiro Nakasone visits Korea.

Feb. 1 Unification Minister Son Jae-shik proposes to North Korea in a statement that a conference of representatives of the South and North Korean governments, political parties and social organizations be held.

Feb. 25 Lee Ung-pyong, a North Korean air force captain, defects flying his MIG-19 fighter to the South Korea.

April 18 A fire breaks out at a discotheque in Daegu, about 300 kilometers southeast of Seoul, resulting in the deaths of 25 people.

May 5 A Chinese airliner with 105 passengers and crew aboard, is hijacked by six Chinese nationals seeking political asylum in Taiwan and makes an emergency landing at an air base northeast of Seoul.

June 30 The state-run Korean Broadcasting System airs a special program, from June 30 to Nov. 14, to help reunite family members separated during the Korean War (1950-1953).

Sept. 1 A Korean Air Lines (KAL) Boeing 747 jetliner with 269 passengers and crew aboard is shot down by a Soviet fighter en route to Seoul from New York via Anchorage, Alaska.

Sept. 25 The 53rd World Travel Congress of the American Society of Travel Agents (ASTA) is held in Seoul.

Oct. 2 The 70th conference of the Inter-Parliamentary Union (IPU) is held in Seoul Oct. 2-13.

Oct. 8 President Chun Doo-hwan embarks on an 18-day tour of six southwest Asian and Oceanian countries.

Oct. 9 A powerful remote-controlled bomb explodes at the Martyrs' Mausoleum in Rangoon, Burma (now Yangon, Myanmar), killing 18 ranking Korean officials, including Deputy Prime Minister Suh Suk-joon, and three other cabinet ministers, and injuring 14 others.

Oct. 17 In a de facto announcement of North Korean responsibility for the Rangoon bombing, the Burmese government confirms that two 'Koreans' captured and another killed by Burmese troops are the culprits of the bombing.

Nov. 12 U.S. President Ronald Reagan makes a state visit to Korea Nov. 12-14.

1984

Jan. 10 U.S. Ambassador to Seoul Richard Walker says that the United States supports the quadripartite talks, including South and North Korea, China, and the United States. North Korea rejected the proposal on Jan. 25.

Feb. 4 Australian Prime Minister Robert Hawke visits Korea Feb. 4-7.

Feb. 25 Eight Koreans visit China for the first time in four decades to participate in the preliminary games of the Davis Cup Tennis Tournament in Kunming.

March 12 Foreign Minister Lee Won-kyung announces before the National Assembly that Korea will intensify non-political exchanges with China, the Soviet Union and other communist nations.

April 2 Korean Olympic Committee chairman Chung Ju-yung proposes to North Korea to hold inter-Korean sports talks April 9 for a discussion of forming the unified Olympic team.

• The Agency for National Security Planning, South Korea's intelligence agency, announces that movie star couple Shin Sang-ok and Choi Eun-hee were abducted by North Korea. The couple later escaped during a visit to Vienna in 1986.

May 3 Pope John Paul II visits Korea.

Aug. 20 President Chun Doo-hwan declares that Seoul is willing to provide North Korea with technology and goods, free of charge.

Aug. 31 The Seoul-Tokyo hotline begins operation.

Sept. 6 President Chun Doo-hwan makes a state visit to Japan Sept. 6-8.

Sept. 14 The Korean National Red Cross accepts an offer by the North Korean Red Cross Society to provide materials to South Korean flood victims.

Sept. 15-19 The Asian-Pacific Parliamentarians' Union holds its 20th general meeting in Seoul.

Sept. 27-31 The Olympic Council of Asia holds its plenary meeting in Seoul.

Oct. 4 President Chun Doo-hwan announces that the government will continue to seek improved relations with East-bloc nations.

Nov. 15 The first ever inter-Korean economic conference is held at the truce village of Panmunjom.

1985

Jan. 9 In his new year's statement, President Chun Doo-hwan calls for an early summit meeting between the top leaders of South and North Korea.

Feb. 8 Opposition leader Kim Dae-jung returns to South Korea after spending 27 months in the United States, purportedly to receive health treatment. Kim later served as president from 1998-2003.

Feb. 12 The 12th National Assembly general elections are held.

March 6 President Chun Doo-hwan lifts a ban on political activity imposed against a number of opposition leaders and other key figures, including Kim Dae-jung, Kim Young-sam and Kim Jong-pil. Kim Young-sam and Kim Dae-jung were both later elected president and Kim Jong-pil served as prime minister under Kim Dae-jung's government in the late 1990s.

April 7 French Prime Minister Laurent Fabius visits Korea.

April 9 North Korea proposes that inter-Korean parliamentary talks be held to discuss ways to ease tensions between the two Koreas.

April 24-29 President Chun Doo-hwan visits the United States.

May 13 The 12th National Assembly is inaugurated.

May 23 A total of 73 university students stage a three-day sit-in at the U.S. Information Service building in Seoul, demanding that the United States apologize to the Korean people for what they call "U.S. involvement in the Gwangju incident five years ago."

May 28 Red Cross officials from South and North Korea agree to arrange mutual visits by 'dispersed family members' and folk art troupes around Aug. 15.

June 20 South and North Korea agree in principle to adopt an agreement on the implementation of commodity trade and economic cooperation, as well as the establishment of an inter-Korean joint economic cooperation committee.

July 23 South Korea proposes at the first preliminary meeting of the inter-Korean parliamentary talks, held in Panmunjom, that a constitution for national reunification be drafted.

July 31 Juan Antonio Samaranch, president of the International Olympic Committee, rejects Pyongyang's proposal for the joint hosting of the 1988 Seoul Summer Olympic Games.

Sept. 20 South and North Korea simultaneously exchange hometown visiting groups and folk art troupes for the first time. The 151-member visiting groups from each side arrive in Seoul and Pyongyang, respectively, for four-day visits.

Oct. 1-5 A total of 145 archers from 32 countries, including the Soviet Union, compete in the 33rd World Archery Championships held in Seoul.

Oct. 11 The World Bank and the International Monetary Fund adopt the 'Seoul Convention.'

Nov. 11-17 The International Men's Volleyball Championships are held in Seoul.

1986

Jan. 7 The president of the South Korean Olympic Committee Kim Chong-ha, his North Korean counterpart Kim Yu-sun and Juan Antonio Samaranch, president of the IOC, produce no progress in Lausanne, Switzerland, toward agreement over North Korea's demand to 'co-host' the 1988 Olympics.

Feb. 18 The first shipment of South Korean cars, consisting of 1,000 units of the Pony model, a compact vehicle produced by Hyundai Motor, arrives in the United States.

Feb. 24 President Chun Doo-hwan tells leaders of political parties that the government intends to rewrite the Constitution in 1989.

March 1 President Chun Doo-hwan in his Samil (March 1) anniversary message reiterates his call for a meeting this year between the 'highest authorities' of South and North Korea.

March 13 Korean movie director Shin Sang-ok and actress Choi Eun-hee defect to the U.S. Embassy in Wien, Austria, after eight years under North Korea's yoke.

April 5 President Chun Doo-hwan embarks on a four-nation European tour for summit talks with leaders of the United Kingdom, West Germany, France and Belgium from April 7 to 18.

April 28 Two student activists at Seoul National University, Kim Se-jin and Lee Je-ho, burn themselves to death as part of an antiwar, anti-nuclear protest.

May 2 British Prime Minister Margaret Thatcher arrives in Seoul for a three-day official visit.

May 7 U.S. Secretary of State George Shultz arrives in Seoul to attend the Korea-U.S. foreign ministers' meeting.

May 12 Brian Mulroney, Canadian Prime Minister, arrives in Seoul for a four-day official visit.

June 25 Singapore's Prime Minister Lee Kuan Yew arrives in Seoul on a four-day visit.

Aug. 3 South and North Korean sports officials agree to form joint Korean teams to compete in the second annual Asia-Europe Table Tennis Competition to be held in Japan in December.

Aug. 15 President Chun Doo-hwan

urges North Korea to agree to reopen all existing channels of dialogue, which it has unilaterally closed.

Aug. 19 The three top opposition leaders -Kim Young-sam, Kim Dae-jung and Lee Min-woo -manifest their opposition to the ruling party's draft for constitutional revision advocating a parliamentary form of government.

Sept. 2 Opposition leaders Kim Dae-jung and Kim Young-sam propose a meeting between President Chun Doo-hwan and the top three opposition leaders, including themselves, to reach a breakthrough in revising the Constitution.

Sept. 20 The tenth Seoul Asian Games open its 16-day run.

• Japanese Prime Minister Yasuhiro Nakasone pays a courtesy call on President Chun Doo-hwan, making an apology for one of his cabinet members' inflammatory remarks on Japan's 1910 annexation of Korea.

Oct. 30 Construction Minister Lee Kyu-hyo strongly demands that North Korea immediately stop construction of a mammoth dam ostensibly intended for a hydroelectric power plant, arguing that it could cause a formidable catastrophe in the South, involving water shortage, ecological destruction as well as a threat to security.

Dec. 27 Leaders of the ruling and opposition parties agree to negotiate a seven-point list of democratic reforms proposed by Yi Min-u, president of the main opposition party, as a prerequisite for considering the ruling party's parliamentary cabinet formula.

1987

Jan. 12 President Chun Doo-hwan urges ruling and opposition parties to resolve the issue of amending the Constitution in the National Assembly as soon as possible.

Feb. 4 Yoon Han-shik and Sohn Tae-hwan, researchers at the Korea Advanced Institute of Science and Technology, succeed in developing the world's first high-density polymer alloy fiber.

Feb. 8 North Korean defector Kim Man-chul and his family arrive in South Korea after fleeing the communist country.

Feb. 13 Opposition leaders Kim Dae-jung and Kim Young-sam propose talks with President Chun Doo-hwan, which they say would be the key to breaking the political deadlock over constitutional revision.

Feb. 30 Ground is broken for the construction of the Peace Dam, designed to block a probable North Korean water-offensive.

March 3 A four-member delegation from the East German Olympic Committee arrives in Seoul for a six-day visit to Korea.

April 6 President Ahmed Abdallah Abderemane of the Comoros visits Seoul for four days.

April 13 President Chun Doo-hwan declares the waiving of the counter-productive debate on constitutional reform, with a pledge to hand the government over to his successor in accordance with the 'current Constitution.'

• Belize Prime Minister Manuel Esquivel arrives in Seoul for a five-day official visit.

May 1 The opposition Reunification Democratic Party (RDP) led by Kim Young-sam is inaugurated with calls for direct presidential election and a 'civilianized government.'

May 6 Korea and the United States agreed to set up a direct communications line linking the offices of the top defense officials of both countries, the Defense Ministry says.

May 27 More than 2,000 opposition politicians, dissidents, religious people and others launch a joint campaign for democratic constitutional reforms.

June 8 Burmese President U San Yu arrives in Seoul for talks with President Chun Doo-hwan.

June 25 Opposition leader Kim Dae-jung is freed from his 78-day house arrest.

June 26 Tens of thousands of people shouting slogans pour into the streets in Seoul and other cities across the nation, and clashing with police as they attempt to take part in the banned 'Grand Peace March' for democracy.

June 29 Democratic Justice Party (DJP) chairman Roh Tae-woo discloses an eight-point proposal for ending the current political stalemate, including the revision of the Constitution to establish direct presidential election.

July 1 President Chun Doo-hwan declares he "fully accepts" proposals for broad democratic reforms including a direct presidential election during his tenure of office.

July 8 The government releases on parole 357 people convicted of anti-government activities and political offenses.

July 9 The government announces a sweeping amnesty and restoration of civil rights for 2,335 people, including opposition leader Kim Dae-jung.

• President of the International Olympic Committee (IOC) Juan Antonio Samaranch says the 1988 Olympic Games will either be in Seoul, South Korea "or will be no Games at all."

July 10 President Chun Doo-hwan resigns as president of the ruling Democratic Justice Party (DJP), renewing his pledge to fairly and impartially administer affairs of state.

July 13 President Chun Doo-hwan appoints Kim Chung-yul, former minister of National Defense, new Prime Minister.

July 21-23 Large residential areas and paddy fields in the central region hit by a record rainfall remains submerged in muddy flood-waters leaving 95 dead and 32 missing.

Aug. 5 Roh Tae-woo is formally elected president of the ruling Democratic Justice Party (DJP).

Aug. 7 An eight-day extraordinary session of the National Assembly opens to deliberate a supplementary budget bill for repairing flood damage and to reactivate a special constitution revision committee..

Aug. 8 Opposition leader Kim Dae-jung joins the main opposition Reunification Democratic Party (RDP) as permanent party adviser.

Aug. 15 The Independence Hall Complex, a sanctuary illuminating the nation's bloody struggle against the Japanese colonialists, opens.

Aug. 30 Vaai Kolone, Prime Minister of Western Samoa, arrives in Seoul.

Aug. 31 Bipartisan constitutional talks are brought to a conclusion as negotiators resolved differences on the few sticky issues that remained. The ruling and opposition parties decide to jointly submit a constitutional reform bill to the National Assembly.

Sept. 2 King Carl XVI Gustaf of Sweden arrives in Seoul at the invitation of the Boy Scouts of Korea.

Sept. 8 Colombian President Virgilo Barco arrives in Seoul for summit talks with President Chun Doo-hwan.

• South Korea's Kang Su-yeon captures the Best Actress Award at the Venice International Film Festival in Italy.

Sept. 13 Ruling Democratic Justice Party leader Roh Tae-woo says in a meeting with U.S. President Ronald Reagan in the White House that Korea would develop into a mature democracy by carrying out without fail a peaceful transfer of power in February.

Sept. 17 Minister of Foreign Affairs Choe Kwang-su says the government allowed South Korean diplomats to have contact with their North Korean counterparts at formal and informal functions around the world.

Oct. 12 The National Assembly passes a constitutional amendment providing for direct presidential election. The new Constitution was approved by an overwhelming majority in a national referendum on Oct. 27.

Oct. 28 Egyptian Foreign Minister Boutros Ghali arrives in Seoul.

Nov. 9 Hu Qili, member of China's Politburo Standing Committee, says China would trade directly with South Korea but only with the consent of the North.

Nov. 29 A Korean Air (KAL) jetliner with 104 passengers and 11 crew members aboard is reported missing over Rangoon, Burma. The woman, thought to have planted a bomb in the missing Korean passenger jetliner, was flown on Dec. 15 to Seoul from Bahrain.

Dec. 16 The nation's nearly 26 million voters go to the polls to vote in the first direct presidential election in 16 years.

Dec. 21 Japanese Prime Minister Noboru Takeshita says his government will fully support Korea in its efforts to establish diplomatic relations with China.

1988

Jan. 15 The Agency for National Security Planning announces that two special North Korean agents acting on instructions of Kim Jong-il, son of President Kim Il-sung, planted a bomb on the Korean Air jetline (KAL Flight 858) that vanished near Burma late in November 1987 to block the participation of other countries in the 1988 Seoul Olympics.

Feb. 17 The state-run King Sejong Station is established on King George Island in Antarctica. About 20 South Korean researchers and officials are now stationed at the Sejong base, studying the environment and natural resources of the Antarctic.

Feb. 25 Roh Tae-woo is inaugurated as the President of the sixth republic.

• The revised constitution comes into effect.

• President Roh Tae-woo and Japanese Prime Minister Noboru Takeshita hold a summit meeting and agree to set up a joint consultative body to prevent terrorist attacks during the upcoming Seoul Olympics.

Feb. 29 Opposition leader Kim Dae-jung makes a six-point demand for democratization which includes a call for the release of all the political dissidents and restoration of their civil rights, the guarantee of press freedom and the overall implementation of a local autonomy system.

April 26 The 13th National Assembly elections are held.

May 12 Kim Dae-jung, president of the Party for Peace and Democracy, demands that former President Chun Doo-hwan be investigated in connection with the bloody military suppression of a 1980 Gwangju civil uprising.

May 30 The 13th National Assembly is launched.

• Juan Antonio Samaranch, president of the International Olympic Committee, says that he cannot accept the North Korean demand for the 'co-hosting' of the Seoul Olympics as it is against the Olympic Charter.

June 2 The Fujinoki tomb in Nara, Japan, yielded a golden crown similar to those worn by kings of the Silla Kingdom (57 B.C.-934) in Korea, the Kashihara Archaeology Institute in Nara says.

June 10 Foreign Minister Choi Kwang-soo presents a three-stage formula in his keynote speech at the United Nations, which would build mutual trust and confidence, conclude a non-aggression pact and begin negotiations on disarmament.

July 7 President Roh Tae-woo declares a six-point plan to ease 40 years of bitter confrontation between Seoul and Pyongyang and clear the way for peaceful reunification of the divided homeland.

July 15 Education Minister Kim Young-shik proposes a good-will students' sports meeting and exchange of pilgrimages between South and North Korea.

July 16 Foreign Minister Choi Kwang-soo says that South Korea would not oppose its allies, including the United States and Japan, initiating exchanges with North Korea in non-political, non-governmental and non-military areas.

July 19 The government removes a ban on the works of about 120 writers who voluntarily defected to North Korea, published before the liberation from Japanese colonial rule in 1945.

• Foreign Minister Choi Kwang-soo says the government would permit Koreans who lived overseas and carried South Korean passports to visit North Korea and overseas Koreans with North Korean nationality to freely visit the South.

Aug. 15 President Roh Tae-woo proposes a summit meeting with North Korean leader Kim Il-sung at the earliest possible date in a speech celebrating the 43rd anniversary of liberation of Korea.

Aug. 21 The World Academic Conference of the Seoul Olympiad opens at the Academy House and Hotel Hilton in Seoul.

Aug. 29 The 52nd Seoul International PEN Congress opens with 900 writers from 37 countries participating.

Sept. 3 The Bolshoi Ballet of the Soviet Union makes its South Korean debut at the Sejong Cultural Center in Seoul.

Sept. 8 North Korean leader Kim Il-sung proposes an inter-Korean summit in Pyongyang to seek reunification on a confederal basis, which could be achieved only after the withdrawal of U.S. forces in Korea and the signing of an inter-Korean non-aggression pact.

Sept. 13 Korea and Hungary exchange ratifications of a pact to exchange permanent missions, which was signed Aug. 26.

Sept. 17 The 24th Summer Olympic Games opens in Seoul with 9,627 athletes from 160 countries participating.

Oct. 7 The government announces a 7-point package plan to open Seoul-

Pyongyang economic exchanges, allowing port calls by North Korean ships carrying trade goods and private firms in the South to trade with North Korea.

Oct. 15 The Korea Trade Promotion Corp. and the Soviet Chamber of Commerce and Industry exchange a memorandum to promote direct economic exchanges between the two countries and open trade offices in the other country's capital.

Oct. 18 Delivering the first address before the U.N. General Assembly by a Korean head of state, President Roh Tae-woo proposes that a six-nation consultative conference be created to discuss a wide range of issues concerning peace, stability, progress and prosperity within Northeast Asia, referring to South and North Korea, China, Japan, the Soviet Union and the United States.

Oct. 20 President Roh Tae-woo and U.S. President Ronald Reagan have talks at White House to ensure peace on the Korean Peninsula.

• The Seoul International Trade Fair (SITRA) '88 opens for a 12-day run with 511 firms from 31 nations participating.

Oct. 25 South Korea opens its permanent mission in Hungary.

Oct. 27 Opposition lawmakers demand an immediate removal of the scandalous legacies of the Fifth Republic, including thorough investigation into corruptions of ex-President Chun Doo-hwan and his relatives, and the truth of forced mergers of news media and ouster of some critical journalists when Chun took power of eight years earlier.

Nov. 3 President Roh Tae-woo leaves for a 12-day state visit to Malaysia, Australia, Indonesia and Brunei.

Nov. 17 President Roh Tae-woo and his predecessor Chun Doo-hwan make an indirect contact to exchange views on ways of liquidating the legacies of the Fifth Republic.

Nov. 21 Lawmakers open their parliamentary hearings into the en masse dismissal of journalists in 1980.

Nov. 23 Former President Chun Doo-hwan leaves Seoul for internal exile at a remote mountainous Buddhist temple after apologizing to the nation for abuses of power during his seven-year rule and surrendering his personal assets to the state.

Dec. 2 Kim Hyun-hui is quoted as saying that she was shown by a cadre of the North Korean Workers (Communist) Party a letter from Kim Jong-il ordering her to destroy a KAL jetliner.

Dec. 28 In a letter to his North Korean counterpart Yon Hyong-muk, Prime Minister Kang Young-hoon proposes inter-Korean talks between high authorities to discuss a possible South-North summit and other inter-Korean confidence-building measures.

1989

Jan. 1 North Korean President Kim Il-sung proposed the South-North talks for political negotiations, composed of South-North leading figures, Pyongyang's North Korean Central News Agency reports.

Jan. 3 Some 612 art works from North Korea arrive in Busan port, the first art to arrive since the division of the Korean Peninsula.

Jan. 11 North Korea orders 55,000 South Korean television sets from Korea's Lucky-Goldstar Trading Co. in Hong Kong.

Jan. 16 North Korean Premier Yon Hyong-muk agrees to hold inter-Korean prime ministerial talks with South Korean Premier Kang Young-hoon, proposing the preparatory meeting for the talks.

Jan. 21 Chung Ju-yung, honorary chairman of the Hyundai Group, leaves for North Korea to discuss overall South-North economic cooperation.

Jan. 23 Lee Sun-ki, president of the Korea Trade Promotion Corp. agrees with Vladimir Golanov, vice president of the Soviet Chamber of Commerce, that the two countries would open trade offices in Seoul and Moscow.

Feb. 1 The government establishes diplomatic relations with Hungary.

• South Korea, for the first time, imports 20,000 tons of coal from North Korea.

Feb. 3 Kim Hyun-hee, a North Korean citizen, is indicted for the 1987 bombing of Korean Air Flight 858. The flight exploded in midair over Myanmar when a bomb planted by North Korean agents was detonated, killing all 115 passengers and crew.

Feb. 8 The preliminary meeting for the South-North high-level talks is held in Panmunjom, ending with no success because of the North Korea's demanding the halt of the Team Spirit exercise.

Feb. 27 U.S. President George Bush visits Korea and agrees to strengthen Korea-U.S. security cooperation in summit talks.

March 9 The first South-North Korean sports talks are held in Panmunjom, closing with no progress.

March 26 The Rev. Moon Ik-whan arrives in Pyongyang by way of Beijing to meet Kim Il-sung.

April 3 The Soviet Chamber of Commerce and Industry opens a trade office in Seoul.

April 25 A Seoul court sentences self-confessed North Korean agent Kim Hyun-hee to death after she is convicted of bombing a Korean Air Lines jetliner near Myanmar, killing all 115 people on board. The death sentence was later commuted to life imprisonment. She was eventually freed in an amnesty because the government said she was duped by the North's communist regime.

June 2 Kim Young-sam, president of the Reunification Democratic Party, arrives in the Soviet Union.

June 13 Kim Young-sam, president of the Reunification Democratic Party, announces he met with Ho Dam, chairman of Pyongyang's Council for Peaceful Reunification of the Fatherland, for two hours in Moscow.

June 20 The U.S. State Department delivers answers to a questionnaire on the Gwangju democratization movement to the Korean National Assembly.

July 9 Korea restores ambassador-level diplomatic relations with Iraq.

July 18 Actress Kang Su-yon wins the Best Actress Award at the 16th Moscow Film Festival for 'Aje Aje Bara Aje,' directed by Lim Kwon-taek.

July 26 The Seoul District Education Board fires 485 elementary, middle and high school teachers for joining the National Teachers Union.

July 29 Major Zuo Xiukai, a Chinese member of the Military Armistice Commission, and his wife cross the Military Demarcation Line in Panmunjom to seek political asylum.

July 31 Reps. Park Chan-jong and Lee Chul claim that Park Chul-un, minister of state for political affairs, visited secretly Pyongyang and met with North Korean officials when he was a presidential adviser.

Aug. 3 The Soviet Red Cross proposes in a telegram to the South Korean Red Cross that they directly discuss the Sakhalin-Korean problem.

Sept. 11 Georgi Arbatov, an adviser on foreign affairs to Soviet President Mikhail Gorbachev, delivers a speech on perestroika and cooperation in the Asian-Pacific region at a symposium in Korea.

• President Roh Tae-woo proposes forming a Korean Commonwealth for Reunification in a special address to the National Assembly.

Sept. 26 The 70th National Sports Games and the World Korean Ethnic Sports Festival open.

Oct. 4 The 44th International Eucharist Congress opens at Olympic Park with approximately 100 countries taking part.

Oct. 7 Pope John Paul II visits Korea.

Oct. 9 Korea is granted membership in the Antarctic Treaty Consultative Party at the ninth Antarctic Treaty Special Committee meeting in Paris.

Oct. 12 The Committee for the Promotion of South-North Faculties and Academic Exchanges is inaugurated.

Oct. 16 Delegates to the South-North Korean Red Cross working-level talks agree to exchange visitors and art troupes.

Oct. 24 Former West German Prime Minister Billy Brandt visits Korea for seven days.

Oct. 30 The 24th Asian-Pacific Parliamentarians' Union General Assembly convenes in Seoul. The Assembly calls on North Korea to try to reunify the Korean Peninsula.

Nov. 1 Korea establishes ambassadorial diplomatic relations with Poland.

Nov. 3 The government begins construction of Daebul Industrial Complex on the west coast.

Nov. 18 President Roh Tae-woo leaves on a European tour of West Germany, Hungary, Switzerland, Britain and France.

Dec. 15 President Roh Tae-woo and the leaders of the three other parties agree to end the liquidation of Fifth Republic wrongdoings. They had a common interest in taking efforts for economic development, settlement of the political crisis and other problems.

Dec. 28 Korea establishes ambassadorial diplomatic ties with Yugoslavia.

Dec. 31 Former President Chun Doo-hwan testifies on 125 problems listed in a written questionnaire to the National Assembly hearing on the Gwangju democratization movement and Fifth Republic scandals.

1990

Jan. 10 President Roh Tae-woo calls for a summit with North Korean President Kim Il-sung to discuss Kim's proposal for free inter-Korean travel.

Jan. 15 South Korea and Algeria set up diplomatic relations.

Jan. 16 Hyundai Business Group receives formal permission from the Soviet Chamber of Commerce and Industry to set up a branch office in Moscow, the first South Korean company to do so.

Feb. 8 As many as 120 Korean workers who were sent to Russia's Sakhalin Island during the Japanese colonial period return home for the first time in 50 years.

Feb. 9 The Democratic Liberal Party (DLP) is inaugurated with the merger of the ruling Democratic Justice and two opposition Reunification Democratic and New Democratic Republican parties.

March 14 North Korea, in a shock move unprecedented in over 40 years of highly tense inter-Korean confrontation, admits tunneling underneath the DMZ into South Korea during the 455th session of the Military Armistice Commission on a joint investigation into the fourth tunnel.

March 22 Kim Young-sam, executive chairman of the ruling DLP, and Soviet President Mikhail Gorbachev meet in the Kremlin for talks on normalization of relations and economic cooperation between South Korea and the Soviet Union.

• South Korea establishes diplomatic relations with Czechoslovakia, which later split into the Czech Republic and Slovakia.

March 23 Seoul establishes diplomatic ties with Bulgaria.

March 26 South Korea and Mongolia establish ambassador-level diplomatic relations.

March 27 A regular flight of Korean Air makes a stop in Moscow for the first time.

March 30 Romania opens ambassador-level diplomatic relations with South Korea in protocol signing ceremony in Seoul.

April 15 Pyunghwa Broadcasting Corp., a Roman Catholic Church-operated television and radio station, opens in Seoul.

April 20 Mikhail Smirnov, in an interview with Radio Moscow, says the Korean War (1950-1953) had been triggered apparently by North Korea's surprise attack against South Korea--the first for a Soviet scholar to acknowledge Pyongyang's invasion of Seoul.

May 18 South Korea and South Yemen establish ambassador-level diplomatic relations.

May 24 President Roh Tae-woo embarks on a three-day state visit to Japan. Japanese Emperor Akihito apologizes to Korea and its people for Japan's wrongdoings in the past, expressing 'deepest regret' in a banquet at the Imperial Palace for visiting President Roh Tae-woo.

• North Korean President Kim Il-sung proposes that South and North Korea share a seat in the United Nations.

June 4 Presidents Roh Tae-woo and Mikhail Gorbachev agree to normalize diplomatic relations between their two countries at an early date in a historic summit, the first ever between South Korea and the Soviet Union, in San Francisco.

June 14 The Paris-based Bureau International des Exposition in a unanimous agreement approves Taejon Expo '93, to be held under the slogan 'The Challenge of a New Road to Development.'

June 16 South Korea and Congo resume diplomatic ties.

June 29 President Roh Tae-woo says that he wants to go beyond politics to exchange merchandise, technology and capital with North Korea, meeting each other's needs and promoting economic cooperation.

July 10 A 4,587km-long fiber optics cable linking South Korea, Japan and Hong Kong(H-J-K Line) is opened.

July 20 President Roh Tae-woo proposes free cross-border travel through Panmunjom by South and North Korean citizens for five days in mid-August but Pyongyang immediately rejects the proposal.

July 26 South and North Korea sign an agreement to hold the first round of inter-Korean prime ministers' talks in Seoul on Sept. 4-7 and the second round in Pyongyang on Oct. 16-19.

Aug. 23 South Korea and Nicaragua normalize diplomatic ties.

Sept. 4 North Korean Prime Minister Yon Hyong-muk, heading seven-member delegation and accompanied by 83 officials and journalists, crosses the military demarcation line (MDL) into the South for talks on reducing tensions and hostility and promoting cooperation between the Koreas. On Sept. 6 President Roh Tae-woo calls for an early inter-Korean summit when North Korean Premier Yon calls on him at Cheong Wa Dae.

• South Korea sets up diplomatic relations with Zambia.

Sept. 20 The government authorizes visits to Pyongyang by 14 musicians and three journalists who had been invited by North Korea to a 'pan-national' concert scheduled for Oct. 18-24.

Sept. 27 Foreign Minister Choi Ho-joong and his Chinese counterpart Qian Qichen hold the first South Korea-China foreign ministers' meeting at the United Nations headquarters.

Sept. 30 South Korea and the Soviet Union open a new chapter of history by establishing diplomatic relations at the ambassadorial level.

Oct. 3 South Korea and Benin establish diplomatic relations at ambassadorial level.

Oct. 18 Prime Ministers Kang Young-hoon of South Korea and Yon Hyong-muk of North Korea announce they had agreed during their meeting in Pyongyang to meet again in Seoul on Dec. 11-14 for the third round of inter-Korean premiers' talks.

Oct. 19 The 145 South Korean musicians give a recital in Pyongyang, becoming the first private group from Seoul to perform in the Feb. 8 House of Culture.

Nov. 8 President Roh Tae-woo and Yugoslavian President Borisav Javic discuss bilateral economic cooperation and other matters of mutual concern in a summit at Chong Wa Dae.

Nov. 14 Greek Prime Minister Constantine Mitsotakis supports Seoul's position regarding its U.N. membership question during summit talks with President Roh Tae-woo in Seoul.

Nov. 15 President Roh Tae-woo and Hungarian President Arpad Goncz discuss ways to promote bilateral cooperation and other matters of mutual concern in summit talks in Seoul.

Dec. 7 Musicians from South and North Korea open the year-end 'Reunification' concert -the first time since Korea was divided in 1945 -that South-North Korean musicians have shared the stage in Seoul.

Dec. 11 North Korean Prime Minister Yon Hyong-muk and a 89-member entourage arrive in Seoul via Panmunjom for the talks with South Korean Prime Minister Kang Young-hoon.

Dec. 14 Presidents Roh Tae-woo of South Korea and Mikhail Gorbachev of the Soviet Union issue a joint declaration in Moscow calling for peace and security in the Asia-Pacific region and bilateral cooperation in political, economic, trade, cultural, scientific and humanitarian areas.

1991

Jan. 10 President Roh Tae-woo and Japan's Premier Toshiki Kaifu agree on three principles to build a future-oriented partnership during Seoul summit.

Jan. 30 South Korea's permanent trade mission in Beijing opens.

Feb. 25 President Roh Tae-woo and German President Richard von Weizsaecker have summit talks at Cheong Wa Dae, during which the two leaders discussed matters of mutual concern.

March 14 The Nakdong River is contaminated by phenol, which leaked from an electronics company in Gumi, a city in North Gyeongsang Province.

March 19 A medical research team led by Lee Hae-bang succeeds in inventing the world's first insulin patch, which allows diabetics to absorb insulin without an injection.

March 20 The Foreign Ministry announces that the government will provide 30 million dollars in cash to Britain for its war efforts in the Gulf War.

March 26 Local elections to choose city, county and provincial council members are held for the first time in 30 years.

April 1 The 47th session of the United Nations Economic and Social Commission for Asia and Pacific (ESCAP) opens in Seoul.

April 10 South Korea approves the first direct trade with North Korea.

April 19-20 Soviet President Mikhail Gorbachev comes to Jeju island. The two presidents pledge active joint efforts to replace confrontation with peace on the Korean Peninsula and upgrade cooperation in the Asia-Pacific region in their summit talks.

April 27 A 25-member South Korean delegation comprising 12 lawmakers and their aides cross the border at Panmunjom to attend an Inter-Parliamentary Union (IPU) meeting in Pyongyang.

May 6 The North Korean soccer delegation arrives in Seoul by crossing Panmunjom for the first of two tryout games to form a single Korean team to be fielded in the Sixth World Youth Championship in Portugal in June.

• South and North Korean unified table tennis team finishes third in a team event at the 41st World Table Tennis Championships in Chiba, Japan.

May 7 A South Korean expedition team conquers the North Pole following a 62-day journey.

June 12 President Roh Tae-woo and Danish Prime Minister Poul Schlueter discuss bilateral trade and investment promotion during a summit conference at Cheong Wa Dae.

June 21 President Roh Tae-woo and Polish Prime Minister Jan Krzysztof Bielecki agree to upgrade civilian and trade exchanges at summit talks in Seoul.

July 2 Korean President Roh Tae-woo and U.S. President George Bush reaffirm their commitment to joint security cooperation and pledge joint diplomatic endeavors to deter North Korean nuclear development during summit talks in Washington.

July 3 President Roh Tae-woo and Canadian Prime Minister Brian Mulroney in their summit in Ottawa agree on a closer regional cooperation through the Asia-Pacific Economic Cooperation (APEC).

July 13 The National Assembly unanimously passes a bill accepting the U.N. Charter, clearing the way for the government to submit an application for admission to U.N. Sec.-Gen. Javier Perez de Cuellar early in August.

Aug. 7 The 17th World Jamboree opens at Goseong, Gangwon Province, on the slopes of Mt. Seorak, close to the heavily fortified border with North Korea. A record 19,062 people came from 129 nations.

Aug. 8 The U.N. Security Council unanimously adopts a resolution recommending South and North Korea be accepted as members of the global body.

Aug. 19 About 300 scientists and technologists of Korean ancestry, including those from South and North Korea, open a world Korean ethnics scientist-technologist conference in Yanji, China.

Aug. 22 The Foreign Ministry says South Korea and Albania have established ambassadorial-level diplomatic relations.

Aug. 29 An international conference on a Tumen River basin development project opens in Changchun, China, with South and North Korea, China, the Soviet Union, the United States, Japan and Mongolia attending.

Sept. 5 A South Korean delegation, led by Vice Foreign Minister Yoo Chong-ha, leaves for Pyongyang to attend the Asian ministerial meeting of the Group of 77 Sept. 7-12.

Sept. 12 The 2nd World Korean Ethnics Sports Festival opens at Seoul's Olympic Stadium, and 1,652 ethnic Koreans from 88 nations gather for eight days of athletic competition, folk art performances, cultural events and academic discussions.

Sept. 13 President Roh Tae-woo and Malaysian King Sultan Azlan Shah pledge in their summit talks at Cheong Wa Dae to upgrade bilateral cooperation for security and prosperity in Asia and the Pacific.

Sept. 18 South and North Korea become full members of the United Nations.

Sept. 24 President Roh Tae-woo proposes in a keynote address to the U.N. General Assembly that South and North Korea replace the armistice treaty with a peace structure, seek arms reduction and open free exchanges of people and information to improve their relations.

Sept. 25 President Roh Tae-woo and Mexican President Carlos Salinas de Gortari agree to boost Korean investment and business advances in Mexico.

Oct. 2 Korean Foreign Minister Lee Sang-ock and his Chinese counterpart Qian Qichen meet in a United Nations conference room, exchanging views on bilateral relations, North Korea's signing of a nuclear safeguards agreement and inter-Korean dialogue.

Oct. 3 South Korea and Burundi normalize diplomatic relations.

Oct. 9 A cabinet meeting approves a motion to accept the charter of the International Labor Organization (ILO) to join the specified United Nations agency.

Oct. 15 The Foreign Ministry says Seoul has set up full ambassadorial diplomatic relations with Lithuania.

Oct. 22 Prime Minister Chung Won-shik, seven other members of the South Korean delegation, 33 officials and 50 journalists arrive in Pyongyang to attend the 4th round of South-North Korean High-Level Talks.

• A 14th Buddhist painting is sold for US$ 76 million at a Sotheby's auction in New York. It was the highest price ever for a Korean fine art item.

Oct. 24 South and North Korea agree to produce an accord on reconciliation, nonaggression, and exchanges and cooperation during their talks between prime ministers in Pyongyang, but fail to narrow differences on nuclear issues.

Nov. 8 President Roh Tae-woo, calling for a 'non-nuclear Korean Peninsula, declares South Korea will not manufacture, store or use nuclear weapons, asking the North to do the same.

Nov. 12 President Roh Tae-woo greets Chinese Foreign Minister Qian Qichen at Cheong Wa Dae to discuss North Korea's nuclear arms development program and prospects for establishing bilateral diplomatic ties.

Nov. 25 The 15-member North Korean delegation to the "Peace in Asia and Women's Role" seminar arrives in Seoul via a truce village of Panmunjom.

Dec. 9 Korea becomes the 151st member of the International Labor Organization (ILO).

Dec. 10-13 North Korean Prime Minister Yon Hyong-muk and his party arrive in Seoul via Panmunjom to attend the inter-Korean prime ministerial talks. They sign an agreement on reconciliation, nonaggression, and exchanges and cooperation to take effect on Feb. 19, 1992.

Dec. 18 President Roh Tae-woo, declaring South Korea free of nuclear weapons, challenges the North to match his move and shut down all nuclear facilities and submit unconditionally to international inspections.

• The Finance Ministry initials an agreement allowing foreign residents and overseas Koreans to change any amount of foreign money into 'won'.

1992

Jan. 6 President Roh Tae-woo and U.S. President George Bush agree at a Cheong Wa Dae summit to upgrade the Korea-U.S. partnership in diplomatic, security and economic areas for the co-prosperity and development of their countries.

Jan. 17 President Roh Tae-woo and visiting Japanese Prime Minister Kiichi Miyazawa agree to have bilateral cooperation committees finish drafting and report on an action plan on trade balancing and technology transfer by the end of June 1992.

Jan. 22 Kim Yong-sun, a close confidant of North Korean leader Kim Jong-il who handled international affairs at the ruling Workers' Party, meets Arnold Kanter, U.S. undersecretary of state for political affairs, in New York to discuss the communist country's nuclear problems. It was the first high-level meeting on the subject between the two countries.

Jan. 25 North Korean leader Kim Il-sung wants an early inter-Korean summit and investment by South Korean firms in the North. Kim Woo-choong, chairman of Seoul's Daewoo Group, tells reporters in Beijing after an 11-day visit to North Korea. According to Kim, the North Korean leader said he hoped to meet the South

Korean president "as soon as possible to discuss unification and other issues." He met with Kim Il-sung on Jan. 20.

Jan. 28 South Korea establishes diplomatic ties with Kazakhstan.

Jan. 29 South Korea establishes diplomatic ties with Uzbekistan.

Jan. 30 North Korea signs the nuclear safeguards agreement with the International Atomic Energy Agency.

Feb. 5 North Korea ratifies the South-North Joint Declaration on the Denuclearization of the Korean Peninsula, an inter-Korean treaty aimed at making the peninsula free of nuclear weapons.

Feb. 7 South and North Korea initial an agreement on the format and operation of political, military and exchanges and cooperation subcommittees, which will implement the inter-Korean accord on reconciliation and nonaggression signed in December.

• South Korea and Turkmenistan forge diplomatic ties.

Feb. 10 South Korea and Ukraine establish diplomatic relations.

Feb. 19 South and North Korea effectuate three agreements on basic relations and a nuclear-free Korean Peninsula between inter-Korean prime ministers in Pyongyang.

March 18 Russian Foreign Minister Andrei Kozyrev, at a Moscow-Seoul foreign ministers' meeting, promises to back Seoul when the North Korean nuclear issue is taken up by the United Nations for possible sanctions against Pyongyang.

March 19 Francesca Donner, the wife of the nation's first president, Rhee Syngman, dies in Seoul. She was 93.

March 24 The nation goes to the polls to pick the 14th National Assemblymen.

March 26 South Korea urges Japan to show sincerity in settling the comfort women issue as part of its efforts to build a sound relationship between the two nations.

April 10 South and North Korea agree in principle to open a shipping route between Incheon and Nampo and remove tariffs on trade between the two sides.

• A nuclear safeguards agreement between North Korea and the International Atomic Energy Agency goes into effect.

April 13 South Korea and China, in their foreign ministers' talks in Beijing, agree to closely cooperate for diplomatic normalization.

April 15 An interview in the Washington Times quotes North Korean President Kim Il-sung as saying he wants early diplomatic normalization with the United States and that his son, Kim Jong-il, is the de facto ruler of North Korea.

April 20 The Foreign Ministry announces South Korea and Vietnam have agreed to exchange "liaison offices" in their capitals around July as an interim step toward diplomatic normalization.

April 26 President Roh Tae-woo and visiting Czechoslovak President Vaclav Havel agree to promote bilateral economic cooperation and work together for peace and stability on and around the Korean Peninsula.

May 3 One Korean immigrant is killed and 46 others are injured in Los Angeles in riots by Black Americans. Korean immigrants suffer property losses amounting to US$ 336 million.

May 7 South and North Korea agree to arrange family reunions around Aug. 15, open liaison offices in Panmunjom and form three joint committees -military, economic exchanges and cooperation, and social-cultural exchanges and cooperation.

• Korea Telecom announces McDonnell Douglas Corp. has been chosen to put South Korea's first communications and broadcasting satellite, Mugunghwa-ho, into orbit.

June 8 The government announces the blueprint for an international airport capable of handling 100 million passengers a year on a 56 million-square meter tidal flat between Yeongjong Island and Yongyu Island, off Incheon.

June 10 Hans Blix, director general of the International Atomic Energy Agency (IAEA), reports that a "radiochemical laboratory" North Korea is building in Yongbyon is in fact a very large nuclear plant that could be converted into nuclear reprocessing facilities.

June 13 Prime Minister Chung Won-shik, in a keynote speech to the Rio de Janeiro Earth Summit, calls for the establishment of a regional institution for environmental cooperation in Northeast Asia.

June 30 The ground breaking is held for the construction of the Seoul-Busan high-speed railway.

July 19 North Korean Deputy Premier Kim Dal-hyon arrives in Seoul via Panmunjom on what South Korean officials describe as a field tour of industrial facilities. On July 24 President Roh Tae-woo, in a meeting with Kim, receives a verbal message from North Korean leader Kim Il-sung in which Kim requested South Korean cooperation for the establishment of a light industrial complex in Nampo near Pyongyang in the North.

July 28 The government says South and North Korea, in the meeting at Panmunjom, agreed the South will open its ports of Incheon and Pohang to direct shipments from North Korea and the North will open Nampo and Wonsan ports to direct shipments from the South.

Aug. 9 Hwang Young-jo of South Korea wins the men's marathon in the Barcelona Olympics of Spain.

Aug. 11 Korea's first satellite, Uribyol (Our Star) No. 1, is launched by a European Space Agency's Arian space rocket with two other satellites from Kourou in French Guinea.

Aug. 17 The South Korean liaison office in Hanoi begins consular functions.

Aug. 20 Delegates of South and North Korea agree to establish a hot line between defense ministers of both sides at a border meeting of the South-North Military Subcommittee under Inter-Korean High-Level Talks, led by the prime ministers.

Aug. 24 Foreign Ministers Lee Sang-ock of Korea and Qian Qichen of China sign a six-point joint communique in Beijing to open full ties between the two countries.

Aug. 28 Kim Young-sam is elected president of the ruling Democratic Liberal Party and becomes the first civilian leader of a Korean ruling party in 31 years.

Sept. 1 A 20-woman South Korean delegation, led by Lee Oo-chung, arrives in Pyongyang via Panmunjom to attend the third forum on "Peace in Asia and Women's Role."

Sept. 3 South and North Korea, at their prime ministers meeting, agree to open an air route between Gimpo Airport in Seoul and Sunan Airport in Pyongyang.

Sept. 17 The Inter-Korean Prime Ministers Meeting in Pyongyang decides the Reconciliation Joint Commission under the basic South-North Korean agreement to have its first meeting Nov. 5; the Military Joint Commission Nov. 12; the Economic Exchange and Cooperation Joint Commission Nov. 19; and the Social Exchange and Cooperation Joint Commission Nov. 26, all at Panmunjom.

Sept. 22 President Roh Tae-woo, in a speech at the United Nations titled "Toward a Peaceful and Prosperous 21st Century," proposes dialogue among all interested parties of Northeast Asia to build trust and prosperity.

Sept. 29 A group of 76 aged Koreans from Sakhalin arrive for permanent settlement in South Korea. They were taken there by the Japanese for forced labor before the end of World War II.

Sept. 30 President Roh Tae-woo winds up a four-day historic visit to China, ending more than 40 years of hostility and providing a "monumental" turning point for closer ties between the two nations.

Oct. 2 Pohang Iron and Steel Co. (POSCO) dedicates its fourth and last phase of Gwangyang Steel Works, enabling Korea's yearly steel production capacity to reach 32 million tons--the sixth biggest steel producing nation in the world.

Oct. 4 The Korean movie, White Badge, wins the best picture and best director awards at the 5th Tokyo International Film Festival.

Oct. 6 A semi-government team leaves for North Korea crossing Panmunjom to conduct a feasibility study for building a light-industrial complex in Nampo, a port city 50km southwest of Pyongyang.

Oct. 12 The Navy launches the nation's first submarine, the Yichun-ham, at the Daewoo Dockyard on Geoje Island.

Nov. 2 Prince Charles and Princess Diana begin their four-day trip to Korea, laying a wreath at the National Cemetery and attending the opening of a new British Embassy in Seoul.

Nov. 12 Ground is broken for South Korea's largest ever construction project, a 10 trillion-won airport on Yeongjong Island west of Incheon.

Nov. 19 President Roh Tae-woo and Russian President Boris Yeltsin sign a treaty on basic relations, establishing cooperative relations between the two countries.

Nov. 27 The Daedeok Science Town, modeled after the Silicon Valley in California, is dedicated capping two decades of work to create the high-tech research center in central Korea.

Dec. 1 Korea takes over the Ground Component Command of the Korea-U.S. Combined Forces from the United States, and the two allies activate the Combined Marine Forces Command.

Dec. 18 Majority party candidate Kim Young-sam wins presidential elections, becoming the nation's first ruler in 32 years who is not a former army general.

Dec. 19 Kim Dae-jung, Korea's most influential opposition leader, resigns as a National Assemblyman, conceding defeat in the presidential election and ending a 40-year political career.

Dec. 22 South Korea and Vietnam restore relations severed in 1975.

1993

Jan. 5 President-elect Kim Young-sam says that drastic reforms will be pressed in such a way as not to destabilize the nation and hamper the people's daily lives.

Jan. 14 Korea Telecom announces it has developed a highly integrated neurochip.

Jan. 19 The committee in charge of power transition for President-elect Kim Young-sam announces that the Agency for National Security Planning will stop meddling in domestic politics and turn affairs related to national unification over to the National Unification Board.

Jan. 26 The Defense Ministry announces the implementation of the South Korea-U.S. joint military exercise Team Spirit with the participation of an estimated 120,000 soldiers, including 50,000 U.S. servicemen.

Feb. 3 The government decides to participate in the Organization for Economic Cooperation and Development (OECD) at an early date to keep pace with the economic opening and internationalization.

Feb. 22 President-elect Kim Young-sam appoints Rep. Hwang In-sung as the first prime minister of his government while naming Lee Hoi-chang as chief of the Board of Audit and Inspection.

Feb. 25 Kim Young-sam, a long-time opposition leader, takes office as South Korea's 14th president, becoming the first civilian president in more than 30 years.

March 1 President Kim Young-sam, in an address to the nation in celebration of the March 1 Independence Movement, stresses that the way to reinstate the movement's spirit is to heal the 'Korean Diseases' and to build a New Korea.

March 12 North Korea announces its decision to withdraw from the Nuclear Nonproliferation Treaty.

March 15 President Kim Young-sam instructs the cabinet to halt economic assistance to the North until the North Korean nuclear question is resolved.

March 18 The government announces that it will completely liberalize the finance, foreign exchange and capital markets by 1997.

• The International Atomic Energy Agency adopts a resolution calling for the inspection of North Korean nuclear facilities.

March 19 South Korea allows Lee In-mo, a former North Korean spy, to return home. Despite 40 years of imprisonment in South Korea, Lee had refused to renounce communism, which was a reason for his repatriation.

March 28 A Busan-bound train from Seoul derails and overturns near Gupo Station, outside the southeastern port city. The accident left 68 people dead and 123 others injured.

April 8 The Foreign Ministry announces that the government will dispatch a 250-man Army Engineering Unit to Somalia for one year as a United Nations Peacekeeping Force.

May 7 The 'Seoul Book Fair' opens with the participation of a number of renowned printing houses from around the world.

May 13 President Kim Young-sam defines the Dec. 12 event as a "coup-d'tat-like incident" by the military.

May 17 The government scraps the military training of highschool students after 24 years.

May 20 The government proposes to hold high-level talks with North Korea to seek a breakthrough in inter-Korean dialogue.

May 22 Hyon Chung-hwa wins the

women's singles in the 42nd World Table Tennis Championship -the first such victory for a Korean.

• The Pacific Basin Economic Council (PBEC) opens its 26th general assembly in Seoul.

June 4 The government launches a satellite over the West Sea for a scientific experiment.

June 12 President Kim Young-sam says that an inter-Korean summit meeting is possible if the North Korean nuclear issue is settled.

June 29 The government dispatches the 'Evergreen Unit' to participate in the U.N. peacekeeping mission in Somalia.

July 10 President Bill Clinton visits South Korea and says he supports the immediate unification of Korea.

July 26 A Boeing 737 operated by Asiana Airlines on the Seoul-Mokpo route crashes near Mokpo Airport, killing 66 people on board.

July 27 The Foreign Ministry announces that Seoul and Taipei have reached an agreement to set up private-level representative offices in both countries.

Aug. 1 The government decides to join in the transfer of technology for a light-water nuclear reactor in an attempt to thrash out the North Korean nuclear problem.

Aug. 4 Prime Minister Hwang In-sung proposes to North Korea that an Inter-Korean Joint Nuclear Control Commission meeting be held on Aug. 10.

Aug. 6 The Daejeon Expo '93 opens with 108 countries and 33 international organizations taking part.

Aug. 7 The Navy launches its second operational submarine.

Aug. 12 President Kim Young-sam announces the effectuation of the real-name financial transaction system.

Aug. 20 The government confirms the selection of TGV of France to supply locomotives and equipment for the high-speed railway.

Aug. 24 The U.S. State Department says it has delivered to the South Korean government materials related to the 'Yulgok' military modernization project at the request of the Korean Board of Audit and Inspection.

Aug. 26 Former Presidents Chun Doo-hwan and Roh Tae-woo issue separate statements in response to questionnaires from the Board of Audit and Inspection regarding the construction of the 'Peace Dam' and the selection of F-16 fighters for the Air Force's next-generation fighter program.

Aug. 31 The Information Ministry selects Yonhap Television News (YTN) and 19 other bidders as successful candidates to provide programming for the mammoth cable television project.

Sept. 1 North Korea proposes to the South to exchange special envoys appointed by their top authorities in order to discuss pending issues between the two countries including the denuclearization matter.

Sept. 2 South Korean Prime Minister Hwang In-sung phones his North Korean counterpart Kang Song-san to discuss holding a vice ministerial-level contact to address the matter of exchanging special envoys.

Sept. 14 President Kim Young-sam meets visiting French President Francois Mitterrand to discuss conditions around the Korean Peninsula and ways of further developing bilateral relations.

Sept. 25 Japan's Mainichi Shimbun quotes South Korean President Kim Young-sam as arguing that it is inevitable for the international community to apply sanctions against North Korea if efforts to thwart that country's plans to develop nuclear weapons fail.

Oct. 5 South and North Korea agree to the timing and methods for exchanging special envoys at a working-level contact but fail to iron out all their differences, as the North demands the cessation of the South Korea-U.S. joint military exercise Team Spirit and international collaboration.

Oct. 14 The Korean movie, Sopyonjae, wins the best director and best actress prizes in the first Shanghai International Film Festival.

Oct. 17 The government confirms that 268 passengers were drowned in the sinking of a ferry boat in the West Sea.

Oct. 25 South and North Korea intensively discuss the matter of terminating the Team Spirit exercise, which constitutes the biggest stumbling block, in the third round of inter-Korean talks on exchanging special envoys.

Oct. 30 Korea Telecom begins laying a 400-km underwater optical fiber cable connecting the western part of South Korea and China.

Nov. 1 The United Nations General Assembly adopts a resolution calling on North Korea to accept nuclear checks by the International Atomic Energy Agency (IAEA).

Nov. 6 Japanese Prime Minister Morihiro Hosokawa pays an official visit to South Korea. On Nov. 7 the two chief executives agree to cooperate to usher in a new future and to overcome the dark past.

Nov. 10 President Kim Young-sam tells a meeting of security-related ministers that the North Korean nuclear problem has entered an important phase.

Nov. 15 Defense Minister Kwon Young-hae tells the National Assembly Defense Committee that North Korea had completed preparations for military provocation against the South by July 27.

Nov. 17 President Kim Young-sam leaves for the United States to participate in the Asia-Pacific Economic Cooperation (APEC) summit.

Nov. 23 President Kim Young-sam and his U.S. counterpart Bill Clinton agree during summit talks that North Korea should accept nuclear inspections by the IAEA and resume inter-Korean negotiations as the two principal preconditions for better relations with Seoul and Washington.

Nov. 25 South Korea and Taiwan agree to set up private-level representative offices on each other's soil.

Dec. 7 President Kim Young-sam, in a telephone conversation with U.S. President Bill Clinton, strongly urges America to make political considerations to reserve the tariffication of rice and liberalization of the rice market.

Dec. 16 President Kim Young-sam names Lee Hoi-chang, director of the Board of Audit and Inspection, as prime minister.

Dec. 22 U.N. Sec.-Gen. Boutros Boutros-Ghali visits South Korea.

Dec. 23 President Kim Young-sam, while meeting with the visiting U.N. secretary-general, underscores that South Korea will push for economic assistance to North Korea if the nuclear problem is solved.

1994

Jan. 11 A South Korean antarctic expedition team successfully reaches the Antarctic Pole by trekking 1,400 kilometers in 44 days.

Jan. 18 The Bidding Committee for the 2002 World Cup soccer finals in Korea is formally inaugurated with Lee Hong-koo as chairman.

Jan. 24 South Korea and China agree on the opening of a direct Seoul-Beijing air route.

Jan. 27 Kim Dae-jung, then head of the now defunct Democratic Party, establishes the Asia-Pacific Peace Foundation.

Feb. 11 President Kim Young-sam delivers a personal message to U.S. President Bill Clinton, calling for close bilateral cooperation over the North Korean nuclear question.

Feb. 17 The government decides to use the occasion of President Kim Young-sam's visit to Beijing to expand Korean industries's advancement to China in the areas of airplanes, automobiles and nuclear energy.

Feb. 25 President Kim Young-sam says at his first-anniversary press conference that he would promote a South-North summit meeting, deeming it helpful for checking North Korea's nuclear development.

March 18 South Korean and Chinese finance ministers agree that Korea will release 40 million dollars in Korea's External Development Cooperation Fund (EDCF) to finance four Chinese projects ahead of schedule.

March 19 An inter-Korean dialogue, which continued off and on, breaks down after a North Korean official made threatening remarks at a border meeting. The North Korean official, Pak Young-soo, said, "If war breaks out, Seoul will become a sea of fire."

March 22 The U.S. Defense Department decides to deploy 192 Patriot missiles to Korea.

March 24 President Kim Young-sam and Japanese Prime Minister Morihiro Hosokawa hold a summit meeting in Tokyo and agree to closely cooperate with each other on the resolution of the North Korean nuclear question.

March 28 President Kim Young-sam

holds a summit meeting with Chinese President Jiang Zemin in Beijing during which they agreed on the need to denuclearize the Korean Peninsula.

April 16 Korea is one of 111 nations to sign the Uruguay Round Agreement. The World Trade Organization (WTO) is launched.

April 18 The 43rd Pacific Area Travel Association (PATA) meeting opens in Seoul.

• South Korea decides to use France's high-speed TGV train technology to build its own bullet train service.

April 30 The family of Yo Man-chol, former North Korean Public Security Ministry captain, defects to the South by way of Hong Kong.

May 11 North Korea's deputy ambassador to the United Nations Kim Jong-su says his country accepted the suggestion offered by the International Atomic Energy Agency to send an additional inspection team to North Korea to look into the Radiochemical Laboratory in Yongbyon.

June 1 President Kim Young-sam visits Russia and holds a summit meeting with President Boris Yeltsin to discuss the North Korean nuclear issue and others.

• Foreign exchange reforms are put into practice by the Finance Ministry.

June 2 President Kim Young-sam says Russia agreed to install a direct telephone line between Seoul and Moscow and to suspend the supply of weapons to North Korea.

June 3 President Kim Young-sam visits the Uzbekistan Republic.

June 13 Former U.S. President Jimmy Carter visits Seoul on his way to North Korea by way of Panmunjom to discuss with North Korean leaders the nuclear question.

June 20 Prime Minister Lee Yung-duk proposes to have preliminary contact with North Korea to discuss a South-North summit meeting. On June 22, North Korean Premier Kang Song-san accepts the South's proposal for preliminary contact.

June 28 A South-North preliminary contact agrees that President Kim Young-sam would visit Pyongyang July 25-27 to have talks with North Korean President Kim Il-sung.

July 2 South and North Korea reach a complete accord on procedural matters related to President Kim Young-sam's visit to Pyongyang.

July 9 Radio Pyongyang announces the death of Kim Il-sung on July 8. The Defense Ministry alerts the Armed Forces in connection with Kim Il-sung's death.

July 11 North Korea informs the South of the postponement of the South-North summit meeting slated for July 25.

July 14 Pak Bo-hi, president of the daily Segye Ilbo, arrives in Pyongyang via Beijing to express condolences over the death of Kim Il-sung.

July 20 The government formally confirms that secret Soviet documents indicate that the Korean War was an aggressive war perpetrated by Kim Il-sung in collusion with Joseph Stalin and Mao Tse-tung.

July 21 South Korea and the United States agree that the cost of the light-water reactors to be supplied to the North would be borne in the form of a consortium among South Korea, the United States and Japan.

July 23 President Kim Young-sam confers with Japanese Prime Minister Tomiichi Murayama at Cheong Wa Dae.

Aug. 13 Samsung Electronics Co. announces the development of 256-mega DRAM chip for the first time in the world.

Aug. 15 President Kim Young-sam says in a Liberation Day message that the light-water reactor project for North Korea will become the first in a number of joint programs for national development.

Aug. 18 South Korea and the United States decide to assign the Seventh U.S. Fleet to the Korea-U.S. Combined Forces Command in case of emergency on the Korean Peninsula.

Aug. 22 The 21st Congress of the Universal Postal Union (UPU) opens in Seoul with 1,600 delegates from 167 UPU member countries attending.

Sept. 5 The International Olympic Committee (IOC), in a meeting held in Paris, approves Taekwondo as an official game of the 2000 Sydney Olympics.

Sept. 12 The Foreign Ministry discloses the nation's entry into the Science-

Technology Policy Committee under the Organization for Economic Cooperation and Development (OECD).

Sept. 20 President Kim Young-sam sends a personal message to former U.S. President Jimmy Carter in which he asks for Carter's mediatory role in improving inter-Korean relations in the wake of the death of Kim Il-sung.

Sept. 21 The Communications Ministry says Korea Mobile Telecom will take part in the Iridium Project designed to link the whole world with a single communications network.

Sept. 22 President Kim Young-sam sends a personal message to U.S. President Bill Clinton saying that Korea would play a central role in the light-water reactor project if North Korean nuclear transparency is ensured.

Oct. 5 Czech Prime Minister Vaclav Klaus arrives in Seoul for a three-day official visit.

Oct. 10 The National Red Cross and several other private organizations donate 433,000 U.S. dollars to Rwanda refugee programs.

Oct. 20 South Korea and China agree to build South Korean-model nuclear power plants in China in 1995.

Oct. 21 The United States and North Korea sign an agreement on North Korea's nuclear problem.

Oct. 29 The prosecution says that an extensive investigation revealed the December 12 incident was a military rebellion perpetrated by a group of army officers in a premeditated plan.

Oct. 31 South Korea and China formally agree on the joint development of 100-seat mid-size airplanes. President Kim Young-sam and Chinese Premier Li Peng have talks at Cheong Wa Dae and decide to cooperate closely in the implementation of the U.S-North Korea Agreed Framework.

Nov. 8 The government announces measures to promote economic cooperation with North Korea, allowing industries to visit the North or set up branch offices in North Korea.

Nov. 13 President Kim Young-sam has a summit meeting with Indonesian President Suharto in Jakarta.

Nov. 14 President Kim Young-sam holds separate summit talks with the top

U.S. and Japanese leaders in Jakarta.

Nov. 21 President Kim Young-sam holds a summit meeting with visiting Chilean President Eduardo Frei at Cheong Wa Dae.

Dec. 5 The government announces a foreign exchange reform plan under which it will completely liberalize the rights to own possessions by individual people of foreign exchanges beginning 1995.

Dec. 10 The Finance Ministry decides to allow people to invest in overseas real estate beginning 1995.

Dec. 14 President Kim Young-sam has a breakfast meeting with visiting Israeli Prime MInister Yitzhak Rabin.

Dec. 16 The National Assembly passes a bill calling for the ratification of the country's entry into the World Trade Organization (WTO).

1995

Jan. 5 South Korea joins the Financial Market Committee of the Organization for Economic Cooperation and Development (OECD) as an observer.

• Korea Telecom successfully dedicates cable television (CATV) transmission networks, facilitating cable TV services for about 20,000 subscribers in 18 areas.

Jan. 12 A Daewoo Group delegation flies into North Korea to conduct an investment feasibility survey there.

Jan. 16 The Samsung Group reaches an agreement with Pyongyang to build an airport and highways in the Rajin-Sonbong area of North Korea.

Jan. 20 The Daewoo Group announces the signing of an agreement with China for the conglomerate's participation in the construction of a grand park in Beijing at 5.2 billion dollars.

Jan. 23 A support group for the construction of light-water nuclear power reactors in North Korea is formed.

Feb. 5 The government decides to take part in the U.S. Theater Missile Defense (TMD) system development project.

Feb. 10 Seoul National University Prof. Hwang Woo-suk becomes the first South Korean to successfully clone a calf by transplanting a nucleus.

Feb. 12 South Korea and Egypt agree to establish ambassadorial relations soon, 34 years after the two countries set up consular ties.

Feb. 17 President Islam Karimov of Uzbekistan visits Seoul.

Feb. 21 The United Liberal Democrats (ULD) is formally inaugurated under the leadership of Kim Jong-pil, who had resigned as ruling Democratic Liberal Party (DLP) chairman.

Feb. 26 The government reports that South Korea would formally graduate from World Bank (IBRD) assistance on March 3, 33 years after it began to receive them.

Feb. 27 South Korea and Angola establish diplomatic relations.

March 1 Twenty cable television channels begin broadcast operations, kicking off the nation's cable TV industry.

March 2 President Kim Young-sam departs for an official tour of France, the Czech Republic, Germany, the United Kingdom and Denmark, and to attend a U.N.-sponsored summit on social development.

March 3 Loans from the International Bank for Reconstruction and Development (IBRD) to Korea end after 33 years.

March 12 President Kim Young-sam meets with Chinese Premier Li Peng in Copenhagen and both agree to have talks on pending Korean Peninsula issues, including the North Korean nuclear question.

March 13 The government allows 13 businessmen from eight firms to visit North Korea.

March 18 An American company ships 54,000 tons of corn to North Korea as food aid, representing the first shipment of its kind from the United States to the North.

March 22 The Foreign Ministry announces South Korea has secured full diplomatic relations with Palau of the South Pacific.

March 23 Lee Hyo-gae, head of the Korea Land Development Corp., reports that his firm has concluded an agreement with Russia on the development of a Korean industrial estate in Nakhodka.

March 28 The domestically built "Cheonma" surface-to-air missile is successfully test-fired.

April 3 President Kim Young-sam confers with visiting Bulgarian President Zhelyu Zhelev at Cheong Wa Dae.

April 5 The Korea Land Development Corp. signs a contract with China to construct a 429,000 square meter Korean industrial estate near Shenyang.

April 10 North Korea opens direct telephone lines with the United States.

April 11 General Secretary Do Muoi of the Vietnamese Communist Party visits Seoul.

April 13 The Foreign Ministry announces that South Korea has agreed to establish full diplomatic relations with Egypt and Kazakhstan.

April 28 A massive gas explosion during morning rush hour at a subway station construction site in Daegu, 302 kilometers southeast of Seoul, kills more than 100 people.

May 3 North Korea announces at a Military Armistice Commission secretaries meeting the closure of the Neutral Nations Supervisory Commission (NNSC) offices it had managed.

May 10 South Korea, the U.S. and Japan reaffirm that the light-water reactors to be provided to North Korea will be a South Korean model and South Korea would play a central role in the project.

May 15 The 44th annual meeting of the International Press Institute (IPI) opens in Seoul with 1,200 foreign journalists attending. The IPI unanimously adopts a resolution calling on North Korea to resume South-North dialogue.

May 21 South Korea and Russia initial a memorandum of understanding on bilateral cooperation in the areas of defense industry and logistics programs.

May 30 An Asia-Pacific Economic Cooperation (APEC) communications ministers' meeting adopts a Seoul declaration calling for stepped-up cooperation in the information and communications area in the region.

June 11 The Defense Ministry reports that the country would produce small remote-controlled pilotless reconnaissance planes by 1997.

June 23 The government allows Daewoo Corp. to remit 5.12 million U.S. dollars to North Korea as an investment fund for the operation of the Nampo Industrial Estate.

June 25 A South Korean freight carrying 2,000 tons of rice leaves for North Korea.

June 29 The government stops shipping rice to North Korea, saying that it would suspend rice shipment until Pyongyang formally apologizes for forcing a South Korean rice vessel to hoist a North Korean flag at Chongjin harbor.

July 3 U.N. Secretary General Boutros Boutros-Ghali names former South Korean Ambassador to the Czech Republic Min Pyong-sok as head of U.N. peacekeeping operations in Croatia.

July 8 South African President Nelson Mandela makes an official visit to Seoul.

July 17 Hyundai Motors Co. concludes a contract with Vietnam for the construction of a joint automobile plant on the outskirts of Ho Chi Minh City.

July 23 North Korea asks the United States through its U.N. mission for 1 million tons of food grain.

July 26 President Kim Young-sam, in his address to a joint U.S. Congressional session in Washington, says durable peace on the Korean Peninsula can be rooted only through inter-Korean dialogue and cooperation.

July 27 President Kim meets with U.S. President Bill Clinton at the White House and the two leaders agree to have a high-level consultative mechanism for policies toward North Korea.

Aug. 5 South Korea's first man-made satellite, Mugunghwa, is successfully launched from Cape Canaveral Air Force Base in the United States.

Aug. 12 The 1995 World Ethnic Koreans Festival takes place at Olympic Park with 1,000 ethnic Koreans from some 100 countries worldwide attending.

Aug. 15 The 50th anniversary of Korea's liberation is celebrated with the removal of the dome of the former Japanese colonial government building at the start of its demolition.

Sept. 2 Defense Minister Lee Yang-ho and his American counterpart, William Perry, agree to establish 'midand long-term security dialogue' to better cope with threat from North Korea.

Sept. 5 The National Congress for New Politics (NCNP) is formally inaugurated and Kim Dae-jung is chosen as its president.

Sept. 14 The government decides to expand the width of its territorial waters along the Korean Strait from 3 nautical miles to 12 nautical miles.

Sept. 20 The first Gwangju Biennale, slated to run through Nov. 20, opens.

Oct. 4 The Defense Ministry dispatches a 188-member Army engineer battalion for U.N. peace-keeping operations in Angola.

Oct. 9 The government signs an agreement with Vietnam under which South Korea is to provide a loan of 38.24 billion won to Hanoi.

Oct. 16 President Kim Young-sam leaves for an official visit to Canada and to attend a special summit to be held in commemoration of the 50th anniversary of the United Nations.

Oct. 22 President Kim Young-sam, in an address at a special U.N. summit meeting, proposes a special U.N. general meeting to discuss new ways of running the world organization.

Oct. 25 South Korea and Laos establish diplomatic relations.

Nov. 8 South Korea is elected to a non-permanent seat on the U.N. Security Council.

Nov. 13 Chinese President Jiang Zemin arrives in Seoul, the first ever visit to South Korea by a Chinese head of state.

Nov. 16 Former President Roh Tae-woo is arrested on suspicion of accepting bribes.

Nov. 19 Four senior Vietnamese Communist Party officials, including a Central Committee secretary, Le Duc To, make a goodwill visit to South Korea.

Dec. 2 The Seoul District Court issues an arrest warrant for former President Chun Doo-hwan on suspicion of being the leader of a military rebellion.

Dec. 6 UNESCO puts Sokkuram, Pulguksa, Chongmyo and the Tripitaka Koreana woodblocks on the World Heritage list.

Dec. 12 President Kim Young-sam says in a statement that the drive to rectify Korea's history is a 'revolution of honor,' stressing the need to expel the nation's 'military culture.'

• The Korean Peninsula Energy Development Organization (KEDO) and North Korea agree on the supply of light-water nuclear reactors.

Dec. 13 Hungarian Prime Minister Gyula Horn arrives in Seoul for an official visit at the invitation of President Kim Young-sam.

Dec. 15 The Foreign Ministry announces the establishment of full diplomatic relations with the Republic of Bosnia and Herzegovina.

Dec. 16 Huh Young-ho succeeds in climbing the highest peak in the Antarctic, thus becoming the first man in the world to conquer the highest peaks in seven continents and reach the North and South poles.

Dec. 18 President Kim Young-sam formally appoints Lee Soo-sung. president of Seoul National University, as Prime Minister.

1996

Jan. 2 The government decides to provide one million U.S. dollars in equipment and supplies to Russia for use in anti-contamination efforts of the East Sea.

Jan. 3 The Trade, Industry and Energy Ministry reports that 1995 exports reached 125,230 million dollars and imports 135,105 million dollars on a customs clearance basis.

Jan. 4 The Korean National Red Cross (KNRC) decides to provide 100,000 packs of instant noodles to North Korea with their producers' labels on.

Jan. 13 The Foreign Ministry reports that Choe Su-bong, the wife of North Korean Embassy Third-Secretary Hyon Song-il in Zambia, sought political asylum at the Seoul Embassy in the African country.

Jan. 14 Korea's Mugunghwa No. 2 communications satellite is successfully launched at the U.S. Cape Canaveral Air Force Base.

Jan. 23 Hyun Sung-il, an official at the North Korean Embassy in Zambia, defects to South Korea.

Jan. 30 The government submits a ratification paper of the U.N. Convention on the Law of the Sea to U.N. Sec.-Gen. to make the country the 85th signatory country of the convention.

Feb. 6 South Korea and Israel sign investment guarantee and double taxation avoidance accords.

Feb. 9 Foreign Ministry spokesman Suh Dae-won, rejecting a Japanese claim to the Dokdo islets, says Dokdo has been and is Korean territory historically or under international law.

Feb. 14 The government and Japan decide to discuss the Exclusive Economic Zone (EEZ) question separate from the Dokdo issue, agreeing that disputes over the isle would greatly undermine bilateral relations.

Feb. 25 A White Paper on the North Korean Human Rights Situation prepared by the Research Institute on National Unification says that since 1955, 3,738 South Koreans had been kidnapped to the North, with 442 of them still being held there and the rest repatriated.

Feb. 26 The European Union (EU) formally decides to contribute 6.25 million dollars to the Korean Peninsula Energy Development Organization (KEDO).

Feb. 27 The Cabinet approves a plan to sign a prerogatives and immunity agreement in connection with the country's planned entry into the Organization for Economic Cooperation and Development (OECD).

Feb. 28 President Kim Young-sam meets Singaporean Prime Minister Goh Chok Tong during his official visit to the city-state.

March 1 The government and the European Union (EU) initial a bilateral basic cooperation agreement.

March 2 The government and China agree to open four new air routes linking Busan to Beijing, Jeju to Shanghai, Jeju to Beijing, and Seoul to Hainan.

March 5 President Kim Young-sam agrees with visiting British Prime Minister John Major at Cheong Wa dae, to expand bilateral exchanges and cooperation.

March 11 The Seoul District Court begins the trial of former Presidents Chun Doo-hwan and Roh Tae-woo for their involvement in the December 1979 coup and 1980 Gwangju massacre.

March 19 The now-defunct U.S.-led Korean Peninsula Energy Development Organization selects the Seoul-based Korea Power Electric Corp. as its main contractor to build two power-generating nuclear reactors in North Korea as a reward for the North's pledge to give up its nuclear weapons program under a 1994 agreement. The project fell through after the U.S. accused North Korea in 2003 of secretly pushing a separate uranium-based nuclear arms program.

March 20 Foreign Minister Gong Ro-myung confers with Chinese counterpart Qian Qichen in Beijing on matters of mutual concern, including the North Korea situation.

April 4 North Korea declares that the (North) Korean People's Army renounced its truce agreement obligations on the maintenance of the Military Demarcation Line (MDL) and Demilitarized Zone (DMZ).

April 6 President Kim Young-sam, calling an emergency National Security Council meeting, asks security officers to be fully prepared against any North Korean provocations.

April 7 The Defense Ministry orders all commander-level officers to be on standby at their respective units in connection with the intrusions by North Korean troops into the Panmunjom area over three consecutive days.

April 10 U.N. Sec.-Gen. Boutros Boutros-Ghali sends a message to the North Korean leadership expressing concern about the rising tension on the Korean Peninsula.

April 11 The 15th National Assembly general elections are held across the country.

April 16 President Kim Young-sam and U.S. President Bill Clinton, in their summit on Jeju Island, jointly propose four-way talks among South and North Korea, the United States and China to discuss a permanent peace on the Korean Peninsula. North Korea initially rejects the four-way meeting proposal.

April 20 Chinese President Jiang Zemin sends a personal message to President Kim Young-sam expressing support for the proposed four-way peace talks.

• The U.N. Command in Korea asks the U.N. Security Council to take steps so that North Korea would not violate the Armistice Agreement again.

April 27 The National Unification Ministry reports it permitted plans of Samsung and Daewoo electronics companies and Taechang Co. to invest 19.2 million dollars in North Korea.

May 1 The government announces a plan to declare a 200-mile Exclusive Economic Zone (EEZ) around the peninsula.

May 4 The Bank of Korea says the country's foreign debts totaled 78,980 million dollars at the end of 1995, up 38.9 percent over the previous year.

May 8 The representatives of three member countries of the Neutral Nations Supervisory Commission (NNSC) urge North Korea to respect the Armistice Agreement in connection with the North's recent intrusions into the Panmunjom Joint Security Area.

May 9 South Korea emerges as the world's fifth-largest steel producer with 9,783,000 tons in the first quarter of 1996.

May 13 Seoul, Washington and Tokyo agree in their assistant minister-level officials meeting not to ease economic sanctions against or provide food aid to North Korea until the North makes a positive response to the proposed four-way meeting.

May 15 South Korea and Cambodia sign a memorandum of understanding on diplomatic normalization between the two countries.

May 20 KEDO and North Korea wind up talks in New York on prerogatives and immunity and consular protection agreements related to the light-water nuclear reactor project.

May 23 The Defense Ministry reports that a North Korean Air Force Capt., Ri Chol-su, flew his MiG-19 fighter into the South to defect.

May 31 FIFA, soccer's world governing body, finally decides to have the 2002 World Cup finals co-hosted by South Korea and Japan.

June 8 The government decides to expand various convenience facilities around exclusive foreign investors' industrial estates as a means of better inducing foreign investment.

June 10 President Kim Young-sam holds a summit meeting with visiting Dutch Prime Minister Wim Kok.

June 14 South Korea and Russia initial an accord on the wording of a treaty on mutual cooperation in criminal cases.

June 17 The government decides to completely lift restrictions to the creation of securities firms and banks by foreigners in 1998 and allow foreign stock investment without limit in 2000.

June 23 President Kim Young-sam holds a summit meeting with Japanese Prime Minister Ryutaro Hashimoto on Jeju Island, agreeing to maintain a Korea-Japan liaison system for the effective joint hosting of the 2002 World Cup soccer finals.

June 26 The Finance Committee of the OECD approves South Korea's application for entry.

June 28 The Foreign Ministry says the government signed the general agreement on services and trade under the World Trade Organization (WTO) convention.

July 10 Korean Peninsula Energy Development Organization (KEDO) and North Korea sign a communications protocol and two others related to the light-water nuclear reactor project.

July 22 President Kim Young-sam confers with visiting Pakistani Prime Minister Benazir Bhutto.

July 23 The government says it plans to repeal the Korea-U.S. missile memorandum prohibiting Seoul from developing missiles with ranges exceeding 180 km.

Aug. 9 The Finance-Economy Ministry says the country's direct overseas investments totaled 20,603 million dollars.

Aug. 31 President Kim Young-sam confers with Gabonese President Omar Bongo during his unofficial visit to Seoul.

• The government decides to promote a Northeast Asia Environment Cooperation System among South Korea, China, Japan and other regional countries to effectively tackle environmental problems in the region.

Sept. 1 President Kim Young-sam leaves for an official tour of Latin America, including Guatemala from Sept. 3-5, Chile from Sept. 5-8, Argentina from Sept. 8-10, Brazil from Sept. 10-12 and Peru from Sept. 12-14.

Sept. 5 President Kim Young-sam proposes in his talks with the heads of state of five Latin American countries the creation of a Korea-Latin America dialogue.

Sept. 12 The Foreign Ministry announces the creation of a permanent South Korean mission in Cambodia effective Sept. 16.

Sept. 13 The Construction and Transportation Ministry says a tentative agreement was reached on the opening of North Korean airspace to international airliners at a working-level meeting

among South and North Korea, Japan and China in Bangkok from Sept. 10-13.

• The first Busan International Film Festival opens.

Sept. 14 The 9th Trade Policy Forum of the Asia-Pacific Economic Cooperation (APEC) Committee adopts the Seoul Declaration calling upon APEC to take a leading role in the realization of trade liberalization in the region by 2020.

Sept. 16 The 96th Inter-Parliamentary Union (IPU) meeting opens in Seoul with 1,044 parliamentary delegates from 122 countries and representatives of 18 global organizations attending.

Sept. 17 The government says a total of 53 billion dollars in foreign capital has been introduced into the country from 1959 through the end of 1995.

Sept. 18 A small North Korean submarine is found aground near Kangnung, Kangwon Province, along the East Coast. One crewman is captured alive and 11 others found to have committed mass suicide.

Sept. 20 The U.N. Security Council, blasting the North Korean submarine intrusion as a grave violation of the Korean Armistice Agreement, asks the council president to demand that the North Korean ambassador to the United Nations explain about the incident.

Sept. 25 The National Unification Ministry says North Korea is capable of turning out about 100 Scud B or C missiles a year.

Oct. 1 South Korean Consul Choi Tok-kun in Vladivostok, Russia, is killed by unidentified persons near his apartment in Vladivostok.

Oct. 2 The Foreign Ministry reports the government joined the Australian Group (AG), a biological and chemical weapons non-proliferation regime.

Oct. 5 A government official says the government will totally freeze inter-Korean economic cooperation for the time being, saying that no cooperation projects can be undertaken under the mounting tension caused by the submarine intrusion.

Oct. 8 Yang Hyong-sop, chairman of the North Korean Supreme People's Assembly, vows to retaliate against the South for the submarine incident, asserting "we will levy a hundredor thousand-time higher price on them by all means."

Oct. 11 Korea joins the Organization for Economic Cooperation and Development (OECD) as the 29th member.

Oct. 13 The U.N. Security Council adopts its president's statement expressing serious concern about the North Korean submarine intrusion and the need to maintain the existing Military Armistice Agreement until a new peace regime is instituted.

Oct. 20 Spanish King Juan Carlos arrives in Seoul for a five-day official visit.

Oct. 21 The cabinet approves a plan for the country's entry into the OECD.

Oct. 24 Colombian President Ernesto Samper arrives in Seoul for a three-day official visit.

Oct. 28 South Korea and the European Union (EU) conclude the Basic Agreement on Trade and Cooperation.

Nov. 4 A Korea-Russia memorandum on bilateral military cooperation is signed in Moscow by visiting Defense Minister Kim Dong-jin and his Russian counterpart, Igor Rodionov.

Nov. 6 The 3rd Asia-Pacific Satellite Communications Conference opens in Seoul with 350 related officials at home and abroad attending.

Nov. 13 The 2nd science and technology APEC ministerial meeting opens in Seoul.

Nov. 19 North Korea says it would withdraw its officials from the South and North Liaison Offices at Panmunjom for the time being in retaliation against the South's decision to freeze South-North cooperation projects due to the submarine incident.

Nov. 20 President Kim Young-sam leaves for official visits to Vietnam, Malaysia and the Philippines, where he would attend the APEC summit meeting on Nov. 25 at Subic.

Nov. 27 President Kim Young-sam, in a Korea-Malaysia summit meeting, agrees with Malaysian Prime Minister Mahathir Mohamad to closely cooperate in the Mekong River basin development and trans-Asia railroad projects.

Nov. 29 President Kim Young-sam meets visiting Mexican President Ernesto Zedillo to discuss matters of common interest.

• The government selects 10 items,

including Hangeul (Korean Alphabet), traditional clothing and kimchi, as things that symbolize Korea.

Dec. 3 South Korea and the United States agree to step up bilateral cooperative system to better cope with North Korea's missile threat.

Dec. 11 North Korean Foreign Minister Kim Young-nam, in an interview with a German television network, concedes that his country's economy is in danger of collapse.

Dec. 12 The government delivers a letter on entry into the OECD to France, the site of OECD headquarters, to become the 29th member of the organization.

Dec. 16 President Kim Young-sam holds a Korea-Ukraine summit meeting at Cheong Wa dae with visiting Ukrainian President Leonid Kuchma.

Dec. 30 The opposition National Congress for New Politics and United Liberal Democrats jointly file an appeal with the Constitutional Court against the unilateral passage of the labor-related laws.

1997

Jan. 2 The Defense Leadership Institute says North Korea has the capability to produce 15 MiGs a year, and is building more than 60 underground tunnels that can store up to 1.4 million tons of food for the military.

Jan. 3 The cabinet approves a bill to open a South Korean representative office at OECD headquarters in Paris.

Jan. 8 The Korean Peninsula Energy Development Organization (KEDO) and North Korea sign protocols on service and approval of location for light water reactor construction.

Jan. 10 South Korea and Canada agree on 'special partner relations' at the summit in Seoul.

Jan. 19 The government announces it will select 100 ethnic Koreans living in Sakhalin and settle them permanently in South Korea.

Jan. 23 South Korean conglomerate Hanbo Group declares bankruptcy due to mounting debt.

Jan. 24 1997 Winter Universiade opens in Muju, North Jeolla Province.

Jan. 28 The 31st session of Asia-Pacific

450

Parliamentary Union in Tokyo adopts a resolution urging inter-Korean dialogue and four-party talks on Korean affairs.

Jan. 31 Prosecutors arrest Hanbo Group Chairman Chung Tae-soo on suspicion of bribery and embezzlement.

Feb. 3 Arirang TV, South Korea's English-only broadcasting company, launches domestic service.

Feb. 12 Hwang Jang-yop, secretary of the North Korean Workers' Party, requests political asylum at the South Korean Consulate General in Beijing.

Feb. 13 The government submits a draft plan for the liberalization of the communication market to WTO.

Feb. 19 The Asia-Pacific Cable Network opens, linking nine Asian countries including South Korea, Japan and Taiwan.

Feb. 22 South Korea-U.S. foreign ministers tell a joint press conference that the two countries will seek strong, combined defense position to counter the volatile political situation in North Korea.

Feb. 24 South Korea and China have their first meeting on discussion of the boundary demarcation for the two countries' exclusive economic zones (EEZ).

Feb. 25 President Kim Young-sam apologizes to the nation with regard to the Hanbo incident.

March 3 The Federation of Korean Industries demands the government allow corporate layoffs and adopt a 'no work, no wage principle.'

March 5 South Korea and the United States explain to North Korea at a briefing session that they would like to discuss food aid, establishing peace on the Korean Peninsula and confidence building at the proposed four-party talks on Korean affairs.

March 11 Chinese foreign ministry says it will handle North Korean defector Hwang Jang-yop's case according to international law and in consideration of peace and stability on the Korean Peninsula.

March 28 Chung Bo-keun, then chairman of Hanbo Group, is arrested on charges of embezzling company funds.

April 4 North Korea proposes high-level contact with South Korea and the United States to discuss opening four-party talks.

April 8 The National Unification Ministry says some 1,500 North Korean escapees are hiding in neighboring countries, and about 500 of them hope to come to South Korea.

April 10 The 97th session of the Inter-Parliamentary Union (IPU) begins in Seoul.

April 12 South Korea and China concur on draft agreement for exclusive economic zones (EEZ).

April 14 South Korea-Japan foreign ministers pledge efforts for early conclusion of new fisheries agreement, in connection to territorial dispute over Dokdo.

April 17 Supreme Court hands down life imprisonment for former President Chun Doo-hwan and 17-year sentence for former President Roh Tae-woo on charges of mutiny.

April 20 North Korean defector Hwang Jang-yop arrives in Seoul and urges Pyongyang to reform and open up to save its people from famine.

April 22 Hwang Jang-yop is quoted as saying North Korea has enough nuclear, chemical and rocket weapons to set South Korea ablaze.

April 28 South Korea-Japan defense ministers agree to strengthen security cooperation so that Japan's relations with North Korea will contribute to peace and stability on the Korean Peninsula.

May 2 South Korea proposes a cooperative system for regional marine environment protection at Asia-Pacific Economic Cooperation (APEC) meeting.

May 3 South and North Korean Red Cross organizations agree in principle at Beijing meeting on direct delivery of food aid to the North.

May 6 Foreign Minister Yoo Jong-ha says North Korea is believed to have the capability of producing 5,000 tons of chemical weapons a year and already owns 5,000 tons of such weapons.

May 10 The Defense Ministry says Russia contacted Seoul to see if it can repay South Korean loans by shipping missiles, fighter jets and submarines, instead of cash.

May 14 U.S. Chairman of the Joint Chiefs of Staff, John Shalikashvili, says Pyongyang's unpredictable regime is the biggest threat to peace on the Korean Peninsula and to the neighboring region.

May 18 The Ministry of Finance and Economy announces an earlier-than-planned opening of the domestic bond market to foreigners, starting June 2.

May 20 The Korean Peninsula Energy Development Organization (KEDO) announces that the European Community has initialed an agreement to join KEDO.

May 30 The Maritime Affairs and Fisheries Ministry says it will divide coastal waters into five zones for extensive development, and will build an international marine center.

June 5 The U.S. House of Representatives urges Taiwan to scrap its plans to transfer nuclear waste to North Korea.

June 8 North Korean defector Kim Dae-ho reveals that Pyongyang possessed six to 10kg of plutonium in 1992, enough to make two nuclear missiles, and that it has a giant underground nuclear factory in Yongbyon.

June 12 Five tons of corn and other grain is handed directly to North Korea. by South Korean Red Cross Society officials.

June 22 Russia and the G-7 adopt a joint statement at a Denver meeting, urging North Korea to halt missile exports and to agree to opening of four-party talks.

June 24 President Kim Young-sam suggests inter-Korean efforts to protect the fauna and flora in the demilitarized zone (DMZ), in his speech at a special U.N. environmental summit.

June 26 South Korea and China decide to work for an agreement first on western seas in negotiating an agreement on overlapping parts of the two countries' exclusive economic zone (EEZ).

June 27 South Korea and U.S. presidents meet in New York and consult about North Korean politics and their policies toward Pyongyang.

June 29 North Korea threatens to blow up Seoul's vernacular daily newspaper Chosun Ilbo, over an editorial urging Pyongyang's de facto leader Kim Jong-il to voluntarily resign.

July 10 North Korean defector Hwang Jang-yop claims that North Korean military commanders proposed an invasion scenario which included attacking South Korea in 1992. He said Supreme leader Kim Jong-il turned down the recommendation.

July 10 The Korean wing at the British National Museum opens.

July 11 The Information and Communications Ministry announces it finalized negotiations on communications market opening with the United States.

July 20 Former U.S. Ambassador to Seoul James Laney, and Sen. Sam Nunn, begin a three-day Pyongyang visit.

July 24 South Korean and Russian foreign ministers agree at a meeting in Seoul to hold regular sessions of a bilateral forum attended by political, economic and scientific representatives.

July 27 The ASEAN Regional Forum (ARF) expresses its support for four-party talks on Korean affairs, and registers concern for Taiwan's plans to ship nuclear waste to North Korea.

July 31 The government allocates 45 million U.S. dollars for reactor construction in North Korea.

Aug. 6 A Korean Air passenger aircraft carrying 254 people crashes into a mountainous region near Guam airport. Official tallies have 29 people surviving the crash.

Aug. 15 North Korean broadcasts report Oh Ik-je, head of South Korea's Chondogyo religious sect, defected to the North and arrived in Pyongyang via train.

Aug. 17 The Joint Chiefs of Staff estimate North Korea has facilities to produce 15 tons of chemical weapons a day, and could attack Seoul and metropolitan areas within seconds with 70 tons of chemical arms.

Aug. 19 KEDO holds a ground-breaking ceremony in the Shinpo-Kumho district in North Korea to begin reactor construction.

Aug. 23 The government announces it will provide 10 million U.S. dollars' worth of food and farm supplies to North Korea via the United Nations.

Aug. 25 Government officials confirm that North Korean Amb. to Egypt Jang Sung-gil and his family, are taking steps to seek asylum under the protection of a third country.

Sept. 1 The Second Gwangju Biennale opens with more than 3,000 foreigners in attendance.

Sept. 5 The White House says it will ensure that the Korean Peninsula is the exception to the global accord banning the use of land mines.

Sept. 7 The Foreign Ministry is concerned at Japanese-Chinese agreement to establish an exclusive economic zone (EEZ) in their adjacent seas, saying the boundary may overlap with South Korea's own exclusive waters.

Sept. 10 The Korea Summit 1997 opens in Seoul with domestic and foreign representatives present from the financial, academic and media sectors.

Sept. 12 Washington appoints KEDO executive director Stephen Bosworth as the new ambassador to South Korea.

Sept. 18 The government declares it cannot abide by an agreement draft that comprehensively bans the use of land mines.

Sept. 22 The North Korean Central News Agency reports Kim Jong-il was nominated as Rodong Party general secretary at a party session in Pyongsong, South Pyongan Province. It is the first concrete signal that Kim is about to assume the party's highest post.

Sept. 25 The Unification Ministry announces that Daewoo Group chairman Kim Woo-choong and company officials visited Pyongyang Sept. 14-19, where they met North Korea's economic officials.

Sept. 26 Government officials say they will allow South Korean businessmen to visit North Korea, and will issue permits on case-by-case study.

Sept. 29 The Foreign Ministry says North Korea sold approximately 400 Scud B and Scud C missiles to Iran and other Arab countries, and even sold missiles to Syria built at its local plant.

Oct. 1 The United States invokes Super 301 trade law to try to gain wider acceptance into South Korea's auto market.

• UNESCO lists Hunmin Jeongum and Joseon Wangjo Shillok (Veritable Records of the Joseon Dynasty) on the Memory of the World Register.

Oct. 6 'Grandma Hun,' who had been forced into sexual slavery as a 'comfort woman' for the Japanese imperialist army during World War II and has been living in Cambodia for 30 years, returns to Korea for the first time in 50 years.

Oct. 7 South and North Korea agree to link their respective flight information regions (FIR) to allow aircraft to fly directly over their air space.

Oct. 10 South Korea and Japan agree to establish a temporary fishing boundary, while continuing negotiations on an exclusive economic zone (EEZ).

Oct. 15 Agency for National Security Planning (NSP) director Kwon Young-hae says North Korea doubled the number of its small-size submarines and reinforced its war scenario against South Korea.

Oct. 20 North Korean defector Hwang Jang-yop advises Seoul not to expect any policy changes in Pyongyang, despite Kim Jong-il formally assuming the top party post.

Oct. 28 The Unification Ministry reveals that five Samsung Co. officials visited North Korea to discuss inter-Korean economic cooperation.

Oct. 30 South Korea and Cambodia normalize relations.

Nov. 6 Japan protests South Korea's construction of quay facilities on Dokdo, an island whose ownership is disputed by the two countries, and demands removal of the facilities.

Nov. 8 The South Korean National Red Cross proposes meeting with North Korean Red Cross to discuss setting up family reunion centers.

Nov. 13 Finance and Economy Ministry officials say the government will seek from 1998 mergers and acquisitions for not only merchant banks but also commercial banks as well, to financially restructure.

Nov. 16 A broadcast on Pyongyang Radio says North Korea will threaten to blow up state-run KBS-2 TV and kill producers of a new drama depicting life of officials and ordinary citizens in North Korea. The drama is based on accounts told by a North Korean female defector.

Nov. 19 The government announces that South and North Korea have opened direct communication lines between airport control towers on both sides; a follow-up to the opening North Korea's airspace to foreign flights.

Nov. 21 The government announces it asked for 20 billion U.S. dollar assistance from the International Monetary Fund to ward off an impending foreign exchange crisis.

Nov. 22 President Kim Young-sam apologizes to the nation for the national economic crisis, and appeals for public unity to overcome the coming hard times.

Nov. 24 The Finance and Economy Ministry orders 12 merchant banks ailing from a foreign currency drought to improve their foreign exchange operations by the end of the year.

Nov. 25 South Korean and Chinese presidents discuss Korean affairs at their meeting during the APEC summit in Vancouver, Canada.

Nov. 27 The Finance and Economy Ministry says the World Bank (IBRD) and Asian Development Bank (ADB) have agreed to participate in the IMF's financial assistance program for South Korea.

Dec. 1 The World Bank says it is negotiating with Seoul and the IMF to muster international support for South Korea's bailout program.

Dec. 3 The government and the International Monetary Fund sign agreement for IMF financial support.

Dec. 9 South Korea and U.S. defense ministers issue joint statement at the 29th Security Consultative Meeting, pledging combined resistance against any possible North Korean invasion.

Dec. 10 The government orders five merchant banks to close down.

Dec. 11 The government decides to draw bridge loans.

Dec. 16 ASEAN adopts a joint statement that includes its support for inter-Korean dialogue and for South Korea's financial restructuring efforts.

Dec. 18 The 15th presidential elections are held.

Dec. 19 The Central Election Management Commission formally proclaims that Kim Dae-jung, head of opposition National Congress for New Politics (NCNP), is the winner of the presidential election.

Dec. 21 The National Statistical Office says that South Korea's population as of July 1997 is 45.991 million (23.17 million men and 22.821 million women).

Dec. 22 The government grants special amnesty to former presidents Chun Doo-hwan and Roh Tae-woo.

Dec. 23 The exchange rate of the won tops 2,000 won to the U.S. dollar for the first time.

Dec. 25 President-elect Kim Dae-jung establishes his transition team, comprised of 12 members each from his NCNP party, and his coalition partner, the United Liberal Democrats.

1998

Jan. 6 President Kim Young-sam and President-elect Kim Dae-jung hold their first weekly meeting and reach a five-point agreement on economic reform steps, including corporate layoffs.

Jan. 7 The 6th general meeting of the Asia-Pacific Parliamentary Forum convenes in Seoul with over 190 participants from 25 countries.

Jan. 9 President-elect Kim Dae-jung meets a U.S. congressional delegation and discusses U.S. support for the nation's economic recovery measures.

Jan. 14 The cabinet approves amendments to the financial industry reform law to allow layoffs in the sector.

Jan. 19 Over 1.45 million citizens donate 97,500 kilograms of gold worth 970 million U.S. dollars in a national campaign to help the country get out of the recession.

Jan. 21 The National Assembly approves a bill on a government guarantee of repayment of 15 billion U.S. dollars of foreign loans by the Bank of Korea and Korea Exchange Bank.

Jan. 23 Japan formally notifies South Korea that it is scrapping the bilateral fisheries pact. South Korea consequently declares that it is suspending the voluntary fishing restriction.

Jan. 24 President-elect Kim Dae-jung advises conglomerates to no longer look to the government for help as in the past, and seek self-rescue measures through reform.

Jan. 29 U.S. President Bill Clinton says Washington will actively cooperate with South Korea in helping it to overcome its economic crisis.

Feb. 1 The government bans business groups from cross-guaranteeing debt repayment and orders them to clear all such guarantees by the end of 1999.

Feb. 4 President Kim Young-sam says

he is wholly responsible for the economic crisis.

Feb. 6 President-elect Kim Dae-jung reaches a five-point agreement on structural reform with representatives from the top 30 conglomerates.

Feb. 7 President Kim Young-sam and World Bank President James Wolfensohn pledge cooperation in solving foreign exchange and economic crisis in the nation and Southeast Asia.

Feb. 12 Presidential transition team announces 100 national tasks of the new government.

Feb. 14 The National Assembly passes agreements by the tripartite committee on labor affairs legalizing layoffs and pledging corporate reform.

Feb. 19 President-elect Kim Dae-jung says he is determined to resume inter-Korean dialogue and open a South-North Korean summit or an exchange of special envoys.

Feb. 24 The cabinet approves the government restructuring bill on cutting down the number of ministries, agencies and administrations and reducing cabinet members from 21 to 17.

Feb. 25 Kim Dae-jung, a lifelong pro-democracy fighter, is inaugurated as the 15th president. Kim won the 2000 Nobel Peace Prize for his efforts to promote pro-democracy movements and reconcile with North Korea.

March 1 Cathay Pacific cargo plane flies through North Korean airspace, the first airplane from a non-communist nation to do so since the 1950-1953 Korean War.

March 4 The Ministry of Finance and Economy announces across-the-board liberalization of the insurance business from April 1.

March 7 The government decides to foot its share in North Korean reactor construction chiefly through Korean won-based costs and construction materials.

March 13 The government pardons over 5.52 million people in the biggest amnesty in the nation's history to mark President Kim Dae-jung's inauguration.

March 14 Buddhists from South and North Korea agree in Beijing to hold a joint peace and unification prayer session in June in Los Angeles.

March 16 The government urges North Korea at four-party talks for progress in inter-Korean dialogue and for implementation of 1992 basic agreement on reconciliation and cooperation.

March 17 The Unification Ministry allows separated family members aged 65 and over to visit North Korea simply by reporting their itinerary and decides to use 45 million won from the national budget to help family reunions in a third country.

March 20 The government announces a new policy towards North Korea, naming peace, reconciliation and cooperation as the ultimate goals and foundation to national reunification.

March 31 President Kim Dae-jung leaves for London to attend the second Asia-Europe Meeting (ASEM).

April 1 An international trade delegation from Taiwan arrives in Seoul, the island nation's first official delegation sent here since diplomatic ties were severed in 1992.

April 2 President Kim Dae-jung holds summit talks with Japanese Prime Minister Ryutaro Hashimoto and Chinese Prime Minister Zhu Rongji during the ASEM in London. Both discuss bilateral relations, North Korea policy and South Korea's economic situation.

April 3 British Prime Minister Tony Blair pledges cooperation for South Korea's economic recovery efforts and expresses support for the government's stance on inter-Korean issues at a summit with President Kim Dae-jung in London.

April 4 North Korea proposes vice minister-level inter-Korean talks in Beijing April 11 to discuss fertilizer aid.

April 8 Prime Minister Kim Jong-pil suggests that Seoul-Busan high-speed railway project must be rescheduled due to the economic crisis.

April 10 The government declares it will overhaul restructuring tasks on national banks, credit funds, insurance companies, security dealers and financial supervisory organizations.

April 11 Vice minister-level inter-Korean talks open in Beijing.

April 21 The prosecution arrests Kwon Young-hae, former director of the Agency for National Security Planning, for masterminding a press conference by a Korean-American to allege that President Kim Dae-jung has close ties with North Korea.

April 22 South Korea and the United States conclude an open-sky agreement, removing restrictions on flight routes and service frequencies.

April 23 The Korea Meteorological Administration proposes joint inter-Korean research and exchange of information to prevent weather-related disasters.

April 27 Officials say the government knows of some 80 South Korean POWs believed to be alive in North Korea.

April 29 Samsung Electronics Co. announces it will start producing 256 mega DRAM for the first time in the world.

April 30 The government completely lifts investment restrictions in North Korea, limited so far to 10 million U.S. dollars, to promote inter-Korean economic cooperation.

May 1 President Kim Dae-jung meets U.S. Secretary of State Madeleine Albright on South Korea's economic situation and his planned visit to Washington in June.

May 2 'Little Angels,' a youth cultural troupe managed by an affiliate of the Unification Church, arrives in Pyongyang for the first inter-Korean cultural event in 10 years.

May 5 The Finance and Economy Ministry decides to revise investment regulations to open 11 businesses to foreign investors.

May 12 The Korean National Red Cross announces it will ship relief aid of 5,509 tons of corn, flour and salt to North Korea.

May 16 Four former officials of the Agency for National Security Planning (NSP) are arrested on charges of trying to bribe North Korea to stage a shootout at the truce village just before the 1997 presidential election.

May 17 Representatives from 17 nations gather in Gwangju for Asian Human Rights Committee meeting and adopts a constitution of human rights in Asia.

May 18 The government decides to liberalize foreign exchange transactions, including measures for opening up foreign currency service market and allowing freer overseas remittances.

May 19 Foreign Affairs and Trade Minister Park Chung-soo and Belgian counterpart Eric Derycke agree in Seoul to make joint efforts to expand trade and investment and to settle peace on the Korean Peninsula.

May 23 The Unification Ministry approves a request by the National Council of Churches on visiting North Korea to discuss building a church inside North Korea's Rajin-Sonbong free economic zone.

May 27 President Kim Dae-jung expresses hope that a visit to North Korea by Chung Ju-yung, honorary chairman of the Hyundai Group, will provide a breakthrough in establishing a new policy of separating economic cooperation from political issues in dealing with the Pyongyang regime.

June 9 President Kim Dae-jung leaves on a state visit to the United States.

June 13 President Kim Dae-jung says he is ready to meet North Korean leader Kim Jong-il anytime and anywhere, saying it is time to discuss preventing war and reducing the number of armaments.

June 16 Hyundai Group founder and honorary chairman Chung Ju-yung enters North Korea via the truce village of Panmunjom with 500 heads of cattle to donate to the North.

June 18 The Financial Supervisory Commission announces a list of 55 companies up for liquidation, including 20 subsidiaries of the top five conglomerates.

June 22 A North Korean submarine, caught in a fishing net, is tugged to a Navy base in South Korea.

June 23 Hyundai Group founder Chung returns from North Korea visit and says he concluded an agreement with North Korea to start a tourism business to Mt. Kumgang in the fall.

June 25 The Korean National Tourism Organization prepares a three-phase plan on inter-Korean tourism exchanges involving the set-up of a joint working-level body, designation of free tour zones and joint development of tourism complexes.

June 29 Defense Minister Chun Yong-taek issues a public statement saying an investigation showed the North Korean submarine that infiltrated South Korean waters

July 6 Ruling and opposition parties agree to allow dual citizenship for ethnic Koreans overseas to attract science experts to work at domestic institutions.

July 8 Russian diplomat Oleg Abramkim is expelled in retaliation to the expulsion of a South Korean diplomat from Moscow as persona non grata.

July 20 South Korea and Russia agree to adjust the number of their intelligence agents in each other's country as a solution to recent diplomatic expulsions.

July 24 The heads of five banks and the Financial Supervisory Commission agree on terms of the bank merger covering loan transfers and employment for workers from closed-down banks.

Aug. 4 Hyundai Group signs an agreement with North Korea on establishing a joint company for tours of the North's Mt. Kumgang.

Aug. 6 South Korea and the United States hold high-level consultations in Hawaii on North Korean issues, including lifting of economic sanctions and food aid.

Aug. 11 The Financial Supervisory Commission orders a three-month business suspension for four life insurers that was seen as a virtual order to close permanently.

Aug. 31 North Korea fires a multi-staged rocket that flies over Japan.

Sept. 1 The government starts consulting Japan, the United States and other allies to counter North Korea's missile test.

Sept. 4 North Korea says the projectile launched Aug. 31 carried a satellite, not a missile, and that the satellite was successfully put into orbit.

Sept. 8 Cheong Wa Dae urges opposition leader Lee Hoi-chang to apologize for the illegal campaign fundraising scandal and that opposition lawmaker Suh Sang-mok appear at the prosecution for questioning.

Sept. 17 President Kim Dae-jung proposes forming an inter-Korean joint team for international competitions at a luncheon for visiting IOC officials.

Sept. 25 South Korea and Japan conclude a new fisheries pact after two years and four months of haggling.

Oct. 8 President Kim Dae-jung and Japanese Prime Minister Keizo Obuchi agree on a joint declaration pledging a new bilateral partnership for the 21st century.

Oct. 23 Culture and Tourism Minister Shin Nak-yun says the government will decide on the pace of opening the country to Japanese pop culture and that the nation's cultural competitiveness will be fully considered.

Oct. 31 South Korea and Iran sign aviation and investment guarantee pacts in Tehran.

Nov. 2 Foreign Minister Hong Soonyoung declares that the Dokdo islets are historically and legally South Korean territory and that they are not subject to dispute.

Nov. 9 Officials wrap up negotiations with China on a bilateral fisheries agreement in Beijing by setting up temporary exclusive zones.

Nov. 12 President Kim Dae-jung and Chinese President Jiang Zemin hold summit talks and agree on establishing "cooperative partner relations for the 21st century."

Nov. 17 President Kim Dae-jung and Canadian Prime Minister Jean Chretien agree on joint advances in reactor construction projects in China and Turkey.

Nov. 19 Charles Kartman, U.S. special envoy on Korean affairs, tells a press conference that Seoul and Washington have strong indications that the underground facility under construction in North Korea is related to nuclear development.

Nov. 21 President Kim Dae-jung and U.S. President Bill Clinton emphasize dialogue and negotiations in resolving North Korea's nuclear and missile suspicions at summit talks.

Nov. 28 Prime Minister Kim Jong-pil proposes to Japanese Prime Minister Keizo Obuchi in Japan an 'Asian Monetary Fund' worth 300 million U.S. dollars to pull Asia out of its economic slump.

Nov. 30 The National Assembly's foreign affairs and national security committee adopts a resolution urging North Korea to allow access to its suspected nuclear underground facility.

Dec. 7 President Kim Dae-jung discusses with William Perry, U.S. policy coordinator for North Korea, the engagement policy and North Korean issues.

Dec. 8 The Defense Ministry says North Korea has over 8,200 underground installations stretching 547 kilometers throughout the country.

Dec. 15 President Kim Dae-jung and Vietnamese President Tran Duc Luong pledge to put behind their unhappy past and strive to nurture friendly and future-oriented bilateral ties.

Dec. 16 President Kim Dae-jung and Japanese Prime Minister Keizo Obuchi decide at summit talks to establish a joint cultural committee in January 1999.

Dec. 17 Hyundai Group founder Chung Ju-yung says he and Kim Yong-sun, head of North Korea's Asia-Pacific Peace Committee, agreed to build an industrial complex along the North's western coast for South Korea's small- and medium-sized companies.

Dec. 21 South Korea and Mongolia initial an extradition treaty and an agreement on mutual assistance on criminal matters.

1999

Jan. 7 South Korean and Japanese defense ministers agree in Seoul to jointly counter missile and other threats from North Korea.

Jan. 11 President Kim Dae-jung briefs U.S. congressmen on Korea's economic reform efforts and security issues and seeks their support.

Jan. 15 South Korean and U.S. defense ministers meet in Seoul. The United States agrees to provide a nuclear umbrella and all other necessary means if North Korea attacks with weapons of mass destruction.

Jan. 24 Russia asks the government to find ways to repay US$ 1.7 billion of its loans from South Korea in kind with military arms.

Jan. 28 The government announces a five-year plan to turn the Demilitarized Zone (DMZ) into a world peace park.

Feb. 5 Working-level officials of South Korea and Japan reach an agreement on the implementation of a bilateral fisheries accord.

Feb. 6 Prime Minister Kim Jong-pil visits Egypt, discusses establishing direct flight service and providing technology for reactor construction.

Feb. 7 South Korea inks investment treaty with Israel.

Feb. 13 President Kim Dae-jung says the government will seek inter-Korean dialogue in the nearest possible time.

Feb. 18 The Foreign Affairs and Trade Ministry sets as diplomatic goals establishing peace and stability on the Korean Peninsula and building a market economy.

Feb. 24 A group of 60 ethnic Koreans from Sakhalin arrive in Seoul to permanently settle in South Korea.

March 1 President Kim Dae-jung says in his Independence Movement Day speech that South Korea must cooperate closely with the United States and Japan to end the Cold War on the Korean Peninsula.

March 3 The government and Japan agree to establish a committee to promote cultural exchanges.

March 9 The National Intelligence Service says 231 prisoners of war and 454 South Korean abduction victims are still detained in North Korea.

March 10 The Thai foreign ministry reveals North Korean counselor Hong Soon-gyong is under custody after seeking asylum in a third country.

March 17 President Kim Dae-jung and opposition leader Lee Hoi-chang meet and produce a set of agreements on political reforms and mending ruling-opposition relations.

March 20 President Kim Dae-jung holds a summit with Japanese Prime Minister Keizo Obuchi at the presidential office Cheong Wa Dae.

March 29 Foreign ministers from member nations of the Asia-Europe Meeting (ASEM) express support for Seoul's engagement policy towards Pyongyang, calling on the international community to prevent proliferation of weapons of mass destruction (WMD) on the Korean Peninsula.

March 31 Commercial vessels from South Korea and North Korea collide in waters off Sri Lanka. The North Korean ship sank and 37 of its crewmen went missing, but two crew members were rescued by the South Korean ship. The North Korean "Manpok-ho" was blamed for the accident since it did not steer clear of the "Hyundai Duke," and experts said a lack of communication between the ships was also a factor.

April 7 IMF Deputy Managing Director Stanley Fischer urges the top five groups to press on with corporate restructuring.

April 9 Hosni Mubarak, the president of Egypt, visits South Korea, becoming the first Egyptian leader to come to Seoul.

April 14 A special investigation team looking into the death of Army 1st Lt. Kim Hoon, whose death was suspected of being linked to his subordinates' unauthorized contact with North Korean soldiers, concludes that Kim committed suicide by firing a bullet into his right temple. Kim was found dead in February 1998 at a bunker inside the Joint Security Area in the truce village of Panmunjom, where he was on guard duty.

April 15 A Korean Air cargo plane crashes minutes after takeoff from Shanghai, killing seven crew members and injuring 40 others.

April 18 Former President Roh Tae-woo reveals in an interview that he was invited to Pyongyang by the late North Korean President Kim Il-sung, and that he pursued an inter-Korean summit through secret exchanges of envoys.

April 19 President Kim Dae-jung and British Queen Elizabeth II discuss promotion of bilateral relations. The queen was the first British monarch to visit Korea since diplomatic normalization in 1883.

April 23 South Korea opens its first futures exchange in Busan, the country's largest port city.

April 26 Korea, United States and Japan agree to form a trilateral coordination oversight group (TCOG) to work together on North Korea policy.

May 3 Former President Chun Doo-hwan says his pursuit of an inter-Korean summit was aborted after North Korea demanded to co-host the 1988 Summer Olympics.

May 10 Doctors and pharmacists announce an agreement on a medical reform bill that divides their roles in prescribing and selling medicine.

May 14 Over 530 university professors nationwide issue a joint statement calling for economic and social reform.

May 18 The Korea Ocean Research and Development Institute says radioactive elements in yellow dust from China has polluted South Korea for decades.

May 28 Korea and Russia summit issues a joint statement featuring Russian support for policy of engagement and dialogue towards North Korea.

May 31 President Kim Dae-jung visits Mongolia. He produces a joint statement on mutual cooperation and partnership after summit talks with Mongolian President Natsagiin Bagabandi.

June 3 National Intelligence Service Director Lim Dong-won says South and North Korea signed an agreement to hold vice minister-level talks in Beijing from June 21.

June 7 Korea and the Philippines agree on future-oriented cooperation and common goals for democracy and market economy in summit talks.

June 15 South and North Korea clash in the West Sea as nine consecutive days of North Korean incursions explode into armed conflict.

June 18 The National Assembly adopts a resolution denouncing North Korea's naval attack and pledges resolute countermeasures.

June 20 G-8 summit leaders express concern over North Korea's missile test and development, reaffirming their commitment to missile technology control regime.

June 26 South and North Korea agree to open vice minister-level talks in Beijing July 1.

June 30 Twenty-three kindergarten students and teachers die in a fire at a summer camp at makeshift structures in Hwaseong-gun, Gyeonggi Province.

July 3 President Kim Dae-jung and U.S. President Bill Clinton reaffirm their solid joint defense posture against North Korean aggression, urging Pyongyang to accept comprehensive proposal to end the Cold War in Korea.

July 12 The Financial Supervisory Commission (FSC) launches a full investigation into financial subsidiaries of the top five conglomerates.

July 18 Intelligence officials say North Korea is bolstering its naval bases along the west coast with armored artillery and multiple rocket launchers.

July 21 Korea and New Zealand agree in summit talks to boost bilateral relations and cooperation through the Asia-Paciic Economic Cooperation (APEC) forum.

Aug. 3 Typhoon Olga, the seventh typhoon of the year, strikes the Korean Peninsula.

Aug. 7 North Korean Vice Foreign Minister Kim Gye-gwan admits that his government exports missiles to earn foreign currency. He adds Pyongyang can suspend the exports if it is given enough financial compensation.

Aug. 11 The Foreign Affairs and Trade Ministry expresses regret over Kazakhstan's sale of MiGs to North Korea, requesting that such an incident does not happen again.

Aug. 12 Inter-Korean friendship soccer matches open in Pyongyang.

Aug. 17 North Korea and the U.N. Command (UNC) meet at the truce village of Panmunjeom to discuss the North's intrusions into the Northern Limit Line (NLL).

Aug. 23 South Korean and Chinese defense ministers meet for the first time since 1945. They agree on exchanges of military personnel and cooperative relations.

Aug. 25 President Kim Dae-jung and representatives of the top five conglomerates discuss corporate reform, and issue an agreed statement on completing the reforms within the year

Sept. 1 North Korea and the U.N. Command meet to discuss the Northern Limit Line, the inter-Korean maritime border, but fail to reach any agreement.

Sept. 2 South and North Korean business leaders agree on six points of cooperation, primarily on exchanges and joint research involving financial reform.

Sept. 5 South Korea's third satellite Mugunghwa III is successfully launched from France.

Sept. 11 The Foreign Affairs and Trade Ministry files an official complaint with the Chinese government for detaining three South Koreans without notice.

Sept. 16 The government decides to dispatch 400 infantry soldiers to the U.N. peace-keeping force in East Timor.

Sept. 17 The Finacial Supervisory Commission (FSC) signs an agreement to sell Korea First Bank to Newbridge Capital of the United States.

Sept. 18 A Defense Ministry white paper for 1999 estimates North Korea's chemical arms stockpile at 2,500 to 5,000 tons in over 10 different kinds of weapons.

Sept. 24 North Korea announces a moratorium on missile tests during high-level contact with the United States.

Sept. 27 The Information and Communication Ministry says it will invest 4.6 trillion won by 2004 on six research and development projects to transform Korea into one of the top five nations in the world in the information industry.

Sept. 29 The Associated Press reports that it confirmed a civilian massacre in Nogeun-ri, North Chungcheong Province by American soldiers in the early years of the Korean War

Oct. 2 Hyundai Group founder Chung Ju-yung returns from Pyongyang. He says he met North Korean top leader Kim Jong-il and agreed to pursue business projects including the Mt. Kumgang tour and industrial complex construction.

Oct. 12 President Kim Dae-jung tells Kyodo News Service in an interview that he welcomes free contact and diplomatic normalization between North Korea and Japan.

Oct. 13 Washington proposes consulting on Nogeun-ri massacre at the Annual Security Consultative Meeting in November after a thorough joint investigation.

Oct. 16 Advance team of 160 Korean forces and staff arrive in East Timor to work with U.N. peacekeeping forces.

Oct. 18 President Kim Dae-jung says Korea and Japan will open each other's markets to each other and eventually cover all areas except for criminal and violent material.

Oct. 22 President Kim Dae-jung says the time has come to consider developing a regional consultative body comprising ASEAN plus South Korea, China and Japan.

Oct. 25 President Kim Dae-jung asks Japanese Foreign Minister Yohei Kono to allow ethnic Korean residents in Japan to participate in local governments.

Oct. 27 Korea Telecom declares a business transformation from telephone operations to Internet, e-commerce and IMT-2000 communications.

Oct. 30 Fifty-seven people, mostly teenagers, die in a fire at a beer hall and a karaoke in Incheon.

Nov. 3 The North Korean Red Cross sends a letter to its South Korean counterpart demanding repatriation of former spies and the release of long-term pro-communist prisoners.

Nov. 5 The U.N. Human Rights Commission recommends that Korea revise the National Security Law on the clause punishing those praising the enemy and eventually repeal it.

Nov. 9 U.S. State Department says it will sell the Patriot missile system and supplementary equipment worth US$ 4.2 billion to South Korea.

Nov. 15 Korea, Japan, Switzerland, the European Union and other major agricultural importing nations agree to establish joint countermeasures against exporting countries at the New Round negotiations.

Nov. 16 U.S. Defense Department claims the spraying of defoliants along the Demilitarized Zone in the late 1960s was agreed to by the South Korean government and military.

Nov. 23 The United States denies any legal responsibility for the use of defoliants in the DMZ, saying the decisions were made by the South Korean government.

Nov. 28 Korea and Japan agree at a summit in Manila to jointly advance into the third market by combining Korean labor and Japanese capital.

Dec. 7 A research team at Pohang University of Science and Technology develops a DNA vaccine that causes a cell to self-generate anti-bodies against the disease AIDs.

Dec. 10 Korean and Chinese foreign ministers agree in Seoul to hold regular talks and continue cooperation for peace and stability on the Korean Peninsula.

Dec. 14 U.S. Ambassador to South Korea Stephen Bosworth says a tripartite consultative body comprising South Korea, China and Japan may be necessary but premature, and would require much time to form.

Dec. 16 Korea urges Japan to allow ethnic Korean residents in Japan to run for local government posts, and hire more of them as public employees.

Dec. 21 The Korea Aerospace Research Institute successfully launches Korea's first multi-purpose satellite from U.S. Vandenberg Air Force Base.

2000

Jan. 13 Park Tae-joon takes office as South Korea's 32nd prime minister.

Feb. 1 The Cabinet approves a legal revision on human organ transplants.

Feb. 13 South Korean marathon runner Lee Bong-ju sets a new South Korean record of 2 hours, 7 minutes and 20 seconds at the Tokyo Marathon.

Feb. 28 The World Bank, the international body that bailed South Korea out of its 1997 financial crisis, announces it will halt aid programs for Seoul as South Korea's financial situation had improved.

March 9 President Kim Dae-jung visits Germany and announces the Berlin Declaration, in which South Korea agreed in principle to provide assistance to rebuild North Korea's economic infrastructure.

April 3 The Citizens' Coalition for the 2000 General Election names 86 candidates as unfit for public service. Of those targeted, 68.6 percent failed to win National Assembly seats. The organization released a list of 108 such candidates this year.

April 10 South and North Korea simultaneously announce an agreement to hold their first-ever summit meeting in Pyongyang on June 15.

April 13 South Korea holds a general election to pick lawmakers for the 16th National Assembly.

April 19 Slugger Lee Seung-yeop becomes the youngest baseball player ever to hit 150 homers.

April 27 French automaker Renault acquires Samsung Motors and renames it Renault Samsung Motors.

May 29 President Kim Dae-jung holds a summit with Japanese Prime Minister Yoshiro Mori in Seoul.

June 8 President Kim Dae-jung attends the funeral of former Japanese Prime Minister Keizo Obuchi during his visit to Tokyo and holds summit talks with Japanese Prime Minister Yoshiro Mori and U.S. President Bill Clinton after the ceremony.

June 14 South Korean President Kim Dae-jung takes part in the first inter-Korean summit with North Korean leader Kim Jong-il in Pyongyang. They released a five-point joint statement aimed at increasing economic and social exchanges and holding reunions of families separated since the division of the country before the Korean War.

June 30 South and North Korean Red Cross sign an agreement to exchange 151 visitors from each side in August for family reunions and for the South to repatriate in September all pro-communist prisoners who wish to return to the North.

July 26 South and North Korea hold their first-ever foreign ministerial talks in Bangkok.

July 30 South and North Korea hold their first ministerial meeting in Seoul. They agreed to have inter-Korean ministerial meetings on a regular basis, reopen liaison offices in the border village of Panmunjom and establish a reconciliation week in honor of Aug. 15, the anniversary of Korea's liberation from Japanese colonial rule in 1945.

July 31 Alpinist Um Hong-gil completes scaling all 14 peaks of the Himalayas, which stand more than 8,000 meters above sea level. He was the first South Korean to achieve the feat.

Aug. 5 The heads of 46 South Korean news organizations visit North Korea at the invitation of its leader, Kim Jong-il. The unprecedented visit was made after a landmark summit between the leaders of the two Koreas in Pyongyang in June.

Aug. 10 North Korea and South Korean conglomerate Hyundai agree to operate a tour program enabling South Koreans to visit the North's scenic Mount Kumgang resort on the country's southeast coast.

Aug. 15 The first reunions of separated families from South and North Korea since the division of the peninsula in 1948 are held in Seoul and the North's capital Pyongyang. The reunions were arranged in accordance with an agreement at the historic inter-Korean summit in Pyongyang in June 2000.

Aug. 19 North Korea's national orchestra holds its first performance in Seoul.

Aug. 25 The government releases a list of 63 prisoners of conscience who will be sent to communist North Korea. Jailed during the 1950-53 Korean War and refusing to accept the capitalist South as their home, they were bused to the North on Sept. 2.

Sept. 1 The second round of inter-Korean ministerial talks ends with the two sides issuing a joint statement.

Sept. 2 South Korea repatriates 63 former North Korean spies as part of Seoul's reconciliation with Pyongyang. The ex-spies were freed after serving prison terms of up to 40 years.

Sept. 7 President Kim Dae-jung meets his U.S. counterpart, Bill Clinton, in New York on the sidelines of the U.N. Millennium Summit. Clinton expressed his complete support for Kim's "sunshine" policy toward North Korea, and they issued a joint statement calling for constructive engagement with Pyongyang.

Sept. 11 A North Korean delegation led by Workers' Party Secretary Kim Yong-sun arrives in Seoul. Its four-day trip followed President Kim Dae-jung's visit to North Korea in June of that year for the inter-Korean summit.

Sept. 15 South and North Korea march together at the opening ceremony of the Sydney Olympic Games, the first time for the two sides to do so.

Sept. 20 South Korean male fencer Kim Young-ho wins a gold medal at the Sydney Olympic Games. Kim's victory marked the first time that South Korea took gold in an Olympic fencing event.

Sept. 25 South and North Korea hold their first-ever defense ministerial talks on Jeju Island.

Oct. 18 South Korea signs an extradition treaty with China.

Oct. 20 The Asia-Europe Meeting opens in Seoul with leaders from 26 member countries tackling political, security, economic and social issues. The meeting adopted the Seoul Declaration for Peace on the Korean Peninsula, a commitment to support peace on the peninsula and dialogue and exchanges with North Korea.

Oct. 28 Unionized pilots at Korean Air, South Korea's leading airline, launch their first-ever strike.

Nov. 11 Representatives of doctors, pharmacists and the government reach an agreement on revising the Pharmacy Law to implement medical reforms aimed at separating the roles of doctors and pharmacists. The revised law denied doctors the right to sell medication and required pharmacists to follow a doctor's prescription before selling drugs above a certain strength.

Nov. 30 Two hundred separated families from South and North Korea hold tearful reunions in Seoul and Pyongyang for the first time since the 1950-53 Korean War. The reunions were one of the crowning achievements from the landmark summit talks between the leaders of the two Koreas earlier in the year.

Dec. 10 South Korean President Kim Dae-jung receives the Nobel Peace Prize in recognition of his work for reconciliation between South and North Korea and for democracy and human rights in East Asia, becoming his country's first Nobel laureate.

Dec. 22 Kookmin Bank and Housing and Commercial Bank agree to merge, creating the nation's largest commercial bank.

Dec. 27 Delegates from South Korea arrive in Pyongyang to hold the first preliminary meeting on the establishment of inter-Korean economic cooperation talks.

Dec. 28 South Korea and the United States complete a revised Status of Forces Agreement (SOFA), which expanded South Korean jurisdiction over U.S. military suspects and set legal grounds for environmental protection on U.S. military bases.

2001

Jan. 12 U.S. President Bill Clinton expresses "regret" over the killing of South Korean citizens by U.S. soldiers during the 1950-1953 Korean War. He acknowledged that U.S. soldiers "killed or injured an unconfirmed number of Korean refugees" in Nogeun-ri, a hamlet in southeastern South Korea, in July 1950, barely a month after the war broke out. Bereaved families claim at least 248 people were killed.

Jan. 16 South Korean golfer Pak Se-ri wins the U.S. LPGA tour, YourLife Vitamins LPGA Classic.

Jan. 17 The Seoul government announces that it sought Washington's consent to allow it to develop and produce missiles with a range of up to 300 kilometers that can carry warheads weighing up to 500 kilograms. Under a 1979 accord with the United States, South Korea is barred from developing missiles with a range of over 180km.

Jan. 18 South Korea and the U.S. sign a revised Status of Forces Agreement (SOFA), which governs legal status of American military forces stationed here. The revised SOFA increases the number of crimes to be ruled by Korean courts to 12 and allows U.S. suspects to be handed over to the Korean side before indictment. It contains clauses increasing the level of respect U.S. forces are required to show Korean environmental laws and creates stricter rules regarding the dismissal of Korean employees from jobs on U.S. bases.

Jan. 26 Lee Su-hyeon, a South Korean studying in Japan, dies when he is hit by a train in a Tokyo subway station after saving a drunken Japanese man who had fallen onto the tracks.

Jan. 29 South and North Korea hold their third Red Cross talks to discuss the reunions of family members separated in the 1950-53 Korean War.

Jan. 31 The two Koreas hold their fourth round of military talks in the truce village of Panmunjom.

Feb. 2 Prosecutors announce Daewoo Group engaged in about 41 trillion won worth of accounting fraud.

Feb. 13 The Ministry of Justice grants refugee status to an Ethiopian seeking asylum in the country, marking the first time for South Korea to grant refugee status.

March 1 North Korea establishes diplomatic ties with Germany.

March 8 President Kim Dae-jung visits the United States for a summit with U.S. President George W. Bush.

March 10 Culture and Tourism Minister Kim Han-gill visits North Korea to discuss culture, tourism and sports exchanges with Pyongyang.

March 21 Chung Ju-yung, the founder and former honorary chairman of the Hyundai Group died at a Seoul hospital. He was 86.

March 26 South Korea joins the Missile Technology Control Regime

(MTCR). The MTCR, established in 1987, bans signatories from exporting technology to non-signatories for missiles with a range of over 300 kilometers and the capacity to carry more than 500 kilograms.

March 29 Incheon International Airport, South Korea's largest airport, is officially opened.

April 11 A court rules that the South Korean government must compensate residents of Maehyangri, a community near a U.S. Air Force shooting range in Gyeonggi Province, for physical and mental damage. After the Koo-ni shooting range was established in 1951 during the Korean War, more than a dozen people died and many others were seriously wounded because of military activity. The residents, mostly farmers, had appealed to South Korean authorities about the issue since the 1980s. The residents didn't receive the compensation of 194 million won (US$169,750) until April 2004.

April 16 Lee Bong-ju wins the Boston Marathon.

April 22 American Paul Muenzen is appointed the head priest of Hyeonjeongsa, a Buddhist temple in North Gyeongsang Province. Muenzen, a former Catholic who became a monk in 1987, became the first foreigner to head a Korean Buddhist temple.

May 11 The Seoul District Court allows Dong-Ah Construction Company to go into bankruptcy.

May 19 The United Nations Educational, Scientific and Cultural Organization (UNESCO) designates Korea's traditional royal ritual honoring deceased kings and queens as a world cultural heritage. The ritual's music was also named a heritage.

July 5 Pitcher Park Chan-ho becomes the first South Korean to be selected as a Major League Baseball all-star in the U.S.

July 19 South Korea's Constitutional Court rules against the nationwide proportional representation system. A revised form of the system was later introduced in which some of the seats in the National Assembly are determined by the proportion of a party's electoral vote.

July 26 North Korean leader Kim Jong-il embarks on a month-long trip to Russia by train.

Aug. 5 South Korea's Pak Se-ri and Kim Mi-hyun take first and second place respectively at the Weetabix Women's British Open, the last major event of the year's LPGA season.

Aug. 17 Bang Sang-hoon, president of the daily Chosun Ilbo, Kim Byung-kwan, former honorary chairman of the daily Dong-A Ilbo, and Cho Hee-jun, former chairman of the Kukmin Daily, are arrested on tax evasion charges after a special tax probe into news organizations. Conservative forces claimed the probe conducted under the Kim Dae-jung administration was a plot to tame news media critical of the government.

Aug. 23 President Kim Dae-jung holds a summit with the visiting Vietnamese head of state Tran Duc Luong.

Sept. 3 The National Assembly approves a motion to dismiss Unification Minister Lim Dong-won.

Sept. 21 General Motors Corp. (GM) signs a memorandum of understanding to take over ailing Korean carmaker Daewoo Motor Co.

Oct. 20 President Kim Dae-jung and Japanese Prime Minister Junichiro Koizumi agree to settle pending issues between their countries, including ones related to Japan's history textbook distortions and South Koreans fishing in waters off the Southern Kuril Islands. At the summit in Shanghai, the two leaders agreed to form a joint history study group.

Nov. 2 The Korea Federation of Teachers' Associations declares that teachers will begin to officially participate in political activities.

Nov. 22 South Korea test-fires a 100km-range missile.

Dec. 7 President Kim Dae-jung agrees with Norwegian Prime Minister Kjell Magne Bondevik to strengthen their economic partnership. The two leaders named shipbuilding, energy and information technology as key areas for cooperation and agreed to seek joint entry into plant construction markets in other countries.

Dec. 21 Pitcher Park Chan-ho signs a five-year contract with the U.S. Major League Baseball team Texas Rangers.

2002

Jan. 24 President Kim Dae-jung holds talks with Norwegian Prime Minister Kjell Magne Bondevik to discuss the latest political situation on the Korean Peninsula and ways to enhance bilateral cooperation.

Feb. 1 A group of 46 ruling and opposition party members submit a resolution to the National Assembly calling for the release of Robert Kim, a Korean-American who was serving a prison sentence in the United States on conviction of passing secret information to South Korea while serving as a U.S. naval intelligence officer. The 65-year-old was released on probation in July 2004 after serving seven years of his nine-year sentence.

Feb. 6 Park Yong-sung, chairman of South Korea's Doosan Group, is elected as a member of the International Olympic Committee at its general assembly.

Feb. 28 Ruling and opposition lawmakers release the names of 708 people who allegedly collaborated with Japan when Korea was under its colonial rule from 1910 to 1945.

March 14 A group of 25 North Korean refugees rushes into the Spanish Embassy in Beijing to seek asylum in South Korea.

March 17 Twenty-five North Koreans who sought asylum at the Spanish Embassy in Beijing arrive in South Korea via Manila.

March 24 A special prosecution team announces the results of its investigation into what is dubbed "Lee Yong-ho-gate," a corruption scandal involving high-level government officials, senior prosecutors and intelligence officials. The prosecution said several top-level officials collaborated with Lee to manipulate the stock market. Lee was later charged with embezzling 68 billion won (US$53.7 million).

March 27 South Korea regains a sovereign credit rating of "A" four years and four months after the 1997 financial crisis.

April 2 Yangyang International Airport opens.

April 3 Lim Dong-won, national security advisor to then-President Kim Dae-jung, visits Pyongyang as a special presidential envoy.

April 8 Speed skater Kim Dong-sung wins six gold medals at the 2002 World Short Track Championship.

April 15 A Chinese passenger plane crashes in Gimhae, South Gyeongsang province, killing 129 people.

April 18 South Korea and Chile sign a double taxation avoidance accord.

April 27 Roh Moo-hyun, a former human rights lawyer, wins the ruling Millennium Democratic Party's nomination to run in the presidential election in December.

April 28 A reunion of separated family members from North and South Korea is held at the Mount Kumgang resort in the North.

May 10 The main opposition Grand National Party elects Lee Hoi-chang as its candidate for the presidential election in December of the year. He narrowly lost to Roh Moo-hyun of the then ruling Millennium Democratic Party.

May 26 Veteran director Im Kwon-taek wins the Best Director award at the Cannes International Film Festival for "Chihwaseon," the story of an eminent Korean painter in the late 19th century. Im became the first Korean to win the prize.

June 3 North Korea starts to discharge waters at Imnam Dam, also referred to as Kumgang-san dam, on the North's section of the Han River. The discharge raised the water level at South Korea's Peace Dam, 38 kilometers to the south, five-fold.

June 4 South Korea's national soccer team defeats Poland 2-0 in a World Cup match in Busan, marking the country's first victory in a World Cup finals match since it first played in the international tournament in 1954. South Korea, which co-hosted the World Cup with Japan, later made history by becoming the first Asian team to advance to the semifinals.

June 13 Two South Korean middle school students are killed by a U.S. military vehicle in Yangju, just north of Seoul.

June 14 South Korea, co-hosting the FIFA World Cup with Japan, advances to the final 16 for the first time by beating Portugal. Korea later reached the semifinal but was defeated by Germany.

June 18 The South Korean national soccer team defeats Italy 2-1 and advances to the quarterfinals of the World Cup. South Korea made it to the semifinals before falling to Germany.

June 22 World Cup co-hosts South Korea defeats Spain in a penalty shoot-out, becoming the first Asian team to advance to the semifinals of the tournament.

June 25 South Korea loses 1-0 to Germany in the semifinals of the World Cup. Led by Dutch coach Guus Hiddink, the South Korean team advanced further than any other Asian team in the history of the quadrennial tournament.

June 29 South Korea has an unexpected 25-minute naval battle with North Korea near Yeonpyeong Island, the inter-Korean maritime border, in the Yellow Sea. The firing exchange leaves four South soldiers killed and 19 others wounded, with one local patrol boat sunk.

July 30 South Korean golfer Gloria Park wins the LPGA's Big Apple Classic in New York, with compatriot Han Hee-won finishing in second place.

July 31 South and North Korea end a Cabinet-level meeting in Seoul after issuing a six-point agreement that called for, among other things, the re-linking of a cross-border railway, the Gyeongui Line.

Aug. 12 South and North Korea hold their seventh round of ministerial talks in Seoul.

Sept. 3 A group of 16 North Korean defectors enters a residential facility for German diplomats in Beijing and requests asylum.

Sept. 5 The government finalizes revisions to labor laws to introduce a five-day workweek by July 2006.

Sept. 7 A friendly soccer match between South and North Korea ends in a scoreless draw. It was the first time for the two to face each other since a pair of friendlies in 1990. The inter-Korean match was held two months after South Korea co-hosted the World Cup with Japan.

Sept. 8 The Red Cross of South and North Korea agree to jointly set up a venue at the North's scenic resort of Mount Kumgang for reunions of families separated since the Korean War.

Sept. 16 The militaries of South and North Korea agree to open a hotline to coordinate, among other tasks, work on re-linking two sets of severed railways and roads across their heavily fortified border. The railways and roads have been reconnected, but they have yet to open for traffic because of political and military tensions between the two sides.

Sept. 17 Japanese Prime Minister Junichiro Koizumi holds a historic summit with North Korean leader Kim Jong-il in Pyongyang.

Sept. 23 North Korean athletes come to Busan, South Korea's largest port city, to participate in the 14th Asian Games.

Sept. 24 The two Koreas open a hotline between military authorities for the first time since the Korean War ended in 1953.

Sept. 29 Oct. 14 The 14th Asian Games open in South Korea's southeastern port city of Busan. South Korea finished second in the number of medals won.

Oct. 25 North Korea officially rejects a U.S. demand for dismantlement of its nuclear program and instead demands that a non-aggression treaty be signed between it and the United States.

Nov. 4 Unionized government workers stage a nationwide walkout for the first time in South Korea's history.

Nov. 5 Rep. Chung Mong-joon, head of the National Integration 21 Party and also chairman of the Korea Football Association, is officially nominated as a presidential candidate at his party's national convention.

Nov. 15 President Kim Dae-jung holds summits with U.S. President Bill Clinton and other heads of state on the sidelines of the Asia-Pacific Economic Cooperation summit in Brunei. Kim and Clinton reaffirmed their commitment to continuing cooperation on relations with North Korea, following U.S. Secretary of State Madeleine Albright's visit to North Korea earlier that year. Kim also expressed his government's intention to revise the Status of Forces Agreement, which governs the legal status of American soldiers in South Korea, and urged the U.S. to investigate civilian massacres by U.S. forces during the Korean War.

Nov. 24 Roh Moo-hyun wins the united presidential candidacy of his Millennium Democratic Party and National Alliance 21, led by Chung Mong-joon, by finishing ahead of Chung in a voter survey that followed a television debate between the two candidates. Roh defeated opposition leader Lee Hoi-chang in the presidential election in December of the year.

Nov. 25 North Korea designates Mount Kumgang as a special attraction for international tourists. Hyundai Asan, an affiliate of the South Korean conglomerate Hyundai Group, began operating tours to the scenic mountain on the North's east coast in 1998.

Nov. 27 On behalf of U.S. President George W. Bush, U.S. Ambassador to Korea Thomas Hubbard apologizes for the accidental deaths of two South Korean schoolgirls in a road accident on June 13 by a U.S. military vehicle.

Nov. 29 Dacom Corp. becomes the new owner of Powercomm Co.

Dec. 2 Kookmin Bank and a new lottery operator, KLS consortium, begin selling lottery tickets.

Dec. 8 South and North Korea agree to open a temporary road between Seoul and Sinuiju.

Dec. 13 U.S. President George W. Bush apologizes to South Korean President Kim Dae-jung by phone for the deaths of two South Korean schoolgirls run over by a U.S. military vehicle.

Dec. 14 Candlelight vigils are held in over 70 cities in 12 countries, including South Korea and the United States, in memory of two South Korean schoolgirls who were killed in an accident involving an armored U.S. military vehicle.

Dec. 15 South and North Korea hold a third round of working-level talks on the North's Mount Kumgang aimed at opening their cross-border railways and roads.

Dec. 17 Red Cross officials of South and North Korea agree to set up a joint panel on the construction of a reunion center for separated families at Mount Kumgang in North Korea and to hold a sixth round of reunions.

Dec. 20 Lee Hoi-chang, leader of the opposition Grand National Party, announces he will retire from politics.

Dec. 25 South and North Korea hold working-level talks to discuss cooperation on maritime affairs.

Dec. 30 The government designates the inner port of Incheon as a duty-free area.

2003

Jan. 3 A Korean postal code is given to Dokdo Island, the twin islets near Ulleung Island at the eastern-most part of the country.

Jan. 5 South Korea and Russia agree to cooperate to solve the North Korean nuclear issue in a peaceful manner.

Jan. 10 North Korea withdraws from the Nuclear Non-Proliferation Treaty (NPT) after the United States accuses it of running a clandestine atomic weapons program in violation of a 1994 treaty.

Jan. 21 A court acquits 18 of 20 former democratic activists convicted of being involved in an alleged rebellion conspiracy, led by former dissident leader Kim Dae-jung, which drove Gwangju citizens to the massive uprising on May 18, 1980.

Jan. 24 Seoul and Pyeongyang pledge to cooperate with each other in resolving the North Korean nuclear issue peacefully at ministerial talks held in South Korea.

Jan. 27 South Korean presidential envoy Lim Dong-won leaves for Pyongyang to discuss with North Korean leaders ways to resolve the North's standoff with the United States over its nuclear weapons program.

Jan. 28 Lee Jong-wook is elected as director-general of the World Health Organization (WHO), becoming the first South Korean to head an international agency.

Jan. 29 Allegations surface that Hyundai Merchant Marine Co., the shipping arm of Hyundai Group, made a secret payment of 224 billion won to Pyongyang shortly before the inter-Korean summit in June 2000 between South Korean President Kim Dae-jung and North Korean leader Kim Jong-il. An independent counsel, named by President Roh Moohyun to investigate the summit scandal, announced in June 2003 that Hyundai Group illegally sent US$500 million to North Korea.

Feb. 5 Hyundai Asan Chairman Chung Mong-hun crosses into North Korea on a pilot tour using an overland route to the North's scenic Mount Kumgang resort, which the company developed for South Korean tourists. The route through the

Demilitarized Zone, which saves time and expenses, has been gradually replacing a sea route that had been used exclusively for the tour.

Feb. 11 The Seoul metropolitan government announces plans for a project to restore the Cheonggyecheon, a stream hidden by an overpass running through downtown Seoul. The stream had been buried under concrete since 1958, when the country was in the early stages of industrialization.

Feb. 14 President Kim Dae-jung makes a public statement admitting his administration helped arrange illegal loans to Hyundai for remittance to North Korea, believing expediting cooperation with the North is in the country's interest.

Feb. 17 Lee Hyung-taik, a South Korean tennis player and his partner Vladimir Voltchkov of Belarus win the doubles competition at the Siebel Open held in the U.S. city of San Jose.

Feb. 18 A fire engulfs a subway station in the southeastern city of Daegu, killing 197 people and injuring hundreds. The blaze was started early in the morning by a mentally disturbed man in his 50s who intended to kill others as well as himself. He was later sentenced to life in prison.

Feb. 22 SK Corp. Chairman Chey Tae-won is arrested on charges of illegal stock trading.

Feb. 25 Roh Moo-hyun, a human rights lawyer-turned-politician, is inaugurated as South Korea's 16th President.

March 1 A North Korean delegation visits Seoul to attend an inter-Korean commemoration of the March 1 Independence Movement.

March 7 Cliff Richard, a British pop star, performs in Seoul for the first time in 34 years.

March 15 The Ministry of National Defense shortens mandatory military service by two months, cutting service periods in South Korea's army, navy and air force to 24, 26 and 28 months, respectively. The changes went into effect in October that year. All South Korean men are required to serve.

March 19 Lee Seok-hee, former deputy chief of the National Tax Service, is repatriated to Seoul from the United States for questioning by prosecutors on charges of raising illegal funds for government candidate Lee Hoi-chang in the 1997 presidential elections. Lee Seok-hee was later sentenced to 18 months in prison.

March 27 The government moves to allow open access to administrative information and replace closed "press rooms" with briefing rooms, to which any journalist of an accredited media organization can be given access.

March 28 The Labor Ministry announces a plan to introduce an "employment permit system" for foreign migrant workers under which they are granted greater labor rights and legal protection equivalent to their Korean peers for up to three years.

April 2 The National Assembly passes a controversial bill on sending non-combat forces to support the U.S.-led military campaign in Iraq.

April 9 South Korea and the United States agree on the early relocation of the American military's Yongsan garrison outside of central Seoul.

April 12 South Korea's lottery picks the numbers for a 47 billion won prize, the country's biggest ever.

April 14 The new leader of "Hanchongnyeon," the Federation of Korean University Student Associations, says he will consider dissolving the organization so it can be reorganized into a more productive body.

April 15 The Seoul government extradites a South Korean who committed a crime in Japan. It was the first South Korean action taken under an extradition treaty signed between the two countries.

April 16 A special counsel begins an inquiry into charges that some aides of President Kim Dae-jung sent money secretly to North Korea before the historic summit meeting between Kim and North Korean leader Kim Jong-il in Pyongyang on June 15, 2000. Five officials and an executive of Hyundai Group, which provided part of the money, were convicted by the Supreme Court on March 29, 2004, of violating the Foreign Exchange Control Law by remitting the money illegally.

April 17 South Korea sends 20 soldiers to Iraq in its first deployment to the war-torn country.

April 24 National Assembly by-elections take place.

April 27 Inter-ministerial meetings between South and North Korea open in Pyongyang.

April 30 In honor of the inauguration of President Roh Moo-hyun, the government releases a total of 1,424 prisoners who had been convicted of violating labor laws.

May 6 The National Assembly passes a revision bill on war veterans and Agent Orange patients to expand government subsidies and free treatment.

May 8 Five North Koreans, who tried to enter the Japanese consulate in the Chinese city of Shenyang in an alleged defection attempt, are arrested by Chinese security forces.

May 14 President Roh Moo-hyun holds a summit meeting with U.S. President George W. Bush at the White House, in which they agree to lift their relationship to a new level and reaffirm their commitment to seeking a peaceful resolution to the North Korean nuclear issue.

May 19 Chung Mong-hun, chairman of Hyundai Asan, is summoned by prosecutors for questioning over his alleged involvement in illicit payments to North Korea. The prosecution said Hyundai provided millions of dollars to the North before its leader agreed to hold a summit meeting with South Korean President Kim Dae-jung in June 2000. In return for the secret payment, Hyundai received permits to promote business projects in the North, prosecutors said. Chung committed suicide in August of that year.

May 20 Lee Keun-young, former head of the Financial Supervisory Commission, is arrested on charges of arranging illegal loans to Hyundai affiliates in 2000 in connection with a scandal involving payoffs to North Korea ahead of the first-ever inter-Korean summit.

May 29 The South Korean government reduces the mandatory military service period for South Korean men by two months to a total of two years. It also reduced the training period for reservists to one year.

June 7 President Roh Moo-hyun holds a summit in Tokyo with Japanese Prime Minister Junichiro Koizumi.

June 13 Chey Tae-won, chairman of SK Group, gets a three-year prison sentence for illegal insider trading and accounting fraud.

June 14 South and North Korea hold ceremonies inside the demilitarized zone near the truce village of Panmunjom to mark the reconnection of railroads that had been severed since the 1950-53 Korean War. Reconstruction of the railroads was one of the agreements made at the inter-Korean summit in Pyongyang in 2000.

July 1 The Seoul Municipal Government breaks ground for the restoration of Cheonggye-cheon, a stream that runs through the heart of downtown Seoul. The stream had been covered over with asphalt and cement during government-led industrialization efforts in the 1970s. The project was completed in 2005.

July 2 South and North Korean officials meet in Paju, a South Korean border city 40 kilometers north of Seoul, to discuss reconnecting severed railways and roads across their heavily fortified border. The transportation links were cut just before the Korean War broke out on June 25, 1950. Construction for two sets of inter-Korean railways and roads was completed in late 2005, but the railways remain closed due to alleged North Korean military opposition.

July 9 The two Koreas hold the 11th ministerial-level meeting in Seoul.

July 15 The Seoul Administrative Court orders the government to suspend a massive tidal flat reclamation project launched in 1991. The Saemangeum project, intended to create farmland by reclaiming tidal flats in North Jeolla Province, had been mired in controversy, with opposition from civic groups and environmentalists who feared the development would wreak havoc on the local ecosystem.

July 21 Han Hee-won wins her first LPGA title, capturing the Sybase Big Apple Classic in New Rochelle, N.Y. She becomes the eighth South Korean woman to win on the U.S. Tour.

Aug. 4 Chung Mong-hun, the head of the Hyundai Group, jumps to his death from his 12th-floor office in Seoul. He was one of the central figures being tried for being involved in a scandal over Hyundai's secret payment of US$500 million to North Korea just before the 2000 inter-Korean summit. Following the political reconciliation, Hyundai expanded its business ties with North Korea, including a tour project to Mount Kumgang.

Aug. 19 The Constitutional Court nominates Chon Hyo-suk as one of its nine justices. In September, Chon became the first woman to take a post on the bench.

Aug. 28 South and North Korea agree to cooperate to ensure the profitability of the troubled Mount Kumgang tour program operated by Hyundai Asan, an affiliate of the Hyundai Group, which provides South Koreans access to the scenic North Korean mountain resort.

Sept. 10 Lee Kyung-hae, 55, a South Korean farmer and former chairman of the Korean Advanced Farmers Federation, stabs himself to death during a street demonstration in Cancun, Mexico, where a World Trade Organization conference was taking place. Lee had flown there with other South Korean activists to protest the international body's move to remove trade barriers around the globe.

Sept. 15 The Ministry of Culture and Tourism announces a blueprint for further opening the South Korean market to Japanese pop culture products. The blueprint took effect in January 2004, allowing imports of Japanese films with a rating of 18 or over, pop songs with Japanese lyrics and video games.

Sept. 22 Dissident Korean-German professor Song Doo-yul arrives in South Korea after 36 years of self-imposed exile in Germany. He was accused of violating the South Korean National Security Law through his pro-North Korean activities during his life in exile and, after arrival, was arrested and sentenced to seven years in prison. But a Seoul appellate court later ruled that there was no evidence to support the charges by state prosecutors. Song and his wife returned to Germany in August 2004.

Sept. 27 A Russian rocket carrying a South Korean scientific research satellite is successfully launched from Russia's Plesetsk Cosmodrome base near the Arctic Ocean.

Oct. 2 South Korean slugger Lee Seung-yeop, then playing for the Samsung Lions, hits his 56th home run of the season, breaking the previous Asian single-season record set by Japan's base-ball hero Sadaharu Oh. Lee later played two seasons for the Chiba Lotte Marines of Japan's Pacific League before signing with the Yomiuri Giants of the Japanese Central League.

Oct. 6 A gymnasium named after the late South Korean business tycoon Chung Ju-yung opens in Pyongyang. Senior figures with the Hyundai business group, the leading South Korean investor in North Korea, and government officials participated in the opening ceremony, held after three years of construction.

Oct. 7 South Korea, China and Japan agree to cooperate to prevent the proliferation of weapons of mass destruction (WMD) throughout the world and to peacefully resolve the standoff over North Korea's nuclear weapons program. The agreement was adopted at a summit between South Korean President Roh Moo-hyun, Japanese Prime Minister Junichiro Koizumi and Chinese Premier Wen Jiabao. They had gathered in Bali for the annual "ASEAN Plus Three" forum, a meeting of the 10 member countries of the Association of Southeast Asian Nations plus South Korea, Japan and China.

Oct. 11 Prime Minister Goh Kun and other Cabinet members offer to resign en masse following the National Assembly's impeachment of President Roh Moo-hyun on charges of illegal electioneering.

Oct. 20 President Roh Moo-hyun and U.S. President George W. Bush issue a four-point joint press statement calling for the early resumption of, and substantive progress in, multilateral talks on North Korea's nuclear arms ambitions. The statement was released in their meeting on the sidelines of the Asia-Pacific Economic Cooperation conference in Bangkok.

Nov. 11 Thousands of supporters of President Roh Moo-hyun launch the Uri Party, emphasizing clean politics and reconciliation with North Korea. Roh had run for the presidency on the then-ruling Millennium Democratic Party ticket the previous year, but left the party in September 2003, citing its waning enthusiasm for reform. He joined the Uri Party in May.

Dec. 4 The National Assembly overrides President Roh Moo-hyun's veto and passes a bill for the appointment of a special counsel to investigate his former aides on corruption charges. The move by the opposition-controlled assembly came just nine days after Roh vetoed the bill, saying that there was already an ongoing investigation by prosecutors into the alleged irregularities.

Dec. 6 President Roh Moo-hyun promulgates a law that calls for the appointment of an independent counsel to probe allegations that his former aides took bribes.

Dec. 8 The parliamentary panel endorses plans to build an administrative capital.

Dec. 17 South Korea finalizes a plan to send an additional 3,000 troops to Iraq on a rehabilitation mission at the request of the United States.

2004

Jan. 7 South Korea welcomes North Korea's offer to freeze its nuclear program.

Jan. 29 Former President Kim Dae-jung is declared not guilty by the Seoul High Court in a retrial of a 1980 case accusing him of treason.

Feb. 3 Reversing itself, North Korea agrees to attend a new six-party meeting on its nuclear weapons program, though South Korean officials say they do not anticipate a dramatic breakthrough in the 15-month row.

Feb. 13 The National Assembly approves a government proposal to send an additional 3,000 troops to help rebuild war-torn Iraq. About 3,600 South Korean troops were sent to northern Iraq, making up the largest foreign contingent in the Middle Eastern country after those of the United States and Britain.

Feb. 16 South Korea's National Assembly ratifies the South Korea-Chile Free Trade Agreement.

Feb. 25 The first round of six-party talks on North Korea's nuclear weapons program opens in Beijing. The disarmament negotiations, which involve the two Koreas, the United States, China, Japan and Russia, recently produced a breakthrough as Pyongyang agreed on denuclearization in exchange for energy and other types of assistance by its negotiating partners.

Feb. 28 The second round of six-way talks on North Korea's nuclear ambitions ends in Beijing, with negotiators only reaching an agreement on the next meeting and a preparatory working group.

March 5 South and North Korea agree to allow South Korean firms to establish full operations in an industrial park that began being constructed in the North Korean border town of Kaesong the previous year. The two sides also agreed to conduct train test runs on newly completed railway sections along the western and eastern parts of their border. The accord was one of the seven points in a joint press statement released at the end of four-day talks in Seoul. The Kaesong complex is one of the most visible products of the historic inter-Korean summit in 2000, which set bilateral rapprochement in motion.

March 9 South Korea's two main opposition parties submit a motion to impeach President Roh Moo-hyun. A total of 159 opposition lawmakers supported the motion.

March 13 SK Telecom launches a digital multimedia broadcasting satellite, intended for the world's first satellite-based broadcasting service, from the John F. Kennedy Space Center in the U.S. state of Florida. The launch of the satellite, dubbed "Hanbyul" and code-named MBSat, signaled the advent of the era of mobile satellite-based broadcasting in South Korea.

March 28 The Supreme Court convicts Lim Dong-won, former chief of the National Intelligence Service, and five others in connection with Hyundai Group's illegal remittance of US$450 million to North Korea just days before the first-ever inter-Korean summit in 2000.

April 1 A free trade agreement (FTA) between South Korea and Chile is implemented, a year and five months after it was signed. It was Korea's first FTA and the first for Chile with an Asian partner.

April 9 Seoul issues a ban on travel to Iraq in the wake of the kidnapping of South Korean missionaries in the war-torn country.

April 12 Chung Dong-young quits as chairman of the ruling Uri Party.

April 16 General elections are held, with the results showing a rising demand for a generational change in politics. The ruling Uri Party emerged as the majority with 152 seats in the 299-member National Assembly, and young and new candidates prevailed. The number of new lawmakers aged 40 or younger was 129, or 43.1 percent of the total, sharply up from the 28.5 percent in the previous election.

April 24 North Korea issues a statement, carried by its state-run Korea Central News Agency, to confirm the April 22 explosion at Ryongchon Railway Station in North Pyongan Province. It claimed the explosion was "caused by an electrical short-circuit due to carelessness during the shunting of wagons loaded with ammonium nitrate fertilizer and tanker wagons," and asked the international community to render humanitarian assistance.

May 7 South and North Korea agree to hold high-level defense talks aimed at averting possible military clashes along their heavily fortified border. The meeting marked the first contact by general-grade officers of the rival Koreas divided along the 38th parallel since the 1950-53 Korean War.

May 8 The prosecution arrests Shin Il-soon, a four-star South Korean general who served as deputy chief of the Korea-U.S. Combined Forces Command, on charges of embezzlement and bribery.

May 11 Hyundai Group Chairwoman Hyun Jung-eun, who succeeded her husband Chung Mong-hun after his suicide in mid-2003, arrives in North Korea to discuss inter-Korean economic projects. During her four-day visit, Hyun met with officials from the Asia-Pacific Peace Committee, Hyundai's North Korean business partner, to exchange views on the Mount Kumgang tourism project and the construction of an industrial complex in Kaesong, a city on the border with South Korea.

May 22 The South Korean movie "Old Boy" wins the Grand Prize at the Cannes Film Festival. The movie, directed by Park Chan-wook, depicts an ordinary man trying to find an unknown person who kidnapped and confined him for 15 years.

May 26 General-grade officers of the two Koreas hold talks on measures aimed at avoiding accidental naval clashes along the disputed western maritime border.

June 11 Park Ji-won, a lifetime aide to former President Kim Dae-jung, is sentenced to 12 years in jail on charges of taking 15 billion won (US$14 million) in illegal slush funds from Hyundai Group right before the historic inter-Korean summit in 2000.

June 15 Warships from South and North Korea exchange radio messages for the first time to express non-hostility. The prearranged 15-minute exchange, which took place at 9 a.m., marked the first direct contact between combat-ready field units of the two states.

June 16 Two Koreas begin dismantling propaganda loudspeakers and signboards.

June 21 The six countries participating in talks over North Korea's nuclear weapons program start a preliminary session before holding main negotiations.

July 9 South Korean President Roh Moo-hyun and visiting U.S. National Security Adviser Condoleezza Rice meet and reaffirm their countries' determination to resolve the North Korean nuclear issue through dialogue and diplomacy.

July 28 The first 200 out of a group of 460 North Korean defectors arrive in Seoul on a chartered flight from a Southeast Asian country in the largest defection by North Koreans since the end of the three-year Korean War in 1953.

Aug. 5 A four-day gathering of South Korean adoptees begins in Seoul, bringing together more than 450 adoptees from 15 different nations. The gathering was the third of its kind after events in Washington, D.C. in 1999 and in Oslo, Norway, in 2001.

Aug. 16 Judo player Lee Won-hee wins South Korea's first gold medal of the Athens Olympics.

Aug. 27 South Korea's parliamentary speaker Kim One-ki conveys concerns to the Chinese Communist Party leader over a controversy surrounding the history of the ancient Korean kingdom of Goguryeo (37 B.C.-A.D. 668). The controversy was sparked by assertions that the kingdom was a vassal state of China.

Sept. 9 South Korea admits to extracting plutonium in 1982.

Sept. 21 South Korean President Roh Moo-hyun and Russian President Vladimir Putin announce a comprehensive partnership between the two nations at a summit held at the Kremlin. They agreed to cooperate regarding the six-party talks on North Korea's nuclear weapons program, the fight against international terrorism and proliferation of weapons of mass destruction, the development of oil and natural gas wells in Siberia, linkage of the Trans-Siberian Railway and the Trans-Korean Railway, and the transfer of Russian space technology to South Korea.

Oct. 6 The United States announces it will significantly delay a plan to reduce the number of its troops stationed in South Korea.

Oct. 21 North Korea's No. 2 leader, Kim Yong-nam, returns to Pyongyang after a visit to China. The goodwill visit provided an opportunity to affirm long-standing friendly relations between the two communist states.

Nov. 9 A Japanese delegation arrives in North Korea for working-level talks on the communist state's abduction of Japanese nationals.

Nov. 26 The International Atomic Energy Agency's governing board decides not to refer South Korea to the U.N. Security Council over its undeclared experiments with nuclear material, but adopts a "chairman's statement" to express concern over Seoul's failure to report them. South Korea acknowledged in September that its scientists secretly extracted and enriched plutonium and uranium, two key ingredients for nuclear weapons, in 1982 and 2000.

Dec. 23 South Korea reports an outbreak of a mild strain of avian influenza at a duck farm in the southwestern part of the country. The Ministry of Agriculture and Forestry said DNA tests found that ducks at the farm in Gwangju, about 330 kilometers south of Seoul, were infected with the low-pathogenic H5N2 virus.

2005

Jan. 17 South Korea declassifies more than a 1,000 pages of decades-old sensitive documents regarding its diplomatic normalization with Japan in 1965. The declassification later spurred a series of compensation lawsuits by victims of Japan's 1910-45 colonial rule.

Feb. 8 The foreign ministers of South Korea and Japan agree to work closely with the United States to jump-start the stalled six-party talks aimed at ending the North Korean nuclear weapons development standoff.

Feb. 10 North Korea vows not to attend future six-way talks on its nuclear arms program unless the United States drops its "hostile" policy toward the communist country.

April 14 The U.N. Human Rights Commission (UNHRC) adopts a resolution on North Korea for a third time to urge the communist state to immediately end its "systemic, widespread and grave violations of human rights."

April 27 The National Assembly passes a special law on the sustainable use and maintenance of the Dokdo islets, following a March 16 ordinance by Japan's Shimane Prefecture to designate Feb. 22 as the day of Takeshima, the Japanese name for the Korean islets in the East Sea. Japan also claims sovereignty over the islets.

May 16 South Korea promises to make a new "important" proposal to help resolve the growing tension over North Korea's nuclear weapons program if the communist country returns to the dialogue table. The nuclear standoff was a key topic at two days of inter-Korean talks which reopened at the North's border city of Kaesong after a 10-month hiatus.

May 28 South Korea completes the overland shipment of 200,000 metric tons of emergency fertilizer aid to North Korea. The shipment is part of an assistance package agreed to by Seoul at high-level inter-Korean talks.

June 1 The flow of water through the restored stream of Cheonggyecheon in central Seoul is successfully tested. Cheonggyecheon, a 5.8 km creek flowing west to east through downtown Seoul, was covered with concrete for roads in 1948 after South Korea was liberalized from Japan. In July 2003, then-Seoul mayor, current President Lee Myung-bak initiated a project to remove the elevated highway and restore the stream.

June 5 South Korean pitcher Park Chan-ho earns his 100th major league win, marking yet another milestone since his U.S. debut in 1994. Park, the first South Korean major league baseball player, became the second Asian to attain the feat after Japanese pitcher Hideo Nomo.

June 7 The number of tourists to Mount Kumgang surpasses 1 million since the scenic resort on North Korea's east coast first opened to South Koreans in 1998.

June 16 Seoul District Court issues arrest warrant for Daewoo Group founder Kim Woo-choong for accounting fraud, illegal borrowing and foreign currency smuggling.

June 17 South Korea's Unification Minister Chung Dong-young meets with North Korean leader Kim Jong-il in Pyongyang. Chung visited the North Korean capital as head of a South Korean delegation for inter-Korean events marking the fifth anniversary of the inter-Korean summit held in June 2000.

July 20 The divided Koreas agree to resume dismantling propaganda facilities along their heavily-fortified border as part of tension-easing measures following the historic inter-Korean summit in 2000. The Koreas had initially agreed to dismantle the loudspeaker facilities in June 2004, but the dismantlement was halted shortly after the agreement amid a prolonged hiatus in military talks.

Aug. 3 A Seoul National University research team, led by Hwang Woo-suk, announces the cloning of a dog, which has been independently verified through genetic testing. The dog, an Afghan hound, was named Snuppy.

Aug. 14 The national football squads of the two Koreas hold a friendly match in Seoul as part of events to celebrate Korea's liberation from Japan's 1910-1945 colonial rule.

Aug. 15 South and North Korea hold a reunion of 40 separated families via video for the first time.

Aug. 23 South Korean pop star Cho Yong-pil gives a concert in Pyongyang, North Korea to mark the 60th anniversary of Korea's liberation from Japan's colonial rule.

Aug. 24 The sixth inter-Korean Red Cross talks open for a three-day run at Mount Kumgang, a tourist resort on the North's east coast. The two sides agreed to hold more reunions of separated families via a high-tech video connection, but failed to narrow differences on the issue of confirming the fate of South Korean prisoners of war and civilians abducted by Pyongyang after the end of the 1950-53 Korean War.

Sept. 6 Typhoon Nabi hits South Korea, after leaving four dead and dozens injured in Japan.

Oct. 28 Busan, South Korea's second-largest city, is named a candidate to host two major International Olympic Committee (IOC) meetings in 2009 -the General Assembly of the IOC and the 13th Olympic General Assembly.

Nov. 2 Olympic committees from the two Koreas reach a tentative agreement to field a unified team for future Asian Games and Olympics.

Nov. 5 The 12th round of reunions is held for families separated by the 1950-1953 Korean War.

Nov. 9 A new round of six-nation talks on North Korea's nuclear program begins in Beijing.

Nov. 16 South Korea and China hold a summit in Seoul.

Dec. 1 South Korea's National Assembly ratifies a free trade agreement with Singapore, Seoul's second free trade pact after one with Chile.

Dec. 30 The National Assembly approves the government's plan to reduce the number of South Korea's 3,200 troops in Iraq by one-third but extend their deployment until the end of the following year.

2006

Feb. 6 Tokyo announces it will waive visas for South Korean visitors as a way of boosting ties, enabling South Korean tourists to stay in Japan for up to 90 days without a visa.

Feb. 21 South and North Korea resume bilateral talks between their Red Cross officials despite the prolonged stalemate in international negotiations over North Korea's nuclear programs.

Feb. 22 Pope Benedict VXI appoints South Korean Archbishop Nicholas Cheong Jin-suk as one of his 15 new cardinals.

Feb. 23 North Korea agrees to help confirm the fate of South Koreans missing during and after the 1950-53 Korean War. The agreement came at the end of three-day talks between the two countries' Red Cross officials.

March 7 South Korean President Roh Moo-hyun and Egyptian President Hosni Mubarak agree to broaden South Korean companies' participation in Egypt's infrastructure construction, defense procurement and expansion of information technology networks.

March 9 South Korean President Roh Moo-hyun holds a summit with Nigerian President Olusegun Obasanjo in Abuja, the Nigerian capital, and discloses details of his Africa initiative.

April 24 North Korea agrees to resolve the issue of abducted South Korean civilians at the 18th round of inter-Korean ministerial talks held in Pyongyang. The agreement followed repeated calls by Seoul for the release of nearly 600 South Korean prisoners of war held since the 1950-53 Korean War and 485 civilians believed to have been kidnapped by the communist state since the war ended.

May 4 KT Corp., South Korea's largest fixed-line and broadband service operator, establishes the first private telephone line in the Dokdo islets in the East Sea. There had previously been a total of 11 telephone lines on Dokdo, a set of small islets located 92 km east of Ulleung Island, but only for patrol forces stationed there and public use. The new line was set up at the house of a married couple who moved there earlier that year to promote awareness of the nation's sovereignty over the easternmost territory and oppose Japan's repeated claim to the islets.

May 13 South and North Korea agree to conduct test runs of two sets of railways that were built across their heavily fortified border.

May 16 South Korea signs a free trade agreement with the Association of Southeast Asian Nations (ASEAN) to cut trade barriers on merchandise. Thailand, however, was excluded from the accord due to disagreements over agricultural goods and that country's political crisis. The agreement with nine of the 10 member countries of ASEAN called for gradual tariff elimination by 2010 on almost 90 percent of goods traded on both sides.

June 8 France agrees to lease to South

Korea a collection of Korean royal texts that were looted by French forces in 1866 from an archive of Korea's Joseon Dynasty (1392-1910). The texts are now being kept at France's national library in Paris, but Seoul wants them to be returned.

June 12 A group of 76 foreign diplomats in Seoul, including U.S. Ambassador Alexander Vershbow, takes a one-day trip to a joint industrial complex developed by South Korea in North Korea's border town of Kaesong. The group was accompanied by then South Korean Foreign Minister Ban Ki-moon.

June 22 South Korea's Supreme Court allows legal gender change for transsexuals.

July 28 South Korea successfully launches a satellite from the Plesetsk Cosmodrome in northern Russia to help the country make timely updates on geographical changes and assist in the search for natural resources.

July 30 Dozens of crewmen aboard a South Korean tuna trawler are released after nearly four months of captivity in Somalia. The 360-ton ship, owned by Dongwon Fisheries Co. and manned by eight Koreans and 17 others from Indonesia, China and Vietnam, was abducted in April by a group of Somali bandits in waters off the East African country.

Oct. 9 North Korea announces through its official Korean Central News Agency that it successfully and safely conducted an underground nuclear test. The South Korean government confirms a 3.58-3.7 magnitude seismic tremor in a remote area of the North's Hamgyeong Province at around 10:36 a.m.

Nov. 17 South Korea signs a deal with Vietnam to provide US$35 million to build a hospital in central Vietnam. The donation, initially pledged during President Roh Moo-hyun's state visit to Hanoi in 2004, is the largest-ever overseas grant by the Seoul government.

Nov. 18 Leaders of South Korea, the U.S. and Japan hold their first three-way summit in four years in Hanoi and re-confirm their close cooperation for regional peace and stability, and the settlement of the North Korean nuclear problem.

Dec. 25 South Korea selects two finalists to compete to become the country's first astronaut. Ko san, a researcher at the Korea Aerospace Research Institute, was selected over Yi So-yeon in September 2007. Ko was later replaced by Yi due to violations of training protocol.

2007

Jan. 3 Ban Ki-moon, a South Korean diplomat, starts work as the eighth secretary-general of the United Nations. Elected by the U.N. General Assembly, he succeeded Kofi Annan and passed several major reforms on peacekeeping and U.N. employment practices.

Jan. 12 North Korea hands over a South Korean fishing boat, with its engineer aboard, that crossed into North Korean waters in December 2006 in the East Sea.

Jan. 23 Top nuclear envoys of the two Koreas hold talks in Beijing and agree that the six-nation negotiations on ending North Korea's nuclear ambitions will be reopened soon. The talks, attended by the two Koreas, the United States, Japan, China and Russia, resumed in February. North Korea agreed to disable its key nuclear facilities and submit a complete list of its nuclear programs under an aid-for-denuclearization deal signed on Feb. 13.

Feb. 11 Nine foreigners are killed and 18 others injured in a pre-dawn fire that engulfed an immigration detention center in the southern city of Yeosu, about 450km south of Seoul. The deceased, mostly Chinese, were being held in the facility after they were caught trying to enter South Korea or were in the country illegally.

Feb. 13 North Korea agrees to shut down its nuclear facilities and invite nuclear inspectors back into the country in return for fuel aid under a deal with South Korea, the United States, China, Russia and Japan.

Feb. 22 President Roh Moo-hyun announces his decision to defect from the ruling Uri Party in order to maintain political neutrality in the run-up to December's presidential election.

Feb. 24 South Korea and the United States announce that Seoul will reclaim wartime operational control of its forces from Washington as of April 17, 2012.

The agreement resolved one of the most controversial bilateral issues as the two countries continue to redefine a military alliance that dates back to the 1950-1953 Korean War, when American soldiers fought with South Korea against North Korea's invasion.

March 22 Host China called the stalled six-nation nuclear disarmament talks into a recess after North Korea withdrew its delegation from Beijing in a dispute over its funds being frozen at a Macau bank.

April 8 Bill Richardson, Democratic governor of the U.S. state of New Mexico, arrives in Pyongyang to discuss reclaiming the remains of American soldiers killed during the 1950-53 Korean War and ending the dispute on North Korea's nuclear weapons program.

April 12 The Supreme Court sentences Jeong Nam-guy to death for murdering 13 people and injuring seven others from January 2004 to April 2006.

April 22 South and North Korea hold their 13th round of economic cooperation talks and agree to conduct test runs of cross-border railways in Kaesong, a North Korean town just north of the inter-Korean border, in May and make efforts to ensure a military guarantee for their safe operations.

May 16 Two South Korean fishing boats and their 24 crew members, including four South Koreans, are captured by a group of insurgents believed to be Somali pirates in waters off of Somalia.

May 17 South and North Korea conduct test-runs of two railways -one linking Seoul with Sinuiju, a North Korean border city with China, and the other linking Wonsan, a city on the eastern coast of the North, to Goseong, an eastern coastal city of the South. The two train lines were cut during the 1950-53 Korean War, but they were partly restored in 2005 under an agreement sealed during the two countries' first summit in 2000.

May 18 North Korea names Pak Ui-chun, 75, a former ambassador to Russia, as its new foreign minister. The post had been vacant since his predecessor, Paek Nam-sun, died in January.

June 5 The 6th Asia Cooperation Dialogue (ACD), attended by 30 regional nations, opens in Seoul to discuss ways to close the information gap and increase economic and security cooperation.

June 14 Macau's Banco Delta Asia transfers more than US$20 million in North Korean funds, which North Korea requested to take place before it would take steps in the denuclearization procedure. The U.S. had earlier frozen the money for nearly two years, accusing the bank of money laundering and counterfeiting for North Korea. After the transfer, the communist North came back to nuclear talks, which it had been for boycotting more than a year.

June 16 The United States formally asked South Korea to renegotiate seven areas of a proposed free trade agreement.

June 30 South Korea signs a free trade agreement with the United States. For South Korea, it is a pact with its second-biggest export market. For the U.S., it is the first FTA with an Asian country and the largest since the North American FTA (NAFTA) of 1994. The deal has yet to be ratified by the legislators of the two countries.

July 10 Golfer Choi Kyung-ju wins the inaugural PGA National, hosted by Tiger Woods. It was Choi's second title of the season and his sixth career U.S. PGA title.

July 20 Taliban insurgents kidnap 18 South Koreans, including 15 women, in Afghanistan, threatening to kill them if Seoul doesn't withdraw its troops from the war-torn country. South Korea had stationed about 210 army engineers and medics in Afghanistan for noncombat, reconstruction missions as part of U.S.-led coalition forces. Two of the captives -both male -were killed in the early stage of negotiations to free them, and the rest returned home safely after Seoul pledged to withdraw the troops by the end of the year as planned.

July 28 A special South Korean presidential envoy meets with Afghan officials in Kabul on a mission to secure the release of 22 South Koreans seized by Taliban insurgents in Afghanistan 10 days prior.

July 30 The Taliban extends the deadline on the execution of 22 South Koreans taken hostage in Afghanistan as the Kabul government refused to accede to a key demand of the kidnappers.

Aug. 9 S. Korea's central bank lifts the key rate for August to 5 percent, the bank's first ever back-to-back rate hike, to curb inflation by controlling ample liquidity.

Aug. 13 Two South Korean women from a 23-member aid group abducted by the Taliban in Afghanistan are freed. Two men in the group, including its 42-year-old leader Bae Hyung-kyu, are executed. The remaining 19 hostages are freed in late August after Seoul announces it will pull out troops from the country by the end of the year and ban all missionary work there.

Sept. 6 Hyundai Motor chairman Chung Mong-koo receives a suspended three-year jail term from an appeals court for embezzlement of company funds, allowing him to actively pursue business activities. The Seoul High Court previously convicted Chung, head of the world's sixth-largest automaker, handing down a five year suspended jail term.

Sept. 11 President Roh Moo-hyun stresses that a new Korean Peninsula peace arrangement to formally end the 1950-53 Korean War will be the most important agenda item at his summit talks with North Korean leader Kim Jong-il slated for Oct. 2-4 in Pyongyang.

Sept. 27 A new round of six-party talks aimed at denuclearizing North Korea opens in Beijing amid the communist country's alleged nuclear cooperation with Syria.

Oct. 2 President Roh Moo-hyun meets with North Korean leader Kim Jong-il in Pyongyang after walking across the heavily fortified border for the second-ever summit between the two Koreas. Kim made a surprise public appearance to greet Roh in a welcoming ceremony in front of the April 25 Hall of Culture. The three-day summit produced a slew of agreements to build a permanent peace regime on the peninsula and enhance economic exchanges, such as reopening cross-border railroads that were closed during the Korean War and expanding the joint industrial park in the North Korean border town of Kaesong. Roh was the first South Korean leader to travel overland to North Korea. His predecessor, Kim Dae-jung, traveled by air across the West Sea for the first inter-Korean summit with Kim Jong-il in 2000.

Oct. 9 U.S. President George W. Bush

says he welcomes the latest inter-Korean summit agreement calling for peace and denuclearization on the Korean Peninsula.

Dec. 7 A Hong-Kong registered oil tanker collides with a barge carrying a crane, causing the largest oil spill in Korean history in waters off South Korea's west coast. About 15,000 tons of oil from the supertanker leaked into waters, blackening the ecologically pristine shorelines of Taean, South Chungcheong Province, and destroying thousands of sea farms. A court battle ensued between Hong Kong-registered Hebei Spirit Shipping and Samsung Heavy Industries (which owned the barge) over the allocation of compensation fees. More than 1.2 million Koreans traveled to Taean to clean up the oil spill area.

Dec. 11 The two Koreas launch a regular cross-border train service for the first time since the end of the 1950-53 Korean War.

2008

Jan. 4 North Korea expresses hope that a six-party deal on the communist country's denuclearization will be smoothly implemented, as it has revealed a complete list of its nuclear programs to the United States.

Jan. 17 The Constitutional Court dismisses President Roh Moo-hyun's petition to allow political comments by government officials before an election, upholding the legality of South Korea's election law.

Feb. 1 A Seoul court finds the U.S. private equity firm Lone Star Funds guilty of stock manipulation in the controversial takeover of the credit card unit of the Korea Exchange Bank in 2003. KEB and its main shareholder, Lone Star, were fined 25 billion won (US$26.5 million) each.

Feb. 10 A fire destroys Seoul's Namdaemun, a historic gate located in the heart of the capital. The landmark, officially called Sungnyemun, or "gate of exalted ceremonies," was the southern gate of an ancient wall that surrounded Seoul during the Joseon Dynasty (1392-1910). A 70-year-old man was later found guilty of setting the fire and destroying South Korea's No. 1 national treasure.

Feb. 25 Lee Myung-bak, a business CEO-turned-politician, is inaugurated as president following a landslide victory in the presidential election in December 2007.

Feb. 26 The New York Philharmonic performs in Pyongyang, North Korea's capital.

April 8 Yi So-yeon, a female astronaut and bio-systems engineer, becomes the first South Korean to reach orbit. On April 10 the Soyuz spacecraft carrying South Korea's first astronaut Yi So-yeon docks with the International Space Station (ISS) two days after blasting off from Earth.

May 5 Park Kyung-ni, one of Korea's best-known contemporary writers, dies of lung cancer at the age of 82. Her epic novel "The Land," regarded by her compatriots as a masterpiece of contemporary Korean literature, has been included in the UNESCO Collection of Representative Works.

May 16 Patrol boats from South Korea and Japan confront each other over an alleged violation of Japan's Exclusive Economic Zone (EEZ) by a Korean fishing boat. The standoff ends a few hours later after Japan concedes that the Korean boat did not violate its waters.

May 26 High-level government officials from South Korea and over 20 resource-rich Arab countries pledge to increase cooperation in energy and other areas amid rising global oil prices.

June 7 South Korean President Lee Myung-bak and U.S. President George W. Bush agree to cooperate to ensure that U.S. beef from cattle older than 30 months is not exported to South Korea.

June 9 North Korea warns it will be forced to bolster its nuclear arsenal and other "war deterrents" if the United States and South Korea continue to threaten it militarily.

June 21 South Korea and the United States agree to ban imports of beef from cattle older than 30 months to address concerns of South Korean people over the safety of U.S. beef.

June 24 The Seoul Appeals Court overturns a guilty verdict against Lone Star Funds for stock manipulation, clearing the way for the U.S. equity fund to complete its sale of Korea Exchange

Bank (KEB) to a British lender. The lawsuit was part of Korea's broader investigation into Lone Star's controversial takeover of the bank in 2003. Prosecutors said government officials artificially understated the bank's financial ill-health to help Lone Star purchase it at a below-market price. KEB was struggling in the aftermath of the 1997 Asian financial crisis when Lone Star approached. The 1.38-trillion-won price Lone Star paid in 2003 was considered to be 20 to 30 percent lower than the bank's market value.

June 28 North Korea blows up a cooling tower at its nuclear facility in Yongbyon as part of a disablement process under an aid-for-denuclearization deal signed at six-party talks in 2007. The event, broadcast worldwide by major U.S. and South Korean news outlets, marked a near-end to the disablement process.

July 10 The six-nation talks aimed at denuclearizing North Korea resume after a nine-month lull. The top agenda item is how to verify North Korea's past and current nuclear activity, in line with a deal signed in September 2005 that calls for the North to disarm in exchange for energy aid and other economic and political benefits.

July 15 South Korea's Ambassador to Japan, Kwon Chul-hyun, is recalled to Seoul in protest of Tokyo's decision to ask teachers to refer to Dokdo as "disputed territory," suggesting the islets belong to Japan, not South Korea.

Aug. 4 Three South Korean climbers who went missing the previous week are found dead on the Himalayan K2, the world's second-highest mountain. The victims are Park Gyeong-hyo, Kim Hyo-gyeong and their leader Hwang Dong-jin.

Aug. 9 South Korean Choi Min-ho wins a gold medal in the men's 60kg judo competition of the Beijing Olympics, bringing his country its first gold medal in the games.

Aug. 16 Jang Mi-ran shatters three world records in a row to win gold in the women's over-75-kilogram weightlifting competition of the Beijing Olympics.

Aug. 25 President Lee Myung-bak holds a summit meeting with Chinese President Hu Jintao in Seoul and asks Beijing to refrain from forcibly repatriating North Korean defectors in consideration of their human rights.

Sept. 11 The South Korean government and private companies announce a plan to invest a combined 3 trillion won to develop clean energy resources over the next five years.

Oct. 6 President Lee Myung-bak proposes a tripartite summit with Japan and China on the sidelines of the Asia-Europe Summit.

Oct. 28 South Korea's currency plunges to an over 10-year low against the U.S. dollar as foreign investors dump local stocks and shrug off the central bank's efforts to calm markets.

Oct. 29 Pak Song-chol, a former North Korean vice president and a key factor in late North Korean leader Kim Il-sung's fight against Japanese colonial rule, dies of chronic disease at age 95.

Nov. 13 The Constitutional Court rules that a law levying heavier taxes on high-end home owners is partly unconstitutional.

Nov. 22 A United Nations committee approves a resolution on North Korean human rights.

Nov. 24 Hyundai Asan, a South Korean company operating a business in North Korea, announces suspension of its tour program to the North's city of Kaesong as Pyongyang halts the program in retaliation against Seoul's hard-line stance toward the communist regime.

Dec. 8 A new round of six-way talks begins in Beijing on North Korea's nuclear weapons program and how to verify its accounting of the program.

Dec. 11 Delegates to the six-party talks on denuclearizing North Korea fail to produce a deal on ways to inspect the North's nuclear facilities, casting clouds over the future of the often-troubled multilateral talks.

Dec. 18 North Korean senior defense official Kim Yong-chol visits the joint Kaesong Industrial Complex to hold talks with South Korean companies over restrictions on travel to the border city imposed earlier in December.

Dec. 20 South Korea completes its four-year troop presence in Iraq by pulling out the last group of its Zaytun contingent that was dispatched to Irbil, a northern city, and an air support unit in neighboring Kuwait in 2004. Korea dispatched a 3,600-strong non-combat force to Iraq on the request of the United States. The Zaytun unit provided medical services and other support to help rebuild the war-torn country.

2009

Jan. 6 Lotte Chilsung Beverage Co., a unit of South Korean conglomerate Lotte Group, says it signed a formal deal to buy a liquor unit of Doosan Corp. for 503 billion won (US$383 million), a deal that helped boost Lotte's beverage business.

Feb. 7 South Korea's Kim Yu-na wins the women's single competition at the Four Continents figure skating competition. Kim scored 116.83 points at the free skating competition held in Vancouver, following a world-record short program performance of 72.24 points.

Feb. 29 President Lee Myung-bak apologizes for the recent confusion caused by his nomination of scandal-ridden figures as Cabinet ministers.

March 9 North Korea severs an inter-Korean military communications channel in protest against a South Korea-U.S. war drill.

March 29 Kim Yu-na, South Korea's figure skating superstar, claims her first women's singles gold medal with a record 207.71 points at the 2009 World Figure Skating Championship in Los Angeles. Kim recorded 131.59 points in the free skate of the championship held at the Staples Center and topped the overall standings with 207.71 points. Kim became the first to receive over 200 points in the women's singles event.

April 5 North Korea fires a long-range rocket which it says carries "communications satellite Kwangmyongsong-2." The North claimed the satellite has successfully entered into orbit. But South Korea and the United States said that the North failed to put the satellite into orbit after its three-stage rocket fell into the Pacific Ocean along with its payload.

April 8 Ssangyong Motor Co. cuts 37 percent of its workforce in a survival bid.

April 15 North Korea says it withdraws from nuclear disarmament talks and restores its nearly disabled nuclear

facilities challenging the U.N. Security Council's condemnation of its rocket launch on April 5. Nine days after North Korea fired a long-range rocket, the U.N. Security Council unanimously adopted a statement accusing Pyongyang of violating an earlier U.N. resolution barring it from engaging in ballistic missile activity.

April 20 A Seoul court acquits a controversial online South Korean pundit known by his Internet alias "Minerva." He was indicted on charges of spreading misleading information on the country's monetary policy.

May 4 A South Korean naval unit rescues a North Korean freighter from being hijacked by suspected pirates in Somali waters. The unit, operating in the Gulf of Aden as part of a U.S.-led multinational anti-piracy campaign, received a distress call from the North Korean vessel, the Dabaksol, and dispatched an anti-submarine attack helicopter to fend off pirates. It also hovered around the North Korean freighter after its crew asked for extended support.

May 13 South Korean President Lee Myung-bak and Kazakh President Nursultan Nazarbayev agree to upgrade their countries' relationship to a "strategic partnership" and launch a number of joint projects to create billions of dollars in benefits for both sides.

May 25 North Korea conducts its second atomic test, sparking international condemnation and U.N. Security Council Resolution 1874, which intensified U.N. sanctions imposed on the communist nation, shortly after its first atomic test in October 2006.

May 26 South Korea decides to fully participate in the U.S.-led campaign aimed at curbing the spread of weapons of mass destruction (WMD) and related materials.

June 16 North Korea claims two jailed U.S. journalists admitted to plotting a "smear campaign" against the communist state.

July 2 South and North Korea fail to make progress in their third round of talks, with their positions remaining wide apart over a joint industrial park and the fate of a detained worker.

July 4 North Korea test-launches seven ballistic missiles off its eastern coast in a stand-off with the U.S. over its nuclear and missile programs. It fires the first two missiles from its East Sea base around 8:30 a.m. and the firing of the seventh missile that appears to be a Scud-type takes place on the east coast at around 5:40 p.m.

July 8 Unidentified cyber hackers renew attacks on seven major South Korean Internet Web sites, including Ahn-Lab Inc., which provides computer virus vaccines and online security services.

July 9 At least seven Web sites operated by government and media organizations report access delays and failures under a third round of DDos attack. The previous two rounds of attacks overwhelmed major Web sites in South Korea and the United States, including the official site of South Korea's presidential office Cheong Wa Dae.

July 28 Kumho Asiana Group says its chairman will resign from his post to pave the way for a professional manager to guide South Korea's eighth-largest conglomerate.

July 29 Lee Charm is named chief of the Korea National Tourism Organization, becoming the first naturalized Korean to take a top government post in South Korea.

July 30 North Korea seizes a stray South Korean fishing boat carrying four crew members and hauls it to a port on its east coast.

Aug. 10 Hyun Jung-eun, chairwoman of Hyundai Group, visits Pyongyang to seek the release of a detained employee of Hyundai Asan Corp., the group's North Korea business arm. Yu Seong-jin was detained on March 30 at a joint industrial park in the North's border town of Kaesong. North Korea accused him of "slandering" the North's political system and trying to persuade a local woman to defect to the South.

Aug. 14 Former Samsung chairman and South Korea's richest man, Lee Kun-hee, is sentenced to a suspended three-year prison term and a 110 billion won fine for illegal bond transactions. He is found guilty of tax evasion and breach of trust.

Aug. 16 North Korean leader Kim Jong-il meets with the visiting chairwoman Hyun Jung-eun of South Korea's Hyundai Group.

Aug. 18 Former President Kim Dae-jung, a lifelong campaigner for democracy and inter-Korean peace, dies at Seoul's Severance Hospital after a long battle with pneumonia and related complications.

Aug. 19 North Korea's leader Kim Jong-il sends condolences on the death of former South Korean President Kim Dae-jung, who died of complications from pneumonia on Aug. 18.

Aug. 23 The state funeral of late President Kim Dae-jung takes place in Seoul, attended by tens of thousands of people, including incumbent President Lee Myung-bak. North Korea sent a group of delegates to the funeral.

Aug. 25 South Korea's first space rocket launch fails to place a scientific satellite into orbit.

Sept. 9 North Korea criticizes the United States and rejects international sanctions over its nuclear program as the communist state marks its 61st founding anniversary.

Sept. 11 North Korea withdraws demands for a hefty wage increase at a South Korean-run industrial park as anger brewed in the South over a deadly flash flood unleashed by the North.

Oct. 6 South Korea expresses concerns that a set of economic deals reached between North Korea and China during Chinese Premier Wen Jiabao's trip to Pyongyang may affect the implementation of U.N. sanctions against the North.

Oct. 9 South Korean President Lee Myung-bak and Japanese Prime Minister Yukio Hatoyama agree to seek a "comprehensive" solution to ending North Korea's nuclear development through a package deal.

Oct. 26 Disgraced cloning scientist Hwang Woo-suk is sentenced to a suspended jail term for embezzling research funds and breaching bioethics laws.

Oct. 28 South Korea's main opposition Democratic Party wins a meaningful victory in parliamentary by-elections by taking three of five contested seats.

Oct. 29 The Constitutional Court rules that disputed media reform laws railroaded by the ruling party are valid, despite violations in the voting process.

Nov. 2 The National Museum of Korea celebrates the 100th anniversary of the establishment of the country's first national museum.

Nov. 19 South Korean President Lee Myung-bak and U.S. President Obama vow efforts to denuclearize N. Korea and ratify the FTA.

Dec. 10 North Korea and the United States reach "common understandings" on the need to resume the six-party nuclear talks and implement a 2005 landmark deal on the North's denuclearization.

Dec. 20 The United Nations General Assembly approves a resolution on North Korean human rights for the fifth straight year, calling on the communist North to improve its dire human rights conditions.

2010

Jan 12 The Araon, South Korea's first dedicated icebreaker, sets out to explore waters off Antarctica and examine candidate sites for a second Korean research station on the frozen continent.

Jan 14 The Supreme Court sentences Roh Gun-pyeong to two and a half years in prison and orders him to forfeit 300 million won for graft and influence peddling. Roh is the elder brother of late former President Roh Moo-hyun.

• A South Korean consortium including a state-run institute is set to sign a deal with Jordan to build the first atomic research reactor in the Middle Eastern country.

Jan 18 South Korea provides over US$10 million worth of emergency relief aid and long-term support to Haiti, one of largest contributions committed to the Caribbean nation since it was hit by a powerful earthquake last week.

Jan 23 Just a little over a month since its release in South Korea, James Cameron's 'Avatar' has become the first-ever foreign movie here to top the 10 million mark in ticket sales.

Jan. 24 South Korean President Lee Myung-bak arrives in New Delhi, India, for a four-day state visit aimed at deepening the two countries' economic cooperation and bolstering bilateral efforts to tackle regional and global challenges, including security threats.

Jan. 26 North Korea declares two maritime areas near the inter-Korean maritime border in the Yellow Sea as "no-sail" zones.

Feb. 17 South Korea's Lee Sang-hwa wins gold in the women's 500-meter speed skating event at the Vancouver Winter Olympics, becoming the first Asian female skater to win an Olympic speed skating event.

Feb. 21 South Korea's Lee Jung-su captures second gold medal at the Vancouver Winter Olympics by winning the men's 1,000 meter short track speed skating event. Lee, who won the 1,500m race on Feb. 14, crossed the finish line a hair faster than his compatriot Lee Ho-seok with a new Olympic record of 1:23.747.

Feb. 24 South Korea's Lee Seung-hoon wins the gold medal at the men's 10,000 meter speed skating event with a new Olympic record at the Vancouver Winter Olympics.

Feb. 26 Figure skater Kim Yu-na wins South Korea's first Olympic figure skating gold medal in Vancouver, setting a world record of 228.56 points.

March 10 The Korean Utility Helicopter, also called "Surion," makes a successful maiden test flight, making the country the world's 11th to turn out an indigenous chopper.

March 11 Pup Jeong, a South Korean Buddhist monk who preached the happiness of a life unbound by desire for possessions in a series of best-selling books, dies. He was 78.

March 17 South Korea says that it has selected Terra Nova Bay for a second research station in the Antarctic, based on the results of thorough analysis and opinion gathering from government and private-sector experts.

March 26 The Cheonan, a South Korean Navy patrol ship, sinks off the Yellow Sea border, causing the deaths of 46 sailors. A team of multinational investigators concluded that North Korea was responsible for the sinking two months later. To this day, Pyongyang has continued to deny its involvement.

March 30 Han Joo-ho, a South Korean military diver, dies after falling unconscious while searching for missing crew members of a sunken naval warship, deepening the tragedy surrounding sinking of 1,200-ton navy ship Cheonan.

April 4 The Samho Dream, a South Korean oil tanker carrying five South Korean crew members and 19 Filipinos, is hijacked in the Indian Ocean by Somali pirates.

April 9 A Seoul district court acquits former Prime Minister Han Myeong-sook of the charge of receiving money from a local businessman while in office.

April 29 South Korea holds a mass funeral for 46 sailors killed in North Korea's sinking of the warship Cheonan.

May 3 North Korean leader Kim Jong-il arrives in the Chinese port city of Dalian aboard a train in his first trip to China since 2006. He leaves the city on the following day for a summit with Chinese President Hu Jintao in Beijing.

May 20 A probe led by an international team of investigators concludes that a North Korean torpedo sank the Cheonan warship on March 26 near the tense inter-Korean border in the Yellow Sea, killing 46 sailors.

May 24 President Lee Myung-bak says the sinking of the warship Cheonan was the result of North Korea's military attack on South Korea. Lee also announces plans to halt Inter-Korean trade and ban the North from using South Korean waterways. North Korea says it will fire at South Korean speakers broadcasting propaganda.

June 10 The Naro-1, South Korea's first locally assembled space rocket carrying a scientific satellite, explodes about two minutes into flight.

July 2 The U.N. Security Council debates the extent to which North Korea should be held responsible for the deadly sinking of a South Korean warship in March.

July 7 A number of South Korean Web sites, including those of the presidential office Cheong Wa Dae and the Foreign Ministry, are hampered by a series of so-called distributed denial-of-service (DDoS) attacks. They were later found to be masterminded by North Korea.

July 21 U.S. Secretary of State Hillary Clinton announces a set of new sanctions against North Korea to punish Pyongyang for the sinking of a South Korean warship and warns the communist regime against further provocations.

July 28 South Korea and the U.S. close out their joint large-scale drills off the South's east coast, with Seoul officials saying the allies accomplished their mission of sending a clear message of deterrence to North Korea.

Aug. 2 The Guinness World Records certifies South Korea's Saemangeum dike as the longest man-made sea barrier in the world, according to the South Korean government. The world's leading authority on record-breaking achievements officially confirmed that the 33.9-kilometer-long seawall is 1.4 km longer than the dike at the Zuiderzee Works in the Netherlands.

Aug. 9 North Korea fires some 130 rounds of artillery into a disputed maritime border with South Korea in the Yellow Sea in an apparent response to South Korea's large-scale navy drills. The artillery causes no damage to South Korean ships.

Aug. 10 Japanese Prime Minister Naoto Kan offers a renewed apology to South Korea over the 1910-45 colonial rule of the Korean Peninsula.

Aug. 14 South Korean baseball slugger Lee Dae-ho sets the world's straight-game home run record in a Korean pro baseball match. The Lotte Giants infielder became the first baseball player in the world to hit a home run in nine consecutive games.

Aug. 18 A North Korean fighter jet crashes in a Chinese border area, killing the pilot aboard who may have been attempting to defect to Russia.

Sept. 2 The ruling Grand National Party (GNP) expels Rep. Kang Yong-seok after he is accused of making derogatory comments about women. Kang came under fire in late July for allegedly making lewd, sexist remarks during a dinner with college students about TV anchorwomen and women's appearances.

Sept. 16 The foreign affairs council of the European Union (EU) approves a free trade agreement with South Korea, aimed at eliminating or phasing out tariffs on 96 percent of EU goods and 99 percent of South Korean goods within three years. The Korea-EU FTA comes into full effect on July 1, 2011.

Oct. 6 South Korea and the EU seal a free trade agreement pact and eye a 'strategic partnership'

Oct. 22 Finance ministers from the Group of 20 major economies open two-day talks in Gyeongju, 371 kilometers southeast of Seoul, to find ways to resolve the sticky global currency row and set the agenda for the Seoul summit held on Nov. 11-12. The economies agreed to avoid competitive currency devaluations and curb excessive trade imbalances in an effort to ease mounting economic tensions.

Nov. 6 Somali pirates release 24 crew members of the South Korean tanker MV Samho Dream after more than seven months of captivity on the Indian Ocean.

Nov. 11 The leaders from the Group of 20 major economies gathered in Seoul for a two-day summit to discuss ways to cooperate in tackling the global financial crisis under the theme of "Shared Growth Beyond Crisis."

Nov. 19 The U.N. General Assembly committee adopts a resolution on North Korea's human rights violations.

Nov. 23 North Korea shells the South Korean border island of Yeonpyeong, killing two marines and two civilians. Tensions peaked on the peninsula following the shelling, which was recorded as one of the worst attacks on the South since the 1950-53 Korean War.

Dec. 28 The Constitutional Court declares the telecommunications law that punishes Internet users for spreading false information online is unconstitutional, a move seen as upholding freedom of expression on the Web. The decision comes after a famous online pundit known by his pen name "Minerva" filed a petition with the top court after being indicted on charges of spreading false information on the Web. He was later acquitted.

2011

Jan. 4 Foot-and-mouth disease (FMD) is spreading throughout the country despite extensive quarantine efforts. The authorities concerned confirmed the number of officially counted FMD cases to 86 after the disease was first detected on Nov. 29, 2010.

Jan. 11 North Korea reopens its Red Cross hotline with South Korea at their joint truce village as promised, as the communist state continues to appeal for talks with Seoul in an apparent attempt to draw much-needed assistance.

Jan. 15 The MV Samho Jewelry, a South Korean chemical freighter with 21 crew members including eight South Koreans, is hijacked by Somali pirates in the Arabian Sea while en route to Sri Lanka from the United Arab Emirates.

Jan. 21 South Korea's special naval forces raid a hijacked freighter in the Arabian Sea, freeing 21 crewmen and killing eight Somali pirates in a secret mission code named "Dawn of Gulf of Aden."

Jan. 22 Park Wan-sue, a well-known South Korean novelist and essayist who delved into post-Korean War realities of everyday people, dies of gallbladder cancer on Saturday. She was 80.

Jan. 24 The number of foreigners naturalized as Koreans surpasses the landmark 100,000, 63 years after the establishment of the South Korean government in 1948.

Feb. 6 South Korea finishes third in the overall medal standings at the Asian Winter Games in Kazakhstan. It won 13 Gold, 12 Silver and 13 Bronze medals.

• Robert King, U.S. special envoy for North Korean human rights issues, visits South Korea to gather information on the North's human rights abuse and discuss strategy to address the problem.

Feb. 8 South Korea's Defense Ministry says that military officers from South and North Korea held preliminary talks to lay groundwork for a higher-level meeting, the first inter-Korean dialogue since the North's deadly bombardment of a South Korean border island. But the preliminary military talks broke down as the North refused to apologize and admit its responsibility for deadly provocations last year.

Feb. 9 A South Korean fishing vessel with 43 sailors aboard, including two South Koreans, is released after four months of captivity in Somalia. All crew members were freed from the 241-ton trawler Keummi 305 after it was hijacked by Somali pirates on Oct. 9.

Feb. 10 South Korea and the U.S. sign their free trade agreement (FTA), paving the way for the pending pact to be ratified in both countries.

Feb. 19 The Financial Services Commission (FSC) suspends operations of four savings banks, including three affiliates of the country's largest savings bank, Busan Savings Bank, citing concerns over liquidity shortage.

Feb. 20 The Korean film "Night Fishing (Paranmanjang)" wins the Golden Bear Award for best short film at the 61st Berlin International Film Festival.

Feb. 21 Government officials say hundreds of Libyans raided a South Korean-run construction site in the capital city of Tripoli, injuring three Koreans and two Bangladeshi workers, amid the rising violence against anti-government protesters in Libya.

Feb. 24 Huh Chang-soo, the chairman of energy & construction giant GS Group, is elected the new Federation of Korean Industries (FKI) chief in a general assembly of the organization.

Feb. 26 A chartered Korean Air plane carrying 235 South Koreans out of strife-torn Libya arrives in Seoul.

March 1 The Pentagon announces the nomination of Gen. James Thurman, commander of Army Forces Command, as the new commander of U.S. Forces in Korea.

March 2 About half of all South Korean schools begin providing free lunches as political parties and municipalities continue debating the need for the expensive program.

March 4 Industry sources say malicious computer codes attacked the Web sites of the presidential office and other major institutions, shutting down some of them temporarily.

• The Defense Ministry says a South Korean warship, the Choi Young, carrying 32 Korean nationals was evacuated from the turmoil-battered Libya and arrived in Malta.

March 8 Korea's Hyundai Motor Group signs a final deal with creditors of Hyundai Engineering & Construction Co. to take over a major stake in the biggest local builder.

March 9 The Foreign Ministry says Korea decided to ban its nationals from traveling to or staying in Libya amid intensifying violence between protesters and government forces there.

• Government officials say multiple Korean diplomats at the consulate in Shanghai were accused of having extramarital affairs with a 33-year-old Chinese woman and providing her with various favors.

March 10 Korea's Supreme Court finds Lone Star Korea's chief guilty of manipulating the stock price of a former credit card firm, in a ruling that overturned a lower court ruling that acquitted its head in a controversial 2003 deal.

March 12 South Korean President Lee Myung-bak starts his four-day visit to the United Arab Emirates, a trip highlighting economic cooperation.

March 13 South Korea clinches its largest-ever oil field development deal, potentially valued at 110 trillion won(US$98 billion), with the United Arab Emirates (UAE).

March 14 A 102-member Korean rescue team departs for Japan aboard Air Force planes to help the neighboring country cope with the massive devastation left by a record earthquake and tsunami.

March 15 Government officials say North Korea agreed to the repatriation of only 27 of its 31 nationals held in South Korea after their boat drifted to the South last month, withdrawing its earlier demand that all of them, including four who had expressed their wish to defect.

March 18 President Lee Myung-bak pays a visit to the Japanese embassy in Seoul to convey a message of condolences for the victims of last week's massive earthquake and tsunami.

March 20 U.S. investor Warren Buffett arrives in South Korea on a trip that includes a meeting with President Lee Myung-bak.

March 21 Korea and Peru sign a free trade deal, Seoul's latest trade pact that could pave the way for Korea to tap deeper into the South American region.

March 24 South Korea's Coast Guard says that nine North Koreans have arrived in South Korea after crossing the Yellow Sea aboard a boat from China in an apparent bid to seek asylum.

March 25 The government concludes that a sex scandal involving several South Korean diplomats in Shanghai and a mysterious Chinese woman is not an espionage incident intended to steal classified state information.

March 27 Twenty-seven among 31 North Koreans are repatriated to their communist nation, 50 days after their boat drifted across the western border into South Korea.

March 28 South Korean director Lee Chang-dong's film "Poetry" is named best picture at the 25th Fribourg International Film Festival in Switzerland.

April 1 South Korea's President Lee Myung-bak offers a public apology for breaking a promise to construct a major airport in the Gyeongsang region, but stresses that his administration's will for balanced regional development remains unchanged.

April 5 The Parliament passes a resolution condemning Japan for its renewed territorial claims to the South Korean islets of Dokdo in a recently approved set of Japanese textbooks.

April 6 South Korean police say that North Korea was behind the massive cyber attacks, so-called distributed denial-of-service (DDoS) that severely slowed and disrupted dozens of South Korean government and business Web sites in March.

April 8 North Korea's Asia Pacific Peace Committee says that it could terminate an exclusive contract with a South Korean conglomerate Hyundai Asan for tourism at Mt. Kumgang, a resort along its east coast.

April 13 The first shipment of ancient Korean royal books (75 books of the 297-volume "Oegyujanggak") are returned to Seoul by plane 145 years after being looted by France.

April 15 South Korea and the United States sign an agreement for the development of a missile defense system against North Korea, which is believed to have developed ballistic missiles carrying nuclear warheads capable of hitting the U.S. mainland.

April 18 Chollian, South Korea's first geostationary communication and weather satellite, starts full commercial operations, 10 months after being launched from the Guiana Space Center in South America on June 27, 2010.

April 22 Korea's Samsung Electronics Co. says it filed lawsuits against Apple Inc. in South Korea, Japan and Germany, accusing the U.S.-based company of violating its patents in producing the iPhone and the iPad.

April 24 Former U.S. President Jimmy Carter embarks on a tour of China and the two Koreas in a "new initiative" to help reduce tensions on the Korean Peninsula amid stalled international dialogue for North Korea's nuclear dismantlement.

April 26 South Korean climber Kim Jae-soo reaches the summit of Annapurna, 8,091 meters tall, in the Himalayas.

April 29 A second batch of ancient Korean royal books that had been stored in France for 145 years arrives in South Korea, two weeks after the first shipment.

May 1 A Singapore-registered chemical tanker with crew that includes four South Koreans has been hijacked by Somali pirates.

May 3 South Korea condemns North Korea for a cyber attack that paralyzed the computer network of a South Korean bank last month, as Seoul's prosecutors said Pyongyang's intelligence organization was responsible for the attack.

May 4 South Korea's National Assembly ratifies the free trade agreement (FTA) with the European Union (EU), allowing it to take effect in July.

May 5 Local police say a South Korean forestry helicopter carrying two people appears to have crashed on the east coast.

May 8 South Korean President Lee Myung-bak arrives in Berlin on the first leg of a three-nation European tour focused on boosting investment and trade with the European economies ahead of the implementation of a free trade agreement between South Korea and the European Union.

May 13 South Korean President Lee Myung-bak and French President Nicolas Sarkozy agree to step up joint efforts to help the G-20 economic forum to deliver its commitment to bring stability to the world economy, including fighting speculation in food and energy markets.

May 20 A retired American soldier pinpoints a heliport inside his former military camp in South Korea as the site where large amounts of leftover toxic chemical Agent Orange were illegally buried in the 1970s.

May 22 Seoul and Washington agree to conduct a joint investigation into allegations that massive amounts of leftover toxic chemical Agent Orange were buried at a U.S. Forces Korea (USFK) base in southeastern South Korea in the 1970s.

May 25 South Korea makes a contract to export its T-50 trainer jets to Indonesia, a deal that will mark the first time the country will export supersonic jets.

May 26 Hanwha Engineering & Construction Co. wins a US$7.25 billion deal from Iraq to construct a new town near its capital city, the largest-ever deal that a South Korean builder has clinched.

May 30 The Korea Meteorological Administration (KMA) says South Korea launched its first meteorological observation ship "Gisang 1," a vessel that is expected to improve precision in the country's weather forecasts.

May 31 The Seoul Metropolitan Government says people will be fined 100,000 won (US$93) if they are caught smoking in major public squares in downtown Seoul, a measure to heighten public awareness of the health hazards from secondhand smoking.

June 3 The government cabinet approves a new ratification bill for the South Korea-U.S. free trade agreement (FTA) after fixing translation errors in the Korean text of the deal.

June 5 South Korean Foreign Minister Kim Sung-hwan departs for Budapest, Hungary, to attend the foreign ministerial meeting of the Asia-Europe Meeting (ASEM).

• Washington sources say the Barack Obama administration tapped South Korean-born Sung Kim as its new Ambassador to Seoul.

June 8 South Korea's Army holds a send-off ceremony for 350 troops set to depart for Afghanistan to replace its military contingent protecting the nation's aid workers on a mission to help rebuild the war-torn nation.

June 9 Yonhap News TV, an all-news cable channel to be launched later this year, signs an agreement with Al Jazeera Satellite Network for exchanges of video news content.

June 10 Thousands of college students and supporters, holding lit candles, rally in central Seoul, demanding that the government take steps to lower escalating tuitions.

June 14 South Korea's military establishes a defense command to better shield five frontline islands near the Yellow Sea border from possible North Korean attacks.

June 17 The North's Korean Central News Agency (KCNA) says the North asked South Korean companies to visit Mount Kumgang by June 30 to discuss the matter of disposing of the frozen and seized properties.

June 20 The prosecution and police reach a last-minute compromise to end a dispute over investigative rights, agreeing to empower police to open investigations on their own under the broad supervision of prosecutors.

June 22 United Nations Secretary General Ban Ki-moon is re-elected to serve a second five-year term in a unanimous decision at the UN General Assembly in New York.

June 24 Apple Inc. files a lawsuit against Samsung Electronics Co., accusing the South Koran company of infringing its patented technologies used in making its iconic smartphone, the iPhone.

June 29 The National Assembly passes a bill on South Korea's free trade agreement (FTA) with Peru, paving the way for trades and investments between the countries to increase.

June 30 The National Assembly passes a contentious bill on redefining investigative rights of the prosecution and police despite strong protests from prosecutors over a last-minute revision that could restrict their control of police investigations.

July 1 A free trade agreement between South Korea and the European Union goes into effect, making Europe South Korea's second-largest trading partner after China. The Korea-EU free trade agreement was signed October 2010.

• North Korea's state news agency (KCNA) says its agreements with The Associated Press, under which the U.S. news agency will be allowed to open a bureau in Pyongyang, will help improve relations between the two countries.

July 4 Prosecutor-General Kim Joon-gyu offers to step down in protest over the recent parliamentary approval of a bill limiting the prosecution's investigatory power.

July 5 A group of seven lawmakers visit South Korea's easternmost islets of Dokdo, seeking to boost the morale of South Korean Coast Guard officers stationed there in the face of Japan's constant territorial claims.

July 6 PyeongChang wins the bid to host the 2018 Winter Olympics in a vote by the International Olympic Committee (IOC) in Durban, South Africa, succeeding in its third attempt to bring the Winter Games to South Korea for the first time.

July 8 South Korea's President Lee Myung-bak and Congolese President Joseph Kabila agree to work together to rebuild the war-torn Congo through a combination of Korea's technologies and Congo's rich national resources.

July 10 South Korea establishes diplomatic relations with South Sudan, expressing congratulations for the formal independence of the world's newest state.

July 14 The Changwon District Court says the local unit of Apple Inc. paid its first ever compensation in South Korea to an iPhone user over a controversial function that tracks users' locations.

July 15 A government official says Somali pirates holding four South Koreans in a hijacked chemical tanker are demanding that Seoul pay ransom for the hostages and release five pirates captured during a January raid of a seized Korean freighter.

July 18 South Korean researchers say that they have discovered the world's largest fossilized tooth marks of a carnivorous dinosaur in Hadong, South Gyeongsang Province.

July 20 The South's Land, Transport and Maritime Affairs Ministry says South Korea introduced its first indigenous private aircraft in a ceremony marking the first flight of the light passenger plane, named "Naraon."

July 24 South Korean swimmer Park Tae-hwan wins the men's 400-meter freestyle race at the 2011 World Aquatics Championships in Shanghai.

July 25 South Korea and India sign a nuclear energy cooperation agreement after a year of negotiations, paving the way for Seoul to export atomic power plants to the fast-developing nation.

July 26 A team of civic group officials delivers 300 tons of flour aid for vulnerable North Koreans in what became the first dispatch of flour since the North's deadly attack on a South Korean island.

July 28 A government official says South Korea has decided to slap an entry ban on two Japanese lawmakers planning to visit an island near the South's easternmost islets of Dokdo, a trip that Seoul calls an attempt to renew Tokyo's territorial claims to the islets.

• The Coast Guard says a cargo plane operated by Asiana Airlines, South Korea's second-largest flagship carrier, crashed into the sea off Jeju Island, leaving its two pilots missing.

• SK Communications Co., the operator of South Korea's third most-visited Internet portal, says that its popular Web sites were hacked, compromising the private information of 35 million users.

July 29 South Korea and Bolivia agree to cooperate on a lithium battery business with the two countries seeking to set up a joint venture in Bolivia to produce parts for rechargeable batteries.

July 31 Rep. Lee Jae-oh, an aide to President Lee Myung-bak, arrives on Ulleung Island in the East Sea in an effort to thwart a planned trip by three Japanese lawmakers seen as an attempt to reassert Tokyo's claim to the Korean territory.

Aug. 1 Three Japanese lawmakers, stuck in an airport waiting room for nine hours after being denied entry to South Korea, drop their plan to visit an eastern island near the South Korean islets of Dokdo and return home.

• An E-737, the country's first airborne early warning and control (AEW&C) aircraft from Boeing, lands at the Air Force base in Gimhae, South Gyeongsang Province.

Aug. 2 The Korean Council for Reconciliation and Cooperation (KCRC) says South Korean civic groups delivered an additional 300 tons of flour to North Korea, following through with their pledge to send a total of 2,500 tons by the end of this month.

Aug. 6 South Korean Foreign Minister Kim Sung-hwan leaves for Russia to hold bilateral talks that are expected to focus on North Korea and other issues concerning the two nations.

Aug. 8 The Korea Meteorological Administration (KMA) says typhoon Muifa passed South Korea's capital of Seoul along the peninsula's west coast, leaving at least four dead and two others missing as it proceeded northward toward China.

Aug. 10 The Joint Chiefs of Staff (JCS) says the South's Navy heard North Korea fire three artillery shots toward the Northern Limit Line (NLL), and then responded with three warning shots.

Aug. 11 SK Communications Co., the operator of the Nate portal and Cyworld social networking service, says last month a hacker broke into its servers and stole user data, including names, birth dates, email addresses, phone number and encrypted social security numbers.

Aug. 12 The Unification Ministry says South Korea returned home all four North Korean fishermen its navy had rescued near the Yellow Sea border who were handed over at the inter-Korean truce village of Panmununjom.

Aug. 17 The Korea Communications Commission (KCC) says LG Uplus Corp. won the "golden" spectrum of 2.1 GHz for its super-fast wireless service, setting the stage for the nation's smallest mobile phone operator to aggressively compete with its two bigger rivals in the soaring market for smartphones.

• The Russian Skating Union (RSU) says Ahn Hyun-soo, a three-time Olympic short track champion for South Korea currently training in Moscow, is seeking Russian citizenship so he can represent the country at the next Winter Olympics.

• A South Korean law firm representing 27,000 iPhone users files a class-action suit against Apple Inc., demanding compensation for privacy violations inflicted by the smartphone's user location tracking.

Aug. 18 The presidential office Cheong Wa Dae says former Supreme Court Justice Yang Sung-tae was named the new chief justice of the Supreme Court.

Aug. 19 North Korea says it has accepted a request by the United States for talks on resuming the remains recovery mission of American troops killed during the 1950-53 Korean War.

Aug. 21 South Korean President Lee Myung-bak arrives in Mongolia as part of a three-nation trip to Central Asia, a region that is rich in resources and business opportunities and carries strategic significance as a bridge between Asia and Europe.

Aug. 22 South Korean President Lee Myung-bak and Mongolian President Tsakhia Elbegdorj agree to significantly boost resources and energy cooperation and elevate their relations to a "comprehensive partnership" in a symbolic commitment to bolster ties in all areas.

Aug. 24 South Korea and Uzbekistan sign a US$4.1 billion package of deals to develop the Surgil gas field near the Aral Sea and build a gas and chemical plant, the largest-ever project between the two countries since they established diplomatic relations in 1992.

• The Seoul Metropolitan Government holds a referendum on whether the city should proceed with its free school lunch program. The referendum was nullified, as voter turnout fell short of the legally required quorum of one-third of all eligible voters.

• Hyundai Heavy Industries Co., South Korea's leading shipbuilder, says that it has developed the world's largest ice-breaking merchant ship (190,000-ton).

• North Korean leader Kim Jong-il holds rare talks with Russian President Dmitry Medvedev in an eastern Siberian city, a meeting that Moscow said would focus on how to revive long-stalled talks on ending Pyongyang's nuclear programs.

Aug. 26 Seoul Mayor Oh Se-hoon announces his resignation, saying he would take responsibility for his failed attempts to block the free lunch program in a referendum earlier this week.

• The International Conference on AIDS in Asia and the Pacific (ICAAP) kick off its congress in Busan, Korea with some 4,000 people from 70 countries taking part in the event.

Aug. 27 Prosecutors say Park Myoung-gee, a professor at Seoul National University of Education, was taken into custody over allegations that he had received 130 million won (US$120,147) from then rival and now education chief Kwak No-hyun.

• The southeastern city of Daegu marks the official start of the 13th World Championships in Athletics through Sept. 4 with a lavish opening ceremony, celebrating the dreams and passion of nearly 2,000 athletes participating in the world's biggest athletics competition, with the U.S. the first place finishing.

Aug. 28 Seoul education chief Kwak No-hyun admits to giving 200 million won (US$184,800) to a college professor who dropped out of last year's election, but denied allegations the money was in return for the professor giving up his candidacy.

Sept. 6 South Korea and Ecuador agree to liberalize air transportation between the countries, allowing the launch of an air route connecting them for the first time in history.

Sept. 8 The Busan District Court sentences a Somali pirate to life in prison after he was convicted of hijacking a South Korean ship and shooting its captain earlier this year, upholding a lower court ruling.

Sept. 12 The North's Korean Central News Agency reports a renowned South Korean orchestra conductor Chung Myung-whun arrived in North Korea, on a trip he said is aimed at promoting cultural exchanges between the two countries.

Sept. 13 Japan's Kyodo News Agency says the nine North Korean people, three men, three women and three children, were found drifting in a small wooden boat in waters near Nanatsu, an island off western Japan facing the Korean Peninsula.

• Samsung Electronics Co., the world's second-biggest mobile phone maker, says that it has filed a complaint in France claiming that Apple Inc.'s iPhone and iPad violated its mobile technology patents.

Sept. 15 An unexpected heat wave leads to temporary massive blackouts. The state-run power distributor, Korea Power Exchange (KPX), said it began alternately cutting power supplies to neighborhoods or districts for up to 30 minutes from 3:30 p.m. onwards as the country's electricity reserve rate fell to as low as 6 percent, far below the 7 percent level that is considered the safe margin.

Sept. 18 The Financial Services Commission (FSC) says it has suspended business operations of seven savings banks, including major players Jeil and Tomato whose asset values exceed 3 trillion won (US$2.7 billion).

Sept. 21 South Korean President Lee Myung-bak in a keynote speech at the U.N. General Assembly urges North Korea to break its self-imposed isolation and join the international community by forsaking its nuclear ambitions, declaring that Seoul is ready to help its impoverished neighbor if it makes the strategic decision.

• Prosecutors indict the Seoul education chief Kwak No-hyun on charges of bribing his rival candidate to win the public post, bringing the election irregularity case against the high-profile official to court.

• South Korean President Lee Myung-bak and Japan's new Prime Minister, Yoshihiko Noda, agree to cooperate closely in dealing with North Korea and moving relations between the two countries forward as they held their first face-to-face talks in New York.

Sept. 22 Samsung Electronics Co., the world's top memory chip supplier, says it had started to mass-produce memory chips based on 20-nanometer class technology in a move to cement its leadership and weather an industry-wide downturn.

Sept. 23 South Korean President Lee Myung-bak meets with Microsoft founder Bill Gates and discusses ways to help people in developing countries in Africa and other parts of the world, a focus of the Bill & Melinda Gates Foundation.

• South Korea is reelected to the executive board of the International Atomic Energy Agency (IAEA).

Sept. 25 A Seoul's Foreign Ministry official says Tokyo is set to transfer nine North Koreans who entered Japan aboard a wooden boat to South Korea this week according to their wishes.

Sept. 27 Prime Minister Kim Hwang-sik holds talks with his Bulgarian counterpart to discuss ways to boost trade and investment, in such fields as renewable energy, infrastructure, e-government and agriculture.

Sept. 28 South Korea's National Assembly speaker Park Hee-tae with Malaysian Prime Minister Mohamed Najib bin Tun Abdul Razak in Malaysia calls for business cooperation between the two countries, especially in such areas as resources and energy.

Sept. 29 The Seoul government says South Korea and Ukraine vowed to push for full-scale bilateral cooperation in science and technology during talks held in Kiev between their prime ministers.

Oct. 1 Seoul's Trade Ministry says South Korea joined a multilateral accord aimed at combating counterfeiting and piracy of intellectual properties, and eight countries including Japan, the U.S., Singapore and New Zealand, signed the accord in Tokyo.

Oct. 3 Lawyer-turned-activist Park Won-soon is picked as the unified opposition-bloc candidate to run in the upcoming Seoul mayoral race.

Oct. 4 The Seoul Metropolitan Government agrees to launch joint city marketing activities with New York City as part of efforts to increase the world's awareness of South Korea and its capital.

• The Seoul Central District Court orders SK Broadband Co., a high-speed Internet service provider, to pay a total of 4 billion won (US$3.35 million) in compensation to its customers for leaking their personal information as concerns about Internet privacy grow in the world's most wired nation.

• The Joint Chiefs of Staff (JCS) says two North Koreans crossed the eastern sea border into South Korea on a small boat.

• A group of nine North Korean defectors arrives in Seoul, after having been under protective custody in Japan for nearly three weeks.

Oct. 5 The Foreign Ministry says South Korea appointed its chief nuclear envoy, Wi Sung-lac, as the new ambassador to Russia, replacing him with a former diplomatic minister to Beijing Lim Sung-nam.

Oct. 9 South Korea wins the seventeenth consecutive championships at the International Vocational Training Competition in London, capturing 13 gold, 5 silver and 6 bronze medals.

Oct. 11 South Korean President Lee Myung-bak leaves for Washington for talks with U.S. President Barack Obama as Congress is set to endorse a long-pending free trade agreement with Seoul.

• A major committee of the U.S. Senate approves a free trade agreement (FTA) with South Korea.

• The 2011 Gwangju Summit of the Urban Environmental Accords (UEA) is held in the city from Oct. 11-13 and hundreds of mayors and environment experts from more than 100 cities across the globe are gathered in this southwestern city of Gwangju for the summit.

• Seoul's Foreign Ministry official says one of two South Koreans detained by Chinese authorities late last month with a group of North Korean defectors has been released and returned home.

Oct. 12 An official says South Korean President Lee Myung-bak and U.S. President Barack Obama celebrated the Congressional ratification of a free trade agreement between the two countries in Washington.

• The presidential office says South Korean President Lee Myung-bak paid an unprecedented visit to the Pentagon and received a briefing from top American military officials on North Korea and other security issues.

• A Foreign Ministry official says South Korea demanded that Japan take "legal responsibility" for aging Korean women forced into sexual slavery for Japan's World War II soldiers, formally raising the issue at a U.N. meeting in New York.

Oct. 14 South Korean President Lee Myung-bak visits an auto plant in Detroit, along with U.S. President Barack Obama, promising American auto workers that a free trade agreement between the two countries will help protect their jobs and create more work for Americans.

• The 2011 Gwangju Summit of the Urban Environmental Accords (UEA) endorses the Gwangju Declaration and the Gwangju Initiative at a closing ceremony that collectively called for participating cities to take practical measures to reduce carbon emissions and strengthen cooperation.

Oct. 15 A group of activists rally in the streets of Seoul to protest what they called "the greed of conglomerates and the widening income gap in South Korea," joining the "Occupy Wall Street" movement that began in the United States.

Oct. 17 A North Korean artist formerly residing in Egypt arrives in South Korea in a rare defection through the South Korean embassy in the Middle East country.

Oct. 19 South Korean President Lee Myung-bak and Japanese Prime Minister Yoshihiko Noda agree to expand their currency swap volume to US$70 billion from the current $13 billion and strengthen working-level discussions on a possible free trade agreement between the two neighbors.

Oct. 20 The Korean Alpine Federation (KAF) says South Korean mountaineer Park Young-seok has apparently gone missing along with two fellow climbers during their climb of a Himalayan peak.

• S-Oil Corp., South Korea's oil refiner, says it has completed the world's biggest paraxylene plant on the country's southeast coast of Ulsan.

Oct. 21 President Lee Myung-bak meets with visiting French Prime Minister Francois Fillon and discusses ways of moving forward relations between the two countries, expanding trade and investment and cooperating at the upcoming summit of the Group of 20 major economies in France.

• The U.S. Defense Department says North Korea and the United States have agreed to resume a joint search for the remains of American soldiers killed in the 1950-53 Korean War.

• U.S. President Barack Obama signs into law a free trade agreement (FTA) with South Korea, completing a long-delayed process in Washington to put the accord, expected to help create jobs, into effect.

Oct. 22 A group of civic and labor activists holds an "Occupy Seoul" rally in Seoul to protest what they called the greed of financial institutions and the growing income disparity in the country.

Oct. 23 North Korea's top negotiator Kim Kye-gwan arrives in Geneva for a second round of bilateral meeting with his U.S. counterpart as part of diplomatic efforts to resume long-stalled negotiations on ending Pyongyang's nuclear weapons programs.

Oct. 25 Washington's chief envoy Stephen Bosworth says two days of talks between North Korea and the United States on how to revive the stalled six-nation talks were "very positive," but the two sides need to hold further talks to narrow outstanding issues.

• A parliamentary trade committee passes a law on the procedures for signing and implementation of a trade pact, considered a first step to ratifying the long-delayed Korea-U.S. free trade agreement (FTA).

Oct. 26 U.S. Defense Secretary Leon Panetta arrives in South Korea on his first official visit for an annual bilateral security meeting. He said that U.S. will not cut its troops in South Korea, reassuring the ally against the threat of provocations by North Korea despite intense budget woes at home.

• South Korea's top nuclear envoy Lim Sung-nam leaves for Russia to coordinate their joint strategy on how to revive the stalled six-party talks on ending North Korea's nuclear weapons programs.

• The Bank of Korea (BOK) says South Korea and China agreed to expand their won-yuan swap line to the equivalent of US$56 billion in a bid to secure foreign exchange liquidity amid growing external economic uncertainty.

Oct. 27 GS Caltex Co., South Korea's refiner, says that it has completed a polymer compound plant in eastern China that will help the company further tap into the world's second-largest economy.

• Opposition-backed civic activist Park Won-soon is elected mayor of Seoul in by-election.

Oct. 28 Defense chiefs of South Korea and the U.S. agree to pursue a joint operational plan to counter potential provocations by North Korea at their annual bilateral security meeting in Seoul.

• The National Assembly passes a revision bill that scraps the statute of limitations for rape against the disabled and children in a move to implement stronger punishments for those who prey on the most vulnerable.

• The foreign ministers of South Korea and Southeast Asia's five Mekong River nations launch their first meeting aimed at boosting economic and development cooperation, as Asia's fourth-largest economy seeks to strengthen its diplomacy with the resource-rich region.

• South Korean fashion-designer Lee Young-hee showcases her collection of hanbok, or traditional Korean attire, on the easternmost islets of Dokdo, in the first-ever fashion event held on the rocky islets.

Oct. 30 Jeju maritime police says the bodies of two pilots of a South Korean cargo plane that crashed into waters off the southern resort island of Jeju were recovered nearly three months after the accident took place.

Oct. 31 The government says South Korea and the United States have agreed to set up a service and investment committee to reduce any fallout from the bilateral free trade pact that may go into effect next year.

Nov. 1 South Korean President Lee Myung-bak arrives in Russia for talks with President Dmitry Medvedev.

• South Korea's nuclear envoy Lim Sung-nam leaves for China for discussions on how to bring North Korea back to the six-nation talks aimed at ending the North's nuclear ambitions.

• The Euijeongbu District Court sentences a U.S. soldier stationed in South Korea to 10 years behind bars for raping a local teenage girl in what could be one of the nation's heaviest punishments for crimes committed by a U.S. soldier.

• Public elementary schools in Seoul offer free meals to all students under an expanded meal program, the first policy change by the new mayor Park Won-soon who took office after his predecessor resigned over the failed attempt to downsize the plan.

Nov. 2 South Korean President Lee Myung-bak and Russian President Dmitry Medvedev agree to work closely together on North Korean nuclear programs and a project to build a gas pipeline linking the two countries via North Korea, saying it would benefit all three countries involved.

• Kim Jong-an, a former trademark examiner of the Intellectual Property Tribunal of Korea has been nominated for a senior position in the World Intellectual Property Organization (WIPO), becoming the first Korean to rise to the agency's higher echelon.

Nov. 3 South Korean President Lee Myung-bak in Cannes, France calls for world leaders to come up with specific plans to restore the fiscal health of their governments and urges debt-laden eurozone countries to carry out thorough restructuring measures.

Nov. 4 Seok Hae-kyun, the heroic captain of a South Korean freighter hijacked by Somali pirates and rescued in a naval operation earlier this year, is released from a local hospital after over nine months of treatment for gunshot wounds.

Nov. 5 Officials say a group of 21 North Koreans was found drifting aboard a boat off South Korea's west coast earlier this week.

Nov. 7 The Education Ministry says it has decided to shut down two local universities, Myungshin University and Sunghwa College, as part of a sweeping drive to weed out nonviable institutions of higher learning and to improve the country's education quality.

Nov. 8 Vietnamese President Truong Tan Sang with South Korean President Lee Myung-bak during summit talks in Seoul agree to seek greater cooperation with South Korea on nuclear power plant construction.

• The Fair Trade Commission says South Korea's major department stores agreed to lower sales commissions for vendors as part of efforts to ease the heavy financial burden of their small business partners.

• A government source says a North Korean man crossed the maritime border into South Korea on a raft late last month, the same day that 21 other North Koreans were found drifting aboard a boat off the South's west coast.

Nov. 10 Unionized workers at Hanjin Heavy Industries & Construction unanimously approve a deal with management to end an 11-month-long dispute triggered by the shipmaker's massive layoffs last year.

Nov. 11 The government says South Korea has reached an agreement with Taiwan to further expand air travel between the two countries.

• A diplomatic source says a group of 19 North Korean defectors being held in China will arrive in South Korea as early as this month in a rare move that goes against Chinese policy.

• South Korean President Lee Myung-bak arrives in Hawaii to attend a summit of Asia-Pacific Economic Cooperation (APEC) aimed at discussing ways to spur the global economy, create jobs, reform regulations and improve energy efficiency and security.

Nov. 13 An official says South Korea and the United States have agreed to step up preparations to provide travelers from each other's country with automated immigration checks instead of face-to-face interviews.

Nov. 14 North Korea's government-run Web site begins linking posts critical of South Korea to popular social networking sites (SNS) to allow netizens to more easily spread their messages online, in its latest effort to step up cyber propaganda.

Nov. 15 Ahn Cheol-soo, anti-virus software firm AhnLab,, announces that he will donate about 150 billion won (US$133 million), or half of his 37 percent stake in the firm, to charity, saying he hopes to use the money to help educate children of low-income families.

Nov. 16 A government source says North Korea flew its IL-28 bomber to test anti-ship missiles in the Yellow Sea waters, adding that the missiles are reportedly the modified versions of the North's Styx ground-to-ship missiles.

Nov. 17 South Korea's President Lee Myung-bak and Indonesian President Susilo Bambang Yudhoyono agree in Bali to strengthen defense industry cooperation and work closely together to carry out Indonesia's major economic development blueprint.

• The Seoul government says the International Finance Center (IFC) opened in Seoul's financial district of Yeouido, part of the city's ambitious project to become a financial hub in Northeast Asia.

Nov. 18 South Korean President Lee Myung-bak and leaders of Southeast Asian nations pledge at an annual cooperation summit in Bali, Indonesia to work closely together to further boost the already brisk trade between the two sides.

Nov. 19 South Korean President Lee Myung-bak at the summit in Bali, Indonesia with Chinese Premier Wen Jiabao and Japanese Prime Minister Yoshihiko Noda says North Korea should halt all illegal nuclear activities and pledge not to restart if the stalled six-party talks are to resume.

Nov. 20 South Korean President Lee Myung-bak arrives in the Philippines for a three-day state visit that will include summit talks with President Benigno Aquino III about improving bilateral ties and boosting trade and investment and other cooperation.

• Hyundai Heavy Industries Co., the world's biggest shipbuilder, says it has completed the construction of a new power transformer plant in the United States.

Nov. 21 South Korean President Lee Myung-bak and Philippine Benigno Aquino III agree to cooperate closely to maximize the effects of Seoul's development aid by putting together assistance strategies supporting Manila's economic development blue print, known as the Philippines Development Plan.

• Special U.N. rapporteur Marzuki Darusman arrives in Seoul for talks with senior South Korean officials and North Korean defectors, aimed at collecting the latest information on the North's human rights record.

• Diplomats say the United Nations General Assembly adopted a draft resolution condemning North Korea's human rights abuses as part of an annual move to put pressure on the communist regime.

Nov. 22 South Korea's National Assembly approves the long-pending free trade agreement with the United States during a chaotic session, after an opposition lawmaker set off tear gas in an attempt to block the passage.

Nov. 23 The opposition Democratic Party (DP) vows to boycott all parliamentary sessions in protest at the ruling party's unilateral passage of the disputed free trade agreement with the U.S.

Nov. 24 South Korea and Macao agree to liberalize air services between the two sides, in a move that could significantly increase bilateral cooperation and exchanges.

Nov. 25 Police officers across the country plan to return their handcuffs to the government in a symbolic gesture to protest modified criminal investigation procedures that they fear will reduce their rights to conduct internal investigations on their own.

• Nexon Korea Corp., a game developer, says that personal information of its online game Maple Story's 13 million subscribers has been leaked, the latest in a series of security breaches that are spurring concern about private data protection.

Nov. 26 More than 1,000 protesters hold a candlelight vigil against the free trade agreement (FTA) with the United States for the fifth day in Seoul, claiming that the deal unfairly favors the United States.

Nov. 28 President Lee Myung-bak agrees with Ethiopian Prime Minister Meles Zenawi to help Ethiopia develop its textile and leather industry through sharing South Korea's development experience and know-how.

• Prosecutors say they have launched an investigation into corruption allegations that a former female prosecutor received a luxury sedan and a designer handbag from a private-practice lawyer in return for peddling her influence in his criminal suit.

• Prosecutors open an investigation into allegations that Shin Jae-min, who served as a vice culture minister from 2008 through 2009, took more than 130 million won (US$112,651) from Lee Kuk-chul, chairman of SLS Group.

• The United Nations Educational, Scientific and Cultural Organization (UNESCO) says three Korean cultural traditions taekkyeon, tightrope walking and weaving of fine ramie in the Hansan region received world intangible heritage status from UNESCO.

Nov. 29 President Lee Myung-bak signs off on a package of bills needed to implement South Korea's free trade agreement with the United States, moving a step closer to putting the landmark pact into effect.

Nov. 30 President Lee Myung-bak and U.N. Secretary-General Ban Ki-moon in Busan call for major donor nations to keep their aid pledges amid concerns that a looming global economic crisis may cut assistance budgets.

• South Korea unveils its latest unmanned aerial vehicle (UAV) that is the world's fastest and also the world's first remote-controlled aircraft capable of taking off and landing vertically.

• North Korea says its enriched uranium production efforts are "progressing apace," rejecting demands from South Korea and the United States that the communist regime immediately halt uranium enrichment if the stalled international nuclear talks are to reopen.

Dec. 1 Five new cable television channels "MBN," "JTBC," "CSTV," "news Y," and "Channel A" begin broadcasting nationwide.

Dec. 2 The Defense Acquisition Program Administration (DAPA) says it has signed a deal with Lockheed Martin to purchase the Sniper Advanced Targeting Pod (ATP) for F-15K fighters.

• Hana Financial Group says that it has agreed with Lone Star Funds to cut the prices of buying Korea Exchange Bank by 11 percent to 3.92 trillion won (US$3.5 billion), paving the way for the U.S. buyout fund to exit from the Korean market.

Dec. 4 Jeonbuk Hyundai Motors captures the championship of South Korean professional football, beating Ulsan Hyundai FC 2-1 in the second leg of the K-League final series.

Dec. 5 The government says South Korea's trade volume exceeded the US$1 trillion mark for the first time in its history this year, becoming the world's ninth country ever to achieve the milepost.

• The Democratic Labor Party, the People's Participatory Party and a nascent party split from the Progressive New Party announce the creation of the new party "Unified Progressive Party."

Dec. 8 South Korea's Korea Exchange says it has signed a preliminary agreement with its Japanese counterpart to begin cross-trading of listed stocks as early as next year, a move that is expected to speed up trading time and lower costs for investors in both countries.

Dec. 9 The ruling Grand National Party head Hong Joon-pyo resigns, yielding to mounting pressure from reformist members seeking desperately to reshape the beleaguered party ahead of next year's general elections.

• South Korea's Navy says it has agreed with the United States to stage submarine drills twice a year beginning next year to strengthen readiness against possible North Korean provocation.

Dec. 10 Thousands of people rally in downtown Seoul in protest of a free trade agreement (FTA) South Korea has signed with the United States, arguing that it unfairly favors Washington.

• A judge of the Seoul Central District Court issues an arrest warrant for an aide to President Lee Myung-bak's brother Lee Sang-deuk in the latest in a string of high-profile corruption scandals.

• South Koreans observe a total eclipse of the moon, beginning from 11:6 p.m. to 2:32 a.m. following day.

Dec. 11 The Seoul Central District

Court issues an arrest warrant for a suspect, an aide to Rep. Choi Gu-sik of the Grand National Party, in the hacking attacks on the National Election Commission Web site that took place on a key election day in October.

Dec. 12 The Coast Guard says one South Korean Coast Guard commando was killed and another was injured in stabbings by Chinese sailors caught for fishing illegally in the Yellow Sea off Incheon.

Dec. 13 Park Tae-joon, honorary chairman of South Korea's top steelmaker POSCO, dies of lung disease on Tuesday. Park was 84.

• South Korea celebrates the return of hundreds of centuries-old Korean royal books, stolen by Japan during its 1910-45 colonial rule over the Korean Peninsula from Japan, with a procession and traditional ceremonies.

Dec. 14 An estimated 1,000 people rally in front of Japan's embassy in Seoul in the landmark 1,000th "Wednesday demonstration" demanding apology and compensation from Tokyo for the country's sexual enslavement of Korean women during World War II.

Dec. 16 The opposition Democratic Party and other liberal forces announce their merger and the creation of a new center-left party, a move aimed at boosting their chances in next year's major polls.

Dec. 19 North's state media reports North Korean leader Kim Jong-il who ruled the communist nation with an iron fist while ceaselessly pursuing nuclear weapons programs dies of a heart attack, leaving behind a nation with a broken economy and an untested young successor. He was 69.

Dec. 19 South Korea's Joint Chiefs of Staff (JCS) places all military units on emergency alert following the news of North Korean leader Kim Jong-il's death, handling crisis management and operations.

• North's Korean Central News Agency says the North Korean military and people have pledged to follow the leadership of the late leader's heir apparent Kim Jong-un to carry on the legacy of the communist state, amid growing uncertainty over the power transition.

Dec. 20 An official says South Korea expressed sympathy to the people of North Korea over the death of leader Kim Jong-il but decided not to send an official condolence delegation to the communist nation.

Dec. 21 South Korean President Lee Myung-bak says he hopes North Korea will overcome the death of leader Kim Jong-il well so that peace on the divided peninsula will be maintained.

Dec. 22 The Supreme Court sentences a Somali pirate to life imprisonment for hijacking a South Korean ship and attempting to kill the ship's captain, upholding a previous ruling.

• North Korea's state media refers to late leader Kim Jong-il's youngest son, Jong-un, as "an outstanding leader and a great sun," a proclamation of the official opening of a new era in the communist country.

Dec. 23 Seoul's nuclear envoy Lim Sung-nam says South Korea and China have agreed to work together to "swiftly reinvigorate" diplomatic efforts to revive the stalled six-party talks on ending North Korea's nuclear weapons program.

• Seoul High Court upholds a 20-year sentence for a medical doctor who killed his pregnant wife during a quarrel, rejecting his appeal to overturn an earlier conviction.

Dec. 26 The Unification Ministry says a former South Korean first lady Lee Hee-ho and the chairwoman of Hyundai Group Hyun Jeong-eun met with Kim Jong-un, North Korea's new leader, during their visit to Pyongyang to pay respects to the late North Korean leader Kim Jong-il.

• The Coast Guard says a trawler carrying 14 crew members sank off South Korea's southeastern coast, leaving one dead and 10 others missing.

• South Korea says it has provided all Coast Guard commandos raiding illegal Chinese fishing boats with firearms and will enact other tough crackdown measures.

• The Seoul High Court allows South Korea's mobile carrier KT Corp. to shut down its second-generation wireless telecommunication service, paving the way for the firm to jump into the popular fourth-generation service.

Dec. 27 South Korean lawmakers pass a resolution calling for the renegotiation of a key clause in the free trade agreement with the United States, expected to go into effect early next year.

• South Korea's antitrust watchdog says it has approved SK Telecom Co.'s bid to take over Hynix Semiconductor Inc., the world's second-largest memory chipmaker.

Dec. 28 The Justice Ministry says South Korea's extradition treaty with 47 European countries will go into effect this week, allowing the transfer of fugitive criminal suspects back to Seoul.

• South Korea's chief nuclear envoy, Lim Sung-nam and U.S. nuclear envoy agree to resume talks with the communist nation if the "right conditions" are created, in their first meeting since the death of North Korean leader Kim Jong-il.

• Taekwang Industrial Co., a South Korean chemical fiber company, says that it will begin commercial production of carbon fiber starting in March of next year for the first time in South Korea.

• North Korea begins a state funeral for its late leader Kim Jong-il at a snow-covered plaza in Pyongyang, with new leader Kim Jong-un walking at the right front of the hearse, followed by the North's military and political elites.

• Ship operators say South Korea's first icebreaker, the Araon, successfully completed its four-day mission to rescue a Russian boat that had been trapped in the Antarctic for nearly two weeks.

Dec. 29 The National Assembly approves a bill that would protect North Korean residents' rights to inherit assets from family members living in South Korea but also strictly limit the transfer of those assets out of the South.

• The Constitutional Court rules that using Twitter and other social networking sites for election campaigns does not violate election laws, a landmark ruling that allows candidates to reach out to voters with online and mobile media before the April general elections.

• The Seoul Central District Court issues the warrant to arrest Chey Jae-won on charges of misappropriating about 100 billion won (US$87 million) from SK affiliates to make up for futures investment losses incurred by his elder brother and group chairman Chey Tae-won.

• The Seoul Central District Court issues an arrest warrant for a former aide to the parliamentary speaker on suspicion of participating in the hacking attacks into the National Election Commission's Web site on a key by-election day two months earlier.

Dec. 30 Kim Geun-tae, a former leading South Korean democracy activist and prominent liberal politician, died from a brain disease. He was 64.

Dec. 31 President Lee Myung-bak sets taming inflation and job creation as two of his top goals for 2012 and vows to reinforce the national defense posture against the hostility shown by North Korea's new leadership.

• The National Assembly approves the government's budget proposal for next year, scaled at 325.4 trillion won (US$282.6 billion), with 171 votes in favor and two votes against.

2012

Jan. 6 Prosecutors conclude that a protocol secretary to a former chief of the National Assembly speaker and a former personal assistant to a former lawmaker colluded to launch the so-called distributed denial-of-access (DDoS) attacks on the Web site of the National Election Commission (NEC).

Jan. 7 Ahn Chang-ho is inducted into the International Civil Rights Walk of Fame in Atlanta for the first time as an Asian.

Jan. 8 A Chinese man who claims his grandmother was forced into sexual slavery for the Japanese military hurls four Molotov cocktails at the Japanese Embassy building in Seoul. The man claims he also set fire to Tokyo's Yasukuni Shrine before leaving that country.

Jan. 9 President Lee Myung-bak embarks on a state visit to Beijing to hold summit talks with his Chinese counterpart Hu Jintao to discuss the situation on the Korean Peninsula and bilateral economic ties.

Jan. 10 The government releases a total of 955 prisoners on a special pardon to celebrate the lunar New Year's day.

Jan. 13 The National Election Commission allows election campaigning through social network service (SNS) such as Facebook and Tweeter.

Jan. 15 Former Prime Minister Han Myeong-sook is elected as the chairman of the main opposition Democatic United Party (DUP).

• A 4191-ton vessel Doola No. 3 carrying oil explodes in waters three miles north of Jawol Island near Incheon, killing five crew members and causing six others to go missing.

Jan. 19 Kwak No-hyun, the suspended Seoul education chief, is fined 30 million won for bribing a rival candidate to get him drop out of the 2010 election for the capital's education superintendent seat.

Jan. 24 South Korea signs a bilateral agreement with Bermuda on the exchange of tax information, which officials said would serve as a stepping stone for the improvement in the two countries' relations.

Jan. 25 Army Gen. Jung Seung-jo, chairman of South Korea's Joint Chiefs of Staff and U.S. Gen. Martin Dempsey sign a new operational plan against potential North Korean provocations, called the Strategic Planning Directive (SPD).

Jan. 26 The Seoul Metropolitan Office of Education proclaims an ordinance on the protection of students' human rights, banning corporal punishment and allowing freedom to choose their own hairstyle and clothing.

• The Board of Audit and Inspection refers Kim Eun-seok, to the prosecution for criminal investigation over playing a key role in inflating stock prices of CNK International by deliberately exaggerating the volume of diamond reserves in a Cameroon mine developed by the KOSDAQ-listed company.

Jan. 27 South Korea's Financial Supervisory Commission gives the final green light next month to Hana Financial Group to buy Korea Exchange Bank (KEB), wrapping up the long-pending deal after concluding that there are no problems with Hana Financial's purchase of country's fifth-largest lender from the U.S. buyout firm Lone Star Fund regardless of Lone Star's eligibility issue

• Korea Communications Commission (KCC) Chairman Choi See-joong resigns amid allegations that his former aide took a bribe from a businessman in return for favors.

Jan. 30 Prosecutors raid the Foreign Ministry in Seoul as they broaden their investigation into allegations a ministry's energy envoy illegally used his influence to reap massive profits in a stock manipulation scheme involving an overseas mining project.

• Unionists of South Korea's public broadcaster MBC go on an indefinite general strike, demanding the resignation of the president and personnel reforms

Feb. 2 The ruling Grand National Party (GNP) unveils its new name, "Saenuri," which means new world in Korean.

Feb. 4 South Korean President Lee Myung-bak departs for a weeklong visit to Turkey. On Feb. 5 the two countries agree to build an atomic power plant on Turkey's Black Sea coast.

Feb. 7 South Korean President Lee Myung-bak departs for Saudi Arabia.

Feb. 8 Five former and current pro league volleyball players, along with a gambling broker, are arrested on suspicions of rigging games in return for financial rewards from the broker.

Feb. 9 South Korea and Saudi Arabia agree in Riyadh to significantly bolster their defense cooperation to elevate relations in non-economic sectors to match those of their prospering business ties.

• Parliamentary Speaker Park Hee-tae resigns, holding himself responsible for the widening investigation into allegations that he bribed fellow lawmakers during campaigns for a 2008 leadership election of the ruling party.

Feb. 10 South Korean President Lee Myung-bak agrees to the establishment of a "High-level Strategic Cooperation Committee" after Qatari Emir Sheikh Hamad bin Khalifa Al-Thani suggested the mechanism to expand the scope of bilateral cooperation to all sectors.

• A group of eight South Korean lawmakers cross the heavily fortified border into North Korea for a rare tour of a joint inter-Korean industrial complex. The parliamentary delegation meets with South Korean company officials in the complex in the North Korean border city of Kaesong.

Feb. 12 Park Tae-hwan of South Korea broke his own record in the men's 1,500m race in 14 minutes, 47.38 seconds at the New South Wales State Open Championships in Sydney.

Feb. 14 Kim Jong-pil, an enduring political figure in South Korean history leaves the ruling Saenuri Party.

Feb. 16 The ruling Saenuri Party scraps a plan to build a new airport near the southern port city of Busan.

Feb. 21 Former National Assembly Speaker Park Hee-tae is indicted without physical detention for bribing fellow ruling party lawmakers before being elected as party chairman in 2008.

Feb. 22 The Special Olympics World Winter Games in PyeongChang kicks off.

Feb. 23 Seoul Mayor Park Won-soon joins the main opposition Democratic United Party (DUP).

Feb. 28 The Cabinet approves the National Assembly's decision to increase the number of parliamentary seats from 299 to 300 in the new parliament. It marks the first time the number of parliamentary seats has reached the 300 mark.

Feb. 29 South Korea defeats Kuwait 2-0 in a World Cup qualifying match at Seoul World Cup Stadium and advances to the fourth and the final round of the Asian qualifying round for the 2014 FIFA World Cup in Brazil.

March 5 South Korea signs its first agreement with the United Arab Emirates (UAE) to develop two inland and one offshore oil fields in the Middle Eastern country.

March 6 Unionists of public broadcaster KBS launch a strike, demanding the resignation of their president.

March 7 South Korea's Navy and a local construction firm blow up part of a rocky coastal area on the southern resort island of Jeju as it starts key construction work for the contentious Jeju naval base project. But the blasting is met with severe protest among activists, Jeju residents and opposition lawmakers who accuse the Navy of destroying an environmental treasure.

March 11 South Korea and Turkey agree on key issues such as tariff concessions and dispute settlement schemes in their free trade talk.

March 13 A scuffle breaks out between a North Korean diplomat and South Korean lawmakers at a U.N. session on the communist nation's human rights abuses after So Se-pyong, the North's ambassador to its mission in Geneva, flatly denied a U.N. report on Pyongyang's human rights record.

March 14 Unionists of Yonhap News Agency go on a strike.

• Prosecutors in Daegu indict 27 professional baseball and volleyball players, gamblers and gambling brokers on charges of rigging matches in search of gambling dividends.

March 15 The Korea-U.S. Free Trade Agreement (FTA) takes effect.

March 25 South Korean female speed skater Lee Sang-hwa and male skater Mo Tae-bun finish first in the 500 meters at the sprint championships, run by the International Skating Union (ISU).

March 26 The two-day Nuclear Security Summit in Seoul, hosted by South Korean President Lee Myung-bak, kicks off. On March 27 concluding the final session of the two-day summit, leaders adopt the document called the "Seoul Communique," which also encourages nations to minimize the use of weapons-usable uranium by the end of 2013.

March 28 South Korea's first overseas voting for the April general elections begins.

April 1 Five defectors, who have been staying in South Korean embassy in China, enter South Korea while China allowed the defectors to leave the country

April 2 42 graduates of law school are named as state prosecutors for the first time.

April 3 Overseas votes for general election end. A total of 56,456 voted out of 123,571 voters, showing a 45.7% turnout.

• The government passes an ordinance to limit business hours of supermarkets run by conglomerates to protect small business owners.

April 6 Super Junior holds a first solo concert in Paris, France, drawing 7,000 attendance.

April 8 Foreign media reporters arrive in Pyongyang to cover North Korea's planned rocket launch.

April 9 Cho Hyeon-oh, commissioner of the National Police Agency, offers resignation, holding responsibility for Suwon murder case.

April 10 The Web site of the election watchdog, the National Election Commission(NEC), comes under the so-called distributed denial-of-service (DDoS) attacks.

April 11 Parliamentary elections are conducted with the ruling party winning 152 seats of the total 300 seats up for grabs against the DUP's 127 seats.

• Lee Jasmine, a 35-year-old naturalized Korean from the Philippines, wins one of 54 proportional representation seats as a candidate of the Saenuri Party in the general elections.

April 13 North Korea defiantly fired off a long-range rocket, the Unha-3 rocket, but the three-stage craft exploded in mid-air and crashed into the sea shortly after takeoff.

• Han Myeong-sook resigns from the chief of the DUP, taking responsibility for the loss in general elections. Moon Seong-keun takes over.

April 17 The United Nations Security Council adopts a presidential statement, condemning North Korea for the launch of a long-range missile only three days earlier. UNSC resolutions 1718 and 1874, which were passed after two North Korean nuclear tests in 2006 and 2009, ban the country from launching any ballistic missile.

April 19 Cheng Dawei, a Chinese boat captain, is sentenced to 30 years in prison for killing a South Korean law enforcement officer during a crackdown on illegal fishing.

April 24 South Korean President Lee Myung-bak and Sri Lankan President Mahinda Rajapaksa hold a summit in Seoul to discuss ways to strengthen economic and other cooperation between the two countries.

April 25 International Association of Educating Cities (IAEC) World Summit kicks off in Changwon with more than 1,420 attendants from 343 cities of 41 countries.

April 26 Hapcheon, South Gyeongsang Province, starts building a hydroelectric power generation.

April 27 Pop star Lady Gaga holds a concert in Seoul, only allowing adults over the age of 18 to watch the concert.

• South Korean fencing team wins 2012 Asia Fencing Competition held in Osaka, Japan with 9 gold, 4 silver, and 4 bronze.

April 28 Korean Air Co. opens route between Incheon and London.

April 29 South Korean rhythmic gymnast Son Yeon-jae wins bronze medal in the hoof event at FIG Worldcup Series in Russia.

May 2 South Korea and China declare to begin Free Trade Agreement talks between the two countries in Bejing, China.

• Kim Ki-yong inaugurates as commissioner of the National Police Agency.

May 4 Shin Uljin nuclear power generators begin construction.

• Park Ji-won is selected as a DUP floor leader.

• Samsung Electronics Co. rolls out Galaxy S in London for the first time.

May 10 South Korean President Lee Myung-bak and Peruvian President Ollanta Humala upgrade their relations to a "comprehensive strategic partnership."

May 11 An extravagant gala, the pre-opening events of the 2012 Yeosu Expo, takes place.

• South Korea and Poland agree on a revised double taxation avoidance agreement to help boost bilateral economic cooperation.

May 14 South Korean President Lee Myung-bak makes a landmark visit to Myanmar for summit talks with President Thein Sein.

May 15 South Korea and the United States hold their first free trade agreement (FTA) joint committee meeting in Washington to discuss rules and procedures for dealing with disputes and other issues.

• The ruling Saenuri Party elects a five-term judge-turned-lawmaker, Hwang Woo-yea, as its new chairman.

• The governments of South Korea and Denmark sign agreements in the fields of alternative energy, shipbuilding and livestock production, aimed at further promoting their bilateral cooperation on "green growth."

• President Lee Myung-bak meets with Suu Kyi in Yangon, Myanmar.

May 17 Samsung Electronics Co. begins mass producing a 20-nanometer based Multi-Level Cell (MLC) NAND flash memory chip.

May 18 South Korea's multipurpose satellite equipped with a high-resolution camera, the Arirang 3 satellite, successfully reaches the earth's orbit after blasting off from a Japanese space center.

May 23 South Korean President Lee Myung-bak and Guinea's President Alpha Conde hold a summit to expand resource development and other economic cooperation.

May 24 South Korea's Supreme Court rules that Japanese enterprises should pay compensation for their former Korean employees who were forcibly drafted into the Japanese workforce during the country's colonial rule of the Korean Peninsula decades ago.

May 25 The "Ara" waterway linking the Han River running through Seoul to the Yellow Sea opens.

May 29 South Korean President Lee Myung-bak and Paraguayan President Fernando Lugo hold summit talks in Blue house and agree to work together to boost trade, investment and development cooperation between the two countries.

May 30 North Korea calls itself a "nuclear-armed state" in its recently revised constitution.

• South Korean President Lee Myung-bak meets with Swedish King Carl XVI Gustaf in Blue house.

June 1 Rep. Kang Chang-hee, the six-term lawmaker, considered loyal to leading presidential hopeful Park Geun-hye, is selected as the new National Assembly speaker.

June 2 Defense Ministers of South Korea, Japan, and the United Sates agree to strengthen their ties at an annual regional security forum in Singapore, known as the Shangri-La security dialogue.

June 3 South Korean swimmer Park Tae-hwan won the 200-meter freestyle event at the Santa Clara International Grand Prix, raising his golds at the event to four.

June 7 Eleven South Koreans went missing in an apparent crash of a tourist helicopter in Peru.

June 8 Unionists of public broadcaster KBS end a 94-day strike.

June 9 Former Prime Minister Lee Hae-chan is elected new chairman of the main opposition Democratic United Party (DUP) in its national convention.

June 13 South Korean travelers become able to pass through U.S. airports without face-to-face interviews with immigration officials. The U.S. put the Smart Entry Service (SES) into operation for Koreans, making them eligible for automated immigration checks to save time and worries over a language barrier. The users are allowed to pass the unmanned immigration check points, called KIOSK, at 25 airports in the U.S.

• Prosecutors presses additional charges against Former Vice Knowledge Economy Minister Park Young-joon and others as they wrap up a reinvestigation into allegations authorities illegally spied on civilians critical of the government. The outcome of the three-month reinvestigation is seen as insufficient as it failed to clear suspicions that higher-level officials could have been involved.

June 14 South Korea starts construction of an international sea port, the new Saemangeum port on the massive plot of reclaimed land on the southwest coast.

June 17 South Korean President Lee Myung-bak leaves for Mexico for a G20 summit. On June 18 President Lee holds summit talks with Mexican President Felipe Calderon.

June 19 A 47-year-old Japanese conservative activist places insulting signs on a symbolic statue of a sex slave in front of the Japanese Embassy in downtown Seoul.

June 22 South Korean President Lee Myung-bak and Peruvian President Ollanta Humala hold summit talks during a meeting in Brazil.

June 23 South Korea joins the ranks of the exclusive "20-50 club," marking a new chapter in the development history of the country as the country's population has passed the 50 million mark and it has been able to maintain a per capita income of over US$20,000.

June 25 South Korea and Colombia announce they have concluded free trade talks, a deal Seoul expects will boost auto and other exports to the fast-emerging market in South America and serve as a foothold for expansion to other parts of the continent.

June 28 A Seoul administrative court rules that a human embryonic stem cell line created by disgraced scientist Hwang Woo-suk in 2003 can be registered with the nation's state public health agency.

July 1 Dr. Jim Yong Kim, Dartmouth College President is formally appointed as the new head of the World Bank.

July 2 South Korea launches a new

administrative hub, Sejong City, in a central region south of Seoul, which will be home to 17 central government offices and 20 subsidiary organizations in or near Seoul by 2014.

July 4 President Lee Myung-bak meets with Laotian Prime Minister Thongsing Thammavong and discusses ways to expand cooperation in energy and resources as well as development aid between the two countries.

July 9 The South Korean dancer Kong Ok-jin, known for her creative one-person song and dance drama, dies.

July 10 Rep. Park Geun-hye of the ruling Saenuri Party officially announces her bid to become South Korea's first female president, pledging to promote a fair economy, expand welfare and improve relations with North Korea.

July 11 The minor Unified Progressive Party elects Rep. Sim Sang-jung, a former labor activist, as its new floor leader.

July 12 Top diplomats from South Korea, the United States and Japan set up a three-way consultative body aimed at building a strong trilateral alliance in the face of North Korean aggression.

• South Korean Prime Minister Kim Hwang-sik agrees with his Mozambican counterpart Aires Bonifacio Ali to strengthen cooperation in energy and resources development during bilateral talks in Maputo.

July 13 Asia's biggest aquarium, Hanwha aqua planet opens on the southern resort island of Jeju.

July 14 China officially opens a consular office on the southern resort island of Jeju.

July 15 The Unified Progressive Party (UPP) elects reformist interim leader Kang Ki-kab as its new chairman.

July 18 Unionists of the public broadcaster MBC decide to call off a 170-day strike and return to work.

• North Korea announces that its young leader Kim Jong-un has been awarded the title of marshal, the top commander of the North's 1.2-million-strong army.

July 19 Fiji officially opens an embassy in South Korea, 40 years after the two nations established diplomatic ties.

July 20 Four South Korean activists who had been detained in China since March after apparently helping North

Korean defectors are released and arrive in Seoul.

• South Korea begins commercial operations of its 22nd nuclear reactor, New Gori 2 reactor.

July 24 President Lee Myung-bak apologizes to the nation over a string of bribery scandals involving his former aides and his elder brother-cum-political mentor, marking the sixth public apology during his single five-year term.

July 25 North Korean media identify the woman named Ri Sol-ju. seen accompanying North Korean leader Kim Jong-un in a recent series of public appearances as his wife, confirming his marriage for the first time.

July 27 South Korean archer Im Dong-hyun sets a world record with a 699 score during an individual ranking round at the London Olympics.

July 28 Pistol shooter Jin Jong-oh captures South Korea's first gold medal at the London Olympics, taking the men's 10-meter air pistol event.

July 29 Park Tae-hwan wins the silver medal in 400-meter freestyle swimming at the London Olympics. On July 31 he grabs the silver in the men's 200-meter freestyle swimming.

July 30 South Korea captures gold medal in the women's team archery at the London Olympics.

Aug. 1 South Korea and Turkey sign their free trade deal, paving the way for South Korean firms to tap deeper into the Eurasian nation.

• South Korean judoka Kim Jae-bum captures gold medal in the men's under-81-kilogram category at the London Olympics.

Aug. 2 Samsung Electronics Co. starts the mass production of the world's fastest 64 gigabyte (GB) embedded memory card to be used for mobile devices.

• Ki Bo-bae wins the gold in women's individual archery at the London Olympics.

• Kim Jang-mi wins gold in the women's 25-meter pistol event at the London Olympics

• Judoka Song Dae-nam wins gold in the men's under-90kg category at the London Olympics.

• Female sabre fencer Kim Ji-yeon captures the gold medal for South Korea's third gold medal.

• Psy's "Gangnam Style" hit 10 million hit at Youtube.

Aug. 4 South Korean team of Gu Bon-gil, Kim Jung-hwan and Won Woo-young, plus substitute Oh Eun-seok, capture the gold medal in men's sabre team event at the London Olympics.

• Oh Jin-hyek wins the gold medal in men's individual archery at the London Olympics.

Aug. 5 South Korea enjoys a one-two finish in men's 50-meter pistol shooting at the London Olympics.

Aug. 6 South Korean Kim Jong-hyun wins the silver medal in the men's 50-meter rifle 3 positions event at the London Olympics.

• South Korea and Vietnam declare the launch of talks on a bilateral free trade agreement (FTA) as part of efforts to strengthen economic ties.

Aug. 7 South Korean gymnast Yang Hak-seon wins the gold medal in men's vault at the London Olympics.

Aug. 8 South Korean wrestler Kim Hyeon-woo wins the gold medal in the men's 66-kilogram Greco-Roman match at the London Olympics.

• Samsung Electronics Co. releases smartphones that support the voice over long-term evolution (VoLTE) service.

Aug. 9 South Korea's government says that at least 14 people have died in South Korea in the past two months due to a record heat wave that has also killed more than 1 million farm animals.

• Lee Dae-hoon wins silver in the men's under-58-kilogram taekwondo competition at the London Olympics.

Aug. 10 President Lee Myung-bak makes a landmark visit to South Korea's easternmost islets of Dokdo.

Aug. 11 U.N. Secretary-General Ban Ki-moon arrives in South Korea for a four-day visit to attend an international maritime conference and the closing ceremony for the World Expo in Yeosu.

• Hwang Kyeong-seon captures the gold medal in the women's under-67-kilogram taekwondo finals at the London Olympics.

• South Korea beats Japan 2-0 to claim the bronze medal in men's football at the London Olympics.

Aug. 12 South Korean boxer Han Soon-chul takes silver in men's light-weight boxing, the final day of the London Olympics, for the country's last medal.

• An international exposition held in South Korea's southern port city of Yeosu drops the curtain after attaining its goal of drawing more than 8 million visitors.

Aug. 13 Four workers were killed and 24 others injured in a fire at a building under construction to house a Seoul branch of the National Museum of Contemporary Art.

• South Korean singer Kim Jang-hoon begins his three-day project to swim the 220 kilometers distance in a relay from an eastern port to Dokdo, South Korea's easternmost islets in the East Sea.

Aug. 15 A group of South Koreans, led by famous rock star Kim Jang-hoon, reaches the country's easternmost islets of Dokdo.

Aug. 16 "The Thieves," breaks the 10 million mark in total audience, becoming the sixth homegrown film to do so in the local movie history.

Aug. 19 South Korea installs a 1.2-meter-tall monument on its easternmost islets of Dokdo.

Aug. 20 Former Saenuri Party leader Park Geun-hye is elected the ruling party's presidential candidate after garnering a landslide victory in its national convention.

Aug. 21 South Korean President Lee Myung-bak and Costa Rican President Laura Chinchilla Miranda reach the agreement during summit talks in Seoul to work together to lay the groundwork for launching free trade talks.

• South Korean Foreign Minister Kim Sung-hwan dismisses a proposal by Japan to jointly refer the issue of Dokdo to the International Court of Justice (ICJ), saying the proposal is "not worth consideration."

Aug. 23 One worker is killed with 13 others injured after a storage drum containing toxic waste exploded at a factory owned by LG Chem. in Cheongju, 137 kilometers south of Seoul.

Aug. 30 South Korea sends a diplomatic document to Japan, dismissing Tokyo's latest proposal to take the sovereignty issue of South Korea's easternmost islets of Dokdo to the International Court of Justice (ICJ).

Sept. 3 Rev. Sun Myung Moon, founder of the Unification Church, dies of complications from pneumonia.

Sept. 4 The music video of South Korean rapper-singer Psy breaks the 100 million mark in YouTube views.

Sept. 6 The 2012 IUCN World Conservation Congress, organized by the International Union for Conservation of Nature (IUCN), begins a 10-day summit on South Korea's southern resort island of Jeju.

• Actress Revalina S. Temat, an Indonesian actress, is appointed as a "Goodwill Ambassador for Public Diplomacy" for South Korea.

Sept. 7 South Korean President Lee Myung-bak leaves for Russia's Far Eastern city of Vladivostok for an annual summit of Pacific Rim economies on a trip that will also take him to Greenland, Norway and Kazakhstan.

• The World Health Organization (WHO) says that it will soon close down its South Korean office after deciding that the country, formerly a beneficiary of foreign aid, is no longer in need of its services.

Sept. 8 South Korean President Lee Myung-bak and Russian President Vladimir Putin agree to work closely together to resolve the North Korean nuclear standoff and continue cooperation on a project to build a gas pipeline stretching from Russia across both Koreas.

Sept. 9 South Korean President Lee Myung-bak and U.S. Secretary of State Hillary Clinton meet and agree on the importance of cooperation between Seoul, Washington and Tokyo in dealing with North Korea and its nuclear programs at the Asia Pacific Economic Cooperation (APEC) forum summit.

• South Korean director Kim Ki-duk's drama "Pieta" wins the Golden Lion for best film at the 69th Venice Film Festival.

Sept. 10 Kang Ki-kab, the chairman of the minor opposition Unified Progressive Party (UPP) steps down to take responsibility for the party's split.

• South Korean President Lee Myung-bak travels to Greenland to take a first-hand look at problems resulting from climate change and to hold talks with Premier Kuupik Kleist of the Danish autonomous territory about green growth.

Sept. 13 South Korean President Lee Myung-bak and Kazakhstan's President Nursultan Nazarbayev celebrate the groundbreaking for a joint power plant project during a summit talk.

• The Seoul High Court delivers a 23-year-prison term and a fine of 20 million won to a Chinese captain for killing a South Korean officer on duty.

Sept. 15 The participants adopt the Jeju Declaration at the end of the IUCN World Conservation Congress.

• South Korean rapper-singer Psy tops the iTunes Chart with his single "Gangnam Style," making him the first Korean artist to reach No. 1 on the U.S. online chart.

Sept. 16 Rep. Moon Jae-in clinches the presidential nomination of the main opposition Democratic United Party after winning all of the party's regional primaries with combined total of 347,183 votes, or 56.5 percent.

Sept. 17 South Korean Shin Ji-yai wins the Ricoh Women's British Open on the LPGA Tour.

Sept. 19 Ahn Cheol-soo, an entrepreneur-turned-professor, says that he will run for presidency, putting an end to long-running speculation about his political ambition and turning this year's presidential race into a three-way competition.

Sept. 21 President Lee Myung-bak endorses a parliamentary motion authorizing an independent investigation into suspicions surrounding his retirement home project.

Sept. 22 Two construction workers are killed and 12 others injured after they fell from a bridge under construction in Paju, Gyeonggi Province.

Sept. 24 The ruling Saenuri Party's presidential hopeful Park Geun-hye expresses remorse and apologizes to all those who suffered under her late father's rule.

Sept. 27 South Korea, the United States, Japan and Australia carry out the U.S.-led Proliferation Security Initiative (PSI) exercise in waters 100 kilometers south of the southern port city of Busan.

• An explosion sparks at the Gumi National Industrial Complex in North Gyeongsang Province, killing four workers and injuring eight others.

• The Supreme Court confirms a one-year prison term for Seoul's education chief Kwak No-hyun for bribery charges, stripping the disgraced liberal educator of his post.

• "Gangnam Style," a song by South Korean rapper and YouTube sensation Psy, jumps to second place on Billboard's Hot 100 chart.

• South Korea's National Assembly authorizes sending about 300 military personnel to South Sudan on a peace-keeping mission that will last until the end of 2013.

Sept. 29 Addressing the U.N. General Assembly, South Korean Foreign Minister Kim Sung-hwan implicitly criticizes Japan for continuing to claim the South Korean islets of Dokdo, saying "no country should abuse" the rule of law to infringe upon another's territorial integrity.

Oct. 1 K-pop viral phenomenon Psy's hit "Gangnam Style" tops the formal British music chart for the first time for a Korean singer.

Oct. 2 South Korea's top baseball league surpasses 7 million fans in single season attendance for the first time in its 30-year history.

Oct. 4 Rapper Psy hits the stage at a public plaza in front of Seoul City Hall for a free concert designed to thank home fans for their support of his global hit song "Gangnam Style."

• Hangeul earns the top honor beating India's Telugu alphabet and the English alphabet at the 2nd World Alphabet Olympics held in Bangkok.

Oct. 6 A North Korean soldier defects to South Korea across the heavily armed border after shooting two superiors to death.

Oct. 7 South Korea announces a new missile agreement, known as the "missile guideline," calling for extending the maximum range of South Korean ballistic missiles from the current 300 kilometers to 800 kilometers, a distance long enough to reach the northern tip of North Korea, with the United States.

• PGA Tour veteran Choi Kyoung-ju wins own tournament at home for a second year this week. The CJ Invitational was hosted by K.J. Choi.

Oct. 8 South Korean President Lee Myung-bak and Myanmar President Thein Sein agree to launch negotiations to forge an investment guarantee pact

between the two countries to lay the foundation for greater economic cooperation.

Oct. 9 South Korea decides not to renew the expiring current swap contract with Japan as the country's capacity to deal with external risks has improved and the overall financial market conditions have been stabilizing.

Oct. 15 The World Bank and the Seoul government agree to open an office in Seoul. They also agree to launch a US$90 million fund with the global lender to step up cooperation in supporting emerging countries for their development.

• A team of independent prosecutors is launched to look into suspicions over a retirement home project of President Lee Myung-bak.

Oct. 16 A Chinese fisherman aboard a boat illegally fishing in South Korean waters in the Yellow Sea is shot dead by a South Korean Coast Guard officer during a raid.

Oct. 17 South Korean President Lee Myung-bak and Zambian President Michael Sata agree to work together to strengthen cooperation in resource development, construction and development assistance.

Oct. 18 President Lee Myung-bak visits the island of Yeonpyeong near the Yellow Sea border with the North.

Oct. 19 South Korea is elected as a non-permanent member of the U.N. Security Council.

Oct. 20 South Korea is selected as a host country of the secretariat of the United Nations climate fund.

• The Korean historical film "Gwanghae: the Man Who Became the King" surpasses the 10 million mark in attendance.

Oct. 21 Around 20,000 people gather at in Milan, Italy to show flash mob for "Gangnam Style" by South Korean rapper-singer Psy.

• Eight-time LPGA Tour winner Kim Mi-hyun of South Korea bids a teary farewell to competitive golf, after completing her final round at the LPGA KEB-HanaBank Championship on her home soil.

Oct. 23 The Global Green Growth Institute (GGGI), the Seoul-led international organization on green growth, is formally launched.

Oct. 24 South Korean Defense Minister Kim Kwan-jin and his American counterpart, Leon Panetta, reach the agreement in the annual Security Consultative Meeting (SCM) at the Pentagon.

• A group of South Koreans forcibly drafted into the Japanese workforce during its colonial rule of the Korean Peninsula decades ago launches a compensation suit against a Japanese firm.

• The King Sejong Institute Foundation, an organization overseeing the management and support of state-sponsored Korean language institutes all over the world, kicks off operations.

Oct. 25 The ruling Saenuri Party and minor Advancement and Unification Party (AUP) agree to merge.

Oct. 29 United Nations Secretary-General Ban Ki-moon receives Seoul Peace Prize.

Nov. 1 The Samsung Lions becomes champions of South Korean baseball in 2012.

Nov. 5 More than 20,000 people participate at a flashmob for Psy's "Gangnam Style' in Paris, France.

Nov. 6 Rep. Moon Jae-in of the main opposition Democratic United Party and independent candidate Ahn Cheol-soo announce a decision to field a unified contender before candidate registration.

Nov. 7 South Korean President Lee Myung-bak departs for Indonesia for a regional democracy forum. On Nov. 8 President Lee holds summit talks with Indonesian President Susilo Bambang Yudhoyono.

• A North Korean defector couple, Kim Kwang-hyok and his wife Ko Jong-nam, who fled to South Korea and lived here for about four years return to their homeland.

Nov. 10 South Korea's Ulsan Hyundai Tigers are crowned the Asian football club champion after beating Al Ahli of Saudi Arabia 3-0.

• South Korean President Lee Myung-bak holds summit talks with Thai Prime Minister Yingluck Shinawatra in Bangkok.

• Rapper Psy's international smash single "Gangnam Style" is certified by the United States record association as "double-platinum" for more than 2 million digital sales.

Nov. 11 South Korean pop phenomenon Psy receives a prize at the MTV Europe Music Awards (EMA) 2012 held in the western German city of Frankfurt.

Nov. 13 South Korea wins another term on the U.N. Human Rights Council.

Nov. 14 South Korea kicks off the inaugural meeting of a senior-level multilateral security forum, the Seoul Defense Dialogue (SDD).

• Special prosecutor Lee Kwang-bum decides against indicting President Lee Myung-bak's son Lee Si-hyung. He wraps up a month-long investigation into a land deal for Lee's now-scrapped retirement home project and refers tax records of the president's son to the National Tax Service (NTS) for possible donation tax imposition.

Nov. 15 A total of 462 people are indicted in connection with alleged irregularities in selecting a left-wing minor party's proportional candidates for April's parliamentary elections.

Nov. 16 Asiana Airlines Inc., South Korea's No. 2 flag carrier, launches a regular flight to the far eastern Russian city of Vladivostok.

Nov. 18 South Korean President Lee Myung-bak departs Cambodia for a series of international summits, including one involving the newly re-elected U.S. president, Barack Obama, about freer trade and other cooperation issues in the region.

Nov. 19 South Korea's pop sensation Psy is honored at the annual American Music Awards (AMA) for the massive cyber success of "Gangnam Style."

• South Korean Choi Na-yeon wins the final LPGA Tour event of the season, CME Group Titleholders at the TwinEagles Club in Naples, Florida.

Nov. 20 South Korea, China and Japan declare the start of free trade talks aimed at boosting their trade.

Nov. 21 South Korean President Lee Myung-bak arrives in the United Arab Emirates (UAE) for a summit with UAE President Sheikh Khalifa Bin Zayed Al Nahyan.

• South Korea achieves a landmark in tourism by attracting more than 10 million foreign tourists.

• FC Seoul clinches the championship for South Korea's top football league.

Nov. 22 An investigation is launched into allegations that a trainee prosecutor was found to have performed sexual acts with a suspect in her 40s while questioning her on suspicion of theft.

• Lone Star Funds files investor state dispute (ISD) arbitration claims against the South Korean government for losses related to its investment in Korea Exchange Bank (KEB).

Nov. 23 Independent presidential candidate Ahn Cheol-soo announces his abrupt withdrawal from the presidential campaign, endorsing Rep. Moon Jae-in of the main opposition Democratic United Party and clearing the way for a two-way race with ruling party hopeful Park Geun-hye in the Dec. 19 polls.

Nov. 24 The music video of "Gangnam Style" by South Korean singer-rapper Psy ranks first on YouTube's all-time list of most-viewed videos, by drawing 803.69 million hits.

• Jeju fully re-opens "Olle" tracking road in five years.

Nov. 27 South Korea's state-run Korea National Oil Corp. (KNOC) and STX Energy Co. agree to join hands in importing natural gas liquid (NGL) and crude oil from Canada.

Nov. 29 Top nuclear envoys of South Korea and China hold talks in Beijing and discuss the recent situation in North Korea. Lim Sung-nam, Seoul's chief negotiator to the six-party talks aimed at ending the North's nuclear ambitions, arrived in Beijing earlier in the day for a two-day trip and held talks with his Chinese counterpart Wu Dawei.

• The South Korean men's national football team is selected the National Team of the Year in the men's category by the Asian Football Confederation (AFC), with forward Lee Keun-ho winning the AFC Asian Player of the Year honors.

Nov. 30 Veteran pitcher Park Chan-ho announces his retirement.

• Prosecutor General Han Sang-dae offers to resign after senior prosecutors refused to comply with his instructions following a string of disgraceful scandals within the powerful investigative body.

Dec. 1 Four South Korean sailors are set free more than 19 months after they were seized by Somali pirates, after paying an unspecified amount of ransom.

• North Korea says it will launch a long-range rocket within weeks.

Dec. 2 Lee Chun-sang, a close aide to Park Geun-hye, the presidential candidate of the ruling Saenuri Party, dies in a car accident on the campaign trail in the eastern city of Hongcheon, with five others being injured.

Dec. 3 FIFA, the international governing body of football, suspends South Korean player Park Jong-woo for two international matches over "Dokdo ceremony," his celebration of the country's bronze medal at the London Olympics.

Dec. 4 South Korean President Lee Myung-bak and Pakistan's President Asif Ali Zardari agree to bolster all-round economic cooperation between the two countries.

• South Korean golfer Lee Dong-hwan becomes the first Asian to finish in sole possession of first place at the PGA Tour's qualifying tournament.

Dec. 5 Samsung Group promotes Lee Jae-yong to vice chairman of Samsung Electronics Co.

• Korea's traditional folk song "Arirang" is added to UNESCO's intangible cultural heritage list.

Dec. 6 Former independent presidential candidate Ahn Cheol-soo joins forces with the main opposition candidate Moon Jae-in.

Dec. 9 South Korean figure skater Kim Yu-na wins victory in her season debut at the NRW Trophy in Germany after sitting out the past one and a half years.

Dec. 10 South Korean All-Star pitcher Ryu Hyun-jin signs with the Los Angeles Dodgers in Major League Baseball (MLB).

Dec. 11 Presidents of nine clubs in the Korea Baseball Organization (KBO) give the green light to add a 10th team to their league at a board meeting.

Dec. 12 North Korea fires off what it claimed was a rocket carrying a satellite, defying international pressure to call off the provocative act.

• South Korean outfielder Choo Shin-soo of the Cleveland Indians in Major League Baseball (MLB) is traded to the Cincinnati Reds.

Dec. 13 South Korean President Lee Myung-bak and Greenland's Premier Kuupik Kleist agree to work closely together for an environment-friendly development of the resources-rich Arctic nation.

Dec. 14 Three construction workers are killed and 11 others missing when a barge laden with a crane capsized off South Korea's southeast coast.

Dec. 15 Three North Korean fishermen found drifting aboard a small boat in South Korean waters are sent back to their communist homeland.

Dec. 17 Four South Korean workers and a Nigerian are abducted by an unidentified armed group at a Korean company's construction site in southern Nigeria.

Dec. 19 Voting begins for South Korea's presidential election with the outcome of the race between ruling Saenuri Party candidate Park Geun-hye and main opposition rival Moon Jae-in.

Dec. 20 Park Geun-hye wins the tightly contested South Korean presidential race.

• Hong Joon-pyo, the former chief of the conservative ruling party, wins a by-election for the governor of South Gyeongsang Province.

• Moon Yong-lin, the former conservative-leaning education minister, is elected Seoul city education superintendent in a by-election.

Dec. 21 North Korea confirms it was holding a U.S. citizen for a "crime" he has admitted committing against the communist country while leading a tour group there. "American citizen Pae Jun Ho who entered Rason City of the DPRK on Nov. 3 for the purpose of tour committed a crime against the DPRK. He was put into custody by a relevant institution," the North's Korean Central News Agency (KCNA) says.

Dec. 22 All four South Korean workers who were abducted earlier this week in Nigeria are released.

• The music video of "Gangnam Style" by South Korean singer-rapper Psy becomes the world's first-ever to get more than 1 billion views on YouTube.

Dec. 26 The National Museum of Korean Contemporary History opens its doors in a ceremony attended by President Lee Myung-bak.

Dec. 27 President-elect Park Geun-hye names Kim Yong-joon, a former Constitutional Court chief to lead her transition team.

• Mount Mudeung, the most famous landmark of the southwestern city of Gwangju, is designated as South Korea's 21st national park.

Dec. 28 The main opposition Democratic United Party (DUP) picks a three-term lawmaker, Rep. Park Ki-choon, as its floor leader.

Dec. 30 Hwang Soo-kwan, a medical doctor known widely for his trademark smile therapy, dies at age 67.

Dec. 31 U.S. Internet company Yahoo Inc. halts its South Korean service, pulling out of one of the world's most wired countries after 15 years.

2013

Jan. 5 Kim Tae-chon, former boss of South Korea's noted criminal syndicates in the 1970s and 1980s dies in hospital at age 64.

Jan. 6 Presidential transition team officially starts work.

Jan. 7 South Korean Army sets up new unit that will conduct humanitarian, rebuilding operations in Sudan

• Google's executive chairman, Eric Schmit visits North Korea.

Jan. 8 Dongbu Group buys Daewoo Electronics for 272.6 billion won.

Jan. 12 People near Gyeongju evacuated after 200 tons of hydrochloric acid is accidentally released into the environment at a silicon plant.

Jan. 14 Agency for Defense Development(ADD) develops kit that turns "dumb bombs" into smart munitions using GPS technology.

Jan. 15 Presidential transition team announces a 17-ministry structure for the incoming government, adding two new ministries to the current make-up and establishing a vice premiership for economic affairs.

• Defense Acquisition Program Administration(DAPA) picks "Lynx Wildcat" as winner of the Navy's multi-purpose helicopter program.

Jan. 16 South Korea's top court confirmed life imprisonment for a Korean-Chinese man for kidnapping and killing a woman in Suwon.

Jan. 17 South Korean groups in U.S. start petition campaign for dual names for East Sea.

Jan. 19 SK Innovation enters electric car battery business.

Jan. 20 Total number of foreign students who have taken Korean language proficiency tests surpass 1 million mark.

• Hyundai Heavy Industries wins US$1.1 billion marine plant order from Norway.

Jan. 21 President-elect Park Geun-hye outlines plans to reorganize presidential staff and creates new national security office.

• Escaped North Korean national who worked as Seoul city official arrested for espionage.

Jan. 22 President Lee Myung-bak vetoes legislation classifying taxis as part of the country's public transportation system.

Jan. 23 North Korea's foreign ministry says it will scrap all denuclearization talks.

Jan. 24 Court posthumously acquits activist Chang Joon-ha imprisoned for campaigning against the military regime of late President Park Chung-hee.

• Lee Sang-deuk, an elder brother of President Lee Myung-bak, is sentenced to two years in prison and ordered to pay a fine of 750 million won for receiving a massive amount of bribes.

Jan. 26 Psy wins recognition at NRJ Music Award in Caen, France.

Jan. 27 Samsung Electronics recognized as world's largest mobile phone maker in 2012, overtaking Nokia. The electronics giant sold 470 million units in the one year period.

Jan. 28 Myanmar opposition leader Aung San Suu Kyi visits South Korea for first time.

Jan. 29 The 10th Special Olympics World Winter Games kicks off in PyeongChang, an alpine town some 180 kilometers east of Seoul and the chosen host for 2018 Winter Olympics. About 3,000 athletes from 106 countries participated in seven sports, such as snowboarding, alpine skiing and figure skating, and one demonstration sport, floorball. The event ran through Feb. 5.

Jan. 30 South Korea successfully launches its first-ever space rocket, the Korea Space Launch Vehicle-1 (KSLV-1), also known as Naro. The satellite carried by the rocket was later confirmed to have entered its intended orbit.

Feb. 1 Myanmar opposition leader Aung San Suu Kyi pays respects at the May 18 Democracy Movement Cemetery in Gwangju.

Feb. 4 South Korean and Chinese chief delegates of six party talks meet in Beijing. China reaffirms commitment to a nuclear-free Korean Peninsula.

Feb. 5 South Korea and Saudi Arabia sign defense cooperation agreement.

Feb. 7 South Korean and U.S. Marine Corps conduct first-ever winter military drills in Gangwon Province.

Feb. 8 President-elect Park Geun-hye taps Chung Hong-won to become her first prime minister. She also picks presidential security chief and appoints Kim Jang-soo, a retired four-star army general as head of the national security office.

Feb. 11 North Korea informs U.S., China and Russia in advance of its plan to conduct its third nuclear test.

Feb. 12 North Korea carries out its third nuclear test.

• International Olympic Committee decides to give South Korean footballer Park Jong-woo his bronze medal despite carrying out Dokdo ceremony during an Olympic football match against Japan in London.

Feb. 13 Defense ministry says it has deployed ship-to-shore missiles with 500 kilometer range.

Feb. 14 National Assembly adopt motion condemning North Korea's nuclear test.

Feb. 18 Gov't regulator revises law that will ban the collection and use of citizens' identification numbers on the Internet.

• President-elect Park Geun-hye names her close political ally and former three-term lawmaker Huh Tae-yeol as presidential chief of staff.

Feb. 19 President Lee Myung-bak holds farewell address at presidential office.

• Opposition leader Rhyu Si-min announces his retirement from politics.

Feb. 20 Court finds former head of police guilty of slandering late President Roh Moo-hyun by claiming that he had opened bank account under false name to hide slush funds.

Feb. 21 South Korea and Columbia formally sign free trade agreement.

Feb. 23 Unified Progressive Party picks Lee Jung-hee as new leader.

Feb. 24 Park In-bee wins Honda LPGA match in Thailand.

Feb. 25 Park Geun-hye, the daughter of former President Park Chung-hee, is inaugurated as South Korea's 18th president, becoming the first female leader.

Feb. 26 Chung Hong-won is sworn in as 42nd prime minister.

Feb. 27 Samsung Electronics sweeps all five awards related to mobile phones at the Mobile World Congress (MWC) in Barcelona, Spain.

March 2 New government appoints Nam Jae-joon as head of National Intelligence Service.

March 3 Rhythmic gymnast Son Yeon-jae wins bronze at Moscow Grand Prix.

March 4 Ssangyong E&C enters workout program.

March 5 North Korea declares null-and-void the armistice agreement that halted the Korean War (1950-53).

March 6 South Korea imports Chilean beef for the first time.

March 7 62.9 percent of women in their 20s are engaged in economic activities. Surpassing numbers for men for the first time.

March 8 North Korea announces it is discarding South-North non-aggression pact. Cuts off Red Cross communication lines that runs through the truce village of Panmunjom.

March 10 Authorities take legal action against 119 doctors who received rebates from Dong A Pharmaceutical.

March 14 Supreme Court acquits Han Myeong-sook, former prime minister of taking bribes.

March 17 Lawmakers agree on new government structure under Park Geun-hye administration.

• Kim Yu-na wins ISU senior event in singles event in Canada.

March 18 Defense minister meets the U.S. Deputy Secretary of Defense Ashton Carter and gets assurances that South Korea will receive top priority in terms of military manpower despite sequestering.

March 19 US B-52s conduct mock bombing runs over Korean Peninsula.

• Prosecutors raid the headquarters of the Korea Exchange Bank to investigate allegations that it deliberately raised lending rates for smaller firms to rake in profits totaling over 18 billion won

March 20 Computer networks at TV stations and banks crash. Police track source.

• U.S. nuclear-powered submarine USS Cheyenne takes part in South Korea-U.S. naval exercise.

March 21 Lawmakers agree on government reorganization.

• Constitutional Court rules emergency decree carried out under Yushin era are unconstitutional.

• KEPCO wins a US$2.3 billion deal to build a 1.2 million kilowatt coal-fired thermal power plant in Vietnam.

March 22 The National Assembly passes government reorganization bill.

• South Korea and U.S. seal the deal that would allow "automatic involvement" of U.S. forces in the event of a South-North Korea clash in the Yellow Sea.

• Acid leak reported at SK hynix plant in Cheongju.

March 23 France's first ethnic Korean cabinet minister Fleur Pellerin visits South Korea.

March 24 KT and Daewoo International Corp win a 23 billion won project to build a broadband network in Poland.

March 25 Police determine malignant computer codes that cause network crash on March 20 originated from IP addresses in the United States, Europe and two other countries. Computer virus companies detect a mutated virus.

• South Korea's single largest solar power generation plant opens for operations.

March 26 South Korea and China hold first FTA talks in Seoul.

• Seoul strongly protests move by Tokyo to include "Dokdo issue" in Japanese highschool textbooks and calls on Japan to fundamentally change its stance on its unfounded claims to the islets.

• Computer networks crash across the country. Authorities try to determine cause.

March 27 Fair Trade Commission start probe on companies that won four rivers refurbishment projects.

• The Financial Supervisory Service(FSS) starts special probe into computer net crash at five financial institutions under Shinhan Bank and Nong-hyup.

• Next generation bullet train HEMU-430x reaches top speed of 401.4 kilometers per hour.

• Seoul city opens first tourism fair in Paris France.

• North Korea says it will sever military hotlines with South Korea and halt military liaison operations.

March 28 Two U.S. B-2 stealth bombers conduct bombing drills over Korean Peninsula.

• Samsung Medical Center in Seoul opens first departments specializing in treating seriously ill patients.

March 29 Gov't launches special fund to help relieve debts incurred by low income earners.

• South Korea completes development of Surion helicopter, making it the 11th country in the world to build its own rotary aircraft.

March 30 Presidential Cheong Wa Dae apologizes for confusion over its selection of senior government officials and pledges to strengthen screening process for government appointees.

March 31 South Korean Curling team wins rights to participate in 2014 Winter Olympics in Sochi.

April 1 Government announces new real estate policy aimed at easing the tax burden for people selling and buying homes.

• North Korea names Pak Pong-ju as new prime minister.

April 2 North Korea declares it will re-start the 5 megawatt graphite moderated nuclear reactor at Yongbyon that was shut down as a result of the six-party talks in 2007.

• The main structure of the 1,200-year-old Buddhist Seokga Pagoda at Bulguk Temple is disassembled for repairs. This was the first exposure of the compartment in 47 years since its last repair in 1966.

April 3 North Korea halts movement into Kaesong Industrial Complex.

April 4 North Korea's Internet propaganda site Uriminzokkiri has been hacked, Anonymous international claims credit.

• U.S. stations chemical warfare battalion in South Korea.

April 5 National Assembly Speaker Kang Chang-hee visits Mexico City to attend the 4th G20 Speaker' Consultation Forum 2013.

April 6 Anonymous international releases names of 6,216 members of Uriminzokkiri site.

• Psy's Gangnam Style generates 1.5 billion hits on Youtube.

April 7 Rhythmic gymnast Son Yeonjae wins bronze at FIG World Cup in Lisbon.

April 8 North Korea says it will shut down Kaesong Industrial Complex, pull out all of its workers.

• KORAIL decides to scrap Yongsan international district project.

April 9 All operations at Kaesong Industrial Complex comes to a halt. 53,000 North Korean workers fail to report to work.

April 10 South Korea and U.S. set Watch Condition 2 as North Korea intensifies saber rattling.

• Seoul claims the March 20 hacking attack was perpetrated by North Korea.

April 11 President Park Geun-hye proposes to North Korea that government-level talks be held to resolve Kaesong Industrial Complex shutdown.

• Hyundai Motor Co. and its affiliate Kia Motors Corp. recall 160,000 cars for problems with brake light switches.

April 12 President Park Geun-hye meets U.S. Secretary of State John Kerry at Cheong Wa Dae and discusses North Korean provocations.

April 13 Psy's new single "Gentleman" is released in 119 countries. Psy holds a concert titled "Happening" at a football stadium in western Seoul.

April 16 Lawmakers agree on government's April 1 real-estate policy initiative that calls for tax cuts in the buying and selling of homes.

• Anonymous International releases names of people that have accounts with North Korean Internet site Paekdu-Hanna.com.

April 17 The Defense Acquisition Program Administration picks the Apache (AH-64E) as South Korea's large attack helicopter. Delivery to begin in 2016 with the last of the 36 choppers to be operational by 2018.

April 18 Police announce findings on

Internet meddling by country's spy agency in 2012 presidential elections. Recommends three agents be charged for illegal activities.

April 22 President Park Geun-hye meets Bill Gates at Cheong Wa Dae.

• Law extending retirement age to 60 passes National Assembly sub-committee. To go into effect in 2016 for businesses with more than 300 employees.

April 23 Music star Cho Yong-pil holds concert at Seoul's Olympic Park to launch his 19th singles album.

April 24 By-elections are held in 12 areas around the country. Independent Ahn Cheol-soo is elected to a parliamentary seat in Seoul.

April 25 Unification Ministry proposes formal talks to reopen Kaesong Industrial Complex. Warns that if the North rejects, it will take grave measures.

April 26 North Korea rejects Kaesong complex talks. Seoul makes decision to pull all workers out of Kaesong Complex.

April 27 126 people at Kaesong Complex return home across DMZ.

• North Korea says Kenneth Bae to be tried by high court for subversive activities.

April 29 National Assembly adopt resolution condemning visit to war shrine by Japanese Cabinet ministers.

• State prosecutors summon former National Intelligence Service (NIS) chief for questioning for his alleged involvement in presidential election meddling.

April 30 43 people at Kaesong Complex return home, seven remain to handle outstanding pay, utility charge issues.

• Parliament passes law raising retirement age to 60.

• State prosecutors raid National Intelligence Service (NIS) to gather evidence on election meddling.

May 1 South Korea's free trade agreement (FTA) with Turkey goes into effect.

May 4 President Park Geun-hye celebrates the reopening of Sungnyemun, an ancient gate in central Seoul, that was destroyed in an arson attack more than five years ago, saying it signifies a path to a new era.

May 5 President Park Geun-hye arrives in New York on the first stop of a visit to the United States that will culminate in a summit with President Barack Obama which is expected focus on how to deal with North Korea.

May 7 President Park Geun-hye meets with South Korean-born U.N. Secretary-General Ban Ki-moon in New York to discuss a range of issues, including North Korea's nuclear program.

May 8 President Park Geun-hye meets with U.S. President Barack Obama in Washington, vowing not to tolerate North Korean threats and provocations. They warned that any bad behavior by North Korea would only deepen its isolation.

May 9 The Bank of Korea lowers the benchmark seven-day repo rate by a quarter percentage point to a two-year low of 2.5 percent for May.

May 10 President Park Geun-hye fires her spokesman, Yoon Chang-joong, who got engulfed in a sex scandal during her official visit to the U.S. The spokesman allegedly assaulted a young Korean-American woman who worked for him during the U.S. trip.

May 11 The U.S. nuclear-powered aircraft carrier USS Nimitz arrives in South Korea to participate in joint naval drills.

May 15 South Korea gains permanent observer status at the Arctic Council.

• Prosecutors raid the offices of nearly 30 local builders as part of a probe into corruption allegations surrounding the previous administration's highly controversial project to refurbish the country's four major rivers.

May 17 South Korean Prime Minister Chung Hong-won arrives in Thailand to participate the 2nd Asia-Pacific Water Summit.

May 19 North Korea fires a projectile off the Korean Peninsula's east coast, a day after it launched three short-range projectiles into the East Sea.

May 20 South Korean rapper Psy wins the award for the most viewed online video at the Billboard Music Awards 2013.

• South Korean mountaineer Kim Chang-ho climbs all 14 Himalayan peaks of more than 8,000 meters without oxygen tanks, becoming the first from his country to do so and setting a world record for completing the climbs in the shortest span of time.

May 21 The government says it will bail out some delinquent borrowers from the 1997-98 Asian financial crisis as part of its program to ease the financial burden of the underprivileged.

May 23 Three Japanese activists, including historians, claim Dokdo belongs to South Korea after visiting South Korea's easternmost islets.

May 25 Artist Hong Kyung-taek's work sold for 6.63 Hong Kong dollars at Christie's evening sales held in Hong Kong, marking the highest amount for a South Korean piece.

May 27 Laos sends nine North Koreans who fled their totalitarian homeland through China last month back to China.

May 28 The nuclear safety commission halts the operation of two nuclear reactors -the Shin Kori Reactor 2 and Shin Wolsong Reactor 1, - while also suspending the scheduled operation of two other reactors for substandard parts used in the reactors.

May 29 South Gyeongsang Province closes the 103-year-old Jinju Medical Center in Jinju, 434 kilometers south of Seoul, despite fierce protests from unionized workers and opposition parties.

May 30 South Korean President Park Geun-hye pledges to expand development cooperation for Uganda to help modernize its economy as she held her first summit at home since taking office in a symbolic outreach to resources-rich Africa.

June 1 South Korean Defense Minister Kim Kwan-jin agrees with his U.S. counterpart to maintain their combined military posture even after the current joint body is dissolved December, 2015 when the wartime operational control (OPCON) of South Korean troops is transferred from the U.S. to South Korea. They met on the sidelines of the Shangri-La Dialogue in Singapore.

June 2 South Korea's Environment Ministry rolls out volume-rate food waste disposal system, adopts the radio frequency identification tag (RFID) system.

June 4 South Korean President Park Geun-hye holds a summit with Mozambique's President Armando Guebuza, focuses on expanding economic cooperation with the African nation.

June 7 Son Yeon-jae wins the individual all-around final at the Asian Rhythmic Gymnastics Championships in Tashkent, Uzbekistan, becoming the first South Korean to win gold at any international event for rhythmic gymnastics.

June 9 South Korea and North Korea holds their first government-level talks in years at the truce village of Panmunjom.

June 10 South Korea and North Korea agrees to hold two-day, high-level talks. Seoul requests the North's United Front Department chief, Kim Yang-gon, to visit South Korea.

June 11 A High-level inter-Korean meeting was called off due to disagreement over the level of their respective chief delegates.

June 13 South Korean Foreign Minister Yun Byung-se leaves for Indonesia to attend a forum of East Asian and Latin American countries.

June 14 Prosecutors indict Won Sei-hoon, the former head of the National Intelligence Service (NIS), on charges of meddling in the 2012 presidential election.

June 15 South Korea's daily newspaper Hankook Ilbo closes down its editorial office, prints downsized editions as its reporters protest against the head's alleged embezzlement.

June 17 The 49th International Insurance Society (IIS) seminar kicks off in Seoul to discuss future strategies on the impact of the aging population and development in technology

June 18 South Korean President Park Geun-hye meets Facebook CEO Mark Zuckerberg, discusses on "creative economy" vision.

• South Korea loses to Iran 1-0 but still advances to the FIFA World Cup finals for the eighth consecutive time. Despite the defeat at Munsu Football Stadium in Ulsan, South Korea secured the four automatic Asian berths to football's global extravaganza in Brazil 2014.

June 19 South Korean President Park Geun-hye President vows to drastically advance government services in an effort to meet the individual needs of the citizens, upgrading her government to version "3.0"

June 21 Cho Tae-yong, Seoul's chief negotiator to the stalled six-party talks, arrives in Beijing for talks with his Chinese counterpart, Wu Dawei, as North Korea expressed its willingness to rejoin talks to resolve its nuclear standoff.

June 23 The 37th session of UNESCO's World Heritage Committee adds historic sites in North Korea's ancient city of Kaesong to the world heritage list of UNESCO.

June 24 The National Intelligence Service (NIS) releases an inter-Korean summit script to ruling Saenuri Party lawmakers, in which the late South Korean President Roh Moo-hyun allegedly called for transforming the disputed Yellow Sea border with North Korea into a "peace-economy zone." Roh met with the then North Korean leader, Kim Jong-il, in Pyongyang in 2007.

June 25 Unidentified hackers attack the websites of South Korea's presidential office, stealing some 100,000 pieces of personal data.

June 26 Samsung Electronics Co. launches the world's first long-term evolution advanced (LTE-A) smartphone, the Galaxy S4 LTE-A.

June 27 South Korean President Park Geun-hye and Chinese President Xi Jinping agree that a nuclear-armed North Korea is unacceptable "under any circumstances" and that ending the North's atomic program serves the national interests of Seoul and Beijing.

June 28 South Korean President Park Geun-hye meets one-on-one with Chinese Premier Li Keqiang and Zhang Dejiang, chairman of the Standing Committee of the National People's Congress, during her trip to Beijing.

June 29 South Korean President Park Geun-hye delivers a speech at Beijing's Tsinghua University, calling for closer relations between the two countries

July 1 The Korea New Exchange (KONEX) market kicks off with the aim of fostering the growth of young venture firms and lend support to the government's "creative economy" vision.

July 2 The National Assembly passes a proposal calling for disclosure of an inter-Korean summit transcript that allegedly contain the late South Korean President Roh Moo-hyun's controversial remarks on the disputed Yellow Sea border with North Korea. Roh visited the North in 2007 for a summit with the then North's leader, Kim Jong-il.

July 3 The Seoul High Court finds the late President Kim Dae-jung, a liberal icon, not guilty in a retrial 36 years after he was imprisoned for campaigning against the military-backed regime led by then President Park Chung-hee.

July 4 The foreign and defense ministers from South Korea and Australia hold their first joint security dialogue in Seoul.

July 5 South Korean Foreign Minister Yun Byung-se and U.S. Secretary of Homeland Security Janet Napolitano hold talks in Seoul.

July 7 South and North Korea agrees in principle to normalize operations at their joint industrial complex in the North's border city of Kaesong. The factory zone has been idle for nearly three months after the North unilaterally withdrew all of its 40,000 nationals working for South Korean companies there.

• An Asiana Airlines passenger jet carrying 307 people crashes upon landing at San Francisco International Airport, killing three people and injuring 180 others.

July 9 South Korea's 25-member advance party for working-level government talks aimed at normalizing the inter-Korean industrial complex crosses the demarcation line that separates the two Koreas.

July 10 The two Koreas end a new round of working-level talks without agreement on detailed measures to reopen a joint industrial complex that has remained shut for more than three months.

• The Seoul Central District Court orders Nobuyuki Suzuki, the member of an ultra-right Japanese party, to provide compensation for defaming Yun Bonggil, a deceased Korean independent activist during the Japanese colonial rule of Korea, in the early part of the 20th century. During his visit to Seoul, the Japanese planted a wooden post next to Yun's monument in an anti-Korean gesture.

July 11 North Korea puts a hold on its proposal to resume programs to reunite families who remain separated since the Korean War and restart a cross-border South Korean sightseeing tour.

• Rep. Hong Ihk-pyo of the Democratic Party, describes the late father of President Park Geun-hye as "gwitae" or a "baby born to a ghost," meaning he should not have been born.

July 12 South Korea's top court partly reverses a lower court ruling that said two U.S. producers of Agent Organge should compensate most of the South Korean Vietnam War veterans who sued the firms, claiming that they are victims of the toxic chemical.

July 15 A team of lawmakers from the ruling and opposition parties begins a review of classified presidential records to verify what late former President Roh Moo-hyun said about the western sea border during his 2007 summit with North Korea.

July 17 South Korea requests another delay in its schedule to regain the wartime operational control (OPCON) of its troops from the United States in the event of war.

July 18 The defense ministry abolishes a controversial unit composed of the so-called "entertainment soldiers" as criticism grew over special treatment of them under a lax system.

July 19 The South Korean metropolitan city of Gwangju is selected as the host of the 2019 World Swimming Championships. However, controversy rises as its mayor allegedly forged the signatures of former Prime Minister Kim Hwang-sik and former Culture Minister Choe Kwang-sik in a document guaranteeing the central government's financial support.

July 20 South Korea's western port city of Incheon is chosen to be the World Book Capital for 2015 by the United Nations Educational, Scientific and Cultural Organization (UNESCO).

July 21 U.S. law enforcement authorities mulls over seeking an arrest warrant for Yoon Chang-joong, the disgraced former spokesman of President Park Geun-hye in connection with his alleged involvement in a high-profile sex scandal.

July 22 The ruling and main opposition parties fail to locate a transcript of South Korea's 2007 summit with North Korea, fueling tensions over who is to blame for the missing document.

July 23 Kim Jong-hak, a well-known 62-year-old TV producer-director whose credits include the '90s smash-hit soap opera "Sandglass," is found dead in an apparent suicide.

July 24 State prosecutors raid the offices of some 30 companies suspected of having been involved in the provision of substandard nuclear reactor parts by falsifying quality warranties.

July 25 South Korea and France agree to ramp up efforts to boost bilateral trade and investment by building a close cooperative network.

• Samsung C&T Corp., a construction and trading arm of Samsung Group, wins a US$225 million order from the Singapore government to build a subway section in the city-state's downtown.

July 26 South Korea President Park Geun-hye holds a summit with New Zealand Prime Minister John Key, discusses issues related to North Korea and ways to bolster bilateral exchanges.

• A 45-year-old male rights activist Sung Jae-gi committed suicide by jumping into the Han River off the Mapo Bridge in western Seoul. A declared anti-feminist, he has led a campaign against South Korean laws which he believed are unfairly favorable to women and advocated equal treatment of men.

July 28 South Korea says it will make a "final offer" to North Korea for talks on normalizing a suspended joint industrial complex in the North's border city of Kaesong.

July 29 SK Engineering & Construction Co., one of South Korea's leading builders, wins a US$417 million order to build a jetty and a seabed oil pipeline in Vietnam.

July 30 Samsung C&T Corp., a major South Korean builder, wins a 2.2 trillion won (US$2 billion) order to build three subway sections in Riyadh.

July 31 South Korean rapper Psy's music video, "Gentleman," surpasses the 500 million view mark on YouTube.

Aug 1 The main opposition Democratic Party (DP) launches an all-out campaign calling on the ruling party to cooperate in a deadlocked parliamentary investigation into the state spy agency's alleged meddling in last year's presidential election.

Aug. 4 The South Korean Navy's anti-piracy unit in Somalia rescues 11 foreign sailors who were drifting near the Gulf of Aden.

Aug. 5 Hyundai Heavy Industries Co., the world's top shipbuilder, clinches a US$3.3 billion deal to build a power plant in Saudi Arabia.

Aug. 6 Samsung Electronics Co. begins mass production of what it claims is an industry first, three-dimensional Vertical NAND flash memory chip.

Aug. 7 The government authorizes 280.9 billion won in insurance payments to South Korean companies that have factories at the inter-Korean industrial complex in North Korea's border city of Kaesong. The factory zone remains closed for four months after North Korea unilaterally withdrew all of its 40,000 workers hired by South Korean plants there.

Aug. 8 The government rolls out a new tax reform package, expanding burdens for those earning more than 300 million won a year and imposing taxes on earnings by monks, priests and other religious leaders starting in 2015.

Aug. 10 South Korean A-lister Lee Byung-hun marries actress Lee Min-jung at the Grand Hyatt Hotel in central Seoul.

Aug. 11 North Korea reveals its own touch smartphone, named Arirang.

Aug. 12 South Korea shuts down air-conditioning at all government and public office buildings in the face of a possible power shortage that could cause a nationwide blackout.

Aug. 13 South Korea's Navy launches its fourth 1,800-ton Type 214 submarine as part of efforts to boost its underwater warfare capabilities against North Korean submarines. The ship, named after Korea's famous independence fighter Kim Jwa-jin (1889-1930), is the fourth of its kind in operation since 2010.

Aug. 14 South and North Korea agree to reopen their troubled joint factory park in the North's border city of Kaesong after Pyongyang promised not to shut it down again "under any circumstances."

Aug. 20 South Korea proposes to North Korea that both sides hold talks in late September for discussions on possible ways to resume suspended tours to Mount Kumgang in North Korea after staging another round of separated family reunions.

Aug. 22 South Korean businessmen visit an inter-Korean joint factory zone in North Korea's border city of Kaesong to check the condition of their plants there. Expectations are high that the complex may reopen soon after several months of closure.

Aug. 25 South Korea's icebreaker Araon commences its travel across the U.S. exclusive economic zone in the Artic Ocean.

Aug. 26 South Korean President Park Geun-hye meets visiting U.S. Senators John McCain and Sheldon Whitehouse, and Rep. Charles Rangel to discuss a range of bilateral issues.

• South Korean movies attract a record number of 20.44 million viewers in August as several big hits dominated the local box office.

Aug. 29 The National Intelligence Service raids the homes and offices of Rep. Lee Seok-ki of the minor opposition Unified Progressive Party charged with plotting to overthrow the Seoul government in the event of an inter-Korean war.

Aug. 30 Maeil Business Newspaper rolls out the country's first pay-online newspaper, providing the service to PC and mobile devices for 15,000 won a month.

Aug. 31 Two passenger trains, involving a KTX bullet train and a Mugung-wha passenger train, collide near Daegu Station, disrupting rail traffic between Seoul and Busan.

Sept. 1 South Korea's pop diva Lee Hyori marries a guitarist on the resort island of Jeju.

Sept. 3 The United States officially returns a century-old currency printing plate to the South Korean government, 62 years after it was illegally taken to the United States during the 1950-53 Korean War.

Sept. 4 The National Intelligency Agency arrests Rep. Lee Seok-ki of the minor opposition Unified Progressive Party on charges of plotting to overthrow the government, putting it a step closer to launching a prosecution probe into the scandal.

• Former President Roh Tae-woo,

convicted of bribery while in office, pays off the remainder of his unpaid fines amounting to 23 billion won.

Sept. 5 South Korean President Park Geun-hye meets U.N. Secretary-General Ban Ki-moon on the sidelines of the G20 summit in Russia. The topics include the crisis in Syria and other global and regional issues.

Sept. 6 South Korean President Park Geun-hye meets Russian President Vladimir Putin for the first time. The topics focus on economic cooperation.

• South and North Korea restore a military hotline as the two sides work toward reopening a shuttered joint industrial park.

Sept. 7 Film director and producer Kimjo Gwang-soo, 48, and 29-year-old Kim Seung-hwan, the head of gay film distributor Rainbow Factory, get married in a plaza near Cheonggye Stream in downtown Seoul with about 1,000 guests and citizens in attendance.

Sept. 8 South Korean President Park Geun-hye arrives in Vietnam for a five-day state visit that she plans to use as the starting point for her "sales diplomacy" drive.

Sept. 9 South Korean President Park Geun-hye meets Vietnamese President Truong Tan Sang. The topics include economic cooperation and development aid projects for Vietnam.

Sept. 10 Two T-50i trainer jets fly to Indonesia in the country's first export of the supersonic trainer, two years after Korea Aerospace Industries Ltd. signed a US$400 million deal to export 16 T-50i trainer jets to the country.

Sept. 11 South and North Korea agree to reopen their shuttered joint industrial complex in the North's border city of Kaesong after a five-month hiatus.

• South Korea unveils its first indigenous 3,500-ton amphibious landing ship, named after Cheonwangbong, the highest peak of Mount Jiri. The ship will be deployed during the Navy's landing and transportation operations in 2015.

Sept. 13 South Korea and North Korea exchange lists of candidates who will take part in planned separated family reunions. The reunions, if held, will be the first of their kind in three years.

Sept. 15 Binggrae Co. opens its first overseas branch in Brazil.

Sept. 16 The Kaesong Industrial Complex begins its trial-run production after a five-month hiatus, as the two Koreas discuss ways to ensure sustainable growth of the joint economic venture.

Sept. 17 North Korea's First Vice Foreign Minister Kim Kye-gwan arrives in Beijing to meet his Chinese counterpart Wu Dawe. Both sides say they share views on ways to resume the six-party talks on ending the Norths' nuclear weapons program.

Sept. 20 The Los Angeles County Museum of Art decides to return a seal used by a queen of Korea's Joseon Dynasty (1392-1910) after confirming it was stolen by an American soldier during the 1950-53 Korean War.

Sept. 21 North Korea unilaterally postpones the planned reunions of separated family members, citing what it called Seoul's confrontational policy.

Sept. 22 POSCO signs a preliminary deal with China's Chongqing Iron & Steel Co. to build a steel mill in the world's second-largest economy.

Sept. 23 Yeoju-gun of Gyeonggi Province earns city status.

Sept. 24 South Korea decides not to select Boeing's F-15SE as its next-generation fighter jet amid concerns that the sole-remaining candidate for the 8.3 trillion won project is not suitable as it lacks stealth features.

• State prosecutors indict a total of 22 incumbent and former executives of 11 major local builders on charges of collusion in the former Lee Myung-bak administration's highly controversial project to refurbish the country's four major rivers.

Sept. 25 State prosecutors begins reclaiming illegally taken wealth by former President Chun Doo-hwan, weeks after he pledged to return the money to the country.

Sept. 26 A South Korean F-5 fighter jet crashes into a mountain in the central part of the country, with the pilot ejecting safely just before impact.

Sept. 27 Health and Welfare Minister Chin Young offers his resignation, holding himself responsible for the government's scaled-back pension plan for senior citizens.

Sept. 28 Culture ministers of South Korea, China, and Japan gather in South Korea's southern city of Gwangju, hold meeting to forge deeper ties in the cultural sector.

Sept. 29 U.S. Secretary of Defense Chuck Hagel arrives in Seoul for an unprecedentedly long, four-day visit to the Asian ally that will include annual talks with his South Korean counterpart and a visit to the border with North Korea.

Sept. 30 Gen. Jung Seung-jo, the chairman of South Korea's Joint Chiefs of Staff, and his U.S. counterpart, Gen. Martin Dempsey, hold a meeting, discusses the timing of the planned transition of wartime operational control (OPCON) of South Korean troops to Seoul in response to rising North Korean nuclear threats.

• South Korea's No. 1 conglomerate Samsung Group inks a memorandum of understanding with the Vietnamese government to cooperate in the fields of power generation, city development, shipbuilding and telecommunications.

Oct. 1 South Korea stages a massive military parade for the first time in five years in downtown Seoul as part of programs marking the 65th Armed Forces Day. About 4,500 soldiers and 105 pieces of military hardware took part.

Shooter Jung Yoo-jin wins a gold medal and sets a new South Korean record by winning 586 points at a 10-meter event at the 29th National Competition of Korea Shooting Federation.

Oct. 2 The South Korea-U.S. Security Consultative Meeting (SCM) kicks off in Seoul, with the allies focusing on ways to curb North Korean nuclear threats and weapons of mass destruction (WMD). The allies also agreed to conclude on going talks on the issue of the proposed transfer of the wartime operational control of South korean troops by the first half of 2014.

• Prosecutors conclude that the missing transcript of the 2007 inter-Korean summit had been filed with the presidential office's electronic archives following the summit, but was later deleted.

Oct. 4 South Korean women forced to work in poor working conditions at a Japanese company during World War II testify before a local court for the first

time in 68 years since the country's liberation. During a district court hearing in the southern city of Gwangju, the victims urged Japan's Mitsubishi Heavy Industries, Ltd. to provide compensations for them.

Oct. 6 South Korea takes top spot at the 2013 World Archery Championships in Turkey, with Lee Seung-yun winning the gold at men's individual. It also took golds in women's and mixed teams. Yoon Ok-hee also won bronze at women's individual.

Oct. 7 President Park Geun-hye attends the Asia-Pacific Economic Cooperation forum in Indonesia's resort island of Bali, urging members to embrace freer trade and fight protectionism.

• President Park Geun-hye meets China's President Xi Jinping in Indonesia's resort island of Bali, with Xi expressing objection to North Korea going nuclear or conducting additional atomic tests.

Oct. 8 The government pushes to reform the method of compiling statistics on employment, costs of living, and income levels to better reflect the views of the general public. It develops 103 new statistics including studies on the youth.

Oct. 9 President Park Geun-hye arrives in Brunei for a set of regional cooperation summits with the Association of Southeast Asian Nations (ASEAN) and its dialogue partners, suggests South Korea-ASEAN security meeting.

• Hangeul Day, observed on Oct. 9 to mark the invention and proclamation of the Korean alphabet in 1446, is re-designated a national holiday in 23 years, with the 567th anniversary ceremony being held at the Saejong Center for the Performing Arts.

Oct. 10 President Park Geun-hye meets bilaterally with U.S. Secretary of State John Kerry on the sidelines of the Association of Southeast Asian Nations (ASEAN) summit, discusses issues between the two countries and North Korea.

Oct. 11 The mother of U.S. missionary Kenneth Bae visits North Korea to meet her son who has been locked up there for nearly a year on unspecified anti-state charges.

Oct. 12 President Park Geun-hye meets Indonesian President Susilo Bambang Yudhoyono in Jakarta, agrees to forge a comprehensive economic partnership agreement (CEPA) by the end of 2013, and expand trade to US$100 billion by 2020.

Oct. 13 South Korea and the United Arab Emirates clinches a three-year won-dirham currency swap deal worth US$5.4 billion.

Oct. 14 A new road stretching 42.1 kilometers opens at the Hallyeo Haesang National Park that covers six major islands such as Mireukdo and Hansando along South Korea's south coast.

Oct. 15 State prosecutors raid the offices of Tong Yang Group as part of their ongoing probe into allegations that the financially troubled family-run conglomerate fraudulently issued commercial papers worth 160 billion won.

Oct. 16 The South Korean Air Force holds a missile shooting contest in South Chungcheong Province, which two PAC-2 missiles with blast-fragmentation warheads used to shoot down a drone at an altitude of 2 kilometers.

Oct. 17 President Park Geun-hye meets Philippine President Benigno Aquino III, agrees to cooperate closely to boost defense industry cooperation between the two countries.

Oct. 19 Seoul and Washington clinches an agreement to forge deeper ties in surveillance over bio-weapon development.

• South Korea signs a nuclear energy cooperation agreement with Hungary, a deal expected to help Seoul export nuclear power plants to the European nation.

• Prime Minister Chung Hong-won leaves for Denmark to participate in the Global Green Growth Forum.

• Pohang Steelers defeats Jeonbuk Hyundai Motors 4-3 at the FA Cup final, marking its fourth victory.

Oct. 20 South Korea and Malaysia signs a won-ringgit currency swap deal worth US$4.7 billion.

• Yang Hee-young makes her first LPGA career victory at the KEB·HanaBank Championship at the Sky72 Golf Club in Incheon.

• South Korea's women football team wins the 2013 AFC U-19 Women's Championship held in Nanjing, China.

Oct. 21 The Ministry of Education recommends publishers of all eight government-approved Korean history textbooks revise 829 factual errors and unfair descriptions found in them.

Oct. 22 President Park Geun-hye meets Polish President Bronislaw Komorowski, agrees to upgrade relations between the two countries to a "strategic partnership."

Oct. 23 Moon Jae-in, a former opposition presidential candidate and rival to President Park Geun-hye demands that Park confront a growing election-meddling scandal involving the state spy agency and other government bodies, claiming that last year's presidential poll was unfair.

Oct. 24 President Park Geun-hye meets General Electric Chairman Jeffrey Immelt, asks the U.S. firm to consider forging ties with South Korean firms and create new business opportunities and jointly enter third-country markets.

• The Ministry of Employment and Labor notifies the Korean Teachers and Education Workers Union (KTU) of its decision to outlaw the organization.

Oct. 25 North Korea hands over six South Korean citizens and the body of a South Korean female at the neutral border village of Panmunjom, with three of them being prosecuted later on Nov. 13 for violating the National Security Law.

• South Korea conducts a defensive drill in waters near the country's easternmost islets of Dokdo. The rare drills involving the Navy and Coast Guard is to raise public awareness of South Korea's sovereignty over the rocky outcroppings.

• Samsung Display Co., a flat-panel unit of Samsung Electronics Co., starts mass production of 8th-generation liquid crystal display (LCD) panels at its new plant in China, as it seeks to meet the demand for large-sized panels from Chinese television manufacturers.

Oct. 27 President Park Geun-hye nominates Kim Jin-tae, a former deputy chief at the Supreme Prosecutors' Office, as the single candidate to become the nation's new chief prosecutor

Oct. 28 Police arrest two gang members, book 122 more on charges of operating an illegal gambling website, through which nearly 200 billion won was wagered.

• Artist Nam Eun-joo becomes the first Asian to open a private exhibition in Kenya, displaying drawings which describes Kenyans lives and animals with vivid color.

Oct. 29 South Korea request the U.S. National Security Agency's formal reply to its query about whether South Korean presidents have been a target of its alleged bugging.

• Prosecutors begin the process of auction for some of the Chun family's jewelry and real estate worth 23 billion won for public sale, while redeeming 5 billion won worth of additional goods.

Oct. 30 The ruling Saenuri Party posts a landslide victory in by-elections, earning two parliamentary seats up for grabs at Hwaseong and Pohang.

• A group of South Korean lawmakers tours the inter-Korean factory park in North Korea's border city of Kaesong that recently reopened after being closed for more than five months, calling for greater cooperation between Seoul and Pyongyang to ensure its sustainable growth.

• The 10th World Council of Churches (WCC), referred to as "the Olympics of christians," kicks off in Busan, with 8,500 participants discussing various topics such as life, justice, and peace, along with issues regarding the Korean Peninsula and the Middle East.

Oct. 31 South Korea is re-elected as a member of the United Nations' Economic and Social Council, which oversees the majority of the international organization's financial resources.

• SK Telecom Co. commences its first wider-bandwidth long-term evolution (LTE) service across Seoul in 1.8GHz band.

Nov. 2 President Park Geun-hye leaves Seoul to visit France, Britain and Belgium to forge deeper ties with key European countries.

Nov. 3 Lee Suk-chae, who heads KT Corp., conveys his intention to resign amid an ongoing prosecution investigation into corruption allegations against him.

Nov. 4 President Park Geun-hye meets French President Francois Hollande, agrees to strengthen cooperation in high-tech and futuristic sectors to develop new growth engines for their economies.

Nov. 5 President Park Geun-hye arrives in London for a four-day state visit that includes an elaborate welcome ceremony at Buckingham Palace, meetings with Queen Elizabeth II and summit talks with Prime Minister David Cameron.

Nov. 6 President Park Geun-hye and British Prime Minister David Cameron agree to double trade and investment volume between the two countries by 2020, strengthen their partnership in nuclear energy projects and work closely together to develop future growth engines.

• Five lawmakers of the leftist Unified Progressive Party begin a hunger strike over the government's decision to file a petition with the Constitutional Court seeking to disband the party.

Nov. 7 President Park Geun-hye and Belgian Prime Minister Elio Di Rupo agree to push for a science and technology pact to lay the groundwork for greater cooperation. On the sideline of Park's visit, major EU firms made investment commitments worth a total of $370 million.

Nov. 9 South Korean speed skater Lee Sang-hwa claims the gold medal at the 500m race with a time of 36.91 at the International Skating Union (ISU) Speed Skating World Cup in Calgary, Canada.

Nov. 10 The Democratic Party ends its 101-day-long "tent protest," but vows to expand its struggle to resolve the controversy surrounding the 2012 presidential race with the help of civic and religious groups.

Nov. 11 South Korean speed skater Lee Seung-hoon sets the national record en route to a third-place finish in the men's 5,000 meters at the Speed Skating World Cup in Canada

Nov. 12 The three-day 2013 Seoul Defense Dialogue (SDD) kicks off, bringing together vice defense ministers and assistant vice defense ministers from 21 nations including the United States, Canada, Australia, Japan, Singapore and the Philippines.

Nov. 13 President Park Geun-hye holds a summit with Russian President Vladimir Putin with a focus on increasing economic cooperation, forging 15 memorandum of understandings.

Nov. 14 The Seoul Central District Prosecutors' Office indicts a total of 21 people, including TV personalities and a former K-pop singer, for illegal sports-themed online gambling. Those indicted included comedian Lee Soo-geun and singers Tak Jae-hoon and Tony An.

Nov. 16 A private helicopter owned by LG Electronics Inc. crashes in dense fog into a high-rise apartment building in southern Seoul, killing two pilots

Nov. 17 Robert King, U.S. special envoy on North Korean human rights issues, arrives in Seoul, as Kenneth Bae, a Christian missionary, remains detained in North Korea since he was caught nearly a year ago.

Nov. 18 President Park Geun-hye makes her first budget speech at the National Assembly, urging lawmakers to lend support to the government's budget plan for 2014.

Nov. 19 South Korea is re-elected as a member state of the UNESCO World Heritage Committee. It marks the third time that South Korea has been elected as one of the 21 state members of the committee following 1997 and 2005. Seoul's new four-year term is set to begin Dec. 1.

• President Park Geun-hye holds a summit with Kyrgyz counterpart Almazbek Atambayev, expand ties in energy, resources, and agricultural sector.

• The South Korean Embassy in Japan finds a few dozen lists containing the identities of Koreans victimized in a nationwide independence movement in 1919 and in Japan's massacre of Koreans after the 1923 earthquake in Kanto, Japan.

Nov. 20 Thomas Bach, president of the International Olympic Committee (IOC), visits South Korea to check preparations for the 2018 Winter Olympics to be held in PyeongChang.

Nov. 21 President Park Geun-hye holds a summit with Lao President Choummaly Sayasone with a focus on enhancing economic cooperation.

• South Korea decides to send some 500 troops composed of doctors and engineers to the Philippines to help with relief efforts in Tacloban following Typhoon Haiyan.

• South Korea launches its first science satellite with infrared radar, the Science and Technology Satellite 3 (STSAT-3), at Russia's Yasny Launch Base.

Nov. 22 South Korea decides to purchase 40 Lockheed Martin's F-35A stealth fighters for four years starting in 2018.

Nov. 24 A tiger attacks a zookeeper, leaving him seriously injured at Seoul Zoo on the southern outskirts of Seoul.

Nov. 25 South Korea expresses "regret" to China through a diplomatic channel after Beijing informed Seoul of its decision to expand its air defense zone over the East China Sea that includes South Korean airspace.

Nov. 27 The International Monetary Fund (IMF) names South Korean Rhee Chang-yong to become its new Asia-Pacific head.

Nov. 28 The ruling Saenuri Party introduces a motion calling for the expulsion of leftist lawmaker Lee Seok-ki who was accused of treason.

Nov. 29 The Ministry of Education orders publishers of seven out of the eight government-approved Korean history textbooks to revise a total of 41 instances, saying that they contain imbalanced descriptions of history.

Dec. 3 President Park Geun-hye and Greek President Karolos Papoulias agree to deepen economic cooperation between the two countries, especially in the shipbuilding and infrastructure sectors.

Dec. 4 The Green Climate Fund (GCF) formally goes into operation in South Korea's Songdo, west of Seoul with the goal of raising money from industrialized nations to help developing countries tackle climate change.

Dec. 5 U.S. Vice President Joe Biden visits Seoul for a three-day trip.

Dec. 6 South Korea is selected as the host of the 2017 FIFA U-20 World Cup. The U-20 World Cup will be the fourth FIFA-sanctioned competition to be held in South Korea.

Dec. 7 North Korea deports Merrill Edward Newman, an 85-year-old U.S. citizen who had been detained in the communist state for more than a month for alleged hostile acts against the regime.

Dec. 8 South Korea announces a new air defense zone to counter China's unilateral decision to expand its own, bolstering Seoul's sovereignty over a reef and other islands off the southern coast of the Korean Peninsula.

Dec. 9 Unionized rail workers launch a strike in protest against what they believed is a government move to privatize the state-run railway operator. The protest considerably disrupted the nation's train services.

Dec. 10 The Ministry of Education gives the final go-ahead to seven Korean history textbooks modified in accordance with its order.

Dec. 11 President Park Geun-hye and Singapore Prime Minister Lee Hsien Loong agree to combine their specialties for joint-venture infrastructure and other projects in Southeast Asian countries.

Dec. 12 South Korean aircraft maker Korea Aerospace Industries signs a US$2.1 billion deal to export 24 FA-50 light attackers to Iraq, paving the way to tap into other Middle East countries.

Dec. 13 South and North Korea agree to hold working-level talks to discuss ways to upgrade their joint factory park in the North Korean border city of Kaesong.

Dec. 15 Hyundai Heavy Industries Co. clinches a $970 million order to construct a power plant in Kuwait.

Dec. 16 President Park Geun-hye orders officials to study ways to revive the secretariat of the National Security Council to cope with the security situation on and around the Korean Peninsula in a more proactive and efficient manner.

• The National Diplomacy Academy, a subsidiary of the Foreign Ministry, accepts the first group of students who wish to become diplomats.

Dec. 18 South Korea and the United States agree to step up joint efforts to prepare for "all possible scenarios" associated with North Korea, in high-level strategic talks in Washington.

• South Korea summons the vice chief of the Japanese Embassy in Seoul to lodge a complaint against Tokyo's renewed territorial claims to Seoul's easternmost islets of Dokdo.

Dec. 19 The Defense Ministry's Central Investigation Command announces the interim result of a two-month probe into the Defense Ministry's cyber command over its alleged attempt to affect the 2012 presidential election. It is ac-

cused of posting numerous online messages to discredit the then opposition presidential candidate.

Dec. 21 Around 3,000 railroad workers hold a protest rally against what they believe is a government move to privatize the state rail operator.

Dec. 22 South Korean outfielder Choo Shin-soo agrees to a US$130 million, seven-year contract with the Texas Rangers.

Dec. 23 Two South Korean military transport planes depart for South Sudan to deliver ammunition and firearms as well as subsidiary foods for South Korean troops deployed there

Dec. 24 South Korea deploys the K-14 sniper rifle developed with domestic technology for armed forces to conduct missions involving precision attacks.

Dec. 25 Hyundai Motor Co. sells 1 million cars annually for the first time in China, 11 years after the carmaker tapped the market.

Dec. 26 South Korea denounces the visit by Japanese Prime Minister Shinzo Abe to the controversial Yasukuni war shrine, saying it is a "lamentable" and "anachronistic act" that will result in diplomatic repercussions.

Dec. 27 South Korea's three top mobile operators were levied a record-setting 106.4 billion won in penalties for doling out illegal subsidies to customers in an attempt attract new subscribers, a persistent practice that is to blame for the overheated market.

Dec. 28 Thousands of rail workers and supporters stage street rallies at Seoul Plaza in downtown Seoul to protest what they called a government move to privatize state rail operations, claiming that it would lead to massive layoffs.

Dec. 29 A cargo ship collides with a chemical-laden tanker off South Korea's southeast coast, causing the tanker to catch fire, but all 91 crew members on the two vessels were rescued safely.

Dec. 30 The four-seat KC-100 plane, manufactured by Korea Aerospace Industries Ltd., wins its first governmental certificate.

Dec. 31 South Korea's trade surplus reaches an all-time high of US$44.2 billion in 2013, with exports reaching $559.7 billion.

Korea in Brief

Yonhap News Agency

KOREAN HISTORY

BEGINNING OF HISTORY

Korea is an ancient country with a history of more than five thousand years. It is therefore hard to pinpoint the origin of the Korean people. The early inhabitants on the Korean Peninsula, according to a theory, were a Tungusic branch of the Ural Altaic family who migrated from the northwestern regions of Asia to the southern Manchuria and the Korean Peninsula some five thousand years ago.

Legend has it that Tangun, the first great ruler of Gojoseon, organized various primitive tribes in the northern region of the country into a kingdom about 24 centuries before the birth of Christ. The Tangun era lasted about 1,200 years, followed by the Kija dynasty which lasted about 99 years.

The Kija dynasty, established by Chinese scholar by that name, was essentially a city state. Meanwhile, in the southern region of the Korean Peninsula three tribe states of Mahan, Chinhan and Byonhan were established at about the same.

They unleashed what historians call the Three Hans period there. The rule of the Kija dynasty came to an end in 194 B.C., when power was seized by Weiman who also came to Pyongyang from China.

In 109 B.C. the Chinese Han dynasty extended its power over the northern Korea and remained there for the next four hundred years, establishing four colonies of Lolang (Nakrang), Chenfan (Chinbon), Hsuantu (Hyondo) and Lintun (Imdun). The Lolang tombs, dating from 108 B.C. to 200 A.D., have revealed some examples of exquisite lacquer work, bronze mirrors and jewelry.

THREE KINGDOMS

It was in the first century B.C. that centralized monarchy began to develop on the Korean Peninsula. But the country was then divided into three parts. There was Goguryeo, which ruled in the northern part of the country as well as greater part of present day Manchuria.

Meanwhile, the southern region of the peninsula was divided into kingdoms Silla and Paekje. Thus began what has been known as the Three kingdoms Period in Korea.

The Kingdom of Goguryeo was the strongest of the three and ruled from Pyongyang until 668 A.D. when it fell before the onslaught of Silla which was allied with Tang Empire of China.

It was Goguryeo Kingdom that introduced Buddhism and Confucianism from China, which were later passed on to Japan. Silla earlier had succeeded in subjugating the neighboring Paekje.

UNIFIED SILLA (668-918)

After Silla unified the Korean Peninsula, she succeeded in driving out the armies of the Tang Empire, achieving political union of the entire Korean Peninsula. Silla had extensive contact with distant countries through its maritime commerce with the outside world.

Traders of that ancient kingdom are known to have established hundreds of settlements along the eastern coast of mainland China. Buddhism flourished as the state religion, becoming a dominant force both in spiritual and cultural life of the kingdom. This is evidenced by many highly refined Buddhist sculptures, paintings and architecture which are found in the temples built during the Silla dynasty.

These are among the most valued artistic treasures of Korea today. However, the kingdom of Silla fell victim to growing power struggles and corruption in its latter years, finally overthrown by Wang Gon in 918 A.D.

GORYEO DYNASTY (918-1392)

Wang Gon founded Goryeo Dynasty which ruled the Korean Peninsula for 475 years. The present English appellation of Korea is derived from Goryeo. Buddhism became its state religion and played a dominant role in the shaping of the kingdom. Buddhist monks held high positions as advisors to the King.

Goryeo came under constant harassment by the Mongols and had at one time to accept the overlordship of the Mongol Khan. The invasions of Mongolian armies, however, served to awaken the country to the advanced cultures of the outside world.

There were frequent exchanges of people and goods between the Mongols

and Koreans. Goryeo was brought into contact with medicines, astronomy, mathematics, arts and other scientific advances of the west as well.

Goryeo inaugurated the civil service examination for the first time in Korea's history. Bronze coins were invented and used, and highly refined porcelains were produced during this period. But the same Buddhism which had played an important role in the development of Goryeo had a decisive role in sealing the fate of the kingdom.

It was a scheming Buddhist monk who instigated the King to send General Yi Seong-gye at the head of an expeditionary force to attack Manchuria. Aware of the impossible task thrust upon him, General Yi instead turned his army back to dethrone the King and usurp power for himself.

JOSEON DYNASTY (1392-1910)

■ **Birth of Joseon Dynasty**

After Lee (Yi) Seong-gye overthrew the Goryeo Kingdom, he enthroned himself as King Taejo and renamed his kingdom as Joseon in 1392 A.D. Upon seizure of power, Lee swiftly moved to effect sweeping reforms. The reforms were mainly aimed at ridding the country of Buddhist influence which had permeated all walks of life in the preceding dynasty, by driving monks and temples out of cities into the mountains.

Thus, he effectively barred religious leaders from interfering with state affairs. He then adopted the Confucian doctrine making it the moral foundation of society for the ensuing 500 years.

Of all the kings of the 500-year Yi Dynasty, the greatest and the most enlightened was King Sejong. His personal interest and initiative led to many scientific inventions and discoveries. He was also responsible for many of the cultural and educational innovations effected during his rule.

Most of all, he was instrumental in inventing Hangeul, the Korean alphabet consisting of 11 vowels and 28 (later reduced to 24) consonants. The Korean alphabet, noted for its phonetic adaptability and scientific accuracy, can be

KINGS OF THE JOSEON DYNASTY

	Name	Period of Reign
1	King Taejo	1392 - 1398
2	King Jeongjong	1398 - 1400
3	King Taejong	1400 - 1418
4	King Sejong	1418 - 1450
5	King Munjong	1450 - 1452
6	King Danjong	1452 - 1455
7	King Sejo	1455 - 1468
8	King Yejong	1468 - 1469
9	King Seongjong	1469 - 1494
10	King Yeonsangun	1494 - 1506
11	King Jungjong	1506 - 1544
12	King Injong	1544 - 1545
13	King Myeongjong	1545 - 1567
14	King Seonjo	1567 - 1608
15	King Kwanghaegun	1608 - 1623
16	King Injo	1623 - 1649
17	King Hyojong	1649 - 1659
18	King Hyeonjong	1659 - 1674
19	King Sukjong	1674 - 1720
20	King Gyeongjong	1720 - 1724
21	King Yeongjo	1724 - 1776
22	King Jeongjo	1776 - 1800
23	King Sunjo	1800 - 1834
24	King Heonjong	1834 - 1849
25	King Cheoljong	1849 - 1863
26	King Gojong	1863 - 1907
27	King Sunjong	1907 - 1910

learned by any Korean in a few days.

Under the rule of King Sejong, the first metal movable printing type was invented, anteceding Gutenberg by 50 years. During his rule scholars were accorded high esteem as a matter of government policy aimed to encourage scientific learning and literary works.

Invention of highly refined astronomical instruments was also credited to King Sejong. In fact, Sejong's interest in astronomical science was legendary. Sun dials, water clocks, orreries of the solar system, celestial globes and astronomical maps were all invented during his rule.

As the Joseon Dynasty was solidifying the foundation of its kingdom, there

developed frictions in its ruling class. It became intensified during the reign of child King Seongjong, when the dynasty reached the height of its prosperity. The partisan strife started when the patriotic scholars of Confucian Chuja School launched a campaign aimed at eliminating the corruptions rampant in the government.

The sanguine partisan war between the two opposing factions of scholars raged for about 50 years. In that turbulent period, those close to the throne who had inevitably won resorted to extreme measures of sending many eminent scholars on exile.

The notorious factional struggle had in effect beneficial to the nation, however. Many scholars, who had thus found unintended leisure, devoted their time to studying and teaching Confucianism. The nation turned out such outstanding scholars as Lee Toe-gye, Lee Yul-gok and Seo Gyeong-deok during this period. It was in fact a golden age for Confucianism in Korea.

■ Japanese Invasion

Japanese army of Hideyoshi Toyotomi launched an all-out invasion of Korea in 1592. The Japanese captured Seoul within three weeks after they landed at the Busan port. The speed with which the Japanese were sweeping the Korean Peninsula caught the Korean court by surprise.

The King and his government moved northward abandoning the capital city of Seoul. Despite the humiliating defeat on land, however, there emerged a great figure, Admiral Lee Sun-shin, who invented the turtle ship, the first ironclad warship ever built.

Lee, with the fleet of his turtle ships, smashed the huge fleet of Japanese vessels. It was this decisive victory at sea that turned the tide of war against the invading forces. Finally, with the aid of Chinese army, Korea succeeded in driving the invaders out of the country.

The seven-year war was touched off when Japan invaded Korea in retaliation against Korea's refusal to grant a free passage of its army on its way to conquer the Chinese mainland. It was the first of successive Japanese invasions to which the nation had since been subjected due to its proximity to Japan.

■ Manchurian Invasion

The Manchu which replaced Ming Dynasty in mainland China in 1627 invaded Korea when Korea barely recovered from the Toyotomi invasion in the 16th century. The Manchu invasion was a demonstration by the newly installed dynasty in China to show off its might in an attempt to make Korea its vassal state.

The army of the Chinese Ching Dynasty left soon without inflicting lasting damage on the Korean Peninsula. But the Korean court whose fortune sagged immensely from the series of invasions was shocked and distressed.

In the wake of these external aggressions, the court adopted a closed-door policy in its foreign stance. Korea shut herself completely from the outside world. It thereby acquired the nickname of "hermit kingdom" and unconsciously adopted a negative mentality of rejecting everything alien as barbarous.

This policy of self-imposed isolation was to last until the turn of the 20th century. Interested in opening Korea as one of their trading partners, the Western nations had started to knock on the closed doors of Korea in the 19th century.

■ Western Power in Korea

In 1866, Prince Daewon, the apostle of Korea's closed-door policy, ruled the country as regent for his 12-year-old son.

At that time, French Jesuits were residing in Korea for missionary work. The regent determined that their preachings, totally alien to the teachings of Confucianism, represented an evil which would contaminate the Korean soul.

He declared that the Jesuit teachings were a menace to the traditional values of Koreans and ordered the Jesuit missionaries to leave the country. But nine of them refused to leave. Thereupon, Prince Daewon moved to persecute them.

Following the persecution, the French government sent a punitive fleet to Korea under Admiral Pierre G. Roze. The French fleet, however, soon had to withdraw from waters off Ganghwa island under a fierce artillery bombardment. In 1870, American Rear Admiral Rodgers led a flotilla to repeat Commodore Perry's exploit in Japan earlier.

When the American ships approached Korean shore, however, a Korean fort fired upon the American fleet through mis-understanding. In the ensuing exchange of fire, over 300 Korean soldiers were killed. When Rodgers disengaged himself and left simply, the court was left to believe Korea was invulnerable against the barbarian aliens.

In 1876, Japan finally succeeded in making a crack at the closed doors of Korea. While the Korean court was engulfed in a power struggle between the regent and his daughter-in-law, Queen Min, the Japanese adroitly played the regent and the Queen off one against the other.

The power struggle at the court was settled in favor of Queen Min, who, with the support of her powerful consort, wrested power from the regent and gained control of the government. But the change of power was closely followed by a vendetta which culminated in the assassination of the Queen by the Japanese in 1895.

Following Queen Min's assassination, Korea was finally brought around to sign a treaty with Japan promising to open Korea. Soon other Western powers made similar demand, and a Treaty of Peace, Amity, Commerce and Navigation was signed with the United States on May 22, 1882.

Under the Korea-Japan treaty, Korea opened the Busan port in 1876 and Incheon in 1883. Subsequently, the Korean kingdom was to become the scene of bitter rivalry between Russia, China, Japan and other foreign powers.

In 1884, a company of enlightened and progressive Koreans such as Kim Ok-kyun and Pak Yeong-hyo, in the belief that Korea was ready to make the same volte-face that Japan had made in 1868, seized momentary control of the government with the help of the Japanese.

Their coup, however, proved to be abortive when the Chinese army intervened. The failure of the coup compelled Japan to make a temporary retreat from the Korean scene.

However, the frequent contacts with foreign powers, though involuntary in nature, were not without their benefits.

Some advances were made in the field of administration during those turbulent periods. Customs service was installed at the Pusan and Inchon ports. The government employed foreign experts in agricultural, educational and military sectors in an attempt to improve administrative management.

▪ Sino-Japanese Rivalry in Korea

In 1894, Japan came to be determined to eliminate Chinese influence from Korea, by military means if necessary. The Japanese decision to embark on a Korean adventure was made on the assumption that the British and American governments would condone it. Just as Japan was waiting for an opportune moment to strike, there broke out what was later known as Donghak Revolution in Korea.

Bands of farmers took up arms in the south of Korea in protest against the unbearable conditions for which the central government was unable to provide relief. The farmers riot soon threatened to spread nationwide. The central government which, racked by prolonged power struggle, found itself helpless, finally asked China for military intervention.

Fearing that this might lead to China gaining a permanent and dominant influence in Korea, Japan swiftly declared war on China accusing China of aggression in Korea. In the ensuing war, Japan won a decisive victory over China, gaining a momentum for progressively consolidating its foothold in Korea.

The Sino-Japanese war provided the occasion for Japan to establish itself as the unchallenged power in Korea receiving international recognition for its daring military exploit against the Chinese giant. Taking advantage of its superior position, Japan began to demand political and economic concessions to which Korea could not comply without seriously compromising its national integrity.

The Japanese demands were met with stiff opposition by Koreans who rallied around Queen Min. Thereupon, the Japanese legation in Seoul mobilized Japanese hoodlums to break into the palace and kill Queen Min, who had been the arch frustrater of their dark scheme. The Japanese then forced King Gojong to organize a pro-Japanese cabinet.

The King, who had been placed under virtual house arrest, could not stand any longer. The King and crown prince escaped from the palace and found refuge in the Russian legation. Caught by this unexpected turn of events, the Japanese were at a loss for the time being. At last, however, they realized that they would have to have another showdown, with Russians this time, in order to bring Korea under their complete control.

Meanwhile, King Gojong returned to his palace in February 1897. Under a new protective umbrella of Russians, in August of that year he renamed the country Daehan Jeguk and crowned himself Emperor to make a fresh start as an independent and sovereign state. He proclaimed a new education law that established elementary schools, high schools and normal schools. He also effected some changes in the administrative structure of his government.

At about the same time, a group of U.S.-educated young men, alarmed by the ominous Russo-Japanese rivalry over the fate of Korea and the consequent erosion of national integrity, launched a movement calling for reassertion of Korea's independence.

The movement was led by Seo Jae-pil and Syngman Rhee. They published the first modern newspaper of the country, the Independence News. Printed in both English and Korean, the paper ran stories and commentaries drumming up the spirit of freedom, civil liberties and national independence, criticizing the government for failing to safeguard the nation's independence.

The government became alarmed by their radical activities and broke up the movement. Its leaders were either imprisoned or sent on exile to foreign countries. On the other hand, fuming under a setback they suffered in Korea, the Japanese were waiting for a chance to strike back.

▪ Russo-Japanese War

Russia was the only country which challenged Japan in Korea then. The expansionist policies of Japan and Russia were at last heading for an inevitable head-on clash. Determined to eliminate Russian presence in Korea and encouraged by her alliance with Britain in 1903, Japan broke off diplomatic relations with Russia the next year.

Shortly afterward, Japan, without a formal declaration of war, attacked Port Arthur and sank a Russian warship off Inchon. The Korean government immediately declared itself neutral in the war. Japan ignored it, however, and landed her troops on Korea. Russia, under the corrupt government of Tsardom, could not wage an effective war and finally conceded defeat before a small but rising power in the Far East.

Through the good offices of U.S. President Theodore Roosevelt, a peace treaty was signed in September 1905 at Portsmouth. Under the treaty, Japan's dominant political, military and economic prerogatives in Korea were recognized.

Russia also ceded the southern half of Sakhalin to Japan and transferred her extraterritorial rights in Port Arthur and Dalny to Japan. While pledging to respect the interests of the two countries in Manchuria, the two countries agreed to withdraw their military forces from Manchuria, promising to respect their mutual interests there.

▪ Protectorate Treaty

On Nov. 17, 1905, Hirobumi Ito broke into the palace with a large retinue to confront Emperor Gojong with demands that virtually amounted to surrendering of Korea's national identity. Prime Minister Han Gyu-sol refused to comply. Thereupon, Ito saw to it that he was separated from the rest of his cabinet who were threatened with physical violence. Then a few cabinet members were brought around to sign it under duress.

Under the treaty, all Korean diplomatic relations would be handled through the Japanese government; Japanese diplomatic and consular missions would look after overseas Koreans and their interests; Japan would assume full responsibility for carrying out all the provisions of treaties and agreements existing between Korea and foreign countries at the time of the treaty; Japan would install a Resident-General under the Korean Emperor to act as the supreme authority in Korean foreign affairs.

The Daehan Empire had virtually ceased to exist. All Korean overseas missions were closed as of March 1906. At the same time, the ministers of Britain, the U.S., China, Germany, France and Belgium also closed their legations in Seoul and returned home.

JAPANESE RULE (1910-1945)

▪ Treaty of Annexation

The Korean people knew nothing about the signing of the protectorate treaty until the Hwangsong News broke the news. The people were shocked. They joined the nationwide resistance movement, set fire on the new Prime Minister's home, and closed all stores in Seoul in protest. Some court officials committed suicide. To compound the situation, the Japanese Resident-General ordered the Korean armed forces dissolved in August 1907.

Korean troops stationed in Seoul immediately took up arms against the Japanese army. Other military units throughout the country followed suit. However, confronted with superior Japanese armed forces, they fled to the countryside and carried on a stubborn resistance for several years. In 1907, the Japanese government saw the need to install a figurehead more amenable as King in place of Gojong who still stood in its way.

Then, it was revealed that Gojong had sent secret emissaries to the international peace conference at the Hague in a move to arouse international attention to the outrageous situation in Korea. The Japanese Resident-General, blaming Gojong for the violation of treaty, forced him to abdicate and put his second son on the throne. This was Sunjong, the second Emperor of the Daehan Empire and 27th and last monarch of the 500-year Joseon Dynasty.

On Aug. 22, 1910, packing the streets of Seoul with Japanese soldiers, the Japanese forced the Korean government to accept yet another humiliating treaty. It was a treaty accepting total outright annexation with Japan. Korean archtraitor Lee Wan-yong, then Prime Minister, and Japanese Resident-Governor Terauchi signed the agreement which sealed the fate of Korea.

Conclusion of the treaty was officially announced on Aug. 29, 1910. The annexation immediately deprived Koreans not only of their political freedom, but currency, and seized the country's transportation and communications systems.

The Japanese semi-governmental Oriental Development Company took over a huge part of Korean farmlands in the course of the so-called land survey programs. Farmlands were systematically expropriated until up to 80 percent of the nation's total rice fields fell under Japanese ownership. Faced with destitution, millions of Koreans migrated to Siberia and Manchuria.

■ Independence Movement

In the face of increasing Japanese suppression, latent spirit of the Koreans found its expression in numerous resistance movements that sprang up throughout the country. In foreign countries including China and the United States, the Koreans living in exile staged active anti-Japanese campaigns. The most dramatic and tragic event representative of Korean resistance to the Japanese imperialism was the nationwide uprising known as the March First Independence Movement.

The spontaneous and peaceful resistance movement, which broke out on March 1, 1919. called on Japan for voluntary withdrawal from her imperialistic course in Korea. The movement was inspired by the principle of self-determination of nations enunciated by U.S. President Woodrow Wilson at the Paris peace conference that followed the end of World War II. When the news of Wilson's 14-point declaration reached the Korean students studying in Tokyo, they published a statement demanding Korea's independence from Japan in February 1919.

This served as a spark for the movement in Korea. Secret plans were drafted and detailed instructions sent out to all the towns and villages via the underground grapevine urging the people to rise up seizing the inspired moment. The movement was timed to be launched on March 1, two days before the date set for the funeral of Emperor Gojong who had just passed away to dramatize the tragic fate of the nation.

At the core of the movement was a group of 33 patriots. On March 1, the 33 men gathered before a large crowd at the Pagoda Park in downtown Seoul and read Korea's declaration of Independence. And then they led the crowd into the streets to stage a peaceful demonstration calling for national independence. Even remote villages joined in the spontaneous nationwide movement.

The exiled patriots in Manchuria, Siberia, Shanghai and the United States also acted in concert, appealing to the governments of their respective host countries to help Korea in her efforts to recover her sovereignty.

However, the movement was ruthlessly put down by the Japanese. The Japanese police arrested the leaders of the movement, tortured and killed many of them. They mercilessly gunned down the crowd who marched in peaceful procession. More than 6,000 demonstrators were killed and about 15,000 others wounded. Some 50,000 others were arrested.

■ Extermination Policy

Japan embarked on a war in Manchuria in 1930. At the same time, Japan started to tighten its grip on Korea. It also embarked on all out efforts to mobilize all available resources, human as well as material, in support of its war efforts. When new Governor-General Minami Jiro arrived, he openly declared that he would adopt a policy of assimilation which was aimed at total eradication of everything Korea. Then he undertook a series of measures for the purpose of assimilating the Korean people to the Japanese.

The Japanese banned Korean language newspapers and magazines. Koreans were forbidden to speak Korean, forcing the students to speak Japanese only in schools and even at home. Students found speaking Korean were severely caned or expelled from schools. Koreans were forced to discard their Korean names to adopt Japanized names.

Members of the Korean Linguistic Society were arrested and put in prison in efforts to discourage Koreans from studying the Korean language. The Japanese stepped up their totalitarian measures more recklessly when they invaded north China. By that time, the powerful financial combines were consolidating their monopolistic control of Korean industries.

In the meantime, Koreans carried on their independence movement against the Japanese rule overseas. On April 17, 1919, a Korean Provisional Government was established in Shanghai with Dr. Syngman Rhee as its head. The government-in-exile was joined by Korean patriots who fled abroad to escape from the Japanese.

In Manchuria and on the Chinese mainland, exiled leaders such as the right wing nationalist Kim Gu and the leftist Kim Won-bong organized Korean youths and student-soldiers who deserted Japanese army into paramilitary units to fight against the Japanese army.

As Japan's defeat appeared inevitable toward the end of World War II, her imperialistic policy took a frenzied turn, and hundreds of thousands of Koreans were taken to Japan and elsewhere for forced labor in coal mines and other war-related industries.

In cities and rural villages the Koreans were forced to surrender almost everything including even the metal kitchenware such as spoons, metal chopsticks and bowls for futile Japanese war efforts, until they were finally liberated by the victorious Western allies in August 1945.

CONTEMPORARY KOREA (1945)

▪ Liberation

Korea was liberated from Japanese rule on Aug. 15, 1945, 36 years after Japan forcibly annexed the country in 1910. At the end of World War II, however, the southern half of Korea was occupied by the U.S. forces and the other half by the Soviet Union.

Thus, the liberation brought with it a tragic division of the country. For the ensuing three years, the nation, halved at the 38th parallel arbitrarily drawn up as a border line, lived under foreign military rule.

▪ Political Upheaval

The postwar political situation in Korea was marked by mushrooming political organizations and their power struggles. The ensuing confusion arising from the clashes of conflicting power groups cast

dark pall over the political horizon of the infant country.

Among political parties emerging, the most cohesive was the Korean Communist Party which, first organized in 1925 as one of the underground anti-Japanese resistance groups, was reinaugurated on Sept. 14, 1945, with Pak Heon-yeong at its helm bringing virtually all leftist groups under its control.

On the other hand, conservative nationalists led by Song Jin-u and Kim Seongsu formed the Korea Democratic Party on Sept. 16, 1945, as a major political force opposed to the Communists. At this point, it became apparent that the nation was divided ideologically as well as territorially under the full impact of a new alignment then shaping up in the world.

While confrontation involving opposing political forces continued unabated, it was a Moscow Foreign Ministers conference of major powers that sparked major violent clash between the Communists and nationalists.

▪ Moscow Conference

Meeting in Moscow in December 1945, the four Great Powers agreed to place Korea under a 4-power trusteeship for five years under the supervision of the United Nations. They also decided to create a U.S.-Soviet Joint Commission to help form a provisional Korean government in consultation with political parties and social organizations in Korea and to work out an arrangement to carry out the trusteeship plan with the participation of the projected Korean provisional government.

The announcement came as a shock to the people in Korea. The nation rose up in unison in the common cause of spurning the humiliating trusteeship by the Big Four Nations including China. The dramatic unity of the nation was soon broken when the Communists, in a sudden about-face, switched their position to declare full support for the trusteeship plan. From then on violent clashes between the two opposed political forces became a daily affair.

Meanwhile, another development helped quicken the pace of events. The U.S.-Soviet Joint Commission, provided for at the four power foreign ministers conference, held its first plenary meeting in Seoul on March 20, 1946. At the meeting the Soviet side insisted that the Commission invite only those parties and organizations accepting the trusteeship.

As everybody except the Communists who were small in number in reality was opposed to the plan, this would be tantamount to leaving the Communists alone qualified. The United States rejected the Soviet bid. The meeting broke off without any agreement after 50 days of heated dispute.

The Commission opened its second and last series of talks on May 21, 1947. The meeting broke off again in 20 days. The breakdown of the meeting served as a signal for the Communists to launch full-fledged subversive campaigns to disrupt and discredit the U.S. military government.

They renamed their party as the South Korea Labor Party on Nov. 23, 1946, absorbing some minor leftist groups. They resorted to every possible means available including assassination, sabotage, strike, riot and rebellion in their all-out subversive campaign. Their aggressive tactics prompted the U.S. military government to outlaw virtually all leftist groups in the southern half of the country.

■ Korean Issue at The U.N.

In the meantime, the United Nations began to deliberate the Korean question at the initiative of the United States in 1947. The United Nations resolved, on Nov. 14, 1947, to hold general elections throughout Korea in May 1948 and to create the U.N. Temporary Commission on Korea to supervise the elections.

The Commission arrived in Korea in January 1948, but the Soviet occupation forces denied the Commission's access to North Korea. The Commission then recommended that the elections be conducted in such parts of Korea as are accessible to the Commission. In compliance with the U.N. resolution, the U.S. military government announced on March 1, 1948 that the elections would be held in South Korea alone on May 10.

The Russian occupation forces and the North Korean Communists led by Kim Il-sung denounced the plan as a plot to turn South Korea into a base for U.S. expansion. The South Korean Communists and middle-of-roaders joined in opposing the projected elections.

Kim Gu, the erstwhile head of the Korean provisional government in exile in Chungking, and his Korea Independence Party also joined the campaign against an independent government in South Korea alone, together with Kim Gyu-shik, then chairman of the Legislative Assembly under the U.S. military government.

This meant that the rightist political groups were split into two, one led by Dr. Syngman Rhee supporting unilateral elections in South Korea and the other advocating negotiated settlement with North Korea, which came to be called South-North Negotiation Group. Top leaders of the group journeyed to Pyongyang for a futile negotiation with the North Korean Communists for the purported goal of achieving a coalition government.

Despite the complete failure of their parley with the North Korean Communists, the negotiationists boycotted the U.N.-sponsored general elections on May 10 in South Korea on the ground that the election would perpetuate the division of the Korean Peninsula. After the elections, Kim Gu was assassinated by an army lieutenant in Seoul.

THE FIRST REPUBLIC

■ First Elections

The elections took place on May 10, 1948 as scheduled. During the elections, the Communists used all obstructionist tactics, attacking polling booths and government offices on 348 occasions and killing 47 candidates and election officials.

Of the 48 parties and organizations taking part in the elections, the National Council for Expediting Independence led by Syngman Rhee won 55 seats, whereas the Korea Democratic Party obtained 29 seats in the 200-seat National Assembly. 85 seats went to independents.

■ Constituent Assembly

The Constituent Assembly, thus elected for a 2-year term, was convoked on May 31, 1948, and decided to reserve 100 seats vacant for prospective representatives

▲ President Syngman Rhee

from the northern half of the nation. Dr. Syngman Rhee was elected speaker and Shin Ik-hui and Kim Dong-won vice speakers.

The Assembly designated the embryo state the Republic of Korea on July 1, and passed draft Constitution on July 12. Dr. Rhee and Lee Si-yeong were elected by the National Assembly President and Vice President, respectively.

The Constitution was promulgated on July 17, 1948 and Rhee and Lee were inaugurated on July 24. President Rhee subsequently appointed Lee Bom-sok as Prime Minister and Kim Byong-no as chief justice with parliamentary consent, while the Assembly elected Shin Ik-hui to speakership. Thus, the Republic of Korea proclaimed itself on Aug. 15, 1948 on the occasion of the third anniversary of the national liberation.

The U.N. General Assembly declared on Dec. 1, 1948 that the Republic of Korea was the sole legitimate government of the Korean Peninsula. Meanwhile, the North Korean Communists proclaimed the establishment of what they called the Democratic People's Republic of Korea on Sept. 9, 1948.

■ Leftist Activities

As the government was struggling to restore order and stability throughout the country after the turbulent period preceding the birth of the new Republic, Communists intensified their campaign of agitation and sabotage to create unrest in the Republic.

On Oct. 20, 1948, a revolt broke out in army units stationed in the cities of Yeosu and Suncheon on the south coast of the country, and the rebels occupied the two cities until they were crushed by government troops. The remnants of the rebels went into mountainous areas and became guerrillas to infest the areas for the next few years.

Subsequently, the government enacted the State Security Law which was instrumental in bringing Communist subversion and other anti-state activities under control. At about the same time, pro-Communist elements in the National Assembly started to demand withdrawal of the U.S. and Soviet occupation forces from Korea and peaceful unification of Korea through negotiations with North Korean leaders.

On Feb. 5, 1949, a formal resolution asking for negotiated unification was introduced in the Assembly by leftist Vice Speaker Kim Yak-su and his fellow travellers. Similar motions were repeatedly tabled until 12 leading leftist lawmakers were arrested between May and June of 1949 to face trial for conspiring with the South Korea Labor (Communists) Party to overthrow the newly formed government in South Korea. This led to the formal outlawing of all leftist parties including the Labor Party on Oct. 16, 1949.

In the meantime, President Syngman Rhee came out with a list of names to fill his new cabinet. President Rhee utterly ignored the Korea Democratic Party, which had played a key role in bringing him to power, in picking his cabinet members.

Leaders of the Korea Democratic Party were infuriated and took an anti-Rhee stance throughout his presidency. In time, its head, Kim Seong-su, aligned with Shin Ik-hui and Lee Cheong-cheon, organized a united opposition by the name of Democratic Nationalist Party (DNP) with Shin as its chairman.

In an attempt to curb the nearly absolute power Syngman Rhee was wielding under the presidential responsibility system, the DNP advocated creation of a cabinet responsibility system patterned after the British system of government. Holding 70 of the 200 seats in the Constituent Assembly against 55 of the pro-Rhee Ilmin Club, DNP began promoting a constitutional amendment in favor of a cabinet system.

This forced pro-Rhee groups to regroup themselves into the Nationalist Party on Nov. 12, 1949, which resulted in the redistribution of Assembly seats to 71 for the Nationalist Party, 69 for DNP, 30 for the Ilmin Club, and 28 Independents. Subsequently, the opposition DNP, in alliance with some of the independents, introduced a constitutional revision stipulating a cabinet system of government. Rhee's supporters, however, succeeded in defeating the amendment bill.

On May 30, 1950, general elections for the second National Assembly were held. Some 2,209 candidates registered for the 210-seat legislature from 39 parties and organizations including 165 from the ruling Nationalist Party, 154 from the Opposition DNP and 1,513 independents.

The voting, conducted amid Communist disturbances, was the first election held without supervision of any outsiders such as the United Nations. Of the 210 seats, 126 went to independents, 24 to the ruling Nationalist Party, 24 to the opposition DNP, and 36 to pro-government splinter groups. The second National Assembly was convoked on June 19, 1950, only six days before the North Korean Communists launched all-out invasion.

- **Korean War**

North is All-out Invasion At dawn Sunday, June 25, 1950, the North Korean Communist army unleashed an all-out invasion across the entire 38th parallel. The well-equipped Communist divisions, spearheaded by a large number of Russian-made tanks, overran Korean defense positions manned without a single tank or a field gun.

The Communist forces occupied Seoul on June 28, and continued their lightening assault southward. The Korean government moved to Daejon on June 27, then to Daegu on July 16, and finally to Busan on the southeastern tip of the peninsula on Aug. 18, 1950.

On June 30, 1950, U.S. President Harry S. Truman ordered U.S. Army General Douglas MacArthur to use U.S. forces in Japan to help defend the Republic of Korea. The first elements of the 24th U.S. Division arrived in Korea from Japan on July 2 and made an initial engagement with North Korean forces at Osan south of Seoul on July 4, 1950.

U.N. Intervention The North Korean invasion, the first full-scale hostility in the world since World War II, shocked the world. The United States promptly brought the matter before the United Nations Security Council, which in an emergency session on June 25, called for immediate cessation of the hostility and withdrawal of the North Korean forces. The veto-wielding Soviet delegate happened to be absent at the session, making adoption of the resolution possible.

On June 27, 1950, the Security Council recommended that the U.N. member nations furnish military and other assistance to help stop the Communist aggression. On July 7, the Security Council established a unified U.N. Command under which the troops provided by the U.S. and other U.N. members were to fight the aggressors. Thus, for the first time in world history, international police force was set up under a single command.

A total of 16 U.N. member nations contributed armed forces to the U.N. forces. They are Australia, Belgium, Canada, Colombia, Ethiopia, France, Greece, Luxembourg, the Netherlands, South Africa, New Zealand, the Philippines, Thailand, Turkey and the United States. Denmark, India, Italy, Norway and Sweden also provided medical and other forms of assistance to Korea.

President Truman appointed U.S. Army Gen. MacArthur as Commander-in-Chief of the U.N. forces. The Korean ground, air and sea forces were also placed under his command. However, the U.N. forces were forced to retreat down to the Naktdong River line. The U.N. and Korean troops had been cornered to a small pocket along the southeast coast of the Korean Peninsula.

The U.N. forces, regrouped and reorganized at Daegu, quickly built up a strong defense line along the Naktdong River, where the Communist advance was halted for more than a month. Then on Sept. 15, 1950, the United Nations forces landed at Inchon, far behind the enemy line, in one of the most successful amphibious assaults in history.

10 days after the landing, the U.N.

forces recaptured Seoul, and from then on marched in close pursuit of the fleeing Red army that offered almost no resistance.

Chinese Intervention On Nov. 2, 1950, nearly 30 divisions of Communist Chinese army began to storm the U.N. forces along the entire front. At the time, the victorious U.N. forces had made a deep thrust into North Korea, some of them reaching the Yalu River that divided Korea from Manchuria.

Pyongyang, the North Korean capital, had been captured on Oct. 19. When the Chinese army intervened in the war, Gen. MacArthur announced that an entirely new war had started.

The heavily outnumbered U.N. forces pulled back, followed by more than 600,000 North Korean refugees seeking freedom in South Korea. The U.N. General Assembly, in a resolution on Feb. 1, 1951, branded Communist China an aggressor.

Seoul fell again to the enemy in early January 1951. The government, in the meantime, again moved to Busan where it stayed for more than three years though the Communists were thrown back beyond the 38th parallel in a month.

Armistice By the end of May 1951, both sides pitched against each other roughly along the 38th parallel. General lull set in across the battle fronts. It was at this time that Soviet delegate Jacob Malik hinted at the United Nations that a negotiated settlement of the conflict would be possible.

The United States responded to the Russian offer and authorized its top commander in Korea to negotiate a truce with his Communist counterpart. The truce talks, which began on July 10, 1951 at Kaesong, ran into difficulties from the outset over the question of setting up a demilitarized zone along the front line.

Both sides also differed on the questions that concerned the exchange of prisoners of war and enforcement and observance of truce. The negotiations were stalemated for months while the bloody fighting went on along the nearly fixed front line.

The U.N. Command proposed that POWs be repatriated according to their free will. But the Communists demanded indiscriminate repatriation of all prisoners. In the meantime, more than half of the 130,000 Communist war prisoners refused to go back to the north.

In April 1953, President Syngman Rhee declared that his government would never accept an armistice short of complete unification of Korea. He threatened to stage a unilateral military action by South Korea alone to achieve unification. His adamant stand against the truce received support from the National Assembly and the general public.

Anti-truce demonstrations organized by the government broke out across the country. Then in a dramatic move, President Rhee defiantly freed 27,000 North Korean anti-Communist prisoners of war who refused to go back to the north from POW camps at Daegu, Yongchon, Busan, Masan, Gwangju, Nonsan and Bupyong.

Rhee's dramatic move shocked the world and caught the U.S. government off balance. U.S. government leaders who were anxious to end war in Korea blamed Rhee for undercutting the U.S. bargaining position at the truce parley. U.S. President Dwight Eisenhower sent Secretary of State John Foster Dulles as special envoy to persuade Rhee to accept truce terms.

President Rhee announced his intention to accept the truce only after he received commitments from the U.S. that she would sign a mutual defense pact with the Republic of Korea. The armistice agreement was signed on July 27, 1953. Both sides folded their war machines at 10 p.m. that day.

The two sides pulled back 2km each from their positions, creating 4kim-wide demilitarized zone. The buffer zone remains unchanged until today. The four-nation Neutral Nations Supervisory Commission began overseeing the armistice.

During the Korean War, over an estimated one million persons were killed in combat. The combat casualty toll included 225,784 Koreans, 57,440 U.N. troops, 294,151 North Koreans, 184,128 Communist Chinese soldiers. Some 244,663 civilians were killed in combat-related actions. In addition, 128,936 Korean citizens were murdered by Communist troops and secret police with 84,523 others abducted to North Korea.

Geneva Conference The Geneva conference opened in accordance with the terms of the Korean armistice agreement to discuss issues related to the reunification of Korea. A total of 19 nations including North Korea and Communist China participated in the meeting which was held in Geneva in April 1954.

The government sent Foreign Minister Pyon Yong-tae to represent the Republic of Korea at the parley. The Communist side submitted a six-point proposal calling for a nationwide election under the supervision of an international commission to be composed of representatives from both North and South Korea and those from neutral countries.

Foreign Minister Pyon at the meeting proposed a 14-point formula that called for a united, independent and democratic Korea through a free election in the whole of Korea under the supervision of the United Nations in accordance with the constitutional provisions of the Republic of Korea. He also suggested that representation in all-Korea legislature be proportionate to the population of the whole country.

Pyon then called for the complete withdrawal of Chinese troops one month in advance of the election date and for continued stationing of U.N. troops in Korea until such time as the unified government of all-Korea was established. The conference was terminated by the U.S. and its allies after two months of futile wranglings.

■ Liberal Party Government

Due to his high-handedness, Syngman Rhee's popularity was sagging among the National Assembly members during the war. And the party lineup in the second National Assembly, which started to function in the wartime capital of Busan on March 15, 1951, was unfavorable to Rhee.

Sensing that he could not win a presidential election through an indirect parliamentary vote as stipulated in the existing Constitution, Rhee decided to change the Constitution to make the President chosen through a popular vote.

On Dec. 23, 1951, President Rhee, who had been first elected in 1948, organized his supporters in the Liberal Party to form a parliamentary majority numerically large enough to pass constitutional revision. When the new party had been organized, the party initiated a constitutional amendment aimed at paving the way for popular election of President.

But the bill was killed in the legislature due to the revolt of some of Rhee's own party members on Jan. 18, 1952. However, using persuasion and arm-twisting, he had it introduced for the third time on June 21, 1952. The amendment finally passed in an unprecedented standing vote on the night of July 4.

The second presidential election was scheduled for Aug. 5, 1952 under the revised Constitution. The Liberal Party renominated Rhee at its national convention held in Daejon on July 19, 1952. The convention also named Lee Beomseok to run as Rhee's running mate.

But seeing Lee as a political menace to himself, Rhee ignored the convention endorsement of Lee and instead picked Ham Tae-yong as his running mate. The major opposition DNP, in the meantime, nominated Lee Si-yeong for presidency and Cho Byong-ok for vice presidency.

In the election, Syngman Rhee was elected for his second four-year term on Aug. 5, 1952, by a large margin over his runner-up Cho Bong-am who ran on the ticket of the Progressive Party. President Rhee wanted to run for another term as his second presidential tenure approached to its end, but found himself unable to do so under the constitutional provision limiting presidential terms to eight years.

Therefore, he set out to change the Constitution again. In June 1954, the Liberal Party formally introduced a constitutional amendment designed to lift, totally this time, any curb on presidential terms. The bill was voted on Nov. 27, 1954, and mustered 135 of the total of 203 votes, whereupon it was declared defeated.

However, the next day the Liberal Party speaker of the National Assembly hurriedly convened the Assembly to announce that he had made a grave mistake in declaring the bill killed the previous day. The constitutional revision bill which required 135.333 votes for its passage had in reality been approved under the mathematical practice of knocking off fractions under 0.5, he declared.

In the face of the scornful jeers, he insisted that affirmative votes of 135 were sufficient for a constitutional amendment. Under the new revised constitution, the government announced that the third presidential election would be conducted on May 15, 1956. The Liberal Party again nominated Rhee for presidency, while picking Lee Gi-bung as its vice presidential candidate.

On the other hand, the opposition Democratic Party nominated Shin Ik-hui as its presidential candidate and Chang Myon was chosen to be its vice presidential nominee. Cho Bong-am announced his presidential aspiration with backing of his Progressive Party.

But Democratic Party nominee Shin Ik-hui died of heart attack at the height of electioneering. This left only Syngman Rhee and Cho Bong-am in the field where Cho was bound to turn out to be the loser. Now with the major rival in the presidential race out of the way, the Liberals were determined to do everything in their power to see that Lee Gi-bung gets enough votes to beat his opponent from the Democratic Party.

They in fact did everything they could to rig the election, mobilizing police force and making use of government officials, because they knew Lee Gi-bung, if left alone, would have no chance of winning against Chang Myon of the popular opposition Democratic Party. On the voting day opposition witnesses at voting booths were terrorized, ballot sheets were forged and in some districts ballot boxes had been stuffed beforehand.

When the votes were tallied, Syngman Rhee scored an easy victory as expected winning 5,046,437 votes or 70 percent of all valid votes, while 2,163,808 votes went to Progressive Party Cho Bong-am. Cho was hanged in late 1959 for allegedly collaborating with North Korean communists. When it came to the vice presidential race, however, the Liberals suffered a humiliating defeat.

Despite all-out efforts to fake the returns, there were simply too many people who cast their votes for Chang Myon of the oppositon. The final vote count revealed, it was announced, Chang defeated Lee Gi-bung by a margin of 200,000

votes. Thus, Syngman Rhee was thrown into an untenable position where he had to accept the top opposition politician as his chief deputy.

The Liberals suffered another setback in the general elections held on May 2, 1958. They failed to win a two-thirds majority as they had hoped for, while the Democrats increased their seats at the cost of Liberals.

In the local elections that closely followed the presidential election, the government party openly attempted to fake the returns. The successive defeats in elections had convinced the Liberal Party that the only way it could win future elections would be to rig the elections and fake the returns.

With this in mind the Liberals started to take a series of measures. The measures included an amendment to the Local Autonomy Law under which they could pack every local government with their own henchmen. The amendment was pushed through the National Assembly.

Another bill was aimed at revising the National Security Law to include a provision warning that those who publish or circulate false or distorted reports to mislead the public shall be subject to heavy punishment. The occasion of passage of this bill came to be known as the Dec. 24 Political Turmoil. On Christmas eve, policemen stormed into the Assembly floor, manhandled opposition legislators to carry them forcibly out of building to enable the Liberals to pass the bill alone.

As the presidential election set for March 15, 1960 approached, the Liberal Party again nominated Syngman Rhee for its presidential candidate and Lee Gi-bung as its vice presidential candidate. The opposition party picked Cho Byong-ok as its presidential candidate and Chang Myon for vice presidency.

But once again, as in 1956, death snatched away from the Democratic Party a chance for power. On Feb. 15, 1960, Democratic Party presidential nominee Cho Byong-ok died in Walter Reed Army Hospital in the United States, leaving Syngman Rhee as the only contestant in the presidential race.

Despite the demise of the opposition candidate, the Liberals would take no chance, however. Opposition observers were thrown out of the polls to allow the Liberals to freely manipulate ballots. Voting booths were left open in some places so that the voters could be watched from outside.

■ April 19 Uprising

The Liberals brazen rigging of elections finally touched off violent demonstrations in Masan just west of Busan. On the election day, March 15, 1960, thousands of citizens and students marched through the streets of Masan and clashed with police.

Police fired on the crowds, killing, according to the official count, eight men and injuring 50 others. About 20 days later, the body of a high school student was found floating in the sea off the port. This triggered another wave of even more violent demonstrations in the city.

On April 18, the students of Korea University swarmed through the streets of Seoul and staged demonstrations outside the National Assembly building. The following day, April 19, they were joined by colleagues from other schools and by noon students from almost all the universities, colleges and high schools in the capital hit the streets.

The government proclaimed martial law as it was apparent that the demonstrations were developing into a popular uprising. In the meantime, demonstrations were also launched in other big cities, threatening to spread throughout the country. Then on the evening of April 25, some university and college professors in the capital marched through the streets of Seoul in support of the students, giving a decisive blow to the faltering Liberal regime.

Next day, President Rhee promised a new election while saying that he was ready to step down if the people so wanted. At the same time, he carried out a partial reshuffle of his cabinet. The National Assembly, however, in an emergency session, resolved that President Rhee resign immediately.

Thereupon, Rhee finally announced his resignation on April 27. On April 28, Lee Gi-bung, together with his wife and two sons, committed suicide evidently to escape public disgrace and trial. After Syngman Rhee stepped down from presidency, Heo Jeong, former acting Prime Minister, was installed as Acting President.

The caretaker government of Heo Jeong started to prepare for new parliamentary election. The National Assembly voted for a consitutional amendment to provide for a bicameral legislature and to replace the presidential system with a parliamentary system which would give the prime minister full responsibility for governing the nation.

THE SECOND REPUBLIC

■ Democratic Party Government

Under the revised Constitution, new election took place on July 29, 1960 for the fifth National Assembly and the newly created House of Councillors. The Democratic Party which had been in opposition under Syngman Rhee scored a landslide victory in the elections.

The Democratic government, led by figurehead President Yun Po-son and Prime Minister Chang Myon, was confronted with numerous difficulties from the start. Students, vociferous and proud of their role in toppling the Syngman Rhee regime, showed little restraint in meddling in politics.

During the period from April 19, 1960 to May 16, 1961, there were more than 500 major demonstrations by university students, and some 110 by students of high school level and under. In the same period, there were also 45 demonstrations by various labor organizations.

On domestic and international political fronts, the Democratic Party regime was staggering under mounting radical development. Among those were mushrooming radical leftist political organizations that clamoured for North-South contact and neutralization of Korea.

The Democratic Party regime called for, as its official policy, reunification of Korea through general elections to be held in South and North Korea under the supervision of the United Nations in accordance with the constitutional procedures of the Republic of Korea.

Earlier, the North Korean communists began to launch propaganda offensive by calling for federation of South and North Korea and neutralization of entire Korea. At about the same time, U.S. Senator Mike Mansfield maintained that the U.S. government should start considering the possibility of reunifying Korea in consultation with other big powers on the basis of the formula that neutralized Austria in 1965. Mansfield's plea emboldened some segments of leftist students and politicians and they began to ask publicly the government to embrace it.

The so-called Inauguration Committee for the National Reunification League at Seoul National University on Nov. 1 called on Prime Minister Chang to visit the United States and the Soviet Union to sound out on the new unification formula. The Inauguration Committee of the Socialist Party on Nov. 28 also issued a statement calling for neutralized reunification.

On Nov. 30, the Progressive Party issued a statement saying permanent neutralization of Korea should be considered. At the same time, a socialistic radical group led by Kim Tal-ho on Dec. 7 demanded that a national referendum be held to decide on the issue of neutralization of the country.

The Democratic Party regime got literally bogged down in the mounting pressure from within and without. Despite the situation which had seemingly run out of control, the DP regime, in its latter days, started to show signs that it was finally succeeding in putting the chaotic situation under control.

At the same time, it had completed drafting a long-term economic development plan, which succeeding governments made use of. And there were signs that the noisy demonstrations by students and some of the unruly labor leaders, lacking in support by the general public, began to subside. However, there were people who would not give the regime the time to prove itself.

■ May 16 Coup

In predawn hours of May 16, 1961, military columns led by Maj. Gen. Park Chung-hee crossed the Han River into Seoul and seized power, overthrowing the Democratic Party regime. Gen. Park then decreed martial law throughout the country, naming Gen. Chang Do-yong, army chief of staff, as chairman of the Military Revolutionary Committee.

When Prime Minister Chang Myon came out from hiding to announce his forced resignation on May 18, the revolutionary committee established the Supreme Council for National Reconstruction which it said would exercise legislative and administrative powers.

The council then went on to enact a law for installing a revolutionary Court and revolutionary Prosecution Office on June 21 under the provisions of another law of its making, the National Reconstruction Extraordinary Measures Law. Its purpose was to root out the old evils. On July 2, 1961, the Supreme Council for National Reconstruction named Gen. Park Chung-hee as its chairman. On March 24, 1962, two days after President Yun Po-seon announced his resignation, the Supreme Council resolved to accept his resignation and named its chairman to act as President until the government was turned over to civilians.

■ Constitutional Amendment

On Dec.17, 1962, the military government conducted a national referendum on a constitutional revision to revive the presidential system of government, and it was announced that the amendment had been approved by 78.78% of the valid votes.

On Dec. 27, 1962, the military leaders, in violation of their own pledge, declared that they would participate in the civilian government to be established the following year. The declaration drew concerted attacks from the civilian politicians and the people.

On top of the resulting confusion, power struggles had developed within the military junta rending the closed ranks of the military officers engaged in self-imposed task of rebuilding the nation. Then charges of corruption and impropriety were leveled against some members of the military junta, and news media reported daily on what was labeled as four major scandals involving the military regime.

Coupled with the serious misdeeds involving some of the junta members, the mounting criticism by civilian politicians and the press threw the nation into a turbulent confusion which demanded some extraordinary step. On Feb. 18, 1963, acting President and Supreme Council Chairman Park Chung-hee publicly came out to renounce his intention to participate in the civilian government he was pledged to install.

The opposition politicians and the general public were quick to welcome it. However, under pressure by his followers who had completed secret organization of a new political party and were ready to come out in the open while all civilian politicians were in fetters, Park changed his mind.

THE THIRD REPUBLIC

▪ Park's First and Second Term

Despite his public pledge to turn over the power to a civilian government, Park, after retirement from the army, ran in the presidential election on Oct. 5, 1963 and won. It was announced that Park had defeated former President Yun Po-son who ran on the ticket of the Minjung Party, by a slim margin of 150,000 votes.

The opposition civilian politicians failed to present a unified front in the election, several splinter parties fielding their own presidential candidates. The transition from military to civilian rule was completed with the general elections held on Nov. 26, 1963 for the sixth National Assembly.

In the parliamentary elections, it was proclaimed, the Democratic Republican

▲ President Park Chung-hee

Party, composed mainly of soldier-turned politicians and their followers, scored victory over the badly split opposition forces. In the subsequent presidential election held on May 3, 1967, President Park Chung-hee was reelected to a second consecutive term with 51.4% of the total valid votes over his chief opponent Yun Po-son.

In the parliamentary elections on June 8, 1967, Park's Democratic Republican Party won 130 seats, 13 seats more than the two-thirds majority required for constitutional revision. The major opposition New Democratic Party, which had been formed just prior to the general elections through the merger of two parties, Minjung and Shinmin, got only 44 seats.

▪ Constitutional Amendment

Kim Jong-pil, the founder-chairman of the ruling Democratic Republican Party, by announcing all of a sudden that he was retiring from politics in the summer of 1968, laid bare the intraparty feud which had obviously been seething for sometime within the ruling party.

The internal bickering within the ruling hierarchy worsened in early 1969 when the so-called non-mainstream faction of the ruling Democratic Republican Party started the move to rewrite the basic law to scrap the two-term limit on presidency.

The opposition politicians, with the backing of public opinion, immediately started a campaign to bar another constitutional amendment initiated for the sole purpose of prolonging the presidential tenure of an individual. President Park's party tabled a constitutional amendment bill on Sept. 14, 1969 which would enable the incumbent President to bid for his third straight term.

The constitutional amendment bill was rammed through the legislature in a special session held at a National Assembly annex building in the absence of opposition lawmakers. The constitutional amendment proposal was put to a national referendum on Oct. 17. The official announcement said 65.1% of the voters throughout the country cast aye votes.

▪ Park's Third Term

In the wake of the railroading of the

constitutional amendment, the legislative function came to a virtual standstill. The opposition New Democratic Party adamantly refused to attend the National Assembly sessions, demanding that ruling Democratic Republican Party accept its five-point preconditions, including a revision of election laws to hold elections for the President and National Assembly at the same time and implementation of local autonomy.

Negotiations dragged on, both sides refusing to give in. However, politicians changed the focus of their attention elsewhere when the next parliamentary election approached early in 1970. And yet, the nation's political world was tense throughout 1970.

The National Assembly bogged down in partisan bickering over every major issue. The political strife took yet another vociferous turn in the closing months of 1970 when the opposition New Democratic Party named Kim Dae-jung, a new generation politician, as its standard-bearer for the oncoming presidential election.

Following his nomination, the opposition leader started to stump the nation attacking President Park and his government for their alleged corruption and strong-arm tactics. President Park, however, was reelected on April 27, 1971 for his third consecutive four-year term, defeating Kim Dae-jung.

Nevertheless, the ruling Democratic Republican Party suffered a major setback in the general elections on May 25 for the 204-seat new National Assembly.

The governing party won 113 seats, 23 seats short of the two-thirds majority, whereas the opposition New Democratic Party had 89 seats, 20 seats more than 69 seats required to block any future attempt to rewrite the basic law.

■ Proclamation of State of National Emergency

President Park proclaimed a state of national emergency throughout the country on Dec. 6, 1971, asking the people, among other things, to be prepared to shoulder increased burdens to tide over the crucial situation surrounding the nation.

The emergency measure was aimed at awakening the people to the international situation which endangered the security and vital interests of the nation. The declaration contained a six-point guideline which Park said should govern the administration's policies and the daily life of the people in the face of the crucial situation surrounding the country.

The Dec. 6 declaration was followed up by a series of concrete measures designed to streamline and strengthen the military preparedness of the nation, which included the passage of Special Measure Law on National Defense. The law empowers the President to exercise, if necessary, the vast powers which he would otherwise be able to invoke only under martial law.

In the meantime, the ruling Democratic Republican Party drafted a special bill on national security to support President Park's efforts to weather through the national emergency. The opposition New Democratic Party immediately came out against the special bill, and its lawmakers resorted to physical resistance on the Assembly floor to block its passage.

The ruling Democratic Republican Party legislators, however, went ahead and passed the bill in a predawn Assembly session on Dec. 27 which was convened in secrecy without the knowledge of the opposition lawmakers. Two months earlier the government had invoked the Garrison Act in the Seoul area to put down anti-government student demonstrations protesting the military training program for colleges.

■ July 4 Joint Communique

On July 4, 1972, South and North Korea simultaneously announced a joint communique pledging mutual collaboration to seek peaceful reunification, stunning the nation. The historic joint communique called for renouncing the use of force in pursuit of reunification.

The agreement was reached after Lee Hu-rak, director of the Korean Central Intelligence Agency, and Pak Song-chol, North Korean Vice Premier, exchanged secret visits to each other's capital. But the agreement became a dead letter as the Red Cross talks between the two sides came to a deadlock in 1973.

Red Cross Talks

The Red Cross talks between South and North Korea started at the initiative of the Korean National Red Cross in 1971 with the specific aim of helping reunite an estimated 10 million divided family members living in separation. Representatives from both sides held a total of four full-fledged meetings alternately in Seoul and Pyongyang in 1972.

In 1973, however, they held only three rounds of full-dress meetings as the talks deadlocked because of North Korea's politically motivated demands which obviously had been raised to wreck the talks from the beginning. The divergence of view between the two sides over the basic approach toward the Red Cross parley led the humanitarian conference to a stand-still.

The impasse was further aggravated in August of 1973 when North Korea demanded replacement of chief South Korea negotiator Lee Hu-rak, accusing him of masterminding the abduction of Korean opposition leader Kim Dae-jung from Tokyo to Seoul in August 1973.

Proclamation of Martial Law

On Oct. 17, 1972, President Park proclaimed martial law which was meant to partially suspending the Constitution and dissolving the National Assembly, while banning political activities. The emergency measure was necessary to effect institutional reforms in the nation's political system to cope with the changing international situation and to carry on with South-North dialogue just initiated with Communist North Korea.

10 days later Park bared another constitutional revision calling for creation of the National Conference for Unification (NCU) whose function it was to pick the President, doing away with a nationwide poll. The proposed Constitution also provided for extension of the tenure for both the President and the National Assembly from the current four to six years.

Also the National Assembly would be composed of a total of 219 members, of which one-third would be picked by the President, leaving the remaining two-thirds to be elected through a popular vote.

THE FOURTH REPUBLIC

Yushin System

The Fourth Republic was created under the new Constitution named Yushin (revitalizing reform). The Constitution was adopted in a national referendum on Nov. 21, 1972. The reform Constitution drafted by the then martial law government of President Park to institute a tougher ruling structure created a novel form of institution called the National Conference for Unification (NCU).

It is essentially an electoral college whose main job is to choose the President through non-popular vote. The NCU is also mandated to act as the supreme deliberative organ of the nation, acting on such important issue as territorial unification. The NCU opened its inaugural session on Dec. 23, 1972 and elected President Park as the 8th President.

President Park was sworn in on Dec. 27. On Feb. 27, 1973, voters went to the polls to elect 146 representatives to the 219-seat National Assembly. It was announced that the ruling Democratic Republican Party won 73 seats while the opposition New Democratic Party garnered 52 seats. The splinter Democratic Unification Party, a political grouping formed by dissident members of NDP, won only two seats. The remaining 19 seats went to independents.

In accordance with the new Constitution, the NCU elected the rest of 73 seats of the National Assembly on the basis of the ticket handpicked by President Park on March 7, 1973.

Promulgation of Emergency Decrees

President Park Chung-hee proclaimed a series of Presidential Emergency Decrees in 1974, invoking Article 53 of the new Constitution which empowered him to take extraordinary measures in time of national crisis.

On Jan. 8, 1974, he issued Presidential Emergency Decree No. 1, banning all activities opposing, distorting or slandering the Yushin Constitution as well as any press reports on those activities. At the same time, he issued Presidential Emergency Decree No. 2 promulgating the establishment of special courts martial to deal with violators of Decree No 1.

The Emergency Decree No. 2 provided for taking into custody all violators of Decree No. 1 without arrest warrants and giving them prison sentences of up to 15 years. On Jan. 14, 1974, President Park promulgated Presidential Emergency Decree No. 3 for the purpose of stabilizing the people livelihood by drastically cutting or exempting taxes for low-income earners.

On April 3, 1974, Presidential Emergency Decree No. 4 was promulgated to outlaw the so-called National Federation of Democratic Youths and Students which Park said was plotting the overthrow of the government through clandestine subversive activities. It also ordered the closure of the schools engaged in anti-state activities.

On April 8, 1975, President Park promulgated Presidential Emergency Decree No. 7 ordering temporary closure of Korea University and banning rallies and demonstrations on its campus. This decree was lifted on May 13.

Another Presidential Emergency Decree, this time No. 9, was issued on May 13, 1975 to consolidate the national consensus as well as to strengthen the total security posture in the wake of the Indo-Chinese debacle.

The decree called for imprisonment of no less than one year plus suspension of civil rights for no more than 10 years for any campaign against the existing Constitution, politically motivated student demonstrations, press reports thereof and a number of specified wrongdoings including bribery and land speculations.

This decree was in reality a revival of emergency decrees issued in early 1974 and lifted in August of the same year. Later that year some 200 students and other dissidents were jailed by the court martial for their anti-government campaigns.

Assassination of Park Chung-hee

President Park Chung-hee and his 18-year rule came to an abrupt, tragic end on Dec. 26, 1979. Park, his two topmost aids, Cha Ji-chol, the top presidential bodyguard, and KCIA Director Kim Jae-kyu, were meeting in a carousal at a KCIA safe house restaurant to discuss the explosive situation in Pusan. A pall

of darkness had descended on what was widely believed to be the securely entrenched regime of Park Chung-hee when a series of serious student demonstrations erupted in Busan and another port city of Masan on the east coast.

THE FIFTH REPUBLIC

On March 3, 1981, Chun Doo-hwan inaugurated his 7-year presidency as the head of the Fifth Republic, by outlining his policies and programs, pledging to build just society guaranteeing welfare of all citizens and to create an era of economic progress and social justice. Chun's ascendance to power, however, was not without its attendant difficulties.

During the transitional period from Park's assassination in October 1979 to his inauguration in March 1981, he had to play a tightrope performance in paving the way for his own rise to power. First, he had to eliminate the general officers within the military who stood in his way.

They included the incumbent army chief of staff, Gen. Chung Sung-hwa and his followers, whom he succeeded in rounding up with a show of force provided by tanks of Maj. Gen. Roh Tae-woo's 9 Division on the ground that Gen. Chung had been involved in the assassination of the late President Park.

Chun then set out to create a terrorized atmosphere in an attempt to silence criticisms and to remove the potential presidential aspirants. To that end, Mar-

▲ President Chun Doo-hwan

tial Law Decree No. 10 was proclaimed to ban all forms of political activities and labor strikes, closed all universities and colleges, and imposed censorship on the press and televisions.

Kim Jong-pil, Lee Hu-rak, Pak Chong-kyu and seven other prominent leaders of the Park era were put under arrest on charge of corruption. Kim Dae-jung was arrested on trumped-up charges of conspiring to overthrow the government, and Kim Yong-sam was placed under house arrest. The National Assembly was also closed.

However, student demonstrations demanding liberalization and ouster of political generals started to escalate in the spring of 1980, which alarmed Chun and his fellow generals. And Kim Dae-jung's arrest touched off violent demonstrations in Gwangju, the traditional stronghold of the politician hailing from that region.

The subsequent 9-day bloody demonstrations were finally put down by all-out assault launched by army paratroopers backed by tanks, which resulted in several hundred casualties by an official count.

During Chun Doo-hwan's administration, many outdated and cumbersome regulations and laws were either eliminated or simplified. The midnight to 4 a.m. curfew which had been in effect for 36 years was lifted and restrictions on international travels were relaxed.

Inflation was brought down to an annual rate of less than 5%. The Fifth 5-Year Economic Development Plan, which was drawn up during his administration to cover the period from 1982 to 1986, projected a growth rate of 7.6% in real GNP.

Perhaps the one most valuable legacy Chun left as Chief of State was his voluntary surrender of power as he had repeatedly sworn to do. Which was quite remarkable in view of the fact that he found no precedent in which a head of state relinquished his power at the end of his term in the 50-year history since the end of World War II.

THE SIXTH REPUBLIC

President Roh Tae-woo took the oath of office ushering in the Sixth Republic in February 1988. President Roh began his

▲ President Roh Tae-woo

term of office by promising that the authoritarian rule of the past would end and that the June 29 Declaration would continue to be adhered to.

Prior to the presidential election of 1987, Roh made a dramatic declaration, now known as the June 29 Declaration, in which he accepted practically all of the opposition demands including choosing of the President through a popular vote which led to his assumption of power as the first popularly elected President in 16 years.

During his term of office, President Roh took many measures and steps with the aim of liberalizing and democratizing the national life and institutions. These included the repeal or revision of non-democratic laws and regulations, release of many political detainees and discontinuation of surveillance of the news rooms of major press organizations including radio and television stations by the government's intelligence agents.

During the Roh administration, International Olympic games were held in Seoul for the first time in the nation's history. The 24th Olympics held in Korea in 1988 was widely hailed as a great success.

President Roh shook the political world of the country in January 1990 by announcing a grand unprecedented alignment in which his ruling Democratic Justice Party merged into a new Democratic Liberal Party with two major opposition political parties, Kim Yong-sam's Reunification Democratic Party and the

New Democratic Republican Party led by Kim Jong-pil.

The unusual political realignment was the direct result of the surprising returns of the National Assembly election held on April 26, 1988. The final vote tallies of the nationwide elections revealed that Roh's ruling Democratic Justice Party failed to muster a working majority in the National Assembly.

On top of that, the Democratic Party for Peace led by Kim Dae-jung came out to be the largest opposition in the National Assembly. Through this grand maneuver, it was Kim Yong-sam who benefitted most in paving the way for his triumphant victory in the presidential race in 1992.

KIM YOUNG-SAM GOVERNMENT

President Kim Young-sam was sworn as president on Feb. 25, 1993 amid upbeat public fanfare, being the first civilian president in three decades. Kim began his five-year term with a pledge to engineer sweeping reforms in all sectors of society, particularly stressing the need to cut once and for all traditional collusive links between politicians and businessmen.

In the early days of his term, Kim enforced a set of reformative programs to public acclaim. For instance, he forced senior public officials and politicians to declare assets of their families and themselves, and expelled politically-minded generals from active service and introduced a real-name financial transactions

▲ *President Kim Young-sam*

system.

However, the chief executive soon faltered in his reform drive, apparently amid resistance from conservatives who formed the main stay of his power base. Moreover, some of his reforms were criticized as being prejudiced and unfair. His waning popularity was evident in the local elections on June 27, 1995, when his ruling party suffered a stunning defeat.

In a symbolic gesture to rejuvenate his sagging party, the president renamed the ruling Democratic Liberal Party, the New Korea Party (NKP). As part of his strategy to win back public support for the NKP and himself, Kim launched a history righting campaign targeted mainly against two former heads of state, Chun Doo-hwan and Roh Tae-woo.

Under the president's initiative, the ruling party huddled together with opposition parties to hammer out a law empowering the prosecution to act against the two ex-presidents, regardless of the statute of limitations.

Prosecutors arrested Chun and Roh and some of their colleagues on charges of rebellion, under the Military Criminal Code, for their roles in the 1979 coup and the Gwangju massacre in May 1980. The two ex-presidents were also charged with graft. The Seoul District Court sentenced Chun to death and Roh to 22-and-half-a-years in prison.

The Seoul Appeals Court reduced Chun's sentence to life imprisonment and Roh's to 17 years, both of which were upheld by the Supreme Court on April 17, 1997.

President Kim's action against Chun and Roh paid off, since public support for him was waning.

No sooner had Kim rejoiced over election victories, when public suspicion surfaced that he had received a large sum of Roh's slush fund as campaign funds in the 1992 presidential elections.

Compounding the campaign fund issue and dealing a crushing blow to his image, the Hanbo scandal erupted at the turn of 1997. Hanbo Group Chairman Chung Tae-soo had attained a huge amount of bank loans to finance the construction of his ironworks company in Dangjin without proper collateral, apparently through influential politicians.

The opposition camp accused Kim Hyun-chul, the second son of President Kim, of being a central figure in the scandal. They said a large portion of the loans must have flowed into the pockets of ruling camp politicians as kickbacks, and a number of ruling and opposition politicians had in fact, received money from Chung.

At a National Assembly hearing on the scandal, the junior Kim denied guilt or any wrongdoing. But the prosecution arrested him on May 17 on charges of allegedly receiving 6.5 billion won from businessmen, 3.2 billion won of it in kickbacks.

Another incident that marred the image of the Kim Young-sam Administration was controversy over the passage of amendments to labor-related laws, and the Law on the Agency for National Security Planning. With public sentiment sizzling, the ruling and opposition parties worked out and adopted new bills on March 10, 1997, to replace the disputed laws.

Meanwhile, the diplomatically-active president saw a personal goal fulfilled with the country's entry into the Organization for Economic Cooperation and Development (OECD). South Korea was admitted as OECD's 29th member country on Oct. 11, 1997, five years after the nation expressed an interest in joining it.

KIM DAE-JUNG GOVERNMENT

President Kim Dae-jung was inaugurated on Feb. 25, 1998, becoming the first chief of state from the opposition camp in the nation's constitutional history. A lifetime opposition leader, President Kim was also the successor to Kim Young-sam, the first civilian president after a series of military juntas. It is still too early to decide whether his five years in office were a success or failure, and the interpretation of his actions will vary depending on the perspective in years to come.

However, on a personal note, he will be remembered positively as the first Korean and the only president to receive the Nobel Peace Prize for his work for democracy and human rights in South Korea and East Asia in general, and for peace and reconciliation with North

▲ President Kim Dae-jung

Korea in particular.

From the beginning, the regime's biggest task was overcoming the financial crisis that shook the nation's economy to its roots in late 1997. "If democracy and a market economy harmonize and develop in tandem, there will be no collusion between government and business circles, no government-controlled finance and no corruption and irregularities," said the president in his inauguration address.

President Kim added that transparent business management would evolve from economic restructuring, and bad practices such as cross-guarantees of debt payments would end. He promised to take tough action against leaders of mismanagement and concentrate on building a sound financial structure.

The government's efforts for a fast economic recovery paid off in August 2001 when the nation completed repayment of bailout loans, amounting to US$19.5 billion, from the International Monetary Fund (IMF) three years ahead of schedule. As of the end of January, 2003, the nation's official foreign exchange reserves stood at 122 billion dollars, a drastic improvement from the four billion at the end of 1997.

His government also concentrated on nurturing the IT industry .and working to improve the national welfare by guaranteeing a basic standard of living. However, its greatest achievement would be the "Sunshine Policy" on inter-Korean relations. President Kim adhered to three principles - blocking any North Korean aggression against the South, promising that South Korea would not absorb the North, and separating politics from the economy - to promote cooperation and exchanges between Seoul and Pyongyang.

As a result, Kim became the first South Korean leader to participate in an inter-Korean summit when he traveled to Pyongyang on June 15, 2000. Since then, there have been continuous dialogues between the two countries, including nine minister-level talks. Prior to the government-level exchanges, civilians began traveling to the North's Mount Kumgang in November 1998.

This could not have been possible without the government's full political support. Nonetheless, there were a few military incidents with North Korea that startled the nation. In June 1998, the South Korean navy captured a North Korean submarine after it became entangled in a fishing net near Sokcho on the eastern coast.

In June of the following year, a North Korean torpedo boat was sunk and two other northern vessels seriously damaged in a fierce battle off the West Coast. But the most casualties occurred in June 2002. Five South Korean sailors were killed and 19 others were wounded, with one still missing, during another exchange of fire in the West Sea. However, cultural and economic exchanges between the two Koreas are continuing.

In the international sports arena, Kim's government was praised for successfully hosting the 2002 Busan Asian Games and co-hosting the 2002 World Cup with Japan. The South Korean team finished fourth in the soccer tournament. Despite all these achievements, President Kim and his government had to endure dark moments.

Although the nation chose Kim Dae-jung as its leader, his party failed to win the majority at the National Assembly, which often resulted in gridlock with the opposition party, led by Lee Hoi-chang.

President Kim's government came under fierce attack when his two sons and a right-hand man, Kwon Roh-gap, were arrested for accepting bribes. The arrests were a serious blow to the Nobel Peace Prize laureate and further tarnished the image of the government, which had yet to fully recover from the "Clothes Lobby" scandal in late 1998.

The Kim administration is also accused of secretly paying North Korea US$100 million to get Pyongyang to agree to the historic summit in 2000. Kim has admitted to approving the transfer and defended the action by saying it was for the sake of peace, and history will decide whether his action was just or not.

ROH MOO-HYUN GOVERNMENT

President Roh Moo-hyun took office on Feb. 25, 2003 with wide public support as shown by voluntary fundraising and campaigning by citizens during his presidential campaign. The transition of power was conducted smoothly with his predecessor Kim Dae-jung's full support and blessing.

But his five-year term in office drew mixed evaluations on a wide range of issues from politics and diplomacy to economy and social issues.

Roh pushed hard for political reforms to root out corruption inside the government and to achieve democracy, and such efforts paid off by leading the general election in 2004 to be one of the most "clean" ones in history with the least number of irregularities and no major ethical scandals during his term.

But his anti-corruption drive that included many administrative reforms such as the prosecution, drew much opposition

▲ *President Roh Moo-hyun*

from his own government officials and political parties. Though he was credited with guaranteeing the independence of the key powerful bodies of the prosecution and the intelligence agency so as to upgrade the country's democratic standards, some criticized his loss of control over them as the head of state.

One of the rockiest moments of his presidency would be when he faced an impeachment bill in 2004 presented by opposition parties who accused Roh of economic mismanagement and election law violations, among other things. But the Constitutional Court put him back in power some two months later.

Putting building a firm foundation for peace on the Korean Peninsula as one of the top policy goals of "the Participatory Government," Roh inherited his predecessor's Sunshine Policy of engagement toward North Korea. The policy, however, drew criticism from the conservative side and caused a rift with the United States, particularly after Pyongyang continued its bellicose actions of detonating a nuclear device and firing a Taepodong-2 missile in 2006.

Inter-Korean relations, badly frayed by the provocations, thawed the following year, as the two Koreas agreed on a range of economic cooperation projects in their second-ever summit in 2007. During the talks, Roh signed a 10-point peace agreement on Oct. 4 with his North Korean counterpart Kim Jong-il as part of effort to boost reconciliation by forging closer economic ties.

But the summit which came in the final months of Roh's term in office failed to bear much-expected tangible fruits, with conservative presidential candidate Lee Myung-bak vowing a tougher stance against the communist country.

Roh won the presidential election in late 2002 largely on the back of anti-U.S. sentiment triggered by the acquittal of two U.S. sergeants charged with negligent homicide after two local schoolgirls were struck and killed by a military armored vehicle.

As a presidential candidate, Roh, who had once demanded the withdrawal of the U.S. military, called for equality in the countries' relations and vowed not to kowtow to Washington. He, however, in general was supportive toward the U.S. while in office: he deployed troops to Iraq in support of the U.S.-led coalition in the Middle Eastern country, saying such commitment was need to draw support from the U.S. in resolving the North Korean nuclear crisis.

In 2005, Roh and then U.S. President George W. Bush expressed their willingness to explore the possibility of an FTA despite strong opposition, and reached the deal in 2007. After a series of both domestic and diplomatic procedures, the free trade deal took into effect in March 2012.

In terms of the economic policy, Roh put an emphasis on a free and fair market order and welfare distribution rather than growth and deregulation as part of effort to achieve the national integration. His long-term economic policy measures to improve the overall structure earned positive evaluations, but skyrocketing housing prices and mounting household debts during his term, among others, served as a drag on the economic growth.

No major ethical scandal involving Roh emerged, but bribery by his aides haunted the president. In 2009 after his retirement, his family members and aides came under prosecution investigations for bribery charges, with his elder brother Roh Gun-pyeong imprisoned. In April 2009, the probe was expanded to summon and question Roh and his wife for their alleged involvement in a corruption scandal in which they allegedly received millions of dollars from a local businessman.

After being distressed by months-long investigations, Roh leaped to his death from a mountainside precipice above his hometown of Bonghwan, southeastern South Korea, on May 23, 2009 at the age of 62. His death led to an outpouring of grief that was followed by days of mourning as people lined up in the thousands nationwide to pay tribute to the late leader.

LEE MYUNG-BAK GOVERNMENT

President Lee Myung-bak was inaugurated on Feb. 25, 2008 amid expectations for his bid to boost national development on the basis of market economy and to spread pragmatic ideals across the society.

▲ *President Lee Myung-bak*

Lee, the former chief executive of Hyundai's construction arm, was elected with the largest margin of votes in the country's history, but saw his approval ratings dip to the 20-something percent range due mainly to widespread perceptions that he was out of touch with the public, the wealth gap widened due to his pro-business policies and the benefits of growth in big businesses did not trickle down to the working class.

Other factors for his fall from favor include his insistent placement of long-term confidants in key posts, his unpopular project to refurbish the nation's four major rivers, a strain in inter-Korean relations escalated by his hard-line policy and a string of corruption scandals involving his close aides and even family members.

The first crisis came just a few months after Lee took office when massive anti-government protests began over mad cow concerns after his decision to resume U.S. beef imports. The months of protests dealt a heavy blow to his fledgling presidency. What followed that same year was a global financial crisis triggered by the U.S. subprime mortgage debacle.

It raised fears that Asia's fourth-largest economy might plunge into a crisis similar to the one that battered the country in the late 1990s, and which took years of painful economic restructuring to overcome. Even before that crisis had eased, South Korea was faced with yet more fiscal turmoil emanating from Europe.

In between the two major economic crises, tensions with North Korea constantly weighed on the South as the communist country sought to shake Seoul with a series of provocations in an attempt to force Lee to soften his policy towards Pyongyang and resume unconditional aid.

In 2009, North Korea carried out a long-range missile launch that was followed by an underground nuclear test, the country's second such test following the first one in 2006. In 2010, the North mounted two deadly attacks on the South, torpedoing a warship in waters near the western sea border between the two in March and launching an artillery attack on the border island of Yeonpyeong in November. The two attacks claimed the lives of 50 people.

In 2011, the autocratic leader Kim Jong-il died unexpectedly, leaving the belligerent regime with a nuclear program in the hands of his untested youngest son and heir, Kim Jong-un. In 2012, Pyongyang carried out two long-range rocket launches -- one in April and the other in December.

The series of North Korean provocations culminated with another nuclear test in February, the country's third, that fueled fears Pyongyang may be getting closer to being able to produce nuclear-tipped long-range missiles.

Presidential officials say these negative images unfairly overshadowed Lee's accomplishments, such as the quick recovery from the global economic crises; a series of massive economic deals, including a nuclear power plant construction project in the United Arab Emirates; and the nation's successful hosting of a G20 summit in 2010 and the Nuclear Security Summit last year.

His accomplishments include the bolstering of relations with the United States after the traditional alliance suffered under Lee's predecessor, the late President Roh Moo-hyun, who pledged not to "kowtow" to Washington and sought a foreign policy more independent of the U.S. Multiple free trade deals with foreign countries are also considered among Lee's feats.

Lee aggressively sought such trade deals to expand what he calls the "economic territory" of South Korea, which is a resource-scarce economy that relies heavily on exports for growth.

His achievements on the domestic economic front, however, fell way short of expectations. One of Lee's trademark campaign pledges was the so-called "747" promise that was named after the Boeing aircraft and calls for attaining 7% annual economic growth, increasing per capita income to US$40,000 and making South Korea the world's seventh-largest economy within a decade.

But South Korea's economy grew only an average of 2.9% during Lee's time. Though South Korea's unemployment rate is relatively low at around 3% when compared with other nations, the jobless rate for those aged 15-29 was at 7.5% as of the end of 2012, the highest level since June 2012 when the rate rose to 7.7%.

He also suffered from a series of ethical lapses with himself, his family members and close aides involved in bribery and other influence-peddling scandals. The latest scandal involved Lee's only son, Si-hyung, and the Presidential Security Service allegedly misusing public funds and violating real estate laws when they jointly bought a plot of land in 2011 for the president's retirement residence, which was to be built in Naegok-dong on the southern edge of Seoul.

The cost was allegedly not shared evenly, with the presidential entity paying too much for the site for security facilities. Though the prosecution stopped short of bringing charges against three former presidential officials for breach of trust, several local civic groups sued Lee for his alleged role in pushing for the project.

GEOGRAPHY

LOCATION

Korea consists of a mountainous peninsula and 3,201 contiguous islands. It is separated from Manchuria by the Yalu River, Mt. Paektu and the Tumen River. The Tumen River separates Korea from Siberia at its mouth. The Korean peninsula is flanked by two oceans, the East Sea to the east and the West (Yellow) Sea to the west.

It lies between 124°11'04" and 131° 52'42" East Longitude and between 33° 06'43" and 43°00'42" North Latitude in the northern temperate zone of the Eastern Hemisphere. The standard time is based on the meridian passing through the center of the peninsula along 135 East Longitude.

As of Jan. 1, 2012, the total area of South and North Korea was 223,171km² - 100,148km² in South Korea, 123,023km² in North Korea. The longest distance in the peninsula from north to south is 600 miles, and the average distance from west to east is 170 miles.

TOPOGRAPHY

▪ Mountains

The major portion of the country is composed of mountains. Only 30% of the total area is flat. There are no vast plains in the country. Most of the more expansive plains lie in the western part of the land. From Mt. Paekdu on the Manchurian border, a huge mountain-range runs southward along the east coast which is often referred to as the backbone of the country.

The slopes on the east coast are steep, while those on the west coast are gentle. Korean mountains are mostly low, and their crests are in most cases shaped like plateaus. The average height of the Kaema, the highest plateau in the country, is only 1,500m. The highest peak of the nation, Mt. Paektu, stands 2,744m high. In South Korea, there are no mountains that exceed 2,000m in hight.

▪ Coastlines and Islands

The entire coastline of the Korean peninsula is 16,323km including its adjacent islands. The west coast is marked by numerous indentations and irregularities, and abounds in islands. On the other hand, the east coast is mostly steep and has only a few islands. The south coast is even more irregular than the west and is considered a most unusual coastline formations in the world.

The east coast has a relatively few good harbors, while the west and the south have them in abundance. However, harbors on the west Coast are handi-capped by big differences in tides. The gap in tides reaches as much as 33 feet at Incheon, while on the east coast near Wonsan, the difference is only a foot.

The major ports along the east coast include Unggi, Cheongjin, Seongjin and Wonsan in North Korea, Mukho and Pohang in the South. Mukho, located halfway between Wonsan and Busan, serves as a base for fisheries. Pohang, which is one of the largest ports on the east coast, houses a large integrated iron and steel mill.

Chinnampo in North Korea and Incheon and Gunsan in South Korea are the ports located on the west coast. Chinnampo, the largest port on the west coast of North Korea, has been the center of trade with China. Incheon, which has become famous since it served as the staging area for the allied amphibious landing during the Korean War, is important as a gateway to Seoul, due to its proximity.

Major ports along the south coast are Ulsan, Busan, Chinhae, Masan, Yeosu and Mokpo. Busan is the oldest and the largest port city in Korea. Ulsan is well known for its industrial complex. Jinhae is important for its naval base, and Yeosu is primarily a fishing port.

■ **Inland Waters**

Korean rivers are mostly short, shallow and swift, due to its topographical characteristics. As the eastern and the northern parts of the country are mountainous while the western and the southern parts abound in narrow plains, the majority of large rivers are in the south and west.

Rivers exceeding 400km in length are the Yalu and the Tumen which form the borders between Korea and Manchuria. Together with Taedong, Kum and Nakdong Rivers, these rivers provide for good waterways. They also provide water to the nation's agriculture, as well as to serve to generate hydroelectric powers.

CLIMATE

■ **Temperature**

Korea's climate has wide variations and differences influenced by monsoons,

the latitudinal position and terrain and the currents running along its coasts. The country spans nine latitudes with the elevations in the north greater than in the south. Due to these geographical factors, the average temperature drops from the south to the north.

The average temperature throughout the year is 13 degrees Celsius along the southern coast and drops as low as 10 degrees Celsius and 8 degrees Celsius respectively over the central and northern zones. The west coast, facing continental Asia, is vulnerable to the influences of cool monsoons during all seasons of the year.

The east coast, on the other hand, is separated from the West by steep mountain ranges that protect it from the northwesterly winds. Furthermore, owing to the warm currents from the east sea, it is about 2 degrees Celsius warmer than the west coast.

Differences in temperature are least conspicuous during the summer months. The average temperature in August in the lower area of the east coast, which is affected by warm currents, is about 25 degrees Celcius, while it falls below this on the northeastern coast and in the Kaema Plateau. The average maximum temperature throughout the country is generally over 40 degrees Celsius.

The hottest period of the year lasts for about one month, beginning in early August. The outstanding feature of winter is a clear temperature difference between the north and the south. The average minimum temperatures along the southern coast, in the interior and on the Kaema Plateau in the north are -5 degrees Celsius, -9 degrees Celsius and -26 degrees Celsius, respectively.

The northern frontier town of Chunggangjin once recorded the lowest temperature in Korea at -43.6 degrees Celsius. The winter lasts six months in the northernmost areas as compared with only three months in the southern provinces.

■ **Rainfall**

Korea is located in the East-Asian Monsoon belt. The summer monsoon brings abundant moisture from the ocean, and produces heavy rainfalls. The average annual precipitation in Korea varies from 500mm in the northeastern inland areas to 1,500mm on the southern coast.

More than half of the land registers an average annual precipitation rate of 800mm to 1,000mm. About 55-56% of the total annual rainfall occurs in June, July and August and often some 30% of the annual rainfall is seen in July alone. There is more rainfall in the western regions than in the east.

Particularly, South Gyeongsang province draws much more than 1,300mm of rainfall a year. The eastern inland areas along the Cheongcheon and Han River basins, mideast coastal areas and western part of the southern coast are where heavy rains are recorded every year. The areas on the upper reaches of the Tumen River registers the scantiest rainfall of 500mm.

PEOPLE AND LANGUAGE

■ People

Koreans are generally considered descendants of two strains-the nomadic tribes of Mongolia and Aryan Migrants from central and western Asia. At any rate, it is believed that the forebears of Koreans are migrants from the north who moved to the peninsula some 4,300 years ago. Koreans are predominantly Mongoloid, but they have both Occidental and Oriental characteristics. They are homogeneous race somewhat distinct from both the Chinese and the Japanese.

They have wide foreheads similar to those of the Shantung Chinese and some Japanese. In this respect, they differ from the Tungus and Mongols. They are, however, brachycephalic, and it is in this respect that the Koreans resemble the Tungus and Mongols more than they do the Shantung Chinese and Japanese.

Koreans have lighter skin than Chinese and Japanese and this suggests the possibility that they are of some strain of white-skinned ethnic stock from the West. It could be inferred that the present-day Koreans descended from several peoples, of whom the Shantung Chinese, Tungus and Mongols were predominant.

The distinctive physical structure of the Koreans appears not to have been affected appreciably by the close contacts with the Chinese over thousands of years. The Koreans also have developed and preserved a distinctive cultural heritage of their own, despite the great cultural influences of the Chinese over the centuries.

■ Language

The origin of the Korean language has not been established definitively, though it derives from the Tungustic branch of the Ural-Altaic family which traces its ancestry to Central Asia. But in as much as the Korean people are primarily of Mongolian origin, having migrated from Siberian and Manchurian regions into the Korean peninsula, it is inferred that Korean language is somewhat related to Manchu or Mongolian.

But the fact is that Korean and Mongolian are found much more apart from each other, both in vocabulary and syntax, than are English and German, or English and French. The generally accepted theory indicates that the archtype of the Korean language was developed in the southern part of the peninsula among agrarian tribes. Another developed among the northern Goguryeo Kingdom when the four colonies of Han of China were established in Korea.

It is certain that Chinese language and letters greatly influenced the language. Korean grammar, however, is entirely different from the Chinese. Korean language has simple forms to express different tenses and modes such as indicative, conditional, imperative and infinitive, etc. It has forms to express all those more delicate verbal relations which in English requires a circumlocution or the use of various adverbs.

The difference between Korean and Chinese language is that Korean is strictly phonetic in writing whereas Chinese is not. The grammatic structure of Korean language is regular and simple. Forms consist of stems plus endings. While a single stem may occur in many forms, it remains almost constant in all of them.

There are also many word endings that cannot be expressed. The use of particles and inflectional endings is wider in Korean than in Manchu or Mongolian.

Even Japanese has fewer particles and different endings than Korean. It should also be noted that the formation of compounds by connecting stems is very extensive.

In the Korean language, there are no articles, i.e. "the" or "a." There is no change in the ending of noun for singular or plural. Neither is there any sharp discrimination of gender in the personal pronoun. Verbs have no special distinction for third person, singular or plural. On the other hand, the Korean adjectives have conjugations like verbs.

Order of words in the clause or sentence in Korean is subject, object and verb; qualifying elements precede the objects qualified; dependent clauses precede independent clauses. The Korean language is rich in sound, and there are 10 primary vowels, as well as secondary or derived vowels.

In the Korean language, the function of euphony is conspicuous. Euphony is the distinctive characteristic of Korean language. The Korean language, however, became complicated by the wide use of "honorifics" in accordance with the complex social order of Korea.

Another characteristic feature of the Korean language is that it possesses a large vocabulary, not only for expressions of concrete things but for presentations of subtle human feelings and sentiments. It is, however, short of words pertaining to abstract reasoning and logical thinking. This renders it extremely difficult for a translator to interpret Korean into a foreign language word for word and vice versa.

The main dialects of Korean are northern Korean and southern Korean. Korean spoken in Seoul is regarded as the standard spoken language. During the past several hundred years, the normal evolution of Korean as an independent and original language has been hindered much by two developments.

Chief among them was the discouragement of the use of native tongue by Confucian influences that encouraged the use of Chinese letters. The other hindrance was the policy of the Japanese colonial rule which attempted systematically to destroy the Korean language. Since liberation in 1945, however, there have been movements aimed at refining and standardizing Hangeul.

■ **Hangeul**

There are historical evidences, though uncorroborated, that suggest that ancient Koreans used their own system of writings. Some scholars regard inscriptions on the stone walls in Namhae inland as ancient Korean characters. The Samguksagi(history of the Three Kingdoms) says: "letters were first used in the beginning of the Goguryeo Kingdom".

Notwithstanding the historical evidence, it is true that the Koreans wrote exclusively in Chinese characters until the 15th century. Then in 1443, King Sejong of the Joseon Dynasty, with the help of several scholars (Chong In-ji, Song Sam-mun and Shin Suk-chu), invented a phonetic alphabet called Han-geul which has since been in use.

▲ *The statue of King Sejong*

The Korean alphabet is so simple that anybody can master it. In a Korean encyclopedia compiled in about 1770, a reference was made to the simplicity of Hangeul, saying that "the possibility of interchanging letters is unlimitedly simple, but that the language is very efficiently neat and comprehensive enough for any combinations."

The Korean alphabet consisted originally of 28 letters, according to Hunmin-

552

jeongeum, the book of the authorized alphabet first promulgated. It was reduced later to 24 letters. In the Korean alphabet there are 10 vowels(originally 11) and 14 consonants. Two principles were followed in devising the forms of vowels and consonants.

The 14 consonants symbolize either the organs of speech or the manner of articulation. The 11 vowels are devised to symbolize heaven, earth and man, the three elements constituting the universe in the Oriental view of the universe.

By taking a consonant sound like K and putting it before each of the vowels, various syllables begin to take shape. If the syllable should begin with a vowel sound, the consonant NG precedes the vowel. The NG has no sound when used in that way. The shape of the vowel determines whether the consonant should be placed above it or to the left of it.

Currently 24 letters are in use. They represent the phonemes of the Korean language. ㄱ(g), ㄴ(n), ㄷ(d), ㄹ(r or l), ㅁ (m), ㅂ(b), ㅅ(s), ㅈ(j), ㅊ(ch), ㅋ(k), ㅌ (t), ㅍ(p), ㅎ(h), ㅇ(ng), ㅏ(a), ㅑ(ya), ㅓ (eo), ㅕ(yeo), ㅗ(o), ㅛ(yo), ㅜ(u), ㅠ(yu), ㅡ(eu), ㅣ(i)

CUSTOMS

▪ Overview

Korea has undergone rapid changes since its once closed society was exposed to western culture about a century ago. Western culture has since influenced the traditions developed by the Korean people since the nation was established on the Korean peninsula some 4,300 years ago.

Today long beards, white costumes and horsehair hats are rare sights, even among elderly people.

In Seoul and other major cities around the country, vast majority wear western suits, shoes and haircuts, and live in western styled houses. Traditional manners and styles are also on the rapid decline. However, many Koreans have made continuous efforts to prevent those priceless, intangible assets from becoming extinct.

▪ Dress

In the past five decades, Korea has experienced remarkable changes affecting virtually all aspects of the nation. Their traditional way of life has been on the wane, due to the impact of western culture and civilization. Traditional costumes have all but vanished from their everyday lives.

▲ Korean traditional dress, Hanbok

Except for some elderly people, especially in the more remote areas of the nation, the preferred mode of fashion has been that of the West. However, this has been a relatively recent phenomena. Before the national liberation in 1945 most Koreans were attired like nowhere else in the world-the traditional Hanbok, a comfortable, loose-fitting gown, had been the norm.

Since then, the tremendous inflow of western culture, accompanied with the nation's remarkable economic development, has changed the way the Koreans dress forever. Koreans have embraced the new western styles for everyday wear, making the Hanbok a ceremonial costume to be worn on special occasions only.

Nowadays, Koreans wear Hanbok only on Lunar New Year's Day and the Korean Thanksgiving Day (Aug. 25, on the lunar calendar), the two most important traditional holidays in Korea. Weddings are another favorite days for wearing Hanbok.

Although the vast majority of Koreans now wear tuxedos and wedding dresses for the actual ceremony, virtually all wear the Hanbok at "Pyebaek", a ceremonial greeting made by the bride to the groom's family right after the wedding.

The original Hanbok for women consists of long full skirt and a short jacket. The designs and styles vary, however according to the age of the person wearing it. The Hankbok is usually cut loosely for comfort, not for style or mobility.

The traditional male costume consists of an overcoat, a loose jacket and a loose pair of trousers that are tied around the ankles. Females wear short, flared blouse over a white undergarment, and a long, high-waisted skirt.

Neither the male or female version contains buttons or hooks, instead, long cloth strings are used to fasten the costumes to the body. Except for the royal courts where colorful decorations with silk fabrics were used, traditional Hanboks were usually made of cotton and linen, and white has been the predominant color.

Koreans were once called the "White-Clad People" for this reason, which invoked an image of purity an innocence. In recent times, however, a variety of fabrics and colors have been used in making the traditional costumes, even for the average Korean.

▲ A fermented vegetable dish, Kimchi

■ Korean Food

Due to its rapid growth, Korea has become an international country in a very short time. Seoul is truly a cosmopolitan city, and one can find restaurants of all palate and national origin. However, Koreans are rather picky about their food, most finding the traditional cuisine preferable to the others which is quite distinctive in several aspects from that of the neighboring China and Japan.

In Korea, as in other Asian nations, rice is the staple of all meals. It is sometimes mixed with other grains, such as barley. Rice is accompanied by a number of side dishes and usually a soup.

Among Koreans favorite side dishes are a variety of vegetables, steamed and seasoned; braised meat or fish; and Kimchi, a fermented vegetable dish that is highly seasoned with red pepper and garlic. Kimchi, which is served at virtually all meals, is probably the best known Korean dish among foreigners.

Vegetables are important ingredients in side dishes, and the most commonly used vegetables are radishes, Chinese cabbage, garlic, hot pepper and leeks. The ingredients are similar to those used in making salads.

The important seasonings include red peppers, red pepper curds, bean curds, sesame oils and soy sauce. Bean curds are most often used in soups, and soy sauce is used in almost all side dishes. Until recently, all of the side dishes have been prepared at home.

However, in these days of instant foods, virtually all of the side dishes can be purchased ready made at the market. Kimchi, however, remains one dish that is almost always prepared at home. Koreans eat three well-balanced meals a day. Breakfast used to be considered the principal meal of the day. Lunch is rather simple, but dinner is considered almost as important as breakfast. While eating, Koreans use a spoon and a pair of chopsticks.

Although food is one area of Korean lifestyle that is least influenced by the Western culture, it has been simplified to fit the more convenient lifestyles. On holidays, birthdays and other festive occasions, special foods are prepared.

■ Housing

The traditional Korean house, with its attractive charm and graceful lines once

▲ The traditional Korean house, Hanok

adorned the cities and villages throughout the country. A typical Korean house is a rectangular, L- or U-shaped single-storied structure made primarily with wood and clay.

The most distinctive aspect of a Korean house is its age-old radiant heating system, Ondol, which carries heat from the kitchen fireplace through stone flues under the floor. Therefore, the fireplace has a dual purpose - A cooking food and heating the floor.

In the olden days, Koreans burned wood in these fireplaces which later gave way to charcoal briquettes. Nowadays most houses and apartments throughout the country use oil and natural gas for central heating. Even in these centrally heated homes, however, the predominant style of heating is done through pipes which carry the heated water beneath the floors, radiating the heat throughout the rooms.

Since beds or chairs were not used in these traditional homes, people sat on mats and cushions and slept on so called "Yo," a padded floor mattress. Recently, however, more and more people live in apartment complexes complete with western furnitures.

Apartments have been the preferred way of living due to the modern conveniences as well as lack of available building sites. Throughout the country, large apartment complexes sprout up everyday, accounting for about 59% of 13,883,571 homes, according to 2010 Census.

■ **Name**

Koreans usually have two names; the family name or surname placed first and a name identifying each individual. This name is mostly comprised of two characters, one common to the generation, therefore common to brothers and sisters, and the other indicating the individual.

When writing their names in the Western or Roman alphabet, Koreans sometimes will invert the order of the names and place the family name last, as Westerners do. This can lead to confusion, however, since many Occidentals know about the traditional order of the Oriental names, and will thus still misidentify the family names by reinverting the inverted order.

If you see the names Kim, Lee, Park, Ahn, Chae, Cho, Chong, Han, Ku, Ko, Ihm, Oh, No, Shin, Yu, or Yun, etc., you can be fairly sure that it is the family name, whether it appears first or last in the sequence of names. There are, however, a total of more than 275 family names in Korea.

A woman retains her family name even after marriage. In English conversation, the wife of Mr. Park may be referred to as Mrs. Park, but this is only for the sake of convenience. In reality, her name will still be Mrs. Lee, or whatever she was prior to the marriage, in both customs and law.

In Korean conversation, she will most likely be called Park's wife or her full legal name to reduce the confusion. Unlike the West, Koreans rarely use their signatures to sign important papers. Virtually all of the legal documents must be sealed with hand-carved seals bearing his or her name, which must be registered with the local civic administrative office for its authenticity.

■ **Family Occasions**

Birthday The two most important birthdays in the life of a Korean are the first and the sixtieth. Each is an occasion for hosting a greatest feast for family and friends. These birthdays are important since infant mortality was high and life expectancy was low in the past, making them highly festive occasions for the average Korean.

Marriage In arranging marriages, Koreans traditionally emphasize the succession of lineage and prosperity of the family. In the traditional Korean family, the choice of one's future husband or wife and the wedding date were entirely up to the parents. After the ceremony, the groom would spend three days at the bride's home and would then take her to his home where another ceremony would be held.

Weddings today have changed over the past decades and now it is almost identical with the marriages of the West. Today, the weddings are held in churches or wedding halls wearing tuxedos and dresses. The important difference, however, is that in Korea, wedding ceremony is considered only as a ceremony, and legally one does not get bound to the each other until a wedding license is filed later at the civic administrative office.

Therefore, no minister or a judge need to preside to do the ceremony. Normally, the bride and the groom together will request one of their respected elders to preside over the ceremony.

▪ Jokbo

The importance of family in Korean society is attested to by the custom of keeping a jokbo, or genealogical record book. These records, which in Korea are among the most comprehensive to be found anywhere in the world, record the name, origin, birth date and year, family relations and social standing of each member of the family, as well as the family's history.

Such genealogies have their roots in Chinese culture, and their publication and distribution is believed to have become widespread in Korea from around the late 15th century on. The oldest one known to have been printed is that of the "Kwon" family from Andong, near Gyeongju, which was printed in 1476.

They were, however, in existence in Korea from the Goryeo Dynasty (918-1392), being used largely as guarantees of the background of those taking the state examinations to become public

officials. The records also encouraged solidarity between those from the same extended family, something that gained increased importance in the Confucianism dominated society of the Joseon Dynasty(1392-1910).

The possession of jokbo was not universal, being regarded as particularly important for the yangban or nobleman class in order to show their aristocratic lineage. With significant social benefits accruing form high-born status, it was inevitable, then, that the forging of jokbo became widespread, culminating in a major investigation and crackdown in 1807.

In modern day Korean society, the practice of meticulously keeping a jokbo continues. Family ties are still regarded as highly important, and there exist many private societies consisting of people with a shared family root. Classified by name, there are 275 distinct family groups in Korea today, the largest being Kim, with over 20% of the population, followed by Lee, Park and Choi.

▪ Holidays

Jan. 1 (New Year's Day) The first day of the year are officially designated as holidays.

Lunar Jan. 1 The Lunar New Year's day (Seollal) is the first day of the first month by the lunar calendar. The days right before and after Seollal also make up this 3-day holiday. Seollal is possibly the greatest holidays of the year. Most Koreans take this time to visit their elders and other relatives.

It is also a time where children get to receive considerable amount of pocket money. Juniors will start the new year by

556

bowing to his or her senior. This bowing involves crouching to one's knees and placing the head on the ground to wish the seniors a healthy and prosperous new year. In return, the juniors almost always receive token sum of money.

Before Korea adopted the Julian Calender like the West, Koreans have traditionally considered the Lunar New Year's as the start of the new year. Therefore, all of the bowings, gatherings of the families that goes on the New Year's day used to have been reserved for this day.

In fact, most Koreans have returned to their traditional past observing this day as the true New Year's day, observing the traditional "harae" (giving thanks to the ancestors that have passed away) the first thing in the morning. Together with Korean Thanksgiving Day (Aug. 15, in the lunar calendar), this is the day that the most traffic jams occur in the highways and other freeways, due to the Koreans returning to their homes.

March 1 (Independence Movement Day) On this day back in 1919, 33 Korean patriots signed and circulated a declaration of independence, and launched a nationwide freedom campaign of nonviolence against the Japanese colonial government. Koreans throughout the country solemnly observe the anniversary of this Independence Movement. Memorial services are held for the deceased patriots at Tapgol Park in Seoul, where the declaration was first proclaimed.

Lunar April 8 (Buddha's Birthday) Solemn rituals are held at temples with throngs of devout Buddhists attending. At night, tens of thousands of people, each holding a glowing amber lanterns hanging from a tall pole, lines the streets leading to the temples across the nation.

May 5 (Children's Day) On Jan, 15, 1975, the government designated May 5 as the Children's Day which is observed as a national holiday. The Children's Day was made a national holiday so that adults would be able to spend the day with their children, making it a good occasion for the whole family to get together.

June 6 (Memorial Day) The nation pays tribute to its war dead. Memorial services are held at the National Cemetery.

Aug. 15 (Liberation Day) This day marks the anniversary of the establishment of the Republic of Korea in 1948. On this day, the Republic of Korea was established after liberating from the 36 years of Japanese colonial rule on this day.

Lunar Aug. 15 ("Chuseok" or Korean Thanksgiving Day) Moon festival or Chuseok literally means "Autumn's Eve" and is a time reserved to give thanks to the ancestors for the year's good crop and harvest. Normally a grand feast and celebrations follow the thanksgiving.

Oct. 3 (National Foundation Day) Literal translation being "The day the Heavens Opened," according to mythology, this is the day that the national founder, Dangun, descended upon the earth on this day more than 4,300 years ago.

Oct. 9 ("Hangeul" or Korean Alphabet Day) The nation observes this holiday in commemoration of the adoption of the Hangeul, the Korean alphabet invented by King Sejong of Yi Dynasty in 1446. Calligraphy contests and other events are held during this day.

Dec. 25 (Christmas) Koreans observe the occasion as in the Western countries.

TAEGEUKGI

(National Flag of S. Korea)

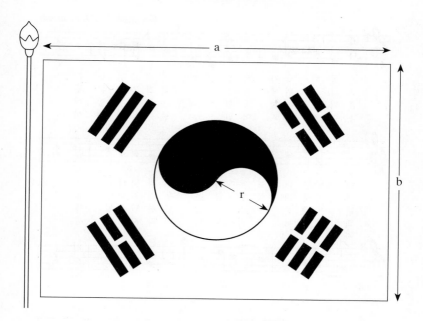

$$a:b = 3:2 \quad r = \frac{1}{4}b$$

Taegeukgi, the Korean National Flag, symbolize peace, unity, creation, brightness and infinity. The symbol, in the center, and sometimes the flag itself, is called *Tagegeuk*. The upper section of the circle in red is the *Yang* and the lower the Um. Locked together in perfect balance, these two opposites symbolize the dualism of the universe. There are good and evil, male and female, night and day, life and death, being and not being, etc.

The central thought in the Taegeuk is said to be that while there is constant movement within the sphere of infinity, there is also balance and harmony.

The three parallel unbroken bars on the upper left-hand corner stand for heaven, and opposite these are the three broken bars representing earth. At the upper right-hand corner are two broken bars with unbroken bar in between, symbolizing moon; and opposite them, a broken bar between a pair of unbroken bars, the symbol for sun.

In short, the *Taegeuk* symbol is described as follows:

"From the unknown comes the everlasting, from the everlasting comes the overcharging. The symbol, *Teague*, means infinity."

White ground: black bars. The upper section of the central circle is red and the lower section is blue. The flag top is in the shape of a bud of *Mugunghwa*(Hibiscus syriacus) - the national flower. The flag top is surrounded with five calyces of Hibiscus.

AEGUKGA

(National Anthem of S. Korea)

Composed by Ahn Eak-tai

1. 동 해 물 과 백 두 산 이 마 르 고 닳 도 록
2. 남 산 위 에 저 소 나 무 철 갑 을 두 른 듯
3. 가 을 하 늘 공 활 한 데 높 고 구 름 없 이
4. 이 기 상 과 이 맘 으 로 충 성 을 다 하 여

하 느 님 이 보 우 하 사 우 리 나 라 만 세
바 람 서 리 불 변 함 은 우 리 기 상 일 세
밝 은 달 은 우 리 가 슴 일 편 단 심 일 세
괴 로 우 나 즐 거 우 나 나 라 사 랑 하 세

(후렴) 무 궁 화 삼 천 리 화 려 강 산

대 한 사 람 대 한 으 로 길 이 보 전 하 세

1. Until that day when the waters of the East Sea run dry and Mount Baekdusan is worn away, God protect and preserve our nation; Hurray to Korea.

2. As the pine atop the near mountain stands firm, unchanged through wind and frost, as if wrapped in armor, so shall our resilient spirit.

3. The autumn sky is void and vast, high and cloudless; the bright moon is our heart, undivided and true.

4. With this spirit and this mind, give all loyalty, in suffering or in joy, to the love of country.

Refrain: Three thousand ri of splendid rivers and mountains covered with mugunghwa blossoms. Great Korean people, stay true to the Great Korean way!

Documents

Yonhap News Agency

NEW YEAR MESSAGE TO THE NATION BY PRESIDENT PARK GEUN-HYE

(Jan. 1, 2014, Seoul)

Fellow Koreans, New Year 2014, the Year of the Blue Horse, has begun. I wish you all a year full of hope and the energy of a galloping horse.

Despite many difficulties in the past year, Your confidence and support helped us pull through. Building on the trust, we were able to nurture the seeds of hope and change.

In the New Year, the Administration will continue to do all it can to reap a bountiful harvest so that every one of you will be able to live a richer and happier life.

My Administration will channel the national capabilities into reinforcing the hard-won gains of economic recovery, so as to invigorate the economy and stabilize the day-to-day lives of the people. I hope all of you will also join forces to prepare for an economic takeoff.

A top priority for reviving the economy as well as a prerequisite to that end is to protect national security and public safety.

The Government will strive to maintain an impregnable security posture and prepare specific contingency plans against any possible provocation by the

North. Building on this, the Government will redouble its efforts to further promote peace on the Korean Peninsula and lay groundwork for peaceful reunification.

My Administration will also continue reforms to set right the wrong practices rooted throughout our society.

As we open a New Year and embrace new changes, I ask all of you to join us. My Administration will do everything it can to ensure 2014 brings greater hope and vitality to you all.

Thank you for your support and encouragement over the past year, and again, a very happy New Year to all.

NEW YEAR'S MESSAGE BY NATIONAL ASSEMBLY SPEAKER KANG CHANG-HEE

(Jan. 1, 2014, Seoul)

Fellow citizens, Korean compatriots abroad, The morning has come to year 2014.

I wish all Koreans at home and abroad, and people all around the world a joyful and hopeful New Year.

Last year, we worked hard to revive our economy and promote the vision of this nation worldwide. And we achieved a lot. Korea has now become one of the strong leaders of the world that make great contributions to prosperity and the peace of humanity.

Many advanced countries view us as a partner walking together towards the future while others from Asia to Africa to South America see us as a model for economic growth.

Korean War veterans from 16 countries visited Korea last year to mark the 60th anniversary of the armistice of the war, and they were all astonished by the economic and cultural miracle that we have accomplished.

Our status as a trade powerhouse has been raised as well by our passion and innovation. I think it is especially meaningful that we ran a trade surplus again last year amid the challenging situations both at home and abroad.

Based on these accomplishments, we should make substantial strides forward this year. As we all know, however, circumstances signal that we are going to have another tough year.

Tension is growing higher than any other time on the Korean Peninsula and in East Asia. As a retrogressive nationalism expands across the region, our neighboring countries are deploying armed forces near the Korean Peninsula.

North Korea continues to develop nuclear weapons and missiles, and given its domestic situation, it is unpredictable what will happen, and how and when it will provoke us.

Fellow Koreans, It is evident that we are now at a crucial watershed moment in history. We achieved remarkable economic development, the so-called "Miracle on the Han River," but this was not because we had much to begin with.

Even though we face difficult situations now, we must make a huge leap forward once again. We must add more jobs, and develop our potential in science, technology and the knowledge industry.

By that means, we must address social polarization and forge a strong foundation for a unified society. Especially, we must create a society where our youth can have dreams, passion and aspirations. That will be the road to sustaining prosperity in the middle of this volatile global economy and politics.

And yet the road ahead of us will be filled with difficulties. That journey will require every sector of our society to reflect on itself. In particular, the political circle must not disappoint the people any more.

Through a severe self-reflection, it must seek the spirit of mutual understanding, concession and compromise.

Political parties must work together with common goals from a broader perspective of security and the future of the nation, economic prosperity, and a peaceful life for the people. This will be the true way to unite as a whole and meet the hopes of the people.

I personally think that for a more secure future of Korea, we should bring to the fore the issue of Constitutional amendment this year. Ever since the establishment of this country, we have made a history that is admired by the rest of the world.

Now many Koreans believe that for our second great leap forward, a new legal system and a new Constitutional framework that fit our society are needed.

As the Speaker of the National Assembly, I will do what I can do to pool the nation's wisdom and knowledge, starting with the Speaker's Advisory Council on the Constitution, which many academics, experts and I are planning to establish soon. We will look forward to your encouragement and support.

Hoping more laughter and vitality will fill Korean society this year, I send you all my best wishes for a healthy and blessed New Year. Thank you.

REMARKS BY PRESIDENT PARK GEUN-HYE AT THE WORLD ECONOMIC FORUM ANNUAL MEETING 2014

(Jan. 22, 2014, Davos)

Distinguished guests, ladies and gentlemen. My warm greetings to all of you. This is an opportune occasion to speak about "entrepreneurship" and the "creative economy." For in our post-crisis era, the global economy is charting a new course. And many of the global leaders in this audience stand at the forefront of that journey.

Thanks to strong national responses coupled with close international coordination, the global economy is gradually escaping from the crisis.

Yet, countries still experience slow growth. High unemployment is weighing economies down. Income inequality continues to linger.

Making growth sustainable is another task all of us face. As our planet eventually becomes home to 9 billion people, the need to deal with climate change and resource depletion has never been more compelling.

The global financial crisis has brought these issues to the fore. As a matter of fact, they are problems that have been with us well before the crisis. And they lay bare the limitations of our existing paradigm.

We must make growth sustainable. We must make growth inclusive. But piecemeal fixes will not do. Macroeconomic policies or labor policies under existing paradigms alone will not do. What we need is nothing short of a paradigm shift. What we now need - and need urgently - is an engine that takes us beyond these constraints; one that transforms the existing order and helps reshape the world.

Korea is seeking that engine in the creative economy.

Ladies and gentlemen, Today, the brilliant idea, creative thought, or new technology of a single individual can help move the world and get nations going.

Since the industrial revolution, the wealth and happiness of nations - of individuals - had been marked by a material divide. Recently, this has given way to a digital divide. The future will be defined by a creative divide.

Whereas existing economies have focused on extracting mineral resources from the ground, creative economies seek to tap into the creativity of the human mind.

We in Korea believe that the only way to solving our problems is to creatively innovate our way out. Hence, our pursuit of a creative economy vision as the new paradigm for driving our economy forward.

A creative economy harnesses the creative ideas of individuals and marries them with science and technology - with IT. It promotes the convergence of different industries and the confluence of industry and culture. And along the way, it creates new markets and new jobs.

Together with creativity, what is key to successfully realizing this vision is entrepreneurship.

Creativity begets innovative ideas. Entrepreneurship puts innovation into action.

Entrepreneurship is what translates an individual's innovative ideas and creative potential into the courage to start a new business.

We have a saying in Korea : "Beads are not considered jewelry unless they are woven together." Entrepreneurship is what weaves together the beads of creative ideas into new markets and into new jobs.

Companies must rise to the challenge of a new era. In doing so, they shouldn't be afraid of failure. Entrepreneurial spirit in the 21st century must be indefatigable.

To support the thriving of entrepreneurship, barriers that stand in its way must be removed. We also need to build a financial system that supports entrepreneurship and spreads risk; a system that helps those that fail get back up.

Another key task is to build a creative economy eco-system, which spurs endless research and constantly churns out new ideas and value. The government needs to support this.

In most cases, it's difficult to do due diligence on ideas. And bringing ideas from the drawing board to the marketplace involves a high degree of uncertainty. This makes it difficult for early-stage startups to raise funds.

To ease this process, we must help transform how startups and venture companies finance capital : away from loans and towards investment capital including through angel investors.

Financing assistance should also be tailored to a company's evolution. Policies should include tax inducements and other steps aimed at encouraging M&As of venture companies.

Where businesses fail despite honest and hard work, their credit-worthiness should be restored promptly, so they could try again.

We need a climate where entrepreneurs can learn from their failure, bounce back and achieve success.

Korea is focusing on building an eco-system where entrepreneurship can flourish. We will use this as a platform for fleshing out our vision of a creative economy.

Last October, we opened a "Creative Economy Town" website. This online platform helps people with great ideas, who have done creative research and sometimes have the technology, but who have quit halfway through because of difficulties in making them marketable.

In the span of a few months, some four thousand creative ideas have already been put forward. Success stories are beginning to appear, as patents are filed, prototypes are produced, and funds are raised to start businesses.

Here is the story of one young man. He developed an application that directly translates any word on a mobile screen and offers the user learning opportunities through a vocabulary book. After submitting the idea to the K-Startup program, he was able - with the help of mentors - to launch a cloud-based language learning application. It now supports twelve languages. In just four months, this application was downloaded four hundred thousand times. Today, it is growing into a venture business.

Creative ideas such as these will help inject fresh vitality to creating jobs and growing the economy. They will underpin our nation's competitiveness.

Starting this year, we will move offline and establish creative economy centers across Korea. Once the system is fully up and running, anyone with a constructive idea will be able to get mentoring from experts and start a business. Companies would not only be linked up with talented people, their competitive edge would also be enhanced through innovative ideas.

To reinforce these efforts, we will set up a "Creative Economy Joint Task Force." This will include venture companies, SMEs, large companies as well as the government. The private sector will be in the driver's seat and lead the creative economy.

Furthermore, to facilitate startups and entrepreneurial risk-taking, we are moving to a negative list approach to regulation. We are drastically cutting red-tape that stands in the way of convergence and in the way of new industries.

We will cap the total economic impact of regulations. Regulations will be relaxed across the board, except for those that are absolutely necessary. A ministerial-meeting that I as president will be chairing will oversee these efforts.

Answers to tackling energy and environmental challenges will also be sought through the creative economy. We will develop policies to build "environment-friendly energy towns" as creative business models.

We will try new ways to site incineration plants and landfills, which local communities tend to reject. Those communities will receive real benefits in the form of clean technology-based energy - energy that will come from biomass co-generation plants or energy storage systems.

We will also make government information more open and accessible for the general public. This "Government 3.0" initiative can also serve as the connective tissue for a wide range of new businesses.

For example, the Korean Government made available its 3D maps, land registration maps and other information on the nation's landscape.

One startup made use of that data and developed a service application that estimates the power capacity and profitability of locating solar equipment in various areas on the map.

Such data and ways to use our nation's landscape will be made publicly available so that anyone could easily use them and develop many different services. As a result, we expect to see some twelve thousand decent jobs created by 2017.

Ladies and gentlemen, Wouldn't it be nice to join Korea's journey towards a creative economy?

Ladies and gentlemen! I believe the creative economy needs to play an important role in the reshaping of our world - the theme of this year's forum.

For it can offer new opportunities for dealing with diverse challenges that can arise in the course of that transformation.

Existing factors of production were the prerogatives of select classes or groups. In contrast, the power to imagine and think up ideas is universal to everyone. It is not conditioned by nationality, ethnicity, wealth or education.

Unlike resources, creativity is non-depletable. Nor does it degrade the environment. It therefore unlocks opportunities for sustainable growth. Creativity is inherent to all people regardless of age, class, race or nationality. It therefore holds promise for inclusive growth.

The promotion of creativity will serve as the wellspring for overcoming unbalanced growth among nations and among different classes. Every member of humanity has the potential to become key players in the success story of a creative economy.

This is why I believe the creative economy can offer a path to resolving the triple pressures of slow growth, high unemployment, and income disparities. Through startups as well as the innovation of existing businesses, a creative economy can generate new engines of growth and can grow jobs. There will also be less income inequality since anyone with a great idea can live out one's dreams by starting a business.

Where there is concern and care for others, there we can see fresh ideas blossom. It is when the desire to improve the human condition - to heal humanity's pain - meets science and technology that solutions are produced... that suffering is eased... that the wellbeing of humanity is served.

Realizing the benefits and goals of a creative economy requires concerted global efforts.

Climate change and environmental challenges are global in nature. As such, the world must act as one in tackling them. Solutions to these problems could be found through the imagination and entrepreneurial drive empowered by a creative economy.

I also hope to see nations that are custodians of the world's cultural heritage amplify creative value through cultural sharing and heart-to-heart exchange through the creative economy.

Culture has the power to connect - to connect people of different languages and different backgrounds.

The world is coming closer together as economic, social, cultural and other barriers are ebbing away. We see this happening with our own eyes.

We see how the culture of one nation is no longer confined to that country alone. It is increasingly being shared and enjoyed beyond borders.

We use the expression Korean Wave to describe the widespread enthusiasm for Korean culture. Today, that wave is spreading rapidly across the globe.

When Korean music recently paired

564

up with Youtube, it became a global sensation. K-POP, Korean dramas and films are being greeted here and there and creating new added value.

When the cultural values of each country are brought together with IT technology, the possibilities for generating greater added value become truly limitless. Indeed, this is another key attribute of the creative economy.

The companies that are welcomed around the world are those that have successfully combined various cultural content with new technology.

May this audience help draw up ideas that enable culture to serve as a vehicle - one that brings affection and joy around the world.

Ladies and gentlemen, Since the global economic crisis, the Washington Consensus has not been regarded as sacred as it once was. The world beckons for something more - something that better meets the calling of our time. But a new consensus has yet to emerge.

May this World Economic Forum lead to what we could call the "Davos Consensus:" the belief in entrepreneurship as the driving force of sustainable, inclusive growth. Indeed, a gathering of global leaders such as this should aim to usher in a new era. I believe you can do so by coming up with practical guidelines toward an economic, social, political and cultural climate that fosters entrepreneurship.

I also hope that Korea's quest for a creative economy can offer the international community a practical, entrepreneurship-driven strategy for shaping a new future.

Our world currently faces countless challenges. But to me, they seem no more than minor bumps on our path to a better world. The indefatigable spirit of entrepreneurship can lift economies up... and lift countries up.

It is now up to us to rise to the challenge and not be afraid to fail. Let us set our sights on making a better world. And let us embark on this journey with tireless entrepreneurial spirit and through a creative economy. Thank you, ladies and gentlemen, for your kind attention.

ADDRESS BY PRESIDENT PARK GEUN-HYE ON THE 95TH MARCH FIRST INDEPENDENCE MOVEMENT DAY

(March 1, 2014, Seoul)

Fellow Koreans, seven million compatriots overseas and our brethren in the North, decorated patriots who fought for the nation's independence and distinguished guests, Today, we celebrate the meaningful 95th March First Independence Movement Day.

Had it not been for the sacrifices of our patriots and martyred forefathers who devoted their lives for the country's independence, the Republic of Korea would not have been possible and it would not have been able to stand tall in the world.

On the occasion of the March First Independence Movement Day today, I bow my head in tribute to their souls. My heartfelt sympathy also goes to our decorated patriots who fought for the nation's independence and to the families of fallen heroes. They have endured suffering and difficulties in their hearts throughout their lives.

Ninety five years ago today, our ancestors rose up resolutely to win back the country's independence and sovereignty. Their conviction and patriotism that their nation's sovereignty should no longer be robbed inspired all people to stand up.

There was no difference between men and women and between young and old. It was not important what their social status or class was, what their religion was, nor where they came from. Regardless of where they were, from Manchuria and the Littoral Province of Siberia to Tokyo and Philadelphia, their passionate patriotism to save the country swelled.

The towering spirit of the March First Independence Movement was passed on through the legitimacy of the Provisional Government in Shanghai to become the spirit of the constitution of the Republic of Korea today. It has become the source of the achievement of prosperity and miracles in Korean history.

Fellow citizens, In the March First Declaration of Korean Independence, our forefathers proclaimed that their task was to build up their own strength, not to destroy others, and that they would build the nation which would contribute to peace in the East and the world as well as happiness for mankind. They also emphasized that their purpose was to restore natural and just conditions by correcting unnatural and unjust conditions.

Today, we are entrusted with the duty of continuing to work to realize the noble ideals and values that our ancestors envisioned. I will begin the task by correcting unnatural and unreasonable conditions rampant in every corner of society for so long and setting right all abnormal practices in and outside the country.

Starting with reforms in the public sector, I will take bold action to eliminate improper and unfair old customs and work to carve out a new Republic of Korea. The Three-year Plan for Economic Innovation will help change our economic fundamentals to lay the foundation for sustainable growth and build a cornerstone to go beyond US$30,000 in per capita income and reach US$40,000.

The successful implementation of this plan necessitates your wisdom and cooperation. I am confident that you will all come forward to render the three-year plan fruitful, thereby making contributions to building a greater and mightier Republic of Korea.

My fellow Koreans, Next year will mark the 50th anniversary of the normalization of diplomatic ties between Korea and Japan. Thus far, upholding shared values on the basis of mutual understanding, the two nations have fostered close cooperative relations for the sake of peace and common progress in Northeast Asia.

A painful history notwithstanding, the two nations were able to develop such relations since there were efforts to promote friendly and good neighborly relations with surrounding countries on the basis of the Peace Constitution. There were also efforts to march toward the future based on Japan's reflection on its colonial rule and invasion through the Kono Statement and the Murayama Statement.

It can be said that a nation's historical consciousness serves as a compass needle pointing to the future direction of the nation. If it fails to look back upon past wrongdoings, it will not be able to open a new era. It goes without saying that a leader who is not ready to acknowledge past wrongs cannot open up a new era in the future.

Courage in the genuine sense is not about negating the past but about facing up to history as it was and teaching undistorted historic facts to future generations.

Now is high time for the Japanese Government to make the right and courageous decisions so that our two nations will be able to overcome our painful history and move forward toward a future of new prosperity. In particular, it is imperative to heal the wounds of the comfort women victims of the Japanese imperial military; after having lived all their lives overwhelmed by indescribable resentment and grief, now only 55 of them survive.

If a nation continues denying past history, it will only end up driving itself into a corner and looking more miserable. People who are still alive are witness to the truth of history. Turning a deaf ear to their testimonies and ignoring them just for the sake of political interests will only result in isolation.

Politics should not stand in the way of the friendship and trust the peoples of our two countries have so far fostered. Even now, they are still sharing mutual understanding by means of culture.

I hope that the Japanese Government, guided by the universal conscience of humanity and the good precedent made by post-war Germany, will be able to break away from its negation of the past and write a new chapter in history characterized by truth and reconciliation for a future of cooperation, peace and shared prosperity.

Fellow citizens, I believe that laying the foundation for peace and unification on the Korean Peninsula is the most important step to strengthening the cornerstone of our economy and building an advanced nation. This is why I plan to create a presidential committee to prepare for unification and begin making provisions for peaceful unification.

The recent reunions of separated families impressed upon all Koreans again the depth of pain and suffering that has been brought by division. The members of these families are now elderly, and not much time remains for them. Reunions must no longer be isolated special events.

I propose to the North that reunions of separated families be regularized so that those who have lived with the sorrows of division may find comfort and peace as soon as possible. There are separated family members living in the North whose pain and suffering must also be eased.

My hope is that the South and North will build trust by keeping small promises, and continue, one step at a time, on the path to unification. A united people and a unified Peninsula will be the culmination of the spirit of the March First Independence Movement which cried out for the self-reliant independence of the Korean people. It will contribute to peace and prosperity not only in Northeast Asia but also around the world.

A unified Korean Peninsula will also become the heart of peace connecting Eurasia and Northeast Asia. In a peaceful and unified Korea, Northeast Asian countries will be able to find new opportunities for growth.

At this crossroads on the way to a new era of peace and cooperation, I call on the North to lay down its nuclear weapons and choose the path to shared progress and peace for the South and North.

Fellow citizens, The proud history of the Republic of Korea was written with the blood and sweat of our martyred patriots. Now, in order that we may pass on to future generations the legacy of a new Korea, we must all join hands together.

With the fortitude of spirit passed down to us by our forefathers, let us set out on a journey of creativity and challenges, achieving greater things for the Korean people and greater change for the world. Let us better cultivate and develop the value and the beauty of our cultural heritage, sharing it with all peoples and building a happier world.

Let us now join hands and go forth with vigor toward a new day of hope and a new era of happiness for the people. Thank you very much.

AN INITIATIVE FOR PEACEFUL UNIFICATION ON THE KOREAN PENINSULA

(March 28, 2014, Dresden)

Professor Hans Mueller-Steinhagen, former Prime Minister Lothar de Maiziere, students and faculty members of the Dresden University of Technology, ladies and gentlemen.

It is my great pleasure to visit this esteemed German institute of higher learning. It is also a unique privilege to receive an honorary doctorate from a university where the presence of history and tradition can be felt.

As the fastest-growing region in the former East Germany, Dresden is an iconic community that has moved beyond division and toward integration. The German people have transformed Dresden into a city brimming with hope - where freedom and abundance suffuse the air.

Those who reach beyond the confines of reality and dream of a better world can draw strength and inspiration from this city.

As I ponder on where a united Germany stands today and where the Korean Peninsula seems headed next year - namely 70 years of division, - I find myself overwhelmed by the sheer weight of history.

We have a saying in Korea that the impact of education lasts for generations and beyond. Looking around your campus today, I am reminded of how a nation's future is often charted and shaped from the likes of Dresden University of Technology.

The words 'Knowledge builds bridges - education binds people' represent the educational vision of this university. And I am sure it is a vision that will be lived out through the passionate strivings of its students and faculty alike, and will help usher in a brighter future.

As one who studied electronic engineering in college, I hold dear the belief that science and technology are the key to unlocking a nation's advancement.

This is why I established the Ministry of Science, ICT and Future Planning early in my presidency and have been highlighting the importance of building a creative economy.

Ours is an era when the ingenuity and innovation of a single individual can move the world. As we enter this new age, I am seeking to generate new business opportunities and jobs through creative endeavors and innovation; to breathe greater vitality and dynamism into the economy by marrying science and technology and ICT to existing industries.

This is what a creative economy is all about.

We will also strengthen collaboration among academia, industry and local communities - very much like what the City of Dresden has been doing - and provide the kind of support that enables a creative economy to spur local renewal and development.

I believe that in our efforts to make Korea's economy more creative, we will continue to find much to draw upon from the future evolution of Dresden and its colleges.

Ladies and gentlemen. Korea and Germany have long been bound by special links. Fifty years ago, Korea was among the poorest nations in the world, with a per capita income of 87 dollars. Many young Koreans fresh out of college came here to Germany to earn money. They came as miners and nurses and dedicated themselves to working in the service of their homeland.

Much as Korea sought to lift its economy out of poverty, no country was willing to offer loans to a small nation in the northeast corner of Asia, let alone to a divided one.

It was in those difficult and forlorn times that Germany stepped up and provided 150 million German Marks in loans, while also offering advanced technology and vocational training programs. Germany's help would prove to be a huge boost to Korea's subsequent modernization and economic development.

The Korean president who visited Germany at the time felt that Germany's rise from the ashes of the Second World War and its Miracle on the Rhine were feats that could be replicated in Korea.

As he was driven on the autobahn and shown the steel mills of German industry, he became convinced that Korea too would need its own autobahn and its own steel industry to effect an economic take-off.

When that president sought to build expressways and steel mills upon his return to Korea, he was met with widespread resistance.

"What use is an expressway when we don't have cars? Building an expressway is a recipe for failure." "What's the point of a steel mill when we're struggling just to get by?"- went the argument.

But the highways that were eventually paved against such opposition became the solid bedrock on which the Korean economy would rise. Those long stretches of concrete helped remove bottlenecks in the nation's distribution and logistical networks.

The steel and automobile industries which had thus begun, join the ranks of the top five, six players in the world today. The desperate country that 50 years ago had been hard-pressed even to obtain loans, has now come of age as the 8th largest trading nation in the world and a major economic partner to Germany.

As President of grateful nation, I thank Germany once again for placing its confidence and trust in the Republic of Korea, helping us pull through those difficult years.

Ladies and gentlemen, Germans and Koreans get going when the going gets tough.

In the years following the Second World War, Germany and Korea both endured the pain of seeing their nation divided. But instead of submitting to despair, Germans and Koreans alike marched forward with hope.

From lands ravaged by war, Germans and Koreans worked as hard as any to rebuild. They refused to let up their determination to pass on a better country to future generations.

Thus came the Miracle on the Rhine and the Miracle on the Han River some years later.

Germany would later go on to achieve unification, but Korea has yet to become whole again.

I believe that just as the Miracle on the Rhine was followed by the Miracle on the Han, so too, will unification in Germany be reenacted on the Korean Peninsula.

I remember the bold courage of the German people as unification and integration unfolded.

Even the Berlin Wall, which had seemed so insuperable, couldn't stop the longing for freedom and peace coming from both sides of the Wall.

Years of preparation by the people of East and West Germany eventually succeeded in turning the great dream of unification into reality and, ultimately, even transformed the future of Europe.

A reunited Germany took its place at the heart of Europe. The years since unification have seen Dresden emerge from a backwater into a world-class city known for its advanced science and technology. Other parts of the former East Germany also made huge strides forward.

These are the images of one Germany that encourage those of us in Korea to cement our hope and our conviction that unification must also come on the Korean Peninsula.

I believe that the Republic of Korea will similarly reach ever greater heights after unification. The northern half of the Korean Peninsula will also experience rapid development. A unified Korea that is free from the fear of war and nuclear weapons will be well positioned to make larger contributions to dealing with a wide range of global issues like international peace-keeping, nuclear non-proliferation, environment and energy, and development.

Furthermore, as a new distribution hub linking the Pacific and Eurasia, it is bound to benefit the economies of East Asia and the rest of the world.

Ladies and gentlemen, It pained me to see a recent footage of North Korean boys and girls in the foreign media. Children who lost their parents in the midst of economic distress were left neglected out in the cold, struggling from hunger.

Even as we speak, there are North Koreans who are risking their lives to cross the border in search of freedom and happiness.

The agony inflicted by division is also captured by the plight of countless people who were separated from their families during the war and who have ever since been yearning to see their loved ones without even knowing whether they were still alive.

Just as the German people secured freedom, prosperity and peace by tearing down the Berlin Wall, we too, must tear down barriers in our march toward a new future on the Korean Peninsula.

Today, a 'wall of military confrontation' runs through the center of the Peninsula. A 'wall of distrust' has also been erected during the war and the ensuing decades of hostility.

Formidable still is a 'socio-cultural wall' that divides southerners and northerners who have long lived under vastly different ideologies and systems in terms of how they think and live.

Then there is a 'wall of isolation' imposed by North Korea's nuclear program, cutting North Korea off from the community of nations.

All of these curtains must be swept away if we are to unite the Korean Peninsula. And in their place we must build a 'new kind of Korean Peninsula:' a peninsula free of nuclear weapons, free from the fear of war, and free to enjoy life, peace and prosperity.

Ladies and gentlemen, I harbor no illusions that these tremendous barriers could be torn down with ease. But the future belongs to those who believe in their dreams and act on them. To make today's dream of peaceful unification tomorrow's reality, we must begin meticulous preparations now.

Nor do I believe that a nation is made whole again simply by virtue of a reconnected territory or the institution of a single system.

It is when those in the south and the north can understand each other and can get along as people of the same nation, that the Korean Peninsula can truly experience renewal as one.

In my view, Germany was able to overcome the after-shocks of unification fairly quickly and achieve the level of integration we see today because of the sustained people-to-people interaction that took place prior to unification.

Now more than ever, South and North

Korea must broaden their exchange and cooperation. What we need is not one-off or promotional events, but the kind of interaction and cooperation that enables ordinary South Koreans and North Koreans to recover a sense of common identity as they help each other out.

And so I hereby present three proposals to North Korean authorities in the hope of laying the groundwork for peaceful unification.

First, we must take up the agenda for humanity - the concerns of everyday people.

For a start, we must help ease the agony of separated families. It makes little sense to talk about solidarity as one nation, when members of the same family are refused their chance to even see each other despite their god-given right to live together.

It has been 70 long years. Last year alone, some three thousand eight hundred people who have yearned a lifetime just to be able to hold their sons' and daughters' hands - just to know whether they're alive - passed away with their dreams unfulfilled.

I am sure the same is true of their fellow family members in North Korea. Allowing reunions should also give family members in North Korea solace.

In order to address problems arising from family separations, East and West Germany permitted family visits in both directions and steadily promoted exchanges.

It is about time South and North Korea allow family reunions to take place regularly so we could ease their anguish and build trust in doing so.

We will reach out to North Korea to discuss concrete ways to achieve this and engage in necessary consultations with international bodies like the International Committee of the Red Cross.

Going forward, the Republic of Korea will expand humanitarian assistance to ordinary North Koreans.

The Korean Government will work with the United Nations to implement a program to provide health care support for pregnant mothers and infants in North Korea through their first 1,000 days. Furthermore, we will provide assistance for North Korean children so they could grow up to become healthy partners in our journey toward a unified future.

Second, we must pursue together an agenda for co-prosperity through the building of infrastructure that support the livelihood of people.

South and North Korea should collaborate to set up multi-farming complexes that support agriculture, livestock and forestry in areas in the north suffering from backward production and deforestation.

Working together from sowing to harvesting will enable South and North Korea not just to share the fruits of our labor, but also our hearts. As the bonds of trust begin to burgeon between the two sides, we can start to look at larger forms of development cooperation.

To help make life less uncomfortable for ordinary North Koreans, Korea could invest in infrastructure-building projects where possible, such as in transportation and telecommunication. Should North Korea allow South Korea to develop its natural resources, the benefits would accrue to both halves of the peninsula.

This would organically combine South Korean capital and technology with North Korean resources and labor and redound to the eventual formation of an economic community on the Korean Peninsula.

In tandem with trilateral projects among the two Koreas and Russia, including the Rajin-Khasan joint project currently in the works, we will push forward collaborative projects involving both Koreas and China centered on the North Korean city of Shinuiju, among others. These will help promote shared development on the Korean Peninsula and in Northeast Asia.

The international community also needs to take greater interest in getting involved if development projects in North Korea are to proceed more efficiently.

I call on those NGOs from Germany and Europe which have extensive experience working with North Korea on agricultural projects and forestry to join us. I also hereby ask international organizations like the United Nations and the World Bank for their support and cooperation.

Third, we must advance an agenda for integration between the people of South and North Korea.

As the state of division persists year after year, the language, culture and living habits of the two sides continue to diverge. If there is to be real connection and integration between the south and the north, we must narrow the distance between our values and our thinking.

To achieve this, those from the south and the north must be afforded the chance to interact routinely. We will encourage exchanges in historical research and preservation, culture and the arts, and sports - all of which could promote genuine people-to-people contact - rather than seek politically-motivated projects or promotional events.

Should North Korea so desire, we would be happy to partner with the international community to share our experience in economic management and developing special economic zones, and to provide systematic education and training opportunities relating to finance, tax administration and statistics.

We could also look at jointly developing educational programs to teach future generations and cultivate talent, for it is in them that the long-term engines to propel a unified Korean Peninsula forward will be found.

I hereby propose to North Korea that we jointly establish an 'inter-Korean exchange and cooperation office' that would be tasked to realize these ideas.

Ladies and gentlemen, The armistice line bisecting the peninsula and the demilitarized zone, which is in fact the most militarized stretch of real estate on the planet, best epitomize the reality of our division today.

My hope is to see South and North Korea, together with the United Nations, moving to build an international peace park inside the DMZ. By clearing barbed-wire fences and mines from parcels of the DMZ, we can start to create a zone of life and peace.

This international peace park will presage the replacement of tension with peace on the DMZ, division with unification, and conflict in Northeast Asia with harmony.

If South and North Korea could shift the adversarial paradigm that exists today, build a railway that runs through the DMZ and connect Asia and Europe, we will see the makings of a genuine 21st century silk road across Eurasia and be able to prosper together.

North Korea must choose the path to denuclearization so we could embark without delay on the work that needs to be done for a unified Korean Peninsula.

I hope North Korea abandons its nuclear aspirations and returns to the Six Party Talks with a sincere willingness to resolve the nuclear issue so it could look after its own people.

Should North Korea make the strategic decision to forgo its nuclear program, South Korea would correspondingly be the first to offer its active support, including for its much needed membership in international financial institutions and attracting international investments. If deemed necessary, we can seek to create a Northeast Asia Development Bank with regional neighbors to spur economic development in North Korea and in surrounding areas.

We could also build on the Northeast Asia Peace and Cooperation Initiative to address North Korea's security concerns through a multilateral peace and security system in Northeast Asia.

Here lies the road to shared prosperity between South and North Korea and here lies the path to peace and prosperity in Northeast Asia.

Korea will aspire to a unification that promotes harmony with its neighbors, that is embraced by the community of nations, and that serves the cause of the international community.

With a view to ushering in an era peaceful unification on the Korean Peninsula, I will soon be launching a committee to prepare for unification - one that reports directly to me as president.

People from inside and outside the government will come together through this committee to muster our collective wisdom as we more fully prepare for the process of unification and integration.

Citizens and students of Dresden, Human history has been an incessant march towards justice and towards peace.

Just as Germany turned the great wheels of history forward from the western end of Eurasia, a new chapter in mankind's progress will start from its eastern tip, namely the Korean Peninsula.

Just as German unification represented the inexorable tide of history, I believe that Korean unification is a matter of historical inevitability. For nothing can repress the human yearning for dignity, freedom and prosperity.

Today I stand behind this podium and observe the faces of young German students bound together by an impassioned quest for truth. And as I do so, I am also picturing the day when young students from both halves of a unified Korean Peninsula are studying side by side and nurturing their dreams together.

Mark my words - that day will come. And when that day arrives, young people from Germany, from the whole of Korea and from all over the world, will exchange their vision of a better world as they travel back and forth between Asia and Europe through a Eurasian railway.

I ask our friends here in Germany to join us on this journey to peaceful unification.

'Wir sind ein Volk!' The day will soon come when these powerful words that united the people of East and West Germany echoes across the Korean Peninsula.

In closing, may a prosperous future await our true friends here in Germany and here at the Dresden University of Technology. Thank you.

ADDRESS TO THE NATION BY PRESIDENT PARK GEUN-HYE ON THE SEWOL FERRY DISASTER

(May 19, 2014, Seoul)

Fellow Koreans, Today is the 34th day since the sinking of the Sewol occurred. All Koreans share in the pain and grief of the families that lost loved ones.

As the President responsible for lives and safety of the people, I apologize from deep in my heart for the pain and suffering you have undergone.

Fellow Koreans, I fully understand why you all have shared pain and outrage over the past weeks.

Many students who could have been saved were not rescued. The fumbling response in the initial stage caused great confusion. Illegal overloading and other factors identified as safety problems were never prevented; I believe you have been frustrated and outraged for this.

I, too, have spent sleepless nights in agony, thinking about the many young students whose lives had yet to blossom, the child left alone now after what became her last family trip and other heartbreaking stories of the victims.

As President, I feel a sense of sorrow and grief over not having been able to protect them, not having been able to make their trip safe. The ultimate responsibility for failing to properly deal with the disaster lies with me.

I will take this opportunity to make this country reborn so that their invaluable sacrifices are not in vain.

The Korea Coast Guard did not live up to its inherent duties in this ferry disaster. Had it performed rescue operations promptly and proactively right after the accident, the number of victims could have been greatly reduced. The Coast Guard's rescue operations were virtually a failure.

The cause of the failure can be found in the chronic structural problems that have persisted since the founding of the Coast Guard. It has, in fact, neglected rescue and salvage operations, focusing on investigation and its external growth. Even though the Coast Guard has continued to grow in size, it has failed to secure necessary manpower and budget for maritime safety. Moreover, it has lacked adequate lifesaving training.

With these structural problems left unattended, we would not be able to prevent another calamity in the future. Thus, I decided to dismantle the Coast Guard after serious consideration. Investigation and intelligence functions will be transferred to the National Police Agency while maritime rescue and salvage as well as coast guard responsibilities will be handed over to a soon-to-be established national safety agency. In so doing, professionalism and responsibility for maritime safety will be significantly bolstered.

The Ministry of Security and Public Administration ultimately responsible for public safety has not fulfilled its duties either. It will be divested of its core duties for safety as well as personnel and organizational issues. Its safety-related mandate will be transferred to the national safety agency and its personnel and organizational functions handed over to an administration reform agency to be created and placed under the Prime Minister. By this, the Ministry of Security and Public Administration will be allowed to concentrate on administration and local autonomy affairs.

The Ministry of Oceans and Fisheries, which takes command of and supervises the Coast Guard, is not free from responsibilities either. Its Vessel Traffic Services Center will be merged into the national safety agency. The Ministry of Oceans and Fisheries will focus on fostering the ocean industry as well as preserving and promoting the fishing industry. In this way, the expertise of individual organizations will be fully leveraged, making it possible to carry out responsible administration of government.

A bill to revise the Government Organization Act reflecting all these contents will be submitted to the National Assembly in the near future.

Fellow Koreans, My Administration has thus far continued with the reform process to normalize abnormal practices and systems in our society.

It rankles deep in my heart that I was not able to hasten the reform process and eliminate such wrong practices earlier, ending up causing great suffering to the people. The ferry disaster attests to how big a catastrophe can be brought on by deep-rooted abnormal practices, such as our cliquish culture and the government-business collusion rampant in our society.

If safety regulations, including ship inspection and safety guidelines, had been adhered to by the book and supervision properly carried out, this tragic disaster would not have happened.

Until now, the Korean Shipping Association, an interest group of marine companies, has been given the authority for marine safety management, and its senior positions have been customarily filled by retired government officials.

As long as the Government, which is supposed to regulate and supervise the safety of ships, and the shipping companies that are the subject of supervision have such a cozy relationship, it is obvious that no proper ship safety management would be possible.

An aged ferry built nearly 20 years ago was purchased and refurbished in defiance of safety. With a fabricated document, the ship was loaded with cargo whose weight was much higher than the permissible limit, but no one responsible for supervising the ship set the wrongs right.

This case of government-business collusion represents a chronic malady that has piled up layer upon layer over decades not only in the shipping industry but in our society in general.

I will do whatever it takes to make my Administration's reform drive for the normalization of the abnormal a success. By doing so, I will certainly sever the collusive links between government officials and business people that promote cover-ups and whitewashing disregarding life. This will resolve the problems of the so-called bureaucratic mafia.

For now, civil servants will not be appointed as heads or auditors for civil service related organizations that are responsible for safety supervision, procurement, or approval-related regulations susceptible to conflicts of interest Employment by other organizations will be more strictly restricted.

Currently, there are regulations putting restrictions on the employment of retired government officials, but they are nothing more than in name only to the extent that only seven percent of the retired officials who were supposed to go through the screening process were prevented from being employed in the past three years.

To make matters worse, the Korea Shipping Association and the Korean Register of Shipping, which are related to the sinking of the ferry, were not even on the list of companies subject to the system that limits the employment of retired government officials.

In the days to come, the Government will significantly increase by more than three times the current number of organizations where the employment of retired government officials is restricted. Consequently, some organizations and associations will be newly subject to the restrictions.

In addition, the period during which employment is restricted after retirement will be extended to three years from the current two years. As part of efforts to check the practices of the bureaucratic mafia, in case of retired senior government officials, the entire duties of their agency, not simply those of their department, will be taken into consideration when judging the correlation with their future duties. By doing so, the Government will greatly enhance the effectiveness in restricting their employment.

The Government will also introduce a new employment history disclosure system for senior government officials, under which their employment period and positions will be made public for ten years following retirement.

The Government will immediately submit to the National Assembly an amendment bill to the Public Service Ethics Act, which will include the aforementioned measures.

Given the significance of severing the collusive ties of former and current government officials, the Government has presented the so-called Kim Young-ran Act, a bill to ban illegal solicitation and to prevent civil servants from getting caught in a conflict of interest, and the bill is under review at the National Assembly.

I urge the National Assembly to pass the bill as early as possible.

Korea's public service sector is now saddled with the problems of a closed organizational culture and complacency.

In order to survive in the competition of the 21st century that is all about creativity, it is necessary to carry out reform aimed at fundamentally overhauling the public service sector.

In order to eliminate the ill practices of the bureaucratic mafia and fundamentally reform the public service, the Government will strive to reestablish the sector as one that is characterized by professionalism and openness from the point of officials' recruitment to their retirement.

To this end, the recruitment system will undergo drastic changes so that an increasing number of experts from the private sector will have opportunities to work for the government.

To facilitate the entry of private experts, the number of grade-5 government officials recruited through the open examinations and experienced professionals recruited from the private sector will be balanced to 5:5. In place of the state examinations that used to select many government officials at once in the past, the Government will ultimately establish a new system through which experts can be recruited when necessary and where needed according to their expertise.

As of now, there exists an open recruitment system that allows civilian professionals to be appointed at positions above the division director level. Notwithstanding, government officials occupy many such positions, and thus the public is criticizing its lack of effectiveness.

The open recruitment system went awry because each ministry and agency has operated its own selection committee. To address this problem, a central examination and selection committee will be newly established to recruit civilian professionals in a fair manner and assign them to ministries and agencies.

Together with this move, the Government will reform the system of job rotation, which has been continuously pointed out as a problem in the public service sector, so that the duty continuity and professionalism will be able to be maintained.

For officials who have expertise and devote themselves to the interests of the people and the nation, a better working environment will be created: due incentives will be provided so that they would be able to continue to work hard with greater self-esteem.

My fellow citizens, The immediate cause of the accident was the dereliction of duty by the captain and some crewmembers as well as the wrongful pursuit of profits through excessive additions to the ferry and overloading.

Cheonghaejin Marine Company, the operator of the ill-fated ferry, entered the shipping industry by taking over an affiliate of Semo Group, which went under in 1997. The company, which went bankrupt because of its debts amounting to 300 billion won 17 years ago, made ill use of the workout program to write off 200 billion won worth of its debts. It was then resold to the original owner at a giveaway price, and the greedy pursuit of profits since then has led to the recent disaster.

This kind of practice must not be tolerated any more.

All profits of businesses accumulated in the process of seeking interests in a greedy manner while doing much damage to the people and their properties will be restituted and used as financial resources to compensate the victims for their loss. Those businesses will be forced to shut down.

To this end, the Government will swiftly legislate a law that makes it possible to seek and get back not only the assets of offenders themselves but also those concealed under the names of family members or third parties.

With regard to this accident, the Government will first promptly compensate the victims and immediately submit a special bill that enables the Government to exercise the right to indemnity against those who are responsible for the sinking.

By doing so, the Government will make sure that those who suffered indescribable sacrifices this time will not undergo additional serious pain in the process of receiving damages from the unethical businesses and offenders.

If the right to indemnity cannot be exercised in a proper manner, we would end up seeing a preposterous situation where tax paid with the sweat and blood of the people are used to compensate for the loss incurred by the wrongdoings of offenders or businesses.

With the many problems of Cheonghaejin Marine Company coming to light this time, many people are casting doubts on various special favors given to the company and its collusive ties with government officials in the course of its growth. If there had been any forces that stood behind the company, they would also be traced to the end. In order for such collusive ties not to threaten the lives and safety of people yet again, the Government will root out corruptive practices in every part of our society.

If needed, a special prosecutor will be appointed to get to the bottom of every detail of the accident and strictly punish those who are responsible for it.

On top of this, I suggest that a special act be legislated, which includes the establishment of a fact-finding commission consisting of theruling and oppositions lawmakers as well as people from the private sector. I hope the commission will serve as a place for ruling and oppositions lawmakers to engage in discussions together over all matters related to the Sewol.

The irresponsible acts of the captain and some members of the crew, who fled first leaving hundreds of passengers trapped in the vessel, are virtually tantamount to homicide. In some advanced nations, those who commit felonies that cause extensive loss of human life are sentenced to hundreds of years behind bars.

In the days ahead, we will propose revisions to our Criminal Act so that, in this country also, strict punishment is given to those whose actions cause grave human losses, or whose malicious tampering with food endangers many. We will thus make certain that wrongfully gained profits are a profit to no one, and that those responsible for disasters of such a magnitude do not get off lightly.

Fellow citizens, So many precious lives were taken from us in this tragedy. It is the duty of the living to make reform and a great transformation for the country so that the sacrifices of the dead are not in vain. If we cannot reform ourselves in a situation like this, we will become a nation that will never be able to achieve reform.

The Government failed to respond promptly and cohesively in this emergency because public safety and disaster management functions were scattered across various government agencies. Other problems arose concerning the central "control tower."

To solve these problems, we will establish a national safety agency that combines the functions of existing safety-related agencies, streamlining the chain of command to allow for coordinated onsite responses to emergencies on land and at sea.

For emergencies on land, a system will be set up to coordinate a speedy and efficient response by the local fire department, local authorities and the related central ministries. For maritime emergencies, onsite rescue and salvage functions will be strengthened through the creation of regional maritime safety offices for the Yellow Sea, the South Sea, the East Sea and Jeju Island.

For disasters in the aviation, energy, chemical and telecommunications sectors, areas that are currently overseen separately by their related ministries, a special disaster management office will be opened to direct disaster responses.

In addition, a special rescue force complete with state-of-the-art equipment and the most advanced technologies will be set up for dispatch to the site of any disaster in any part of the country. This team will undergo

repeated training of the kind used in the military or special police force and thereby strengthen significantly its capacity to take effective action during the "golden time" of rescue operations.

To ensure practically that all of these functions can be performed, the national safety agency will be given the right to prior consultation concerning the national safety budget and be allowed to allocate special revenue funds for disaster prevention.

Moreover, in order to make the national safety agency an organization of disaster and safety experts, it will operate an open recruitment policy. With strict limitations on job rotation, this agency will be fostered as a model for the changes that can be realized in the public sector through a partnership of experts and the people. I ask for the active participation of willing experts and other interested citizens throughout the country.

When the new agency is created, we will carry out an extensive survey for suggestions from the public and from related experts that will then provide a basis for the creation of a safety innovation master plan. We will also speed up the conclusion of the project to build a national disaster and safety communications network, which has continued for eleven years without progress. This way, all of the disaster response organizations will be able to work within a single communications network to mount a unified response and solidify cooperative efforts.

Fellow citizens, In preparing to come before you today to speak about measures for public safety and government reform, I listened to the concerns and views of numerous people. I spent past weeks in agony and painstaking contemplation.

The sinking of the Sewol will be recorded as a painful wound in this country's history that will not be easily removed. Yet if we can go on, in the aftermath of this tragedy, to build a truly safe Republic of Korea, this will mark a new history. Such heavy responsibilities are given to all of us.

We possess the fortitude and experience of having united together, whenever our country faced difficulty, to overcome whatever crises lay before us. Now we must rise up from our despair and go forward. We must set our country right and make it new.

I will work to rectify the wrong practices and the irregularities of the past and present and devote myself completely and fully to building a new Korea. I will take firm strides to enact what I have promised - the Three Year Plan for Economic Innovation, normalization of past abnormal practices, public service reforms and elimination of corruption.

The problems before us will not be resolved easily. But we will not cease our efforts. Together with the people, we will make a better tomorrow, and we will build a country that our children will be proud of.

In the days after the Sewol capsized, countless people dropped everything and rushed to the scene. Fishermen and civilian divers as well as donors and volunteers from every walk of life put their lives and work on hold in hopes that they could help to save even one more life.

After giving his life vest to his younger sister and getting her off the boat, Kwon Hyeok-gyu disappeared among the missing. High school student Jeong Cha-wung took off his life vest for his friend and then went back into the water to save another friend. Choi Deok-ha was the student who made the first call notifying 119 emergency services of the accident, but he did not come back.

Teachers Nam Yun-cheol and Choi Hye-jeong did everything they could for their students until the very last. Crew members Pak Ji-yeong, Kim Gi-wung and Jeong Hyeon-seon, chief officer Yang Dae-hong, and civilian rescue diver Lee Gwang-wuk spent their final moments helping to save lives. In the actions of all of these, I see the hope of this country. They are the true heroes of our time.

In order that we may honor the memory of the victims and be ever reminded of the importance of safety, I propose that a memorial be raised and April 16 observed as National Safety Day.

I pray once again for the eternal rest of those who were lost, and I extend deepest condolences to all of the grieving families. Thank you very much.

REMARKS AT THE CLIMATE SUMMIT BY PRESIDENT OF THE REPUBLIC OF KOREA

(Sept. 23, 2014, New York)

Mr. Secretary-General, fellow leaders, The climate crisis is real. The earth is warming. Scorching heat waves, severe rains and frigid colds - such extreme weather events are affecting human life in so many ways.

As Secretary-General Ban stated, "climate change is the great challenge of the 21st century." And we must rise to the challenge.

Ladies and gentlemen, Escaping poverty was once our top priority. But even then, Korea made sure the Miracle on the Han River didn't come at the cost of our environment.

Our annual Arbor Day and Forestry Day campaigns completely reforested our once barren landscape.

These efforts continue to this day. Driven by a new paradigm, Korea is seeking a creative economy. Nurturing new energy industries to deal with climate change is a key part of this initiative.

Energy storage systems that supply electricity around-the-clock; smart grid technologies that let plug-ins feed power back into the grid - these are key examples.

Carbon capture and storage, and zero-energy buildings are spurring new industries. Eco-friendly towns are being set up that produce solar power and bio-gas from cattle and food waste.

Next year, we will become the first Asian country to implement a nation-wide Emissions Trading Scheme.

We will also let frugal consumers sell saved electricity back to the grid. So we're doing our best to enlist everyone in reducing our carbon footprint.

Ladies and gentlemen, Tackling climate change needs to proceed on several fronts.

First, we need to see climate action not as a burden, but as an opportunity.

The tiniest change in how we think can later make a world of difference. How we view the climate agenda - as boon or bane - will bring huge differences.

Investing in the chance to unlock new energy industries and jobs, can ignite fresh engines of future growth.

It has been said that the stone age didn't end because we ran out of stones.

Second, technology and market-based solutions should be at the center.

Innovations can't come from government alone. To encourage the private sector to lead, markets should reward carbon-cutting innovations.

Third, all countries need to be on board. For developing countries, however, cutting CO_2 can be a burden. To help them invest in needed capabilities and build markets, the developed world should transfer technology and know-how.

Distinguished guests, All countries need to do their share if we are to limit global warming to 2 degrees by this century's end.

Korea will work to submit next year our plan to support the Post-2020 climate regime.

We will also work with bodies like the Green Climate Fund, and the GGGI, to share and spread our experience.

The early capitalization of the GCF is vital to the launch of a new climate regime next year. So we look to your contributions to the Fund.

The Korean government pledges up to 100 million dollars to the GCF, including the 50 million we are currently paying.

Distinguished Leaders, The human race has but one earth. We must save our planet from warming. And the time to act is NOW. Thank you.

ADDRESS BY PRESIDENT PARK GEUN-HYE AT THE 69TH SESSION OF THE GENERAL ASSEMBLY OF THE UNITED NATIONS

(Sept. 24, 2014, New York)

Mr. President, Mr. Secretary-General, fellow delegates, Let me start by congratulating you, Mr. Kutesa, on your election as President of the 69th Session of the UN General Assembly. I am confident that this session will make meaningful progress under your able leadership.

I would also like to express my appreciation to Secretary-General Ban Ki-moon for his tireless efforts to tackle the numerous challenges breaking out across the globe.

Next year marks the 70th anniversary of the founding of the United Nations.

I am prompted by the state of our world today, to reflect once again upon the noble dreams and ideals that inspired the founders of the United Nations seventy years ago.

The founders aspired to build a new world that places people at the center, as the opening words of the UN Charter, 'We the Peoples,' remind us.

Throughout the ensuing decades of the Cold War and post-Cold War era, the UN has been tackling countless crises, striving as it did so, to fulfill its purpose of maintaining international peace, promoting development, and upholding human rights.

Yet, our world continues to be beset with widespread disputes and conflicts - both large and small - despite the efforts of the UN.

Civil conflicts raging on in Syria, Libya and South Sudan are leading to the deaths of untold numbers of innocent women and children.

In Iraq and surrounding areas, the activities of foreign terrorist fighters are posing new threats to peace internationally, not to mention in the Middle East.

The fragile ceasefire in Gaza and Ukraine call for a more fundamental and lasting solution.

The recent Ebola outbreak in Africa, widespread poverty and natural disasters, together underscore how humanity is under threat from multiple challenges.

The need to push back against these harmful challenges to peace and development beckons us to return to the UN's founding spirit of putting people first and promoting cooperation among the family of nations.

And to meet the aspirations of the international community for justice and common prosperity, the UN needs to continue playing a central role for arranging more rapid and efficient responses.

Ladies and Gentlemen, The Republic of Korea was founded in 1948 with the blessing of the UN. It was able to safeguard freedom and democracy during the Korean War that broke out two years later, again with the help of the UN.

Once a country that barely managed to survive with the UN's assistance, the Republic of Korea is today a nation that has achieved both an advanced market economy and democracy.

And in the course of that journey, the Republic of Korea came to espouse the values upheld by the UN - peace, development and human rights - as its own vision.

Given its history, the Republic of Korea is no stranger to the agonies of civil war, aggression, poverty and humanitarian disasters that are unfolding around the world.

This is why Korea is actively working to serve international peace, promote human rights and sustainable development, as a member of the three major councils of the UN - the Security Council, Human Rights Council, and Economic and Social Council.

Developments unfolding in the Middle East, Eurasia, and Northeast Asia are a far cry from the peaceful and just world that was envisioned by the UN's founders.

Overcoming the instability and chaos we see today must start with our adherence to the fundamental order and norms of the international community.

That is, respect for sovereignty and territorial integrity, refraining from the threat or use of force in violation of the UN Charter, and respect for human rights and humanitarian values.

We need to prevent the development and proliferation of weapons of mass destruction like nuclear weapons, which pose a fundamental threat to international peace and security.

In this regard, we welcome the elimination of Syria's chemical weapons through the joint efforts of the UN and the Organization for the Prohibition of Chemical Weapons (OPCW), as well as the progress being made in addressing the Iranian nuclear issue.

By the same token, I would underline the urgency of resolving the North Korean nuclear issue, which presents the single-greatest threat to peace on the Korean Peninsula and in Northeast Asia.

The DPRK is the only country to have conducted a nuclear test in the 21st century.

Its nuclear program is not only a serious threat to international peace, but also amounts to a total rejection of the Non-Proliferation Treaty, the backbone of the global nuclear non-proliferation regime.

The DPRK must make the decision to give up its nuclear weapons. The DPRK should follow in the footsteps of other countries that have abandoned their nuclear weapons in favor of reform and opening, and choose a different path that supports its economic development and improves the lives of its people.

Should it choose to do so, the Republic of Korea, together with the international community, will provide our strong support for developing the DPRK economy.

In addition to this serious challenge on the Korean Peninsula, Northeast Asia is undergoing a difficult transition.

There are growing tensions in the region surrounding issues of history, territory and maritime security. Yet, unlike other regions, Northeast Asia lacks a mechanism for dealing with these problems through multilateral consultations.

It is against this backdrop that I am seeking to advance a Northeast Peace and Cooperation Initiative that is aimed at building an order of trust and cooperation in the region.

In my view, building up habits of cooperation in practical areas, such as climate action, disaster relief, nuclear safety, and tackling transnational crime, can materialize into a multilateral process of cooperation along the lines of what we see in Europe.

In this context, I have also proposed creating a Northeast Asia nuclear safety consultative body to discuss nuclear safety issues - a topic of shared interest for the countries in the region.

At the same time, we are reaching beyond Northeast Asia and seeking to build transportation and energy networks across an economically inter-dependent Eurasia, which would help strengthen political and security trust across the continent.

Ladies and Gentlemen, This year marks 20 years since the Rwanda genocide - the world's greatest humanitarian tragedy of the late 20th century.

The international community had pledged 'never again' in the aftermath of the genocides in the former Yugoslavia and Rwanda in the 1990s. Yet, we are witnessing today a different type of humanitarian disaster unfolding in Syria and Iraq.

The Republic of Korea is actively participating in the efforts of the UN to prevent such humanitarian tragedies.

The Republic of Korea strongly supports UN policies to protect human rights, such as, in particular, the Rights up Front initiative and Open Gate Policy that the Secretary-General is leading.

Even as we speak, Korean troops are taking part in UN peacekeeping missions in South Sudan and Lebanon, helping with peace-building, reconstruction, and the protection of civilians and human rights.

The Republic of Korea also attaches great importance to preventing the humanitarian suffering of women and children, in particular, who are most vulnerable in conflict situations.

In this context, during its presidency of the UN Security Council in February 2013, Korea chaired an open session on civilian protection in conflict situations and helped raise global awareness. Korea is also participating in the Preventing Sexual Violence Initiative (PSVI) as a champion state. Sexual violence against women during armed conflicts is a clear violation of human rights and humanitarian norms, regardless of how far back or where it occurred.

The human rights situation in the DPRK is also the subject of profound interest and concern for the international community.

Last March, the UN Human Rights Council adopted the recommendations in the report of the Commission of Inquiry (COI) on human rights in the DPRK. The DPRK and the international community should take the necessary measures to implement these recommendations.

In this regard, the UN office that will soon be set up in the Republic of Korea to investigate human rights abuses in the DPRK is expected to reinforce such efforts.

The international community should also pay greater attention to the human rights situation of North Korean defectors. Relevant UN agencies and countries should provide the necessary support so that defectors can freely choose their resettlement destinations.

Ladies and Gentlemen, The challenges facing humanity today, such as absolute poverty and climate change, can only be addressed through concerted international response, given their complexity and intertwined character.

Less than 500 days remain until the target date of the Millennium Development Goals (MDGs), which was launched with the goal of eradicating absolute poverty and increasing social and economic opportunities.

The Republic of Korea is ready to play a bridging role between developed and developing countries as the post-2015 development goals are being set, by harnessing our unique historical experience.

In this regard, the decision was made to develop the Busan Global Partnership into an international development cooperative mechanism at the Ministerial Meeting that was held last April in Mexico.

The Republic of Korea will seek to enhance the quality of its overseas assistance. We will continue to share our development experience, by globally promoting the Saemaul movement model, which conduced to eradicating rural poverty in Korea through the spirit of diligence, self-reliance and cooperation.

Having seen the power of education in propelling its own development, the Republic of Korea strongly supports - as a Champion - the Secretary-General's Global Education First Initiative (GEFI).

Korea will share its lessons-learned and provide substantive support to the UN's initiatives on education, which is one of the main themes of the post-2015 development goals.

To this end, Korea will host the World Education Forum (WEF) in 2015 and make efforts to reach an agreement on the new education objectives for the next fifteen years.

Climate change is no less an existential threat to humanity than the question of war and peace.

At yesterday's Climate Summit, leaders rallied their collective resolve to reach a consensus on the post-2020 new climate regime.

Going forward, an agreement must be reached on a new climate regime by the 2015 Conference of the Parties to the UNFCCC in Paris.

As the host country of the Green Climate Fund (GCF) and the Green Growth Global Institute (GGGI), Korea is committed to supporting international efforts to strengthen developing countries' mitigation and adaptation capacities.

Above all, we will continue to work for the full and early operationalization of the GCF and for the expansion of GGGI's assistance to developing countries.

Korea views the climate challenge, not as a burden, but an opportunity to unleash new value, markets and jobs through technology innovation. We are nurturing new energy industries.

And we hope to share the fruits of our efforts with other developing countries.

Mr. President, Fellow delegates, The Korean people gained independence 69 years ago, but the subsequent division of the Korean Peninsula precluded its membership in the UN as a single sovereign state.

The two Koreas were separately admitted as member states to the UN in

1991. Having two separate seats despite a single language, culture and history is clearly not normal.

This year marks the 25th anniversary of the fall of the Berlin Wall. But the Korean Peninsula remains stifled by a wall of division.

Countless separated families have been spending decades in agony, longing to see their loved ones.

I call on the international community to stand with us in tearing down the world's last remaining wall of division.

Not long ago, I proposed to the DPRK that we build corridors that can connect our environment, our livelihoods, and our culture.

In my view, a genuine community that can heal the wounds of division and move the both sides forward together, will only come about when people from the South and the North are able to live in natural harmony within a single ecosystem, when separated families are able to come together and ease their agony, and when culture is shared.

Today, the Korean Peninsula is divided by a 4km wide and 250km long demilitarized zone (DMZ). This DMZ, built around the military demarcation line to prevent renewed conflict, in reality ended up preventing the back-and-forth of people for some sixty years.

But from the stretches of the DMZ would emerge, in those decades, a treasure trove of nature's wildlife.

The DMZ's eco-system is a testament to the fact that the South and North are part of a single whole, one which both sides should work together to restore. And so I hope to build inside the very symbol of our division a World Eco-Peace Park that would start reconnecting the Peninsula's divided nature and divided people.

If we sweep away barbed-wire fences from small tracts inside the DMZ and thereby allow people from both sides to live in natural harmony, the World Eco-Peace Park will emerge as a corridor of life and peace.

I call on the UN to spearhead these efforts. Building a park that embodies respect for international norms and values, and doing so under UN auspices with all the parties to the war on board - the two

Koreas, the US and China - would serve the cause of easing tensions and peaceful reunification of the two Koreas.

A unified Korea will be the starting point for a world without nuclear weapons, offer a fundamental solution to the North Korean human rights issue, and help unlock a stable and cooperative Northeast Asia.

Just as the unification of Germany laid the grounds for a new Europe by integrating Europe, a unified Korea will set in motion a new Northeast Asia.

I am confident that a peacefully reunified Korean Peninsula will contribute to realizing the founding purposes and values espoused by the UN.

Mr. President, Mr. Secretary-General, Ladies and Gentlemen, The founders of the UN were not deterred by the heat of war from looking to the future and planning for a peaceful post-war world.

The Republic of Korea is committed to a vision of diplomacy that seeks lasting peace and unification in the Peninsula, peace and development in Northeast Asia, and contributes to building a happier world.

The Republic of Korea will do its part in the noble journey to ensure that the UN continues to safeguard our common values and cements its place at the center of global governance. Thank you.

ADDRESS BY PRESIDENT PARK GEUN-HYE AT THE NATIONAL ASSEMBLY ON GOVERNMENT PROPOSAL FOR FY 2015 BUDGET PLAN AND FISCAL OPERATIONS

(Oct. 29, 2014, Seoul)

Fellow Koreans, Honorable Speaker Chung Ui-hwa and distinguished members of the National Assembly, I am pleased to be here to explain to you, as I promised last year, the government's budget plan for next year. My Administration has made all-out efforts for national innovation and economic revival over the past year centering on four administrative priorities.

As a result, the economy has been making gradual headway. Economic growth is forecast to rise to the mid-3 percent level from last year's 3 percent. With a steady increase in jobs, the employment rate is also projected to climb 1 percent from last year to 65 percent.

The economy, however, is still in crisis. According to the third-quarter statistics on GDP growth released last week by the Bank of Korea, manufacturing output has decreased 0.9 percent and exports have dropped by a great margin. Capital investment in August slipped to its lowest point in 11 years and seven months.

Low growth, low prices and a weaker Japanese yen currently challenge the economy. Owing to these, the competitiveness of Korean businesses has been drastically undermined and global economic uncertainties, including the possibility of an interest rate hike in the United States sometime soon, have escalated as well. The most severe problem, however, is the fact that the country's working age population will begin to dwindle from 2017 due to Korea being the world's fastest aging society, inevitably lowering growth potential.

Inappropriate responses to these challenges from within and without will cause a prolonged recession and cause the economy to lose its momentum.

We are standing at a crossroads, facing our last golden opportunity; which road we take will determine whether our economy takes off or stagnates. Now is the time for the National Assembly, the Administration, businesses and the people to come together as one and make dedicated efforts to resuscitate the economy. With such an understanding, I will speak to you about the basic direction for running state affairs, the principles for fiscal operations and the budget plan for next year, and I would like to ask for your cooperation.

Fellow citizens and distinguished members of the National Assembly, The Government has placed economic revitalization as the top administrative priority for next year and accordingly increased the government budget by 20 trillion won from this year's.

The Government is already now working on a stimulus package totaling 46 trillion won - 12 trillion won for the reinforcement of finance in the latter half of the year, 5 trillion won for expanding investments in public corporations and 29 trillion won for supporting policy financing. The expansionary budget added to these will infuse great vitality into our economy.

The Government is well aware of the fact that the fiscal deficit and national debt will increase in the process of implementing the budget.

Yet at a time when households and businesses cannot afford to spend, if even the Government tightens its purse strings, it will be difficult for our economy to lift itself out of low growth.

When a family is in need, if all family members sit on their hands doing nothing, they cannot unfetter themselves from difficulties. They need to work together to tackle the difficulties head on. As such, when the nation is facing economic challenges, all its people should cope with them actively and wisely.

We must make painstaking efforts to get out of the crisis by investing in reviving the economy even if the fiscal deficit increases.

If a timely injection of finance serves as priming water and leads to a rebound in the economy and the settlement of a virtuous cycle expanding the tax revenue base, our financial fundamentals will be strengthened and the fiscal deficit and national debt will be reduced.

The Government has put in place a mid-term financial plan up to 2018. According to the plan, the foundation for a balanced budget will be laid and the national debt will be stably managed at the level of mid-30 percent of the GDP.

My Administration will at least have created a better financial situation for the next administration than it had when it was launched. Along with efforts to revitalize the economy, we can never ease up on the structural reform drive aimed at improving economic fundamentals and expanding the growth potential.

Marking the first anniversary of my inauguration last February, I announced the Three Year Plan for Economic Innovation and have continuously checked on the progress of its implementation. All-out efforts have been channeled into making economic fundamentals stronger by rectifying lax management and inefficiency in the public sector, turning our economy into a dynamic and innovative economy by helping a creative economy take deep root, and achieving an economy with balanced domestic demand and exports through deregulation.

Next year is the first year that the budget will be allocated in accordance with the three-year plan for economic innovation. My Administration will work to the best of its ability to ensure that the results of the three-year plan will be genuinely felt by the people next year. To this end, I will explain to you the three core tasks of the three-year plan for economic innovation and how they have been reflected in the next year's budget.

Fellow Koreans and distinguished Assembly members, It is imperative to make our economic fundamentals stronger by taking sweeping action to set right abnormal institutions and practices as well as long-running evils of the past in order to help our economy make a giant leap forward.

First, I will begin with making sure that the Government will uphold its basic responsibility of safeguarding public safety. To achieve this goal, the budget for safety has been expanded 17.9 percent, the highest increase across all sectors, to reach 14.6 trillion won. The Government will make investments not only in hardware to renovate school safety facilities and improve dangerous roads but also in software to enhance safety education and unify the telecommunication networks for the national disaster response system.

At the same time, it will pursue an across-the-board national safety assessment, which will be conducted by both specialists and ordinary people who voluntarily participate using mobile applications. On the basis of findings of such safety screenings, the Government will inject safety investment funds or apply the relevant budget to thoroughly repair and reinforce unsafe facilities.

In accordance with such measures, it is expected that accidents at major public facilities, including school buildings, will be prevented and that safety awareness will also be greatly raised in society in general.

Especially, increased investments in safety facilities are anticipated to help revive the economy and induce investments from the private sector that will develop state-of-the-art safety products and foster professional workers, thereby nurturing the safety industry into a high-value-added industry.

The Government will also step up efforts for public sector reforms to help reduce deficits. More than anything else, there is an urgent need to reform the government employees' pension. The seriousness of the deficit in this pension had already been expected for the past 20 years, but previous administrations stopped short of coming up with a solution that could get to the root of the matter, bringing about today's crisis. If pension reform is not appropriately carried out this time either, the next administrations and future generations will end up with a tremendous debt and a hefty burden.

The situation has changed significantly since 1960 when the civil servants' pension was first designed. Compared to that time, the average life expectancy has increased nearly 30 years, and between 1983 and 2013, the number of pension beneficiaries jumped more than 60-fold from 6,000 to 370,000.

As a result, the shortage in the pension is forecast to swell from 15 trillion won under the current administration to 33 trillion won in the next administration and to more than 53 trillion won in the following one, causing the public burden to snowball.

To be honest, any administration would be afraid of carrying out pension reform and would want to avoid it because it will require sacrifice from the civil servants who have devoted themselves to the country. However, the current situation, in which a colossal amount of tax money has to be funneled each year to shore up the pension plan, cannot be left unattended. If left unaddressed, the country - our children and grandchildren - will be handed a huge debt, and the pension itself might fail. For these reasons and out of desperation, we must complete pension reform.

Civil servants have long served as the crossbeam of the country. I recognize their meritorious service and have a high regard for their sense of duty. But the economy is now in a downturn and the lives of low-income people are especially hard. I hope that the civil servants will regard their sacrifice as a way to save the very foundation of the Republic of Korea for posterity. I ask for their sacrifice and concessions.

Calling for their deep understanding on this issue, I plead with them to join our reform efforts. I also call upon the National Assembly to actively cooperate so that the government employees' pension reform will be finalized by the end of this year.

The Government will continue to reform public organizations and cut their debts. Seamless implementation of normalization plans for state-run organizations this year helped significantly rectify their chronic lax management practices, and thus their debts are expected to be reduced by over 33 trillion won by the end of this year.

Building on this achievement, the Government will place focus on boosting their productivity and efficiency in the days to come. To this end, the functions of each organization will be examined to eliminate superfluity.

To strengthen the fundamentals of the economy, it is necessary to redouble our efforts to strengthen the social safety net for those who are left out in the cold. Next year's welfare budget of 115.5 trillion won - up 8.5 percent from this year - exceeds 30 percent of the total budget for the first time.

Above all, basic pension benefits will be distributed to 4.64 million senior citizens to enhance their post-retirement income. A 105.3 billion won energy voucher scheme has been newly introduced to ensure that the 960,000 households headed by the low-income elderly, those with disabilities and adolescents get through winter without worrying about heating costs.

To give greater health protection to all people, national health insurance coverage for four serious illnesses has been scaled up significantly. On top of this, three costs incurred by the selection of a doctor, the use of a ward with fewer than six beds and the need for care-giving services, which are not covered by the national health insurance, will be lowered to drastically reduce the burden of medical expenses.

More than anything else, the budget for emergency welfare support has more than doubled compared to this year, reaching 101.3 billion won. This is intended to prevent the recurrence of the tragic incident of a mother and her two daughters taking their own lives because of severe financial difficulties.

In line with the changes in the National Basic Living Security program that will make it possible to provide necessary basic living assistance tailored to the different need of recipients, housing allowances for the vulnerable have also increased by a large margin. The related budget has increased 50 percent to 1.1 trillion won to cover a total of 970,000 households, an increase of 240,000 from this year, and to provide an additional 240,000 won in rent for a year.

Since the Government even expanded the budget by increasing national debt to revive the economy next year, it will make sure that not even a single won will be wasted. The increase in the welfare budget this time is indispensable in eliminating blind spots in the welfare system, giving hope to those who face difficulties in earning a living and making the lives of retirees more stable.

I look forward to your cooperation in the budget planning to bring new hope to those in need. For its part, the Government will reinforce the monitoring of the whole process from the selection of welfare recipients and provision of services to post management to ensure that limited funds do not fall into the wrong hands. It will also thoroughly prevent a leakage of welfare funds by strictly punishing unqualified recipients as a warning to others.

My fellow citizens and members of the National Assembly, Currently competition in the global economy is getting ever fiercer, and new ideas and technologies are generating significant added value. In this situation, it is necessary for our nation to shift to a dynamic and innovative economy to jump over the pit of low growth and make yet another leap forward.

I believe the starting point lies in a creative economy. When our people's limitless creativity and potential are utilized to create growth engines, it will be possible to win the competition with other nations. The Government has so far made efforts to create an environment where anyone with ideas and technology can seek an opportunity to start a business and an ecosystem characterized by a virtuous cycle within which starting a business can lead to growth, returns and reinvestment.

As a consequence, over 40,000 businesses have been newly established in the first half of this year, an all-time high, and the number of registered angel investors increased by 150 percent compared to that of the end of 2012.

Some foreign press outlets have reported that a new wave is being generated in the world of startups in Korea. As such, a silent revolution is taking place at universities and industrial sites.

In addition, Korea came in fifth among 189 nations in the World Bank's global ranking on the ease of doing business released today, its highest ranking. It ranked first and third among G20 and OECD member nations, respectively, which points to our nation's unmatched business environment.

This also proves that the world is paying attention to Korea and that many global businesses regard Korean companies as partners. Among other things, in the category of starting a business, Korea ranked 17th, a jump from 34th last year. This shows that the Korean Government's focus on the creative economy is bearing fruit and that a foothold has been prepared to open an era of globalization. In order to reinforce that foothold, the Government is planning to inject 8.3 trillion won next year, an increase of 17.1 percent from this year's budget, into the creative economy sector so that changes in the field will spread to the overall economy.

To ensure that the embers of a creative economy kindled with some difficulty become the flame of creativity and innovation illuminating our economy as a whole, the Government is opening Centers for Creative Economy and Innovation. The first such Centers have been opened in Daegu and Daejeon, and others will be up and running in all 17 provinces and cities. Making the most of each region's unique features and strengths, the Government will place emphasis on helping make tailored creative economy models take root.

For instance, numerous technologies developed by government-funded research institutes in Daejeon will be commercialized. For Sejong city, a creative village model has been proposed; new added value in agriculture could be generated through smart farms where ICT is applied in farming. In Daegu, conventional industries such as textiles and auto parts will become more advanced through the convergence with ICT.

To turn many brilliant ideas that are posted on the Creative Economy Town website into businesses, the Government will inject 10 billion won into establishing a comprehensive support framework to help manufacture test products and provide legal and consulting services.

In addition, a total of 30.8 billion won will be invested in the creative economy valley project to provide one-stop services for identifying ideas, manufacturing test products, starting a business, business incubation and the entry into overseas markets, thereby helping create a Korean version of Silicon Valley.

Research and development constitutes a pillar sustaining the creative economy. Starting in 13 major growth engine areas, the Government will raise R&D investments to reach 5 percent of the GDP by 2017. Specifically, a total of 18.8 trillion won, an increase of 5.9 percent from this year, will be injected next year.

The efficiency of R&D investments will be enhanced, and efforts will be redoubled to help them produce tangible results. In particular, assistance by the government-funded research institutes to small and medium-sized businesses that are in urgent need of technological support will be enhanced. The Government will also strive to make sure that the outcomes of technological development will be turned into new products and businesses, instead of being kept in the laboratory.

To further boost the dynamism of the economy, businesses have to redouble their efforts to develop foreign markets. Thanks to continued endeavors to address difficulties in exporting, the proportion of exports by SMEs and enterprises of middle standing has been on a steady rise, reaching a record-high 37.7 percent of the total in September this year.

The Government will further step up its efforts to nurture leading SMEs into global small-but-strong businesses. Next year it will select 500 promising technology businesses and invest 250 billion won, a 150 percent increase from this year, to assist R&D for and commercialization of technologies in promising areas. In so doing, the competitive edge of SMEs and enterprises of middle standing will be further sharpened, and their entry into overseas markets will be accelerated.

In addition, a total of 73.3 billion won, an increase of 160 percent from this year, will be injected into enhancing export capabilities tailored to diverse needs; supporting sales in global online shopping malls, facilitating the acquisition of overseas standard certifications, securing overseas distribution channels and marketing.

For about 500 selected fast-growing gazelle companies that also create many job opportunities, policy funds worth 300 billion won will be provided to help them grow into specialized global businesses.

The Government will implement in earnest the Manufacturing Industry Innovation 3.0 Strategy to help Korea's key manufacturers emerge as leaders in the global market where competition is intensifying.

To facilitate entry into overseas markets, it is necessary to continuously expand the FTA network.

The signing of FTAs with Australia and Canada, which had been long delayed, was finalized after I personally persuaded the Prime Ministers of the two nations. As a result, our FTA network has expanded to cover North America and Oceania, going beyond Asia and Europe.

The Government will further strive to conclude FTA negotiations with China, New Zealand and Vietnam as early as possible. FTAs constitute the firm foundation for increasing the exports of domestic businesses and attracting increased foreign investments in the face of the global economic downturn.

I urge you to quickly pass the ratification bills on pending FTAs so that Korean businesses will be able to benefit from first-mover advantages conferred by tariff reductions ahead of their competitors.

My fellow citizens and members of the National Assembly, For the sustainable growth of our economy, it is necessary to pursue balanced growth between domestic demand and exports, companies and households and the manufacturing industry and the service industry.

As a first step to invigorating domestic demand, we must continue efforts to increase business investment through deregulation. Over the course of several ministerial meetings on regulatory reform as well as trade and investment promotion meetings, we have developed tailored solutions to address current obstacles, which have resulted in new investments of 15 trillion won to date. In addition, we have received over 15,000 suggestions about regulations this year from the public since launching the online regulatory reform portal, which provides detailed information on government regulations and allows for real-time citizen oversight and involvement. The Government will continue to make thorough checks to remove unconstructive regulations.

To increase domestic demand, we must also ensure that the fruits of growth reach all households by means of jobs. In order to provide a stable basis for household incomes, the Government has expanded next year's budget for job support to a record 14.3 trillion won. Of this, 109.7 billion won will go to strengthening support for irregular and other disadvantaged workers in order to promote employment stability and establish a secure income base. For companies that move to give irregular workers regular employment status and raise wages, we will provide support of up to 600,000 won per month. We will also implement an unemployment credit system that subsidizes a portion of the national pension insurance contributions for the unemployed. In order to actively encourage the adoption of retirement pensions by microbusinesses and SMEs, we will subsidize a portion of the employer contribution for retirement pensions for low-income workers as well.

To ensure that women can work without concern over career interruptions or childcare obligations, approximately 804.7 billion won has been allocated for childcare support, 15.3 percent more than for this year. Besides expanding public daycare centers as well as private workplace daycare programs, the Government will strengthen financial incentives to allow women to work shorter hours during primary child-rearing years and be assured of their jobs when they return from childcare leave.

In a 40 percent increase from this year, approximately 32.6 billion won has been allocated to create quality flexible-hour jobs, which allow individuals to choose the working arrangements that best meet their needs. By subsidizing consulting services and labor costs for companies, the Government will facilitate reforms to the current work system and thereby promote the creation of such jobs. We will also work to prevent wrongful discrimination against flexible-hour job holders by making changes to the provisions in the current social insurance system that exclude such workers from eligibility for coverage.

Another key to revitalizing domestic demand is concentrated cultivation of the service industries, which, in comparison to the manufacturing industries, have fallen behind. To this end, the Government plans to strategically develop the most promising among these, namely the "five plus two," which encompasses seven high-potential industries, including healthcare, tourism, finance and content.

To boost the international expansion of the healthcare industry, the Government will put 30 billion won into starting a new global healthcare fund for across-the-board investments in such sectors as pharmaceuticals, healthcare devices and healthcare systems. We will also actively nurture creative tourism companies by increasing investment in the develop-

ment of creative tourism packages and the sharing of tourism information by public organizations.

For the cultivation of content industries like music, film and animation, we will increase related funding by 50 percent from this year for a total 120 billion won. We will also expand initiatives like the Content Korea Labs as well as game development centers and story creation centers in order to strengthen support for early-stage startups and related employment. Such efforts will also undergird the creation of new growth engines and additional quality jobs.

Distinguished members of the Assembly, As you all know, government spending alone cannot revive both the economy and the people's livelihoods. For this to be possible, the Government, the National Assembly and the Korean people must work together, each doing their best. Legislation to abolish regulations and strengthen livelihoods must be enacted promptly by the National Assembly for the policies concerned to have maximum effectiveness.

Unfortunately, even now, legislation to improve the people's livelihoods and create jobs await approval. The proposed revision to the National Basic Living Security Act, in particular, has been continuously delayed; as a result, the 230 billion allocated to cover 130,000 new recipients remains unspent. This situation is no doubt bewildering to the waiting beneficiaries.

The World Bank's Doing Business report I mentioned earlier identified "getting credit" as Korea's weakest area. It is particularly unfortunate that crowdfunding, which is widely accepted abroad as a key way for creative entrepreneurs to secure funding, has not become established here. At the same time, few countries offer capital-deficient entrepreneurs the kind of business environment that Korea does, especially with our world-renowned Internet infrastructure. In order to improve conditions for financing businesses, the revised bill to the Capital Markets Act, which will launch a crowdfunding system, must be passed.

Similarly, the housing market normalization bill is necessary in order to make appropriate improvements to the existing system, introduced during a housing price hike many years ago, so that it reflects present conditions. It is also important for reinvigorating the housing market for the long term. As the bill also includes a provision to return taxes equivalent to a month's rent to home renters and so reduce the burden of housing costs for lower- to middle-class households, it must be passed as soon as possible.

As all of you also know, unless we get the service industries up and moving, we cannot create new jobs, nor can we find solutions to the pressing issue of youth unemployment. In order to foster these into high-value-added, high-potential industries, we must provide systematic support for R&D and human resources development. We must also change the unreasonable regulation that allows medical advertising to locals but not to foreigners.

If crucial legislative reforms are not enacted in time, the costs will be borne in their entirety by the people and the national economy. I ask you today, ruling and opposition party members alike, to put your heads together in a spirit of collaboration for mutual benefit and make sure that these bills are passed as soon as possible.

Fellow Koreans, members of the National Assembly, In the coming year, the Government will continue to pursue, with all steadfastness and resolve, the national innovation it has promised to the Korean people. As you pointed out during the recent audit, corruption and wrongdoings still plague the public sector and Korean society as a whole.

The corruption in defense industry procurement projects and military supply contracts brought up repeatedly in recent days, and similar unlawful actions taken in the course of budget execution, will be equated with aiding the enemy by undermining national security. We will purge these practices completely, striking at their very root and punishing those responsible, making them examples for the future.

In order to achieve a new takeoff for the economy and leave future generations with a country they can be proud of, our efforts must take place at a more fundamental level. Recent experiences have taught us that though time may pass, the traces of deeply-rooted past wrongs can remain as painful wounds for our children. If we fail to reform the public sector and eliminate corruption, we cannot know what kind of suffering we will pass on to the next generation; our efforts now will be like water poured into a bottomless well.

The law must be the foundation of all of our efforts. To uproot corruption and misconduct at a fundamental level, the Kim Young-ran Bill, Yoo Byung-eun Bill and other reform bills that have been moored in the National Assembly must be passed with no further delay.

Revising the Government Organization Act and establishing a unified, field-focused disaster and safety system, which would include the planned national safety agency, is also urgent. Since these bills have not passed, the ministries concerned have not found their proper places and there has been no overhaul of the national safety system.

I ask you once more for your active cooperation.

Fellow citizens and members of the National Assembly, This budget was expanded and finalized in recognition of the imperative to take bold, preemptive action for economic revitalization in the midst of serious difficulties as well as challenges with the economy and government finance. I will make every effort to revive the economy and set it again on a firm foundation. I ask that you will work to pass the budget in the prescribed period so that it can fulfill its purpose, priming the pump for economic revitalization and laying a path toward greater happiness for the people.

Fellow Koreans, The Korean people possess a strength and power of will that has raised up the economy in other times of great difficulty. Once again, I ask all members of the National Assembly, civil servants, and the Korean people to come together and contribute their insights to help pave the way for a new Republic of Korea. Through innovation, we will be reborn, and through a push to new heights, we will soar again.

Let us work together with one mind to open a new future for the Republic of Korea. Thank you very much.

Statistics

Yonhap News Agency

Area and Administrative Unit by City, County and District[1]

	Area(km²)[2]	Composition (%)	Eup	Myeon	Dong[3]		Area(km²)[2]	Composition (%)	Eup	Myeon	Dong[3]
Seoul	605.20	100.0	-	-	423	Daegu	883.48	100.0	3	6	130
Jongno-gu	23.91	4.0	-	-	17	Jung-gu	7.06	0.8	-	-	12
Jung-gu	9.96	1.6	-	-	15	Dong-gu	182.16	20.6	-	-	20
Yongsan-gu	21.87	3.6	-	-	16	Seo-gu	17.35	2.0	-	-	17
Seongdong-gu	16.85	2.8	-	-	17	Nam-gu	17.44	2.0	-	-	13
Gwangjin-gu	17.06	2.8	-	-	15	Buk-gu	94.08	10.6	-	-	23
Dongdaemun-gu	14.21	2.3	-	-	14	Suseong-gu	76.46	8.7	-	-	23
Jungnang-gu	18.50	3.1	-	-	16	Dalseo-gu	62.34	7.1	-	-	22
Seongbuk-gu	24.58	4.1	-	-	20	Dalseong-gun	426.59	48.3	3	6	-
Gangbuk-gu	23.60	3.9	-	-	13						
Dobong-gu	20.70	3.4	-	-	14	Incheon	1,040.88	100.0	1	19	127
Nowon-gu	35.44	5.9	-	-	19	Jung-gu	131.29	12.6	-	-	11
Eunpyeong-gu	29.70	4.9	-	-	16	Dong-gu	7.19	0.7	-	-	11
Seodaemun-gu	17.61	2.9	-	-	14	Nam-gu	24.84	2.4	-	-	21
Mapo-gu	23.84	3.9	-	-	16	Yeonsu-gu	45.57	4.4	-	-	12
Yangcheon-gu	17.40	2.9	-	-	18	Namdong-gu	57.01	5.5	-	-	19
Gangseo-gu	41.43	6.8	-	-	20	Bupyeong-gu	32.00	3.1	-	-	22
Guro-gu	20.12	3.3	-	-	15	Gyeyang-gu	45.57	4.4	-	-	11
Geumcheon-gu	13.02	2.2	-	-	10	Seo-gu	114.01	11.0	-	-	20
Yeongdeungpo-gu	24.53	4.1	-	-	18	Ganghwa-gun	411.33	39.5	1	12	-
Dongjak-gu	16.35	2.7	-	-	15	Ongjin-gun	172.07	16.5	-	7	-
Gwanak-gu	29.57	4.9	-	-	21						
Seocho-gu	47.00	7.8	-	-	18	Gwangju	501.18	100.0	-	-	95
Gangnam-gu	39.50	6.5	-	-	22	Dong-gu	49.20	9.8	-	-	13
Songpa-gu	33.87	5.6	-	-	26	Seo-gu	47.79	9.5	-	-	18
Gangdong-gu	24.59	4.1	-	-	18	Nam-gu	60.99	12.2	-	-	16
						Buk-gu	120.30	24.0	-	-	27
Busan	769.86	100.0	2	3	205	Gwangsan-gu	222.90	44.5	-	-	21
Jung-gu	2.83	0.4	-	-	9						
Seo-gu	13.93	1.8	-	-	13	Daejeon	540.24	100.0	-	-	78
Dong-gu	9.73	1.3	-	-	14	Dong-gu	136.67	25.3	-	-	16
Yeongdo-gu	14.13	1.8	-	-	11	Jung-gu	62.13	11.5	-	-	17
Busanjin-gu	29.69	3.9	-	-	23	Seo-gu	95.47	17.7	-	-	23
Dongnae-gu	16.63	2.2	-	-	13	Yuseong-gu	177.28	32.8	-	-	10
Nam-gu	26.81	3.5	-	-	17	Daedeok-gu	68.68	12.7	-	-	12
Buk-gu	39.37	5.1	-	-	13						
Haeundae-gu	51.47	6.7	-	-	18	Ulsan	1,060.46	100.0	4	8	44
Saha-gu	41.73	5.4	-	-	16	Jung-gu	37.00	3.5	-	-	13
Geumjeong-gu	65.27	8.5	-	-	17	Nam-gu	72.70	6.9	-	-	14
Gangseo-gu	181.63	23.6	-	-	7	Dong-gu	36.03	3.4	-	-	9
Yeonje-gu	12.08	1.6	-	-	12	Buk-gu	157.34	14.8	-	-	8
Suyeong-gu	10.21	1.3	-	-	10	Ulju-gun	757.39	71.4	4	8	-
Sasang-gu	36.09	4.7	-	-	12						
Gijang-gun	218.28	28.4	2	3	-	Sejong	464.90	100.0	1	9	1

590

	Area(km²)²⁾		Eup, Myeon and Dong³⁾				Area(km²)²⁾		Eup, Myeon and Dong³⁾		
		Composition (%)	Eup	Myeon	Dong			Composition (%)	Eup	Myeon	Dong
Gyeonggi-do	10,172.63	100.0	32	108	410	Cheorwon-gun	889.43	5.3	4	7	-
Suwon-si	121.05	1.2	-	-	40	Hwacheon-gun	908.97	5.4	1	4	-
Seongnam-si	141.69	1.4	-	-	48	Yanggu-gun	661.90	3.9	1	4	-
Uijeongbu-si	81.54	0.8	-	-	15	Inje-gun	1,645.15	9.8	1	5	-
Anyang-si	58.46	0.6	-	-	31	Goseong-gun	660.94	3.9	2	4	-
Bucheon-si	53.44	0.5	-	-	36	Yangyang-gun	629.86	3.7	1	5	-
Gwangmyeong-si	38.51	0.4	-	-	18						
Pyeongtaek-si	457.46	4.5	3	6	13	**Chungcheongbuk-do**	7,407.19	100.0	15	87	51
Dongducheon-si	95.66	0.9	-	-	8	Cheongju-si	153.44	2.1	-	-	30
Ansan-si	149.40	1.5	-	-	25	Chungju-si	983.67	13.3	1	12	12
Goyang-si	268.05	2.6	-	-	39	Jecheon-si	883.43	11.9	1	7	9
Gwacheon-si	35.87	0.4	-	-	6	Cheongwon-gun	786.84	10.6	3	10	-
Guri-si	33.31	0.3	-	-	8	Boeun-gun	584.25	7.9	1	10	-
Namyangju-si	458.05	4.5	5	4	7	Okcheon-gun	537.09	7.3	1	8	-
Osan-si	42.73	0.4	-	-	6	Yeongdong-gun	845.58	11.4	1	10	-
Siheung-si	135.01	1.3	-	-	15	Jincheon-gun	407.26	5.5	1	6	-
Gunpo-si	36.46	0.4	-	-	11	Goesan-gun	842.44	11.4	1	10	-
Uiwang-si	53.99	0.5	-	-	6	Eumseong-gun	520.30	7.0	2	7	-
Hanam-si	93.03	0.9	-	-	10	Danyang-gun	781.06	10.5	2	6	-
Yongin-si	591.33	5.8	1	6	24	Jeungpyeong-gun	81.83	1.1	1	1	-
Paju-si	672.77	6.6	4	9	7						
Icheon-si	461.36	4.5	2	8	4	**Chungcheongnam-do**	8,204.51	100.0	24	137	46
Anseong-si	553.44	5.4	1	11	3	Cheonan-si	636.07	7.8	4	8	18
Gimpo-si	276.63	2.7	3	3	6	Gongju-si	864.29	10.5	1	9	6
Hwaseong-si	689.66	6.8	3	10	10	Boryeong-si	569.39	6.9	1	10	5
Gwangju-si	431.00	4.2	3	4	3	Asan-si	542.18	6.6	2	9	6
Yangju-si	310.36	3.1	1	4	6	Seosan-si	740.78	9.0	1	9	5
Pocheon-si	826.73	8.1	1	11	2	Nonsan-si	554.78	6.8	2	11	2
Yeoju-si	608.32	6.0	1	8	3	Gyeryong-si	60.71	0.7	-	3	1
Yeoncheon-gun	675.83	6.6	2	8	-	Dangjin-si	695.48	8.5	2	9	3
Gapyeong-gun	843.59	8.3	1	5	-	Geumsan-gun	576.71	7.0	1	9	-
Yangpyeong-gun	877.78	8.6	1	11	-	Buyeo-gun	624.33	7.6	1	15	-
						Seocheon-gun	358.13	4.4	2	11	-
Gangwon-do	16,829.81	100.0	24	95	74	Cheongyang-gun	479.21	5.8	1	9	-
Chuncheon-si	1,116.41	6.6	1	9	15	Hongseong-gun	443.99	5.4	2	9	-
Wonju-si	872.41	5.2	1	8	16	Yesan-gun	542.33	6.6	2	10	-
Gangneung-si	1,040.38	6.2	1	7	13	Taean-gun	516.13	6.3	2	6	-
Donghae-si	180.20	1.1	-	-	10						
Taebaek-si	303.44	1.8	-	-	8	**Jeollabuk-do**	8,066.44	100.0	14	145	82
Sokcho-si	105.63	0.6	-	-	8	Jeonju-si	205.62	2.5	-	-	33
Samcheok-si	1,186.64	7.1	2	6	4	Gunsan-si	394.85	4.9	1	10	16
Hongcheon-gun	1,819.67	10.8	1	9	-	Iksan-si	506.61	6.3	1	14	14
Hoengseong-gun	997.76	5.9	1	8	-	Jeongeup-si	692.77	8.6	1	14	8
Yeongwol-gun	1,127.63	6.7	2	7	-	Namwon-si	752.23	9.3	1	15	7
Pyeongchang-gun	1,463.70	8.7	1	7	-	Gimje-si	544.81	6.8	1	14	4
Jeongseon-gun	1,219.70	7.2	4	5	-	Wanju-gun	821.19	10.2	2	11	-

	Area(km²)[2]		Eup, Myeon and Dong[3]				Area(km²)[2]		Eup, Myeon and Dong[3]		
		Composition (%)	Eup	Myeon	Dong			Composition (%)	Eup	Myeon	Dong
Jinan-gun	789.12	9.8	1	10	-	Sangju-si	1,254.79	6.6	1	17	6
Muju-gun	631.87	7.8	1	5	-	Mungyeong-si	911.62	4.8	2	7	5
Jangsu-gun	533.29	6.6	1	6	-	Gyeongsan-si	411.70	2.2	2	6	7
Imsil-gun	597.20	7.4	1	11	-	Gunwi-gun	614.21	3.2	1	7	-
Sunchang-gun	495.93	6.1	1	10	-	Uiseong-gun	1,175.17	6.2	1	17	-
Gochang-gun	607.87	7.5	1	13	-	Cheongsong-gun	846.08	4.4	1	7	-
Buan-gun	493.07	6.1	1	12	-	Yeongyang-gun	815.17	4.3	1	5	-
						Yeongdeok-gun	741.10	3.9	1	8	-
Jeollanam-do	12,303.92	100.0	33	196	67	Cheongdo-gun	693.78	3.6	2	7	-
Mokpo-si	50.60	0.4	-	-	23	Goryeong-gun	384.10	2.0	1	7	-
Yeosu-si	504.31	4.1	1	6	20	Seongju-gun	616.14	3.2	1	9	-
Suncheon-si	910.43	7.4	1	10	13	Chilgok-gun	450.97	2.4	3	5	-
Naju-si	608.54	4.9	1	12	6	Yecheon-gun	661.16	3.5	1	11	-
Gwangyang-si	460.06	3.7	1	6	5	Bonghwa-gun	1,201.47	6.3	1	9	-
Damyang-gun	455.05	3.7	1	11	-	Uljin-gun	989.43	5.2	2	8	-
Gokseong-gun	547.46	4.4	1	10	-	Ulleung-gun	72.86	0.4	1	2	-
Gurye-gun	443.24	3.6	1	7	-						
Goheung-gun	807.33	6.6	2	14	-	**Gyeongsangnam-do**	10,537.32	100.0	20	176	119
Boseong-gun	663.53	5.4	2	10	-	Changwon-si	747.12	7.1	2	6	54
Hwasun-gun	786.87	6.4	1	12	-	Jinju-si	712.95	6.8	1	15	16
Jangheung-gun	622.41	5.1	3	7	-	Tongyeong-si	239.22	2.3	1	6	8
Gangjin-gun	500.96	4.1	1	10	-	Sacheon-si	398.59	3.8	1	7	6
Haenam-gun	1,013.08	8.2	1	13	-	Gimhae-si	463.36	4.4	1	6	12
Yeongam-gun	603.49	4.9	2	9	-	Miryang-si	798.59	7.6	2	9	5
Muan-gun	448.94	3.6	3	6	-	Geoje-si	402.06	3.8	-	9	10
Hampyeong-gun	392.26	3.2	1	8	-	Yangsan-si	485.35	4.6	1	4	8
Yeonggwang-gun	474.95	3.9	3	8	-	Uiryeong-gun	482.90	4.6	1	12	-
Jangseong-gun	518.33	4.2	1	10	-	Haman-gun	416.64	4.0	1	9	-
Wando-gun	396.29	3.2	3	9	-	Changnyeong-gun	532.82	5.1	2	12	-
Jindo-gun	440.13	3.6	1	6	-	Goseong-gun	517.69	4.9	1	13	-
Sinan-gun	655.67	5.3	2	12	-	Namhae-gun	357.54	3.4	1	9	-
						Hadong-gun	675.52	6.4	1	12	-
Gyeongsangbuk-do	19,028.98	100.0	36	202	93	Sancheong-gun	794.84	7.5	1	10	-
Pohang-si	1,129.84	5.9	4	10	15	Hamyang-gun	725.47	6.9	1	10	-
Gyeongju-si	1,324.51	7.0	4	8	11	Geochang-gun	803.17	7.6	1	11	-
Gimcheon-si	1,009.09	5.3	1	14	6	Hapcheon-gun	983.51	9.3	1	16	-
Andong-si	1,521.91	8.0	1	13	10						
Gumi-si	615.39	3.2	2	6	19	**Jeju-do**	1,849.26	100.0	7	5	31
Yeongju-si	669.09	3.5	1	9	9	Jeju-si	978.33	52.9	4	3	19
Yeongcheon-si	919.39	4.8	1	10	5	Seogwipo-si	870.93	47.1	3	2	12

Source : Ministry of Land, Infrastructure and Transport,
Ministry of Government Administration and Home Affairs

Note : 1) There are two kinds of local government. Large district local government(Metropolitan City,
Province) and fundamental local government(City, District, County).
Dong, Eup and Myeon are the lowest hierarchical offices under City, District and County.
2) As of December 31. 2013
3) As of January 1. 2014

Meteorological Observation

	Gang-neung	Seoul	Incheon	Ulleungdo	Chupung-nyeong	Daegu	Jeonju	Ulsan	Gwangju	Busan	Mokpo	Jeju
Mean air pressure(sea level : hPa)												
2009	1,014.7	1,015.6	1,015.7	1,014.2	1,015.4	1,015.4	1,016.6	1,015.1	1,016.2	1,015.1	1,015.9	1,015.9
2010	1,015.3	1,016.1	1,016.3	1,014.8	1,015.9	1,016.0	1,017.3	1,015.8	1,016.9	1,015.8	1,016.3	1,016.2
2011	1,015.9	1,016.6	1,016.8	1,015.3	1,016.6	1,016.9	1,017.3	1,016.1	1,017.2	1,016.1	1,016.8	1,016.8
2012	1,015.2	1,015.8	1,015.9	1,014.9	1,016.1	1,016.5	1,016.1	1,015.5	1,016.2	1,015.4	1,016.1	1,015.8
2013	1,014.8	1,015.9	1,015.8	1,014.6	1,016.0	1,016.4	1,016.3	1,015.4	1,016.5	1,015.4	1,016.4	1,016.2
Mean air temperature(℃)												
2009	13.4	12.9	12.6	12.5	12.0	14.8	13.6	14.3	14.6	15.2	13.8	16.0
2010	13.0	12.1	12.3	12.6	11.6	14.4	13.5	14.0	14.2	14.9	13.5	15.6
2011	12.6	12.0	12.0	12.1	11.5	14.3	13.1	13.7	13.7	14.6	13.0	15.6
2012	12.6	12.2	12.1	11.9	11.2	14.1	13.2	13.7	13.7	14.5	13.1	15.7
2013	13.6	12.5	11.9	12.7	11.8	15.0	13.8	14.8	14.2	15.3	13.8	16.5
Mean relative humidity(%)												
2009	59	61	67	72	66	54	64	64	66	61	78	63
2010	62	63	68	71	70	56	66	66	69	62	81	66
2011	60	60	66	72	67	55	66	65	69	60	78	69
2012	59	57	69	73	68	56	65	63	67	58	76	71
2013	57	60	77	69	67	56	67	60	66	57	81	72
Precipitation(mm)												
2009	1,183.0	1,564.0	1,382.1	1,616.1	1,010.7	832.5	1,163.9	1,133.2	1,448.2	1,772.9	1,088.4	1,304.8
2010	1,102.8	2,043.5	1,777.7	1,448.3	1,260.4	1,204.5	1,462.3	1,161.6	1,573.1	1,441.9	1,335.7	1,584.9
2011	1,810.5	2,039.3	1,725.5	1,795.8	1,401.8	1,430.4	1,621.8	1,233.2	1,300.3	1,478.6	982.1	1,478.6
2012	1,321.4	1,646.3	1,415.1	1,777.1	1,465.8	1,189.9	1,359.7	1,458.1	1,626.8	1,983.3	1,577.5	2,248.3
2013	921.7	1,403.8	1,186.6	1,265.9	920.6	996.4	1,264.7	858.3	1,245.4	1,130.1	1,089.7	859.1

	Suwon	Sokcho	Chun-cheon	Cheongju	Daejeon	Seosan	Gunsan	Yeosu	Pohang	Tong-yeong	Seogwipo	Uljin
Mean air pressure(sea level : hPa)												
2009	1,015.9	1,015.1	1,015.8	1,015.8	1,015.3	1,016.0	1,016.4	1,016.3	1,015.0	1,015.1	1,015.2	1,014.8
2010	1,016.4	1,015.8	1,016.3	1,016.3	1,015.8	1,016.4	1,017.0	1,016.9	1,015.8	1,015.8	1,015.7	1,015.3
2011	1,017.0	1,016.1	1,016.9	1,016.8	1,016.7	1,017.2	1,017.3	1,016.7	1,016.3	1,016.2	1,015.9	1,015.9
2012	1,016.0	1,015.1	1,016.2	1,016.1	1,016.2	1,016.6	1,016.3	1,015.4	1,015.6	1,015.5	1,014.9	1,015.4
2013	1,016.1	1,014.6	1,016.1	1,016.1	1,016.3	1,016.7	1,016.4	1,015.6	1,015.3	1,015.7	1,015.4	1,015.0
Mean air temperature(℃)												
2009	12.6	12.8	11.5	13.0	12.8	12.3	13.0	14.6	14.8	14.9	17.2	13.0
2010	12.2	12.3	11.0	13.0	12.7	11.7	12.9	14.3	14.6	14.0	16.9	12.3
2011	11.8	12.1	10.7	12.8	12.6	11.6	12.2	14.0	14.3	13.8	16.7	12.0
2012	12.1	12.0	10.7	12.7	12.6	11.5	12.3	14.0	14.1	13.7	16.7	11.9
2013	12.3	12.9	11.1	13.3	13.1	11.8	12.6	14.7	14.9	14.5	17.4	12.8
Mean relative humidity(%)												
2009	71	61	69	61	63	73	77	63	63	71	66	66
2010	73	62	70	65	66	74	78	66	65	73	69	68
2011	70	62	69	65	64	73	75	64	63	69	71	69
2012	69	67	69	64	68	76	76	68	65	68	70	68
2013	72	66	73	65	73	81	81	68	60	68	70	67
Precipitation(mm)												
2009	1,541.2	1,420.1	1,446.9	1,019.8	1,090.4	1,074.3	1,022.7	1,247.7	885.5	1,548.6	2,006.8	851.7
2010	1,470.6	1,283.6	1,581.4	1,422.4	1,419.7	2,141.8	1,347.5	1,733.1	927.4	1,397.8	2,393.3	784.9
2011	1,975.9	1,656.1	2,029.3	1,805.6	1,943.4	1,704.4	1,634.2	1,650.4	1,089.9	1,524.9	2,010.2	1,376.6
2012	1,748.3	1,217.7	1,324.3	1,387.6	1,409.5	1,642.6	1,659.5	1,825.1	1,333.7	1,611.2	2,700.8	1,101.3
2013	1,240.1	1,115.7	1,738.9	1,240.7	1,120.2	1,018.7	1,092.4	1,200.8	905.2	1,161.9	1,086.6	994.1

Source : Korea Meteorological Administration
* Mean air pressure, mean air temperature and mean relative humidity are arithmetic means of the figures derived from 8 observations at 3,6,9,12,15,18,21 and 24 o'clock a day

Population Trend

Unit : thousand persons

	Census population[1]	Midyear population projections according to the medium-growth scenario[2]			Population increase rate[3] (%)	Sex ratio (per 100 females)	Population density (persons per sq.km)	Land area[4](km²)	Population of North Korea[5]
		Total	Male	Female					
1972		33,505	16,955	16,550	1.89	102.4	340	98,484	15,683
1973		34,103	17,235	16,868	1.78	102.2	345	98,758	16,080
1974		34,692	17,514	17,178	1.73	102.0	351	98,824	16,388
1975		35,281	17,766	17,515	1.70	101.4	357	98,807	16,646
1975 (11.1)	34,707	-	(17,461)	(17,245)	-	(101.3)	(351)	98,807	-
1976		35,849	18,059	17,790	1.61	101.5	363	98,799	16,871
1977		36,412	18,349	18,062	1.57	101.6	374	97,459	-
1978		36,969	18,637	18,332	1.53	101.7	379	97,542	-
1979		37,534	18,929	18,605	1.53	101.7	384	97,775	-
1980		38,124	19,236	18,888	1.57	101.8	389	98,011	-
1980 (11.1)	37,436	-	(18,767)	(18,669)	-	(100.5)	(382)	-	-
1981		38,723	19,536	19,188	1.57	101.8	395	98,079	-
1982		39,326	19,837	19,489	1.56	101.8	401	98,158	-
1983		39,910	20,129	19,781	1.49	101.8	406	98,240	-
1984		40,406	20,375	20,031	1.24	101.7	411	98,278	-
1985		40,806	20,576	20,230	0.99	101.7	415	98,349	-
1985 (11.1)	40,448	-	(20,244)	(20,205)	-	(100.2)	(411)	-	-
1986		41,214	20,772	20,442	1.00	101.6	419	98,389	-
1987		41,622	20,960	20,662	0.99	101.4	423	98,499	-
1988		42,031	21,155	20,876	0.98	101.3	426	98,679	-
1989		42,449	21,357	21,092	0.99	101.3	430	98,707	-
1990		42,869	21,568	21,301	0.99	101.3	434	98,730	-
1990 (11.1)	43,411		(21,782)	(21,629)	-	(100.7)	(440)	-	-
1991		43,296	21,784	21,512	0.99	101.3	437	98,975	-
1992		43,748	22,014	21,734	1.04	101.3	442	99,010	-
1993		44,195	22,243	21,952	1.02	101.3	446	99,184	21,103
1994		44,642	22,472	22,169	1.01	101.4	450	99,203	21,412
1995		45,093	22,705	22,388	1.01	101.4	454	99,286	21,715
1995 (11.1)	44,609	-	(22,389)	(22,219)	-	(100.8)	(449)	-	-
1996		45,525	22,925	22,600	0.96	101.4	458	99,313	21,991
1997		45,954	23,148	22,805	0.94	101.5	462	99,373	22,208
1998		46,287	23,296	22,991	0.72	101.3	466	99,408	22,355
1999		46,617	23,458	23,159	0.71	101.3	469	99,434	22,507
2000		47,008	23,667	23,341	0.84	101.4	473	99,461	22,702
2000 (11.1)	46,136	-	(23,159)	(22,978)	-	(100.8)	(464)	-	-
2001		47,357	23,843	23,514	0.74	101.4	476	99,538	22,902
2002		47,622	23,970	23,652	0.56	101.3	478	99,585	23,088
2003		47,859	24,090	23,770	0.50	101.3	481	99,601	23,254
2004		48,039	24,165	23,874	0.38	101.2	482	99,617	23,411
2005		48,138	24,191	23,947	0.21	101.0	483	99,646	23,561
2005 (11.1)	47,279	-	(23,624)	(23,655)	-	(99.9)	(474)	-	-
2006		48,372	24,303	24,069	0.49	101.0	485	99,678	23,707
2007		48,598	24,410	24,188	0.47	100.9	487	99,720	23,849
2008		48,949	24,576	24,373	0.72	100.8	490	99,828	23,934
2009		49,182	24,665	24,518	0.48	100.6	492	99,897	24,062
2010		49,410	24,758	24,653	0.46	100.4	494	100,033	24,187
2010 (11.1)	48,580	-	(24,167)	(24,413)	-	(99.0)	(486)	-	-
2011		49,779	24,942	24,837	0.75	100.4	497	100,148	24,308
2012		50,004	25,040	24,965	0.45	100.3	499	100,188	24,427
2013		50,220	25,133	25,087	0.43	100.2	501	100,266	24,545
2014		50,424	25,220	25,204	0.41	100.1	-	-	24,662

Source : Statistics Korea,
Ministry of Land, Infrastructure and Transport
Note : 1) Including foreigners   2) The figures to 2010 are fixed, but those after 2011 can be revised
3) Rates of increase over the last year   4) Figures are the land areas used in population density calculation
5) Estimates of mid-year population based on 1993, 2008 Census of North Korea

Vital Statistics

	Live births (persons)	Deaths (persons)	Crude birth rate (per 1000 population)	Crude death rate (per 1000 population)	Total fertility rate (persons)	Sex ratio at birth (persons)	Marriages (cases)	Divorces (cases)
2005	435,031	243,883	8.9	5.0	1.08	107.8	314,304	128,035
2006	448,153	242,266	9.2	5.0	1.12	107.5	330,634	124,524
2007	493,189	244,874	10.0	5.0	1.25	106.2	343,559	124,072
2008	465,892	246,113	9.4	5.0	1.19	106.4	327,715	116,535
2009	444,849	246,942	9.0	5.0	1.15	106.4	309,759	123,999
2010	470,171	255,405	9.4	5.1	1.23	106.9	326,104	116,858
2011	471,265	257,396	9.4	5.1	1.24	105.7	329,087	114,284
2012	484,550	267,221	9.6	5.3	1.30	105.7	327,073	114,316
2013	436,455	266,257	8.6	5.3	1.19	105.3	322,807	115,292

Source : Statistics Korea

Arrivals of Foreigners by Nationality[1]

Unit : person

	Total	Asia							
		Japan	China	HongKong	Taiwan	Philippines	Thailand	Singapore	
2009	7,817,533	6,074,513	3,053,311	1,342,317	215,769	380,628	271,962	190,972	96,622
2010	8,797,658	6,838,514	3,023,009	1,875,157	228,582	406,352	297,452	260,718	112,855
2011	9,794,796	7,766,292	3,289,051	2,220,196	280,849	428,208	337,268	309,143	124,565
2012	11,140,028	9,009,323	3,518,792	2,836,892	360,027	548,233	331,346	387,441	154,073
2013	12,175,550	9,978,587	2,747,750	4,326,869	400,435	544,662	400,686	372,878	174,567
2014	14,201,516	11,863,784	2,280,434	6,126,865	558,377	643,683	434,951	466,783	201,105

	Asia			Middle East[2]		Europe				
	Malaysia	Indonesia	India			Russian Federation	United Kingdom	Germany	France	Nether-lands
2009	80,105	80,988	72,779	49,615	597,762	137,054	91,165	97,691	61,426	20,358
2010	113,675	95,239	86,547	67,912	645,753	150,730	97,510	98,119	66,192	22,669
2011	156,281	124,474	92,047	80,601	681,025	154,835	104,644	99,468	69,459	23,279
2012	178,082	149,247	91,700	14,996	717,315	166,721	110,172	102,262	71,140	25,886
2013	207,727	189,189	123,235	19,900	768,185	175,360	120,874	100,803	75,947	28,916
2014	244,520	208,329	147,736	26,274	848,530	214,366	131,080	100,624	80,518	30,204

	Europe					America		Oceania
	Italy	Poland	Greece	Sweden	Spain	United States	Canada	Australia
2009	22,894	10,598	7,885	11,941	10,691	751,697	611,327	109,249	130,446	99,153
2010	25,686	11,555	7,975	13,351	12,590	813,860	652,889	121,214	146,089	112,409
2011	26,442	13,451	8,802	14,228	12,884	827,383	661,503	122,223	155,654	122,494
2012	28,941	13,656	8,600	15,495	15,833	876,149	697,866	128,431	166,304	128,812
2013	38,715	13,300	8,585	17,711	17,513	915,622	722,315	133,640	160,047	123,560
2014	48,350	14,895	8,281	17,055	19,247	974,021	770,305	146,429	177,934	141,208

	Oceania	Africa			by purpose					
	New Zealand		Egypt	Others[3]	Total	Tourist	Business	Crew	Students	Others
2009	23,953	28,501	3,852	234,614	7,817,533	5,685,194	312,133	893,234	123,012	803,960
2010	26,973	33,756	5,138	319,686	8,797,658	6,366,884	311,117	991,505	137,896	990,256
2011	26,608	36,979	5,845	327,463	9,794,796	7,203,107	270,594	1,099,052	149,723	1,072,320
2012	29,546	41,236	5,753	329,701	11,140,028	8,656,818	245,540	1,007,031	145,633	1,085,006
2013	29,105	43,414	6,585	309,695	12,175,550	9,075,688	327,892	1,521,637	152,100	1,098,233
2014	30,805	44,053	7,270	293,194	14,201,516	10,927,480	315,277	1,582,174	163,446	1,213,139

Source : Korea Tourism Organization
Note : 1) Monthly figures are the total amount from Jan. to the corresponding month
2) From January 2012, data contains only 6 GCC countries(U.A.E., Saudi Arabia, Kuwait, Oman, Qatar and Bahrain)
3) Others include the number of Korean national abroad

Summary Table of Economically Active Population

Unit : thousand persons

	Population 15 years and over[1]				Economically inactive population	Participation rate[%]	Employment/ population ratio[%]	Unemploy- ment rate[%]
		Economically active population						
			Employed persons	Unemployed persons				
						Total			
2009	40,092	24,394	23,506	889	15,698	60.8	58.6	3.6
2010	40,590	24,748	23,829	920	15,841	61.0	58.7	3.7
2011	41,052	25,099	24,244	855	15,953	61.1	59.1	3.4
2012	41,582	25,501	24,681	820	16,081	61.3	59.4	3.2
2013	42,096	25,873	25,066	807	16,223	61.5	59.5	3.1
2014	42,513	26,536	25,599	937	15,977	62.4	60.2	3.5
					Male			
2009	19,596	14,319	13,734	584	5,278	73.1	70.1	4.1
2010	19,849	14,492	13,915	577	5,356	73.0	70.1	4.0
2011	20,076	14,683	14,153	530	5,393	73.1	70.5	3.6
2012	20,328	14,891	14,387	504	5,437	73.3	70.8	3.4
2013	20,583	15,071	14,573	498	5,512	73.2	70.8	3.3
2014	20,795	15,387	14,839	548	5,409	74.0	71.4	3.6
					Female			
2009	20,496	10,076	9,772	304	10,420	49.2	47.7	3.0
2010	20,741	10,256	9,914	342	10,485	49.4	47.8	3.3
2011	20,976	10,416	10,091	325	10,561	49.7	48.1	3.1
2012	21,254	10,609	10,294	316	10,645	49.9	48.4	3.0
2013	21,513	10,802	10,494	309	10,710	50.2	48.8	2.9
2014	21,718	11,149	10,761	389	10,568	51.3	49.5	3.5

Source : Statistics Korea
Note : 1) Soldiers, auxilary police, defence corps, prisoners are excluded.

Employed Persons by Industry[1]

Unit : thousand persons

	Total	Agriculture, forestry & fishing	Mining and manufacturing		Social overhead capital and other services				
				Manu- facturing		Con- struction	Wholesale & retail trade, hotels & restaurants	Electricity, transport, telecom & finance	Business, personal, public service & others
					Total				
2009	23,506	1,648	3,859	3,836	17,998	1,720	5,536	2,761	7,981
2010	23,829	1,566	4,049	4,028	18,214	1,753	5,469	2,834	8,158
2011	24,244	1,542	4,108	4,091	18,595	1,751	5,492	2,956	8,396
2012	24,681	1,528	4,120	4,105	19,033	1,773	5,595	2,997	8,668
2013	25,066	1,520	4,200	4,184	19,347	1,754	5,630	3,059	8,903
2014	25,599	1,452	4,343	4,330	19,805	1,796	5,889	3,041	9,079
					Male				
2009	13,734	910	2,697	2,676	10,127	1,557	2,610	2,092	3,868
2010	13,915	884	2,811	2,791	10,220	1,587	2,588	2,143	3,903
2011	14,153	859	2,834	2,817	10,460	1,595	2,660	2,216	3,990
2012	14,387	870	2,850	2,837	10,668	1,626	2,706	2,238	4,098
2013	14,573	870	2,942	2,928	10,761	1,614	2,695	2,286	4,165
2014	14,839	837	3,049	3,037	10,954	1,645	2,857	2,268	4,183
					Female				
2009	9,772	738	1,162	1,160	7,872	163	2,926	669	4,114
2010	9,914	683	1,238	1,237	7,994	166	2,882	691	4,255
2011	10,091	683	1,274	1,273	8,134	156	2,832	740	4,407
2012	10,294	659	1,270	1,268	8,365	147	2,889	759	4,570
2013	10,494	650	1,258	1,256	8,586	139	2,935	774	4,738
2014	10,761	615	1,294	1,293	8,851	151	3,032	773	4,896

Source : Statistics Korea
Note : 1) Based on the 9th revision of Korean Standard Industrial Classification.

Principal Indicators on National Accounts

	Unit	2009	2010	2011	2012	2013[P]
National Income(at current prices)						
Gross Domestic Product	Bill. won	1,151,708	1,265,308	1,332,681	1,377,457	1,428,295
	100mill. $	9,023	10,943	12,027	12,224	13,043
Gross National Income	Bill. won	1,148,982	1,266,580	1,340,530	1,391,596	1,441,064
	100mill. $	9,002	10,954	12,097	12,349	13,160
Per capita G N I	10thou. won	2,336	2,563	2,693	2,783	2,870
	$	18,303	22,170	24,302	24,696	26,205
Growth rate by kind of economic activity (at chained 2010 year prices)						
Gross domestic product	%	0.7	6.5	3.7	2.3	3.0
Agriculture, forestry and fishing	%	3.2	-4.3	-2.0	-0.9	5.8
Mining, quarrying and manufacturing	%	-0.5	13.5	6.5	2.4	3.3
(Manufacturing)	%	-0.5	13.7	6.5	2.4	3.3
Electricity, gas and water supply	%	5.0	5.9	0.2	4.0	1.4
Construction	%	2.3	-3.7	-5.5	-1.8	3.6
Services	%	1.5	4.4	3.1	2.8	2.9
Taxes less subsidies on products[1]	%	-2.5	7.6	5.2	1.8	1.9
Gross national income	%	2.5	7.0	1.6	2.7	4.0
Growth rate by kind of expenditure (at chained 2010 year prices)						
Final consumption expenditure	%	1.3	4.3	2.7	2.2	2.2
Private	%	0.2	4.4	2.9	1.9	2.0
Government	%	5.2	3.8	2.2	3.4	2.7
Gross fixed capital formation	%	0.3	5.5	0.8	-0.5	4.2
Exports of goods and services	%	-0.3	12.7	15.1	5.1	4.3
Imports of goods and services	%	-6.8	17.3	14.3	2.4	1.6
Gross saving and investment (at current prices)						
Gross saving ratio	%	32.9	35.0	34.6	34.2	34.4
Private	%	25.2	27.1	26.6	26.6	27.7
Government	%	7.6	7.8	8.0	7.6	6.8
Gross domestic investment ratio	%	28.6	32.1	32.9	30.8	28.8
(Gross domestic fixed investment ratio)	%	31.5	30.6	30.2	29.4	29.5
GDP deflator	2010=100	96.9	100.0	101.6	102.6	103.4
(Rate of change)	%	3.5	3.2	1.6	1.0	0.7

Source : The Bank of Korea
Note : 1) Taxes (less) subsidies on products
   * Preliminary annual estimate : within 3 months after the end of the year concerned
   * Final annual estimate : within 15 months after the end of the year concerned

Farm Households and Farm Population by Full and Part-Time

	Farm household (household)				Farm population (person)				
		Full-time	Class 1 part-time[1]	Class 2 part-time[2]		Male	Composi-tion(%)	Female	Composi-tion(%)
2008	1,212,050	707,056	159,568	345,426	3,186,753	1,542,337	48.4	1,644,417	51.6
2009	1,194,715	692,993	150,714	351,007	3,117,322	1,510,297	48.4	1,607,025	51.6
2010	1,177,318	627,460	193,438	356,420	3,062,956	1,501,064	49.0	1,561,892	51.0
2011	1,163,209	630,118	181,476	351,614	2,962,113	1,455,777	49.1	1,506,336	50.9
2012	1,151,116	625,376	169,272	356,468	2,911,540	1,423,685	48.9	1,487,855	51.1
2013	1,142,029	607,385	172,310	362,335	2,847,435	1,386,679	48.7	1,460,756	51.3

Source : Statistics Korea
Note : 1) Class 1 part-time : Farm households recording more agricultural receipts than non-agricultural ones
   2) Calss 2 part-time : Farm households recording less agricultural receipts than non-agricultural ones

Farm Households, Farm Population and Cultivated Land

	Farm house-hold (house-hold)	Farm popula-tion (person)	Population per farm household	Area of cultivated land(ha)			Area per farm household(a)		
					Paddy field	Upland field		Paddy field	Upland field
2006	1,245,083	3,304,173	2.65	1,800,470	1,084,024	716,446	144.6	87.1	57.5
2007	1,231,009	3,274,091	2.66	1,781,579	1,069,932	711,647	144.7	86.9	57.8
2008	1,212,050	3,186,753	2.63	1,758,795	1,045,991	712,804	145.1	86.3	58.8
2009	1,194,715	3,117,322	2.61	1,736,798	1,010,287	726,511	145.4	84.6	60.8
2010	1,177,318	3,062,956	2.60	1,715,301	984,140	731,161	145.7	83.6	62.1
2011	1,163,209	2,962,113	2.55	1,698,040	959,914	738,126	146.0	82.5	63.5
2012	1,151,116	2,911,540	2.53	1,729,982	966,076	763,905	150.3	83.9	66.4
2013	1,142,029	2,847,435	2.49	1,711,436	963,876	747,560	149.9	84.4	65.5

Source : Statistics Korea

Major Indicators of Farm Household Economy(Average per Household)[1]

Unit : won

	Farm household income	Agricultural income		Farm expenses	Non-farm income			
			Gross farm receipts			Business income		
							Receipts	Expenses
2008	30,522,624	9,654,302	25,843,026	16,188,723	11,352,588	2,899,830	6,346,755	3,446,925
2009	30,813,662	9,697,897	26,621,461	16,923,564	12,127,682	3,295,899	7,654,506	4,358,607
2010	32,120,816	10,098,008	27,220,716	17,122,708	12,946,311	3,466,809	8,444,553	4,977,744
2011	30,148,071	8,752,709	26,457,112	17,704,403	12,948,896	3,652,876	8,695,395	5,042,519
2012	31,031,135	9,127,448	27,588,671	18,461,224	13,585,485	3,966,296	9,358,468	5,392,173
2013	34,523,966	10,034,697	30,647,935	20,613,238	15,705,029	4,182,306	9,431,501	5,249,195

	Non-business income			Transfer income	Irregular income	Expenditure		Disposable F. H.income	Surplus (or deficit)
		Receipts	Expenses			Consumption expenditure	Non-consumption expenditure		
2008	8,452,758	8,532,435	79,677	5,289,227	4,226,507	20,328,235	6,773,475	23,749,149	3,420,913
2009	8,831,782	8,944,265	112,483	5,480,584	3,507,500	20,017,130	6,556,700	24,256,962	4,239,832
2010	9,479,502	9,597,585	118,083	5,609,592	3,466,904	21,263,572	6,408,469	25,712,346	4,448,774
2011	9,296,020	9,471,737	175,717	5,453,395	2,993,071	22,155,829	5,750,002	24,398,069	2,242,240
2012	9,619,189	9,738,528	119,340	5,613,545	2,704,658	22,314,555	5,175,757	25,855,378	3,540,823
2013	11,522,722	11,675,663	152,941	5,843,883	2,940,358	24,183,637	6,080,337	28,443,629	4,259,992

Source : Statistics Korea
Note : 1) 2008 results had time-series block due to revision of samples, and thus its continuity was blocked, and therefore, this should be kept in mind when making direct comparisons and analyses

Agricultural Production(Food Grains)

Unit : t

	Rice[1]	Barley[1]				Miscellaneous grains		Pulses		
		Common barley	Naked barley	Beer barley	Wheat	Corn	Buck wheat	Soy beans	Red beans	Green beans
2008	4,843,478	22,142	82,013	65,898	10,359	92,830	2,545	132,674	5,995	1,589
2009	4,916,080	18,112	76,962	53,550	18,782	76,975	2,210	139,251	5,814	1,599
2010	4,295,413	12,444	42,584	26,188	39,116	74,339	1,954	105,345	4,561	1,543
2011	4,224,019	11,595	43,752	20,173	43,677	73,612	2,370	129,394	3,896	1,644
2012	4,006,186	11,650	35,458	10,109	37,014	83,210	2,512	122,519	4,563	1,885
2013	4,230,012	18,429	29,986	12,046	27,130	80,465	1,923	154,067	7,628	2,345

Source : Statistics Korea
Note : 1) Polished corps

Agricultural Production(Potatoes, Vegetables, Fruits, etc)

Unit : t

	Potatoes		Vegetables							
	White potatoes	Sweet potatoes	Chinese cabbage	Cabbage	Water melons	Melons (chamwei)	Cucumbers	Pumpkins	Tomatoes	White radish
2007	574,396	352,269	2,217,149	320,466	741,880	205,416	330,225	330,040	479,851	1,194,327
2008	604,592	329,351	2,584,908	317,031	856,755	220,385	383,921	327,502	408,170	1,402,187
2009	590,375	350,661	2,528,966	319,043	846,921	227,832	352,018	341,163	383,768	1,256,423
2010	616,707	298,930	1,783,010	252,685	678,810	207,747	306,164	302,868	324,806	1,039,345
2011	622,202	255,284	2,680,847	368,486	608,986	180,013	303,805	300,400	368,224	1,236,797
2012	607,534	342,668	1,816,021	302,909	642,945	186,693	288,071	325,113	432,779	844,732
2013	727,438	329,516	2,120,393	314,022	672,914	176,622	254,576	323,364	388,624	1,001,130

	Vegetables			Fruits				Oilseed crop	
	Green onions	Onions	Garlics	Apples	Asian pears	Grapes	Tangerines	Persi-mmons	Sesame	Perilla seeds
2007	488,814	1,213,375	347,546	435,686	467,426	328,680	777,547	395,614	17,506	28,300
2008	505,056	1,035,076	375,463	470,865	470,745	333,596	636,413	430,521	19,472	24,205
2009	446,991	1,372,291	357,278	494,491	418,368	332,978	752,837	416,705	12,780	28,479
2010	417,229	1,411,646	271,560	460,285	307,820	305,543	614,786	390,630	12,703	33,941
2011	482,143	1,520,016	295,002	379,541	290,494	269,150	680,507	390,820	9,515	30,533
2012	356,734	1,195,737	339,113	394,596	172,599	227,917	692,186	401,049	9,690	28,916
2013	430,580	1,294,009	412,250	493,701	282,212	260,280	682,801	351,990	12,392	33,347

Source : Statistics Korea

Number of Livestock and Poultry

Unit : head

	Beef cattle	Dairy cattle	Horses	Pigs	Goats	Deer	Rabbits	Chickens[1]	Ducks[2]	Geese
2008	2,430,389	445,754	27,881	9,087,434	266,240	78,853	237,510	119,783,943	9,702,215	6,898
2009	2,634,705	444,648	28,718	9,584,903	249,855	75,272	256,086	138,767,543	12,733,275	6,402
2010	2,921,844	429,547	30,402	9,880,632	243,520	64,927	245,158	149,199,689	14,397,301	9,369
2011	2,949,664	403,689	30,058	8,170,979	247,943	51,411	205,544	149,511,309	12,735,187	9,077
2012	3,058,601	420,113	29,698	9,915,935	257,262	48,463	189,146	146,835,639	11,161,324	15,229
2013	2,917,929	424,202	29,342	9,912,204	242,787	41,874	137,186	151,337,054	10,898,806	12,101

Source : Ministry of Agriculture, Food and Rural Affairs
Note : 1) From 2006, complete enumeration was made for all the households breeding 3 thousand chickens or more
2) From 2011, data covered only for the households breeding 2 thousand ducks or more, based on complete enumeration

Forest Land Area by Forest Type

Unit : ha

	Total	Forest land area				
		Conifers	Non-Conifers	Mixed	Bamboo Stand	Un-stocked
2005	6,393,949	2,698,574	1,659,128	1,874,586	7,040	154,621
2006	6,389,393	2,695,398	1,660,019	1,868,951	7,039	157,986
2007	6,382,449	2,686,649	1,661,535	1,961,655	7,039	165,571
2008	6,374,875	2,679,803	1,659,173	1,853,447	7,039	175,413
2009	6,370,304	2,671,924	1,657,271	1,844,205	7,039	189,865
2010	6,368,843	2,580,629	1,718,916	1,864,925	7,039	197,334

Source : Korea Forest Service
Note : The next edition of Forest Basic Statistics will be released when the sixth National Forest Inventory is completed in 2015 over a period of five years

Fish Catches by Type of Fisheries

	Total	Adjacent waters fisheries	Shallow-sea cultures	Distant waters fisheries	Inland waters fisheries
	Quantities(M/T)				
2008	3,361,255	1,284,890	1,381,003	666,182	29,180
2009	3,182,342	1,226,966	1,313,355	611,950	30,071
2010	3,110,634	1,132,536	1,355,000	592,116	30,982
2011	3,255,929	1,235,489	1,477,546	510,624	32,270
2012	3,183,424	1,091,034	1,488,950	575,308	28,131
2013	3,135,250	1,044,697	1,515,210	549,928	25,414
	Amount(thousand won)				
2008	6,345,058,101	3,222,256,094	1,520,122,116	1,327,394,939	275,284,952
2009	6,924,248,502	3,640,436,977	1,846,310,734	1,163,750,724	273,750,067
2010	7,425,685,572	3,911,681,208	1,815,645,793	1,364,524,490	333,834,081
2011	8,072,860,450	4,444,105,662	1,784,244,398	1,467,044,368	377,466,022
2012	7,689,050,760	3,951,034,494	1,759,270,530	1,655,406,229	323,339,507
2013	7,226,886,951	3,747,607,063	1,725,808,459	1,408,034,170	345,437,258

Source : Statistics Korea

Exports and Imports of Fishery Products(New Classification)

	Total	Live fish	Fresh or chilled	Frozen	Smoked	Dried	Salted or in brine	Others	In airtight containers	Other prepared
	Exports(1,000 dollars)									
2009	1,511,230	71,624	174,345	897,662	1,540	80,968	16,989	79,304	29,597	159,201
2010	1,798,162	85,641	192,678	1,074,204	1,331	105,728	19,655	102,814	39,383	176,729
2011	2,308,155	78,357	221,909	1,437,191	1,666	135,651	27,814	115,721	46,504	243,341
2012	2,362,050	81,579	249,750	1,399,867	3,630	153,098	25,397	120,509	46,225	281,996
2013	2,151,951	74,959	183,929	1,239,240	1,952	138,109	19,875	119,572	49,640	324,584
	Exports(ton)									
2009	652,214	6,686	30,744	499,151	316	8,225	6,028	73,233	6,112	21,720
2010	793,045	6,471	30,129	608,826	143	9,336	9,571	98,972	7,467	22,130
2011	686,930	5,948	25,348	492,229	103	10,156	15,031	104,447	8,052	25,615
2012	708,638	5,722	28,239	519,322	113	11,055	13,884	97,615	5,857	26,830
2013	687,569	5,420	22,115	488,486	82	10,087	14,723	109,999	6,452	30,206
	Imports(1,000 dollars)									
2009	2,895,495	171,377	284,904	1,788,739	3,451	64,275	25,563	301,944	8,442	246,799
2010	3,458,400	250,683	302,771	2,084,306	4,185	110,225	25,835	381,433	10,788	288,174
2011	4,191,944	268,571	336,996	2,651,802	5,736	121,260	37,598	366,682	16,396	386,902
2012	3,974,627	255,847	312,394	2,473,246	29,505	114,157	33,335	346,238	29,870	380,034
2013	3,894,740	299,636	315,291	2,323,666	53,302	120,377	25,627	341,117	33,604	382,119
	Imports(ton)									
2009	4,080,425	31,635	99,298	850,294	623	9,338	27,105	2,997,621	2,365	62,146
2010	4,715,726	33,635	102,143	905,970	686	15,587	25,013	3,563,725	2,179	66,787
2011	4,845,662	26,956	114,329	1,013,154	615	14,412	34,981	3,562,774	3,114	75,329
2012	4,829,157	23,905	107,795	947,228	2,130	13,650	27,799	3,626,284	5,420	74,946
2013	5,387,008	26,585	98,514	904,816	3,380	13,382	17,603	4,244,259	6,092	72,377

Source : Ministry of Oceans and Fisheries
* Data to use HSK of item code

600

Manufacturing Operation Ratio Index[1]

2010=100

	Manu-facturing	Food products	Bever-ages	Tobacco products	Textiles, except apparel	Wearing apparel, clothing accessories and fur articles	Tanning and dressing of leather, luggage and footwear	Wood and products of wood & cork	Pulp, paper & paper products	Coke, hard-coal & lignite fuel briquettes & refined	Chemicals & chemical products	Rubber & plastic products
Weight	10,000.0	469.3	89.1	46.7	173.3	16.2	45.5	34.2	137.1	508.8	916.5	455.1
2010	100.0	100.0	100.0	100.0	100.0	100.0	100.0	100.0	100.0	100.0	100.0	100.0
2011	100.2	99.3	98.7	101.3	99.6	90.6	91.5	99.5	100.5	104.9	99.1	101.4
2012	97.5	100.0	101.9	108.9	97.8	88.0	89.6	96.3	100.3	105.8	99.1	99.6
2013	95.1	101.6	102.3	100.5	97.6	96.8	93.5	101.4	101.1	100.0	98.3	99.6
2014	94.2	99.9	102.9	105.3	95.6	87.5	84.1	102.8	100.4	99.6	97.5	98.7

	Other non-metallic mineral products	Basic metal products	Fabricated metal products	Electronic components, computer, radio, television & communications equipment	Medical, precision & optical instruments, watches	Electrical equipment	Other machinery and equipment	Motor vehicles, trailers and semitrailers	Other transport equipment	Furniture	Other manu-facturing
Weight	293.9	894.0	602.8	1,939.3	160.1	518.0	868.5	1,163.3	547.4	75.0	45.9
2010	100.0	100.0	100.0	100.0	100.0	100.0	100.0	100.0	100.0	100.0	100.0
2011	98.3	99.9	106.1	93.1	98.9	96.7	103.0	106.5	105.6	99.9	99.3
2012	94.6	99.2	103.6	88.6	97.0	94.1	99.4	102.9	95.0	90.1	100.4
2013	96.7	98.1	102.1	85.9	97.8	90.5	91.6	102.0	86.8	87.5	96.9
2014	90.8	100.5	102.9	84.2	85.7	90.0	91.3	103.3	80.4	95.4	95.6

Source : Statistics Korea
* Data are the results of Manufacturing. The Survey covers 314 commodities in the field of manufacturing

Manufacturing Production Capacity Index[1]

2010=100

	Manu-facturing	Food products	Bever-ages	Tobacco products	Textiles, except apparel	Wearing apparel, clothing accessories and fur articles	Tanning and dressing of leather, luggage and footwear	Wood and products of Wood & Cork	Pulp, paper & paper products	Coke, hard-coal & lignite fuel briquettes & refined	Chemicals & chemical products	Rubber & plastic products
Weight	10,000.0	505.8	97.2	53.5	171.3	28.5	46.1	37.8	127.1	428.7	845.9	454.7
2010	100.0	100.0	100.0	100.0	100.0	100.0	100.0	100.0	100.0	100.0	100.0	100.0
2011	104.7	101.2	103.7	100.1	103.3	98.6	104.8	96.7	102.4	102.8	103.3	105.2
2012	106.9	102.7	105.9	97.1	104.4	82.6	104.1	89.5	103.7	104.1	106.1	108.9
2013	108.6	101.5	106.7	95.9	101.6	77.7	101.6	88.7	104.4	105.0	110.4	110.6
2014	110.3	103.5	108.1	98.5	101.4	77.8	103.3	87.5	105.2	109.6	111.9	113.3

	Other non-metallic mineral products	Basic metal products	Fabricated metal products	Electronic components, computer, radio, television & communication equipment	Medical, precision & optical instruments, watches	Electrical equipment	Other machinery and equipment	Motor vehicles, trailers and semitrailers	Other transport equip-ment	Furniture	Other manu-facturing
Weight	422.6	868.8	659.8	1,686.5	164.0	512.4	989.6	1,124.7	653.3	69.8	51.9
2010	100.0	100.0	100.0	100.0	100.0	100.0	100.0	100.0	100.0	100.0	100.0
2011	100.6	107.0	102.2	109.4	107.0	104.7	107.4	101.6	101.7	108.0	101.8
2012	101.8	108.7	103.5	112.6	110.1	106.0	112.7	101.6	105.5	109.6	104.6
2013	104.0	109.7	105.6	115.1	120.5	105.2	117.0	101.2	107.4	110.7	105.6
2014	107.3	113.9	104.5	118.6	123.0	105.0	117.6	100.7	107.6	109.3	106.7

Source : Statistics Korea
* Data are the results of Manufacturing. The Survey covers 314 commodities in the field of manufacturing

Length of Roads

Unit : km

	Total				National expressway
	Length of roads	Paved	Unpaved	Unimproved	
2007	103,019.0	80,642.2	11,109.3	11,267.5	3,367.8
2008	104,236.1	81,829.4	10,914.3	11,492.4	3,447.1
2009	104,983.3	83,196.2	10,630.0	11,157.1	3,775.7
2010	105,565.1	84,196.2	10,034.2	11,334.7	3,859.5
2011	105,930.9	85,120.4	9,536.0	11,274.5	3,912.8
2012	105,703.0	88,183.1	8,765.3	8,754.6	4,043.6
2013	106,413.5	87,798.4	8,619.8	9,995.4	4,111.5
Seoul	8,222.9	8,222.9	-	-	25.0
Busan	3,101.2	3,022.4	72.8	5.9	51.7
Daegu	2,626.6	2,626.6	-	-	97.6
Incheon	2,742.8	2,605.1	111.6	26.1	100.3
Gwangju	1,806.1	1,798.5	-	7.6	26.4
Daejeon	2,077.5	2,077.5	-	-	76.1
Ulsan	1,759.8	1,723.9	22.6	13.3	62.8
Sejong	411.6	333.7	39.8	38.1	18.5
Gyeonggi-do	12,823.8	11,330.3	302.3	1,191.2	669.3
Gangwon-do	10,147.2	7,317.2	1,216.4	1,613.6	348.8
Chungcheongbuk-do	6,577.9	5,429.3	574.6	573.9	342.8
Chungcheongnam-do	7,003.5	5,775.3	950.6	277.6	430.0
Jeollabuk-do	8,040.2	5,950.0	1,152.9	937.4	423.4
Jeollanam-do	10,532.4	8,291.8	1,110.0	1,130.6	414.6
Gyeongsangbuk-do	12,290.3	9,291.4	1,765.9	1,233.0	535.6
Gyeongsangnam-do	13,053.4	9,323.9	1,092.3	2,637.2	488.7
Jeju-do	3,196.4	2,678.5	208.1	309.8	-

	National highway				Special/metropolitan city road			
		Paved	Unpaved	Unimproved		Paved	Unpaved	Unimproved
2007	13,831.8	13,466.8	59.5	305.5	18,109.1	17,998.9	110.0	0.2
2008	13,905.1	13,549.9	60.2	295.0	18,516.8	18,403.6	95.7	17.5
2009	13,819.7	13,464.3	56.5	298.8	18,749.1	18,634.6	98.0	16.5
2010	13,812.4	13,474.5	57.3	280.6	18,878.4	18,763.9	98.0	16.5
2011	13,797.5	13,459.6	57.3	280.6	19,072.5	18,960.0	96.0	16.5
2012	13,765.9	13,431.7	57.3	276.9	19,464.5	19,298.1	117.3	49.1
2013	13,842.7	13,526.7	57.3	258.8	4,879.7	4,821.4	20.3	38.1
Seoul	171.9	171.9	-	-	1,017.7	1,017.7	-	-
Busan	99.7	99.7	-	-	762.3	762.3	-	-
Daegu	144.8	144.8	-	-	715.1	715.1	-	-
Incheon	74.9	74.9	-	-	620.2	620.2	-	-
Gwangju	86.6	86.6	-	-	558.0	558.0	-	-
Daejeon	83.9	83.9	-	-	490.4	490.4	-	-
Ulsan	164.2	150.1	0.8	13.3	474.5	474.5	-	-
Sejong	64.1	64.1	-	-	241.6	183.2	20.3	38.1
Gyeonggi-do	1,553.6	1,519.3	-	34.3	-	-	-	-
Gangwon-do	1,960.8	1,921.9	37.2	1.7	-	-	-	-
Chungcheongbuk-do	935.0	935.0	-	-	-	-	-	-
Chungcheongnam-do	1,264.7	1,205.8	-	58.9	-	-	-	-
Jeollabuk-do	1,434.2	1,397.1	-	37.1	-	-	-	-
Jeollanam-do	2,036.1	1,948.3	12.5	75.3	-	-	-	-
Gyeongsangbuk-do	2,214.5	2,204.6	-	9.9	-	-	-	-
Gyeongsangnam-do	1,553.7	1,518.6	6.8	28.3	-	-	-	-
Jeju-do	-	-	-	-	-	-	-	-

	Provincial road				Si/Gun road			
		Paved	Unpaved	Unim-proved		Paved	Unpaved	Unim-proved
2007	18,174.7	14,652.3	2,138.0	1,384.5	49,535.6	31,156.4	8,801.8	9,577.4
2008	18,192.6	14,753.6	2,072.2	1,366.9	50,174.5	31,675.3	8,686.2	9,813.0
2009	18,138.0	14,851.6	1,966.7	1,319.6	50,500.9	32,470.0	8,508.8	9,522.2
2010	18,179.7	14,977.6	1,805.0	1,397.1	50,835.1	33,120.7	8,073.9	9,640.5
2011	18,196.3	15,080.9	1,709.3	1,406.1	50,951.8	33,707.1	7,673.4	9,571.4
2012	18,162.0	15,230.0	1,590.9	1,341.2	50,267.0	36,179.8	6,999.8	7,087.4
2013	18,082.4	15,243.0	1,528.7	1,310.7	65,497.2	50,095.9	7,013.5	8,387.8
Seoul	14.0	14.0	-	-	6,994.4	6,994.4	-	-
Busan	29.7	29.7	-	-	2,157.8	2,079.0	72.9	5.9
Daegu	11.6	11.6	-	-	1,657.5	1,657.5	-	-
Incheon	45.5	19.4	-	26.1	1,901.9	1,790.3	111.6	-
Gwangju	23.7	16.1	-	7.6	1,111.5	1,111.5	-	-
Daejeon	30.4	30.4	-	-	1,396.7	1,396.7	-	-
Ulsan	-	-	-	-	1,058.3	1,036.5	21.8	-
Sejong	87.4	67.9	19.5	-	-	-	-	-
Gyeonggi-do	2,712.3	2,300.5	42.2	369.5	7,888.7	6,841.2	260.0	787.4
Gangwon-do	1,641.0	1,454.7	119.9	66.5	6,196.6	3,591.8	1,059.3	1,545.4
Chungcheongbuk-do	1,472.8	1,391.6	48.9	32.3	3,827.2	2,759.9	525.7	541.6
Chungcheongnam-do	1,660.5	1,432.1	163.2	65.2	3,648.3	2,707.4	787.4	153.5
Jeollabuk-do	1,897.1	1,552.0	228.3	116.8	4,285.6	2,577.6	924.5	783.5
Jeollanam-do	2,297.9	1,761.3	305.4	231.2	5,783.7	4,167.5	792.1	824.1
Gyeongsangbuk-do	3,011.2	2,517.0	405.6	88.5	6,529.1	4,034.2	1,360.2	1,134.7
Gyeongsangnam-do	2,414.0	1,964.5	195.7	253.9	8,597.0	5,352.2	889.8	2,355.0
Jeju-do	733.4	680.2	-	53.2	2,463.0	1,998.3	208.1	256.6

Source : Ministry of Land, Infrastructure and Transport

Permits Authorized for Building Construction[1]

	Total	By use					By building material			
		Dwellings	Commercial	Factory	Educational and social	Others	Ferro-concrete	Masonry	Wooden	Others
					Number of buildings					
2009	212,347	72,891	63,776	19,407	14,784	56,273	178,182	22,225	11,022	918
2010	227,509	81,793	64,198	22,539	13,350	45,629	195,370	19,924	10,922	1,295
2011	239,836	99,074	67,789	22,353	12,558	38,062	208,302	19,357	11,686	491
2012	230,928	98,898	65,987	21,000	11,771	33,272	201,135	17,398	11,826	569
2013	225,002	93,592	65,553	22,132	11,916	31,809	196,498	16,101	11,710	693
2014	236,804	101,894	68,830	20,956	9,817	35,307	206,806	16,100	13,062	836
					Floor area (1,000㎡)					
2009	105,137	41,917	24,399	11,542	11,262	27,279	102,487	1,755	839	56
2010	125,447	51,464	26,617	15,484	12,062	19,820	122,840	1,680	868	59
2011	137,868	56,557	34,002	16,499	10,452	20,358	135,229	1,611	997	33
2012	137,141	59,256	32,334	15,940	10,459	19,152	134,749	1,388	961	43
2013	127,065	50,238	33,719	16,092	10,319	16,697	124,727	1,291	995	53
2014	141,347	60,935	37,420	15,655	9,350	17,987	138,824	1,260	1,200	63

Source : Ministry of Land, Infrastructure and Transport
* Includes new construction, reconstruction, alteration, extention, and repair
Note : 1) Excludes bogeumjari

Housing Construction Records

Unit : dwelling

	Total[1]			
		Detached House (Incl. multiple dwellings)	Apartment	Multi-family house[2]
2007	555,792	51,450	476,462	27,880
2008	371,285	53,667	263,153	54,465
2009	381,787	54,665	297,183	29,939
2010	386,542	62,173	276,989	47,380
2011	549,594	73,097	356,762	119,735
2012	586,884	71,255	376,086	139,543
2013	440,116	69,759	278,739	91,618
Seoul	77,621	1,444	45,104	31,073
Busan	29,922	960	20,445	8,517
Daegu	18,078	1,753	15,331	994
Incheon	18,907	1,196	14,373	3,338
Gwangju	8,454	1,546	5,682	1,226
Daejeon	5,180	841	3,794	545
Ulsan	5,344	1,542	3,213	589
Sejong	17,844	1,132	16,219	493
Gyeonggi-do	96,082	12,749	54,333	29,000
Gangwon-do	12,964	5,141	6,958	865
Chungcheongbuk-do	19,267	5,308	12,073	1,886
Chungcheongnam-do	32,343	6,613	23,354	2,376
Jeollabuk-do	13,179	4,404	7,257	1,518
Jeollanam-do	20,061	5,511	13,207	1,343
Gyeongsangbuk-do	23,878	8,569	12,276	3,033
Gyeongsangnam-do	34,683	8,779	23,963	1,941
Jeju-do	6,309	2,271	1,157	2,881

Source : Ministry of Land, Infrastructure and Transport
Note : 1) Based on construction permits and approval of construction plan
2) Includes row house

Energy Production, Consumption and Import & Export by Source[1]

Unit : 1,000TOE

	Production						Consumption			
		Anthr-acite	LNG[2]	Hydro	Nuclear	Renew-ables		Coal	LNG	Hydro
2009	40,133	1,171	498	1,213	31,771	5,480	243,311	68,604	33,908	1,213
2010	40,912	969	539	1,391	31,948	6,064	263,805	77,092	43,008	1,391
2011	42,987	969	451	1,684	33,265	6,618	276,636	83,640	46,284	1,684
2012	42,748	942	436	1,615	31,719	8,036	278,698	80,978	50,185	1,615
2013	41,321	817	463	1,771	29,283	8,987	280,290	81,915	52,523	1,771
2014[P]	45,442	786	322	1,651	33,002	9,681	281,920	84,797	47,773	1,651

	Nuclear	Petroleum	Renew-able	Imports				Exports	Bunkers[3]
				Coal	Petroleum	LNG	Petroleum		
2009	31,771	102,336	5,480	257,143	63,431	160,144	33,568	46,758	7,229
2010	31,948	104,301	6,064	279,649	72,576	164,689	42,384	48,224	7,844
2011	33,265	105,146	6,618	301,425	79,861	173,875	47,690	57,541	7,811
2012	31,719	106,165	8,036	304,116	77,546	179,387	47,184	61,454	7,805
2013	29,283	105,811	8,987	308,806	79,230	177,578	51,998	59,665	8,187
2014[P]	33,002	105,016	9,681	309,479	80,459	180,633	48,388	62,315	8,521

Source : Korea Energy Economics Institute
Note : 1) From 2012, are based on the revised calorific value
2) Production at Donghae-1 gas field
3) Deliveres to foreign-flag ships and planes.

Crude Oil Imports by Country of Origin

Unit : thousand barrel

	Total			Saudi Arabia	Kuwait	Indonesia	Iran	U.A.E	Others
		Rate of Change [%]	1,000kℓ						
2003	804,809	1.7	127,952	250,473	65,885	33,672	63,682	138,869	252,228
2004	825,790	2.6	131,287	253,849	64,659	38,104	64,974	145,598	258,606
2005	843,203	2.1	134,056	249,337	79,679	37,703	70,767	150,608	255,109
2006	888,794	5.4	141,304	261,563	92,620	23,359	75,058	158,865	277,329
2007	872,541	-1.8	138,720	249,887	94,031	17,603	85,793	141,887	283,340
2008	864,872	-0.9	137,501	262,637	104,593	16,308	73,016	158,109	250,209
2009	835,085	-3.4	132,765	254,799	100,090	20,115	81,437	114,592	264,052
2010	872,415	4.5	138,700	276,787	103,079	29,668	72,605	105,656	284,620
2011	927,044	6.3	147,385	291,348	117,370	21,008	87,184	87,234	322,900
2012	947,292	2.2	150,604	303,049	137,647	20,588	56,146	86,536	343,326
2013	915,075	-3.4	145,482	286,588	139,853	13,242	48,214	110,809	316,369

Source : Korea Energy Economics Institute

Summary of Electricity

	Generating facilities[1]			Gross generation[1]			Auxiliary use	Pumping storage	Net generation	T&D losses
		KEPCO & subsidiaries	Other Co.		KEPCO & subsidiaries	Other Co.				
	MWh			GWh			GWh			
2004	59,961	53,907	6,054	342,148	327,191	14,511	15,268	1,994	324,885	14,490
2005	62,258	55,956	6,302	364,639	349,758	14,612	16,452	1,980	346,207	15,615
2006	65,514	58,142	7,373	381,181	362,447	18,355	15,812	2,315	363,054	14,587
2007	68,268	60,269	8,000	403,125	380,201	22,093	16,614	1,817	384,693	15,345
2008	72,491	63,529	8,961	422,355	394,930	26,696	17,374	3,243	401,726	16,106
2009	73,470	63,962	9,508	433,604	406,780	25,968	18,258	3,713	411,631	16,770
2010	76,078	65,560	10,519	474,660	435,384	38,434	19,372	3,663	451,433	18,034
2011	79,342	67,006	12,336	496,893	443,409	52,671	19,689	4,257	472,650	17,430
2012	81,806	68,848	12,957	509,574	448,516	58,964	20,154	4,789	484,334	17,292
2013	86,969	70,845	16,124	517,148	448,757	66,710	20,463	5,408	491,003	18,311

	Power sold	Peak load	Average load	Average revenues per kWh sold	Customers	Employees	Paid-in capital	Total assets	Generation per capita	Consumption per capita
	GWh	MW		Won/ kWh	Household	person	Milion won	Milion won	kWh/ Person	kWh/ Person
2004	312,096	51,264	39,058	74.58	17,061,591	18,081	3,203,743	58,917,324	7,116	6,491
2005	332,413	54,631	41,625	74.46	17,329,494	18,261	3,207,839	61,626,841	7,550	6,883
2006	348,719	58,994	43,514	76.43	17,624,836	18,341	3,207,839	63,536,201	7,893	7,191
2007	368,605	62,285	46,019	77.85	18,038,810	18,599	3,207,839	65,642,590	8,319	7,607
2008	385,070	62,794	48,082	78.76	18,419,048	18,534	3,207,839	66,868,176	8,689	7,922
2009	394,475	66,797	49,498	83.59	18,727,411	17,885	3,207,839	69,985,451	8,895	8,092
2010	434,160	71,308	54,185	86.12	19,229,450	17,486	3,207,839	74,398,204	9,712	8,883
2011	455,070	73,137	56,723	89.32	19,814,866	17,095	3,209,820	94,769,898	9,982	9,142
2012	466,593	75,987	58,012	99.10	20,475,899	17,117	3,209,820	96,234,698	10,191	9,331
2013	474,849	76,522	59,035	106.33	21,017,693	17,517	3,209,820	98,249,927	10,112	9,285

Source : Korea Electric Power Corporation
Note : 1) Excludes purchased power of private power stations for commercial use

Electric Power Sold

Unit : GWh

	Total	Residential	Public	Service	Agriculture, forestry and fishery	Mining	Manufacturing
2005	332,413	50,873	13,741	100,987	7,007	1,317	158,489
2006	348,719	52,522	14,589	106,948	7,296	1,393	165,972
2007	368,605	54,174	15,579	112,601	7,795	1,484	176,973
2008	385,070	56,228	16,577	117,635	8,389	1,446	184,795
2009	394,475	57,596	17,932	121,203	9,145	1,350	187,249
2010	434,160	61,194	19,872	129,923	10,042	1,683	211,447
2011	455,070	61,564	20,539	130,762	10,575	1,928	229,701
2012	466,593	63,536	21,422	132,499	12,074	1,616	235,445
2013	474,849	63,971	21,982	132,055	13,062	1,478	242,301
2014	477,592	62,675	21,669	128,630	13,557	1,571	249,490

Source : Korea Electric Power Corporation

Number of Licensed Drivers[1]

Unit : persons

	Total	First grade				Second grade		
		Large	Ordinary	Light	Special	Ordinary	Light	Motorcycle
2002	21,223,010	1,270,504	10,400,477	41	3,404	9,001,680	8,089	538,815
2003	22,062,457	1,325,825	11,102,708	37	3,268	9,109,779	7,812	513,028
2004	22,735,053	1,405,017	11,715,778	35	3,267	9,107,720	8,101	495,135
2005	23,497,657	1,497,985	12,474,621	30	3,470	9,030,307	8,619	482,625
2006	24,088,229	1,569,687	13,289,729	26	3,342	8,752,021	8,943	464,481
2007	24,681,440	1,643,468	13,950,803	24	3,332	8,620,142	9,435	454,236
2008	25,268,379	1,723,357	14,517,649	24	3,478	8,561,731	10,157	451,983
2009	25,822,149	1,803,216	15,076,953	21	3,451	8,485,597	10,340	442,571
2010	26,402,364	1,866,443	15,521,417	20	3,324	8,571,612	10,289	429,259
2011	27,251,153	1,923,220	15,973,639	20	3,315	8,927,910	9,688	413,361
2012	28,263,317	1,972,010	16,419,173	19	3,311	9,452,989	9,166	406,649
2013	28,848,040	2,024,228	16,687,957	17	3,288	9,730,627	9,186	392,737
2014	29,764,939	19,200,096	17,115,160	17	3,232	10,178,636	9,264	376,943

Source : Korean National Police Agency
Note : 1) Date are different from the number of persons with driving licenses due to a person with two kinds or more of licenses.

Summary of Railway Operation

	Unit	2008	2009	2010	2011	2012	2013
Railway-km	km	3,391	3,378	3,557	3,559	3,572	3,590
Passengers traffic	thousand persons	1,018,977	1,020,319	1,060,941	1,118,622	1,151,523	1,224,820
Freight traffic	thousand tons	46,806	38,398	39,217	40,012	40,309	39,822
Engine-km	1,000km	876,871	885,084	902,666	968,684	984,874	994,602
Train-km	1,000km	120,728	119,242	122,447	128,599	131,088	133,131
Converted car-km	1,000km	1,660,167	1,605,338	1,631,733	1,711,301	1,751,266	1,751,266
Track Installation							
Track length	km	7,980,847	7,990,816	8,425,974	8,427,581	8,419,014	8,456,442
Normal bridge	km	302,854	360,949	404,538	410,892	415,533	429,184
Station	Number	639	639	652	652	662	666
Revenue[1]	million won	2,787,973	2,628,096	2,805,206	3,418,567	3,340,015	3,532,271
Passenger	million won	2,123,510	2,020,479	2,168,846	2,693,476	2,663,912	2,815,844
Freight	million won	321,739	272,592	312,304	406,115	333,170	331834

Source: Korea Railroad
Note: 1) Includes baggages and other operating revenue

Passenger Traffic of Railway

Unit : thousand persons, thousand passengers-km

| | Total | | Commuters | KTX | General | | | |
	Intercity	SMESRS			Samaeul	Mugunghwa	Commuter	Other
Number of passenger								
2005	950,995	115,002	835,993	8,565	31,337	10,483	53,261	10,486	870
2006	969,145	114,331	854,814	8,762	35,017	9,458	50,637	9,579	879
2007	989,294	110,631	878,664	8,797	35,550	9,667	49,415	6,046	1,156
2008	1,018,977	113,098	905,879	10,034	36,105	10,415	50,606	4,890	1,049
2009	1,020,319	107,733	912,586	10,281	35,340	10,297	47,824	2,918	1,073
2010	1,060,941	112,093	948,848	9,992	39,063	10,226	50,694	1,154	965
2011	1,118,621	121,769	996,852	10,681	47,463	9,615	52,313	685	1,013
2012	1,149,340	125,817	1,023,523	9,418	49,693	8,852	56,121	712	1,020
2013	1,224,820	132,033	1,092,786	11,927	51,465	8,506	58,217	1,023	896
Passenger-km								
2005	31,004,212	19,076,105	11,928,106	468,389	8,777,254	2,229,192	6,967,860	400,167	233,243
2006	31,415,976	19,078,533	12,337,443	500,828	9,674,341	1,915,405	6,388,190	374,647	225,121
2007	31,595,987	18,680,339	12,915,648	525,560	9,732,288	1,806,423	6,141,232	211,806	263,029
2008	32,026,528	18,671,356	13,355,172	585,788	9,858,806	1,766,317	6,073,612	151,569	235,263
2009	31,299,106	17,816,751	13,482,355	638,822	9,609,209	1,638,688	5,590,264	86,742	253,026
2010	33,012,479	19,018,617	13,993,862	621,866	10,652,094	1,611,050	5,882,340	30,644	220,622
2011	36,784,264	21,603,203	15,181,061	684,214	13,160,915	1,422,004	6,075,988	17,531	242,551
2012	42,492,561	22,244,053	20,380,580	717,746	13,696,875	1,205,772	6,358,426	19,670	245,565
2013	38,531,500	22,626,433	15,905,066	745,182	14,011,686	1,140,410	6,482,962	30,884	215,309

Source : Korea Railroad

Marine Freight Transportation[1]

Unit : thousand R/T

	Total	Grains	Oil	Cement	Bituminous coal	Lumber	Iron ore	Iron material	Others
Unloaded									
2008	723,821	9,368	243,283	18,565	88,460	8,887	59,519	49,811	245,928
2009	680,318	8,396	240,358	17,734	93,201	7,979	46,075	41,834	224,741
2010	766,062	10,588	252,614	15,677	105,502	9,388	59,449	50,828	262,015
2011	824,798	9,766	270,805	15,062	123,033	11,644	66,316	56,362	271,810
2012	839,422	9,521	277,760	15,574	113,947	10,133	67,626	58,802	286,059
2013	853,714	8,868	280,229	15,138	115,775	12,505	64,787	59,396	297,014
2014	892,255	8,803	280,489	15,250	120,290	16,239	74,534	61,312	315,338
Loaded									
2008	415,265	210	95,280	22,644	189	1,776	899	37,312	256,956
2009	396,223	132	92,970	21,200	153	2,218	1,172	36,056	242,323
2010	438,006	155	93,427	22,347	96	3,362	1,182	42,366	275,071
2011	486,392	511	111,594	24,332	159	7,891	1,331	50,284	290,290
2012	499,167	382	114,054	23,672	106	5,820	1,278	52,114	301,740
2013	505,212	260	109,067	23,361	10	5,372	1,198	51,276	314,667
2014	523,649	283	109,587	23,822	136	6,485	963	53,706	328,667

Source : Ministry of Oceans and Fisheries

Note : 1) Sum of domestic and international transport

* Including coastwise vessels, excluding passenger vessels

Aviation Traffics[1]

	International line						Domestic Line		
	In bound			Out bound					
	Passengers (number)	Freight (ton)	Mail (ton)	Passenger (number)	Freight (ton)	Mail (ton)	Passenger (number)	Freight (ton)	Mail (ton)
2001	9,816,967	821,991	5,930	9,904,958	946,444	19,283	21,495,715	423,512	4,098
2002	10,933,222	919,451	8,154	10,943,162	1,050,362	20,467	20,754,386	423,941	3,754
2003	10,260,584	962,301	7,111	10,296,017	1,127,257	20,180	20,802,254	416,385	832
2004	12,379,349	1,070,383	7,717	12,395,736	1,277,400	20,882	18,594,251	404,876	672
2005	13,715,185	1,109,018	8,349	13,789,914	1,273,730	20,560	16,690,887	364,367	2,771
2006	15,165,162	1,259,855	10,483	15,194,525	1,324,891	22,506	16,641,159	347,892	1,842
2007	17,757,723	1,469,839	13,238	17,692,112	1,493,992	23,861	16,202,240	309,563	373
2008	17,203,025	1,342,713	12,792	17,108,135	1,459,943	29,893	16,133,618	247,289	314
2009	16,428,780	1,232,343	13,194	16,461,988	1,443,147	39,916	17,584,158	263,390	538
2010	19,462,135	1,463,241	14,470	19,414,670	1,616,340	44,073	19,585,897	256,735	585
2011	20,782,751	1,398,013	15,538	20,630,416	1,451,845	47,441	20,357,717	274,819	611
2012	23,047,548	1,403,384	16,656	22,999,164	1,512,734	51,526	20,526,700	256,617	358
2013	24,383,075	1,454,184	20,114	24,309,657	1,550,741	57,922	21,471,586	246,085	229

Source : Ministry of Land, Infrastructure and Transport
Note : 1) Scheduled flight only

Motor Vehicle Registration
Unit : number

	Total[1]		Car			Van and Bus	
			Government	Private	Commercial		Government
2003	14,586,795	10,278,923	17,361	9,941,907	319,655	1,246,629	11,488
2004	14,934,092	10,620,557	17,933	10,273,673	328,951	1,204,313	11,606
2005	15,396,715	11,122,199	18,932	10,759,393	343,874	1,124,645	11,914
2006	15,895,234	11,606,971	19,817	11,219,435	367,719	1,105,636	12,358
2007	16,428,177	12,099,779	20,714	11,674,085	404,980	1,104,949	12,650
2008	16,794,219	12,483,809	21,388	12,025,715	436,706	1,096,698	13,269
2009	17,325,210	13,023,819	22,267	12,551,833	449,719	1,080,687	14,177
2010	17,941,356	13,631,769	22,872	13,124,972	483,925	1,049,725	15,039
2011	18,437,373	14,136,478	24,244	13,601,821	510,413	1,015,391	15,667
2012	18,870,533	14,577,193	25,295	14,010,618	541,280	986,833	16,428
2013	19,400,864	15,078,354	25,409	14,459,653	593,292	970,805	17,270

	Van and Bus		Truck				Special car
	Private	Commercial		Government	Private	Commercial	
2003	1,153,511	81,630	3,016,407	24,092	2,677,451	314,864	44,836
2004	1,111,979	80,728	3,062,314	24,638	2,716,572	321,104	46,908
2005	1,030,763	81,968	3,102,171	24,480	2,755,991	321,700	47,700
2006	1,007,723	85,555	3,133,201	24,855	2,781,552	326,794	49,426
2007	999,807	92,492	3,171,351	25,230	2,811,537	334,584	52,098
2008	987,448	95,981	3,160,338	25,535	2,796,092	338,711	53,374
2009	967,890	98,620	3,166,512	25,970	2,798,797	341,745	54,192
2010	931,740	102,946	3,203,808	26,306	2,831,697	345,805	56,054
2011	893,717	106,007	3,226,421	26,680	2,848,544	351,197	59,083
2012	860,074	110,331	3,243,924	27,177	2,862,737	354,010	62,583
2013	837,173	116,362	3,285,707	27,768	2,890,373	367,566	65,998

Source : Ministry of Land, Infrastructure and Transport
Note : 1) Excluding motor cycle

Number of Facilities of Wired and Wireless Telecommunication

Unit : line

		Wired telecom.						
		Subscriber telephone						
		Local telephone	Long distance telephone	International telephone	Public payphone	ISDN	Internet Phone	Premise telecom
2007	43,289,479	20,118,214	1,926,028	34,671	198,792	18,612	236,134	288,250
2008	44,061,394	21,148,653	1,675,434	34,671	160,996	15,769	1,266,730	302,663
2009	44,195,982	19,701,025	1,424,119	34,671	143,645	26,423	3,185,078	287,530
2010	43,973,990	19,109,994	1,281,707	34,671	127,361	30,386	4,140,601	316,283
2011	43,902,348	18,918,894	1,153,536	34,671	101,278	30,538	4,554,661	317,548
2012	43,643,904	18,729,705	1,142,001	34,671	101,658	30,233	4,645,754	314,373

		Wired telecom.				
		High-speed network service			Telex & telegram	Value added comm. Network
	Leased line	High-speed internet service	High-speed subscriber network service	Other high-speed network		
2007	707,712	19,533,485	14,255	-	3,868	209,458
2008	707,792	18,480,688	14,334	1,050	3,050	249,564
2009	627,750	18,510,269	13,395	-	-	242,077
2010	640,305	18,029,814	13,529	-	-	249,339
2011	646,708	17,878,477	14,205	-	-	251,832
2012	653,175	17,723,637	14,347	-	-	254,350

		Wireless telecom.						
		Mobile telecom.	Trunked radio system(TRS) mobile phone	Wireless data comm.	Pager & messaging	Other mobile telecom.	Satellite comm.	Wireless high-speed internet service
2007	92,528,049	91,767,181	1,317	401	700,165	1,000	1,157	56,828
2008	109,560,625	108,807,181	1,391	406	700,165	1,000	1,336	49,146
2009	122,470,156	121,595,381	1,377	722	560,132	-	1,363	311,181
2010	119,270,601	118,382,843	1,418	718	532,125	-	1,390	352,107
2011	112,116,808	111,173,456	1,409	682	524,143	-	1,397	415,721
2012	107,519,251	106,538,212	1,479	662	524,667	-	1,411	452,820

Source : Korea Association for ICT Promotion · Korea Electronics Association

Overseas Direct Investments[1]

Unit : thousand U. S. dollars

		Total Invested						
		Asia	North America	Latin America	Europe	Middle East	Africa	Oceania
2005	7,323,076	4,342,598	1,296,524	606,326	661,305	132,232	129,751	154,340
2006	11,867,148	6,447,308	2,283,019	1,091,475	1,233,104	397,740	206,766	207,737
2007	22,336,015	11,738,739	3,754,743	1,226,920	4,464,781	368,441	238,919	543,474
2008	23,975,330	11,854,019	5,276,070	2,077,013	3,407,393	264,096	320,246	776,493
2009	20,709,847	7,119,332	6,018,933	989,993	5,337,808	321,581	373,603	548,597
2010	24,637,846	10,174,700	4,681,067	2,225,581	6,186,460	306,936	284,329	778,771
2011	29,001,042	11,116,450	8,629,587	2,557,393	4,390,737	385,549	371,650	1,549,676
2012	28,423,078	11,474,984	6,402,038	3,342,295	4,191,811	296,499	366,540	2,348,911
2013	29,799,177	11,071,207	6,192,801	3,331,867	5,367,085	334,025	222,046	3,280,148
2014	24,701,184	8,722,903	6,139,695	3,489,876	3,272,369	1,024,457	314,910	1,736,974

Source : The Export-Import Bank of Korea
Note : 1) The figures for the latest year are preliminary

Foreign Direct Investments[1][2]

Unit : thousand U. S. dollars

	Investment from abroad by country(Notification cases)									
	U.S.A	Japan	Germany	Hong Kong	Netherlands	Switzerland	United Kingdom	France	China	Other
2004	12,795,638	4,706,993	2,262,620	487,030	89,486	1,309,083	70,354	652,754	179,962	1,164,760	1,872,596
2005	11,565,543	2,689,764	1,880,795	704,812	819,795	1,140,928	40,254	2,316,458	85,179	68,414	1,819,144
2006	11,247,441	1,705,495	2,111,046	483,907	165,161	791,717	241,143	706,556	1,173,434	37,887	3,831,095
2007	10,515,625	2,328,750	990,290	438,902	132,284	1,965,426	224,563	363,853	439,300	384,131	3,248,126
2008	11,711,873	1,328,190	1,423,941	685,418	223,369	1,228,067	63,885	1,232,792	537,889	335,601	4,652,721
2009	11,484,139	1,486,367	1,934,253	569,813	773,486	1,897,667	60,836	1,952,895	109,551	159,607	2,539,664
2010	13,071,463	1,974,549	2,082,692	268,260	92,527	1,184,839	85,030	648,956	159,919	414,178	6,160,513
2011	13,673,089	2,371,796	2,289,134	1,471,035	572,405	1,011,004	188,341	918,614	236,282	650,853	3,963,625
2012	16,285,905	3,674,116	4,541,610	407,864	1,669,800	634,621	144,288	360,811	221,701	726,952	3,904,142
2013	14,548,344	3,525,455	2,689,660	359,951	976,484	618,008	70,253	115,876	529,928	481,186	5,181,543

Source : Ministry of Trade, Industry & Energy
Note: 1) The figures for the latest year are preliminary
2) When a project is invested by more than one country, the figures for notification (permission) cases by the respective countries will differ from other tables

Arbitrated Basic Exchange Rate of Major Currencies[1]

Unit : won per currency

	United Kingdom £	U.S. $	Japan Per 100 ¥	Canada Can. $	China Yuan	Singapore S. $	HongKong H.K. $	EURO EURO	Australia A. $	Saudi-Arabia S.R
2007	1,874.10	938.20	833.33	956.91	128.45	648.94	120.26	1,381.26	822.85	250.21
2008	1,817.65	1,257.50	1,393.89	1,038.31	184.09	875.54	162.25	1,776.22	870.00	335.07
2009	1,877.73	1,167.60	1,262.82	1,106.99	171.06	831.27	150.56	1,674.28	1,045.06	311.29
2010	1,757.72	1,138.90	1,397.08	1,138.67	172.50	884.00	146.35	1,513.60	1,157.92	303.68
2011	1,777.24	1,153.30	1,485.16	1,129.74	182.51	886.44	148.38	1,494.10	1,169.27	307.54
2012	1,730.95	1,071.10	1,247.50	1,076.05	171.88	875.48	138.18	1,416.26	1,111.43	285.59
2013	1,740.66	1,055.30	1,004.66	990.85	174.09	832.75	136.09	1,456.26	939.96	281.38
2014	1,710.47	1,099.20	920.14	946.53	177.23	831.75	141.70	1,336.52	899.09	292.92

Source : The Bank of Korea
Note : 1) Arbitrated rates based on basic rate of Won
2) Data up to 1998 are arbitrated rates of ECU, available from 1994-04-01

International Reserves

Unit : million U.S. dollars

	Total	Gold[1]	Special drawing rights	IMF Reserve Position	Foreign currency reserves
2002	121,412.5	69.2	11.8	520.2	120,811.4
2003	155,352.4	70.9	21.0	751.6	154,508.8
2004	199,066.1	72.3	32.7	785.8	198,175.4
2005	210,390.7	73.6	43.6	305.8	209,967.7
2006	238,956.1	74.2	54.0	440.0	238,387.9
2007	262,224.1	74.3	68.6	310.5	261,770.7
2008	201,223.4	75.7	86.0	582.6	200,479.1
2009	269,994.7	79.0	3,731.9	981.6	265,202.3
2010	291,570.7	79.6	3,539.9	1,024.7	286,926.4
2011	306,402.5	2,166.6	3,446.7	2,566.2	298,232.9
2012	326,968.4	3,761.4	3,525.6	2,783.6	316,897.7
2013	346,459.6	4,794.5	3,489.9	2,527.7	335,647.5
2014	363,592.7	4,794.7	3,280.5	1,917.1	353,600.5

Source : The Bank of Korea
Note : 1) Domestic-owned gold is valued at US $42.22 per troy ounce (31.1035grams)
Overseas-deposited gold is valued at purchased cost

External Assets in Debt Instruments and External Debt Position[1] *Unit : million U.S. dollars*

	Gross External Assets									Net external assets
		General government	Central Bank	Deposit taking corporations			Other Sectors			
					Domestic banks	Domestic branches of foreign banks		Other financial corporations	Nonfinancial corporations, households, and NPISHs	
2009	415,083.5	13,499.5	269,994.7	74,962.5	63,056.3	11,906.2	56,626.8	19,218.8	37,408.0	70,476.1
2010	450,580.9	17,675.7	291,570.7	82,508.1	68,737.3	13,770.8	58,826.4	17,436.7	41,389.7	94,669.9
2011	498,668.2	18,342.0	306,402.5	100,844.6	83,918.0	16,926.6	73,079.2	19,825.0	53,254.1	98,634.3
2012	538,579.1	19,769.1	326,968.4	106,699.5	89,363.0	17,336.5	85,142.1	25,775.7	59,366.5	129,651.0
2013	608,888.7	21,356.8	346,954.5	137,666.8	107,587.7	30,079.2	102,910.6	34,727.2	68,183.4	185,384.0
2014[p]	678,925.3	23,327.9	364,076.5	162,262.8	116,642.6	45,620.2	129,258.2	51,269.3	77,988.9	253,476.1

	Gross External Debt								
		General government	Central Bank	Deposit taking corporations			Other Sectors		
					Domestic banks	Domestic branches of foreign banks		Other financial corporations	Nonfinancial corporations, households, and NPISHs
2009	344,607.4	34,190.7	33,068.5	179,786.9	102,512.3	77,274.6	97,561.4	27,088.7	70,472.7
2010	355,911.0	50,700.1	28,736.4	172,858.7	105,725.2	67,133.5	103,615.7	27,773.9	75,841.8
2011	400,033.9	60,313.5	23,070.3	196,296.6	129,702.4	66,594.2	120,353.5	33,306.6	87,046.9
2012	408,928.0	60,822.3	36,140.9	183,106.6	120,801.2	62,305.4	128,858.2	32,643.9	96,214.3
2013	423,504.7	62,979.3	40,011.2	180,093.4	124,302.3	55,791.1	140,420.7	32,630.3	107,790.5
2014[p]	425,449.2	65,226.1	38,085.8	186,044.2	122,372.3	63,671.9	136,093.2	29,341.2	106,751.9

Source : The Bank of Korea
Note : 1) Data are revised due to the implementation of BPM6 (2014.5.)

Balance of payments[1][2] *Unit : million U.S. dollars*

	Current account								
		Goods				Services		Primary income	Secondary income
			Exports	Imports		Credit	Debit		
2009	33,593.3	47,814.0	363,900.9	316,086.9	-9,589.9	72,752.1	82,342.0	-2,436.2	-2,194.6
2010	28,850.4	47,915.4	463,769.6	415,854.2	-14,238.4	83,260.3	97,498.7	489.9	-5,316.5
2011	18,655.8	29,089.9	587,099.7	558,009.8	-12,279.1	90,900.1	103,179.2	6,560.6	-4,715.6
2012	50,835.0	49,406.0	603,509.2	554,103.2	-5,213.6	103,533.2	108,746.8	12,116.7	-5,474.1
2013	81,148.2	82,781.0	618,156.9	535,375.9	-6,499.2	103,739.2	110,238.4	9,055.7	-4,189.3
2014[p]	89,220.1	92,687.6	621,298.9	528,611.3	-8,163.4	106,855.3	115,018.7	10,197.7	-5,501.8

	Capital and financial account								Net errors and omissions
		Capital account	Financial account						
				Direct investment	Portfolio investment	Financial derivatives	Other investment	Reserve assets	
2009	-28,953.6	-69.6	-28,884.0	-8,414.0	49,469.4	-3,093.0	1,820.0	-68,666.4	-4,639.7
2010	-23,253.2	-63.2	-23,190.0	-18,782.5	42,364.7	828.9	-20,630.5	-26,970.6	-5,597.2
2011	-24,427.8	-112.0	-24,315.8	-19,931.7	13,142.7	-1,031.3	-2,542.7	-13,952.8	5,772.0
2012	-51,624.1	-41.7	-51,582.4	-21,136.2	6,747.8	2,627.8	-26,637.3	-13,184.5	789.1
2013	-80,131.6	-27.0	-80,104.6	-15,593.2	-9,344.5	4,410.3	-43,281.1	-16,296.1	-1,016.6
2014[p]	-90,392.3	-9.0	-90,383.3	-20,659.5	-33,605.3	3,704.9	-21,937.9	-17,885.5	1,172.2

Source : The Bank of Korea
Note : 1) Due to the implementation of a new international standard (BPM6) (the change in the method to calculate processing trade, the reflection of the reinvestment rate and the change in coverage, etc.), past time-series data was revised
2) After 2014 figures are preliminary

Exports by Principal Country

Unit : thousand U.S. dollars

	Total	U.S.A.	Japan	HongKong	China	Germany	Singapore	Taiwan
2009	363,533,561	37,649,854	21,770,839	19,661,055	86,703,245	8,820,863	13,616,994	9,501,115
2010	466,383,762	49,816,058	28,176,281	25,294,346	116,837,833	10,702,180	15,244,202	14,830,499
2011	555,213,656	56,207,703	39,679,706	30,968,405	134,185,009	9,500,927	20,839,005	18,205,965
2012	547,869,792	58,524,559	38,796,057	32,606,189	134,322,564	7,509,691	22,887,919	14,814,856
2013	559,632,434	62,052,488	34,662,290	27,756,308	145,869,498	7,907,865	22,289,028	15,699,099
2014	572,664,607	70,284,872	32,183,788	27,256,402	145,287,701	7,570,926	23,749,882	15,077,398

	Indonesia	Philippines	United Arab Emirates	India	Netherlands	Vietnam	France	Denmark
2009	5,999,880	4,567,278	4,977,751	8,013,290	4,527,507	7,149,477	2,910,564	478,704
2010	8,897,299	5,837,983	5,487,047	11,434,596	5,306,208	9,652,073	3,004,291	561,525
2011	13,564,498	7,338,902	7,267,754	12,654,078	4,626,981	13,464,922	5,707,388	437,664
2012	13,955,030	8,210,714	6,861,716	11,922,037	5,058,782	15,945,975	2,598,779	349,836
2013	11,568,178	8,783,427	5,737,664	11,375,792	5,512,228	21,087,582	3,487,970	1,273,631
2014	11,360,656	10,032,489	7,211,628	12,782,490	5,296,459	22,351,690	2,639,283	2,232,440

	Russia	Saudi Arabia	Panama	Thailand	United Kingdom	Liberia	Malaysia	Canada
2009	4,194,066	3,856,582	4,476,617	4,528,169	3,796,553	4,884,557	4,324,822	3,439,570
2010	7,759,836	4,556,673	4,053,509	6,459,776	5,555,094	5,401,658	6,114,823	4,101,864
2011	10,304,880	6,964,299	3,798,253	8,458,966	4,969,095	7,389,345	6,275,131	4,927,656
2012	11,097,138	9,112,041	3,977,303	8,221,082	4,896,879	3,803,650	7,723,494	4,828,116
2013	11,149,103	8,827,722	3,484,594	8,071,656	4,727,085	3,512,923	8,587,757	5,202,855
2014	10,129,249	8,287,511	2,764,664	7,599,142	5,782,610	2,976,249	7,582,611	4,916,629

	Mexico	Australia	Brazil	Italy	Spain	Argentina	Bangladesh	Belgium
2009	7,132,760	5,243,144	5,311,210	2,797,342	1,737,082	494,269	1,063,848	2,189,249
2010	8,845,549	6,641,624	7,752,579	3,569,135	1,857,955	909,449	1,554,317	2,028,477
2011	9,729,059	8,163,845	11,821,399	4,107,495	1,856,558	1,081,071	1,627,620	2,255,376
2012	9,042,360	9,250,485	10,286,065	3,261,663	1,668,338	972,906	1,458,891	2,257,450
2013	9,727,377	9,563,090	9,688,236	3,125,722	1,682,123	1,074,647	1,427,204	2,240,758
2014	10,846,018	10,282,512	8,922,091	3,473,076	2,068,471	753,793	1,235,935	2,454,703

	Chile	Pakistan	Egypt	Sweden	South Africa	Sri Lanka	Israel	Turkey
2009	2,229,062	729,814	1,528,199	472,105	1,082,071	170,323	725,818	2,660,688
2010	2,947,054	780,871	2,240,439	637,649	1,668,191	245,884	1,059,432	3,752,906
2011	2,381,457	818,096	1,726,874	1,042,835	2,254,760	343,615	1,817,867	5,070,997
2012	2,469,337	847,195	1,806,970	788,768	2,188,273	320,313	1,532,297	4,551,618
2013	2,458,198	818,990	1,534,529	872,971	2,697,795	299,315	1,464,116	5,657,826
2014	2,083,323	769,963	2,363,828	871,068	1,475,573	314,125	1,224,845	6,664,732

	Poland	Iran	Uzbekistan	Colombia	Switzerland	Austria	Norway	New Zealand
2009	4,146,741	3,991,897	1,149,783	797,029	341,404	643,020	1,606,344	890,761
2010	4,381,011	4,596,721	1,438,644	1,388,553	369,501	951,754	2,801,149	918,464
2011	4,100,788	6,068,276	1,718,758	1,613,984	1,130,414	838,490	666,394	1,103,835
2012	3,677,297	6,256,525	1,766,516	1,467,701	401,766	838,481	1,061,510	1,465,066
2013	3,600,729	4,480,902	1,968,036	1,342,312	872,192	606,904	1,539,407	1,490,532
2014	3,849,508	4,162,243	2,032,460	1,509,399	313,643	937,826	1,669,793	1,730,305

Source : Korea International Trade Association

Imports by Principal Country

Unit : thousand U.S. dollars

	Total	Japan	U.S.A.	China	Germany	Saudi Arabia	Australia	Indonesia
2009	323,084,521	49,427,515	29,039,451	54,246,056	12,298,461	19,736,848	14,756,068	9,264,135
2010	425,212,160	64,296,117	40,402,691	71,573,603	14,304,896	26,820,002	20,456,219	13,985,848
2011	524,413,090	68,320,170	44,569,029	86,432,238	16,962,579	36,972,612	26,316,304	17,216,374
2012	519,584,473	64,363,080	43,340,962	80,784,595	17,645,374	39,707,051	22,987,917	15,676,272
2013	515,585,515	60,029,355	41,511,916	83,052,877	19,335,968	37,665,214	20,784,616	13,189,998
2014	525,514,506	53,768,313	45,283,254	90,082,226	21,298,750	36,694,536	20,413,019	12,266,260

	Canada	Italy	Malaysia	France	Taiwan	Vietnam	United Kingdom	Singapore
2009	3,535,329	3,512,913	7,574,059	4,006,099	9,851,388	2,369,970	2,895,758	7,871,779
2010	4,350,930	3,723,304	9,530,964	4,283,490	13,647,080	3,330,815	3,265,544	7,849,530
2011	6,611,934	4,373,924	10,467,817	6,314,947	14,693,589	5,084,246	3,818,089	8,966,683
2012	5,247,371	4,828,203	9,796,411	4,924,008	14,011,960	5,719,246	6,366,770	9,676,408
2013	4,717,331	5,383,466	11,095,821	6,012,939	14,632,594	7,175,193	6,193,715	10,369,435
2014	5,442,591	6,260,922	11,097,901	6,823,519	15,689,769	7,990,325	7,446,596	11,303,182

	Iran	Russia	United Arab Emirates	Brazil	Switzerland	Kuwait	Netherlands	Oman
2009	5,745,749	5,788,759	9,310,021	3,743,503	1,662,784	7,991,513	2,059,777	4,124,492
2010	6,940,236	9,899,456	12,170,134	4,712,085	2,003,169	10,850,149	4,189,300	4,095,900
2011	11,358,379	10,852,171	14,759,366	6,342,934	2,555,059	16,959,617	4,425,509	5,362,787
2012	8,544,429	11,354,318	15,115,287	6,085,364	2,581,096	18,297,149	3,994,092	5,305,683
2013	5,564,403	11,495,500	18,122,897	5,573,117	2,715,495	18,725,097	4,213,728	4,783,308
2014	4,578,119	15,669,238	16,194,256	4,907,128	2,755,335	16,892,033	4,605,487	4,596,803

	South Africa	Chile	Belgium	Philippines	Finland	Denmark	Austria	Qatar
2009	1,171,788	3,103,300	892,681	2,651,633	850,893	586,303	862,709	8,386,492
2010	2,272,295	4,221,395	1,154,766	3,488,104	1,003,799	574,507	1,014,709	11,915,450
2011	3,105,467	4,857,963	1,450,330	3,571,472	935,224	714,520	1,330,007	20,749,364
2012	2,128,947	4,676,463	1,385,935	3,283,935	1,053,236	748,643	1,261,890	25,504,675
2013	1,729,269	4,657,503	1,585,905	3,706,235	1,283,177	918,943	1,382,572	25,873,843
2014	1,623,905	4,810,134	1,830,528	3,331,239	1,355,995	994,309	1,344,329	25,723,055

	Spain	New Zealand	HongKong	Thailand	Sweden	Panama	India	Yemen
2009	875,670	879,361	1,487,173	3,238,628	1,169,497	1,090,543	4,141,622	52,734
2010	955,144	1,175,909	1,945,933	4,168,786	1,414,899	573,460	5,674,456	420,695
2011	1,161,712	1,474,143	2,315,073	5,413,360	2,143,525	393,860	7,893,573	1,126,526
2012	1,293,246	1,339,176	2,058,419	5,353,245	1,455,723	594,848	6,920,826	1,101,839
2013	1,597,030	1,395,172	1,929,242	5,231,003	1,624,890	516,357	6,180,172	1,663,255
2014	2,887,540	1,526,481	1,749,889	5,344,776	1,799,801	495,355	5,274,668	2,391,853

	Pakistan	Mexico	Ireland	Bahrain	Egypt	Israel	Norway	Turkey
2009	382,133	971,992	644,950	317,953	462,978	691,180	2,868,704	434,435
2010	399,661	1,521,027	631,219	589,233	937,560	769,140	3,673,025	516,290
2011	736,984	2,315,698	718,983	656,042	690,854	683,496	2,594,863	804,624
2012	776,018	2,591,566	765,683	801,785	802,111	861,286	5,094,367	672,311
2013	522,060	2,300,742	833,344	598,647	1,015,832	856,219	3,655,683	691,870
2014	401,916	3,268,495	935,408	615,508	531,711	959,741	2,841,303	655,159

Source : Korea International Trade Association

Summary of Exports and Imports

Unit : millions U.S. dollars, %

	Total		Exports		Imports		Excess of exports and imports(-)
		Over the same month of last year		Over the same month of last year		Over the same month of last year	
2006	634,847.5	16.3	325,464.8	14.4	309,382.6	18.4	16,082.2
2007	728,334.8	14.7	371,489.1	14.1	356,845.7	15.3	14,643.4
2008	857,282.1	17.7	422,007.3	13.6	435,274.7	22.0	-13,267.4
2009	686,618.1	-19.9	363,533.6	-13.9	323,084.5	-25.8	40,449.0
2010	891,595.9	29.9	466,383.8	28.3	425,212.2	31.6	41,171.6
2011	1,079,626.7	21.1	555,213.7	19.0	524,413.1	23.3	30,800.6
2012	1,067,454.3	-1.1	547,869.8	-1.3	519,584.5	-0.9	28,285.3
2013	1,075,217.9	0.7	559,632.4	2.1	515,585.5	-0.8	44,046.9
2014	1,098,179.1	2.1	572,664.6	2.3	525,514.5	1.9	47,150.1

Source : Korea International Trade Association

Revenue & Expenditure of Central Gov't & Consolidated Public Sector

Unit : billion won

		Revenue			Expenditure & net lending			Consolidated budget balance
			Current revenue	Capital revenue		Expenditure	Net lending	
2009	Total	250,810.6	248,278.6	2,532.0	268,430.8	205,381.5	18,049.3	-17,620.1
	Central Gov't	247,992.4	245,476.8	2,515.6	264,883.5	246,834.1	18,049.3	-16,891.1
	NFPEs	2,818.3	2,801.8	16.5	3,547.3	3,547.3	-	-729.1
2010	Total	270,992.7	268,540.0	2,382.7	254,231.0	251,146.5	3,084.5	16,691.7
	Central Gov't	268,153.4	265,779.7	2,373.7	251,156.2	248,071.7	3,084.5	16,997.2
	NFPEs	2,769.3	2,760.3	9.0	3,074.8	3,074.8	-	-305.5
2011	Total	292,323.3	289,796.6	2,526.7	273,694.1	269,768.4	3,925.6	18,629.2
	Central Gov't	289,920.0	287,403.6	2,516.4	270,655.1	266,729.4	3,925.6	19,265.0
	NFPEs	2,403.3	2,393.0	10.3	3,039.0	3,039.0	-	-635.7
2012	Total	311,455.8	307,754.3	3,701.5	292,977.2	286,920.8	6,056.4	18,478.6
	Central Gov't	308,795.9	305,146.8	3,649.1	289,083.7	283,027.2	6,056.4	19,712.2
	NFPEs	2,660.0	2,607.6	52.4	3,893.5	3,893.5	-	-1,233.6
2013	Total	314,437.6	311,135.7	3,301.9	300,237.6	302,035.8	-1,798.3	14,200.0
	Central Gov't	311,375.6	308,114.4	3,261.1	296,556.6	298,354.8	-1,798.3	14,819.0
	NFPEs	3,062.0	3,021.2	40.7	3,681.0	3,681.0	-	-619.0

Source : Ministry of Strategy and Finance

Bank Notes and Coins in Circulation by Denomination

Unit : million won

	Total		Bank notes					Coins[1]
			50,000 won	10,000 won	5,000 won	1,000 won	500 won & below	
2005	26,135,776	24,552,470	-	22,655,734	825,017	1,058,204	13,516	1,583,305
2006	27,843,113	26,183,604	-	23,923,102	1,153,133	1,093,854	13,515	1,659,510
2007	29,321,854	27,540,872	-	25,306,524	1,058,013	1,162,821	13,514	1,780,982
2008	30,758,260	28,915,163	-	26,699,942	1,033,312	1,168,395	13,514	1,843,097
2009	37,346,212	35,414,582	9,922,992	23,259,166	1,018,191	1,200,720	13,512	1,931,630
2010	43,307,163	41,280,991	18,996,243	20,012,191	1,016,731	1,242,314	13,512	2,026,172
2011	48,657,565	46,557,716	25,960,296	18,247,202	1,046,696	1,290,012	13,511	2,099,850
2012	54,334,430	52,176,316	32,766,487	16,966,019	1,097,126	1,333,173	13,510	2,158,114
2013	63,365,910	61,135,221	40,681,239	17,878,083	1,184,856	1,377,533	13,509	2,230,689
2014	74,944,785	72,643,797	52,003,417	17,946,287	1,249,766	1,430,818	13,509	2,300,988

Source : The Bank of Korea
Note : 1) Includes commemorative coins

614

Depository Corporations Survey[1][7]

Assets — Domestic claims

		Net claims on central government			Claims on local government & social security org.[2]	Claims on other financial corp.[3]		
			Claims on central government	Less: Liabilities to central government			Loans	Securities other than shares
2009	1,793,131.4	-71,286.8	102,513.5	173,800.3	6,792.9	184,234.5	19,876.2	99,312.2
2010	1,874,199.1	-81,911.9	109,093.3	191,005.2	7,254.2	221,780.9	19,580.5	118,047.0
2011	1,988,339.6	-102,380.3	101,182.2	203,562.5	8,747.7	232,780.9	27,855.0	123,347.2
2012	2,072,117.9	-99,847.9	113,521.3	213,369.1	12,513.4	271,921.0	26,838.5	149,673.1
2013	2,135,927.5	-106,525.2	122,096.5	228,621.7	13,925.0	292,262.4	23,911.7	165,999.2
2014	2,299,674.9	-112,642.8	130,195.3	242,838.1	19,065.7	330,353.6	24,004.5	181,801.3

Assets — Domestic claims / Net foreign assets

	Claims on nonfin. corp.sector[4]			Claims on households		Net foreign assets	Foreign assets	Foreign liabilities
		Loans	Securities other than shares		Loans			
2009	1,027,895.7	729,647.7	164,617.3	645,495.1	639,281.2	245,832.3	496,405.6	250,573.3
2010	1,051,852.9	755,941.3	169,944.0	675,121.0	673,879.6	275,573.9	504,717.0	229,143.1
2011	1,137,216.2	801,086.1	185,869.3	711,975.0	710,590.0	289,622.5	532,356.8	242,734.3
2012	1,159,480.2	813,262.0	189,765.4	728,051.2	727,514.4	334,378.9	612,036.3	277,657.3
2013	1,186,403.9	844,172.4	184,708.0	749,861.3	749,379.2	385,445.9	647,377.6	261,931.7
2014	1,256,769.6	903,827.6	174,407.0	806,128.9	805,662.9	427,673.5	730,312.4	302,639.0

Liabilities — Broad money

	Total assets or liabilities & net worth	Broad money	Currency in circulation	Transferable deposits		Other deposits			
				Demand deposits	Other transferable deposits	MMF (Money market funds)	Time & savings deposits below 2Y	Certificates of deposits	Beneficiary certificates
2009	2,052,498.5	1,566,850.0	29,205.9	99,027.3	261,161.3	54,280.9	647,778.6	91,303.5	159,105.8
2010	2,169,640.8	1,660,530.0	34,948.8	104,124.2	288,718.6	54,885.8	776,284.6	35,943.4	142,047.0
2011	2,302,630.2	1,751,458.4	39,609.1	108,573.1	293,895.3	40,886.8	849,960.3	26,935.2	151,592.5
2012	2,406,496.9	1,835,641.6	44,173.8	112,677.0	313,159.8	45,763.5	875,874.5	20,337.2	150,357.2
2013	2,521,373.4	1,920,795.0	53,316.2	125,991.7	336,335.5	44,232.6	867,040.9	21,542.2	152,463.4
2014	2,727,348.4	2,077,234.0	64,438.5	142,632.3	378,751.8	58,061.1	885,198.3	15,100.2	161,094.3

Liabilities

	Broad money			Deposits excluded from M2	Securities other than shares excluded from M2	Loans etc.[6]	Other items(net)	Shares and other equity	Consolidation adjustment, net
	Other deposits		Securities other than shares included in M2						
	Money in trusts below 2Y	Other items[5]							
2009	75,998.9	94,447.0	54,540.8	158,394.7	123,712.3	42,412.8	3,461.8	136,675.1	20,991.8
2010	75,908.4	86,695.4	60,973.7	181,817.1	120,266.2	37,923.4	41,503.2	142,186.4	-14,585.5
2011	93,499.5	86,073.3	60,433.3	199,581.4	120,101.1	40,429.9	21,596.5	149,125.9	20,337.1
2012	123,837.2	88,852.4	60,609.0	218,577.2	217,041.8	45,951.7	-9,643.0	160,542.6	28,384.9
2013	147,171.9	101,542.5	71,158.1	238,590.9	138,152.4	46,350.9	-20,939.9	159,035.7	39,388.5
2014	172,807.2	113,287.1	85,863.1	273,100.9	173,018.8	41,884.1	-35,463.1	175,051.6	22,522.1

Source : The Bank of Korea

Note : 1) Covers central bank (CB), other depository corporations (ODCs)
2) National pension fund, unemployment insurance fund, industrial accident prevention fund, etc
3) Life and non-life insurance corporation, securities companies, finance companies, etc
4) Public nonfinancial corporations, private nonfinancial corporations
5) Repurchase Agreement, CMA, Bills Issued, Bills sold, Deposites in Foreign Currency bellow 2 years
6) Loans, financial derivatives, etc
7) Due to the change of accounting rules, some series are revised

Cleared and Dishonored Checks and Bills[1]

Unit : Number-thousand bills, Value-billion won

	Cleared[2]		Average value per bill (1,000won)	Daily average clearings		Dishonored[2]		Dishonored ratio (%)	
	Number	Value		Number	Value	Number	Value	Number	Value
2009	641,266.2	5,399,803.3	8,421	2,532	21,258.7	147.0	7,578.9	0.02	0.14
2010	512,155.0	5,811,846.2	11,348	2,032	23,062.9	114.2	8,479.7	0.02	0.15
2011	413,777.0	5,301,060.9	12,811	1,662	21,289.4	93.6	5,688.1	0.02	0.11
2012	306,060.1	4,341,081.7	14,184	1,229	17,434.1	92.2	5,168.7	0.03	0.12
2013	239,322.0	3,771,402.3	15,759	965	15,207.3	63.8	5,238.4	0.03	0.14
2014	202,688.6	3,178,250.5	15,680	824	12,919.7	56.8	6,023.2	0.03	0.19

	Cleared and dishonored value by type							
	Cashier's checks		Household checks		Current account checks		Promissory notes	
	Cleared	Dishonored	Cleared	Dishonored	Cleared	Dishonored	Cleared	Dishonored
2009	821,152.3	31.7	6,858.3	64.6	794,711.2	500.4	1,983,120.8	5,827.2
2010	776,431.1	35.8	6,341.4	43.7	780,997.3	376.3	3,150,829.2	6,096.5
2011	760,495.6	14.5	5,878.6	39.6	819,138.0	302.2	2,751,558.4	3,481.7
2012	587,334.8	14.9	5,387.8	41.2	818,649.1	209.9	2,068,910.0	2,272.6
2013	499,818.0	21.0	4,620.8	29.8	782,241.5	141.7	1,764,215.8	2,741.8
2014	459,017.8	13.1	4,322.1	22.3	698,119.0	496.4	1,279,795.6	2,619.6

Source : The Bank of Korea

Note : 1) Excludes electronic settlement   2) Includes electronic bills from jan. 2009

Dealing in Securities

Unit : number-million shares, amount-billion won

	Securities transaction				Weighted stock price average[1]	Turnover ratio of based on trading volume	KOSPI[2]		KOSDAQ[3]	
	Stocks		Bond[4]							
	Trading volumes	Trading value	Trading volume (par value)	Trading value	KRW	%	Closing	Average	Closing	Average
2008	88,149	1,287,165	376,373	374,007	26,509	296.70	1,124.47	1,529.49	332.1	525.6
2009	122,871	1,466,275	504,382	510,194	24,798	408.74	1,682.77	1,429.04	513.6	473.6
2010	95,596	1,410,562	584,268	585,206	29,492	292.11	2,051.00	1,764.99	510.7	503.6
2011	87,732	1,702,060	815,152	824,827	32,596	254.09	1,825.74	1,983.42	500.2	498.3
2012	120,647	1,196,263	1,351,281	1,376,365	31,335	338.51	1,997.05	1,930.37	496.3	502.4
2013	81,096	986,375	1,312,827	1,321,989	32,617	230.74	2,011.34	1,960.50	500.0	531.0
2014	68,130	975,977	1,373,214	1,394,893	33,459	192.63	1,915.59	1,982.16	543.0	545.4

Source : Korea Exchange

Note : 1) Stock price average of year   2) Jan. 4. 1980 = 100   3) Jul. 1. 1996 = 1,000
4) Foreign currency-denominated bonds and won-denominated foreign bonds have been excluded

Listed Stocks by Ownership

	Listed stocks					
	Total stocks (million shares)	Composition(%)				
		Gov't & public bodies	Banks	Private corps[1]	Individuals	Foreigners
2007	28,261.8	4.4	6.0	34.1	36.5	18.9
2008	28,641.5	4.6	4.0	29.5	45.8	16.1
2009	31,278.0	1.5	9.1	23.3	49.9	16.3
2010	32,866.4	4.7	6.5	35.8	36.6	16.5
2011	34,548.7	3.2	6.1	38.5	36.3	15.9
2012	35,823.0	5.7	4.1	36.8	37.9	15.5
2013	35,217.3	5.6	3.9	36.4	38.3	15.9

Source: Korea Exchange

Note: 1) Includes securities companies, insurance companies, collective investment vehicle, merchant & mutual saving banks, pension funds and other corporations

Summary of Price Indexes

	Producer price[1]				Consumer price[2]		
		Agricultural, forest & marine products	Manufacturing products	Services		Food & nonalcoholic beverages	Housing, water, electricity, gas & other fuels	Restaurants & hotels
2002	78.5	73.0	76.4	85.3	78.2	69.3	80.3	78.5
2003	80.2	77.2	77.7	87.2	80.9	72.5	83.7	81.4
2004	85.1	86.5	83.6	89.7	83.8	78.3	86.4	84.5
2005	86.9	83.3	86.3	90.9	86.1	80.8	88.0	86.5
2006	87.7	81.3	86.4	92.9	88.1	81.2	90.6	88.2
2007	88.9	83.5	87.1	95.0	90.3	83.2	92.6	89.8
2008	96.5	84.4	97.6	97.5	94.5	87.4	96.6	94.1
2009	96.3	91.8	95.9	98.3	97.1	94.0	97.7	97.7
2010	100.0	100.0	100.0	100.0	100.0	100.0	100.0	100.0
2011	106.7	107.4	109.0	102.5	104.0	108.1	104.5	104.3
2012	107.5	108.3	108.6	104.2	106.3	112.4	109.3	105.5
2013	105.7	101.9	105.3	104.5	107.7	113.4	113.2	107.2
2014	105.2	102.5	103.1	106.1	109.0	113.7	116.5	108.7

	Received by farmers				Paid by farmers		Export & import price	
		Grain	Vegetables & fruits			Household goods	Farm supplies	Export	Import
2002	-	-	-	-	-	-	96.9	59.8
2003	-	-	-	-	-	-	94.8	60.9
2004	-	-	-	-	-	-	100.7	67.0
2005	92.5	101.5	88.5	81.8	85.0	73.8	94.0	69.0
2006	91.8	96.9	91.0	83.3	87.0	74.4	86.3	69.6
2007	93.8	101.7	93.6	85.7	89.1	77.4	84.4	72.7
2008	91.9	109.4	81.7	94.4	94.1	94.9	102.8	99.1
2009	93.4	101.5	84.9	98.5	96.8	102.2	102.6	95.0
2010	100.0	100.0	100.0	100.0	100.0	100.0	100.0	100.0
2011	107.6	113.5	111.4	103.5	104.6	101.3	100.2	111.6
2012	117.5	120.8	139.0	106.1	105.5	106.0	97.9	110.8
2013	113.2	124.0	124.4	107.1	105.5	107.7	93.7	102.7
2014	111.3	115.7	116.2	108.4	106.7	108.3	88.1	94.9

Source : Statistics Korea
Note : 1) Includes services from 1995   2) All cities

Hospitals and Clinics

Unit : Establishment

	Total	Hospitals and clinics			Specialized hospital			Dental hospitals and clinics		Oriental medicine hospitals and clinics		Dispen-saries[1]	Midwifery clinics
		General hospital	Hospital[2]	Clinic	Tuber-culosis hospital	Leprosy hospital	Mental hospital	Dental hospital	Dental clinic	Oriental medicine hospitals	Oriental medicine clinics		
2007	52,914	302	1,538	26,265	3	1	107	151	13,280	138	10,895	182	52
2008	54,165	313	1,754	26,581	3	1	118	184	13,618	139	11,248	175	31
2009	55,769	312	1,891	27,104	3	1	130	178	14,071	151	11,705	185	38
2010	56,244	312	2,003	27,334	3	1	143	188	14,074	159	11,804	186	37
2011	58,496	319	2,220	27,909	3	1	144	199	15,002	178	12,305	180	36
2012	59,519	323	2,414	28,762	3	1	156	202	14,800	199	12,440	184	35
2013	60,899	324	2,559	28,816	3	1	160	200	15,579	203	12,816	191	47

Source : Ministry of Health & Welfare Statistical Yearbook
Note : 1) Belongs to clerical & industrial establishments for employees based on 'Medical Act' Article 35
2) Hospital + Long term care hospital

Licensed Medical Personnel and Pharmacists[1]

Unit : person

	Physicians	Dentists	Oriental medical doctors	Midwives	Nurses	Dietitians[2]	Medical technicians	Pharmacists
2007	91,475	23,126	16,732	8,587	235,687	107,832	195,332	57,176
2008	95,088	23,924	17,541	8,565	246,840	112,071	208,780	58,363
2009	98,434	24,639	18,401	8,603	258,568	116,283	222,131	59,717
2010	101,443	25,390	19,132	8,578	270,274	121,679	236,117	60,956
2011	104,397	26,098	19,912	8,562	282,656	124,924	250,782	62,245
2012	107,295	26,804	20,668	8,528	295,254	128,807	265,692	63,647
2013	109,563	27,409	21,355	8,422	307,797	132,663	281,958	63,292

Source : Ministry of Health & Welfare
Note : 1) Includes those living abroad   2) Excluding those dead from 2011

Summary of Schools

Unit : each, person

	Schools			Classes & departments			Students
	2012	2013	2014	2012	2013	2014	2012
Total	20,569	20,781	20,973	300,883	301,772	303,476	11,113,958
Kindergarten[1]	8,538	8,678	8,826	28,386	30,597	33,041	613,749
Elementary school[2]	5,895	5,913	5,934	121,393	119,896	119,894	2,951,995
Middle school	3,162	3,173	3,186	57,086	56,843	56,305	1,849,094
General high school	1,529	1,525	1,520	40,415	40,417	40,538	1,381,130
Special-purposed high school	128	138	143	1,643	2,604	2,674	64,468
Specialized high school	499	494	499	7,829	11,626	11,661	330,797
Autonomous high school	147	165	164	2,951	4,758	4,723	143,692
Special school[3]	156	162	166	4,086	4,274	4,374	24,785
Civic school	-	-	-	-	-	-	-
Civic high school	4	4	4	13	16	5	170
Trade high school	9	9	7	46	43	44	1,137
Miscellaneous school[6]	30	34	43	326	323	358	9,291
Open middle school	-	2	6	-	5	30	-
Open high school	40	40	42	417	422	414	14,480
Junior college[6][7]	142	140	139	6,601	6,489	6,242	769,888
University of education[6]	10	10	10	139	140	140	18,789
University[6]	189	188	189	11,124	11,126	11,018	2,103,958
Others[8]	91	107	95	1,666	1,633	1,534	506,991
Graduate school[4][5][6]	1,177	1,200	1,209	10,523	10,560	10,511	329,544

	Students		Teachers			Entrants & graduates(2014)	
	2013	2014	2012	2013	2014	Entrants	Graduates
Total	10,891,364	10,655,034	561,015	569,365	576,547	2,735,519	2,985,746
Kindergarten1)	658,188	652,546	42,235	46,126	48,530	313,673	532,212
Elementary school2)	2,784,000	2,728,509	181,435	181,585	182,672	479,304	530,819
Middle school	1,804,189	1,717,911	111,004	112,690	113,349	528,611	606,494
General high school	1,356,070	1,314,073	89,538	89,469	90,174	430,079	453,046
Special-purposed high school	67,099	66,928	6,289	6,678	6,934	22,562	23,842
Specialized high school	320,374	313,449	27,283	26,759	26,938	105,011	106,521
Autonomous high school	149,760	144,922	9,843	10,508	10,442	48,411	49,574
Special school3)	25,161	25,317	7,654	8,012	8,297	8,682	8,600
Civic school	-	-	-	-	-	-	-
Civic high school	175	117	18	17	11	96	63
Trade high school	1,031	1,026	91	90	93	456	421
Miscellaneous school6)	7,857	8,356	675	752	923	3,088	2,498
Open middle school	160	826	-	-	-	661	-
Open high school	13,320	12,136	-	-	-	3,643	4,510
Junior college6)7)	757,721	740,801	13,078	13,015	12,920	221,750	183,557
University of education6)	17,500	17,500	842	835	834	3,868	4,690
University6)	2,120,296	2,120,296	61,993	63,042	64,378	363,655	301,606
Others8)	484,641	484,801	2,338	2,351	2,375	74,873	81,557
Graduate school4)5)6)	329,822	329,822	6,699	7,436	7,677	127,757	95,736

Source : Ministry of Education, Korean Educational Development Institute

Note : 1) The number of Reentrants of Kindergarten are not included in the number of entrants of Kindergarten

2) Earlier entrants are included in the entrants of elementary school

3) The graduates of the special schools include kindergarten, elementary school, middle school, high school students who completed educational process.

4) Graduate schools are not included in the total number of schools. The Total number of graduate schools indicates the numerical sum of 'graduate schools' and 'graduate school college', and indicates the number of 'graduate school colleges'. The Total number of schools includes sole-standing 'graduate school colleges'

5) The number of departments in graduate schools indicates that of master's degree programs.

6) The number of faculty members of institutions of higher education is sum of all the presidents/deans and full-time professors

7) Since 2008, the bachelor's degree-conferring intensive course programs have been included in the number of academic departments of junior colleges

8) Air & Corr. University, Industrial University, Technical College, Miscellaneous School, Cyber University, Distance University, College in the Company, Specialization College, Polytechnic College

Publication by Field[1]

Unit : kind, thousand volumes

	Total	Generalities	Philosophy	Religion	Social Sciences	Natural Sciences
				Kinds		
2006	38,035	254	826	1,749	6,488	694
2007	33,804	515	1,066	1,980	5,579	565
2008	36,588	822	946	2,009	6,335	593
2009	36,456	805	915	2,177	6,483	542
2010	35,515	703	1,055	1,899	6,017	541
2011	37,603	715	1,152	1,925	5,919	647
2012	34,342	613	1,237	1,889	6,089	521
2013	37,838	822	1,335	1,899	7,097	645
				Volumes		
2006	92,408	458	1,696	3,359	9,942	1,536
2007	114,407	1,006	2,125	1,539	9,303	787
2008	89,605	1,616	1,729	4,393	10,853	761
2009	92,951	1,514	1,488	4,368	10,937	907
2010	96,833	1,405	1,980	3,790	10,765	727
2011	100,387	1,336	2,153	3,997	9,364	1,113
2012	79,388	1,190	2,162	3,328	9,774	675
2013	79,968	1,448	2,240	3,384	9,618	783

	Science for technology	Art	Language	Literature	History	Children's book	Reference book
				Kinds			
2006	4,493	1,731	2,277	9,667	1,326	6,700	1,830
2007	3,135	1,441	1,667	7,572	1,048	7,307	1,749
2008	2,754	1,451	1,823	8,482	1,139	8,417	1,787
2009	3,054	1,407	1,660	8,718	1,008	7,884	1,803
2010	3,206	1,382	1,625	8,192	1,031	7,352	2,512
2011	3,628	1,354	1,385	8,184	989	9,546	2,159
2012	3,552	1,329	1,192	7,963	1,083	7,495	1,379
2013	3,880	1,402	1,399	9,296	1,283	7,424	1,356
				Volumes			
2006	6,378	2,930	5,917	21,133	2,460	21,103	15,496
2007	4,637	2,075	3,581	17,324	1,873	56,747	13,409
2008	3,641	2,265	4,048	17,641	2,151	26,885	13,621
2009	3,902	2,202	3,591	18,644	1,826	29,275	14,297
2010	4,397	2,116	4,338	17,280	1,829	26,200	22,007
2011	4,977	2,151	2,720	15,837	1,816	37,705	17,217
2012	4,634	2,007	1,871	14,796	1,866	26,537	10,547
2013	4,872	1,936	2,185	15,945	2,064	24,863	10,630

Source : Korean Publication Association

Note : 1) The figures includes only first-edition

Designated Cultural Heritage

Unit : each

	State designated						
	Tangible cultural heritage		Important intangible cultural heritage	Monument			
	National treasure	Treasure		Historic site	Historic site & scenic-area	Scenic-area	
2008	3,178	309	1,573	114	478	10	51
2009	3,237	313	1,588	114	490	-	67
2010	3,326	313	1,667	114	491	-	72
2011	3,385	314	1,710	114	479	-	82
2012	3,459	315	1,758	116	483	-	89
2013	3,513	315	1,774	119	485	-	106

	National monument	Important folklore materials		Tangible cultural heritage	Intangible cultural heritage	Monument	Folklore materials	Cultural property materials
			City · Province designated heritage					
2008	389	254	6,775	2,426	356	1,500	320	2,173
2009	404	261	6,964	2,528	364	1,513	321	2,238
2010	407	262	7,351	2,647	412	1,559	335	2,398
2011	422	264	7,543	2,711	446	1,593	342	2,451
2012	429	269	7,687	2,823	435	1,601	361	2,467
2013	424	280	7,855	2,915	497	1,588	388	2,467

Source : Cultural Heritage Administration

Air Quality in Major Cities

	Seoul	Busan	Daegu	Incheon	Gwangju	Daejeon	Ulsan
	SO_2[1] (ppm)						
2009	0.005	0.005	0.005	0.007	0.004	0.005	0.008
2010	0.005	0.006	0.005	0.007	0.003	0.004	0.008
2011	0.005	0.006	0.005	0.007	0.003	0.004	0.008
2012	0.005	0.006	0.004	0.007	0.004	0.004	0.008
2013	0.006	0.007	0.004	0.007	0.005	0.004	0.008
	PM-10[2] (µg/m³)						
2009	54	49	48	60	46	43	49
2010	49	49	51	55	45	44	48
2011	47	47	47	55	43	44	49
2012	41	43	42	47	38	39	46
2013	45	49	45	49	42	42	47
	O_3[3] (ppm)						
2009	0.021	0.027	0.023	0.024	0.026	0.023	0.024
2010	0.019	0.026	0.022	0.021	0.024	0.021	0.023
2011	0.019	0.027	0.025	0.022	0.026	0.022	0.025
2012	0.021	0.029	0.026	0.024	0.027	0.024	0.026
2013	0.022	0.029	0.025	0.025	0.029	0.024	0.028
	NO_2[4] (ppm)						
2009	0.035	0.021	0.024	0.030	0.021	0.022	0.022
2010	0.034	0.021	0.025	0.030	0.020	0.023	0.023
2011	0.033	0.020	0.024	0.030	0.019	0.021	0.023
2012	0.030	0.020	0.021	0.027	0.019	0.021	0.023
2013	0.033	0.021	0.023	0.028	0.020	0.021	0.024

Source : Ministry of Environment, National Institute of Environmental Research
Note : 1) The air quality standard of SO_2 is 0.02ppm or less
2) From 2001 to 2006, the air quality standard of particulate matter was 70µg/m³. Since 2007, it has been 50µg/m³
3) The air quality standard of O_3 is 0.06ppm or less on average for eight hours
4) Until 2006, the air quality standard of NO_2 was 0.05ppm or less on annual average. Since 2007, it has been 0.03ppm or less

Status of Film

	Number of new films[1] (each)	Number of screen (each)	Number of attendance (10,000 persons)			Share (%)	
				Korean film	Foreign film	Korean film	Foreign film
2007	124	1,975	15,877	7,939	7,938	50.0	50.0
2008	113	2,004	15,083	6,354	8,729	42.1	57.9
2009	138	2,055	15,696	7,641	8,055	48.7	51.3
2010	152	2,003	14,918	6,940	7,978	46.5	53.5
2011	216	1,974	15,972	8,287	7,686	51.9	48.1
2012	229	2,081	19,489	11,461	8,028	58.8	41.2

	Korean films exported[2]				foreign films imported(each)[3]		
	Number of films exported (each)	Average price per film (US$)	Total exports(US$)		Number of direct distribution(each)	Average price per film (US$)	Total imports (US$)[4]
2007	321	38,266	24,396,215	404	62	167,146	67,526,855
2008	361	56,901	21,036,540	362	48	217,611	78,775,016
2009	251	54,499	14,122,143	311	53	236,803	73,645,664
2010	276	47,704	13,582,850	381	47	140,088	53,373,711
2011	366	40,479	15,828,662	500	51	92,710	46,355,237
2012	331	42,811	20,174,950	721	48	82,398	59,409,280

Source : Korean Film Council
Note : 1) The number of full-length films which were graded according to the criteria by the Korea Media Rating Board
2) Total exports after 2007 include additional earnings. The average for exports of Korean film is calculated by excluding additional earnings
3) Based on the data regarding import recommendation of foreign films by the Korea Media Rating Board until 2005. Based on the data regarding foreign Films that were graded from 2006
4) Based on the value of imports that was reported by applicants for film grading. There might be discrepancies between the actual value and the reported value. It's because most import companies pay for just print prices of films and then the actual prices of films are decided according to net profits of films after releases

Participation in Overseas Film Festivals

Unit : case

	Total	Asia	North America	Central and South America	Europe	Oceania	Others
2006	158	25	32	10	73	10	8
2007	181	21	42	7	96	7	8
2008	134	20	28	5	72	4	5
2009	196	31	49	5	93	7	11
2010	139	25	34	5	63	6	6
2011	208	35	41	10	113	8	1
2012	211	42	43	11	100	12	3

Source : Korean Film Council

Tourism Balance[1][2]

Unit : million U.S. dollars, %, U.S. dollars

	Tourism receipts			Tourism expenditures			Balance
		Growth rate[3]	Average expenditure per capita		Growth rate[3]	Average expenditure per capita	
2008	9,696.1	59.7	1,407	14,571.7	-13.9	1,215	-4,875.6
2009	9,767.2	0.7	1,249	11,035.7	-24.3	1,162	-1,268.5
2010	10,290.5	5.4	1,170	14,277.7	29.4	1,143	-3,987.2
2011	12,347.2	20.0	1,261	15,530.8	8.8	1,224	-3,183.6
2012	13,358.4	8.2	1,199	16,494.5	6.2	1,201	-3,136.1
2013	14,524.8	8.7	1,175	17,340.7	5.1	1,202	-2,815.9
2014[p]	18,062.1	24.4	1,272	19,763.1	14.0	1,229	-1,701.0

Source : Korea Tourism Organization
Note : 1) After 2014 figures are preliminary   2) Excluding expense of students studying overseas from 1993
3) Over the same period last year

Directories

Yonhap News Agency

---III GOVERNMENT DIRECTORY III---

• As of June 12, 2015

THE EXECUTIVE

PRESIDENT

Park Geun-hye

Office of the President
(Cheong Wa Dae, The Blue House)

Add:1, Cheongwadae-ro, Jongno-gu, Seoul
Tel:(02)730-5800 http://www.president.go.kr
Chief of Staff   *Lee Byung-ki*
Senior Secretary to the President for State
 Affairs Planning   *Hyun Jung-taek*

Senior Secretary to the President for Political
 Affairs   *(a Vacancy)*
Senior Secretary to the President for Civil Affairs
                                        Woo Byung-woo
Senior Secretary to the President for Foreign
 Affairs and National Security   *Ju Chul-ki*
Senior Secretary to the President for Public
 Relations   *Kim Sung-woo*
Senior Secretary to the President for Economic
 Affairs   *An Chong-bum*
Senior Secretary to the President for Future
 Strategy   *Cho shin*
Senior Secretary to the President for Education
 and Culture   *Kim Sang-ryul*
Senior Secretary to the President for Employment
 and Welfare   *Choi Won-young*
Senior Secretary to the President for Personnel
 Affairs   *Jung Jin-chul*

Office of National Security

Director   *Kim Kwan-jin*
Deputy Director I   *Kim Kyou-hyun*
Deputy Director II   *Ju Chul-ki*

Presidential Security Service

http://www.pss.go.kr
Chief   *Park Heung-ryul*
Deputy Director   *Park Jong-joon*

National Intelligence Service

http://www.nis.go.kr
Director   *Lee Byung-ho*
Deputy Director I   *Han Ki-bum*
Deputy Director II   *Kim Soo-min*
Deputy Director III   *Kim Kyu-suk*
Planning and Coordination Office

Board of Audit and Inspection

Add:112, Bukchon-ro, Jongno-gu, Seoul
Tel:(02)2011-2114 http://www.bai.go.kr
Chairman   *Hwang Chan-hyun*
Commissioner   *Kim Byoung-chul,*
          Chin Young-kon, Kwak Sang-wook,
          Ryu Jin-hee, Choe Jae-hae,
          Wang Jung-hong
Secretary General   *Kim Young-ho*
Financial Management and Economy Audit
  Bureau
Industry and Finance Audit Bureau
Land and Maritime Affairs Audit Bureau
Public Institutions Audit Bureau
Strategic Programs Audit Group
Social and Welfare Audit Bureau
Public Administration and Security Audit Bureau
Provincial and Local Governments Audit Bureau
National Defense Audit Group
Local Construction Audit Group
Special Audit Group for Defense Corruption
Special Investigations Bureau
Audit Requests Investigation Bureau
IT Audit Group
Internal Audit Support Group
Advaced Audit Support Group
Inspector General
Legal Services and Quality Management Office
Director General for Claims Review
Training Administration Office
Audit and Inspection Research Institute

Korea Communications Commission

Add:47, Gwanmun-ro, Gwacheon-si,
Gyeonggi-do Tel:(02)2110-2114 http://www.
kcc.go.kr
Chairman   *Choi Sung-joon*
Vice Chairperson   *Hur Won-je*
Planning and Coordination Office
Broadcasting Policy Bureau
Consumer Policy Bureau
Broadcasting Infrastructure Bureau

PRIME MINISTER

(a Vacancy)

Office for Government Policy Coordination

Add:261, Dasom-ro, Sejong-si Tel:(044)200-
2114 http://www.pmo.go.kr
Minister   *Choo Kyeong-ho*
Vice Minister I   *Hong Yun-sik*
Vice Minister II   *Cho Kyeong-Gyu*
National Agenda Office
Government Performance Evaluation Office
Regulatory Reform Office
Economic Policy Coordination Office
Social Policy Coordination Office
<Affiliated Organizations>
Tax Tribunal

Prime Minister's Secretariat

Add:261, Dasom-ro, Sejong-si Tel:(044)200-
2114 http://www.pmo.go.kr
Chief of Staff   *(a Vacancy)*
Political Affairs Office
Civil Affairs Office
Public Information and Press Office

Ministry of Public Safety and Security

Add:209, Sejong-daero, Jongno-gu, Seoul
Tel:(02)2100-2114 http://www.mpss.go.kr
Minister   *Park In-yong*
Vice Minister   *Lee Seong-ho*
Safety Audit and Inspection Bureau
National Disaster and Safety Status Control
  Center
Planning and Coordination Office
Public Safety Policy Office
Disaster Management Office

Special Disaster Management Office
Central Fire Service
Korea Coast Guard
<Affiliated Organizations>
National Civil Defense and Disaster Management
 Training Institute
Central Fire Service Academy
Central 119 Rescue Headquarters
Korea Coast Guard Academy
Maritime Special Rescue Division
Regional Headquarters, Korea Coast
 Guard(5)
National Disaster Management Institute
Korea Coast Guard Maintenance Workshop

Ministry of Personnel Management

Add:209, Sejong-daero, Jongno-gu, Seoul
Tel:110 http://www.mpm.go.kr
Minister   Lee Geun-myun
Deputy minister   Hwang Seo-jong
Bureau of Human Resource Information
Civil Service Labor-Management Cooperation
 Bureau
Planning and Coordination Office
Human Resource Development Bureau
Bureau of Personnel Management Reform
Bureau of Personnel Management
Government Ethics and Discipline Bureau
<Affiliated Organizations>
Central Officials Training Institute
Appeals Commission

Ministry of Government Legislation

Add:20, Doum 5-ro, Sejong-si Tel:(044)200-
6900 http://www.moleg.go.kr
Minister   Je Jeong-boo
Bureau of Planning and Coordination
Legislation Bureau of Administrative Affairs
Legislation Bureau of Economic Affairs
Legislation Bureau of Social and Cultural
 Affairs
Bureau of Statutory Interpretation Information
Bureau of Legislation Support

Ministry of Patriots and Veterans Affairs

Add:9, Doum 4-ro, Sejong-si Tel:1577-0606
http://www.mpva.go.kr
Minister   Park Sung-choon
Assistant Minister for Planning and Coordination
Benefits Bureau
Burial and Commemoration Bureau
Welfare and Healthcare Bureau

Veterans Policy Bureau
<Affiliated Organizations>
Regional Administrations(5)
Regional Offices(19)
National Cemeteries(8)
Board of Patriots and Veterans Entitlement

Ministry of Food and Drug Safety

Add:187, Osongsaengmyeong 2-ro,
Osong-eup, Heungdeok-gu, Cheongju-si,
Chungcheongbuk-do Tel:1577-1255 http://
www.mfds.go.kr
Minister   Kim Seung-hee
Director General for Planning and Coordination
Customer Risk Prevention Bureau
Food Safety Policy Bureau
Food Nutrition and Dietary Safety Bureau
Agro-Livestock and Fishery Products Safety
 Bureau
Pharmaceutical Safety Bureau
Biopharmaceuticals and Herbal Medicine
 Bureau
Medical Device Safety Bureau
<Affiliated Organizations>
National Institute of Food and Drug Safety
 Evaluation
Regional FDSs(6)

Korea Fair Trade Commission

Add:95, Dasom-3ro, Sejong-si Tel:(044)200-
4010 http://www.ftc.go.kr
Chairman   Jeong Jae-chan
Vice Chairman   Kim Hack-hyun
General Counsel
Director General for Planning and Coordina-
 tion
Competition Policy Bureau
Director General for Market Structure Policy
Consumer Policy Bureau
Anti-Monopoly Bureau
Cartel Investigation Bureau
Business Cooperation Bureau
Task Force for Regulatory Reform
Regional Offices(5)

Financial Services Commission

Add:124, Sejong-daero, Jung-gu, Seoul
Tel:(02)2156-8000 http://www.fsc.go.kr
Chairman   Yim Jong-yong
Vice Chairman   Jeong Chan-woo
Planning and Coordination Bureau
Financial Policy Bureau
International Cooporation Office

Financial and Corporate Restruring Policy Bureau
Banking and Insurance Bureau
Consumer Finance and Protection Bureau
Capital Markets Bureau
Capital Market Investigation Unit
<Affiliated Organizations>
Financial Intelligence Unit
Financial Consumer Protection Bureau

Anti-Corruption and Civil Rights Commission

Add:20, Doum 5-ro, Sejong-si Tel:110 http://www.acrc.go.kr
Chairperson   *Lee Sung-bo*
Vice Chairpersons   *Kim In-su,*
            Kwak Jin-yong, Hong Seong-chil
Planning and Coordination Office
Institutional Improvement Bureau
Ombudsman Bureau
Anti-Corruption Bureau
Administrative Appeals Bureau
<Affiliated Organizations>
ACRC Seoul Complaints Center
Anti-Corruption Training Institute

Nuclear Safety and Security Commission

Add:178, Sejong-daero, Jongno-gu, Seoul
Tel:(02)397-7300 http://www.nssc.go.kr
Chairman   *Lee Un-chul*
Planning and Coordination Office
Nuclear Regulatory Bureau
Radiation Emergency Bureau
<Affiliated Organizations>
Regional Site Offices(4)

EXECUTIVE MINISTRIES

(17 ministries, 16 agencies)

Ministry of Strategy and Finance

Add:477, Galmae-ro, Sejong-si Tel:(044)215-2114 http://www.mosf.go.kr
Deputy Prime Minister and Minister
                          Choi Kyung-hwan
Vice Minister Ⅰ   *Joo Hyung-hwan*
Vice Minister Ⅱ   *Bang Moon-gyu*
Tax and Customs Office
Economic Policy Bureau
Policy Coordination Bureau
Future and Social Policy Bureau
International Finance Bureau

International Finance Cooperation Bureau
International Economic Affairs Bureau
Planning and Coordination Office
Budget Office
Treasury Bureau
Fiscal Policy Bureau
Fiscal Management Bureau
Public Institutions Policy Bureau
Korea Lottery Commission

National Tax Service

Add:8-14, Noeul 6-ro, Sejong-si Tel:126
http://www.nts.go.kr
Commissioner   *Lim Hwan-soo*
Planning and Coordination Bureau
Information System Bureau
Taxpayer Advocacy Bureau
International Taxation Bureau
Collection, Legal Affairs and PR Bureau
Individual Taxation Bureau
Corporate Taxation Bureau
Property Taxation Bureau
Investigation Bureau
Earned Income Tax Bureau
Innovating Information System Bureau
<Affiliated Organizations>
Regional Tax Offices(6)
District Tax Offices(117)
National Tax Officials Training Institute
NTS Liquors Licence Aid Center
NTS Customer Satisfaction Center

Korea Customs Service

Add:189, Cheongsa-ro, Seo-gu, Daejeon
Tel:125 http://www.customs.go.kr
Commissioner   *Kim Nak-hoe*
Director General for Planning and Coordination
Clearance Facilitation Bureau
Audit Policy Bureau
Investigation and Surveillance Bureau
Information Management and International
  Affairs Bureau
National Comprehensive Customs Information
  Network Task Force
<Affiliated Organizations>
Main Customs(6)
Customs Border Control Training Center
Central Customs Laboratory and Scientific
  Service
Customs Valuation and Classification Institute
Overseas Customs Attaches(9)
Customs Offices under the Direct Control of
  KCS

Public Procurement Service

Add:189, Cheoungsa-ro, Seo-gu, Daejeon
Tel:1588-0800 http://www.pps.go.kr
Administrator   *Kim Sang-kyu*
Director General for Planning and Coordination
e-Procurement Service Bureau
International Goods Bureau
Procurement Service Bureau
New Technologies and Services Bureau
Construction Works Bureau
<Affiliated Organizations>
Procurement Quality Management Office
Public Procurement Training Institute
Regional Offices(11)
Overseas Offices(2)

Statistics Korea

Add:189, Cheongsa-ro, Seo-gu, Daejeon
Tel:(042)481-4114   http://www.kostat.go.kr
Commissioner   *Yoo Gyeong-joon*
Director General for Planning and Coordination
Statistics Policy Bureau
Survey Management Bureau
Economic Statistics Bureau
Social Statistics Bureau
Informatics and Service Bureau
<Affiliated Organizations>
Statistical Training Institute
Statistical Research Institute
Regional Statistics Offices(5)
Regional Branch Offices(49)

Ministry of Education

Add:408, Galmae-ro, Sejong-si Tel:(044)203-
6118 http://www.moe.go.kr
Deputy Prime Minister and Minister
                                 Hwang Woo-yea
Vice Minister   *Gim Chae-chun*
Office of Planning and Coordination
School Policy Office
University Policy Office
Local Education Support Bureau
Lifelong and Vocational Education Bureau
Educational Safety Information Bureau
<Affiliated Organizations>
National Institute of Korean History
National Institute for International Education
National Institute for Special Education
National Institute for Educational Research
  and Training
Appeal Commission for Teachers
National Academy of Sciences

Offices of Education(17)

Ministry of Science, ICT and Future Planning

Add:47, Gwanmun-ro, Gwacheon-si, Gyeonggi-
do Tel:1355 http://www.msip.go.kr
Minister   *Choi Yang-hee*
Vice Minister I   *Lee Suk-joon*
Vice Minister II   *Choi Jae-you*
Office of Planning and Coordination
Office of R&D Policy
Creative Economy Policy Bureau
Science and Technology Policy Bureau
Science, ICT and Future HR Policy Bureau
R&D Investment Coordination Bureau
Evaluation Innovation Bureau
Office of ICT Policy
Cyber Security Policy Bureau
Broadcasting Promotion Policy Bureau
Telecommunications Policy Bureau
Radio Policy Bureau
<Affiliated Organizations>
National Radio Research Agency
Central Radio Management Office
Korea Post
National Science Museum
Gwacheon National Science Museum

Ministry of Foreign Affairs

Add:60, Sajik-ro 8-gil, Jongno-gu, Seoul
Tel:(02)2100-2114   http://www.mofa.go.kr
Minister   *Yun Byung-se*
Vice Minister I   *Cho Tae-yong*
Vice Minister II   *Cho Tae-yul*
Office of Planning and Coordination
Northeast Asian Affairs Bureau
South Asian and Pacific Affairs Bureau
North American Affairs Bureau
Latin American and Caribbean Affairs Bureau
European Affairs Bureau
African and Middle Eastern Affairs Bureau
International Organizations Bureau
Development Cooperation Bureau
International Legal Affairs Bureau
Cultural Affairs Bureau
Overseas Koreans and Consular Affairs Bureau
Multilateral Economic Affairs Bureau
Bilateral Economic Affairs Bureau
Global Economic Affairs Bureau
Office of Korean Peninsula Peace and Security
  Affairs
Korea National Diplomatic Academy
<Affiliated Organizations>
Overseas Missions(161)

Korea International Cooperation Agency
Korea Foundation
Overseas Koreans Foundation

Ministry of Unification

Add:209, Sejong-daero, Jongno-gu, Seoul
Tel:1577-1365 http://www.unikorea.go.kr
Minister   Hong Yong-pyo
Vice Minister   Hwang Boo-gi
Planning and Coordination Office
Unification Policy Office
Intelligence Analysis Bureau
Inter-Korean Exchange and Cooperation
  Bureau
Inter-Korean Cooperation District Policy Planning
  Directorate
<Affiliated Organizations>
Special Office for Inter-Korean Dialogue
Institute for Unification Education
Settlement Support Center for North Korean
  Refugees(Hana-won)
Inter-Korean Transit Office
Inter-Korean Exchange and Cooperation
  Consultation Office
The National Committee on Investigating
  Abductions during the Korean War

Ministry of Justice

Add:47, Gwanmun-ro, Gwacheon-si, Gyeonggi-
do Tel:(02)2110-3000 http://www.moj.go.kr
Minister   Hwang Kyo-ahn
Vice Minister   Kim Ju-Hyeon
Planning and Coordination Bureau
Legal Affairs Bureau
Criminal Affairs Bureau
Crime Prevention Policy Bureau
Human Rights Bureau
Korea Correctional Service
Korea Immigration Service
<Affiliated Organizations>
Institute of Justice
Probation and Parole Committees(5)
Probation Offices(18)
Probation Branch Offices(38)
Central Electronic Monitoring Center(2)
Juvenile Training Schools(10)
Juvenile Classification and Examination
  Center
Juvenile Delinquency Prevention Centers(16)
Institute of Forensic Psychiatry
Regional Corrections Headquarters(4)
Correctional Institutions(37)
Detention Centers(11)
Correctional Branches(3)

Immigration Offices(19)
Immigration Branch Offices(21)
Immigration Detention Centers(2)

Supreme Prosecutors' Office

Add:157, Banpo-daero, Seocho-gu, Seoul
Tel:(02)3480-2000 http://www.spo.go.kr
Prosecutor General   Kim Jin-tae
Planning and Coordination Department
Anti-Corruption Department
Criminal Department
Violent Crime Inverstigation Department
Public Security Department
Criminal Trial and Civil Litigation Department
Forensic Science Investigation Department
Inspection Headquarters
Administration Bureau
<Affiliated Organizations>
High Prosecutors' Offices(5)
  Seoul High Prosecutors' Office
  Daejeon High Prosecutors' Office
  Daegu High Prosecutors' Office
  Busan High Prosecutors' Office
  Gwangju High Prosecutors' Office
District Prosecutors' Offices(18)
  Seoul Central District Prosecutors' Office
  Seoul Eastern District Prosecutors' Office
  Seoul Southern District Prosecutors' Office
  Seoul Northern District Prosecutors' Office
  Seoul Western District Prosecutors' Office
  Uijeongbu District Prosecutors' Office
  Incheon District Prosecutors' Office
  Suwon District Prosecutors' Office
  Chuncheon District Prosecutors' Office
  Daejeon District Prosecutors' Office
  Cheongju District Prosecutors' Office
  Daegu District Prosecutors' Office
  Busan District Prosecutors' Office
  Changwon District Prosecutors' Office
  Ulsan District Prosecutors' Office
  Gwangju District Prosecutors' Office
  Jeonju District Prosecutors' Office
  Jeju District Prosecutors' Office
Branch Offices(40)

Ministry of National Defense

Add:22, Itaewon-ro, Yongsan-gu, Seoul
Tel:(02)748-1111 http://www.mnd.go.kr
Minister   Han Min-koo
Vice Minlster   Baek Seung-joo
Defense Reform Office
Office of Planning and Coordination
Office of National Defense Policy
Office of Personnel and Welfare

Office of Military Force and Resources Management
Joint Chiefs of Staff   http://www.jcs.mil.kr
Army   http://www.army.mil.kr
Navy   http://www.navy.mil.kr
Air Force   http://www.airforce.mil.kr
Marine Corps   http://www.rokmc.mil.kr
<Affiliated Organizations>
Seoul National Memorial Board
Defense Media Agency
National Defence Computer Center

Military Manpower Administration

Add:189, Cheongsa-ro, Seo-gu, Daejeon
Tel:1588-9090 http://www.mma.go.kr
Commissioner   Park Chang-myung
Planning and Coordination Officer
Military Service Resources Bureau
Active and Mobilization Bureau
Social Service Bureau
<Affiliated Organizations>
Regional Military Manpower Offices(11)
Military Manpower Branch Offices(2)
Central Physical Examination Agency
Call-Center of MMA

Defense Acquisition Program Administration

Add:54-99, Duteopbawi-ro, Yongsan-gu,
Seoul Tel:1577-1118 http://www.dapa.go.kr
Administrator   Chang Myoung-jin
Planning and Cooridination Bureau
Acquisition Planning Bureau
Defense Industry Promotion Bureau
Analysis, Test and Evaluation Bureau
Program Management Agency
Contract Management Agency

Ministry of Government Administration and Home Affairs

Add:209, Sejong-daero, Jongno-gu, Seoul
Tel:(02)2100-3399 http://www.mogaha.go.kr
Minister   Chong Jong-sup
Vice Minister   Chung Chae-gun
Planning and Coordination Office
Creative Government and Organization Management Office
e-Government Bureau
Local Administration Office
Local Finance and Taxation Office
<Affiliated Organizations>
National Archives of Korea
Government Building Management Service

National Computing and Information Agency
Local Government Officials Development Institute
Committee for the Five Northern Korean Provinces
National Forensic Service
National Police Commission

Korean National Police Agency

Add:97, Tongil-ro, Seodaemun-gu, Seoul
Tel:182 http://www.police.go.kr
Commissioner General   Kang Sin-myeong
Director General for Planning and Coordination
Public Safety Bureau
Criminal Investigation Bureau
Cyber Bureau
Traffic Bureau
Public Security Bureau
Intelligence Bureau
National Security Bureau
Foreign Affairs Bureau
<Affiliated Organizations>
Korean National Police University
Police Training Institute
Central Police Academy
Police Investigation Academy
National Police Hospital
Local Police Agencies(16)
Police Stations(250)

Ministry of Culture, Sports and Tourism

Add:388, Galmae-ro, Sejong-si Tel:(044)203-2000   http://www.mcst.go.kr
Minister   Kim Jong-deok
Vice Minister I   Park Min-Kwon
Vice Minister II   Kim Chong
Planning and Coordination Office
Cultural and Arts Policy Office
Culture Content Industry Bureau
Sports and Tourism Policy Bureau
Public Communication Office
Religious Affairs Office
Hub City of Asian Culture Bureau
Winter Olympic Games Special Zone Planning Department
<Affiliated Organizations>
National Academy of Arts of The Republic of Korea
Korean National University of Arts
Gukak National Middle·High School
National Museum of Korea
National Institute of the Korean Language
National Library of Korea
Korean Culture and Information Service

National Gugak Center
National Folk Museum of Korea
National Museum of Korean Contemporary History
National Theater of Korea
National Museum of Modern and Contemporary Art

Cultural Heritage Administration

Add:189, Chungsa-ro, Seo-gu, Daejeon
Tel:1600-0064 http://www.cha.go.kr
Administrator   *Rha Sun-hwa*
Director General for Planning and Coordination
Heritage Policy Bureau
Heritage Conservation Bureau
Heritage Promotion Bureau
<Affiliated Organizations>
Korean National University of Cultural Heritage
National Research Institute of Cultural Heritage
National Palace Museum of Korea
National Research Institute of Maritime Cultural Heritage
Hyeonchungsa Shrine Office
King Sejong Shrine Office
Chilbaeguichong Shrine Office
Royal Palaces and Royal Shrine Management Offices(5)
National Intangible Heritage Center

Ministry of Agriculture, Food and Rural Affairs

Add:94, Dasom 2-ro, Sejong-si Tel:110 http://www.mafra.go.kr
Minister   *Lee Dong-phil*
Vice Minister   *Yeo In-hong*
Planning and Coordination Office
Rural Policy Bureau
Agricultural Policy Bureau
International Cooperation Bureau
Livestock Policy Bureau
Food Industry Policy Office
<Affiliated Organizations>
Animal and Plant Quarantine Agency
National Agricultural Products Quality Management Service
Food and Agriculture Officials Training Institute
Korea National College of Agriculture and Fisheries
Korea Seed and Variety Service

Rural Development Administration

Add:300, Nongsaengmyeong-ro, Wansan-gu, Jeonju-si, Jeollabuk-do Tel:(063)238-

1000 http://www.rda.go.kr
Administrator   *Lee Yang-ho*
Director General for Planning and Coordination
Research Policy Bureau
Extension Service Bureau
Technology Cooperation Bureau
<Affiliated Organizations>
National Academy of Agricultural Science
National Institute of Crop Science
National Institute of Horticulture and Herbal Science
National Institute of Animal Science

Korea Forest Service

Add:189, Cheongsa-ro, Seo-gu, Daejeon
Tel:1588-3249 http://www.forest.go.kr
Administrator   *Shin Won-sop*
Planning and Coordination Bureau
International Affairs Bureau
Forest Resources Bureau
Forest Utilization Bureau
Forest Protection Bureau
<Affiliated Organizations>
National Institute of Forest Science of the Korea Forest Service
Korea National Arboretum
Forest Training Institute of the Korea Forest Service
Forest Aviation Headquarters
Korea Forest Seed and Variety Center
National Recreation Forest Management Office
Regional Forest Service(5)

Ministry of Trade, Industry and Energy

Add:402, Hannuri-daero, Sejong-si Tel:1577-0900 http://www.motie.go.kr
Minister   *Yoon Sang-jick*
Vice Minister I   *Lee Kwan-sup*
Vice Minister II   *Moon Jae-do*
Office of Planing and Coordination
Office of International Trade and Investment
Office of Industrial Policy
Office of Industrial Creativity and Innovation
Bureau of Trade Policy
Bureau of Trade Cooperation
Office of FTA Negotiations
Office of Energy and Resources
<Affiliated Organizations>
Korean Agency for Technology and Standards
Administration Agencies of Regional Free Trade Zone(7)
Korea Trade Commission

Planning Office of Free Economic Zone
Mine Registration Office
Mine Security Offices(4)
Korean Electricity Commission

Small and Medium Business Administration

Add:189, Cheongsa-ro, Seo-gu, Daejeon
Tel:1357 http://www.smba.go.kr
Administrator   *Han Jung-wha*
Planning and Coordination Bureau
SME Policy Bureau
Micro-Enterprise Policy Bureau
High Potential Enterprise Bureau
Business Start-up and Venture Bureau
Business Marketing Bureau
Productivity and Technology Bureau
<Affiliated Organizations>
Regional Administrations(11)
Regional Offices(3)
Meister High Schools(3)

Korean Intellectual Property Office

Add:189, Cheongsa-ro, Seo-gu, Daejeon
Tel:1544-8080 http://www.kipo.go.kr
Commissioner   *Choi Dong-kyu*
Planning and Coordination Bureau
Intellectual Property Policy Bureau
Intellectual Property Protection and International
   Cooperation Bureau
Information and Customer Service Bureau
Trademark and Design Examination Bureau
Patent Examination Policy Bureau
Patent Examination Bureau I
Patent Examination Bureau II
Patent Examination Bureau III
<Affiliated Organizations>
Intellectual Property Tribunal
International Intellectual Property Training
   Institute

Ministry of Health and Welfare

Add:13, Doum 4-ro, Sejong-si Tel:129 http://
www.mw.go.kr
Minister   *Moon Hyung-pyo*
Vice Minister   *Chang Ok-ju*
Office for Planning and Coordination
Office for Healthcare Policy
Office for Social Welfare Policy
Office for Population Policy
Bureau of Health Insurance Policy
Bureau of Health Policy
Bureau of Health Industry

Bureau of Policy for Persons with Disabilities
Bureau of Pension Policy
<Affiliated Organizations>
Korea Center for Disease Control and Prevention
National Rehabilitation Center
Administration for the Osong Bio Technopolis
National Mang-hyang Cemetery
National Hospitals(8)
National Quarantine Stations(13)

Ministry of Environment

Add:11, Doum 6-ro, Sejong-si Tel:1577-8866
http://www.me.go.kr
Minister   *Yoon Seong-kyu*
Vice Minister   *Jeong Yeon-man*
Planning and Coordination Office
Environmental Policy Office
Water Environment Policy Bureau
Nature Conservation Bureau
Resource Recirculation Bureau
<Affiliated Organizations>
National Institute of Environmental Research
National Institute of Environmental Human
   Resources Development
Greenhouse Gas Inventory and Research
   Center
National Institute of Chemical Safety
National Environmental Dispute Resolution
   Commission
National Institute of Biological Resources
Basin Environmental Offices(4)
Regional Environmental Offices(3)
Metropolitan Air Quality Management Office

Korea Meteorological Administration

Add:61, Yeouldeabang-ro 16-gil, Dongjak-
gu, Seoul Tel:(02)2181-0900   http://www.
kma.go.kr
Administrator   *Ko Yun-hwa*
Director General for Planning and Coordina-
   tion
Forecast Bureau
Observation Infrastructure Bureau
Climate Science Bureau
Meteorological Industry and Information
   Technology Bureau
<Affiliated Organizations>
National Institute of Meteorological Research
Korea Aviation Meteorological Agency
Regional Meteorological Administrations(6)
National Meteorological Satellite Center
Weather Radar Center

Ministry of Employment and Labor

Add:422, Hannuri-daero, Sejong-si Tel:1350
http://www.moel.go.kr
Minister   *Lee Ki-kweon*
Vice Minister   *Koh Young-sun*
Planning and Coordination Office
Employment Policy Office
Labor Policy Office
Vocational Skills Policy Bureau
Industrial Accident Prevention and Compensation
  Bureau
<Affiliated Organizations>
Regional Labor Administrations(6)
Regional Labor Offices(40)
Regional Labor Branch Office
National Labor Relations Commission
Regional Labor Relations Commissions(11)
Minimum Wage Council
Industrial Accident Deliberation Commission
Employment Insurance Deliberation Com-
  mission

Ministry of Gender Equality and Family

Add:209, Sejong-daero, Jongno-gu, Seoul
Tel:(02)2100-6000 http://www.mogef.go.kr
Minister   *Kim Hee-jung*
Vice Minister   *Kwon Yong-hyun*
Planning and Coordination Office
Women's Policy Bureau
Youth and Family Policy Bureau
Women's and Youth Rights Promotion Bureau

Ministry of Land, Infrastructure and Transport

Add:11, Doum 6-ro, Sejong-si Tel:1599-0001
http://www.molit.go.kr
Minister   *Yoo Il-ho*
Vice Minister I   *Kim Kyung-hwan*
Vice Minister II   *Yeo Hyung-ku*
Planning and Coordination Office
Territorial and Urban Development Office
Housing and Land Office
Construction Policy Bureau
Water Resources Policy Bureau
Transport and Logistics Office
Civil Aviation Office
Road Bureau
Railway Bureau
<Affiliated Organizations>
Training Institute for Land Transport and
  Maritime Affairs
Regional Construction and Management

Administrations(5)
Flood Control Offices(4)
Railroad Special Judicial Police
Regional Aviation Offices(3)
Aviation and Railway Accident Investigation
  Board
National Geographic Information Institute
Central Land Tribunal

Multifunctional Administrative City Construction Agency

Add:11, Doum 6-ro, Sejong-si Tel:(044)200-
3000 http://www.macc.go.kr
Chairman   *Lee Choong-jae*
Planning and Coordination Bureau
Urban Planning Bureau
Infrastructure Bureau
Public Architecture Bureau

Korea Agency for Saemangeum Development and Investment

Add:31, Dasom 1-ro, Sejong-si Tel:(044)415-
1000 http://www.saemangeum.go.kr
Commissioner   *Lee Byoung-gook*
Planning and Coordination Bureau
Investment Strategy Bureau
Development Project Bureau

Ministry of Oceans and Fisheries

Add:94, Dasom 2-ro, Sejong-si Tel:110 http://
  www.mof.go.kr
Minister   *Yoo Ki-june*
Vice Minister   *Kim Young-suk*
Planning and Coordination Office
Marine Policy Office
Fisheries Policy Office
Shipping and Logistics Bureau
Maritime Affairs and Safety Policy Bureau
Ports and Harbors Bureau
Hebei Spirit Incident Compensation Bureau
Sewol Incident Compensation Bureau
<Affiliated Organizations>
Regional Maritime Affairs and Port Administra-
  tions(11)
Busan Maritime High School
Incheon National Maritime High School
Oceans and Fisheries HRD Institute
National Fisheries Research and Development
  Institute
Korea Hydrographic and Oceanographic
  Administration
Korean Maritime Safety Tribunal
National Fishery Products Quality Management

Service
Fisheries Management Services(2)

LOCAL GOVERNMENTS

Seoul Metropolitan Government
Add:110, Sejong-daero, Jung-gu, Seoul Tel:(02)120 http://www.seoul.go.kr
Mayor *Park Won-soon*

Busan Metropolitan Government
Add:1001, Jungang-daero, Yeonje-gu, Busan Tel:(051)120 http://www.busan.go.kr
Mayor *Suh Byung-soo*

Daegu Metropolitan Government
Add:88, Gongpyeong-ro, Jung-gu, Daegu Tel:(053)120 http://www.daegu.go.kr
Mayor *Kwon Young-jin*

Incheon Metropolitan Government
Add:29, Jeonggak-ro, Namdong-gu, Incheon Tel:(032)120 http://www.incheon.go.kr
Mayor *Yoo Jeong-bok*

Gwangju Metropolitan Government
Add:111, Naebang-ro, Seo-gu, Gwangju Tel:(062)120 http://www.gwangju.go.kr
Mayor *Yoon Jang-hyun*

Daejeon Metropolitan Government
Add:100, Dunsan-ro, Seo-gu, Daejeon Tel:(042)120 http://www.daejeon.go.kr
Mayor *Kwon Sun-taek*

Ulsan Metropolitan Government
Add:201, Jungang-ro, Nam-gu, Ulsan Tel:(052)120 http://www.ulsan.go.kr
Mayor *Kim Gi-hyeon*

Sejong Metropolitan Autonomous City Government
Add:93, Guncheong-ro, Jochiwon-eup, Sejong-si Tel:(044)300-3114 http://www.sejong.go.kr
Mayor *Lee Choon-hee*

Gyeonggi-Do Government
Add:1, Hyowon-ro, Paldal-gu, Suwon-si, Gyeonggi-do Tel:(031)120 http://www.gg.go.kr
Governor *Nam Kyung-pil*

Gangwon-Do Government
Add:1, Jungang-ro, Chuncheon-si, Gangwon-do Tel:(033)120 http://www.provin.gangwon.kr
Governor *Choi Moon-soon*

Chungcheongbuk-Do Government
Add:82, Sangdang-ro, Sangdang-gu, Cheongju-si, Chungcheongbuk-do Tel:(043)220-2114 http://www.cb21.net
Governor *Lee Si-jong*

Chungcheongnam-Do Government
Add:21, Chungnam-daero, Hongbuk-myeon, Hongseong-gun, Chungcheongnam-do Tel:(041)635-2000 http://www.chungnam.net
Governor *Ahn Hee-jung*

Jeollabuk-Do Government
Add:225, Hyoja-ro, Wansan-gu, Jeonju-si, Jeollabuk-do Tel:(063)280-2114 http://www.jeonbuk.go.kr
Governor *Song Ha-jin*

Jeollanam-Do Government
Add:1, Oryong-gil, Samhyang-eup, Muan-gun, Jeollanam-do Tel:(061)247-0011 http://www.jeonnam.go.kr
Governor *Lee Nak-Yon*

Gyeongsangbuk-Do Government
Add:40, Yeonam-ro, Buk-gu, Daegu Tel:(053)959-0114 http://www.gb.go.kr
Governor *Kim Kwan-yong*

Gyeongsangnam-Do Government
Add:300, Jungang-daero, Uichang-gu, Changwon-si, Gyeongsangnam-do Tel:(055)211-2114 http://www.gsnd.net
Governor *Hong Joon-pyo*

Jeju Special Self-Governing Province Government
Add:6, Munnyeon-ro, Jeju-si, Jeju-do Tel:(064)120 http://www.jeju.go.kr
Governor *Won Hee-ryong*

<OFFICES OF EDUCATION>

Seoul Metropolitan Office of Education
Add:48, Songwol-gil, Jongno-gu, Seoul Tel:(02)1396 http://www.sen.go.kr
Superintendent *Cho Hee-yeon*

632

Busan Metropolitan Office of Education
Add:12, Hwaji-ro, Busanjin-gu, Busan
Tel:(051)860-0114 http://www.pen.go.kr
Superintendent   Kim Seok-joon

Daegu Metropolitan Office of Education
Add:11, Suseong-ro 76-gil, Suseong-gu, Daegu Tel:(053)231-0000 http://www.dge.go.kr
Superintendent   Woo Tong-ki

Incheon Metropolitan Office of Education
Add:9, Jeonggak-ro, Namdong-gu, Incheon
Tel:(032)423-3303 http://www.ice.go.kr
Superintendent   Lee Cheong-yeon

Gwangju Metropolitan Office of Education
Add:93, Hwawoon-ro, Seo-gu, Gwangju
Tel:(062)380-4500 http://www.gen.go.kr
Superintendent   Jang Hui-guk

Daejeon Metropolitan Office of Education
Add:89, Dunsan-ro, Seo-gu, Daejeon Tel:
(042)480-7979 http://www.dje.go.kr
Superintendent   Sul Dong-Ho

Ulsan Metropolitan Office of Education
Add:375, Bukbusunhwan-doro, Jung-gu, Ulsan
Tel:(052)210-5400 http://www.use.go.kr
Superintendent   Kim Bok-man

Sejong City Office of Education
Add:2154, Hannuri-daero, Sejong-si
Tel:(044)320-1000 http://www.sje.go.kr
Superintendent   Choi Gyo-jin

Gyeonggi-Do Provincial Office of Education
Add:18, Jowon-ro, Jangan-gu, Suwon-si,
Gyeonggi-do Tel:(031)1396 http://www.goe.go.kr
Superintendent   Lee Jae-jung

Gangwon-Do Office of Education
Add:2854, Yeongseo-ro, Chuncheon-si,
Gangwon-do Tel:(033)258-5114 http://www.gwe.go.kr
Superintendent   Min Byeong-hee

Chungcheongbuk-Do Office of Education
Add:1929, Cheongnam-ro, Heungdeok-gu, Cheongju-si, Chungcheongbuk-do
Tel:(043)290-2000 http://www.cbe.go.kr
Superintendent   Kim Byeong-woo

Chungcheongnam-Do Office of Education
Add:22, Seonhwa-ro, Hongbuk-myeon, Hongseong-gun, Chungcheongnam-do Tel:
(041)640-7777 http://www.cne.go.kr
Superintendent   Kim Ji-cheol

Jeollabuk-Do Office of Education
Add:111, Hongsan-ro, Wansan-gu, Jeonju-si, Jeollabuk-do Tel:(063)239-3114 http://www.jbe.go.kr
Superintendent   Kim Seung-hwan

Jeollanam-Do Office of Education
Add:10, Eojinnuri-gil, Samhyang-eup, Muan-gun, Jeollanam-do Tel:(061)260-0114 http://www.jne.go.kr
Superintendent   Jang Man-chae

Gyeongsangbuk-Do Office of Education
Add:40, Yeonam-ro, Buk-gu, Daegu
Tel:(053)603-3800 http://www.gbe.kr
Superintendent   Lee Young-woo

Gyeongsangnam-Do Office of Education
Add:241, Jungang-daero, Uichang-gu, Changwon-si, Gyeongsangnam-do Tel:
(055)268-1100 http://www.gne.go.kr
Superintendent   Park Jong-hoon

Jeju Special Self-Governing Provincial Office of Education
Add:5, Munyeon-ro, Jeju-si, Jeju-do
Tel:(064)710-0114 http://www.jje.go.kr
Superintendent   Lee Seok-moon

LEGISLATURE

NATIONAL ASSEMBLY

Add:1, Uisadang-daero, Yeongdeungpo-gu,
Seoul Tel:(02)788-2114 http://www.assembly.go.kr
Speaker   Chung Ui-hwa
Deputy Speakers   Jeong Kab-yoon,
                              Lee Seok-hyun

Standing Committees And Special Committees

House Steering Committee
Legislation and Judiciary Committee
National Policy Committee
Strategy and Finance Committee
Science, ICT, Future Planning, Broadcasting and Communications Committee
Education, Culture, Sports and Tourism Committee
Foreign Affairs and Unification Committee
National Defense Committee
Security and Public Administration Committee
Agriculture, Food, Rural Affairs, Oceans and Fisheries Committee
Trade, Industry and Energy Committee
Health and Welfare Committee
Environment and Labor Committee
Land, Infrastructure and Transport Committee
Intelligence Committee
Gender Equality and Family Committee
Special Committee on Budget and Accounts
Special Committee on Ethics

National Assembly Secretariat

Add:1, Uisadang-daero, Yeongdeungpo-gu, Seoul Tel:(02)788-2114
http://nas.na.go.kr
Secretary General   *Park Heong-joon*
Legislative Counseling Office
Proceedings Bureau
Broadcast Bureau
Office of the Security Planning
Legislative Request and Petition Center
Planning and Coordination Office
International Affairs and Protocol Bureau
Management and Maintenance Bureau
Parliamentary Training Office
Personnel Division
Management Support Division

National Assembly Library

Add:1, Uisadang-daero, Yeongdeungpo-gu, Seoul Tel:(02)788-4211 http://www.nanet.go.kr
Chief Librarian   *Lee Eun-chul*
Planning and Management Office
Parliamentary Information Office
Law Library
Information Management Bureau
Information Services Bureau
National Assembly Archives

National Assembly Budget Office

Add:1, Uisadang-daero, Yeongdeungpo-gu, Seoul Tel:(02)2070-3114 http://www.nabo.go.kr
Chief   *Kim Jun-ki*
Planning and Management Office
Budget Analysis Office
Economic Analysis Office
Program Evaluation Bureau

National Assembly Research Service

Add:1, Uisadang-daero, Yeongdeungpo-gu, Seoul Tel:(02)788-4510 http://www.nars.go.kr
Chief   *Lim Seong-ho*
Planning and Management Office
Politics and Administration Research Office
Economy and Industry Research Office
Society and Culture Research Office

JUDICIARY

SUPREME COURT

Add:219, Seocho-daero, Seocho-gu, Seoul Tel:(02)3480-1100 http://www.scourt.go.kr
Chief Justice   *Yang Sung-tae*
Justices   *Min Il-young, Lee In-bok, Lee Sang-hoon, Park Byong-dae, Kim Yong-deok, Park Poe-young, Ko Young-han, Kim Chang-suk, Kim Shin, Kim So-young, Jo Hee-de, Kwon Soon-il, Park Sang-ok*

High Courts(5)
  Seoul High Court
  Daejeon High Court
  Daegu High Court
  Busan High Court
  Gwangju High Court
Patent Court
District Courts(18)
  Seoul Central District Court
  Seoul Eastern District Court
  Seoul Southern District Court
  Seoul Northern District Court
  Seoul Western District Court
  Uijeongbu District Court
  Incheon District Court

Suwon District Court
Chuncheon District Court
Daejeon District Court
Cheongju District Court
Daegu District Court
Busan District Court
Ulsan District Court
Changwon District Court
Gwangju District Court
Jeonju District Court
Jeju District Court
Branch District Courts(40)
Family Courts(5)
Seoul Family Court
Daejeon Family Court
Daegu Family Court
Busan Family Court
Gwangju Family Court
Branch Family Courts(16)
Seoul Administrative Court

National Court Administration

Add:219, Seocho-ro, Seocho-gu, Seoul Tel:
(02)3480-1100 http://www.scourt.go.kr
Minister   Park Byong-dae
Vice Minister   Kang Hyung-ju
Planning and Coordination Office
Judicial Procedure Office
Judicial Policy Office
Administrative Management Office
Registration Bureau
Judicial IT Bureau
Supreme Court Litigation Bureau

Judical Research and Training Institute

Add:550, Hosu-ro, Ilsandong-gu, Goyang-si,
Gyeonggi-do Tel:(031)920-3114 https://jrti.
scourt.go.kr
Chief   Cho Yong-ku

Judical Policy Research Institute

Add:550 Hosu-ro, Ilsandong-gu, Goyang-si
Tel:(031)920-3550 http://jpri.scourt.go.kr
President   Choi Song-wha

Training Institute for Court Officials

Add:523, Hosu-ro, Ilsandong-gu, Goyang-si,
Gyeonggi-do Tel:(031)920-5114 https://edu.
scourt.go.kr
President   Koo Yon-mo

Supreme Court Library

Add:219, Seocho-daero, Seocho-gu, Seoul
Tel:107 https://library.scourt.go.kr
President   Kim Chan-don

INDEPENDENT ORGANS

CONSTITUTIONAL COURT

Add:15, Bukchon-ro, Jongno-gu, Seoul
Tel:(02)708-3456 http://www.ccourt.go.kr
President   Park Han-chul
Justices   Lee Jung-mi , Kim Yi-su,
Lee Jin-sung, Kim Chang-jong,
Ahn Chang-ho, Kang Il-won,
Suh Ki-seog, Cho Yong-ho
Planning and Coordination Office
Administration Management Bureau
Judgement Affairs Bureau
Information and Materials Bureau
<Affiliated Organizations>
Constitutional Research Institute

NATIONAL ELECTION COMMISSION

Add:44, Hongchonmal-ro, Gwacheon-si, Gyeong-
gi-do Tel:(02)503-1114 http://www.nec.go.kr
Chairperson   Lee In-bok
Standing Commissioner   Lee Jong-woo
Commissioners   Lee Han-goo,
Cho Byoung-hyun, Lee Sang-hwan,
Kim Jung-ki, Choi Yoon-hee,
Kim Yong-ho, Cho Yong-koo
Planning and Coordination Office
Election Policy Office
Internet Election News Deliberation Commission
National Election Survey Deliberation
Commission
National Election Broadcasting Debates
Commission
Si(Special Metropolitan, Metropolitan City)/
Do(Province) ECs(17)
Gu(Ward)/Si(City)/Gun(County) ECs(251)
Eup/Myeon/Dong Ecs(3,487)

⫶⫶ HEADS OF LOCAL GOVERNMENT ⫶⫶

Note

* *There are two kinds of local government. Regional local government(Metropolitan City, Province) and Basic local government(City, District, County).*
* *For the name of local government, two different names are used as belows;*
  do=Province, si=City, gu=District, gun=County
* ** = Winners from a By-election or Re-election*
* *As of June 12, 2015*

<LOCAL SITUATION TO HOLD ELECTIONS EVER>

* 1st Nationwide Local Elections : June 27, 1995
* 2nd Nationwide Local Elections : June 4, 1998
* 3rd Nationwide Local Elections : June 13, 2002
* 4th Nationwide Local Elections : May 31, 2006
* 5th Nationwide Local Elections : June 2, 2010
* 6th Nationwide Local Elections : June 4, 2014

* From june 1995, heads of local government elected by popular vote.

REGIONAL LOCAL GOVERNMENT

(Order)	(Name)	(Term of Office)	

Mayors of Seoul Metropolitan City

1st	Cho Soon	July	1995-Sept.	1997
2nd	Goh Kun	July	1998-June	2002
3rd	Lee Myung-bak	July	2002-June	2006
4th	Oh Se-hoon	July	2006-June	2010
5th	Oh Se-hoon	July	2010-Aug.	2011
5th*	Park Won-soon	Oct.	2011-June	2014
6th	Park Won-soon	July	2014-*present*	

Mayors of Busan Metropolitan City

1st	Moon Jung-soo	July	1995-June	1998
2nd	Ahn Sang-young	July	1998-June	2002
3rd	Ahn Sang-young	July	2002-Feb.	2004
3rd*	Hur Nam-sik	June	2004-June	2006
4th	Hur Nam-sik	July	2006-June	2010
5th	Hur Nam-sik	July	2010-June	2014
6th	Suh Byung-soo	July	2014-*present*	

Mayors of Daegu Metropolitan City

1st	Moon Hi-gab	July	1995-June	1998
2nd	Moon Hi-gab	July	1998-June	2002
3rd	Cho Hae-nyoung	July	2002-June	2006
4th	Kim Bum-il	July	2006-June	2010
5th	Kim Bum-il	July	2010-June	2014
6th	Kwon Young-jin	July	2014-*present*	

Mayors of Incheon Metropolitan City

1st	Choi Ki-sun	July	1995-June	1998
2nd	Choi Ki-sun	July	1998-June	2002
3rd	Ahn Sang-soo	July	2002-June	2006
4th	Ahn Sang-soo	July	2006-June	2010
5th	Song Young-gil	July	2010-June	2014
6th	Yoo Jeong-bok	July	2014-*present*	

Mayors of Gwangju Metropolitan City

1st	Song Eon-jong	July	1995-June	1998
2nd	Koh Jae-yoo	July	1998-June	2002
3rd	Park Kwang-tae	July	2002-June	2006
4th	Park Kwang-tae	July	2006-June	2010
5th	Kang Un-tae	July	2010-June	2014
6th	Yoon Jang-hyun	July	2014-*present*	

Mayors of Daejeon Metropolitan City

1st	Hong Sun-kee	July	1995-June	1998
2nd	Hong Sun-kee	July	1998-June	2002
3rd	Yum Hong-chul	July	2002-June	2006
4th	Park Seoung-hyo	July	2006-June	2010
5th	Yum Hong-chul	July	2010-June	2014
6th	Kwon Sun-taik	July	2014-*present*	

Mayors of Ulsan Metropolitan City

▸ *Promoted to Ulsan Metropolitan City on July 15, 1997.*

(Mayor of Ulsan City)

1st	Shim Wan-gu	July	1995-July	1997
1st	Shim Wan-gu	July	1997-June	1998
2nd	Shim Wan-gu	July	1998-June	2002
3rd	Bak Maeng-woo	July	2002-June	2006
4th	Bak Maeng-woo	July	2006-June	2010
5th	Bak Maeng-woo	July	2010-March	2014
6th	Kim Gi-hyeon	July	2014-*present*	

Mayors of Sejong Metropolitan Autonomous City

▸ *Sejong Metropolitan Autonomous City was launched on July 1, 2012.*

1st	Yu Han-sik	July	2012-June	2014
2nd	Lee Choon-hee	July	2014-*present*	

Governors of Gyeonggi-do

1st	Rhee In-je	July	1995-Sept.	1997
2nd	Lim Chang-yuel	July	1998-June	2002
3rd	Sohn Hak-kyu	July	2002-June	2006
4th	Kim Moon-soo	July	2006-June	2010
5th	Kim Moon-soo	July	2010-June	2014
6th	Nam Kyung-pil	July	2014-*present*	

Governors of Gangwon-do

1st	Choi Gak-kyu	July	1995-June	1998
2nd	Kim Jin-sun	July	1998-June	2002
3rd	Kim Jin-sun	July	2002-June	2006
4th	Kim Jin-sun	July	2006-June	2010
5th	Lee Kwang-jae	July	2010-Jan.	2011
5th*	Choi Moon-soon	April	2011-June	2014
6th	Choi Moon-soon	July	2014-*present*	

Governors of Chungcheongbuk-do

1st	Joo Byong-duck	July	1995-June	1998
2nd	Lee Won-jong	July	1998-June	2002
3rd	Lee Won-jong	July	2002-June	2006
4th	Chung Woo-taik	July	2006-June	2010
5th	Lee Si-jong	July	2010-June	2014
6th	Lee Si-jong	July	2014-*present*	

Governors of Chungcheongnam-do

1st	Sim Dae-pyung	July	1995-June	1998
2nd	Sim Dae-pyung	July	1998-June	2002
3rd	Sim Dae-pyung	July	2002-March	2006
4th	Lee One-koo	July	2006-Dec.	2009
5th	Ahn Hee-jung	July	2010-June	2014
6th	Ahn Hee-jung	July	2014-*present*	

Governors of Jeollabuk-do

1st	You Jong-keun	July	1995-June	1998
2nd	You Jong-keun	July	1998-June	2002
3rd	Kang Hyon-wook	July	2002-June	2006
4th	Kim Wan-ju	July	2006-June	2010
5th	Kim Wan-ju	July	2010-June	2014
6th	Song Ha-jin	July	2014-*present*	

Governors of Jeollanam-do

1st	Huh Kyung-man	July	1995-June	1998
2nd	Huh Kyung-man	July	1998-June	2002
3rd	Park Tae-young	July	2002-April	2004
3rd*	Park Joon-young	June	2004-June	2006
4th	Park Joon-young	July	2006-June	2010
5th	Park Joon-young	July	2010-June	2014
6th	Lee Nak-yon	July	2014-*present*	

Governors of Gyeongsangbuk-do

1st	Lee Eui-geun	July	1995-June	1998
2nd	Lee Eui-geun	July	1998-June	2002
3rd	Lee Eui-geun	July	2002-June	2006
4th	Kim Kwan-yong	July	2006-June	2010
5th	Kim Kwan-yong	July	2010-June	2014
6th	Kim Kwan-yong	July	2014-*present*	

Governors of Gyeongsangnam-do

1st	Kim Hyuk-kyu	July	1995-June	1998
2nd	Kim Hyuk-kyu	July	1998-June	2002
3rd	Kim Hyuk-kyu	July	2002-Dec.	2003
3rd*	Kim Tae-ho	June	2004-June	2006
4th	Kim Tae-ho	July	2006-June	2010
5th	Kim Doo-gwan	July	2010-July	2012
5th*	Hong Joon-pyo	Dec.	2012-June	2014

| 6th | Hong Joon-pyo | July | 2014-present | |

Governors of Jeju Special Self-Governing Province

▸ *Jeju Special Self-governing Province was launched on July 1, 2006.*

(Governors of Jeju Province)

1st	Shin Koo-bum	July	1995-June	1998
2nd	Woo Keun-min	July	1998-June	2002
3rd	Woo Keun-min	July	2002-April	2004
3rd*	Kim Tae-hwan	June	2004-May	2006
4th	Kim Tae-hwan	July	2006-June	2010
5th	Woo Keun-min	July	2010-June	2014
6th	Won Hee-ryong	July	2014-present	

BASIC LOCAL GOVERNMENT

Seoul Metropolitan City

25 Districts(gu)

· Dobong-gu · Dongdaemun-gu · Dongjak-gu
· Eunpyeong-gu · Gangbuk-gu · Gangdong-gu
· Gangnam-gu · Gangseo-gu · Geumcheon-gu
· Guro-gu · Gwanak-gu · Gwangjin-gu
· Jongno-gu · Jung-gu · Jungnang-gu
· Mapo-gu · Nowon-gu · Seocho-gu
· Seodaemun-gu · Seongbuk-gu
· Seongdong-gu · Songpa-gu · Yangcheon-gu
· Yeongdeungpo-gu · Yongsan-gu

Mayors of Dobong-gu

1st	Ryu Chon-su	July	1995-June	1998
2nd	Lim Ik-keun	July	1998-June	2002
3rd	Choi Sun-kil	July	2002-June	2006
4th	Choi Sun-kil	July	2006-June	2010
5th	Lee Dong-jin	July	2010-June	2014
6th	Lee Dong-jin	July	2014-present	

Mayors of Dongdaemun-gu

1st	Park Hoon	July	1995-June	1998
2nd	Yoo Deok-yeol	July	1998-June	2002
3rd	Hong Sa-rip	July	2002-June	2006
4th	Hong Sa-rip	July	2006-May	2009
5th	Yoo Deok-yeol	July	2010-June	2014
6th	Yoo Deok-yeol	July	2014-present	

Mayors of Dongjak-gu

1st	Kim Ki-ok	July	1995-March	1998
2nd	Kim Woo-joong	July	1998-June	2002
3rd	Kim Woo-joong	July	2002-June	2006
4th	Kim Woo-joong	July	2006-June	2010
5th	Moon Chung-sill	July	2010-June	2014
6th	Lee Chang-woo	July	2014-present	

Mayors of Eunpyeong-gu

1st	Lee Bae-young	July	1995-June	1998
2nd	Lee Bae-young	July	1998-Feb.	2001
2nd*	Roh Jae-dong	April	2001-June	2002
3rd	Roh Jae-dong	July	2002-June	2006
4th	Roh Jae-dong	July	2006-June	2010
5th	Kim Woo-young	July	2010-June	2014
6th	Kim Woo-young	July	2014-present	

Mayors of Gangbuk-gu

1st	Chang Jung-shik	July	1995-June	1998
2nd	Chang Jung-shik	July	1998-June	2002
3rd	Kim Hyun-poong	July	2002-June	2006
4th	Kim Hyun-poong	July	2006-June	2010
5th	Park Gyum-soo	July	2010-June	2014
6th	Park Gyum-soo	July	2014-present	

Mayors of Gangdong-gu

1st	Kim Choong-whan	July	1995-June	1998
2nd	Kim Choong-whan	July	1998-June	2002
3rd	Kim Choong-whan	July	2002-Dec.	2003
3rd*	Shin Dong-woo	June	2004-June	2006
4th	Shin Dong-woo	July	2006-Dec.	2007
4th*	Lee Hae-sik	June	2008-June	2010
5th	Lee Hae-sik	July	2010-June	2014
6th	Lee Hae-sik	July	2014-present	

Mayors of Gangnam-gu

1st	Kwon Moon-yong	July	1995-June	1998
2nd	Kwon Moon-yong	July	1998-June	2002
3rd	Kwon Moon-yong	July	2002-Feb.	2006
4th	Maeng Jung-ju	July	2006-June	2010
5th	Shin Yeon-hee	July	2010-June	2014
6th	Shin Yeon-hee	July	2014-present	

Mayors of Gangseo-gu

| 1st | Yoo Young | July | 1995-June | 1998 |

2nd	Ro Hyun-song	July	1998-June	2002
3rd	Yoo Young	July	2002-June	2006
4th	Kim Do-hyun	July	2006-Oct.	2007
4th*	Kim Jae-hyun	Dec.	2007-June	2010
5th	Ro Hyun-song	July	2010-June	2014
6th	Ro Hyun-song	July	2014-*present*	

Mayors of Geumcheon-gu

1st	Ban Sang-kewn	July	1995-June	1998
2nd	Ban Sang-kewn	July	1998-June	2002
3rd	Han In-soo	July	2002-June	2006
4th	Han In-soo	July	2006-June	2010
5th	Cha Sung-soo	July	2010-June	2014
6th	Cha Sung-soo	July	2014-*present*	

Mayors of Guro-gu

1st	Park Won-chul	July	1995-June	1998
2nd	Park Won-chul	July	1998-June	2002
3rd	Yang Dae-woong	July	2002-June	2006
4th	Yang Dae-woong	July	2006-June	2010
5th	Lee Sung	July	2010-June	2014
6th	Lee Sung	July	2014-*present*	

Mayors of Gwanak-gu

1st	Jin Jin-hyong	July	1995-June	1998
2nd	Kim Hee-chull	July	1998-June	2002
3rd	Kim Hee-chull	July	2002-June	2006
4th	Kim Hyo-kyeum	July	2006-Nov.	2009
5th	Yoo Jong-pil	July	2010-June	2014
6th	Yoo Jong-pil	July	2014-*present*	

Mayors of Gwangjin-gu

1st	Chung Yeung-sup	July	1995-June	1998
2nd	Chung Yeung-sup	July	1998-June	2002
3rd	Chung Yeung-sup	July	2002-June	2006
4th	Jeong Song-hag	July	2006-June	2010
5th	Kim Ki-dong	July	2010-June	2014
6th	Kim Ki-dong	July	2014-*present*	

Mayors of Jongno-gu

1st	Jeong Heung-jin	July	1995-June	1998
2nd	Jeong Heung-jin	July	1998-Feb.	2002
3rd	Kim Chung-yong	July	2002-June	2006
4th	Kim Chung-yong	July	2006-June	2010
5th	Kim Young-jong	July	2010-June	2014
6th	Kim Young-jong	July	2014-*present*	

Mayors of Jung-gu

1st	Kim Dong-il	July	1995-June	1998
2nd	Kim Dong-il	July	1998-June	2002
3rd	Kim Dong-il	July	2002-Dec.	2003
3rd*	Sung Nak-hap	June	2004-March	2006
4th	Jeong Dong-il	July	2006-June	2010
5th	Park Hyung-sang	July	2010-Feb.	2011
5th*	Choi Chang-sik	April	2011-June	2014
6th	Choi Chang-sik	July	2014-*present*	

Mayors of Jungnang-gu

1st	Lee Moon-jae	July	1995-June	1998
2nd	Jung Jin-taek	July	1998-June	2002
3rd	Mun Byung-kwon	July	2002-June	2006
4th	Mun Byung-kwon	July	2006-June	2010
5th	Mun Byung-kwon	July	2010-June	2014
6th	Ra Jin-goo	July	2014-*present*	

Mayors of Mapo-gu

1st	Roh Sung-hwan	July	1995-June	1998
2nd	Roh Sung-hwan	July	1998-June	2002
3rd	Park Hong-sup	July	2002-June	2006
4th	Shin Young-seob	July	2006-June	2010
5th	Park Hong-sup	July	2010-June	2014
6th	Park Hong-sup	July	2014-*present*	

Mayors of Nowon-gu

1st	Choi Sun-kil	July	1995-July	1996
1st*	Kim Yong-chae	Sept.	1996-March	1998
2nd	Lee Ki-jae	July	1998-June	2002
3rd	Lee Ki-jae	July	2002-June	2006
4th	Lee No-keun	July	2006-June	2010
5th	Kim Sung-whan	July	2010-June	2014
6th	Kim Sung-whan	July	2014-*present*	

Mayors of Seocho-gu

1st	Cho Nam-ho	July	1995-June	1998
2nd	Cho Nam-ho	July	1998-June	2002
3rd	Cho Nam-ho	July	2002-June	2006
4th	Park Sung-joong	July	2006-June	2010
5th	Jin Ik-chul	July	2010-June	2014
6th	Cho Eun-hee	July	2014-*present*	

Mayors of Seodaemun-gu

1st	Lee Chung-kyu	July	1995-June	1998
2nd	Lee Chung-kyu	July	1998-June	2002
3rd	Hyun Dong-hoon	July	2002-June	2006
4th	Hyun Dong-hoon	July	2006-Feb.	2010
5th	Mun Seok-jin	July	2010-June	2014
6th	Mun Seok-jin	July	2014-*present*	

Mayors of Seongbuk-gu

1st	Chin Young-ho	July	1995-June	1998

2nd	Chin Young-ho	July	1998-June	2002
3rd	Seo Chan-kyo	July	2002-June	2006
4th	Seo Chan-kyo	July	2006-June	2010
5th	Kim Young-bae	July	2010-June	2014
6th	Kim Young-bae	July	2014-present	

Mayors of Seongdong-gu

1st	Goh Jae-deuk	July	1995-June	1998
2nd	Goh Jae-deuk	July	1998-June	2002
3rd	Goh Jae-deuk	July	2002-June	2006
4th	Lee Ho-jo	July	2006-June	2010
5th	Goh Jae-deuk	July	2010-June	2014
6th	Chong Won-o	July	2014-present	

Mayors of Songpa-gu

1st	Kim Sung-soon	July	1995-June	1998
2nd	Kim Sung-soon	July	1998-Feb.	2000
2nd*	Lee Yoo-taek	June	2000-June	2002
3rd	Lee Yoo-taek	July	2002-June	2006
4th	Kim Young-soon	July	2006-June	2010
5th	Park Chun-hee	July	2010-June	2014
6th	Park Chun-hee	July	2014-present	

Mayors of Yangcheon-gu

1st	Yang Jae-ho	July	1995-June	1998
2nd	Huh Wan	July	1998-June	2002
3rd	Chu Jae-yeop	July	2002-June	2006
4th	Lee Hoon-gu	July	2006-Jan.	2007
4th*	Chu Jae-yeop	April	2007-June	2010
5th	Lee Je-hack	July	2010-June	2011
5th*	Chu Jae-yeop	Oct.	2011-April	2013
6th	Kim Soo-young	July	2014-present	

Mayors of Yeongdeungpo-gu

1st	Kim Doo-ki	July	1995-June	1998
2nd	Kim Soo-il	July	1998-Oct.	2001
3rd	Kim Yong-il	July	2002-Oct.	2003
3rd*	Kim Hyung-soo	June	2004-June	2006
4th	Kim Hyung-soo	July	2006-June	2010
5th	Cho Gil-hyung	July	2010-June	2014
6th	Cho Gil-hyung	July	2014-present	

Mayors of Yongsan-gu

1st	Seol Song-woong	July	1995-June	1998
2nd	Sung Jang-hyun	July	1998-April	2000
2nd*	Park Jang-kyu	June	2000-June	2002
3rd	Park Jang-kyu	July	2002-June	2006
4th	Park Jang-kyu	July	2006-June	2010
5th	Sung Jang-hyun	July	2010-June	2014
6th	Sung Jang-hyun	July	2014-present	

Busan Metropolitan City

15 Districts(gu), 1 County(gun) ─────

- Buk-gu · Busanjin-gu · Dong-gu
- Dongnae-gu · Gangseo-gu · Geumjeong-gu
- Gijang-gun · Haeundae-gu · Jung-gu
- Nam-gu · Saha-gu · Sasang-gu
- Seo-gu · Suyeong-gu · Yeongdo-gu
- Yeonje-gu

Mayors of Buk-gu

1st	Kwon Ik	July	1995-June	1998
2nd	Kwon Ik	July	1998-June	2002
3rd	Bae Sang-do	July	2002-June	2006
4th	Lee Seong-sik	July	2006-June	2010
5th	Hwang Jae-gwan	July	2010-June	2014
6th	Hwang Jae-gwan	July	2014-present	

Mayors of Busanjin-gu

1st	Ha Kye-yeol	July	1995-June	1998
2nd	An Young-il	July	1998-June	2002
3rd	An Young-il	July	2002-June	2006
4th	Ha Kye-yeol	July	2006-June	2010
5th	Ha Kye-yeol	July	2010-June	2014
6th	Ha Kye-yeol	July	2014-present	

Mayors of Dong-gu

1st	Kwak Yoon-sup	July	1995-June	1998
2nd	Chung Hyun-ok	July	1998-June	2002
3rd	Chung Hyun-ok	July	2002-June	2006
4th	Chung Hyun-ok	July	2006-June	2010
5th	Park Han-jae	July	2010-July	2011
5th*	Jung Young-suk	Oct.	2011-June	2014
6th	Park Sam-seok	July	2014-present	

Mayors of Dongnae-gu

1st	Lee Kyu-sang	July	1995-June	1998
2nd	Lee Kyu-sang	July	1998-June	2002
3rd	Lee Jin-bok	July	2002-June	2006
4th	Choi Chan-ki	July	2006-June	2010
5th	Jo Kil-woo	July	2010-June	2014
6th	Jeon Kwang-woo	July	2014-present	

Mayors of Gangseo-gu

1st	Bae Yeong-ki	July	1995-June	1998
2nd	Bae Yeong-ki	July	1998-June	2002
3rd	Ahn Byung-hae	July	2002-Feb.	2005

3rd*	Kang In-gil	May 2005-June	2006
4th	Kang In-gil	July 2006-June	2010
5th	Kang In-gil	July 2010-June	2014
6th	Roh Ki-tae	July 2014-*present*	

Mayors of Geumjeong-gu

1st	Yoon Suk-chun	July 1995-June	1998
2nd	Yoon Suk-chun	July 1998-Nov.	2000
2nd*	Kim Moon-gon	April 2001-June	2002
3rd	Kim Moon-gon	July 2002-June	2006
4th	Ko Bong-bok	July 2006-June	2010
5th	Won Jeong-hee	July 2010-June	2014
6th	Won Jeong-hee	July 2014-*present*	

Mayors of Gijang-gun

1st	Oh Kyu-suk	July 1995-April	1998
2nd	Choi Hyun-dol	July 1998-June	2002
3rd	Choi Hyun-dol	July 2002-June	2006
4th	Choi Hyun-dol	July 2006-June	2010
5th	Oh Kyu-suk	July 2010-June	2014
6th	Oh Kyu-suk	July 2014-*present*	

Mayors of Haeundae-gu

1st	Suh Suk-in	July 1995-June	1998
2nd	Shin Jung-bok	July 1998-Nov.	1999
2nd*	Suh Byung-soo	Jan. 2000-Feb.	2002
3rd	Hur Oc-kyong	July 2002-Dec.	2003
3rd*	Bae Duk-kwang	June 2004-June	2006
4th	Bae Duk-kwang	July 2006-June	2010
5th	Bae Duk-kwang	July 2010-March	2014
6th	Baek Seon-gi	July 2014-*present*	

Mayors of Jung-gu

1st	Byun Jong-kil	July 1995-June	1998
2nd	Lee In-jun	July 1998-June	2002
3rd	Lee In-jun	July 2002-June	2006
4th	Lee In-jun	July 2006-Nov.	2007
4th*	Kim Eun-sook	Dec. 2007-June	2010
5th	Kim Eun-sook	July 2010-June	2014
6th	Kim Eun-sook	July 2014-*present*	

Mayors of Nam-gu

1st	Lee Young-geun	July 1995-June	1998
2nd	Lee Young-geun	July 1998-June	2002
3rd	Jeon Sang-soo	July 2002-June	2006
4th	Lee Jong-cheol	July 2006-June	2010
5th	Lee Jong-cheol	July 2010-June	2014
6th	Lee Jong-cheol	July 2014-*present*	

Mayors of Saha-gu

1st	Park Jae-young	July 1995-June	1998
2nd	Park Jae-young	July 1998-June	2002
3rd	Park Jae-young	July 2002-June	2006
4th	Cho Jeong-hwa	July 2006-June	2010
5th	Lee Kyung-hoon	July 2010-June	2014
6th	Lee Kyung-hoon	July 2014-*present*	

Mayors of Sasang-gu

1st	Suh Kyung-won	July 1995-March	1998
2nd	Yoon Deok-jin	July 1998-June	2002
3rd	Yoon Deok-jin	July 2002-June	2006
4th	Yoon Deok-jin	July 2006-June	2010
5th	Song Suk-hee	July 2010-June	2014
6th	Song Suk-hee	July 2014-*present*	

Mayors of Seo-gu

1st	Byun Ik-kyu	July 1995-June	1998
2nd	Kim Young-oh	July 1998-June	2002
3rd	Kim Young-oh	July 2002-June	2006
4th	Park Geok-je	July 2006-June	2010
5th	Park Geok-je	July 2010-June	2014
6th	Park Geok-je	July 2014-*present*	

Mayors of Suyeong-gu

1st	Shin Jong-kwan	July 1995-June	1998
2nd	Shin Jong-kwan	July 1998-Feb.	2000
2nd*	Yoo Jae-jung	June 2000-June	2002
3rd	Yoo Jae-jung	July 2002-April	2006
4th	Park Hyun-wook	July 2006-June	2010
5th	Park Hyun-wook	July 2010-June	2014
6th	Park Hyun-wook	July 2014-*present*	

Mayors of Yeongdo-gu

1st	Park Dae-seok	July 1995-June	1998
2nd	Park Dae-seok	July 1998-June	2002
3rd	Park Dae-seok	July 2002-June	2006
4th	Eo Yoon-tae	July 2006-June	2010
5th	Eo Yoon-tae	July 2010-June	2014
6th	Eo Yoon-tae	July 2014-*present*	

Mayors of Yeonje-gu

1st	Park Dae-hae	July 1995-June	1998
2nd	Park Dae-hae	July 1998-June	2002
3rd	Park Dae-hae	July 2002-April	2006
4th	Lee Wie-joon	July 2006-June	2010
5th	Lee Wie-joon	July 2010-June	2014
6th	Lee Wie-joon	July 2014-*present*	

Daegu Metropolitan City

7 Districts(gu), 1 County(gun)

· Buk-gu · Dalseo-gu · Dalseong-gun
· Dong-gu · Jung-gu · Nam-gu
· Seo-gu · Suseong-gu

Mayors of Buk-gu

1st	Lee Myung-gyu	July	1995-June	1998
2nd	Lee Myung-gyu	July	1998-June	2002
3rd	Lee Myung-gyu	July	2002-Dec.	2003
3rd*	Lee Jong-hwa	June	2004-June	2006
4th	Lee Jong-hwa	July	2006-June	2010
5th	Lee Jong-hwa	July	2010-March	2014
6th	Bae Kwang-sik	July	2014-*present*	

Mayors of Dalseo-gu

1st	Hwang Dae-hyun	July	1995-June	1998
2nd	Hwang Dae-hyun	July	1998-June	2002
3rd	Hwang Dae-hyun	July	2002-Sept.	2005
4th	Kwak Dae-hoon	July	2006-June	2010
5th	Kwak Dae-hoon	July	2010-June	2014
6th	Kwak Dae-hoon	July	2014-*present*	

Mayors of Dalseong-gun

1st	Yang Si-yeong	July	1995-June	1998
2nd	Park Kyung-ho	July	1998-June	2002
3rd	Park Kyung-ho	July	2002-June	2006
4th	Lee Jong-jin	July	2006-June	2010
5th	Kim Moon-oh	July	2010-June	2014
6th	Kim Moon-oh	July	2014-*present*	

Mayors of Dong-gu

1st	Oh Kee-hwan	July	1995-June	1998
2nd	Lim Dae-yoon	July	1998-June	2002
3rd	Lim Dae-yoon	July	2002-Dec.	2003
3rd*	Lee Hoon	June	2004-June	2006
4th	Lee Jae-man	July	2006-June	2010
5th	Lee Jae-man	July	2010-Feb.	2014
6th	Kang Dae-sik	July	2014-*present*	

Mayors of Jung-gu

1st	Kang Hyeon-joong	July	1995-Feb.	1998
2nd	Kim Joo-hwan	July	1998-June	2002
3rd	Jung Jae-won	July	2002-June	2006
4th	Yoon Sun-young	July	2006-June	2010
5th	Yoon Sun-young	July	2010-June	2014
6th	Yoon Sun-young	July	2014-*present*	

Mayors of Nam-gu

1st	Lee Jae-yong	July	1995-June	1998
2nd	Lee Jae-yong	July	1998-April	2002
3rd	Lee Shin-hak	July	2002-June	2006
4th	Lim Byung-heon	July	2006-June	2010
5th	Lim Byung-heon	July	2010-June	2014
6th	Lim Byung-heon	July	2014-*present*	

Mayors of Seo-gu

1st	Lee Eui-sang	July	1995-June	1998
2nd	Lee Eui-sang	July	1998-June	2002
3rd	Yun Jin	July	2002-June	2006
4th	Yun Jin	July	2006-Jan.	2008
4th*	Seo Jung-hyun	June	2008-June	2010
5th	Seo Jung-hyun	July	2010-Sept.	2011
5th*	Kang Sung-ho	Oct.	2011-June	2014
6th	Ryoo Han-guk	July	2014-*present*	

Mayors of Suseong-gu

1st	Kim Kyu-taik	July	1995-June	1998
2nd	Kim Kyu-taik	July	1998-June	2002
3rd	Kim Kyu-taik	July	2002-June	2006
4th	Kim Hyeong-ryeol	July	2006-June	2010
5th	Lee Jin-hoon	July	2010-June	2014
6th	Lee Jin-hoon	July	2014-*present*	

Incheon Metropolitan City

8 Districts(gu), 2 Counties(gun)

· Bupyeong-gu · Dong-gu · Ganghwa-gun
· Gyeyang-gu · Jung-gu · Nam-gu
· Namdong-gu · Ongjin-gun · Seo-gu
· Yeonsu-gu

Mayors of Bupyeong-gu

1st	Choi Yong-gue	July	1995-March	1998
2nd	Park Soo-mook	July	1998-June	2002
3rd	Park Yoon-bae	July	2002-June	2006
4th	Park Yoon-bae	July	2006-June	2010
5th	Hong Mi-young	July	2010-June	2014
6th	Hong Mi-young	July	2014-*present*	

Mayors of Dong-gu

1st	Kim Chang-soo	July	1995-June	1998
2nd	Kim Chang-soo	July	1998-June	2002
3rd	Lee Hwa-yong	July	2002-June	2006

4th	Lee Hwa-yong	July	2006-June	2010
5th	Cho Tack-sang	July	2010-June	2014
6th	Lee Heung-su	July	2014-present	

Mayors of Ganghwa-gun

1st	Kim Sun-hung	July	1995-June	1998
2nd	Kim Sun-hung	July	1998-June	2002
3rd	Yoo Byeong-ho	July	2002-June	2006
4th	Ahn Duck-soo	July	2006-June	2010
5th	Ahn Duck-soo	July	2010-Dec.	2011
5th*	Yoo Chun-ho	April	2012-June	2014
6th	Lee Sang-bog	July	2014-present	

Mayors of Gyeyang-gu

1st	Lee Hun-jin	July	1995-June	1998
2nd	Lee Ik-jin	July	1998-June	2002
3rd	Park Hee-ryong	July	2002-June	2006
4th	Lee Ik-jin	July	2006-June	2010
5th	Park Hyung-woo	July	2010-June	2014
6th	Park Hyung-woo	July	2014-present	

Mayors of Jung-gu

1st	Rhee Se-young	July	1995-June	1998
2nd	Rhee Se-young	July	1998-Feb.	2000
2nd*	Kim Hong-sub	June	2000-June	2002
3rd	Kim Hong-sub	July	2002-April	2006
4th	Park Seung-suk	July	2006-June	2010
5th	Kim Hong-bok	July	2010-Sept.	2012
5th*	Kim Hong-sub	Dec.	2012-June	2014
6th	Kim Hong-sub	July	2014-present	

Mayors of Nam-gu

1st	Min Bong-gi	July	1995-June	1998
2nd	Chung Myung-hwan	July	1998-June	2002
3rd	Park Woo-sub	July	2002-June	2006
4th	Lee Young-soo	July	2006-June	2010
5th	Park Woo-sub	July	2010-June	2014
6th	Park Woo-sub	July	2014-present	

Mayors of Namdong-gu

1st	Kim Yong-mo	July	1995-March	1998
2nd	Lee Hun-bok	July	1998-Nov.	1999
2nd*	Yoon Tae-jin	Jan.	2000-June	2002
3rd	Yoon Tae-jin	July	2002-June	2006
4th	Yoon Tae-jin	July	2006-March	2010
5th	Bae Jin-kyo	July	2010-June	2014
6th	Jang Seok-hyeon	July	2014-present	

Mayors of Ongjin-gun

1st	Cho Gun-ho	July	1995-June	1998
2nd	Cho Gun-ho	July	1998-June	2002
3rd	Cho Gun-ho	July	2002-June	2006
4th	Cho Youn-gil	July	2006-June	2010
5th	Cho Youn-gil	July	2010-June	2014
6th	Cho Youn-gil	July	2014-present	

Mayors of Seo-gu

1st	Kweon Jung-kwang	July	1995-June	1998
2nd	Park Hyun-yang	July	1998-June	2002
3rd	Lee Hak-jae	July	2002-June	2006
4th	Lee Hak-jae	July	2006-Dec.	2007
4th*	Lee Hoon-kook	June	2008-June	2010
5th	Jeon Nyun-sung	July	2010-June	2014
6th	Kang Bum-suck	July	2014-present	

Mayors of Yeonsu-gu

1st	Shin Won-chul	July	1995-June	1998
2nd	Shin Won-chul	July	1998-June	2002
3rd	Chung Ku-un	July	2002-June	2006
4th	Nam Moo-kyu	July	2006-June	2010
5th	Go Nam-seok	July	2010-June	2014
6th	Lee Jae-ho	July	2014-present	

Gwangju Metropolitan City

5 Districts(gu)
· Buk-gu · Dong-gu · Gwangsan-gu
· Nam-gu · Seo-gu

Mayors of Buk-gu

1st	Kim Tae-hong	July	1995-March	1998
2nd	Kim Jae-kyun	July	1998-June	2002
3rd	Kim Jae-kyun	July	2002-March	2006
4th	Song Kwang-woon	July	2006-June	2010
5th	Song Kwang-woon	July	2010-June	2014
6th	Song Kwang-woon	July	2014-present	

Mayors of Dong-gu

1st	Park Jong-chul	July	1995-June	1998
2nd	Park Jong-chul	July	1998-June	2002
3rd	Yoo Tae-myung	July	2002-June	2006
4th	Yoo Tae-myung	July	2006-June	2010
5th	Yoo Tae-myung	July	2010-Sept.	2012
5th*	Roh Hee-yong	Dec.	2012-June	2014
6th	Roh Hee-yong	July	2014-present	

Mayors of Gwangsan-gu

1st	Koh Jae-yoo	July	1995-March	1998
2nd	Song Byong-tae	July	1998-June	2002
3rd	Song Byong-tae	July	2002-June	2006
4th	Jeon Kab-kil	July	2006-Feb.	2010
5th	Min Hyung-bae	July	2010-June	2014
6th	Min Hyung-bae	July	2014-*present*	

Mayors of Nam-gu

1st	Chung Doo-chae	July	1995-May	1998
2nd	Park Yong-kweon	July	1998-July	1999
2nd*	Chong Dong-nyun	Sept.	1999-April	2002
3rd	Hwang Il-bong	July	2002-June	2006
4th	Hwang Il-bong	July	2006-June	2010
5th	Choi Young-ho	July	2010-June	2014
6th	Choi Young-ho	July	2014-*present*	

Mayors of Seo-gu

1st	Lee Jeong-il	July	1995-June	1998
2nd	Lee Jeong-il	July	1998-April	2002
3rd	Kim Jong-sik	July	2002-June	2006
4th	Jeon Joo-eon	July	2006-June	2010
5th	Jeon Joo-eon	July	2010-Aug.	2010
5th*	Kim Jong-sik	Oct.	2010-June	2014
6th	Lim Woo-jin	July	2014-*present*	

Daejeon Metropolitan City

5 Districts(gu)

· Daedeok-gu · Dong-gu · Jung-gu
· Seo-gu · Yuseong-gu

Mayors of Daedeok-gu

1st	Oh Hee-jung	July	1995-June	1998
2nd	Oh Hee-jung	July	1998-June	2002
3rd	Oh Hee-jung	July	2002-Dec.	2003
3rd*	Kim Chang-soo	June	2004-June	2006
4th	Jeong Yong-ki	July	2006-June	2010
5th	Jeong Yong-ki	July	2010-March	2014
6th	Park Soo-beom	July	2014-*present*	

Mayors of Dong-gu

1st	Park Byung-ho	July	1995-June	1998
2nd	Lim Young-ho	July	1998-June	2002
3rd	Lim Young-ho	July	2002-Dec.	2003
3rd*	Park Byung-ho	June	2004-June	2006

4th	Lee Jang-woo	July	2006-June	2010
5th	Han Hyoun-tak	July	2010-June	2014
6th	Han Hyoun-tak	July	2014-*present*	

Mayors of Jung-gu

1st	Chon Sung-hwan	July	1995-June	1998
2nd	Kim Sung-kee	July	1998-June	2002
3rd	Kim Sung-kee	July	2002-June	2006
4th	Lee Eun-kwan	July	2006-June	2010
5th	Park Yong-kab	July	2010-June	2014
6th	Park Yong-kab	July	2014-*present*	

Mayors of Seo-gu

1st	Lee Hun-koo	July	1995-June	1998
2nd	Lee Hun-koo	July	1998-Aug.	2000
2nd*	Ga Gi-san	Oct.	2000-June	2002
3rd	Ga Gi-san	July	2002-June	2006
4th	Ga Gi-san	July	2006-June	2010
5th	Park Hwan-yong	July	2010-June	2014
6th	Chang Jong-tae	July	2014-*present*	

Mayors of Yuseong-gu

1st	Song Seok-chan	July	1995-June	1998
2nd	Song Seok-chan	July	1998-Feb.	2000
2nd*	Lee Byung-ryung	June	2000-June	2002
3rd	Lee Byung-ryung	July	2002-Dec.	2003
3rd*	Jhin Dong-kyu	June	2004-June	2006
4th	Jhin Dong-kyu	July	2006-June	2010
5th	Heo Tae-jeong	July	2010-June	2014
6th	Heo Tae-jeong	July	2014-*present*	

Ulsan Metropolitan City

▸ *Promoted to Ulsan Metropolitan City on July 15, 1997.*
▸ *From 2nd Nationwide Local Elections(june 1998), heads of local government elected by popular vote.*

4 Districts(gu), 1 County(gun)

· Buk-gu · Dong-gu · Jung-gu
· Nam-gu · Ulju-gun

Mayors of Buk-gu

1st	Joe Sueng-su	July	1998-June	2002
2nd	Lee Sang-bum	July	2002-May	2006
3rd	Gang Seog-gu	July	2006-June	2010
4th	Yoon Jong-o	July	2010-June	2014
5th	Park Cheon-dong	July	2014-*present*	

Mayors of Dong-gu

1st	Kim Chang-hyun	July	1998-Sept.	1999
1st*	Lee Young-soon	Oct.	1999-June	2002
2nd	Lee Gap-yong	July	2002-May	2006
3rd	Jung Cheon-seok	July	2006-June	2010
4th	Jung Cheon-seok	July	2010-Dec.	2010
4th*	Kim Jong-hoon	April	2011-June	2014
5th	Kwon Myung-ho	July	2014-*present*	

Mayors of Jung-gu

1st	Jun Na-myeong	July	1998-June	2002
2nd	Cho Yong-soo	July	2002-June	2006
3rd	Cho Yong-soo	July	2006-June	2010
4th	Cho Yong-soo	July	2010-Dec.	2010
4th*	Park Seong-min	April	2011-June	2014
5th	Park Seong-min	July	2014-*present*	

Mayors of Nam-gu

1st	Lee Che-ik	July	1998-June	2002
2nd	Lee Che-ik	July	2002-Feb.	2006
3rd	Kim Du-kyum	July	2006-June	2010
4th	Kim Du-kyum	July	2010-Feb.	2014
5th	Seo Dong-wook	July	2014-*present*	

Mayors of Ulju-gun

1st	Park Jin-koo	July	1998-June	2002
2nd	Um Chang-sub	July	2002-June	2006
3rd	Um Chang-sub	July	2006-Sept.	2008
3rd*	Shin Jang-yeol	Oct.	2008-June	2010
4th	Shin Jang-yeol	July	2010-June	2014
5th	Shin Jang-yeol	July	2014-*present*	

Gyeonggi-do

28 Cities(si), 3 Counties(gun)

- Ansan-si · Anseong-si · Anyang-si
- Bucheon-si · Dongducheon-si
- Gapyeong-gun · Gimpo-si · Goyang-si
- Gunpo-si · Guri-si · Gwacheon-si · Gwangju-si
- Gwangmyeong-si · Hanam-si · Hwaseong-si
- Icheon-si · Namyangju-si · Osan-si
- Paju-si · Pocheon-si · Pyeongtaek-si
- Seongnam-si · Siheung-si · Suwon-si
- Uijeongbu-si · Uiwang-si · Yangju-si
- Yangpyeong-gun · Yeoju-si · Yeoncheon-gun
- Yongin-si

Mayors of Ansan-si

1st	Song Jin-sup	July	1995-June	1998
2nd	Park Seong-kyu	July	1998-June	2002
3rd	Song Jin-sup	July	2002-June	2006
4th	Park Joo-won	July	2006-June	2010
5th	Kim Cheol-min	July	2010-June	2014
6th	Je Jong-geel	July	2014-*present*	

Mayors of Anseong-si

▶ *Promoted Anseong-gun to Anseong-si on April 1, 1998.*

<Mayor of Anseong-gun>

1st	Lee Jong-geon	July	1995-March	1998
1st	Lee Jong-geon	April	1998-June	1998
2nd	Han Young-sik	July	1998-Oct.	1999
2nd*	Lee Dong-hee	Dec.	1999-June	2002
3rd	Lee Dong-hee	July	2002-June	2006
4th	Lee Dong-hee	July	2006-Feb.	2010
5th	Hwang Eun-sung	July	2010-June	2014
6th	Hwang Eun-sung	July	2014-*present*	

Mayors of Anyang-si

1st	Lee Souk-yong	July	1995-June	1998
2nd	Lee Souk-yong	July	1998-Feb.	1999
2nd*	Shin Joong-dai	March	1999-June	2002
3rd	Shin Joong-dai	July	2002-June	2006
4th	Shin Joong-dai	July	2006-Oct.	2007
4th*	Lee Phil-woon	Dec.	2007-June	2010
5th	Choi Dae-ho	July	2010-June	2014
6th	Lee Phil-woon	July	2014-*present*	

Mayors of Bucheon-si

1st	Lee Hae-seon	July	1995-June	1998
2nd	Won Hye-young	July	1998-June	2002
3rd	Won Hye-young	July	2002-Dec.	2003
3rd*	Hong Gun-pyo	June	2004-June	2006
4th	Hong Gun-pyo	July	2006-June	2010
5th	Kim Man-soo	July	2010-June	2014
6th	Kim Man-soo	July	2014-*present*	

Mayors of Dongducheon-si

1st	Bang Jae-hwan	July	1995-June	1998
2nd	Bang Jae-hwan	July	1998-June	2002
3rd	Choi Yong-soo	July	2002-June	2006
4th	Choi Yong-soo	July	2006-March	2007
4th*	Oh Sae-chang	April	2007-June	2010
5th	Oh Sae-chang	July	2010-June	2014
6th	Oh Sae-chang	July	2014-*present*	

Mayors of Gapyeong-gun

1st	Lee Hyun-jik	July	1995-June	1998
2nd	Lee Hyun-jik	July	1998-June	2002
3rd	Yang Jai-soo	July	2002-June	2006
4th	Yang Jai-soo	July	2006-March	2007
4th*	Lee Jin-yong	April	2007-June	2010
5th	Lee Jin-yong	July	2010-Jan.	2013
5th*	Kim Seong-gi	April	2013-June	2014
6th	Kim Seong-gi	July	2014-*present*	

Mayors of Gimpo-si

▸ *Promoted Gimpo-gun to Gimpo-si on April 1, 1998.*

\<Mayor of Gimpo-gun\>

1st	Yoo Jeong-bok	July	1995-March	1998
1st	Yoo Jeong-bok	April	1998-June	1998
2nd	Yoo Jeong-bok	July	1998-June	2002
3rd	Kim Dong-sik	July	2002-June	2006
4th	Kang Kyung-ku	July	2006-June	2010
5th	Yoo Young-rok	July	2010-June	2014
6th	Yoo Young-rok	July	2014-*present*	

Mayors of Goyang-si

1st	Shin Dong-young	July	1995-June	1998
2nd	Shin Dong-young	July	1998-June	1999
2nd*	Hwang Kyo-sun	Aug.	1999-June	2002
3rd	Kang Hyun-suk	July	2002-June	2006
4th	Kang Hyun-suk	July	2006-June	2010
5th	Choi Sung	July	2010-June	2014
6th	Choi Sung	July	2014-*present*	

Mayors of Gunpo-si

1st	Cho Won-keuk	July	1995-June	1998
2nd	Kim Yoon-joo	July	1998-June	2002
3rd	Kim Yoon-joo	July	2002-June	2006
4th	Ro Jae-young	July	2006-June	2010
5th	Kim Yoon-joo	July	2010-June	2014
6th	Kim Yoon-joo	July	2014-*present*	

Mayors of Guri-si

1st	Lee Moo-sung	July	1995-June	1998
2nd	Park Young-sun	July	1998-June	2002
3rd	Lee Moo-sung	July	2002-June	2006
4th	Park Young-sun	July	2006-June	2010
5th	Park Young-sun	July	2010-June	2014
6th	Park Young-sun	July	2014-*present*	

Mayors of Gwacheon-si

1st	Lee Sung-whan	July	1995-June	1998
2nd	Lee Sung-whan	July	1998-June	2002
3rd	Yeo In-kook	July	2002-June	2006
4th	Yeo In-kook	July	2006-June	2010
5th	Yeo In-kook	July	2010-June	2014
6th	Shin Gye-yong	July	2014-*present*	

Mayors of Gwangju-si

▸ *Promoted Gwangju-gun to Gwangju-si on March 21, 2001.*

\<Mayors of Gwangju-gun\>

1st	Park Jong-jin	July	1995-June	1998
2nd	Park Jong-jin	July	1998-March	2001
2nd	Park Jong-jin	March	2001-June	2002
3rd	Kim Young-kyu	July	2002-Jan.	2006
4th	Jo Eok-dong	July	2006-June	2010
5th	Jo Eok-dong	July	2010-June	2014
6th	Jo Eok-dong	July	2014-*present*	

Mayors of Gwangmyeong-si

1st	Jeon Jae-hee	July	1995-June	1998
2nd	Baek Jae-hyun	July	1998-June	2002
3rd	Baek Jae-hyun	July	2002-June	2006
4th	Lee Hyo-sun	July	2006-June	2010
5th	Yang Ki-dae	July	2010-June	2014
6th	Yang Ki-dae	July	2014-*present*	

Mayors of Hanam-si

1st	Son Yeung-chae	July	1995-June	1998
2nd	Son Yeung-chae	July	1998-Feb.	2002
3rd	Lee Kyo-bum	July	2002-June	2006
4th	Kim Hwang-sik	July	2006-June	2010
5th	Lee Kyo-bum	July	2010-June	2014
6th	Lee Kyo-bum	July	2014-*present*	

Mayors of Hwaseong-si

▸ *Promoted Hwaseong-gun to Hwaseong-si on March 21, 2001.*

\<Mayors of Hwaseong-gun\>

1st	Kim Il-su	July	1995-June	1998
2nd	Kim Il-su	July	1998-Oct.	1999
2nd*	Woo Ho-tae	Dec.	1999-March	2001
2nd	Woo Ho-tae	March	2001-June	2002
3rd	Woo Ho-tae	July	2002-Jan.	2005
3rd*	Choi Young-keun	April	2005-June	2006
4th	Choi Young-keun	July	2006-June	2010
5th	Chae In-seok	July	2010-June	2014
6th	Chae In-seok	July	2014-*present*	

Mayors of Icheon-si

▸ *Promoted Icheon-gun to Icheon-si on March 1, 1996.*

<Mayor of Icheon-gun>

1st	Yoo Seung-woo	July	1995-Feb.	1996
1st	Yoo Seung-woo	March 1996-June		1998
2nd	Yoo Seung-woo	July	1998-June	2002
3rd	Yoo Seung-woo	July	2002-June	2006
4th	Cho Byung-don	July	2006-June	2010
5th	Cho Byung-don	July	2010-June	2014
6th	Cho Byung-don	July	2014-*present*	

Mayors of Namyangju-si

1st	Kim Young-hee	July	1995-June	1998
2nd	Kim Young-hee	July	1998-June	2002
3rd	Lee Kwang-kil	July	2002-June	2006
4th	Lee Suk-woo	July	2006-June	2010
5th	Lee Suk-woo	July	2010-June	2014
6th	Lee Suk-woo	July	2014-*present*	

Mayors of Osan-si

1st	You Tae-hyoung	July	1995-Sept.	1996
1st*	Yoo Kwan-chin	Nov.	1996-June	1998
2nd	Yoo Kwan-chin	July	1998-June	2002
3rd	Park Shin-won	July	2002-June	2006
4th	Lee Ki-ha	July	2006-June	2010
5th	Kwak Sang-wook	July	2010-June	2014
6th	Kwak Sang-wook	July	2014-*present*	

Mayors of Paju-si

▸ *Promoted Paju-gun to Paju-si on March 1, 1996.*

<Mayor of Paju-gun>

1st	Song Dal-yong	July	1995-Feb.	1996
1st	Song Dal-yong	March 1996-June		1998
2nd	Song Dal-yong	July	1998-June	2002
3rd	Lee Joon-won	July	2002-June	2004
3rd*	Ryoo Hwa-sun	Oct.	2004-June	2006
4th	Ryoo Hwa-sun	July	2006-June	2010
5th	Lee In-jae	July	2010-June	2014
6th	Lee Jae-hong	July	2014-*present*	

Mayors of Pocheon-si

▸ *Promoted Pocheon-gun to Pocheon-si on October 19, 2003.*

<Mayors of Pocheon-gun>

1st	Lee Jin-ho	July	1995-June	1998
2nd	Lee Jin-ho	July	1998-June	2002
3rd	Park Youn-kook	July	2002-Oct.	2003
3rd	Park Youn-kook	Oct.	2003-June	2006
4th	Park Youn-kook	July	2006-Dec.	2007
4th*	Seo Jang-wone	June	2008-June	2010
5th	Seo Jang-wone	July	2010-June	2014
6th	Seo Jang-wone	July	2014-*present*	

Mayors of Pyeongtaek-si

1st	Kim Sun-ki	July	1995-June	1998
2nd	Kim Sun-ki	July	1998-June	2002
3rd	Kim Sun-ki	July	2002-Dec.	2003
3rd*	Song Myung-ho	June	2004-June	2006
4th	Song Myung-ho	July	2006-June	2010
5th	Kim Sun-ki	July	2010-June	2014
6th	Kong Jae-kwang	July	2014-*present*	

Mayors of Seongnam-si

1st	Oh Seong-soo	July	1995-June	1998
2nd	Kim Byung-ryang	July	1998-June	2002
3rd	Lee Dae-yub	July	2002-June	2006
4th	Lee Dae-yub	July	2006-June	2010
5th	Lee Jae-myung	July	2010-June	2014
6th	Lee Jae-myung	July	2014-*present*	

Mayors of Siheung-si

1st	Chung On-yang	July	1995-June	1998
2nd	Baek Chung-soo	July	1998-June	2002
3rd	Jung Jong-heun	July	2002-June	2006
4th	Lee Yeun-soo	July	2006-Jan.	2009
4th*	Kim Yun-sig	April 2009-June		2010
5th	Kim Yun-sig	July	2010-June	2014
6th	Kim Yun-sig	July	2014-*present*	

Mayors of Suwon-si

1st	Sim Jae-duck	July	1995-June	1998
2nd	Sim Jae-duck	July	1998-June	2002
3rd	Kim Yong-seo	July	2002-June	2006
4th	Kim Yong-seo	July	2006-June	2010
5th	Yeom Tae-young	July	2010-June	2014
6th	Yeom Tae-young	July	2014-*present*	

Mayors of Uijeongbu-si

1st	Hong Nam-yong	July	1995-June	1998
2nd	Kim Kee-hyoung	July	1998-June	2002
3rd	Kim Mun-won	July	2002-June	2006
4th	Kim Mun-won	July	2006-June	2010
5th	Ahn Byung-yong	July	2010-June	2014
6th	Ahn Byung-yong	July	2014-*present*	

Mayors of Uiwang-si

1st	Shin Chang-hyun	July 1995-June	1998
2nd	Kang Sang-sup	July 1998-June	2002
3rd	Lee Hyung-koo	July 2002-June	2006
4th	Lee Hyung-koo	July 2006-June	2010
5th	Kim Sung-jei	July 2010-June	2014
6th	Kim Sung-jei	July 2014-*present*	

Mayors of Yangju-si

▶ *Promoted Yangju-gun to Yangju-si on October 19, 2003.*

<Mayors of Yangju-gun>

1st	Yoon Myoung-no	July 1995-June	1998
2nd	Yoon Myoung-no	July 1998-June	2002
3rd	Im Chung-bin	July 2002-Oct.	2003
3rd	Im Chung-bin	Oct. 2003-June	2006
4th	Im Chung-bin	July 2006-June	2010
5th	Hyun Sam-shik	July 2010-June	2014
6th	Hyun Sam-shik	July 2014-*present*	

Mayors of Yangpyeong-gun

1st	Min Byung-chae	July 1995-June	1998
2nd	Min Byung-chae	July 1998-June	2002
3rd	Han Taek-su	July 2002-June	2006
4th	Han Taek-su	July 2006-Dec.	2006
4th*	Kim Sun-gyo	April 2007-June	2010
5th	Kim Sun-gyo	July 2010-June	2014
6th	Kim Sun-gyo	July 2014-*present*	

Mayors of Yeoju-si

▶ *Promoted Yeoju-gun to Yeoju-si on September 23, 2013.*

<Mayors of Yeoju-gun>

1st	Park Yong-kuk	July 1995-June	1998
2nd	Park Yong-kuk	July 1998-June	2002
3rd	Lim Chang-sun	July 2002-June	2006
4th	Lee Ki-su	July 2006-June	2010
5th	Kim Chun-seok	July 2010-Sept.	2013
5th	Kim Chun-seok	Sept. 2013-June	2014
6th	Won Kyong-hee	July 2014-*present*	

Mayors of Yeoncheon-gun

1st	Lee Jung-ik	July 1995-June	1998
2nd	Lee Jung-ik	July 1998-June	2002
3rd	Kim Kyu-bae	July 2002-June	2006
4th	Kim Kyu-bae	July 2006-June	2010
5th	Kim Kyu-sun	July 2010-June	2014
6th	Kim Kyu-sun	July 2014-*present*	

Mayors of Yongin-si

▶ *Promoted Yongin-gun to Yongin-si on March 1, 1996.*

<Mayor of Yongin-gun>

1st	Youn Byung-hee	July 1995-Feb.	1996
1st	Youn Byung-hee	March 1996-June	1998
2nd	Youn Byung-hee	July 1998-July	1999
2nd*	Yea Kang-hwan	Sept. 1999-June	2002
3rd	Lee Jung-mun	July 2002-June	2006
4th	Seo Jung-suk	July 2006-June	2010
5th	Kim Hak-kyu	July 2010-June	2014
6th	Jung Chan-min	July 2014-*present*	

Gangwon-do

7 Cities(si), 11 Counties(gun)

- · Cheorwon-gun · Chuncheon-si · Donghae-si
- · Gangneung-si · Goseong-gun
- · Hoengseong-gun · Hongcheon-gun
- · Hwacheon-gun · Inje-gun · Jeongseon-gun
- · Pyeongchang-gun · Samcheok-si
- · Sokcho-si · Taebaek-si · Wonju-si
- · Yanggu-gun · Yangyang-gun · Yeongwol-gun

Mayors of Cheorwon-gun

1st	Kim Ho-youn	July 1995-June	1998
2nd	Lee Soo-hwan	July 1998-June	2002
3rd	Kim Ho-youn	July 2002-May	2004
3rd*	Moon Kyoung-hyun	Oct. 2004-June	2006
4th	Jung Ho-jo	July 2006-June	2010
5th	Jung Ho-jo	July 2010-June	2014
6th	Lee Hyeon-jong	July 2014-*present*	

Mayors of Chuncheon-si

1st	Bai Ke-sup	July 1995-June	1998
2nd	Bai Ke-sup	July 1998-June	2002
3rd	Ryu Chong-su	July 2002-June	2006
4th	Lee Gwang-joon	July 2006-June	2010
5th	Lee Gwang-joon	July 2010-Dec.	2013
6th	Choi Dong-yong	July 2014-*present*	

Mayors of Donghae-si

1st	Kim In-ki	July 1995-June	1998
2nd	Kim In-ki	July 1998-Sept.	2001
3rd	Kim Jin-dong	July 2002-June	2006
4th	Kim Hak-ki	July 2006-June	2010

5th	Kim Hak-ki	July	2010-Aug.	2013
6th	Shim Gyu-eon	July	2014-*present*	

Mayors of Gangneung-si

1st	Shim Ki-seob	July	1995-June	1998
2nd	Shim Ki-seob	July	1998-June	2002
3rd	Shim Ki-seob	July	2002-March	2006
4th	Choi Myeng-hee	July	2006-June	2010
5th	Choi Myeng-hee	July	2010-June	2014
6th	Choi Myeng-hee	July	2014-*present*	

Mayors of Goseong-gun

1st	Lee Young-koo	July	1995-June	1998
2nd	Hwang Jong-kook	July	1998-June	2002
3rd	Ham Hyeng-gu	July	2002-June	2006
4th	Ham Hyeng-gu	July	2006-March	2008
4th*	Hwang Jong-kook	June	2008-June	2010
5th	Hwang Jong-kook	July	2010-Sept.	2013
6th	Yoon Seung-keun	July	2014-*present*	

Mayors of Hoengseong-gun

1st	Cho Tae-jin	July	1995-June	1998
2nd	Cho Tae-jin	July	1998-June	2002
3rd	Cho Tae-jin	July	2002-June	2006
4th	Han Kyu-ho	July	2006-June	2010
5th	Ko Seok-yong	July	2010-June	2014
6th	Han Kyu-ho	July	2014-*present*	

Mayors of Hongcheon-gun

1st	Lee Chun-seob	July	1995-June	1998
2nd	Lee Chun-seob	July	1998-June	2002
3rd	Roh Seung-chul	July	2002-June	2006
4th	Roh Seung-chul	July	2006-June	2010
5th	Hur Pil-hong	July	2010-June	2014
6th	No Seung-rak	July	2014-*present*	

Mayors of Hwacheon-gun

1st	Hong Eun-pyo	July	1995-June	1998
2nd	Hong Eun-pyo	July	1998-June	2002
3rd	Jung Gap-chul	July	2002-June	2006
4th	Jung Gap-chul	July	2006-June	2010
5th	Jung Gap-chul	July	2010-June	2014
6th	Choi Moon-soon	July	2014-*present*	

Mayors of Inje-gun

1st	Lee Seung-ho	July	1995-June	1998
2nd	Lee Seung-ho	July	1998-June	2002
3rd	Kim Jang-jun	July	2002-June	2006
4th	Park Sam-rae	July	2006-June	2010
5th	Lee Ki-soon	July	2010-Aug.	2011

5th*	Lee Soon-sun	Oct.	2011-June	2014
6th	Lee Soon-sun	July	2014-*present*	

Mayors of Jeongseon-gun

1st	Kim Weon-chang	July	1995-June	1998
2nd	Kim Weon-chang	July	1998-June	2002
3rd	Kim Weon-chang	July	2002-June	2006
4th	Yoo Chang-sik	July	2006-June	2010
5th	Choi Seung-jun	July	2010-June	2014
6th	Jeon Jeong-hwan	July	2014-*present*	

Mayors of Pyeongchang-gun

1st	Kim Yong-wook	July	1995-June	1998
2nd	Kwon Hyuk-seung	July	1998-June	2002
3rd	Kwon Hyuk-seung	July	2002-June	2006
4th	Kwon Hyuk-seung	July	2006-June	2010
5th	Lee Seok-rae	July	2010-June	2014
6th	Sim Jae-guk	July	2014-*present*	

Mayors of Samcheok-si

1st	Kim Ill-dong	July	1995-June	1998
2nd	Kim Ill-dong	July	1998-June	2002
3rd	Kim Ill-dong	July	2002-June	2006
4th	Kim Dae-soo	July	2006-June	2010
5th	Kim Dae-soo	July	2010-June	2014
6th	Kim Yang-ho	July	2014-*present*	

Mayors of Sokcho-si

1st	Dong Moon-sung	July	1995-June	1998
2nd	Dong Moon-sung	July	1998-June	2002
3rd	Dong Moon-sung	July	2002-June	2006
4th	Chae Yong-saeng	July	2006-June	2010
5th	Chae Yong-saeng	July	2010-June	2014
6th	Lee Byung-seon	July	2014-*present*	

Mayors of Taebaek-si

1st	Hong Soon-il	July	1995-June	1998
2nd	Hong Soon-il	July	1998-June	2002
3rd	Hong Soon-il	July	2002-June	2006
4th	Park Jong-ki	July	2006-June	2010
5th	Kim Yeon-sik	July	2010-June	2014
6th	Kim Yeon-sik	July	2014-*present*	

Mayors of Wonju-si

1st	Kim Gi-yeol	July	1995-June	1998
2nd	Han Sang-cheol	July	1998-June	2002
3rd	Kim Gi-yeol	July	2002-June	2006
4th	Kim Gi-yeol	July	2006-June	2010
5th	Won Chang-mug	July	2010-June	2014
6th	Won Chang-mug	July	2014-*present*	

Mayors of Yanggu-gun

1st	Im Kyung-soon	July	1995-June	1998
2nd	Im Kyung-soon	July	1998-June	2002
3rd	Im Kyung-soon	July	2002-June	2006
4th	Joun Chang-boum	July	2006-June	2010
5th	Joun Chang-boum	July	2010-June	2014
6th	Joun Chang-boum	July	2014-*present*	

Mayors of Yangyang-gun

1st	Oh In-tack	July	1995-June	1998
2nd	Oh In-tack	July	1998-June	2002
3rd	Lee Jin-ho	July	2002-June	2006
4th	Lee Jin-ho	July	2006-June	2010
5th	Lee Jin-ho	July	2010-Feb.	2011
5th*	Jeong Sang-cheol	April	2011-June	2014
6th	Kim Jin-ha	July	2014-*present*	

Mayors of Yeongwol-gun

1st	Kim Tae-soo	July	1995-June	1998
2nd	Kim Tae-soo	July	1998-June	2002
3rd	Kim Sin-ui	July	2002-June	2006
4th	Park Sun-kyu	July	2006-June	2010
5th	Park Sun-kyu	July	2010-June	2014
6th	Park Sun-kyu	July	2014-*present*	

Chungcheongbuk-do

3 Cities(si), 8 Counties(gun) ————————

· Boeun-gun · Cheongju-si · Chungju-si
· Danyang-gun · Eumseong-gun
· Goesan-gun · Jecheon-si
· Jeungpyeong-gun · Jincheon-gun
· Okcheon-gun · Yeongdong-gun

Mayors of Boeun-gun

1st	Kim Jong-cheol	July	1995-June	1998
2nd	Kim Jong-cheol	July	1998-June	2002
3rd	Bak Jong-gi	July	2002-June	2006
4th	Lee Hang-rae	July	2006-June	2010
5th	Jung Sang-hyuck	July	2010-June	2014
6th	Jung Sang-hyuck	July	2014-*present*	

Mayors of Cheongju-si

▸ *Cheongju-si and Cheongwon-gun incorporated into the unified Cheongju city on July 1, 2014.*

1st	Kim Hyun-soo	July	1995-March 1998	
2nd	Na Ki-jeong	July	1998-June	2002
3rd	Han Dae-soo	July	2002-March 2006	
4th	Nam Sang-woo	July	2006-June	2010
5th	Han Beum-deuk	July	2010-June	2014
6th	Lee Sung-hun	July	2014-*present*	

\<Mayors of Cheongwon-gun\>

1st	Byun Jong-suk	July	1995-June	1998
2nd	Byun Jong-suk	July	1998-Aug.	2001
3rd	Oh Hyo-jhin	July	2002-March 2006	
4th	Kim Jae-ook	July	2006-Dec.	2009
5th	Lee Jong-yun	July	2010-June	2014

Mayors of Chungju-si

1st	Lee Si-jong	July	1995-June	1998
2nd	Lee Si-jong	July	1998-June	2002
3rd	Lee Si-jong	July	2002-Dec.	2003
3rd*	Han Chang-hee	June	2004-June	2006
4th	Han Chang-hee	July	2006-Sept.	2006
4th*	Kim Ho-bok	Oct.	2006-June	2010
5th	Woo Keon-do	July	2010-July	2011
5th*	Lee Jong-bae	Oct.	2011-March 2014	
6th	Cho Gil-hyoung	July	2014-*present*	

Mayors of Danyang-gun

1st	Jung Ha-mo	July	1995-June	1998
2nd	Lee Keon-pyo	July	1998-June	2002
3rd	Lee Keon-pyo	July	2002-Feb.	2006
4th	Kim Dong-sung	July	2006-June	2010
5th	Kim Dong-sung	July	2010-June	2014
6th	Leu Han-u	July	2014-*present*	

Mayors of Eumseong-gun

1st	Jung Sang-hern	July	1995-June	1998
2nd	Jung Sang-hern	July	1998-June	2002
3rd	Lee Gun-yong	July	2002-April	2003
3rd*	Park Soo-kwang	Oct.	2003-June	2006
4th	Park Soo-kwang	July	2006-Dec.	2009
5th	Lee Pil-yong	July	2010-June	2014
6th	Lee Pil-yong	July	2014-*present*	

Mayors of Goesan-gun

1st	Kim Hwan-mook	July	1995-June	1998
2nd	Kim Hwan-mook	July	1998-April	2000
2nd*	Kim Moon-bae	June	2000-June	2002
3rd	Kim Moon-bae	July	2002-June	2006
4th	Lim Gak-soo	July	2006-June	2010
5th	Lim Gak-soo	July	2010-June	2014
6th	Lim Gak-soo	July	2014-*present*	

Mayors of Jecheon-si

1st	Kwon Hee-pil	July	1995-June	1998
2nd	Kwon Hee-pil	July	1998-June	2002
3rd	Eom Tae-young	July	2002-June	2006
4th	Eom Tae-young	July	2006-June	2010
5th	Choi Myeong-hyun	July	2010-June	2014
6th	Lee Keun-kyu	July	2014-*present*	

Mayors of Jeungpyeong-gun

▸ *Inaugurated Jeungpyeong-gun on August 30, 2003.*

1st	Yu Myung-ho	Oct.	2003-June	2006
2nd	Yu Myung-ho	July	2006-June	2010
3rd	Hong Seong-yeol	July	2010-June	2014
4th	Hong Seong-yeol	July	2014-*present*	

Mayors of Jincheon-gun

1st	Kim Young-wan	July	1995-June	1998
2nd	Kim Kyong-hoe	July	1998-June	2002
3rd	Kim Kyong-hoe	July	2002-June	2006
4th	Yu Young-hoon	July	2006-June	2010
5th	Yu Young-hoon	July	2010-June	2014
6th	Yu Young-hoon	July	2014-*present*	

Mayors of Okcheon-gun

1st	Yu Bong-yeol	July	1995-June	1998
2nd	Yu Bong-yeol	July	1998-June	2002
3rd	Yu Bong-yeol	July	2002-June	2006
4th	Han Yong-taek	July	2006-June	2010
5th	Kim Young-man	July	2010-June	2014
6th	Kim Young-man	July	2014-*present*	

Mayors of Yeongdong-gun

1st	Park Wan-jin	July	1995-June	1998
2nd	Park Wan-jin	July	1998-June	2002
3rd	Son Mun-ju	July	2002-June	2006
4th	Jeong Gu-bok	July	2006-June	2010
5th	Jeong Gu-bok	July	2010-June	2014
6th	Park Se-bok	July	2014-*present*	

Chungcheongnam-do

8 Cities(si), 7 Counties(gun)

· Asan-si · Boryeong-si · Buyeo-gun
· Cheonan-si · Cheongyang-gun · Dangjin-si
· Geumsan-gun · Gongju-si · Gyeryong-si
· Hongseong-gun · Nonsan-si
· Seocheon-gun · Seosan-si · Taean-gun
· Yesan-gun

Mayors of Asan-si

1st	Lee Kil-young	July	1995-June	1998
2nd	Lee Kil-young	July	1998-May	2002
3rd	Kang Hee-bok	July	2002-June	2006
4th	Kang Hee-bok	July	2006-June	2010
5th	Bok Ki-wang	July	2010-June	2014
6th	Bok Ki-wang	July	2014-*present*	

Mayors of Boryeong-si

1st	Kim Hak-hyun	July	1995-June	1998
2nd	Shin Jun-hee	July	1998-June	2002
3rd	Rhee Si-woo	July	2002-June	2006
4th	Shin Jun-hee	July	2006-June	2010
5th	Rhee Si-woo	July	2010-June	2014
6th	Kim Dong-il	July	2014-*present*	

Mayors of Buyeo-gun

1st	Yoo Byoung-don	July	1995-June	1998
2nd	Yoo Byoung-don	July	1998-June	2002
3rd	Kim Moo-hwan	July	2002-June	2006
4th	Kim Moo-hwan	July	2006-June	2010
5th	Rhi Ryong-woo	July	2010-June	2014
6th	Rhi Ryong-woo	July	2014-*present*	

Mayors of Cheonan-si

1st	Lee Keun-young	July	1995-June	1998
2nd	Lee Keun-young	July	1998-June	2002
3rd	Sung Moo-yong	July	2002-June	2006
4th	Sung Moo-yong	July	2006-June	2010
5th	Sung Moo-yong	July	2010-June	2014
6th	Ku Bon-young	July	2014-*present*	

Mayors of Cheongyang-gun

1st	Jung Won-young	July	1995-June	1998
2nd	Jung Won-young	July	1998-June	2002
3rd	Kim Si-hwan	July	2002-June	2006
4th	Kim Si-hwan	July	2006-June	2010
5th	Lee Seok-hwa	July	2010-June	2014
6th	Lee Seok-hwa	July	2014-*present*	

Mayors of Dangjin-si

▸ *Promoted Dangjin-gun to Dangjin-si on January 1, 2012.*

\<Mayors of Dangjin-gun\>

1st	Kim Nak-sung	July	1995-June	1998
2nd	Kim Nak-sung	July	1998-June	2002
3rd	Kim Nak-sung	July	2002-Dec.	2003
3rd*	Min Jong-gi	June	2004-June	2006
4th	Min Jong-gi	July	2006-June	2010
5th	Lee Cherl-hwan	July	2010-Dec.	2011
5th	Lee Cherl-hwan	Jan.	2012-June	2014
6th	Kim Hong-jang	July	2014-*present*	

Mayors of Geumsan-gun

1st	Kim Hyun-gun	July	1995-Feb.	1998
2nd	Kim Hang-kee	July	1998-June	2002
3rd	Kim Hang-kee	July	2002-June	2006
4th	Park Dong-chell	July	2006-June	2010
5th	Park Dong-chell	July	2010-June	2014
6th	Park Dong-chell	July	2014-*present*	

Mayors of Gongju-si

1st	Jeon Byung-yong	July	1995-June	1998
2nd	Jeon Byung-yong	July	1998-Nov.	2001
3rd	Yoon Wan-joong	July	2002-Nov.	2002
3rd*	Oh Young-hee	April	2003-June	2006
4th	Lee Jun-won	July	2006-June	2010
5th	Lee Jun-won	July	2010-June	2014
6th	Oh Si-duck	July	2014-*present*	

Mayors of Gyeryong-si

▸ *Gyeryong-si was launched on September 19, 2003.*

1st	Choi Hong-mook	Oct.	2003-June	2006
2nd	Choi Hong-mook	July	2006-June	2010
3rd	Lee Ki-won	July	2010-June	2014
4th	Choi Hong-mook	July	2014-*present*	

Mayors of Hongseong-gun

1st	Lee Jong-keun	July	1995-June	1998
2nd	Lee Sang-sun	July	1998-June	2002
3rd	Chae Hyun-byung	July	2002-June	2006
4th	Lee Jong-ken	July	2006-Dec.	2009
5th	Kim Seok-hwan	July	2010-June	2014
6th	Kim Seok-hwan	July	2014-*present*	

Mayors of Nonsan-si

▸ *Promoted Nonsan-gun to Nonsan-si on March 1, 1996.*

\<Mayor of Nonsan-gun\>

1st	Jeon Il-soon	July	1995-Feb.	1996
1st	Jeon Il-soon	March	1996-June	1998
2nd	Jeon Il-soon	July	1998-Nov.	2000
2nd*	Lim Sung-kyu	April	2001-June	2002

3rd	Lim Sung-kyu	July	2002-June	2006
4th	Lim Sung-kyu	July	2006-June	2010
5th	Hwang Myeong-seon	July	2010-June	2014
6th	Hwang Myeong-seon	July	2014-*present*	

Mayors of Seocheon-gun

1st	Park Hyung-soon	July	1995-June	1998
2nd	Park Hyung-soon	July	1998-June	2002
3rd	Na So-yeol	July	2002-June	2006
4th	Na So-yeol	July	2006-June	2010
5th	Na So-yeol	July	2010-May	2014
6th	Noh Pak-rae	July	2014-*present*	

Mayors of Seosan-si

1st	Kim Gee-heung	July	1995-June	1998
2nd	Kim Gee-heung	July	1998-June	2002
3rd	Jo Kyu-seon	July	2002-June	2006
4th	Jo Kyu-seon	July	2006-Feb.	2007
4th*	Yoo Sang-gon	April	2007-June	2010
5th	Yoo Sang-gon	July	2010-Aug.	2011
5th*	Lee Wan-seob	Oct.	2011-June	2014
6th	Lee Wan-seob	July	2014-*present*	

Mayors of Taean-gun

1st	Yoon Hyung-sang	July	1995-June	1998
2nd	Yoon Hyung-sang	July	1998-June	2002
3rd	Jin Tae-ku	July	2002-June	2006
4th	Jin Tae-ku	July	2006-June	2010
5th	Kim Se-ho	July	2010-March	2011
5th*	Jin Tae-ku	April	2011-June	2014
6th	Han Sang-ki	July	2014-*present*	

Mayors of Yesan-gun

1st	Kwon Ou-chang	July	1995-June	1998
2nd	Kwon Ou-chang	July	1998-June	2002
3rd	Park Jong-soon	July	2002-June	2006
4th	Choi Seung-woo	July	2006-June	2010
5th	Choi Seung-woo	July	2010-June	2014
6th	Hwang Seon-bong	July	2014-*present*	

Jeollabuk-do

6 Cities(si), 8 Counties(gun) ————

- · Buan-gun · Gimje-si · Gochang-gun
- · Gunsan-si · Iksan-si · Imsil-gun
- · Jangsu-gun · Jeongeup-si · Jeonju-si
- · Jinan-gun · Muju-gun · Namwon-si
- · Sunchang-gun · Wanju-gun

Mayors of Buan-gun

1st	Kang Soo-weon	July	1995-May	1998
2nd	Choi Kyu-hwan	July	1998-June	2002
3rd	Kim Jong-gyu	July	2002-June	2006
4th	Lee Byung-hak	July	2006-Oct.	2007
4th*	Kim Ho-su	Dec.	2007-June	2010
5th	Kim Ho-su	July	2010-June	2014
6th	Kim Jong-gyu	July	2014-*present*	

Mayors of Gimje-si

1st	Kwak In-hee	July	1995-June	1998
2nd	Kwak In-hee	July	1998-June	2002
3rd	Kwak In-hee	July	2002-June	2006
4th	Lee Gun-sik	July	2006-June	2010
5th	Lee Gun-sik	July	2010-June	2014
6th	Lee Gun-sik	July	2014-*present*	

Mayors of Gochang-gun

1st	Lee Ho-chong	July	1995-June	1998
2nd	Lee Ho-chong	July	1998-June	2002
3rd	Lee Kang-soo	July	2002-June	2006
4th	Lee Kang-soo	July	2006-June	2010
5th	Lee Kang-soo	July	2010-June	2014
6th	Park Woo-jung	July	2014-*present*	

Mayors of Gunsan-si

1st	Kim Gil-jun	July	1995-June	1998
2nd	Kim Gil-jun	July	1998-March	2001
2nd*	Kang Keun-ho	April	2001-June	2002
3rd	Kang Keun-ho	July	2002-April	2005
4th	Moon Dong-shin	July	2006-June	2010
5th	Moon Dong-shin	July	2010-June	2014
6th	Moon Dong-shin	July	2014-*present*	

Mayors of Iksan-si

1st	Cho Han-yong	July	1995-June	1998
2nd	Cho Han-yong	July	1998-June	2002
3rd	Chae Kyu-jung	July	2002-June	2006
4th	Lee Han-su	July	2006-June	2010
5th	Lee Han-su	July	2010-June	2014
6th	Park Kyung-chul	July	2014-*present*	

Mayors of Imsil-gun

1st	Lee Hyeong-ro	July	1995-June	1998
2nd	Lee Hyeong-ro	July	1998-Nov.	2000
2nd*	Lee Chul-kyu	April	2001-June	2002
3rd	Lee Chul-kyu	July	2002-Feb.	2004
3rd*	Kim Jin-ouk	June	2004-June	2006
4th	Kim Jin-ouk	July	2006-Jan.	2010

5th	Kang Wan-muk	July	2010-Aug.	2013
6th	Sim Min	July	2014-*present*	

Mayors of Jangsu-gun

1st	Kim Sang-doo	July	1995-June	1998
2nd	Kim Sang-doo	July	1998-June	2002
3rd	Choi Yong-deuk	July	2002-Nov.	2002
3rd*	Jang Jae-yeong	Dec.	2002-June	2006
4th	Jang Jae-yeong	July	2006-June	2010
5th	Jang Jae-yeong	July	2010-June	2014
6th	Choi Yong-deuk	July	2014-*present*	

Mayors of Jeongeup-si

1st	Guk Sung-rock	July	1995-June	1998
2nd	Guk Sung-rock	July	1998-June	2002
3rd	You Sung-yop	July	2002-Feb.	2006
4th	Kang Kwang	July	2006-June	2010
5th	Kim Saeng-ki	July	2010-June	2014
6th	Kim Saeng-ki	July	2014-*present*	

Mayors of Jeonju-si

1st	Lee Chang-seung	July	1995-May	1996
1st*	Yang Sang-ryoul	July	1996-June	1998
2nd	Kim Wan-ju	July	1998-June	2002
3rd	Kim Wan-ju	July	2002-March	2006
4th	Song Ha-jin	July	2006-June	2010
5th	Song Ha-jin	July	2010-Feb.	2014
6th	Kim Seung-su	July	2014-*present*	

Mayors of Jinan-gun

1st	Lim Su-jin	July	1995-June	1998
2nd	Lim Su-jin	July	1998-June	2002
3rd	Lim Su-jin	July	2002-June	2006
4th	Song Young-sun	July	2006-June	2010
5th	Song Young-sun	July	2010-June	2014
6th	Lee Hang-ro	July	2014-*present*	

Mayors of Muju-gun

1st	Kim Se-ung	July	1995-June	1998
2nd	Kim Se-ung	July	1998-June	2002
3rd	Kim Se-ung	July	2002-March	2006
4th	Hong Nak-pyo	July	2006-June	2010
5th	Hong Nak-pyo	July	2010-June	2014
6th	Hwang Jeong-su	July	2014-*present*	

Mayors of Namwon-si

1st	Lee Jeong-kyu	July	1995-June	1998
2nd	Choi Jin-young	July	1998-June	2002
3rd	Choi Jin-young	July	2002-June	2006
4th	Choi Jung-kuen	July	2006-June	2010

5th	Yun Seung-ho	July	2010-June	2011
5th*	Lee Hwan-ju	Oct.	2011-June	2014
6th	Lee Hwan-ju	July	2014-*present*	

Mayors of Sunchang-gun

1st	Lim Duk-chun	July	1995-June	1998
2nd	Lim Duk-chun	July	1998-June	2002
3rd	Kang In-hyung	July	2002-June	2006
4th	Kang In-hyung	July	2006-June	2010
5th	Kang In-hyung	July	2010-June	2011
5th*	Hwang Sook-joo	Oct.	2011-June	2014
6th	Hwang Sook-joo	July	2014-*present*	

Mayors of Wanju-gun

1st	Lim Myung-hwan	July	1995-June	1998
2nd	Lim Myung-hwan	July	1998-June	2002
3rd	Choi Chong-il	July	2002-June	2006
4th	Rym Chung-yeap	July	2006-June	2010
5th	Rym Chung-yeap	July	2010-March	2014
6th	Park Sung-il	July	2014-*present*	

Jeollanam-do

5 Cities(si), 17 Counties(gun)

- Boseong-gun · Damyang-gun · Gangjin-gun
- Goheung-gun · Gokseong-gun · Gurye-gun
- Gwangyang-si · Haenam-gun · Hampyeong-gun
- Hwasun-gun · Jangheung-gun · Jangseong-gun
- Jindo-gun · Mokpo-si · Muan-gun
- Naju-si · Shinan-gun · Suncheon-si
- Wando-gun · Yeongam-gun
- Yeonggwang-gun · Yeosu-si

Mayors of Boseong-gun

1st	Moon Kwang-woong	July	1995-June	1998
2nd	Ha Seung-wan	July	1998-June	2002
3rd	Ha Seung-wan	July	2002-June	2006
4th	Jeong Jong-hae	July	2006-June	2010
5th	Jeong Jong-hae	July	2010-June	2014
6th	Lee Yong-boo	July	2014-*present*	

Mayors of Damyang-gun

1st	Mun Kyeng-gyu	July	1995-June	1998
2nd	Mun Kyeng-gyu	July	1998-June	2002
3rd	Choe Hyeong-sik	July	2002-June	2006
4th	Lee Jung-seob	July	2006-Sept.	2009
5th	Choe Hyeong-sik	July	2010-June	2014
6th	Choe Hyeong-sik	July	2014-*present*	

Mayors of Gangjin-gun

1st	Kim Jae-hong	July	1995-June	1998
2nd	Yoon Young-soo	July	1998-June	2002
3rd	Yoon Dong-hwan	July	2002-Aug.	2004
3rd*	Hwang Ju-hong	Oct.	2004-June	2006
4th	Hwang Ju-hong	July	2006-June	2010
5th	Hwang Ju-hong	July	2010-Dec.	2011
5th*	Gang Jin-won	April	2012-June	2014
6th	Gang Jin-won	July	2014-*present*	

Mayors of Goheung-gun

1st	Yoo Sang-chul	July	1995-June	1998
2nd	Yoo Sang-chul	July	1998-June	2002
3rd	Jin Jong-geun	July	2002-June	2006
4th	Bak Byeong-jong	July	2006-June	2010
5th	Bak Byeong-jong	July	2010-June	2014
6th	Bak Byeong-jong	July	2014-*present*	

Mayors of Gokseong-gun

1st	Cho Hyung-rae	July	1995-June	1998
2nd	Koh Hyun-seok	July	1998-June	2002
3rd	Koh Hyun-seok	July	2002-June	2006
4th	Cho Hyung-rae	July	2006-June	2010
5th	Heo Nam-seok	July	2010-June	2014
6th	Yoo Geun-gi	July	2014-*present*	

Mayors of Gurye-gun

1st	Lee Dong-seung	July	1995-June	1998
2nd	Jeon Kyong-tae	July	1998-June	2002
3rd	Jeon Kyong-tae	July	2002-June	2006
4th	Seo Gi-dong	July	2006-June	2010
5th	Seo Gi-dong	July	2010-June	2014
6th	Seo Gi-dong	July	2014-*present*	

Mayors of Gwangyang-si

1st	Kim Ok-hyun	July	1995-June	1998
2nd	Kim Ok-hyun	July	1998-June	2002
3rd	Lee Seong-woong	July	2002-June	2006
4th	Lee Seong-woong	July	2006-June	2010
5th	Lee Seong-woong	July	2010-June	2014
6th	Jeong Hyeon-bok	July	2014-*present*	

Mayors of Haenam-gun

1st	Kim Chang-il	July	1995-June	1998
2nd	Min Hwa-shik	July	1998-June	2002
3rd	Min Hwa-shik	July	2002-May	2004
3rd*	Park Hee-hyun	Oct.	2004-June	2006
4th	Park Hee-hyun	July	2006-Oct.	2007
4th*	Kim Choong-sik	Dec.	2007-April	2010

5th	Park Chul-hwan	July	2010-June	2014
6th	Park Chul-hwan	July	2014-*present*	

Mayors of Hampyeong-gun

1st	Jeong Won-kang	July	1995-June	1998
2nd	Lee Seug-hyung	July	1998-June	2002
3rd	Lee Seug-hyung	July	2002-June	2006
4th	Lee Seug-hyung	July	2006-Jan.	2010
5th	Ahn Byeong-ho	July	2010-June	2014
6th	Ahn Byeong-ho	July	2014-*present*	

Mayors of Hwasun-gun

1st	Lim Heung-lak	July	1995-June	1998
2nd	Lim Heung-lak	July	1998-June	2002
3rd	Lim Ho-kyoung	July	2002-Jan.	2004
3rd*	Lee Young-nam	June	2004-June	2006
4th	Jeon Hyung-joon	July	2006-Sept.	2006
4th*	Jun Owan-joon	Oct.	2006-June	2010
5th	Jun Owan-joon	July	2010-Feb.	2011
5th*	Hong Lee-sik	April	2011-June	2014
6th	Koo Choong-gon	July	2014-*present*	

Mayors of Jangheung-gun

1st	Kim Jae-jong	July	1995-June	1998
2nd	Kim Jae-jong	July	1998-June	2002
3rd	Kim In-kyu	July	2002-June	2006
4th	Kim In-kyu	July	2006-July	2007
4th*	Lee Myeong-heum	Dec.	2007-June	2010
5th	Lee Myeong-heum	July	2010-June	2014
6th	Kim Sung	July	2014-*present*	

Mayors of Jangseong-gun

1st	Kim Heung-sik	July	1995-June	1998
2nd	Kim Heung-sik	July	1998-June	2002
3rd	Kim Heung-sik	July	2002-June	2006
4th	Yoo Du-seok	July	2006-Oct.	2007
4th*	Lee Chung	Dec.	2007-June	2010
5th	Kim Yang-soo	July	2010-June	2014
6th	Yoo Du-seok	July	2014-*present*	

Mayors of Jindo-gun

1st	Park Seung-man	July	1995-June	1998
2nd	Park Seung-man	July	1998-June	2002
3rd	Yang In-sup	July	2002-Oct.	2003
3rd*	Kim Kyung-boo	June	2004-June	2006
4th	Park Yun-soo	July	2006-Nov.	2009
5th	Lee Dong-jin	July	2010-June	2014
6th	Lee Dong-jin	July	2014-*present*	

Mayors of Mokpo-si

1st	Kwon Yi-dam	July	1995-June	1998
2nd	Kwon Yi-dam	July	1998-June	2002
3rd	Jeon Tae-hong	July	2002-Jan.	2005
3rd*	Chung Chong-dug	May	2005-June	2006
4th	Chung Chong-dug	July	2006-June	2010
5th	Chung Chong-dug	July	2010-June	2014
6th	Park Hong-ryull	July	2014-*present*	

Mayors of Muan-gun

1st	Lee Jae-hyun	July	1995-June	1998
2nd	Lee Jae-hyun	July	1998-June	2002
3rd	Seo Sam-seog	July	2002-June	2006
4th	Seo Sam-seog	July	2006-June	2010
5th	Seo Sam-seog	July	2010-Dec.	2011
5th*	Kim Cheal-zoo	April	2012-June	2014
6th	Kim Cheal-zoo	July	2014-*present*	

Mayors of Naju-si

1st	Na In-soo	July	1995-June	1998
2nd	Kim Dae-dong	July	1998-June	2002
3rd	Shin Jeong-hun	July	2002-June	2006
4th	Shin Jeong-hun	July	2006-Feb.	2010
5th	Lim Seong-hoon	July	2010-June	2014
6th	Kang In-kyu	July	2014-*present*	

Mayors of Shinan-gun

1st	Son Jang-jo	July	1995-June	1998
2nd	Choi Gong-in	July	1998-June	2002
3rd	Go Gil-ho	July	2002-June	2006
4th*	Park Woo-ryang	Oct.	2006-June	2010
5th	Park Woo-ryang	July	2010-May	2014
6th	Go Gil-ho	July	2014-*present*	

Mayors of Suncheon-si

1st	Bahng Seong-ryong	July	1995-June	1998
2nd	Shin Joon-shik	July	1998-March	2002
3rd	Cho Choong-hoon	July	2002-June	2006
4th	Roh Kwan-kyu	July	2006-June	2010
5th	Roh Kwan-kyu	July	2010-Dec.	2011
5th*	Cho Choong-hoon	April	2012-June	2014
6th	Cho Choong-hoon	July	2014-*present*	

Mayors of Wando-gun

1st	Cha Kwan-hoon	July	1995-June	1998
2nd	Cha Kwan-hoon	July	1998-May	2002
3rd	Kim Jong-sik	July	2002-June	2006
4th	Kim Jong-sik	July	2006-June	2010
5th	Kim Jong-sik	July	2010-June	2014

6th   Shin Woo-chul   July   2014-*present*

Mayors of Yeongam-gun

1st	Park Il-jae	July	1995-June	1998
2nd	Kim Cheol-ho	July	1998-June	2002
3rd	Kim Cheol-ho	July	2002-June	2006
4th	Kim Il-tae	July	2006-June	2010
5th	Kim Il-tae	July	2010-June	2014
6th	Joun Dong-pyoung	July	2014-*present*	

Mayors of Yeonggwang-gun

1st	Kim Bong-ryul	July	1995-June	1998
2nd	Kim Bong-ryul	July	1998-June	2002
3rd	Kim Bong-ryul	July	2002-June	2006
4th	Kang Jong-man	July	2006-March	2008
4th*	Jung Ki-ho	June	2008-June	2010
5th	Jung Ki-ho	July	2010-June	2014
6th	Kim Jun-sung	July	2014-*present*	

Mayors of Yeosu-si

▸ *Yeosu-si, Yeocheon-si and Yeocheon-gun incorporated into the unified Yeosu city on April 1, 1998.*

1st	Kim Kwang-hyun	July	1995-March	1998
2nd	Joo Seung-yong	July	1998-June	2002
3rd	Kim Chung-seog	July	2002-June	2006
4th	Oh Hyun-sup	July	2006-June	2010
5th	Kim Chung-seog	July	2010-June	2014
6th	Ju Chul-hyun	July	2014-*present*	

\<Mayor of Yeocheon-si>

1st	Chung Chae-ho	July	1995-March	1998

\<Mayors of Yeocheon-gun>

1st	Chung Keun-jin	July	1995-June	1996
1st*	Joo Seung-yong	Aug.	1996-March	1998

Gyeongsangbuk-do

10 Cities(si), 13 Counties(gun) ───────

· Andong-si · Bonghwa-gun · Cheongdo-gun
· Cheongsong-gun · Chilgok-gun
· Gimcheon-si · Goryeong-gun · Gumi-si
· Gunwi-gun · Gyeongju-si · Gyeongsan-si
· Mungyeong-si · Pohang-si · Sangju-si
· Seongju-gun · Uiseong-gun · Uljin-gun
· Ulleung-gun · Yecheon-gun · Yeongcheon-si
· Yeongdeok-gun · Yeongju-si
· Yeongyang-gun

Mayors of Andong-si

1st	Chung Dong-ho	July	1995-June	1998
2nd	Chung Dong-ho	July	1998-June	2002
3rd	Kim Hwi-dong	July	2002-June	2006
4th	Kim Hwi-dong	July	2006-June	2010
5th	Kwon Young-sae	July	2010-June	2014
6th	Kwon Young-sae	July	2014-*present*	

Mayors of Bonghwa-gun

1st	Um Tae-hang	July	1995-June	1998
2nd	Um Tae-hang	July	1998-June	2002
3rd	Ryu In-hee	July	2002-June	2006
4th	Kim Hee-moon	July	2006-Jan.	2007
4th*	Um Tae-hang	April	2007-June	2010
5th	Park No-wook	July	2010-June	2014
6th	Park No-wook	July	2014-*present*	

Mayors of Cheongdo-gun

1st	Kim Sang-soun	July	1995-June	1998
2nd	Kim Sang-soun	July	1998-June	2002
3rd	Kim Sang-soun	July	2002-Oct.	2004
3rd*	Lee Won-dong	May	2005-June	2006
4th	Lee Won-dong	July	2006-July	2007
4th*	Jung Han-tae	Dec.	2007-April	2008
4th*	Lee Jung-gun	June	2008-June	2010
5th	Lee Jung-gun	July	2010-June	2014
6th	Lee Seung-yool	July	2014-*present*	

Mayors of Cheongsong-gun

1st	Ahn Eui-jong	July	1995-June	1998
2nd	Ahn Eui-jong	July	1998-April	2000
2nd*	Park Jong-kap	June	2000-June	2002
3rd	Bae Dae-yun	July	2002-June	2006
4th	Yun Gyeong-hui	July	2006-Sept.	2007
4th*	Han Dong-soo	Dec.	2007-June	2010
5th	Han Dong-soo	July	2010-June	2014
6th	Han Dong-soo	July	2014-*present*	

Mayors of Chilgok-gun

1st	Choi Jae-yung	July	1995-June	1998
2nd	Choi Jae-yung	July	1998-May	2001
3rd	Bae Sang-do	July	2002-June	2006
4th	Bae Sang-do	July	2006-June	2010
5th	Jang Se-ho	July	2010-July	2011
5th*	Baek Sun-ki	Oct.	2011-June	2014
6th	Baek Sun-ki	July	2014-*present*	

Mayors of Gimcheon-si

1st	Park Pal-yong	July	1995-June	1998

2nd	Park Pal-yong	July	1998-June	2002
3rd	Park Pal-yong	July	2002-June	2006
4th	Park Bo-saeng	July	2006-June	2010
5th	Park Bo-saeng	July	2010-June	2014
6th	Park Bo-saeng	July	2014-*present*	

Mayors of Goryeong-gun

1st	Lee Jin-hwan	July	1995-June	1998
2nd	Lee Tae-keun	July	1998-June	2002
3rd	Lee Tae-keun	July	2002-June	2006
4th	Lee Tae-keun	July	2006-June	2010
5th	Kwak Yong-hwan	July	2010-June	2014
6th	Kwak Yong-hwan	July	2014-*present*	

Mayors of Gumi-si

1st	Kim Kwan-yong	July	1995-June	1998
2nd	Kim Kwan-yong	July	1998-June	2002
3rd	Kim Kwan-yong	July	2002-Feb.	2006
4th	Nam Yoo-chin	July	2006-June	2010
5th	Nam Yoo-chin	July	2010-June	2014
6th	Nam Yoo-chin	July	2014-*present*	

Mayors of Gunwi-gun

1st	Hong Soon-hong	July	1995-June	1998
2nd	Park Young-eon	July	1998-June	2002
3rd	Park Young-eon	July	2002-June	2006
4th	Park Young-eon	July	2006-June	2010
5th	Jang Wook	July	2010-June	2014
6th	Kim Young-man	July	2014-*present*	

Mayors of Gyeongju-si

1st	Lee Won-sik	July	1995-June	1998
2nd	Lee Won-sik	July	1998-June	2002
3rd	Baek Sang-seung	July	2002-June	2006
4th	Baek Sang-seung	July	2006-June	2010
5th	Choi Yang-sik	July	2010-June	2014
6th	Choi Yang-sik	July	2014-*present*	

Mayors of Gyeongsan-si

1st	Choi Hee-wook	July	1995-June	1998
2nd	Choi Hee-wook	July	1998-June	2002
3rd	Yoon Young-jo	July	2002-Nov.	2004
3rd*	Choi Byoung-kuk	May	2005-June	2006
4th	Choi Byoung-kuk	July	2006-June	2010
5th	Choi Byoung-kuk	July	2010-Nov.	2012
5th*	Choi Young-jo	Dec.	2012-June	2014
6th	Choi Young-jo	July	2014-*present*	

Mayors of Mungyeong-si

| 1st | Kim Hak-mun | July | 1995-June | 1998 |

2nd	Kim Hak-mun	July	1998-June	2002
3rd	Park In-won	July	2002-June	2006
4th	Shin Hyun-kook	July	2006-June	2010
5th	Shin Hyun-kook	July	2010-Dec.	2011
5th*	Ko Yun-hwan	April	2012-June	2014
6th	Ko Yun-hwan	July	2014-*present*	

Mayors of Pohang-si

1st	Park Ki-hwan	July	1995-June	1998
2nd	Chung Jang-sik	July	1998-June	2002
3rd	Chung Jang-sik	July	2002-Feb.	2006
4th	Park Seung-ho	July	2006-June	2010
5th	Park Seung-ho	July	2010-March	2014
6th	Lee Kang-deok	July	2014-*present*	

Mayors of Sangju-si

1st	Kim Keun-soo	July	1995-June	1998
2nd	Kim Keun-soo	July	1998-June	2002
3rd	Kim Keun-soo	July	2002-June	2006
4th	Lee Jung-baek	July	2006-June	2010
5th	Sung Beck-young	July	2010-June	2014
6th	Lee Jung-baek	July	2014-*present*	

Mayors of Seongju-gun

1st	Kim Keon-yeong	July	1995-June	1998
2nd	Kim Keon-yeong	July	1998-Oct.	2001
3rd	Lee Chang-woo	July	2002-June	2006
4th	Lee Chang-woo	July	2006-June	2010
5th	Kim Hang-gon	July	2010-June	2014
6th	Kim Hang-gon	July	2014-*present*	

Mayors of Uiseong-gun

1st	Choung Hae-gul	July	1995-June	1998
2nd	Choung Hae-gul	July	1998-June	2002
3rd	Choung Hae-gul	July	2002-June	2006
4th	Kim Bok-kyu	July	2006-June	2010
5th	Kim Bok-kyu	July	2010-June	2014
6th	Kim Joo-soo	July	2014-*present*	

Mayors of Uljin-gun

1st	Chon Kwang-sun	July	1995-June	1998
2nd	Shin Jeong	July	1998-June	2002
3rd	Kim Yong-soo	July	2002-June	2006
4th	Kim Yong-soo	July	2006-June	2010
5th	Im Kwang-won	July	2010-June	2014
6th	Im Kwang-won	July	2014-*present*	

Mayors of Ulleung-gun

| 1st | Jeong Jong-tae | July | 1995-June | 1998 |
| 2nd | Jeong Jong-tae | July | 1998-July | 2001 |

3rd	Oh Chang-keun	July	2002-June	2006
4th	Jung Yoon-yul	July	2006-June	2010
5th	Jung Yoon-yul	July	2010-June	2011
5th*	Choi Soo-il	Oct.	2011-June	2014
6th	Choi Soo-il	July	2014-*present*	

Mayors of Yecheon-gun

1st	Kwon Sang-kook	July	1995-June	1998
2nd	Kim Soo-nam	July	1998-June	2002
3rd	Kim Soo-nam	July	2002-June	2006
4th	Kim Soo-nam	July	2006-June	2010
5th	Lee Hyun-joon	July	2010-June	2014
6th	Lee Hyun-joon	July	2014-*present*	

Mayors of Yeongcheon-si

1st	Jeung Jae-kyoon	July	1995-June	1998
2nd	Jeung Jae-kyoon	July	1998-July	2000
2nd*	Park Jin-kyu	Oct.	2000-June	2002
3rd	Park Jin-kyu	July	2002-March	2005
3rd*	Son Yi-mok	May	2005-June	2006
4th	Son Yi-mok	July	2006-June	2007
4th*	Kim Young-seok	Dec.	2007-June	2010
5th	Kim Young-seok	July	2010-June	2014
6th	Kim Young-seok	July	2014-*present*	

Mayors of Yeongdeok-gun

1st	Kim Woo-youn	July	1995-June	1998
2nd	Kim Woo-youn	July	1998-June	2002
3rd	Kim Woo-youn	July	2002-Nov.	2004
3rd*	Kim Byung-mok	May	2005-June	2006
4th	Kim Byung-mok	July	2006-June	2010
5th	Kim Byung-mok	July	2010-June	2014
6th	Lee Hee-jin	July	2014-*present*	

Mayors of Yeongju-si

1st	Kim Chin-yong	July	1995-June	1998
2nd	Kim Chin-yong	July	1998-June	2002
3rd	Kwon Yeong-chang	July	2002-June	2006
4th	Kim Joo-young	July	2006-June	2010
5th	Kim Joo-young	July	2010-June	2014
6th	Jang Wook-hyeon	July	2014-*present*	

Mayors of Yeongyang-gun

1st	Kwon Yong-han	July	1995-June	1998
2nd	Lee Rye-hyung	July	1998-June	2002
3rd	Kim Yong-am	July	2002-June	2006
4th	Kwon Yeong-taek	July	2006-June	2010
5th	Kwon Yeong-taek	July	2010-June	2014
6th	Kwon Yeong-taek	July	2014-*present*	

Gyeongsangnam-do

8 Cities(si), 10 Counties(gun)

- Changnyeong-gun · Changwon-si
- Geochang-gun · Geoje-si · Gimhae-si
- Goseong-gun · Hadong-gun · Haman-gun
- Hamyang-gun · Hapcheon-gun · Jinju-si
- Miryang-si · Namhae-gun · Sacheon-si
- Sancheong-gun · Tongyeong-si
- Uiryeong-gun · Yangsan-si

Mayors of Changnyeong-gun

1st	Kim Jin-baek	July	1995-June	1998
2nd	Kim Jin-baek	July	1998-June	2002
3rd	Kim Jong-kyu	July	2002-June	2006
4th	Kim Jong-kyu	July	2006-July	2006
4th*	Ha Jong-geun	Oct.	2006-Oct.	2007
4th*	Kim Choong-sik	Dec.	2007-June	2010
5th	Kim Choong-sik	July	2010-June	2014
6th	Kim Choong-sik	July	2014-*present*	

Mayors of Changwon-si

▸ *Changwon-si, Masan-si and Jinhae-si incorporated into the unified Changwon city on July 1, 2010.*

1st	Kong Min-bae	July	1995-June	1998
2nd	Kong Min-bae	July	1998-June	2002
3rd	Bae Han-sung	July	2002-March	2004
3rd*	Park Wan-soo	June	2004-June	2006
4th	Park Wan-soo	July	2006-June	2010
5th	Park Wan-soo	July	2010-Feb.	2014
6th	Ahn Sang-soo	July	2014-*present*	

<Mayors of Masan-si>

1st	Kim In-gyu	July	1995-June	1998
2nd	Kim In-gyu	July	1998-March	2001
2nd*	Hwang Cheol-gon	April	2001-June	2002
3rd	Hwang Cheol-gon	July	2002-June	2006
4th	Hwang Cheol-gon	July	2006-June	2010

<Mayors of Jinhae-si>

1st	Kim Byoung-ro	July	1995-June	1998
2nd	Kim Byoung-ro	July	1998-June	2002
3rd	Kim Byoung-ro	July	2002-June	2006
4th	Lee Jae-bok	July	2006-Dec.	2009

Mayors of Geochang-gun

1st	Jung Ju-hwan	July	1995-June	1998
2nd	Jung Ju-hwan	July	1998-June	2002
3rd	Kim Tae-ho	July	2002-May	2004
3rd*	Kang Seog-jin	Oct.	2004-June	2006

4th	Kang Seog-jin	July	2006-Dec.	2007
4th*	Yang Dong-in	June	2008-June	2010
5th	Lee Hong-gi	July	2010-June	2014
6th	Lee Hong-gi	July	2014-*present*	

Mayors of Geoje-si

1st	Jo Sang-do	July	1995-June	1998
2nd	Yang Jeong-sik	July	1998-June	2002
3rd	Yang Jeong-sik	July	2002-Jan.	2003
3rd*	Kim Han-gyeom	April	2003-June	2006
4th	Kim Han-gyeom	July	2006-June	2010
5th	Kwon Min-ho	July	2010-June	2014
6th	Kwon Min-ho	July	2014-*present*	

Mayors of Gimhae-si

1st	Song Eun-book	July	1995-June	1998
2nd	Song Eun-book	July	1998-June	2002
3rd	Song Eun-book	July	2002-Feb.	2006
4th	Kim Jong-gan	July	2006-June	2010
5th	Kim Maeng-kon	July	2010-June	2014
6th	Kim Maeng-kon	July	2014-*present*	

Mayors of Goseong-gun

1st	Lee Kab-young	July	1995-June	1998
2nd	Lee Kab-young	July	1998-June	2002
3rd	Lee Hak-lul	July	2002-June	2006
4th	Lee Hak-lul	July	2006-June	2010
5th	Lee Hak-lul	July	2010-June	2014
6th	Ha Hak-yeol	July	2014-*present*	

Mayors of Hadong-gun

1st	Chung Ku-yong	July	1995-June	1998
2nd	Chung Ku-yong	July	1998-June	2002
3rd	Jo Yu-haeng	July	2002-June	2006
4th	Jo Yu-haeng	July	2006-June	2010
5th	Jo Yu-haeng	July	2010-June	2014
6th	Youn Sang-ki	July	2014-*present*	

Mayors of Haman-gun

1st	Cho Sung-hwi	July	1995-June	1998
2nd	Cho Sung-hwi	July	1998-July	1999
2nd*	Jin Seok-kyu	Sept.	1999-June	2002
3rd	Jin Seok-kyu	July	2002-June	2006
4th	Jin Seok-kyu	July	2006-Nov.	2007
4th*	Cho Yeong-kyoo	Dec.	2007-June	2010
5th	Ha Sung-sik	July	2010-June	2014
6th	Cha Jeong-sup	July	2014-*present*	

Mayors of Hamyang-gun

1st	Jung Yong-kyu	July	1995-June	1998

2nd	Jung Yong-kyu	July	1998-June	2002
3rd	Chun Sar-yeong	July	2002-June	2006
4th	Chun Sar-yeong	July	2006-June	2010
5th	Rhee Chul-woo	July	2010-July	2011
5th*	Choi Wan-sik	Oct.	2011-Feb.	2013
5th*	Rim Chang-ho	April	2013-June	2014
6th	Rim Chang-ho	July	2014-*present*	

Mayors of Hapcheon-gun

1st	Kang Seok-jung	July	1995-June	1998
2nd	Kang Seok-jung	July	1998-June	2002
3rd	Sim Eui-jo	July	2002-June	2006
4th	Sim Eui-jo	July	2006-June	2010
5th	Ha Chang-hwan	July	2010-June	2014
6th	Ha Chang-hwan	July	2014-*present*	

Mayors of Jinju-si

1st	Baek Seung-doo	July	1995-June	1998
2nd	Baek Seung-doo	July	1998-June	2002
3rd	Jeong Young-suk	July	2002-June	2006
4th	Jeong Young-suk	July	2006-June	2010
5th	Lee Chang-hee	July	2010-June	2014
6th	Lee Chang-hee	July	2014-*present*	

Mayors of Miryang-si

1st	Lee Sang-jo	July	1995-June	1998
2nd	Lee Sang-jo	July	1998-June	2002
3rd	Lee Sang-jo	July	2002-June	2006
4th	Um Yong-soo	July	2006-June	2010
5th	Um Yong-soo	July	2010-June	2014
6th	Park Il-ho	July	2014-*present*	

Mayors of Namhae-gun

1st	Kim Doo-gwan	July	1995-June	1998
2nd	Kim Doo-gwan	July	1998-April	2002
3rd	Ha Young-je	July	2002-June	2006
4th	Ha Young-je	July	2006-Dec.	2007
4th*	Jung Hyun-tae	June	2008-June	2010
5th	Jung Hyun-tae	July	2010-June	2014
6th	Park Young-il	July	2014-*present*	

Mayors of Sacheon-si

1st	Ha Il-cheong	July	1995-June	1998
2nd	Ha Il-cheong	July	1998-Sept.	1998
2nd*	Chong Man-kyu	Nov.	1998-Nov.	2000
2nd*	Kim Soo-young	April	2001-June	2002
3rd	Kim Soo-young	July	2002-June	2006
4th	Kim Soo-young	July	2006-June	2010
5th	Chong Man-kyu	July	2010-June	2014
6th	Song Do-gun	July	2014-*present*	

Mayors of Sancheong-gun

1st	Kwon Sun-young	July	1995-June	1998
2nd	Kwon Sun-young	July	1998-June	2002
3rd	Kwon Chul-hyun	July	2002-June	2006
4th	Lee Jae-kun	July	2006-June	2010
5th	Lee Jae-kun	July	2010-June	2014
6th	Her Ki-do	July	2014-*present*	

Mayors of Tongyeong-si

1st	Ko Dong-joo	July	1995-June	1998
2nd	Ko Dong-joo	July	1998-June	2002
3rd	Kim Dong-jin	July	2002-Sept.	2003
3rd*	Jin Euy-jang	Oct.	2003-June	2006
4th	Jin Euy-jang	July	2006-June	2010
5th	Kim Dong-jin	July	2010-June	2014
6th	Kim Dong-jin	July	2014-*present*	

Mayors of Uiryeong-gun

1st	Jeon Won-yong	July	1995-June	1998
2nd	Jeon Won-yong	July	1998-June	2002
3rd	Han Woo-sang	July	2002-June	2006
4th	Kim Chae-yong	July	2006-June	2010
5th	Kwon Tae-woo	July	2010-Sept.	2010
5th*	Kim Chae-yong	Oct.	2010-June	2014
6th	Oh Young-ho	July	2014-*present*	

Mayors of Yangsan-si

▸ *Promoted Yangsan-gun to Yangsan-si on March 1, 1996.*

<Mayor of Yangsan-gun>

1st	Shon Yoo-seob	July	1995-Feb.	1996
1st	Shon Yoo-seob	March	1996-June	1998
2nd	Ahn Jong-kil	July	1998-June	2002
3rd	Ahn Jong-kil	July	2002-March	2004
3rd*	Oh Geun-sub	June	2004-June	2006
4th	Oh Geun-sub	July	2006-Nov.	2009
5th	Na Dong-yean	July	2010-June	2014
6th	Na Dong-yean	July	2014-*present*	

Jeju Special Self-Governing Province

2 Administrative cities(si)
· Jeju-si · Seogwipo-si

Mayors of Jeju-si

▸ *Unified Jeju city(Jeju-si and Bukjeju-gun) was launched on July 1, 2006.*

· **Elected by popular vote mayor**

1st	Ko Min-soo	July	1995-June	1998
2nd	Kim Tae-hwan	July	1998-June	2002
3rd	Kim Tae-hwan	July	2002-May	2004
3rd*	Kim Yung-hoon	June	2004-May	2006

· **Appointed mayor**

1st	Kim Yung-hoon	July	2006-June	2008
2nd	Kang Taek-sang	July	2008-March	2010
3rd	Kim Bang-hun	March	2010-June	2010
4th	Kim Byoung-lib	July	2010-Dec.	2011
5th	Kim Sang-oh	Dec.	2011-June	2014
6th	Lee Ji-hoon	July	2014-Aug.	2014
7th	Kim Byoung-lib	Dec.	2014-*present*	

<Mayors of Bukjeju-gun>

1st	Shin Chul-ju	July	1995-June	1998
2nd	Shin Chul-ju	July	1998-June	2002
3rd	Shin Chul-ju	July	2002-June	2005

Mayors of Seogwipo-si

▸ *Unified Seogwipo city(Seogwipo-si and Namjeju-gun) was launched on July 1, 2006.*

· **Elected by popular vote mayor**

1st	Oh Kwang-hyub	July	1995-June	1998
2nd	Kang Sang-joo	July	1998-June	2002
3rd	Kang Sang-joo	July	2002-March	2006

· **Appointed mayor**

1st	Lee Young-du	July	2006-Nov.	2006
2nd	Kim Hyoung-soo	Dec.	2006-Dec.	2008
3rd	Park Young-boo	Dec.	2008-June	2010
4th	Ko Chang-hu	July	2010-Dec.	2011
5th	Kim Jae-bong	Dec.	2011-Aug.	2013
6th	Han Dong-joo	Aug.	2013-Nov.	2013
7th	Yang Byung-sik	Dec.	2013-June	2014
8th	Lim Byung-heon	July	2014-*present*	

<Mayors of Namjeju-gun>

1st	Kang Tae-hoon	July	1995-June	1998
2nd	Kang Tae-hoon	July	1998-Aug.	1999
2nd*	Kang Ki-kwon	Oct.	1999-June	2002
3rd	Kang Ki-kwon	July	2002-May	2006

⫿ DIPLOMATIC DIRECTORY ⫿

KOREAN OVERSEAS MISSIONS

EMBASSIES

<ASIA-PACIFIC>

Afghanistan *Amb. Cha Young-cheol* Add:House No.34, Street No.10, Wazir Akbar Khan, Kabul, Afghanistan Tel:(93-20)210-2481 http://afg.mofa.go.kr
Australia *Amb. Kim Bong-hyun* Add:113 Empire Circuit, Yarralumla ACT 2600, Australia Tel:(61-2)6270-4100 http://aus-act.mofa.go.kr
Bangladesh *Amb. Lee Yun-young* Add:4 Madani Avenue, Baridhara, Dhaka-1212, Bangladesh Tel:(880-2)881-2088 http://bgd.mofa.go.kr
Brunei *Amb. Cho Won-Myung* Add:No. 17, Simpang 462 Kg. Sg. Hanching Baru, Jln Muara, B.S.B BC 2115, Brunei Tel:(673)233-0248 http://brn.mofa.go.kr
Cambodia *Amb. Kim Weon-jin* Add:#50-52, St. No. 214, Phnom Penh, P.O. Box 2433, Kingdom of Cambodia Tel:(855-23)211-900 http://khm.mofa.go.kr
China *Amb. Kim Jang-soo* Add:No.20, Dong Fang Dong Lu Chaoyang District, Beijing, 100600, China Tel:(86-10)8531-0700 http://chn.mofa.go.kr
Fiji *Amb. Kim Seong-in* Add:8th Floor Vanua House, Victoria Parade, Suva, Fiji Tel:(679)330-0977 http://fji.mofa.go.kr
India *Amb. Lee Joon-kyu* Add:9, Chandragupta Marg, Chanakyapuri Extension, New Delhi-110021, India Tel:(91-11)4200-7000 http://ind.mofa.go.kr
Indonesia *Amb. Cho Tai-young* Add:Jalan Jenderal Gatot Subroto Kav. 57 Jakarta Selatan 12950 Tel:(62-21)2992-2500 http://idn.mofa.go.kr
Japan *Amb. Yoo Heung-soo* Add:1-2-5 Minami-Azabu Minato-ku Tokyo Japan Tel:(81-3)3452-7611 http://jpn-tokyo.mofa.go.kr
Laos *Amb. Kim Soo-gwon* Add:Lao-Thai Friendship Road, Ban Watnak, Sisettanak District, P.O. Box 7567, Vientiane, Lao P.D.R. Tel:(856)21-352-031 http://lao.mofa.go.kr
Malaysia *Amb. Cho Byung-jae* Add:No. 9&11, Jalan Nipah, Off Jalan Ampang, 55000 Kuala Lumpur, Malaysia Tel:(603)4251-2336 http://mys.mofa.go.kr
Mongolia *Amb. Oh Song* Add:P.O. Box-1039, 14220, Embassy Street-19, Sukhbaatar District, Ulaanbaatar, Mongolia Tel:(976-11)32-1548 http://mng.mofa.go.kr
Myanmar *Amb. Lee Baek-soon* Add:No. 97, University Avenue Road, Bahan Township, P.O.Box 1408, Yangon, Union of Myanmar Tel:(95-1)527-142 http://mmr.mofa.go.kr
Nepal *Amb. Choe Yong-jin* Add:1058 Ravi bhawan Tahachal, Kathmandu, Nepal Tel:(977-1)427-0172 http://npl.mofa.go.kr
New Zealand *Amb. Kim Hae-yong* Add:11th Floor, ASB Bank Tower, 2 Hunter Street, Wellington 6011, New Zealand Tel:(64-4)473-9073 http://nzl-wellington.mofa.go.kr
Pakistan *Amb. Song Jong-hwan* Add:Block 13, Street 29, G-5/4, Diplomatic Enclave II, Islamabad, Pakistan, G.P.O. Box 1087 Tel:(92-51)227-9380 http://pak-islamabad.mofa.go.kr
Papua New Guinea *Amb. Kim Seong-choon* Add:P.O. Box 381, POM, 4th Floor, Pacific MMI Building Section 21 Allotments 2&3, Champion Parade, Granville, Port Moresby, Papua New Guinea Tel:(675)321-5822 http://png.mofa.go.kr
Philippines *Amb. Kim Jae-shin* Add:122 Upper McKinley Road, McKinley Town Center, Fort Bonifacio, Taguig city 1634, Philippines Tel:(63-

2)856-9210 http://embassy_philippines.mofa.go.kr

Singapore *Amb. Suh Chung-ha* Add:47 Scotts Road, #08-00 Goldbell Tower Singapore 228233 Tel:(65)6256-1188 http://sgp.mofa.go.kr

Sri Lanka *Amb. Chang Won-sam* Add:No.98 Dharmapala Mawatha, Colombo 7, Sri Lanka Tel:(94-11)269-9036 http://lka.mofa.go.kr

Thailand *Amb. Jeon Jae-man* Add:23 Thiam-Ruammit Road, Ratchadapisek, Huay-Kwang, Bangkok 10310, Thailand Tel:(66-2)247-7537 http://tha.mofa.go.kr

Timor-Leste *Amb. Kim Ki-nam* Add:P.O. Box 230, Avenida de Portugal, Campo Alor, Dom Aleixo, Dili, Timor-Leste Tel:(670)332-1635 http://tls.mofa.go.kr

Vietnam *Amb. Jun Dae-joo* Add:28th Fl., Lotte Center Hanoi, 54 Lieu Giai St., Ba Dinh District, Hanoi, Vietnam Tel:(84-4)3831-5110 http://vnm-hanoi.mofa.go.kr

\<AMERICA\>

Argentina *Amb. Choo Jong-youn* Add:Av. del Libertador 2395, Ciudad Autonoma de Buenos Aires, (1425) Argentina Tel:(54-11)4802-8865 http://arg.mofa.go.kr

Bolivia *Amb. Lee Jong-cheol* Add:Calacoto calle #13, Edificio Torre Lucia 4-5 Piso, La Paz, Bolivia Tel:(591)2211-0361 http://bol.mofa.go.kr

Brazil *Amb. Lee Jeong-gwan* Add:SEN-Av. das Nacoes, Lote 14 Asa Norte, 70800-915, Brasilia-DF, Brazil Tel:(55-61)3321-2500 http://bra-brasilia.mofa.go.kr

Canada *Amb. Jo Dae-shik* Add:150 Boteler Street, Ottawa, Ontario, Canada K1N 5A6 Tel:(613)244-5010 http://can-ottawa.mofa.go.kr

Chile *Amb. Yu Ji-eun* Add:Av. Alcatara 74, Las Condes, Santiago, Chile Tel:(56-2)228-4214 http://chl.mofa.go.kr

Colombia *Amb. Jang Myung-soo* Add:Calle 94 No.9-39, Bogota, Colombia Tel:(571)616-7200 http://col.mofa.go.kr

Costa Rica *Amb. Chun Young-wook* Add:400 metros norte y 200 metros oeste, del Restaurante Rostipollos, Urbanizacion Trejos Montealegre, San Rafael de Escazu, San Jose, Costa Rica Tel:(506)2220-3160 http://cri.mofa.go.kr

Dominican Republic *Amb. Oh Han-gu* Add:Torre Empresarial Forum, Piso 14, Avenida 27 de Febrero No.495, El Millon, Santo Domingo, Republica Dominicana Tel:(1-809)482-6505 http://dom.mofa.go.kr

Ecuador *Amb. Lee Eun-chul* Add:12 de Octubre 1942 y Cordero Edificio World Trade Center, Torre B, Piso 3, Quito, Ecuador Tel:(593-2)290-9227 http://ecu.mofa.go.kr

El Salvador *Amb. Kim Byong-seop* Add:Calle El Mirador y 87 Av. Nte. Edificio Torre Futura, Nivel 14, Local 5, Col. Escalon, San Salvador, El Salvador Tel:(503)2263-9145 http://slv.mofa.go.kr

Guatemala *Amb. Choo Yeon-gon* Add:5 Avenida 5-55 Zona 14, Edificio Europlaza, Torre 3, Nivel 7, Ciudad de Guatemala, Guatemala C.A Tel:(502)2382-4051 http://gtm.mofa.go.kr

Honduras *Amb. Kim Rai-hyug* Add:Metropolis Torre 2, piso 15, Blvd. Suyapa, frente a Televicentro, Tegucigalpa, Honduras Tel:(504)2235-5561 http://hnd.mofa.go.kr

Jamaica *Amb. Agent. Lim Jong-seon* Add:5 Oakridge Kingston 8 Jamaica W.I.. Tel:(1-876)924-2731 http://jam.mofa.go.kr

Mexico *Amb. Chun Bee-ho* Add:Lopez Diaz de Armendariz 110, Col. Lomas de Virreyes C.P 11000, Mexico D.F. Tel:(52-55)5202-9866 http://mex.mofa.go.kr

Nicaragua *Amb. Kim Doo-sik* Add:Edificio Invercasa Torre III 5to Piso Frente al Hospital Monte España, Managua, Nicaragua Tel:(505)2267-6777 http://nic.mofa.go.kr

Panama *Amb. Cho Byoung-lip* Add:Calle 50, Torre Global Bank, Piso 30, Oficina 3002, Obario, Panama, Republica de Panama Tel:(507)264-8203 http://pan.mofa.go.kr

Paraguay *Amb. Hahn Myung-jae* Add:Av. Republica Argentina 678 esq. Pacheco Asuncion, Paraguay Tel:(595-21)605-606 http://pry.mofa.go.kr

Peru *Amb. Jang Keun-ho* Add:Calle Guillermo Marconi 165, San Isidro, Lima, Peru Tel:(51-1)632-5000 http://per.mofa.go.kr

Trinidad and Tobago *Amb. Lee Doo-young* Add:36th Elizabeth Street, St.Clair,Port of Spain Tel:(1-868)622-9081 http://tto.mofa.go.kr

United States of America *Amb. Ahn Ho-young* Add:2450 Massachusetts Avenue N.W. Washington, D.C. 20008 Tel:(202)939-5600 http://usa.mofa.go.kr

Uruguay *Amb. Yoo Han-jun* Add:Av. Luis Alberto de Herrera 1248, Torre II, Piso 10 WTC, C.P. 11300, Montevideo, Uruguay Tel:(598)2628-9374 http://ury.mofa.go.kr

Venezuela *Amb. Maeng Dal-young* Add:Av. Francisco de Miranda, Centro Lido, Torre B, Piso 9, Ofic.91-92-B, El Rosal, Caracas, Venezuela PO box. Apartado Postal 62.586-Chacao Tel:(58-212)954-1270 http://ven.mofa.go.kr

<EUROPE>

Austria *Amb. Song Young-wan* Add:Gregor Mendel Strasse 25, A-1180, Vienna, Austria Tel:(43-1)478-1991 http://aut.mofa.go.kr

Azerbaijan *Amb. Choi Suk-inn* Add:H.Aliyev str., Cross 1, House 12, Baku, Republic of Azerbaijan Tel:(994-12)596-7901 http://aze.mofa.go.kr

Belarus *Amb. Yang Joong-mo* Add:Ave. Pobediteley 59, Minsk, Belarus Tel:(375-17)306-0147 http://blr.mofa.go.kr

Belgium *Amb. Ahn Chong-ghee* Add:Chaussee de la Hulpe 173-175, 1170 Brussels(Watermael-Boitsfort), Belgium Tel:(32-2)675-5777 http://bel.mofa.go.kr

Bulgaria *Amb. Shin Maeng-ho* Add:World Trade Center, 7A Floor, 36 Dragan Tsankov Blvd, 1040 Sofia, Bulgaria Tel:(359-2)971-2181 http://bgr.mofa.go.kr

Croatia *Amb. Suh Hyung-won* Add:Ksaverska cesta 111/A-B, 10000 Zagreb, Croatia Tel:(385-1)4821-282 http://hrv.mofa.go.kr

Czech *Amb. Moon Ha-yong* Add:Slavickova 5, 160 00 Praha 6-Bubenec, Czech Republic Tel:(420)234-090-411 http://cze.mofa.go.kr

Denmark *Amb. Ma Young-sam* Add:Svanem Φllevej 104, 2900 Hellerup, Denmark Tel:(45)3946-0400 http://dnk.mofa.go.kr

Finland *Amb. Chang Dong-hee* Add: Erottajankatu 7A, 00130 Helsinki, Finland Tel:(358-9)251-5000 http://fin.mofa.go.kr

France *Amb. Mo Chul-min* Add:125 rue de Grenelle 75007 Paris, France Tel:(33-01)4753-0101 http://fra.mofa.go.kr

Germany *Amb. Lee Kyung-soo* Add:Botschaft der Republik Korea Stülerstr. 10, 10787 Berlin, Germany Tel:(49-30)260-650 http://deu.mofa.go.kr

Greece *Amb. Shin Gil-Sou* Add:Athens Tower A' building, 19th Floor, 2-4 Messogion Avenue, 115 27, Athens, Greece Tel:(30-210)698-4080 http://grc.mofa.go.kr

Holy See *Amb. Kim Kyung-surk* Add:Via Della Mendola 109, 00135, Rome, Italy, Holy see Tel:(39-06)331-4505 http://ita-vatican.mofa.go.kr

Hungary *Amb. Yim Geun-hyeong* Add:1062 Andrassy ut. 109. Budapest, Hungary Tel:(36-1)462-3080 http://hun.mofa.go.kr

Ireland *Amb. Park Hae-yun* Add:15 Clyde Road, Ballsbridge, Dublin 4, Ireland Tel:(353-1)660-8800 http://irl.mofa.go.kr

Italy *Amb. Lee Yong-joon* Add:Via Barnaba Oriani, 30-00197 Roma, Italy Tel:(39-06)802461 http://ita.mofa.go.kr

Kazakhstan *Amb. Cho Yong-chun* Add: Office No.91, 92, 93 Kaskad business-centre, Kabanbai Batyr Av.6/1 Astana, 010000 Kazakhstan Tel:(7-7172)925-591 http://kaz.mofa.go.kr

Kyrgyz Republic *Amb. Jung Byeong-hoo* Add:35, Str. Akhunbaev, Bishkek, Kyrgyz Republic, 720005 Tel:(996)312-579-771 http://kgz.mofa.go.kr

Netherlands *Amb. Choe Jong-hyun* Add:Verlengde Tolweg 8, 2517 JV The Hague, Netherlands Tel:(31-70)740-0200 http://nld.mofa.go.kr

Norway *Amb. Lee Byung-hwa* Add: Inkognitogaten 3, 0244 Oslo, Norway Tel: (47)2254-7090 http://nor.mofa.go.kr

Poland *Amb. Hong Ji-in* Add:ul. Szwolezerow 6, 00-464 Warssaw, Poland Tel:(48-22)559-2900 http://pol.mofa.go.kr

Portugal *Amb. Lee Yoon* Add:Av. Miguel Bombarda 36-7, 1051-802 Lisboa, Portugal Tel:(351-21)793-7200 http://prt.mofa.go.kr

Romania *Amb. Park Hyo-sung* Add:2nd Floor, Blvd. Primaverii, Nr.29, Sector 1, Bucharest, Romania Tel:(40-21)230-7198 http://rou.mofa.go.kr

Russia *Amb. Park Ro-byug* Add:St. Plyushchikha 56 bldg 1, Moscow Russia Tel:(7-495)783-2727 http://rus-moscow.mofa.go.kr

Serbia *Amb. Lee Do-hoon* Add:Milosa Savcica 4, 11040 Belgrade, Serbia Tel:(381-11)3674-225 http://srb.mofa.go.kr

Slovakia *Amb. Park Sang-hoon* Add:Dunajska 4, 811 08, Bratislava, Slovakia Tel:(421-2)3307-0711 http://svk.mofa.go.kr

Spain *Amb. Park Hee-kwon* Add:C/Gonzalez Amigo 15, 28033 Madrid, Spain Tel:(34-91)353-2000 http://esp.mofa.go.kr

Sweden *Amb. Son Sung-hwan* Add: Laboratoriegatan 10, 115 27 Stockholm, Sweden Tel:(46-8)5458-9400 http://swe.mofa.go.kr

Switzerland *Amb. Bae Young-han* Add: Kalcheggweg 38, P.O. Box 301, 3000 Bern 15, Switzerland Tel:(41-31)356-2444 http://che-berne.mofa.go.kr

Tajikistan *Amb. Agent. Yom Kee-young* Add:61, Ghani Abdullo street, Dushanbe, Republic of Tajikistan Tel:(992-44) 600-2114 http://tjk.mofa.go.kr

Turkey *Amb. Cho Yun-soo* Add:Alacam Sok No.5, Cinnah Caddesi, Ankara 06690, Turkey Tel:(90-312)468-4821 http://tur-ankara.mofa.go.kr

Turkmenistan *Amb. Chung Tae-in* Add:

744005, Azadi str., 17a, Ashgabat, Turkmenistan Tel:(993-12)94-72-86 http://tkm.mofa.go.kr

Ukraine *Amb. Sul Kyung-hoon* Add: Volodymyrska St.,01001, Kyiv, Ukriane Tel:(38-044)246-3759 http://ukr.mofa.go.kr

United Kingdom *Amb. Lim Sung-nam* Add: 60 Buckingham Gate, London SW1E 6AJ, U.K Tel:(44-20)7227-5500 http://gbr.mofa.go.kr

Uzbekistan *Amb. Lee Wook-heon* Add: Afrosiab st. 7, Tashkent, 100029, Uzbekistan Tel:(998-71)252-3151 http://uzb.mofa.go.kr

<MIDDLE EAST-AFRICA>

Algeria *Amb. Park Sang-jin* Add:23 Chemin de la madeleine chekiken, Hydra, Alger Tel:(213)21-546555 http://dza.mofa.go.kr

Angola *Amb. Lee Kyong-yul* Add:Centro de Convencoes(chalet A101) Talatona, Luanda-Sul, Angola Tel:(244)222-006-067 http://ago.mofa.go.kr

Bahrain *Amb. Yu Joon-ha* Add:Villa 401, Road 915, Al Salmaniya 309, Manama, Kingdom of Bahrain Tel:(973)1753-1120 http://nma.mofa.go.kr

Cameroon *Amb. Lim Jae-hoon* Add:P.O.Box 13286, Yaounde, Cameroon Tel:(237)2220-3756 http://cmr.mofa.go.kr

Congo(D.R.) *Amb. Kwon Ki-Chang* Add:63 Ave. de la Justice, Gombe, Kinshasa, Democratic Republic of Congo Tel:(243-1)503-5001 http://congo.mofa.go.kr

Cote d'ivoire *Amb. Surh Sung-yol* Add:01BP 3950 Abidjan 01, Rue Saint Marie, Lot 18~19, Cocody Sud, Abidjan, Cote d'ivoire Tel:(225)2248-6701 http://civ.mofa.go.kr

Egypt *Amb. Chung Kwang-kyun* Add:3 Boulos Hanna St, Dokki, Cairo, A.R.E Tel:(20-2)3761-1234 http://egy.mofa.go.kr

Ethiopia *Amb. Kim Moon-hwan* Add:P.O.Box 2047, Addis Ababa, Ethiopia Tel:(251-113)728111 http://eth.mofa.go.kr

Gabon *Amb. Choe Cheol-kyu* Add:B.P.2620, Libreville, Gabon Tel:(00241)0173-4000 http://gab.mofa.go.kr

Ghana *Amb. Lyeo Woon-Ki* Add:P.O. BOX. GP 13700, No.3 Abokobi Rd. East Cantonments Accra, Ghana Tel:(233-30)277-6157 http://gha.mofa.go.kr

Iran *Amb. Song Woong-yeob* Add:No. 2, West Daneshvar St, Sheikhbahai Ave, Vanak Sq, Tehran, Iran Tel:(98-21)8805-4900 http://irn.mofa.go.kr

Iraq *Amb. Cho Jung-won* Add:M915 St.10 H11 Babilon Street, Al-Jadria, Baghdad Tel:(964-77)0725-2006 http://irq.mofa.go.kr

Israel *Amb. Lee Gun-tae* Add:3rd Fl. 4 Hasadnaot St., Herzliya Pituach 46728 Tel:(972)9-951-0318 http://isr.mofa.go.kr

Jordan *Amb. Choi Hong-ghi* Add:P.O. Box 3060, Amman 11181, Jordan Tel:(962-6)593-0745 http://jor.mofa.go.kr

Kenya *Amb. Choi Dong-gyou* Add:1st&2nd Floor, Misha Tower, Westlands Road, P.O. Box 30455-00100, Nairobi, Kenya Tel:(254-20)361-5000 http://ken.mofa.go.kr

Kuwait *Amb. Shin Boo-nam* Add:Plot 6, Block 7A, Diplomatic Zone 2, Mishref, Kuwait Tel:(965)2537-8621 http://kwt.mofa.go.kr

Lebanon *Amb. Choi Jong-il* Add:Diplomat Bld.2F, Presidential Palace street, Baabda P.O.Box 40-290 Baabda, Lebanon Tel:(961-5)953167 http://lbn.mofa.go.kr

Libya *Amb. Kim Young-chae* Add:P.O. Box 4781/5160, Abounawas Area, Gargaresh St., Tripoli, Libya Tel:(218-21)483-1322 http://lby.mofa.go.kr

Morocco *Amb. Park Dong-sil* Add:41 Av. Mehdi Ben Barka, Souissi, Rabat. Morocco Tel:(212-537)75-1767 http://mar.mofa.go.kr

Nigeria *Amb. Noh Kyu-duk* Add:No9 Ovia Crescent Off Pope John Paul II Street Maitama, P.O. Box 6870, Abuja, Federal Republic of Nigeria Tel:(234-9)461-2701 http://nga-abuja.mofa.go.kr

Oman *Amb. Kim Dae-sik* Add:P.O.Box 377, Madinat Qaboos, Postal Code 115, Sultan-ate of Oman Tel:(968)2469-1490 http://omn.mofa.go.kr

Qatar *Amb. Park Heung-kyeong* Add:P.O. BOX 3727, West Bay, Diplomatic Area, Doha, Qatar Tel:(974)4483-2238 http://qat.mofa.go.kr

Rwanda *Amb. Park Yong-min* Add:Plot No. 10050, Nyarutarama, Kigali, Rwanda, P.O. BOX 6404 Tel:(250)252-577-577 http://rwa.mofa.go.kr

Saudi Arabia *Amb. Kim Jin-soo* Add:P.O. Box 94399, Riyadh 11693, Saudi Arabia Tel:(966-11)488-2211 http://sau.mofa.go.kr

Senegal *Amb. Shin Jong-won* Add:Villa Hamoudy, Rue Aime Cesaire, Fann Residence, Dakar, Senegal Tel:(221-33)824-0672 http://sen.mofa.go.kr

South Africa *Amb. Choi Yeon-ho* Add:Greenpark Estates #3, 27 George Storrar Drive, Groenkloof, Pretoria 0181 Tel:(012)460-2508 http://zaf.mofa.go.kr

Sudan *Amb. Park Won-sup* Add:House No.55, Al-Jazira Street 56, Khartoum2, P.O. Box 2414 Khartoum, Sudan Tel:(249)1-8358-0031 http://sdn.mofa.go.kr

Tanzania *Amb. Chung Il* Add:19th floor, Golden Jubilee Towers, Ohio Street, City Centre, P.O.Box 1154, Dar es Salaam Tel:(255-22)211-6086 http://tza.mofa.go.kr

Tunisia *Amb. Kim Jong-seok* Add:3 Rue de l'Alhambra, Mutuelleville, B.P.297, 1002 Tunis, Tanzania Tel:(216)71-799-905 http://tun.mofa.go.kr

Uganda *Amb. Park Jong-dae* Add:Plot 14, Ternan Road, Nakasero, Kampala, Uganda Tel:(256-414)500-197

United Arab Emirates *Amb. Kwon Hae-ryong* Add:P.O.Box 3270, Abu Dhabi, United Arab Emirates Tel:(971-2)441-1520 http://are.mofa.go.kr

Yemen *Amb. Lee Young-ho* Add:House No.4(Off Iran St), Sana'a, Yemen Tel:(967-1)431-801 http://yem.mofa.go.kr

Zimbabwe *Amb. Kwon Yong-kyu* Add:3rd Floor, Redbridge, Eastgate Building, 3rd Street, Robert Mugabe Road, Harare, Zimbabwe Tel:(263-4)756-541 http://zwe.mofa.go.kr

<PERMANENT MISSIONS>

ASEAN *Amb. Suh Jeong-in* Add:Jalan Jenderal Gatot Subroto Kav. 57, Jakarta Selatan 12950 Tel:(62-21)2967 2570 http://asean.mofa.go.kr

EU *Amb. Ahn Chong-ghee* Add:Chaussee de la Hulpe 173-175, 1170 Brussels, Belgium Tel:(32-2)675-5777 http://missiontoeu.mofa.go.kr

Geneva *Amb. Choi Seok-young* Add:1 Avenue de l'Ariana, Case Postale 42, 1211 Geneva 20, Switzerland Tel:(41-22)748-0000 http://che-geneva.mofa.go.kr

ICAO *Amb. Hur Jin* Add:1250 Rene-Levesque Boulevard West, Suite 3600, Montreal H3B 4W8 Tel:(514)845-2555 http://can-montreal.mofa.go.kr

Taipei *Amb. Cho Baek-sang* Add:Rm.1506, 15F. No. 333, Sec.1, KeeLung Road, Taipei Tel:(886-2)2758-8320 http://taiwan.mofa.go.kr

OECD *Amb. Lee Si-hyung* Add:4, place de la porte de passy 75016 Paris, France Tel:(33-1)4405-2050 http://oecd.mofa.go.kr

UN *Amb. Oh Joon* Add:335 East, 45th Street, New York, NY10017, U.S.A. Tel:(212) 439-4000 http://un.mofa.go.kr

UNESCO *Amb. Lee Byong-hyun* Add:33 Avenue de Maine 75015 Paris, France Tel:(33-1)4410-2400 http://unesco.mofa.go.kr

CONSULATES GENERAL

<ASIA-PACIFIC>

Chengdu *Con.-Gen. Ahn Sung-kook* Add:19F, Paradise Oasis Mansion, No.6 Xia Nan Da Jie Avenue, Chengdu, Sichuan 610016 P.R. China Tel:(028)8616-5800 http://chn-chengdu.mofa.go.kr

Chennai *Con.-Gen. Kim Kyung-soo* Add:5th Floor, Bannari Amman Towers, Dr. Radha Krishnan Road, Mylapore, Chennai 600 004 Tel:(91-44)4061-5500 http://ind-chennai.mofa.go.kr

Fukuoka *Con.-Gen. Park Jin-woong* Add:1-1-3 Jigyohama Chuo-ku Fukuoka, Japan 810-0065 Tel:(81-92)771-0461 http://jpn-fukuoka.mofa.go.kr

Guangzhou *Con.-Gen. Hwang Soon-taik* Add:No.18, Youlin Road3, Chigang Consulate Area, Haizhu District, Guangzhou, 510310, P.R.China Tel:(86-20)2919-2999 http://chn-guangzhou.mofa.go.kr

Hiroshima *Con.-Gen. Seo Jang-eun* Add:4-22, Higashikouzin-Machi Minami-Ku, Hiroshima-Shi Japan Tel:(81-82)568-0502 http://jpn-hiroshima.mofa.go.kr

Hochiminh *Con.-Gen. Park Noh-wan* Add:107 Nguyen Du, Dist 1, hochiminh, Vietnam Tel:(84-8)3822-5757 http://vnm-hochiminh.mofa.go.kr

Hong kong *Con.-Gen. Kim Kwang-dong* Add:5-6/F, Far East Finance Centre, 16 Harcourt Road, Hong Kong Tel:(852)2529-4141 http://hkg.mofa.go.kr

Kobe *Con.-Gen. Lee Seong-kweun* Add:2-21-5, Hyogo-ken, Kobe-shi, Chuo-Ku, Nakayamatedori, Japan Tel:(81-78)221-4853 http://jpn-kobe.mofa.go.kr

Mumbai *Con.-Gen. Jang Seok-gu* Add:Kanchanjunga Bldg., 9th Floor, 72, Peddar Road, Mumbai 400026, India Tel:(91-22)2388-6743 http://ind-mumbai.mofa.go.kr

Nagoya *Con.-Gen. Park Whan-seon* Add:1-19-12, Meieki Minami, Nakamura-ku, Nagoya, Japan Tel:(81-52)586-9221 http://jpn-nagoya.mofa.go.kr

Niigata *Con.-Gen. Cho Kun-hee* Add:8th Floor, Bandaijima Building, Bandaijima 5-1, Niigata-city, Niigata, Japan Tel:(81-25)255-5555 http://jpn-niigata.mofa.go.kr

Osaka *Con.-Gen. Ha Tae-yun* Add:2-3-4, Nishi-sinsaibashi, Chuo-ku, Osaka, Japan Tel:(81-6)6213-1401 http://jpn-osaka.

Qingdao *Con.-Gen. Lee Soo-john* Add:#101 Hongkong East Rd., Qingdao 266061, China Tel:(86-532)8897-6001 http://qingdao.mofa.go.kr

Sapporo *Con.-Gen. Han Hye-jin* Add:1-4, Nishi 12, Kita2, Chuo-ku, Sapporo, Hokkaido, Japan Tel:(81-11)218-0288 http://jpn-sapporo.mofa.go.kr

Sendai *Con.-Gen. Yang Gae-hwa* Add:1-4-3 Kamisugi, Aoba-Ku, Sendai, Miyagi, Japan Tel:(81-22)221-2751 http://jpn-sendai.mofa.go.kr

Shanghai *Con.-Gen. Han Suk-hee* Add:60 WanShan Road, Shanghai, China Tel:(86-21)6295-5000 http://chn-shanghai.mofa.go.kr

Shenyang *Con.-Gen. Shin Bong-sup* Add:No. 37, South 13 Latitude Road, Heping District, Shenyang, Liaoning, 110003 P.R China Tel:(86-24)2385-3388 http://chn-shenyang.mofa.go.kr

Sydney *Con.-Gen. Lee Whie-jin* Add:Level 13, 111 Elizabeth St, Sydney NSW 2000 Australia Tel:(61-2)9210-0200 http://aus-sydney.mofa.go.kr

Wuhan *Con.-Gen. Chung Jae-nam* Add:4F, Pudong Development Bank B/D, 218, Xinhua-Road, Jianghan-District, Wuhan, Hubei 430022 P.R.China Tel:(027)8556-1085 http://chn-wuhan.mofa.go.kr

Xian *Con.-Gen. Lee Kang-kuk* Add:19F, HIBC, 33# Keji Road, GaoXin Hi-Tech Industries Development Zone, Xian, Shaanxi, China 710075 Tel:(86-29)8835-1001 http://chn-xian.mofa.go.kr

Yokohama *Con.-Gen. Joo Joong-chul* Add:118, Yamate-cho, Naka-ku, Yokohama, Japan Tel:(81-45)621-4531 http://jpn-yokohama.mofa.go.kr

<AMERICA>

Atlanta *Con.-Gen. Kim Seong-jin* Add:229 Peachtree Street Ne, Suite 2100, Interantion Tower, Atlanta, GA 30303, U.S.A Tel:(1-404)522-1611 http://usa-atlanta.mofa.go.kr

Boston *Con.-Gen. Ohm Song-jun* Add:300 Washington Street(One Gateway Center), Suite 251, 300 Washington Street, Newton, MA 02458, U.S.A Tel:(1-617)641-2830 http://usa-boston.mofa.go.kr

Chicago *Con.-Gen. Kim Sang-il* Add:NBC Tower 2700, 455 N. Cityfront Plaza Dr. Chicago, IL 60611, U.S.A Tel:(1-312)822-9485 http://usa-chicago.mofa.go.kr

Honolulu *Con.-Gen. Paik Ki-yup* Add:2756 Pali Highway Honolulu, Hawaii 96817, U.S.A Tel:(1-808)595-6109 http://usa-honolulu.mofa.go.kr

Houston *Con.-Gen. Baik Joo-hyeon* Add:1990 Post Oak Blvd. #1250, Houston, Texas 77056, U.S.A Tel:(1-713)961-0186 http://usa-houston.mofa.go.kr

Los Angeles *Con.-Gen. Kim Hyun-myung* Add:3243 Wil-shire Blvd., Los Angeles, CA 90010, U.S.A Tel:(1-213)385-9300 http://usa-losangeles.mofa.go.kr

Montreal *Con.-Gen. Hur Jin* Add:1250 Rene-Levesque Boulevard West, Suite 3600, Montreal H3B 4W8 Tel:(1-514)845-2555 http://can-montreal.mofa.go.kr

New York *Con.-Gen. Kim Ghee-whan* Add:460 Park Ave.(bet.57th&58th St.) 6th Fl.New York, NY 10022, U.S.A Tel:(1-646)674-6000 http://usa-newyork.mofa.go.kr

San Francisco *Con.-Gen. Han Dong-man* Add:3500 Clay Street, San Francisco, CA 94118, U.S.A Tel:(1-415)921-2251 http://usa-sanfrancisco.mofa.go.kr

Sao Paulo *Con.-Gen. Hong Young-jong* Add:Av. Paulista 37, 9 andar cj. 91-Bela Vista, Sao Paulo-SP, Brasil 01311-902 Tel:(55-11)3141-1278 http://bra-saopaulo.mofa.go.kr

Seattle *Con.-Gen. Moon Duk-ho* Add:2033 6th Avenue #1125, Seattle, WA 98121, U.S.A Tel:(1-206)441-1011 http://usa-settle.mofa.go.kr

Toronto *Con.-Gen. Kang Jeong-sik* Add:555 Avenue Road, Toronto, Ontario, Canada, M4V2J7 Tel:(1-416)920-3809 http://can-toronto.mofa.go.kr

Vancouver *Con.-Gen. Lee Kie-cheon* Add:Suite 1600, 1090 West Georgia Street Vancouver, British Columbia, Canada V6E 3V7 Tel:(1-604)681-9581 http://can-vancouver.mofa.go.kr

<EUROPE>

Frankfurt *Con.-Gen. Kim Young-hoon* Add:Lyoner Str. 34, 60528 Frankfurt am Main, Germany Tel:(49-69)956-7520 http://deu-frankfurt.mofa.go.kr

Hamburg *Con.-Gen. Chang See-jeong* Add:Kaiser-Wilhelm-Str 9, 20355 Hamburg. Germany Tel:(49-40)650-677-600 http://deu-hamburg.mofa.go.kr

Irkutsk *Con.-Gen. Park Chung-nam* Add:3F, st.Gagarin Blvd., 44, Irkutsk Russia Tel:(7-3952)250-301 http://rus-irkutsk.mofa.go.kr

Istanbul *Con.-Gen. Chun Tae-dong* Add:Kaptapasa Mah. Piyalepasa Bulvari No.73 Ortadogu Plaza K:18 Okmeydani 34484 Sisli, Istanbul, Turkey Tel:(90-212)368-8368 http://tur-istanbul.mofa.go.kr

Milano *Con.-Gen. Chang Jae-bok* Add:Piazza Cavour 3, 20121, Milano, ITALIA Tel:(39)02-2906-2641 http://ita-milano. mofa.go.kr

Stpetersburg *Con.-Gen. Lee Jin-hyun* Add:St. Nekrasova 32-A, St. Petersburg, 191014, Russia Tel:(7-812)448-1909 http:// rus-stpetersburg.mofa.go.kr

Vladivostok *Con.-Gen. Lee Sok-bae* Add:Pologaya St. 19 Vladivostok 690091 Russia Tel:(7-423)240-2222 http://rus-vladivostok.mofa.go.kr

<MIDDLE EAST-AFRICA>

Dubai *Con.-Gen. Ahn Seong-doo* Add:Villa #39, Street 24b, Area 342, Jumeirah 2, Dubal Tel:(971-4)344-9200 http://are-dubai.mofa.go.kr

Jeddah *Con.-Gen. Oh Nak-young* Add:P. O.Box 55503 Jeddah 21544 Kingdom of Saudi Arabia Tel:(966-12)668-1990 http:// sau-jeddah.mofa.go.kr

CONSULATE AGENCIES

Almaty *Con.-Gen. Son Chi-keun* Add:050059, 52A, Ivanilov St. Gornyi Gigant, Almaty, 010000 Kazakhstan Tel:(7-727)246-8897 http://kaz-almaty.mofa.go.kr

Anchorage *Head of Consular Office Jeon Seung-min* Add:800 E. Dimond Blvd., STE 3-695, Anchorage, AK 99515, U.S.A Tel:(907)339-7955 http://usa-anchorage. mofa.go.kr

Auckland *Con.-Gen. Pak Yil-ho* Add:Level 12, Tower 1, 205 Queen Street, Auckland Central , New Zealand Tel:(64-9)379-0818 http://nzl-auckland.mofa.go.kr

Bonn *Con.-Gen. Kwon Sae-young* Add:Godesberger Allee 142-148, 3. Obergeschoss, 53175 Bonn, Bundesrepublik Deutschland Tel:(49-228)943-790 http:// deu-bonn.mofa.go.kr

Dalian *Head of Consular Office Bek Bum-hym* Add:FL Hongyuan building, Renmin Road, Zhongshan district, Dalian, 116001, China Tel:(86-411)8235-6288 http://chn-dalian.mofa.go.kr

Dallas *Head of Consular Office Kim Dong-chan* Add:14001 N. Dallas Parkway Ste.450, Dallas, TX 75240, U.S.A Tel:(972)701-0180 http://usa-dallas.mofa.go.kr

Hagatna *Head of Consular Office Yoon Sang-don* Add:125C Tun Jose Camacho St., Tamuning, Guam 96913 U.S.A Tel:(1-671)647-6488 http://usa-hagatna.mofa. go.kr

Karachi *Con.-Gen. Lee Chang-hee* Add:101, 29th Street(Off. Khayaban-e-Mohafiz) Phase VI, DHA, Karachi, Pakistan Tel:(92-21)3585-3950 http://pak-karachi. mofa.go.kr

Lagos *Con.-Gen. Kim Gyu-young* Add:Plot 10A&B, Layi Ajayi Bembe Street, Parkview, Ikoyi, Lagos, Nigeria Tel:(234-1)271-6295 http://nga-lagos.mofa.go.kr

Las Palmas *Con.-Gen. Lee Jum-soo* Add:Luis Doreste Silva 60-1, 35004 Las Palmas de Gran Canaria, Spain Tel:(34-928)23-0499 http://esp-las.mofa.go.kr

Melbourne *Con.-Gen. JO Hong-ju* Add:Level 10, 636 St Kilda Rd, Melbourne VIC 3004, Australia Tel:(61-3)9533-3800 http://mel.mofa.go.kr

Yuzhno-Sakhalinsk *Head of Consular Office Sagong Jang-taek* Add:283 Bm Lenin St., Yuzhno-Sakhalinsk, Russia Tel:(7-4242)462-430

DIPLOMATIC MISSIONS IN KOREA

EMBASSIES

Afghanistan *Amb. Agent. Mohammad Saleem Sayeb* Add:Rm.101 Hyoungwoo Bestvill 90, Dokseodang-ro, Yongsan-gu, Seoul Tel:(02)793-3535

Algeria *Amb. DERRAGUI Mohammed Elamine* Add:81, Hoenamu-ro, Yongsan-gu, Seoul Tel:(02)794-5034 http://www. algerianemb.or.kr

Angola *Amb. Albino Malungo* Add:102, Dokseodang-ro, Yongsan-gu, Seoul Tel:(02)792-8463 http://www.angolaembassy.or.kr

Argentina *Amb. Jorge roballo* Add:5F, Cheonwoo Bldg., 206, Noksapyeong-daero, Yongsan-gu, Seoul Tel:(02)796-8144

Austria *Amb. Elisabeth Bertagnoli* Add:21F,

Kyobo Bldg., 1, Jong-ro, Jongno-gu, Seoul Tel:(02)732-9071 http://www.bmeia.gv.at

Australia Amb. *William Paterson* Add:19F, Kyobo Bldg., 1, Jong-ro, Jongno-gu, Seoul Tel:(02)2003-0100 http://www.southkorea. embassy.gov.au

Azerbaijan *Amb. Agent. Ramzi Teymurov* Add:14, Hannam-daero 27-gil, Yongsan-gu, Seoul Tel:(02)797-1765 http://www. azembassy.co.kr

Bangladesh *Amb. Md. Khandker Masudul Alam* Add:17, Jangmun-ro 6-gil, Yongsan-gu, Seoul Tel:(02)796-4056 http://www. bdembseoul.org

Belarus *Amb. Natallia Zhylevich* Add:252-21, Dongho-ro 17-gil, Jung-gu, Seoul Tel:(02)2237-8171 http://www.belarus. or.kr

Belgium *Amb. Francois Bontemps* Add:23, Itaewon-ro 45-gil, Yongsan-gu, Seoul Tel:(02)749-0381 http://www.diplomatie. be/seoulfr

Bolivia *Amb. Guadalupe Palomeque De Taboada* Add:6, Eulji-ro, Jung-gu, Seoul Tel:(02)318-1767

Brazil *Amb. Edmundo Sussumu Fujita* Add:4~5F, Ihn Gallery Bldg., 73, Cheongwadae-ro, Jongno-gu, Seoul Tel:(02)738-4970 http://seul.itamaraty.gov.br/pt-br

Brunei *Amb. Agent. Amalina Bakar* Add:133, Jahamun-ro, Jongno-gu, Seoul Tel:(02)790-1078

Bulguria *Amb. Petar Andonov* Add:102-8, Hannam-daero, Yongsan-gu, Seoul Tel:(02)794-8625

Cambodia *Amb. Suth Dina* Add:12, Daesagwan-ro 20-gil, Yongsan-gu, Seoul Tel:(02)3785-1041

Canada *Amb. Eric Walsh* Add:21, Jeongdong-gil, Jung-gu, Seoul Tel:(02)3783-6000 http:// www.korea.gc.ca

Chile *Amb. Hernan Brantes Glavic* Add:97, Toegye-ro, Jung-gu, Seoul Tel:(02)779-2610 http://www.coreachile.org

China *Amb. Qiu Guohong* Add:27, Myeong-dong 2-gil, Jung-gu, Seoul Tel:(02)738-1038 http://www.chinaemb.or.kr

Colombia *Amb. Tito Saul Pinilla Pinilla* Add:11F, Kyobo Bldg., 1, Jong-ro, Jongno-gu, Seoul Tel:(02)720-1369

Congo(D.R.) *Amb. Ngwey Ndambo Christophe* Add:30, Saemunan-ro 3-gil, Jongno-gu, Seoul Tel:(02)722-7958

Costa Rica *Amb. Agent. Jario Lopez* Add:45, Mapo-daero, Mapo-gu, Seoul Tel:(02)707-9249 http://www.ecostarica.or.kr

Cote d'ivoire *Amb. Sylvestre Kouassi Bile* Add:31 Hannam-daero, Yongsan-gu, Seoul Tel:(02)3785-0561 http://cotedivoireembassy. or.kr

Czech Republic *Amb. Tomas Husak* Add:17, Gyeonghuigung 1-gil, Jongno-gu, Seoul Tel:(02)720-6453 http://www.mzv.cz

Denmark *Amb. Thomas Lehmann* Add:5F, Namsong Bldg., 272, Sowol-ro, Yongsan-gu, Seoul Tel:(02)795-4187 http://sydkorea. um.dk

Dominica Republic *Amb. Grecia F. Pichardo Polanco* Add:F19, Taepyeong Bldg., 73, Sejong-daero, Jung-gu, Seoul Tel:(02)756-3513 http://www.embadom.or.kr

Ecuador *Amb. Oscar Gustavo Herrera Gilbert* Add:19F, Standard Chartard Bank Bldg., 47, Jong-ro, Jongno-gu, Seoul Tel:(02)739-2401 http://www.ecuadorkorea.or.kr

Egypt *Amb. Hany Moawad Selim Labib* Add:114, Dokseodang-ro, Yongsan-gu, Seoul Tel:(02)749-0787

El salvador *Amb. Agent. Jason Manuel Castro Olivares* Add:20F, Samsunglife Bldg., 55, Sejong-daero, Jung-gu, Seoul Tel:(02)753-3432 http://cafe.daum.net/elsalvadorencorea

Ethiopia *Amb. Dibaba Abdetta* Add:20, Hoenamu-ro 44-gil, Yongsan-gu, Seoul Tel:(02)790-9766

Fiji *Amb. Filimone Kau* Add:64, Hoenamu-ro, Yongsan-gu, Seoul Tel:(02)792-6396

Finland *Amb. Matti Helmonen* Add:18F, Kyobo Bldg., 1, Jong-ro, Jongno-gu, Seoul Tel:(02)732-6737 http://www.finland.or.kr

France *Amb. Jerome Pasquier* Add:43-12, Seosomun-ro, Seodaemun-gu, Seoul Tel: (02)3149-4300 http://www.ambafrance-kr.org

Gabon *Amb. Carlos Victor Boungou* Add:4F, Yousung Bldg., 239, Itaewon-ro, Yongsan-gu, Seoul Tel:(02)793-9575

Georgia *Amb. Nikoloz Apkhazava* Add:30, Itaewon-ro 27-gil, Yongsan-gu, Seoul Tel:(02)792-7118

Germany *Amb. Rolf Mafael* Add:32, 8F, Seoul Square, 416 Hangang-daero, Jung-gu, Seoul Tel:(02)748-4114 http://www. seoul.diplo.de

Ghana *Amb. Elizabeth Nicol* Add:120, Dokseodang-ro, Yongsan-gu, Seoul Tel:(02)3785-1427 http://www.ghanaembassy.or.kr

Greece *Amb. Dionysios Sourvanos* Add:F27, Hanwha Bldg., 86, Cheonggyecheon-ro, Jung-gu, Seoul Tel:(02)729-1401

Guatemala *Amb. Gustavo Adolfo Lopez Calderon* Add:614ho Lotte Bldg., 30, Eulji-ro, Jung-gu, Seoul Tel:(02)771-7582

Holy See *Amb. Archbishop Osvaldo Padilla* Add:19, Jahamun-ro 26-gil, Jongno-gu, Seoul Tel:(02)736-5725

Honduras *Amb. Michel Idiaquez Baradat* Add:22F, Jongno Tower Bldg., 51, Jong-ro, Jongno-gu, Seoul Tel:(02)738-8402

Hungary *Amb. Gabor Csaba* Add:58, Jangmun-ro, Yongsan-gu, Seoul Tel:(02)792-2105 http://www.mfa.gov.hu

India *Amb. Vikram Kumar Doraiswami* Add:101, Dokseodang-ro, Yongsan-gu, Seoul Tel:(02)798-4257 http://www.indembassy.or.kr

Indonesia *Amb. John Aristianto Prasetio* Add:380, Yeouidaebang-ro, Yeongdeungpo-gu, Seoul Tel:(02)783-5675 http://kbriseoul.kr/kbriseoul

Iran *Amb. Hassan Taherian* Add:45, Jangmun-ro, Yongsan-gu, Seoul Tel:(02)793-7751 http://seoul.mfa.ir

Iraq *Amb. Khalil Ismail Abdul Sahib Al-Mosawi* Add:55, Jangmun-ro, Yongsan-gu, Seoul Tel:(02)790-4202

Ireland *Amb. Aingeal O'Donoghue* Add:13F, Leema Bldg., 42, Jong-ro 1-gil, Jongno-gu, Seoul Tel:(02)721-7200 http://www.embassyofireland.or.kr

Israel *Amb. Uri Gutman* Add:18F, Cheongye11 Bldg., 11, Cheonggyecheon-ro, Jongno-gu, Seoul Tel:(02)3210-8500 http://seoul.mfa.gov.il

Italy *Amb. Sergio Mercuri* Add:3F, Ilshin Bldg, 98, Hannam-daero, Yongsan-gu, Seoul Tel:(02)796-0491 http://www.ambseoul.esteri.it

Japan *Amb. Koro Bessho* Add:22, Yulgok-ro 2-gil, Jongno-gu, Seoul Tel:(02)2170-5200 http://www.kr.emb-japan.go.jp

Jordan *Amb. Omar Al Nahar* Add:B-dong 6F, Twin Tree Bldg., 6, Yulgok-ro, Jongno-gu, Seoul Tel:(02)318-2897 http://www.jordankorea.gov.jo

Kazakhstan *Amb. Dulat Bakishev* Add:24, UN village-gil, Yongsan-gu, Seoul Tel:(02)394-9716 http://www.kazembassy.org

Kenya *Amb. Mohamed Abdi Gello* Add:38, Hoenamu-ro 44-gil, Yongsan-gu, Seoul Tel:(02)3785-2903 http://www.kenya-embassy.or.kr

Kuwait *Amb. Jasem Mohammad Albudaiwi* Add:34, Jangmun-ro, Yongsan-gu, Seoul Tel:(02)749-3688

Kyrgyz Republic *Amb. Duishonkul Chotonov* Add:Rm.403 Namsong Bldg., 272, Sowol-ro,

Yongsan-gu, Seoul Tel:(02)379-0951

Laos *Amb. Khamla Xayachack* Add:Han Starvil, 30-4, Daesagwan-ro 11-gil, Yongsan-gu, Seoul Tel:(02)796-1713

Lebanon *Amb. Elias Nicolas* Add:29, Jangmun-ro, Yongsan-gu, Seoul Tel:(02)794-6482

Libya *Amb. Otman S. Saad Ahbara* Add:24, UN village-gil, Yongsan-gu, Seoul Tel:(02)797-6001

Malaysia *Amb. Dato' Rohana Binti Ramli* Add:129, Dokseodang-ro, Yongsan-gu, Seoul Tel:(02)795-9203 http://www.malaysia.or.kr

Marshall Island *Amb. Kejjo Bien* Add:109, Mapo-daero, Mapo-gu, Seoul Tel:(02)714-7175

Mexico *Amb. Jose Luis Bernal Rodriguez* Add:93, Dokseodang-ro, Yongsan-gu, Seoul Tel:(02)798-1694 http://embamex.sre.gob.mx

Mongolia *Amb. Baasanjav Ganbold* Add: 95, Dokseodang-ro, Yongsan-gu, Seoul Tel: (02)798-3464 http://www.mongolembassy.com

Morocco *Amb. Mohammed Chraibi* Add:4F, Hannam Tower, 14, Hannam-daero 27-gil, Yongsan-gu, Seoul Tel:(02)793-6249

Myanmar *Amb. Soe Lwin* Add:12, Hannam-daero 28-gil, Yongsan-gu, Seoul Tel:(02)790-3814

Nepal *Amb. Kaman Singh Lama* Add:19, Seonjam-ro 2-gil, Seongbuk-gu, Seoul Tel: (02)3789-9770 http://www.nepembseoul.gov.np

Netherland *Amb. Aloijsius Johannes Adrianus Embrechts* Add:10F, Jeongdong Bldg., 21-15, Jeongdong-gil, Jung-gu, Seoul Tel:(02)311-8600 http://southkorea.nlembassy.org

New zealand *Amb. Clare Patricia Fearnley* Add:8F, Jeongdong Bldg., 21-15, Jeongdong-gil, Jung-gu, Seoul Tel:(02)3701-7700 http://www.nzembassy.com

Nigeria *Amb. Desmond Akawor* Add:13, Jangmun-ro 6-gil, Yongsan-gu, Seoul Tel:(02) 797-2370 http://www.nigerianembassy.or.kr

Norway *Amb. Torbjorn Holthe* Add:13F, Jeongdong Bldg., 21-15, Jeongdong-gil, Jung-gu, Seoul Tel:(02)727-7100 http://www.norway.or.kr

Oman *Amb. Mohamed Salim Hamood Alharthy* Add:9, Saemunan-ro 3-gil, Jongno-gu, Seoul Tel:(02)790-2431

Pakistan *Amb. Zahid Nasrullah Khan* Add:39, Jangmun-ro 9ga-gil, Yongsan-gu, Seoul Tel:(02)796-8252 http://www.pkembassy.or.kr

Panama *Amb. Ruben Eloy Arosemena Valdes* Add:14, Hannam-daero 27, Yongsan-gu, Seoul Tel:(02)734-8610

Papua New Guinea *Amb. Bill Veri* Add: Rm.210 Doosan we've pavilion, 81, Sambong-ro, Jongno-gu, Seoul Tel:(02)2198-5771 http://www.papuanewguineaembassy.kr

Paraguay *Amb. Ceferino Adrian Valdez Peralta* Add:3F, Hannam Tower, 14, Hannam-daero 27-gil, Yongsan-gu, Seoul Tel:(02)792-8335 http://www.embaparcorea.org

Peru *Amb. Jaime Antonio Pomareda Montenegro* Add:Rm.2002 Daeyeongak Bldg., 97, Toegye-ro, Jung-gu, Seoul Tel:(02)757-1735

Philippines *Amb. Raul S. Hernandez* Add:12, Hoenamu-ro 42-gil, Yongsan-gu, Seoul Tel:(02)796-7387 http://www.philembassy-seoul.com

Poland *Amb. Krzysztof Ignacy Majka* Add:20-1, Samcheong-ro, Jongno-gu, Seoul Tel:(02)723-9681 http://seul.msz.gov.pl

Portugal *Amb. Antonio Quinteiro Nobre* Add:2F, Wonseo Bldg., 13, Changdeokgung 1-gil, Jongno-gu, Seoul Tel:(02)3675-2251 http://www.portugalseoul.com

Qatar *Amb. Mohammed Bin Abdalla Obaid Al-Dohaimi* Add:48, Jangmun-ro, Yongsan-gu, Seoul Tel:(02)798-2444

Rumania *Amb. Calin Fabian* Add:50, Jangmun-ro, Yongsan-gu, Seoul Tel:(02)797-4924

Russia *Amb. Konstantin Vasilievich Vnukov* Add:43, Seosomun-ro 11-gil, Jung-gu, Seoul Tel:(02)318-2116 http://russian-embassy.org

Rwanda *Amb. Emma-Francoise Isumbingabo* Add:Rm.503 Suyeong Bldg., 13, Hannam-daero 20-gil, Yongsan-gu, Seoul Tel:(02)798-1052 http://www.rwanda-embassy.or.kr

Saudi Arabia *Amb. Ahmad Younos Al-Barrak* Add:37, Noksapyeong-daero 26-gil, Yongsan-gu, Seoul Tel:(02)739-0631

Senegal *Amb. Mamadou Ndiaye* Add:Rm.501 Daeyeongak Bldg., 97, Toegye-ro, Jung-gu, Seoul Tel:(02)745-5554

Serbia *Amb. Zoran Kazazovic* Add:14, Hannam-daero 27-gil, Yongsan-gu, Seoul Tel:(02)797-5109 http://www.embserb.or.kr

Sierra Leone *Amb. Omrie Michael Golley* Add:54, Seonjam-ro 2ra-gil, Seongbuk-gu, Seoul Tel:(02)741-0038 http://gsdemo230.giantsoft.co.kr

Singapore *Amb. Yip Wei Kiat* Add:28F, Seoul Finance Center, 136, Sejong-daero, Jung-gu, Seoul Tel:(02)774-2464 http://www.mfa.gov.sg

Slovakia *Amb. Milan Laiciak* Add:28, Hannam-daero 10-gil, Yongsan-gu, Seoul Tel:(02)794-3981

South Africa *Amb. Nozuko Gloria Bam* Add:104, Dokseodang-ro, Yongsan-gu, Seoul Tel:(02)792-4855 http://www.south-africa-embassy.or.kr

Spain *Amb. Gonzalo Ortiz* Add:17, Hannam-daero 36-gil, Yongsan-gu, Seoul Tel:(02)794-3581 http://www.exteriores.gob.es

Sri lanka *Amb. Watte Walawwe Tissa Wijeratne* Add:39, Dongho-ro 10-gil, Jung-gu, Seoul Tel:(02)735-2966

Sudan *Amb. Mohamed Abdelaal* Add:3F, Vivien Bldg., 52, Seobinggo-ro 51-gil, Yongsan-gu, Seoul Tel:(02)793-8692 http://www.sudanseoul.net

Sweden *Amb. Lars Gunnar Danielsson* Add:8F, Danam Bldg, 10, Sowol-ro, Jung-gu, Seoul Tel:(02)3703-3700 http://www.swedenabroad.com

Switzerland *Amb. Jorg Alois Reding* Add:20-16, Daesagwan-ro 11-gil, Yongsan-gu, Seoul Tel:(02)739-9511 http://www.eda.admin.ch

Tajikistan *Amb. Agent. Kiromov Salohiddin* Add:63, Mapo-daero, Mapo-gu, Seoul, Korea

Thailand *Amb. Kulkumut Singhara Na Ayudhaya* Add:33, Daesagwan-ro 42-gil, Yongsan-gu, Seoul Tel:(02)795-3098 www.thaiembassy.org

Timor Leste *Amb. Hernani F. Coelho Da Silva* Add:Rm.405 Hannam Tower, 14, Hannam-daero 27-gil, Yongsan-gu, Seoul Tel:(02)797-6151

Tunisia *Amb. Mohamed Ali Nafti* Add:8, Jangmun-ro 6-gil, Yongsan-gu, Seoul Tel:(02)790-4334

Turkey *Amb. Arslan Hakan Okcal* Add:4F, Vivien Bldg., 52, Seobinggo-ro 51-gil, Yongsan-gu, Seoul Tel:(02)3780-1600

Turkmenistan *Amb. Myrat Mammetalyyev* Add:31, Itaewon-ro 45-gil, Yongsan-gu, Seoul Tel:(02)796-9975

United Arab Emirates *Amb. Abdulla Al Romaithi* Add:118, Dokseodang-ro, Yongsan-gu, Seoul Tel:(02)790-3235 http://uae-embassy.ae

United Kingdom *Amb. Charles John Hay* Add:24, Sejong-daero 19-gil, Jung-gu, Seoul Tel:(02)3210-5500 http://www.gov.uk/government/world

United States of America *Amb. Mark W. Lippert* Add:188, Sejong-daero, Jongno-gu, Seoul Tel:(02)397-4114 http://seoul.usembassy.gov
Ukraine *Amb. Vasyl Marmazov* Add:21, Itaewon-ro 45-gil, Yongsan-gu, Seoul Tel:(02)790-5696 http://korea.mfa.gov.ua
Uruguay *Amb. Alba Florio Legnani* Add:Rm.402 Hannam Hiil Side , 8, Daesagwan-ro 12-gil, Yongsan-gu, Seoul Tel:(02)6245-3180 http://www.embrou.or.kr
Uzbekistan *Amb. Alisher Kurmanov* Add:Rm.701 Diplomatic Center, 2558, Nambusunhwan-ro, Seocho-gu, Seoul Tel:(02)574-6554 http://www.uzbekistan.or.kr
Venezuela *Amb. Agent. Yadira Hidalgo de Ortiz* Add:16F, Standard Chartard Bank Bldg., 47, Jong-ro, Jongno-gu, Seoul Tel:(02)732-1546 http://www.venezuelaemb.or.kr
Vietnam *Amb. Pham Huu Chi* Add:123, Bukchon-ro, Jongno-gu, Seoul Tel:(02)739-2065 http://www.travelvietnam.co.kr
Zambia *Amb. Mumba Smyth Kapumba* Add:2, Hoenamu-ro 44-gil, Yongsan-gu, Seoul, Korea Tel:(02)-793-1961

CONSULATES GENERAL

China(Busan) *Con.-Gen. YAN Fenglan* Add:25, Haeun-daero 394beon-gil, Haeun-dae-gu, Busan Tel:(051)743-7990 http://busan.china-consulate.org
China(Gwangju) *Con.-Cen. Wang Xian-min* Add:413, Daenam-daero, Nam-gu, Gwangju Tel:(062)385-8874 http://gwangju.china-consulate.org
China(Jeju) *Con.-Cen. Zhang Xin* Add:10, Cheongsa-ro 1-gil, Jeju-si, Jeju-do Tel:(064)900-8830 http://jeju.china-consulate.org
Japan(Busan) *Con.-Gen. Sadao Matsui* Add:18, Gogwan-ro, Dong-gu, Busan Tel:(051)465-5101 www.busan.kr.emb-japan.go.jp
Japan(Jeju) *Con.-Gen. Mitsuo Suzuki* Add:3351, 1100-ro, Jeju-si, Jeju-do Tel:(064)710-9500 http://www.jeju.kr.emb-japan.go.jp
United States of America(Busan) *Con.-Gen. Jonathan L. Yoo* Add:Rm.612 Lotte Gold Rose Bldg.,993, Jungang-daero, Busanjin-gu, Busan Tel:(051)863-0731 http://korean.busan.usconsulate.gov

Russia(Busan) *Con.-Gen. Vostrikov Alexander Sergeevich* Add:8F, Korea Exchange Bank Bldg., 94, Jungang-daero, Jung-gu, Busan Tel:(051)441-9904

REPRESENTATIVES

EU *Amb. Tomasz Kozlowski* Add:16F, S-Tower,82, Saemunan-ro, Jongno-gu, Seoul Tel:(02)3704-1700 http://eeas.europa.eu
Taipei *Con.-Gen. Ting Joseph Shih* Add:6F, Gwanghwamun Bldg., 149, Sejong-daero, Jongno-gu, Seoul Tel:(02)399-2760 http://www.roc-taiwan.org

HONORARY CONSULATES

Albania *Hon. Con.-Gen. Lee Kyung-won* Add:Rm.1114 24, Sinmunno 1-ga, Jongno-gu, Seoul Tel:(02)720-8690
Angola *Hon. Con. Kwon Yung-ho* Add:8F Inter-Burgo Bldg., 99 Samhaksa-ro, Songpa-gu, Seoul Tel:(02)413-5146
Antigua and Barbuda *Hon. Con. Rhee Sung-hee* Add:9F Hyunma Bldg., 40 Jongno 39gil, Jongno-gu, Seoul Tel:(02)742-9770
Australia *Hon. Con. Choi Yong-suk* Add:Rm.802 Samhwan Officetel, 11 jasung-ro 141beon-gil, Dong-gu, Busan Tel:(051)647-4006
Austria *Hon. Con. Cho Sung-je* Add:1817 Jungang-daero, Geumjeong-gu, Busan Tel:(051)519-2000
Bangladesh *Hon. Con.-Gen. Kim Gwang-ho* Add:Rm.409 ACE hitech city 775, Gyeongin-ro, Yeongdeungpo-gu, Seoul Tel:(02)888-8609 / *Hon. Con.-Gen. Lee Yong-yi* Add:Rm.914 Ocean Tower Bldg., 203, Haeundaehaebyeon-ro, Haeundae-gu, Busan Tel:(051)522-3500
Belarus *Hon. Con. Yoon Kyung-duk* Add:Rm.503 DMC Bldg., 330, Seongam-ro, Mapo-gu, Seoul Tel:(02)3153-7090
Belgium *Hon. Con. Choi Seung-bong* Add:100, Ijin-ro, Onsan-eup, Ulju-gun, Ulsan Tel:(052)231-0001
Belize *Hon. Con.-Gen. Pan Gi-ro* Add:8F, Bookook Securities Bldg., 17, Gukjegeu-myung-ro 6-gil, Yeongdeungpo-gu, Seoul

Tel:(02)799-2266

Benin *Hon. Con.-Gen. Kim Deok-sil* Add:Rm.301 Sukjung Bldg., 16, Nohae-ro 61-gil, Dobong-gu, Seoul Tel:070-7676-5226

Bhutan *Hon. Con.-Gen. Kim Han-young* Add:Rm.401 MES Bldg., 7 Hakdong-ro 6-gil, Gangnam-gu, Seoul Tel:(02)3444-5961

Bolivia *Hon. Con. Seo Seok-hae* Add:4F Donghwa Plaza Bldg., Baekseok-ro, Uijeongbu-si, Gyeonggi-do Tel:(031)826-0001

Botswana *Hon. Con. Kim Jong-chun* Add:158-15, Wanjusandan 3-ro, Bongdong-eup, Wanju_Gun, Jeollabuk-do Tel:(063)261-7555

Brazil *Hon. Con. Hyun Jeong-eun* Add:12F 194, Yulgok-ro, Jongno-gu, Seoul Tel:(02)3706-5005 / *Hon. Con. Choi Shin-won* Add:13F Naewei Bldg., 51 Eulji-ro, Jung-gu, Seoul Tel:(02)779-2036

Bulgaria *Hon. Con. Kim Hi-yong* Add:2~3F Daeyong Bldg., 7 Eonju-ro 133-gil, Gangnam-gu, Seoul Tel:(02)3014-2700 / *Hon. Con. Choi Kang-yong* Add:Rm.802 Baegang Bldg., 801, Seolleung-ro, Gangnam-gu, Seoul Tel:(02)542-2533

Cambodia *Hon. Con. Ku Jung-sook* Add:5F Bando Bldg., 59-1 Haegwan-ro, Jung-gu, Busan Tel:(051)465-1331 / Hon. Con. Seo Kyung-suk

Cameroon *Hon. Con. Cho Dong-soon* Add:Rm.1004 Renaissance Tower, 14 Mallijae-ro, Mapo-gu, Seoul Tel:(02)3272-2011

Canada *Hon. Con. Baek Jeong-ho* 44, Bibong-ro, Saha-gu, Busan Tel:(051)200-4533

Republic of Chad *Hon. Con. Adam Adji Ibrahim* Add:1F, 34, Itaewon-ro 36-gil, Yongsan-gu, Seoul Tel:(02)793-9564

Chile *Hon. Con. Kim Sung-tae* Add:391 Wonyang-ro, Saha-gu, Busan, Korea Tel:(051)200-1110 / *Hon. Con. Koo Cha-myung* Add:20F AsemTower, 524 Bongeunsa-ro, Gangnam-gu, Seoul Tel:(02)2189-9800

Colombia *Hon. Con. Goo Bon-sang* Add:10F, Prudential Tower Bldg., 298, Gangnam-daero, Gangnam-gu, Seoul Tel:(02)2033-0650

Congo *Hon. Con. Cho Don-young* Add:4F, Baegang Bldg., 801, Seolleung-ro, Gangnam-gu, Seoul Tel:(02)541-7700

Cote D'Ivoire *Hon. Con. Kim In-geuk*

Add:Juganinmulsa Bldg, 36 Jungang-daero 1778beon-gil, Geumjeong-gu, Busan Tel:(051)518-0051

Croatia *Hon. Con. Yang In-mo* Add:Rm.1002 Gangnam Bldg., 396, Seocho-daero, Seocho-gu, Seoul Tel:(02)3488-5102

Denmark *Hon. Con. Suhr Young-hwa* Add:1117 Byucksan e-Centum Class One, 99 Centum dong-ro, Haeundae-gu, Busan Tel:(051)244-9697

Djibouti *Hon. Con.-Gen. Lee Tae-young* Add:12F 34, Sangamsan-ro, Mapo-gu, Seoul Tel:(02)320-6103

Dominican Republic *Hon. Con.-Gen. Jun Byung-hyun* Add:27, Wiryeseong-daero 22-gil, Songpa-gu, Seoul Tel:(02)2146-5773 / *Hon. Con. Hwang Chul-soo* Add:216, Yeoksam-ro, Gangnam-gu, Seoul Tel:(02)563-7997

El Salvador *Hon. Con. Koo Cha-too* Add:13F Shin-an Bldg., 512 Teheran-ro, Gangnam-gu, Seoul Tel:(02)3467-0518 / *Hon. Con. Do Yong-bok* 5, Jungang-daero 691beonga-gil, Busanjin-gu, Busan Tel:(051)803-3311

Ecuador *Hon. Con. Kim Young-tae* Add:11F, Dcubecity Bldg., 662, Gyeongin-ro, Guro-gu, Seoul Tel:(02)735-3417 / *Hon. Con. Kim Eun-sun* Add:Boryung Bldg., 136, Changgyeonggung-ro, Jongno-gu, Seoul Tel:(02)708-8199

Eritrea *Hon. Con. Kim Eui-jae*

Estonia *Hon. Con. Kwon Young-soo* Add:17F LG Twin Towers., 128, Yeoui-daero, Yeongdeungpo-gu, Seoul Tel:(02)3777-0700

Ethiopia *Hon. Con.-Gen. Sung Woan-jong* Add:Rm.420 1, Uisadang-daero, Yeong-deungpo-gu, Seoul Tel: (02)784-8640

Fiji *Hon. Vice-Con. Lee Young-gi* Add:5F, Dukyoung Bldg., 64, Sapyeong-daero, Seocho-gu, Seoul Tel:1599-2227

Finland *Hon. Con. Cho Dong-seong* Add:6F Daehyun Bldg., 46 Ewhayeodae 2gil, Seodaemun-gu, Seoul Tel:(02)390-4511 / *Hon. Con. Yoo Sung-bok* Add:15-36, Gangbyeon-daero 456beon-gil, Sasang-gu, Busan Tel:(051)329-0502

France *Hon. Con. Kim Hyung-soo* Add:10, Jungdong 1-ro 37beon-gil, Haeundae-gu, Busan Tel:(051)747-9000

Germany *Hon. Con. Kim Jung-soon* Add:162 Dasan-ro, Saha-gu, Busan Tel:(051)261-7073

Greece *Hon. Con.-Gen. Kim Seung-youn* Add:Hanwha Bldg., 86, Cheonggyecheon-ro, Jung-gu, Seoul Tel:(02)729-1001

Grenada *Hon. Con. Lee Chung-gu* Add:6F UNIX Bldg., 252 Wonhyo-ro, Yongsan-gu, Seoul Tel:(02)716-3112

Guatemala *Hon. Con. Chung Hee-ja* Add:23F, Hilton Hotel, 50, Sowol-ro, Jung-gu, Seoul Tel:(02)753-3535

Guinea-Bissau *Hon. Con. Kim Tae-jeong* Add:Rm.801 Seonghae Bldg. 36 Saebyeoksijanggil, Seo-gu, Busan Tel:(051)256-1597

Guyana *Hon. Con. Kim Wan-hee* Add:Rm.402 Hyungin Bldg., 195 Sungmisan-ro, Mapo-gu, Seoul Tel:(02)784-7202

Haiti *Hon. Con. Yu Seung-pil* Add:5F Yuyu Bldg., 197 Dongho-ro, Jung-gu, Seoul Tel:(02)2253-6300

Honduras *Hon. Con. Choue Chung-won* Add:1329, Seongnam-daero, Sujeong-gu, Seongnam-si, Gyeonggi-do Tel:(02)539-1752

Hungary *Hon. Con. Sohn Bong-rak* Add:Dongyang Tower, 543, Gukhoe-daero, Yeongdeungpo-gu, Seoul Tel:(02)2639-1712 / *Hon. Con. Cho Hyun-shick* Add:Hankook Tire Bldg., 133 Teheran-ro, Gangnam-gu, Seoul Tel:(02)2222-1011

Iceland *Hon. Con.-Gen. Cho Hae-hyeong* Add:1F, Nara Bldg., 8 Itaewon-ro 49-gil, Yongsan-gu, Seoul Tel:(02)549-5671 / Hon. Vice-Con. Kim Hui

Iraq *Hon. Con. Shin Se-won* Add:19F Golden-vill, 39 Bongeunsa-ro 113-gil, Gangnam-gu, Seoul Tel:(02)548-4775

Ireland *Hon. Con.-Gen. Cho Yang-ho* Add:260 Haneul-gil, Gangseo-gu, Seoul Tel:(02)2656-7031

Israel *Hon. Con. Bae Jung-hwa* Add:Rm.302 2nd, Seocho Town Trapalace, 23 Seocho-daero 74-gil, Seocho-gu, Seoul Tel:(02)525-7301

Italy *Hon. Con. Ha Chun-soo* Add:Daegu Head Bank Office Bldg., 2310 Dalgubeol-daero, Suseong-gu, Daegu Tel:(053)740-2001

Jamaica *Hon. Con.-Gen. Yoon Yung-woo* Add:5F Daegwang Bldg., 23 Bongeunsa-ro 108-gil, Gangnam-gu, Seoul Tel:(02)554-1915

Jordan *Hon. Con. Jchung Mong-yoon* Add:14F Hyundai Marine&Fire Insurance Bldg., 178 Sejong-daero, Jongno-gu, Seoul Tel:(02)732-1133

Kyrgyz *Hon. Con. Kim Jong-gu* Add:Rm.402 Modne Venture Town Bldg., 562, Gamasan-ro, Yeongdeungpo-gu, Seoul Tel:(02)844-1101

Laos *Hon. Con. Kim Chang-min* Add:Rm.401 Centralview Bldg., 5 Geoje-sijang-ro 22beon-gil, Yeonje-gu, Busan Tel:(051)861-4430 / *Hon. Con. Cho Won-guon* Add:59, Baengnyong-ro, Dong-gu, Daejeon Tel:(042)630-9247

Latvia *Hon. Con.-Gen. Kwon Kyoung-hoon* Add:4F, Dongwon Bldg., 7 Teheran-ro 77-gil, Gangnam-gu, Seoul Tel:(02)3460-4980

Luxembourg *Hon. Con. Hong Young-chul* Add:20F, Janggyo Bldg., 363 Samil-daero, Jung-gu, Seoul Tel:(02)316-6113

Madagascar *Hon. Con. Lee Yoong-yeul* Add:10F, Lotte Center Bldg., 179, Gasan digital 2-ro, Geumcheon-gu, Seoul Tel:(02)2028-9299 / *Hon. Con. Kim Yun-seek* Add:Rm.902 Daeo Bldg., 53-1 Yeouinaru-ro, Yeongdeungpo-gu, Seoul Tel:(02)761-6530

Maldive *Hon. Con. Kim Eui-bae* Add:8F, Dongbang Bldg., 76 Jungang-daero, Jung-gu, Busan Tel:(051)464-9494

Mali *Hon. Con. Kim Suk-hee* Add:12F SAM-E Bldg., 435 Dosan-daero, Gangnam-gu, Seoul Tel:(02)515-6725

Malta *Hon. Con. Ly Kwang-yong* Add:Rm.311 Seong-chang Bldg., 299 Samil-daero, Jung-gu, Seoul Tel:(02)778-9201

Marshall *Hon. Con. Harold Park* Add:15F, Partners Tower Bldg., 83, Gasan digital 1-ro, Geumcheon-gu, Seoul Tel:070-4486-9442

Mauritanie *Hon. Con. Lee Woo-sok* Add:6F, Kolon Tower Bldg., 13, Kolon-ro, Gwacheon-si, Gyeonggi-do Tel:(02)2120-8310

Mexico *Hon. Con. Park Soon-ho* Add:158 Muhaksong-ro, Geumjeong-gu, Busan Tel:(051)510-5008 / *Hon. Con. Yoon June-sick* Add:8F Inter-Burgo Bldg., 99 Samhaksa-ro, Songpa-gu, Seoul Tel:(02)413-5146

Micronesia *Hon. Con.-Gen. Shin Myoung-jin* Add:6F, 1st, Ace Twin Tower, 285 Digital-ro, Guro-gu, Seoul Tel:(02)2109-6930

Monaco *Hon. Con. Hong Seok-joh* Add:11F, BGF Co.Bldg., 405, Teheran-ro, Gangnam-gu, Seoul Tel:(02)528-7001

Mongolia *Hon. Con. Kim Yoon-kwang* Add:7F Sungae General Hospital, 22 Yeouidaebang-ro 53-gil, Yeongdeungpo-gu, Seoul Tel:(02)840-7101 / *Hon. Con. Park Jong-jin* Add:Rm.604 Shindong Bldg., 267, Jungang-daero, Dong-gu, Busan Tel:(051)465-9996 / *Hon. Con. Kang Seong-il* Add:5F, Handu Bldg., 49, Hangang-daero, Yongsan-gu, Seoul

Myanmar *Hon. Con.-Gen. Dahn Won-bae* Add:33, Marine city 2-ro, Haeundae-gu, Busan Tel:(051)466-0785

Nepal *Hon. Con. Yoon Sung-do* Add:56, Dalseong-ro, Jung-gu, Daegu Tel:(053)250-8287

New Zealand *Hon. Con. Kim Jae-chul* Add:Dongwon Industries Co.Bldg., 68 Mabang-ro, Seocho-gu, Seoul Tel:(02)589-3101

Nicaragua *Hon. Con. Koo Cha-joon* Add:LIG Tower, 334, Teheran-ro, Gangnam-gu, Seoul Tel:(02)6900-2003

Niger *Hon. Con. Lee Hyuck-bae* Add: Dongwon Bldg., 3F 15 Saemunan-ro 3-gil, Jongno-gu, Seoul Tel:(02)736-5262

Pakistan *Hon. Con.-Gen. Kim Young-il* Add:JS Bldg., 20, Nonhyeon-ro 128-gil, Gangnam-gu, Seoul Tel:(02)783-8548

Panama *Hon. Con. Chu Myung-hee* Add:5F Bando Bldg., 59-1, Haegwan-ro, Jung-gu, Busan Tel:(051)465-6101

Peru *Hon. Con. Han Young-chul* Add:7F, 77 Banpo-daero, Seocho-gu, Seoul Tel:(02)3475-9101

Poland *Hon. Con.-Gen. Synn Il-hi* Add: Kyemyung Univ., 1095 Dalgubeol-daero, Dalseo-gu, Daegu Tel:(053)580-5000

Portugal *Hon. Con. Kang Eui-ku* Add:Bando Bldg., 59-1 Haegwan-ro, Jung-gu, Busan Tel:(051)441-2988

Romania *Hon. Con. Shin Pyung-jai* Add:4, Sajik-ro 8-gil, Jongno-gu, Seoul Tel:(02)720-3657 / *Hon. Con. Sun Kyung-hoon* Add:645, Daejong-ro, Jung-gu, Daejeon Tel:(042)220-8007

Russia *Hon. Con.-Gen. Jung Heon* Add:4F, Top Bldg., 6, Nonhyeon-ro 38-gil, Gangnam-gu, Seoul Tel:(02)533-0101

San Marino *Hon. Con.-Gen. Paik Nam-hyuk* Add:16F Deokheung Bldg., 363 Gangnam-daero, Seocho-gu, Seoul Tel:(02)522-8171

Seychelles *Hon. Con.-Gen. Jeong Dong-chang* Add:Rm.411 Doosan We've Pavilion, 81 Sambong-ro, Jongno-gu, Seoul Tel:(02)737-3235

Slovenia *Hon. Con. Yoon Byong-hwa* Add:Rm.501 Yeongcho Bldg., 53 Nam-busunhwan-ro 347-gil, Seocho-gu, Seoul Tel:(02)569-3535

Solomon Islands *Hon. Con.-Gen. Park Young-ju* Add:16F Seoul Mobile Telecomunication Bldg., 233-3 Mokdongdong-ro, Yangcheon-gu, Seoul Tel:(02)2007-2208

Spain *Hon.Con.Yang Yong-chee* Add:20 Jogakgongwon-ro, Nam-gu, Busan

Tel:(051)625-8115

Srilanka *Hon. Con. Shin Jung-taek* Add:3F Seuninovil, 23 Hwangnyeong-daero, Busan-jin-gu, Busan Tel:(051)647-8142

Suriname *Hon. Con. Wang Ki-ju* Add:Rm.501 Bongseong Bldg., 345-6, Hyoryeong-ro 55-gil, Seocho-gu, Seoul Tel:(02)557-1955

Sweden *Hon. Con. Yoo Jae-jin* Add:Rm.301 505, Hwangnyeong-daero, Suyeong-gu, Busan Tel:(051)709-6203 / *Hon. Con. Sun Seung-hoon* Add:Sun Hospital, 29 Mokjung-ro, Jung-gu, Daejeon Tel:(042)220-8007 / *Hon. Con. Lee Dong-koo* Add:331, Dong-daegu-ro, Suseong-gu, Daegu Tel:(053)755-7775 / *Hon. Vice-Con. Yoo Chang-jong* Add:277 Haeun-daero, Haeundae-gu, Busan Tel:(051)709-6211

Thailand *Hon. Con.-Gen. Kim Il-kyoun* Add:Rm.1109 1470, U-dong, Haeundae-gu, Busan Tel:(052)277-7723

Timor-Leste *Hon. Con. Park Tae-woo* Add:Rm.1401 Gwanghwamun Officia 92, Saemunan-ro, Jongno-gu, Seoul Tel:(02)737-1905

Trinidad & Tobago *Hon. Con. Choi Seung-woong* Add:5F Samsung Bldg., 623 Teheran-ro, Gangnam-gu, Seoul Tel:(02)508-1180

Turkey *Hon. Con. Park Sa-ick* Add:12F Gyeongbu Bldg., 1412 Nakdongnam-ro, Saha-gu, Busan Tel:(051)206-6432

Tuvalu *Hon. Con.-Gen. Kim Seung-ho* Add:18F Boryung Bldg., 136 Changgyeong-gung-ro, Jongno-gu, Seoul Tel:(02)708-8108

United Kingdom *Hon. Con. Kim Moon-ik* Add:Rm.1707 Ocean Tower Bldg., 203, Haeundaehaebyeon-ro, Haeundae-gu, Busan Tel:(051)740-5787

Vietnam *Hon. Con.-Gen. Park Soo-kwan* Add:45 Gimhae-daero 2596beon-gil, Gimhae-si, Gyeongsangnam-do Tel:(055)336-7300 / *Hon. Con.-Gen. Kim Sang-yeol* Add:Rm.502 1495-2, Seocho 3-dong, Seocho-gu, Seoul Tel:(02)2007-7119

Zambia *Hon. Con. Lee Jong-woo* Add:10F Paradise Venture Tower, 21 Teheran-ro 52-gil, Gangnam-gu, Seoul Tel:(02)557-3240

Zimbabwe *Hon. Con. Baik Young-chul* Add:2F Taeseong Bldg., 12 Samjeon-ro 8-gil, Songpa-gu, Seoul Tel:(02)425-0252

⊪ CULTURAL AND SOCIAL DIRECTORY ⊪

INTERNATIONAL ORGANIZATIONS AND AMITY

<Organizations>

Amnesty International Korea Add:31, Donggyo-ro 8an-gil, Mapo-gu, Seoul Tel:(02)730-4755 http://www.amnesty.or.kr

ASEAN-Korea Centre Add:8F, Press Center Bldg., 124, Sejong-daero, Jung-gu, Seoul Tel:(02)2287-1115 http://www.aseankorea.org

Asian Federation of Biotechnology Add:#1906 Get-Pearl Tower, 12, Gaetbeol-ro, Yeonsu-gu, Incheon Tel:(032)260-0066 http://www.afob.org

Association of World Election Bodies(A-WEB) Add:24F, G Tower Bldg., 175, Art center-daero, Yeonsu-gu, Incheon Tel:(032)455-7200 http://www.aweb.org

Civitan International Korea District Add:82, Yeonhui-ro, Seodaemun-gu, Seoul Tel:(02)364-7804 http://www.civitankorea.com

East Asian-Australasian Flyway Partnership Add:3F, G Tower Bldg., 175, Art center-daero, Yeonsu-gu, Incheon Tel:(032)458-6509 http://www.eaaflyway.net

Global Civic Sharing Add:84, Yulgok-ro, Jongno-gu, Seoul Tel:(02)747-7044 http://www.gcs.or.kr

Global Green Growth Institute Add:19F, Jeongdong Bldg., 21-15, Jeongdong-gil, Jung-gu, Seoul Tel:(02)2096-9991 http://www.gggi.org

Green Climate Fund Add:12F, G Tower Bldg., 175, Art center-daero, Yeonsu-gu, Incheon Tel:(032)458-6059 http://www.gcfund.org

International Organization for Migration Add:12F, Hyoryeong Bldg., 32, Mugyo-ro, Jung-gu, Seoul Tel:(02)6925-1360 http://www.iom.int

International PEN Korean Centre Add:18, Gukhoe-daero 76-gil, Yeongdeungpo-gu, Seoul Tel:(02)782-1337 http://www.penkorea.or.kr

International Vaccine Institute Add:SNU Research Park, 1 Gwanak-ro, Gwanak-gu, Seoul Tel:(02)872-2801 http://www.ivi.int/korean

Kiwanis Korea Add:32, Janggi-ro, Gyeyang-gu, Incheon Tel:(032)555-4580 http://한국키와니스.kr

Korea Chamber of Commerce and Industry Add:39, Sejongdaero, Jung-gu, Seoul Tel:(02)6050-3114 http://www.korcham.net

Korea FAO Association Add:187, Simin-daero, Dongan-gu, Anyang-si, Gyeonggi-do Tel:(031)440-9080 http://www.fao.or.kr

Korea Foundation Add:2558, Nambu-sunhwan-ro, Seocho-gu, Seoul Tel:(02)2046-8500 http://www.kf.or.kr

Korea National Headquarters People to People International Add:#1501 Donghwa Bldg., 71, Yeouinaru-ro, Yeongdeungpo-gu, Seoul Tel:(02)761-5241 http://www.ptpkorea.or.kr

Moral Re-Armament Initiatives of change Movement Korea Add:234, Geumnanghwa-ro, Gangseo-gu, Seoul Tel:(02)2662-7360 http://www.mrakorea.or.kr

UN Asian and Pacific Training Centre for Information and Communication Technology for Development Add:5F, G-Tower Bldg., 175, Art center-daero, Yeonsu-gu, Incheon Tel:(032)458-6650 http://www.unapcict.org

UN Association of the Rep. of Korea Add:141, Seosomun-ro, Jung-gu, Seoul Tel:(02)774-0456 http://www.unarok.org

UN Commission on International Trade Law Regional Centre for Asia and the Pacific Add:3F, G Tower Bldg., 175, Art center-daero, Yeonsu-gu, Incheon Tel:(032)458-6540 http://www.uncitral.org

UN Development Programme Seoul Policy Centre Add:Korea Univ. international Studies Hall, 145, Anam-ro, Seongbuk-gu, Seoul Tel:(02)3290-1391 http://www.undp.org/uspc

UN Economic and Social Commission for Asia and the Pacific Add:7F, G Tower Bldg., 175, Art center-daero, Yeonsu-gu, Incheon Tel:(032)458-6600 http://northeast-sro.unescap.org

UN Educational, Scientific and Cultural Organization Add:26, Myeongdong-gil, Jung-gu, Seoul Tel:(02)6958-4100 http://www.unesco.or.kr

UN Environment Programme National Committee for the Republic of Korea Add:46, Maeheon-ro, Seocho-gu, Seoul Tel:(02)720-1011 http://www.unep.or.kr

UN Environment Programme Northwest Pacific Action Plan Add:216, Gijanghaean-ro, Gijang-eup, Gijang-gun, Busan Tel:(051)720-3001 http://www.nowpap.org

UN Industrial Development Organization Investment and Technology Promotion Office Add:#201, Hanman Tower annex Bldg., 14, Hannam-daero 27-gil, Yongsan-gu, Seoul Tel:(02)794-8191 http://unidoseoul.org

UN International Children's Emergency Fund Add:49, Hyoja-ro, Jongno-gu, Seoul Tel:(02)735-2315 http://www.unicef.or.kr

UN International Strategy for Disaster Reduction Add:4F, G Tower Bldg., 175, Art center-daero, Yeonsu-gu, Incheon Tel:(032)458-6551 http://www.unisdr.org/incheon

UN Korean War Allies Association Add:33, Gukjegeumyung-ro 6-gil, Yeongdeungpo-gu, Seoul Tel:(02)782-3643

UN Memorial Cemetery in Korea Add:93, UN pyeonghwa-ro, Nam-gu, Busan Tel:(051)625-0625 http://www.unmck.or.kr

UN North-East Asian Subregional Programme for Environmental Cooperation Add:7F, G Tower Bldg., 175, Art center-daero, Yeonsu-gu, Incheon Tel:(032)458-6603 http://www.neaspec.org

UN Office for Sustainable Development Add:#205 Libertas Hall A, Yonsei University International Campus 85, Songdogwahak-ro, Yeonsu-gu, Incheon Tel:(032)822-9088 http://www.unosd.org

UN Project Office on Governance Add:#1721 Changgang Bldg., 86, Mapo-daero, Mapo-gu, Seoul Tel:(02)2100-4276 http://www.unpog.org

UN Refugee Agency Add:7F, Geumsegi Bldg., 6, Mugyo-ro, Jung-gu, Seoul Tel:(02)773-7011 http://www.unhcr.or.kr

World Bank Group Add:37F, PoscoE&C Tower Bldg., 241, Incheon tower-daero, Yeonsu-gu, Incheon Tel:(032)713-7000 http://www.worldbank.org

World Food Programme Add:#301 Lotte International Education Hall, Seoul

University 1, Gwanak-ro, Gwanak-gu, Seoul Tel:(02)722-9579 http://ko.wfp.org

World Health Organization Add:#512 Seoul National University College Of Medicine, 103, Daehak-ro, Jongno-gu, Seoul Tel:(02)740-8361 http://www.who.int

World Taekwondo Federation Add: 1329, Seongnam-daero, Sujeong-gu, Seongnam-si, Gyeonggi-do Tel:(02)566-2505 http://www.wtf.org

Y's Men International Korea Area Add:69, Jong-ro, Jongno-gu, Seoul Tel:(02) 735-2395 http://www.ysmenkoreaarea.org

<Amity>

Korean-American Association Add:87, Nonhyeon-ro, Seocho-gu, Seoul Tel:(02)589-0005 http://www.koram.or.kr

Korean American Friendship Association Add:8, Teheran-ro 8-gil, Gangnam-gu, Seoul Tel:(02)757-3011 http://kafa-kafa.com

Korea America Friendship Society Add:96, Sajik-ro, Jongno-gu, Seoul Tel:(02)730-3595 http://www.kafs.or.kr

Korea China Cultural Association Add:175, Bangbae-ro, Seocho-gu, Seoul Tel:(02)785-3117 http://www.k-cca.or.kr

Korea China Economy Association Add:130, Sajik-ro, Jongno-gu, Seoul Tel:(02)3210-6022 http://www.kceco.or.kr/

Korea-China Friendship Association Add:75, Saemunan-ro, Jongno-gu, Seoul Tel:(02)6303-1961 http://www.korea-china.or.kr

Korean Council on Latin America & the Caribbean Add:11, Yangpyeong-ro, Yeongdeungpo-gu, Seoul Tel:(02)539-4871 http://www.latinamerica.or.kr

Koreanisch-Deutsche Gesellschaft e. V. Add:132, Teheran-ro, Gangnam-gu, Seoul Tel:(02)527-5197 http://www.koreagermany.com

Korean Japanese Association Add:381, Gangnam-daero, Seocho-gu, Seoul Tel:(02)3452-5999 http://www.koja.or.kr

Korea-Japan Cooperation Foundation for Industry and Technology Add:18-4, Seolleung-ro 131-gil, Gangnam-gu, Seoul Tel:(02)3014-9898 http://www.kjc.or.kr

Korea-Japan Economic Association Add:18-4, Seolleung-ro 131-gil, Gangnam-gu, Seoul Tel:(02)3014-9888 http://www.kje.or.kr

Korea Japan Women's Association Add:297, Dongho-ro, Jung-gu, Seoul Tel: (02)2273-7645

Trilateral Cooperation Secretariat Add:20F, S Tower Bldg., 82, Saemunan-ro, Jongno-gu, Seoul Tel:(02)733-4700 http:// kr.tcs-asia.org

POLITICAL PARTIES

Green Party Korea Add:32, Jahamun-ro, Jongno-gu, Seoul Tel:(02)737-1711 http:// www.kgreens.org

Justice Party Add:7, Gukhoe-daero 70-gil, Yeongdeungpo-gu, Seoul Tel:(02)2038-0103 http://www.justice21.org

Labor Party Add:664, Gukhoe-daero, Yeongdeungpo-gu, Seoul Tel:(02)6004-2000 http://www.laborparty.kr/

Saenuri Party Add:18, Gukhoe-daero 70-gil, Yeongdeungpo-gu, Seoul Tel:(02)3786-3000 http://www.saenuriparty.kr

The New Politics Alliance for Democracy Add:14, Gukhoe-daero 68-gil, Yeongdeungpo-gu, Seoul Tel:1577-7667 http://npad.kr

JURIDICAL SOCIETIES

Korea Legal Aid Center for Family Relations Add:14, Gukhoe-daero 76ga-gil, Yeongdeungpo-gu, Seoul Tel:1644-7077 http://www.lawhome.or.kr

Korea Patent Attorneys Association Add:107, Myeongdal-ro, Seocho-gu, Seoul Tel:(02)3486-3486 http://www.kpaa.or.kr

Korean Bar Association Add:124, Teheran-ro, Gangnam-gu, Seoul Tel:(02)3476-4000 http://www.koreanbar.or.kr

Korea Association Of Beommusa Lawyer Add:651, Nonhyeon-ro, Gangnam-gu, Seoul Tel:(02)511-1906 http://www.kjaa.or.kr

Korean Lawyers Association Add:47, Gwanmun-ro, Gwacheon-si, Gyeonggi-do Tel:(02)2110-3622 http://www.bupjo.or.kr

Korea Legal Center Add:34, Seosomun-ro 11-gil, Jung-gu, Seoul Tel:(02)752-7481 http://www.legalcenter.or.kr

Korean Notaries Association Add:21, Beobwon-ro 1-gil, Seocho-gu, Seoul Tel:(02) 3477-5007 http://www.koreanotary.or.kr

Legal Ethics & Professional Conduct Council Add:20, Seocho-daero 45-gil, Seocho-gu, Seoul Tel:(02)3476-4061 http:// www.lepcc.or.kr

MINBYUN-Lawyers for a Democratic Society Add:34, Banpo-daero 30-gil, Seocho-gu, Seoul Tel:(02)522-7284 http:// www.minbyun.org

GENERAL

Association of Commemorative Services for Patriot Kim Koo Add:26, Imjeong-ro, Yongsan-gu, Seoul Tel:(02)799-3400 http://www.kimkoo.or.kr

Association of Meritorious Supporters of Korea Independence Add:46, Seongji-gil, Mapo-gu, Seoul Tel:(02)722-8400 http://www.815family.or.kr

Central Association for National Unification of Korea Add:4, Cheonjung-ro 15ga-gil, Gangdong-gu, Seoul Tel:(02)476-8194 http://www.mintong.or.kr

Citizens' Coalition for Economic Justice Add:26-9, Dongsung 3-gil, Jongno-gu, Seoul Tel:(02)765-9731 http://www.ccej.or.kr

Consumers Korea Add:42, Saemunan-ro, Jongno-gu, Seoul Tel:(02)739-5441 http://www.consumerskorea.org

Consumers Union of Korea Add:1-7, Dokseodang-ro 20-gil, Yongsan-gu, Seoul Tel:(02)795-1042 https://www.cuk.or.kr

Dosan Ahn Chang Ho Memorial Foundation Add:20, Dosan-daero 45-gil, Gangnam-gu, Seoul Tel:(02)541-1800 http://www.ahnchangho.org

Friends of National Museum of Korea Add:137, Seobinggo-ro, Yongsan-gu, Seoul Tel:(02)2077-9790 http://fnmk.org

Green Environment Centers Association Add:215, Jinheung-ro, Eunpyeong-gu, Seoul Tel:(02)357-4401 http://www.geca.or.kr

Green Korea Add:15, Seongbuk-ro 19-gil, Seongbuk-gu, Seoul Tel:(02)747-8500 http://www.greenkorea.org

Hung Sa Dan(Young Korean Academy) Add:122, Daehak-ro, Jongno-gu, Seoul Tel:(02)743-2511 http://www.yka.or.kr

Junior Chamber International Korea Add:368, Cheonho-daero, Seongdong-gu, Seoul Tel:1566-5883 http://www.koreajc.or.kr

Korea Consumer Agency Add:246, Yangjae-daero, Seocho-gu, Seoul Tel:(02)3460-3000 http://www.kca.go.kr

Korean Council on Foreign Relations Add:33, Nambusunhwan-ro 294-gil, Seocho-gu, Seoul Tel:(02)2186-3600 http://www.kcfr.or.kr

Korea Disabled Veterans Organization Add:33, Gukhoe-daero 76-gil, Yeongdeungpo-gu, Seoul Tel:(02)782-2263 http://www.kdvo.or.kr

Korea Disaster Relief Association Add:52, Sinsu-ro, Mapo-gu, Seoul Tel:(02)3272-0123 http://www.relief.or.kr

Korea Environment Association Add:1163, Ori-ro, Guro-gu, Seoul Tel:(02)2689-2681 http://www.koae.org

Korea Environmental Preservation Association Add:320-2, Gwangnaru-ro, Seongdong-gu, Seoul Tel:(02)3407-1500 http://www.epa.or.kr

Korea Freedom Federation Add:72, Jangchungdan-ro, Jung-gu, Seoul Tel:(02)2238-1037 http://www.koreaff.or.kr

Korea Liberation Association Add:13, Gukhoe-daero 62-gil, Yeongdeungpo-gu, Seoul Tel:(02)780-9661 http://www.kla815.or.kr

Korea National Council of Consumer Organizations Add:20, Myeongdong 11-gil, Jung-gu, Seoul Tel:(02)774-4050 http://www.consumer.or.kr

Korean National Police Veterans Association Add:407, Wangsimni-ro, Jung-gu, Seoul Tel:(02)2234-1881 http://www.ex-police.or.kr

Korea Retired Generals & Admirals Association Add:115, Wangsimni-ro, Seongdong-gu, Seoul Tel:(02)417-5415 http://www.starflag.or.kr

Korea Saemaul Undong Center Add:316, Youngdong-daero, Gangnam-gu, Seoul Tel:(02)2600-3600 http://www.saemaul.com

Korea Social Service, Inc. Add:70, Samyang-ro 162ga-gil, Dobong-gu, Seoul Tel:(02)908-9191 http://www.kssinc.org

Korean Association on Smoking or Health Add:22, Gukhoe-daero 72-gil, Yeongdeungpo-gu, Seoul Tel:(02)2632-5190 http://www.kash.or.kr

Korean Federation for Environment Movement Add:23, Pirundae-ro, Jongno-gu, Seoul Tel:(02)735-7000 http://www.kfem.or.kr

Korean National Union For Conservation of Nature Add:18, Toegye-ro, Jung-gu, Seoul Tel:(02)757-0008 http://www.knccn.org

Korean Senior Citizens Association Add:54, Imjeong-ro, Yongsan-gu, Seoul Tel:(02)715-2928 http://www.koreapeople.co.kr

Korean Veterans Association Add:115, Wangsimni-ro, Seongdong-gu, Seoul Tel:(02)417-0641 http://www.korva.or.kr

Parliamentarian's Society of The Republic of Korea Add:1, Uisadang-daero, Yeongdeungpo-gu, Seoul Tel:(02)757-6612 http://www.rokps.or.kr

People's Solidarity for Participatory Democracy Add:16, Jahamun-ro 9-gil, Jongno-gu, Seoul Tel:(02)723-5300 http://www.peoplepower21.org

Society For A Better Tomorrow Add: 151, Dogok-ro, Gangnam-gu, Seoul Tel: (02)719-8111 http://www.sfbt.or.kr

Unification Korea Federation Add:34, Mapo-daero, Mapo-gu, Seoul Tel:(02)704-2013 http://www.onekorea.or.kr

Women's Korean Veterans Association Add:3, Wangsimni-ro 5-gil, Seongdong-gu, Seoul Tel:(02)417-1383 http://www.wkorva.or.kr

RESEARCH INSTITUTES

Academy of Korean Studies Add:323, Haogae-ro, Bundang-gu, Seongnam-si, Gyeonggi-do Tel:(031)709-8111 http://www.aks.ac.kr

Architecture &Urban Research Institute Add:230, Simin-daero, Anyang-si, Gyeonggi-do Tel:(031)478-9600 http://www.auri.re.kr

Busan Development Institute Add:955, Jungang-daero, Busanjin-gu, Busan Tel:(051)860-8619 http://www.bdi.re.kr

Center for Korean Women & Politics Add:196, Mapo-daero, Mapo-gu, Seoul Tel:(02)706-6761 http://ckwp.feminet.or.kr

Chungnam Development Institute Add:73-26, Yeonsuwon-gil, Gongju-si, Chungcheongnam-do Tel:(041)840-1114 http://www.cni.re.kr

Chungbuk Research Institute Add:102-1, Daeseong-ro, Sangdang-gu, Cheongju-si, Chungcheongbuk-do Tel:(043)220-1141 http://www.cri.re.kr

Company Policy Research Institute Add:163, Nonhyeon-ro, Seocho-gu, Seoul Tel:(02)577-8816 http://www.wonga.or.kr

Construction Economy Research Institute of Korea Add:163, Eonju-ro, Gangnam-gu, Seoul Tel:(02)3441-0600 http://www.cerik.re.kr

DaeguGyeongbuk Development Institute Add:43, Cheongsu-ro, Suseong-gu, Daegu Tel:(053)770-5000 http://www.dgi.re.kr

Daejeon Development Institute Add:85, Jungang-ro, Jung-gu, Daejeon Tel:(042)530-3500 http://www.djdi.re.kr

Daishin Economic Research Institute Add:16, Gukjegeumyung-ro 8-gil, Yeongdeungpo-gu, Seoul Tel:(02)769-2000 http://www.deri.co.kr

Electronics and Telecommunications Research Institute Add:218, Gajeong-ro, Yuseong-gu, Daejeon Tel:(042)860-6114 http://www.etri.re.kr

Gallup Korea Add:70, Sajik-ro, Jongno-gu, Seoul Tel:(02)3702-2100 http://www.gallup.co.kr

Green Technology Center Add:173, Toegye-ro, Jung-gu, Seoul Tel:(02)3393-3900 http://www.gtck.re.kr

Gwangju Developmet Institute Add:53-27, Sochon-ro 152beon-gil, Gwangsan-gu, Gwangju Tel:062-940-0500 http://www.gji.re.kr

Gwangju Institute of Science and Technology Add:123, Cheomdangwagi-ro, Buk-gu, Gwangju Tel:(062)715-2114 http://www.gist.ac.kr

Gyeonggi Research Institute Add:1150, Gyeongsu-daero, Jangan-gu, Suwon-si, Gyeonggi-do Tel:(031)250-3114 http://www.gri.re.kr

Gyeongnam Development Institute Add:248, Yongji-ro, Uichang-gu, Changwon-si, Gyeongsangnam-do Tel:(055)266-2076 http://www.gndi.re.kr

Hana Institute of Finance Add:82, Uisadang-daero, Yeongdeungpo-gu, Seoul Tel:(02)2002-2200 http://www.hanaif.re.kr

Hankyoreh Economic Research Institute Add:6, Hyochangmok-gil, Mapo-gu, Seoul Tel:(02)710-0074 http://heri.kr

Hyundai Research Institute Add:194, Yulgok-ro, Jongno-gu, Seoul Tel:(02)2072-6305 http://www.hri.co.kr

Incheon Developmet Institute Add:98, Simgok-ro, Seo-gu, Incheon Tel:(032)260-2600 http://www.idi.re.kr

Institute for Advanced Engineering Add:175-28, Goan-ro 51beon-gil, Baegam-myeon, Cheoin-gu, Yongin-si, Gyeonggi-do Tel:(031)330-7114 http://www.iae.re.kr

Institute for Basic Science Add:70, Yuseong-daero 1689beon-gil, Yuseong-gu, Daejeon Tel:(042)8788-114 http://www.ibs.re.kr

Institute for Far Eastern Studies Add:2, Bukchon-ro 15-gil, Jongno-gu, Seoul Tel:(02)3700-0700 http://ifes.kyungnam.ac.kr

Institute for Global Economics Add:511, Yeongdong-daero, Gangnam-gu, Seoul

Tel:(02)551-3334 http://www.igenet.com

Institute for Industrial Policy Studies
Add:203, Sinchon-ro, Seodaemun-gu,
Seoul Tel:(02)456-5588 http://www.ips.
or.kr

Institute for Peace Affairs Add:373,
Eungam-ro, Eunpyeong-gu, Seoul Tel:(02)358-
0612 http://www.ipa.re.kr

Institute of Global Management
Add:11-16, Jangchungdan-ro 8-gil, Jung-
gu, Seoul Tel:(02)2036-8300 http://www.
igm.or.kr

Institute of Korean Studies Add:22,
Hyochangwon-ro 64-gil, Yongsan-gu, Seoul
Tel:(02)569-5574 http://www.iks.or.kr

Institute of North Korean Studies
Add:21, Janghan-ro, Dongdaemun-gu,
Seoul Tel:(02)2248-2392 http://www.
nkorea.or.kr

Jeju Development Institute Add:253,
Ayeon-ro, Jeju-si, Jeju-do Tel:(064)726-
0500 https://www.jdi.re.kr

Jeonbuk Development Institute
Add:1696, Kongjwipatjwi-ro, Wansan-gu,
Jeonju-si, Jeollabuk-do Tel:(063)280-7100
http://www.jthink.kr

Jeonnam Research Institute Add:242,
Hugwang-daero, Samhyang-eup, Muan-
gun, Jeollanam-do Tel:(061)280-3900
http://www.jeri.re.kr

Korean Academy of Science Technology
Add:42, Dolma-ro, Bundang-gu, Seongnam-
si, Gyeonggi-do Tel:(031)726-7900 http://
www.kast.or.kr

Korea Accounting Standards Board
Add:39, Sejong-daero, Jung-gu, Seoul
Tel:(02)6050-0150 http://www.kasb.or.kr

**Korea Advanced Institute of Science
and Technology** Add:291, Daehak-ro,
Yuseong-gu, Daejeon Tel:(042)350-2114
http://www.kaist.ac.kr

Korea Aerospace Research Institute
Add:169-84, Gwahak-ro, Yuseong-gu,
Daejeon Tel:(042)860-2114 http://www.
kari.re.kr

**Korea Astronomy and Space Science
Institute** Add:776, Daedeok-daero,
Yuseong-gu, Daejeon Tel:(042)865-
3332 http://www.kasi.re.kr

Korea Atomic Energy Research Institute
Add:111, Daedeok-daero 989beon-gil,
Yuseong-gu, Daejeon Tel:(042)868-2000
http://www.kaeri.re.kr

Korea Basic Science Institute Add: 169-
148, Gwahak-ro, Yuseong-gu, Daejeon
Tel:(042)865-3500 http://www.kbsi.re.kr

Korea Construction Institute Add:
1200, Jungbu-daero, Cheoin-gu, Yongin-
si, Gyeonggi-do Tel:(031)322-5301 http://
www.cik.re.kr

Korea Culture & Tourism Institute Add:
154, Geumnanghwa-ro, Gangseo-gu, Seoul
Tel:(02)2669-9800 http://www.kcti.re.kr

Korea Development Institute Add:263,
Namsejong-ro Sejong-si Tel:(044)550-4114
http://www.kdi.re.kr

Korea Economic Research Institute
Add:24, Yeoui-daero, Yeongdeungpo-gu,
Seoul Tel:(02)3771-0001 http://www.keri.
org

Korea Educational Development Institute
Add:35, Baumoe-ro 1-gil, Seocho-gu, Seoul
Tel:(02)3460-0114 http://www.kedi.re.kr

Korea Electronics Technology Institute
Add:25, Saenari-ro, Bundang-gu, Seongnam-
si, Gyeonggi-do Tel:(031)789-7000 http://
www.keti.re.kr

**Korea Electrotechnology Research
Institute** Add:12, Bulmosan-ro 10beon-gil,
Seongsan-gu, Changwon-si Tel:(055)280-
1114 http://www.keri.re.kr

Korea Energy Economics Institute
Add:405-11, Jongga-ro, Jung-gu, Ulsan
Tel:(052)714-2114 http://www.keei.re.kr

Korea Environment Institute Add:370,
Sicheong-daero, Sejong Tel:(044)415-7777
http://www.kei.re.kr

**Korea Environmental Industry &
Technology Institute** Add:215, Jinheung-
ro, Eunpyeong-gu, Seoul Tel:(02)3800-500
http://www.keiti.re.kr

Korea Food Research Institute Add:
62, Anyangpangyo-ro 1201beon-gil,
Bundang-gu, Seongnam-si, Gyeonggi-do
Tel:(031)780-9114 http://www.kfri.re.kr

Korea Human Development Institute
Add:536, Yeoksam-ro, Gangnam-gu, Seoul
Tel:(070)7500-9500 http://www.khdi.or.kr

Korea Industrial Development Institute
Add: 13, Nambusunhwan-ro 319-gil,
Seocho-gu, Seoul Tel:(02)2023-9700 http://
www.kid.re.kr

Korea Industrial Economics Policy
Add:45-2, Jibeom-ro, Suseong-gu, Daegu
Tel:(053)767-3111 http://www.kiiep.or.kr

Korea Industrial Marketing Institute
Add:70, Banpo-daero 26-gil, Seocho-gu, Seoul
Tel:(02)588-2480 http://www.kimikorea.com

**Korea Information Society Development
Institute** Add:18, Jeongtong-ro, Deoksan-
myeon, Jincheon-gun, Chungcheongbuk-do
Tel:(043)531-4114 http://www.kisdi.re.kr

Korea Institute for Curriculum and Evaluation Add:21-15, Jeongdong-gil, Jung-gu, Seoul Tel:(02)3704-3704 http://www.kice.re.kr

Korea Institute for Defense Analyses Add:37, Hoegi-ro, Dongdaemun-gu, Seoul Tel:(02)967-4911 http://www.kida.re.kr

Korea Institute for Health and Social Affairs Add:370, Sicheong-daero, Sejong Tel:(044)287-8000 http://www.kihasa.re.kr

Korea Institute for Industrial Economics & Trade Add:370, Sicheong-daero, Sejong Tel:(044)287-3188 http://www.kiet.re.kr

Korea Institute for Industrial Research Add:173, Digital-ro, Geumcheon-gu, Seoul Tel:(02)588-2162 http://www.kiir.or.kr

Korea Institute for International Economic Policy Add:370, Sicheong-daero, Sejong Tel:(044)414-1114 http://www.kiep.go.kr

Korea Institute for National Unification Add:217, Banpo-daero, Seodho-gu, Seoul Tel:(02)2023-8000 http://www.kinu.or.kr

Korea Institute for Research in the Behavioral Sciences Add:21, Teheran-ro 52-gil, Gangnam-gu, Seoul Tel:(02)538-6912 http://www.kirbs.re.kr

Korean Institute for Women & Politics Add:309, Gangnam-daero, Seocho-gu, Seoul Tel:(02)3474-0738 http://www.kiwp.or.kr

Korea Institute of Civil Engineering and Building Technology Add:283, Goyang-daero, Ilsanseo-gu, Goyang-si, Gyeonggi-do Tel:(031)9100-114 http://www.kict.re.kr

Korea Institute of Child care and Education Add:2558, Nambusunhwan-ro, Seocho-gu, Seoul Tel;(02)398-7700 http://www.kicce.re.kr

Korean Institute of Criminology Add:114, Taebong-ro, Seocho-gu, Seoul Tel:(02)575-5282 http://www.kic.re.kr

Korea Institute of Energy Research Add:152, Gajeong-ro, Yuseong-gu, Daejeon Tel:(042)860-3114 http://www.kier.re.kr

Korea Institute of Finance Add:19, Myeongdong 11-gil, Jung-gu, Seoul Tel:(02)3705-6300 http://www.kif.re.kr

Korea Institute of Firm Advice Add: 43, Daehak-ro 76beonan-gil, Yuseong-gu, Daejeon Tel:(042)823-8611 http://www.kifa.or.kr

Korea Institute of Geoscience and Mineral Resources Add:124, Gwahak-ro, Yuseong-gu, Daejeon Tel:(042)868-3114 http://www.kigam.re.kr

Korea Institute of Industrial Technology Add:89, Yangdaegiro-gil, Ipjang-myeon, Seobuk-gu, Cheonan-si Tel:(041)589-8114 http://www.kitech.re.kr

Korean Institute of Legislation Studies, Inc. Add:259, Hangang-daero, Yongsan-gu, Seoul Tel:(02)6325-3149 http://www.assembly.re.kr

Korea Institute of Machinery & Materials Add:156, Gajeongbuk-ro, Yuseong-Gu, Daejeon Tel:(042)861-7401 http://www.kimm.re.kr

Korea Institute of Materials Sciences Add:797, Changwon-daero, Seongsan-gu, Changwon-si, Gyeongsangnam-do Tel:(055)280-3000 http://www.kims.re.kr

Korea Institute of Nuclear Safety Add:62, Gwahak-ro, Yuseong-gu, Daejeon Tel:(042)868-0000 http://www.kins.re.kr

Korea Institute of Ocean Science & Technology Add:787, Haean-ro, Sangnok-gu, Ansan-si, Gyeonggi-do Tel:(031)400-6000 http://www.kiost.ac

Korea Institute of Oriental Medicine Add:1672, Yuseong-daero, Yuseong-gu, Daejeon Tel:(042)861-1994 http://www.kiom.re.kr

Korea Institute of Public Administration Add:508, Eonju-ro, Gangnam-gu, Seoul Tel:(02)564-2000 http://www.kipa.re.kr

Korea Institute of Public Finance Add:1924, Hannuri-daero, Sejong Tel:(044)414-2114 http://www.kipf.re.kr

Korea Institute of S&T Evaluation and Planning Add:68, Mabang-ro, Seocho-gu, Seoul Tel:(02)589-2200 http://www.kistep.re.kr

Korea Institute of Science and Technology Add:5, Hwarang-ro 14-gil, Seongbuk-gu, Seoul Tel:(02)958-5114 http://www.kist.re.kr

Korea Institute of Science and Technology Information Add:245, Daehak-ro, Yuseong-gu, Daejeon Tel:(042)869-1004 http://www.kisti.re.kr

Korea Institute of Sport Science Add:727, Hwarang-ro, Nowon-gu, Seoul Tel:(02)970-9500 http://www.sports.re.kr

Korea Institute of Toxiology Add:141, Gajeong-ro, Yuseong-gu, Daejeon Tel:(042)610-8250 http://www.kitox.re.kr

Korea Insurance Development Institute Add:38, Gukjegeumyung-ro 6-gil, Yeongdeungpo-gu, Seoul Tel:(02)368-4000 http://www.kidi.or.kr

Korea Internet & Security Agency Add:109, Jungdae-ro, Songpa-gu, Seoul Tel:(02)405-4118 http://www.kisa.or.kr

Korean Labor Force Development Institute for the Aged Add:67, Seocho-daero, Seocho-gu, Seoul Tel:(02)6007-9100 http://www.kordi.go.kr

Korea Labor Institute Add:370, Sicheong-daero, Sejong Tel:(044)287-6114 http://www.kli.re.kr

Korea Labour & Society Institute Add:169-9, Baekbeom-ro, Mapo-gu, Seoul Tel:(02)393-1457 http://www.klsi.org

Korea Legislation Research Institute Add:1934, Hannuri-daero, Sejong-si Tel:(044)861-0300 http://www.klri.re.kr

Korea Local Government Development Institute Add:358-39, Hosu-ro, Ilsandong-gu, Goyang-si, Gyeonggi-do Tel:(031)925-3001 http://www.kgdi.re.kr

Korea Management Institute Add:129, Jungbu-daero, Paldal-gu, Suwon-si, Gyeonggi-do Tel:(031)223-9234 http://www.kmics.com

Korea Maritime Institute Add:26, Haeyang-ro 301beon-gil, Yeongdo-gu, Busan Tel:(051)797-4800 http://www.kmi.re.kr

Korea Maritime Research Institute Add:54, Sejong-daero 23-gil, Jongno-gu, Seoul Tel:(02)776-9153 http://www.komares.re.kr

Korea Medical Institute Add:54, Sejong-daero 23-gil, Jongno-gu, Seoul Tel:(02)3702-9000 http://www.kmi.or.kr

Korea Railroad Research Institute Add:176, Cheoldobangmulgwan-ro, Uiwang-si, Gyeonggi-do Tel:(031)460-5000 http://www.krri.re.kr

Korea Research Institute for Human Settlements Add:254, Simin-daero, Dongan-gu, Anyang-si, Gyeonggi-do Tel:(031)380-0114 http://www.krihs.re.kr

Korea Research Institute for Local Administration Add:12-6, Banpo-daero 30-gil, Seocho-gu, Seoul Tel:(02)3488-7300 http://www.krila.re.kr

Korea Research Institute for Strategy Add:40, Cheongpa-ro, Yongsan-gu, Seoul Tel:(02)705-1301 http://www.kris.or.kr

Korea Research Institute for Vocational Education & Training Add:370, Sicheong-daero, Sejong Tel:(044)415-5000 http://www.krivet.re.kr

Korea Research Institute of Bioscience & Biotechnology Add:125, Gwahak-ro, Yuseong-gu, Daejeon Tel:(042)860-4114 http://www.kribb.re.kr

Korea Research Institute of Chemical Technology Add:141, Gajeong-ro, Yuseong-gu, Daejeon Tel:(042)860-7114 http://www.krict.re.kr

Korea Research Institute of Standards and Science Add:267, Gajeong-ro, Yuseong-gu, Daejeon Tel:(042)868-5114 http://www.kriss.re.kr

Korea Rural Economic Institute Add:117-3, Hoegi-ro, Dongdaemun-gu, Seoul Tel:(02)3299-4000 http://www.krei.re.kr

Korea Small Business Institute Add:189, Seongam-ro, Mapo-gu, Seoul Tel:(02)707-9800 http://www.kosbi.re.kr

Korea Social Economic Institute Add:205, Dongsuwon-ro 146beon-gil, Gwonseon-gu, Suwon-si, Gyeonggi-do Tel:(031)225-2548 http://www.ksei.org

Korean Social Policy Institute Add:9, Chungmu-ro, Jung-gu, Seoul Tel:(02)2278-1068 http://www.kspi.kr

Korea Testing & Research Institute Add:155, Beodeunaru-ro, Yeongdeungpo-gu, Seoul Tel:(02)2164-0011 http://www.ktr.or.kr

Korea Testing Certification Add:22, Heungan-daero 27beon-gil, Gunpo-si, Gyeonggi-do Tel:1899-7654 http://www.ktc.re.kr

Korea Transport Institute Add:370, Sicheong-daero, Sejong Tel:(044)211-3114 http://www.koti.re.kr

Korean Women's Development Institutue Add:225, Jinheung-ro, Eunpyeong-gu, Seoul Tel:(02)3156-7000 http://www.kwdi.re.kr

Korea Women's Studies Institute Add:6, Gukhoe-daero 55-gil, Yeongdeungpo-gu, Seoul Tel:(02)877-6206 http://www.kwsi.or.kr

KOTITI Testing & Researching Institute Add:111, Sagimakgol-ro, Jungwon-gu, Seongnam-si, Gyeonggi-do Tel:(02)3451-7171 http://www.kotiti.re.kr

LG Economic Research Institute Add:128, Yeoui-daero, Yeongdeungpo-gu, Seoul Tel:(02)3777-1114 http://www.lgeri.com

Lotte R&D Center Add:19, Yangpyeong-ro 19-gil, Yeongdeungpo-gu, Seoul Tel:(02)2169-3600 http://www.lotternd.com

National Academy of Arts of The Republic of Korea Add:59, Banpo-daero 37-gil, Seocho-gu, Seoul Tel:(02)3479-7223 http://www.naa.go.kr

National Academy of Sciences, Republic of Korea Add:59, Banpo-daero 37-gil, Seocho-gu, Seoul Tel:(02)3400-5250 http://www.nas.go.kr

National Fusion Research Institute Add:169-148, Gwahak-ro, Yuseong-gu, Daejeon Tel:(042)879-6000 http://www. nfri.re.kr

National Information Society Agency Add:14, Cheonggyecheon-ro, Jung-gu, Seoul Tel:(02)2131-0114 http://www.nia. or.kr

National Institute for Mathematical Sciences Add:70, Yuseong-daero 1689beon-gil, Yuseong-gu, Daejeon Tel:(042)864-5700 https://www.nims.re.kr

National Institute of Korean History Add:86, Gyoyukwon-ro, Gwacheon-si, Gyeonggi-do Tel:(02)500-8282 http:// www.history.go.kr

National Institute of The Korean Language Add:154, Geumnanghwa-ro, Gangseo-gu, Seoul Tel:(02)2669-9775 http://www.korean.go.kr

National Research Institute of Cultural Heritage Add:132, Munji-ro, Yuseong-gu, Daejeon Tel:(042)860-9114 http://www. nrich.go.kr

National Security Research Institute Add:1559, Yuseong-daero, Yuseong-gu, Daejeon Tel:(042)870-2114

National Strategy Institute Add:53-1, Yeouinaru-ro, Yeongdeungpo-gu, Seoul Tel:(02)786-7799 http://www.nsi.or.kr

National Youth Policy Institute Add:370, Sicheong-daero, Sejong Tel:(044)415-2114 http://www.nypi.re.kr

Nonghyup Economic Research Institute Add:92, Tongil-ro, Jung-gu, Seoul Tel:(02)6399-6127 http://www.nheri.re.kr

Posco Research Institute Add:514, Bongeunsa-ro, Gangnam-gu, Seoul Tel:(02)3457-8000 https://www.posri.re.kr

Research Institute for Gangwon Add:5, Jungang-ro, Chuncheon-si, Gangwon-do Tel:(033)250-1340 http://www.rig.re.kr

Samsung Advanced Institute of Technology Add:130, Samsung-ro, Yeongtong-gu, Suwon-si, Gyeonggi-do Tel:(031)8061-1114 http://www.sait. samsung.co.kr

Samsung Economic Research Institute Add:4, Seocho-daero 74-gil, Seocho-gu, Seoul Tel:(02)3780-8000 http://www.seri. org

Science and Technology Policy Institute Add:370, Sicheong-daero, Sejong Tel:(044)287-2000 http://www.stepi.re.kr

Sejong Institute Add:20, Daewangpangyo-ro 851beon-gil, Sujeong-gu, Seongnam-si, Gyeonggi-do Tel:(031)750-7500 http:// www.sejong.org

Seoul Institute Add:57, Nambusunhwan-ro 340-gil, Seocho-gu, Seoul Tel:(02)2149-1234 http://www.si.re.kr

Seoul Institute of Economic and Social Studies Add:102, Sajik-ro, Jongno-gu, Seoul Tel:(02)598-4652 http://www.sies. re.kr

Seoul National University Institute on Aging Add:1, Gwanak-ro, Gwanak-gu, Seoul Tel:(02)880-2511 http://ioa.snu.ac.kr

SK Research Institute for SUPEX Management Add:136, Sejong-daero, Jung-gu, Seoul Tel:(02)6323-2505 http:// www.skri.re.kr

Ulsan Developmet Institute Add:915, Saneop-ro, Buk-gu, Ulsan Tel:(052)283-7700 http://www.udi.re.kr

World Institute of Kimchi Add:86, Kimchi-ro, Nam-gu, Gwangju Tel:(062)610-1700 http://www.wikim.re.kr

ACADEMIC SOCIETIES

Association of Korean Education Add:96, Seochojungang-ro, Seocho-gu, Seoul Tel:(02)3475-2425 http://www. korean-lang.com

Architectural Institute of Korea Add:87, Hyoryeong-ro, Seocho-gu, Seoul Tel:(02)525-1841 http://www.aik.or.kr

Art History Association of Korea Add:1794, Nambusunhwan-ro, Gwanak-gu, Seoul Tel:(02)884-0271 http://korea-art. or.kr

Journal of Korea History Add:84, Heukseok-ro, Dongjak-gu, Seoul Tel:(02)2245-0746 http://www.hanguk-sa.org

Ecological Society of Korea Add:22, Teheran-ro 7-gil, Gangnam-gu, Seoul Tel:(02)555-1647 http://www.ecosk.org

Ergonomics Society of Korea Add:45, Yongso-ro, Nam-gu, Busan http://www. esk.or.kr

Genetics Society of Korea Add:22, Teheran-ro 7-gil, Gangnam-gu, Seoul Tel:(02)554-3328 http://www.kgenetics.or.kr

Geological Society of Korea Add:22, Teheran-ro 7-gil, Gangnam-gu, Seoul Tel:(02)3453-1550 http://www.gskorea.or.kr

Institute of Electronics And Information Engineers Add:22, Teheran-ro 7-gil, Gangnam-gu, Seoul Tel:(02)553-0255 http://www.ieek.or.kr

Korea Commercial Law Association
Add:50, Yonsei-ro, Seondaemun-gu, Seoul
Tel:(02)2123-3008 http://www.korcla.net

Korea Contents Association Add:31,
Daehak-ro, Yuseong-gu, Daejeon Tel:(042)
825-8829 http://www.koreacontents.
or.kr

Korea Information Processing Society
Add:109, Hangang-daero, Yongsan-gu,
Seoul Tel:(02)2077-1414 http://www.kips.
or.kr

Korea Language & Literature Society
Add:309, Pilmun-daero, Dong-gu, Gwangju
Tel:(063)230-7327 http://www.koreall.or.kr

Korea Logistics Research Association
Add:72, Choerubaek-ro, Bongdam-eup,
Hwaseong-si, Gyeonggi-do Tel:(031)299-
0861 http://www.klra21.org

Korea Money and Finance Association
Add:82, Dohwadong 4-gil, Mapo-gu, Seoul
Tel:(02)3273-6325 http://www.kmfa.or.kr

**Korea Private International Law
Association** Add:41, Sungkyunkwan-ro,
Jongno-gu, Seoul Tel:(02)760-0596 http://
www.kopila.re.kr/

**Korean Academic Society of Business
Administration** Add:178, Baekbeom-ro,
Mapo-gu, Seoul Tel:(02)2123-9206 http://
www.kasba.or.kr

Korean Academic Society of Taxation
Add:12, Chungjeong-ro 7-gil, Seodaemun-
gu, Seoul Tel:(02)365-4366 http://www.
koreataxation.org

**Korean Academy of International
Commerce .Inc** Add:255, Jungang-ro,
Suncheon-si, Jeollanam-do http://www.
kaic87.or.kr

Korean Academy of Medical Sciences
Add:33, Ichon-ro 46-gil, Yongsan-gu, Seoul
Tel:(02)798-3807 http://www.kams.or.kr

Korean Accounting Association Add:12,
Chungjeong-ro 7-gil, Seodaemun-gu, Seoul
Tel:(02)363-1648 http://www.kaa-edu.
or.kr

Korean Archeological Society Add:1666,
Yeongsan-ro, Cheonggye-myeon, Muan-
gun, Jeollanam-do Tel:(010)2474-9737
http://www.kras.or.kr

**Korean Association for Local Government
Studies** Add:53, Chungjeong-ro, Seodaemun-
gu, Seoul Tel:(02)567-3372 http://www.
kalgs.or.kr

Korean Association for Public Administration
Add:28, Saemunan-ro 5ga-gil, Jongno-
gu, Seoul Tel:(02)736-4977 http://www.
kapa21.or.kr

Korean Association for Religious Studies
Add:35, Baekbeom-ro, Mapo-gu, Seoul
Tel:(02)705-8361 http://www.kahr21.org

Korean Association of Anatomists
Add:50, Yonsei-ro, Seodaemun-gu, Seoul
Tel:(02)2228-1640 http://www.anatomy.
re.kr

Korean Association of Christian Studies
http://www.kacs.or.kr

Korean Association of Immunologists
Add:22, Teheran-ro 7-gil, Gangnam-gu,
Seoul Tel:(02)797-0975 http://www.ksimm.
or.kr

**Korean Association of International
Studies** Add:4, Donggyo-ro 15-gil, Mapo-
gu, Seoul Tel:(02)325-0372 http://www.
kaisnet.or.kr

Korean Association of Public Finance
Add:49, Myeongdong-gil, Jung-gu, Seoul
Tel:(02)777-0128 http://www.kapf.or.kr

Korean Association of Rusists Add:22,
Samdeok-ro 37beon-gil, Manan-gu,
Anyang-si, Gyeonggi-do Tel:(031)467-0801
http://www.russian.or.kr

Korean Astronomical Society Add:776,
Daedeok-daero, Yuseong-gu, Daejeon
Tel:(042)865-3395 http://www.kas.org

**Korean Association of North Korean
Studies** Add:2, Bukchon-ro 15-gil, Jongno-
gu,
Seoul Tel:(02)3700-0857 http://www.
kanks.org

Korean Breast Cancer Society
Add:92, Saemunan-ro, Jongno-gu, Seoul
Tel:(02)3461-6060 http://www.kbcs.or.kr

Korean Educational Research Association
Add:35, Baumoe-ro 1-gil, Seocho-gu, Seoul
Tel:(02)572-4696 http://www.ekera.org

Korean Society and Information Science
Add:99, Daehak-ro, Yuseong-gu, Daejeon
Tel:(042)821-8689 https://kslis.jams.or.kr

Korean Society of Civil Engineers Add:3-
16, Jungdae-ro 25-gil, Songpa-gu, Seoul
Tel:(02)407-4115 http://www.ksce.or.kr

Korean Society for the Study of Obesity
Add:53, Chungjeong-ro, Seodaemun-gu,
Seoul Tel:(02)364-0886 http://www.kosso.
or.kr

Korea Society of Waste Management
Add:217-1, Susaek-ro, Eunpyeong-gu, Seoul
Tel:(02)353-9805 http://www.kswm.or.kr

Korea Trade Research Association
Add:511, Yeongdong-daero, Gangnam-gu,
Seoul Tel:(02)6000-5182 http://www.ktra.
org

Korean Cancer Association Add:92, Saemunan-ro, Jongno-gu, Seoul Tel:(02)792-1486 http://www.cancer.or.kr

Korean Classical Literature Association Add:280, Daehak-ro, Gyeongsan-si, Gyeongsangbuk-do Tel:(010)6506-8238 http://www.hangomun.org

Korean Dermatological Association Add:44, Seocho-daero 78-gil, Seocho-gu, Seoul Tel:(02)3473-0284 http://www.derma.or.kr

Korean Earth Science Society Add:250, Taeseongtabyeon-ro, Cheongwon-gun, Chungcheongbuk-do Tel:(043)231-7415 http://www.kess64.net

Korean Economic Association Add:28, Saemunan-ro 5ga-gil, Jongno-gu, Seoul Tel:(02)3210-2522 http://www.kea.ne.kr

Korean Endocrine Society Add:14, Mallijae-ro, Mapo-gu, Seoul Tel:(02)714-2428 http://www.endocrinology.or.kr

Korean Environmental Sciences Society Add:13, Jungang-daero 1719beon-gil, Geumjeong-gu, Busan Tel:(051)514-1752 http://www.kenss.or.kr

Korean Finance Association Add:67-8, Yeouinaru-ro, Yeongdeungpo-gu, Seoul Tel:(02)2003-9921 http://www.korfin.org

Korean Folklore Society Add:41, Tojeong-ro 25-gil, Mapo-gu, Seoul http://www.kofos.or.kr

Korean Forest Society Add:57, Hoegi-ro, Dongdaemun-gu, Seoul Tel:(02)965-0454 http://www.kfs21.or.kr

Korean Geographical Society Add:213-12, Saechang-ro, Yongsan-gu, Seoul Tel:(02)875-1463 http://www.kgeography.or.kr

Korean History Research Association Add:52, Saechang-ro, Mapo-gu, Seoul Tel:(02)586-4854 http://www.koreanhistory.org

Korean Home Economics Association Add:22, Teheran-ro 7-gil, Gangnam-gu, Seoul Tel:(02)561-6446 http://www.khea.or.kr

Korean Industrial Economic Association Add:20, Changwondaehak-ro, Uichang-gu, Changwon-si, Gyeongsangnam-do Tel:(055)213-3350 http://www.kiea.ne.kr

Korean Institute of Communications and Information Sciences Add:42, Seocho-daero 78-gil, Seocho-gu, Seoul Tel:(02)3453-5555 http://www.kics.or.kr

Korean Institute of Electrical Engineers Add:22, Teheran-ro 7-gil, Gangnam-gu, Seoul Tel:(02)553-0151 http://www.kiee.or.kr

Korea Institute of Information and Communication Engineering Add:27, Seomyeonmunhwa-ro, Busanjin-gu, Busan Tel:(051)463-3683 http://www.kiice.org

Korean Institute of Information Scientists and Engineers Add:76, Bangbae-ro, Seocho-gu, Seoul Tel:1588-2728 http://www.kiise.or.kr

Korean Institute of Landscape Architecture Add:22, Teheran-ro 7-gil, Gangnam-gu, Seoul Tel:(02)565-2055 http://www.kila.or.kr

Korean Language Society Add:7, Saemunan-ro 3-gil, Jongno-gu, Seoul Tel:(02)738-2236 http://www.hangeul.or.kr

Korean Magnetics Society Add:22, Teheran-ro 7-gil, Gangnam-gu, Seoul Tel:(02)3452-7363 http://www.komag.org

Korean Mathematical Society Add:22, Teheran-ro 7-gil, Gangnam-gu, Seoul Tel:(02)565-0361 http://www.kms.or.kr

Korean Meteorological Society Add:14, Mallijae-ro, Mapo-gu, Seoul Tel:(02)835-1619 http://www.komes.or.kr

Korean Neurological Association Add:12, Insadong-gil, Jongno-gu, Seoul Tel:(02)737-6530 http://www.neuro.or.kr

Korean NeuroPsychiatric Association Add:27, Seochojungang-ro 24-gil, Seocho-gu, Seoul Tel:(02)537-6171 http://www.knpa.or.kr

Korean Nuclear Society Add:794, Yuseong-daero, Yuseong-gu, Daejeon Tel:(042)826-2613 http://www.kns.org

Korean Nutrition Society Add:22, Teheran-ro 7-gil, Gangnam-gu, Seoul Tel:(02)3452-0432 http://www.kns.or.kr

Korean Oil Chemists' Society Add:1, Chungdae-ro, Seowon-gu, Cheongju-si, Chungcheongbuk-do Tel:(043)263-3516 http://www.kocsa.or.kr

Korean Ophthalmological Society Add:50-1, Jungnim-ro, Jung-gu, Seoul Tel:(02)583-6520 http://www.ophthalmology.org

Korean Orthopaedic Association Add:32, 63-ro, Yeongdeungpo-gu, Seoul Tel:(02)780-2765 http://www.koa.or.kr

Korean Pediatric Society Add:19, Seounro, Seocho-gu, Seoul Tel:(02)3473-7305 http://www.pediatrics.or.kr

Korean Philosophical Association Add:42, Seocho-daero 78-gil, Seocho-gu,

Seoul Tel:(070)7762-7741 http://www.hanchul.org

Korean Physical Society Add:22, Teheran-ro 7-gil, Gangnam-gu, Seoul Tel:(02)556-4737 http://www.kps.or.kr

Korean Physiological Society Add:14, Teheran-ro 83-gil, Gangnam-gu, Seoul Tel:(02)568-8026 http://www.koreaphysiol.org

Korean Political Science Association Add:183-11, Donggyo-ro, Mapo-gu, Seoul Tel:(02)3452-9555 http://www.kpsa.or.kr

Korean Public Law Association Add:107, Imun-ro, Dongdaemun-gu, Seoul Tel:(02)880-5621 http://www.kpla.or.kr

Korean Publishing Science Society Add:6, Hyochangwon-ro 64-gil, Yongsan-gu, Seoul Tel:(02)712-9169 http://www.kpss.or.kr

Korean Regional Science Association Add:1, Gwanak-ro, Gwanak-gu, Seoul Tel:(02)880-4638 http://www.krsa83.or.kr

Korean Securities Association Add:143, Uisadang-daero, Yeongdeungpo-gu, Seoul Tel:(02)783-2615 http://www.iksa.or.kr

Korean Society for Aeronautical & Space Sciences Add:22, Teheran-ro 7-gil, Gangnam-gu, Seoul Tel:(02)552-4795 http://www.ksas.or.kr

Korean Society for Applied Biological Chemistry Add:22, Teheran-ro 7-gil, Gangnam-gu, Seoul Tel:(02)568-0799 http://www.ksabc.or.kr

Korean Society for Atmospheric Environment Add:102, Sajik-ro, Jongno-gu, Seoul Tel:(02)387-1400 http://www.kosae.or.kr

Korean Society for Biochemistry and Molecular Biology Add:22, Teheran-ro 7-gil, Gangnam-gu, Seoul Tel:(02)508-7436 http://www.ksbmb.or.kr

Korean Society for Biotechnology and Bioengineering Add:22, Teheran-ro 7-gil, Gangnam-gu, Seoul Tel:(02)556-2164 http://www.ksbb.or.kr

Korean Society for Chemotherapy Add:17, Teheran-ro 87-gil, Gangnam-gu, Seoul Tel:(02)557-1755 http://www.ksac.or.kr

Korean Society for Cultural Anthropology Add:1, Gwanak-ro, Gwanak-gu, Seoul Tel:(02)887-4356 http://www.koanthro.or.kr

Korean Society for Horticultural Science Add:100, Nongsaengmyeong-ro, Wanju-gu, Jeollabuk-do Tel:(063)226-6885 http://www.horticulture.or.kr

Korean Society for Journalism & Communication Studies Add:19, Jongro, Jongno-gu, Seoul Tel:(02)762-6833 http://www.comm.or.kr

Korean Society for Legal Medicine Add:42, Jebong-ro, Dong-gu, Gwangju Tel:(062)220-4090 http://www.legalmedicine.or.kr

Korean Society for Microbiology Add:22, Teheran-ro 7-gil, Gangnam-gu, Seoul Tel:(02)887-3062 http://www.ksmkorea.org

Korean Society for Microbiology and Biotechnology Add:22, Teheran-ro 7-gil, Gangnam-gu, Seoul Tel:(02)552-4733 http://www.kormb.or.kr

Korean Society for Philosophy East-West Add:99, Daehak-ro, Yuseong-gu, Daejeon Tel:(042)821-6321 http://www.kspew.org

Korean Society for Plant Biotechnology Add:28, Daehak-ro, Yuseong-gu, Daejeon Tel:(042)862-0986 http://www.kspbt.or.kr

Korean Society for Precision Engineering Add:50-1, Jungnim-ro, Jung-gu, Seoul Tel:(02)518-0722 http://www.kspe.or.kr

Korean Society for Preventive Medicine Add:222, Banpo-daero, Seocho-gu, Seoul Tel:(02)2258-7379 http://www.prevent.richis.org

Korean Society for Western History Add:100, Cheongpa-ro 47-gil, Yongsan-gu, Seoul Tel:(02)710-9357 http://www.westernhistory.or.kr

Korean Society of Aesthetics Add:1, Gwanak-ro, Gwanak-gu, Seoul Tel:(02)880-6255 http://www.aesthetics.or.kr

Korean Society of American History Add:63-8, Mapo-daero, Mapo-gu, Seoul Tel:(02)714-6217 http://www.americanhistory.or.kr

Korean Society of Analytical Sciences Add:127, Mapo-daero, Mapo-gu, Seoul Tel:(070)8744-9473 http://www.koanal.or.kr

Korean Society of Anesthesiologists Add:109, Hangang-daero, Yongsan-gu, Seoul Tel:(02)792-5128 http://www.anesthesia.or.kr

Korean Society of Animal Sciences and Technology Add:22, Teheran-ro 7-gil, Gangnam-gu, Seoul Tel:(02)562-0377 http://www.ksast.org

Korean Society of Automotive Engineers Add:21, Teheran-ro 52-gil, Gangnam-gu, Seoul Tel:(02)564-3971 http://www.ksae.org

Korean Society of Blood Transfusion
Add:33, Ichon-ro 46-gil, Yongsan-gu, Seoul
Tel:(02)795-7911 http://www.transfusion.
or.kr

Korean Society of Breeding Science
Add:125, Suin-ro, Gwonseon-gu, Suwon-
si, Gyeonggi-do Tel:(031)296-6898 http://
www.breeding.or.kr

Korean Society of Cardiology Add:331,
Dongmak-ro, Mapo-gu, Seoul Tel:(02)3275-
5258 http://www.circulation.or.kr

Korean Society of Dance Add:20,
Hongjimun 2-gil, Jongno-gu, Seoul
Tel:(070)4694-6654 http://www.ksdance.
org

**Korean Society of Environment and
Ecology** Add:36, World Cup-ro 3-gil, Mapo-
gu, Seoul Tel:(070)4194-7488 http://www.
enveco.org

Korean Society of Environmental Biology
Add:22, Teheran-ro 7-gil, Gangnam-gu,
Seoul Tel:(070)8825-5449 http://www.
koseb.org

**Korean Society of Environmental
Engineers** Add:309, Gangnam-daero,
Seocho-gu, Seoul Tel:(02)383-9652 http://
www.kosenv.or.kr

Korean Society of Epidemiology
Add:222, Wangsimni-ro, Seongdong-gu,
Seoul Tel:(02)2220-4262 http://www.kepis.
org

**Korean Society of Food Science and
Technology** Add:22, Teheran-ro 7-gil,
Gangnam-gu, Seoul Tel:(02)566-9937
http://www.kosfost.or.kr

Korean Society of Hematology Add:24,
Sajik-ro 8-gil, Jongno-gu, Seoul Tel:(02)516-
6581 http://www.hematology.or.kr

Korean Society of Infectious Diseases
Add:17, Teheran-ro 87-gil, Gangnam-gu,
Seoul Tel:(02)2055-1441 http://www.ksid.
or.kr

Korean Society of Limnology Add:22,
Teheran-ro 7-gil, Gangnam-gu, Seoul
Tel:(02)569-0744 http://www.ksl.or.kr

Korean Society of Mechanical Engineers
Add:22, Teheran-ro 7-gil, Gangnam-gu,
Seoul Tel:(02)501-3646 http://www.ksme.
or.kr

**Korean Society of Mineral and Energy
Resources Engineers** Add:22, Teheran-ro
7-gil, Gangnam-gu, Seoul Tel:(02)566-8744
http://www.ksge.or.kr

Korean Society of Mycology Add:145,
Anam-ro, Seongbuk-gu, Seoul Tel:(02)953-
8355 http://www.mycology.or.kr

Korean Society of Nuclear Medicine
Add:29, Jibong-ro, Jongno-gu, Seoul
Tel:(02)745-2040 http://www.ksnm.or.kr

**Korean Society of Nuclear Medicine
Technology** Add:82, Gumi-ro 173beon-gil,
Bundang-gu, Seongnam-si, Gyeonggi-do
Tel:(031)787-3905

Korean Society of Nursing Science Add:
22, Teheran-ro 7-gil, Gangnam-gu, Seoul
Tel:(02)567-7236 http://www.kan.or.kr

**Korean Society of Obstetrics And
Gynecology** Add:36, Gangnam-
daero 132-gil, Gangnam-gu, Seoul
Tel:(02)3445-2262 http://www.ksog.org

Korean Society of Oceanography
Add:60, Mabang-ro, Seocho-gu, Seoul
Tel:(02)589-6590 http://www.ksocean.
or.kr

**Korean Society of Otorhinolaryngology-
Head and Neck Surgery** Add:67, Seobinggo-
ro, Yongsan-gu, Seoul Tel:(02)3487-9091 http://
www.korl.or.kr

Korean Society of Pathologists
Add:92, Saemunan-ro, Jongno-gu, Seoul
Tel:(02)795-3094 http://www.pathology.
or.kr

Korean Society of Pharmacognosy
Add:1, Gwanak-ro, Gwanak-gu, Seoul
Tel:(02)765-4768 http://www.ksp.or.kr

Korean Society of Pharmacology
Add:87, Seongmisan-ro, Mapo-gu, Seoul
Tel:(02)326-0370 http://www.kosphar.org

Korean Society of Plant Biologists
Add:295-1, Bongcheon-ro, Gwanak-gu,
Seoul Tel:(02)884-0384 http://www.kspb.
kr

Korean Society of Plant Pathology
Add:92, Suseong-ro, Paldal-gu, Suwon-
si, Gyeonggi-do Tel:(031)291-5442 http://
www.kspp.org

**Korean Society of Plastic and Reconstructive
Surgeons** Add:19, Seoun-ro, Seocho-gu, Seoul
Tel:(02)3472-4252 http://www.plasticsurgery.
or.kr

Korean Society of Poultry Science Add:
114, Sinbang 1-gil, Seonghwan-eup, Seobuk-gu, Cheonan-si, Chungcheongnam-do
Tel:(041)580-6712 http://www.ksops.org

Korean Society of Radiology Add:71,
Yangjaecheon-ro, Seocho-gu, Seoul
Tel:(02)578-8003 http://www.radiology.
or.kr

Korean Society of Rheology Add:22,
Teheran-ro 7-gil, Gangnam-gu, Seoul
Tel:(02)3452-5117 http://www.rheology.
or.kr

Foundation for the Rural Youth Add: 354, Gangnam-daero, Gangnam-gu, Seoul Tel:(02)6259-1232 http://www.fry.or.kr

Korea Association for Community Education Add:5-29, Olympic-ro 34-gil, Songpa-gu, Seoul Tel:(02)424-8377 http://kace.or.kr/

Korea Association of Hakwon Add:9-3, Hangang-daero 40-gil, Yongsan-gu, Seoul Tel:(02)798-8881 http://www.kaoh.or.kr

Korea Elementary School Principal's Association Add:713, Yangcheon-ro, Gangseo-gu, Seoul Tel:(02)433-9328 http://www.kespa.or.kr

Korea Federation of Teacher's Association Add:114, Taebong-ro, Seocho-gu, Seoul Tel:(02)570-5500 http://www.kfta.or.kr

Korea Foundation for Advanced Studies Add:211, Teheran-ro, Gangnam-gu, Seoul Tel:(02)552-3641 http://www.kfas.or.kr

Korea Foundation for the Advancement of Science and Creativity Add: 602, Seol-leung-ro, Gangnam-gu, Seoul Tel:(02)555-0701 http://www.kofac.re.kr

Korea Foundation For the Promotion of Private School Add:345, Hyeoksin-daero, Dong-gu, Daegu Tel:(053)770-2500 http://www.kfpp.or.kr

Korea Heart Foundation Add:11, Olympic-ro 35ga-gil, Songpa-gu, Seoul Tel:(02)414-5321 http://www.heart.or.kr

Korea Humanistic Education Association Add:376, Gonghang-daero, Gangseo-gu, Seoul Tel:(02)782-5678 http://www.edu-net.or.kr

Korea Maritime Foundation Add:101, YeouiGongwon-ro, Yeongdeungpo-gu, Seoul Tel:(02)741-5278 http://korea maritimefoundation.or.kr

Korea Association of Secondary Education Principal Add:114, Taebong-ro, Seocho-gu, Seoul Tel:(02)576-0035 http://www.kyojang.or.kr

Korea Nuclear Energy Promotion Agency Add:1418, Nambusunhwan-ro, Geumcheon-gu, Seoul Tel:(02)859-0011 http://www.konepa.or.kr

Korea Sanhak Foundation Add:329, Gang-nam-daero, Seocho-gu, Seoul Tel:(02)3415-1234 http://www.sanhakfund.or.kr

Korea Scholarship Foundation for the Future Leaders Add:199, Seochojungang-ro, Seocho-gu, Seoul Tel:(02)595-6810 http://www.kosffl.or.kr

Korean Association for Special Education Add:22, Uisadang-daero, Yeongdeungpo-gu, Seoul Tel:(02)719-1622 http://www.kase.or.kr

Korean Association of Private Secondary School Principals Add:113, Sajik-ro, Jongno-gu, Seoul Tel:(02)739-6950 http://www.sahack.or.kr

Korean Association of Public Kindergarten Teachers Add:114, Taebong-ro, Seocho-gu, Seoul, Korea Tel:(02)577-4865 http://www.kapkt.info

Korean Council for University College Education Add:38, Seosomun-ro, Jung-gu, Seoul Tel:(02)364-1540 http://www.kcce.or.kr

Korean Council for University Education Add:606, Seobusaet-gil, Geumcheon-gu, Seoul Tel:(02)6919-3800 http://www.kcue.or.kr

Korea Cultural Heritage Foundation Add: 406, Bongeunsa-ro, Gangnam-gu, Seoul Tel:(02)566-6300 http://www.chf.or.kr

Federation of Korea Private School and University Foundation Associations Add:7, Yeouidaebang-ro 69-gil, Yeongdeungpo-gu, Seoul Tel:(02)783-8418 http://sahak21.or.kr

Korean Teachers and Education Workers Union Add:82, Kyonggidae-ro, Seodaemun-gu, Seoul Tel:(02)2670-9300 http://www.eduhope.net

Korean Teachers' Credit Union Add:50, 63-ro, Yeongdeungpo-gu, Seoul Tel:1577-3400 http://www.ktcu.or.kr

Kumho Asiana Cultural Foundation Add:75, Saemunan-ro, Jongno-gu, Seoul Tel:(02)6303-1977 http://www.kacf.net

Kumkang Scholarship Foundation Add:25, World Cup buk-ro, Mapo-gu, Seoul Tel:(02)771-7892

Lotte Foundation Add:81, Namdaemun-ro, Jung-gu, Seoul Tel:(02)776-6723 http://www.lottefoundation.or.kr

Namgang Cultural Foundation Add:17, Bogwang-ro 7-gil, Yongsan-gu, Seoul Tel:(02)790-1786 http://www.namgang.or.kr

National Research Foundation of Korea Add:25, Heolleung-ro, Seocho-gu, Seoul Tel:(02)3460-5500 http://www.nrf.re.kr

Ok-po Scholarship & Cultural Foundation Add:2154, Gyeonggang-ro, Gangneung-si, Gangwon-do Tel:(033)641-5901 http://www.okposnc.or.kr

Sam-il Cultural Foundation Add:77, Jahamun-ro, Jongno-gu, Seoul Tel:(02)735-3132 http://www.31cf.or.kr

Sammi Foundation Add:333, Yeongdong-daero, Gangnam-gu, Seoul Tel:(02)2222-4116 http://www.sammi.or.kr

Samsung Dream Scholarship Foundation Add:107, Huam-ro, Yongsan-gu, Seoul Tel:(02)727-5400 http://www.sdream.or.kr

Samsung Foundation Add:60-16, Itaewon-ro 55-gil, Yongsan-gu, Seoul Tel:(02)2014-6990 http://www.samsung-foundation.org

Samsung Scholarship Add:64, Itaewon-ro 55-gil, Yongsan-gu, Seoul Tel:(02)2014-6790 http://www.ssscholarship.com

SBS Foundation Add:442, Yangcheon-ro, Gangseo-gu, Seoul Tel:(02)2113-5352 http://foundation.sbs.co.kr

Seonam Foundation Add:13, Baekbeom-ro 90da-gil, Yongsan-gu, Seoul Tel:(02)3770-3850 http://www.seonam.org

Seoul Peace Prize Cultural Foundation Add:424, Olympic-ro, Songpa-gu, Seoul Tel:(02)2203-4096 http://www.spp.or.kr

Teachers' Pension Add:245, Munhwa-ro, Naju-si, Jeollanam-do Tel:(061)338-0000 http://www.tp.or.kr

POSCO TJ Park Foundation Add:422, Teheran-ro, Gangnam-gu, Seoul Tel:(02)562-0398 http://www.postf.org

LG Foundation Add:10, Gukjegeumyung-ro, Yeongdeungpo-gu, Seoul Tel:(02)6137-9450 http://foundation.lg.or.kr

Youlchon Foundation Add:112, Yeouidaebang-ro, Dongjak-gu, Seoul Tel:(02)820-8873 http://www.youlchon.org

Yuhan Corporation Add:74, Noryangjin-ro, Dongjak-gu, Seoul Tel:(02)828-0181 http://www.yuhan.co.kr

PRESS SOCIETIES

Association of Korean Journalists Add:30, Gukjegeumyung-ro 6-gil, Yeongdeungpo-gu, Seoul Tel:(02)3775-3733 http://www.akj21.org

Association of National Local Newspaper Add:139, Dangsan-ro, Yeongdeungpo-gu, Seoul Tel:(02)2632-1260 http://www.anln.org

Bang Il-Young Foundation Add:30, Sejong-daero 21-gil, Jung-gu, Seoul Tel:(02)724-5040 http://www.bangfound.org

Grassroots Media Add:1719, Gyebaek-ro, Jung-gu, Daejeon Tel:(070)7013-9995 http://www.bjynews.com

Korean Producers And Directors Association Add:233, Mokdongdong-ro, Yangcheon-gu, Seoul Tel:(02)3219-5613 http://www.pdjournal.com

Foundation for Broadcast Culture Add:20, Gukjegeumyung-ro, Yeongdeungpo-gu, Seoul Tel:(02)780-2491 http://www.fbc.or.kr

Journalists Association of Korea Add:124, Sejong-daero, Jung-gu, Seoul Tel:(02)734-9321 http://www.journalist.or.kr

Journalists Association of Korean Language Add:124, Sejong-daero, Jung-gu, Seoul Tel:(02)732-7367 http://www.malgeul.net

Korea Audit Bureau of Circulations Add:137, Olympic-ro 35-gil, Songpa-gu, Seoul Tel:(02)783-4983 http://www.kabc.or.kr

Korea Broadcasting Engineers & Technicians Association Add:233, Mokdongdong-ro, Yangcheon-gu, Seoul Tel:(02)3219-5635 http://www.kobeta.com

Korean Broadcasting Actors Association Add:7, Yeouidaebang-ro 69-gil, Yeongdeungpo-gu, Seoul Tel:(02)783-7830 http://www.koreatv.or.kr

Korea Broadcasting Camera Directors Association Add:233, Mokdongdong-ro, Yangcheon-gu, Seoul Tel:(02)3219-5624 http://www.tvcamera.or.kr

Korea Broadcasting Journalists Club Add:233, Mokdongdong-ro, Yangcheon-gu, Seoul Tel:(02)782-0002 http://www.kbjc.net

Korea Cable Television and Tele-communications Association Add:21, Seosomun-ro, Seodaemun-gu, Seoul Tel:(02)735-6511 http://www.kcta.or.kr

Korea Copy Editors Association Add:124, Sejong-daero, Jung-gu, Seoul Tel:(02)732-1267 http://www.edit.or.kr

Korea Independent Productions Association Add:233, Mokdongdong-ro, Yangcheon-gu, Seoul Tel:(02)3219-5645 http://www.kipa21.com

Korea Internet Newspaper Association Add:17, Teheran-ro 86-gil, Gangnam-gu, Seoul Tel:(02)730-7748 http://www.kina.or.kr

Korea Internet-Media Journalists Association Add:80, Beodeunaru-ro, Yeongdeungpo-gu, Seoul Tel:(070)4411-5452 http://www.kija.org

Korea Journalists Club Add:124, Sejong-daero, Jung-gu, Seoul Tel:(02)732-4797 http://www.kjclub.or.kr

Korea Local News Association Add:455, Bongeunsa-ro, Gangnam-gu, Seoul Tel:02)851-8582 http://klpa.net

Korea Magazine Association Add: 11, Yeouidaebang-ro 67-gil, Yeongdeungpo-gu, Seoul Tel:(02)360-0000 http://www.magazine.or.kr

Korea News Editors' Association Add: 124, Sejong-daero, Jung-gu, Seoul Tel:(02)732-1726 http://www.editor.or.kr

Korea Online Newspaper Association Add:29, Chungjeong-ro, Seodaemun-gu, Seoul Tel:(02)360-0345 http://www.kona.or.kr

Korea Press Ethics Commission Add:124, Sejong-daero, Jung-gu, Seoul Tel:(02)734-3081 http://www.ikpec.or.kr

Korea Press Foundation Add:124, Sejong-daero, Jung-gu, Seoul Tel:(02)2001-7114 http://www.kpf.or.kr

Korea Press Photographers Association Add:124, Sejong-daero, Jung-gu, Seoul Tel:(02)733-9576 http://www.kppa.or.kr

Korea Publication Ethics Commission Add:154, Geumnanghwa-ro, Gangseo-gu, Seoul Tel:(02)2669-0700 http://www.kpec.or.kr

Korea Science Journalists Association Add:22, Teheran-ro 7-gil, Gangnam-gu, Seoul Tel:(02)501-3630 http://www.scinews.co.kr

Korea Specialized Newspapers Association Add:5, Seongmisan-ro, Mapo-gu, Seoul Tel:(02)334-7251 http://www.kosna.or.kr

Korean TV News Cameraman Association Add:233, Mokdongdong-ro, Yangcheon-gu, Seoul Tel:(02)3219-6477 http://tvnews.or.kr

Korea Woman Journalists Association Add:124, Sejong-daero, Jung-gu, Seoul Tel:(02)313-3556 http://www.womanjournalist.or.kr

Korean Association of Newspapers Add:124, Sejong-daero, Jung-gu, Seoul Tel:(02)733-2251 http://www.presskorea.or.kr

Korean Broadcasters Association Add:233, Mokdongdong-ro, Yangcheon-gu, Seoul Tel:(02)3219-5560 http://www.kba.or.kr

Korean Television Directors of Photography Association Add:233, Mokdongdong-ro, Yangcheon-gu, Seoul Tel:(02)3219-5660 http://tvcam.or.kr/KTPA

Kwanhun Club Add:124, Sejong-daero, Jung-gu, Seoul Tel:(02)732-0876 http://www.kwanhun.com

LG Sangnam Press Foundation Add: 128, Yeoui-daero, Yeongdeungpo-gu, Seoul Tel:(02)3773-0191 http://www.lgpress.org

National Union of Mediaworkers Add:124, Sejong-daero, Jung-gu, Seoul Tel:(02)739-7285 http://media.nodong.org

People's Coalition for Media Reform Add:46, Tojeong-ro 37-gil, Mapo-gu, Seoul Tel:(02)732-7077 http://www.mediareform.co.kr

Samsung Press Foundation Add:4, Seocho-daero 74-gil, Seocho-gu, Seoul Tel:(02)597-4201 http://www.ssmedianet.org

Seoul Foreign Correspondents' Club Add:124, Sejong-daero, Jung-gu, Seoul Tel:(02)734-3272 http://www.sfcc.or.kr

SPORTS

Korean Olympic Committee Add:424, Olympic-ro, Songpa-gu, Seoul Tel:(02)2144-8114 http://www.sports.or.kr

<Member Associations>

Badminton Korea Association Add:424, Olympic-ro, Songpa-gu, Seoul Tel:(02)421-2724 http://www.koreabadminton.org

Boxing Association of Korea Add:424, Olympic-ro, Songpa-gu, Seoul Tel:(02)420-4251 http://boxing.sports.or.kr

Korea Biathlon Union Add:424, Olympic-ro, Songpa-gu, Seoul Tel:(02)423-1129 http://www.korbia.or.kr

Federation of Korean Aeronautics Add:26, Tongil-ro, Jung-gu, Seoul Tel:(02)424-5933 http://www.fkaero.or.kr

Korea Alpine Federation Add:424, Olympic-ro, Songpa-gu, Seoul Tel:(02)414-2750 http://new.kaf.or.kr

Korea Amateur Baduk Association Add:424, Olympic-ro, Songpa-gu, Seoul Tel:(02) 3407-3880 http://www.kbaduk.or.kr

Korea Archery Association Add:424, Olympic-ro, Songpa-gu, Seoul Tel:(02)420-4263 http://www.archery.or.kr

Korea Association of Athletics Federations Add:25, Olympic-ro, Songpa-gu, Seoul Tel:(02)414-3032 http://www.kaaf.or.kr

Korea Baseball Association Add:278, Gangnam-daero, Gangnam-gu, Seoul Tel:(02)572-8411 http://www.korea-baseball.com

Korea Basketball Association Add:424, Olympic-ro, Songpa-gu, Seoul Tel:(02)420-4221 http://www.koreabasketball.or.kr

Korea Billiards Federation Add:424, Olympic-ro, Songpa-gu, Seoul Tel:(02)2203-4674 http://kbf.sports.or.kr

Korea Bobsleigh & Skeleton Federation Add:424, Olympic-ro, Songpa-gu, Seoul Tel:(02)420-1120 http://봅슬레이.한국

Korea Bodybuilding & Fitness Federation Add:424, Olympic-ro, Songpa-gu, Seoul Tel:(02)3431-4523 http://bodybuilding.sports.or.kr

Korea Bowling Congress Add:424, Olympic-ro, Songpa-gu, Seoul Tel:(02)420-4279 http://www.bowling.or.kr

Korea Canoe Federation Add:424, Olympic-ro, Songpa-gu, Seoul Tel:(02)420-4282 http://www.canoe.or.kr

Korea Cricket Association Add:2066, Seobu-ro, Jangan-gu, Suwon-si, Gyeonggi-do Tel:(031)299-6903 http://blog.daum.net/koreacricket

Korea Curling Federation Add:424, Olympic-ro, Songpa-gu, Seoul Tel:(02)419-6281 http://curling.sports.or.kr

Korea Cycling Federation Add:424, Olympic-ro, Songpa-gu, Seoul Tel:(02)420-4247 http://www.cycling.or.kr

Korea Equestrian Federation Add:424, Olympic-ro, Songpa-gu, Seoul Tel:(02)422-7563 http://kef.sports.or.kr

Korea Federation of Dancesport Add:424, Olympic-ro, Songpa-gu, Seoul Tel:(02) 415-2090 http://www.kfds.or.kr

Korea Football Association Add:46, Gyeonghuigung-gil, Jongno-gu, Seoul Tel:(02)2002-0707 http://www.kfa.or.kr

Korea Golf Association Add:174, Hoedong-gil, Paju-si, Gyeonggi-do Tel:(031)955-2255 http://www.kgagolf.or.kr

Korea Gymnastics Association Add:424, Olympic-ro, Songpa-gu, Seoul Tel:(02)420-4266 http://www.gymnastics.or.kr

Korea Handball Federation Add:424, Olympic-ro, Songpa-gu, Seoul Tel:(02)6200-1414 http://www.handballkorea.com

Korea Hockey Association Add:424, Olympic-ro, Songpa-gu, Seoul Tel:(02)420-4267 http://www.koreahockey.co.kr

Korea Ice Hockey Association Add:424, Olympic-ro, Songpa-gu, Seoul Tel:(02)425-7001 http://www.kiha.or.kr

Korea Judo Association Add:424, Olympic-ro, Songpa-gu, Seoul Tel:(02)422-0581 http://judo.sports.or.kr

Korea Kabaddi Association Add:27, Nakdong-daero 536beon-gil, Saha-gu, Busan Tel:(051)207-0900 http://kabaddi.sports.or.kr

Korea Karatedo Federation Add:424, Olympic-ro, Songpa-gu, Seoul Tel:(02)413-0154 http://www.karatedo.or.kr

Korea Kumdo Association Add:424, Olympic-ro, Songpa-gu, Seoul Tel:(02)420-4258 http://www.kumdo.org

Korea Luge Federation Add:424, Olympic-ro, Songpa-gu, Seoul Tel:(02)413-9917 http://luge.sports.or.kr

Korea Modern Pentathlon Federation Add:424, Olympic-ro, Songpa-gu, Seoul Tel:(02)423-3057 http://www.pentathlon.or.kr

Korea National Archery Association Add:424, Olympic-ro, Songpa-gu, Seoul Tel:(02)420-4261 http://kungdo.sports.or.kr

Korea Orienteering Federation Add: 40, Cheonggyecheon-ro, Jung-gu, Seoul Tel:(02)318-1867 http://www.orienteering.or.kr

Korea Racquetball Federation Add: 25, Olympic-ro, Songpa-gu, Seoul Tel:(070)7405-7882 http://www.korearacquetball.com

Korea Roller Sports Federation Add:424, Olympic-ro, Songpa-gu, Seoul Tel:(02)420-4277 http://www.krsf.or.kr/rb

Korea Rowing Association Add:424, Olympic-ro, Songpa-gu, Seoul Tel:(02)420-4275 http://rowing.sports.or.kr

Korea Rugby Union Add:424, Olympic-ro, Songpa-gu, Seoul Tel:(02)420-4244 http://www.rugby.or.kr

Korea Sailing Federation Add:424, Olympic-ro, Songpa-gu, Seoul Tel:(02)420-4390 http://www.ksaf.org

Korea Sepaktakraw Association Add:424, Olympic-ro, Songpa-gu, Seoul Tel:(02) 420-4288 http://sepaktakraw.sports.or.kr

Korea Shooting Federation Add:653, Hwarang-ro, Nowon-gu, Seoul Tel:(02)972-5654 http://www.shooting.or.kr

Korea Skating Union Add:424, Olympic-ro, Songpa-gu, Seoul Tel:(02)2203-2018 http://www.skating.or.kr

Korea Ski Association Add:424, Olympic-ro, Songpa-gu, Seoul Tel:(02)420-4219 http://ski.sports.or.kr

Korea Soft Tennis Association Add:424, Olympic-ro, Songpa-gu, Seoul Tel:(02) 420-4057 http://softtennis.sports.or.kr

Korea Softball Federation Add:424, Olympic-ro, Songpa-gu, Seoul Tel:(02)420-4316 http://www.softball.or.kr

Korea Squash Federation Add:424, Olympic-ro, Songpa-gu, Seoul Tel:(02)419-6454 http://www.koreasquash.or.kr

Korea Ssireum Association Add:424, Olympic-ro, Songpa-gu, Seoul Tel:(02)420-4256 http://ssireum.sports.or.kr

Korea Swimming Federation Add:424, Olympic-ro, Songpa-gu, Seoul Tel:(02) 420-4236 http://swimming.sports.or.kr

Korea Taekkyon Federation Add:424, Olympic-ro, Songpa-gu, Seoul Tel:(02)516-2707 http://www.taekkyon.or.kr

Korea Taekwondo Association Add:424, Olympic-ro, Songpa-gu, Seoul Tel:(02) 420-4271 http://www.koreataekwondo.org

Korea Table Tennis Association Add:424, Olympic-ro, Songpa-gu, Seoul Tel:(02) 420-4240 http://www.koreatta.or.kr

Korea Tennis Association Add:424, Olympic-ro, Songpa-gu, Seoul Tel:(02)420-4285 http://www.kortennis.co.kr

Korea Underwater Association Add:424, Olympic-ro, Songpa-gu, Seoul Tel:(02) 420-4293 http://kua.sports.or.kr

Korea Volleyball Association Add:218, Dogok-ro, Gangnam-gu, Seoul Tel:(02)578-9025 http://www.kva.or.kr

Korea Waterski and Wakeboard Association Add:424, Olympic-ro, Songpa-gu, Seoul Tel:(02)2203-0488 http://www.waterskinet.org

Korea Weightlifting Federation Add: 424, Olympic-ro, Songpa-gu, Seoul Tel:(02) 420-4260 http://www.weightlifting.or.kr

Korea Wrestling Federation Add:424, Olympic-ro, Songpa-gu, Seoul Tel:(02)420-4255 http://www.wrestling.or.kr

Korea Wushu Association Add:424, Olympic-ro, Songpa-gu, Seoul Tel:(02)412-6381 http://wushu.sports.or.kr

Korean Fencing Federation Add:424, Olympic-ro, Songpa-gu, Seoul Tel:(02)420-4289 http://fencing.sports.or.kr

Triathlon Korea Add:424, Olympic-ro, Songpa-gu, Seoul Tel:(02)3431-6798 http://www.triathlon.or.kr

World Association of Kickboxing Organization Korea Add:42, Daehak-gil, Gwanak-gu, Seoul Tel:(02)732-8826 http://www.wako.or.kr

<Etc.>

Korea Aerobic Association Add:16, Sungkyunkwan-ro 3-gil, Jongno-gu, Seoul Tel:(02)734-1110 http://www.aerobics.co.kr

Korea Baseball Organization Add: 278, Gangnam-daero, Gangnam-gu, Seoul Tel:(02)3460-4600 http://www.koreabaseball.com

Korea Boxing Commission Add:298, Gwanak-daero, Dongan-gu, Anyang-si, Gyeonggi-do Tel:(031)689-5441 http://www.koreaboxing.co.kr

Korea Council of Sport for All Add:424, Olympic-ro, Songpa-gu, Seoul Tel:(02)2152-7330 http://www.sportal.or.kr

Korea e-Sports Association Add:109, Cheongpa-ro, Yongsan-gu, Seoul Tel:(02)737-3710 http://www.e-sports.or.kr

Korea Ladies Professional Golf Association Add:13, Yeongdong-daero 85-gil, Gangnam-gu, Seoul Tel:(02)587-2929 http://www.klpga.com

Korea Professional Football League Add:46, Gyeonghuigung-gil, Jongno-gu, Seoul Tel:(02)2002-0663 http://www.kleague.com

Korea Professional Golfers' Association Add:121, Unjung-ro, Bundang-gu, Seongnam-si, Gyeonggi-do Tel:(02)414-8855 http://www.koreapga.com

Korea Sports Promotion Foundation Add:424, Olympic-ro, Songpa-gu, Seoul Tel:(02)410-1114 http://www.kspo.or.kr

Korea University Basketball Federation Add:424, Olympic-ro, Songpa-gu, Seoul Tel:(02)424-1941 http://www.kubf.or.kr

Korea University Football Confederation Add:46, Gyeonghuigung-gil, Jongno-gu, Seoul Tel:(02)2002-0717 http://www.kufc.or.kr

Korea University Ssireum Federation Add:424, Olympic-ro, Songpa-gu, Seoul Tel:(02)783-0534 http://www.ksuf.com

Korean Association of Sport for All Add:32, Gosan-gil, Mapo-gu, Seoul Tel:(02)3272-8307 http://www.kasfa.or.kr

Korean Basketball League Add:110, Dosan-daero, Gangnam-gu, Seoul Tel:(02)2106-3000 http://www.kbl.or.kr

Korean Volleyball Federation Add:402, World Cup buk-ro, Mapo-gu, Seoul Tel:(02)422-0110 http://www.kovo.co.kr

Kukkiwon Add:32, Teheran-ro 7-gil,

Gangnam-gu, Seoul Tel:(02)567-1058 http://www.kukkiwon.or.kr

Taereung National Training Center Add:727, Hwarang-ro, Nowon-gu, Seoul Tel:(02)970-0114 http://www.sports.or.kr/player

Women's Korean Basketball League Add:355, Gonghang-daero, Gangseo-gu, Seoul Tel:(02)752-7493 http://www.wkbl.or.kr

MEDICINE

Association of Korean Medicine Add:91, Heojun-ro, Gangseo-gu, Seoul Tel:(02) 2657-5000 http://www.akom.org

Corporation Aggregate Korea Atopy Association Add:510, Yangcheon-ro, Gangseo-gu, Seoul Tel:(02)3663-3236 http://www.atopykorea.or.kr

Diabetic Association of Korea Add: 9-3, Eonju-ro 98-gil, Gangnam-gu, Seoul Tel:(02)771-8542 http://www.dangnyo.or.kr

Health Insurance Review & Assessment Service Add:267, Hyoryeong-ro, Seocho-gu, Seoul Tel:1644-2000 http://www.hira.or.kr

Korea Association of Health Promotion Add:350, Hwagok-ro, Gangseo-gu, Seoul Tel:(02)2601-6141 http://www.kahp.or.kr

Korea Blood Cancer Association Add:393, Hangang-daero, Yongsan-gu, Seoul Tel:(02)3432-0807 http://www.bloodcancer.or.kr

Korean Cancer Society Add:13, Chungmu-ro, Jung-gu, Seoul Tel:(02)2263-5110 http://www.kcscancer.org

Korea Federation for HIV/AIDS Prevention Add:209, Dongsomun-ro, Seongbuk-gu, Seoul Tel:(02)927-4071 http://www.kaids.or.kr

Korea Hypertension Management Association Add:508, Samseong-ro, Gangnam-gu, Seoul Tel:(02)557-2941 http://www.khma.or.kr

Korean Medical Association Add:33, Ichon-ro 46-gil, Yongsan-gu, Seoul Tel:(02) 794-2474 http://www.kma.org

Korea Midwives Association Add:86, Cheonggu-ro, Jung-gu, Seoul Tel: (02)2279-1972 http://www.midwife.or.kr

Korea Oriental Drug Association Add:122, Wangsan-ro, Dongdaemun-gu, Seoul Tel:(02)960-5185 http://kherb.org

Korean Medicine Hospitals' Association Add:128, BangbaeJungang-ro, Seocho-gu, Seoul Tel:(02)596-4245 http://www.komha.or.kr

Korea Pharmaceutical Manufacturers Association Add:161, Hyoryeong-ro, Seocho-gu, Seoul Tel:(02)581-2101 http://www.kpma.or.kr

Korean Association for Radiation Application Add:77, Seongsuil-ro, Seongdong-gu, Seoul Tel:(02)3490-7111 http://www.ri.or.kr

Korea School Health Association Add:23, Gukhoe-daero 66-gil, Yeongdeungpo-gu, Seoul Tel:(02)785-7529 http://www.ksha.or.kr

Korean Alliance to Defeat AIDS Add:11, Jowonjungang-ro, Gwanak-gu, Seoul Tel:(02)861-4114 http://www.aids.or.kr

Korean Association for Children with Leukemia and Cancer Add:37, Donggyo-ro 17-gil, Mapo-gu, Seoul Tel:1544-1415 http://soaam.or.kr

Korean Association for Dementia Add:32, 63-ro, Yeongdeungpo-gu, Seoul Tel:(02)762-0710 http://www.silverweb.or.kr

Korean Dental Association Add:257, Gwangnaru-ro, Seongdong-gu, Seoul Tel:(02)2024-9100 http://www.kda.or.kr

Korean Hansen Welfare Association Add:59, Wongol-ro, Uiwang-si, Gyeonggi-do Tel:(031)452-7091 http://www.khwa.or.kr

Korean Hospital Association Add:15, Mapo-daero, Mapo-gu, Seoul Tel:(02)705-9200 http://www.kha.or.kr

Korean National Tuberculosis Association Add:57, Baumoe-ro 6-gil, Seocho-gu, Seoul Tel:1544-1050 http://www.knta.or.kr

Korean Nurses Association Add:314, Dongho-ro, Jung-gu, Seoul Tel:(02)2260-2511 http://www.koreanurse.or.kr

Korean Pharmaceutical Association Add:194, Hyoryeong-ro, Seocho-gu, Seoul Tel:(02)581-1201 http://www.kpanet.or.kr

Korea Public Health Association Add:121, Bomun-ro, Seongbuk-gu, Seoul Tel:(02)921-9520 http://www.kpha.or.kr

Korean Radiological Technologists Association Add:18, Mabang-ro 4-gil, Seocho-gu, Seoul Tel:(02)576-6524 http://www.krta.or.kr

Korean Research-Based Pharmaceutical Industry Association Add:320, Gangnam-daero, Gangnam-gu, Seoul Tel:(02)456-8553 http://www.krpia.or.kr

Korean Veterinary Medical Association Add:8-6, Hwangsaeul-ro 319beon-gil, Bundang-gu, Seongnam-si, Gyeonggi-do Tel:(031)702-8686 http://www.kvma.or.kr

National Health Insurance Service Add:311, Dongmak-ro, Mapo-gu, Seoul Tel:1577-1000 http://www.nhic.or.kr

Planned Population Federation of Korea Add:20, Beodeunaru-ro 14ga-gil, Yeongdeungpo-gu, Seoul Tel:(02)2634-8212 http://www.ppfk.or.kr

RELIGION

\<Christianity\>

Academia Christiana of Korea Add: 30, Kimsangok-ro, Jongno-gu, Seoul Tel:(02)764-0376 http://www.instit.ac

Anglican Church of Korea Add:15, Sejong-daero 21-gil, Jung-gu, Seoul Tel:(02)738-6597 http://www.skh.or.kr

Assemblies of God of Korea Add:134, Tongil-ro, Jongno-gu, Seoul Tel:(02)720-6832 http://www.kihasung.org

Christian Council of Korea Add:30, Kimsangok-ro, Jongno-gu, Seoul Tel:(02)741-2782 http://www.cck.or.kr

Christian Literature Society of Korea Add: 14, Teheran-ro 103-gil, Gangnam-gu, Seoul Tel:(02)553-0870 http://www.clsk.org

Christian Work Mission Add:129, Bongeunsa-ro, Gangnam-gu, Seoul Tel:(02)3446-5070 http://www.workmission.net

Connecting Business and Marketplace to Christ Add:75, Keunumul-ro, Mapo-gu, Seoul Tel:(02)717-0111 http://www.cbmc.or.kr

Council of Presbyterian Churches in Korea Add:19, Daehak-ro, Jongno-gu, Seoul Tel:(02)764-0950 http://www.cpck.kr

General Assembly of Presbyterian Church in Korea Add:330, Yeongdong-daero, Gangnam-gu, Seoul Tel:(02)559-5600 http://www.gapck.org

Korea Baptist Convention Add:10, Gukhoe-daero 76-gil, Yeongdeungpo-gu, Seoul Tel:(02)2683-6693 http://www.korea-baptist.or.kr/

Korea Campus Crusade for Christ Add:2-8, Baekseokdong 1ga-gil, Jongno-gu, Seoul Tel:(02)397-6200 http://www.kccc.org

Korea Christian Leaders Association Add:21-11, Sowol-ro 2-gil, Yongsan-gu, Seoul Tel:(02)795-7952 http://www.c-l.or.kr

Korea Evangelical Church Add:264, Yulgok-ro, Jongno-gu, Seoul Tel:(02)762-7529 http://www.kec21.or.kr

Korea Evangelical Holiness Church Add:17, Teheran-ro 64-gil, Gangnam-gu, Seoul Tel:(02)3459-1071 http://www.kehc.org

Korea Harbor Evangelism Inc. Add:211, Hangang-daero, Yongsan-gu, Seoul Tel:(02)335-3445 http://www.khewck.org

Korea World Missions Association Add:76, Gamasan-ro, Geumcheon-gu, Seoul Tel:(02)3280-7981 http://www.kwma.org

Korean Bible Society Add:2569, Nambusunhwan-ro, Seocho-gu, Seoul Tel:(02)2103-8700 http://www.bskorea.or.kr

Korean Methodist Church Add:149, Sejong-daero, Jongno-gu, Seoul Tel:1688-1008 http://www.kmc.or.kr

Presbyterian Church in the Republic of Korea Add:30, Kimsangok-ro, Jongno-gu, Seoul Tel:(02)3499-7600 http://www.prok.org

The Salvation Army Korea Territory Add:130, Deoksugung-gil, Jung-gu, Seoul Tel:(02)6364-4000 http://www.salvationarmy.or.kr

\<Buddhism\>

Association of Korean Buddhist Orders Add:45-19, Ujeongguk-ro, Jongno-gu, Seoul Tel:(02)732-4885 http://www.kboa.or.kr

Cheontae Order Add:73, Guinsa-gil, Yeongchun-myeon, Danyang-gun, Chungcheong-buk-do Tel:(043)423-7100 http://www.cheontae.org

Chonghwajong Add:7, Changsin 5ma-gil, Jongno-gu, Seoul http://www.chonghwajong.org

Buddhist Chongji Order Add:35, Dogok-ro 25-gil, Gangnam-gu, Seoul Tel:(02)552-1080 http://www.chongji.or.kr

Korean Buddhist Jingak Order Add:17, Hwarang-ro 13-gil, Seongbuk-gu, Seoul Tel:(02)913-0751 http://www.jingak.or.kr

Jodongjong Add:103, Deongneung-ro 145-gil, Nowon-gu, Seoul Tel:(02)2091-0408 http://www.조동종.kr

Jogye Order of Korean Buddhism Add: 55, Ujeongguk-ro, Jongno-gu, Seoul Tel: (02)2011-1700 http://www.buddhism.or.kr

Korea Buddhism Il Seung Order Add:14-6, Gyeongchun-ro 16beon-gil, Guri-si, Gyeonggi-do Tel:(031)562-2751 http://www.ilseung.or.kr

Korea Buddhism Promotion Foundation Add:20, Mapo-daero, Mapo-gu, Seoul Tel:(02)719-1855 http://www.kbpf.org

Korea Yeombul Ilseung Order Add:213-47, Okcheon-ro, Dong-gu, Daejeon Tel:(042)282-6936 http://www.yeombul.org

Korea Buddhist Daeseung Jong Add:85, Dasan-ro 24-gil, Jung-gu, Seoul Tel:(02)2234-2198

Korea Buddhist Ilbung Seonkyo Order Add:76-9, Segeomjeong-ro 6-gil, Jongno-gu, Seoul Tel:(02)991-8175 http://www.ilbung.org

Korean Buddhist Kwanum order Add: 31, Jong-ro 63ga-gil, Jongno-gu, Seoul Tel: (02)763-0054 http://www.kwanum.or.kr

Korean Buddhist Mita Order Add: 133, Mangu-ro, Dongdaemun-gu, Seoul Tel:(02)2242-1049 http://www.mitajong.or.kr

Korean Buddhist Taego Order Add:31, Yulgok-ro 1-gil, Jongno-gu, Seoul Tel:(02)739-3450 http://www.taego.or.kr

Wawoo Buddhist Temple Add:89-19, Haesil-ro, Cheoin-gu, Yongin-si, Gyeonggi-do Tel:(031)332-2472 http://www.wawoo-temple.org

<Catholic>

Catholic Bishops' Conference of Korea Add:74, Myeonmok-ro, Gwangjin-gu, Seoul Tel:(02)460-7500 http://www.cbck.or.kr

<Dioceses>

Archdiocese of Gwangju Add:980, Sangmu-daero, Seo-gu, Gwangju Tel:(062)380-2809 http://www.gjcatholic.or.kr

Archdiocese of Seoul Add:74, Myeong-dong-gil, Jung-gu, Seoul Tel:(02)727-2114 http://aos.catholic.or.kr

Catholic Diocese of Daejeon Add:86, Songchonnam-ro 11beon-gil, Dong-gu, Daejeon Tel:(042)630-7700 http://www.djcatholic.or.kr

Catholic Diocese of Cheju Add:14, Gwandeok-ro 8-gil, Jeju-si, Jeju-do Tel:(064) 751-0145 http://www.diocesejeju.or.kr

Catholic Diocese of Cheongju Add:135-35, Juseong-ro, Sangdang-gu, Cheongju-si, Chungcheongbuk-do Tel:(043)210-1700 http://www.cdcj.or.kr

Catholic Archdiocese of Daegu Add:112, Namsan-ro 4-gil, Jung-gu, Daegu Tel:(053) 250-3000 http://www.daegu-archdiocese.or.kr

Catholic Diocese of Andong Add:36-15, Jeongbaegigol-gil, Andong-si, Gyeongsangbuk-do Tel:(054)858-3114 http://www.acatholic.or.kr

Catholic Diocese of Busan Add:39, Suyeong-ro 427beon-gil, Suyeong-gu, Busan Tel:(051)629-8700 http://www.catholicbusan.or.kr

Catholic Diocese of Chunchon Add:300, Gongji-ro, Chuncheon-si, Gangwon-do Tel:(033)240-6000 http://www.cccatholic.or.kr

Catholic Diocese of Incheon Add:2, Uhyeon-ro 50beon-gil, Jung-gu, Incheon Tel:(032)765-6961 http://www.caincheon.or.kr

Catholic Diocese of Jeonju Add:100, Girin-daero, Wansan-gu, Jeonju-si, Jeollabuk-do Tel:(063)230-1004 http://www.jcatholic.or.kr

Catholic Diocese of Masan Add:27, Odongbuk 16-gil, Masanhappo-gu, Changwon-si, Gyeongsangnam-do Tel:(055)249-7000 http://cathms.kr

Catholic Diocese of Suwon Add:39, Imok-ro, Jangan-gu, Suwon-si, Gyeonggi-do Tel:(031)244-5001 http://www.casuwon.or.kr

Catholic Diocese of Uijeongbu Add:261, Sinheung-ro, Uijeongbu-si, Gyeonggi-do Tel:(031)850-1400 http://www.ucatholic.or.kr

Catholic Diocese of Wonju Add:28, Wo-nil-ro, Ilsanseo-gu, Goyang-si, Gyeonggi-do Tel:(033)765-4221 http://www.wjcatholic.or.kr

Military Ordinariate in Korea Add:P. O.Box 31, 118, Hangang-daero, Yongsan-gu, Seoul Tel:(02)749-1921 http://www.gunjong.or.kr

LABOR

Korean Confederation of Trade Unions Add:3, Jeong-gil, Jung-gu, Seoul Tel:(02)2670-9100 http://www.nodong.org

Member Unions : Chemical and Textile Workers, Clerical and Financial Labour, Construction Industry, Democracy and

Federacy Workers, Government Employees, Health and Medical Workers, Irregular University Professors, IT Workers, Private Service Workers, Media workers, Metal Workers, Professors, Public & Social Services and Transportation workers, Teachers and Education Workers, University Workers, Women Workers

Federation of Korean Trade Unions Add:26, Gukjegeumyung-ro 6-gil, Yeongdeungpo-gu, Seoul Tel:(02)6277-0000 http://www.inochong.org

Member Unions : Automobile and Transport Workers, Apartment Workers, Chemical Workers, Construction Industry, Financial Industry, Food Industry Workers, Foreign Organization Employees, Government Workers, Information Technology Office Service Workers, Medical Industry Workers, Metal workers, Mine Workers, Port & Transport Workers, Postal Workers, Private University Workers, Printing Workers, Public Industry, Public Trade, Railway Industry, Rubber Workers, Seafarers, Taxi Workers, Textile and Distribution Workers, Tobacco and Ginseng Workers, Tourism and Service Industry Workers, United Workers

WOMEN AND YOUTH

Big Brothers and Big Sisters of Korea Add:12, Gukhoe-daero 70-gil, Yeongdeungpo-gu, Seoul Tel:(02)3494-1800 http://www.bbskorea.or.kr

Central Women's Association Add:51, Jibong-ro 23-gil, Seongbuk-gu, Seoul Tel:(02)928-4735 http://www.jw21.org

Girl Scouts Korea Add:47, Yulgok-ro, Jongno-gu, Seoul Tel:(02)733-6801 http://www.girlscout.or.kr

Hostelling International Korea Add:7, Chungjeong-ro, Seodaemun-gu, Seoul Tel:(02)725-3031 http://www.kyha.or.kr

Korea 4-H Association Add:31, Dongnam-ro 73-gil, Gangdong-gu, Seoul Tel:(02)428-0451 http://www.korea4-h.or.kr

Korea Association for Youth Service Add:23, Eulji-ro 11-gil, Jung-gu, Seoul Tel:(02)2273-3030 http://www.kays.or.kr

Korea Association of Welfare Promotion for Youth Add:234, Geumnanghwa-ro, Gangseo-gu, Seoul Tel:(02)2662-6152 http://www.kawpy.org

Korea Federation of Women's Welfare Add:14, Mallijae-ro, Mapo-gu, Seoul Tel: (02)712-0713 http://www.womenbokji.or.kr

Korea Foundation for Women Add:13, World Cup buk-ro 5-gil, Mapo-gu, Seoul Tel:(02)336-6364 http://www.womenfund.or.kr

Korea Rotary Youth Association Add:19, Saemunan-ro 5-gil, Jongno-gu, Seoul Tel:(02)738-1501 http://www.rotarykorea.org

Korea Scout Association Add:14, Gukhoe-daero 62-gil, Yeongdeungpo-gu, Seoul Tel:(02)6335-2000 http://www.scout.or.kr

Korea Student Christian Federation Add:19, Daehak-ro, Jongno-gu, Seoul Tel:(02)763-8776 http://www.kscf.or.kr

Korea Women Inventors Association Add:131, Teheran-ro, Gangnam-gu, Seoul Tel:(02)538-2710 http://www.inventor.or.kr

Korea Women's Hot Line Add:8-4, Jinheung-ro 16-gil, Eunpyeong-gu, Seoul Tel:(02)3156-5400 http://www.hotline.or.kr

Korea Youth Association Add:33, Yeouidaebang-ro 20-gil, Dongjak-gu, Seoul Tel:(02)2181-7417 http://www.koya.or.kr

Korea Youth Buddhist Association Add:67, Ujeongguk-ro, Jongno-gu, Seoul Tel:(02)738-1920 http://www.kyba.org

Korea Youth Edify Association Add:120, Supyo-ro, Jongno-gu, Seoul Tel: (02)735-8165 http://www.yeba.or.kr

Korea Youth Protection & Upbringing Association Add:16-1, Mokdong-ro 9-gil, Yangcheon-gu, Seoul Tel:(02)922-3388 http://www.youthboy.net

Korea Youth Loyalty and Filial Piety A Group League Add:19, Sangdang-ro 190beon-gil, Sangdang-gu, Cheongju-si, Chungcheongbuk-do Tel:(043)221-2918 http://www.chunghyo.or.kr

Korean Etiquette Institute Add:89, Segeomjeong-ro, Seodaemun-gu, Seoul Tel:(02)391-1988 http://www.etiquette.or.kr

Korean League of Women Voters Add:11, Olympic-ro 35ga-gil, Songpa-gu, Seoul Tel:(02)423-5355 http://www.womenvoters.or.kr

Korean National Council of Women Add: 25, Hangang-daero 21-gil, Yongsan-gu, Seoul Tel:(02)794-4560 http://www.kncw.or.kr

Korean National Mothers' Association Add:46, Eonju-ro 146-gil, Gangnam-gu, Seoul Tel:(02)512-0488 http://www.koreamother.or.kr

Korean Women Entrepreneurs Association Add:221, Yeoksam-ro, Gangnam-gu, Seoul Tel:(02)369-0900 http://www.womanbiz.or.kr

Korean Womenlink Add:39, World Cup-ro 26-gil, Mapo-gu, Seoul Tel:(02)737-5763 http://www.womenlink.or.kr

Korean Women's Association Add: 35, Huiujeong-ro, Mapo-gu, Seoul Tel:(02)701-7321 http://www.womankorea.or.kr

Korean Women's Association United Add:6, Gukhoe-daero 55-gil, Yeongdeungpo-gu, Seoul Tel:(02)313-1632 http://www.women21.or.kr

Korean Women's Federation For Consumer Add:30, Namdaemun-ro, Jung-gu, Seoul Tel:(02)752-4227 http://www.jubuclub.or.kr

Language Laboratory Add:7, Chungjeongno, Seodaemun-gu, Seoul Tel:(02)736-0521 http://www.labo.or.kr

National Council of Homemakers' Classes Add:7, Toegye-ro 45-gil, Jung-gu, Seoul Tel:(02)2265-3628 http://www.nchc.or.kr

National Council of YMCA's of Korea Add:68, Jandari-ro, Mapo-gu, Seoul Tel:(02)754-7891 http://www.ymcakorea.org

National Council of Youth Organizations in Korea Add:234, Geumnanghwa-ro, Gangseo-gu, Seoul Tel:(02)2667-0471 http://www.ncyok.or.kr

National Youth Policy Institute Add:370, Sicheong-daero, Sejong-si Tel:(044)415-2114 http://www.nypi.re.kr

Korea YMCA Add:73, Myeongdong-gil, Jung-gu, Seoul Tel:(02)774-9702 http://www.ywca.or.kr

Research Center for Korean Youth Culture Add:42, Dongho-ro 20-gil, Jung-gu, Seoul Tel:(02)2238-0702 http://www.youth.re.kr

Samdong Youth Association Add: 1058, Muwang-ro, Iksan-si, Jeollabuk-do Tel:(063)834-0676 http://www.sdya.or.kr

Sea Explorers of Korea Add:1935, Nambusunhwan-ro, Gwanak-gu, Seoul Tel:(02)886-8522 http://www.sekh.or.kr

Yejiwon Cultural Institute Add:72, Jangchungdan-ro, Jung-gu, Seoul Tel:(02)2234-3325 http://www.yejiwon.or.kr

Young Astronauts Korea Add:46, Hyehwa-ro, Jongno-gu, Seoul Tel:(02)739-6369 http://www.yak.or.kr

WELFARE

Beautiful Foundation Add:6, Jahamun-ro 19-gil, Jongno-gu, Seoul Tel:(02)766-1004 http://www.beautifulfund.org

Community Chest Of Korea Add:39, Sejong-daero 21-gil, Jung-gu, Seoul Tel:(02)6262-3000 http://www.chest.or.kr

Good Neighbors Add:13, Beodeunaru-ro, Yeongdeungpo-gu, Seoul Tel:(02)6717-4000 http://www.goodneighbors.kr

HelpAge Korea Add:53, Yangsan-ro, Yeongdeungpo-gu, Seoul Tel:(02)849-6588 http://www.helpage.or.kr

Holt Children's Services Inc. Add:19, Yanghwa-ro, Mapo-gu, Seoul Tel:(02)331-7078 http://www.holt.or.kr

Join Together Society Add:7, Hyoryeong-ro 51-gil, Seocho-gu, Seoul Tel:(02)587-8756 http://www.jts.or.kr

Korea Association in Community Care for the Elderly Add:16, Baekbeom-ro 37-gil, Mapo-gu, Seoul Tel:(02)3273-8646 http://www.kacold.or.kr

Korea Federation of Senior Welfare Add:14, Mallijae-ro, Mapo-gu, Seoul Tel:(02)712-9763 http://www.elder.or.kr

Korea Food for the Hungry International Add:109, Gonghang-daero 59da-gil, Gangseo-gu, Seoul Tel:(02)544-9544 http://www.kfhi.or.kr

Korea International Cooperation Agency Add:825, Daewangpangyo-ro, Sujeong-gu, Seongnam-si, Gyeonggi-do Tel:(031)7400-114 http://www.koica.go.kr

Korea National Council on Social Welfare Add:14, Mallijae-ro, Mapo-gu, Seoul Tel:(02)2077-3908 http://kncsw.bokji.net

Korea Polio Association Add:93, Walkerhill-ro, Gwangjin-gu, Seoul Tel:(070)7457-8518 http://www.kpa1966.or.kr

Korea Society of Civil Volunteer Add:17, Samseong-ro 104-gil, Gangnam-gu, Seoul Tel:(02)2663-4163 http://www.civo.net

Korea Women's Home Add:63, Seongmisan-ro 19-gil, Mapo-gu, Seoul Tel:(02)333-7511 http://www.hanyeou.or.kr

Korean Red Cross Add:145, Sopa-ro, Jung-gu, Seoul Tel:(02)3705-3705 http://www.redcross.or.kr

Korean Society for Rehabilitation of Persons with Disabilities Add:161, Hyoryeong-ro, Seocho-gu, Seoul Tel:(02)3472-3556 http://www.freeget.net

Korean Society for the Cerebral Palsied Add:69, Banghwa-daero 45-gil, Gangseo-gu, Seoul Tel:(02)932-4292 http://www.kscp.net

Rotary Korea Add:19, Saemunan-ro 5-gil, Jongno-gu, Seoul Tel:(02)738-1501 http://www.rotarykorea.org

Salvation Army Korea Territory Add:130, Deoksugung-gil, Jung-gu, Seoul Tel:(02)6364-

4000 http://www.salvationarmy.or.kr

Save the Children Korea Add:174, Tojeong-ro, Mapo-gu, Seoul Tel:(02)6900-4400 http://www.sc.or.kr

Sisters of Mary Add:20-11, Baengnyeonsan-ro 14-gil, Eunpyeong-gu, Seoul Tel:(02)351-2020 http://www.sistersofmary.or.kr

Social Welfare Society, Inc. Add:21, Nonhyeon-ro 86-gil, Gangnam-gu, Seoul Tel:(02)552-1017 http://www.sws.or.kr

World Vision Korea Add:77-1, Yeouinaru-ro, Yeongdeungpo-gu, Seoul Tel:(02)2078-7000 http://www.worldvision.or.kr

ART AND CULTURE

Federation of Korean Artistic and Cultural Organizations Add:225, Mokdong-seo-ro, Yangcheon-gu, Seoul Tel:(02)2655-3000 http://www.yechong.or.kr

Member Associations : Korean Institute of Architects, Korean Traditional Music Association, Dance Association of Korea, Korean Writers Association, Korean Fine Arts Association, Photo Artist Society of Korea, National Theater, Korean Entertainment Artist Federation, Motion Pictures Association of Korea, Music Association of Korea

Arts Council Korea Add:640, Bitgaram-ro, Naju-si, Jeollanam-do Tel:(061)900-2100 http://www.arko.or.kr

Galleries Association of Korea Add:461, Samil-daero, Jongno-gu, Seoul Tel:(02)733-3706 http://www.koreagalleries.or.kr

Institute of Traditional Culture Add:428, Samil-daero, Jongno-gu, Seoul Tel:(02) 762-8401 http://www.juntong.or.kr

King Sejong the Great Memorial Society Add:56, Hoegi-ro, Dongdaemun-gu, Seoul Tel:(02)969-8851 http://www.sejongkorea.org

Korea Ballet Association Add:20, Teheran-ro 25-gil, Gangnam-gu, Seoul Tel:(02)538-0505 http://www.koreaballet.or.kr

Korea Cartoonists Association Add:130, Sopa-ro, Jung-gu, Seoul Tel:(02)757-8485 http://www.cartoon.or.kr

Korea Pansori Preservation Society Add:406, Bongeunsa-ro, Gangnam-gu, Seoul Tel:(02)566-9457 http://www.korea-pansori.com

Korea Voice Performance Association Add:23, Gukhoe-daero 62-gil, Yeong-deungpo-gu, Seoul Tel:(02)784-0422 http://kvpa.kr

Korean Broadcasting Actors Association Add:7, Yeouidaebang-ro 69-gil, Yeongdeungpo-gu, Seoul Tel:(02)783-7830 http://www.koreatv.or.kr

Korean Film Council Add:55, Centum jungang-ro, Haeundae-gu, Busan Tel:(051)720-4700 http://www.kofic.or.kr

Korean Modern Poet Association Add:18, World Cup buk-ro 9-gil, Mapo-gu, Seoul Tel:(02)323-2227 http://www.kmpoet.com

Korean People Artist Federation Add:60, Jandari-ro, Mapo-gu, Seoul Tel:(02)739-6851 http://kpaf.kr

Korean Society of Interior Architects/Designers Add:377, Sowol-ro, Yongsan-gu, Seoul Tel:(02)508-8038 http://www.kosid.or.kr

Korean Society of Translators Add: 12, Saemunan-ro 3-gil, Jongno-gu, Seoul Tel:(02)725-0506 http://www.kstinc.or.kr

Korean TV&Radio Writers Association Add:750, Gukhoe-daero, Yeongdeungpo-gu, Seoul Tel:(02)782-1696 http://www.ktrwa.or.kr

Saekdong Add:29, Sinchon-ro, Seodaemun-gu, Seoul Tel:(02)3141-5504 http://www.saekdong.or.kr

Society of Korean Poets Add:36, Yulgok-ro 6-gil, Jongno-gu, Seoul Tel:(02)764-4596 http://www.koreapoet.org

\<Dance and Music\>

Changmu Arts Center Add:148, Wausan-ro, Mapo-gu, Seoul Tel:(02)337-5961 http://www.changmu.co.kr

Gloria Opera Company Add:24, Nonhyeon-ro 168-gil, Gangnam-gu, Seoul Tel:(02)543-2351 http://www.gloriaopera.co.kr

Grand Opera Company Add:32, Samseong-ro 71-gil, Gangnam-gu, Seoul Tel:(02)2238-1002 http://www.grandopera.or.kr

KBS Symphony Orchestra Add:13, Yeouigongwon-ro, Yeongdeungpo-gu, Seoul Tel:(02)6099-7410 http://www.kbssymphony.org

Korea National Opera Add:2406, Nambusunhwan-ro, Seocho-gu, Seoul Tel:(02)586-5282 http://www.nationalopera.org

Korea Opera Group Add:225, Mokdongseo-ro, Yangcheon-gu, Seoul Tel:(02)584-5021 http://www.kopera.co.kr

Korean Chamver Orchestra Add:9, Nambusunhwan-ro 325-gil, Seocho-gu, Seoul Tel:(02)592-5728 http://www.kco.or.kr

Korean National Ballet Add:2406, Nambusunhwan-ro, Seocho-gu, Seoul Tel:(02)587-6181 http://www.kballet.org

Little Angels Add:664, Cheonho-daero, Gwangjin-gu, Seoul Tel:(070)7124-1762 http://www.littleangels.or.kr

National Changguk Compoany Of Korea Add:59, Jangchungdan-ro, Jung-gu, Seoul Tel:(02)2280-4114 http://www.ntok.go.kr/changguk

National Chorus of Korea Add:2406, Nambusunhwan-ro, Seocho-gu, Seoul Tel:(02)587-8111 http://www.nationalchorus.or.kr

National Dance Company of Korea Add:59, Jangchungdan-ro, Jung-gu, Seoul Tel:(02)2280-4114 http://www.ntok.go.kr/dance

National Orchestra of Korea Add: 59, Jangchungdan-ro, Jung-gu, Seoul Tel:(02)2280-4114 http://www.ntok.go.kr/orchestra

Seoul Metropolitan Traditional Music Orchestra Add:175, Sejong-daero, Jongno-gu, Seoul Tel:(02)339-1114 http://sjartgroups.or.kr/intro/tradition

Seoul Performing Arts Company Add:2406, Nambusunhwan-ro, Seocho-gu, Seoul Tel:(02)523-0984 http://www.spac.or.kr

Seoul Philharmonic Orchestra Add: 175, Sejong-daero, Jongno-gu, Seoul Tel: 1588-1210 http://www.seoulphil.or.kr

Universal Ballet Add:664, Cheonho-daero, Gwangjin-gu, Seoul Tel:(070)7124-1737 http://www.universalballet.com

World Vision Korea Children's Choir Add:85, Gangseo-ro 47ma-gil, Gangseo-gu, Seoul Tel:(02)2662-1803 http://www.wvchoir.or.kr

\<Museums and Art Museums\>

Alternative Space LOOP Add:20, Wausan-ro 29na-gil, Mapo-gu, Seoul Tel:(02)3141-1074 http://www.galleryloop.com

Art Center Nabi Add:26, Jong-ro, Jongno-gu, Seoul Tel:(02)2121-1031 http://www.nabi.or.kr

Artsonje Center Add:87, Yulgok-ro 3-gil, Jongno-gu, Seoul Tel:(02)733-8945 http://www.artsonje.org

Asan Gallery Add:83-15, Buksu-ro, Baebang-eup, Asan-si, Chungcheongnam-do Tel:(041)531-7470 http://www.asangallery.co.kr

Buyeo National Museum Add:5, Geumseong-ro, Buyeo-eup, Buyeo-gun, Chungcheongnam-do Tel:(041)833-8562 http://buyeo.museum.go.kr

Chuncheon National Museum Add:70, Useok-ro, Chuncheon-si, Gangwon-do Tel:(033)260-1500 http://chuncheon.museum.go.kr

Daecheongho Art Museum Add:721, Daecheonghoban-ro, Munui-myeon, Cheongwon-gun, Chungcheongbuk-do Tel:(043)201-0911 http://museum.puru.net

Daegu National Museum Add:321, Cheongho-ro, Suseong-gu, Daegu Tel: (053)768-6051 http://daegu.museum.go.kr

Daejeon Museum of Art Add:155, Dunsan-daero, Seo-gu, Daejeon Tel:(042)602-3225 http://dmma.daejeon.go.kr

Daelim Museum Add:21, Jahamun-ro 4-gil, Jongno-gu, Seoul Tel:(02)720-0667 http://www.daelimmuseum.org

Gail Art Museum Add:1549, Bukhangang-ro Cheongpyeong-myeon, Gapyeong-gun, Gyeonggi-do Tel:(031)584-4722 http://www.gailart.org

Gallery Hyundai Add:14, Samcheong-ro, Jongno-gu, Seoul Tel:(02)2287-3500 http://www.galleryhyundai.com

Gana Art Gallery Add:28, Pyeongchang 30-gil, Jongno-gu, Seoul Tel:(02)720-1020 http://www.ganaart.com

Gidang Art Museum Add:15, Namseongjung-ro 153beon-gil, Seogwipo-si, Jeju-do Tel:(064)733-1586 http://gidang.seogwipo.go.kr

Gimhae National Museum Add:190, Gayaui-gil, Gimhae-si, Gyeongsangnam-do Tel:(055)320-6800 http://gimhae.museum.go.kr

Gwangju Museum of Art Add:52, Haseo-ro, Buk-gu, Gwangju Tel:(062)613-7100 http://www.artmuse.gwangju.go.kr

Gwangju National Museum Add:110, Haseo-ro, Buk-gu, Gwangju Tel:(062)570-7000 http://gwangju.museum.go.kr

Gyeonggi Museum of Modern Art Add:268, Dongsan-ro, Danwon-gu, Ansan-si, Gyeonggi-do Tel:(031)481-7007 http://www.gmoma.or.kr

Gyeongju National Museum Add:186, Iljeong-ro, Gyeongju-si, Gyeongsangbuk-do Tel:(054)740-7500 http://gyeongju.museum.go.kr

Gyeongnam Art Museum Add:296, Yongji-ro, Uichang-gu, Changwon-si, Gyeongsangnam-do Tel:(055)254-4600 http://www.gam.go.kr

Hangaram Design Museum Add:2406, Nambusunhwan-ro, Seocho-gu, Seoul Tel:(02)580-1300 http://www.sac.or.kr

Hoam Art Museum Add:38, Everland-ro 562beon-gil, Pogok-eup, Cheoin-gu, Yongin-si, Gyeonggi-do Tel:(031)320-1801 http://www.hoammuseum.org

Jeju National Museum Add:17, Iljudong-ro, Jeju-si, Jeju-do Tel:(064)720-8000 http://jeju.museum.go.kr

Jeonbuk Museum of Art Add:111-6, Moaksan-gil, Gui-myeon, Wanju-gun, Jeollabuk-do Tel:(063)290-6888 http://www.jma.go.kr

Jeonju National Museum Add:249, Ssukgogae-ro, Wansan-gu, Jeonju-si, Jeollabuk-do Tel:(063)223-5651 http://jeonju.museum.go.kr

Jinju National Museum Add:626-35, Namgang-ro, Jinju-si, Gyeongsangnam-do Tel:(055)742-5951 http://jinju.museum.go.kr

Korea National Arboretum Add:415, Gwangneungsumogwon-ro, Sohol-eup, Pocheon-si, Gyeonggi-do Tel:(031)540-2000 http://www.kna.go.kr

Korea Railroad Museum Add:142, Cheoldobangmulgwan-ro, Uiwang-si, Gyeonggi-do Tel:(031)461-3610 http://www.railroadmuseum.co.kr

Korean National Police Heritage Museum Add:41, Saemunan-ro, Jongno-gu, Seoul Tel:(02)3150-3681 http://www.policemuseum.go.kr

Kukje Gallery Add:54, Samcheong-ro, Jongno-gu, Seoul Tel:(02)735-8449 http://www.kukje.org

Kyung-In Museum of Fine Art Add:11-4, Insadong 10-gil, Jongno-gu, Seoul Tel:(02)733-4448 www.kyunginart.co.kr

Leeum Add:60-16, Itaewon-ro 55-gil, Yongsan-gu, Seoul Tel:(02)2014-6900 http://www.leeum.org

Moran Museum of Art Add:8, Gyeongchun-ro 2110beon-gil, Hwado-eup, Namyangju-si, Gyeonggi-do Tel:(031)594-8001 http://www.moranmuseum.org

Namsong Art Museum Add:322, Baekdun-ro, Buk-myeon, Gapyeong-gun, Gyeonggi-do Tel:(031)581-0772 http://www.namsongart.com

National Folk Museum of Korea Add:37, Samcheong-ro, Jongno-gu, Seoul Tel:(02)3704-3114 http://www.nfm.go.kr

National Lighthouse Museum Add:20, Haemaji-ro 150beon-gil Homigot-myeon, Nam-gu, Pohang-si, Gyeongsangbuk-do Tel:(054)284-4857 http://www.lighthouse-museum.or.kr

National Maritime Museum Add:45, Haeyang-ro 301beon-gil, Yeongdo-gu, Busan Tel:(051)309-1900 http://www.knmm.or.kr

National Museum of Mordern and Contemporary Art, Korea Add:313, Gwangmyeong-ro, Gwacheon-si, Gyeonggi-do Tel:(02)2188-6000 http://www.moca.go.kr

National Museum of Korea Add: 137, Seobinggo-ro, Yongsan-gu, Seoul Tel: (02)2077-9000 http://www.museum.go.kr

National Palace Museum of Korea Add: 12, Hyoja-ro, Jongno-gu, Seoul Tel:(02)3701-7500 http://www.gogung.go.kr

National Science Museum Add:481, Daedeok-daero, Yuseong-gu, Daejeon Tel:(042)601-7894 http://www.science.go.kr

Plateau Add:55, Sejong-daero, Jung-gu, Seoul Tel:1577-7595 http://www.plateau.or.kr

Pohang Museum of Steel Art Add:10, Hwanhogongwon-gil, Buk-gu, Pohang-si, Gyeongsangbuk-do Tel:(054)250-6000 http://www.poma.kr

Project Space Sarubia Add:4, Jahamun-ro 16-gil, Jongno-gu, Seoul Tel:(02)733-0440 http://www.sarubia.org

Seoul Museum of Art Add:61, Deoksugung-gil, Jung-gu, Seoul Tel:(02)2124-8800 http://sema.seoul.go.kr

Seoul Museum of History Add:55, Saemunan-ro, Jongno-gu, Seoul Tel:(02)724-0274 http://www.museum.seoul.kr

Seoul National Science Museum Add:215, Changgyeonggung-ro, Jongno-gu, Seoul Tel:(02)3668-2200 http://www.ssm.go.kr

Sungkok Art Museum Add:42, Gyeonghuigung-gil, Jongno-gu, Seoul Tel:(02)737-7650 http://www.sungkokmuseum.com

Total Museum of Contemporary Art Add:8, Pyeongchang 32-gil, Jongno-gu, Seoul Tel:(02)379-3994 http://www.totalmuseum.org

Leeungno Museum Add:157, Dunsan-daero, Seo-gu, Daejeon Tel:(042)611-9821 http://ungnolee.daejeon.go.kr

War Memorial of Korea Add:29, Itaewon-ro, Yongsan-gu; Seoul Tel:(02)709-3139 http://www.warmemo.or.kr

Zaha Art Museum Add:46, Changuimun-ro 5ga-gil, Jongno-gu, Seoul Tel:(02)395-3222 http://www.zahamuseum.com

<Theaters and Art Centers>

3.15 Art Center Add:135, Samho-ro, MasanHoiwon-gu, Changwon-si, Gyeong-sangnam-do Tel:(055)286-0315 http://www.cwcf.or.kr/facility/facility_315art.asp

Aekwan Theater Add:63-2, Gaehang-ro, Jung-gu, Incheon Tel:(032)761-7177 http://www.ak5.co.kr

Ansan Arts Center Add:312, Hwarang-ro, Danwon-gu, Ansan-si, Gyeonggi-do Tel:(031)481-4000 http://www.ansanart.com

Arirang Cine & Media Center Add: 82, Arirang-ro, Seongbuk-gu, Seoul Tel:(02)3291-5540 http://cine.arirang.go.kr

Art House MOMO Add:52, Ewhayeodae-gil, Seodaemun-gu, Seoul Tel:(02)363-5333 http://www.cineart.co.kr

Blue Square Add:294, Itaewon-ro, Yongsan-gu, Seoul Tel:1544-1591 http://www.bluesquare.kr

Busan Cinema Center Add:120, Suyeonggangbyeon-daero, Haeundae-gu, Busan Tel:(051)780-6000 http://www.dureraum.org

Busan Citizen's Hall Add:16, Jaseong-ro 133beon-gil, Dong-gu, Busan Tel:(051)630-5200 http://citizenhall.bisco.or.kr

Busan Culture Center Add:1, UN pyeonghwa-ro 76beon-gil, Nam-gu, Busan Tel:(051)120 http://culture.busan.go.kr

Chongong Theater Add:43, Jeongdong-gil, Jung-gu, Seoul Tel:(02)751-1500 http://www.chongdong.com

Chuncheon Culture & Art Center Add:13, Hyojasang-gil 5beon-gil, Chuncheon-si, Gangwon-do Tel:(033)259-5841 http://www.ccac.or.kr

Chungmu Art Hall Add:387, Toegye-ro, Jung-gu, Seoul Tel:(02)2230-6600 http://www.cmah.or.kr

CGV Add:434, World Cup buk-ro, Mapo-gu, Seoul Tel:1544-1122 http://www.cgv.co.kr
Branches : Gangnam, Gangdong, Gang-byeon, Guro, Gunja, Gimpo Airport, Daehak-ro, Doksan, Myeong-dong, Myeong-dong Station, Mok-dong, Mia, Bulgwang, Sangam, Sungshin Women's University, Songpa, Sindorim, Sinchon Artren, Apgujeong-dong, Yeouido, Yeongdeungpo, Wangsimni, Yongsan, Junggye, Chungdam Cinecity, Hagye, Cine de Chef Apgujeong, Gwangmyeong, Gwangmyeong Cheolsan, Gimpo, Gimpo Pungmu, Dongbaek, Dong-suwon, Dongtan, Dongtan Star, Beomgye, Buche, Buksuwon, Sopung, Suwon, Si-heung, Ansan, Anyang, Yatap, Yeokgok, Ori, Uijeongbu, Uijeongbu Taehung, Ilsan, Jukjeon, Pyeongchon, Pyeongtaek, Pyeong-taek Bijeon, Hwajeong, Gyeyang, Bupyeong, Incheon, Incheon Airport, Incheon Nonhy-eon, Incheon Yeonsu, Incheon Terminal, Juan, Nampo, Daeyeon, Daehan, Dongnae, Busan University, Seomyun, Centum City, Asiad, Hwamyeong, Cine de Chef Centum, Ulsan Samsan, Daegu, Daegu Suseong, Daegu Stadium, Daegu Academy, Daegu Esia, Daegu Chilgok, Daegu Hanil, Daegu Hyundai, Daejeon, Daejeon Gao, Daejeon Dunsan, Daejeon Terminal, Gwangju, Gwangju Yongbong, Gwangju Chomdan, Gwangju Terminal, Gangneung, Wonju, Chuncheon, Chuncheon Myeongdong, Geoje, Gimhae, Masan, Jinju, Changwon, Changwon the City, Tongyeong, Gumi, Bukpohang, Pohang, Gunsan, Mokpo, Sun-cheon, Iksan, Junju, Jeongeup, Cheonan, Cheonan Pentaport, Cheongju Bukmun, Cheongju Summun, Hongseong, Jeju

Cinecube Add:68, Saemunan-ro, Jongno-gu, Seoul Tel:(02)2002-7770 http://www.icinecube.com

COEX Add:513, Yeongdong-daero, Gangnam-gu, Seoul Tel:(02)6000-0114 http://www.coex.co.kr

Ganainsa Art Center Add:41-1, Insadong-gil, Jongno-gu, Seoul Tel:(02)736-1020 http://www.insaartcenter.com

Gwanghwamun Art Hall Add:21, Inwangsan-ro 1-gil, Jongno-gu, Seoul Tel:(02)722-3416 http://www.ghmarthall.co.kr

Gwangju Culture & Art Center Add:60, Bungmun-daero, Buk-gu, Gwangju Tel:(062)613-8333 http://www.gjart.net

Gyeonggi Arts Center Add:20, Hyowon-ro 307beon-gil, Paldal-gu, Suwon-si, Gyeonggi-do Tel:(031)230-3200 http://www.ggac.or.kr

Gyeongju Arts Center Add:1, Alcheonbuk-ro, Gyeongju-si, Gyeongsangbuk-do Tel:1588-4925 http://www.gjartcenter.kr

Gyeongnam Culture & Arts Center Add:215, Gangnam-ro, Jinju-si, Gyeongsangnam-do Tel:1544-6711 http://www.gncac.com

Incheon Culture & Arts Center Add: 149, Yesul-ro, Namdong-gu, Incheon Tel: (032)427-8401 http://art.incheon.go.kr

Jeju Arts Center Add:231, Onam-ro, Jeju-si, Jeju-do Tel:(064)753-2209 http://arts.jeju.go.kr

Jeonju Cinema Town Add:67, Jeonju-gaeksa 3-gil, Wansan-gu, Jeonju-si, Jeollabuk-do Tel:(063)283-7722 http://www.jcinema.co.kr

KEPCO Art Center Add:60, Hyoryeong-ro 72-gil, Seocho-gu, Seoul Tel:(02)2105-8133 http://www.kepco.co.kr/artcenter

Kumho Art Hall Add:75, Saemunan-ro, Jongno-gu, Seoul Tel:(02)6303-1977 http://www.kumhoarthall.com

LG Arts Center Add:508, Nonhyeon-ro, Gangnam-gu, Seoul Tel:(02)2005-0114 http://www.lgart.com

Lotte Cinema Add:269, Olympic-ro, Songpa-gu, Seoul Tel:1544-8855 http://www.lottecinema.co.kr

Branches : Gasan digital, Gasan Hyhill, Gangdong, Konkuk University, Gimpo Airport, Nowon, Nurikkum, LotteWorld, Broadway, Seoul University, Sillim, Yongsan, Sindorim, City Gangnam, Avenuel, Yeong-deungpo, Jangan, Cheongnyangri, Picca-dilly, Hapjeong, Hongik University, Hwang-hak, Geomdan, Gwangju Terminal, Guri, Lafesta, Maseok, Byeongjeom, Bucheon, Bucheon Station, Bupyeong, Bupyeong Station, Sanbon, Seongnam, Seongnam Sinheung, CentralRock, Songtan, Sihwa, Asan LotteMart, Anyang, Yangju Goeup, Anseong, Indeogwon, Yongin, Incheon, Jinjeop, Juyeop, Paju, Pyeongchon, Dae-jeon, Boryung, Seosan, Seocheongju, Asan Terminal, Cheongju, Cheongju Chungbuk University, Gyeongju, Gunsan, Mokpo, Mokpo Central, Suwan, Sangmu, Yeosu, Jeonju, Chungjangro, Jeonju Pyeonghwa, Gimhae Outlet, Gumi, Gumi Gongdan, Gyeongju, Gyeongsan, Daegu, Daegu Gwangjang, Daeguyulha, Dongnae, Dong-seongro, Masan, Masan Terminal, Busan Head Store, Sasang, Seomyun, Seongseo, Centum City, Andong, Yangsan, Ulsan, Ulsanseongnam, Jinju, Jinhae, Changwon, Tongyeong ZoomOutlet, premium Chilgok, Pohang, Haeundae, Namwonju, Donghae, Seogwipo, Jeju

MEGA Box Add:215, Tancheon-ro, Bundang-gu, Seongnam-si, Gyeonggi-do Tel:1544-0070 http://www.megabox.co.kr

Branches : Gangnam, Dongdaemun, Mok-dong, Sangbong, Central, Sinchon, Eunpyeong, Isu, COEX, Suyu, EOE4, Art Nine, Namyangju, Bundang, Suwon, An-san, Yeonsu, Yeongtong, Pajubookcity, Ilsan, KINTEX, Pyeongtaek, Yangju, Backsuk, Onemount, Suwon Nammoon, Gimpo, Gongju, Daejeon, Sejong, Cheonan, Jecheon, Chungju, Kyongnam University, Gyeongju, Daegu, Busan Theater, Seo-myun, O2, Ulsan, Changwon, Bukdaegu, Haeundae, Jangsan, Gumi Gangdong, Deokcheon, Gumi, Andong, Gwangju, Namwon, Songcheon, Suncheon, Yeosu, Jeondae, Jeonju, Sangmu, Hanam, Chom-dan, Sokcho, Wonju, Jeju, Jejuara

MMC Megaplex Cinema Add:547, Gukchaebosang-ro, Jung-gu, Daegu Tel:1577-1015 http://www.immc.co.kr

Branches : Mangyengkwan, Samyoungfilm

Mokpo Culture & Arts Center Add:102, Namnong-ro, Mokpo-si, Jeollanam-do Tel:(061)270-8484 http://art.mokpo.go.kr

Myeongdong Theater Add:35, Myeong-dong-gil, Jung-gu, Seoul Tel:1644-2003 http://www.mdtheater.or.kr

Myungbo Art Hall Add:47, Mareunnae-ro, Jung-gu, Seoul Tel:(02)2274-2121 http://www.myungbo.com

NamJunePaik Art Center Add:10, Paiknamjune-ro, Giheung-gu, Yongin-si, Gyeonggi-do Tel:(031)201-8500 http://www.njpartcenter.kr

National Theater of Korea Add:59, Jang-chungdan-ro, Jung-gu, Seoul Tel:(02)2280-4114 http://www.ntok.go.kr

Pohang Culture and Arts Center Add:850, Huimang-daero, Nam-gu, Pohang-si, Gyeongsangbuk-do Tel:(054)280-9350 http://phart.phsisul.org

Primus Cinema Add:434, World Cup buk-ro, Mapo-gu, Seoul Tel:1544-1122 http://www.primuscinema.com

Branches : Gimcheon, Mokpo, Ansan, Osan

Sangsangmadang Add:65, Eoulmadang-ro, Mapo-gu, Seoul Tel:(02)330-6200 http://www.sangsangmadang.com

Sejong Center Add:175, Sejong-daero, Jongno-gu, Seoul Tel:(02)399-1114 http://www.sejongpac.or.kr

Seongnam Arts Center Add:808, Seongnam-daero, Bundang-gu, Seongnam-si, Gyeonggi-do Tel:(031)783-8000 http://www.snart.or.kr

Seoul Arts Center Add:2406, Nambu-sunhwan-ro, Seocho-gu, Seoul Tel:(02)580-

1300 http://www.sac.or.kr

Seoul Art Cinema Add:13, Donhwamun-ro, Jongno-gu, Seoul Tel:(02)741-9782 http://www.cinematheque.seoul.kr

Seoul Cinema Add:13, Donhwamun-ro, Jongno-gu, Seoul Tel:(02)2277-3011 http://www.seoulcinema.com

Sori Arts Center of Jeollabuk-do Add:31, Sori-ro, Deokjin-gu, Jeonju-si, Jeollabuk-do Tel:(063)270-8000 http://www.sori21.co.kr

Sowol ArtHall Add:281, Wangsimni-ro, Seongdong-gu, Seoul Tel:(02)2204-6400 http://sowol.sdmc.go.kr

Sungsan Arts Hall Add:181, Jungang-daero, Uichang-gu, Changwon-si, Gyeongsangnam-do Tel:(055)268-7900 http://www.cwcf.or.kr/facility/facility_sungsan

Suseong Artpia Add:180, Muhak-ro, Suseong-gu, Daegu Tel:(053)668-1800 http://www.ssartpia.kr

Suwon Art Center Add:19, Songjeong-ro, Jangan-gu, Suwon-si, Gyeonggi-do Tel:(031)243-3647 http://www.suwonartcenter.org

Uijeongbu Arts Center Add:1, Uijeong-ro, Uijeongbu-si, Gyeonggi-do Tel:(031)828-5841 https://www.uac.or.kr

Ulsan Culture Art Center Add:200, Beonyeong-ro, Nam-gu, Ulsan Tel:(052)275-9623 http://www.ucac.or.kr

Universal Art Center Add:664, Cheonho-daero, Gwangjin-gu, Seoul Tel:(070)7124-1740 http://www.uac.co.kr

Yawoori Cinema Add:43, Mannam-ro, Dongnam-gu, Cheonan-si, Chungcheongnam-do Tel:(041)640-6200 http://www.yawooricinema.com

Yoondang ArtHall Add:844, Eonju-ro, Gangnam-gu, Seoul Tel:(02)546-8095 http://www.ydart.co.kr

UNIVERSITIES AND COLLEGES

PUBLIC UNIVERSITIES AND COLLEGES

Andong National Univ. Add:1375, Gyeongdong-ro, Andong-si, Gyeongsangbuk-do Tel:(054)820-5114 http://www.andong.ac.kr

Armed Forces Nursing Academy Add:90, Jaun-ro, Yuseong-gu, Daejeon Tel:1688-9171 http://www.afna.ac.kr

Busan National Univ. of Education Add:24, Gyodae-ro, Yeonje-gu, Busan Tel:(051)500-7114 http://www.bnue.ac.kr

Changwon National Univ. Add:20, Changwondaehak-ro, Uichang-gu, Changwon-si, Gyeongsangnam-do Tel:(055)213-2114 http://www.changwon.ac.kr

Cheongju National Univ. of Education Add:2065, Cheongnam-ro, Seowon-gu, Cheongju-si, Chungcheongbuk-do Tel:(043)299-0800 http://www.cje.ac.kr

Chinju National Univ. of Education Add:3, Jinnyangho-ro 369beon-gil, Jinju-si, Gyeongsangnam-do Tel:(055)740-1114 http://www.cue.ac.kr

Chonbuk National Univ. <Jeonju Campus> Add:567, Baekje-daero, Deokjin-gu, Jeonju-si, Jeollabuk-do Tel:(063)270-2114 <Specialized Campus> Add:79, Gobong-ro, Iksan-si, Jeollabuk-do Tel:(063)270-4114 <Gochang Campus> Add:361, Taebong-ro Gochang-eup, Gochang-gun, Jeollabuk-do Tel:(063)562-2621 http://www.jbnu.ac.kr

Chonnam National Univ. <Gwangju Campus> Add:77, Yongbong-ro, Buk-gu, Gwangju Tel:(062)530-5114 <Yeosu Campus> Add:50, Daehak-ro, Yeosu-si, Jeollanam-do Tel:(061)659-6114 http://www.jnu.ac.kr

Chuncheon National Univ. of Education Add:126, Gongji-ro, Chuncheon-si, Gangwon-do Tel:(033)260-6000 http://www.cnue.ac.kr

Chungbuk National Univ. Add:1, Chungdae-ro, Seowon-gu, Cheongju-si, Chungcheongbuk-do Tel:(043)261-2114 http://www.chungbuk.ac.kr

Chungnam National Univ. Add:99, Daehak-ro, Yuseong-gu, Daejeon Tel:(042)821-5114 <Boun Campus> Add:55, Munhwa-ro, Jung-gu, Daejeon Tel:(042)580-8115 http://www.cnu.ac.kr

Daegu Gyeongbuk Institue of Science & Technology Add:333, Techno jungang-daero Hyeonpung-myeon, Dalseong-gun, Daegu Tel:(053)785-0114 http://www.dgist.ac.kr

Daegu National Univ. of Education Add:219, Jungang-daero, Nam-gu, Daegu Tel:(053)620-1114 http://www.dnue.ac.kr

Gangneung-Wonju National Univ. <Gangneung Campus> Add:7, Jukheon-gil, Gangneung-si, Gangwon-do Tel:(033)642-7001 <Wonju Campus> Add:150, Namwon-ro, Heungeop-myeon, Wonju-si, Gangwon-do Tel:(033)760-8114 http://www.gwnu.ac.kr

Gongju National Univ. of Education
Add:27, Ungjin-ro, Gongju-si, Chungcheong-nam-do Tel:(041)850-1114 http://www.gjue.ac.kr

Gwangju Institute of Science and Technology Add:123, Cheomdangwagi-ro, Buk-gu, Gwangju Tel:(062)715-2114 http://www.gist.ac.kr

Gwangju National Univ. of Education Add:55, Pilmun-daero, Buk-gu, Gwangju Tel:(062)520-4114 http://www.gnue.ac.kr

Gyeongin National Univ. of Education Add:62, Gyesan-ro, Gyeyang-gu, Incheon Tel:(032)540-1114 〈Gyeonggi Campus〉 Add:155, Sammak-ro, Manan-gu, Anyang-si, Gyeonggi-do Tel:(031)470-6114 http://www.ginue.ac.kr

Gyeongnam National Univ. of Science and Technology Add:33, Dongjin-ro, Jinju-si, Gyeongsangnam-do Tel:(055)751-3114 http://www.gntech.ac.kr

Gyeongsang National Univ. 〈Gajwa Campus〉 Add:501, Jinju-daero, Jinju-si, Gyeongsangnam-do Tel:(055)772-0114 〈Chiram Campus〉 Add:15, Jinju-daero 816beon-gil, Jinju-si, Gyeongsangnam-do Tel:(055)772-8020 〈Tongyeong Campus〉 Add:38, Cheondaegukchi-gil, Tongyeong-si, Gyeongsangnam-do Tel:(055)772-9099 http://www.gnu.ac.kr

Hanbat National Univ. Add:125, Dongseo-daero, Yuseong-gu, Daejeon Tel:(042)821-1114 〈Daedeok Campus〉 Add:75, Techno 1-ro, Yuseong-gu, Daejeon Tel:(042)939-4800 http://www.hanbat.ac.kr

Hankyong National Univ. Add:327, Jungang-ro, Anseong-si, Gyeonggi-do Tel:(031)670-5114 http://www.hankyong.ac.kr

Incheon National Univ. Add:119, Academy-ro, Yeonsu-gu, Incheon Tel:(032)835-8114 〈Jemulpo Campus〉 Add:165, Seokjeong-ro, Nam-gu, Incheon Tel:(032)835-8114 〈Michuhol Campus〉 Add:12, Gaetbeol-ro, Yeonsu-gu, Incheon Tel:(032)835-8653 http://www.incheon.ac.kr

Jeju National Univ. 〈Ara Campus〉 Add:102, Jejudaehak-ro, Jeju-si, Jeju-do Tel:(064)754-2114 〈Sara Campus〉 Add:61, Iljudong-ro, Jeju-si, Jeju-do Tel:(064)754-4800 http://www.jejunu.ac.kr

Jeonju National Univ. of Education Add:50, Seohak-ro, Wansan-gu, Jeonju-si, Jeollabuk-do Tel:(063)281-7114 http://www.jnue.ac.kr

Kangwon National Univ. 〈Chuncheon Campus〉 Add:1, Gangwondaehak-gil, Chuncheon-si, Gangwon-do Tel:(033)250-6114 〈Dogye Campus〉 Add:346, Hwangjo-gil, Dogye-eup, Samcheok-si, Gangwon-do Tel:(033)540-3114 〈Samcheok Campus〉 Add:346, Jungang-ro, Samcheok-si, Gangwon-do Tel:(033)570-6114 http://www.kangwon.ac.kr

Kongju National Univ. Add:56, Gongju-daehak-ro, Gongju-si, Chungcheongnam-do Tel:(041)850-8114 〈Cheonan Campus〉 Add:1223-24, Cheonan-daero, Seobuk-gu, Cheonan-si, Chungcheongnam-do Tel:(041)521-9114 〈Yesan Campus〉 Add:54, Daehak-ro, Yesan-eup, Yesan-gun, Chungcheongnam-do Tel:(041)330-1011 http://www.kongju.ac.kr

Korea Advanced Institute of Science and Technology Add:291, Daehak-ro, Yuseong-gu, Daejeon Tel:(042)350-2114 http://www.kaist.ac.kr

Korea Maritime and Ocean Univ. Add:727, Taejong-ro, Yeongdo-gu, Busan Tel:(051)410-4114 http://www.kmou.ac.kr

Korea Military Academy Add:574, Hwarang-ro, Nowon-gu, Seoul Tel:(02)2197-0114 http://www.kma.ac.kr

Korea National Defense Univ. Add:33, Je2jayu-ro, Deogyang-gu, Goyang-si, Gyeonggi-do Tel:(02)300-2114 http://www.kndu.ac.kr

Korea National Open Univ. Add:86, Daehak-ro, Jongno-gu, Seoul Tel:1577-9995 http://www.knou.ac.kr

Korea National Police Univ. Add:74, Eonnam-ro, Giheung-gu, Yongin-si, Gyeonggi-do Tel:(031)620-2114 http://www.police.ac.kr

Korea National Univ. of Arts Add:146-37, Hwarang-ro 32-gil, Seongbuk-gu, Seoul Tel:(02)746-9000 〈Daehak-ro Campus〉 Add:215, Changgyeonggung-ro, Jongno-gu, Seoul 〈Seocho-dong Campus〉 Add:2374, Nambusunhwan-ro, Seocho-gu, Seoul Tel:(02)746-9000 http://www.karts.ac.kr

Korea National Univ. of Cultral Heritage Add:367, Baekjemun-ro, Gyuam-myeon, Buyeo-gun, Chungcheongnam-do Tel:(041)830-7114 http://www.nuch.ac.kr

Korea National Univ. of Education Add:250, Taeseongtabyeon-ro, Gangnae-myeon, Cheongwon-gun, Chungcheongbuk-do Tel:(043)230-3114 http://www.knue.ac.kr

Korea National Univ. of Transportation 〈Chungju Campus〉 Add:50, Daehak-ro, Daesowon-myeon, Chungju-si, Chungcheongbuk-do Tel:(043)841-5114 〈Jeungpyeong Campus〉 Add:61, Daehak-ro, Jeungpyeong-eup, Jeungpyeong-gun, Chungcheongbuk-do Tel:(043)820-5114 〈Uiwang Campus〉 Add:157, Cheoldo-bangmulgwan-ro, Uiwang-si, Gyeonggi-do Tel:(070)8855-1699 http://www.ut.ac.kr

Korea National Sport Univ. Add:1239, Yangjae-daero, Songpa-gu, Seoul Tel:(02)410-6700 http://www.knsu.ac.kr

Kumoh National Institute of Technology Add:61, Daehak-ro, Gumi-si, Gyeongsangbuk-do Tel:(054)478-7114 〈Sinpyeong-dong Campus〉 Add:350-27, Gumi-daero, Gumi-si, Gyeongsangbuk-do http://www.kumoh.ac.kr

Kunsan National Univ. Add:558, Daehak-ro, Gunsan-si, Jeollabuk-do Tel:(063)469-4114 http://www.kunsan. ac.kr

Kyungpook National Univ. Add:80, Daehak-ro, Buk-gu, Daegu Tel:(053)950-5114 〈Sangju Campus〉 Add:2559, Gyeongsang-daero, Sangju-si, Gyeong-sangbuk-do Tel:(054)532-6000 http://www.knu.ac.kr

Mokpo National Univ. Add:1666, Yeongsan-ro, Cheonggye-myeon, Muan-gun, Jeollanam-do Tel:(061)450-2114 〈Daebul Campus〉 Add:1703-17, Yongang-ri, Samho-eup, Yeongam-gun, Jeollanam-do 〈Namak Campus〉 Add:2540, Namak-ri, Samhyang-eup, Muan-gun, Jeollanam-do 〈Mokpo Campus〉 Add:11, Songnim-ro 41beon-gil, Mokpo-si, Jeollanam-do Tel:(061)450-2114 http://www.mokpo.ac.kr

Mokpo National Maritime Univ. Add:91, Haeyangdaehak -ro, Mokpo-si, Jeollanam-do Tel:(061)240-7114 http://www.mmu.ac.kr

Pukyong National Univ. Add:45, Yongso-ro, Nam-gu, Busan Tel:(051)629-4114 〈Yongdang Campus〉 Add:365, Sinseon-ro, Nam-gu, Busan Tel:(051)629-4114 http://www.pknu.ac.kr

Pusan National Univ. Add:2, Busandaehak-ro 63beon-gil, Geumjeong-gu, Busan Tel:(051)512-0311 〈Miryang Campus〉 Add:1268-50, Samnangjin-ro, Samnangjin-eup, Miryang-si, Gyeongsangnam-do Tel:(055)350-5100 〈Yangsan Campus〉 Add:49, Busandaehak-ro, Mulgeum-eup, Yangsan-si, Gyeongsangnam-do Tel:(051)512-0311 http://www.pusan.ac.kr

Republic of Korea Air Force Academy Add:P.O. Box 335-1, 635, Danjae-ro, Namil-myeon, Sangdang-gu, Cheongju-si, Chun-gcheongbuk-do Tel:(043)290-6114 http://www.afa.ac.kr

Republic of Korea Naval Academy Add:1, Jungwon-ro, Jinhae-gu, Changwon-si, Gyeongsangnam-do Tel:(055)549-1367 http://www.navy.ac.kr

Seoul National Univ. Add:1, Gwanak-ro, Gwanak-gu, Seoul Tel:(02)880-5114 http://www.snu.ac.kr 〈Yeongeon Campus〉 Add:103, Daehak-ro, Jongno-gu, Seoul Tel:(02)740-8114 http://www.snu.ac.kr 〈Pyeongchang Campus〉 Add:1447, Pyeongchang-daero Daehwa-myeon, Pyeongchang-gun, Gangwon-do Tel:(033)339-5500 http://greenbio.snu.ac.kr/

Seoul National Univ. of Education Add:96, Seochojungang-ro, Seocho-gu, Seoul Tel:(02)3475-2114 http://www.snue.ac.kr

Seoul National Univ. of Science and Technology Add:232, Gongneung-ro, Nowon-gu, Seoul Tel:(02)970-6114 http://www.seoultech.ac.kr

Sunchon National Univ. Add:255, Jungang-ro, Suncheon-si, Jeollanam-do Tel:(061)750-3114 http://www.sunchon.ac.kr

Ulsan National Institute of Science and Technology Add:50, UNIST-gil, Eonyang-eup, Ulju-gun, Ulsan Tel:(052)217-0114 http://www.unist.ac.kr

Univ. of Seoul Add:163, Seoulsiripdae-ro, Dongdaemun-gu, Seoul Tel:(02)6490-6114 http://www.uos.ac.kr

PRIVATE UNIVERSITIES AND COLLEGES

Ajou Univ. Add:206, World cup-ro, Yeongtong-gu, Suwon-si, Gyeonggi-do Tel:(031)
219-2114 http://www.ajou.ac.kr

Anyang Univ. Add:22, Samdeok-ro 37beon-gil, Manan-gu, Anyang-si, Gyeonggi-do Tel:(031)467-0700 〈Ganghwa Campus〉 Add:602-14, Jungang-ro, Bureun-myeon, Ganghwa-gun, Incheon Tel:(032)930-6000 http://www.anyang.ac.kr

Asia United Theological Univ. Add:1276, Gyeonggang-ro, Okcheon-myeon, Yangpyeong-gun, Gyeonggi-do Tel:(031)770-7700 http://www.acts.ac.kr

Baekseok Univ. Add:76, Munam-ro, Dong-nam-gu, Cheonan-si, Chungcheongnam-do Tel:(041)550-9114 〈Seoul Campus〉 Add:69, Bangbae-ro, Seocho-gu, Seoul Tel:(02)520-0712 http://www.bu.ac.kr

Busan Presbyterian Univ. Add:1894-68, Gimhae-daero, Gimhae-si, Gyeongsangnam-do Tel:(055)320-2500 http://www.bpu.ac.kr

Busan Univ. of Foreign Studies Add:65, Geumsaem-ro 485beon-gil, Geumjeong-gu, Busan Tel:(051)509-5000 http://www.bufs.ac.kr

Calvin Univ. Add:184, Mabuk-ro, Giheung-gu, Yongin-si, Gyeonggi-do Tel:(031)284-4752 http://www.calvin.ac.kr

Catholic Kwandong Univ. Add:24, Beomil-ro 579beon-gil, Gangneung-si, Gangwon-do Tel:(033)649-7114 http://www.cku.ac.kr

Catholic Univ. of Daegu Add:13-13, Hayang-ro, Hayang-eup, Gyeongsan-si, Gyeongsangbuk-do Tel:(053)850-3114 〈Luke Campus〉 Add:33, Duryugongwon-ro 17-gil, Nam-gu, Daegu Tel:(053)650-4455 〈Justin Campus〉 Add:47, Myeongnyun-ro 12-gil, Jung-gu, Daegu Tel:(053)660-5100 〈Gamsam-dong Campus〉 Add: 17, Yongsan-ro 24-gil, Dalseo-gu, Daegu Tel:(053)660-5552 http://www.cu.ac.kr

Catholic Univ. of Korea Add:43, Jibong-ro, Wonmi-gu, Bucheon-si, Gyeonggi-do Tel:(02)2164-4114 〈Songeui Campus〉 Add:222, Banpo-daero, Seocho-gu, Seoul Tel:(02)2258-7114 〈Songsin Campus〉 Add:296-12, Changgyeonggung-ro, Jongno-gu, Seoul Tel:(02)740-9714 http://www.catholic.ac.kr

Catholic Univ. of Pusan Add:57, Oryundae-ro, Geumjeong-gu, Busan Tel:(051)515-5811 〈Maryknoll Campus〉 Add:74-9, Oryundae-ro, Geumjeong-gu, Busan Tel:(051)510-0729 〈Theology Campus〉 Add: 56-7, Gichal-ro 102beon-gil, Geumjeong-gu, Busan Tel:(051)519-0432 http://www.cup.ac.kr

CHA Univ. Add:120, Haeryong-ro, Pocheon-si, Gyeonggi-do Tel:1899-2010 〈Bundang Campus〉 Add:43, Beolmal-ro 30beon-gil, Bundang-gu, Seongnam-si, Gyeonggi-do Tel:1899-2010 〈Gangnam Campus〉 Add:158, Bongeunsa-ro, Gangnam-gu, Seoul Tel:(02)3468-3344 http://www.cha.ac.kr

Changshin Univ. Add:262, Paryong-ro, Masanhoewon-gu, Changwon-si, Gyeong-sangnam-do Tel:(055)250-3001 http://www.cs.ac.kr

Cheongju Univ. Add:298, Daeseong-ro, Sangdang-gu, Cheongju-si, Chungcheong-buk-do Tel:(043)229-8114 http://www.chongju.ac.kr

Chosun Univ. Add:309, Pilmun-daero, Dong-gu, Gwangju Tel:(062)230-7114 http://www.chosun.ac.kr

Chodang Univ. Add:380, Muan-ro, Muan-eup, Muan-gun, Jeollanam-do Tel:(061)453-4960 http://www.chodang.ac.kr

Chongshin Univ. Add:143, Sadang-ro, Dongjak-gu, Seoul Tel:(02)3479-0200 〈Yangji Campus〉 Add:110, Hakchon-ro, Yangji-myeon, Cheoin-gu, Yongin-si, Gyeonggi-do Tel:(031)679-1700 http://www.chongshin.ac.kr

Chugye Univ. For The Arts Add:7, Bugahyeon-ro 11ga-gil, Seodaemun-gu, Seoul Tel:(02)362-5700 http://www.chugye.ac.kr

Chungwoon Univ. Add:25, Daehak-gil, Hongseong-eup, Hongseong-gun, Chung-cheongnam-do Tel:(041)630-3114 http://www.chungwoon.ac.kr 〈Incheon Campus〉 Add:113, Sukgol-ro, Nam-gu, Incheon Tel:(032)770-8114

Chung-Ang Univ. Add:84, Heukseok-ro, Dongjak-gu, Seoul Tel:(02)820-5114 〈Anseong Campus〉 Add:4726, Seodong-daero, Daedeok-myeon, Anseong-si, Gyeonggi-do Tel:(031)670-3114 http://www.cau.ac.kr

Daegu Univ. Add:201, Daegudae-ro, Jillyang-eup, Gyeongsan-si, Gyeongsangbuk-do Tel:(053)850-5000 〈Daemyeongdong Campus〉 Add:33, Seongdang-ro 50-gil, Nam-gu, Daegu Tel:(053)650-8405 http://www.daegu.ac.kr

Daegu Univ. of Foreign Studies Add:730, Namcheon-ro, Namcheon-myeon, Gyeongsan-si, Gyeongsangbuk-do Tel:(053)810-7000 http://www.dufs.ac.kr

Daegu Art Univ. Add:202, Dabugeomun 1-gil, Gasan-myeon, Chilgok-gun, Gyeongsang-buk-do Tel:(054)973-5311 http://www.dgau.ac.kr

Daegu Haany Univ. Add:1, Hanuidae-ro, Gyeongsan-si, Gyeongsangbuk-do Tel: (053)819-1000 〈Oseong Campus〉 Add:285-10, Eobongji-gil, Gyeongsan-si, Gyeongsangbuk-do Tel:(053)802-0066 〈Suseong Campus〉 Add:136, Sincheon-dong-ro, Suseong-gu, Daegu Tel:(053)770-2233 http://www.dhu.ac.kr

Daejeon Univ. Add:62, Daehak-ro, Dong-gu, Daejeon Tel:(042)280-2114 http://www.dju.ac.kr

Daejeon Catholic Univ. Add:30, Catholicdaehak-ro, Jeonui-myeon, Sejong-si Tel:(044)861-7101 http://www.dcatholic.ac.kr

Daejeon Theological Univ. Add:41, Hannam-ro, Daedeok-gu, Daejeon Tel:(042)606-0114 http://www.daejeon.ac.kr

Daejin Univ. Add:1007, Hoguk-ro, Pocheon-si, Gyeonggi-do Tel:(031)539-1114 http://www.daejin.ac.kr

Daeshin Univ. Add:33, Gyeongcheong-ro 222-gil, Gyeongsan-si, Gyeongsangbuk-do Tel:(053)810-0701 http://www.daeshin.ac.kr

Dankook Univ. Add:152, Jukjeon-ro, Suji-gu, Yongin-si, Gyeonggi-do Tel:1899-3700 ‹Cheonan Campus› Add:119, Dandae-ro, Dongnam-gu, Cheonan-si, Chungcheongnam-do Tel:1899-3700 http://www.dankook.ac.kr

Dong-A Univ. Add:37, Nakdong-daero 550beon-gil, Saha-gu, Busan Tel:(051)200-7000 http://www.donga.ac.kr ‹Bumin Campus› Add:225, Gudeok-ro, Seo-gu, Busan ‹Gudeok Campuus› Add:32, Daesingongwon-ro, Seo-gu, Busan

Dongduk Women's Univ. Add:60, Hwarang-ro 13-gil, Seongbuk-gu, Seoul Tel:(02)940-4000 http://www.dongduk.ac.kr

Dong-Eui Univ. Add:176, Eomgwang-ro, Busanjin-gu, Busan Tel:(051)890-1114 http://www.deu.ac.kr ‹Yangjung Campus› Add:52-57, Yangjeong-ro, Busanjin-gu, Busan Tel:(051)850-8632

Dongguk Univ. Add:30, Pildong-ro 1-gil, Jung-gu, Seoul Tel:(02)2260-3114 http://www.dongguk.edu ‹Bio-Medi Campus› Add:32, Dongguk-ro, Ilsandong-gu, Goyang-si, Gyeonggi-do Tel:(031)961-5203 http://www.dongguk.edu ‹Gyeongju Campus› Add:123, Dongdae-ro, Gyeongju-si, Gyeongsangbuk-do Tel:(054)770-2114 http://web.dongguk.ac.kr

Dongseo Univ. Add:47, Jurye-ro, Sasang-gu, Busan Tel:(051)313-2001 http://www.dongseo.ac.kr ‹Centum Campus› Add:55, Centum jungang-ro, Haeundae-gu, Busan Tel:(051)950-6542 http://art.dongseo.ac.kr

Dongshin Univ. Add:185, Geonjae-ro, Naju-si, Jeollanam-do Tel:(061)330-3114 http://www.dsu.ac.kr

Dongyang Univ. Add:145, Dongyangdae-ro, Punggi-eup, Yeongju-si, Gyeongsangbuk-do Tel:(054)630-1114 http://www.dyu.ac.kr

Duksung Women's Univ. Add:33, Samyang-ro 144-gil, Dobong-gu, Seoul Tel:(02)901-8000 http://www.duksung.ac.kr ‹Jongno Campus› Add:78, Yulgok-ro, Jongno-gu, Seoul

Eulji Univ. Add:77, Gyeryong-ro 771beon-gil, Jung-gu, Daejeon Tel:1899-0001 ‹Seongnam Campus› Add:553, Sanseong-daero, Sujeong-gu, Seongnam-si, Gyeonggi-do Tel:1899-0001 http://www.eulji.ac.kr

Ewha Women's Univ. Add:52, Ewhayeo-dae-gil, Seodaemun-gu, Seoul Tel:(02)3277-2114 http://www.ewha.ac.kr

Far East Univ. Add:76-32, Daehak-gil, Gamgok-myeon, Eumseong-gun, Chungcheongbuk-do Tel:(043)879-3500 http://www.kdu.ac.kr

Gachon Univ. Add:1342, Seongnam-daero, Sujeong-gu, Seongnam-si, Gyeonggi-do Tel:(031)750-5114 ‹Medical Campus› Add: 191, Hambangmoe-ro, Yeonsu-gu, Incheon Tel:(032)820-4000 http://www.gachon.ac.kr

Geumgang Univ. Add:522, Sangwol-ro, Sangwol-myeon, Nonsan-si, Chungcheongnam-do Tel:(041)731-3114 http://www.ggu.ac.kr

Gimcheon Univ. Add:214, Daehak-ro, Gimcheon-si, Gyeongsangbuk-do Tel:(054)420-4000 http://www.gimcheon.ac.kr

Gwangju Univ. Add:277, Hyodeok-ro, Nam-gu, Gwangju Tel:(062)670-2114 http://www.gwangju.ac.kr

Gwangju Catholic Univ. Add:12-25, Jungnam-gil, Nampyeong-eup, Naju-si, Jeollanam-do Tel:(061)337-2181 http://www.gjcatholic.ac.kr

Gyeongju Univ. Add:188, Taejong-ro, Gyeongju-si, Gyeongsangbuk-do Tel:(054)770-5114 http://www.gju.ac.kr

Halla Univ. Add:28, Halladae-gil, Heungeop-myeon, Wonju-si, Gangwon-do Tel:(033)760-1114 http://www.halla.ac.kr

Hallym Univ. Add:1, Hallimdaehak-gil, Chuncheon-si, Gangwon-do Tel:(033)248-1000 http://www.hallym.ac.kr

Handong Global Univ. Add:558, Handong-ro, Heunghae-eup, Buk-gu, Pohang-si, Gyeongsangbuk-do Tel:(054)260-1111 http://www.handong.edu

Hanil Univ. and Presbyterian Theological Seminary Add:726-15, Waemok-ro, Sanggwan-myeon, Wanju-gun, Jeollabuk-do Tel:(063)230-5400 http://www.hanil.ac.kr

Hanlyo Univ. Add:94-13, Hallyeodae-gil, Gwangyang-eup, Gwangyang-si, Jeollanam-do Tel:(061)760-1114 http://www.hanlyo.ac.kr

Hannam Univ. Add:70, Hannam-ro, Daedeok-gu, Daejeon Tel:(042)629-7114 http://www.hannam.ac.kr

Hansei Univ. Add:30, Hanse-ro, Gunpo-si, Gyeonggi-do Tel:(031)450-5114 http://www.hansei.ac.kr

Hanseo Univ. Add:46, Hanseo 1-ro, Haemi-myeon, Seosan-si, Chungcheongnam-do Tel:(041)660-1144 ⟨Taean Campus⟩ Add:236-49, Gomseom-ro Nam-myeon, Taean-gun, Chungcheongnam-do Tel:(041)671-6122 http://www.hanseo.ac.kr

Hanshin Univ. Add:137, Hanshindae-gil, Osan-si, Gyeonggi-do Tel:(031)379-0114 ⟨Seoul Campus⟩ Add:159, Insubong-ro, Gangbuk-gu, Seoul Tel:(02)2125-0114 http://www.hs.ac.kr

Hansung Univ. Add:116, Samseongyo-ro 16-gil, Seongbuk-gu, Seoul Tel:(02)760-4114 http://www.hansung.ac.kr

Hanyang Univ. Add:222, Wangsimni-ro, Seongdong-gu, Seoul Tel:(02)2220-0114 ⟨ERICA Campus⟩ Add:55, Hanyangdaehak-ro, Sangnok-gu, Ansan-si, Gyeonggi-do Tel:(031)400-5114 http://www.hanyang.ac.kr

Hanyoung Theological Univ. Add: 290-42, Gyeongin-ro, Guro-gu, Seoul Tel:(02)2067-4500 http://www.hytu.ac.kr

Hanzhong Univ. Add:200, Jiyang-gil, Donghae-si, Gangwon-do Tel:(033)520-9900 http://www.hanzhong.ac.kr

Honam Univ. Add:417, Eodeung-daero, Gwangsan-gu, Gwangju Tel:(062)940-5114 http://www.honam.ac.kr ⟨Ssangchon Campus⟩ Add:231, Naebang-ro, Seo-gu, Gwangju

Honam Theological Univ. and Seminary Add:77, Jejung-ro, Nam-gu, Gwangju Tel:(062)650-1552 http://www.htus.ac.kr

Hongik Univ. Add:94, Wausan-ro, Mapo-gu, Seoul Tel:(02)320-1114 http://home.hongik.ac.kr ⟨Sejong Campus⟩ Add:2639, Sejong-ro, Jochiwon-eup, Sejong-si Tel:(044)860-2114 http://sejong.hongik.ac.kr

Hoseo Univ. Add:20, Hoseo-ro 79beon-gil, Baebang-eup, Asan-si, Chungcheongnam-do Tel:(041)540-5114 ⟨Cheonan Campus⟩ Add:12, Hoseodae-gil, Dongnam-gu, Cheon-an-si, Chungcheongnam-do Tel:(041)560-8114 http://www.hoseo.ac.kr

Hyupsung Univ. Add:72, Choerubaek-ro, Bongdam-eup, Hwaseong-si, Gyeonggi-do Tel:(031)299-0900 http://www.uhs.ac.kr

Howon Univ. Add:64, Howondae 3-gil, Impi-myeon, Gunsan-si, Jeollabuk-do Tel:(063)450-7114 http://www.howon.ac.kr

Incheon Catholic Univ. Add:12, Haesong-ro, Yeonsu-gu, Incheon Tel:(032)830-7000 ⟨Ganghwa Campus⟩ Add:53, Goryeowang-neung-ro Yangdo-myeon, Ganghwa-gun, Incheon Tel:(032)930-8000 http://www.iccu.ac.kr

Inha Univ. Add:100, Inha-ro, Nam-gu, Incheon Tel:(032)860-7114 http://www.inha.ac.kr

Inje Univ. Add:197, Inje-ro, Gimhae-si, Gyeongsangnam-do Tel:(055)334-7111 ⟨Busan Campus⟩ Add:75, Bokji-ro, Busanjin-gu, Busan Tel:(051)894-3421 ⟨Seoul Campus⟩ Add:31, Supyo-ro, Jung-gu, Seoul Tel:(02)2270-0515 http://www.inje.ac.kr

International Univ. of Korea Add:965, Dongbu-ro, Munsan-eup, Jinju-si, Gyeongsangnam-do Tel:(055)751-8114 http://www.iuk.ac.kr

Jeju International Univ. Add:2870, 516-ro, Jeju-si, Jeju-do Tel:(064)754-0200 http://www.jeju.ac.kr

Jeonju Univ. Add:303, Cheonjam-ro, Wansan-gu, Jeonju-si, Jeollabuk-do Tel:1577-7177 http://www.jj.ac.kr

Jesus Univ. Add:383, Seowon-ro, Wansan-gu, Jeonju-si, Jeollabuk-do Tel:(063)230-7700 http://www.jesus.ac.kr

Joong-Ang Sangha Univ. Add:123, Seungga-ro, Gimpo-si, Gyeonggi-do Tel:(031)980-7777 http://www.sangha.ac.kr

Joongbu Univ. Add:201, Daehak-ro, Chubu-myeon, Geumsan-gun, Chungcheongnam-do Tel:(041)750-6500 http://www.joongbu.ac.kr ⟨Goyang Campus⟩ Add:22-4, Dongheon-ro 307beon-gil, Deogyang-gu, Goyang-si, Gyeonggi-do Tel:(031)8075-1000

Jungwon Univ. Add:85, Munmu-ro, Goesan-eup, Goesan-gun, Chungcheongbuk-do Tel:(043)830-8114 http://www.jwu.ac.kr

Kangnam Univ. Add:40, Gangnam-ro, Giheung-gu, Yongin-si, Gyeonggi-do Tel:(031)280-3114 http://www.kangnam.ac.kr

Kaya Univ. Add:208, Samgye-ro, Gimhae-si, Gyeongsangnam-do Tel:(055)330-1000

⟨Goryeong Campus⟩ Add:1103, Daegaya-ro, Goryeong-eup, Goryeong-gun, Gyeong-sangbuk-do Tel:(054)956-3100 http://www.kaya.ac.kr

Keimyung Univ. Add:1095, Dalgubeol-daero, Dalseo-gu, Daegu ⟨Daemyung Campus⟩ Add:104, Myeongdeok-ro, Nam-gu, Daegu Tel:(053)580-5114 http://www.kmu.ac.kr

Kkottongnae Univ. Add:133, Sangsam-gil, Hyeondo-myeon, Cheongwon-gun, Chungcheongbuk-do Tel:(043)270-0114 http://www.kkot.ac.kr

Konkuk Univ. Add:120, Neungdong-ro, Gwangjin-gu, Seoul Tel:(02)450-3114 http://www.konkuk.ac.kr ⟨Glocal Campus⟩ Add:268, Chungwon-daero, Chungju-si, Chungcheongbuk-do Tel:(043)840-3114 http://www.kku.ac.kr

Konyang Univ. Add:121, Daehak-ro, Nonsan-si, Chungcheongnam-do Tel:(041)730-5114 ⟨Daejoen Medical Campus⟩ Add:158, Gwanjeodong-ro, Seo-gu, Daejeon Tel:(042)600-6310 http://www.konyang.ac.kr

Kookmin Univ. Add:77, Jeongneung-ro, Seongbuk-gu, Seoul Tel:(02)910-4114 http://www.kookmin.ac.kr

Korea Univ. Add:145, Anam-ro, Seongbuk-gu, Seoul Tel:(02)3290-1114 http://www.korea.ac.kr ⟨Sejong Campus⟩ Add:2511, Sejong-ro, Jochiwon-eup, Sejong-si Tel:(044)860-1114 http://sejong.korea.ac.kr

Hankuk Univ. of Foreign Studies Add:107, Imun-ro, Dongdaemun-gu, Seoul Tel:(02)2173-2114 ⟨Global Campus⟩ Add:81, Oedae-ro, Mohyeon-myeon, Cheoin-gu, Yongin-si, Gyeonggi-do Tel:(031)330-4114 http://www.hufs.ac.kr

Korea Univ. of Technology and Education Add:1600, Chungjeol-ro, Byeongcheon-myeon, Dongnam-gu, Cheonan-si, Chungcheongnam-do Tel:(041)560-1114 http://www.koreatech.ac.kr

Korea Aerospace Univ. Add:76, Hanggongdaehak-ro, Deogyang-gu, Goyang-si, Gyeonggi-do Tel:(02)300-0114 http://www.kau.ac.kr

Korea Baptist Theological Univ. and Seminary Add:190, Bugyuseong-daero, Yuseong-gu, Daejeon Tel:(042)828-3114 http://www.kbtus.ac.kr

Korea Bible Univ. Add:32, Dongil-ro 214-gil, Nowon-gu, Seoul Tel:(02)950-5401 http://www.bible.ac.kr

Korea Christian Univ. Add:47, Kkachisan-ro 24-gil, Gangseo-gu, Seoul Tel:(02)2600-2400 http://www.kcu.ac.kr

Korea Nazarene Univ. Add:48, Wolbong-ro, Seobuk-gu, Cheonan-si, Chungcheongnam-do Tel:(041)570-7700 http://www.kornu.ac.kr

Korea Polytechnic Univ. Add:237, Sangidaehak-ro, Siheung-si, Gyeonggi-do Tel:(031)8041-1000 http://www.kpu.ac.kr

Kosin Univ. Add:194, Wachi-ro, Yeongdo-gu, Busan Tel:(051)990-2114 ⟨Cheonan Campus⟩ Add:535-31, Chungjeol-ro, Dong-nam-gu, Cheonan-si, Chungcheongnam-do Tel:(041)560-1999 ⟨Songdo Campus⟩ Add:262, Gamcheon-ro, Seo-gu, Busan Tel:(051)990-6406 http://web.kosin.ac.kr

Kwangju Women's Univ. Add:201, Yeodae-gil, Gwangsan-gu, Gwangju Tel:(062)956-2500 http://www.kwu.ac.kr

Kwangshin Univ. Add:36, Yangsan-taekjiso-ro, Buk-gu, Gwangju Tel:(062)605-1004 http://www.kwangshin.ac.kr

Kwangwoon Univ. Add:20, Gwangun-ro, Nowon-gu, Seoul Tel:(02)940-5114 http://www.kw.ac.kr

Kyonggi Univ. Add:154-42, Gwanggyo-san-ro, Yeongtong-gu, Suwon-si, Gyeonggi-do Tel:(031)249-9114 ⟨Seoul Campus⟩ Add:24, Kyonggidae-ro 9-gil, Seodaemun-gu, Seoul Tel:(02)390-5114 http://www.kyonggi.ac.kr

Kyungdong Univ. Add:46, Bongpo 4-gil, Toseong-myeon, Goseong-gun, Gangwon-do Tel:(033)631-2000 ⟨Sorak Campus(Sokcho)⟩ Add:5, Doriwon-gil, Sokcho-si, Gangwon-do Tel:(033)632-6551 ⟨Wonjumunmak Medical Campus⟩ Add:815, Gyeonhwon-ro, Munmak-eup, Wonju-si, Gangwon-do Tel:(033)742-1200 ⟨Yangju Metropol Campus⟩ Add:27, Gyeongdongdaehak-ro, Yangju-si, Gyeonggi-do Tel:(031)869-9500 http://kduniv.ac.kr

Kyunghee Univ. Add:26, Kyungheedae-ro, Dongdaemun-gu, Seoul Tel:(02)961-0114 http://www.khu.ac.kr ⟨Global Campus⟩ Add:1732, Deogyeong-daero, Giheung-gu, Yongin-si, Gyeonggi-do Tel:(031)201-2114 ⟨Gwangneung Campus⟩ Add:195, Gwangneungsumogwon-ro, Jinjeop-eup, Namyangju-si, Gyeonggi-do

Kyungil Univ. Add:50, Gamasil-gil, Hayang-eup, Gyeongsan-si, Gyeongsangbuk-do Tel:(053)600-4000 http://www.kiu.ac.kr

Kyungnam Univ. Add:7, Kyungnam-daehak-ro, Masanhappo-gu, Changwon-si, Gyeongsangnam-do Tel:(055)245-5000 http://www.kyungnam.ac.kr

Kyungsung Univ. Add:309, Suyeong-ro, Nam-gu, Busan Tel:(051)663-4114 http://ks.ac.kr

Kyungwoon Univ. Add:730, Gangdong-ro, Sandong-myeon, Gumi-si, Gyeongsang-buk-do Tel:(054)479-1114 http://www.ikw.ac.kr 〈Daegu Education Center〉 Add:180, Chilgokjungang-daero, Buk-gu, Daegu Tel:(053)310-7200

Luther Univ. Add:20, Geumhwa-ro 82 beon-gil, Giheung-gu, Yongin-si, Gyeonggi-do Tel:(031)679-2300 http://www.ltu.ac.kr

Methodist Theological Univ. Add:56, Dongnimmun-ro, Seodaemun-gu, Seoul Tel:(02)361-9114 http://www.mtu.ac.kr

Mokpo Catholic Univ. Add:697, Yeongsan-ro, Mokpo-si, Jeollanam-do Tel:(061)280-5000 http://www.mcu.ac.kr

Mokwon Univ. Add:88, Doanbuk-ro, Seo-gu, Daejeon Tel:(042)829-7114 http://www.mokwon.ac.kr

Myongji Univ. Add:34, Geobukgol-ro, Seodaemun-gu, Seoul 〈Natural Science Campus〉 Add:116, Myongji-ro, Cheoin-gu, Yongin-si, Gyeonggi-do Tel:1577-0020 http://www.mju.ac.kr

Nambu Univ. Add:23, Cheomdanj ungang-ro, Gwangsan-gu, Gwangju Tel:(062)970-0001 http://www.nambu.ac.kr

Namseoul Univ. Add:91, Daehak-ro, Seonghwan-eup, Seobuk-gu, Cheonan-si, Chungcheongnam-do Tel:(041)580-2000 http://www.nsu.ac.kr

Paichai Univ. Add:155-40, Baejae-ro, Seo-gu, Daejeon Tel:(042)520-5114 http://www.pcu.ac.kr 〈Daedeok Campus〉 Add:11-3, Techno 1-ro, Yuseong-gu, Daejeon Tel:(042)520-5818 https://sancam.pcu.ac.kr

Pohang Univ. of Science and Technology Add:77, Cheongam-ro, Nam-gu, Pohang-si, Gyeongsangbuk-do Tel:(054)279-0114 http://www.postech.ac.kr

Presbyterian University and Theological Seminary Add:25-1, Gwangjang-ro 5-gil, Gwangjin-gu, Seoul Tel:(02)450-0700 http://www.puts.ac.kr

Pyeongtaek Univ. Add:3825, Seodong-daero, Pyeongtaek-si, Gyeonggi-do Tel:(031)659-8114 http://www.ptu.ac.kr

Sahmyook Univ. Add:815, Hwarang-ro, Nowon-gu, Seoul Tel:(02)3399-3636 http://www.syu.ac.kr

Sangji Univ. Add:83, Sangjidae-gil, Wonju-si, Gangwon-do Tel:(033)730-0114 http://www.sangji.ac.kr

Sangmyung Univ. Add:20, Hongjimun 2-gil, Jongno-gu, Seoul Tel:(02)2287-5114 〈Cheonan Campus〉 Add:31, Sangmyeongdae-gil, Dongnam-gu, Cheonan-si, Chung cheongnam-do Tel:(041)550-5114 http://www.smu.ac.kr

Sehan Univ. Add:1113, Noksaek-ro, Samho-eup, Yeongam-gun, Jeollanam-do Tel:(061)469-1114 http://www.sehan.ac.kr 〈Dangjin Campus〉71-200, Namsan-gil, Sinpyeong-myeon, Dangjin-si, Chungcheong nam-do Tel:(041)359-6114

Sejong Univ. Add:209, Neungdong-ro, Gwangjin-gu, Seoul Tel:(02)3408-3114 http://www.sejong.ac.kr

Semyung Univ. Add:65, Semyeong-ro, Jecheon-si, Chungcheongbuk-do Tel:(043)645-1125 http://www.semyung.ac.kr

Seokyeong Univ. Add:124, Seogyeong-ro, Seongbuk-gu, Seoul Tel:(02)940-7114 http://www.skuniv.ac.kr

Seonam Univ. Add:439, Chunhyang-ro, Namwon-si, Jeollabuk-do Tel:(063)620-0114 〈Asan Campus〉 Add:7-111, Pyeongchon-gil, Songak-myeon, Asan-si, Chungcheongnam-do Tel:(041)539-5511 http://www.seonam.ac.kr

Seoul Christian Univ. Add:26-2, Galhyeon-ro 4-gil, Eunpyeong-gu, Seoul Tel:(02)380-2500 http://www.scu.ac.kr

Seoul Jangsin Univ. Add:145, Gyeongan-ro, Gwangju-si, Gyeonggi-do Tel:(031)799-9000 http://www.sjs.ac.kr

Seoul Theological Univ. Add:52, Hoh yeon-ro 489beon-gil, Sosa-gu, Bucheon-si, Gyeonggi-do Tel:(032)340-9114 http://www.stu.ac.kr

Seoul Women's Univ. Add:621, Hwar ang-ro, Nowon-gu, Seoul Tel:(02)970-5114 http://www.swu.ac.kr

Seowon Univ. Add:377-3, Musimseo-ro, Heungdeok-gu, Cheongju-si, Chungcheong buk-do Tel:(043)299-8114 http://www.seowon.ac.kr

Shingyeong Univ. Add:400-5, Namya ngjungang-ro Namyang-eup, Hwaseong-si, Gyeonggi-do Tel:(031)369-9112 http://www.sgu.ac.kr

Shinhan Univ. Add:95, Hoam-ro, Uij eongbu-si, Gyeonggi-do Tel:(031)870-3114 〈The 2nd Campus〉 Add:30, Beolmadeul-ro 40beon-gil, Dongducheon-si, Gyeonggi-do Tel:(031)870-2900 http://www.shinhan.ac.kr

Silla Univ. Add:140, Baegyang-daero 700beon-gil, Sasang-gu, Busan Tel:(051)999-5000 http://www.silla.ac.kr

Sogang Univ. Add:35, Baekbeom-ro, Mapo-gu, Seoul Tel:(02)705-8114 http://www.sogang.ac.kr

Songwon Univ. Add:73, Songam-ro, Nam-gu, Gwangju Tel:(062)360-5700 http://www.songwon.ac.kr

Sookmyung Women's Univ. Add:100, Cheongpa-ro 47-gil, Yongsan-gu, Seoul Tel:(02)710-9114 http://www.sookmyung.ac.kr

Soonchunhyang Univ. Add:22, Soon-chunhyang-ro, Sinchang-myeon, Asan-si, Chungcheongnam-do Tel:(041)530-1114 http://homepage.sch.ac.kr

Soongsil Univ. Add:369, Sangdo-ro, Dongjak-gu, Seoul Tel:(02)820-0114 http://www.ssu.ac.kr

Sungkonghoe Univ. Add:320, Yeondong-ro, Guro-gu, Seoul Tel:320, Yeondong-ro, Guro-gu, Seoul Tel:(02)2610-4114 http://www.skhu.ac.kr

Sungkyul Univ. Add:53, Sungkyuldaehak-ro, Manan-gu, Anyang-si, Gyeonggi-do Tel:(031)467-8114 http://www.sungkyul.ac.kr

Sungkyunkwan Univ. Add:25-2, Sung-kyunkwan-ro, Jongno-gu, Seoul Tel:(02)760-0114 ⟨Natural Science Campus⟩ Add:2066, Seobu-ro, Jangan-gu, Suwon-si, Gyeonggi-do Tel:(031)290-5114 http://www.skku.edu

Sungshin Women's Univ. Add:2, Bomun-ro 34da-gil, Seongbuk-gu, Seoul Tel:(02)920-7114 ⟨Miaunjung Campus⟩ Add:55, Dobong-ro 76ga-gil, Gangbuk-gu, Seoul Tel:(02)920-7870 http://www.sungshin.ac.kr

Sunmoon Univ. Add:70, Sunmoon-ro 221beon-gil, Tangjeong-myeon, Asan-si, Chungcheongnam-do Tel:(041)530-2114 ⟨Cheonan Campus⟩ Add:277, Cheonan-daero, Dongnam-gu, Cheonan-si, Chungcheongnam-do Tel:(041)559-1214 http://www.sunmoon.ac.kr

Suwon Catholic Univ. Add:67, Wangnim 1-gil, Bongdam-eup, Hwaseong-si, Gyeonggi-do Tel:(031)290-8800 http://www.suwoncatholic.ac.kr

Tongmyong Univ. Add:428, Sinseon-ro, Nam-gu, Busan Tel:(051)629-1000 http://www.tu.ac.kr

Uiduk Univ. Add:261, Donghae-daero, Gangdong-myeon, Gyeongju-si, Gyeongsang-buk-do Tel:(054)760-1114 http://www.uu.ac.kr

Univ. of Suwon Add:17, Wauan-gil, Bongdam-eup, Hwaseong-si, Gyeonggi-do Tel:(031)220-2114 http://www.suwon.ac.kr

Univ. of Ulsan Add:93, Daehak-ro, Nam-gu, Ulsan Tel:(052)277-3101 http://www.ulsan.ac.kr

Wonkwang Univ. Add:460, Iksan-daero, Iksan-si, Jeollabuk-do Tel:(063)850-5114 http://www.wonkwang.ac.kr

Woosong Univ. Add:171, Dongdaejeon-ro, Dong-gu, Daejeon Tel:(042)630-9600 http://www.wsu.ac.kr

Woosuk Univ. Add:443, Samnye-ro, Samnye-eup, Wanju-gun, Jeollabuk-do Tel:(063)290-1114 http://www.woosuk.ac.kr ⟨Jincheon Campus⟩ Add:66, Daehak-ro Jincheon-eup, Jincheon-gun, Chungcheongbuk-do Tel:(043)531-2700 http://jc.woosuk.ac.kr

Yeungnam Univ. Add:280, Daehak-ro, Gyeongsan-si, Gyeongsangbuk-do Tel:(053)810-2114 http://www.yu.ac.kr ⟨Daegu Campus⟩ Add:170, Hyeonchung-ro, Nam-gu, Daegu Tel:(053)620-4302 http://yumc.yu.ac.kr

Yewon Art Univ. Add:117, Changin-ro, Sinpyeong-myeon, Imsil-gun, Jeollabuk-do Tel:(063)640-7114 ⟨Jeonju Campus⟩ Add:20, Chopodari-ro, Deokjin-gu, Jeonju-si, Jeollabuk-do Tel:(063)253-7071 ⟨Yangju Campus⟩ Add:110, Hwahap-ro 1134beon-gil Eunhyeon-myeon, Yangju-si, Gyeonggi-do Tel:(031)869-0577 http://www.yewon.ac.kr

Yongin Univ. Add:134, Yongindaehak-ro, Cheoin-gu, Yongin-si, Gyeonggi-do Tel:(031)332-6471 http://www.yongin.ac.kr

Yonsei Univ. Add:50, Yonsei-ro, Seodaemun-gu, Seoul ⟨International Campus⟩ Add:85, Songdogwahak-ro, Yeonsu-gu, Incheon ⟨Wonju Campus⟩ Add:1, Yonsedae-gil, Heungeop-myeon, Wonju-si, Gangwon-do Tel: 1599-1885 http://www.yonsei.ac.kr

Youngdong Univ. Add:310, Daehak-ro, Yeongdong-eup, Yeongdong-gun, Chungcheongbuk-do Tel:(043)740-1114 http://www.youngdong.ac.kr

Youngnam Theological Univ. and Seminary Add:26, Bonghoe 1-gil, Jillyang-eup, Gyeongsan-si, Gyeongsangbuk-do Tel:(053)850-0500 http://www.ytus.ac.kr

Youngsan Univ. Add:288, Junam-ro, Yangsan-si, Gyeongsangnam-do Tel:(055)380-9114 ⟨Haeundae Campus⟩ Add:142, Bansongsunhwan-ro, Haeundae-gu, Busan Tel:(051)540-7000 http://www.ysu.ac.kr

Youngsan Univ. of Son Studies Add: 1357, Seongji-ro, Baeksu-eup, Yeonggwang-gun, Jeollanam-do Tel:(061)350-6015 http://www.youngsan.ac.kr

MASS MEDIA

NEWSPAPERS

\<National Newspapers\>

Asia Economy Daily Add:29, Chungmuro, Jung-gu, Seoul Tel:(02)2200-2114 http://
www.asiae.co.kr

Chosun Ilbo Add:52, Sejong-daero 21-gil, Jung-gu, Seoul Tel:(02)724-5114 http://www.chosun.com

Daily Sports Add:56, Sejong-daero 7-gil, Jung-gu, Seoul Tel:(02)2031-1111 http://isplus.joinsmsn.com

Digital Times Add:22, Saemunan-ro, Jung-gu, Seoul Tel:(02)3701-5500 http://www.dt.co.kr

Dong-A Ilbo Add:29, Chungjeong-ro, Seodaemun-gu, Seoul Tel:(02)2020-0114 http://www.donga.com

Electronic Times Add:51, Beodeunaru-ro 12ga-gil, Yeongdeungpo-gu, Seoul Tel:(02)2168-9200 http://www.etnews.com

Financial News Add:81, Yeouinaru-ro, Yeongdeungpo-gu, Seoul Tel:(02)2003-7114 http://www.fnnews.com

Hankyoreh Add:6, Hyochangmok-gil, Mapo-gu, Seoul Tel:1566-9595 http://www.hani.co.kr

Hankook Ilbo Add:63, Namdaemun-ro, Jung-gu, Seoul Tel:(02)724-2114 http://news.hankooki.com

Herald Corporation Add:10, Huam-ro 4-gil, Yongsan-gu, Seoul Tel:(02)727-0114 http://www.heraldm.com

Joongang Ilbo Add:100, Seosomun-ro, Jung-gu, Seoul Tel:(02)751-9114 http://www.joongang.co.kr

Korea Economic Daily Add:463, Cheongpa-ro, Jung-gu, Seoul Tel:(02)360-4114 http://www.hankyung.com

Korea Times Add:81, Tongil-ro, Seodaemun-gu, Seoul Tel:(02)724-2359 http://www.korea-times.co.kr

Kukmin Ilbo Add:101, Yeouigongwon-ro, Yeongdeungpo-gu, Seoul Tel:(02)781-9114 http://www.kmib.co.kr

Kyunghyang Shinmun Add:3, Jeongdong-gil, Jung-gu, Seoul Tel:(02)3701-1114 http://www.khan.co.kr

Maeil Business Newspaper Add:190, Toegye-ro, Jung-gu, Seoul Tel:(02)2000-2114 http://www.mk.co.kr

Munhwa Ilbo Add:22, Saemunan-ro, Jung-gu, Seoul Tel:(02)3701-5114 http://www.munhwa.com

Naeil Shinmoon Add:43, Saemunan-ro, Jongno-gu, Seoul Tel:(02)2287-2300 http://www.naeil.com

Segye Times Add:26, Gyeonghuigung-gil, Jongno-gu, Seoul Tel:(02)2000-1234 http://www.segye.com

Seoul Economic Daily Add:9F, 13F, imkwang Bldg., 81, Tongil-ro, Seodaemun-gu, Seoul Tel:(02)724-2200 http://economy.hankooki.com

Seoul Shinmoon Add:124, Sejong-daero, Jung-gu, Seoul Tel:(02)2000-9000 http://www.seoul.co.kr

Sports Chosun Add:20F, Dream Tower, 233-1, Mokdongdong-ro, Yangcheon-gu, Seoul Tel:(02)3219-8114 http://sports.chosun.com

Sports Dong-A Add:1, Cheonggyecheon-ro, Jongno-gu, Seoul Tel:(02)2020-1010 http://sports.donga.com

Sports Seoul Add:775, Gyeongin-ro, Yeongdeungpo-gu, Seoul Tel:(02)2001-0021 http://www.sportsseoul.com

Sports World Add:26, Gyeonghuigung-gil, Jongno-gu, Seoul Tel:(02)2000-1800 http://www.sportsworldi.com

\<Local Newspapers\>

Busan Ilbo Add:365, Jungang-daero, Dong-gu, Busan Tel:(051)461-4114 http://www.busan.com

Jeonbuk Domin Ilbo Add:54, Beotkkot-ro, Deokjin-gu, Jeonju-si, Jeollabuk-do Tel:(063)259-2170 http://www.domin.co.kr

Chungcheong Daily News Add:735, Jikji-daero, Heungdeok-gu, Cheongju-si, Chungcheongbuk-do Tel:(043)277-5555 http://www.ccdn.co.kr

Chungbuk Ilbo Add:715, Musimseo-ro, Heungdeok-gu, Cheongju-si, Chungcheongbuk-do Tel:(043)277-2114 http://www.inews365.com

Chungbukin News Add:17, Sangdang-ro 144beon-gil, Sangdang-gu, Cheongju-si, Chungcheongbuk-do Tel:(043)250-0040 http://www.cbinews.co.kr

Chungcheong Today Add:67, Galmajung-ro 30beon-gil, Seo-gu, Daejeon Tel:(042)380-7000 http://www.cctoday.co.kr

Chungcheong Ilbo Add:769, Jikji-daero, Heungdeok-gu, Cheongju-si, Chungcheongbuk-do Tel:(043)279-2000 http://www.ccdailynews.com

Jeonnam Maeil Add:322, Jebong-ro, Buk-gu, Gwangju Tel:(062)720-1000 http://www.jndn.com

Daegu Ilbo Add:330, Dongdaegu-ro, Suseong-gu, Daegu Tel:(053)757-5700 http://www.idaegu.com

Daegu Shinmun Add:94, Dongbu-ro, Dong-gu, Daegu Tel:(053)424-0004 http://www.idaegu.co.kr

Daehan Ilbo Add:212-11, Toegye-ro, Jung-gu, Seoul Tel:(02)2277-7675 http://www.daehanilbo.co.kr

Daejon Ilbo Add:314, Gyeryong-ro, Seo-gu, Daejeon Tel:(042)251-3311 http://www.daejonilbo.com

Dongyang Daily News Add:103, Chungcheong-daero, Sangdang-gu, Cheongju-si, Chungcheongbuk-do Tel:(043)218-7117 http://www.dynews.co.kr

Gwangnam Ilbo Add:154, Wolsan-ro, Nam-gu, Gwangju Tel:(062)370-7000 http://www.gwangnam.co.kr

Gyeong-gi Shinmun Add:55, Songwon-ro, Jangan-gu, Suwon-si, Gyeonggi-do Tel:(031)268-8114 http://www.kgnews.co.kr

Halla Ilbo Add:154, Seosa-ro, Jeju-si, Jeju-do Tel:(064)750-2114 http://www.ihalla.com

Honam Maeil Add:166, Mudeung-ro, Buk-gu, Gwangju Tel:(062)363-8800 http://www.honammaeil.co.kr

Incheon Ilbo Add:226, Injung-ro, Jung-gu, Incheon Tel:(032)452-0114 http://news.itimes.co.kr

Jeju Daily News Add:4, Taeseong-ro 3-gil, Jeju-si, Jeju-do Tel:(064)740-6114 http://www.jejunews.com

Jemin Ilbo Add:2700, Pyeonghwa-ro Aewol-eup, Jeju-si, Jeju-do Tel:(064)741-3111 http://www.jemin.com

Jeolla Ilbo Add:75, Jeollagamyeong-ro, Wansan-gu, Jeonju-si, Jeollabuk-do Tel:(063)232-3132 http://www.jeollailbo.com

Jeonbuk Ilbo Add:418, Girin-daero, Deokjin-gu, Jeonju-si, Jeollabuk-do Tel:(063)250-5500 http://www.jjan.kr

Jeonbuk Joongang Shinmun Add:6, Handupyeong 2-gil, Wansan-gu, Jeonju-si, Jeollabuk-do Tel:(063)230-9100 http://www.jjn.co.kr

Jeonbuk Maeil Sinmun Add:38, Hongsanjungang-ro, Wansan-gu, Jeonju-si, Jeollabuk-do Tel:(063)232-9301 http://www.mjbnews.com

Jeonnam Ilbo Add:324, Jebong-ro, Buk-gu, Gwangju Tel:(062)527-0015 http://www.jnilbo.com

Joongboo Ilbo Add:733, Gwonseon-ro, Paldal-gu, Suwon-si, Gyeonggi-do Tel:(031)230-2114 http://www.joongboo.com

Joongbu Maeil Add:22, 1sunhwan-ro 436beon-gil, Heungdeok-gu, Cheongju-si, Chungcheongbuk-do Tel:(043)275-2001 http://www.jbnews.com

Joongdo Ilbo Add:832, Gyeryong-ro, Jung-gu, Daejeon Tel:(042)220-1114 http://www.joongdo.co.kr

Kang Won Domin Ilbo Add:22, Huseok-ro 462beon-gil, Chuncheon-si, Gangwon-do Tel:(033)260-9000 http://www.kado.net

Kangwon Ilbo Add:23, Jungang-ro, Chuncheon-si, Gangwon-do Tel:(033)258-1000 http://www.kwnews.co.kr

Kiho Ilbo Add:5, Injung-ro, Nam-gu, Incheon Tel:(032)761-0007 http://www.kihoilbo.co.kr

Kookje Shinmun Add:1217, Jungang-daero, Yeonje-gu, Busan Tel:(051)500-5114 http://www.kookje.co.kr

Kwangju Ilbo Add:238, Geumnam-ro, Dong-gu, Gwangju Tel:(062)222-8111 http://www.kwangju.co.kr

Kwangju Maeil Shinmun Add:16, Cheonbyeonjwa-ro 338beon-gil, Nam-gu, Gwangju Tel:(062)650-2000 http://www.kjdaily.com

Kyeonggi Ilbo Add:6, Gyeongsu-daero 973beon-gil, Jangan-gu, Suwon-si, Gyeonggi-do Tel:(031)250-3300 http://www.kyeonggi.com

Kyeonggi Maeil Add:10F AceTower, 54, Gojan-ro, Danwon-gu, Ansan-si, Gyeonggi-do Tel:(031)235-1111 http://www.kgmaeil.net

Kyeongin Ilbo Add:299, Hyowon-ro, Paldal-gu, Suwon-si, Gyeonggi-do Tel:(031)231-5114 http://www.kyeongin.com

Gyeongnam Maeil Add:1125, Geumgwan-daero, Gimhae-si, Gyeongsangnam-do Tel:(055)323-1000 http://www.gnmaeil.com/

Gyeongnam Ilbo Add:1065, Namgang-ro, Jinju-si, Gyeongsangnam-do Tel:(055)751-1000 http://www.gnnews.co.kr

Kyongbuk Ilbo Add:93, Jungheung-ro, Nam-gu, Pohang-si, Gyeongsangbuk-do Tel:(054)289-2215 http://www.kyongbuk.co.kr

Kyongbukdomin Ilbo Add:66-1, Jungang-ro, Nam-gu, Pohang-si, Gyeongsangbuk-do Tel:(054)283-8100 http://www.hidomin.com/

Kyongbuk Maeil Add:289, Jungang-ro, Buk-gu, Pohang-si, Gyeongsangbuk-do Tel:(054)289-5000 http://www.kbmaeil.com/

Kyungnam Shinmun Add:3, Jungang-daero 210beon-gil, Uichang-gu, Changwon-si, Gyeongsangnam-do Tel:(055)210-6000 http://www.knnews.co.kr

Kyongnamdomin Ilbo Add:38, Samho-ro, Masanhoewon-gu, Changwon-si, Gyeongsangnam-do Tel:(055)250-0100 http://www.idomin.com

Kyungsang Ilbo Add:17, Bukbusunhwando-ro, Nam-gu, Ulsan Tel:(052)220-0515 http://www.ksilbo.co.kr

Moodeung Ilbo Add:9F, Skyland Bldg., 213, Uncheon-ro, Seo-gu, Gwangju Tel:(062) 606-7760 http://www.moodeungilbo.co.kr

Maeil Shinmun Add:20, Seoseong-ro, Jung-gu, Daegu Tel:(053)255-5001 http://www.imaeil.com

Namdo Ilbo Add:323, Daenam-daero, Nam-gu, Gwangju Tel:(062)670-1000 http://www.namdonews.com

Saejeonbuk Shinmun Add:728, Baekje-daero, Deokjin-gu, Jeonju-si, Jeollabuk-do Tel:(063)230-5700 http://www.sjbnews.com

Sudokwon Ilbo Add:3~5F, Irum Bldg., 79, Maesan-ro, Paldal-gu, Suwon-si, Gyeonggi-do Tel:(031)248-8700 http://www.sudokwon.com

Ulsan Daily Newspaper Add:9F, 10F, Tempo Bldg., 4, Suam-ro, Nam-gu, Ulsan Tel:(052)243-1001 http://www.iusm.co.kr

Ulsan Shinmun Add:86, Dotjil-ro, Nam-gu, Ulsan Tel:(052)273-4300 http://www.ulsanpress.net

Yeongnam Ilbo Add:441, Dongdaegu-ro, Dong-gu, Daegu Tel:(053)756-8001 http://www.yeongnam.com

NEWS AGENCY

Yonhap News Agency Add:25, Yulgok-ro 2-gil, Jongno-gu, Seoul Tel:(02)398-3114 http://www.yonhapnews.co.kr

Newsis News Agency Add:12F, Nam-sanspuare Bldg., 173, Toegye-ro, Jung-gu, Seoul Tel:(02)721-7400 http://www.newsis.com

News1 Korea Add:17F, Standard Chartered Bank Korea Limited Bldg., 47, Jong-ro, Jongno-gu, Seoul Tel:(02)397-7000 http://www.news1.kr

TELEVISION STATIONS

Buddhist Broadcasting System Add:20, Mapo-daero, Mapo-gu, Seoul Tel:(02)705-5114 http://www.bbsi.co.kr

Channel A Add:1, Cheonggyecheon-ro, Jongno-gu, Seoul Tel:(02)2020-3114 http://www.ichannela.com

Christian Broadcasting System Add:159-1, Mokdongseo-ro, Yangcheon-gu, Seoul Tel:(02)2650-7000 http://www.cbs.co.kr

CJB Add:59-1, Saun-ro, Heungdeok-gu, Cheongju-si, Chungcheongbuk-do Tel:(043)265-7000 http://www.cjb.co.kr

Educational Broadcasting System Add:35, Baumoe-ro 1-gil, Seocho-gu, Seoul Tel:(02)526-2000 http://www.ebs.co.kr

Far East Broadcasting Comapany Add:56, Wausan-ro, Mapo-gu, Seoul Tel:(02)320-0114 http://www.febc.net

Gangwon No.1 Broadcasting Add: 274, Soyanggan-ro, Dong-myeon, Chuncheon-si, Gangwon-do Tel:(033)248-5000 http://www.g1tv.co.kr

Jeonju Television Corporation Add:1083, Jeongyeorip-ro, Deokjin-gu, Jeonju-si, Jeollabuk-do Tel:(063)250-5200 http://www.jtv.co.kr

Jeju Free International City Broadcasting System Add:95, Yeonsam-ro, Jeju-si, Jeju-do Tel:(064)740-7800 http://www.jibstv.com

JTBC Add:48-6, Sangamsan-ro, Mapo-gu, Seoul Tel:(02)751-6000 http://www.jtbc.co.kr

KT Skylife Corporation, Ltd. Add:75, Maebongsan-ro, Mapo-gu, Seoul Tel:(02)2003-3000 http://www.skylife.co.kr

KNN Add:30, Centum seo-ro, Haeundae-gu, Busan Tel:(051)850-9000 http://www.knn.co.kr

Korea Broadcasting System Add:13, Yeouigongwon-ro, Yeongdeungpo-gu, Seoul Tel:(02)781-1000 http://www.kbs. co.kr

Local Network : Andong, Busan, Changwon, Cheongju, Chuncheon, Chungju, Daegu, Daejeon, Gangneung, Gwangju, Jeju, Jeonju, Jinju, Mokpo, Pohang, Suncheon, Ulsan, Wonju

Korea Business News Corporation, Ltd. Add:84, Beodeunaru-ro, Yeongdeungpo-gu, Seoul Tel:(02)6676-0000 http://www. wowtv.co.kr

Kwangju Broadcasting Company Add:87, Jungang-ro, Nam-gu, Gwangju Tel:(062)650-3114 http://www.ikbc.co.kr

Kyonggi FM Add:111, Maeyeong-ro 345beon-gil, Yeongtong-gu, Suwon-si, Gyeonggi-do, Korea Tel:(031)210-0999 http://www.kfm.co.kr

Maeil Broadcasting Network Add: 190, Toegye-ro, Jung-gu, Seoul Tel:(02)2000-3114 http://www.mbn.co.kr

Munhwa Broadcasting Corporation Add:267, Seongam-ro, Mapo-gu, Seoul Tel:(02)789-0011 http://www.imbc.com

Local Network : Andong, Busan, Changwon, Cheongju, Chuncheon, Chungju, Daegu, Daejeon, Gangneung, Gwangju, Gyeongnam, Jeju, Jeonju, Jinju, Mokpo, Pohang, Samcheok, Ulsan, Wonju, Yeosu

OBS Gyeongin TV Add:233, Ojeong-ro, Ojeong-gu, Bucheon-si, Gyeonggi-do Tel:(032)670-5000 http://www.obs.co.kr

Pyeonghwa Broadcasting Corporation Add:330, Samil-daero, Jung-gu, Seoul Tel:(02)2270-2114 http://web.pbc.co.kr

Local Network : Andong, Busan, Daegu, Daejeon, Gwangju, Pohang, Yeosu

Seoul Broadcasting System Add:161, Mokdongseo-ro, Yangcheon-gu, Seoul Tel:(02)2061-0006 http://www.sbs.co.kr

Seoul Traffic Broadcasting System Add:36, Toegye-ro 26-gil, Jung-gu, Seoul Tel:(02)311-5114 http://www.tbs.seoul.kr

TaeJon Broadcasting Company, Ltd. Add:131, Expo-ro, Yuseong-gu, Daejeon Tel:(042)281-1101 http://www.tjb.co.kr

TV Chosun Add:C-Square Bldg., 40, Sejong-daero 21-gil, Jung-gu, Seoul Tel:1661-0190 http://tv.chosun.com

Taegu Broadcasting Company Add:23, Dongdaegu-ro, Suseong-gu, Daegu Tel:(053)760-1900 http://www.tbc.co.kr

Traffic Broadcasting System Add:407, Wangsimni-ro, Jung-gu, Seoul Tel:(02)2230-6114 http://www.tbn.or.kr

Ulsan Broadcasting Corporation Add: 41, Gugyo-ro, Jung-gu, Ulsan Tel:(052)228-6000 http://www.ubc.co.kr

Won-Buddhism Broadcasting System Add:75, Hyeonchung-ro, Dongjak-gu, Seoul Tel:(02)2102-7700 http://www.wbsi.kr

Yonhapnews TV Add:25, Yulgok-ro 2-gil, Jongno-gu, Seoul Tel:(02)398-3114 http:// www.news-y.co.kr

YTN Corporation, Ltd. Add:76, Sangamsan-ro, Mapo-gu, Seoul Tel:(02)398-8000 http:// www.ytn.co.kr

ECONOMIC ASSOCIATIONS

Construction Association of Korea Add:711, Eonju-ro, Gangnam-gu, Seoul Tel:(02)1588-6912 http://www.cak.or.kr

Construction Guarantee Add:711, Eonju-ro, Gangnam-gu, Seoul Tel:(02)3449-8888 http://www.cgbest.co.kr

Credit Finance Association Add:43, Dadong-gil, Jung-gu, Seoul Tel:(02)2011-0700 http://www.crefia.or.kr

Federation of Construction Associations Add:711, Eonju-ro, Gangnam-gu, Seoul Tel:(02)3485-8392 http://www.fcas.or.kr

Federation of Korean Industries Add:24, Yeoui-daero, Yeongdeungpo-gu, Seoul Tel: (02)3771-0114 http://www.fki.or.kr

Federation of Korean Information Industries Add:396, World cup buk-ro, Mapo-gu, Seoul Tel:(02)780-0201 http:// www.fkii.or.kr

General Insurance Association of Korea Add:68, Jong-ro 5-gil, Jongno-gu, Seoul Tel:(02)3702-8500 http://www.knia.or.kr

International Contractors Association of Korea Add:42, Sejong-daero 9-gil, Jung-gu, Seoul Tel:(02)3406-1114 http://kor.icak. or.kr

Korea Advertisers Association Add:24, Yeoui-daero, Yeongdeungpo-gu, Seoul Tel:(02)2055-4000 http://www.kaa.or.kr

Korea Association for ICT Promotion Add:350, Seocho-daero, Seocho-gu, Seoul Tel:(02)580-0580 http://www.kait.or.kr

Korea Association of Advertising Agencies Add:137, Olympic-ro 35-gil, Songpa-gu, Seoul Tel:(02)733-3500 http:// kaaa.co.kr

Korea Association of Machinery Industry Add:37, Eunhaeng-ro, Yeongdeungpo-gu, Seoul, Korea Tel:(02)369-8600 http://www. koami.or.kr

Korea Automobile Association Add:165, Sinbanpo-ro, Seocho-gu, Seoul Tel:(02)565-7001 http://www.kaa21.or.kr

Korea Automobile Manufacturers Association Add:25, Banpo-daero, Seocho-gu, Seoul Tel:(02)3660-1800 http://www.kama.or.kr

Korea Business Women's Federation Add:9, Baumoe-ro 25-gil, Seocho-gu, Seoul Tel:(02)540-4207 http://www.kbwf.or.kr

Korea Cement Association Add:14, Dogok-ro 1-gil, Gangnam-gu, Seoul Tel:(02)538-8230 http://www.cement.or.kr

Korea Chamber of Commerce & Industry Add:39, Sejong-daero, Jung-gu, Seoul Tel:(02)6050-3114 http://www.korcham.net

Korea Chemical Fibers Association Add:130, Sajik-ro, Jongno-gu, Seoul Tel:(02)734-1191 http://www.kcfa.or.kr

Korea Coal Association Add:58, Jongro 5-gil, Jongno-gu, Seoul Tel:(02)734-8891 http://www.kcoal.or.kr

Korea Construction Consulting Engineers Association Add:2714, Nambusunhwan-ro, Gangnam-gu, Seoul Tel:(02)3460-8600 http://www.gamri.or.kr

Korea Construction Engineers Association Add:650, Eonju-ro, Gangnam-gu, Seoul Tel:1577-5445 http://www.kocea.or.kr

Korea Construction Equipment Association Add:54, Seocho-daero 42-gil, Seocho-gu, Seoul Tel:(02)501-5701 http://www.kcea.or.kr

Korea Construction Equipment Manufacturers Association Add:48, Soetgol-ro, Bundang-gu, Seongnam-si, Gyeonggi-do Tel:(02)2052-9300 http://www.kocema.org

Korea Cosmetic Association Add:750, Gukhoe-daero, Yeongdeungpo-gu, Seoul Tel:(02)785-7984 http://www.kcia.or.kr

Korea Customs Logistics Association Add:16-91, Hangang-ro 3-ga, Yongsan-gu, Seoul Tel:(02)701-1455 http://www.kcla.kr

Korea Dairy & Beef Farmers Association Add:88, Myeongdal-ro, Seocho-gu, Seoul Tel:(02)588-7055 http://www.naknong.or.kr

Korea Dairy Industries Association Add:43, Bangbae-ro, Seocho-gu, Seoul Tel:(02)584-3631 http://www.koreadia.or.kr

Korea Defense Industry Association Add:49, Mapo-daero, Mapo-gu, Seoul Tel:(02)3270-6000 http://www.kdia.or.kr

Korea Department Stores Association Add:46, Chilpae-ro, Jung-gu, Seoul Tel:(02)754-6054

Korea Electric Association Add:72-13, Supyo-ro, Jung-gu, Seoul Tel:(02)3393-7600 http://www.electricity.or.kr

Korea Electrical Contractors Association Add:8, Gonghang-daero 58ga-gil, Gangseo-gu, Seoul Tel:(02)3219-0404 http://www.keca.or.kr

Korea Electrical Manufacturers Association Add:10-3, Bangbae-ro 10-gil, Seocho-gu, Seoul Tel:(02)581-8601 http://www.koema.or.kr

Korea Electronics Association Add: 11, World Cup buk-ro 54-gil, Mapo-gu, Seoul Tel:(02)6388-6000 http://www.gokea.org

Korea Employers Federation Add: 88, Baekbeom-ro, Mapo-gu, Seoul Tel:(02)3270-7300 http://www.kefplaza.com

Korea Exchange Add:40, Munhyeongeumyung-ro, Nam-gu, Busan Tel:(051)662-2000 http://www.krx.co.kr

Korea Fashion Association Add:18, Achasan-ro 7na-gil, Seongdong-gu, Seoul Tel:(02)460-8357 http://www.koreafashion.org

Korea Federation of Construction Contractors Add:109, Mapo-daero, Mapo-gu, Seoul Tel:(02)771-7939 http://www.kfcc.or.kr

Korea Federation of Advertising Associations Add:137, Olympic-ro 35-gil, Songpa-gu, Seoul Tel:(02)2144-0750 http://www.kfaa.org

Korea Federation of Banks Add:19, Myeongdong 11-gil, Jung-gu, Seoul Tel:(02)3705-5000 http://www.kfb.or.kr

Korea Federation of Furniture Industry Cooperative Add:79, Janghan-ro, Dongdaemun-gu, Seoul Tel:(02)2215-8838 http://www.kffic.kr

Korea Federation of Textile Industries Add:518, Teheran-ro, Gangnam-gu, Seoul Tel:(02)528-4030 http://www.kofoti.or.kr

Korea Federation of Machinery Industry Cooperatives Add:207, Bangbae-ro, Seocho-gu, Seoul Tel:(02)3481-9900 http://www.komico.or.kr

Korea Federation of Savings Banks Add: 37, Saemunan-ro 5-gil, Jongno-gu, Seoul Tel:(02)3978-600 http://www.fsb.or.kr

Korea Federation of Small and Medium Business Add:30, Eunhaeng-ro, Yeongdeungpo-gu, Seoul Tel:(02)2124-3114 http://www.kbiz.or.kr

Korea Feed Association Add:76, Banpo-daero, Seocho-gu, Seoul Tel:(02)581-5721 http://www.kofeed.org

Korea Fertilizer Association Add:15, Teheran-ro 113-gil, Gangnam-gu, Seoul Tel:(02)552-2812 http://www.fert-kfia.or.kr

Korea Financial Investment Association Add:143, Uisadang-daero, Yeongdeungpo-gu, Seoul Tel:(02)2003-9000 http://www.kofia.or.kr

Korean Fire Protection Association Add:38, Gukjegeumyung-ro 6-gil, Yeongdeungpo-gu, Seoul Tel:(02)3780-0200 http://www.kfpa.or.kr

Korea Fire Safety Association Add: 170, Yeongjung-ro, Yeongdeungpo-gu, Seoul Tel:(02)2671-8695 http://www.kfsa.or.kr

Korea Fisheries Association Add:83, Nonhyeon-ro, Seocho-gu, Seoul Tel:(02)589-0601 http://www.korfish.or.kr

Korea Fisheries Infrastructure Promotion **Association** Add:53, Gasan digital 2-ro, Geumcheon-gu, Seoul Tel:(02)6098-0700 http://www.fipa.or.kr

Korea Flour Mills Industrial Association Add:118, Namdaemunno 5-ga, Jung-gu, Seoul Tel:(02)777-9451 http://www.kofmia.org

Korea Food Industry Association Add: 2423, Nambusunhwan-ro, Seocho-gu, Seoul Tel:(02)585-5052 http://kfia.or.kr

Korea FoodService Industry Association Add:87, Dongho-ro 12-gil, Jung-gu, Seoul Tel:(02)2232-7911 http://www.foodservice.or.kr

Korea Glass Industry Cooperative Add: 18, Ewhayeodae 2ga-gil, Seodaemun-gu, Seoul Tel:(02)364-7799 http://www.glass-korea.org

Korea Grain Association Add:59, Jijok-ro 364beon-gil, Yuseong-gu, Daejeon Tel:(042)826-3116 http://www.gokhyup.or.kr

Korea Housing Association Add:711, Eonju-ro, Gangnam-gu, Seoul Tel:(02)517-1804 http://www.housing.or.kr

Korea Housing Builders Association Add:25, Gukjegeumyung-ro 8-gil, Yeongdeungpo-gu, Seoul Tel:(02)785-0990 http://khba.or.kr

Korea Importers Association Add:76, Sapyeong-daero, Seocho-gu, Seoul Tel:(02)792-1581 http://www.koima.or.kr

Korea Industrial Technology Association Add:37, Baumoe-ro 37-gil, Seocho-gu, Seoul Tel:(02)3460-9114 http://www.koita.or.kr

Korea Information & Comm. Contractors Association Add:308, Hangang-daero, Yongsan-gu, Seoul Tel:(02)3488-6000 http://www.kica.or.kr

Korea Integrated Logistics Association Add:432, Cheonho-daero, Seongdong-gu, Seoul Tel:(02)786-6112 http://www.koila.or.kr

Korea International Trade Association Add:511, Yeongdong-daero, Gangnam-gu, Seoul Tel:1566-5114 http://www.kita.net

Korea Internet Association Add:423, Teheran-ro, Gangnam-gu, Seoul Tel:(02)563-4114 http://www.kinternet.org

Korea Iron & Steel Association Add:135, Jungdae-ro, Songpa-gu, Seoul Tel:(02)559-3500 http://www.kosa.or.kr

Korea IT Business Women's Association Add:81, Sambong-ro, Jongno-gu, Seoul Tel:(02)2198-5511 http://www.kibwa.org

Korea Life Insurance Association Add:173, Toegye-ro, Jung-gu, Seoul Tel:(02)2262-6600 http://www.klia.or.kr

Korea Listed Companies Association Add:76, Yeouinaru-ro, Yeongdeungpo-gu, Seoul Tel:(02)2087-7000 http://www.klca.or.kr

Korea Lubricating Oil Industries Association Add:70, Seonyu-ro, Yeongdeungpo-gu, Seoul Tel:(02)2068-6043 http://www.kloia.or.kr

Korea Machine Tool Manufactures' Association Add:13, Iljink-ro 12beon-gil, Gwangmyeong-si, Gyeonggi-do Tel:(02)565-2721 http://www.komma.org

Korea Management Association Add: 22, Uisadang-daero, Yeongdeungpo-gu, Seoul Tel:(02)3274-9200 http://www.kma.or.kr

Korea Mech Const Contractors Association Add:429, Hakdong-ro, Gangnam-gu, Seoul Tel:(02)6240-1100 http://www.kmcca.or.kr

Korea Nonferrous Metal Association Add:11, Yeoksam-ro 3-gil, Gangnam-gu, Seoul Tel:(02)567-2313 http://www.nonferrous.or.kr

Korea Offshore & Shipbuilding Association Add:308, Gangnam-daero, Gangnam-gu, Seoul Tel:(02)2112-8181 http://www.koshipa.or.kr

Korea Oil Association Add:354, Gangnam-daero, Gangnam-gu, Seoul Tel:(02)555-8322 http://www.koreaoil.or.kr

Korea Overseas Fisheries Association Add:83, Nonhyeon-ro, Seocho-gu, Seoul Tel:(02)589-1621 http://www.kosfa.org

Korea Petrochemical Industry Association Add:190, Yulgok-ro, Jongno-gu, Seoul Tel:(02)3668-6100 http://www.kpia.or.kr

Korea Petroleum Association Add:27, Yeouinaru-ro, Yeongdeungpo-gu, Seoul Tel:(02)3775-0520 http://www.petroleum.or.kr

Korea Pharmaceutical Traders Association Add:511, Yeongdong-daero, Gangnam-gu, Seoul Tel:(02)6000-1841 http://www.kpta.or.kr

Korea Pharmaceutical Wholesalers Association Add:30, Bangbaejungang-ro 29-gil, Seocho-gu, Seoul Tel:(02)522-2921 http://www.kpwa.kr

Korea Photonics Industry Association Add:14, Sadang-ro 6-gil, Dongjak-gu, Seoul Tel:(02)3481-8931 http://www.kophia.or.kr

Korea Ports & Harbours Association Add:53, Yangsan-ro, Yeongdeungpo-gu, Seoul Tel:(02)2165-0092 http://www.koreaports.or.kr

Korea Port Logistics Association Add:35, Bomun-ro, Seongbuk-gu, Seoul Tel:(02)924-2113 http://www.kopla.or.kr

Korea Price Research Center Add:98, Gasan digital 2-ro, Geumcheon-gu, Seoul Tel:(02)799-0700 http://www.kprc.or.kr

Korean Printers Association Add:12, Yanghwa-ro 15-gil, Mapo-gu, Seoul Tel:(02)335-5881 http://www.print.or.kr

Korea Productivity Center Add:32, Saemunan-ro 5ga-gil, Jongno-gu, Seoul Tel:(02)724-1114 http://www.kpc.or.kr

Korea Semiconductor Industry Association Add:182, Pangyoyeok-ro, Bundang-gu, Seongnam-si, Gyeonggi-do Tel:(02)576-3472 http://www.ksia.or.kr

Korea Sericultural Association Add: 26, Uisadang-daero, Yeongdeungpo-gu, Seoul Tel:(02)783-6071 http://ksa.silktopia.or.kr

Korea Shipowners' Association Add:17, Gukhoe-daero 68-gil, Yeongdeungpo-gu, Seoul Tel:(02)739-1551 http://www.shipowners.or.kr

Korea Shipping Association Add:379, Gonghang-daero, Gangseo-gu, Seoul Tel:(02)6096-2000 http://www.haewoon.or.kr

Korea Speciality Chemical Industry Association Add:29, Digital-ro 32-gil, Guro-gu, Seoul Tel:(02)2088-7245 http://www.kscia.or.kr

Korea Specialty Contractors Association Add:15, Boramae-ro 5-gil, Dongjak-gu, Seoul Tel:(02)3284-1010 http://www.kosca.or.kr

Korea Statistics Promotion Institute Add:85, Sujeong-ro, Sujeong-gu, Seongnam-si, Gyeonggi-do Tel:(031)759-0167 http://www.stat.or.kr

Korea Sugar Association Add:49-17, Chungmu-ro 2-ga, Jung-gu, Seoul Tel:(02)2275-6071 http://www.sugar.or.kr

Korea Textile Machinery Association Add:27, Sampung-ro, Gyeongsan-si, Gyeongsangbuk-do Tel:(053)817-5954 http://www.kotma.org

Korea Tire Manufactures Association Add:511, Yeongdong-daero, Gangnam-gu, Seoul Tel:(02)551-1901 http://www.kotma.or.kr

Korea Tourism Association Add:40, Cheonggyecheon-ro, Jung-gu, Seoul Tel:(02)757-7485 http://www.koreatravel.or.kr

Korea Venture Business Association Add:28, Digital-ro 30-gil, Guro-gu, Seoul Tel:(02)6331-7000 http://venture.or.kr

Korea Venture Business Women's Association Add:16, Seocho-daero 45-gil, Seocho-gu, Seoul Tel:(02)2156-2160 http://www.kovwa.or.kr

Korean Women Entrepreneurs Association Add:221, Yeoksam-ro, Gangnam-gu, Seoul Tel:(02)369-0900 http://www.womanbiz.or.kr

Korean Apparel Industry Association Add:518, Teheran-ro, Gangnam-gu, Seoul Tel:(02)528-0114 http://kaia.or.kr

Korean Association of Surveying & Mapping Add:543, Gukhoe-daero, Yeongdeungpo-gu, Seoul Tel:(02)2670-7100 http://www.kasm.or.kr

Korean Commercial Arbitration Board Add:511, Yeongdong-daero, Gangnam-gu, Seoul Tel:(02)551-2000 http://www.kcab.or.kr

Korean Federation of Community Credit Cooperatives Add:20, Bongeunsa-ro 114-gil, Gangnam-gu, Seoul Tel:(02)2145-9114 http://www.kfcc.co.kr

Korean Footwear Industries Association Add:55, Noksansandan 382-ro 14beon-gil, Gangseo-gu, Busan Tel:(051)317-5202 http://www.footwear.or.kr

Korean Ginseng Products Manufacturer's Association Add:8, Changgyeonggung-ro 16ga-gil, Jongno-gu, Seoul Tel:(02)3672-8502 http://www.koreaginseng.or.kr

Korean Institute of Architects Add:225, Mokdongseo-ro, Yangcheon-gu, Seoul Tel:(02)744-8050 http://www.kia.or.kr

Korean Professional Engineers Association Add:22, Teheran-ro 7-gil, Gangnam-gu, Seoul Tel:(02)2098-7111 http://www.kpea.or.kr

Korean Publishers Cooperative Add: 222, Tojeong-ro, Mapo-gu, Seoul Tel: (02)716-5616 http://www.koreabook.or.kr

Korean Shipper's Council Add:511, Yeongdong-daero, Gangnam-gu, Seoul Tel:(02)6000-5114 http://shippersgate.kita.net

Korean Standards Association Add:305, Teheran-ro, Gangnam-gu, Seoul Tel:(02)6009-4114 http://www.ksa.or.kr

Korean Venture Capital Association Add:16, Seocho-daero 45-gil, Seocho-gu, Seoul Tel:(02)2156-2100 http://www.kvca.or.kr

KOSDAQ Listed Companies Association Add:76, Yeouinaru-ro, Yeongdeungpo-gu, Seoul Tel:(02)368-4500 http://www.kosdaqca.or.kr

Mining Korea Add:21-5, Jahamun-ro 4-gil, Jongno-gu, Seoul Tel:(02)736-2501 http://www.miningkorea.or.kr

National Credit Union Federation of Korea Add:745, Hanbat-daero, Seo-gu, Daejeon Tel:(042)720-1000 http://www.cu.co.kr

Spinners & Weavers Association of Korea Add:47-1, Samil-daero 17-gil, Jongno-gu, Seoul Tel:(02)735-5741 http://www.swak.org

Telecommunications Technology Association Add:47, Bundang-ro, Bundang-gu, Seongnam-si, Gyeonggi-do Tel:(031)724-0114 http://www.tta.or.kr

BANKS

Busan Bank Add:30, Munhyeongeumyung-ro, Nam-gu, Busan Tel:1588-6000 http://www.pusanbank.co.kr

Citibank Korea Add:24, Cheonggyecheon-ro, Jung-gu, Seoul Tel:1588-7000 http://www.citibank.co.kr

Hana Bank Add:35, Eulji-ro, Jung-gu, Seoul Tel:1599-1111 http://www.hanabank.co.kr

Industrial Bank of Korea Add:79, Eulji-ro, Jung-gu, Seoul Tel:1566-2566 http://www.ibk.co.kr

Jeju Bank Add:90, Ohyeon-gil, Jeju-si, Jeju-do Tel:1588-0079 http://www.e-jejubank.com

Jeon Buk Bank Add:566, Baekje-daero, Deokjin-gu, Jeonju-si, Jeollabuk-do Tel:1588-4477 http://www.jbbank.co.kr

Kookmin Bank Add:84, Namdaemun-ro, Jung-gu, Seoul Tel:1599-9999 http://www.kbstar.com

Korea Exchange Bank Add:66, Eulji-ro, Jung-gu, Seoul Tel:1544-3000 http://www.keb.co.kr

Kwangju bank Add:225, Jebong-ro, Dong-gu, Gwangju Tel:1588-3388 http://www.kjbank.com

Kyongnam Bank Add:642, 3·15-daero, MasanHoewon-gu, Changwon-si, Gyeong-sangnam-do Tel:1588-8585 http://www.kyongnambank.co.kr

National Agricultural Cooperative Federation Add:16, Saemunan-ro, Jung-gu, Seoul Tel:1588-2100 http://www.nonghyup.com

National Credit Union Federation of Korea Add:745, Hanbat-daero, Seo-gu, Daejeon Tel:(042)720-1000 http://www.cu.co.kr

National Federation of Fisheries Cooperatives Add:62, Ogeum-ro, Songpa-gu, Seoul Tel:1588-1515 http://www.suhyup.co.kr

Shinhan Bank Add:20, Sejong-daero 9-gil, Jung-gu, Seoul Tel:1599-8000 http://www.shinhanbank.co.kr

Standard Chartered Bank Korea Limited Add:47, Jong-ro, Jongno-gu, Seoul Tel:1588-1599 http://www.standardchartered.co.kr

The Bank Of Korea Add:39, Namdaemun-ro, Jung-gu, Seoul Tel:(02)759-4114 http://www.bok.or.kr

The Daegu Bank Add:2310, Dalgubeol-daero, Suseong-gu, Daegu Tel:1566-5050 http://www.daegubank.co.kr

The Export-Import Bank of Korea Add:38, Eunhaeng-ro, Yeongdeungpo-gu, Seoul Tel:3779-6114 http://www.koreaexim.go.kr

The Korea Development Bank Add:14, Eunhaeng-ro, Yeongdeungpo-gu, Seoul Tel:1588-1500 http://www.kdb.co.kr

Woori Bank Add:51, Sogong-ro, Jung-gu, Seoul Tel:1599-5000 http://www.wooribank.co.kr

INSURANCE COMPANIES

AIG Insurance Add:10, Gukjegeumyung-ro, Yeongdeungpo-gu, Seoul Tel:080-208-0365 http://www.aig.co.kr

Alianz Life Insurance Add:147, Uisadang-daero, Yeongdeungpo-gu, Seoul Tel:1588-6500 http://www.aliantzlife.co.kr

Dongbu Insurance Add:432, Teheran-ro, Gangnam-gu, Seoul Tel:1588-0100 http://www.idongbu.com

Dongbu Life Insurance Add:432, Teheran-ro, Gangnam-gu, Seoul Tel:1588-3131 http://www.dongbulife.co.kr

Hanwha General Insurance Add:56, Yeoui-daero, Yeongdeungpo-gu, Seoul Tel:1566-8000 http://www.hwgeneralins.com

Hanwha Life Insurance Add:50, 63-ro, Yeongdeungpo-gu, Seoul Tel:1588-6363 http://www.hanwhalife.com

Heungkuk Fire & Marine Insurance Add:68, Saemunan-ro, Jongno-gu, Seoul Tel:1688-1688 http://www.heungkukfire.co.kr

Heungkuk Life Insurance Add:68, Saemunan-ro, Jongno-gu, Seoul Tel:1588-2288 http://www.hungkuk.co.kr

Hyundai Marine & Fire Insurance Add:163, Sejong-daero, Jongno-gu, Seoul Tel:1588-5656 http://www.hi.co.kr

ING Life Insurance Add:37, Sejong-daero 7-gil, Jung-gu, Seoul Tel:1588-5005 http://www.inglife.co.kr

Kyobo Life Insurance Add:1, Jong-ro, Jongno-gu, Seoul Tel:1588-1001 http://www.kyobo.co.kr

LIG Insurance Add:117, Teheran-ro, Gangnam-gu, Seoul Tel:1544-0114 http://www.lig.co.kr

Lotte Non-Life Insurance Add:3, Sowol-ro, Jung-gu, Seoul Tel:1588-3344 http://www.lotteins.co.kr

Meritz Fire & Marine Insurance Add:382, Gangnam-daero, Gangnam-gu, Seoul Tel:1566-7711 http://www.meritzfire.com

MG Non-Life Insurance Add:335, Teheran-ro, Gangnam-gu, Seoul Tel:1588-5959 http://www.greeninsu.com

Mirae Asset Life Insurance Add:507, Teheran-ro, Gangnam-gu, Seoul Tel:1588-0220 http://life.miraeasset.com

Prudential Corporation Asia Life Insurance Add:302, Teheran-ro, Gangnam-gu, Seoul Tel:1588-4300 http://www.pcakorea.co.kr

Prudential Life Insurance Add:298, Gangnam-daero, Gangnam-gu, Seoul Tel:1588-3374 http://www.prudential.co.kr

Samsung Fire & Marine Insurance Add:29, Eulji-ro, Jung-gu, Seoul Tel:1588-5114 http://www.samsungfire.com

Samsung Life Insurance Add:55, Sejong-daero, Jung-gu, Seoul Tel:1588-3114 http://www.samsunglife.com

Seoul Guarantee Insurance Add:29, Kimsangok-ro, Jongno-gu, Seoul Tel:1670-7000 http://www.sgic.co.kr

Shinhan Life Insurance Add:54, Cheon-ggyecheon-ro, Jung-gu, Seoul Tel:1588-5580 http://www.shinhanlife.co.kr

Tong Yang Life Insurance Add:33, Jong-ro, Jongno-gu, Seoul Tel:1577-1004 http://www.myangel.co.kr

SECURITIES COMPANIES

Bookook Securities Add:17, Gukjegeumyung-ro 6-gil, Yeongdeungpo-gu, Seoul Tel:1588-7744 http://www.bookook.co.kr

Daishin Securities Add:16, Gukjegeumyung-ro 8-gil, Yeongdeungpo-gu, Seoul Tel:1588-4488 http://www.daishin.com

Dongbu Securities Add:32, Gukjegeumyung-ro 8-gil, Yeongdeungpo-gu, Seoul Tel:1588-4200 http://www.dongbuhappy.com

eBEST Investment & Securities Add:14, Yeoui-daero, Yeongdeungpo-gu, Seoul Tel:1588-2428 http://www.ebestsec.co.kr

Eugene Investment & Securities Add:28, Gukjegeumyung-ro 2-gil, Yeongdeungpo-gu, Seoul Tel:1588-6300 http://www.eugenefn.com

Fides Investment advisory Add:97, Uisadang-daero, Yeongdeungpo-gu, Seoul Tel:(02)567-8400 http://www.fides.co.kr

Golden Bridge Investment & Securities Add:50, Chungjeong-ro, Seodaemun-gu, Seoul Tel: 1566-0900 http://www.bridgefn.com

Hana Daetoo Securities Add:66, Yeoui-daero, Yeongdeungpo-gu, Seoul Tel:1588-3111 http://www.hanaw.com

Hanwha Investment & Securities Add:56, Yeoui-daero, Yeongdeungpo-gu, Seoul Tel:1544-8282 http://www.koreastock.co.kr

Hanyang Securities Add:7, Gukjegeumyung-ro 6-gil, Yeongdeungpo-gu, Seoul Tel:1588-2145 http://www.hygood.co.kr

Hi Investment & Securities Add:61, Yeouinaru-ro, Yeongdeungpo-gu, Seoul Tel:1588-7171 http://www.hi-ib.com

HMC Investment & Securities Add:32, Gukjegeumyung-ro 2-gil, Yeongdeungpo-gu, Seoul Tel:1588-6655 http://www.hmcib.com

Hyundai Securities Add:21, Yeouinaru-ro 4-gil, Yeongdeungpo-gu, Seoul Tel:1566-6611 http://www.youfirst.co.kr

IBK Securities Add:11, Gukjegeumyung-ro 6-gil, Yeongdeungpo-gu, Seoul Tel:1588-0030 http://www.ibks.com

I'M Investment & Securities Add:17, Yeouidaebang-ro 69-gil, Yeongdeungpo-gu, Seoul Tel:(02)3770-9200 http://www.iminvestib.com

KB Investment & Securities Add:70, Yeoui-daero, Yeongdeungpo-gu, Seoul Tel:1599-7000 http://www.kbsec.co.kr

KDB Daewoo Securities Add:56, Gukjegeumyung-ro, Yeongdeungpo-gu, Seoul Tel:1588-3322 http://www.kdbdw.com

Kiwoom Securities Add:18, Yeouinaru-ro 4-gil, Yeongdeungpo-gu, Seoul Tel:1544-9000 http://www.kiwoom.com

Korea Asset Investment & Securities Add:57, Yeouinaru-ro, Yeongdeungpo-gu, Seoul Tel:(02)550-6200 http://www.kasset.co.kr

Korea Investment & Securities Add:88, Uisadang-daero, Yeongdeungpo-gu, Seoul Tel:1544-5000 http://www.truefriend.com

Kyobo Securities Add:97, Uisadang-daero, Yeongdeungpo-gu, Seoul Tel:1544-0900 http://www.iprovest.com

Leading Investment & Securities Add:26, Gukjegeumyung-ro 6-gil, Yeongdeungpo-gu, Seoul Tel:(02)2009-7000 http://www.leading.co.kr

Meritz Securities Add:15, Gukjegeumyung-ro 6-gil, Yeongdeungpo-gu, Seoul Tel:(02)785-6611 http://www.imeritz.com

Mirae Asset Securities Add:26, Eulji-ro 5-gil, Jung-gu, Seoul Tel:1588-9200 http://www.smartmiraeasset.com

NH Investment & Securities Add:60, Yeoui-daero, Yeongdeungpo-gu, Seoul Tel:1588-4285 http://www.nhwm.com

Samsung Securities Add:67, Sejong-daero, Jung-gu, Seoul Tel:1544-1544 http://www.samsungpop.com

Shingyoung Securities Add:16, Gukjegeumyung-ro 8-gil, Yeongdeungpo-gu, Seoul Tel:1588-8588 http://www.shin-young.com

Shinhan Investment Add:70, Yeoui-daero, Yeongdeungpo-gu, Seoul Tel:1588-0365 http://www.shinhaninvest.com

SK Securities Add:24, Gukjegeumyung-ro 2-gil, Yeongdeungpo-gu, Seoul Tel:1599-8245 http://www.sks.co.kr

Woori Investment & Securities Add:152, Teheran-ro, Gangnam-gu, Seoul Tel:1544-0000 http://www.wooriwm.com

Yuanta Securities Korea Add:76, Eulji-ro, Jung-gu, Seoul Tel:1588-2600 http://www.yuantakorea.com

Yu Hwa Securities Add:36, Gukjegeumyung-ro 2-gil, Yeongdeungpo-gu, Seoul Tel:(02)3770-0100 http://www.yhs.co.kr

CREDIT CARD COMPANIES

BC Card Add:275, Hyoryeong-ro, Seocho-gu, Seoul Tel:1588-4000 http://www.bccard.com

Citi Card Add:24, Cheonggyecheon-ro, Jung-gu, Seoul Tel:1566-1000 http://www.citicard.co.kr

Hyundai Card Add:3, Uisadang-daero, Yeongdeungpo-gu, Seoul Tel:1577-6000 http://www.hyundaicard.com

KB Kookmin Card Add:30, Saemunan-ro 3-gil, Jongno-gu, Seoul Tel:1588-1688 http://www.kbcard.com

KEB Hana Card Add:24, Namdaemun-ro 9-gil, Jung-gu, Seoul Tel:1800-1111 http://www.yescard.com

Lotte Card Add:3, Sowol-ro, Jung-gu, Seoul Tel:1588-8100 http://www.lottecard.co.kr

Samsung Card Add:67, Sejong-daero, Jung-gu, Seoul Tel:1588-8700 http://www.samsungcard.com

Shinhan Card Add:70, Sogong-ro, Jung-gu, Seoul Tel:1544-7000 http://www.shinhancard.com

Woori Card Add:50, Jong-ro 1-gil, Jongno-gu, Seoul Tel:1588-9955 http://www.wooricard.com

HOSPITALS

Ajou University Medical Center Add:164, World cup-ro, Yeongtong-gu, Suwon-si, Gyeonggi-do Tel:1688-6114 http://hosp.ajoumc.or.kr

Andong Medical Group Add:11, Angsil-ro, Andong-si, Gyeongsangbuk-do Tel:(054)840-1004 http://andonghospital.co.kr

Asan Medical Center Add:88, Olympic-ro 43-gil, Songpa-gu, Seoul Tel:1688-7575 http://medical.amc.seoul.kr

Bundang Cha Medical Center Add:59, Yatap-ro, Bundang-gu, Seongnam-si, Gyeonggi-do Tel:(031)780-5000 http://bundang.chamc.co.kr

Busan Medical Center Add:359, World cup-daero, Yeonje-gu, Busan Tel:(051)507-3000 http://www.busanmc.or.kr

Catholic University of Korea, Bucheon ST. Mary's Hospital Add:327, Sosa-ro, Wonmi-gu, Bucheon-si, Gyeonggi-do Tel:1577-0675 http://www.cmcbucheon.or.kr

Catholic University of Korea, Daejeon ST. Mary's Hospital Add:64, Daeheung-ro, Jung-gu, Daejeon Tel:(042)220-9114 http://www.cmcdj.or.kr

Catholic University of Korea, Seoul ST. MARY's Hospital Add:222, Banpo-daero, Seocho-gu, Seoul Tel:1588-1511 http://www.cmcseoul.or.kr

Catholic University of Korea, ST. PAUL's Hospital Add:180, Wangsan-ro, Dongdaemun-gu, Seoul Tel:(02)958-2114 http://www.cmcbaoro.or.kr

Catholic University of Korea, ST. Vincent's Hospital Add:93, Jungbu-daero, Paldal-gu, Suwon-si, Gyeonggi-do Tel:1577-8588 http://www.cmcvincent.or.kr

Catholic University of Korea, Uijeongbu ST. Mary's Hospital Add:271, Cheonbo-ro, Uijeongbu-si, Gyeonggi-do Tel:1661-7500 http://www.cmcujb.or.kr

Catholic University of Korea, Yeouido ST. MARY's Hospital Add:10, 63-ro, Yeongdeungpo-gu, Seoul Tel:(02)3779-1114 http://www.cmcsungmo.or.kr

Changwon Hospital Add:721, Changwon-daero, Seongsan-gu, Changwon-si, Gyeong-sangnam-do Tel:(055)282-5111 http://www.kcomwel.or.kr/hospital/changwon

Cheju Halla General Hospital Add:65, Doryeong-ro, Jeju-si, Jeju-do Tel:(064)740-5000 http://www.hallahosp.co.kr

Cheongju hospital Add:163, Sangdang-ro, Sangdang-gu, Cheongju-si, Chungcheongbuk-do Tel:(043)220-1251 http://www.cjhospital.kr

Chonbuk National University Hospital Add:20, Geonji-ro, Deokjin-gu, Jeonju-si, Jeollabuk-do Tel:1577-7877 http://www.cuh.co.kr

Chonnam Hospital Add:49, Jwasuyeong-ro, Yeosu-si, Jeollanam-do Tel:(061)640-7575 http://www.yscnhosp.com

Chonnam National University Hospital Add:42, Jebong-ro, Dong-gu, Gwangju Tel:1899-0000 http://www.cnuh.com

Chosun University Hospital Add:365, Pilmun-daero, Dong-gu, Gwangju Tel:(062)220-3114 http://hosp.chosun.ac.kr

Chung-Ang University Hospital Add:102, Heukseok-ro, Dongjak-gu, Seoul Tel:1800-1114 http://ch.cauhs.or.kr

Chungbuk National University hospital Add:776, 1sunhwan-ro, Heungdeok-gu, Cheongju-si, Chungcheongbuk-do Tel:(043)269-6666 http://www.cbnuh.or.kr

Chungju ST. Mary's Hospital Add: 173-19, Juseong-ro, Sangdang-gu, Cheongju-si, Chungcheongbuk-do Tel:(043)219-8000 http://www.ccmc.or.kr

Chungnam National University Hospital Add:282, Munhwa-ro, Jung-gu, Daejeon Tel:(042)280-7114 https://www.cnuh.co.kr

Daegu Catholic Univ. Medical Center Add:33, Duryugongwon-ro 17-gil, Nam-gu, Daegu Tel:(053)650-3000 http://www.dcmc.co.kr

Daegu Fatima Hospital Add:99, Ayang-ro, Dong-gu, Daegu Tel:(053)940-7114 http://www.fatima.or.kr

Daegu Veterans Hospital Add:60, Wolgok-ro, Dalseo-gu, Daegu Tel:(053)630-7000 http://daegu.bohun.or.kr

Daerim Saint Mary's Hospital Add:657, Siheung-daero, Yeongdeungpo-gu, Seoul Tel:(02)829-0000 http://www.drh.co.kr

Daewoo General Hospital Add:16, Dumo-gil, Geoje-si, Gyeongsangnam-do Tel:(055)680-8114 http://www.dwho.or.kr

Dankook University Hospital Add:201, Manghyang-ro, Dongnam-gu, Cheonan-si, Chungcheongnam-do Tel:1588-0063 http://www.dkuh.co.kr

Dong-A University Hospital Add:26, Daesingongwon-ro, Seo-gu, Busan Tel:(051)240-2000 https://www.damc.or.kr

Dongguk University Medical Center Add:27, Dongguk-ro, Ilsandong-gu, Goyang-si, Gyeonggi-do Tel:1577-7000 http://www.dumc.or.kr

Donghae Dongin Medical Center Add:26, Hapyeong-ro, Donghae-si, Gangwon-do Tel:(033)530-0114 http://www.dhdongin.or.kr

Dongkang Medical Center Add:239, Taehwa-ro, Jung-gu, Ulsan Tel:(052)241-1114 http://www.dkmc.or.kr

Eulji General Hsopital Add:68, Hangeulbiseong-ro, Nowon-gu, Seoul Tel:1899-0001 http://www.eulji.or.kr

Eulji University Hospital Add:95, Dunsanseo-ro, Seo-gu, Daejeon Tel:1899-0001 http://www.emc.ac.kr

Ewha Womans University Medical Center Add:1071, Anyangcheon-ro, Yangcheon-gu, Seoul Tel:(02)2650-5114 http://www.eumc.ac.kr

Gachon University Gil Medical Center Add:21, Namdong-daero 774beon-gil,

Namdong-gu, Incheon Tel:1577-2299
http://www.gilhospital.com

Gangnam Severance Hospital Add:211, Eonju-ro, Gangnam-gu, Seoul Tel:1599-6114 http://gs.iseverance.com

Gongju National Hospital Add:623-21, Gobunti-ro, Gongju-si, Chungcheongnam-do Tel:(041)850-5700 http://www.knmh.go.kr

Gunsan Medical Center Add:27, Uiryowon-ro, Gunsan-si, Jeollabuk-do Tel:(063)472-5000 http://www.kunmed.or.kr

Gwangju Veterans Hospital Add:99, Cheomdanwolbong-ro, Gwangsan-gu, Gwangju Tel:(062)602-6114 http://gwangju.bohun.or.kr

Gyeongsang National University Hospital Add:79, Gangnam-ro, Jinju-si, Gyeongsangnam-do Tel:(055)750-8000 http://www.gnuh.co.kr

Hallym Univ. chuncheon Sacred Heart Hospital Add:77, Sakju-ro, Chuncheon-si, Gangwon-do Tel:(033)240-5000 http://chuncheon.hallym.or.kr

Hallym Univ. Gangdong Sacred Heart Hospital Add:150, Seongan-ro, Gangdong-gu, Seoul Tel:1588-4100 http://kangdong.hallym.or.kr

Hallym Univ. Gangnam Sacred Heart Hospital Add:1, Singil-ro, Yeongdeungpo-gu, Seoul Tel:1577-5587 http://kangnam.hallym.or.kr

Hallym Univ. Hangang Sacred Heart Hospital Add:12, Beodeunaru-ro 7-gil, Yeongdeungpo-gu, Seoul Tel:(02)2639-5114 http://hangang.hallym.or.kr

Hanyang University Guri Hospital Add: 153, Gyeongchun-ro, Guri-si, Gyeonggi-do Tel:(031)560-2114 https://guri.hyumc.com

Hanyang University Seoul Hospital Add:222-1, Wangsimni-ro, Seongdong-gu, Seoul Tel:(02)2290-8114 http://seoul.hyumc.com

Incheon Christian Hospital Add:10, Dapdong-ro 30beon-gil, Jung-gu, Incheon Tel:(032)270-8000 http://www.goich.co.kr

Incheon Medican Center Add:217, Bangchuk-ro, Dong-gu, Incheon Tel:(032)580-6000 http://www.icmc.or.kr

Inha University Hospital Add:27, Inhang-ro, Jung-gu, Incheon Tel:(032)890-2114 http://www.inha.com

Inje University Busan Paik Hospital Add:75, Bokji-ro, Busanjin-gu, Busan Tel:(051)890-5001 http://www.paik.ac.kr/busan

Inje University Sanggye Paik Hospital Add :1342, Dongil-ro, Nowon-gu, Seoul Tel:(02)950-1114 http://www.paik.ac.kr/sanggye

Inje University Seoul Paik Hospital Add:9, Mareunnae-ro, Jung-gu, Seoul Tel:(02)2770-0114 http://www.paik.ac.kr/seoul

Jeju National University Hospital Add:15, Aran 13-gil, Jeju-si, Jeju-do Tel:(064)717-1114 https://www.jejunuh.co.kr

Jeongeup Asan Hospital Add:606-22, Chungjeong-ro, Jeongeup-si, Jeollabuk-do Tel:(063)530-6114 http://www.jeh.or.kr

Kangbuk Samsung Medical Center Add:29, Saemunan-ro, Jongno-gu, Seoul Tel:(02)2001-2001 http://www.kbsmc.co.kr

Kangnam CHA Hospital Add:566, Nonhyeon-ro, Gangnam-gu, Seoul Tel:(02)3468-3000 http://kangnam.chamc.co.kr

Keimyung University Dongsan Medical Center Add:56, Dalseong-ro, Jung-gu, Dae gu Tel:(053)250-7114 http://www.dsmc.or.kr

KEPCO Medical Center Add:308, Uicheon-ro, Dobong-gu, Seoul Tel:(02)901-3114 https://www.kepcomedi.co.kr

Konkuk University Chungju Hospital Add:82, Gugwon-daero, Chungju-si, Chung cheongbuk-do Tel:(043)840-8200 http://www.kuh.co.kr ·

Konkuk University Medical Center Add:120-1, Neungdong-ro, Gwangjin-gu, Seoul Tel:1588-1533 http://www.kuh.ac.kr

Korea Institute of Radiological & Medical Sciences Add:75, Nowon-ro, Nowon-gu, Seoul Tel:(02)970-2114 http://www.kirams.re.kr

Korea University Anam Hospital Add:73, Inchon-ro, Seongbuk-gu, Seoul Tel:1577-0083 http://anam.kumc.or.kr

Korea University Guro Hospital Add: 148, Gurodong-ro, Guro-gu, Seoul Tel: (02)2626-1114 http://guro.kumc.or.kr

Kosin University Gospel hospital Add:262, Gamcheon-ro, Seo-gu, Busan Tel:(051)990-6114 http://www.kosinmed.or.kr

Kwangju Christian Hospital Add:37, Yangnim-ro, Nam-gu, Gwangju Tel:(062)650-5000 http://www.kch.or.kr

KyungHee University Medical Center Add:23, Kyungheedae-ro, Dongdaemun-gu, Seoul Tel:(02)958-8114 http://www.khmc.or.kr

Kyungpook National University Hospital Add:130, Dongdeok-ro, Jung-gu, Daegu Tel:(053)200-5114 http://knuh.knu.ac.kr

Marynoll Medical Center Add:121, Junggu-ro, Jung-gu, Busan Tel:(051)465-8801 http://www.maryknoll.co.kr

Masan National Hospital Add:215, Gapo-ro, Masanhappo-gu, Changwon-si, Gyeongsangnam-do Tel:(055)246-1141 http://www.nmh.go.kr

Metro Hospital Add:8, Myeonghak-ro 33beon-gil, Manan-gu, Anyang-si, Gyeonggi-do Tel:(031)467-9000 http://www.metrohospital.co.kr

Myongji Hospital Add:55, Hwasu-ro 14beon-gil, Deogyang-gu, Goyang-si, Gyeonggi-do Tel:(031)810-5114 http://www.mjh.or.kr

National Medical Center Add:245, Euljiro, Jung-gu, Seoul Tel:1588-1775 https://www.nmc.or.kr

National Police Hospital Add:123, Songiro, Songpa-gu, Seoul Tel:(02)3400-1114 http://www.nph.go.kr

Oriental Hospital of Daejeon University Add:138, Daeheung-ro, Jung-gu, Daejeon Tel:(042)255-9366 http://www.djumc.or.kr

Pohang St. Mary Hospital Add:17, Daejamdong-gil, Nam-gu, Pohang-si, Gyeongsangbuk-do Tel:(054)272-0151 https://www.pohangsmh.co.kr

Presbyterian Medical Center Add:365, Seowon-ro, Wansan-gu, Jeonju-si, Jeollabuk-do Tel:(063)230-8114 http://www.jesushospital.com

Pusan National University Hospital Add:179, Gudeok-ro, Seo-gu, Busan Tel:(051)240-7000 http://www.pnuh.co.kr

Samsung Changwon Hospital Add:158, Paryong-ro, MasanHoiwon-gu, Changwon-si, Gyeongsangnam-do Tel:(055)290-6000 https://smc.skku.edu:442

Samsung Medical Center Add:81, Irwon-ro, Gangnam-gu, Seoul Tel:(02)3410-2114 http://www.samsunghospital.com

Samyook Medical Center Add:82, Manguro, Dongdaemun-gu, Seoul Tel:1577-3675 http://www.symcs.co.kr

Seoul Medical Center Add:156, Sinnaero, Jungnang-gu, Seoul Tel:(02)2276-7000 http://www.seoulmc.or.kr

Seoul national Northwestern hospital Add:49, Galhyeon-ro 7-gil, Eunpyeong -gu, Seoul Tel:(02)3156-3000 http://sbhosp.seoul.go.kr

Seoul National University Bundang Hospital Add:82, Gumi-ro 173beon-gil, Bundang-gu, Seongnam-si, Gyeonggi-do Tel:1588-3369 http://www.snubh.org

Seoul National University Hospital Add:101, Daehak-ro, Jongno-gu, Seoul Tel:(02)2072-2114 http://www.snuh.org

Seoul Red Cross Hospital Add:9, Saemunan-ro, Jongno-gu, Seoul Tel:(02)2002-8000 http://www.rch.or.kr/seoul

SNU Boramae Medical Center Add:20, Boramae-ro 5gil, Dongjak-gu, Seoul Tel:(02)870-2114 http://www.brmh.org

Sohwa Children's Hospital Add:383, Cheongpa-ro, Yongsan-gu, Seoul Tel:(02)705-9000 http://www.swch.co.kr

Soonchunghyang University Bucheon Hospital Add:170, Jomaru-ro, Wonmi-gu, Bucheon-si, Gyeonggi-do Tel:(032)621-5114 http://www.schmc.ac.kr/bucheon

Soonchunhyang University Cheonan Hospital Add:31, Suncheonhyang 6-gil, Dongnam-gu, Cheonan-si, Chungcheongnam-do Tel:(041)570-2114 http://www.schmc.ac.kr/cheonan

Soonchunhyang University Gumi Hospital Add:179, 1gongdan-ro, Gumi-si, Gyeongsangbuk-do Tel:(054)468-9114 http://www.schmc.ac.kr/gumi

Soonchunhyang University hospital Add:59, Daesagwan-ro, Yongsan-gu, Seoul Tel:(02)709-9114 http://www.schmc.ac.kr/seoul

Sun Medical Center Add:29, Mokjungro, Jung-gu, Daejeon Tel:1588-7011 http://www.sunhospital.com

Sungae Hospital Add:22, Yeouidaebang-ro 53-gil, Yeongdeungpo-gu, Seoul Tel:(02)8407-114 http://www.ksungae.co.kr

Ulsan Hospital Add:13, Wolpyeong-ro 171, beon-gil, Nam-gu, Ulsan Tel:(052)259-5000 http://www.ush.co.kr

Ulsan University Hospital Add:877, Bangeojinsunhwan-doro, Dong-gu, Ulsan Tel:(052)250-7000 http://www.uuh.ulsan.kr

Busan Veterans Hospital Add:420, Baegyang-daero, Sasang-gu, Busan Tel:(051)601-6000 http://busan.bohun.or.kr

VHS Medical Center Add:53, Jinhwangdoro 61-gil, Gangdong-gu, Seoul Tel:(02)2225-1111 http://seoul.bohun.or.kr

Wallace Memorial Baptist Hospital Add:200, Geumdan-ro, Geumjeong-gu, Busan Tel:(051)580-2000 http://www.wmbh.co.kr

Wonju Severance Christian Hospital Add:20, Ilsan-ro, Wonju-si, Gangwon-do

Tel:(033)741-0114 http://www.wch.or.kr

Wonkwang University School of Medicine & Hospital Add:895, Muwang-ro, Iksan-si, Jeollabuk-do Tel:1577-3773 http://www.wkuh.org

Yeungnam University Medical Center Add:170, Hyeonchung-ro, Nam-gu, Daegu Tel:(053)623-8001 http://www.yumc.ac.kr

Yonsei University Health System, Severance Hospital Add:50-1, Yonsei-ro, Seodaemun-gu, Seoul Tel:1599-1004 http://sev.iseverance.com

HOTELS

<Seoul>

Grand Ambassador Seoul Add:287, Dongho-ro, Jung-gu, Seoul Tel:(02)2275-1101 http://grand.ambatel.com

Grand Hilton Seoul Add:353, Yeonhui-ro, Seodaemun-gu, Seoul Tel:(02)3216-5656 http://www.grandhiltonseoul.com

Grand Hyatt Seoul Add:322, Sowol-ro, Yongsan-gu, Seoul Tel:(02)797-1234 http://seoul.grand.hyatt.kr

Grand Intercontinental Parnas Add:521, Teheran-ro, Gangnam-gu, Seoul Tel:(02)555-5656 http://www.grandicparnas.com

Hotel Capital Add:23, Jangmun-ro, Yongsan-gu, Seoul Tel:(02)6399-2000 http://www.hotelcapital.co.kr

Hotel President Add:16, Eulji-ro, Jung-gu, Seoul Tel:(02)753-3131 http://www.hotelpresident.co.kr

Hotel Riviera Seoul Add:737, Yeongdong-daero, Gangnam-gu, Seoul Tel:(02)541-3111 http://www.hotelriviera.co.kr

Hotel Shilla Add:249, Dongho-ro, Jung-gu, Seoul Tel:(02)2233-3131 http://www.hotelshilla.net

Imperial Palace Seoul Add:640, Eonju-ro, Gangnam-gu, Seoul Tel:(02)3440-8000 http://www.imperialpalace.co.kr

JW Marriott Hotel Seoul Add:176, Sinbanpo-ro, Seocho-gu, Seoul Tel:(02)6282-6262 http://www.jw-marriott.co.kr

Intercontinental Seoul COEX Add:524, Bongeunsa-ro, Gangnam-gu, Seoul Tel:(02)3452-2500 http://www.iccoex.com

Koreana Hotel Add:135, Sejong-daero, Jung-gu, Seoul Tel:(02)2171-7000 http://www.koreanahotel.com

Lotte Hotel Seoul Add:30, Eulji-ro, Jung-gu, Seoul Tel:(02)771-1000 http://www.lottehotelseoul.com

Lotte Hotel World Add:240, Olympic-ro, Songpa-gu, Seoul Tel:(02)419-7000 http://www.lottehotelworld.com

Millennium Seoul Hilton Hotel Add:50, Sowol-ro, Jung-gu, Seoul Tel:(02)753-7788 http://www.seoul.hilton.co.kr

Novotel Ambassador Doksan Add:378, Siheung-daero, Geumcheon-gu, Seoul Tel:(02)838-1101 http://novotel.ambatel.com/doksan

Novotel Ambassador Gangnam Add:130, Bongeunsa-ro, Gangnam-gu, Seoul Tel:(02)567-1101 http://novotel.ambatel.com/gangnam

Pacific Hotel Add:2, Toegye-ro 20-gil, Jung-gu, Seoul Tel:(02)777-7811 http://www.thepacifichotel.co.kr

Plaza Hotel Seoul Add:119, Sogong-ro, Jung-gu, Seoul Tel:(02)771-2200 http://www.hoteltheplaza.com

Ramada Seoul Hotel Add:410, Bongeunsa-ro, Gangnam-gu, Seoul Tel:(02)6202-2000 http://www.ramadaseoul.co.kr

Renaissance Seoul Hotel Add:237, Teheran-ro, Gangnam-gu, Seoul Tel:(02)555-0501 http://www.renaissance-seoul.com

Ritz-Carlton, Seoul Add:120, Bongeunsa-ro, Gangnam-gu, Seoul Tel:(02)3451-8000 http://www.ritzcarltonseoul.com

Sejong Hotel Add:145, Toegye-ro, Jung-gu, Seoul Tel:(02)773-6000 http://www.sejong.co.kr

Seoul Palace Hotel Add:160, Sapyeong-daero, Seocho-gu, Seoul Tel:(02)532-5000 http://www.seoulpalace.co.kr

Seoul Garden Hotel Add:58, Mapo-daero, Mapo-gu, Seoul Tel:(02)710-7111 http://www.seoulgarden.co.kr

Seoul Royal Hotel Add:61, Myeongdong-gil, Jung-gu, Seoul Tel:(02)756-1112 http://www.royal.co.kr

Sheraton Grande Walkerhill Hotel Add:177, Walkerhill-ro, Gwangjin-gu, Seoul Tel:(02)455-5000 http://www.sheraton-walkerhill.co.kr

Westin Chosun Seoul Add:106, Sogong-ro, Jung-gu, Seoul Tel:(02)771-0500 http://www.echosunhotel.com

<Local>

Bugok Hawai Add:77, Oncheonjungang-ro Bugok-myeon, Changnyeong-gun, Gyeongsangnam-do Tel:(055)536-6331 http://www.bugokhawaii.co.kr

Chonju Core Riviera Hotel Add:85, Girindaero, Wansan-gu, Jeonju-si, Jeollabuk-do Tel:(063)232-7000 http://www.core-riviera.co.kr

Commodore Hotel Busan Add:151, Junggu-ro, Jung-gu, Busan Tel:(051)466-9101 http://www.commodore.co.kr

Commodore Hotel Gyeongju Add:422, Bomun-ro, Gyeongju-si, Gyeongsangbuk-do Tel:(054)745-7701 http://www.commodorehotel.co.kr

Commodore Hotel Pohang Add:71, Songdo-ro, Nam-gu, Pohang-si, Gyeongsangbuk-do Tel:(054)241-1400 http://www.commodorepohang.co.kr

Daegu Prince Hotel Add:150, Myeongdeok-ro, Nam-gu, Daegu Tel:(053)628-1001 http://www.princehotel.co.kr

Gyeongju Hilton Hotel Add:484-7, Bomun-ro, Gyeongju-si, Gyeongsangbuk-do Tel:(054)745-7788 http://www.kyongjuhilton.co.kr

Haeundae Grand Hotel Add:217, Haeundaehaebyeon-ro, Haeundae-gu, Busan Tel:(051)740-0114 http://www.haeundaegrandhotel.com

Hotel Concorde Add:404, Bomun-ro, Gyeongju-si, Gyeongsangbuk-do Tel:(054)745-7000 http://www.concorde.co.kr

Hotel Hyundai Gyeongju Add:338, Bomun-ro, Gyeongju-si, Gyeongsangbuk-do Tel:(054)748-2233 http://www.hyundaihotel.com/gyeongju

Hotel Hyundai Ulsan Add:875, Bangeojinsunhwan-doro, Dong-gu, Ulsan Tel:(052)251-2233 http://www.hyundaihotel.com/ulsan

Hotel Inter-Burgo Daegu Add:212, Palhyeon-gil, Suseong-gu, Daegu Tel:(053)602-7114 http://daegu.ibhotel.com

Hotel Inter-Burgo Exco Add:80, Yutongdanji-ro, Buk-gu, Daegu Tel:(053)380-0114 http://exco.ibhotel.com

Hotel Inter-Burgo Wonju Add:200, Dongbusunhwan-ro, Wonju-si, Gangwon-do Tel:(033)769-8114 http://wonju.ibhotel.com

Hotel Inter-Burgo Ansan Add:81, Dongsan-ro, Danwon-gu, Ansan-si, Gyeonggi-do Tel:(031)490-2000 http://ansan.inter-burgo.com

Hotel Miranda Add:45, Jungnicheon-ro 115beon-gil, Icheon-si, Gyeonggi-do Tel:(031)639-5000 http://www.mirandahotel.com

Hotel Riviera Yuseong Add:7, Oncheonseo-ro, Yuseong-gu, Daejeon Tel:(042)823-2111 http://www.shinan.co.kr/yusong

Hotel Sorak Park Add:852-15, Seoraksan-ro, Sokcho-si, Gangwon-do Tel:(033)636-7711 http://www.hotelsorakpark.co.kr

Hyatt Regency Add:114, Jungmungwangwang-ro 72beon-gil, Seogwipo-si, Jeju-do Tel:(064)733-1234 http://www.jeju.regency.hyatt.kr

Jeju Grand Hotel Add:80, Noyeon-ro, Jeju-si, Jeju-do Tel:(064)747-4900 http://www.grand.co.kr

Jeju Aerospace Hotel Add:216, Nokchabunjae-ro, Seogwipo-si, Jeju-do Tel:(064)798-5500 http://ora.oraresort.com

Jeju Oriental Hotel Add:47, Tapdong-ro, Jeju-si, Jeju-do Tel:(064)752-8222 http://www.oriental.co.kr

Jeju Pacific Hotel Add:20, Seosa-ro, Jeju-si, Jeju-do Tel:(064)758-2500 http://www.jejupacific.co.kr

KAL Hotel Jeju Add:151, Jungang-ro, Jeju-si, Jeju-do Tel:(064)724-2001 http://www.kalhotel.co.kr/jeju

KAL Hotel Seogwipo Add:242, Chilsimni-ro, Seogwipo-si, Jeju-do Tel:(064)733-2001 http://www.kalhotel.co.kr/seogwipo

Kolong Hotel Add:289-17, Bulguk-ro, Gyeongju-si, Gyeongsangbuk-do Tel:(054)746-9001 http://www.kolonhotel.co.kr

Lotte Hotel Busan Add:772, Gaya-daero, Busanjin-gu, Busan Tel:(051)810-1000 http://www.lottehotelbusan.com

Lotte Hotel Jeju Add:35, Jungmungwangwang-ro 72beon-gil, Seogwipo-si, Jeju-do Tel:(064)731-1000 http://www.lottehoteljeju.com

Naksan Beach Hotel Add:73, Naksansa-ro, Ganghyeon-myeon, Yangyang-gun, Gangwon-do Tel:(033)672-4000

Novotel Ambassador Busan Add: 292, Haeundaehaebyeon-ro, Haeundae-gu, Busan Tel:(051)743-1234 http://www.novotelbusan.com

Onyang Grand Hotel Add:7, Chungmu-ro 20beon-gil, Asan-si, Chungcheongnam-do Tel:(041)543-9711 http://www.grandhotel.co.kr

Paradise Hotel Busan Add:296, Haeundaehaebyeon-ro, Haeundae-gu, Busan Tel:(051)742-2121 http://www.busanparadisehotel.co.kr

Paradise Hotel Incheon Add:257,

Jemullyang-ro, Jung-gu, Incheon Tel:(032)762-5181 http://incheon.paradisehotel.co.kr

Ramada Songdo Add:29, Neungheodae-ro 267beon-gil, Yeonsu-gu, Incheon Tel:(032)832-2000 http://www.ramada-songdo.co.kr

Shilla Jeju Add:75, Jungmungkwangwang-ro 72beon-gil, Seogwipo-si, Jeju-do Tel:(064)735-5114 http://www.shilla.net/kr/jeju

T.H.E. Hotel Jeju Add:67, Sammu-ro, Jeju-si, Jeju-do Tel:(064)741-8000 http://www.thehotelasia.com

Westin Chosun Busan Add:67, Dongbaekro, Haeundae-gu, Busan Tel:(051)749-7000 http://twcb.echosunhotel.com

Yongpyong Resort Add:715, Olympicro, Daegwanryeong-myeon, Pyeongchanggun, Gangwon-do Tel:1588-0009 http://www.yongpyong.co.kr

Yousung Hotel Add:9, Oncheon-ro, Yuseong-gu, Daejeon Tel:(042)820-0100 http://www.yousunghotel.com

DEPARTMENT STORES

AK Plaza Add:152, Gurojungang-ro, Guro-gu, Seoul Tel:(02)818-1000 http://www.akplaza.com

Daegu Dept. Store Add:30, Dongseongro, Jung-gu, Daegu Tel:(053)423-1234 http://www.debec.co.kr

DongA Dept. Store Add:171, Gyeongsanggamyeong-gil, Jung-gu, Daegu Tel:1577-0111 http://www.dong100.com

Galleria Dept. Store Luxury Hall Add:92, Sejong-daero, Jung-gu, Seoul Tel:(02)410-7114 http://dept.galleria.co.kr

Grand Dept. Store Ilsan Branch Add: 1436, Jungang-ro, Ilsanseo-gu, Goyangsi, Gyeonggi-do Tel:(031)917-0101 http://www.granddept.co.kr

Shinsegae Dept. Store Add:63, Sogongro, Jung-gu, Seoul Tel:1588-1234

Hyundai Dept. Store Add:165, Apgujeongro, Gangnam-gu, Seoul Tel:(02)547-2233 http://www.ehyundai.com

Kunyoungomni Dept. Store Add:258, Seombat-ro, Nowon-gu, Seoul Tel:(02)971-9000

Lotte Dept. Store Add:81, Namdaemunro, Jung-gu, Seoul Tel:(02)771-2500 http://www.ellotte.com

Say Dept. Store Add:1700, Gyebaek-ro, Jung-gu, Daejeon Tel:(042)226-1234 http://www.saydept.com

Index

Yonhap News Agency

Q~R

S